The Cambridge Handbook of Consumer Psychology

Why do consumers make the purchases they do, and which ones make them truly happy? Why are consumers willing to spend huge sums of money to appear high status? This handbook addresses these key questions and many more. It provides a comprehensive overview of consumer psychology, examining cutting-edge research at the individual, interpersonal, and societal levels. Leading scholars summarize past and current findings and consider future lines of inquiry to deepen our understanding of the psychology behind consumers' decision making, their interactions with other consumers, and the effects of societal factors on consumption. *The Cambridge Handbook of Consumer Psychology* will act as a valuable guide for faculty as well as graduate and undergraduate students in psychology, marketing, management, sociology, and anthropology.

MICHAEL I. NORTON is a Professor of Business Administration in the Marketing Unit at Harvard Business School. He is the coauthor, with Elizabeth Dunn, of *Happy Money: The Science of Smarter Spending* (2013).

DEREK D. RUCKER is the Sandy and Morton Goldman Professor of Entrepreneurial Studies in Marketing at Northwestern University's Kellogg School of Management. His articles have appeared in numerous publications, including the *Journal of Personality and Social Psychology*, the *Journal of Consumer Research*, the *Journal of Marketing Research*, and the *Journal of Consumer Psychology*.

CAIT LAMBERTON is an Associate Professor and Fryrear Faculty Fellow in Marketing at the Katz Graduate School of Business at the University of Pittsburgh. Her work has been published in the *Journal of Consumer Research*, the *Journal of Consumer Psychology*, the *Journal of Marketing Research*, the *Journal of Marketing*, and the *Journal of Public Policy and Marketing*.

The Cambridge Handbook of Consumer Psychology

Edited by

Michael I. Norton
Derek D. Rucker
Cait Lamberton

CAMBRIDGE
UNIVERSITY PRESS

CAMBRIDGE
UNIVERSITY PRESS

32 Avenue of the Americas, New York NY 10013-2473, USA

Cambridge University Press is part of the University of Cambridge.

It furthers the University's mission by disseminating knowledge in the pursuit of education, learning and research at the highest international levels of excellence.

www.cambridge.org
Information on this title: www.cambridge.org/9781107641426

© Cambridge University Press 2015

First published 2015
Reprinted 2016
First paperback edition 2016

A catalogue record for this publication is available from the British Library

Library of Congress Cataloguing in Publication data
The Cambridge handbook of consumer psychology / [edited by] Michael I. Norton,
Harvard Business School, Harvard University, Derek D. Rucker, Kellogg School of
Management, Northwestern University, Cait Lamberton, Katz Graduate School of
Business, University of Pittsburgh.
    pages   cm. – (Cambridge handbooks in psychology)
Includes bibliographical references and index.
ISBN 978-1-107-06920-6 (Hardback)
1. Consumers–Psychology.   2. Consumer behavior.   I. Norton, Michael I.,
1975– editor.   II. Rucker, Derek D., 1977– editor.   III. Lamberton, Cait, 1975– editor.
HF5415.32.C36 2015
658.8′342–dc23   2015006129

ISBN 978-1-107-06920-6 Hardback
ISBN 978-1-107-64142-6 Paperback

Contents

Figures

Tables

Contributors

NIDHI AGRAWAL, University of Washington

EDUARDO B. ANDRADE, Brazilian School of Public and Business Administration, FGV, Rio de Janeiro

J. CRAIG ANDREWS, Marquette University

KARL AQUINO, University of British Columbia

JILL AVERY, Harvard Business School

JONAH BERGER, University of Pennsylvania

PABLO BRIÑOL, Universidad Autónoma de Madrid

SCOT BURTON, University of Arkansas

CINDY CHAN, University of Toronto

LAN NGUYEN CHAPLIN, University of Illinois at Chicago

SHIRLEY Y. Y. CHENG, Hong Kong Baptist University

PAUL M. CONNELL, Stony Brook University

DAVID DUBOIS, INSEAD

ADAM DUHACHEK, Indiana University

KRISTINA M. DURANTE, Rutgers University

JEREMY FRIMER, University of Winnipeg

DAVID GAL, University of Illinois at Chicago

ADAM D. GALINSKY, Columbia University

ANDREW D. GERSHOFF, University of Texas at Austin

VLADAS GRISKEVICIUS, University of Minnesota

DAHEE HAN, McGill University

HAL E. HERSHFIELD, University of California at Los Angeles

JULIE R. IRWIN, University of Texas at Austin

LESLIE K. JOHN, Harvard University

ULRIKE KAISER, Institute for Marketing Management, WU Vienna

UMA R. KARMARKAR, Harvard Business School

JEREMY KEES, Villanova University

ANAT KEINAN, Harvard Business School

KIRK KRISTOFFERSON, University of British Columbia

DIDEM KURT, Boston University

CAIT LAMBERTON, University of Pittsburgh

VIKAS MITTAL, Rice University

CASSIE MOGILNER, University of Pennsylvania

CAREY K. MOREWEDGE, Boston University

ASHESH MUKHERJEE, McGill University

MICHAEL I. NORTON, Harvard Business School

CHRISTOPHER Y. OLIVOLA, Carnegie Mellon University

NAILYA ORDABAYEVA, Boston College

HILKE PLASSMANN, INSEAD

REBECCA WALKER RECZEK, Ohio State University

DEREK D. RUCKER, Northwestern University

MARTIN SCHREIER, Institute for Marketing Management, WU Vienna

JANET A. SCHWARTZ, Tulane University

ANUJ K. SHAH, University of Chicago

ABIGAIL B. SUSSMAN, University of Chicago

CARLOS J. TORELLI, University of Minnesota

ZAKARY L. TORMALA, Stanford University

CLAUDIA TOWNSEND, University of Miami

MORGAN K. WARD, Southern Methodist University

KATHERINE WHITE, University of British Columbia

KAREN PAGE WINTERICH, Pennsylvania State University

Introduction

Understanding Consumers in the Here, the Now,
and the Tomorrow

Michael I. Norton, Derek D. Rucker, and Cait Lamberton

> Study the past if you would divine the future.
>
> – Confucius

The words of Confucius define the architecture of this handbook. As editors, we made a decision to seek out a set of scholars that we agreed had conducted some of the most exciting and novel research in their areas of expertise in recent years, and who we felt were likely to play a leading role in shaping the agenda for consumer behavior research in the years to come.

Although we left details of the chapter contents to our authors, as editors we gave all authors the same core blueprint to build the foundation of their chapters. First, we asked our authors to look backward into the literature to offer a discussion of key developments, theoretical arguments, and empirical findings to provide readers with a critical summary of a subject central to consumer psychology – with a focus on research conducted over the last decade, to make each chapter a tour of those research papers likely to become "classics" in the years to come. Second, we asked each author to set a research agenda to address unanswered questions and topics of study that they felt should become part of the future canon of their research area. As a result, while each chapter has its own particular feel and design, the volume as a whole is linked by the common motifs of both the past and future of a research area.

In this introduction, we provide a brief overview of the chapters to come. The handbook is divided and organized by three central lenses on consumer psychology: individual, social, and societal.

Chapters in Part I of the volume emphasize consumer decision making and behavior at the level of the individual. The first five chapters explore the building blocks of consumer behavior from a variety of theoretical orientations, from understanding consumer well-being (Mogilner and Norton), to persuasion (Tormala and Briñol), to predictions about the future (Morewedge and Hershfield), to emotions (Andrade), to evolutionary perspectives (Griskevicius and Durante). Two chapters focus on promising, yet underutilized, approaches to consumer psychology, from neuroscientific techniques (Plassmann and Karmarkar) to developmental approaches (Chaplin and Connell). The final two chapters discuss novel developments in two areas of marketing with rapidly changing landscapes: branding (Avery and Keinan) and co-creation (Townsend, Kaiser, and Schreier).

Part II emphasizes interpersonal and social aspects of consumer psychology. Here the focus shifts to understanding how consumer behavior is affected by the real or even imagined presence of others. Discussions of how others are central to self-definition are introduced with implications for consumption as a means of signaling one's desired identity to others (Gal) and for coping with threat (Han, Duhachek, and Agrawal). This section also recognizes hierarchy – the ranking of individuals – as a fundamental aspect of social relations. To understand the implications of hierarchy for consumer behavior, perspectives are provided with regard to both power (Rucker and Galinsky) and status (Dubois and Ordabayeva). The section continues with an examination of social dynamics regarding the sharing of information between consumers (Berger), the giving of gifts (Ward and Chan), and interpersonal influence (Kristofferson and White). Finally, several emerging perspectives are brought to bear with regard to the role of agentic versus communal orientations (Kurt and Frimer) and online consumer interaction (Gershoff and Mukherjee).

In Part III, authors focus on consumers' embeddedness in – and, often, definition in terms of – broader societal structures. Chapters suggest that rather than consisting of individually constructed identities, consumers' self-definitions are radically shaped by the cultures in which they live (Torelli and Cheng), the economic constraints they face (Shah), the political and moral forces with which they align (Winterich, Mittal, and Aquino), and the experiences of public and collective spending by which they are legally constrained (Olivola and Sussman). At the same time, consumers are not passive actors in their culture – they can choose to purchase in ways that create positive outcomes for others (Reczek and Irwin) or to pool resources in ways that lead not only to survival but to creativity and production (Lamberton). Further, they can make active decisions about their own well-being, whether physical, as in the case of healthcare decisions (Schwartz), or psychological, as they create boundaries between themselves and others (John). Finally, the ways that government works to both protect the individual and empower better decision making are explored (Kees, Burton, and Andrews).

As the chapters reveal, understanding consumers – from individual to social to societal – necessitates drawing on a wide range of theory and approach, ranging from anthropology to behavioral decision theory to neuroscience to economics to developmental psychology. Our authors have done an impressive job of beginning the process of integrating these disparate perspectives; this integration will be crucial in exploring and understanding consumer phenomena as they continue to evolve. We hope this this volume, by bridging both the past and looking to the far horizon of the future, will serve not simply as an archive but as an inspiration for research that will form the building blocks of future handbooks.

PART I

Individual Consumer Decision Making and Behavior

1 Consumer Happiness and Well-Being

Cassie Mogilner and Michael I. Norton

What has consumer research taught us about how to make our lives better? By "better," we mean according to *us* consumers, in terms of how happy we feel in our lives and with the choices we make: our subjective sense of well-being. Having surveyed the research, it is our pleasure to report that over the past ten years, consumer research has taught us quite a lot in terms of things we can do, choices we can make, and ways that we can think to increase our happiness. Still, for as much as we have learned, there is even more yet to learn, which makes consumer happiness a ripe topic for future research.

We can attribute much of the impetus for consumer happiness research to two sources: Martin Seligman's American Psychological Association Presidential Address in 1998 and David Mick's Association of Consumer Research Presidential Address in 2005. Both of these speeches implored their respective fields, Seligman's psychology and Mick's consumer research, to shift the research agenda toward improving subjective well-being. In Seligman's 1998 address, he redefined the mission of psychology to "making the lives of all people better," and in doing so carved out the subfield known as Positive Psychology: "a science and profession whose aim is the building of what makes life most worth living." In Mick's 2005 address, he suggested that the field should pursue "investigations that are framed by a fundamental problem or opportunity, and that strive to respect, uphold, and improve life in relation to the myriad conditions, demands, potentialities, and effects of consumption," terming this pursuit "transformative consumer research."

This chapter reviews research over the past decade that heeded these urgings and sought to transform consumers' lives by increasing their happiness and well-being. This research has typically taken one of two approaches: investigating the happiness consumers feel in their lives at a broad level, or investigating the happiness consumers feel with respect to more specific consumption episodes. The chapter is organized as such. To begin our review, since consumption typically relies on the expenditure of either or both of our two fundamental resources – money and time – we first discuss research (including some of our own) that relates these resources to happiness in general. For instance, we review research that addresses whether having money contributes to happiness, and research that identifies particular ways of spending money that contribute to happiness. We also review research that examines what happens when consumers shift their attention away from money and toward time, and research that explores particularly happy ways of spending time. We wrap up this first section by highlighting work that shows the effect of feeling happy on subsequent thinking and behavior. The second section then surveys research examining the happiness that consumers feel from their choices and consumption experiences more specifically. Finally, we conclude the chapter by identifying some of the many unanswered questions that remain for future research.

Since the two presidential addresses that urged discoveries in this area, a notable body of research has emerged, filling the pages of such books as Aaker and Smith's (2010) *The Dragonfly Effect* and Dunn and Norton's (2013) *Happy Money*. And even though it keeps the two of us very busy reviewing papers and conference submissions, we are thrilled to see the increasing enthusiasm, especially among junior scholars, for this topic of consumer happiness and well-being. It is tremendously encouraging to observe the efforts within our field to provide empirical insights into the age-old question of what makes people happy.

Life Happiness

Happiness from Money

Despite people's intuitions to the contrary, it turns out that more money does not tend to be associated with much more happiness, particularly after people's basic needs are met (Aknin, Norton, & Dunn, 2009; Kahneman & Deaton, 2010; Kahneman, Krueger, Schkade, Schwarz, & Stone, 2006). To be sure, more money has not been shown to make people *less* happy – it is simply the case that the relationship tends to be modest (Diener & Biswas-Diener, 2002; Frey & Stutzer, 2000). But do these correlational studies suggest that money cannot buy happiness, or rather that people are not using their money in ways that maximize their "happiness bang for the buck"? Recent research suggests that when people shift from spending their money on material possessions to other categories – such as prosocial spending and buying experiences – money can in fact pay off in more happiness.

Prosocial Spending

What would make consumers happier – receiving a $5 windfall and being instructed to spend it on themselves, or receiving that same $5 windfall and being asked to spend it on someone else, say, by taking a friend to lunch, or donating to charity? Despite people's strong belief that spending on themselves would make them happier, research shows that people who engage in prosocial spending are reliably happier than those who spend on themselves

(Dunn, Aknin, & Norton, 2008; Hill & Howell, 2014; for a review, see Dunn, Aknin, & Norton, 2014). Moreover, people who chronically spend on others are happier people overall: the more people give, even controlling for how much money they make, the higher their well-being (Dunn, Aknin, & Norton, 2008). These results are not limited to affluent consumers in the United States. Indeed, in countries ranging from Canada to Uganda, from India to South Africa, spending on others is both correlated with happiness and causes people to become happier (Aknin et al., 2013). Happiness from giving even occurs among toddlers – a consumer segment seemingly full of "mine-o-saurs" whom we do not expect to be particularly generous (Aknin, Hamlin, & Dunn, 2012).

Why does prosocial spending pay off more than personal spending? Several studies offer hints by identifying critical moderators that enhance the emotional benefits of giving. First, spending on strong ties leads to more happiness than spending on weak ties. Although both lead to more happiness than spending on the self, spending on a friend tends to lead to more happiness than spending on a charity (Aknin, Sandstrom, Dunn, & Norton, 2011). Relatedly, seeing the recipient of one's generosity increases the happiness gained from giving, which underscores the "social" value of prosocial spending (Aknin, et al., 2013). So, are charities and non-profits doomed to have unhappy donors? Luckily, research suggests another critical moderator: the feeling of having had a specific impact. As a result, framing charitable donations as impacting a specific recipient leads to more happiness (Aknin, et al., 2013).

Buying Experiences

A growing set of findings in psychology and consumer research advises that despite the allure of acquiring material possessions, people should acquire experiences to enjoy greater happiness (for a review, see Gilovich, Kumar, & Jampol, in press). Researchers have shown that positive experiences tend to bring greater enduring happiness than positive material purchases (Howell & Hill, 2009; Nicolao, Irwin, & Goodman, 2009; Van Boven & Gilovich, 2003). Compared to material purchases, experiential purchases are more self-defining (Carter & Gilovich, 2012), more interpersonally connecting (Chan & Mogilner, 2014), harder to compare against forgone alternatives (Carter & Gilovich, 2010), more unique (Rosenzweig & Gilovich, 2012), and subject to slower rates of hedonic adaptation (Nicolao, Irwin, & Goodman, 2009). Indeed, even the experience of waiting for an experience is superior to that of waiting for a material good: whereas the former feels like excitement, the latter feels more like impatience (Kumar, Killingsworth, & Gilovich, 2014). Lastly, shared experiences tend to be more enjoyable than solitary experiences (Caprariello & Reis, 2013), suggesting – as with spending on others – the hedonic benefits of using money to create social connection.

Happiness from Time

Thinking about Time

In his famous adage, "Time is money," Benjamin Franklin equates time to money as a scarce resource. Like money, time can be saved, budgeted, wasted, and spent. Although a considerable amount of research in the fields of marketing and psychology focuses on money, dealing with questions of price, willingness to pay, materialism, and wealth; and although searches on Google reveal consumers to be similarly absorbed with money (Gino & Mogilner, 2014), recent research argues for a shift in attention toward time by showing the positive downstream consequences of thinking about time rather than money. This work doesn't look at the effect of *having* money or *having* time, but instead at the arguably broader and more controllable impact of merely thinking about one resource versus the other.

In her 2010 paper, Mogilner demonstrated that directing attention to time instead of money increases individuals' happiness (by motivating them to socialize more and work less). This effect was shown among typical Americans and low-income Americans planning their days, and among café patrons' visiting a local coffee shop. In this latter experiment, people entering a café were asked to take part in a questionnaire that involved unscrambling a series of sentences that surreptitiously exposed them to time-related words, money-related words, or only neutral words. Unbeknownst to them, these participants were then observed to see how they spent their time in the café (i.e., socializing with fellow patrons or doing work), and when exiting the café were asked to complete a second questionnaire about how happy and satisfied they felt. Those who had been primed with time upon entering the café spent a greater proportion of their time socializing and left happier, whereas people who had been primed with money spent more time with their noses buried in books and left less happy. So, even though focusing on money motivates people to work more (which is useful to know when looking for that extra push to meet a looming deadline), passing the hours working does not translate into greater happiness. Spending time with loved ones does, and a shift in attention toward time proves an effective means to motivate this happy behavior.

Gino and Mogilner (2014) later tested how focusing on time (vs. money) influences morality, and in so doing provided insight into the mechanism underlying the positive effect of thinking about time on happiness. Whereas thinking about money makes people more likely to cheat, thinking about time makes people less likely to cheat, which happens because thinking about time pushes people to reflect more on themselves. The researchers showed this through both the mediating role of self-reflection and the presence of a mirror, which elicited the same effect as priming time. Thus, drawing attention to time seems to nudge people to consider their time in life as ultimately finite, which encourages them to act in ways they can be happy with when holding up this figurative mirror to who they are.

The self-reflecting quality of time also impacts the happiness consumers enjoy from their products. Activating the concept of time leads consumers to be both more likely to purchase and more likely to enjoy products than when the concept of money is activated. Mogilner and Aaker (2009) demonstrated this effect among customers purchasing a cup of lemonade from a lemonade stand, university students thinking about their iPods, restaurant patrons asked about eating out, and typical consumers evaluating their cars. As an example, students first asked how much time they had spent on their iPod liked their iPod significantly more than students who were first asked how much money they had spent on their iPod. This was because thinking about their temporal investment made the students feel that the product said more about who they are than did thinking about their financial investment. (Notably, activating money leads to a more favorable effect than activating time for prestige possessions and highly materialistic consumers – where instead of one's experience with the product, one's possession of the product is a clearer reflection of the self.) The benefits of directing consumers' attention to time rather than money have also been documented in the context of charitable giving (Liu & Aaker, 2008). Because thinking about giving time to a charitable cause evokes greater happiness than thinking about giving money to that cause, donation solicitations that first ask for time produce greater donations – both in the form of time and money.

Not only can thinking about the broad construct of time influence happiness, but so can the *way* people think about time. In particular, how much time people feel like they have left in life and their associated appreciation of the present moment influence how happiness is experienced. Mogilner, Kamvar, & Aaker (2011) studied the emotions expressed on millions of personal blogs in order to understand how people experience feeling happy. This analysis, along with a series of laboratory experiments and surveys, identified two primary forms of happiness: one associated with feeling excited and the other associated with feeling calm. Moreover, through using the bloggers' profile information, the researchers could examine who was expressing each type of happiness and identified a gradual, age-based shift, such that people in their teens and twenties were more likely to experience happiness as excitement, but as people got older, they became more likely to experience happiness as calm.

These researchers' subsequently dug into the psychology underlying this shift and examined how it plays out to influence the choices consumers make (Mogilner, Aaker, & Kamvar, 2012). They concluded that because younger people typically have a longer future ahead of them, the more future-oriented emotion of excitement tends to feel more positive in its alignment with these youngsters' eagerness for that future. However, as people get older, their future becomes more limited and calm starts to feel more positive in its alignment with these more "mature" adults' appreciation of the present moment. Therefore, in pursuit of products that will make them feel happy, younger consumers (or those who eagerly await their futures) are more likely to choose exciting options, whereas older consumers (or those who appreciate the present) are more likely to choose calming options. Notably, an individual's temporal orientation toward the future or present can be manipulated such that young people can instead pursue and experience happiness from calm, and older people can instead pursue and experience happiness from excitement. This means that although the way people experience happiness is dynamic and naturally shifts over the course of life, it is also malleable. Furthermore, whether people experience happiness more from excitement or calm plays into the choices they make, such as the music they listen to, the type of tea they drink, and the brand of water they buy.

Even though young people generally view the remainder of their lives to be relatively long (Carstensen, Isaacowitz, & Charles, 1999), when asked the question, "Is life short or long?" the majority of people (irrespective of age) answer that life is short. They also tend to believe that life is hard rather than easy, which puts the majority of people in agreement with Hobbes's view of life as "nasty, brutish, and short." Norton, Anik, Aknin, and Dunn (2011) tested whether such a philosophy of life relates to happiness. They asked people two binary choice questions – "Is life short or long?" and "Is life easy or hard?" – and measured their happiness. The results revealed that holding the short-hard philosophy is associated with less happiness compared to a long-easy philosophy. Larsen and McKibban (2008) investigated another philosophy proposed by Rabbi Hyman Schachtel in 1954: "Happiness is not having what you want, but wanting what you have." To test this maxim, the researchers asked people whether or not they had, and the extent to which they wanted, fifty-two material items. This allowed the researchers to quantify how much their participants wanted what they had and how much they had what they wanted. The results showed that both variables had distinct and positive effects on happiness, and wanting what you have helps explain the positive effect of gratitude on happiness.

Together these findings suggest that focusing on the broad notion of time increases happiness and that thinking about time in a particular way (as long or short, and with respect to the future or the present) can influence not only how much happiness people feel but also how they experience happiness.

Spending Time

How does spending time influence happiness, and are there particular ways of spending time that produce greater happiness? A group of papers examining the former showed that investing time in product creation can increase how happy consumers subsequently are with that product. Two papers by Norton, Mochon, and Ariely in 2012 uncovered what they called the "IKEA effect." Their findings showed that individuals who built IKEA boxes, folded origami frogs, or constructed sets of Legos were willing to pay more for their finished product than were individuals who had been presented with these same products already assembled by an expert. Whether a self-proclaimed "do-it-yourselfer" or not, it turns out that spending time to successfully assemble a product makes people feel competent and accomplished. The sense of accomplishment tied to these self-assembled products drives people's value for the products. A similar "I designed it myself" effect uncovered by Franke, Schreier, and Kaiser (2010) shows that the benefits of product assembly also pertain to product design. Individuals who designed their own T-shirt or set of skis were willing to pay more for these products than individuals presented with "off-the-shelf" versions of these products. This may not initially seem all that surprising, since designing one's own T-shirt allows consumers to customize their shirts to fit their individual tastes; however, the researchers showed that participants were willing to pay more for a T-shirt that they had designed themselves, even when it looked (and was) exactly the same as the off-the-shelf version. As with the IKEA effect, an increased sense of accomplishment played an underlying role. In both cases, investing time into a product provides feelings of accomplishment, which afford consumers greater happiness from these products. Buechel and Janiszewski (2014) more recently noticed that such benefits may be specific to cases in which design and assembly are combined. When consumers are tasked with designing and assembling their products but these activities are separated, the time that consumers are required to spend becomes onerous. In related work, Moreau, Bonney, and Herd (2011) showed that customization of products is particularly positive when the product is intended as a gift for someone else. In a study among women tasked with designing a tote bag either for herself or for a friend using a real customization website, the researchers found that the women who created their tote bag as a gift were willing to pay significantly more than those who created their tote bag for themselves.

Both the IKEA effect and the "I designed it myself" effect were driven by an increased sense of accomplishment from spending time on a product. This happiness from "doing" may be tapping into something even more fundamental. Hsee, Yang, and Wang (2010) found that although people tend to choose to remain idle, busy people are happier than their idle counterparts. The researchers found across two studies that among college students who had a spare fifteen minutes between two surveys, those who spent the time walking to deliver their first survey to a faraway location felt happier than those who delivered their first survey to a nearby location and idly waited for the next survey to begin.

Mogilner, Chance, and Norton (2012) also noted that despite people's inclination not to exert themselves in their temporal expenditures, doing so can have surprisingly positive ramifications. In particular, although time-constrained people tend to be stingy with their time, if they were to instead give some of their time away, they might feel *less* constrained by time. Four experiments showed that individuals who spent between five and thirty minutes on someone else subsequently felt as though they had more time than did individuals who had wasted that time, spent that time on themselves, or received that time as a windfall. One study, for instance, asked participants to recall a recent expenditure of time that was either for someone else or for themselves. The researchers then asked these individuals how much time they felt like they had and how that expenditure made them feel. The results indicated that although giving time made participants feel more connected to others, it was actually their increased sense of efficacy that was responsible for the positive effect on time affluence. Spending time to help others makes people feel as though they have accomplished more within a given amount of time, such that they can do more with their time in general. This makes time seem more expansive. Therefore, when feeling time-constrained, people should become more generous with their time, despite their inclinations to be less so.

While these papers speak to the potential happiness that can come from investing one's time into products and other people, there is also work that has looked at whether there are temporal expenditures that tend to be happier in and of themselves. Do some experiences tend to be happier than others? Keinan and Kivetz (2011) found that even though staying at a freezing ice hotel or eating such a peculiar food as bacon ice cream may not be particularly pleasant in the moment, people are motivated to collect unusual and extreme experiences in an effort to build their "experiential CV." Additionally, Zauberman, Ratner, and Kim (2009) found that people are motivated to protect their special experiences by not repeating them. Bhattacharjee and Mogilner (2014) examined the happiness derived from different types of experiences more directly. They compared the happiness associated with extraordinary experiences (those that are infrequent and go beyond the realm of everyday life – like incredible vacations and life milestones, such as graduations and weddings) and ordinary experiences (those that are frequent and within the realm of everyday life – like indulging in a delicious treat or having lunch with a friend). Bhattacharjee and Mogilner measured the happiness produced by over 1,800 self-reported experiences that people recalled, imagined, or posted on Facebook and found that the amount of happiness enjoyed from ordinary and extraordinary experiences depended on people's age – more specifically, how much time they felt they had left in life. Whereas younger people enjoyed greater happiness from extraordinary experiences, ordinary experiences became increasingly associated with happiness as people got older, such that ordinary experiences produced as much happiness as extraordinary experiences when people felt they had limited time remaining. An exploration into the multiple factors that might explain this age-based effect produced evidence for the underlying role of self-definition. Irrespective of age, self-defining experiences produce greater happiness, but the type of experiences people use to define themselves seems to change with age. Whereas extraordinary experiences are particularly self-defining for young people, older people are more likely to define themselves using the ordinary things that fill their daily lives.

By measuring people's happiness immediately before and after their attendance of religious services and going to the gym, Mochon, Norton, and Ariely (2008) also noted the potential happiness from frequent, ordinary experiences. They found not only that people were happier exiting the experience than entering it, but the frequency with which people engaged in these experiences was positively related to their overall happiness. Through frequent positive boosts, these seemingly minor experiences promise a long-lasting impact on happiness.

Aaker, Rudd, and Mogilner (2011) proposed five principles of happy ways to spend time to complement Dunn and Norton's (2013, and Dunn, Gilbert, & Wilson's, 2011) principles of happy ways to spend money. These principles include spending time on the right activities, expanding your time, and being aware that happiness changes over time.

Effects of Happiness

Having discussed factors that influence happiness, we now turn to factors that are influenced by happiness. A review paper in 2005 in *Psychological Bulletin* by Lyubomirsky, King, and Diener delineated results revealing happiness to have positive consequences across our three domains of life: work, interpersonal relationships, and health. For instance, in the workplace, happiness was found to make employees more creative, more collaborative, and more flexible in their problem solving. In social settings, happiness was found to make people more liked by others and more liking of others, more outgoing and in-tune with others' feelings, and more prosocial with an increased tendency to volunteer. In the health domain, happiness was found to increase people's thresholds for pain, to make them more likely to follow treatment regimes, and to increase immune functioning. This list includes just experimental results that allow for a causal inference, but the review also included myriad correlational and longitudinal results, which further identify the benefits of feeling happy, such as living longer.

There have since been more papers investigating how happiness influences consumers' thinking and behavior. A nice example by Labroo and Patrick (2009) shows how being in a good mood elevates people's thinking so that they see the big picture. They reasoned that being in a positive mood signals the situation to be benign, which allows people to distance themselves psychologically from the situation. Feeling happy thus increases abstract construal and high-level thinking. On the other hand, a negative mood signals that danger may be imminent. This leads people to take a more proximal perspective that results in a concrete low-level construal. Indeed, participants who were made to feel happy (either through something as subtle as exposure to smiley-face bullet points or as vivid as intricately describing the happiest day of their life) were more likely to (1) generate abstract descriptions of activities (e.g., painting a room was described as beautifying the environment rather than choosing a favorite paint color), (2) endorse abstract goals (e.g., studying for an exam was more important when thinking about why they should study rather than how they should study), and (3) prefer products advertised with abstract messages (e.g., an orange juice was better liked when framed as helping you "invest in your future health" rather than "ensure your health today").

Happiness influences not only the way consumers think but also the way consumers behave. For instance, people put in a good mood were more likely to prefer the first option presented to them (except when instructed to withhold their judgments until all options had been presented, in which case they preferred the last option (Qiu & Yeung, 2008), to perform worse on tasks subject to predecisional distortion or overconfidence (Meloy, Russo, & Miller, 2006), to engage in emotion regulation when holding the belief that emotion is fleeting (Labroo & Mukhopadhyay, 2009), and to be less suspicious of persuasion attempts (DeCarlo & Barone, 2009). Notably, not all of these are positive outcomes.

In an effort to identify ways to increase consumers' happiness, the bulk of the research covered in this chapter treats happiness as the dependent variable. The research covered in this section, however, treats happiness as the independent variable to identify the consequences of feeling happy. A recent paper by Aknin, Dunn, and Norton (2012) took yet another approach and employed happiness as both the independent variable and the dependent variable, which allowed them to identify a positive feedback loop between prosocial spending and happiness. With their prior work showing that spending money on others boosts happiness, here they manipulated happiness by instructing half of their participants to recall an occasion in which they had spent money on others. All participants then reported their happiness and their propensity to spend money on others in the future. The results offered a potential path to sustainable happiness whereby prosocial spending increases happiness, which in turn encourages the happy behavior of spending prosocially. This suggests that one potential outcome of happiness is more happiness.

Consumption Happiness

Although consumers all strive to live happy lives, this is admittedly a fairly lofty pursuit. Consumer researchers have therefore tended to instead focus on understanding the more specific and perhaps attainable goal of feeling happy with the individual choices consumers make and the more discrete experiences that comprise consumers' lives. In this portion of the chapter, we highlight recent work that examines factors that influence the happiness consumers enjoy from their choices and experiences.

Choice Satisfaction

A longstanding and important literature has shown that people *want* choice (e.g., Deci & Ryan, 1985; Ryan & Deci, 2000). Due to the sense of freedom and autonomy that choosing affords, outcomes that are personally selected are often associated with greater task enjoyment and evaluations (Langer 1975; Langer & Rodin 1976). More recently, however, there has been a growing stream of research exploring *when* choosing leads to greater happiness with one's chosen outcome, as well as when the responsibility of choosing can be taxing and lead to *less* happiness. For instance, Botti and McGill (2006) found that when consumers cannot perceive differences between their options, choosing has little effect on their ultimate choice satisfaction. Indeed, consumers have a particularly difficult time perceiving variety within their choice set when there is an overwhelmingly large number of options (Mogilner, Rudnick, & Iyengar, 2008). However, when consumers are able to see the differentiation among their options, choosing increases satisfaction with one's choice when selecting from a set of positive outcomes (e.g., gourmet coffees or chocolates), but decreases satisfaction with one's choice when selecting from a set of negative outcomes (e.g., gross smells; Botti & McGill, 2006). Unless consumers see their options as differentiated, they do not feel as though they have really made a choice and thus do not enjoy the credit (or suffer the blame) from arriving at a positive (or negative) outcome.

Although consumers typically insist on exercising choice, choosing can lead to less happy outcomes. Botti and Hsee (2010) showed this among undergrads presented with ten multiple choice questions from the quantitative section of the General Records Examinations (GRE). Participants were given twenty minutes and told that they would get 40 cents for each correct answer, lose 10 cents for each incorrect answer, and get 20 cents for each minute remaining after they had answered all ten questions. Half of the participants were allowed to choose which ten questions out of a larger set of fifty they would answer, whereas the other half were assigned their ten questions. Students who were free to choose their questions spent more time, felt worse while taking the test, and were not more accurate than those who had not been given a choice. Still, additional studies showed that participants expect to enjoy tasks more and to do better on those tasks when given the freedom to choose, which suggests that consumers' preference for choice may partly stem from their tendency to underweight the temporal costs of searching for the best option relative to the benefits provided by that option.

A set of studies conducted by Mogilner, Shiv, and Iyengar (2013) similarly showed that consumers' satisfaction with whatever they choose can be undermined when consumers hold out hope for a more perfect option. Indeed, comparing the satisfaction and commitment levels between choosers presented with their options simultaneously (all at once) or sequentially (one at a time), the researchers found that sequentially presented options elicit a focus on the future and hope for a better option to come, which leaves choosers less satisfied with and ultimately less committed to whichever option they had selected. Although this effect was demonstrated among individuals choosing a piece of gourmet chocolate, a nail polish color for a salon manicure, or a bottle of Italian red wine from a wine tasting, it has implications for individuals who will likely be presented with their options one at a time for such critical outcomes as a job, house, or spouse. These findings advise that to enjoy greatest happiness from choice, consumers should give up hoping for what is to come and remain focused on that which they currently have. Gu, Botti, and Faro (2013) offer an easy method by which to psychologically conclude the decision-making process so as to increase satisfaction with one's choice: do a physical act that communicates "choice closure," like closing the menu after deciding which option you'll order.

Although consumers think they want choice – preferring to compare their options side-by-side (Hsee & Zhang, 2004) and to be fully informed about the specifications of their options (Hsee, Yang, Gu, & Chen, 2009) – consumers may end up happier with their chosen outcome if they had evaluated each option separately and were not provided with specification information. Yang, Hsee, Liu, & Zhang (2011) showed this among college students who chose between two bath towels: one that looked nicer and one that was 7 millimeters thicker. Since participants would be using their chosen towel for a week in their communal dorm, and millimeter differences in towel thickness are difficult to subjectively assess, a towel's appearance should be more critical to students' happiness while using the towel than its thickness. Indeed, when asked a week later, the students who had selected the better-looking towel were happier with their chosen towel than those who had selected the thicker towel, but the better-looking towel was less likely to have been selected when the thickness specifications were presented at the time of choice and when the two towels had been presented side by side.

Research has also shown that the size of an assortment and the way it is categorized influences consumers' happiness with their chosen option, irrespective of the objective outcome. For instance, Diehl and Poynor (2010) built on prior literature that showed overly large assortments to reduce consumers' happiness with their choices (Chernev, 2003; Gourville & Soman, 2005; Iyengar & Lepper, 2000; Lehmann 1998) by identifying an explanation for why this choice overload effect might occur. It has to do with expectations. When selecting a birthday card for a colleague, those who chose from one hundred cards had higher expectations to be able to precisely match their card preferences than did those who chose from only ten cards. The disconfirmation of their high expectations resulted in choosers in the one hundred assortment size condition to be less satisfied with their chosen birthday card than choosers in the ten assortment size condition (Diehl & Poynor, 2010). Fortunately for consumers, Mogilner, Rudnick, and Iyengar (2008) showed that such choice overload can be offset through option categorization. The researchers found that consumers selecting a magazine from a vast supermarket magazine aisle or a cup of coffee from an extensive menu of blends were more satisfied with their chosen option when the assortment was divided into more (vs. fewer) categories, regardless of whether the category labels contained information. This "mere categorization effect" was stronger among consumers unfamiliar with the choice set – those who were unable to perceive differences among the vast array of options without some help. Poynor and Wood (2010) later found that the *way* options are categorized can also have an effect. For knowledgeable consumers, unexpected categorization provides a newness cue, which engages them in the decision process, thereby increasing their satisfaction with their chosen option. For less know-ledgeable consumers, however, such unexpected categorization reduces choosers' satisfaction.

All of these papers highlight how one's experience during the decision-making process can influence how happy one is with his or her choice, regardless of the objective qualities of that outcome. Even after the choice has been made and the decision-making process is complete, the way consumers engage with prod-ucts can also influence their happiness with those products. Vohs, Wang, Gino, and Norton (2013) found that when consumers perform a ritual before consum-ing a product, they enjoy the product more. They showed this effect among students consuming such tasty products as chocolate and lemonade, as well as the more healthful snack of carrots. It seems that enacting a ritual draws people further into the consumption experience, such that they are more involved and savor the product more. As noted previously, investing time into products and attending to that time spent makes consumers feel more connected to those products, and thus happier with them (Mogilner & Aaker, 2009).

Experience Enjoyment

A growing body of work identifies factors – such as uncertainty, segregation of positive and negative features, and the presence of other consumers – that influence how much happiness consumers enjoy from a consumption experience.

Although people are driven to understand events in order to make them more predictable and replicable, increased understanding can also make these events less enjoyable. That is to say that *un*certainty can increase enjoyment. Norton, Frost, and Ariely (2007) demonstrated this in what they called the "less is more effect." In one of their studies, online daters were given a list of traits describing a potential person to date and were asked how much they liked the person. The number of traits presented varied between one and ten. Although daters believed that more information would lead to greater liking, the study results showed the opposite relationship. Knowing more led to liking less. Uncertainty also benefits romance with respect to knowing how a potential partner feels in return. Whitchurch, Wilson, and Gilbert (2010) found that people like their crush more when they are uncertain about whether their crush likes them back. Uncertainty apparently holds people's attention and keeps them from fully making sense of and adapting to a particular outcome. Even outside the realm of dating, this logic helps explain why uncertainty prolongs the enjoyment of experiences. For instance, students who received a gift of $1 were happier when the description on the gift card was hard to figure out, and movie viewers enjoyed a film for longer when they were unsure of which of two alternate endings was true (Wilson, Centerbar, Kermer, & Gilbert, 2005). Uncertainty is particularly positive when a potential positive outcome is easy to imagine, such as winning a lucky draw (Lee & Qiu, 2009). Even though the human mind is designed to reduce uncertainty to help make sense of the world, maintaining some degree of uncertainty allows consumers to enjoy their positive experiences for a bit longer.

Experience enjoyment is not only influenced by projecting forward but also by reflecting back. When consumers have the chance to reflect on their past experiences, they are motivated to frame them in a positive light. Cowley (2008) documented this tendency, which she termed "hedonic editing." She found that gamblers use this to justify their behavior, and it entails segregating large gains from negative experiences (i.e., focusing on the silver lining) and combining large losses with large gains from positive experiences (i.e., hiding the less than fully pleasant truth). More generally, the way consumers remember their experiences determines their continued enjoyment.

Lastly, the extent to which consumers enjoy an experience is largely influenced by others – others who selected the experience and others who shared in the experience. With respect to the former, Chan and Mukhopadhyay (2010) showed that when choosing an experience for oneself (e.g., which of two concerts to attend), evaluation of the chosen experience initially increases, but then levels out over time. On the other hand, when someone else chooses that same experience for you, any delay leads to less favorable evaluations. With respect to the latter, Caprariello and Reis (2013) suggest that shared experiences lead to greater happiness than solo experiences. They specifically found that experiences are more likely to be shared than material possessions, which they argued explains the greater happiness produced by experiential than material purchases. Whether sharing an experience leads to greater happiness, however, depends on if those sharing in the experience see themselves as in agreement with each other (Raghunathan & Corfman, 2006). Whereas congruence in opinions enhances the enjoyment of the shared experience (both by engendering a feeling of belonging and increasing confidence in the accuracy of one's views), incongruence in opinions diminishes such enjoyment. Ramanathan and McGill (2007) similarly found that consumers' enjoyment of an experience moves in accordance with others' enjoyment when they are able to observe the others' facial expressions. Furthermore, the resulting coherence leads to more positive retrospective evaluations of the experience. Thus, it is not just whether an experience is shared that determines enjoyment, but also the extent to which the level of enjoyment is shared.

Where to Go from Here

While the body of research we have reviewed here offers a glimpse into the immense progress that has been made in understanding the psychology of consumer happiness and well-being, the relative newness of the field means that many critical, interesting, and generative questions remain to be explored. In the following subsections, we offer several avenues that we believe are likely to be fruitful – though, of course, our list is far from comprehensive.

Varieties of Well-being

The focus of much of the research we have reviewed is on happiness – often assessed using a simple scale that asks consumers to state their happiness from "not at all" to "a great deal" (or something similar). Of course, a construct of such centrality to human life as *happiness* is bound to be more multifaceted and complex. Are people looking to maximize the happiness they feel in the moment, or are they looking to maximize the happiness they feel as they reflect back on an experience or their life overall (Mogilner & Norton, 2015)? Although the behaviors that contribute to each will frequently be the same, there are important cases where they diverge, thus pitting the "experiencing self" against the "remembering self" (Kahneman, 2011). Going forward, researchers should more specifically measure each in order to identify consumption behaviors that differently influence these temporally distinct forms of happiness. Another path is to start deconstructing our understanding of what "happiness" means to consumers. One step in this direction can be seen in the research by Mogilner, Kamvar, and Aaker (2011), which demonstrates how different consumers experience happiness differently, preferring either calm or excitement. Relatedly, Rudd, Vohs, and Aaker (2012) assessed and manipulated a specific positive emotion – awe – offering a compelling example of how drilling more deeply into one aspect of happiness offers insight into consumer behavior.

It is also important to remember that feeling happy is but one aspect of overall well-being. Baumeister, Vohs, Aaker, and Garbinsky (2013) highlight meaningfulness as another. While happiness is a critical element of consumer well-being, consumers' search for meaning and purpose deserves far more attention. Diener and colleagues have further proposed *flourishing* and *thriving* as two forms of a more encompassing construct of well-being (Diener et al., 2010; Su, Tay, & Diener, 2014). It is likely that each will be affected by different consumption experiences. Therefore, another area for future research is to begin to unpack the different aspects and varieties of consumer well-being in the hopes of developing a more complete view.

Aside from identifying specific constructs to explore, recent research also suggests that a different approach to emotion – one that focuses not on one emotion but on the range and variety of emotions that consumers experience – may also offer novel insight into consumer well-being. Certainly, consumer behavior researchers have examined consumers' preferences for product variety (e.g., Simonson, 1990) and the ways in which product variety affects consumption and satiation (e.g., Redden, 2008), but the effect of diversity and variety of emotions on consumption has yet to be explored. Simply put, what movie or product is more desirable: one that elicits many emotions or one that elicits few? Research suggests that for overall well-being, greater emodiversity – the variety and relative abundance of the emotions people experience – is an independent and integral component of the human emotional ecosystem that predicts both mental and physical health (Quoidbach et al., 2014). Interestingly, this research suggests that greater diversity of negative emotions also improves well-being, such that it is better to feel sad and angry than simply angry. Future research should explore the implications of emodiversity for consumer satisfaction and happiness.

Building on this question of the role of variety, future research should look to uncover optimal ways for consumers to piece together their behaviors and experiences. We reviewed recent work that identifies which individual experiences are more conducive to happiness (Bhattacharjee & Mogilner, 2014; Caprariello & Reis, 2013). Although there is still much more that can be done on that question alone, another approach is to identify which combinations of experiences are particularly conducive to happiness. For instance, Etkin and Mogilner (2015) have started to investigate whether filling one's day with a greater variety of activities leads to more or less happiness. They have found that whereas variety over the course of a day (or week, or month) increases happiness, incorporating more variety into shorter time intervals has the reverse effect, and instead reduces happiness because of a thwarted sense of progress. Relatedly, Shah and Alter (2014) have found that the way consumers categorize a series of experiences influences their sense of progress, which compels different strategies for categorizing positive and negative events. Such insights into the best ways for consumers to schedule their time offer a promising avenue through which to educate consumers on things that they can actively implement in their lives to increase their daily well-being. A good example is the work by Sellier and Avnet (2014), which shows that people who follow an event-time scheduling style (where tasks are organized based on their order of completion) are better able to savor positive experiences than people who follow a clock-time scheduling style (where tasks are organized based on a clock).

Well-being from Consumer Behaviors

In addition to delving deeper into the impact of different aspects of well-being and the role of variety, consumer behavior researchers should more carefully consider how many of the typical consumer behaviors under investigation – such as word of mouth, social networking, and conspicuous consumption – affect not only behavior but also consumer emotions. In other words, in addition to documenting ways in which various factors increase consumers' propensity to consume, researchers should consider how those consumption decisions affect consumer happiness – for better and for worse – in an effort to design marketing interventions that do not merely change behavior but also increase happiness.

Social Networking and Word of Mouth

Researchers studying word of mouth – both online and offline – have primarily been interested in understanding the factors that increase the likelihood that a piece of information will be passed along to others (e.g., Godes & Mayzlin, 2004, 2009). At the same time, however, some research suggests that usage of online social networking sites is associated with declines in consumer well-being (e.g., Kross et al., 2013). As a result, consumer behavior researchers should be more careful in balancing whether interventions that increase word of mouth – and time on social networking sites – may be decreasing consumer happiness. Recent research hints at the power of emotion in online social networks; for example, the emotional valence of online content shapes its likelihood of being passed on to others (Berger & Milkman, 2012), and consumers' Facebook newsfeeds can be manipulated to impact consumer happiness (Kramer, Guillory, & Hancock, 2014). We suggest that researchers should search for interventions that both increase desired marketing outcomes (such as increased engagement) as well as consumer well-being. One such opportunity arises from recent research documenting the emotional benefits of matchmaking – of connecting two unacquainted people to each other (Anik & Norton, 2014). By encouraging users of online social networks to play matchmaker, marketers may be able to increase engagement and network density while simultaneously improving well-being.

Conspicuous Consumption

Consumer researchers have become increasingly interested in issues of power and status as shapers of consumer behavior (for a review, see Chapter 12 in this volume). In one intriguing set of studies, for example, Ordabayeva and Chandon (2011), showed that – in contrast to existing theory – consumers are most likely to engage in conspicuous consumption when in environments where most of their neighbors have similar possessions. In such cases, one purchase has the power to leapfrog a consumer ahead of more neighbors, making conspicuous consumption a more effective means of attaining status. In another investigation, consumers placed near the bottom of an income distribution displayed "last place aversion," becoming more likely to gamble in an effort to escape being in last place (Kuziemko, Buell, Reich, & Norton, 2014; see also Haisley, Mostafa, & Loewenstein, 2008). And in Bellezza, Gino, and Keinan (2014), consumers selectively chose to dress down in some contexts in order to demonstrate their higher status. But what are the emotional consequences of such status-seeking behaviors? A large body of research suggests that social comparison, status seeking, and inequality can be detrimental to emotional health (e.g., Adler, Marmot, McEwen, & Stewart, 1999; Wilkinson & Pickett, 2010). Researchers should therefore examine how raising status concerns for consumers affects not only their consumption decisions but also their well-being. One early and notable example is the work by Rucker, Dubois, and Galinsky (2011), which examines the impact of different levels of power not only on consumers' spending decisions but also on their subsequent happiness.

Conclusion

The seventeenth-century philosopher and mathematician Blaise Pascal observed that "All men seek happiness. Whatever different means they employ, they all tend to this end." This motivation to be happy is readily observable among consumers centuries later. Quite simply, consumers *want* to be happy. We are proud to be members of a field that is beginning to dedicate its efforts and talents to empirically inform this fundamental human pursuit. We hope that Seligman and Mick are similarly proud to see that their calls for such research have been enthusiastically answered. Over the past decade, a notable body of work has emerged that not only documents the different means consumers tend to employ in their search for happiness but also helps guide consumers to their desired end. Note, however, that even though tremendous strides have been made, there is much more to be done. Because consumer experience and the experience of happiness, let alone well-being more broadly, are so complex (and some would say nebulous), every compelling finding produces even more questions. We have mentioned a mere sampling of such questions, and only hope that this chapter serves to spark further interest, efforts, and questions pertaining to the meaningful improvement of consumer happiness and well-being.

References

Aaker, J., Rudd, M., & Mogilner, C. (2011). If money does not make you happy, consider time. *Journal of Consumer Psychology, 21*(2), 126–130.

Aaker, J. & Smith, A. (2010). *The Dragonfly Effect*. San Francisco, CA: Jossey-Bass.

Adler N. E., Marmot, M., McEwen, B. S., & Stewart, J. (1999). *Socioeconomic Status and Health in Industrial Nations: Social, Psychological and Biological Pathways*. New York: Ann NY Acad Sci.

Aknin, L. B., Barrington-Leigh, C. B., Dunn, E. W., Helliwell, J. F., Burns, J., Biswas-Diener, R., Kemeza, I., Nyende, P., Ashton-James, C. E., & Norton, M. I. (2013). Prosocial spending and well-being: Cross-cultural evidence for a psychological universal. *Journal of Personality and Social Psychology, 104*(4), 635–652.

Aknin, L. B., Dunn, E. W., & Norton, M. I. (2012). Happiness runs in a circular motion: Evidence for a positive feedback loop between prosocial spending and happiness. *Journal of Happiness Studies, 13*(2), 347–355.

Aknin, L. B., Dunn, E. W., Sandstrom, G. M., & Norton, M. I. (2013). Does social connection turn good deeds into good feelings? On the value of putting the "social" in prosocial spending. *International Journal of Happiness and Development, 1*(2), 155–171.

Aknin, L. B., Hamlin, J. K., & Dunn, E. W. (2012). Giving leads to happiness in young children. *PLoS One, 7*(6), e39211.

Aknin, L. B., Norton, M. I., & Dunn, E. W. (2009). From wealth to well-being? Money matters, but less than people think. *Journal of Positive Psychology, 4*(6), 523–527.

Aknin, L. B., Sandstrom, G. M., Dunn, E. W., & Norton, M. I. (2011). It's the recipient that counts: Spending money on strong social ties leads to greater happiness than spending on weak social ties. *PLoS One, 6*(2), e17018.

Aknin, L. B., Dunn, E. W., Whillans, A. V., Grant, A. M., & Norton, M. I. (2013). Making a difference matters: Impact unlocks the emotional benefits of prosocial spending. *Journal of Economic Behavior and Organization, 88*, 90–95.

Anik, L., & Norton, M. I. (2014). Matchmaking promotes happiness. *Social Psychological and Personality Science, 5*, 644–652.

Baumeister, R. F., Vohs, K. D., Aaker, J. L., & Garbinsky, E. N. (2013). Some key differences between a happy life and a meaningful life. *Journal of Positive Psychology, 8*(6), 505–516.

Bellezza, S., Gino, F., & Keinan, A. (2014). The red sneakers effect: Inferring status and competence from signals of nonconformity. *Journal of Consumer Research, 41*(1), 35–54.

Berger, J., & Milkman, K. L. (2012). What makes online content viral? *Journal of Marketing Research, 49*(2), 192–205.

Bhattacharjee, A., & Mogilner, C. (2014). Happiness from ordinary and extraordinary experiences. *Journal of Consumer Research, 41*(1), 1–17.

Botti, S., & Hsee, C. K. (2010). Dazed and confused: How the temporal costs of choice freedom lead to undesirable outcomes. *Organizational Behavior and Human Decision Processes, 112*(2), 161–171.

Botti, S., & McGill, A. L. (2006). When choosing is not deciding: The effect of perceived responsibility on satisfaction. *Journal of Consumer Research, 33*(2), 211–219.

Buechel, E. C., & Janiszewski, C. (2014). A lot of work or a work of art: How the structure of a customized assembly task determines the utility derived from assembly effort. *Journal of Consumer Research, 40*(5), 960–972.

Caprariello, P. A., & Reis, H. T. (2013). To do, to have, or to share? Valuing experiences over material possessions depends on the involvement of others. *Journal of Personality and Social Psychology, 104*(2), 199–215.

Carstensen, L. L., Isaacowitz, D. M., & Charles, S. T. (1999). Taking time seriously: A theory of socioemotional selectivity. *American Psychologist, 54*(3), 165–181.

Carter, T. J., & Gilovich, T. (2010). The relative relativity of material and experiential purchases. *Journal of Personality and Social Psychology, 98*(1), 146–159.

Carter, T. J., & Gilovich, T. (2012). I am what I do, not what I have: The differential centrality of experiential and material purchases to the self. *Journal of Personality and Social Psychology, 102*(6), 1304–1317.

Chan, C., & Mogilner, C. (2014). Experiential gifts are more socially connecting than material gifts. (Working paper.)

Chan, E., & Mukhopadhyay, A. (2010). When choosing makes a good thing better: Temporal variations in the valuation of hedonic consumption. *Journal of Marketing Research, 47*(3), 497–507.

Chernev, A. (2003). When more is less and less is more: The role of ideal point availability and assortment in consumer choice. *Journal of Consumer Research, 30*(2), 170–183.

Cowley, E. (2008). The perils of hedonic editing. *Journal of Consumer Research, 35*(1), 71–84.

DeCarlo, T. E., & Barone, M. J. (2009). With suspicious (but happy) minds: Mood's ability to neutralize the effects of suspicion on persuasion. *Journal of Consumer Psychology, 19*(3), 326–333.

Deci, E. L., & Ryan, R. M. (1985). The general causality orientations scale: Self-determination in personality. *Journal of Research in Personality, 19*(2), 109–134.

Diehl, K., & Poynor, C. (2010). Great expectations?! Assortment size, expectations, and satisfaction. *Journal of Marketing Research, 47*(2), 312–322.

Diener, E., & Biswas-Diener, R. (2002). Will money increase subjective well-being? A literature review and guide to needed research. *Social Indicators Research, 57*(2), 119–169.

Diener, E., Wirtz, D., Tov, W., Kim-Prieto, C., Choi, D., Oishi, S., & Biswas-Diener, R. (2010). New well-being measures: Short scales to assess flourishing and positive and negative feelings. *Social Indicators Research, 97*(2), 143–156.

Dunn, E. W., Aknin, L. B., & Norton, M. I. (2008). Spending money on others promotes happiness. *Science, 319*(5870), 1687–1688.

Dunn, E. W., Aknin, L. B., & Norton, M. I. (2014). Prosocial spending and happiness: Using money to benefit others pays off. *Current Directions in Psychological Science, 23*(1), 41–47.

Dunn, E., & Norton, M. (2013). *Happy Money: The Science of Smarter Spending*. New York: Simon & Schuster.

Dunn, E. W., Gilbert, D. T., & Wilson, T. D. (2011). If money doesn't make you happy, then you probably aren't spending it right. *Journal of Consumer Psychology, 21*(2), 115–125.

Etkin, J. & Mogilner, C. (2015). Does variety increase happiness? (Working paper.)

Franke, N., Schreier, M., & Kaiser, U. (2010). The "I designed it myself" effect in mass customization. *Management Science, 56*(1), 125–140.

Frey, B. S., & Stutzer, A. (2000). Happiness, economy and institutions. *The Economic Journal, 110*(446), 918–938.

Gilovich, T., Kumar, A., & Jampol, L. (in press). A wonderful life: Experiential consumption and the pursuit of happiness. *Journal of Consumer Psychology.*

Gino, F., & Mogilner, C. (2014). Time, money, and morality. *Psychological Science, 25*(2), 414–421.

Godes, D., & Mayzlin, D. (2004). Using on-line conversations to study word-of-mouth communication. *Marketing Science, 23*(4), 545–560.

Godes, D., & Mayzlin, D. (2009). Firm-created word-of-mouth communication: Evidence from a field test. *Marketing Science, 28*(4), 721–739.

Gourville, J. T., & Soman, D. (2005). Overchoice and assortment type: When and why variety backfires. *Marketing Science, 24*(3), 382–395.

Gu, Y., Botti, S., & Faro, D. (2013). Turning the page: The impact of choice closure on satisfaction. *Journal of Consumer Research, 40*(2), 268–283.

Haisley, E., Mostafa, R., & Loewenstein, G. (2008). Subjective relative income and lottery ticket purchases. *Journal of Behavioral Decision Making, 21*(3), 283–295.

Hill, G., & Howell, R. T. (2014). Moderators and mediators of pro-social spending and well-being: The influence of values and psychological need satisfaction. *Personality and Individual Differences, 69*, 69–74.

Howell, R. T., & Hill, G. (2009). The mediators of experiential purchases: Determining the impact of psychological needs satisfaction and social comparison. *The Journal of Positive Psychology, 4*(6), 511–522.

Hsee, C. K., Yang, Y., Gu, Y., & Chen, J. (2009). Specification seeking: How product specifications influence consumer preferences. *Journal of Consumer Research, 35*(6), 952–966.

Hsee, C. K., Yang, A. X., & Wang, L. (2010). Idleness aversion and the need for justified busyness. *Psychological Science, 21*(7), 926–930.

Hsee, C. K., & Zhang J. (2004). Distinction bias: Misprediction and mischoice due to joint evaluation. *Journal of Personality and Social Psychology, 86*(5), 680–695.

Iyengar, S. S., & Lepper, M. R. (2000). When choice is demotivating: Can one desire too much of a good thing? *Journal of Personality and Social Psychology, 79*(6), 346–357.

Kahneman, D. (2011). *Thinking, Fast and Slow*. New York: Farrar, Straus and Giroux.

Kahneman, D., & Deaton, A. (2010). High income improves evaluation of life but not emotional well-being. *Proceedings of the National Academy of Sciences, 107* (38), 16489–16493.

Kahneman, D., Krueger, A. B., Schkade, D., Schwarz, N., & Stone, A. A. (2006). *Would you be happier if you were rich? A focusing illusion. Science, 312*(5782), 1908–1910.

Keinan, A., & Kivetz, R. (2011). Productivity orientation and the consumption of collectable experiences. *Journal of Consumer Research, 37*(6), 935–950.

Kramer, A. D., Guillory, J. E., & Hancock, J. T. (2014). Experimental evidence of massive-scale emotional contagion through social networks. *Proceedings of the National Academy of Sciences, 111*(24), 8788–8790.

Kross, E., Verduyn, P., Demiralp, E., Park, J., Lee, D. S., Lin, N., & Shablack, H. (2013). Facebook use predicts declines in subjective well-being in young adults. *PLoS One, 8*(8), e69841.

Kumar, A., Killingsworth, M. A., & Gilovich, T. (2014). Waiting for Merlot: Anticipatory consumption of experiential and material purchases. *Psychological Science, 25*(10) 1924–1931.

Kuziemko, I., Buell, R. W., Reich, T., & Norton, M. I. (2014). Last-place aversion: Evidence and redistributive implications. *Quarterly Journal of Economics, 129*, 105–149.

Labroo, A. A., & Mukhopadhyay, A. (2009). Lay theories of emotion transience and the search for happiness: A fresh perspective on affect regulation. *Journal of Consumer Research, 36*(2), 242–254.

Labroo, A. A., & Patrick, V. M. (2009). Psychological distancing: Why happiness helps you see the big picture. *Journal of Consumer Research, 35*(5), 800–809.

Langer, E. J. (1975). The illusion of control. *Journal of Personality and Social Psychology, 32*(2), 311–328.

Langer, E. J., & Rodin, J. (1976). The effects of choice and enhanced personal responsibility for the aged: A field experiment in an institutional setting. *Journal of Personality and Social Psychology, 34*, 191–198.

Larsen, J. T., & McKibban, A. R. (2008). Is happiness having what you want, wanting what you have, or both? *Psychological Science, 19*(4), 371–377.

Lee, Y. H., & Qiu, C. (2009). When uncertainty brings pleasure: The role of prospect imageability and mental imagery. *Journal of Consumer Research, 36*(4), 624–633.

Lehmann, D. R. (1998). Customer reactions to variety: Too much of a good thing? *Journal of the Academy of Marketing Science, 26*(1), 62–65.

Liu, W., & Aaker, J. (2008). The happiness of giving: The time-ask effect. *Journal of Consumer Research, 35*(3), 543–557.

Lyubomirsky, S., King, L., & Diener, E. (2005). The benefits of frequent positive affect: Does happiness lead to success? *Psychological Bulletin, 131*(6), 803–855.

Meloy, M. G., Russo, E., & Miller, E. G. (2006). Monetary incentives and mood. *Journal of Marketing Research, 43*(2), 267–275.

Mick, D. (2005, September). *The Presidential Address: Meaning and Mattering through Transformative Consumer Research*. Speech presented at the North American Conference of the Association for Consumer Research, San Antonio, TX.

Mochon, D., Norton, M. I., & Ariely, D. (2008). Getting off the hedonic treadmill, one step at a time: The impact of regular religious practice and exercise on well-being. *Journal of Economic Psychology, 29*(5), 632–642.

Mochon, D., Norton, M. I., & Ariely, D. (2012). Bolstering and restoring feelings of competence via the IKEA effect. *International Journal of Research in Marketing, 29*(4), 363–369.

Mogilner, C. (2010). The pursuit of happiness: Time, money, and social connection. *Psychological Science, 21*(9), 1348–1354.

Mogilner, C., & Aaker, J. (2009). "The time vs. money effect": Shifting product attitudes and decisions through personal connection. *Journal of Consumer Research, 36* (2), 277–291.

Mogilner, C., Aaker, J., & Kamvar, S. D. (2012). How happiness affects choice. *Journal of Consumer Research, 39*(2), 429–443.

Mogilner, C., Chance, Z., & Norton, M. I. (2012). Giving time gives you time. *Psychological Science, 23*(10), 1233–1238.

Mogilner, C., Kamvar, S. D., & Aaker, J. (2011). The shifting meaning of happiness. *Social Psychological and Personality Science, 2*, 395–402.

Mogilner, C., & Norton, M. (2015). Choice of happiness: Experienced versus remembered. (Working paper.)

Mogilner, C., Rudnick, T., & Iyengar, S. S. (2008). The mere categorization effect: How the presence of categories increases choosers' perceptions of assortment variety and outcome satisfaction. *Journal of Consumer Research, 35*(2), 202–215.

Mogilner, C., Shiv, B., & Iyengar, S. S. (2013). Eternal quest for the best: Sequential (vs. simultaneous) option presentation undermines choice commitment. *Journal of Consumer Research, 39*(6), 1300–1312.

Moreau, C. P., Bonney, L., & Herd, K. B. (2011). It's the thought (and the effort) that counts: How customizing for others differs from customizing for oneself. *Journal of Marketing, 75*(5), 120–133.

Nicolao, L., Irwin, J. R., & Goodman, J. K. (2009). Happiness for sale: Do experiential purchases make consumers happier than material purchases? *Journal of Consumer Research, 36*(2), 188–198.

Norton, M. I., Anik, L., Aknin, L. B., & Dunn, E. W. (2011). Is life nasty, brutish, and short? Philosophies of life and well-being. *Social Psychological and Personality Science, 2*(6), 570–575.

Norton, M. I., Frost, J. H., & Ariely, D. (2007). Less is more: The lure of ambiguity, or why familiarity breeds contempt. *Journal of Personality and Social Psychology, 92*(1), 97–105.

Norton, M. I., Mochon, D., & Ariely, D. (2012). The IKEA effect: When labor leads to love. *Journal of Consumer Psychology, 22*(3), 453–460.

Ordabayeva, N., & Chandon, P. (2011). Getting ahead of the Joneses: When equality increases conspicuous consumption among bottom-tier consumers. *Journal of Consumer Research, 38*(1), 27–41.

Poynor, C., & Wood, S. (2010) Smart subcategories: How assortment formats influence consumer learning and satisfaction. *Journal of Consumer Research, 37*(1), 159–175.

Qiu, C., & Yeung, C. W. (2008). Mood and comparative judgment: Does mood influence everything and finally nothing? *Journal of Consumer Research, 34*(5), 657–669.

Quoidbach, J., Gruber, J., Mikolajczak, M., Kogan, A., Kotsou, I. & Norton, M. I. (2014). Emodiversity and the emotional ecosystem. *Journal of Experimental Psychology: General, 143*, 2057–2066.

Raghunathan, R., & Corfman, K. (2006). Is happiness shared doubled and sadness shared halved? Social influence on enjoyment of hedonic experiences. *Journal of Marketing Research, 43*(3), 386–394.

Ramanathan, S., & McGill, A. L. (2007). Consuming with others: Social influences on moment-to-moment and retrospective evaluations of an experience. *Journal of Consumer Research, 34*(4), 506–524.

Redden, J. P. (2008). Reducing satiation: The role of categorization level. *Journal of Consumer Research, 34*(5), 624–634.

Rosenzweig, E., & Gilovich, T. (2012). Buyer's remorse or missed opportunity? Differential regrets for material and experiential purchases. *Journal of Personality and Social Psychology, 102*(2), 215–223.

Rucker, D. D., Dubois, D., & Galinsky, A. D. (2011). Generous paupers and stingy princes: Power drives consumer spending on self versus others. *Journal of Consumer Research, 37*(6), 1015–1029.

Rudd, M., Vohs, K., & Aaker, J. (2012). Awe expands people's perception of time, alters decision making and enhances well-being. *Psychological Science, 23*(10), 1130–1136.

Ryan, R. M., & Deci, E. (2000). Self-determination theory and the facilitation of intrinsic motivation, social development, and well-being. *American Psychologist, 55*(1), 68–78.

Seligman, M. E. P. (1998, September). *The President's Address (Annual Report)*. Speech presented at the National Press Club, Washington, DC.

Sellier, A. L., & Avnet, T. (2014). So what if the clock strikes? Scheduling style, control, and well-being. *Journal of Personality and Social Psychology: Attitudes and Social Cognition, 107*(5), 791–808.

Shah, A. K., & Alter, A. L. (2014). Consuming experiential categories. *Journal of Consumer Research, 41*(4).

Simonson, I. (1990). The effect of purchase quantity and timing on variety seeking behavior. *Journal of Marketing Research, 27*(2), 150–162.

Su, R., Tay, L., & Diener, E. (2014). The development and validation of Comprehensive Inventory of Thriving (CIT) and Brief Inventory of Thriving (BIT). *Applied Psychology: Health and Well-Being.*

Van Boven, L., & Gilovich, T. (2003). To do or to have? That is the question. *Journal of Personality and Social Psychology, 85*(6), 1193–1202.

Vohs, K. D., Wang, Y., Gino, F., & Norton, M. I. (2013). Rituals enhance consumption. *Psychological Science, 24*(9), 1714–1721.

Whitchurch, E. R., Wilson, T. D., & Gilbert, D. T. (2010). "He loves me, he loves me not ...": Uncertainty can increase romantic attraction. *Psychological Science, 22*, 172–175.

Wilkinson, R., & Pickett, K. (2010). *The Spirit Level: Why Equality Is Better for Everyone*. London: Penguin.

Wilson, T. D., Centerbar, D. B., Kermer, D. A., & Gilbert, D. T. (2005). The pleasures of uncertainty: Prolonging positive moods in ways people do not anticipate. *Journal of Personality and Social Psychology, 88*(1), 5–21.

Yang, A. X., Hsee, C. K., Liu, Y., & Zhang, L. (2011). The supremacy of singular subjectivity: Improving decision quality by removing objective specifications and comparisons. *Journal of Consumer Psychology, 21*(4), 393–404.

Zauberman, G., Ratner, R. K., & Kim, K. (2009). Memories as assets: Strategic memory protection in choice over time. *Journal of Consumer Research, 35*(5), 715–728.

2 Attitude Change and Persuasion

Past, Present, and Future Directions

Zakary L. Tormala and Pablo Briñol

A fundamental goal of consumer psychology research is to shed light on the underlying psychological factors that drive consumer behavior. With this objective in mind, consumer psychologists have long emphasized the importance of understanding *attitudes*. Attitudes refer to the general and relatively enduring evaluations people have of other people, objects, or ideas. Stated differently, attitudes represent the extent to which one likes or dislikes something – for example, a product, company, or brand. Because attitudes can be one of the core drivers of consumer behavior (e.g., choosing one product over another, purchasing now versus later, spending more versus less, and so on), they have been the subject of considerable scrutiny in consumer psychology. Not surprisingly, perhaps, consumer psychologists have been especially interested in understanding the means by which consumers' attitudes can be shaped or changed, particularly in the context of persuasive messages.

In this chapter, we provide an overview of past, present, and future research on attitude change and persuasion. More specifically, we (1) review some of the classic research on persuasion to provide an overview of this area, (2) highlight what we view as some of the crucial recent developments in this field, and then (3) discuss several unanswered questions and opportunities for future research. Our goal is not to be exhaustive in our coverage of any of one of these topics, but rather to offer an illustrative review of the field and, hopefully, some encouragement to pursue what we see as some of the novel and important next steps. Before turning to our review, it is useful to consider some general background issues.

Attitudes

As noted, attitudes refer to our general evaluations of people (e.g., politicians), objects (e.g., new products), or issues (e.g., social policies). Attitudes can vary in a number of important ways. First, of course, they can vary in *valence*. Some attitudes are positive, some are negative, and others are relatively neutral. Consumers' attitudes toward a particular car, for instance, might range from positive (liking it) to neutral (neither liking nor disliking it) to negative (disliking it). Moreover, attitudes can differ in their *extremity*, or the extent to which they deviate from neutral (Abelson, 1995). Indeed, two consumers could both report liking a car (i.e., have attitudes of the same valence), but differ in the extent to which they like it, such that one has a mild liking for the car and the other a more extreme liking. Given the well-documented link between attitudes and behavior (e.g., Fishbein & Ajzen, 1975), these individuals could be expected to behave differently toward the car despite both holding positive attitudes.

In addition to varying in valence and extremity, attitudes can differ in their underlying *bases*. According to the classic tripartite theory (Rosenberg & Hovland, 1960; Zanna & Rempel, 1988), attitudes can be based to varying degrees on affect or feelings (e.g., "this car feels fun to drive"), cognition or beliefs (e.g., "this car is fuel efficient"), and past or current behavior (e.g., "we have always driven this kind of car in my family"). Interestingly, people's perceptions of their attitude bases can be as important as their actual attitude bases in determining their future thoughts and actions (e.g., See, Petty, & Fabrigar, 2008). Generally speaking, persuasive messages are more effective at inducing attitude change when they match (e.g., an emotional appeal targeting an affect-based attitude) rather than mismatch (e.g., a rational appeal targeting an affect-based attitude) the actual or perceived basis of the target attitude (e.g., Edwards, 1990; Fabrigar & Petty, 1999; Mayer & Tormala, 2010; See, Petty, & Fabrigar, 2008; See, Fabrigar, & Petty, 2013). As noted, people can base their attitudes not only on affect and cognition, but also on behavioral information (see Briñol & Petty, 2008). We will address this embodiment approach in the present review by describing research showing that people's physical postures, facial expressions, and bodily movements can all play an important role in attitude formation and change.

Attitudes can also differ in their underlying strength. *Attitude strength* refers to the durability and impact of an attitude (Petty & Krosnick, 1995). Durability encapsulates an attitude's resistance to change, such that strong (relative to weak) attitudes generally persist longer over time and are more resistant in the face of attack. Impact refers to the attitude's influence over thoughts and behavior; in general, strong attitudes exert greater influence on thoughts (e.g., produce more attitude-consistent thinking) and behavior (e.g., produce more attitude-consistent behavior) than do their weaker counterparts. Thus, attitude strength can be a crucial moderator of persuasion effects – making it harder to change attitudes in some cases than in others – and also a crucial target of influence (e.g., strategically increasing consumers' attitude strength when they already hold the desired position).

Over the years, attitude strength has been construed, and operationally defined, in a number of different ways (see Bassili, 1996; Petty & Kronsick, 1995). Some indicators of strength have been viewed as relatively objective in nature. For instance, attitude extremity (distance from neutrality; Abelson, 1995), attitude accessibility (the speed with which an attitude comes to mind; Fazio, 1995), and attitude ambivalence (the presence of conflicting positive and negative evaluations of the same object, which tends to weaken an attitude; Thompson, Zanna, & Griffin, 1995) can all be viewed as somewhat objective in that they do not require people to introspect and report their perception of their own strength. Indeed, people can be ambivalent and not even know it if, for example, they have just a single consciously endorsed attitude that is univalent (e.g., "I do not like scary movies at all") but contradicted by opposing cultural associations ("scary movies are quite popular") or even a former attitude that is now rejected ("I used to like them"). In such cases, people can show signs of *implicit ambivalence* that weakens their attitudes even though they do not perceive or endorse having any attitude conflict (Petty & Briñol, 2012; Petty, Briñol, & DeMarree, 2007; Petty, Tormala, Briñol, & Jarvis, 2006).

Other strength indicators are more subjective in nature in that they revolve around people's perceptions of their own attitudes and whether they are personally important (Boninger, Krosnick, Berent, & Fabrigar, 1995), backed by extensive knowledge (Davidson, Yantis, Norwood, &Montano, 1985), and held with confidence or certainty (for reviews, see Rucker, Tormala, Petty, & Briñol, 2014; Tormala & Rucker, 2007). Of importance, regardless of the particular operationalization of strength in a study, and whether it is viewed as objective or subjective, the dominant perspective is that each dimension or type of strength matters because it shapes the attitude's durability and impact.

Finally, attitudes themselves, and the measures used to study them, have been viewed as varying along a continuum ranging from explicit to implicit. Indeed, after a long tradition of assessing the impact of influence treatments, such as persuasive messages, on attitudes using deliberative self-report measures (Eagly & Chaiken, 1993; Petty & Wegener, 1998), recent work has also used measures that tap the more automatic evaluations associated with objects, issues, and people. Techniques that assess automatic evaluative associations without directly asking people to report their attitudes are often referred to as *implicit measures*, whereas assessments that tap more deliberative and acknowledged evaluations are referred to as *explicit measures* (see Gawronski & Payne, 2010; Petty, Fazio, & Briñol, 2009, for reviews). Although implicit and explicit measures sometimes appear discrepant (e.g., Briñol, Petty, & Wheeler, 2006), they do often yield the same outcome (e.g., both revealing that a person likes a particular brand). In the present review, we will focus mainly on deliberative, self-report attitudes as those have been the primary focus of researchers in consumer psychology, though recent research has begun to test the effects of persuasive messages on implicit attitudes as well (Briñol, Petty, & McCaslin, 2009; Perkins & Forehand, 2010; Smith, De Houwer, & Nosek, 2013).

Persuasion: Source, Message, and Recipient Factors

There are many ways to organize the literature on attitude change and persuasion. One way, which we follow in the current chapter, revolves around the basic distinction among source, message, and recipient variables. Stated differently, researchers often think about persuasion in terms of *who* says *what* to *whom*. Indeed, classic persuasion research essentially viewed these categories as the "3 Ws" of persuasion, whereby maximizing relevant variables within these buckets would facilitate successful persuasion outcomes. In the 1950s, when persuasion became a central focus of social and consumer psychology research, this was the prevailing view on the factors determining a given message's likely success or failure. Since then, we have learned much more about the underlying psychological mechanisms driving persuasion and the interactions among source, message, and recipient factors, but it remains a useful trichotomy for organizing the literature. For the remainder of this chapter, we will briefly review some of the classic research on persuasion, dive deeper into recent developments in this field, and then highlight open questions and new directions, using the source-message-recipient framework as a guide for organizing and understanding the literature.

Classic Conceptualizations: Who Says What to Whom?

Source Factors

Source factors in persuasion refer to aspects of the individual or company that crafts and delivers the persuasive message. There is a voluminous body of research examining the many dimensions of message sources that can play a role in persuasion (for a review, see Briñol & Petty, 2009a). These dimensions include source credibility, attractiveness, and numerical status, among many others. The classic view on these source dimensions is that because they are positively valenced, more of them – for example, more credibility or more attractiveness – fosters more persuasion. Thus, the conventional persuasive prescription was to increase favorable source factors as a means to persuasion. For a historical review on this main effect approach to persuasion, we refer readers to Petty and Briñol (2008).

Perhaps the most frequently studied source factor is source credibility (Kelman & Hovland, 1953; for reviews see Petty & Wegener, 1998; Pornpitak-pan, 2004). Source credibility is an umbrella construct that captures both the expertise and trustworthiness of the source of a message. *Expertise* generally refers to the amount of knowledge one has or one's perceived ability to provide accurate and truthful information. *Trustworthiness* describes one's perceived honesty or motivation to provide accurate and truthful information. In general, whether credibility is operationalized in terms of expertise (Rhine & Severance, 1970) or trustworthiness (Mills & Jellison, 1967), the classic finding is that the more credibility the source of a message has, the more persuaded his or her audience will be. As noted by Petty and colleagues (e.g., Petty, 1997; Petty & Briñol, 2008), early theories of persuasion often suggested that there was likely to be just one mechanism or process that was responsible for whichever outcome was produced. For example, an expert source was thought to increase persuasion by getting a person to learn or internalize the message arguments (Kelman, 1958).

In addition to credibility, other source dimensions such as attractiveness have proven important to persuasion. In general, the more the audience likes the source, the more persuasion there tends to be. As one example, physically attractive sources have been found to be more persuasive than physically unattractive sources (Snyder & Rothbart, 1971). Relatedly, a source's celebrity status has been shown to influence persuasion (e.g., Petty, Cacioppo, & Schumann, 1983); under some conditions, celebrities are more persuasive than unfamiliar sources. Furthermore, consistent with the widely documented similarity-attraction effect (i.e., the notion that people tend to like similar others more than dissimilar others; Byrne, 1971), more persuasion tends to occur when the source of a message is similar to the audience. And importantly, source similarity can increase persuasion regardless of whether the similar dimension is important (e.g., when the source and recipient share important values) or unimportant (e.g., when the source simply mimics the recipient's subtle non-verbal behaviors; Fleming & Petty, 2000). Importantly, while source credibility has been argued to induce agreement because of increased acceptance of the message arguments, the traditional view of attractiveness was that it increases persuasion by boosting identification with the message source (Kelman, 1958).

Potentially related to the dimensions of credibility and attractiveness, a source's numerical status – that is, the degree to which the source is in the statistical majority or minority on a topic – can play an important role in persuasion. All else being equal, people have been shown to be more influenced by numerical majorities than by numerical minorities (see Wood et al. 1994; Tormala, Petty, & DeSensi, 2010). For instance, a persuasive message that ostensibly represents 75 percent of surveyed consumers' views tends to be more effective at inducing attitude change than a message representing only 25 percent of consumers' views. Traditionally, majorities were thought to be more persuasive because people seek to belong to and be accepted by the majority group (Moscovici, 1980, 1985).

Finally, source power can be important as well. Power typically involves an individual's perceived ability to control others' outcomes by providing or withholding rewards or punishments (see Chapter 12 in this volume). In general, powerful sources have been found to produce more attitude change and persuasion than powerless sources (e.g., Festinger & Thibaut, 1951; French & Raven, 1959). Classic work on this topic suggested that this effect stems from mere compliance and should be attenuated in the absence of the powerful source (e.g., Kelman, 1958).

Message Factors

In addition to source factors, message factors are crucial to persuasion. Message factors refer to characteristics of the message itself; for example, what is written or spoken in an advertisement, product review, or restaurant recommendation. Viewed differently, whereas source factors refer to features of the person or company delivering the message, message factors pertain to what that person or company actually says. Broadly speaking, message factors can be viewed in terms of what the source says (e.g., what position they take, how compelling the arguments are), how much of it they say (e.g., number of arguments), and how often they say it (e.g., argument repetition).

Perhaps the most fundamental aspect of a persuasive message is its position, or direction. That is, does the message argue against or in favor of the attitude object? Even more crucial in some ways is whether the message is proattitudinal or counterattitudinal, meaning it is congruent or incongruent with recipients' initial attitudes, respectively (Clark & Wegener, 2013). All else equal, proattitudinal messages tend to be more convincing and persuasive than counterattitudinal messages (e.g., Lord, Ross, & Lepper, 1979). The traditional explanation for this effect is that proattitudinal messages fall within the recipient's latitude of acceptance (Sherif & Hovland, 1961) and, thus, are evaluated more favorably.

A related distinction is whether a message is one-sided or two-sided (Hovland, Lumsdaine, & Sheffield, 1949). Whereas one-sided messages contain arguments that advocate exclusively in the direction of the advocated position or product, two-sided messages contain arguments both against and in favor of it. A considerable amount of research has shown that two-sided messages can be more persuasive than one-sided messages, and this has been thought to occur because considering both sides increases the source's perceived trustworthiness (Crowley & Hoyer, 1994; Etgar & Goodwin, 1982; Pechmann, 1992). Even simply acknowledging minor blemishes or product flaws has been found to boost persuasion under some conditions by making the remaining positive features seem even more positive (Ein-Gar, Shiv, & Tormala, 2012).

Beyond the direction or valence of arguments in a message, there are many other message features that play an important role in persuasion. For example, argument quality – or message strength – refers to how compelling or convincing the arguments in a message are. For instance, a strong message that advocates changing a particular behavior (such as exercising) might highlight consequences of that behavior that are highly desirable, highly likely, and extremely important. A weaker message, by contrast, would highlight consequences that are less desirable, likely, or important. A voluminous body of research suggests that people tend to be more persuaded by strong rather than weak arguments (see Petty & Cacioppo, 1986; Petty & Wegener, 1998), because strong arguments elicit more favorable message-relevant thoughts.

The sheer number of arguments presented in a message can impact persuasion as well. Specifically, messages with more arguments often lead to more persuasion than messages with fewer arguments (Calder, Insko, & Yandell, 1974; Josephs, Giesler, & Silvera, 1994; Petty & Cacioppo, 1984). Similarly, in product evaluation studies, it has been shown that products with more attributes sometimes appear more desirable to consumers than products with fewer attributes (e.g., Sela & Berger, 2012). This effect is consistent with the notion of a general numerosity heuristic (Pelham, Sumarta, & Myaskovsky, 1994), in which people operate according to a "more is better" rule.

As a final example, research has found that simply repeating a message can increase persuasion. This effect was originally explained by the fact that repetition facilitates learning the message arguments. As it turned out, the number of repetitions and other contextual factors were critical to this effect. For example, a few repetitions enhances persuasion, but many repetitions can undo and even reverse this effect (Cacioppo & Petty, 1979; 1989; Gorn & Goldberg, 1980; Miller, 1976). The logic is similar to that articulated in the literature on mere repeated exposure (e.g., Bornstein, 1989; Grush, 1976; Zajonc, 1968), where initial repetition enhances positive associations but overexposure can attenuate this effect.

Recipient Factors

Finally, recipient factors also are a critical determinant of persuasion. These refer to features or characteristics of the target audience – that is, the individuals who will receive the persuasive message. Recipient factors can be stable or situational (e.g., intelligence or current mood, respectively) and can vary along numerous dimensions. Of central import in early persuasion research were variables that affect motivation and the ability to process and understand persuasive messages, as well as variables that directly affect interpretations of those messages. Consider intelligence. Past research shows that that as an audience's intelligence increases, the audience becomes more difficult to persuade (Rhodes & Wood, 1992). The initial explanation for this effect was that intelligence provides individuals with the ability both to evaluate the persuasiveness of an appeal and to counter the information presented.

Of course, there are numerous recipient factors relevant to persuasion beyond intelligence, such as self-esteem, personality, knowledge, and many others. Perhaps the most studied recipient variable concerns the emotional state of the recipient of the persuasion attempt (Petty & Briñol, 2015). As one classic example, happiness has been shown to increase persuasion as a result of classical conditioning (i.e., people associating their current happiness with the message or attitude object). Another prominent recipient factor that has received considerable attention pertains to the recipient's overt physical behavior, or what they are currently doing with their bodies (see Briñol & Petty, 2008). For instance, Cacioppo, Priester, and Berntson (1993) found that neutral Chinese ideographs (irrelevant stimuli for the sample of participants) presented during arm flexion (a pulling or approach behavior) were subsequently evaluated more favorably than ideographs presented during arm extension (a pushing or avoidance behavior). Similarly, Wells and Petty (1980) found that inducing mere head nodding could influence one's agreement with a persuasive message. Like mood effects, one reason these embodiment effects could occur is through classical conditioning, whereby positive behaviors become directly associated with the attitude object (Staats & Staats, 1958).

Another recipient factor, which we devote more attention to later in this chapter, includes recipients' "cognitive feelings" (Clore & Parrott, 1994), such as processing ease or fluency. In general, ease is associated with more persuasion than difficulty; that is, people form more favorable attitudes toward stimuli that feel easy to process (e.g., Labroo, Dhar, & Schwarz, 2008; Lee & Labroo, 2004) and are more persuaded when they can easily generate supportive reasons (e.g., because just a few are requested; Wänke, Bohner, & Jurkowitsch, 1997). The original account for this effect made reference to an availability heuristic whereby people infer that there were more reasons available when it was easy rather than difficult to generate examples (Schwarz et al., 1991).

Contextual Factors: When and Why

After a few decades of research focusing on understanding source, message, and recipient factors as a prescription for successful persuasion, researchers in the 1980s turned their attention away from asking *whether* these variables affected persuasion and instead began to emphasize *when* and *why* they affect persuasion (for a more thorough discussion of the reasons for this shift, see Petty, 1997). This new wave of research provided deeper insight into a number of puzzling issues in the field, including why some factors (e.g., an expert source) sometimes increased persuasion but in other cases undermined it, as well as why attitude change sometimes seemed durable and impactful (e.g., producing attitudes that guide behavior) but other times seemed rather transitory or ephemeral.

The result of this shifted focus was the development of new theories capable of accounting for multiple effects, processes, and consequences of persuasion. Of particular import were the elaboration likelihood model (ELM; Petty & Briñol, 2012; Petty & Cacioppo, 1986), and the heuristic-systematic model (HSM; Chaiken & Ledgerwood, 2012; Chaiken, Liberman, & Eagly, 1989). These frameworks helped shed new light on the multiple ways a given variable could affect attitude change in different contexts. One crucial insight, first articulated in the ELM, was that the psychological processes mediating the effects of any persuasion variable on attitude change could be organized into a finite set that operate at different points on an elaboration continuum. That is, the process guiding a given variable's effect on persuasion – determining the presence or absence of the effect, the direction of the effect, and the durability and downstream impact of the effect – depended critically on the amount of thinking the recipient was likely to engage in. Under low thinking conditions, variables can affect persuasion by operating as a simple cue or heuristic. Under relatively high thinking conditions, the same variables might impact persuasion through more thoughtful means such as by affecting the direction of thoughts that come to mind or serving as a piece of evidence (i.e., an argument) to be scrutinized. When thinking is not constrained to be low or high, the same variables can shape persuasion by affecting the amount of message-relevant thinking that occurs. In the parlance of the ELM, the processes engaged at the low end of the elaboration continuum are referred to as the *peripheral route*, whereas processes engaged at the high end of the continuum are referred to as the *central route*. The more persuasion is based on thoughtful processing – that is, the more central route the process is – the more it tends to persist over time, resist attempts at change, and have consequences for other judgments and behavior (Petty, Haugtvedt, & Smith, 1995).

To offer one example of the organizational and predictive utility of this multiprocess framework, consider source credibility. Traditional views held that credible sources were more persuasive because people have a heuristic that, "if an expert says it, it must be true" (Chaiken, 1980). Consistent with this perspective, early research revealed that source credibility effects on persuasion are more prominent when people are not very motivated or able to think carefully (Petty, Cacioppo, & Goldman, 1981). However, subsequent studies suggested that source credibility does not always operate according to a simple cue or heuristic. Also, more credibility does not always foster more persuasion. That may be the dominant effect, but a more nuanced look indicates that source credibility can produce different effects in different circumstances.

For example, when thinking is not initially constrained to be high or low, credibility can influence persuasion by affecting the amount of thinking people do. When people are unsure whether a message warrants or needs scrutiny, they can use the credibility of the source as a guide – for instance, thinking more about a message from a knowledgeable source than a source lacking in knowledge (e.g., Heesacker, Petty, & Cacioppo, 1983). Furthermore, if high credibility entices someone to think more about a message but that message has weak arguments, then high credibility can be associated with *reduced* persuasion, the opposite of its effect when serving as a simple heuristic. Consistent with this logic, having an expert source sometimes increases persuasion when message arguments are strong but decreases it when message arguments are weak (Bohner, Ruder, & Erb, 2002; Heesacker, Petty, & Cacioppo, 1983).

When processing motivation and ability are high, such as when the message feels highly relevant (Petty & Cacioppo, 1979) and recipients are undistracted (Petty, Wells, & Brock, 1976), people think more carefully about a message. Nevertheless, that thinking can be quite biased – for example, by source credibility. Chaiken and Maheswaran (1994) found that when a message topic was personally important but ambiguous, meaning that recipients were motivated to think about the message but it was not clearly cogent or specious in its own right, an expert (vs. non-expert) source produced more persuasion by biasing the direction of people's thoughts. Under very similar conditions, Tormala, Briñol, and Petty (2006) also found that credible sources could increase persuasion by biasing the valence of recipients' message-relevant thinking.

By now, considerable research has demonstrated that numerous variables beyond source credibility can have this same complexity of effects and mechanisms depending on recipients' initial motivation to process (see Petty & Wegener, 1998). As one additional example, a message recipient's happiness can act as a simple cue to persuasion under low thinking conditions (Slovic, Finucane, Peters, & Macgregor, 2002), be analyzed as an argument (Martin, Ward,

Achee, & Wyer, 1993) or bias the direction of thoughts (Petty, Schumann, Richman, & Strathman, 1993) under high thinking conditions, and influence his or her amount of thinking when that thinking is initially unconstrained to be high or low (Schwarz, Bless, & Bohner, 1991). Based on its ability to integrate this diversity of effects and processes, the ELM emerged as the dominant theory of persuasion, specifying the processes by which source, message, recipient, and context factors shape persuasive outcomes and processes (for historical reviews of the ELM, see Briñol & Petty, 2012; Petty & Briñol, 2012).

Current Developments: A Metacognitive Reconceptualization

As just described, following the first few decades of research on persuasion, we gained much insight into the complexity of source, message, and recipient effects with the development of multiprocess theories such as the ELM and HSM. Research guided by these frameworks shed light on the multiple roles that source, message, and recipient variables play in persuasion. Continuing in this vein, research in the past two decades years has made great strides in deepening our understanding of the processes through which persuasion variables exert their impact and expanding our insight into their diverse and previously unidentified outcomes. Perhaps the greatest shift in this domain has been the new focus on metacognitive factors in persuasion. *Metacognition* refers to thinking about thinking – that is, people's thoughts about their own or other people's thoughts, judgments, and mental processes (for a review, see Briñol & DeMarree, 2012; Petty, Briñol, Tormala, & Wegener, 2007). Recently, there has been an enormous influx of research investigating metacognitive inputs, mechanisms, and outcomes in persuasion.

One of the most influential demonstrations that people's thoughts about their thoughts can be consequential came from research on the *ease of retrieval* paradigm. In the original study on this topic, Schwarz, Bless, Strack, and colleagues (1991) asked participants to list either six (which was easy) or twelve (which was difficult) examples of their own assertiveness. Interestingly, people asked to retrieve fewer examples subsequently viewed themselves as *more* assertive, because their experience of generating or retrieving relevant cognitions was subjectively easier. This cognitive ease, in turn, can lead people to infer that many more such cognitions are likely to be available (Schwarz, 2004) or that those cognitions that came to mind are valid and can be held with confidence (Tormala, Petty, & Briñol, 2002). As we will discuss, this basic idea and finding have fostered numerous and important insights in attitude change and persuasion.

Rucker and Tormala (2012) recently reviewed other metacognitive approaches relevant to the consumer domain. As just as one example, the persuasion knowledge model (Friestad & Wright, 1994, 1995; Kirmani & Campbell, 2004) proposes that consumers hold lay theories about persuasion involving the agent of persuasion, the target of persuasion, and their interaction. Moreover, consumers use these theories to evaluate persuasion attempts (e.g., advertisements and sales pitches), assess their validity and sincerity, and determine whether it is appropriate or inappropriate to be influenced by them. These perceptions, or lay theories, are then used as a basis for responding and yielding to or resisting the influence attempt (for a recent empirical example of naive theories about consumer persuasion, see Briñol, Rucker, & Petty, 2015). Other examples of metacognitive approaches in consumer research that are relevant to understanding attitude and persuasion processes include the accessibility-diagnosticity model (Feldman & Lynch, 1988; Lynch, 2006) and the multiple pathway anchoring and adjustment model (Cohen & Reed, 2006).

In this new wave of metacognition research, particular emphasis has been placed on studying the sense of certainty people have about their own thoughts and attitudes. In general, being certain about a thought or attitude means that one holds the thought or attitude with confidence or conviction and believes it is valid (Rucker et al., 2014). This feeling of confidence or conviction can stem from one's perception that the thought or attitude is correct or simply that it is clear in one's mind (Petrocelli, Tormala, & Rucker, 2007). In either case, certainty can have crucial implications for persuasion and other attitude-relevant outcomes.

For the most part, recent insights into the role of psychological certainty in persuasion has emanated from two research streams. One, termed the self-validation hypothesis (Briñol, Petty, & Tormala, 2004; Petty, Briñol, & Tormala, 2002), has focused on the role of *thought confidence* in persuasion. Conventional research in persuasion largely focused on the amount and valence of people's thinking when they receive persuasive messages. In addition to these two dimensions of thought, the self-validation hypothesis introduced the notion of thought confidence. In essence, the notion is that when individuals receive persuasive messages, it is not only the number and direction of their thoughts that matter but also the confidence with which they hold those individual thoughts (and the extent to which they like their thoughts). Thoughts that are liked and held with high confidence exert more impact on persuasion than thoughts that are disliked or held with low confidence.

In fact, some studies have revealed that having more thoughts in one direction (e.g., positive) can push attitudes in the other direction (e.g., negative) if those thoughts are held with low confidence (e.g., Tormala, Petty & Briñol, 2002). Similarly, rsearch has demonstrated that increasing positive dimensions of a given persuasion variable (e.g., using a source with greater credibility) can sometimes undermine persuasion if doing so boosts confidence in negative thoughts (e.g., because the message contains weak arguments; Tormala, Briñol, & Petty, 2006). These effects are particularly likely to emerge if people are engaged in thoughtful processing and have both the motivation and ability to reflect on their own thinking. Thus, like the ELM, the self-validation hypothesis identifies conditions under which, and new and unique processes through which, normally positive factors can have negative persuasion effects and vice versa.

Another metacognitive factor that has received considerable scrutiny in recent persuasion research is *attitude certainty*. Although attitude certainty has a storied history in attitudes research (see Gross, Holtz, & Miller, 1995), its emergence as a central variable in persuasion is a more recent development (see Rucker et al., 2014). This emergence began with research on resistance to persuasion (Tormala, Clarkson, & Petty, 2006; Tormala & Petty, 2002; see also Petty, Tormala, & Rucker, 2004; Tormala, 2008), where it was observed that, contrary to previous assumptions, when people resisted persuasive attacks on their attitudes, those attitudes did not remain literally unchanged. On the contrary, when people resist persuasion (meaning they received a persuasive message, but their attitude valence and extremity were unchanged), they can perceive and reflect upon this resistance and then make upward or downward adjustments to attitude certainty. Consequently, persuasive messages that seem on the surface to have had no effect on attitude change can actually have an important impact on attitude certainty, which has implications for future behavior, future openness to persuasion, and so on.

Based on these kinds of findings, a great deal of persuasion research has turned from the traditional focus on the amount and direction of thoughts, or even on attitudes per se, to understanding changes in the certainty people associate with those thoughts and attitudes. This metacognitive shift has expanded existing understandings of the effects of persuasion variables on attitudinal outcomes, and it has deepened our insight into the mechanisms driving those effects. In this section, we revisit the source-message-recipient trichotomy to highlight some of the novel insights we have gained as a result of this new metacognitive emphasis. In some areas (e.g., source factors), there has been considerable research on both thought confidence and attitude certainty. In other areas, the attention has been relatively more focused on either attitude certainty (e.g., message factors) or thought confidence (e.g., recipient factors). Thus, it is a developing area of research with much work to be done. In this section, we review relevant work on psychological certainty following the source-message-recipient trichotomy.

Source Effects on Certainty

Consider source effects on metacognitive certainty. These effects have been examined in the context of both thought confidence (and the self-validation hypothesis) and attitude certainty, but in both domains the common emphasis has been on understanding the ways in which classic source variables in persuasion affect metacognitive certainty.

First, various source factors have been shown to influence people's perceptions of their own thoughts. For example, in addition to providing a simple heuristic to persuasion or influencing the amount or valence of thoughts people generate while processing a message, source credibility is now known to influence the confidence with which people hold their thoughts that come to mind during persuasive messages. Consistent with the logic that credibility influences the perceived validity of information contained in a message (Kaufman, Stasson, & Hart, 1999), people tend to have more confidence in their message-relevant thoughts when source expertise and trustworthiness are high rather than low (e.g., Briñol, Petty, & Tormala, 2004). Moreover, because of this effect, source credibility can under some conditions backfire and undermine persuasion. Specifically, when people receive a message containing weak arguments and have negative thoughts about it, high source credibility can increase confidence in those negative thoughts (Tormala, Briñol, & Petty, 2006) and undermine persuasion. Thus, the metacognitive perspective allows us to predict and understand further instances in which normally positive persuasion variables have negative implications for persuasion.

Importantly, this metacognitive effect of source credibility depends on two critical moderators. First, source credibility affects persuasion through thought confidence only under high thinking conditions, such as when participants are relatively high rather than low in need for cognition (Cacioppo & Petty, 1982). Indeed, considering the validity of one's own thoughts requires both motivation and ability to process (Petty, Briñol, & DeMarree, 2007). Under low thinking conditions, source credibility operates as a simple cue to persuasion, as in past research (Petty, Cacioppo, & Goldman, 1981). Second, Tormala, Briñol, and Petty (2007) demonstrated that source credibility affects thought confidence only when the source information follows rather than precedes the persuasive message. When source information precedes a message under high thinking conditions, it biases the direction or valence of thoughts, as reviewed earlier (Chaiken & Maheswaran, 1994). In short, elaboration and timing are two important moderators of self-validation effects.

Like source credibility, majority versus minority source status can affect persuasion by influencing the confidence with which people hold their individual thoughts. In one study, Horcajo, Petty, and Briñol (2010) presented participants with a persuasive message introducing a new company. The message was composed of either strong or weak arguments. Subsequently, source status was manipulated by attributing the message to a source in the numerical minority or majority. As predicted, thought confidence was higher when the source had majority rather than minority status. As a consequence, the majority endorsement increased persuasion when participants had positive thoughts (strong argument condition), but decreased persuasion when participants had negative thoughts (weak argument condition). Again, though, the effect of source status on thought confidence occurred only when source information followed information processing and when elaboration was high (Horcajo, Briñol, & Petty, 2014).

In addition to affecting the confidence people have in their thoughts about a message, source factors can affect the certainty with which people hold their attitudes following a message. For example, recent work indicates that attitude certainty is greater following persuasive messages from high rather than low credibility sources (e.g., Clarkson, Tormala, & Rucker, 2008), even when people resist those messages (Tormala & Petty, 2004a). For instance, if a consumer receives a counterattitudinal message from an expert (as opposed to a non-expert), the consumer can infer that he or she now has access to the best information on the topic. Regardless of whether the consumer counterargues or accepts the message, having access to the most accurate or valid information on the topic tends to augment attitude certainty. Thus, even in the absence of attitude change as it is traditionally defined (in terms of valence and extremity), the credibility of the source of a message can shape meaningful attitudinal outcomes.

The numerical status of a source also affects attitude certainty. For example, although people typically resist persuasive messages from numerical minorities, research by Tormala, DeSensi, and Petty (2007) suggests that this resistance can mask underlying decreases in attitude certainty. The logic is that derogating (or writing off) a message source simply because that source is in the minority is perceived to be an illegitimate thing to do. Therefore, when people resist for that reason, their attitudes remain intact (e.g., they opposed some policy or product, received a message from a minority source, and then continue to oppose it), but they feel less certain about the attitude because they perceive that they have resisted attitude change for an illegitimate reason (see Rucker et al., 2014, for further discussion of legitimacy and certainty).

Message Effects on Certainty

As noted earlier, whether a message argues against or in favor of a given position is one of the most basic dimensions along which it can vary. Although there has not been much consideration of whether positive or negative messages generate greater certainty, there is some evidence that inducing people to think of their attitudes in terms of what or who they oppose, rather than support, leads to greater attitude certainty and more resistance to subsequent change (Bizer, Larsen, & Petty, 2011; Bizer & Petty, 2005). In addition, there is a considerable body of work examining the effects of learning that others oppose or support one's opinion. In particular, people feel more certain about their thoughts and attitudes when they receive high as opposed to low social consensus feedback – that is, when they learn that others agree rather than disagree with their thoughts and evaluations (e.g., Petrocelli, Tormala, & Rucker, 2007; Petty, Briñol, & Tormala, 2002; Visser & Mirabile, 2004). Interestingly, though, recent research suggests that this well-established effect of social consensus on certainty is moderated by one's need for assimilation versus uniqueness (Clarkson, Tormala, Rucker, & Dugan, 2013). Specifically, high consensus fosters greater certainty when people want to belong with or assimilate to others, but low consensus can foster greater certainty when people desire more uniqueness or differentiation.

Relatedly, people also hold tend to hold their attitudes with greater certainty when they perceive them to be based on consideration of both sides of an issue – that is, on both the pros and the cons (Rucker & Petty, 2004; Rucker, Petty, & Briñol, 2008). Even when the valence and extremity of their attitudes are no different (e.g., because considering the cons did not uncover any negatives), merely perceiving that both sides of an issue have been weighed boosts the perception that one's information is more complete. At the same time, if considering both sides of an issue actually reveals conflicting information, such as a favorable product attribute but also a negative customer review, attitude certainty can be lowered as the accuracy of any individual piece of information becomes more questionable (e.g., Koriat, 2012; Smith, Fabrigar, MacDougall, & Wiesenthal, 2008). Thus, perceived consideration of both sides can foster greater certainty as long as that consideration does not yield too much contradictory evidence on a topic.

Argument quality also has been shown to influence attitude certainty. For example, Tormala and Petty (2002; 2004b) found that when people resisted persuasion, the stronger the persuasive message appeared to be, the more certain recipients felt of their original attitudes. In essence, resisting a compelling message is more impressive than resisting a weak or feeble message, leading people to feel more certain about the validity of their original attitudes when those attitudes withstand a strong rather than weak attack. In fact, this effect emerged even when participants across conditions resisted identical messages, but were led to believe that it was strong or weak.

Finally, the amount of information contained in a persuasive message can affect attitude certainty as well. In general, the more information people believe they have received from a message, the more certain they are of their post-message attitudes (Smith et al. 2008). This result has also been observed in research on omission neglect (e.g., Sanbonmatsu, Kardes, & Herr, 1992), which reveals that alerting people to potentially missing information from a message reduces the certainty with which they hold their attitudes. Reduced certainty, in turn, can foster a reluctance to act on one's attitude in the future (see Rucker et al., 2014).

Recipient Effects on Certainty

Just as characteristics of the source and message can affect psychological certainty, so too can characteristics of the target or recipient of the message. Unlike message factors, however, where the bulk of the research attention was on attitude certainty, with recipient factors the lion's share has been focused on understanding the confidence with which people hold their individual message-relevant thoughts.

One prominent feature of message recipients that has received attention is how people behave physically, or what they do with their bodies (see Briñol & Petty, 2008). To summarize, research shows that recipients' body postures, facial expressions, and physical movements can influence persuasion not only by serving as simple cues or affecting the direction and amount of thoughts, but also by affecting thought confidence. As with other sources of thought confidence, the confidence that emerges from behaviors or bodily states can moderate the effect of just about any thought that is currently available or on one's mind (for a review on embodied validation, see Briñol, Petty, & Wagner, 2012). For instance, in a series of studies Briñol and Petty (2003) found that under high thinking conditions, head movements (e.g., nodding or shaking) affected the confidence people had in their thoughts, which mediated the effect of head movements on persuasion. Consequently, when people generated positive thoughts toward a proposal (e.g., while listening to strong arguments), vertical head movements (i.e., head nodding) led to more favorable attitudes than horizontal head movements (i.e., head shaking). However, when people listened to weak arguments and generated mostly negative thoughts toward the proposal, head nodding led to less favorable attitudes than head shaking. Subsequent research replicated these findings using body postures associated with confidence (e.g., pushing the chest out) versus doubt (e.g., hunching forward with a back curved; Briñol, Petty, & Wagner, 2009).

Research has revealed that emotions can play a similar role in persuasion by affecting thought confidence. For example, Briñol, Petty, and Barden (2007) found that when placed in a happy (versus sad) state following message processing, people felt more confident about their thoughts and relied on them more closely in forming their attitudes and behavioral intentions. Importantly, happiness can validate thoughts by increasing confidence in or liking of them. Thus, happiness increased persuasion when people had positive thoughts, but it decreased persuasion when people had negative thoughts. Replicating other self-validation studies, Briñol, Petty, and Barden (2007) also found support for the idea that emotion effects on thought confidence were restricted to high elaboration conditions (e.g., high need for cognition) and situations in which the emotion induction followed rather than preceded one's thinking. In contrast, under low elaboration conditions (e.g., low need for cognition), emotions had just a main effect on attitudes such that happy participants agreed with the message more than did sad participants. Subsequent research has replicated these findings with more unpleasant emotions that are also associated with confidence, such as anger and disgust (Petty & Briñol, 2015).

Bodily movements, behaviors, and emotions are not the only recipient variables relevant to persuasion. As introduced earlier, more cognitive feelings can also play an important role. For example, the subjective sense of ease with which new information can be perceived or generated has been shown to play an important role in persuasion. Indeed, ease effects – in particular, increased persuasion following the generation of two rather than ten positive arguments on a topic – can also be driven by thought confidence under high elaboration conditions (Tormala, Falces, Briñol, & Petty, 2007; Tormala, Petty, & Brinol, 2002). Moreover, other recipient variables have been studied with regard to self-validation, including self-affirmation, self-confidence, and power (see Briñol & Petty, 2009b, for a review). The confidence that emerges from the fit or matching of two related variables (e.g., Clark, et al., 2013; Huntsinger, 2013) and the confidence that sometimes is associated with responses to threat and aggression (Blankenship, Nesbit, & Murray, 2013; Briñol, Petty, & DeMarree, 2015) can also validate thoughts. As noted, in all of these cases, confidence in positive thoughts increases persuasion while confidence in negative thoughts reduces persuasion.

In addition to the work just reviewed on thought confidence, there was some research exploring recipient factors that affect attitude certainty. As just one example, there is now considerable evidence that perceived thoughtfulness can influence the certainty with which people hold their attitudes. In general, the more people believe they have thought about or analyzed an object or issue, the more certain they are of their attitude toward it (Barden & Petty, 2008; Barden & Tormala, 2014; Wan, Rucker, Tormala, & Clarkson, 2010). For instance, Wan and colleagues (2010) presented participants with advertisements under conditions of regulatory depletion or non-depletion. Results indicated that when participants were depleted (versus non-depleted), they inferred that they had processed the ads more deeply, and this fostered greater attitude certainty. Interestingly, though, these effects can be moderated by other factors. For instance, Tormala, Clarkson, and Henderson (2011) found that attitude certainty increases when people perceive that they have taken their time and evaluated something slowly as long as the attitude object is unfamiliar. For familiar objects, people may have a different lay theory that reverses the weight given to slow versus fast evaluation.

Remaining Questions and Future Directions

As we have reviewed, attitude change research has a very rich history dating back many decades. Nonetheless, the field continues to evolve, particularly in our collective understanding of the varied and nuanced effects of classic persuasion variables and the mechanisms they trigger. Indeed, over the years, we have moved from the consideration of singular main effect predictions (e.g., that source credibility boosts persuasion) to more complex interaction predictions stemming from new insights around the cognitive processes driving persuasion (e.g., that source credibility can increase or decrease persuasion due to its effect on information processing) to still higher-order predictions for new outcomes based on the discovery of important metacognitive factors in this domain (e.g., showing that thought confidence and attitude certainty can be affected by people's perceptions of source credibility even when their attitude valence and extremity hold constant). Despite, or perhaps because of, this long history and constant evolution, there remain many open questions and opportunities for future research. In this final section of the chapter, we highlight what we see as some of the more interesting and promising next steps.

Before we do, we acknowledge that there have been other recent calls for future research. For example, Briñol and Petty (2012) described four areas of future research in attitudes and persuasion: (1) identifying more moderating conditions for effects and processes (e.g., moving from elaboration and timing to new contextual features), (2) studying new potential consequences of the different mechanisms of attitude change, (3) discovering new underlying processes of persuasion, and (4) moving from single measures to multiple measures of attitude change. In the latter area, as noted earlier, the impact of persuasion treatments on attitudes first used deliberative measures, whereas now attitude change can also be assessed using automatic measures (Briñol, Petty, & McCaslin, 2009; Smith, De Houwer, & Nosek, 2013). Future research is likely to continue to explore this topic and take advantage of technological advances to understand attitudes. One area that is likely to see an exponential increase in interest concerns how attitudinal processes can be charted with new brain imaging techniques (e.g., Cunningham, Packer, Kesek, & Van Bavel, 2009).

In the remainder of the chapter, we focus on substantive areas and conceptual questions that we see as important to explore in the near future. Interestingly, these questions also key in on the source-message-recipient trichotomy outlined earlier. In particular, we submit that some of the more intriguing directions for new research relate to understanding source-message-recipient dynamics – that is, the interdependent and shifting nature of these variables. For instance, what happens to the source's attitude after delivering a persuasive message? Under what circumstances, and through what mechanisms, do message recipients become future message sources (e.g., advocates for a cause)? When and why do people deliberately act as both source and recipient and design messages to persuade themselves? What determines the kinds of messages that sources elect to deliver to others? We elaborate on these and other questions next.

Source–Recipient Dynamics

One important question that has received some but not nearly enough attention in past research relates to the interdependent relationships between message sources and recipients. For instance, how is the source of a message influenced by the apparent success or failure of that message in changing the recipient's attitude? Building on recent work investigating metacognitive factors in resistance and persuasion (Tormala, 2008), it stands to reason that when the source of a message can perceive the success or failure of his or her persuasion attempt, that perception could influence his or her attitude certainty, openness to future persuasion, and so on. Consistent with this logic, in a classic study in the communications domain, Infante (1976) found that after succeeding (versus failing) to persuade someone, people became more resistant to subsequent counterattitudinal proposals. More recently, Prislin and colleagues (2011) found that a source's initial success or failure in persuading others affected not only his or her certainty, but also his or her actual persuasive efficacy in subsequent persuasion attempts.

We see this area as ripe for further inquiry. As one possibility, just like one's own persuasion or resistance experience can lead one to reflect on one's attitude and adjust certainty upward or downward, we presume there are factors that foster certainty increases and decreases following both successful and unsuccessful attempts at persuading others. Perhaps if one can attribute one's success to the cogency of one's message, for instance, one gains certainty. If one attributes one's success to situational factors (e.g., the recipient's good mood, or known status as a "yes man"), this effect might disappear or even induce doubt. Also interesting to explore is whether there are interpersonal effects of successful and unsuccessful persuasion attempts. Imagine that a source succeeds in persuading a recipient. Could this success be interpreted as reflecting that the source and recipient share core values and/or think in similar ways? If so, it seems reasonable to surmise that the source might like the recipient more after a successful (versus failed) persuasion attempt. In any case, the downstream consequences of persuasion attempts for the source, and perhaps his or her relationship with the recipient, are interesting and understudied topics in persuasion research.

Viewing source–recipient relations in a different light, persuasion can also be construed in terms of the dynamic relationship between two or more people. As noted, the bulk of the literature on persuasion to date has focused on how either an individual source or an individual recipient generates or responds to a persuasive message. One new and potentially important direction is to investigate how source and recipient variables interact with each other. Consider the work on power. On the face of it, given that high power represents a position of dominance over low power, it seems reasonable to expect more persuasion when the source has power over the recipient (e.g., compliance; Kelman, 1958) and less persuasion when the recipient has power over the source. While this certainly is possible (see Lammers, Dubois, Rucker, & Galinsky, 2013), it is also possible that greater persuasion arises when there is a match between the power of the source and recipient.

Consistent with this latter notion, Dubois, Rucker, and Galinsky (2014) recently found that high power sources are sometimes more persuasive when delivering their messages to high power recipients, whereas low power sources tend to be more persuasive when delivering their messages to low power recipients. In other words, Dubois and colleagues observed a matching effect with power and persuasion. Importantly, matching, like any other variable, can operate through multiple processes (e.g., affecting processing, validating thoughts), thus increasing or decreasing persuasion depending on the circumstances (Briñol, Tormala, & Petty, 2013).

Recipient (Source) Variables as Source (Recipient) Variables

Also germane to understanding that sources and recipients can vary along the same dimensions, there are a multitude of variables that have been examined primarily with respect to the recipient but also apply to the source, and that have been examined primarily with respect to the source but also apply to the recipient. Future research would benefit from expanding current conceptualizations of recipient variables to source variables and vice versa.

As one example, individual differences in need for cognition (the tendency to enjoy and engage in effortful thought; Cacioppo & Petty, 1982) have been studied almost exclusively as a recipient variable. Some recipients think more than others, and this difference influences the way they process persuasive messages (see Cacioppo, Petty, Feinstein, & Jarvis, 1996). However, sources presumably vary in need for cognition as well. How does this variation affect their persuasiveness? Briñol et al. (2005) found that although high (versus low) need for cognition individuals were able to generate more convincing arguments in a group setting, they were less efficient at reaching group consensus as the size of the group increased. The authors observed that high need for cognition individuals tended to easily persuade those low in need for cognition because of their greater arsenal of arguments and enhanced resistance to counterarguments (Shestowsky, Wegener, & Fabrigar, 1998), but they had no persuasive advantage against others who shared their high need for cognition, unless they received training on group dynamics (see Petty, Briñol, Loersch, & McCaslin, 2009, for a review).

On a related note, Kupor, Tormala, Norton, and Rucker (2014) recently suggested that although thoughtfulness traditionally has been studied as a recipient variable (e.g., more thoughtfulness creates stronger attitudes; see Barden & Petty, 2008), it can also be explicitly high or low in a message source (e.g., "I have given this a lot of thought and. . ." or "My quick gut reaction is. . ."). In a series of studies, Kupor et al. (2014) found that people liked others more, and were more influenced by their decisions, when those others calibrated their level of thoughtfulness to the demands of the situation. When making a difficult decision, for instance, more source thoughtfulness fostered greater influence and liking. When making an easy decision, however, less thoughtfulness fostered greater influence and liking.

Recent work has taken a similar approach to attitude certainty. Again, although certainty has been studied almost exclusively with respect to message recipients (e.g., high certainty increases resistance to persuasion; Tormala & Rucker, 2007), it can vary on the source side as well. How does a source's expressed certainty or uncertainty affect persuasion? In a recent series of studies, Karmarkar and Tormala (2010) presented participants with restaurant reviews that explicitly incorporated some statement of certainty or uncertainty. For instance, some reviews gave the restaurant a "confident 4 out of 5 stars," whereas others gave the restaurant a "tentative 4 out of 5 stars." Interestingly, results indicated that although non-expert sources could increase their persuasiveness by expressing certainty rather than uncertainty, the opposite was true for expert sources. That is, experts gained persuasiveness by expressing less rather than more attitude certainty. The authors found that when expert (non-expert) sources expressed less (more) certainty, that struck recipients as surprising or unexpected, causing them to tune in and process the message more deeply, which gave it more impact.

Going forward, there is a great opportunity for researchers to continue this line of inquiry. Theoretically, any variable that traditionally has been viewed as a recipient variable could also be studied as a source variable. This might include other forms of attitude strength such as attitude importance, accessibility, or ambivalence; mood states; personality variables; and so on. Similarly, any variable that traditionally has been studied as a source variable could be subject to research as a recipient variable, including expertise, trustworthiness, attractiveness, likeability, and the like. Illustration of this latter possibility come from work on epistemic authority in which source credibility is examined as a recipient rather than a source variable (Kruglanski et al., 2005), research on individual differences in self-monitoring, which have been studied as both a recipient and a source variable (Shavitt, Lowrey, & Han, 1992), and work on numerical status, with minority status being relevant as both a source and recipient variable (Morrison, 2011). We see this as an interesting and fruitful direction for future work.

Turning Recipients into Sources: Creating Advocacy

Another important yet understudied topic in the persuasion literature pertains to the generation of persuasive advocacy. Stated differently, what factors determine whether the recipient of a persuasive message will become a future *source* of a related message? What transforms an attitude holder into an attitude advocate? This topic has remained relatively underdeveloped over the years despite its obvious importance, particularly in consumer psychology, where word of mouth and sharing behavior have emerged as central topics (see Berger, 2014). However, there has been some classic and contemporary work that is of at least indirect relevance, including research on attitude bolstering (Briñol, Rucker, Tormala, & Petty, 2004; Lydon, Zanna, & Ross, 1988; Xu and Wyer, 2012), research on supportive resistance strategies (McGuire, 1964; Visser, Krosnick, & Simmons, 2003), studies on the persuasive effect of the transmitter (Echterhoff, Higgins, Kopietz, & Groll, 2008), work on the "saying is believing" effect (Hausmann, Levine, & Higgins, 2008), and research on proselytizing (Festinger, Riecken, & Schachter, 1956; Gal & Rucker, 2010).

In one recent study exploring the determinants of advocacy, Akhtar, Paunesku, and Tormala (2013) examined the potential effects of message strength. The authors presented prospective voters with a strong or weak persuasive message endorsing their preferred candidate in the 2012 presidential election (e.g., pro-Obama participants received a message in favor of reelecting Barack Obama), and subsequently asked about their advocacy intentions – for instance, their willingness to help the Obama campaign and to try to persuade others to share their view on Obama. Ironically, results indicated that recipients expressed greater advocacy intentions, and actually wrote more in an advocacy message, when they first received weak rather than strong arguments supporting their existing positions. In essence, weak proattitudinal messages induced recipients to believe that they had something important and unique to contribute to the cause, which turned them into advocates, or more willing and energized sources of future messages in the same direction.

Further research that delineates the key contributors to advocacy would help illuminate the factors that transform message recipients (e.g., supporters of a cause) into message sources (e.g., advocates for that cause). In so doing, future studies could help deepen our insight into the numerous important outcomes stemming from persuasive messages that reach beyond attitudes themselves. Indeed, in the Akhtar, Paunesku, and Tormala (2013) research, weak arguments were not more *persuasive* than strong ones. In fact, because participants already held relatively firm attitudes toward Barack Obama, message strength had no effect on attitudes in those studies. Importantly, though, it had a clear and consistent effect on attitudinal *advocacy*. Thus, by better understanding the subtle and previously hidden effects of persuasion variables, we can better predict and apply those effects in the service of important attitude-relevant objectives beyond traditionally identified metrics of persuasion (e.g., attitude measures).

Also important, once an individual decides to advocate for a cause, or attempt to persuade someone else, what determines the strategy he or she employs? As reviewed in this chapter, we know much about the effects of different persuasion strategies on the effectiveness of a given appeal, but we know very little about the determinants of the strategies that sources elect to implement. We assume this decision is guided at least in part by people's lay theories and persuasion knowledge (Briñol, Rucker, & Petty, 2015; Friestad & Wright, 1994, 1995; Kirmani & Campbell, 2004), but what are those theories and how do they vary by person and context? This question is wide open for future exploration and could be of tremendous theoretical and practical import.

Partly related to our previous discussion, how do sources' persuasion strategies affect their own attitudes and self-perceptions? An interesting line of research by Kipnis and colleagues suggests that using different social influence strategies can have different effects. For example, when people rely on their authority or power to influence others, they tend to feel worse about themselves, about their persuasive attempts, and about the recipients than they do when they convince others using arguments or other impression formation strategies that do not exploit their power or authority (Kipnis, Schmidt, & Wilkinson, 1980; O'Neal, Kipnis, & Craig, 1994; Rind & Kipnis, 2002). In general, it could be that some persuasion strategies are perceived as more legitimate than others, and that sources feel more certain about their own attitudes, and about themselves, when they use seemingly legitimate means (for a related discussion, see Tormala DeSensi, & Petty, 2007). Future research could enhance our understanding of both source and recipient persuasion dynamics by exploring these issues.

Turning Sources into Recipients: Self-Persuasion

Finally, one of the classic and most indispensable topics in attitude change and persuasion research is that of self-persuasion: understanding the situations, motives, and mechanisms that lead people to persuade themselves to adopt a new attitude. At its core, self-persuasion is about inducing people to serve as the source of a message aimed at themselves (see Maio & Thomas, 2007). In this respect, self-persuasion is about turning message recipients into their own message sources. One classic study of self-persuasion explored the effects of role playing on attitude change (Janis & King, 1954). In this initial work, participants were induced to act out a specified role (e.g., convince a friend to stop smoking or listen to an appeal to stop smoking). Famously, participants were more persuaded in the direction of the message when they generated it themselves compared to when they passively observed its delivery or listened to the information. One account for this effect is that self-generated messages are more persuasive because creating them leads people to engage in biased scanning of the arguments that they find to be especially compelling (e.g., Greenwald & Albert, 1968).

More recently, self-persuasion research has adopted a metacognitive perspective. For instance, Briñol, McCaslin, and Petty (2012) found that people put more effort into generating persuasive messages when they had doubts rather than confidence in a point of view (see also Gal & Rucker, 2010; cf. Akhtar, Paunesku, & Tormala, 2013; Matthes, Morrison, & Schemer, 2010; Rios, DeMarree, & Statzer, 2014). Greater effort in generating the message led to more self-persuasion. Also germane, recent research on the mere thought effect – the phenomenon whereby merely thinking about an object or issue can foster attitude polarization because people bring attitude-consistent thoughts to mind (e.g., Tesser, 1978) – suggests that self-persuasion effects can be amplified under conditions in which people feel greater confidence. For example, Clarkson, Tormala, and Leone (2011) varied the amount of time people had to think about an issue on which they initially held moderate attitudes. When participants had more time to think, they held their (attitude-consistent) thoughts with more confidence, and thus showed greater self-generated attitude change. Interestingly, though, too much time to think undid this effect, as people began to doubt their own thoughts and depolarize their attitudes (see also Clarkson, Valente, Leone, & Tormala, 2013).

Particularly in the domain of consumer behavior, we believe this classic topic of self-persuasion is ready for a rebirth. Indeed, it is now widely reported that consumers are growing increasingly skeptical of conventional marketing and advertising messages, relying more and more on word of mouth and other consumers for their information and opinions (see Dubois, Rucker, & Tormala, 2011). Accordingly, marketers have made more and more use of social networks, customer reviews, and alternative information sources to spread their messages. A natural next step, we postulate, is to create the conditions under which consumers will be persuaded by themselves or their own thinking. Consider an example in which an individual consumer selects an item (e.g., a pair of shoes) from an online retailer and then transfers to a checkout or purchase page. Based on the findings of Clarkson, Tormala, and Leone (2011), there might be some advantage to getting this consumer to wait briefly, which could allow him or her to generate more attitude-consistent thoughts (e.g., "those shoes really will be great for going out at night"), which in turn boosts his or her likelihood of completing the purchase and ordering the shoes (see Clarkson, Tormala, & Duhachek, 2010).

Relatedly, it is well known that merely completing a customer satisfaction survey can enhance customer satisfaction (Dholakia & Morwitz, 2002). Perhaps customer satisfaction surveys represent opportunities for customer influence via self-persuasion. If, for example, customers were asked to articulate the reasons for their purchase or explain the ways in which the product has been useful to them, a self-persuasion process may be engaged in which customers selectively focus on favorable arguments supporting their purchase and thereby convince themselves that it was a good one. Indeed, inducing people to list positive or negative thoughts on a topic can foster more positive and negative attitudes, respectively (Killeya & Johnson, 1998; Xu & Wyer, 2012). Exploring these kinds of effects in customer survey scenarios could be a useful next step in this domain.

More broadly, we see self-persuasion as an extremely important and still underexplored area in the attitudes literature. Although it had a prominent position in early attitudes research, it has been relatively neglected by recent scholars. There remain many open questions. For instance, when and why do people seek to persuade themselves? Is it when they have discrepancies between their actual and desired attitudes (DeMarree, Wheeler, Briñol, & Petty, 2014)? What strategies do people use? Are some strategies more effective than others? What contextual factors turn these strategies on and off? There are, of course, many more questions that could be raised. For now, we simply highlight self-persuasion as an area of future growth, with many open questions of both a basic and an applied nature.

Coda

Attitude change and persuasion are at the heart of consumer behavior. Research in this area dates back to the middle of the twentieth century. Since that time, attitudes, attitude change, and persuasion have been among the most studied topics in social and consumer psychology, and perhaps in psychology more generally. In this chapter, we sought to provide a broad overview of the persuasion literature, covering classic views of important variables and their effects, discussing modern metacognitive reconceptualizations, and highlighting unanswered or just partially answered questions deserving of new and deeper consideration. Over the years, researchers have made great strides in advancing our basic understanding of persuasion variables and when and how they exert their influence. Nevertheless, the field is constantly evolving and there remain many exciting paths forward. Attitudes are and will continue to be one of the most indispensable constructs in consumer research, and we hope the current chapter can serve as at least a partial guide, and strong encouragement, to pursue some of the important and exciting next steps.

References

Abelson, R. P. (1995). Attitude extremity. In R. E. Petty & J. A. Krosnick (eds.), *Attitude Strength: Antecedents and Consequences* (pp. 25–42). Mahwah, NJ: Erlbaum.

Akhtar, O., Paunesku, D., & Tormala, Z. L. (2013). Weak > strong: The ironic effect of argument strength on supportive advocacy. *Personality and Social Psychology Bulletin, 39*, 1214–1226.

Barden, J., & Petty, R. E. (2008). The mere perception of elaboration creates attitude certainty: Exploring the thoughtfulness heuristic. *Journal of Personality and Social Psychology, 95*, 489–509.

Barden, J., & Tormala, Z. L. (2014). Elaboration and attitude strength: The new meta-cognitive perspective. *Social and Personality Psychology Compass, 8*, 17–29.

Bassili, J. N. (1996) Meta-Judgmental versus operative indices of psychological properties: The case of measures of attitude strength. *Journal of Personality and Social Psychology, 71*, 637–653.

Berger, J. (2014). Word-of-mouth and interpersonal communication: An organizing framework and directions for future research. *Journal of Consumer Psychology, 24*, 586–607.

Bizer, G. Y., Larsen, J. T., & Petty, R. E. (2011). Exploring the valence-framing effect: Negative framing enhances attitude strength. *Political Psychology, 32*, 59–80.

Bizer, G. Y., & Petty, R. E. (2005). How we conceptualize our attitudes matters: The effects of valence framing on the resistance of political attitudes. *Political Psychology, 26*, 553–568.

Blankenship, K. L., Nesbit, S. M., & Murray, R. A. (2013). Driving anger and meta-cognition: The role of thought confidence on anger and aggressive driving intentions. *Aggressive Behavior, 39*, 323–334.

Bohner, G., Ruder, M., & Erb, H.-P. (2002). When expertise backfires: Contrast and assimilation effects in persuasion. *British Journal of Social Psychology, 41*, 495–519.

Boninger, D. S., Krosnick, J. A., Berent, M. K., & Fabrigar, L. R. (1995). The causes and consequences of attitude importance. In R. E. Petty & J. A. Krosnick (eds.), *Attitude Strength: Antecedents and Consequences* (pp. 159–190). Mahwah, NJ: Erlbaum.

Bornstein, R. F. (1989). Exposure and affect: Overview and meta-analysis of research, 1968–1987. *Psychological Bulletin, 106*, 265–289.

Briñol, P., Becerra, A., Díaz, D., Horcajo, J., Valle, C., & Gallardo, I. (2005). The impact of need for cognition on interpersonal influence. *Psicothema, 17*, 666–671.

Briñol, P. & DeMarree, K. G., eds. (2012) *Social Metacognition*. New York: Psychology Press.

Briñol, P., McCaslin, M. J., & Petty, R. E. (2012). Self-generated persuasion: Effects of the target and direction of arguments. *Journal of Personality and Social Psychology, 102*, 925–940.

Briñol, P. & Petty, R. E (2003) Overt head movements and persuasion: A self-validation analysis. *Journal of Personality and Social Psychology, 84*, 1123–1139.

Briñol, P. & Petty, R. E (2005). Individual differences in persuasion. In D. Albarracín, B. T. Johnson, & M. P. Zanna (eds.), *The Handbook of Attitudes and Attitude Change* (pp. 575–616). Hillsdale, NJ: Erlbaum.

Briñol, P. & Petty, R. E (2008). Embodied persuasion: Fundamental processes by which bodily responses can impact attitudes. In G. R. Semin & E. R. Smith (eds.), *Embodiment Grounding: Social, Cognitive, Affective, and Neuroscientific Approaches* (pp. 184–207). Cambridge: Cambridge University Press.

Briñol, P. & Petty, R. E (2009a). Source factors in persuasion: A self-validation approach. *European Review of Social Psychology, 20*, 49–96.

Briñol, P. & Petty, R. E (2009b). Persuasion: Insights from the self-validation hypothesis. In M. P. Zanna (ed.), *Advances in Experimental Social Psychology, 41*, (pp. 69–118). New York: Academic Press.

Briñol, P. & Petty, R. E (2012). The history of attitudes and persuasion research. In A. Kruglanski & W. Stroebe (eds.), *Handbook of the History Of Social Psychology* (pp. 285–320). New York: Psychology Press.

Briñol, P., Petty, R. E., & Barden, J. (2007). Happiness versus sadness as determinants of thought confidence in persuasion: A self-validation analysis. *Journal of Personality and Social Psychology, 93*, 711–727.

Briñol, P., Petty, R. E, & DeMarree, K. (2015). Being threatened and being a threat can increase reliance on thoughts: A self-validation approach. In P. J. Carroll, R. M. Arkin, & A. Wichman (eds.), *Handbook on Personal Security* (pp. 37–54). New York: Psychology Press.

Briñol, P., Petty, R. E., & McCaslin, M. (2009). Changing attitudes on implicit versus explicit measures: What is the difference? In R. E. Petty, R. H. Fazio, & P. Briñol (eds.). *Attitudes: Insights from the New Implicit Measures* (pp. 285–326). New York: Psychology Press.

Briñol, P., Petty, R. E., & Tormala, Z. L. (2004). The self-validation of cognitive responses to advertisements. *Journal of Consumer Research, 30*, 559–573.

Briñol, P., Petty, R. E. & Wagner, B. C. (2009) Body postures effects on self-evaluation: A self-validation approach. *European Journal of Social Psychology 39*, 1053–64.

Briñol, P., Petty, R. E. & Wagner, B. C. (2012). Embodied validation: Our body can change and also validate our thoughts. In P. Briñol & K. G. DeMarree (eds.), *Social Metacognition* (pp. 219–240). New York: Psychology Press.

Briñol, P., Petty, R. E., & Wheeler, S. C. (2006). Discrepancies between explicit and implicit self-concepts: Consequences for information processing. *Journal of Personality and Social Psychology, 91*, 154–170.

Briñol, P., Rucker, D. D., & Petty, R. E. (2015). Naïve theories about persuasion: Implication for information processing and consumer attitude change. *International Journal of Advertising, 34*, 85–106.

Briñol, P., Rucker, D., Tormala, Z. L., & Petty, R. E. (2004). Individual differences in resistance to persuasion: The role of beliefs and meta-beliefs. In E. S. Knowles & J. A. Linn (eds.), *Resistance and Persuasion* (pp. 83–104). Mahwah, NJ: Erlbaum.

Briñol, P., Tormala, Z. L., & Petty, R. E. (2013). Ease and persuasion: Multiple processes, meanings, and effects. In C. Unkelbach & R. Greifeneder (eds.), *The Experience of Thinking: How the Fluency of Mental Processes Influences Cognition and Behavior* (pp. 101–118). London: Psychology Press.

Byrne, D. (1971). *The Attraction Paradigm*. New York: Academic Press

Cacioppo, J. T., & Petty, R. E. (1979). The effects of message repetition and position on cognitive responses, recall, and persuasion. *Journal of Personality and Social Psychology, 37*, 97–109.

Cacioppo, J. T., & Petty, R. E. (1982). The need for cognition. *Journal of Personality and Social Psychology, 42*, 116–131.

Cacioppo, J. T., & Petty, R. E. (1989). Effects of message repetition on argument processing, recall, and persuasion. *Basic and Applied Social Psychology, 10*, 3–12.

Cacioppo, J. T., Petty, R. E., Feinstein, J. A., & Jarvis, W. B. G. (1996). Dispositional differences in cognitive motivation: The life and times of individuals varying in need for cognition. *Psychological Bulletin, 119*, 197–253.

Cacioppo, J. T., Priester, J. R., & Berntson, G. G. (1993). Rudimentary determinants of attitudes II: Arm flexion and extension have differential effects on attitudes. *Journal of Personality and Social Psychology, 65*, 5–17.

Calder, B. J., Insko, C., & Yandell, B. (1974). The relation of cognitive and memorial processes to persuasion in a simulated jury trial. *Journal of Applied Social Psychology, 4*, 62–93.

Chaiken, S. (1980). Heuristic versus systematic information processing in the use of source versus message quest in persuasion. *Journal of Personality and Social Psychology, 39*, 752–766.

Chaiken, S., & Ledgerwood, A. (2012). A theory of heuristic and systematic information processing. In P. A. M. van Lange, A. W. Kruglanski, & E. T. Higgins (eds.), *Handbook of Theories of Social Psychology* (pp. 246–266). Thousand Oaks, CA: Sage.

Chaiken, S. L., Liberman, A., & Eagly, A. H. (1989). Heuristic and systematic processing within and beyond the persuasion context. In J. S. Uleman y J. A. Bargh (eds.), *Unintended Thought* (pp. 212–252). New York: Guilford Press.

Chaiken, S., & Maheswaran, D. (1994). Heuristic processing can bias systematic processing: Effects of source credibility, argument ambiguity, and task importance on attitude judgment. *Journal of Personality and Social Psychology, 66*, 460–473.

Clark, J. K., & Wegener, D. T. (2013). Message position, information processing, and persuasion: The Discrepancy Motives Model. In P. Devine & A. Plant (eds.), *Advances in Experimental Social Psychology* (vol. 47, pp. 189–232). San Diego, CA: Academic Press.

Clark, J. K., Wegener, D. T., Sawicki, V., Petty, R. E., & Briñol, P. (2013). Evaluating the message or the messenger? Implications for self-validation in persuasion. *Personality and Social Psychology Bulletin, 39*, 1571–1584.

Clarkson, J. J., Tormala, Z. L., & Duhachek, A. L. (2010). Seeking optimality in the consumer waiting experience: The good and bad of waiting time. Paper presented at the annual meeting of the Society for Consumer Psychology, St. Petersburg, FL.

Clarkson, J. J., Tormala, Z. L., & Leone, C. (2011). A self-validation perspective on the mere thought effect. *Journal of Experimental Social Psychology, 47*, 449–454.

Clarkson, J. J., Tormala, Z. L., & Rucker, D. D. (2008). A new look at the consequences of attitude certainty: The amplification hypothesis. *Journal of Personality and Social Psychology, 95*, 810–825.

Clarkson, J. J., Tormala, Z. L., Rucker, D. D., & Dugan, R. G. (2013). The malleable influence of social consensus on attitude certainty. *Journal of Experimental Social Psychology, 49*, 1019–1022.

Clarkson, J. J., Valente, M. J., Leone, C., & Tormala, Z. L. (2013). Motivated reflection on attitude-inconsistent information: An exploration of the role of fear of invalidity in self-persuasion. *Personality and Social Psychology Bulletin, 29,* 1559–1570.

Clore, G. L., & Parrott, W. G. (1994). Cognitive feelings and metacognitive judgments. *European Journal of Social Psychology (Special Issue), 24,* 101–115.

Cohen, J. B., & Reed, A. (2006). A multiple pathway anchoring and adjustment (MPAA) model of attitude generation and reinforcement. *Journal of Consumer Research, 33,* 1–15.

Crowley, A. E., & Hoyer, W. D. (1994). An integrative framework for understanding two-sided persuasion. *Journal of Consumer Research, 20,* 561–574.

Cunningham, W. A., Packer, D. J., Kesek, A., & Van Bavel, J. J. (2009). Implicit measurement of attitudes: A physiological approach. In R. E. Petty, R. H. Fazio, & P. Briñol (eds.), *Attitudes: Insights from the New Implicit Measures* (pp. 485–512). New York: Psychology Press.

Davidson, A. R., Yantis, S., Norwood, M., & Montano, D. E. (1985). Amount of information about the attitude object and attitude–behavior consistency. *Journal of Personality and Social Psychology, 49,* 1184–1198.

DeMarree, K. G., Wheeler, C. S., Briñol, P., & Petty, R. E. (2014). Wanting other attitudes: Actual–desired attitude discrepancies predict feelings of ambivalence and ambivalence consequences. *Journal of Experimental Social Psychology, 53,* 5–18.

Dholakia, U. M., & Morwitz, V. G. (2002). The scope and persistence of mere measurement effects: Evidence from a field study of customer satisfaction measurement. *Journal of Consumer Research, 29,* 159–167.

Dubois, D., Rucker, D. D., & Galinsky, A. D. (2014). The power matching effect: Psychological attunement between communicator and audience power enhances persuasion. Unpublished manuscript. INSEAD.

Dubois, D., Rucker, D. D., & Tormala, Z. L. (2011). From rumors to facts, and facts to rumors: The role of certainty decay in consumer communications. *Journal of Marketing Research, 48,* 1020–1032.

Eagly A. H., & Chaiken, S. (1993). *The Psychology of Attitudes.* Fort Worth, TX: Harcourt, Brace, Jovanovich.

Echterhoff, G., Higgins, T. E., Kopietz, R., & Groll, S. (2008). How communication goals determine when audience tuning biases memory. *Journal of Experimental Psychology: General, 137,* 3–21.

Edwards, K. (1990). The interplay of affect and cognition in attitude formation and change. *Journal of Personality and Social Psychology, 59,* 202–216.

Ein-Gar, D., Shiv, B., & Tormala, Z. L. (2012). When blemishing leads to blossoming: The positive effect of negative information. *Journal of Consumer Research, 38,* 846–859.

Etgar, M., & Goodwin, S. A. (1982). One-Sided versus two-sided comparative message appeals for new brand introduction. *Journal of Consumer Research, 8,* 460–465.

Fabrigar, L. R., & Petty, R. E. (1999). The role of the affective and cognitive bases of attitudes in susceptibility to affectively and cognitively based persuasion. *Personality and Social Psychology Bulletin, 25,* 363–381.

Fazio, R. H. (1990). Multiple processes by which attitudes guide behaviour: The MODE model as an integrative framework. In M. P. Zanna (ed.), *Advances in Experimental Social Psychology* (vol. 23, pp. 75–109). San Diego, CA: Academic Press.

Fazio, R. H. (1995). Attitudes as object-evaluation associations: Determinants, consequences, and correlates of attitude accessibility. In R. E. Petty & J. A. Krosnick (eds.), *Attitude Strength: Antecedents and Consequences* (pp. 247–282). Hillsdale, NJ: Erlbaum.

Feldman, J. M., & Lynch, J. (1988). Self-generated validity and other effects of measurement on belief, attitude, intention, and behavior. *Journal of Applied Psychology, 73*, 421–435.

Festinger, L., Riecken, H. W., & Schachter, S. (1956). *When Prophecy Fails.* Minneapolis, MN: University of Minnesota Press.

Festinger, L., & Thibaut, J. (1951). Interpersonal communications in small groups, *Journal of Abnormal and Social Psychology, 46*, 92–100.

Fishbein, M., & Ajzen, I. (1975). *Belief, Attitude, Intention, and Behavior.* Reading, MA: Addison-Wesley.

Fleming, M. A., & Petty, R. E. (2000). Identity and persuasion: An elaboration likelihood approach. In D. J. Terry & M. A. Hogg (eds.), *Attitudes, Behavior, and Social Context: The Role of Norms and Group Membership* (pp. 171–199). Mahwah, NJ: Lawrence Erlbaum.

French, J. R. P., Jr., & Raven, B. H. (1959). The bases of social power. In D. Cartwright (ed.), *Studies in Social Power* (pp. 150–167). Ann Arbor, MI: Institute for Social Research.

Friestad, M., & Wright, P. (1994). The Persuasion Knowledge Model: How people cope with persuasion attempts. *Journal of Consumer Research, 21*, 1–31.

Friestad, M., & Wright, P. (1995). Persuasion knowledge: Lay people's and researches' beliefs about the psychology of persuasion. *Journal of Consumer Research, 27*, 123–156.

Gal, D., & Rucker, D. D. (2010). When in doubt, shout! Paradoxical influences of doubt on proselytizing. *Psychological Science, 20*, 1–7.

Gawronski, B., & Payne, B. K. (2010) (eds.). *Handbook of Implicit Social Cognition: Measurement, Theory, and Applications.* New York: Guilford Press.

Gorn, G., & Goldberg, M. (1980). Children's responses to repetitive TV commercials. *Journal of Consumer Research, 6*, 421–425.

Greenwald, A. G., & Albert, R. D. (1968). Acceptance and recall of improvised arguments. *Journal or Personality and Social Psychology, 8*, 31–34.

Gross, S. R., Holtz, R., & Miller, N. (1995). Attitude certainty. In R. E. Petty & J. A. Krosnick (eds.), *Attitude Strength: Antecedents and Consequences* (pp. 215–245). Hillsdale, NJ: Erlbaum.

Grush, J. E. (1976). Attitude formation and mere exposure phenomena: A non-artificial explanation of empirical findings. *Journal of Personality and Social Psychology, 33*, 281–290.

Hausmann, L. R. M., Levine, J. M., & Higgins, E. T. (2008). Communication and group perception: Extending the "saying is believing" effect. *Group Processes and Intergroup Relations, 11*, 539–554.

Heesacker, M. H., Petty, R. E., & Cacioppo, J. T. (1983). Field dependence and attitude change: Source credibility can alter persuasion by affecting message-relevant thinking. *Journal of Personality, 51*, 653–666.

Horcajo, J., Briñol, P., & Petty, R. E. (2014). Multiple roles for majority versus minority source status on persuasion when source status follows the message. *Social Influence, 9*, 37–51.

Horcajo, J., Petty, R. E., &, Briñol, P. (2010). The effects of majority versus minority source status on persuasion: A self-validation analysis. *Journal of Personality and Social Psychology, 99*, 498–512.

Hovland, C. I., Lumsdaine, A. A., & Sheffield, F. D. (1949). *Experiments on Mass Communication.* Princeton, NJ: Princeton University Press.

Huntsinger, J. R. (2013). Incidental experiences of affective coherence and incoherence influence persuasion. *Personality and Social Psychology Bulletin, 39*, 792–802.

Infante, D. A. (1976). Persuasion as a function of the receiver's prior success or failure as a message source. *Communication Quarterly, 24*, 21–26.

Janis, I. L., & King, B. T. (1954). The influence of role-playing on opinion change. *Journal of Abnormal and Social Psychology, 49*, 211–218.

Josephs, R. A., Giesler, R. B., & Silvera, D. H. (1994). Judgment by quantity. *Journal of Experimental Psychology: General, 123*, 21–32.

Karmarkar, U.R., & Tormala, Z.L. (2010). Believe me, I have no idea what I'm talking about: The effects of source certainty on consumer involvement and persuasion. *Journal of Consumer Research, 46*, 1033–1049.

Kaufman, D. Q., Stasson, M. F., & Hart, J. W. (1999). Are the tabloids always wrong or it that just what we think? Need for cognition and perceptions of articles in print media. *Journal of Applied Social Psychology, 29*, 1984–1997.

Kelman, H. C. (1958). Compliance, identification and internalization: Three processes of attitude change. *Journal of Conflict Resolution, 2*, 51–60.

Kelman, H. C., & Hovland, C. I. (1953). "Reinstatement" of the communicator in delayed measurement of opinion change. *Journal of Abnormal and Social Psychology, 48*, 327–335.

Killeya, L. A. & Johnson, B. T. (1998). Experimental induction of biased systematic processing: The directed-thought technique. *Personality and Social Psychology Bulletin, 24*, 17–33.

Kipnis, D., Schmidt, S. M., & Wilkinson, I. (1980). Intraorganizational influence tactics: Explorations in getting one's way. *Journal of Applied Psychology, 65*, 440–452.

Kirmani, A., & Campbell, M. C. (2004). Goal seeker and persuasion sentry: How consumer targets respond to interpersonal marketing persuasion. *Journal of Consumer Research, 31*, 573–582.

Koriat, A. (2012). The self-consistency model of subjective confidence. *Psychological Review, 119*, 80–113.

Krosnick, J. A., & Petty, R. E. (1995). Attitude strength: An overview. In R. E. Petty & J. A. Krosnick (eds.), *Attitude Strength: Antecedents and Consequences* (pp. 1–24). Mahwah, NJ: Erlbaum.

Kruglanski, A. W., Raviv, A., Bar-Tal, D., Raviv, A., Sharvit, K., Ellis, S., Bar, R., Pierro, A., & Mannetti, L. (2005). Says who? Epistemic authority effects in social judgment. In M. P. Zanna (ed.), *Advances in Experimental Social Psychology* (vol. 37, pp. 346–392). San Diego, CA: Academic Press.

Kupor, D., Tormala, Z. L., Norton, M. I., & Rucker, D. D. (2014). Thought calibration: How thinking just the right amount increases one's influence and appeal. *Social Psychological and Personality Science, 5*, 263–270.

Labroo, A. A., Dhar, R., & Schwarz, N. (2008). Of frog wines and frowning watches: Semantic priming, perceptual fluency, and brand evaluation. *Journal of Consumer Research, 34*, 819–831.

Lammers, J., Dubois, D., Rucker, D. D., & Galinsky, A. D. (2013). Power gets the job: Priming power improves interview outcomes. *Journal of Experimental Social Psychology, 49*, 776–779.

Lee, A. Y., & Labroo, A. A. (2004). The effect of conceptual and perceptual fluency on brand evaluation. *Journal of Marketing Research, 41*, 151–165.

Lord, C., Ross, L., & Lepper, M. (1979). Biased assimilation and attitude polarization: The effects of prior theories on subsequently considered evidence. *Journal of Personality and Social Psychology, 37*, 2098–2109.

Lydon, J., Zanna, M. P., & Ross, M. (1988). Bolstering attitudes by autobiographical recall: Attitude persistence and selective memory. *Personality and Social Psychology Bulletin, 14*, 78–86.

Lynch, J. G. Jr. (2006). Accessibility-diagnosticity and the multiple pathway anchoring and adjustment model. *Journal of Consumer Research, 33*, 25–27.

Maio, G. R., & Thomas, G. (2007). The epistemic–teleologic model of deliberate self-persuasion. *Personality and Social Psychology Review, 11*, 46–67.

Martin, L. L., Ward, D. W., Achee, J. W., & Wyer, R. S. (1993). Mood as input: People have to interpret the motivational implications of their moods. *Journal of Personality and Social Psychology, 64*, 317–326.

Mayer, N. D., & Tormala, Z. L. (2010). "Think" versus "feel" framing effects in persuasion. *Personality and Social Psychology Bulletin, 36*, 443–454.

McGuire, W. J. (1964). Inducing resistance to persuasion: Some contemporary approaches. In L Berkowitz (ed.), *Advances in Experimental Social Psychology* (vol. *19*, pp. 191–229). New York: Academic Press.

Miller, R. C. (1976). Mere exposure, psychological reactance, and attitude change. *Public Opinion Quarterly, 40*, 229–233.

Mills, J., & Jellison, J. M. (1967). Effect on opinion change of how desirable the communication is to the audience the communicator addressed. *Journal of Personality and Social Psychology, 6*, 98–101.

Morrison, K. R. (2011). A license to speak up: Outgroup minorities and opinion expression. *Journal of Experimental Social Psychology, 47*, 756–766.

Morrison, K. R., & Wheeler, S. C. (2010). Nonconformity defines the self: The role of minority opinion status in self-concept clarity. *Personality and Social Psychology Bulletin, 36*, 297–308.

Moscovici, S. (1980). Toward a theory of conversion behavior. In L. Berkowitz (ed.), *Advances in Experimental Social Psychology* (vol. 13, pp. 209–239). New York: Academic Press.

Moscovici, S. (1985). Social influence and conformity. In G. Lindsey & E. Aronson (eds.), *The Handbook of Social Psychology* (vol. 2, 3rd ed., pp. 347–412). New York: Random House.

O'Neal, E. C., Kipnis, D., & Craig, K. M. (1994). Effects on the persuader of employing a peripheral route technique. *Basic and Applied Social Psychology, 15*, 225–238.

Pechmann, C. (1992). Predicting when two-sided ads will be more effective than one-sided ads: The role of correlational and correspondent inferences. *Journal of Marketing Research, 29*, 441–453.

Pelham, B. W., Sumarta, T. T., & Myaskovsky, L. (1994). The easy path from many to much: The numerosity heuristic. *Cognitive Psychology, 26*, 103–133.

Perkins, A. W., & Forehand, M. R. (2010). Implicit social cognition and indirect measures in consumer behavior. In B. Gawronski & B. K. Payne (eds.),

Handbook of Implicit Social Cognition: Measurement, Theory, and Applications (pp. 535–547). New York: Guilford Press.

Petrocelli, J. V., Tormala, Z. L., & Rucker, D. D. (2007). Unpacking attitude certainty: Attitude clarity and attitude correctness. *Journal of Personality and Social Psychology, 92*, 30–41.

Petty, R. E. (1997). The evolution of theory and research in social psychology: From single to multiple effect and process models. In C. McGarty & S. A. Haslam (eds.), *The Message of Social Psychology: Perspectives on Mind in Society* (pp. 268–290). Oxford: Blackwell.

Petty, R. E., & Briñol, P. (2008). Persuasion: From single to multiple to meta-cognitive processes. *Perspectives on Psychological Science, 3*, 137–147.

Petty, R. E., & Briñol, P. (2012). The Elaboration Likelihood Model. In P. A. M. Van Lange, A. Kruglanski, & E. T. Higgins (eds.), *Handbook of Theories of Social Psychology* (vol. 1, pp. 224–245). London: Sage.

Petty, R. E., & Briñol, P. (2015). Emotion and persuasion: Cognitive and meta-cognitive processes impact attitudes. *Cognition and Emotion, 29*, 1–26.

Petty, R. E., Briñol, P., & DeMarree, K. G. (2007). The Meta-Cognitive Model (MCM) of attitudes: Implications for attitude measurement, change, and strength. *Social Cognition, 25*, 609–642.

Petty, R. E., Briñol, P., Loersch, C., & McCaslin, M. J. (2009). The Need for cognition. In M. R. Leary & R. H. Hoyle (eds.), *Handbook of Individual Differences in Social Behavior* (pp. 318–329). New York: Guilford Press.

Petty, R. E., Briñol, P. & Tormala, Z. L. (2002) Thought confidence as a determinant of persuasion: The self-validation hypothesis. *Journal of Personality and Social Psychology, 82*, 722–741.

Petty, R. E., Briñol, P., Tormala, Z. L., & Wegener, D. T. (2007). The role of meta-cognition in social judgment. In E. T. Higgins & A. W. Kruglanski (eds.) *Social Psychology: A Handbook of Basic Principles* (2nd ed., pp. 254–284). New York: Guilford Press.

Petty, R. E., & Cacioppo, J. T. (1979). Issue involvement can increase or decrease persuasion by enhancing message-relevant cognitive responses. *Journal of Personality and Social Psychology, 37*, 1915–1926.

Petty, R. E., & Cacioppo, J. T. (1984). The effects of involvement on responses to argument quantity and quality: Central and peripheral routes to persuasion. *Journal of Personality and Social Psychology, 46*, 69–81.

Petty, R. E., & Cacioppo, J. T. (1986). *Communication and Persuasion: Central and Peripheral Routes to Attitude Change.* New York: Springer-Verlag.

Petty, R. E., Cacioppo, J. T. & Goldman, R. (1981). Personal involvement as a determinant of argument-based persuasion. *Journal of Personality and Social Psychology, 41*, 847–855.

Petty, R. E., Cacioppo, J. T., & Schumann, D. (1983). Central and peripheral routes to advertising effectiveness: The moderating role of involvement. *Journal of Consumer Research, 10*, 135–146.

Petty, R. E., & Fazio, R. H., & Briñol, P., (2009). The new implicit measures: An overview. In R. E. Petty, R. H. Fazio, & P. Briñol (eds.), *Attitudes: Insights from the New Implicit Measures* (pp. 3–18). New York: Psychology Press.

Petty, R. E., Haugtvedt, C. P., & Smith, S. M. (1995). Elaboration as a determinant of attitude strength: Creating attitudes that are persistent, resistant, and predictive of behavior. In R. E. Petty & J. A. Krosnick (eds.), *Attitude Strength: Antecedents and Consequences.* (pp. 93–130). Mahwah, NJ: Erlbaum.

Petty, R. E., & Krosnick, J. A. (1995) (eds.). *Attitude Strength: Antecedents and Consequences.* Hillsdale, NJ: Erlbaum.

Petty, R. E., Schumann, D. W., Richman, S. A., & Strathman, A. J. (1993). Positive mood and persuasion: Different roles for affect under high and low elaboration conditions. *Journal of Personality and Social Psychology, 64*, 5–20.

Petty, R. E., Tormala, Z. L., Briñol, P., & Jarvis, W. B. G. (2006). Implicit ambivalence from attitude change: An exploration of the PAST model. *Journal of Personality and Social Psychology, 90*, 21–41.

Petty, R. E., Tormala, Z. L., & Rucker, D. D. (2004). Resisting persuasion by counterarguing: An attitude strength perspective. In J. T. Jost, M. R. Banaji, & D. A. Prentice (eds.), *Perspectivism in Social Psychology: The Yin and Yang of Scientific Progress* (pp. 37–51). Washington, DC: American Psychological Association.

Petty, R. E., & Wegener, D. T. (1998). Attitude change: Multiple roles for persuasion variables. In D. Gilbert, S. Fiske, & G. Lindzey (eds.), *The Handbook of Social Psychology* (4th ed., vol. 1, pp. 323–390). New York: McGraw-Hill.

Petty, R. E., Wells, G. L., & Brock, T. C. (1976). Distraction can enhance or reduce yielding to propaganda: Thought disruption versus effort justification. *Journal of Personality and Social Psychology, 34*, 874–884.

Pornpitakpan, C. (2004). The persuasiveness of source credibility: A critical review of five decades' evidence. *Journal of Applied Social Psychology, 34*, 243–281.

Prislin, R., Boyle, S., Davenport, C., Farley, A., Jacobds, E.,,ichalak, J., Uehara, K., Zandian, F., & Xu, Y. (2011). On being influenced while trying to persuade: The feedback of persuasion outcomes to the persuader. *Social Psychological and Personality Science, 2*, 51–58.

Rhine, R., & Severance, L. (1970). Ego-involvement, discrepancy, source credibility, and attitude change. *Journal of Personality and Social Psychology, 16*, 175–190.

Rhodes, N., & Wood, W. (1992). Self-esteem and intelligence affect influenciability: The mediating role of message reception. *Psychological Bulletin, 111*, 156–171.

Rind, B., & Kipnis, D. (2002). Changes in self-perceptions as a result of successfully persuading others. *Journal of Social Issues, 55*, 141–156.

Rios, K., DeMarree, K. G., & Statzer, J. (2014). Attitude certainty and conflict style: Divergent effects of correctness and clarity. *Personality and Social Psychology Bulletin, 40*, 819–830..

Rosenberg, M. J., & Hovland, C. I.(1960). Cognitive, affective, and behavioral components of attitudes. In C. I. Hovland, & M. J. Rosenberg (eds.), *Attitude Organization and Change: An Analysis of Consistency among Attitude Components.* New Haven, CT: Yale University Press

Rucker, D. D., & Galisnky, A. D. (this volume). Power and consumer behavior. In M. I. Norton, D. D. Rucker, & C. Lamberton (eds.), *Cambridge Handbook of Consumer Psychology.* New York: Cambridge University Press.

Rucker, D. D., & Petty, R. E. (2004). When resistance is futile: Consequences of failed counterarguing for attitude certainty. *Journal of Personality and Social Psychology, 86*, 219–235.

Rucker, D. D., Petty, R. E., & Briñol, P. (2008). What's in a frame anyway? A meta-cognitive analysis of the impact of one versus two sided message framing on attitude certainty. *Journal of Consumer Psychology, 18*, 137–149.

Rucker, D. D., & Tormala, Z. L. (2012). Meta-cognitive theory in consumer research. In P. Briñol & K. DeMarree (eds.), *Social Metacognition* (pp. 303–321). New York: Psychology Press.

Rucker, D. D., Tormala, Z. L., Petty, R. E., & Briñol, P. (2014). Consumer conviction and commitment: An appraisal-based framework for attitude certainty. *Journal of Consumer Psychology, 24*, 119–36.

Sanbonmatsu, D. M., Kardes, F. R., & Herr, P. M. (1992). The role of prior knowledge and missing information in multiattribute evaluation. *Organizational Behavior and Human Decision Processes, 51*(1), 76–91.

Schwarz, N. (2004). Meta-cognitive experiences in consumer judgment and decision making. *Journal of Consumer Psychology, 14*, 332–348.

Schwarz, N., Bless, H., & Bohner, G. (1991). Mood and persuasion: Affective status influence the processing of persuasive communications. In M. P. Zanna (ed.), *Advances in Experimental Social Psychology* (vol. 24, pp. 161–197). San Diego, CA: Academia Press.

Schwarz, N., Bless, H., Strack, F., Klumpp, G., Rittenauer-Schatka, H., & Simons, A. (1991). Ease of retrieval as information: Another look at the availability heuristic. *Journal of Personality and Social Psychology, 61*, 195–202.

See, Y. H. M., Fabrigar, L. R., & Petty, R. E. (2013). Affective-cognitive meta-bases versus structural bases of attitudes predict processing interest versus efficiency. *Personality and Social Psychology Bulletin, 39*, 1111–1123.

See, Y. H. M., Petty, R. E., & Fabrigar, L. R. (2008). Affective and cognitive meta-bases of attitudes: Unique effects on information interest and persuasion. *Journal of Personality and Social Psychology, 94*, 938–955.

Sela, A., & Berger, J. (2012). How attribute quantity influences option choice. *Journal of Marketing Research, 49*, 942–953.

Shavitt, S., Lowrey, T., Han, S., (1992). Attitude functions in advertising: The interactive role of products and self-monitoring. *Journal of Consumer Psychology, 1*, 337–364.

Sherif, M., & Hovland, C. I. (1961). *Social Judgment: Assimilation and Contrast Effects in Communication and Attitude Change*. New Haven, CT: Yale University Press.

Shestowsky, D., Wegener, D. T., & Fabrigar, L. R. (1998). Need for cognition and interpersonal influence: Individual differences in impact on dyadic decisions. *Journal of Personality and Social Psychology, 74*, 1317–1328.

Slovic, P., Finucane, M. L., Peters, E., & Macgregor, D. G. (2002). The Affect Heuristic. In T. Gilovich, D. Griffin, & D. Kahneman (eds.), *Heuristics and Biases: The Psychology of Intuitive Judgment* (pp. 397–420). New York: Cambridge University Press.

Smith, C. T., De Houwer, J., & Nosek, B. A. (2013). Consider the source: Persuasion of implicit evaluations is moderated by manipulations of source credibility. *Personality and Social Psychology Bulletin, 39*, 193–205.

Smith, S. M., Fabrigar, L. R., MacDougall, B. L., & Wiesenthal, N. L. (2008). The role of amount cognitive elaboration, and structural consistency of attitude-relevant knowledge in the formation of attitude certainty. *European Journal of Social Psychology, 38*, 280–295.

Snyder, M., & Rothbart, M. (1971). Communicator attractiveness and opinion change. *Canadian Journal of Behavioural Science, 3*, 377–387.

Staats, A. W., & Staats, C. (1958). Attitudes established by classical conditioning. *Journal of Abnormal and Social Psychology, 67*, 159–167.

Tesser, A. (1978). Self-generated attitude change. In I. Berkowitz (ed.), *Advances in Experimental Social Psychology* (vol. 11, pp. 289–338). New York: Academic Press.

Thompson, M. M., Zanna, M. P., & Griffin, D. W. (1995). Let's not be indifferent about (attitudinal) ambivalence. In R. E. Petty & J. A. Krosnick (eds.), *Attitude Strength: Antecedents and Consequences.* Hillsdale, NJ: Erlbaum.

Tormala, Z. L. (2008). A new framework for resistance to persuasion: The resistance appraisals hypothesis. In W. D. Crano & R. Prislin (eds.), *Attitudes and Attitude Change* (pp. 213–234). New York: Psychology Press.

Tormala, Z. L., Briñol, P., & Petty, R. E. (2006). When credibility attacks: The reverse impact of source credibility on persuasion. *Journal of Experimental Social Psychology, 42*, 684–691.

Tormala, Z. L., Briñol, P., & Petty, R. E. (2007). Multiple roles for source credibility under high elaboration: It's all in the timing. *Social Cognition, 25*, 4, 536–552.

Tormala, Z. L, Clarkson, J. J., & Henderson, M. D. (2011). Does fast or slow evaluation foster greater certainty? *Personality and Social Psychology Bulletin, 37*, 422–434.

Tormala, Z. L., Clarkson, J. J., & Petty, R. E. (2006). Resisting persuasion by the skin of one's teeth: The hidden success of resisted persuasive messages. *Journal of Personality and Social Psychology, 91* (3), 423–435.

Tormala, Z. L., DeSensi, V. L., & Petty, R. E. (2007). Resisting persuasion by illegitimate means: A meta-cognitive perspective on minority influence. *Personality and Social Psychology Bulletin, 33*, 354–367.

Tormala, Z.L., Falces, C., Briñol, P., & Petty, R.E. (2007). Ease of retrieval effects in social judgment: The role of unrequested cognitions. *Journal of Personality and Social Psychology, 93*, 143–157.

Tormala, Z. L., & Petty, R. E. (2002). What doesn't kill me makes me stronger: The effects of resisting persuasion on attitude certainty. *Journal of Personality and Social Psychology, 83*, 1298–1313.

Tormala, Z. L., & Petty, R. E. (2004a). Source credibility and attitude certainty: A metacognitive analysis of resistance to persuasion. *Journal of Consumer Psychology, 14*, 427–442.

Tormala, Z. L., & Petty, R. E. (2004b). Resistance to persuasion and attitude certainty: The moderating role of elaboration. *Personality and Social Psychology Bulletin, 30*, 1446–1457.

Tormala, Z. L., Petty, R. E., & Briñol, P. (2002). Ease of retrieval effects in persuasion: A self-validation analysis. *Personality and Social Psychology Bulletin, 28*, 1700–1712.

Tormala, Z. L., Petty, R. E., & DeSensi, V. L. (2010). Multiple roles for minority sources in persuasion and resistance. In R. Martin & M. Hewstone (eds.), *Minority Influence and Innovation: Antecedents, Processes, and Consequences* (pp. 105–131). London: Psychology Press.

Tormala, Z. L., & Rucker, D. D. (2007). Attitude certainty: A review of past findings and emerging perspectives. *Social and Personality Psychology Compass, 1*, 469–492.

Visser, P. S., & Mirabile, R. R. (2004). Attitudes in the social context: The impact of social network composition on individual-level attitude strength. *Journal of Personality and Social Psychology, 87*, 779–795.

Wan, E. W., Rucker, D. D., Tormala, Z. L., & Clarkson, J. J. (2010). The effect of regulatory depletion on attitude certainty. *Journal of Marketing Research, 47*, 531–541.

Wänke, M., Bohner, G., & Jurkowitsch, A. (1997). There are many reasons to drive a BMW: Does imagined ease of argument generation influence attitudes? *Journal of Consumer Research, 24*, 170–177.

Wells, G. L., & Petty, R. E. (1980). The effects of overt head movements on persuasion: Compatibility and incompatibility of responses. *Basic and Applied Social Psychology, 1*, 219–230.

Wood, W., Lundgren, S., Quellette, J. A., Busceme, S., & Blackstone, T. (1994). Minority influence: A meta-analytic review of social influence processes. *Psychological Bulletin, 115*, 323–345.

Xu, A. J., & Wyer, R. S. (2012). The role of bolstering and counterarguing mindsets in persuasion. *Journal of Consumer Research, 38*, 920–932.

Zajonc, R. B. (1968). Attitudinal effects of mere exposure. *Journal of Personality and Social Psychology, 9*, 1–27.

Zanna, M. P, & Rempel, J. K. (1988). Attitudes: A new look at an old concept. In D. Bar-Tal & A. W. Kruglanski (eds.), *The Social Psychology of Attitudes* (pp. 315–334). New York: Cambridge University Press.

3 Consumer Prediction

Forecasted Utility, Psychological Distance, and Their Intersection

Carey K. Morewedge and Hal E. Hershfield

Consumer prediction encompasses the cognitive, affective, and motivational psychological processes by which consumers anticipate (and subsequently produce) the future. Prediction is a pervasive factor in consumer decision making, from everyday decisions such as which lunch one should purchase to major decisions about how much one will need to save for retirement. More generally, predictions are the method by which consumers determine which choice options will bring them the greatest satisfaction in the present and by which they anticipate their needs and wants in the near and distant future. In this chapter, we examine the processes by which consumers infer whether and what will happen in the future, the accuracy of their predictions, their antecedents, and consequents. We (i) review the two dimensions of prediction that have been most studied, utility and psychological distance, and how they combine to determine the perceived value of prospects (choice options). We (ii) discuss innovative research on these topics over the last decade, and (iii) end with important open questions and promising future directions.

I. Dimensions of Prediction

Guided by the evaluation of prospective (future) events in terms of their expected value (Kahneman & Tversky, 1979; Von Neumann & Morgenstern, 1947), the two dimensions of prediction typically studied by consumer psychologists are (a) the utility of future events and (b) their probability of occurrence. In this chapter, we discuss these two dimensions of prediction in terms of their recently refined and expanded definitions. Specifically, we review the concept of utility in terms of a refined definition that distinguishes between indirect and direct measures of utility. We review the concept of probability as an instance of a broader dimension of psychological distance, which also includes time, physical space, and more abstract forms of distance such as social connection.

Utility

Utility is a measure of the value of a stimulus that typically connotes the total pleasure or pain associated with its anticipation, experience, and recollection.

Consumer prediction research typically examines two kinds of utility associated with a future event: its *decision utility* and its *predicted utility* (Kahneman, Wakker, & Sarin, 1997; Morewedge, in press; Shiv & Huber, 2000). *Decision utility* refers to relative preference that people exhibit for different stimuli, measured through indirect methods such as observing which stimulus they choose when given a choice of stimuli and their willingness to pay for a stimulus. A bagel presumably has higher decision utility for a person than a banana, for example, if she chooses the bagel when given a choice of the two, or she is willing to pay more for the bagel than the banana. If one observes enough choices [e.g., (bagel > banana) + (banana > granola bar)], one can determine the decision utility of stimuli for that person by building an ordinal map of her rank-ordered preferences (bagel > banana > granola bar). Theoretically, there can be no error in decision utility. A person is assumed to always make choices in a way that will maximize her utility – what she chooses is presumably the choice option that will bring her the most utility (e.g., Bruni & Sugden, 2007; Pareto, 1906; Samuelson, 1937). Consequently, one cannot determine whether any of her choices are made in error. In other words, one cannot determine if the option with the highest decision utility is not the choice option that provides the highest *experienced utility* – the pleasure and pain actually derived from the option she chose (Kahneman, Wakker, & Sarin, 1997).

Predicted utility refers to the pleasure and pain that a person anticipates will be evoked by a future event or stimulus (a prediction of the experienced utility that the stimulus will provide). It is typically measured by asking a person to make an affective forecast – to predict how good or bad she will feel at a specific moment if the event occurs. A safari in Africa has greater predicted utility than wine tasting in France if a person believes that she will experience more pleasure if she vacations in Africa. Most forecasts are made for specific moments (How happy will you be while watching a lion taking down a wildebeest?) rather than of the *total utility* that an experience provides – the sum pleasure and pain of anticipating, having, and remembering the whole vacation. Predicted utility thus usually entails a forecast of one component of experienced utility, *instant utility*, which is the pleasure and pain experienced a single moment of an experience. The temporal inverse is *remembered utility*, which is a retrospective judgment of the pleasure and pain that one had during an experience (Kahneman, 1999; Kahneman, Wakker, & Sarin, 1997; Morewedge, in press). Predicted utility is a means by which to make choices between options, such as which to consume (Alba & Williams, 2013). It can also motivate behavior (Morewedge & Buechel, 2013) as people expend effort to produce the outcomes that they anticipate they will enjoy and to avoid the outcomes they believe will be unpleasant.

The accuracy of predicted utility can be determined by comparing affective forecasts of an experience to the instant utility reported by people currently having the forecasted experience ("experiencers"). For example, one can have one group of consumers predict how much they will enjoy eating a chocolate ice cream cone, have another group report their enjoyment of it while they are eating it, and compare the forecasts made by the former group to the reports made by the latter. These comparisons between predicted and instant utility allow one to test whether, when, and why forecasters err. Forecasters usually get the valence of the experience correct, but do make mistakes when inferring predicted utility. Forecasters usually recognize which experiences will be pleasurable and which will be unpleasant (Mathieu & Gosling, 2012), but they typically overestimate the intensity and duration of the pleasure and pain that experiences will induce. People overestimate how much they will enjoy an unexpected cash bonus or a greater salary (Buechel, Zhang, Morewedge, & Vosgerau, 2014; Aknin, Norton, & Dunn, 2009), for example, and for how long they will enjoy a newly acquired good (Wang, Novemsky & Dhar, 2009).

Decision utility and predicted utility are usually but not necessarily related. Both are assumed to adhere to the prospect theory value function (Kahneman & Tversky, 1979), which is asymmetric with respect to losses and gains and nonlinear with respect to the utility of increasing units of a stimulus. In both cases, a loss is assumed to have a greater psychological impact than an equivalent gain, and both losses and gains to have diminishing marginal utility. Moreover, people typically choose what that they believe will bring them the most pleasure. Most people would choose to eat a bagel rather than a banana if they thought it would bring them more pleasure to eat the bagel, and would choose to eat the banana if they thought it would bring them more pleasure than eating the bagel. Occasionally, however, decision utility inferred from choices does not reflect predicted utility, which we review in section two of this chapter.

Psychological Distance

A second dimension of consumer prediction is the concept of psychological distance. Recent work by Liberman, Trope, and colleagues (e.g., Liberman & Trope, 2014) proposes that the ability to traverse distances mentally – whether those distances are social, temporal, geographic, or hypothetical – is a general human ability that should potentially replace expectancy in models of expected utility. Although we question whether it should fully replace expectancy, we believe there are many ways that considering distance can help in refining models of consumer prediction.

People spend much of their lives outside of the here and now, recalling the past, imagining and planning for the future, and considering others' points of view. These various forms of traversing the present moment require the ability to assess and account for psychological distance. A considerable amount of new research suggests that the different domains of distance are processed automatically and are correlated with one another.

As evidence for automatic processing of this distance dimension, Bar-Anan, Liberman, Trope, and Algom (2007) used a picture-word version of the Stroop paradigm and showed participants landscape images with an arrow that either pointed at a nearby or faraway point on the image. Next to each arrow was a word that varied in terms of its meaning related to distance (e.g., *tomorrow, we,* or *sure* versus *year, others,* or *maybe*). Participants were faster to identify the spatial distance of words when there was distance congruence, that is, when the implicit distance conveyed by the word matched the distance between the arrow and point indicated in the image.

Regarding correlations between distances, Stephan, Liberman, and Trope (2011) found that experimentally inducing distance on one level (e.g., hypotheticality) primed thoughts about distance on another level (e.g., social distance). Moreover, Fiedler, Jung, Wanke, and Alexopoulous (2012) systematically examined correlations between all four distances and demonstrated that when people imagined themselves performing an activity that was either distal or proximal on one dimension (e.g., on time: winning a lottery tomorrow rather than in a year) they were more likely to assume a similar distance on another dimension (e.g., on probability: their chance of winning was estimated to be better in a lottery played tomorrow than in a lottery played next year).

Liberman and Trope (2014) suggest that the ability to project oneself beyond one's present perspective begins early in life. Infants exhibit a capacity for object permanence (Baillargeon, Spelke, & Wasserman, 1985), the understanding that when an object disappears it continues to exist. Object permanence represents a form of abstraction, thinking in high-level terms about the state of the world. And it is through abstract thought that people can effectively traverse psychological distance. Any given event can be represented at different levels of abstraction. Moving from New York to Los Angeles could be construed in high-level, abstract terms: "moving," "changing cities," "changing one's lifestyle." This same move can also be represented in low-level, concrete terms: "packing boxes," "hiring movers," "replacing bagels and Biggie with tacos and Tupac."

One of the basic premises of the theoretical work (construal level theory; Trope & Liberman, 2010) that underlies these predictions about distance is that the more distant a specific event is, the more abstract the construal of that event will be. Indeed, temporally distant events are construed in high-level terms whereas temporally near events are thought of in concrete terms (e.g., Liberman, Sagristano, & Trope, 2002), and similar results have been found for the domains of spatial distance (e.g., Fujita et al., 2006), social distance (Liviatan, Trope, & Liberman, 2008), and hypothetical distance (i.e., probability; Wakslak & Trope, 2009). This positive correlation between distance and abstraction stems in part from the relationship between direct experience and the amount of information that people possess about an event (Trope, Liberman, & Wakslak, 2007). Events occurring in the here and now provide one with many specific, concrete details (e.g., the lobster roll I am eating is red, the bread is crunchy and slightly buttered, the restaurant smells faintly of beer). But if that same event occurs at some faraway point in the distant future or in a faraway city, then one has less available information about the event and instead must rely on a more schematic abstraction of it (e.g., the lobster roll one anticipates cues thoughts of the summer and beach vacations).

Given this shift in the mental representation of events that are near and far, happening to oneself or another person, or are certain and uncertain, consumer prediction can be affected in important ways as a function of whether a predicted event occurs distally or proximally, and accordingly, whether that event is construed in abstract or concrete terms. In section two, we review recent findings illustrating these different effects.

Utility and Distance

Early research on the relationship between utility and distance focused on the discounting effect that uncertainty has on the decision utility of choice options. Lottery tickets, for example, cost a small fraction of their potential payout because they are partially discounted by the probability of winning the lottery (i.e., winning is not guaranteed). In this *expected-value* framework, the value of a stimulus is conditional not only on the utility that it would provide if it is obtained but also on the probability of obtaining it (EV = utility * probability; Von Neumann & Morgenstern, 1947). A gamble in which a person has a 10 percent chance to win $100 has an expected value of $10 (.10 * $100 = $10), for example, and has a lower expected value than a gamble in which that person has a 20 percent chance to win $100 (for which EV = $20).

More recent research has examined whether this relationship and the discounting effect extends to other instantiations of psychological distance. In other words, whether the value of a stimulus is contingent on both the utility of the stimulus and its psychological distance. This work has found that for temporal, spatial, and social distance, the value of a stimulus is discounted with its distance from the judge's origin: now, here, herself. Good and bad events have a greater hedonic impact if they are happening now, nearby, and to oneself than if they are happening in the distant future, far away, or to a stranger (Caruso, Gilbert, & Wilson, 2008; Jones & Rachlin, 2006; Williams & Bargh, 2008). An example of this work in psychology and economics is that of *temporal discounting*. Many people prefer to receive a smaller reward immediately ($10 now) than a larger reward later ($11 in one week). The discounting effects of different instantiations of distance appear to be (at least partially) interchangeable. Events occurring to a future self, for example, are in some cases treated like events happening right now to a different person (Bartels & Rips, 2010; Bryan & Hershfield, 2012; Parfit, 1971; Pronin, Olivola, & Kennedy, 2008; Schelling, 1984).

Discounting is not the only effect that varieties of distance can have on the value of future events. Uncertainty can have the opposite effect on the predicted utility of future events. Surprising, low-probability events tend to elicit a stronger hedonic response than events that are expected (Shepperd & McNulty, 2002). The actual probability of events is not the only way that an event may seem surprising. The *mutability* of an experience, the extent to which an event could have or seems like it could have occurred, similarly amplifies the pleasure or pain it evokes. Mutability can be assessed in advance. Highly uncertain outcomes such as winning the lottery or unlikely medical test results can be labeled as mutable events in advance. Events that were expected in advance, however, can also be perceived as highly mutable while or after they occur if a person can easily generate *counterfactual alternatives*. Counterfactuals are alternative ways that the past could have unfolded that would have produced a different present than the one that was or is being experienced (Kahneman & Miller, 1986). If one is in a car accident that could not have been avoided, for example, it may seem mutable if it is easy to imagine having left home earlier or later or if there were other routes that one might have taken to one's destination (Kahneman & Varey, 1990).

II. Recent Advances

Utility

Research in the past decade on consumers' predictions of utility has attempted to discern why people make errors in their predictions and fail to make choices that reflect their predictions when they are accurate (e.g., Alba & Williams, 2013; Dunn, Gilbert, & Wilson, 2011; Hsee & Hastie, 2006; Morewedge, in press). In the domain of decision utility, this research has focused on why people make choices that fail to maximize their utility – choose the option that would provide them with the most pleasure. In the domain of predicted utility, this research has focused on elucidating the process by which predicted utility is inferred and why and when predicted utility is most susceptible to "affective forecasting" errors.

Theoretically, decision utility is not subject to error. Most (economic) models of decision utility assume that an informed consumer chooses what would best maximize her utility (Bruni & Sugden, 2007). Postmortems of decision making reveal that people often do not maximize their utility, however, as revealed by the considerable number of decisions that people regard to have been regrettable or self-control failures (Baumeister, 2002; Morewedge, in press; Simonson, 1992). Research examining why consumers make choices that do not maximize their utility has generally sorted their mistakes into two categories: (1) failing to accurately predict the consequences of choice options (predicted utility) and (2) failing to select the choice option identified by prediction as maximizing utility (e.g., Hsee & Hastie, 2006). A consumer fails to maximize her utility due to prediction errors, for example, if she incorrectly predicts that she would enjoy eating a banana more than a bagel and chooses the banana on the basis of this false belief. Even if she does correctly predict that she would enjoy eating the bagel more, she may succumb to the second kind of error. Impulsivity may get the better of her, and she may decide to eat the banana because she does not have the patience to wait for the bagel to be toasted (Hsee & Hastie, 2006; Morewedge, in press; Wittman & Paulus, 2008).

Errors in Prediction

Two general accounts have been proposed by which consumers make predictions about how much pleasure or pain future experiences will evoke. A theory-based account suggests that people attempt to anticipate the consequences of future events and then anticipate how those consequences will make them feel (Loewenstein & Lerner, 2003; Tversky & Griffin, 1991). A simulation-based account suggests that people mentally simulate the future event, note how that simulation makes them feel in the present, and make corrections for any differences in context between the future and the present of which they are aware. People then use this corrected "pre-feeling" as a proxy for their response to the future event (Gilbert & Wilson, 2007).

Errors according to the theory-based account stem from inaccurate theories about the consequences of future events, the emotional impact of those consequences, or the influence of incidental (irrelevant) emotions on their actual predictions (Loewenstein & Lerner, 2003). Gym goers predicting whether they would be worse off if they packed insufficient food or water on a hike, for example, were more likely to predict they would regret forgetting food if they had yet to exercise than if they had already exercised. After working out, they were more likely to anticipate accurately how much more thirsty they would be than hungry (Van Boven & Loewenstein, 2003). People may also fail to anticipate accurately how the consequences of an event will make them feel if they are in a state that is not aligned with the preferences they will have in the future. Students, for example, are more likely to underestimate how uncomfortable they will feel telling a joke to their class when they are in a state of calm relaxation than when making their prediction in a state of negative arousal (Van Boven, Loewenstein, Welch, & Dunning, 2012).

Errors according to the simulation-based account occur when people fail to correctly simulate the future experience and when people fail to sufficiently correct for differences in the context in which the experience is forecasted and had (Gilbert & Wilson, 2007). Simulations of future experiences may be flawed because they are based on unrepresentative past experiences. When predicting how much they will enjoy a baseball game they are about to watch, for example, baseball fans tend to recall the best game they can remember and base their prediction on their memory of that unusually good game (Morewedge, Gilbert, & Wilson, 2005).

People also simulate unrepresentative portions of experiences. When people simulate future experiences or remember the past, they tend to focus most closely on the moments from those experiences that are nearest to the present (the beginning or end, respectively). When imagining how happy they will feel after acquiring a new gadget or car, people think about how they will feel in the moments right after it has been purchased rather than how they will feel a week or a month later after they have adapted to their acquisition. They thus overestimate how long new consumer goods will make them happy (Wang, Novemsky, & Dhar, 2009). In other words, people base their predictions on the experience of acquiring the good rather than on a typical moment during its consumption (Hsee, Hastie, & Chen, 2008). Predictions for the future also rely on memories of the past, and interference in memory leads people to best remember the last moments of recent past consumption experiences (Garbinsky,

Morewedge, & Shiv, 2014a). As a consequence, enjoyment of the latter moments of a consumption experience is overweighted when people decide how soon to repeat that consumption experience again in the future (Garbinsky, Morewedge, & Shiv, 2014b).

Even when forecasters accurately simulate future events, they may fail to correct for differences between the circumstances under which forecasts are made and experiences occur. Forecasters tend to overestimate the extent to which they will be tempted and able to compare experiences to their alternatives. As a consequence, they overestimate the extent to which their enjoyment of an experience will be influenced by its comparative value and by the likelihood of experiencing an alternative (Buechel et al., 2014; Gilbert, Morewedge, Risen, & Wilson, 2004; Hsee & Zhang, 2004; Morewedge et al., 2010; Morewedge, Kassam, Hsee, & Caruso, 2009).

Differences in circumstances may also be due to different goals or preferences that are salient or important when making a forecast and having an experience. Intense emotions or cravings may change how one values experiences, and those changes appear to be difficult to anticipate (e.g., Lerner, Small, & Loewenstein, 2004; Sayette, Loewenstein, Griffin, & Black, 2008). People believe that the person they are now is the person who they will always be. Although they recognize how much they have changed from the past, they think that their personality and preferences will remain stable in the future and consequently overpay to enjoy the things they enjoy now in that future (Quoidbach, Gilbert, & Wilson, 2013).

Errors in Execution

Even when people do correctly predict which choice options will bring them the most utility, impulsivity or an overreliance on heuristics may lead them to select options that fail to maximize their utility. People make impulsive decisions when choosing options that have fewer benefits in the long term than their alternatives but more benefits in the present. Immediate rewards may have more salient benefits, or options with greater future reward may seem less appealing because those future rewards are discounted. As impulsive choice options become near in time or space, their incentive value increases to the extent that they can be more tempting than larger future rewards (Ainslie, 2001; Caruso, Gilbert, & Wilson, 2008; Kivetz, Urminsky, & Zheng, 2006). A candy bar is most difficult to resist when it is in one's desk or within arms' reach in the checkout aisle. In some cases, motivational urges can be strong enough to prompt actions that are experienced as unpleasant. Smokers may experience strong cravings to smoke even when they have a negative attitude toward smoking (De Houwer, Custers, & De Clercq, 2006). Future rewards may also be overly discounted because of irregularities in the subjective perception of temporal or social distance (Hershfield, 2011; Zauberman, Kim, Malkoc, & Bettman, 2009), obtaining them seems more uncertain (Keren & Roelofsma, 1995), or the default is to receive the immediate reward rather than the delayed reward unless action is taken (Weber et al, 2007).

Relying too much on heuristics or decision rules may also lead people to fail to choose options that would maximize their utility because those rules fail to capture preferences that are implicit or difficult to articulate (e.g., Maison, Greenwald, & Bruin, 2004), are inappropriate to apply to the present context, or are simply wrong. People have difficulty saving and thus generally try to maximize their earnings when given the opportunity. Sometimes they over apply this rule, however, and end up *overearning* – working to acquire more resources than they can possibly consume (Hsee, Zhang, Cai, & Zhang, 2013). Reason-based choice may more generally lead people to make decisions that can be justified with results that are less satisfactory than decisions that are more difficult to justify. People believe that it is generally beneficial to have variety and more choice options (Botti, 2004). When making choices in advance, however, people may overestimate how much variety they will want in the future and underestimate how soon they will want their favorite option again (Simonson, 1992).

Having many choices can result in having options that better match one's preferences, but too many choices may be demotivating and lead one to delay or avoid choosing any of a set of desirable options (Iyengar & Lepper, 2000). Moreover, satisfaction with chosen options is not only a function of the utility those options provide, but also what those options lack that would have been provided by their alternatives. Consequently, the more, and more varied, choice options that one rejected when choosing, the less one enjoys the option that one chose, even it was indeed the best option (Diehl & Poynor, 2010; Sagi & Friedland, 2007).

Psychological Distance

By definition, a consumer can make predictions only about events that will occur in the future. Yet, the future comprises many different points in time. A consumer can make a prediction about how much he or she will enjoy a given meal in the next hour, the next day, or even years away. Recent advances in consumer psychology research have found that predictions are influenced by the psychological distance of a relevant target, regardless of whether that target is an event or a person. As noted earlier, distance does not have to be solely confined to the temporal domain, and can additionally be conceptualized in terms of geographic, social, and hypothetical distance. All of these perceived distances can affect consumer prediction, and they can do so in terms of confidence judgments, probability estimates, and planning for the future.

Confidence

Construal level theory (CLT) holds that distant events evoke an abstract mindset whereas events that are closer elicit more of a concrete mindset (Trope & Liberman, 2010). Indeed, evaluations and decisions regarding distant future events are more based on high-level aspects of alternatives (e.g., temporal, social, spatial, and hypothetical distance increases the weight given to ends versus means; Liberman & Trope, 1998; Liviatan, Trope, & Liberman, 2008; Sagristano, Trope, & Liberman, 2002; Todorov, Goren, & Trope, 2007). Accordingly, *predictions* made about a distant event should be based more on abstract or high-level construals compared to concrete or low-level construals. To test this possibility, Henderson, Fujita, Trope, and Liberman (2006) had research participants at New York University's Washington Square campus view a series of graphs that depicted events (e.g., number of inches of rainfall) over a five-year period from 1999 to 2004. The events were described as either occurring in New York (spatially near) or at NYU's Florence campus (spatially distant), and in each case there was a general trend for the first four years, followed by a deviation in the final year. Participants then predicted whether the following year's event would follow the general trend or be more in line with the previous year's aberration. In line with predictions made by CLT, participants in the spatially distant condition were more likely to base their predictions off of the high-level general trend (which represents an abstract rule), whereas participants in the spatially near condition were more likely to base their predictions off of the most recent year's aberrant event (a low-level, concrete piece of information).

Temporal distance and information format should subsequently affect confidence judgments about future events as well. Consider a student who is asked to make a confidence judgment about his or her performance on a test in the near or distant future. With more temporal distance between now and the date of the test, we would expect the student to rely more on abstract, high-level information (e.g., general knowledge of the subject matter) when making a prediction about his or her performance than on low-level concrete information (e.g., the format of the test). Along these lines, Nussbaum, Liberman, and Trope (2006) had research participants make predictions about their performance on an upcoming trivia quiz, either in the near or distant future (i.e., fifteen minutes or one month later). Additionally, half of the participants were told that the format was multiple-choice and half were told that it was open-ended, the latter being harder and more likely to tap into general knowledge. Participants who were led to believe that the quiz would take place in the near future were more confident in their ability to do well, but only if they were told that the quiz was a multiple-choice one compared to when it was described as open-ended. A more difficult format, in other words, engendered lower confidence for the near-future quiz. However, both question formats resulted in similarly high levels of confidence when the quiz was framed as taking place in the distant future. Temporal distance reduced the amount of weight assigned to low-level information (e.g., question format) and accordingly prevented the reduction in confidence that went along with this low-level information.

Probability

The hypotheticality of an event is correlated with other distances. For example, people are more likely to say that something "seems to be the case" than something "is the case" when addressing a socially distal person (Stephan et al., 2011). To what extent, however, is the distance of an event related to the likelihood – or probability – of an event's occurrence? Earlier research, which speaks tangentially to this question, demonstrated that people believe that frequent events are more likely to occur to the self and rare events more likely to happen to others, in both positive and negative domains (e.g., Chambers, Windschitl, & Suls, 2003; Kruger & Burrus, 2004). More recently, Wakslak (2012) proposed that unlikely events would be seen as intuitively more likely to occur in distal contexts and likely events seen as more likely to occur in more proximal contexts. This prediction is based on construal level theory insomuch as distant events are thought about abstractly (which is more in line with an "improbable" occurrence) and near events are thought about concretely (which is more in line with a "probable" occurrence). Indeed, earlier work has conceptualized likelihood as a dimension of psychological distance (Wakslak, Trope, Liberman, & Aloni, 2006). Events are seen as more distant (that is, more removed from one's direct experience) if they are hypothetical rather than actual.

Applying this logic to prediction, Wakslak (2012) found that research participants were more likely to think that a rare protein would be found in a friend's pet if the friend lived far away rather than close, would bet more on a boxing underdog if the fight were occurring across the country rather than nearby, were more likely to believe that a rare hand in poker would occur at the end of the night rather than the beginning, and that an unlikely but insurable event would be more likely to occur in a year rather than in a day. The latter finding has particular relevance for consumer prediction to the extent that consumers must regularly make probability judgments when deciding whether and how much insurance to purchase (Kunreuther, Pauly, & McMorrow, 2013). With greater distance (temporal or geographical in this case), consumers are more likely to assume that a relatively low-likelihood event actually has a relatively higher likelihood of occurring, which could cause them to enroll in insurance plans from which they are unlikely to benefit.

Planning

When it comes to making predictions about future behavior, one pervasive problem plaguing consumers is their tendency to exceptionalize the present and fail to connect past behavior to future outcomes. People, for example, fail to budget appropriately because they easily write off big-ticket expenses from each month as "special" expenditures that are unlikely to occur again (Sussman & Alter, 2012). Consumers are also prone to perceiving resource slack in the future (Zauberman & Lynch, 2005), insomuch as they are overly optimistic in thinking about how much they will save in a specific upcoming month (Tam & Dholakia, 2011). Along similar lines, people underestimate how much they will spend in a coming week, even if they know that they typically spend more than the predicted amount (Peetz & Buehler, 2009). These findings are in line with a host of studies on the planning fallacy, many of which suggest that people grossly underestimate the amount of time a given future task will take because they fail to adequately take into account past task completion times (e.g., Buehler, Griffin, & Peetz, 2010; Buehler, Griffin, & Ross, 1994).

In understanding the reasons underlying the planning fallacy, Buehler, Griffin, and Peetz (2010) have suggested that people are likely to take one of two approaches to making predictions: the inside view and the outside view (e.g., Kahneman & Lovallo, 1993). When adopting the "inside view," people are likely to consider the specific aspects of a given case at hand, making it all the more likely that they will see that particular instance as unique. Taking the "outside view," on the other hand, results in a less extreme planning fallacy because people are more likely to consider how a target event fits into a broader pattern of other events.

Peetz and Buehler (2012) recently proposed that one way to induce an outside perspective – and therefore, one way to help consumers make more accurate planning predictions – is to encourage an abstract construal, given that abstract construals tend to help people see events as part of a pattern rather than as unique occurrences (e.g., Fujita & Roberts, 2010; Ledgerwood, Wakslak, & Wang, 2010). To this end, when consumers were primed to be in an abstract rather than a concrete mindset, they made less optimistic (i.e., more realistic) spending predictions for the subsequent week (Peetz & Buehler, 2012). Furthermore, when consumers were asked to make spending predictions for the distant rather than near future, leading to a more abstract rather concrete construal, their predictions were more realistic.

Utility and Distance

Consumers assess utility for decisions that have immediate as well as more distant consequences. Indeed, many, if not all, purchasing decisions can in some way be related back to an estimation of future utility (Dunn, Gilbert, & Wilson, 2011; MacInnis, Patrick, & Park, 2006; Morewedge, in press). Despite the importance of these types of intertemporal spending predictions, consumers often fail to identify with the person who they will become (e.g., Bartels & Rips, 2010; Bartels & Urminsky, 2011; Hershfield, 2011) leading to decisions that can be considered suboptimal over time when enough temporal (and by extension, social) distance exists between the present self and the future self.

Parfit (1971), Schelling (1984), and others (e.g., Thaler & Shefrin, 1981) have suggested that people often act as if their future selves are different people altogether. With enough temporal distance, the distant self actually feels, on an emotional level, as if it is a stranger. This theoretical prediction is grounded in recent empirical work that has found that greater emotional intensity can reduce perceived psychological distance (Van Boven, Kane, McGraw, & Dale, 2010). People who feel more connected and similar to their future selves discount future rewards less (Bartels & Rips, 2010; Ersner-Hershfield et al., 2009; Pronin, Olivola, & Kennedy, 2008). One way, then, to help consumers identify with their future selves (and therefore make more accurate assessments of distant utility) is to heighten the emotional intensity of thoughts about those later selves.

In one recent study, retirement messages that appealed to a sense of social duty to one's future self were most effective among consumers who already feel a strong sense of emotional connection to those distant selves (Bryan & Hershfield, 2012). Participants who read vignettes about people with disrupted identities over time (e.g., from a divorce) discounted future rewards less (Bartels & Urminsky, 2011). Moreover, Hershfield and colleagues (2011) found that research participants who were exposed to vivid, visual images of their future selves allocated more hypothetical money to a long-term savings account compared to participants who simply saw images of their present selves. In follow-up work, Brown, Hershfield, Kouri, and Bryant (under review) found that this relationship between exposure to the future self and heightened saving was due to great episodic future thinking and an intensified emotional connection to the future self.

With more temporal distance, the future self becomes more socially distant as well. In fact, both forms of distance can lead to heightened discounting of rewards. When research participants were asked how much money they would forgo in order to give $75 to another person, the amount decreased hyperbolically along with social distance (Jones & Rachlin, 2006; see also Simon, 1995). Reducing the social distance between the current and future self, then, can lead to more accurate predictions and decisions regarding what the future self might want (to the extent that adults do in fact want more wealth later in life; Carstensen, 2011).

III. Open Questions

The last decade has been one of considerable advance in the study of consumer prediction. Faulty predictions and suboptimal choices have been identified and elucidated. The causes, consequences, and relationships among various forms of psychological distance have begun to be explored. Interactions among these dimensions beyond utility and probability have begun to be explored. Yet, as each dimension and their relationship has become better specified, more questions arise and many remain.

Utility

A major question for future research is how predicted utility and decision utility are related. People usually choose experiences that they believe will bring them more pleasure and less pain than their alternatives (Gilbert & Wilson, 2007; Hsee & Hastie, 2006), and how pleasurable they believe an experience will be influences how hard they work to experience it (Morewedge & Buechel, 2013). How people translate the predicted utility they anticipate in each moment of an experience into an assessment of its total utility and decision utility, however, is less well understood. Past research in this area has primarily focused on biases in the translation of predicted utility to decision utility. Given the choice between experiences that should increase in the utility they provide or decrease in the utility that they provide, for example, people prefer sequences with increasing levels of utility (Loewenstein & Prelec, 1993). Most people would prefer a job with a salary that will increase over time to a job with a salary that will decrease over time, even if both will pay them the same total amount of money.

Much research on the relationship between decision utility and remembered utility (which shares many similarities with predicted utility) has been studied in this vein, focusing on how biases in memory lead the utility provided by peak and end moments to be overweighted in retrospective evaluations of utility and decisions based on those evaluations (e.g., Frederickson & Kahneman, 1993; Kahneman, Fredrickson, Redelmeier, & Schrieber, 1993). When eating a food, for instance, memory for enjoyment of the last bites of the meal interfere with recollection of memory for enjoyment of the initial bites, which leads end enjoyment to be better remembered later and to determine when that food will be consumed again (Garbinksy, Morewedge, & Shiv, 2014a).

Promising new research in this area has developed models to create profiles of the *total utility* of experiences (the sum of all experienced utility they would provide) based on their component features (Baucells & Sarin, 2013). These models, even if subject to some error, are important because they provide a new normative standard for consumer predictions. In other words, these models will allow researchers to test whether consumers are able to forecast accurately the total utility of an experience – to predict accurately how much benefit to their life, on the whole, an experience will bring them. At the present, these comparisons will have to be very basic in nature – comparing the model predictions to consumer choices. This is because no normative way to measure predictions of total utility has been widely adopted that does not rely on methods used to elicit decision utility (e.g., maximum willingness to pay or choice). Kahneman (1999) suggested one duration-weighted method that shares many similarities with the quality-adjusted life years method that is used in medicine, but, to our knowledge, no comparisons between total predicted utility and experienced total utility have been directly tested (Morewedge, in press).

It is possible that people do not attempt to predict the total utility of future experiences. They may only anticipate how they will feel in particular moments. They may focus on the experienced utility associated with an event and under-weight the pleasure they will feel from its anticipation or recollection. Or they may only take anticipation and recollection into account for very brief experiences that provide considerable (dis)utility from anticipation and recollection, such as an electric shock or a kiss (Loewenstein, 1987). Indirect methods of utility elicitation are likely to help understand where biases in these predictions are present and absent, but the development of more direct measures is needed to compare the accuracy of predictions and experiences.

Another major question is whether consumers use predicted utility as the primary determinant of decision utility. Other features of experiences, such as the moral and societal consequences of the experience or the religious and secular ideals and beliefs of the consumer, may contribute more to decision utility than the total pleasure the experience might yield (e.g., Dunn, Aknin, & Norton, 2008; Rucker & Galinsky, 2009). An important example of this is the decision to have children. Most adults decide to have children, yet the evidence that the decision to have children maximizes one's experienced utility is ambiguous at best (Bhargava, Kassam, Loewenstein, 2014). When making moral decisions, people also often choose according to their moral principles and beliefs rather than according to principles of utility maximization (Greene, 2013). It is possible that for many choices, both important and mundane, the total utility that choice options provide has relatively little to do with the option that is chosen.

This question is particularly relevant for consumer decision making, as consumers often are forced to make trade-offs between the utility they imagine they will derive from a good and other attributes such as its price (and opportunity costs). Whether people choose a good because of a sophisticated calculation that takes into account overall utility or because of a particular feature is a crucial question that is difficult to answer. Indeed, consumers seem to neglect important features of the utility of alternatives such as opportunity costs (Frederick et al., 2009). Those consumers who do attempt to engage in utility maximization (maximizers) often appear to struggle with choices during and after decisions. They even are less satisfied in some cases with the (better) choices they have made than satisficers (i.e., consumers who simply choose the first option that surpassed a basic threshold of acceptability; Iyengar, Wells, & Schwartz, 2006).

Distance

Seeing into the Future

Much of our society overeats, undersaves, and mistreats the environment. Given these ubiquitous problems with intertemporal (present vs. future) decision making, it is perhaps not surprising that a large body of research has examined the many ways that people interact with the future. People make fundamentally different decisions for the present than for the future, for example, and these decisions are often erroneous. These suboptimal decisions can arise when people commit one of several different "errors of prospection" (Gilbert & Wilson, 2007), such as failing to simulate the future accurately. Such prospection requires mental time travel (Suddendorf & Corballis, 2007) from one state (the present) to another (the future), crossing a dividing line that separates the two. A major determinant of impulsivity and self-control failure, whether people prefer a smaller reward sooner to a larger reward later, is whether the smaller reward will be received immediately (Hsee & Hastie, 2006; McClure, Laibson, Loewenstein, & Cohen, 2004).

Surprisingly, the literature to date has offered little insight by way of defining this dividing line. In other words, *when is the future?* People perceive time as a sequence of episodes (Newtson, Engquist, & Bois, 1977), but when does the present end and the future begin, and what determines this end and beginning?

Maglio and Hershfield (2014) have begun exploring this question on a general level, and more specifically, whether people differ in their perceptions of when the present ends, if such perceptions are linked to intertemporal decision making, and whether the sense of when the present ends (and the future starts) can be altered. Preliminary results suggest that consumers who perceive a sooner end to the present are more likely to make more patient long-term decisions. If the present ends sooner, the future will bleed more into the "now," causing it to be viewed as starting sooner, and in turn, receiving more weight than it would otherwise receive. This general question is not confined to temporal distance. It is ambiguous how people determine what is not the "origin": what is here and what is there, socially close and distant, and the malleability of these conceptual boundaries.

Beyond the basic distinction of now and later, even less is known about whether people differently perceive the near and far future. In other words, at what point does the future move from being a detailed, vivid scene to a vague and essentialized one? How far can we see into the future before an event ceases to be a realistic picture and becomes more of a cartoonish representation or unfathomable? When is an event so distant that we are unable to picture it, an event sufficiently unlikely that it seems impossible, or a person so different that we cannot imagine what it is like to be her?

Relationships with Different Selves

Consumers are marked by different relationships to different selves in time. People tend to think that their future self will be more similar to their present self than the degree of similarity between their past self and their present self (Quoidbach, Gilbert, & Wilson, 2013). With a great deal of temporal distance, however, we suspect that a young enough past self will be thought of in positive terms, whereas a much older future self might be imbued with negativity. Early childhood, after all, is marked by potential, which can be more valued than actual outcomes (Tormala, Jia, & Norton, 2012), and older adulthood sometimes suffers from negative stereotypes (North & Fiske, 2012). But not all past selves are considered equally: people often denigrate recent past versions of themselves in an effort to feel better about their current selves (Wilson & Ross, 2001), and yet at the same time they idealize slightly earlier versions of themselves and frequently experience nostalgia for a past that is no longer present (Wildschut, Sedikides, Arndt, & Routledge, 2006). An open question, then, concerns the ways in which differing relationships to past selves predict the sense of connection one feels toward the future self.

Relationships with Uncertainty

Consumers and professionals both have difficulty conceptualizing uncertain future events, whether the origin of their uncertainty is their own lack of knowledge or a random process determining whether the future event will happen. Better differentiating these different kinds of uncertainty and designing better elicitation techniques are two promising new areas of development in consumer prediction. Both forms of uncertainty are different, but also share common sources of bias. When judging their relative abilities or likelihood of experiencing a future event, for example, people overweight their own abilities or likelihood of experiencing the event and underweight distributional information such as the general ability level of the population or how frequently other people experience similar events (Kruger & Dunning, 1999; Moore & Healy, 2008; Price, Pentecost, & Voth, 2002). More generally, new elicitation methods are being developed to improve the precision of judgments about the likelihood or prevalence of future events, such as having judges complete subjective probability interval estimates (SPIES; Haran, Moore, & Morewedge, 2010), which explicitly remind judges to consider the full range of possible outcomes of an uncertain future before eliciting their confidence in an uncertain future event.

Utility and Distance

The various instantiations of distance appear to similarly discount utility, but it is not clear whether a common mechanism(s) or different mechanisms underlie discounting by uncertainty, space, time, and social distance. One factor may underlie all of these instances, or each instance may be singly or multiply determined. Discounting by time, for example, appears to be influenced by several factors. Both the nonlinear perception of the passage of time (Zauberman et al., 2009) and the perception that the same event in the future will provide less pleasure than it would in the present appear to lead to temporal discounting (Caruso, Gilbert, & Wilson, 2008; Van Boven, White, & Huber, 2009). Time delay and the uncertainty of future rewards are also deeply interrelated. Foregoing an immediate reward for a larger future reward introduces the risk that one may not receive the reward in the future, and discount rates are sensitive to the amount of risk that the larger future reward will not be paid (Keren & Roelofsma, 1995).

Williams, Huang, and Bargh (2009) have argued that physical distance is the form of psychological distance that most children first experience. Consequently, physical distance may provide the foundation for the mental representation of distance. The other, more abstract, instantiations of distance may then be "scaffolded" upon this initial representation built upon physical interaction with objects in the outside world in childhood. Indeed, asymmetric priming effects among the instantiations of distance are observed such that priming spatial distance constructs (e.g., "local" versus "foreign") appear to have a stronger priming effect on judgments in other dimensions of psychological distance (spatial, temporal, or uncertainty) than does priming the other dimensions of psychological distance on judgments of spatial distance (Zhang & Wang, 2009). Thus, one possibility is that the common discounting effect observed across various forms of distance is due to some facet of the mental representation of physical distance.

A second possible source of the common discounting effect has been suggested by Liberman, Trope, and Halamish (in prep), who propose it is due to the greater dilution of states of the world in which one will experience the focal outcome that occurs as the psychological distance to that outcome increases. More specifically, they suggest that introducing psychological distance increases the number of imagined possible outcome-less states, counterfactual states of the world in which one would not experience the pleasant or unpleasant event. Increasing the distance from a reward increases the number of states in which one would not get to experience it: for temporal distance, the number of distinct selves until the reward is received; for spatial distance, the number of states through which one must travel until the reward is reached; for uncertainty, the number of counter-factual states in which the reward may not be experienced; and for social distance, the states in which some share of the reward may not be experienced (e.g., shared with the self). In support of their theory, the authors find that the same span of time delay results in greater discounting for the values of gains and losses when it cues thoughts of more outcome-less states of the world (e.g., days in which one would not receive a reward or have to pay a penalty).

We suggest that uncertainty is a third possible source of these similar forms of discounting. All forms of distance introduce the uncertainty that an event will be experienced, as distance from the present self becomes larger. Time, space, and social distance all reduce the probability that future rewards and punishments will be experienced. Experiences that happen to one now have a greater guarantee to affect one than experiences that happen in the future, elsewhere, or to another person. Introducing a temporal delay introduces the chance that one may not live to have the experience (or that the party responsible for providing the experience will not be around to produce it). Introducing spatial distance introduces the uncertainty that an event happening somewhere else will also affect where one is. An earthquake farther away is less likely to hurt people one knows and damage homes and infrastructure if it happens thousands of miles away rather than nearby. Introducing social distance increases the uncertainty that one will experience the event or its consequences. The chance of receiving some share of a lottery win is likely to be greater if the person who won the lottery is oneself, one's spouse, or a close family member rather than a distant relation or stranger.

It is possible that any one, all, or none of these mechanisms may drive the common pattern of discounting that is evoked by the various instantiations of distance. Much more research is needed to explain how different forms of psychological distance lead people to discount the perceived value of future experiences, and how truly comparable are the processes underlying these discounting effects.

Conclusion

The last fifteen years of research on consumer prediction has seen greater distinctions drawn between forms of utility and more connections drawn between instantiations of distance. In the coming years, these directions are likely to reverse, with more attention being paid to the overlap between predicted and decision utility to better integrate the research on each from marketing, psychology, and economics and apply these findings to problems faced by consumers and practitioners in the field. It is possible that forecasts of predicted utility that are simulation-based or theory-based may better reflect decision utility, or it may be estimated according to a completely different process. It is likely that more research will be done to connect and differentiate the various instantiations of psychological distance. Most predictions involve multiple forms of distance. A better understanding of how each dimension overlaps with and affects other dimensions will increase the precision of our understanding of how consumers envision the future. Finally, the prospect of expanding the expected value framework from the interaction of utility and probability to that of utility and other instantiations of distance is a potential major advance in the conceptualization of consumer prediction and worthy of considerable testing and attention.

References

Ainslie, G. (2001). *Breakdown of Will*. Cambridge: Cambridge University Press.

Aknin, L. B., Norton, M. I., & Dunn, E. W. (2009). From wealth to well-being? Money matters, but less than people think. *Journal of Positive Psychology, 4*, 523–527.

Alba, J. W., & Williams, E. F. (2013). Pleasure principles: A review of research on hedonic consumption. *Journal of Consumer Psychology, 23*, 2–18.

Baillargeon, R., Spelke, E.S., & Wasserman, S. (1985). Object permanence in five-month old infants. *Cognition, 20*, 191–208.

Bar-Anan, Y., Liberman, N., Trope, Y., & Algom, D. (2007). Automatic processing of psychological distance: Evidence from a stroop task. *Journal of Experimental Psychology: General, 136*, 610–622.

Bartels, D. M. & Rips, L. J. (2010). Psychological connectedness and intertemporal choice. *Journal of Experimental Psychology: General, 139*, 49–69.

Bartels, D.M. & Urminsky, O. (2011). On intertemporal selfishness: The perceived instability of identity underlies impatient consumption. *Journal of Consumer Research, 38*, 182–198.

Baucells, M. & Sarin, R. K. (2013) Determinants of experienced utility: Laws and implications. *Decision Analysis, 10*, 135–151.

Baumeister, R. F. (2002). Yielding to temptation: Self-control failure, impulsive purchasing, and consumer behavior. *Journal of Consumer Research, 28*, 670–676.

Bhargava, S., Kassam, K. S., & Loewenstein, G. (2014). A reassessment of the defense of parenthood. *Psychological Science, 25*, 299–302.

Botti, S. (2004). The psychological pleasure and pain of choosing: when people prefer choosing at the cost of subsequent outcome satisfaction. *Journal of Personality and Social Psychology, 87*, 312.

Boven, L. V., Loewenstein, G., Welch, E., & Dunning, D. (2012). The illusion of courage in self-predictions: Mispredicting one's own behavior in embarrassing situations. *Journal of Behavioral Decision Making, 25*, 1–12.

Brown, A. D., Hershfield, H. E., Kouri, N. A., & Bryant, R. A. (Under review). Old man you're a lot like me: Similarity between current and future self mediates the relationship between episodic future thinking and temporal discounting.

Bruni, L., & Sugden, R. (2007). The road not taken: How psychology was removed from economics, and how it might be brought back. *Economic Journal, 117*, 146–173.

Bryan, C. J., & Hershfield, H. E. (2012). You owe it to yourself: Boosting retirement saving with a responsibility-based appeal. *Journal of Experimental Psychology: General, 141*, 429–432.

Buechel, E. C., Zhang, J., Morewedge, C. K., & Vosgerau, J. (2014). More intense experiences, less intense forecasts: Why affective forecasters overweight probability specifications. *Journal of Personality and Social Psychology, 106*, 20–36.

Buehler, R., Griffin, D., & Peetz, J. (2010). The planning fallacy: Cognitive, motivational, and social origins. In M. P. Zanna & J. M. Olson (eds.), *Advances in Experimental Social Psychology* (vol. 43, pp. 1–62). San Diego, CA: Academic Press.

Buehler, R., Griffin, D., Ross, M. (1994). Exploring the "planning fallacy": Why people underestimate their task completion times. *Journal of Personality and Social Psychology, 67*, 366–81.

Carstensen, L. L. (2011). *A Long Bright Future.* New York: Random House.

Caruso, E. M., Gilbert, D. T., & Wilson, T. D. (2008). A wrinkle in time: Asymmetric valuation of past and future events. *Psychological Science, 19*, 796–801.

Chambers, J. R., Windschitl, P. D., & Suls, J. (2003). Egocentrism, event frequency, and comparative optimism: When what happens frequently is "more likely to happen to me." *Personality and Social Psychology Bulletin, 29*, 1343–1356.

De Houwer, J., Custers, R., & De Clercq, A. (2006). Do smokers have a negative implicit attitude toward smoking? *Cognition and Emotion, 20*, 1274–1284.

Diehl, K., & Poynor, C. (2010). Great expectations?! Assortment size, expectations, and satisfaction. *Journal of Marketing Research, 47*, 312–322.

Dunn, E. W., Aknin, L. B., & Norton, M. I. (2008). Spending money on others promotes happiness. *Science, 319*, 1687–168.

Dunn, E. W., Gilbert, D. T., & Wilson, T. D. (2011). If money doesn't make you happy, then you probably aren't spending it right. *Journal of Consumer Psychology, 21*, 115–125.

Ersner-Hershfield, H., Garton, M.T., Ballard, K., Samanez-Larkin, G.R., & Knutson, B. (2009). Don't stop thinking about tomorrow: Individual differences in future self-continuity account for saving. *Judgment and Decision Making, 4*, 280–286.

Fiedler, K., Jung, J., Wänke, M., Alexopoulos, T. (2012). On the Relations between Distinct Aspects of Psychological Distance: An Ecological Basis of Construal-Level Theory. *Journal of Experimental Social Psychology, 48*, 1014–1021.

Frederick, S., Novemsky, N., Wang, J., Dhar, R., & Nowlis, S. (2009). Opportunity cost neglect. *Journal of Consumer Research, 36*, 553–561.

Fredrickson, B. L., & Kahneman, D. (1993). Duration neglect in retrospective evaluations of affective episodes. *Journal of Personality and Social Psychology, 65*, 45–55.

Fujita, K., & Roberts, J. C. (2010). Promoting prospective self-control through abstraction. *Journal of Experimental Social Psychology, 46*, 1049–1054.

Fujita, K., Henderson, M., Eng, J., Trope, Y., & Liberman, N. (2006). Spatial distance and mental construal of social events. *Psychological Science, 17*, 278–282.

Garbinsky, E. N., Morewedge, C. K., & Shiv, B. (2014a). Interference of the end: Why recency bias in memory determines when a food is consumed again. *Psychological Science, 25*, 1466–1474.

Garbinsky, E. N., Morewedge, C. K., & Shiv, B. (2014b). Does liking or wanting determine repeat consumption delay? *Appetite, 72*, 59–65.

Gilbert, D. T., Morewedge, C. K., Risen, J. L., & Wilson, T. D. (2004). Looking forward to looking backward: The misprediction of regret. *Psychological Science 15*, 346–350.

Gilbert, D. T., & Wilson, T. D. (2007). Prospection: Experiencing the future. *Science, 317*, 1351–1354.

Greene, J. (2013). *Moral Tribes: Emotion, Reason, and the Gap between Us and Them.* New York: Penguin Press.

Haran, U., Moore, D. A., & Morewedge, C. K. (2010). A simple remedy for over-precision in judgment. *Judgment and Decision Making, 5*, 467–476.

Henderson, M. D., Fujita, K., Trope, Y., & Liberman, N. (2006). Transcending the "here": The effect of spatial distance on social judgment. *Journal of Personality and Social Psychology, 91*, 845–856.

Hershfield, H. E. (2011). Future self-continuity: How conceptions of the future self transform intertemporal choice. *Annals of the New York Academy of Sciences, 1235*, 30–43.

Hershfield, H. E., Goldstein, D. G., Sharpe, W. F., Fox, J., Yeykelvis, L., Carstensen, L. L., & Bailenson, J. (2011). Increasing saving behavior through age-progressed renderings of the future self. *Journal of Marketing Research, 48*, S23–S27.

Hsee, C. K., & Hastie, R. (2006). Decision and experience: Why don't we choose what makes us happy? *Trends in Cognitive Sciences, 10*, 31–37.

Hsee, C. K., Hastie, R., & Chen, J. (2008). Hedonomics: Bridging decision research with happiness research. *Perspectives on Psychological Science, 3*, 224–243.

Hsee, C. K. & Zhang, J. (2004). Distinction bias: Misprediction and mischoice due to joint evaluation. *Journal of Personality and Social Psychology, 86*, 680–695.

Hsee, C. K., Zhang, J., Cai, C. F., & Zhang, S. (2013). Overearning. *Psychological Science, 24*, 852–859.

Iyengar, S. S., & Lepper, M. R. (2000). When choice is demotivating: Can one desire too much of a good thing? *Journal of Personality and Social Psychology, 79*, 995–1006.

Iyengar, S. S., Wells, R. E., & Schwartz, B. (2006). Doing better but feeling worse: Looking for the "best" job undermines satisfaction. *Psychological Science, 17*, 143–150.

Jones, B., & Rachlin, H. (2006). Social discounting. *Psychological Science, 17*, 283–286.

Kahneman, D. (1999). Objective happiness. In D. Kahneman, E. Diener, & N. Schwartz (eds.), *Well-being: The Foundations of Hedonic Psychology* (pp. 3–26). New York: Russell Sage.

Kahneman, D., Fredrickson, B. L., Schreiber, C. A., & Redelmeier, D. A. (1993). When more pain is preferred to less: Adding a better end. *Psychological science, 4*, 401–405.

Kahneman, D., & Lovallo, D. (1993). Timid choices and bold forecasts: A cognitive perspective on risk taking. *Management Science, 39*, 17–31.

Kahneman, D., & Miller, D. T. (1986). Norm theory: Comparing reality to its alternatives. *Psychological Review, 93,* 136–153.

Kahneman, D., & Tversky, A. (1979). Prospect theory: An analysis of decision under risk. *Econometrica, 47,* 263–291.

Kahneman, D., & Varey, C. A. (1990). Propensities and counterfactuals: The loser that almost won. *Journal of Personality and Social Psychology, 59,* 1101–1110.

Kahneman, D., Wakker, P. P., & Sarin, R. (1997). Back to Bentham? Explorations of experienced utility. *Quarterly Journal of Economics, 112,* 375–405.

Keren, G., & Roelofsma, P. (1995). Immediacy and certainty in intertemporal choice. *Organizational Behavior and Human Decision Processes, 63,* 287–297.

Kivetz, R., Urminsky, O., & Zheng, Y. (2006). The goal-gradient hypothesis resurrected: Purchase acceleration, illusionary goal progress, and customer retention. *Journal of Marketing Research, 43,* 39–58.

Kruger, J., & Burrus, J. (2004). Egocentrism and focalism in unrealistic optimism (and pessimism). *Journal of Experimental Social Psychology, 40,* 332–40.

Kruger, J., & Dunning, D. (1999). Unskilled and unaware of it: How difficulties in recognizing one's own incompetence lead to inflated self-assessments. *Journal of Personality and Social Psychology, 77,* 1121–1134.

Kunreuther, H., Pauly, M. V., & McMorrow, S. (2013). *Insurance and Behavioral Economics: Improving Decisions in the Most Misunderstood Industry.* New York: Cambridge University Press.

Ledgerwood, A., Wakslak, C. J., and Wang, M. A. (2010) Differential information use for near and distant decisions. *Journal of Experimental Social Psychology, 46,* 638–642.

Lerner, J. S., Small, D. A., & Loewenstein, G. (2004). Heart strings and purse strings: Carryover effects of emotions on economic decisions. *Psychological Science, 15,* 337–341.

Liberman, N., Sagristano, M. D., & Trope, Y. (2002). The effect of temporal distance on level of mental construal. *Journal of Experimental Social Psychology, 38,* 523–534.

Liberman, N. & Trope, Y. (2014). Traversing psychological distance. *Trends in Cognitive Science, 18,* 364–369.

Liberman, N. & Trope, Y. (1998). The role of feasibility and desirability in near and distant future decisions: A test of temporal distance on level of construal. *Journal of Personality and Social Psychology, 75,* 5–18

Liberman, N., Trope, Y., & Halamish, V. (in preparation). A Proximity x Value Theory of Utility and Motivation. Tel Aviv University.

Liviatan, I., Trope, Y., & Liberman, N. (2008). Interpersonal similarity as a social distance dimension: Implications for perception of others' actions. *Journal of Experimental Social Psychology, 44,* 1256–1269.

Loewenstein, G. (1987). Anticipation and the valuation of delayed consumption. *Economic Journal, 97,* 666–684.

Loewenstein, G., & Lerner, J. S. (2003). The role of affect in decision making. In R. J. Davidson, K. R. Scherer, & H. H. Goldsmith (eds.), *Handbook of Affective Sciences* (pp. 619–642). New York: Oxford University Press.

Loewenstein, G. F., & Prelec, D. (1993). Preferences for sequences of outcomes. *Psychological Review, 100,* 91–108.

MacInnis, D. J., Patrick, V., and Park, C. W. (2006). Looking through the crystal ball: Affective forecasting and misforecasting in consumer behavior. *Review of Marketing Research, 2*, 43–80.

Maglio, S. & Hershfield, H.E. (2014). *When Does the Future Start?* Paper presented at the Society for Personality and Social Psychology Annual Conference, Austin, TX.

Mathieu, M.T. & Gosling, S.D. (2012). The accuracy or inaccuracy of affective forecasts depends on how accuracy is indexed: A meta-analysis of past studies. *Psychological Science, 23*, 161–162.

Maison, D., Greenwald, A. G., & Bruin, R. H. (2004). Predictive validity of the Implicit Association Test in studies of brands, consumer attitudes, and behavior. *Journal of Consumer Psychology, 14*, 405–415.

McClure, S. M., Laibson, D. I., Loewenstein, G., & Cohen, J. D. (2004). Separate neural systems value immediate and delayed monetary rewards. *Science, 306*, 503–507.

Moore, D. A., & Healy, P. J. (2008). The trouble with overconfidence. *Psychological Review, 115*, 502.

Morewedge, C. K. (In press). Utility: Anticipated, experienced, and remembered. In G. Keren and G. Wu (eds.), *Blackwell Handbook of Judgment and Decision Making,* 2nd ed. Malden, MA: Blackwell Press.

Morewedge, C. K., & Buechel, E. C. (2013). Motivated underpinnings of the impact bias in affective forecasts. *Emotion, 13*, 1023–1029.

Morewedge, C. K., Gilbert, D. T., & Wilson, T. D. (2005). The least likely of times: How remembering the past biases forecasts of the future. *Psychological Science, 16*, 626–630.

Morewedge, C. K., Gilbert, D. T., Myrseth, K. O. R., Kassam, K. S., & Wilson, T. D. (2010). Consuming experiences: Why affective forecasters overestimate comparative value. *Journal of Experimental Social Psychology, 46*, 986–992.

Morewedge, C. K., Kassam, K. S., Hsee, C. K., & Caruso, E. M. (2009). Duration sensitivity depends on stimulus familiarity. *Journal of Experimental Psychology: General, 138*, 177–186.

Newtson, D., Engquist, G. A., & Bois, J. (1977). The objective basis of behavior units. *Journal of Personality and Social Psychology, 35*, 847–862.

North, M. S., & Fiske, S. T. (2012). An inconvenienced youth? Ageism and its potential intergenerational roots. *Psychological Bulletin, 138*, 982–997.

Nussbaum, S., Liberman, N., & Trope, Y. (2006). Predicting the near and distant future. *Journal of Experimental Psychology: General, 135*, 152–161.

Pareto, Vilfredo (1906). *Manuale di economia politica, con una introduzione alla scienza sociale.* Milan: Societa Editrice Libraria.

Parfit, D. (1971). Personal identity. *Philosophical Review, 80*, 3–27.

Peetz, J., & Buehler, R. (2009). Is there a budget fallacy? The role of savings goals in the prediction of personal spending. *Personality and Social Psychology Bulletin, 35*, 1579–1591

Peetz, J., & Buehler, R. (2012). When distance pays off: The role of construal level in spending predictions. *Journal of Experimental Social Psychology, 48*, 395–398.

Price, P. C., Pentecost, H. C., & Voth, R. D. (2002). Perceived event frequency and the optimistic bias: Evidence for a two-process model of personal risk judgments. *Journal of Experimental Social Psychology, 38*, 242–252.

Pronin, E., Olivola, C. Y., & Kennedy, K. A. (2008). Doing unto future selves as you would do unto others: Psychological distance and decision making. *Personality and Social Psychology Bulletin, 34*, 224–236.

Quoidbach, J., Gilbert, D., & Wilson, T. (2013). The end of history illusion. *Science, 339*, 96–98.

Rucker, D. D., & Galinsky, A. D. (2009). Conspicuous consumption versus utilitarian ideals: How different levels of power shape consumer behavior. *Journal of Experimental Social Psychology, 45*, 549–555.

Sagi, A., & Friedland, N. (2007). The cost of richness: the effect of the size and diversity of decision sets on post-decision regret. *Journal of Personality and Social Psychology, 93*, 515–524.

Sagristano, M. D., Trope, Y., & Liberman, N. (2002). Time-dependent gambling: Odds now, money later. *Journal of Experimental Psychology: General, 131*, 364–376.

Samuelson, P. A. (1937). A note on measurement of utility. *Review of Economic Studies, 4*, 155–161.

Sayette, M. A., Loewenstein, G., Griffin, K. M., & Black, J. J. (2008). Exploring the cold-to-hot empathy gap in smokers. *Psychological Science, 19*, 926–932.

Schelling, T.C. (1984). Self-command in practice, in policy, and in theory of rational choice. *American Economic Review, 74*, 1–11.

Shepperd, J. A., & McNulty, J. K. (2002). The affective consequences of expected and unexpected outcomes. *Psychological Science, 13*, 85–88.

Shiv, B., & Huber, J. (2000). The impact of anticipating satisfaction on consumer choice. *Journal of Consumer Research, 27*, 202–216.

Simon, J. L. (1995). Interpersonal allocation continuous with intertemporal allocation: Binding commitments, pledges, bequests. *Rationality and Society, 7*, 367–392.

Simonson, I. (1992). The influence of anticipating regret and responsibility on purchase decisions. *Journal of Consumer Research, 19*, 105–118.

Stephan, E., Liberman, N., & Trope, Y. (2011). The effects of time perspective and level of construal on social distance. *Journal of Experimental Social Psychology, 47*, 397–402.

Suddendorf, T. & Corballis, M. C. (2007). The evolution of foresight: What is mental time travel and is it unique to humans? *Behavioral and Brain Sciences, 30*, 299–313.

Sussman, A. B., & Alter, A. L. (2012). The exception is the rule: Underestimating and overspending on exceptional expenses. *Journal of Consumer Research, 39*, 800–814.

Tam, L. & Dholakia, U. M. (2011). Delay and duration effects of time frames on personal savings estimates and behavior. *Organizational Behavior and Human Decision Processes, 114*, 142–152.

Thaler, R. H. & Shefrin, H. M. (1981). An economic theory of self-control. *Journal of Political Economy, 89*, 392–406.

Todorov, A., Goren, A., & Trope, Y. (2007). Probability as a psychological distance: Construal and preferences. *Journal of Experimental Social Psychology, 43*, 473–482.

Tormala, Z. L., Jia, J. S., & Norton, M. I. (2012). The preference for potential. *Journal of Personality and Social Psychology, 103*, 567–583.

Trope, Y. & Liberman, N. (2010). Construal Level Theory of Psychological Distance. *Psychological Review, 117*, 440–463.

Trope, Y., Liberman, N., & Wakslak, C. (2007). Construal levels and psychological distance: Effects on representation, prediction, evaluation, and behavior. *Journal of Consumer Psychology, 17*, 83–95.

Tversky, A., & Griffin, D. (1991). Endowment and contrast in judgments of wellbeing. In F. Strack, M. Argyle, & N. Schwartz (eds.), *Subjective Well-being: An Interdisciplinary Perspective* (pp. 101–118). Oxford: Pergamon Press.

Van Boven, L., Kane, J., McGraw, A. P., & Dale, J. (2010). Feeling close: Emotional intensity reduces perceived psychological distance. *Journal of Personality and Social Psychology, 98*, 872–885.

Van Boven, L., & Loewenstein, G. (2003). Social projection of transient drive states. *Personality and Social Psychology Bulletin, 29*, 1159–1168.

Van Boven, L., Loewenstein, G., Welch, E., & Dunning, D. (2012). The illusion of courage in self-predictions: Mispredicting one's own behavior in embarrassing situations. *Journal of Behavioral Decision Making, 25*, 1–12.

Van Boven, L., White, K., & Huber, M. (2009). Immediacy bias in emotion perception: Current emotions seem more intense than previous emotions. *Journal of Experimental Psychology: General, 138*, 368–382.

Von Neumann, J., & Morgenstern, O. (1947). *Theory of Games and Economic Behavior.* Princeton, NJ: Princeton University Press.

Wakslak, C. J. (2012) The experience of cognitive dissonance in important and trivial domains. *Journal of Experimental Social Psychology, 48*, 1361–1364.

Wakslak, C. J., & Trope, Y. (2009). Cognitive consequences of affirming the self: The relationship between self-affirmation and object construal. *Journal of Experimental Social Psychology, 45*, 927–932.

Wakslak, C. J., Trope, Y., Liberman, N., & Aloni, R. (2006). Seeing the forest when entry is unlikely: Probability and the mental representation of events. *Journal of Experimental Psychology: General, 135*, 641–653.

Wang, J., Novemsky, N., & Dhar, R. (2009). Anticipation adaptation to products. *Journal of Consumer Research, 36*, 149–159.

Weber, E. U., Johnson, E. J., Milch, K. F., Chang, H., Brodscholl, J. C., & Goldstein, D. G. (2007). Asymmetric discounting in intertemporal choice a query-theory account. *Psychological Science, 18*, 516–523.

Wildschut, T., Sedikides, C., Arndt, J., & Routledge, C. (2006). Nostalgia: Content, triggers, functions. *Journal of Personality and Social Psychology, 91*, 975–993.

Williams, L. E., & Bargh, J. A. (2008). Keeping one's distance: The influence of spatial distance cues on affect and evaluation. *Psychological Science, 19*, 302–308.

Wilson, A. E., & Ross, M. (2001). From chump to champ: People's appraisals of their earlier and current selves. *Journal of Personality and Social Psychology, 80*, 572–584.

Wittmann, M., & Paulus, M. P. (2008). Decision making, impulsivity and time perception. *Trends in Cognitive Sciences, 12*, 7–12.

Zauberman, G., Kim, B. K., Malkoc, S. A., & Bettman, J. R. (2009). Discounting time and time discounting: Subjective time perception and intertemporal preferences. *Journal of Marketing Research, 46*, 543–556.

Zauberman, G. & Lynch, J.G. (2005). Resource slack and propensity to discount delayed investments of time versus money. *Journal of Experimental Psychology, 134*, 23–37.

Zhang, M., & Wang, J., (2009). Psychological distance asymmetry: The spatial dimension vs. other dimensions. *Journal of Consumer Psychology, 19*, 497–507.

4 Consumer Emotions

Eduardo B. Andrade

Consumer researchers have often pondered the relevance of the research published in the field (Pham, 2013; Sheth, 1982). This concern is exemplified by the recent remarks of the editors of the *Journal of Consumer Research*: "We encourage the authors to 'make it meaningful' by being specific about the relevance of their work to particular audiences, including but not limited to fellow academics" (Dahl, Fischer, Johar, & Morwitz, 2014, p. iii). This chapter therefore begins with a simple but important question: Why should we care about consumer emotions? In other words, are consumer emotions relevant to our understanding of consumer psychology?

Why Consumer Emotions Matter: Prevalence and Power

The answer to the preceding question is a resounding "yes," for two main reasons: prevalence and power. Emotions are ubiquitous in consumer-related contexts. Companies systematically try to induce emotional reactions in consumers through incidental (e.g., store ambience; Kaltcheva & Weitz, 2006) and integral (e.g., brands; Thomson, MacInnis, & Park, 2005) sources. Additionally, positive and negative emotions are present at every step of the consumer behavior cycle, from search (Teixeira, Wedel, & Pieters, 2012), to evaluation (Holbrook & Batra, 1987), to choice (Luce, Payne, & Bettman, 1999), to consumption (Chan, van Boven, Andrade, & Ariely, 2013), and finally, to disposal (Grasmick, Bursik, & Kinsey, 1991). Emotions are not only prevalent but also powerful. For instance, in comparing reason-based and feeling-based evaluations of advertising material, Pham, Cohen, Pracejus, and Hughes (2001) found that feeling-based evaluations produced faster and more consistent judgments and that they were better predictors of the number and valence of thoughts about the target. Feeling-based assessments have also been shown to override (a) the impact of magnitude (e.g., number of items) on evaluations (Hsee & Rottenstreich, 2004), (b) the impact of cognitive assessments on risky decisions (Loewenstein, Weber, Hsee, & Welch, 2001), and (c) the long-term benefits of a given option (Hoch & Loewenstein, 1991; Van den Bergh, Dewitte, & Warlop, 2008).

A critic might argue that most studies on the role of emotions in consumer behavior have addressed relatively inconsequential decisions. If the consequences of the decisions increase, the impact of emotions may fade. This argument can be challenged on empirical and logical grounds. First, many daily consumer choices are of little consequence in the short term (e.g., how frequently do we buy a bottle of water vs. a house?). But even in this case, emotional choices may lead to meaningful consequences in the long run. Food intake is a classic example. Negative emotions not only increase junk food consumption (e.g., Tice, Baumeister, & Bratslavsky, 2001) but are also causally linked to obesity (Blaine, 2008). Second, the more consequential the decision is, the more emotional it becomes, and the challenge associated with such an emotional decision may in turn affect consumer choices (Luce, 1998). Therefore, emotions may be powerful precisely because they are likely to arise when consequential decisions are at stake (Andrade & Iyer, 2009). Further, there are examples of the impact of emotions on highly consequential decisions. For example, in a field experiment in rural India, Soman and Cheema (2011) indirectly showed that guilt can increase savings. In the study, participants kept more money in a savings envelope if the envelope had photographs of their children printed on them. They were also more likely to save if, in order to spend more than 50 percent of the savings for the week, they would have to break the savings commitment twice (i.e., open two envelopes) instead of breaking it only once (i.e., open only one envelope). Similarly, growing evidence in the finance literature suggests that exogenous emotion-inducing events, such as those related to weather or major sports, are associated consequential investment decisions (Edmans, García, & Norli, 2007; Hirshleifer & Shumway, 2003). Still, the understanding of the power of emotions in high-stake decision contexts remains limited. Opportunities abound for consumer researchers to investigate systematically the impact of emotions on consumer behavior, particularly if intense emotional reactions arise from the meaningfulness of the decision context itself.

What Emotions Mean: Properties and Opportunities

Although disagreement remains on what an emotion is and what it is not, a few key properties of an emotion experience stand out in the literature. Building on these properties, emotions are here defined as consciously felt experiences (Elster, 1999) characterized by valence and arousal (i.e., *core affect*; Russell & Barrett, 1999), cognitive appraisal (Smith & Ellsworth, 1985), and action readiness (Frijda, 1987). For the sake of simplicity, the terms emotions, affect, and feelings are used interchangeably in this chapter.

A Note on Mood

Mood seems to represent a unique feeling state, because it lacks a clear source (daily language is revealing in that respect: compare "I'm angry *at/with* you" with "I'm *in* a bad mood"), lasts for a relatively long time, and often comes about gradually (Morris, 1989; Schwarz & Clore, 2007). However, it must be noted that given these characteristics, mood may be difficult to induce in the lab. Although participants are usually unaware of the impact of the induced emotional state on a subsequent or concurrent task, they are often fully aware of the source of the emotion. For example, participants clearly know that the video clip or the autobiographical recall made them feel happy or sad. What they often do not realize is that this incidentally induced state may be impacting their subsequent judgments and decisions. Additionally, mood inductions in the lab do not necessarily "come about gradually." Quite often, the induction is meant to be sudden and short (e.g., pleasant and unpleasant stimuli) and, as important, rapidly followed by the dependent variable of interest. A few minutes at most separate them. Finally, the term "mood" is often used simply because the researchers want to focus on the valence property of the emotion (e.g., "mood (in)congruency"; Lee, Andrade, & Palmer, 2013), not because the induction captures the unique properties of a mood state. We therefore conjecture that the purportedly good and bad mood inductions that are widely reported in literature often induce mild levels of specific emotions, most likely happiness and sadness. In fact, systematically distinguishing the unique effects of mood from those of related specific emotions represents an interesting (and challenging) research opportunity.

In line with this argument, unless a clear mood induction is at stake (e.g., Schwarz & Clore, 1983), it seems more appropriate to report either specific emotions (e.g., happiness, pride, fear, sadness, or disgust) or unspecified emotional states (i.e., feelings and affect), as is done in this chapter.

Consciously Felt States

Defining emotions as a feeling state has two important consequences. On the one hand, such a definition limits the discussion to conscious emotions. Although empirical evidence and theoretical arguments support the existence of unconscious emotions (Winkielman & Berridge, 2004), unconscious emotions make it difficult to distinguish emotions conceptually and empirically from sheer cognitive priming. This distinction has often been a source of concern among emotion researchers (Dunn & Schweitzer, 2005; Keltner, Ellsworth, & Edwards, 1993).

On the other hand, defining emotions as a conscious feeling state broadens the scope of analysis to encompass feeling states that arise from biological drives that are directly related to survival and reproduction, such as hunger, thirst, body temperature, sexual arousal, and pain (Bhatia & Loewenstein, 2013). These "biological feelings" generally share the same properties of an emotion, as defined previously. Most often, hunger is an unpleasant feeling, is arousing, is cognitively appraised as a hungry state (owing to internal and/or external cues), and motivates the body to look for food. Biological feelings are unique in that they push the individual in one very precise direction. In other words, the action readiness they prompt is much narrower in scope. A sad consumer and a thirsty consumer may both be motivated to change the status quo. But whereas the former can attenuate the negative feeling by eating, helping, or taking risks (Andrade & Cohen, 2007a), the latter will want water (Atance & Meltzoff, 2006). For the thirsty consumer, only consumption of fluid will fulfil his or her active goal.

This narrowing of attention has been observed across multiple contexts. For instance, Brendl, Markman, and Messner (2003) showed that food deprivation causes consumers not only to value food but also to devalue items unrelated to food. Van den Bergh, Dewitte, and Warlop (2008) showed that sexual arousal makes consumers more present-focused, as sexually aroused consumers devalue the future to a greater extent than controls (see also Ariely & Loewenstein, 2006). Similarly, thirsty children prefer water to pretzels even when the choice is for future consumption (Atance & Meltzoff, 2006). This evidence shows that "under the influence" of a drive, consumers narrow their attention in general (Bhatia & Loewenstein, 2013; Loewenstein, 1996).

However, many questions remain to be investigated. First, the consequences of attention narrowing are not straightforward. Although people narrow their attention toward food when they feel hungry, the type of food that they desire may vary substantially. For instance, growing evidence suggests that unhealthy food becomes disproportionally more valued among hungry consumers (Wansink, Tal, & Shimizu, 2012; Tal & Wansink, 2013). This finding may also have interesting managerial and policy implications. Feelings of hunger or thirst during product evaluation may affect consumers' attention to, and interpretation of, different product attributes (e.g., price, brand, nutrition facts). Further, biological feelings are triggered by internal (e.g., a homeostatic imbalance) and external (e.g., a tasty burger) cues (Wansink & Chandon, 2014; Wansink, Payne, & Chandon 2007). A deeper understanding of the role of these two types of triggers is needed. Similarly, the understanding of the interplay between the drive itself and the feeling that arises from it remains limited. Although drives and feelings are often positively correlated, this may not always be the case (e.g., Brendl, Markman, & Messner, 2003).

While biological feelings are ubiquitous and influential in consumer decision making, research on biological feelings is relatively scant in the consumer behavior literature (Cheema & Patrick, 2012). An exception is recent research on embodied cognition (Krishna & Schwarz, 2014), in which biological feelings – e.g., body temperature – are misattributed, sometimes metaphorically, to unrelated evaluation targets (Huang, Zhang, Hui, & Wyer, 2014; Zwebner, Lee, & Goldenberg, 2013).

Valence

Valence and arousal are the dominant dimensions of any given emotional experience (Lang, Greenwald, Bradley, & Hamm, 1993). Despite the existence and critical role of additional dimensions (Smith & Ellsworth, 1985), valence and arousal capture most of the physiological, subjective, and behavioral variance in people's emotional reactions and are often characterized as the core of any emotional experience (Barrett, 2006; Russell & Barrett, 1999).

The main impact of valence on evaluation is rather straightforward. The target of evaluation tends to be more positively (negatively) evaluated when people feel good (bad) (Andrade & Cohen 2007a). It is actually difficult to think of a construct that is simpler than emotional valence, that is, the extent to which an emotion is consciously perceived as good or bad. On the basis of the same logic, an emotional episode should be easy to categorize as positive or negative. Interestingly, growing evidence suggests that consumers experience mixed feelings, such that emotional reactions may have opposite valence at the same time or at very close points in time (Schimmack, 2001; Williams & Aaker, 2002). Larsen, McGraw, and Cacioppo (2001) showed that people retrospectively reported feeling happy *and* sad while watching a comedy-drama. Hemenover and Schimmack (2007) found evidence that people have mixed feelings after being exposed to amusing but disgusting movie clips. Even humor comprises negative and positive reactions (McGraw & Warren, 2010; McGraw, Warren, Williams, & Leonard, 2012). Andrade and Cohen (2007b) showed that horror movie fans not only felt good and bad while watching horror movie clips, but also considered the scariest scenes to be the most pleasant. Similar findings were observed in a quasi-experiment in which people were exposed to intense dramas. High empathizers felt sadder during the movie, yet enjoyed the movie to a greater extent than low empathizers (de Wied, Zillmann & Ordman, 1995). Finally, mixed feelings are present even when the negative feeling arises from physical discomfort (e.g., the pleasure of mouth burn from chili peppers; Rozin, 1990).

This body of research has led researchers to tackle a more fundamental question: When and why do consumers choose to expose themselves to consumption experiences that are known to trigger aversive feelings (e.g., red peppers, horror movies, and bungee jumping)? Some consensus has been reached regarding the answer to the "when" question. To experience mixed feelings, a person must find the event sufficiently threatening to experience it as unpleasant but sufficiently safe to derive pleasantness from it. Changes in the "protective frame" or "psychological distance" have been shown to moderate the presence of mixed feelings and to affect the overall appeal of the consumption experience (Andrade & Cohen, 2007b; Apter, 1992; McGraw et al,. 2012; Rozin et al., 2013). For example, consumers who dislike the horror movie genre do so in part because they are "too much into" the consumption experience. Detach these consumers just enough from the scary scenes (e.g., by reminding them that the scene merely involves actors playing a role), and they will derive pleasure from the scary experience (Andrade & Cohen, 2007b; see also Schramm & Wirth 2010).

But why do people consume something that triggers both bad and good feelings (e.g., chili peppers) rather than seek experiences that elicit only good feelings (e.g., milk chocolate)? Multiple possible accounts have been advanced, although they may vary across consumption experiences. Being able to endure the bad can make one feel proud. Thus, mastery and self-signalling may be part of the explanation (Keinan & Kivetz, 2011; Loewenstein, 1999), or what has been termed the "pleasure at mind over body" (Rozin et al. 2013). Such an explanation is possibly more applicable to a big wave surfer than to a horror movie fanatic, though it may be applicable to chili pepper consumers as well (Rozin et al. 2013). Pride may also be felt for the exact opposite reason. Instead of being proud of her ability to control or master a negative situation, the consumer may derive pride from her own empathic reactions to the negative event (e.g., "If I cried, it means that I care"). This explanation may help elucidate why people are so drawn to dramatic aesthetic experiences (e.g., dramas, tragic plays). It is sad, ergo it is meaningful (Wirth, Hofer, & Schramm, 2012). Information and curiosity may also provide a partial explanation. Many of the negative experiences that accompany positive experiences are rather unique. One might derive pleasure from vicariously or actually experiencing these negative events.

Finally, and perhaps most intriguing, is the possibility that consumption enjoyment may often be more a function of *variance* than of *means*. Constant pleasure can rapidly become boring. Thus, if the psychological distance is appropriate, high variance (the rapid interplay between good and bad; Apter, 1992) within a given emotional episode can make consumers feel "more alive," and this feeling can in turn substantially influence consumers' preference for mixed over singular emotional events. Research nevertheless is needed to systematically address all the preceding possibilities.

Arousal

Arousal represents another key property of any emotional experience. Whether a given emotion is positive (relaxing, exciting) or negative (boring, scary), people spontaneously assess the intensity of the emotion. Further, arousal has been shown to affect attention, memory, persuasion, and evaluative judgments. Arousing stressors can reduce cognitive capacity and narrow attention to salient or goal-relevant cues (Eastbrook, 1959; Wells and Matthews 1994). For relevant information, integral arousal enhances memory. Although the valence and arousal of an emotional stimulus (e.g., a picture) can be rapidly encoded, arousal often represents a more reliable predictor of short- and long-term memory performance (Bradley, Greenwald, Petry, & Lang, 1992; Mather & Sutherland, 2009). Because of selective attention, arousal has also been shown to affect message persuasion (Pham 1996; Sanbonmatsu & Kardes, 1988). Finally, the growing consensus is that arousal also systematically affects evaluations. Whereas valence can bias judgment in a congruent manner (e.g., happy people make positive evaluations), arousal makes positive *and* negative evaluations more extreme (Pham, Gorn, & Sin, 2001; Vosgerau, 2010).

A few areas of investigation deserve further scrutiny in the consumer behavior literature. Marketers often wonder about the optimal level of arousal for a given emotional experience (e.g., "how viscerally disgusting should the cigarette picture be?"). Unfortunately, little research in the literature has systematically assessed the differential impact of multiple levels of arousal (e.g., Smith, Wilson, & Jones, 1983) on judgment and decision making. Second, although arousal is conceptually independent from emotion, it is rarely (or never) "left alone." People spontaneously label the arousing experience (Dutton & Aron, 1974; Schachter & Singer, 1962), turning it into a full-blown emotional experience. Therefore, consumer researchers should aim to (a) identify the consumer contexts that are likely to trigger and as a result (re)label arousal, (b) better understand the process of "arousal labelling" (e.g., which cues are more likely to induce individuals to (re)label a given arousing experience and when), and (c) assess the subsequent impact of arousal on consumer decision making.

Cognitive Appraisal and Action Tendency

An emotional experience largely reflects an individual's cognitive appraisal of the environment (Roseman, 1984; Scherer, 1982; Smith & Ellsworth, 1985). Although multiple dimensions beyond valence and arousal have been proposed, a few of them have been quite meaningful. Along the same lines, research has also highlighted the importance of action readiness (i.e., a natural inclination/ motive), given that these dimensions are also inherently linked to a particular motivational state (DeSteno, Petty, Wegener, & Rucker, 2000). Three of these dimensions are worth noting: certainty (Lerner & Keltner 2001; Tiedens & Linton 2001), attribution of responsibility (Schindler, 1998), and orientation (i.e., approach/avoidance; Labroo & Rucker, 2010). For instance, fear and anxiety have been associated with high uncertainty (the certainty dimension), which in turn can make consumers more prone to dodging uncertain environments, such as those involving risky choices (Lee & Andrade, 2011). Disgust is associated with high avoidance (the orientation dimension; Oaten, Stevenson, & Case, 2009) and tends to induce consumers to devalue products that have been subjectively "contaminated" by disgusting items (Morales & Fitzsimons, 2007). Finally, when attributing a price discount to oneself (the attribution of responsibility dimension), consumers are more likely to experience pride and to report a higher repurchase intention (Schindler, 1998). In short, holding constant valence and arousal, emotion specificity (i.e., cognitive appraisal and action readiness), can significantly impact consumer judgment and decision making.

But how do specific emotions interact? If events that trigger emotional reactions that have positive and negative valences are known to be experienced, it follows that identifying events that trigger two or more specific emotions of the *same* valence should be even more plausible. Fear and disgust, sadness and anger, and happiness and pride are all emotional reactions that are likely to emerge from a single source. Interestingly, very little research has aimed to elucidate how dual or multiple emotional reactions of the same valence operate. If two different emotions of the same valence are triggered concomitantly (or at very close points in time) during a given event, how do they interact? Does one dominate the other? Does action readiness of one emotional state fuel the other?

If so, when and why do these interactions occur? An interesting example within this limited body of research is Morales, Wu, and Fitzsimons' (2012) recent research on the interplay between fear and disgust in fear appeals. The authors showed that disgust increases the persuasiveness of fear appeals, and it does so mainly because of the high-avoidance tendency triggered by disgust.

In short, considerable research exists on the main properties of the emotion construct (conscious feeling, valence, arousal, appraisal, and action readiness). However, as this section has highlighted, many questions about each of these properties remain unanswered and deserve further scrutiny.

What Emotions Do: Sources and Outcomes

Emotions arise from multiple sources and affect multiple psychological aspects of decision making. In this section, the major sources and outcomes of emotions are discussed.

Emotion Sources

Conceptually, the sources of emotions vary by the extent to which the source is inherent to the evaluation target (Cohen, Pham, & Andrade, 2008). At one extreme, store ambience is an *incidental* source of emotion when a consumer is judging the quality of a product in that store (Spangenberg, Crowley, & Henderson, 1996), whereas at the other extreme a chocolate cake represents an *integral* source of emotion when the consumer is deciding whether to eat that dessert (Shiv & Fedorikin, 1999). *Task-related* sources lie somewhere in the middle of the continuum for this dimension. Emotion arising from task-related sources is generated not from the evaluation target but from the challenges inherent to the evaluative and/or decision-making process, such as trade-off difficulties among options (Luce, 1998), option attachment after significant choice deliberation (Carmon, Weternbroch, & Zeelenberg, 2003), and time pressure (Stone & Kadous, 1997).

Methodologically, the source of emotion can also vary by the extent to which the source is ecologically (i.e., realistic) and externally valid (i.e., generalizable). For instance, Chebat and Michon (2003) varied store ambience to assess its impact on emotions and spending (high ecological validity), whereas Lee and Andrade (2011) varied people's prior exposure to a movie clip to assess, in a purportedly independent subsequent study, the impact of fear of financial risk taking (low ecological validity).

A common approach in consumer behavior has been to use incidental sources with low ecological validity (for a few recent examples, see Chang & Pham, 2013; Lee, Andrade, & Palmer, 2013; Salermo, Laran, & Janiszewski, 2014). The dominance of this approach is not necessarily surprising given the field's focus on internal validity and theoretical contributions (namely, underlying processes). To understand and test the role of emotions in any aspect of consumer behavior, researchers must detach the emotion construct from other properties of the stimulus to avoid confounds. This challenge is methodologically easier to overcome when the evaluation target remains constant (incidental manipulation) than when the target has to be modified (integral manipulation). Internal validity is also generally easier to achieve if a study is conducted in a contrived environment than if the study is conducted in the real world, as the former most often allows the experimenter to have greater control over the source of emotion itself. Thus, researchers generally adopt procedures that best manipulate emotions in a contrived environment and that best assess underlying processes rather than procedures that best reflect the real-world experience of consumers.

Ecological validity tends to increase with the use of integral sources of emotions (actual ads, actual food, and so forth). For instance, when the research question focuses on the relative contribution of affect-versus cognitive-rich stimuli, the source of emotion is often integral to the evaluation target, as well as more realistic (e.g., chocolate cake vs. fruit salad; Shiv & Fedorikhin, 1999). Likewise, in contexts in which the target itself is the key phenomenon of interest (e.g., advertisements, consumption experience), sources of emotion are also integral and more realistic (Berger and Milkman, 2012; Lee & Tsai, 2014; Teixeira, Wedel, & Pieters, 2012).

That said, the use of lab-induced incidental sources of emotions with low external validity in the consumer behavior literature is widespread. As the field moves toward developing more "relevant" research agendas, consumer researchers may find adopting a bottom-up approach useful – that is, deriving their research questions by being attentive to the daily yet underinvestigated sources of emotions available in the marketplace.

Emotion Outcomes

Integral, task-related, and/or incidental emotions have been shown to affect multiple psychological processes of interest to consumer researchers. The effect of emotion on the psychological processes and preferences is discussed next.

The Effect of Emotion on Attention

The influence of emotions on what individuals direct and hold attention to, or deviate attention from, has received considerable interest from psychologists, neuroscientists, and psychophysiologists. Regarding integral emotions (e.g., exposure to emotional pictures), the findings are relatively consistent. Individuals most often prioritize emotion-inducing over non-emotion-inducing cues. Emotion-inducing cues are better able to draw and/or hold people's attention (Fox, Russo, Bowles, & Dutton, 2001; LaBar, Mesulam, Gitelman & Weintraud, 2000; Ohman, Flykt, & Esteves, 2001; Rosler et al. 2005). The literature has also identified a two-stage process through which emotions affect attention:

a pre-attentive evaluation of the stimulus' emotional significance followed by a selective attentive process (Compton, 2003).

However, more nuanced effects have been found for the influence of incidental sources of emotion on individuals' attention to subsequent unrelated stimuli. Although it has been suggested and demonstrated that happier individuals have a broader attention focus than sadder individuals (Frederickson & Branigan, 2005; Moriya & Nittono, 2011; Rowe, Hirsh, & Anderson, 2007), recent evidence has challenged this view. Rather than varying their attentional scope in a systematic and fixed manner (i.e., negative [positive] affect leads to a narrow [broad] focus of attention), participants' emotional states may simply confer positive or negative value to the dominant perceptual orientation (Huntsinger, 2012). In short, while research has elucidated the impact of emotional cues integral to the evaluation target on attention, further research is needed to understand the role of participants' previously and incidentally induced emotional states in directing their attentional scope.

Recent research in consumer behavior has examined the influence of emotions on pre-attentive and attentive processes. For instance, Teixeira, Wedel, and Pieters (2012) used eye tracking to assess the role of joy and surprise in consumers' attention and retention levels to Internet video advertisements. The authors found that surprise was better able to increase concentrated *attention* than joy, whereas joy was better able to increase *retention* than surprise. Nielsen, Stewart, and Mason (2010) showed that highly emotional semantic cues (e.g., an advertisement with the title "Feeling Selfish") can shift attention away from the focal cue (e.g., the article) and onto the ad.

Additional research, however, is clearly needed to understand the nature and role of incidental and integral emotions in consumers' basic pre-attentive and attentive processes. For instance, although marketers often strategically use emotional cues to draw consumers' attention to an ad, they also have to determine strategically the frequency of exposure. The relationship among emotion, attention, and habituation (e.g., Bradley, Lang, & Cuthbert, 1993) in consumer contexts is therefore worth investigating. Further, interest in the influence of visual emotional cues has generally been greater than the influence of other sensory stimuli on attention. Given that all five senses are clearly relevant to marketers and to our understanding of consumer psychology (Krishna, 2012), elucidating the influence of emotions on non-visual sensory stimuli and identifying the interplay between them are plausible research avenues (e.g., Krishna, Morrin, & Sayin, 2014; Zeelenberg & Bocanegra, 2010).

The Effect of Emotion on Memory

The literature on emotions and memory can again be conceptually distinguished into two groups. The first research stream has investigated the impact of integral emotional versus non-emotional cues on memory. Because emotions are prioritized in attention processes, the significant impact of emotions on memory is not surprising. Indeed, the general findings follow the same pattern observed in the literature on attention: individuals can generally better recall emotional than non-emotional events (e.g., Thorson & Friestad, 1989). Although the dimension responsible for enhanced memory has been debated (Kensinger, 2009; Mather, 2007), there is growing agreement that arousal is the key one. When valence is controlled for, the impact of arousal on enhanced memory remains, whereas when arousal is controlled for, the impact of valence on memory disappears (Mather and Nesmith, 2008). Both dimensions can be rapidly encoded, but arousal often represents a more reliable predictor of short- and long-term memory performance (Bradley et al., 1992). Because negative stimuli are generally more arousing than positive stimuli, individuals can generally better recall negative events than positive ones (Mather & Sutherland, 2009). The types of cues that benefit or suffer from the increase in emotional arousal have been debated to some extent. Earlier evidence and theorizing suggested that a narrowing of attention (Easterbrook 1959) explains the recurrent finding that arousal enhances memory for central cues at the expense of peripheral cues (Burke, Heuer, & Reisberg, 1992; Kensinger, Garoff-Eaton, & Schacter, 2007). This phenomenon was famously exemplified by the so-called "weapon-focus effect," in which eyewitness identification worsens when the wrongdoer holds a weapon (Steblay, 1992). In a similar vein, emotional arousal has also been shown to enhance memory for gist and schematic memory but not for details (Adolphs, Tranel, & Buchanan, 2005; Mather & Johnson, 2003). However, recent findings and theoretical arguments provide a more nuanced view in which arousal enhances memory not necessarily for central cues or gist but for the most perceptually salient or goal-relevant stimuli (Mather & Sutherland, 2011). Given that salience/relevance is often correlated with centrality/ gist, people seem to prioritize central and gist processing. A few reported findings support this rationale. For instance, the detrimental impact of competing arousing cues weakens when the visually peripheral cues are more salient (Mather, Gorlick, & Nesmith, 2009). Likewise, when the specific details are as relevant as the gist, both benefit from emotional arousal (Kensinger, Garoff-Eaton, & Schacter, 2007). Note, however, only a few recent studies have systematically investigated the role of goal relevance and perceptual salience in emotional arousal (Sakati, Fryer, & Mather, 2014; Sutherland & Mather, 2012). Given that marketers often make decisions about the design, content, and degree of emotionality of messages such as advertisements (Chandy, Tellis, MacInnis, & Thaivanich, 2001), consumer researchers have a clear opportunity to rely on such consumer-related contexts to address fundamental questions about the role of emotions and attention priority in memory.

A second and somewhat independent research stream has investigated the role of pre-induced incidental emotions in the subsequent recognition and recall of emotional and non-emotional cues (Bower, 1981; Isen, Shalker, Clark, & Karp, 1978). Two findings are notable. The first suggests that people are more likely to recall emotional cues and episodes that are congruent with the affective state that they experience at the moment of retrieval – that is, mood congruence

(Ehrlichman & Halpen, 1988; Isen et al., 1978). However, this effect is asymmetric: people in a good mood are more likely to recall positive events than people in a bad mood are to recall negative events (Bower & Forgas, 2000; Blaney, 1986). Emotion regulation may at least partially account for the asymmetry (Isen, 1984). Specifically, people who feel bad might be motivated to think of positive events in order to improve their current emotional states (Rusting & DeHart, 2000). The second finding suggests that memory may be enhanced when people encode *and* retrieve events in the same rather than in different mood states – that is, mood-state-dependent memory (Bower, 1981), a special case of context-state dependency (Godden & Baddeley, 1980). The robustness of the mood-state dependency has been vigorously debated, and multiple moderating variables seem to play an important role (Eich, 1995; Kenealy, 1997).

Research on the psychology of consumers' emotions and memory is surprisingly not as widespread as one might expect. Some studies have relied on mood-state dependency to help explain marketing-related phenomena (Stayman & Batra, 1991) or have assessed the robustness of mood congruency in consumer-related contexts and its impact on consumer evaluation (Lawson, 1985). However, perhaps because of consumer researchers' growing interest in behavioral measures (e.g., choice), relatively little recent research has aimed to answer empirical and theoretical questions about emotions and memory (e.g., Baumgartner, Sujan, & Bettman, 1992).

The Effect of Emotion on Processing Style

Feelings are known also to change the way that people process information. The association between emotions and processing style has been widely investigated, and under the feelings-as-information hypothesis (Schwarz and Clore, 1983), a somewhat general consensus has emerged. By signaling a more threatening milieu, negative feelings tend to induce a more careful and bottom-up processing of the environment. Conversely, by signaling a safer situation, positive feelings lead to a less detailed and more top-down processing style (Schwarz, 1990, 2001). The consequences of these changes in processing style can be observed in many consumer contexts. For example, top-down processing leads happy individuals to form broader and more flexible categories (Isen & Daubman, 1984; Lee & Sternthal, 1999), which can in turn influence brand extension evaluations (Barone, Miniard, & Romeo, 2000). Similarly, positive feelings have also been shown to lead consumers to focus on and/or prefer more abstract and future goals, whereas negative feelings have led consumers to focus on and/or prefer more concrete and short-term goals (Labroo & Patrick, 2009). Top-down processing may also increase consumers' reliance on heuristic cues in advertisements (Batra & Stayman, 1990), but contextual and motivational aspects (e.g., type of task or initial interest of participants) may mitigate or even reverse this effect (Schwarz, 2001).

The Effect of Emotion on Estimates

Consumers often estimate some properties of future events. Two of these properties have been extensively investigated in the literature: the likelihood of the occurrence of a given event (i.e., risk estimates) and the emotional reactions to the event (i.e., affective forecasting).

The link between feelings and expected outcomes is well established. To understand how people estimate probabilities, one must learn how they *feel* about the possible outcomes (Finucane, Alhakami, Slovic, & Johnson, 2000; Loewenstein et al. 2001; Slovic, 2010). In a seminal paper, Johnson and Tversky (1983) provided a straightforward demonstration of this phenomenon. In a series of experiments, the authors showed that the subjective probability of the occurrence of future events varied in a manner congruent with the valence of the emotional reaction: positive (negative) events were perceived to be more likely when people were feeling good (bad). Similar findings were obtained in other studies (Constans & Matthews, 1993; Mayer, Gaschke, Braveman, & Evans, 1992; Pietromonaco & Rook, 1987; Wright & Bower, 1982). However, a more nuanced effect emerged when specific emotions were investigated. For instance, holding constant valence and arousal, high-uncertainty emotions (e.g., fear) increase risk perception to a greater extent than low-uncertainty emotions (e.g., anger) (DeSteno et al., 2000; Lerner & Keltner, 2001).

Another research stream has focused on how people estimate their own emotional reactions to future events. Given that many of our consumption experiences contain a hedonic component (Holbrook & Hirschman, 1982) and that the choice process often encompasses affective estimates of the options (Mellers, Schwartz, & Ritov, 1999), the so-called affective forecasting literature has received substantial interest from consumer researchers (e.g., Patrick, McInnis, & Park, 2007). A general finding is that people tend to overestimate the duration of positive and negative emotional experiences – that is, the emotional reactions to the event fade much more quickly than people expect prior to the event (the so-called *duration bias*; Gilbert et al., 1998; Wilson et al., 2000). Interestingly, consumers often fail to consider adaptation in estimates of product enjoyment (Wang, Novemsky, & Dhar, 2009). This phenomenon can lead to some interesting mistakes. For instance, consumers tend to avoid breaking a pleasant consumption experience (Nelson & Meyvis, 2008) or to consume too quickly (Galak, Krueger, & Loewenstein, 2013) even when a more paced consumption reduces adaptation and leads to an overall more pleasant experience. Additionally, given that people tend to misremember their forecasts as being consistent with their experience, they are often incapable of learning and correcting this bias (Meyvis, Ratner, & Levav, 2010). Yet consumers do seem to consider adaptation in certain contexts. For instance, when deciding whether to have "more of the same" (e.g., putting a second Snickers in the shopping basket), consumers are more likely to take satiation into consideration, which in turn increases variety seeking (McAlister 1982). Future research could thus examine consumer contexts in which adaptation may be unlikely to occur as well as situations in which *sensitization* might be experienced (e.g., noise; Weinstein, 1982).

A second often reported finding is that people also overestimate the intensity of the emotional event – that is, prior to a pleasant (unpleasant) event, people anticipate feeling better (worse) than they actually feel *right after* the event (Buehler & McFarland, 2001). However, the so-called *intensity bias* has been a source of controversy. Recent findings suggest that this apparent phenomenon may largely represent a methodological artifact rather than a systematic bias (Levine, Lench, Kaplan, & Safer, 2012). Levine and colleagues (2012) argued that people interpret the forecasting question to be about the focal event and the experience question to be about their feelings in general. These authors show that when this methodologically driven discrepancy is corrected, the intensity bias disappears (see also Levine, Lench, Kaplan, & Safer, 2013). Beyond methodological issues, the intensity bias may conflict with the so-called *empathy gap* phenomenon – that is, people's tendency to underestimate (in a "cold" state) the impact of their own emotions (the "hot" state) on decision making (Loewenstein, 1996). That is, whereas the *intensity bias* indicates that people in a cold state overestimate their future emotional states, the *empathy gap* posits that people in a cold state underestimate the behavioral impact of their future emotional states. More research is needed to understand and integrate the apparent discrepancies between the findings from these two research streams.

Finally, with regard to predicting the future, the literature is relatively silent on a potential *type bias* – that is, the extent to which people systematically experience certain emotions that *qualitatively* differ from what they expected to feel. Many events induce a blend of multiple emotional reactions, particularly in consumer contexts (e.g., feeling both pleasure and guilt after the first bite of chocolate). Salience and inaccurate lay theories may lead consumers to, in advance, disregard emotional reactions that are likely to be experienced after the event. Andrade and van Boven (2010), for instance, asked participants in a gambling task to wager and to estimate the intensity of their general feelings after the outcome. The results showed that people who decided not to gamble underestimated how bad they would feel right after they learned that they would have won. A possible reason for this reversal in the intensity bias is that the participants in that particular context disregarded the role regret would play after the outcome.

The emotional state itself cannot be stored and retrieved; it can simply be (re) experienced (Robinson & Clore, 2002). Thus, the attempt to remember a past emotional state is conceptually similar to the attempt to project a future emotion: it is an approximation (i.e., an estimate). Contrary to current emotions, past emotions are influenced by salient episodic memories as well (Kahneman, 1999). However, (a) attentional focus (Wilson et al., 2000), (b) beliefs about how emotions (should) work (Labroo & Mukhopadhyay, 2009; Wood & Bettman, 2007), (c) current feelings (Loewenstein, 2000), (d) ulterior motives (Gilbert et al., 1998), and (e) personality traits (Rusting, 1998) can all influence both prospective and retrospective emotional reports (Levine & Safer, 2002;

Robinson & Clore, 2002; Wilson & Gilbert, 2003; Wood & Bettman, 2007; Xu & Schwarz, 2009). This argument resonates with the findings that consumers' predictions and memories of pleasant emotional events are more similar to one another, and more positive, than the emotions reported during the emotional event – that is, the so-called *rosy view* effect (Mitchell, Thompson, Peterson, & Cronk, 1997; see also Wirtz, Kruger, Scollon, & Diener, 2003). Substantial research has already been conducted in this area. However, further research is needed to demonstrate and elucidate the relationships among the aforementioned sources of biases, the retrospectively assessed emotional reactions, and, most important, actual choice (e.g., repeated purchase). This discussion leads us to the final topic of interest: consumer preferences.

The Effect of Emotion on Preferences

Emotions affect what consumers focus their attention on and remember, how consumers process information, and how they anticipate feeling after a decision. Accordingly, emotions' systematic influence on consumer preference is not surprising. Integral and incidental emotions are known to influence attitudes, intentions, willingness to pay, and hypothetical and actual choices. (For reviews, see Cohen & Areni, 1991; Cohen, Pham, & Andrade, 2008) In the 1980s and 1990s, consumer researchers devoted a significant amount of effort to clarifying the role of integral affect (i.e., basic positive and negative affective reactions) on attitudes toward advertisements (A_{ad}) and toward the brands being advertised (A_{br}). The evidence consistently suggests that integral affect influences A_{ad} in a congruent manner – that is, positive (negative) affect induced by the ad tends to increase (decrease) liking of the ad more than the cognitive-based assessments of the ad. A weaker and more indirect effect is also observed for A_{br} (Aaker, Stayman, & Hagerty 1986; Batra & Ray, 1986; Brown, Homer, & Inman 1998; Brown & Stayman 1992; Burke & Edell 1989; Edell & Burke 1987). Equally important, the phenomenon goes beyond attitudinal measures. Integral affect has also been shown to congruently influence preferences for, inter alia, AIDS prevention behaviors (Bodur, Brinberg, & Coupey, 2000), product satisfaction (Oliver, 1993), investment options (MacGregor, Slovic, Dreman, & Berry, 2000), and blood donation (Allen, Machleit, & Kleine, 1992). That said, mood-incongruent effects have also been observed under certain circumstances. For instance, a sad facial expression may increase, rather than discourage, donations (Small & Verocchi, 2009).

The role of incidental affect in consumer preference has also been extensively investigated. Axelrod (1963) demonstrated that consumers provided worse product evaluations after (vs. before) watching a sad documentary. Since then, the congruent impact of affect has been consistently observed on different attitudinal and behavioral measures in multiple consumer-related contexts (e.g., Barone, Miniard, and Romeo, 2000; Dommermuth & Millard, 1967; Goldberg & Gorn, 1987; Pham, 1998). Nevertheless, there has also been clear evidence of incongruent effects in which negative feelings encourage consumption-related behaviors and in which positive feelings discourage consumption-related behaviors (Andrade 2005; Labroo & Mukhopadyay, 2009). Finally, preferences can also vary when emotions are triggered by the task itself (Carmon, Wertenbrock, & Zeelenberg, 2003; Luce, 1998). Luce (1998) demonstrated that the difficulty inherent to trade-offs among options increases consumers' preference for options that reduce the negative feelings associated with the task (e.g., increased preference for the status quo).

Although researchers now better understand the role of emotions on consumer preference, two research gaps are worth noting. First, the majority of studies have focused on the short-term consequences of consumer emotions. However, emotions can directly or indirectly have a long-term impact on consumer preference through behavioral consistency (Andrade & Ariely, 2009) and/or memory-based evaluations (Pocheptsova & Novemsky, 2010; see also Ottati & Isbell, 1996). Further research should thus be conducted to understand the role of consumer emotions in long-term preferences and welfare. Second, researchers have focused mostly on individual consumer decision-making contexts. This focus is rather surprising given that (a) emotions serve a social function (Morris & Keltner, 2000) and (b) consumer decision making often involves interpersonal interactions (e.g., Richins, 1983). Understanding the role of emotions on consumer preference in interpersonal contexts is therefore a substantively and theoretically rich research avenue. The role of social exclusion (Ward & Dahl, 2014) and embarrassment (Dahl, Manchanda, & Argo 2001; Lau-Gesk & Drolet, 2008) in consumer decision making and the strategic use of emotions (Andrade & Ho, 2009) in consumer complaints or negotiations are potential research topics.

How Emotions Operate: Evaluation and Regulation

Although initially focused on more substantive aspects, research in the past twenty years has focused on more theoretically driven questions to understand the mechanisms through which emotions affect consumer preference.

Mechanisms for Valence-Congruent Effects

As already noted, valence-congruent judgment – most often called mood-congruent judgment – is a well-established phenomenon: positive (negative) feelings lead to better (worse) assessments of the target. A few explanations have been proposed to elucidate the phenomenon, varying essentially in the quantity and quality of cognitive participation during the affective evaluation. A behaviorist approach suggests that congruent judgments result from an automatic process, a "direct-affect transfer" from the source of affect to the evaluation target. From this perspective, no inferential processes or changes in beliefs are required for emotions to congruently influence evaluations (Kim, Allen, & Kardes, 1996). This rationale resonates with the notion that "preferences need no inferences" (Zajonc, 1980), and it has been used to explain the impact of ad-evoking feelings on attitudes (Machleit & Wilson, 1988) as well as the effect of pleasant and unpleasant background features (e.g., music) on consumer preference (Bierley, McSweeney, & Vannieuwkerk, 1985; Gorn, 1982).

On the other extreme, Isen and colleagues (1978) proposed a highly cognitive, memory-based argument to explain valence-congruent judgments. These authors proposed that a given emotional state is more likely to bring valence-congruent material to mind, which in turn is more likely to influence evaluative judgments and subsequent behaviors in a valence-congruent manner (see also Bower 1981; Forgas, Bower, & Krantz, 1984). Somewhere in middle of this "cognitive-based assessment spectrum," a third explanation suggesting a relatively simple inferential process emerged. Building on Wyer and Carlston's (1979) initial intuition, Schwarz and Clore (1983) proposed that people spontaneously ask, "How do I feel about it?" when they judge a particular target. As they do so, current affective states are then (mis)attributed to the target. This inferential process then influences evaluative judgments, most often in a congruent manner (but see Martin, Abend, Sedikides, & Green, 1997). Evidence for the affect or feelings-as-information hypothesis has accumulated over the past decades. Supporting this theory is, for instance, the evidence that feelings play a weaker role if the affective information is perceived to be relatively less relevant or diagnostic (Avnet, Pham, & Stephen, 2012; Kim, Park, & Schwarz, 2010; Ottati & Isbell, 1996; Pham, 1998; Schwarz & Clore, 1983).

Independent of the exact underlying mechanism, valence-congruent judgments are important in consumer behavior given that positive (negative) feelings not only will lead to more positive (negative) evaluations of products and services, but also, as a result, can encourage (discourage) buying, consumption, and repeated purchases. Interestingly, however, a somewhat independent research stream, to which we turn next, has observed the exact opposite effects.

Mechanisms for Valence-*In*congruent Effects

Assuming that congruent judgments influence behavior in a similar manner – that is, positive (negative) feelings encourage (discourage) the target behavior – one would expect that as consumers' feelings worsen, their willingness to buy, consume, take risks, or help others also decreases. As it turns out, under certain circumstances, the exact opposite effect has been observed: when consumers feel bad (good), they will do more (less). Many labels have been used to explain these incongruent effects: affect regulation (Andrade, 2005), emotion-focused coping (Folkman and Lazarus, 1988), emotion regulation (Gross 1998), mood maintenance (Isen, 1984), mood management (Zillmann, 1988), mood regulation (Erber & Erber, 2001), and negative state relief (Cialdini, Darby, & Vincent, 1973). They all refer to a similar underlying mechanism whereby consumers spontaneously try to attenuate a negative feeling and/or to maintain a positive one, unless a stronger competing goal is at stake (Cohen & Andrade, 2004; Tamir, 2009).

The desire to attenuate negative mood has been used to explain why, under certain circumstances, negative feelings induce individuals to help more, eat more, and take more risks. Likewise, the desire to maintain a positive mood has been used to explain why, under certain circumstances, positive feelings discourage people from helping others, eating, and taking risks (Andrade & Cohen, 2007a). Further, these effects are not limited to behavior. People in a bad (good) mood have been shown to devote more (less) cognitive effort in an attempt to attenuate (maintain) their current feelings (Clark & Isen, 1982; Sedikides, 1994). Similarly, negative feelings can produce valence-incongruent recall owing to affect regulation (Rusting & DeHart, 2000).

An Integrative Framework

Briefly, an overall review of the literature leads to a simple conclusion: positive and negative feelings can both encourage and discourage behavior. Andrade (2005) and Andrade and Cohen (2007a) proposed and tested a unified theoretical conceptualization that systematically incorporated both general mechanisms and that could therefore account for the main apparent discrepancies in the literature (see also Forgas, 1995). The framework adopts a dual-process model in which emotions, on the one hand, inform and color judgment and decision making, most often in a congruent manner through an *affective evaluation* (AE) mechanism, and, on the other hand, motivate individuals to attenuate the bad and to protect the good, producing incongruent effects through an *affect regulation* (AR) mechanism. The interaction between these two often-opposing forces determines how and in which direction emotions influence consumer behavior. Equally important, the perceived "mood-changing" properties of the upcoming activities (i.e., the belief that the action or mental process will change one's current affective state) determine whether affect regulation will override the coloring impact of the affective evaluation on individuals' judgments and decision making. For instance, sad individuals become *more* likely to help or to eat when they perceive that the behavioral activity will attenuate their negative feelings. If they are led to believe that their affective state is "frozen" or if they simply do not consider the action to be a "mood-lifting" opportunity, the effect tends to be reversed (Andrade, 2005; Blechert, Goltsche, Herbert, & Wilhelm, 2014; Cialdini & Kenrich, 1976; Grunberg & Straub, 1992; Tice, Bratslavsky, & Baumeister, 2001). The same logic applies for happy individuals. They are *less* (*more*) likely to help or take risks when "mood-threatening" cues are salient (absent) in the environment (Andrade, 2005; Isen, Nygren, & Ashby, 1988; Isen & Simmonds, 1978).

Because the AE-AR framework highlights the importance of affect regulation as a core mechanism that is capable of overriding valence-congruent effects, it has attracted the attention of consumer researchers (Arnold & Reynolds, 2009; Cai, Tang, & Jia, 2009; Di Muro & Murray, 2012; Fedorikhin & Patrick, 2010; Garg, Wansink, & Inman, 2007; Labroo & Mukopadhyay, 2009; Shen & Wyer, 2008). Nevertheless, many aspects of the initial framework deserve further scrutiny. For instance, Garg, Wansink, and Inman (2007) properly noted that emotions may not only increase a consumer's proclivity to attenuate or maintain a given affective state, but also change the consumer's initial perception of how mood-lifting or mood-threatening a given cue is, which in turn should influence, according to the model's rationale, the consumer's subsequent judgments and decisions. Additional work should further investigate how the affective evaluation mechanism interferes with the perceived mood-changing properties of the stimulus and how it consequently alters the influence of affect regulation on consumer decision making.

The informational value of a given affective state should influence both the affective evaluation and the affect regulation mechanisms. However, much more is known about the impact of the information relevance and diagnosticity on affective evaluation than on affect regulation. Shen and Wyer (2008), for instance, showed that calling attention to the source of affect can also interfere with, and mitigate the impact of, the affect regulation mechanism. More research is needed to understand the interplay between the perceived relevance and diagnosticity of the affective information on both affective evaluation and affect regulation as well as its subsequent behavioral consequences. Finally, most of the documented research in this domain has focused on valence. Di Muro and Murray (2012) showed that consumers may aim to regulate, in addition to emotional valence, their level of arousal, which can in turn influence consumer preferences (see also Mogilner, Aaker, & Kamvar, 2012). Additional dimensions such as the level of certainty or orientation (i.e., approach/avoidance) could and should be explored within the AE-AR framework.

Beyond the WEIRD

The majority of studies published in the leading journals in psychology are conducted on so-called WEIRD people – participants from Western, Educated, Industrialized, Rich, and Democratic societies (Henrich, Heine, & Norenzayan, 2010). The use of such participants may thus constrain the generalizability of these studies and cast doubt on our understanding of human behavior. Unfortunately, research on consumer emotions shares this same limitation. Given that emotional reactions vary significantly across culture (Tsai, Knutson, & Fung, 2006), age (Charles, Mather, & Carstensen, 2003; Gross, Carstensen, Pasupathi, & Tsai, 1997), and income (Côté, Gyurak, & Levenson, 2010), among other characteristics, moving beyond the WEIRD participants represents a critical step to further our understanding of the psychology of consumer emotions.

Conclusion

The study of emotions in general, and of consumer emotions in particular, has grown exponentially in the past twenty years. Research in this field has elucidated what the properties of emotions are, where they come from, and how they influence consumer attention, memory, processing, estimates, and preferences. Nonetheless, this chapter also highlights many research avenues that remain to be explored. Given the power and prevalence of emotions in the marketplace, studying consumer emotions is *sine qua non* to our understanding of consumer behavior.

References

Aaker, D. A., Stayman, D. M., & Hagerty, M. R. (1986). Warmth in advertising – measurement, impact, and sequence effects. *Journal of Consumer Research, 12* (4), 365–381.

Adolphs, R., Tranel, D., & Buchanan, T. W. (2005). Amygdala damage impairs emotional memory for gist but not details of complex stimuli. *Nature Neuroscience, 8,* 512–518.

Allen, C. T., Machleit, K. A., & Kleine, S. S. (1992). A comparison of attitudes and emotions as predictors of behavior at diverse levels of behavioral experience. *Journal of Consumer Research, 18*(4), 493–504.

Andrade, E. B. (2005). Behavioral consequences of affect: Combining evaluative and regulatory mechanisms. *Journal of Consumer Research, 32*(3), 355–362.

Andrade, E. B. & Ariely, D. (2009). The enduring impact of transient emotions on decision making. *Organizational Behavior and Human Decision Processes, 9* (May), 1–8.

Andrade, E. B. & Cohen, J. B. (2007a). Affect-based evaluation and regulation as mediators of behavior: The role of affect in risk-taking, helping and eating patterns. In K. D. Vohs, R. F. Baumeister, & G. Loewenstein (eds), *Do Emotions Help or Hurt Decision Making? A Hedgefoxian Perspective.* New York: Russell Sage, 35–68.

Andrade, E.B. & Cohen, J. B. (2007b). On the consumption of negative feelings. *Journal of Consumer Research, 34*(3), 283–300.

Andrade, E. B. & Ho, T. H. (2009). Gaming emotions in social interactions. *Journal of Consumer Research, 36*(4), 539–552.

Andrade, E. B. & Iyer, G. (2009). Planned versus actual betting in sequential gambles. *Journal of Marketing Research, XLVI* (June), 372–383.

Andrade, E.B. & van Boven, L. (2010). Feelings not foregone: Underestimating affective reactions to what does not happen. *Psychological Science, 21*(5), 706–711.

Apter, M. J. (1992). *The Dangerous Edge: The Psychology of Excitement.* New York: Free Press.

Arnold, M. J. & Reynolds, K. E. (2009). Affect and retail shopping behavior: Understanding the role of mood regulation and regulatory focus. *Journal of Retailing, 85*(3), 308–320.

Atance, C. M. & Meltzoff, A. N. (2006). Preschoolers' current desires warp their choice for the future. *Psychology Science, 17*(7), 583–587.

Avnet, T., Pham, M. T. & Stephen, A. T. (2012). Consumers' trust in feelings as information. *Journal of Consumer Research, 39*(4), 720–735.

Axelrod, J. N. (1963). Induced moods and attitudes toward products. *Journal of Advertising Research, 3*(2), 19–24.

Barone, M. J. Miniard, P. W., & Romero, J. B. (2000). The influence of positive mood on brand extension evaluations. *Journal of Consumer Research, 26,* 386–400.

Barrett, L.F. (2006). Are emotions natural kinds? *Perspectives in Psychological Science, 1*(1), 28–58.

Batra, R., & Ray, M. L. (1986). Affective responses mediating acceptance of advertising. *Journal of Consumer Research, 13*(2), 234–249.

Batra, R., & Stayman, D. M. (1990). The role of mood in advertising effectiveness. *Journal of Consumer Research, 17*(2), 203–214.

Baumgartner, H., Sujan, M., & Bettman, J. R. (1992). Autobiographical memories, affect, and consumer information processing. *Journal of Consumer Psychology, 1*(1), 53–82.

Berger, J., & Milkman, K. L. (2012). What makes online content viral? *Journal of Marketing Research, 49*(2), 192–205.

Bhatia, S., & Loewenstein, G. (2013). Drive states. In E. Diener & R. Biswas-Diener (eds.), *Noba Textbook Series: Psychology.* Champaign, IL: Diener Education Fund.

Bierley, C., McSweeney, F. K., & Vannieuwkerk, R. (1985). Classical conditioning of preference for stimuli. *Journal of Consumer Research, 12*(3), 316–323.

Blaine, B. (2008). Does depression cause obesity? A meta-analysis of longitudinal studies of depression and weight control. *Journal of Health Psychology, 13*(8), 1190–1197.

Blaney, P. H. (1986). Affect and memory – a review. *Psychological Bulletin, 99*(2), 229–246.

Blechert, J., Goltsche, J. E., Herbert, B. M., & Wilhelm, F. H. (2014). Eat your troubles away: Electrocortical and experiential correlates of food image processing are related to emotional eating style and emotional state. *Biological Psychology, 96,* 94–101.

Bodur, H. O., Brinberg, D., & Coupey, E. (2000). Belief, affect, and attitude: Alternative models of the determinants of attitude. *Journal of Consumer Psychology, 9*(1), 17–28.

Bower, G. H. (1981). Mood and memory. *American Psychologist, 36*(2), 129–148.

Bower, G. H., & Forgas, J. P. (2000). Affect, memory, and social cognition. In E.K. Eich, G.H. Bower, J.P. Forgas, & P.M. Niedenthal (eds.), *Cognition and emotion* (pp. 87-168). New York: Oxford University Press

Bradley, C. M., Cuthbert, B. N., & Lang, P. J. (1993). Pictures as prepulse – attention and emotion in startle modification. *Psychophysiology, 30*(5), 541–545.

Bradley, M. M., Greenwald, M. K., Petry, M. C., & Lang, P. L. (1992). Remembering pictures – pleasure and arousal in memory. *Journal of Experimental Psychology-Learning Memory and Cognition, 18*(2), 379–390.

Brendl, C. M., Markman, A. B., & Messner, C. (2003). The devaluation effect: Activating a need devalues unrelated choice options. *Journal of Consumer Research. 29*(4), 463–473.

Brown, S. P., & Stayman, D. M. (1992). Antecedents and consequences of attitude toward the ad – a meta-analysis. *Journal of Consumer Research, 19*(1), 34–51.

Brown, S. P., Homer, P. M., & Inman, J. J. (1998). A meta-analysis of relationships between ad-evoked feelings and advertising responses. *Journal of Marketing Research, 35*(1), 114–126.

Buehler, R., & McFarland, C. (2001). Intensity bias in affective forecasting: The role of temporal focus. *Personality and Social Psychology Bulletin, 27*(11), 1480–1493.

Burke, A., Heuer, F., & Reisberg, D. (1992). Remembering emotional events. *Memory & Cognition, 20*(3), 277–290.

Burke, M. C., & Edell, J. A. (1989). The impact of feelings on ad-based affect and cognition. *Journal of Marketing Research, 26*(1), 69–83.

Cai, F., Tang, F., & Jia, J.-M. (2009). The interaction effect of mood and price level on purchase intention. In A. L. McGill & S. Shavitt (eds.), *Advances in Consumer Research* (vol. 36, pp. 963–964). Duluth, MN: Association for Consumer Research.

Carmon, Z., Wertenbroch, K., & Zeelenberg, M. (2003). Option attachment: When deliberating makes choosing feel like losing. *Journal of Consumer Research, 30*(1), 15–29.

Chan, C., van Boven, L., Andrade, E. B., & Ariely, D. (2013). Moral violations reduce oral consumption. *Journal of Consumer Psychology*, online first, DOI: 10.1016/j.jcps.2013.12.003.

Chandy, R. K., Tellis, G. J., MacInnis, D. J., Thaivanich, P. (2001). What to say when: Advertising appeals in evolving markets. *Journal of Marketing Research, 38*(4), 399–414.

Chang, H. & Pham, M. T. (2013). Affect as a decision making system of the present. *Journal of Consumer Research, 40*(6), 42–63.

Charles, S. T., Mather, M. & Carstensen, L. L. (2003). Aging and emotional memory: The forgettable nature of negative images for older adults. *Journal of Experimental Psychology: General, 132*(2), 310–324.

Chebat, J-C, & Michon, R. (2003). Impact of ambient odors on mall shoppers' emotions, cognitions, and spending: A test of competitive causal theories. *Journal of Business Research, 56*, 529–539.

Cheema, A. and Patrick, V. (2012). Influence of warm versus cool temperatures on consumer choice: A resource depletion account. *Journal of Marketing Research, 49*(6), 984–995.

Cialdini, R. B., Darby, B. L., & Vincent, J. E. (1973). Transgression and altruism: Case for hedonism. *Journal of Experimental Psychology, 9*(6), 502–516.

Cialdini, R. B., & Kenrick, D. T. (1976). Altruism as hedonism: Social-development perspective on relationship of negative mood state and helping. *Journal of Personality and Social Psychology, 34*(5), 907–914.

Clark, M. S., & Isen, A. M. (1982). Toward understanding the relationship between feeling states and social behavior. In L. Berkowitz (ed.), *Cognitive Psychology* (pp. 73–108). New York: Elsevier/North-Holland.

Cohen, J. B., & Andrade, E. B. (2004). Affective intuition and task-contingent affect regulation. *Journal of Consumer Research, 31*(2), 358–367.

Cohen, J. B., & Areni, C. S. (1991). Affect and consumer behavior. In T. S. Robertson & H. H. Kassarjian (eds.), *Handbook of Consumer Behavior* (pp. 188–240). Englewood Cliffs, NJ: Prentice Hall.

Cohen, J. B., Pham, M. T. & Andrade, E. B. (2008). The nature and role of affect in consumer behavior. In C. Haugtvedt, F. Kardes, & P. Herr. Mahway, *Handbook of Consumer Psychology*. Mahwah, NJ: Erlbaum, 297–348.

Compton, R.J. (2003). The interface between emotion and attention: A review of evidence from psychology and neuroscience. *Behavioral and Cognitive Neuroscience Reviews, 2*(2), 115–129.

Constans, J. I., & Matthews, A. M. (1993). Mood and subjective risk of future events. *Cognition and Emotion, 7*(6), 545–560.

Cote, S., Gyurak, A., & Levenson, R. W. (2010). The ability to regulate emotion is associated with greater well-being, income, and socioeconomic status. *Emotion, 10*(6), 923–933.

Dahl, D., Fischer, E., Johar, G., & Morwitz, V., (2014). From the editors-elect: Meaningful consumer research, *Journal of Consumer Research, 41*(1), iii–v.

Dahl, D. W. Manchanda, R. V, & Argo, J. J. (2001). Embarrassment in consumer purchase: The roles of social presence and purchase familiarity. *Journal of Consumer Research, 28* (December), 473–481.

de Wied, M., Zillmann, D., & Ordman, V. (1995). The role of empathic distress in the enjoyment of cinematic tragedy. *Poetics. 23*(1–2), 91–106.

DeSteno, D., Petty, R. E., Wegener, D. T., & Rucker, D. D. (2000). Beyond valence in the perception of likelihood: The role of emotion specificity. *Journal of Personality and Social Psychology, 78*(3), 397–416.

Di Muro, F. & Murray, K. B. (2012). An arousal regulation explanation of mood effects on consumer choice. *Journal of Consumer Research, 39*(3), 574–584.

Dommermuth, W. P., & Millard, W. J. (1967). Consumption coincidence in product evaluation. *Journal of Marketing Research, 4,* 388–390.

Dunn, J. R. & Schweitzer, M. E. (2005). Feeling and believing: The influence of emotion on trust. *Journal of Personality and Social Psychology, 88*(5), 736–748.

Dutton, D. G. & Aron, A. P. (1974). Some evidence for heightened sexual attraction under conditions of high anxiety. *Journal of Personality and Social Psychology, 30*(4), 510–517.

Easterbrook, J. A. (1959). The effect of emotion on cue utilization and the organization of behavior. *Psychological Review, 66*(3), 183–201.

Edell, J. A., & Burke, M. C. (1987). The power of feelings in understanding advertising effects. *Journal of Consumer Research, 14*(3), 421–433.

Edmans, A., García, D., & Norli, O. (2007). Sports sentiment and stock returns. *Journal of Finance, 62*(4), 1967–1998.

Ehrlichman, H., & Halpern, J. N. (1988). Affect and memory: Effects of pleasant and unpleasant odors on retrieval of happy and unhappy memories. *Journal of Personality and Social Psychology, 55*(5), 769–779.

Eich, E. (1995). Searching for mood dependent memory. *Psychological Science, 6*(2), 67–75.

Elster, J. (1999). *Strong Feelings: Emotions, Addiction, and Human Behavior.* Cambridge, MA: MIT Press.

Erber, M. W., & Erber, R. (2001). The role of motivated social cognition in the regulation of affective states. In J. P. Forgas (ed.), *Affect and Social Cognition* (pp. 275–289). Mahwah, NJ: Erlbaum.

Fedorikhin, A., & Patrick, V. M. (2010). Positive mood and resistance to temptation: The interfering influence of elevated arousal. *Journal of Consumer Research, 37* (4), 698–711.

Finucane, M. L., Alhakami, A., Slovic, P., & Johnson, S. M. (2000). The affect heuristic in judgments of risks and benefits. *Journal of Behavioral Decision Making. 13* (1), 1–17.

Folkman, S., & Lazarus, R. S. (1988). Coping as a mediator of emotion. *Journal of personality and social psychology, 54*(3), 466.

Forgas, J. P. (1995). Mood and judgment: The affect infusion model (AIM). *Psychological Bulletin, 117*(1), 39.

Forgas, J. P., Bower, G. H., & Krantz, S. E. (1984). The influence of mood on perceptions of social interactions. *Journal of Experimental Social Psychology, 20*, 497–513.

Fox, E., Russo, R., Bowles, R., & Dutton, K. (2001). Do threatening stimuli draw or hold visual attention in subclinical anxiety? *Journal of Experimental Psychology: General, 130*(4), 681–700.

Frederickson. B. L. & Branigan, C. (2005). Positive emotions broaden the scope of attention and thought-action repertoires. *Cognition & Emotion, 19*(3), 313–332.

Friestad, M. & Thorson, E. (1993). Remembering ads: The effects of encoding strategies, retrieval, and emotional response. *Journal of Consumer Psychology, 2*(1), 1–23.

Frijda, N. H. (1987). Emotion, cognitive structure, and action tendency. *Cognition & Emotion, 1*(2), 115–143.

Galak, J., Krueger, J., & Loewenstein, G. (2013). Slow down! Insensitivity to rate of consumption leads to avoidable satiation. *Journal of Consumer Research, 39*(5), 993–1009.

Garg, N., Wansink, B., & Inman, J. (2007). The influence of incidental affect on consumers' food intake. *Journal of Consumer Research, 71*(1), 194–206.

Gilbert, D. T., Pinel, E. C., Wilson, T. D., & Blumberg, S. J., Wheatley, T. P. (1998). Immune neglect: A source of durability bias in affective forecasting. *Journal of Personality and Social Psychology, 75*(3), 617–638.

Godden, D. & Baddeley, A. (1980). When does context influence recognition memory? *British Journal of Psychology, 71*(1), 99–104.

Goldberg, M. E., & Gorn, G. J. (1987). Happy and sad TV programs: How they affect reactions to commercials. *Journal of Consumer Research, 14*(3), 387–403.

Gorn, G. J. (1982). The effects of music in advertising on choice behavior: A classical conditioning approach. *Journal of Marketing, 46*(1), 94–101.

Gorn, G. J., Pham, M. T., & Sin, L. Y. (2001). When arousal influences ad evaluation and valence does not (and vice versa). *Journal of Consumer Psychology, 11*(1), 43–55.

Grasmick, H. G., Bursik, R., & Kinsey, K. A. (1991). Shame and embarrassment as deterrents to noncompliance with the law: The case of an antilittering campaign. *Environment & Behavior, 23*(2), 233–251.

Greene, T. R., & Noice, H. (1988). Influence of positive affect upon creative-thinking and problem-solving in children. *Psychological Reports, 63*(3), 895–898.

Gross, J. J. (1998). The emerging field of emotion regulation: An integrative review. *Review of General Psychology, 2*(3), 271–299.

Gross, J. J., Carstensen, L. L., Pasupathi, M., & Tsai, J. (1997). Emotion and aging: Experience, expression, and control. *Psychology & Aging, 12*(4), 590–599.

Grunberg, N. E., & Straub, R. O. (1992). The role of gender and taste class in the effects of stress on eating. *Health Psychology, 11*, 97–100.

Hemenover, S. H. & Schimmack, U. (2007). That's disgusting!...But very amusing: Mixed feelings. *Cognition & Emotion, 21*(5), 1102–1113.

Henrich, J., Heine, S. J., & Norenzayan, A. (2010). Most people are not WEIRD. *Nature, 466*(7302), 29.

Hirshleifer, D., & Shumway, T. (2003). Good day sunshine: Stock returns and the weather. *Journal of Finance, 58*(3), 1009–1032.

Hoch, S. J., & Loewenstein, G. F. (1991). Time-Inconsistent preferences and consumer self-control. *Journal of Consumer Research, 17*(March), 492–507.

Holbrook, M. B., & Batra, R. (1987). Assessing the role of emotions as mediators of consumer responses to advertising. *Journal of Consumer Research, 14*(3), 404–420.

Holbrook, M. B. & Hirschman, E. C. (1982). The experiential aspects of consumption: Consumer fantasies, feelings, and fun. *Journal of Consumer Research, 9*(2), 132–140.

Hsee, C. K., & Rottenstreich, Y. (2004). Music, pandas, and muggers: On the affective psychology of value. *Journal of Experimental Psychology: General, 133*(1), 23–30.

Huang, X., Zhang, M., Hui, M. K., & Wyer, R. S. (2014). Warmth and conformity: The effects of ambient temperature on product preferences and financial decisions, *Journal of Consumer Psychology, 24*, 241–250.

Huntsinger, J.R. (2012). Does positive affect broaden and negative affect narrow attentional scope? New answer to an old question. *Journal of Experimental Psychology: General, 141*(4), 595–600.

Isen, A. M. (1984). Toward understanding the role of affect in cognition. In R. S. Wyer & T. K. Srull (eds.), *Handbook of Social Cognition* (vol. 3, pp. 179–236). Hillsdale, NJ: Lawrence Erlbaum Associates.

Isen, A. M., & Daubman, K. A. (1984). The influence of affect on categorization. *Journal of personality and social psychology, 47*(6), 1206.

Isen, A. M., & Simmonds, S. F. (1978). The effect of feeling good on a helping task that is incompatible with good mood. *Social Psychology, 41*(4), 346–349.

Isen, A. M., Daubman, K. A., & Nowicki, G. P. (1987). Positive affect facilitates creative problem-solving. *Journal of Personality and Social Psychology, 52*(6), 1122–1131.

Isen, A. M., Nygren, T. E., & Ashby, F. G. (1988). Influence of positive affect on the subjective utility of gains and losses: It is just not worth the risk. *Journal of Personality and Social Psychology, 55*(5), 710–717.

Isen, A. M., Shalker, T. E., Clark, M., & Karp, L. (1978). Affect, accessibility of material in memory, and behavior: A cognitive loop? *Journal of Personality and Social Psychology, 36*(1), 1–12.

Johnson, E. J., & Tversky, A. (1983). Affect, generalization, and the perception of risk. *Journal of Personality and Social Psychology, 45*(1), 20–31.

Kahneman, D. (1999). Objective happiness. In D. Kahneman, E. Diener, & N. Schwarz (eds.), *Well-being: The Foundations of Hedonic Psychology* (pp. 3–25). New York: Russell Sage.

Kaltcheva, V. D. & Weitz, B. A. (2006). When should a retailer create an exciting store environment? *Journal of Marketing, 70*(January), 107–118.

Keinan, A., & Kivetz, R. (2011). Productivity orientation and the consumption of collectable experiences. *Journal of Consumer Research, 37*(6), 935–950.

Keltner, D., Ellsworth, P. C., & Edwards, K. (1993). Beyond simple pessimism: Effects of sadness and anger on social perception. *Journal of Personality and Social Psychology, 64*(5), 740–752.

Kenealy, P.M. (1997). Mood state-dependent retrieval: The effects of induced mood on memory reconsidered. *Quarterly Journal of Experimental Psychology, Section A: Human Experimental Psychology, 50*(2), 290–317.

Kensinger, E. A. (2009). Remembering the details: Effects of emotion. *Emotion Review, 1*(2), 99–113.

Kensinger, E. A., Garoff-Eaton, R. J., & Schacter, D. L. (2007). Effects of emotion on memory specificity in young and older adults. *Journal of Gerontology B, Psychological Sciences and Social Sciences, 62*(4), 208–215.

Kim, H., Park, K., and Schwarz, N. (2010). Will this trip really be exciting? The role of incidental emotions in product evaluations. *Journal of Consumer Research, 36* (6), 983–991.

Kim, J., Allen, C. T., & Kardes, F. R. (1996). An investigation of the meditational mechanisms underlying attitudinal conditioning. *Journal of Marketing Research, 33*(3), 318–328.

Krishna, A. (2012). An integrative review of sensory marketing: Engaging the senses to affect perception, judgment and behavior. *Journal of Consumer Psychology, 22* (3), 332–351.

Krishna, A., Morrin, M., & Sayin, E. (2014). Smellizing cookies and salivating: A focus on olfactory imagery. *Journal of Consumer Research, 40*(April), doi:10.1086/674664.

Krishna, A., & Schwarz, N. (2014). Sensory marketing, embodiment, and grounded cognition: A review and introduction. *Journal of Consumer Psychology, 24*(2), 159–168.

LaBar, K. S., Mesulam, M.-M., Gitelman, D. R., & Weintraud, S. (2000). Emotional curiosity: Modulation of visuospatial attention by arousal is preserved in aging and early-stage Alzheimer's disease. *Neuropsychologia, 38*(13), 1734–1740.

Labroo, A. A., & Mukhopadhyay, A. (2009). Lay theories of emotion transience and the search for happiness: A fresh perspective on affect regulation. *Journal of Consumer Research, 36*(2), 242–254.

Labroo, A. A., & Patrick, V. M. (2009). Psychological distancing: Why happiness helps you see the big picture. *Journal of Consumer Research, 35*(5), 800–809.

Labroo, A. A., & Rucker, D. D. (2010). The orientation-matching hypothesis: An emotion-specificity approach to affect regulation. *Journal of Marketing Research, 47*(5), 955–966.

Lang, P. J., Greenwald, M. K., Bradley, M. M., & Hamm, A. O. (1993). Looking at pictures: Affective, facial, visceral, and behavioral reactions. *Psychophysiology, 30*(3), 261–273.

Larsen, J. T., McGraw, P. A., & Cacioppo, J. T. (2001). Can people feel happy and sad at the same time? *Journal of Personality and Social Psychology, 81*(4), 684–696.

Lau-Gesk, L., & Drolet, A. (2008). The publicly self-consciousness consumer: Prepared to be embarrassed. *Journal of Consumer Psychology, 18* (2), 127–136.

Lawson, R. (1985). The effects of mood on retrieving consumer product information. In E. C. Hirschman & M. B. Holbrook (eds.), *Advances in Consumer Research* (vol. 12, pp. 399–403). Provo, UT: Association for Consumer Research.

Lee, A. Y., & Sternthal, B. (1999). The effects of positive mood on memory. *Journal of Consumer Research, 26*(2), 115–127.

Lee, C. J. & Andrade, E. B. (2011). Fear, social projection, and financial decision making. *Journal of Marketing Research, 48*(SPL), S121–S129.

Lee, C. J., Andrade, E. B., and Palmer, S. E. (2013). Interpersonal relationships and preferences for mood-congruency in aesthetic experiences. *Journal of Consumer Research, 40*(August), 382–391.

Lee, L., & Tsai, C. (2014). How price promotions influence postpurchase consumption experience over time. *Journal of Consumer Research, 40*(5), 943–959.

Lerner, J. S., & Keltner, D. (2001). Fear, anger, and risk. *Journal of Personality & Social Psychology, 81*(1), 146–159.

Levine, L. J., & Safer, M. A. (2002). Sources of bias in memory for emotions. *Current Directions in Psychological Science, 11*(5), 169–173.

Levine, L. J., Lench, H. C., Kaplan, R. L., & Safer, M.A. (2012). Accuracy and artifact: Reexamining the intensity bias in affective forecasting. *Journal of Personality and Social Psychology, 103*(4), 584–605.

Levine, L. J., Lench, H. C., Kaplan, R. L., & Safer, M. A. (2013). Like Schrödinger's cat, the impact bias is both dead and alive: Reply to Wilson and Gilbert (2013). *Journal of Personality and Social Psychology,105*(5), 749–756.

Loewenstein, G. (1996). Out of control: Visceral influences on behavior. *Organizational Behavior and Human Decision Processes, 65*(3), 272–292.

Loewenstein, G. (1999) Because it is there: The challenge of mountaineering... for utility theory. *Kyklos, 52,* 315–344.

Loewenstein, G. (2000). Emotions in economic theory and economic behavior. *American Economic Review: Papers and Proceedings, 90,* 426–432.

Loewenstein, G., Weber, E. U., Hsee, C. K., & Welch, N. (2001). Risk as feelings. *Psychological Bulletin, 127*(2), 267–286.

Luce, M. F. (1998). Choosing to avoid: Coping with negatively emotion-laden consumer decisions. *Journal of Consumer Research, 24*(4), 409–433.

Luce, M. F., Payne, J. W., & Bettman, J. R. (1999). Emotional trade-off difficulty and choice. *Journal of Marketing Research, 36*(2), 143–159.

MacGregor, D. G., Slovic, P., Dreman, D., & Berry, M. (2000). Imagery, affect, and financial judgment. *Journal of Psychology and Financial Markets, 1*(2), 104–110.

Machleit, K. A., & Wilson, R. D. (1988). Emotional feelings and attitudes toward the advertisement: The roles of brand familiarity and repetition. *Journal of Advertising, 17*(3), 27–35.

Martin, L. L., Abend, T., Sedikides, C., & Green, J. D. (1997). How would it feel if...? Mood as input to a role fulfillment evaluation process. *Journal of Personality & Social Psychology, 73*(2), 242.

Mather, M., Gorlick, M. A., & Nesmith, K. (2009). The limits of arousal's memory impairing effects on nearby information. *American Journal of Psychology, 122,* 349–370.

Mather, M. (2007). Emotional arousal and memory binding: An object-based framework. *Perspectives on Psychological Science, 2,* 33–52.

Mather, M., & Johnson, M. K. (2003). Affective review and schema reliance in memory in older and younger adults. *American Journal of Psychology, 116,* 169–189.

Mather, M., & Nesmith, K. (2008). Arousal-enhanced location memory for pictures. *Journal of Memory and Language, 58,* 449–464.

Mather, M., & Sutherland, M. (2009). Disentangling the effects of arousal and valence on memory for intrinsic details. *Emotion Review, 1,* 118–119.

Mather, M., & Sutherland, M. R. (2011). Arousal-biased competition in perception and memory. *Perspectives on Psychological Science, 6,* 114–133.

Mayer, J. D., Gaschke, Y. N., Braveman, D. L., & Evans, T. W. (1992). Mood-congruent judgment is a general effect. *Journal of Personality and Social Psychology, 63*(1), 119–132.

McAlister, L. (1982). A dynamic attribute satiation model of variety-seeking behavior. *Journal of Consumer Research, 9*(2), 141–150.

McGraw, A. P. & Warren, C. (2010). Benign violations: Making immoral behavior funny. *Psychological Science, 21*, 1141–1149.

McGraw, A. P., Warren, C., Williams, L., & Leonard, B. (2012). Too close for comfort, or too far to care? Finding humor in distant tragedies and close mishaps. *Psychological Science, 25*, 1215–1223.

Mellers, B. A., Schwartz, A., & Ritov, I. (1999). Emotion-based choice. *Journal of ExperimentalPsychology: General, 128*(3), 332–345.

Meyvis, T., Ratner, R. and Levav, J. (2010). Why don't we learn to accurately forecast feelings? How misremembering our predictions blinds us to past forecasting errors. *Journal of Experimental Psychology: General, 139*(November), 579–589.

Mitchell, T.R., Thompson, L., Peterson, E. & Cronk, R. (1997). Temporal adjustments in the evaluation of events: The "rosy view." *Journal of Experimental Social Psychology, 33*(4), 421–448.

Mogilner, C., Aaker, J., & Kamvar, S. (2012). How happiness affects choice. *Journal of Consumer Research, 39*(2), 429–443.

Morales, A. C., & Fitzsimons, G. J. (2007). Product contagion: Changing consumer evaluations through physical contact with "disgusting" products. *Journal of Marketing Research, 44*(2), 272–283.

Morales, A. C., Wu, E. C., and Fitzsimons, G. J. (2012). How disgust enhances the effectiveness of fear appeals. *Journal of Marketing Research, 49*(3), 383–393.

Moriya, H., & Nittono, H. (2011). Effect of mood states on the breadth of spatial attentional focus: An event-related potential study. *Neuropsychologia, 49*(5), 1162–1170.

Morris, M. W., & Keltner, D. (2000). How emotions work: An analysis of the social functions of emotional expression in negotiations. *Review of Organizational Behavior, 22*, 1–50.

Morris, W. N. (1989). *Mood: The Frame of Mind.* New York: Springer-Verlag.

Nelson, L. D., & Meyvis, T. (2008). Interrupted consumption: Adaptation and the disruption of hedonic experience. *Journal of Marketing Research, 45*, 654–664.

Nielsen, J. H., Shapiro, S. A., & Mason, C. H. (2010). Emotionality and semantic onsets: Exploring orienting attention responses in advertising. *Journal of Marketing Research: December, 47*(6), 1138–1150.

Oaten, M., Stevenson, R. J., & Case, T. I. (2009). Disgust as a disease-avoidance mechanism, *Psychological Bulletin, 135*(2), 303–321.

Ohman, A., Flykt, A., & Esteves, F. (2001). Emotion drives attention: Detecting the snake in the grass. *Journal of Experimental Psychology: General, 130*(3), 466–478.

Oliver, R. (1993). Cognitive, affective, and attribute bases of the satisfaction response. *Journal of Consumer Research, 20*(December), 418–430.

Ottati, V. C., & Isbell, L. M. (1996). Effects of mood during exposure to target information on subsequently reported judgments: An on-line model of misattribution and correction. *Journal of Personality and Social Psychology, 71*(1), 39–53.

Patrick, V. M., MacInnis, D. J., & Park, C. W. (2007). Not as happy as I thought I'd be? Affective misforecasting and product evaluations. *Journal of Consumer Research, 33*(4), 479–489.

Pham, M. T. (1996). Cue representation and selection effects of arousal on persuasion. *Journal of Consumer Research, 22*(4), 373–387.

Pham, M. T. (1998). Representativeness, relevance, and the use of feelings in decision making. *Journal of Consumer Research, 25*(2), 144–159.

Pham, M.T. (2013). The seven sins of consumer psychology. *Journal of Consumer Psychology, 23* (Oct), 411–423.

Pham, M. T., Cohen, J. B., Pracejus, J. W., & Hughes, G. D. (2001). Affect monitoring and the primacy of feelings in judgment. *Journal of Consumer Research, 28*(2), 167–188.

Pham, M. T., Gorn, G., & Sin, L. Y. (2001). When arousal influences ad evaluation and valence does not (and vice versa). *Journal of Consumer Psychology, 11*(1), 43–55.

Pietromonaco, P. R., & Rook, K. S. (1987). Decision style in depression: The contribution of perceived risks versus benefits. *Journal of Personality and Social Psychology, 52*(2), 399–408.

Pocheptsova, A., & Novemsky, N. (2010). When do incidental mood effects last? Lay beliefs versus actual effects. *Journal of Consumer Research, 36*(6), 992–1001.

Richins, M. L. (1983). An analysis of consumer interaction styles in the marketplace. *Journal of Consumer Research, 10*(1), 73–82.

Robinson, M. D., & Clore, G. L. (2002). Belief and feeling: evidence for an accessibility model of emotional self-report. *Psychological bulletin, 128*(6), 934.

Roseman, I. J. (1984). Cognitive determinants of emotion: A structural theory. *Review of Personality & Social Psychology, 5*, 11–36.

Rosler, A., Ulrich, C., Billino, J., Sterzer, P., Weidauer, S., Bernhardt, T., Steinmetz, H., Frolich, L., & Kleinschmidt, A. (2005). Effects of arousing emotional scenes on the distribution of visuospatial attention: Changes with aging and early subcortical vascular dementia. *Journal of the Neurological Sciences, 229–30* (March 15), 109–116.

Rowe, G., Hirsh, J. B., & Anderson, A. K., (2007). Positive affect increases the breadth of attentional selection. *Proceedings of the National Academy of Sciences, 104* (1), 383–388.

Rozin, P. (1990). Getting to like the burn of chili pepper: Biological, psychological and cultural perspectives. In B. G. Green, J. R. Mason, & M. R. Kare (eds.), *Chemical Senses* (vol. *2, Irritation*; pp. 231–269). New York: Marcel Dekker.

Rozin, P., Guillot, L., Fincher, K., Rozin, A., & Tsukayama, E. (2013). Glad to be sad, and other examples of benign masochism. *Judgment and Decision Making, 8* (4), 439–447.

Russell, J. A., & Barrett, L. F. (1999). Core affect, prototypical emotional episodes, and other things called emotion: Dissecting the elephant. *Journal of Personality and Social Psychology, 76*(5), 805–819.

Rusting, C.L. (1998). Personality, mood, and cognitive processing of emotional information: Three conceptual frameworks. *Psychological Bulletin, 124*(2), 165–196.

Rusting, C. L., & DeHart, T. (2000). Retrieving positive memories to regulate negative mood: Consequences for mood-congruent memory. *Journal of Personality and Social Psychology, 78*(4), 737–752.

Sakaki, M., Fryer, K., & Mather, M. (2014). Emotion strengthens high priority memory traces but weakens low priority memory traces. *Psychological Science, 25*(2), 387–395.

Salermo, A., Laran, J., & Janiszewski, C. (2014). Hedonic eating goals and emotion: When sadness decreases the desire to indulge. *Journal of Consumer Research, 41*(June), 135–151.

Sanbonmatsu, D. M., & Kardes, F. R. (1988). The effects of physiological arousal on information-processing and persuasion. *Journal of Consumer Research, 15*(3), 379–385.

Schachter, S., & Singer, J. E. (1962) Cognitive, social, and physiological determinants of emotional state. *Psychological Review, 69*(September), 379–399.

Scherer, K. R. (1982). Emotion as a process: Function, origin, and regulation. *Social Science Information, 21*(4–5), 555–570.

Schimmack, U. (2001). Pleasure, displeasure, and mixed feelings? Are semantic opposites mutually exclusive? *Cognition and Emotion, 15*, 81–97.

Schindler, R.M. (1998). Consequences of perceiving oneself as responsible for obtaining a discount: Evidence for smart-shopper feelings. *Journal of Consumer Psychology, 7*(4), 371–392.

Schramm, H., & Wirth, W. (2010). Exploring the paradox of sad-film enjoyment: The role of multiple appraisals and meta-appraisals. *Poetics, 38*, 319–335.

Schwarz, N. (1990). Feelings as information: Informational and motivational functions of affective states. In R. M. Sorrentino & E. T. Higgins (eds.), *Handbook of Motivation and Cognition* (vol. 2, pp. 521–561). New York: Guilford Press.

Schwarz, N. (2001). Feelings as information: Implications for affective influences on information processing. In L. L. Martin & G. Clore (eds.), *Theories of Mood and Cognition: A User's Guidebook* (vol. 8, pp. 159–172). New York: Psychology Press.

Schwarz, N., & Clore, G. L. (1983). Mood, misattribution, and judgments of well-being: Informative and directive functions of affective states. *Journal of Personality and Social Psychology, 45*(3), 513–523.

Schwarz, N., & Clore, G. L. (2007). Feelings and phenomenal experiences. In A. Kruglanski & E. T. Higgins (eds.), *Social Psychology: Handbook of Basic Principles* (2nd ed., pp. 385–407). New York: Guilford.

Sedikides, C. (1994). Incongruent effects of sad mood on self-conception valence: It's a matter of time. *European Journal of Social Psychology, 24*(1), 161–172.

Shen, H., & Wyer, R.S. (2008). Procedural priming and consumer judgments: Effects on the impact of positively and negatively valenced information. *Journal of Consumer Research, 34*(5), 727–737.

Sheth, J. N. (1982). Consumer behavior: Surpluses and shortages. *Advances in Consumer Research* (vol. 19, pp. 13–16), Provo, UT: Association for Consumer Research.

Shiv, B., & Fedorikhin, A. (1999). Heart and mind in conflict: The interplay of affect and cognition in consumer decision making. *Journal of Consumer Research, 26*(3), 278–292.

Slovic, P. (2010). *The Feeling of Risk: New Perspectives on Risk Perception.* New York: Earthscan.

Small, D. & Verocchi, N. M. (2009). The face of need: Facial emotion expression on charity advertisements. *Journal of Marketing Research, 46*(6), 777–787.

Smith, B. D., Wilson, R. J., & Jones, B. E. (1983). Extraversion and multiple levels of caffeine-induced arousal: Effects on overhabituation and dishabituation. *Psychophysiology, 20*(1), 29–34.

Smith, C. A., and Ellsworth, P. C. (1985), Patterns of cognitive appraisal in emotion. *Journal of Personality and Social Psychology, 48*(4), 813–838.

Soman, D. & Cheema, A. (2011). Earmarking and partitioning: increasing saving by low-income households. *Journal of Marketing Research, 48*(SPL), S14–S22.

Spangenberg, E. R., Crowley, A. E., & Henderson, P. W. (1996). Improving the store environment: Do olfactory cues affect evaluations and behaviors? *Journal of Marketing, 60*(2), 67–80.

Stayman, D. M. & Batra, R. (1991). Encoding and retrieval of ad affect in memory. *Journal of Marketing Research, 28*(2), 232–239.

Steblay, N. M. (1992). A meta-analytic review of the weapon focus effect. *Law and Human Behavior, 16*(4), 413–424.

Stone, D. N., & Kadous, K. (1997). The joint effects of task-related negative affect and task difficulty in multiattribute choice. *Organizational Behavior and Human Decision Processes, 70*(2), 159–174.

Sutherland, M. R., & Mather, M. (2012). Negative arousal amplifies the effects of saliency in short-term memory. *Emotion, 12*, 1367–1372.

Tal, A., & Wansink, B. (2013). Fattening fasting: Hungry grocery shoppers buy more calories, not more food. *JAMA Internal Medicine, 173*(12), 1146–1148.

Tamir, M. (2009). What do people want to feel and why? Pleasure and utility in emotion regulation. *Current Directions in Psychological Science, 18*(2), 101–105.

Teixeira, T., Wedel, M., & Pieters, R. (2012). Emotion-induced engagement in internet video advertisements. *Journal of Marketing Research, 49*(2), 144–159.

Thomson, M., MacInnis, D. J., & Park, C. W. (2005). The ties that bind: Measuring the strength of consumers' emotional attachments to brands. *Journal of Consumer Psychology, 15*(1), 77–91.

Thorson, E., & Friestad, M. (1989). The effects of emotion on episodic memory for television commercials. In P. Cafferata & A. M. Tybout (eds.), *Cognitive and Affective Responses to Advertising* (pp. 305–325). Lexington, MA: D.C. Heath and Company.

Tice, D. M., Bratslavsky, E., & Baumeister, R. F. (2001). Emotional distress regulation takes precedence over impulse control: If you feel bad, do it! *Journal of Personality and Social Psychology, 80*(1), 53–67.

Tiedens, L. Z., & Linton, S. (2001). Judgment under emotional certainty and uncertainty: The effects of specific emotions on information processing. *Journal of Personality and Social Psychology, 81*(6), 973–988.

Tsai, J. L., Knutson, B., & Fung, H. H. (2006). Cultural variation in affect valuation. *Journal of Personality and Social Psychology, 90*(2), 288–307.

Van den Bergh, B., Dewitte, S., and Warlop, L. (2008). Bikinis instigate generalized impatience in intertemporal choice. *Journal of Consumer Research, 35*(1), 85–97.

Vosgerau, J. (2010). How prevalent is wishful thinking? Misattribution of arousal causes optimism and pessimism in subjective probabilities. *Journal of Experimental Psychology: General, 139*(1), 32–48.

Wang, J., Novemsky, N., & Dhar, R. (2009). Anticipating adaptation to products. *Journal of Consumer Research, 36*(August), 149–159.

Wansink, B., & Chandon, P. (2014). Slim by design: Redirecting the accidental drivers of mindless overeating. *Journal of Consumer Psychology*, DOI: 10.1016/j.jcps.2014.03.006.

Wansink, B., Payne, C. R., & Chandon, P. (2007). Internal and external cues of meal cessarion: The French paradox redux? *Obesity, 15*(12), 2920–2924.

Wansink, B., Tal, A., & Shimizu, M. (2012). First foods most: After 18-hour fast, people drawn to starches first and vegetables last, *JAMA Internal Medicine, 172*(12), 961–963.

Ward, M. H., & Dahl, D. W. (2104). Should the devil Sell Prada? Retail rejection increases aspiring consumers' desire for the brand. *Journal of Consumer Research*, 41(3), 590-609.

Wells, A., & Matthews, G. (1994). Attention and emotion: A clinical perspective. Hillsdale, NJ: Laurence Erlbaum Associates.

Weinstein, N. D. (1982). Community noise problems: Evidence against adaptation. *Journal of Environmental Psychology, 2*(2), 87–97.

Williams, P., & Aaker, J. L. (2002). Can mixed emotions peacefully coexist? *Journal of Consumer Research, 28*(4), 636–649.

Wilson, T. D., & Gilbert, D. T. (2003). Affective forecasting. In M. Zanna (ed.), *Advances in Experimental Social Psychology* (vol. 35, pp. 345–411). New York: Elsevier.

Wilson, T. D., Wheatley, T., Meyers, J. M., Gilbert, D. T., & Axsom, D. (2000). Focalism: A source of durability bias in affective forecasting. *Journal of Personality and Social Psychology, 78*(5), 821–836.

Winkielman P, & Berridge, K. 2004. Unconscious emotion. *Current Directions Psychological Science, 13*, 120–123.

Wirth, W., Hofer, M., & Schramm, H. (2012). Beyond pleasure: Exploring the eudaimonic entertainment experience. *Human Communication Research, 38* (4), 406–428.

Wirtz, D., Kruger, J., Scollon, C. N., & Diener, E. (2003).What to do on spring break? The role of predicted, on-line, and remembered experience in future choice. *Psychological Science, 14*(5), 520–524.

Wood, S. L., & Bettman, R. B. (2007). Predicting happiness: How normative feeling rules influence (and even reverse) durability bias. *Journal of Consumer Psychology, 17*(3), 188–201.

Wright, W. F., & Bower, G. H. (1982). Mood effects on subjective probability assessment. *Organizational Behavioral and Human Decision Processes, 52*(2), 276–291.

Wyer, R. S., & Carlston, D. (1979). *Social Cognition, Inference and Attribution.* Hillsdale, NJ: Erlbaum.

Xu, J., & Schwarz, N. (2009). Do we really need a reason to indulge? *Journal of Marketing Research, 46*(1), 25–36.

Zajonc, R. B. (1980). Feeling and thinking: Preferences need no inferences. *American Psychologist, 35*(2), 151–175.

Zeelenberg. R., & Bocanegra, B. R. (2010). Auditory emotional cues enhance visual perception. *Cognition, 115*(1), 202–206.

Zillmann, D. (1988). Mood management through communication choices. *American Behavioral Scientist, 31*(3), 327–340.

Zwebner, Y., Lee, L., & Goldenberg, J. (2013). The temperature premium: Warm temperatures increase product valuation. *Journal of Consumer Psychology, 24* (2), 251–259.

5 Evolution and Consumer Behavior

Vladas Griskevicius and Kristina M. Durante

Imagine if Charles Darwin walked into a modern shopping mall. How would he react? From the dazzling sights and sounds to the dizzying array of smells and behaviors, Darwin would likely find many of the things he sees quite puzzling. In fact, Darwin was similarly puzzled by many of the strange characteristics and behaviors of the animals he encountered in his travels around the world. Decades of detective work and such observations led Darwin to formulate the theory of natural selection (Darwin, 1859). Darwin's theory became the unifying framework of the life sciences, helping understand the characteristics and behaviors of all living organisms, including humans. Today this interdisciplinary framework is the bridge between the social and the natural sciences, regularly incorporated into modern psychology, anthropology, and other behavioral sciences.

So how would Darwin seek to make sense of the behaviors in a twenty-first-century shopping mall? In the same way he sought to understand all living organisms – by starting with a simple question: What adaptive function might these behaviors serve?

This question is the starting point for a Darwinian detective – anyone seeking to understand modern behavior in an evolutionarily informed way. The purpose of this chapter is to elucidate what it means to take an evolutionary approach to consumer research. In so doing, we highlight the value of incorporating this approach in consumer research, discuss relevant theories and findings, and offer suggestions for easy ways to incorporate an evolutionary perspective into any area of study.

An Evolutionary Approach to Consumer Behavior

An evolutionary approach to studying behavior can be summarized in the following way:

- All human behavior includes an evolutionary explanation.
- Evolutionary explanations concern the adaptive function of behavior.

All Behaviors Include an Evolutionary Explanation

If you're a social scientist who hasn't been exposed to evolutionary biology, it might seem reasonable to assume that a few human behaviors might be related to evolution, but that many others are probably unrelated to evolution. Unfortunately, this assumption is blatantly false. In reality, all behaviors *include* an evolutionary explanation. This is because any behavior has multiple explanations at different levels of analysis.

For a concrete example, consider the question, why do babies cry? One way to answer this question is that babies cry because they feel distress (e.g., pain, discomfort, hunger, or separation). Another way to answer this question is that babies cry because this behavior functions to elicit care from a caregiver. But it is also equally accurate to explain that babies cry because they are born with a specific crying mechanism. This mechanism follows a relatively fixed developmental trajectory in the first three months of life, but crying then becomes influenced by learning as the baby matures cognitively. And more broadly, babies cry because this is typical behavior for all primate infants and can be traced back to a common ancestor.

There are multiple ways to answer the question of why babies cry. All of the answers are correct, but each one provides a fundamentally different type of explanation for the behavior. This is because all behavior – from crying and coughing to conservation and conspicuous consumption – has multiple explanations. The most widely used method for categorizing explanations was developed by Nobel Prize–winning ethologist Niko Tinbergen (1963). Commonly referred to as "the four questions," Tinbergen grouped explanations into four categories, whereby each explanation is associated with a different type of question:

- **Proximate Mechanism:** What are the triggers (causes) of the behavior?
- **Development:** How does the behavior come about during one's lifetime?
- **Adaptive Function**: What adaptive problem(s) does the behavior ultimately function to solve?
- **Evolutionary History**: How did the behavior arise in the species?

The first two explanations concern processes that occur within the lifetime of the individual. The latter two explanations reside within the deeper realm of evolutionary biology. Table 5.1 provides a deeper overview of the four types of explanations.

When seeking to understand a given behavior, a researcher can begin by starting at any of the four types of explanations. Consumer researchers tend to focus primarily on the first type of explanation – the proximate mechanism. For example, the overwhelming majority of articles in the *Journal of Consumer Research* and the *Journal of Marketing Research* focus exclusively on the proximate mechanism as the sole explanation for behavior. Focusing on the proximate mechanism makes good sense and provides valuable insight into behavior, but to fully understand any behavior it is useful to consider it at more than merely one level of explanation.

Table 5.1 *Four Types of Explanations for Behavior*

Type of Explanation	Central Question and Potential Answers	Example: Why Do Babies Cry?
Proximate Mechanism (Causation) *How does it work?*	**What are the relatively immediate causes of a behavior?** Most behaviors have multiple proximate causes, including environmental cues, social cues, physical state, psychological state, hormones, pheromones, genes, neurological firing, etc.	Babies cry because of distress (e.g., pain, discomfort, hunger, or separation). These explain the proximate mechanism of the behavior because they pertain to the immediate triggers (causes) of the behavior.
Development (Ontogeny) *How does it come about?*	**How does a behavior come about during one's lifetime?** Possibilities include learning, specified developmental trajectory, imprinting, cognitive maturation, environmentally contingent expression of genes, etc.	Babies cry because infant crying follows a relatively fixed developmental trajectory in the first 3 months of life. It then becomes influenced by learning (e.g., when a child is able to form mental representations, crying can be induced by the mere threat of maternal separation).
Ultimate Function (Adaptation) *Why did it evolve?*	**What adaptive problem(s) does a behavior ultimately function to solve?** Some behaviors function to solve one adaptive problem, whereas others can solve multiple problems such as how to obtain food, avoid disease, decrease danger, make friends, attain status, attract mates, care for family, etc.	Babies cry because this behavior has reliably elicited care from a caregiver (e.g., food, holding). These are the ultimate functions of the behavior because they explain how the behavior has enhanced fitness throughout evolutionary history.
Evolutionary History (Phylogeny) *How did it evolve?*	**How did a behavior arise in the species?** Possibilities include that a behavior can be traced to a common ancestor, behavior evolved independently in multiple species, behavior is unique to humans, etc.	Babies cry because it is typical for babies in all primate species to cry. This suggests that multiple species share a similar crying mechanism with a common function that resulted from the same selection pressure.

The Adaptive Function of Behavior

An evolutionary psychological approach focuses on Tinbergen's third type of explanation – the adaptive function. This approach dates back to Darwin's (1859) theory of natural selection. Natural selection is the process by which biologically influenced characteristics become either more or less common in a population depending on how those characteristics affect an individual's reproductive fitness – the passing of genes onto future generations. Characteristics that enhanced reproductive fitness were passed on to future generations, whereas those that impeded it were not. Natural selection therefore maintains particular characteristics because they have (or once had) fitness benefits. The process of natural selection can result in three products:

- **Adaptations:** Characteristics that reliably solved adaptive problems better than competing alternatives during evolutionary history (example: fear of poisonous snakes)
- **By-products:** Artifacts without adaptive value that persist because they are inherently coupled with adaptations (example: fear of harmless snakes)
- **Noise:** Variations in a given characteristic that are due to random environmental events or genetic mutations (example: most rare types of fears, such as fear of flowers)

The principles of natural selection have long been applied to the study of human anatomy and physiology. However, there is now widespread recognition that these principles are powerful tools for understanding psychology and behavior in human and non-human animals (Alcock, 2001; Buss, 2005; Dunbar & Barrett, 2009; Barkow, Tooby, & Cosmides, 1992).

An evolutionary psychological perspective stresses that the human mind is a complex integrated assembly of psychological adaptations – a premise shared widely by evolutionary biologists in understanding animal behavior (Alcock, 2005; Barash, 1977; Wilson, 2000). *Psychological adaptations* are information-processing circuits that take in units of information (from both our external environments and our internal physiological systems) and transform that information into outputs designed to solve a particular adaptive problem (Barrett, 2012; Barrett & Kurzban, 2006; Cosmides, Barrett, & Tooby, 2010).

Psychological adaptations enhanced fitness by solving distinct adaptive problems. Just like physiological adaptations evolved to solve distinct problems in the service of survival and reproduction (think about the distinct problems solved by the heart, liver, lungs, etc.), psychological adaptations also evolved as solutions to qualitatively distinct adaptive problems.

Adaptive problems are many in number. To enhance fitness successfully, we need to obtain food and water. We must also obtain shelter, avoid disease, evade physical harm, make friends, attain status, find a mate, and care for family. Those humans who became our ancestors were the ones who were most successful at solving these problems and enhanced their fitness. Those who were less successful at solving these distinct adaptive problems failed to become anyone's ancestors.

Implication #1: Behavior Has Proximate *and* Ultimate Explanations

As highlighted in Tinbergen's four types of explanations, an evolutionary approach draws an important distinction between proximate reasons for behavior (the first type of explanation) and ultimate reasons for behavior (the third type of explanation). Consider a simple example. Let's say a colleague just bought a triple-chocolate fudge brownie, and you want to know the reason behind her purchase. So you ask her: "Why did you buy that?" She might simply respond "I was hungry." If she were feeling more analytical, she might mention that she loves the taste of chocolate and couldn't resist the delectable scent of a warm baked brownie.

Your colleague's explanations all represent proximate reasons. Proximate reasons are important, but they don't address the deeper question of why brownies taste good to humans in the first place. Understanding these deeper reasons requires an ultimate explanation. Ultimate explanations focus not on the relatively immediate triggers of a behavior, but on its adaptive function. In the brownie case, humans have psychological mechanisms that respond positively to the sight, smell, and taste of foods rich in sugars and fats. These mechanisms exist because an attraction to such calorie-dense foods helped motivate our ancestors to obtain calories and survive in an environment that was often scarce in calories (Lieberman, 2003). So whereas the proximate reason your friend bought a brownie may be because she was hungry for a brownie, the ultimate reason is because a desire for sugary and fatty foods helped solve the critical evolutionary challenge of survival.

Sometimes the ultimate and proximate reason for a behavior might be closely connected. In the brownie case, the proximate reason (feeling hunger) is directly connected to the ultimate function of obtaining calories to survive. But most of the time, the connection between proximate and ultimate reasons will not be that clear. Consider, for example, why birds migrate each year.

The proximate reason birds migrate is because days get shorter; day length is the immediate cue that triggers the motivation to begin the bird's journey. But the ultimate reason for bird migration has nothing to do with day length. Instead, the ultimate reason birds migrate is because the locations of the best food sites and the best mating sites change with the seasons (Cocker & Mabey, 2005; Lincoln, 1999).

Like other animals, human beings do not need to know consciously the connections between the proximate triggers of their behavior and the ultimate reasons behind those behaviors. In fact, people are especially poor at recognizing the ultimate reasons for their actions (Barrett & Kurzban, 2006; Kenrick, Griskevicius, Neuberg, & Schaller, 2010a; Tooby & Cosmides, 2005). But an important insight is that behavior has both proximate and ultimate causes. People often have multiple reasons for a behavior, even if they are not always aware of the ultimate reasons for their choices. For example, a person can be consciously motivated to buy a sporty luxury car because its expensive leather interior and peppy acceleration makes him feel good (a proximate reason), and at the same time be subconsciously motivated to buy that luxury car because owning such a car can increase his desirability as a potential mate and thereby enhances his reproductive fitness (an ultimate reason) (Griskevicius et al., 2007; Sundie et al., 2011).

Implication #2: Evolution Is *Not* the Opposite of Learning

Just because behaviors are rooted in psychological adaptations does not mean that the environment plays no role in the behavior. Consider the fear of snakes.

A programmatic series of studies has shown that fear of snakes stems from a specific psychological adaptation (Mineka & Öhman, 2002; Nesse, 1990; Öhman & Mineka, 2003). Poisonous snakes have persistently posed a threat throughout evolutionary history, leading humans to possess adaptations designed to solve this adaptive problem.

However, this does not mean that people are born with a hardwired fear of snakes. Instead, humans and other primates have specialized learning mechanisms that prepare them to learn this particular association after they are born. Individuals rapidly condition to fear snake-like objects, often acquiring an intense fear in only one trial. For example, witnessing another person respond to a snake with fear just once can instil an intense phobia of snakes. The fear of snakes is extremely difficult to extinguish (it's easy to learn but difficult to unlearn), and it can be traced to specialized neural circuitry (Öhman & Mineka, 2001).

The important takeaway is that evolution is *not* the opposite of learning, socialization, or culture. An evolutionary approach dissolves false dichotomies such as "nature versus nurture," "innate versus learned," and "biological versus cultural." For instance, it does not make sense to ask whether fear of snakes or infant crying are "evolved" or "learned" or due to "nature" or "nurture." Most psychological adaptations require some sort of environmental input for their activation. Because all behavior is produced by the mind, and because the mind evolved via natural selection, all behavior is biologically influenced and has some evolutionary component.

In summary, all human behavior includes an evolutionary explanation. It does not make sense to ask whether a behavior is evolutionary or not. Asking such a question is the equivalent of pitting Tinbergen's four types of explanations against each other. All four types of explanations are complementary, and all four are needed to fully understand any behavior. An evolutionary psychological perspective focuses on Tinbergen's third type of explanation, asking about the adaptive function of behavior. It focuses on how a given behavioral or psychological tendency would have helped our ancestors solve some adaptive problem. Sometimes the answer is obvious, and people are consciously aware of how a given tendency helps solve an adaptive problem. But many times, the answer is not obvious because a given behavior can be concurrently driven by very different proximate reasons and ultimate reasons.

Core Theories and Findings

A common misconception about an evolutionary perspective is that it relies on one single theory. This is false. In the same way that consumer researchers don't base all predictions on a single theory called "social science theory," an evolutionary approach is not based on a single theory called "evolutionary theory." Instead, natural selection is a meta-theory that encompasses hundreds of different theories. Table 5.2 presents a small sampling of evolutionarily informed theories about various domains (for more details, see Saad, 2007). In

Table 5.2 *Sampling of Evolutionarily Informed Theories*

Theory	Domain	Sample Insight	Key References
Kin Selection	Interactions among family members	People help family because of shared genes	Hamilton (1963)
Trivers-Willard Hypothesis	How parents treat sons and daughters	Harsh conditions lead parents to favor daughters over sons	Trivers & Willard (1973)
Parent-Offspring Conflict	Interactions between parents and children	Children seek to extract more resources than parents are willing to give	Maestripieri (2002); Trivers (1974)
Reciprocal Altruism	Interactions among non-relatives	People help non-family to get rewards from them later	Hamilton (1964); Trivers (1971)
Indirect Reciprocity	Interactions among non-relatives	People help non-family to build a good reputation	Alexander (1987); Nowak & Sigmund (1998)
Sexual Selection	Gender differences	Men and women differ in competitiveness	Andersson (1994); Emlen & Oring (1977); Trivers (1972)
Parental Investment Theory	Gender differences	Women are choosier than men in sex partners	Trivers (1972)
Tend and Befriend	Gender differences	Men and women behave differently under stress	Taylor et al. (2000)
Paternity Uncertainty	Gender differences	Fathers are more likely to mistreat their children than mothers	Møller (2000); Westneat & Sherman (1993)
Sexual Strategies Theory	Mating and relationships	Men and women differ in what they seek in a mate	Buss & Schmitt (1993)
Strategic Pluralism	Mating and relationships	People can follow very different types of mating strategies	Gangestad & Simpson (2000)
Attachment Theory	Mating and relationships	Bond between mother and infant influences bonds with others later in life	Bowlby (1969); Simpson & Belsky (2008)
Costly Signaling Theory	Costly show-off behavior	People spend a lot of resources on signals to ensure that signals are honest	Miller (2000); Zahavi & Zahavi (1997)

Theory	Domain	Key idea	References
Fundamental Motives	Context effects on behavior	People's evolutionary goals change depending on situation	Kenrick et al. (2010a); Griskevicius & Kenrick (2013)
Environmental Mismatch	Differences between ancestral and current environment	Some tendencies adaptive in ancestral environments are maladaptive today	Nesse & Williams (1994); Ornstein & Ehrlich (1989)
Life History Theory	Individual differences	Childhood environment calibrates people to differ in adaptive ways	Chisholm (1993); Kaplan & Gangestad (2005); Roff (2002); Stearns (1992)
Error Management Theory	Errors in judgment and decision making	People make errors in adaptive ways	Haselton & Buss (2000); Haselton & Nettle (2006)
Darwinian Gastronomy	Food preferences	People prefer spicier foods in hotter climates	Sherman & Billing (1999)
Adaptive Memory Theory	Memory	People have better memory for survival-related content	Nairne & Pandeirada (2008)
Ovulatory Shift Hypothesis	Hormones	Women's behavior changes during the ovulatory phase of the cycle	Gangestad & Thornhill (1998)

this section, we describe a few of these theories that are particularly relevant for consumer researchers.

Mismatch Theory

All living humans are descendants of ancestors who were nomadic hunter-gathers. Our ancestors lived in roving small bands of about fifty to one hundred individuals, many of whom were members of a few kin groups (Dunbar, 1993, 1998). For hundreds of thousands of years, natural selection shaped human psychology and behavior to solve adaptive problems specifically in this kind of environment. However, our modern-day environment is a bit different from the environment in which humans evolved.

Mismatch theory (Nesse & Williams, 1994; Ornstein & Ehrlich, 1989) highlights that brain evolution often takes many thousands of years, but our environment has changed much more rapidly. This means that people interact with their present-day world using brains that evolved to confront ancestral problems. Although our Stone Age brains are designed to produce adaptive behaviors in the ancestral environment, this does not mean that they will always produce adaptive behaviors today. For example, the evolved desire for sexual gratification can lead to modern behavior with no evolutionary benefits, such as watching pornography, which is sexually arousing but does little to help people's reproductive fitness.

Consider modern eating behavior. We evolved in a world where calories and nutrients were scarce. This produced a desire for foods high in sugar and fat. But whereas this desire was adaptive in our past environment, this proclivity can have downsides in the modern world of affordable caloric abundance. Instead of producing adaptive outcomes, it can instead lead to obesity and Type 2 diabetes (Hu et al., 2001; Meyer et al., 2000; Srinivasan et al., 2005).

Mismatch theory suggests that some of the behaviors we observe today are by-products of psychological mechanisms that were adaptive in the ancestral environment. For example, our ancestors did not have television. If they saw a person come into their living space every day, this person was likely a friend. In the modern world, however, people come daily into our living space via television and other media. Although we obviously "know" that such people are not real people who are physically present, at some level our brain continues to classify these people as "friends" (Barkow, 1989, 1992; De Backer et al., 2007; Kanazawa, 2002). In fact, we end up wanting to know gossip about these "friends," even though we are unlikely to ever meet them.

Mismatch theory provides a useful lens through which to look at modern behavior. For example, in the modern world, we are awash in numerically expressed statistical information. You may have spent enough years in math classes to cognitively understand that a 0.07 probability and a 7 percent likelihood mean the same thing, but many of us will still furrow our brows and squint our eyes when digesting a statement about a 0.07 probability. Probabilities and likelihood estimates are a common way to present statistical information, but they are also an evolutionarily recent invention, arising in Europe in the mid-1600s. Because presenting information in the form of probabilities is evolutionarily novel, this format can lead to a lot of problems and take many years of explicit education to fully comprehend.

Instead of presenting information as conditional probabilities or likelihood estimates, research has demonstrated that people are much better at computing statistical information if it is presented as *natural frequencies,* which represent the way ancestral humans encoded information (Gigerenzer & Hoffrage, 1995; Hoffrage, Gigerenzer, Krauss, & Martignon, 2002; Hoffrage, Lindsey, Hertwig, & Gigerenzer, 2000). For instance, when our ancestor would try to determine whether it was wise to go hunting in red canyon, he could consider what happened the last twenty times people went hunting in red canyon. The person observes natural frequencies – five out of the last twenty hunts in the red canyon were successful. Our ancestors did not observe probabilities in their natural environment. As a consequence, our brains do not process probabilities ("0.25 probability of success") in the same way as natural frequencies ("five out of twenty were successful"). Years of formal math training have taught most of us that these two statistical statements mean the same thing, but one is intuitive and the other one is not. In fact, people show dramatic improvements when hard questions are asked in terms of natural frequencies rather than probabilities (Galesic, Gigerenzer, & Straubinger, 2009; Hoffrage & Gigerenzer, 1998).

In summary, it is useful to think about the kind of environment in which our ancestors evolved and for which our psychology is geared. As in the case of pornography and celebrity gossip, this ancestral psychology can sometimes be "hijacked" by modern contraptions.

Error Management Theory

Imagine that you are hiking in the woods and you notice a rustle under the leaves in front of you. You must decide whether this rustle is the result of the wind or whether there is a snake or other dangerous creature afoot. Making this decision can result in two types of errors: (1) deciding that the rustle is the result of wind when it is actually a snake (a *false negative*) and (2) deciding that the rustle is a snake when it is actually wind (a *false positive*).

Error management theory (EMT; Haselton & Buss, 2000; Haselton & Nettle, 2006) posits that these two errors posed asymmetric costs to fitness across evolutionary history. Assuming the rustle is a snake when it is actually wind (the false positive) can result in a moderate expenditure of energy to run or jump away. But assuming the rustle is wind when it is actually a poisonous snake (the false negative) can result in death. Because the potential cost of the false negative is much greater, EMT predicts that natural selection should have forged cognitive and behavioral biases that lead us to err in favor of the judgment that poses a lower potential cost to fitness.

Error management theory has led researchers to formulate predictions about several errors in judgment and behavior. For example, if an object is moving toward you at 20 feet per second and the object is currently 120 feet away, how long will it take for the object to hit you? The accurate answer is about 6 seconds. It would certainly be inaccurate if people thought the answer is 4 seconds – this would be a clear demonstration of an error in judgment. Yet the mind is wired to intentionally make this error. When our eyes see an approaching object, our brains tell us that this object will hit us *sooner* than it actually will. In fact, merely hearing the sound of an approaching object (the swooshing of a diving bird through the air, the rustling of someone in the bushes) will result in the same error. The bias to sense that approaching sounds will arrive sooner than they really do is known as *auditory looming* (Hall & Moore, 2003; Neuhoff, 2001; Seifritz et al., 2002). One study found that this "error" was made by 100 percent of people.

Like many errors and biases that seem irrational on the surface, auditory looming turns out, on closer examination, to be pretty smart. Other animals, such as rhesus monkeys, have evolved to have the same bias (Ghazanfar, Neuhoff, & Logothetis, 2002; Maier, Neuhoff, Logothetis, & Ghazanfar, 2004). This intentional error functions as an advance warning system, providing individuals with a margin of safety when confronted with potentially dangerous approaching objects. If you spot a rhinoceros or hear an avalanche speeding your way, auditory looming will motivate you to jump out of the way sooner rather than wait until the last second. The evolutionary benefits of immediately getting out of the way of approaching dangers were so strong that natural selection endowed us – and other mammals – with brains that intentionally see and hear the world inaccurately.

Consumer researchers have identified myriad decision errors, biases, and distortions. But they have mostly provided a laundry list of blunders, without offering a theory for the underlying causes behind why people make these mistakes. Error management theory provides a theory of mistakes. This adaptive theory of mistakes not only helps us appreciate the hidden wisdom of our otherwise senseless decisions, it also allows us to predict in advance what particular mistakes people will make and when. For example, recent research has used this approach to understand the overconfidence bias (Forbes, 2005; Johnson & Fowler, 2011; Scott, Stumpp, & Xu, 2003). The tendency to be overly confident might produce errors in judgment, but it turns out that this mistake produces evolutionary benefits by helping solve the adaptive problem of status and resource acquisition.

Fundamental Motives Framework

When people think about "evolutionary success," they may think only about survival and reproduction. Although these are important, there are a number of distinct evolutionary challenges that had to be surmounted to achieve reproductive success. Like all other animals, at a base level our ancestors needed nourishment and shelter. But because humans are intensely social animals, we also faced a set of central and recurrent social challenges (Ackerman & Kenrick, 2008; Griskevicius & Kenrick, 2013; Kenrick et al., 2010a). These fundamental ancestral challenges included (1) evading physical harm, (2) avoiding disease, (3) making friends, (4) attaining status, (5) acquiring a mate, (6) keeping a mate, and (7) caring for family.

The fundamental motives framework maintains that the specific ancestral social challenges faced by humans map onto fundamental motivational systems that function to help solve each challenge. A fundamental motive can be activated or primed by external or internal cues indicating threats or opportunities related to a specific evolutionary challenge (Kenrick et al., 2010a). For example, a person can activate the mate acquisition system by interacting with a desirable member of the opposite sex, or by being in the same room with such a person, being exposed to an image involving such a person, or merely imagining a desirable romantic encounter. The system can also be activated when a person is confronted with a decision that concerns potential mates, as opposed to a decision that pertains to family, status, disease, affiliation, or danger.

When a fundamental motivational system has been activated, it produces a specific set of consequences for attention, memory, cognition, and preferences (Kenrick et al., 2010b; Neuberg, Kenrick, & Schaller, 2011). This coordinated cascade of responses functions to solve the ultimate problem associated with the currently active system. For example, the activation of the mate acquisition system leads a person to prefer and seek products that facilitate achieving the ultimate need of acquiring a mate, as in the case of ovulating women.

An important implication of the fundamental motives framework is that a person's preferences can change quite dramatically depending on which motivational system is currently active. This is because what constitutes adaptive behavior to further one ultimate need may be very different from – and sometimes even completely opposing to – what is adaptive to further another. For example, activating the self-protection system leads people to conform and follow the masses (Griskevicius et al., 2006). When this motive is active, such as when watching a crime-filled television program, people are more attracted to products advertised as best-selling and popular while being less attracted to the same products when they are advertised as unique and different (Griskevicius et al., 2009). Like wildebeests in the presence of a leopard, cues of physical threat motivate people to be part of a larger group.

In contrast, activating the mate acquisition system leads people to want to stand out from the crowd. When this motive is active, such as when watching a romantic or sexy program, people are more attracted to products advertised as unique and different while being repulsed when the same products are advertised as popular or best-selling (Griskevicius et al., 2009). Like an animal on the prowl looking to put on a display for a mate, cues of the opposite sex motivate people to stand out. The important implication of the fundamental motives framework is that the same person might make different – and sometimes entirely inconsistent – choices depending on which fundamental motive is currently active.

Just as fundamental motives can alter preferences, they can also alter decision-making processes – how one goes about maximizing his or her preferences. This has important ramifications for understanding how our decision biases and errors wax and wane. Consider loss aversion, the tendency for people to weigh losses more heavily than equivalent gains (Kahneman & Tversky, 1979). Whereas this tendency is traditionally viewed as irrational, an evolutionary perspective suggests that loss aversion may be an adaptive bias that helped humans solve survival-related ancestral challenges. Consistent with this idea, activating the self-protection system makes people particularly loss averse (Li, Kenrick, Griskevicius, & Neuberg, 2012). When motivated to protect themselves from danger, people are especially concerned about losses. In contrast, activating the mate-acquisition system can lead loss aversion to vanish (Li et al., 2012). In fact, for men, triggering the motive to attract a mate can cause this bias to reverse itself, leading gains to loom larger than losses.

In summary, the fundamental motives framework highlights the adaptive social problems that the mind is geared to solve. It then shows how, why, and when people's preferences and behavior change depending on which adaptive problem they are currently seeking to solve.

Ovulatory Shift Hypothesis

Imagine the next twenty-eight days. For each of these twenty-eight days, how often do you think the desire to have sex will cross your mind? If you are a man, you might think about sex roughly equally across each of the twenty-eight days. If you are a woman, however, you might think about sex a little during days one through seven, a lot on days eight through fourteen, and very little on days fifteen through twenty-eight. Why would women's pattern of sexual thoughts and motivations look different from men's?

To answer this question, assume that the twenty-eight days are not random but map onto the length of a woman's ovulatory cycle. Most women experience an ovulatory cycle that spans twenty-eight days. And, unlike men, women's sexual behavior can result in pregnancy only near ovulation (days eight through fourteen of the cycle). The ovulatory phase is characterized by a steep increase in the ovarian hormone estrogen, which triggers the release of a single sex cell known as an ovum or egg (Jones, 1997; Lipson & Ellison, 1996). Because over evolutionary history women could only reproduce when they ovulate, women's motivations and behavior evolved to shift adaptively specifically at this time. This notion is known as the ovulatory shift hypothesis (Gangestad & Thornhill, 1998; Gangestad, Thornhill, & Garver, 2002; Thornhill & Gangestad, 2008).

The ovulatory shift hypothesis posits that women should experience a shift in mating-related motivation and behavior near ovulation (Gangestad & Thornhill, 1998; Gangestad, Thornhill, & Garver-Apgar, 2005). Supporting this notion, research has since found that women experience an increase in sexual desire near ovulation (Bullivant et al., 2004; Gangestad, Thornhill, & Garver, 2002). For example, ovulation increases women's sexual attraction toward men who possess indicators of genetic fitness such as facial symmetry and attractiveness, masculinity, and social dominance (Cantú et al., 2013; Durante et al., 2012; Gangestad et al., 2004; Gangestad, Garver-Apgar, Simpson, & Cousins,

2007; Gangestad & Thornhill, 1998; Gangestad, Thornhill, & Garver-Apgar, 2005; Penton-Voak et al., 1999).

Research also shows that ovulation has a large effect on women's desire to dress in sexier outfits (Durante et al., 2011). Whether women are selecting outfits directly from their own closet, drawing a desired outfit on a paper doll, or selecting clothing from a fashion website, women consistently choose outfits that are sexier, more fashionable, and more revealing near ovulation – when estrogen levels are high (Durante, Li, & Haselton, 2008; Durante et al. 2011; Saad & Stenstrom, 2012). In fact, the ovulatory shift doesn't just help women optimize the choice of a sexual partner, it also helps them outcompete other women for access to the best men available. For example, ovulation has the strongest effect on women's desire for sexier clothing when women know that there are many other attractive women in their local environment (Durante et al., 2011) – that is, when there is lots of competition for mates.

Research in non-human primates shows that ovulation has a direct effect on female competitive behaviors. For example, female rhesus monkeys become more aggressive and competitive during the ovulatory phase (Walker, Wilson, & Gordon 1983; Wallen, 2000). And indeed, ovulation in women influences their competitive tendencies (Durante, Griskevicius, Cantú, & Simpson, 2014). For example, in one study, ovulating and non-ovulating women made product choices that could either maximize absolute gains or maximize gains relative to other women (Durante et al., 2014). The findings showed that ovulation made women more competitive with regard to other women. Near ovulation, women were willing to accept lesser versions of a product (a $5,000 diamond ring in lieu of a $7,000 diamond ring) as long as they had better products than other women. Also, ovulating women kept more money for themselves in the Dictator Game rather than give it to another woman.

In summary, similar to the effects of testosterone in men, the hormones that regulate fertility drive women's preferences and behaviors (Durante & Li, 2009; Mazur & Booth, 1998). In addition to hormones regulating fertility, there are various other hormones that influence people's behavior in other domains (Nelson, 2005). For example, cortisol drives our responses to stressful situations (Dickerson & Kemeny, 2004), and oxytocin and vasopressin drive our desire to bond with family and friends (Young & Insel, 2002). Each of these hormones is likely to influence consumer behavior in important ways. Understanding how hormones influence behavior provides a unique window into the psychological underpinnings of consumer behavior.

Incorporating an Evolutionary Perspective into Research

How can you incorporate an evolutionary perspective into your research? In the subsections that follow, we discuss three ways that consumer researchers can incorporate an evolutionary perspective into their research.

Read beyond Your Discipline

Taking an evolutionary perspective means thinking a little differently about behavior than is typically thought about in consumer research. If you read only journals in marketing and consumer behavior, you are unlikely to encounter the plethora of evolutionarily informed theory and research relevant to your research area. One way to access this knowledge is by venturing off the beaten path and reading beyond the *Journal of Consumer Research* (*JCR*).

Imagine you're interested in food and eating behavior, and you're looking for novel research questions in this area. Consider searching for previous work on food and evolution. For example, type in the term "evolutionary psychology" next to whatever area you're studying. If you search for research in the domain of food and eating behavior, you will discover a theory called Darwinian gastronomy (Sherman & Billing, 1999). This theory helps explain why humans eat spices. Spices such as salt, garlic, onions, and chili peppers help kill poisonous bacteria and fungi that can contaminate food. Spices thus helped solve the adaptive challenge of disease avoidance, whereby developing a taste for spicy food enhanced fitness across evolutionary time, specifically in places where pathogens were a larger threat, such as warmer, tropical climates where bacteria are more diverse, plentiful, and fast growing. This theory helps explain why spicy meals tend to be found in warmer climates (e.g., Mexico, India, Thailand, the southern United States), while bland meals tend to be found in colder climates (e.g., Norway, England, Germany, the northern United States).

Now that you know more about the function of spicy foods, use these insights to derive hypotheses about the conditions under which people might have an increased desire for spices. If spices function to protect us from food-borne pathogens, one possibility is that environmental cues to pathogens might spur a desire for spicier food. For example, hearing a nearby person coughing and sneezing while ordering lunch might lead people to choose spicier food. By doing a little reading and considering the adaptive function of spicy food, you have just derived a novel and testable hypothesis.

Note that if your study were to find support for the hypothesis, it would not "prove" evolution. Likewise, if your study did not find support for the hypothesis, it would not "disprove" evolution. Instead, you have simply used an evolution-informed theory to derive a novel hypothesis – a hypothesis that you might not have thought of if you didn't venture off the beaten path. Table 5.2 provides an overview of some theories that you will discover in your search, but know that many more theories are already out there (see Saad, 2007, 2013). If you seek to access those theories to develop fresh hypotheses in your research area, all you need is a little curiosity and some courage to venture beyond *JCR*.

When Observing Behavior, Ask about Adaptive Function

Many novel ideas come from observing behavior. You have likely wondered about the reasons why people do a variety of things. But the next time you observe a puzzling behavior, ask yourself the following questions: Why would the brain have been designed to produce that behavior? What adaptive problem might this behavior function to solve?

Imagine you are at the local shopping mall and you see a flock of women admiring the latest Louis Vuitton handbag. You are curious about why women spend so much money on these kinds of luxury products. There are clearly many proximate reasons for this behavior. For instance, the bag makes women feel good, provides them with a sense of identity, and enhances their self-esteem. But this behavior is also likely to serve some adaptive function(s), even if some consumers might be completely unaware of it.

Consider, for example, whether luxury products such as a handbag might serve some mating function. Past research has found that activating a motive to attract a mate leads men to seek luxury products, suggesting that many male luxury goods function to attract mates (Griskevicius et al., 2007; Sundie et al., 2011). What about women? Activating a motive to attract a mate does *not* lead women to seek luxury products (Griskevicius et al., 2007; Sundie et al., 2011). However, activating a motive to guard a mate does lead women to seek luxury products (Wang & Griskevicius, 2014). In fact, women often use luxury goods to send signals specifically to other women, telling them to "back off my man." Just as in the spicy foods example earlier, considering the adaptive function of a behavior led researchers to formulate novel hypotheses that otherwise might have remained hidden from view.

Go to the Zoo

The two authors of this chapter are personally fascinated by animal behavior. In fact, we meet many consumer scientists who love to go to the zoo or watch television programs about the clever ways that animals solve adaptive problems. But whereas most consumer researchers think of animal behavior as being a separate world from their own research, the reality is that human and animal behavior have much more in common than we think. After all, natural selection applies to both animal *and* human behavior.

Evolutionarily informed theories have been used to study animal behavior for much longer than human behavior. This makes theory and research on animal behavior one of the richest sources for inspiring hypotheses about human behavior. Indeed, the zoo is not only a great place to learn about animals; it's a great place to learn more about ourselves. For instance, imagine that you are at the zoo and you notice that in one exhibit there are six chimpanzees – two females and four males. You watch in amusement as the males are extremely active, swinging from branch to branch, knocking each other over, and wrestling each other to the ground. The females, by contrast, are sitting together quietly. Next door at the orangutan exhibit, you notice the opposite pattern. Here there is one male and three females. And, this time, it is the females who are active, wrestling each other for a spot on the top of the rock where the male is sitting. What is going on here? And might it have implications for humans?

If you do a quick search, you will find a large literature on how animal behavior is influenced by sex ratio – the ratio of males to females in the local environment (Kvanermo & Ahnesjö, 1996; Taylor & Bulmer, 1980). Across different animal species, a scarcity of the opposite sex makes members of the more plentiful sex more competitive. And it turns out that sex ratio also has similar effects on human behavior (Durante et al., 2012). For example, when women are scarce, men become more competitive and impulsive (Griskevicius et al., 2012). As with many evolutionarily directed effects, people usually have no idea that their behavior is being influenced by the local sex ratio. Nevertheless, one way researchers could identify such effects in humans is by first considering research and theory in animal behavior.

Roadmap for Future Research

Evolutionary psychology is not a field or an area of research. Instead, an evolutionary perspective is a broad way of thinking about behavior in any domain. Because all human behavior includes an evolutionary explanation, an evolutionary perspective can be useful for generating theories and ideas for any area of consumer behavior (Saad 2007, 2013). For example, an evolutionary perspective is useful for helping make sense of the many errors and biases people make, including helping predict when and why people will make specific types of errors (Kenrick & Griskevicius, 2013). This approach is also highly relevant for understanding environmental behavior and conservation. By better understanding how our evolved tendencies contribute to modern-day problems, we can create better interventions to solve these problems (Griskevicius, Cantú, & van Vugt, 2012). Whatever topic you're interested in, an evolutionary perspective can help you think more broadly about that topic and help generate novel ideas. In the subsections that follow, we highlight a few consumer areas in which an evolutionary perspective is likely to be particularly useful for future research.

Consumption in Relationships and the Family

It begins with dinner and a movie. With any luck, an engagement ring follows. Before we know it, we are buying our first home, deciding on vacation destinations, filling out a will, and saving for our children's college tuition and eventually our retirement. Spending decisions permeate our close relationships. However, little consumer research has examined the factors that can impact the financial decisions we make in our dating, marriage, and family life. For example, we know surprisingly little about the factors that influence how our romantic partners affect our spending and even less about how parents make spending decisions on behalf of their children. Because family and romantic relationships have long been a part of human life, an evolutionary perspective is highly useful for understanding behavior in these domains. In fact, Table 5.2 highlights many evolutionarily informed theories central to the domains of kin, family, and romantic relationships.

Most research on consumer choice assumes that decisions are usually made by individuals and that these decisions are based on an individual's personal attitudes, beliefs, and preferences. Yet, much consumer behavior – from joint decisions to individual choices – is directly or indirectly shaped by people with whom we have some relationship (Simpson, Griskevicius, & Rothman, 2012). An evolutionary perspective highlights that there are fundametally different goals in a relationship (e.g., mate attraction vs. mate retention), and that people pursue different types of mating strategies (e.g., long-term vs. short-term strategy) (Buss & Schmitt, 1993; Gangestad & Simpson, 2000). For instance, one partner might be more committed to maintaining the relationship than the other. Conditions that alter the quality and availability of alternative mates should shift the value of certain consumer products that relationship partners use to signal their value as a mate. For men, this could include products that signal their commitment, willingness, and ability to invest resources in a partner (e.g., jewelry, exotic vacations, designer clothes). For women, this could include products that signal youth and fertility (e.g., botox, cosmetics, diet plans).

The central evolutionary function of romantic relationships is that they facilitate the rearing of children by enabling two individuals to pool their resources and forge a long-term alliance. Doing so improved the survival and long-term reproductive fitness of offspring during evolutionary history (Geary, 2000). Indeed, field research on hunter-gatherer groups that resemble our ancestors' way of life has shown that children are significantly more likely to survive and thrive when they are raised by two cooperative parents than by one single parent (Hill & Hurtado, 1996; Hurtado & Hill, 1992; Hurtado, Hill, Kaplan, & Hurtado, 1992). Therefore, decisions about investment in children were likely critical across human history, yet little consumer research has considered the factors that influence parental spending.

As one example, evolutionary models predict that investment in offspring should differ depending on the offspring's *reproductive value*, which is the child's ability to convert parental resources into reproductive success by having children of their own (Daly & Wilson, 1988). The Trivers-Willard hypothesis suggests that parents should invest more in one gender over the other depending on whether resources are scarce or abundant (Trivers & Willard, 1973). Indeed, findings show that poor economic conditions lead people to spend more money on daughters compared to sons (Durante, Griskevicius, Redden, & White, in press). Future reseach is poised to examine the many ways our ancestral history shapes modern family spending.

Men's and Women's Consumption across the Lifespan

An evolutionary perspective highlights that males and females share important similarities and have important differences. For example, men and women have historically solved some evolutionary problems such as disease avoidance in similar ways, meaning that the sexes are expected to differ little when it comes to their psychology of avoiding pathogens. But males and females have historically solved other evolutionary problems, such as mate acquisition, in very different ways, suggesting that the sexes are likely to differ in predictable ways when it comes to mating (Buss & Schmitt, 1993).

Many behavioral sex differences are rooted in the biological sex difference of minimum parental investment (Kenrick, Sadalla, Groth, & Trost, 1990; Trivers, 1972). In any mammalian species such as humans, reproduction requires females to invest more biologically than males. Whereas females must *at a minimum* carry an energetically hungry fetus for several months and then nurse it afterward, males do not. Instead, males have historically contributed to successful reproduction in other ways. This sex difference in parental investment produces a universal sex difference in mate preferences. Whereas women place more value on men's resources, men place more value on women's cues to fertility, such as attractiveness and youth. One implication is that men should be more interested in products that display their wealth and ability to obtain resources, whereas women should seek products that advertise their youth and attractiveness.

Higher parental investment by females also means that females will be choosier about which males will suffice as mates, especially if the male might not stick around to contribute any resources. As a consequence, males have to compete more vigorously to be selected as mates by a choosy female. This suggests that males should generally be more willing to take risks and more strongly discount the future, especially when doing so could attain status or a mate.

Surprisingly little research has considered systematic similarities and differences in men's and women's consumer behavior. An evolutionary perspective provides a theoretical foundation for examining how, why, and when men and women should differ – and should be similar – in their consumption tendencies and decision making.

An evolutionary perspective is also useful for understanding how consumer behavior changes across the lifespan. This approach highlights that organisms proceed through three distinct stages across the lifespan: (1) a somatic growth stage lasting from birth to puberty, (2) a mating stage lasting from puberty until parenthood, and (3) a parenting stage that (for humans) includes grandparenting. Because individuals need to solve specific evolutionary challenges during each life stage, preferences and behavior are likely to change in systematic ways as a function of life stage. For example, to the extent that men's conspicuous consumption functions to help solve the evolutionary challenges of status and mate acquisition (Griskevicius et al., 2007; Sundie et al., 2011), we would expect that men have the strongest desire for flashy luxury products in the mating stage. This desire for conspicuous luxuries should decrease as men age and become parents. But if an older man finds himself back on the mating market (and hence back in the mating stage), his desire for conspicuous luxury products may increase once again.

Surprisingly little research has considered changes in consumer behavior across the lifespan. An evolutionary perspective provides a fruitful theoretical foundation for examining how, why, and when consumption tendencies and decision making change across the lifespan.

Childhood Environment and Personality

Not all people are the same. An evolutionary perspective highlights that many important individual differences between people are linked to a person's life history strategy (Ellis, Figueredo, Brumbach, & Schlomer, 2009; Griskevicius et al., 2013). Across species, life history strategies vary on a fast–slow continuum. Some individuals follow faster strategies, and others follow slower strategies. Life history strategies are related to important differences in mating. Fast strategists start puberty at earlier ages, have sex at earlier ages, and have more sexual partners. By contrast, slow strategists tend to start puberty at later ages, have sex later in life, and have fewer sexual partners, preferring monogamous relationships. But fast and slow strategies are also associated with vastly different psychologies and orientations to decision making. Whereas fast strategists tend to be short-term opportunists and take immediate benefits with little regard for long-term consequences, slow strategists tend to be long-term planners who delay immediate gratification to increase future payoffs (Griskevicius, Tybur, Delton, & Robertson, 2011; Griskevicius et al., 2013).

Research shows that the nature of one's *environment early in life* is a critical determinant of adult life history strategy (Griskevicius et al., 2011, 2013). Similar to how a person's childhood environment is a critical period for acquiring a language, a person's childhood environment is a critical period for calibrating his or her life history strategy (Belsky, Schlomer, & Ellis, 2012; Simpson et al., 2012). Resource-abundant environments tend to be safer and more stable, making a slow strategy adaptive because such environments are relatively predictable and are not expected to change dramatically over time. By contrast, resource-deprived environments calibrate a faster strategy (Ellis et al., 2009; Griskevicius et al., 2011, 2013). Resource-deprived environments tend to be harsh and unpredictable, making a fast strategy adaptive, because in such constantly fluctuating environments it is difficult to know what tomorrow will bring or whether tomorrow will come at all.

Being a fast or a slow life history strategist is a fundamental evolutionary individual difference. This individual difference has a plethora of implications for decision making and consumer behavior. For example, fast and slow strategists might seek very different types of luxury products. Fast strategists might desire flashy luxury goods, seeking loud brands and readily visible goods, such as bright sports cars. By contrast, slow strategists might desire inconspicuous luxury products, seeking quiet brands and products that attract less attention, such as a beige luxury sedan. In summary, an evolutionary perspective provides powerful theories for studying how consumer behavior is shaped by important individual differences.

Strengths, Limitations, and Conclusion

Strengths

Incorporating an evolutionary perspective provides several benefits. First, it provides consumer researchers with a key to unlock hypotheses about behavior that might have never been generated. Indeed, many of the findings discussed in this chapter were generated because an evolutionary perspective provided ideas about new effects or new moderators. For example, an evolutionary perspective on emotions highlights that different emotions serve different adaptive functions (Neufeld & Griskevicius, 2014). By using the theorized function of each emotion as a starting point, it is possible to derive novel hypotheses regarding how and why specific emotions should influence psychology and behavior (Griskevicius, Shiota, & Neufeld, 2010). For instance, previous research shows that positive emotions produce a "rose-colored-glasses" effect by making products more attractive. However, different positive emotions have unique effects, and specific positive emotions can actually decrease the desirability of some products (Griskevicius, Shiota, & Nowlis, 2010). Consider the emotion of pride. The evolutionary function of pride is to motivate public displays to draw positive attention to oneself. Consistent with this function of pride, feelings of pride enhance attractiveness of products useful for public positive differentiation. However, pride does not enhance the attractiveness of products used primarily around the house – and sometimes even decreases their desirability. Thus, rather than positive emotions always producing a rose-colored-glasses effect, different positive emotions produce an emotion-specific and evolutionarily functional pattern of perceptions and evaluations.

Second, an evolutionary perspective can help explain and build on well-established behavioral phenomena. Take, for example, classic findings on conformity. People are found to be heavily influenced by the actions and beliefs of others and often pattern their own behavior and choices after those around them (Asch, 1956; Cialdini, Reno, & Kallgren, 1990; Sherif, 1936). When considering conformity through the lens of the fundamental motives framework (see Table 5.2), it was found that conformity effects are even stronger when people are motivated to protect themselves from danger (Griskevicius et al., 2006). However, activating mating motives led to a reversal of classic conformity effects, leading men to go against the group when they were motivated to attract a mate.

An evolutionary perspective also helps avoid isolated islands of research by helping scholars think about the bigger scientific picture. For example, researchers working only at one level of analysis (such as by focusing only on Tinbergen's first question) can end up building isolated islands of research that have little connection to other research. However, by thinking about multiple levels of analysis – and by realizing that all findings have to fit together logically across different types of explanations – researchers are more likely to do research that better connects to the work of other scholars within and outside their field. At the end of the day, the theories and findings published in the *Journal of Consumer Research* have to fit together with the theories and findings published in the journal *Evolution and Human Behavior*. Evolutionarily informed theories provide an underlying logic that helps connect all the pieces of the puzzle of human behavior.

Limitations

Although an evolutionary approach provides multiple benefits, it is also important to highlight its limitations. One limitation is that an evolutionary perspective has difficulty explaining certain phenomena. For example, consider homosexual orientation, which is a Darwinian paradox. Exclusive homosexual orientation seems to defy evolutionary logic since it seems to fail to increase an individual's reproductive success. Although evolutionary hypotheses have been proposed for homosexuality, none have received empirical support thus far (e.g., Bobrow & Bailey, 2001).

Another limitation is that we lack detailed knowledge of many selection pressures that humans faced over the millions of years of their evolution. We do not possess a time machine or a video of deep time that would reveal in precise detail all of the selective events over millions of years that have led to the current design of the human body and mind. Nonetheless, this limitation is not total. There is a surprisingly abundant amount of information about the human ancestral environment that we do know to a reasonable degree of certainty (Confer et al., 2010). For example, ancestral humans "had two sexes; chose mates; had color vision calibrated to the spectral properties of sunlight; lived in a biotic environment with predators; were predated on; bled when wounded; were incapacitated from injuries; were vulnerable to a large variety of parasites and pathogens; had deleterious recessives rendering them subject to inbreeding depression if they mated with siblings" (Tooby & Cosmides, 2005, pp. 23–24).

Scientists also know that fertilization occurred internally within females, not within males; that females, not males, bore the metabolic costs of breastfeeding; that our ancestors engaged in hunting for at least the past one million years; that our ancestors lived in small groups, ranging in size from a few dozen to 150; and that our ancestors made and used tools for hunting, gathering, cooking, and warfare. We also know that bipedal locomotion, extended childhood, long-term pair bonds, biparental investment, and relatively concealed ovulation distinguish our ancestors from their closest primate relative, the chimpanzee.

Evolutionary psychologists also use evidence from anthropology, archaeology, primatology, comparative biology, and ethology to elucidate some aspects of an otherwise scientifically uncertain ancestral past. For example, the paleontological evidence is rife with ancient caches of skulls and skeletons showing patterned lethal injuries, corresponding in size and shape to ancient weapons discovered in the vicinity. When combined with cave art depictions of fighting and many other sources of evidence, the cumulative findings yield reasonable inferences that human warfare was a potent hostile force of nature for human ancestors, that males were far more often perpetrators and victims of homicide than females, and that the majority of ancestral attackers were right handed (Duntley & Buss, 2012).

In summary, although convergent evidence from independent data sources yields especially reasonable inferences about *some* past selection pressures, evolutionary psychology, and indeed the entire field of psychology, will always be limited by incomplete knowledge of past selection pressures.

Conclusion

On university campuses, there is a long-standing division between the social and the natural sciences. Generations of researchers studying ecology and biology have been physically divided from those studying psychology and economics. Although scholars on both sides are studying behavior, this wall has led people on one side to be generally unaware of the theory and research on the other side. This division has spawned continued isolation, leading various fields to become ever more insulated.

It is time to tear down this wall. Charles Darwin wrote that, "In the distant future, I see open fields for more important researches. Psychology will be based on a new foundation" (Darwin, 1859). It has been over one hundred years, but Darwin's vision is beginning to be realized by scholars across the behavioral sciences. The current generation of scholars is poised to tear down this wall by incorporating evolutionarily informed thinking into their research. As the bridge between the natural and social sciences becomes stronger, future generations of researchers are poised to build a truly interdisciplinary science of behavior.

References

Ackerman, J. M., & Kenrick, D. T. (2008). The costs of benefits: Help-refusals highlight key trade-offs of social life. *Personality and Social Psychology Review, 12,* 118–140.

Alcock, J. (2001). *The Triumph of Sociobiology*. Oxford: Oxford University Press.

Alcock, J. (2005). *Animal Behavior: An Evolutionary Approach*. Massachusetts: Sinauer Associates.

Alexander, R. D. (1987). *The Biology of Moral Systems*. Piscataway, NJ: Transaction.

Andersson, M. B. (1994). *Sexual Selection*. Princeton, NJ: Princeton University Press.

Asch, S. E. (1956). Studies of independence and conformity: A minority of one against a unanimous majority. *Psychological Monographs: General and Applied, 70(9),* 1–70.

Barash, D. P. (1977). *Sociobiology and Behavior*. Amsterdam: Elsevier North-Holland.

Barkow, J. (1989). *Darwin, Sex, and Status: Biological Approaches to Mind and Culture*. Toronto: University of Toronto Press.

Barkow, J. (1992). Beneath new culture is old psychology: Gossip and social stratification. In J. H. Barkow, L. Cosmides, & J. Tooby (eds.), *The Adapted Mind:*

Evolutionary Psychology and the Generation of Culture (pp. 627–637). Oxford: Oxford University Press.

Barkow, J. H., Cosmides, L. E., & Tooby, J. E. (1992). *The Adapted Mind: Evolutionary Psychology and the Generation of Culture*. Oxford: Oxford University Press.

Barrett, H. C. (2012). A hierarchical model of the evolution of human brain specializations. *Proceedings of the National Academy of Sciences, 109*(Supplement 1), 10733–10740.

Barrett, H. C., & Kurzban, R. (2006). Modularity in cognition: Framing the debate. *Psychological Review, 113*(3), 628.

Belsky, J., Schlomer, G. L., & Ellis, B. J. (2012). Beyond cumulative risk: Distinguishing harshness and unpredictability as determinants of parenting and early life history strategy. *Developmental Psychology, 48*(3), 662–673.

Billings, J., & Sherman, P. W (1999). Darwinian gastronomy: why we use spices. *BioScience, 49*, 453–463.

Bobrow, D., & Bailey, J. M. (2001). Is male homosexuality maintained via kin selection? *Evolution and Human Behavior, 22*(5), 361–368.

Bowlby, J. (1969). *Attachment and Loss*, vol. *1*. Attachment. New York: Basic Books.

Brown, D. E. (2004). Human universals, human nature, & human culture. *Daedalus, 133* (4), 47–54.

Bullivant, S. B., Sellergren, S. A., Stern, K., Spencer, N. A., Jacob, S., Mennella, J. A., & McClintock, M. K. (2004). Women's sexual experience during the menstrual cycle: Identification of the sexual phase by noninvasive measurement of luteinizing hormone. *Journal of Sex Research, 41*, 82–93.

Buss, D. M. (ed.). (2005). *The Handbook of Evolutionary Psychology*. Hoboken, NJ: John Wiley & Sons.

Buss, D. M., & Schmitt, D. P. (1993). Sexual strategies theory: An evolutionary perspective on human mating. *Psychological Review, 100*, 204.

Cantú, S. M., Simpson, J. A., Griskevicius, V., Weisberg, Y. J., Durante, K. M., & Beal, D. J. (2013). Fertile and selectively flirty: Women's behavior toward men changes across the ovulatory cycle. *Psychological Science, 25*, 431–438

Chisholm, J. S. (1993). Death, hope, and sex: Life-history theory and the development of reproductive strategies. *Current Anthropology, 34*, 1–24.

Cialdini, R. B., Reno, R. R., & Kallgren, C. A. (1990). A focus theory of normative conduct: Recycling the concept of norms to reduce littering in public places. *Journal of Personality and Social Psychology, 58*, 1015.

Cocker, M., & Mabey, R. (2005). *Birds Britannica* (pp. 418–425). London: Chatto & Windus.

Confer, J. C., Easton, J. A., Fleischman, D. S., Goetz, C. D., Lewis, D. M., Perilloux, C., et al. (2010). Evolutionary psychology: Controversies, questions, prospects, and limitations. *American Psychologist, 65*, 110–126.

Cosmides, L., Barrett, H. C., & Tooby, J. (2010). Adaptive specializations, social exchange, and the evolution of human intelligence. *Proceedings of the National Academy of Sciences, 107*(Supplement 2), 9007–9014.

Daly, M., & Wilson M. (1988). Evolutionary social psychology and family homicide. *Science, 242*, 519–524.

Darwin, C. (1859). *On the Origin of Species*. London: Murray.

De Backer, C. J., Nelissen, M., Vyncke, P., Braeckman, J., & McAndrew, F. T. (2007). Celebrities: From teachers to friends. *Human Nature, 18*, 334–354.

Dickerson, S. S., & Kemeny, M. E. (2004). Acute stressors and cortisol responses: A theoretical integration and synthesis of laboratory research. *Psychological Bulletin, 130*, 355–391.

Draper, P., & Harpending, H. (1982). Father absence and reproductive strategy: An evolutionary perspective. *Journal of Anthropological Research, 38*, 255–273.

Dunbar, R. I. (1993). Coevolution of neocortical size, group size and language in humans. *Behavioral and Brain Sciences, 16*, 681–694.

Dunbar, R. I. (1998). The social brain hypothesis. *Brain, 9*, 178–190.

Dunbar, R., & Barrett, L. (2009). *Oxford Handbook of Evolutionary Psychology.* Oxford: Oxford University Press.

Duntley, J. D., & Buss, D. M. (2012). The evolution of stalking. *Sex Roles, 66*, 311–327.

Durante, K. M., Griskevicius, V., Redden, J. P., & White, A. E. (in press). Spending on daughters versus sons in economic recessions. *Journal of Consumer Research.*

Durante, K. M., Griskevicius, V., Cantú, S. M., & Simpson, J. A. (2014). Money, status, and the ovulatory cycle. *Journal of Marketing Research, 51*, 27–39.

Durante, K. M., Griskevicius, V., Hill, S. E., Perilloux, C., & Li, N. P. (2011). Ovulation, female competition, and product choice: Hormonal influences on consumer behavior. *Journal of Consumer Research, 37*, 921–934.

Durante, K. M., Griskevicius, V., Simpson, J. A., Cantú, S. M., & Li, N. P. (2012). Ovulation leads women to perceive sexy cads as good dads. *Journal of Personality and Social Psychology, 103*, 292.

Durante, K. M., Griskevicius, V., Simpson, J. A., Cantú, S. M., & Tybur, J. M. (2012). Sex ratio and women's career choice: Does a scarcity of men lead women to choose briefcase over baby? *Journal of Personality and Social Psychology, 103*, 121.

Durante, K. M., & Li, N. P. (2009). Oestradiol level and opportunistic mating in women. *Biology Letters, 5*, 179–182.

Durante, K. M., Li, N. P., & Haselton, M. G. (2008). Changes in women's choice of dress across the ovulatory cycle: Naturalistic and laboratory task-based evidence. *Personality and Social Psychology Bulletin, 34*, 1451–1460.

Ellis, B. J., Figueredo, A. J., Brumbach, B. H., & Schlomer, G. L. (2009). Fundamental dimensions of environmental risk. *Human Nature, 20*, 204–268.

Emlen, S. T., & Oring, L. W. (1977). Ecology, sexual selection, and the evolution of mating systems. *Science, 197*, 215–223.

Forbes, D. P. (2005). Are some entrepreneurs more overconfident than others? *Journal of Business Venturing, 20*, 623–640.

Galesic, M., Gigerenzer, G., & Straubinger, N. (2009). Natural frequencies help older adults and people with low numeracy to evaluate medical screening tests. *Medical Decision Making, 29*, 368–371.

Gangestad, S. W., Garver-Apgar, C. E., Simpson, J. A., & Cousins, A. J. (2007). Changes in women's mate preferences across the ovulatory cycle. *Journal of Personality and Social Psychology, 92*, 151–163.

Gangestad, S. W., & Simpson, J. A. (2000). The evolution of human mating: Trade-offs and strategic pluralism. *Behavioral and Brain Sciences, 23*(04), 573–587.

Gangestad, S. W., Simpson J. A., Cousins A. J., Garver-Apgar, C. E., & Christensen, P. N. (2004). Women's preferences for male behavioral displays across the menstrual cycle. *Psychological Science, 15*, 203–27.

Gangestad, S. W., & Thornhill, R. (1998). Menstrual cycle variation in women's preferences for the scent of symmetrical men. *Proceedings of the Royal Society of London. Series B: Biological Sciences, 265*(1399), 927–933.

Gangestad, S. W., Thornhill, R., & Garver, C. E. (2002). Changes in women's sexual interests and their partners' mate retention tactics across the menstrual cycle: Evidence for shifting conflicts of interest. *Proceedings of the Royal Society of London B, 269*, 975–982.

Gangestad, S. W., Thornhill, R., & Garver-Apgar, C. E. (2005). Women's sexual interest across the ovulatory cycle depending on primary partner fluctuating asymmetry. *Proceedings of the Royal Society of London B, 272*, 2023–2027.

Geary, D. (2000). Evolution and proximate expression of human paternal investment. *Psychological Bulletin, 126*, 55–77.

Ghazanfar, A. A., Neuhoff, J. G., & Logothetis, N. K. (2002). Auditory looming perception in rhesus monkeys. *Proceedings of the National Academy of Sciences, 99*(24), 15755–15757.

Gigerenzer, G., & Hoffrage, U. (1995). How to improve Bayesian reasoning without instruction: Frequency formats. *Psychological Review, 102*, 684–704.

Griskevicius, V., Ackerman, J. A., Cantú, S. M., Delton, A. W., & Robertson, T. E., Simpson, J. A., Thomson, M. E., & Tybur, J. M. (2013). When the economy falters do people spend or save? Responses to resource scarcity depend on childhood environments. *Psychological Science, 24*, 197–205.

Griskevicius, V., Cantú, S. M., & van Vugt, M. V. (2012). The evolutionary bases for sustainable behavior: Implications for marketing, policy, and social entrepreneurship. *Journal of Public Policy & Marketing, 31*, 115–128.

Griskevicius, V., Goldstein, N. J., Mortensen, C. R., Cialdini, R. B., & Kenrick, D. T. (2006). Going along versus going alone: When fundamental motives facilitate strategic (non)conformity. *Journal of Personality and Social Psychology, 91*, 281–294.

Griskevicius, V., Goldstein, N. J., Mortensen, C. R., Sundie, J. M., Cialdini, R. B., & Kenrick, D. T. (2009). Fear and loving in Las Vegas: Evolution, emotion, and persuasion. *Journal of Marketing Research, 46*, 384–395.

Griskevicius, V., & Kenrick, D. T. (2013). Fundamental motives for why we buy: How evolutionary needs influence consumer behavior. *Journal of Consumer Psychology, 23*, 372–386.

Griskevicius, V., Shiota, M. N., & Neufeld, S. (2010). Influence of different positive emotionson persuasion processing: A functional evolutionary approach. *Emotion, 10*, 190–206.

Griskevicius, V., Shiota, M. N., & Nowlis, S. M. (2010). The many shades of rose-colored glasses: An evolutionary approach to the influence of different positive emotions. *Journal of Consumer Research, 37*, 238–250.

Griskevicius, V., Tybur, J. M., Ackerman, J. M., Delton, A. W., Robertson, T. E., & White, A. E. (2012). The financial consequences of too many men: Sex ratio effects on saving, borrowing, and spending. *Journal of Personality and Social Psychology, 102*, 69.

Griskevicius, V., Tybur, J. M., Delton, A. W., & Robertson, T. E. (2011). The influence of mortality and socioeconomic status on risk and delayed rewards: A life history theory approach. *Journal of Personality and Social Psychology, 100*, 1015–1026.

Griskevicius, V., Tybur, J. M., Sundie, J. M., Cialdini, R. B., Miller, G. F., & Kenrick, D. T. (2007). Blatant benevolence and conspicuous consumption: When romantic motives elicit strategic costly signals. *Journal of Personality and Social Psychology, 93*, 85.

Hall, D. A., & Moore, D. R. (2003). Auditory neuroscience: The salience of looming sounds. *Current Biology, 13*, R91–R93.

Hamilton, W. D. (1963). The evolution of altruistic behavior. *American Naturalist, 97*, 354–356.

Hamilton, W. D. (1964). The genetical evolution of social behavior. *Journal of Theoretical Biology, 7*, 1–52.

Haselton, M. G., & Buss, D. M. (2000). Error management theory: A new perspective on biases in cross-sex mind reading. *Journal of Personality and Social Psychology, 78*, 81–91.

Haselton, M. G., & Buss, D. M. (2003). Biases in social judgment: Design flaws or design features? In J. Forgas, K. Williams, & B. von Hippel (eds.), *Responding to the Social World: Implicit and Explicit Processes in Social Judgments and Decisions.* New York: Cambridge University Press.

Haselton, M. G., & Nettle, D. (2006). The paranoid optimist: An integrative evolutionary model of cognitive biases. *Personality and Social Psychology Review, 10*, 47–66.

Hill, K. R., & Hurtado, A. M. (1996). *Ache Life History: The Ecology and Demography of a Foraging People.* Piscataway, NJ: Aldine Transactions.

Hoffrage, U., & Gigerenzer, G. (1998). Using natural frequencies to improve diagnostic inferences. *Academic Medicine, 73*, 538–540.

Hoffrage, U., Gigerenzer, G., Krauss, S., & Martignon, L. (2002). Representation facilitates reasoning: What natural frequencies are and what they are not. *Cognition, 84*, 343–352.

Hoffrage, U., Lindsey, S., Hertwig, R., & Gigerenzer, G. (2000). Communicating statistical information. *Science, 290*, 2261–2262.

Hu, F. B., Manson, J. E., Stampfer, M. J., Colditz, G., Liu, S., Solomon, C. G., & Willett, W. C. (2001). Diet, lifestyle, and the risk of type 2 diabetes mellitus in women. *New England Journal of Medicine, 345*, 790–797.

Hurtado, A. M., & Hill, K. R. (1992). Paternal effect on offspring survivorship among Ache and Hiwi hunter-gatherers. In B. S. Hewlett (ed.), *Father–Child Relations: Cultural and Biosocial Contexts* (pp. 31–55). New York: Aldine de Gruyter.

Hurtado, A. M., Hill, K., Kaplan, H., & Hurtado, I. (1992). Trade-offs between female food acquisition and child care among Hiwi and Ache foragers. *Human Nature, 3*, 185–216.

Johnson, D. D. P, & Fowler, J. H. (2011.) The evolution of overconfidence. *Nature, 477*, 317–320.

Jones, R. E. (1997). *Human Reproductive Biology* 2nd ed. New York: Academic Press.

Kahneman, D., & Tversky, A. (1979). Prospect theory: An analysis of decision under risk. *Econometrica: Journal of the Econometric Society*, 263–291.

Kanazawa, S. (2002). Bowling with our imaginary friends. *Evolution and Human Behavior, 23*(3), 167–171.

Kaplan, H. S., & Gangestad, S. W. (2005). Life history theory and evolutionary psychology. In D. M. Busse (ed.), *The Handbook of Evolutionary Psychology* (pp. 68–95). Hoboken, NJ: John Wiley & Sons.

Kenrick, D. T., Griskevicius, V., Neuberg, S. L., & Schaller, M. (2010a). Renovating the pyramid of needs contemporary extensions built upon ancient foundations. *Perspectives on Psychological Science, 5*, 292–314.

Kenrick, D. T., Groth, G. E., Trost, M. R., & Sadalla, E. K. (1993). Integrating evolutionary and social exchange perspectives on relationships: Effects of gender, self-appraisal, and involvement level on mate selection criteria. *Journal of Personality and Social Psychology, 64*, 951–969.

Kenrick, D. T., Li, N. P., & Butner, J. (2003). Dynamical evolutionary psychology: Individual decision rules and emergent social norms. *Psychological Review, 110*, 3.

Kenrick, D. T., Neuberg, S. L., Griskevicius, V., Becker, D. V., & Schaller, M. (2010b). Goal-driven cognition and functional behavior: The fundamental-motives framework. *Current Directions in Psychological Science, 19*, 63–67.

Kenrick, D. T., Sadalla, E. K., Groth, G., & Trost, M. R. (1990). Evolution, traits, and the stages of human courtship: Qualifying the parental investment model. *Journal of Personality, 58*, 97–116.

Kvarnemo, C., & Ahnesjo, I. (1996). The dynamics of operational sex ratios and competition for mates. *Trends in Ecology & Evolution, 11*, 404–408.

Li, Y. J., Kenrick, D. T., Griskevicius, V., & Neuberg, S. L. (2012). Economic decision biases and fundamental motivations: How mating and self-protection alter loss aversion. *Journal of Personality and Social Psychology, 102*, 550.

Lieberman, L. S. (2003). Dietary, evolutionary, and modernizing influences on the prevalence of type 2 diabetes. *Annual Review of Nutrition, 23*, 345–377.

Lincoln, F. C. (1999). *Migration of Birds* (No. 16). Washington, DC: Government Printing Office.

Lipson, S. F., & Ellison, P. T. (1996). Endocrinology comparison of salivary steroid profiles in naturally occurring conception and non-conception cycles. *Human Reproduction, 11*, 2090–2096.

Maestripieri, D. (2002). Parent–offspring conflict in primates. *International Journal of Primatology, 23*, 923–951.

Maier, J. X., Neuhoff, J. G., Logothetis, N. K., & Ghazanfar, A. A. (2004). Multisensory integration of looming signals by rhesus monkeys. *Neuron, 43*, 177–181.

Mazur, A., & Booth, A. (1998). Testosterone and dominance in men. *Behavioral and Brain Sciences, 21*, 353–363.

Meyer, K. A., Kushi, L. H., Jacobs, D. R., Slavin, J., Sellers, T. A., & Folsom, A. R. (2000). Carbohydrates, dietary fiber, and incident type 2 diabetes in older women. *American Journal of Clinical Nutrition, 71*, 921–930.

Miller, G. F. (2000). *The Mating Mind: How Sexual Selection Shaped the Evolution of Human Nature.* New York: Doubleday.

Mineka, S., & Öhman, A. (2002). Phobias and preparedness: The selective, automatic, and encapsulated nature of fear. *Biological Psychiatry, 52*, 927–937.

Møller, A. P. (2000). Male parental care, female reproductive success, and extrapair paternity. *Behavioral Ecology, 11*, 161–168.

Nairne, J. S., & Pandeirada, J. N. S. (2008). Adaptive memory: Remembering with a Stone-Age brain. *Current Directions in Psychology, 17*, 239–243.

Nelson, R. J. (2005). *An Introduction to Behavioral Endocrinology.* Sunderland, MA: Sinauer Associates.

Nesse, R. M. (1990). Evolutionary explanations of emotions. *Human Nature, 1*, 261–289.

Nesse, R. M., & Williams, G. C. (1994). *Why We Get Sick: The New Science of Darwinian Medicine*. New York: Times Books.

Neuberg, S. L., Kenrick, D. T., & Schaller, M. (2011). Human threat management systems: Self-protection and disease avoidance. *Neuroscience & Biobehavioral Reviews, 35*, 1042–1051.

Neufeld, S. & Griskevicius, V. (2014). Positive emotions, marketing, and social influence. In M. M. Tugade, M. N. Shiota, & L. D. Kirby (eds.), *Handbook of Positive Emotions* (pp. 463–478). New York: Guilford Press.

Neuhoff, J. G. (2001). An adaptive bias in the perception of looming auditory motion. *Ecological Psychology, 13*, 87–110.

Nowak, M. A., & Sigmund, K. (1998). The dynamics of indirect reciprocity. *Journal of Theoretical Biology, 194*, 561–574.

Öhman, A., & Mineka, S. (2001). Fears, phobias, and preparedness: Toward an evolved module of fear and fear learning. *Psychological Review, 108*, 483–522.

Öhman, A., & Mineka, S. (2003). The malicious serpent snakes as a prototypical stimulus for an evolved module of fear. *Current Directions in Psychological Science, 12*, 5–9.

Ornstein, R. E., & Ehrlich, P. R. (1989). *New World, New Mind: Changing the Way We Think to Save Our Future*. London: Methuen.

Penton-Voak, I. S., Perrett, D. I., Castles, D. L., Kobayashi, T., Burt, D. M., Murray, L. K., & Minamisawa, R. (1999). Menstrual cycle alters face preference. *Nature, 399*, 741–742.

Roff, D. A. (2002). *Life History Evolution* (vol. 7). Sunderland, MA: Sinauer Associates.

Saad, G. (2007). *The Evolutionary Bases of Consumption*. Mahwah, NJ: Lawrence Erlbaum.

Saad, G. (2013). Evolutionary consumption. *Journal of Consumer Psychology, 23*, 351–371.

Saad, G., & Stenstrom, E. (2012). Calories, beauty, and ovulation: The effects of the menstrual cycle on food and appearance-related consumption. *Journal of Consumer Psychology, 22*, 102–113.

Scott, J., Stumpp, M., & Xu, P. (2003). Overconfidence bias in international stock prices. *Journal of Portfolio Management, 29*, 80–89.

Seifritz, E., Neuhoff, J. G., Bilecen, D., Scheffler, K., Mustovic, H., Schächinger, H., & Di Salle, F. (2002). Neural processing of auditory looming in the human brain. *Current Biology, 12*, 2147–2151.

Sherif, M. (1936). *The Psychology of Social Norms*. New York: Harper.

Sherman, P. W., & Billing, J. (1999). Darwinian gastronomy: Why we use spices. *Bioscience, 49*, 453–463.

Simpson, J. A., & Belsky, J. (2008). Attachment theory within a modern evolutionary framework. In P. R. Shaver & J. Cassidy (eds.), *Handbook of Attachment: Theory, Research, and Clinical Applications*, 2nd ed. (pp. 131–157). New York: Guilford Press.

Simpson, J. A., Griskevicius, V., Kuo, S. I. C., Sung, S., & Collins, W. A. (2012). Evolution, stress, and sensitive periods: The influence of unpredictability in early versus late childhood on sex and risky behavior. *Developmental Psychology, 48*(3), 674–686.

Simpson, J. A., Griskevicius, V., & Rothman, A. J. (2012). Consumer decisions in relationships. *Journal of Consumer Psychology, 22*, 304–314.

Srinivasan, K., Viswanad, B., Asrat, L., Kaul, C. L., & Ramarao, P. (2005). Combination of high-fat diet-fed and low-dose streptozotocin-treated rat: a model for type 2 diabetes and pharmacological screening. *Pharmacological Research, 52*, 313–320.

Stearns, S. C. (1992). *The Evolution of Life Histories* (vol. 249). Oxford: Oxford University Press.

Sundie, J. M., Kenrick, D. T., Griskevicius, V., Tybur, J. M., Vohs, K. D., & Beal, D. J. (2011). Peacocks, Porsches, and Thorstein Veblen: Conspicuous consumption as a sexual signaling system. *Journal of Personality and Social Psychology, 100*, 664.

Taylor, P. D., & Bulmer, M. G. (1980). Local mate competition and the sex ratio. *Journal of Theoretical Biology, 86*, 409–419.

Taylor, S. E., Klein, L. C., Lewis, B. P., Gruenewald, T. L., Gurung, R. A. R., & Updegraff, J. A. (2000). Biobehavioral responses to stress in females: Tend-and-befriend, not fight-or-flight. *Psychological Review, 107*, 411–29.

Thornhill, R., & Gangestad, S. W. (2008). *The Evolutionary Biology of Human Female Sexuality*. New York: Oxford University Press.

Tinbergen, N. (1963). On aims and methods of ethology. *Zeitschrift für Tierpsychologie, 20*, 410–433.

Tooby, J., & Cosmides, L. (2005). Conceptual foundations of evolutionary psychology. In David M. Buss (ed.), *The Handbook of Evolutionary Psychology* (pp. 5–67). Hoboken, NJ: John Wiley & Sons.

Trivers, R. L. (1971). The evolution of reciprocal altruism. *Quarterly Review of Biology, 46*, 35–57.

Trivers, R. L. (1972). Parental investment and sexual selection. In B. G. Campbell (ed.), *Sexual Selection and the Decent of Man, 1871–1971* (pp. 136–179). Chicago: Aldine.

Trivers, R. L. (1974). Parent-offspring conflict. *American Zoologist, 14*, 249–264.

Trivers, R. L., & Willard, D. E. (1973). Natural selection of parental ability to vary the sex ratio of offspring. *Science, 179*, 90–92.

Walker, M. L., Wilson, M. E., & Gordon, T. P. (1983). Female rhesus monkey aggression during the menstrual cycle. *Animal Behavior, 31*, 1047–1054.

Wallen, K. (2000). Risky business: Social context and hormonal modulation of primate sexual desire. In K. Wallen and J. E. Schneider (eds.), *Reproduction in Context*, (pp. 289–323) Cambridge, MA: MIT Press.

Wang, Y., & Griskevicius, V. (2014). Conspicuous consumption, relationships, and rivals: Women's luxury products as signals to other women. *Journal of Consumer Research, 40*, 834–854.

Westneat, D. F., & Sherman, P. W. (1993). Parentage and the evolution of parental behavior. *Behavioral Ecology, 4*, 66–77.

Wilson, E. O. (2000). *Sociobiology: The New Synthesis*. Cambridge, MA: Harvard University Press.

Young, L. J., & Insel, T. R. (2002). Hormones and parental behavior. In J. B. Becker, M. S. Breedlove, D. Crews, & M. M. McCarthy (eds.), *Behavioral Endocrinology*, 2nd ed. (pp. 331–369). Cambridge, MA: MIT Press.

Zahavi, A., & Zahavi, A. (1997). *The Handicap Principle: A missing Piece of Darwin's Puzzle*. New York: Oxford University Press.

6   Consumer Neuroscience

Revealing Meaningful Relationships between Brain and
Consumer Behavior

Hilke Plassmann and Uma R. Karmarkar

Introduction

In 2004, the journal *Neuron* published a paper titled "Neural Correlates of Behavioral Preferences for Culturally Familiar Drinks." But the work was already generating significant buzz under the somewhat less scientific title of "the Coke-Pepsi study." Using functional magnetic resonance imaging (fMRI), the authors had examined how various areas in the brain reacted to the experience of drinking cola with or without the knowledge of its brand name. Unexpectedly, their results suggested that people have a more complex cognitive interaction with Coke's branding than with Pepsi's (McClure et al., 2004). By finding evidence for brand-dependent neural activity, they also found evidence that neuroscientific methods could offer useful insights about how consumers think.

Since that paper, consumer neuroscience research – which applies tools and theories from neuroscience to better understand decision making and related processes – has generated quite a bit of excitement in marketing and in neighboring disciplines (Ariely & Berns, 2010; Camerer, Loewenstein, & Prelec, 2004; 2005; Plassmann, Ramsøy, & Milosavljevic, 2012; Plassmann, Yoon, Feinberg, & Shiv, 2010; Venkatraman, Clithero, Fitzsimons, & Huettel, 2012). For example, a survey of the most productive marketing professors found that consumer neuroscience was considered one of the top five cutting-edge areas in the field of marketing (Ladik, 2008).

Practitioners' interest in applying neuroscientific methods for conducting company-specific market research, generally referred to as "neuromarketing," has also been increasing. Many of the largest marketing research companies and advertising agencies currently have neuromarketing divisions or partnerships (e.g., Nielsen, Millward Brown). In addition, the number of neuromarketing research companies has been growing steadily (Plassmann, Ramsøy, & Milosavljevic, 2012), with an impressive list of client brands across a variety of product categories (e.g., Google, Campbell Soup, Estée Lauder, Fox News).

Building on this, it's useful to consider both *why* and *how* neuroscience techniques such as fMRI can improve our understanding of consumer psychology beyond more traditional methods. Studies of decision making have commonly relied on asking people about their thoughts, observing their behavior directly in various controlled situations, or observing their behavior indirectly using empirical analysis of large data sets. One way that neural and physiological methods can expand this view is by simply adding distinct types of data, such as those from brain correlates of emotion or affective processing. Such feelings are clearly important in decision making but are difficult to access and express via surveys or revealed preferences. Indeed, because many neurophysiological methods require no conscious effort or response, they offer some access to automatic and unconscious processes more generally.

By measuring brain and body signals related to the mechanisms of thought that individuals cannot consciously control, neuroscience can help build process-related models with a more nuanced understanding of how behavior is generated. Since these measures do not have to rely on verbal or linguistic processing, they also help avoid the biases in attitudes and behavioral intentions that can be introduced by explicit tests of attribute perceptions, such as surveys (Feldman & Lynch, 1988). In addition, while behavioral methods offer "snapshots" of preferences and choices, it can be a challenge to examine how different decision elements develop and change over time. fMRI and other techniques have the ability to gather data relating to multiple constructs dynamically, as a decision or consumption experience unfolds. This also means that the contributions of the same mechanisms can be examined at different stages in the decision process.

The goal of this chapter is to give an overview of the nascent field of consumer neuroscience and discuss when and how it is useful to integrate the "black box" of the consumer's brain into consumer psychology. To reach this goal, we first briefly outline several methods that are part of the consumer neuroscience toolkit and how they are currently used. We then provide an overview of the research that has laid the foundation of consumer neuroscience, showcasing studies that highlight the concrete promises of applying neuroscience to consumer psychology. Building from this, we focus on using brain data to predict consumer behaviour, a topic that has recently generated a lot of excitement from academics and practitioners alike. Last, we take a look at some of the newest developments we think will have an important future impact on our understanding of consumer psychology.

The Consumer Neuroscience Toolkit

Empirical studies in consumer neuroscience and neuromarketing alike employ neuroimaging tools as biomarkers to assess responses before, during, and after the decision-making processes. Table 6.1 gives a brief description of several of these methods and how they have been used in past research (see Cacioppo, Tassinary, & Berntson, 2007 for a detailed scientific review and Plassmann, Ambler, & Braeutigam, 2007 for a more applied review).

In 2014, we conducted a survey about the state of the field among leading academics (N = 59) and practitioners (N = 64) who currently use neuroscience to investigate marketing questions. The results reveal that for academics, the

Table 6.1 *Summary of Neuroscience Methods*

Tool	What Is Measured	Benefits	Limitations	Typical Use
Electroencephalogram (EEG)*	- Average electrical (neural) activity occurring locally in the cortex under the scalp, measured by multiple contacts (electrodes) on the head. - Analysis mostly compares of left vs. right hemispheric differences in EEG signal	- Can be used to measure signals faster than fMRI - Minimal setup, participants able to move around	- Spatial localization of brain activity very limited (hard to pinpoint specific brain areas) - Does not measure from deep brain structures	- Copy testing - Instore experience - Detection of positive/ negative arousal, decision conflict, attention, language processing, some memory effects. - Common in neuromarketing research
Functional magnetic resonance imaging (fMRI)	- Signal is correlated with changes in brain activity, localized with a spatial resolution of 1–10 mm, and a temporal resolution of 1–10 s. - Analysis is commonly linear regression models identifying activity in specific brain areas correlated with treatments or stimuli of interest	- Can resolve activity in small structures - Differentiates signal from neighboring areas. - Measures activity in structures across the whole brain, not just surface	- physically restrictive, participants lie on their backs in the scanner and cannot move around - Expensive; equipment intensive	- Response to marketing stimuli such as brands and price - Localization of neural processing during consumer choices, consumption experiences, and value learning - More sophisticated multivariate approaches promise higher predictive power
Transcranial magnetic stimulation (TMS)/ transcranial direct-current stimulation (TDCS)	- Uses a coil applied on the head that creates a magnetic field disrupting or "turning off" neural activity in specific areas. Creates "temporary lesions." - Monitors changes in behavior or other physiological response	- Unlike correlational measures (fMRI, EEG), can be used to show causality	- Is limited to investigating function of surface brain areas. - Lowers (or enhances) neural activity generally, cannot be used to test "levels" of activity.	- Studying causality of specific brain regions for specific mental processes (e.g., preferences, brand choice) by temporarily taking them "offline"

Method	Description			Application
	after manipulation of brain activity in the target area - Usually decreases neural activity (TMS), but facilitation/increasing activity is possible (TDCS)		- Loses localization, not as clearly identifiable (TDCS)	
Eye tracking	- Eye movements (e.g. where a person is looking, and for how long) - Pupil dilation, correlated with arousal	- Offers strong nuanced data on what aspects of an image are grabbing attention and in what order	- Does not measure inferences, thoughts, or emotions	- Evidence of overt attention - Shelf layout - Packaging and advertising design - Website usability - Product placement
Biometrics: skin conductance response (SCR); heart rate; pupil dilation	- Various physiological signals of arousal	- Simple, well-validated experimental setups - Unobtrusive equipment, allows for more natural interactions with the environment	- Cannot distinguish valence (e.g., positive vs. negative arousal)	- Response to marketing stimuli, in particular commercials - Inferences of emotional engagement / arousal during choice processes
Facial electromyography (fEMG), facial affective recoding using video and automated encoding algorithms	- Minute changes in facial muscles (microexpressions) related to various emotions	- Dynamic tracking of emotional (potentially unconscious) responses to ongoing stimuli/information	- fEMG requires attaching electrodes directly to the face (in a lab) - Application of video encoding is limited for subtle effects	- Valence of response to marketing stimuli, in particular commercials - Inferences of emotional valence of information processing during choice
Lesions	- Behavior on wide variety of tasks with participants who have naturally occurring or trauma-induced lesions in focal brain areas.	- Can establish causality/necessity of a brain area for a specific function	- Requires access to patient populations - Varies in affected areas, and affects functionality across individuals	- Choice behavior, particularly in risky/uncertain decision contexts - discriminating conscious vs. unconscious choice elements.

155

Table 6.1 (*cont.*)

Tool	What Is Measured	Benefits	Limitations	Typical Use
Single neuron recording	- Electrical signals from individual neurons in brain areas of interest to decision making, recorded with microwire electrodes implanted directly in the individual's brain	- Insight into how the most basic units of information are coded - Most direct representation of how and when the brain responds to specific stimuli	- Invasive – in humans, it requires working with medical team on neurosurgery patients - In animals, it requires extensive training and/or laboratory support	- Direct measure of neural activity - Ability to be used to study a variety of questions, as with the aforementioned methods
Pharmacology	- Can measure changes in neuromodulators (e.g., oxytocin, testosterone, dopamine, cortisol) due to specific behaviors or contexts - Can manipulate neuromodulators to examine effects on specific behaviors	- Allows better understanding of (physiological) state-dependent effects	- The method cannot measure fast/immediate changes - Individual chemicals have multiple effects that can be difficult to isolate and specific effects can be unclear	- Oxytocin – stress, cooperation, social interactions - Testosterone – impulsiveness, risk behavior, aggression, social interactions, power - Cortisol – stress, conflict, general arousal - Dopamine – reward processing, learning, motivation, movement

*A very similar but more expensive technique not mentioned here is magnetencephalography (MEG). We do not provide details because the method is of limited application in consumer research, but see Plassmann, Ambler, & Braeutigam, 2007, for more details.

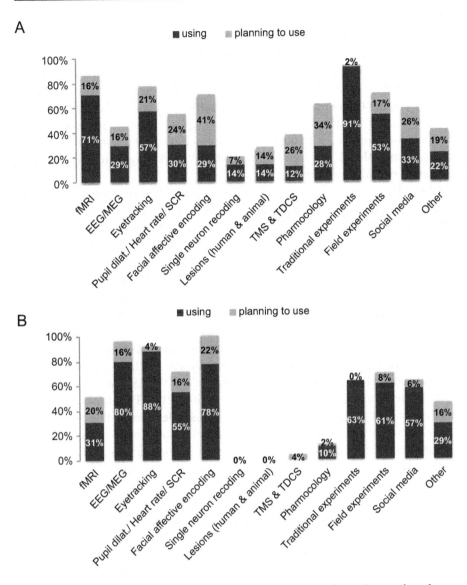

Figure 6.1 *Use of Neuroscientific Tools in (A) Academic Research and (B) Practitioner Research.*

most commonly used neuroscience tool is currently fMRI (71 percent; see Figure 6.1A), followed by eye tracking (57 percent). In contrast, the practitioners responding to this survey primarily use eye tracking (88 percent) and EEG/MEG (80 percent), followed by psychophysiological measures of arousal (i.e., skin conductance response (SCR), heart rate response, and pupil dilation, 55 percent) and measurements of emotional valence (i.e., facial affective encoding, 78 percent; see Figure 6.1B).

Given the similarity of the questions these groups are interested in, why might such striking differences arise? First, fMRI is a complex methodology that requires in-depth training to pursue and is quite expensive (scanner rental costs range from US$100–800 per hour). These experiments also require participants to lie on their backs and to hold very still while in the fMRI scanner, which can diminish their ecological or external validity. However, the benefit of fMRI lies in its ability to visualize a tremendous range of information processes underlying consumer behavior. From that perspective, it is one of the most powerful tools available. Better understanding underlying information processes, or decision mechanisms, is important in understanding *why* a specific behavior arises. Hence fMRI is a central method for marketing academics building consumer psychology theories.

EEG/MEG and eye tracking are more common for neuromarketing companies, in part because they allow for mobile measurement. For example, some EEG configurations can be used when participants are shopping in a real supermarket as opposed to a laboratory environment. Mobile versions of EEG/MEG and eye-tracking tools raise their ecological validity, which is very important from a practitioner's standpoint. However, this improved connection to real-life situations can come at the cost of decreased internal and external statistical validity since (a) sampling neurophysiological measurements while test participants are moving around causes confounds in the recorded data and (b) in-store studies usually do not employ repeated-measures designs (in which participants are exposed to the same stimuli multiple times). Repeated measure designs are important for the robustness of the data, since they are able to decrease measurement noise (Ariely & Berns, 2010). That is also why when academics use eye tracking, as noted in several studies cited in this chapter, they often do so in the lab rather than in the field. Since both types of validity (internal and external) are important, we hope that in the future, academia and industry will establish more collaborations to better combine their viewpoints.

The survey results illustrated in Figure 6.1 further indicate that academic researchers may approach the use of neuroscientific tools in a different manner than neuromarketing practitioners. Academic researchers expressed more of an aim to combine neuroscience tools with traditional behavioral lab experiments than those in industry (91 percent vs. 63 percent). Interestingly, our survey also revealed that going forward, academic researchers are more likely to seek out additional methods to broaden the scope of their research, such as applying psychophysiological measures of valence (i.e., facial affective encoding, +41 percent compared to practitioners) and arousal (i.e., SCR, heart rate response, and pupil dilation, +24 percent) as well as measuring or manipulating pharmacological responses to marketing behavior (+34 percent). These differences may arise because neuromarketing firms put their focus on developing deep competencies in specific methodologies or because they pursue a broader portfolio of techniques by partnering with other firms.

Taken together, the survey findings suggest that consumer neuroscience researchers regard neuroscientific tools less as substitutes for traditional methods and more as complements that can add important new insights to further develop marketing theories.

Foundations of Consumer Neuroscience Research

Research categorized in disciplines such as neuroeconomics, decision neuroscience, and consumer neuroscience over the past decade has worked to establish a better understanding of how specific brain circuits contribute to decision making. Very early consumer neuroscience studies focused on identifying neural correlates of marketing relevant behavior in particular. Figure 6.2 illustrates a number of these areas. Indeed, the question of which brain areas encode preferences for products or specific product feature such as brand label, price information, and product category has received considerable attention.

For instance, Erk and colleagues (2002) investigated preferences for sports cars versus other types of cars (i.e., limousines, small cars) and found that viewing pictures of the more attractive cars resulted in increased activity in mesolimbic brain areas, such as nucleus accumbens (NAcc) and ventromedial prefrontal cortex (vmPFC; Erk et al., 2002). Deppe and colleagues (2005) investigated brand preferences and found that favored brands activated significantly more the vmPFC compared to other brands from the same category that were less liked. Knutson and colleagues (2007) investigated which brain areas had activity correlated with different elements of a shopping decision, such as the product or its price. They found that activity in the NAcc correlated with liking for the product while it was being viewed, while activity in medial prefrontal cortex was associated with perceptions of monetary value when viewing product and price information. In addition, insula activity increased when participants viewed a price and product pairing that they felt was a "rip-off" or bad value, suggesting that it might represent negative emotions associated with price (Knutson et al., 2007). Last, studies by Plassmann, O'Doherty, and Rangel (2007, 2010) investigated which brain areas coded for a decision maker's willingness to pay (WTP) using a second price auction mechanism adopted from behavioral economics (a so-called Becker-DeGroot-Marschak auction; Becker, DeGroot, & Marschak, 1964). They found that activity in the vmPFC and the dorsolateral prefrontal cortex (dlPFC) encoded participants' WTP (Plassmann, O'Doherty, & Rangel, 2007, 2010).

This research, taken together with several other studies that followed on packaging attractiveness (Reimann et al., 2010) and brand preferences (Esch et al., 2012; Schaefer, Berens, Heinze, & Rotte, 2006; Schaefer & Rotte, 2007; for a review, see Plassmann, Ramsøy, & Milosavljevic, 2012), demonstrated the important role of the mesolimbic system, specifically the vmPFC and striatum/NAcc for encoding the preferences and values that individuals assign to products or product features. A meta-analysis of these and other studies involving the neuroscience of decision making further supported the importance of these areas (Bartra, McGuire, & Kable, 2010).

These findings provide a necessary first step in understanding how decision elements are coded in the brain and thus a strong background on how neural methods can be used in future work. However, like the Coke and Pepsi research by McClure and colleagues (2004), their direct contributions add more to an

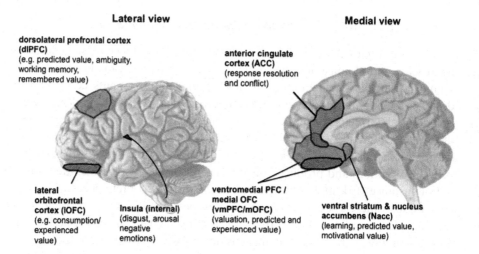

Figure 6.2 *Brain Areas Involved in Consumer Decision Making, Adapted from Plassmann, Ramsøy, & Milosavljevic, 2012.*

understanding of the brain than to our understanding of consumers. While a better understanding of the brain is important from a neuroscientific perspective, it is not the focus of a consumer psychology perspective. This distinction is reflected in our survey of consumer neuroscience academics, in which "understanding the brain" was rated as the least important promise of this field going forward.

Instead, the two top areas of "major promise" were (1) "dissociating competing theories about information processing underlying decision making" and (2) "confirming existing theories about mechanisms underlying decision making." A close third was "identifying new processes in decision making." In other words, consumer neuroscience research may best be seen as a powerful accompaniment to existing methodologies, allowing us to strengthen the foundations of consumer psychology as well as offering avenues for new discoveries and advancing its boundaries. In the following, we highlight studies that exemplify each of these three top promises of consumer neuroscience.

Promise 1: Dissociating Competing Theories about Information Processing

Neuroscientific tools can demonstrate dissociations between psychological processes in at least three ways. First, methods such as fMRI can help to dissociate competing hypotheses that that cannot be distinguished on a behavioral level (because they result in the same behavior) by showing that they are dissociated in the brain. For example, a common finding in the marketing literature is that marketing actions such as pricing and branding induce expectations about the product's quality that in turn alter choices (Lee, Frederick, & Ariely, 2006) or liking for otherwise identical products during consumption (Allison & Uhl, 1964). Marketing actions can even influence the efficacy or impact of otherwise identical products, such as the ability of a discounted versus a normal-priced energy drink to aid in solving mental puzzles (for review, see Plassmann & Wager, 2014). These effects could be explained by three possible mechanisms: (1) the existence of reporting biases due to social desirability, (2) motivated reasoning, or (3) that marketing-induced expectations do indeed change how features such as the taste of the product are perceived. Plassmann, O'Doherty, Shiv, and Rangel (2008) tested these competing theories by scanning participants' brains while they consumed identical wines with different price tags and found that higher prices enhanced the actual taste experience, that is, how the product quality is perceived.

Second, neuroscientific tools can test competing formal models of the information processes underlying consumer decision making (Willemsen & Johnson, 2011). For example Reutskaja, Nagel, Camerer, and Rangel (2011) used eye tracking to compare different models of how consumers conduct dynamic information search over the set of feasible items under conditions of extreme time pressure and choice overload. They found that to terminate the search process, participants use a stopping rule that is qualitatively consistent with a hybrid model (informed by neurological data) but not with the satisficing or optimal search models from economic theory.

A third example is the investigation of the common assumption in social psychology that hypothetical choices and/or purchase intentions are good approximations for real behavior. This assumption is in stark contrast to revealed preference theory in economics, which relies on real choices as a preference measure. A study by Kang, Rangel, Camus, and Camerer (2011) investigated the neural correlates of these two competing preference measures by using fMRI to compare whether hypothetical and real choices recruit similar or distinct neural systems. They found that indeed hypothetical and real choices recruit overlapping neural systems. However, they also showed that the activation patterns were stronger for real as compared to hypothetical choices.

Promise 2: Confirming or Refining Existing Theories about Mechanisms Underlying Decision Making

In the following, we offer several examples of how neuroscientific methods can provide evidence that argues for or against existing psychological theories in marketing and also how neural data can improve our understanding of the phenomena these theories describe.

Prominent research on brand perception suggests that brands have personalities in a way that is analogous to human personalities, but also has revealed dimensions that are unique to brands (Aaker, 1997). The question of whether brand personalities are indeed perceived in the same way as human ones was examined in an fMRI study comparing the neural activity related to judgments in the two categories (Yoon, Gutchess, Feinberg, & Polk, 2006). They found that judgments about brands and people recruited mostly dissociable neural systems. This suggests that despite apparent similarities in the constructs, individuals process information about brands and humans using fundamentally different mechanisms.

Beyond branding, marketers also often use celebrity endorsements to endow a product with the ability to engage consumers socially. However, it remains unclear why these individuals might be more persuasive than other equally attractive spokespeople. A neuroimaging study examining the use of celebrities when they were (or were not) credible experts on a product provided a deeper understanding of the benefits of expertise, controlling for celebrity. When celebrity spokespeople were credible experts, they could create deeper processing, trust, and possibly deeper encoding for the target product than non-expert celebrities could (Klucharev, Smidts, & Fernández, 2008). A subsequent study by Stallen and colleagues (2010) was able to confirm that the benefits of celebrity itself arise from a transfer of positive affect from the individual to the product, arising from (positive) memories and thoughts about the person.

Moving into the domain of choice, a well-known and well-studied pillar of the marketing literature is the attraction effect (Huber & Puto, 1983). By measuring neural signals during this type of task, Hedgcock and Rao (2009) were able to show evidence that the attraction effect is driven by trade-off aversions, thus providing new links between theories even within the existing consumer psychology literature.

Neuroscience can also support consumer behavior theories related to the question of whether consumers' preferences for an item rely on the awareness of a decision-making context or the need to make a choice. Research in more traditional psychological disciplines has suggested that individuals form and/or retrieve preferences immediately and automatically (e.g., Duckworth, Bargh, Garcia, & Chaiken, 2002; Fazio, Sanbonmatsu, Powell, & Kardes, 1986; Zajonc, 1980). That implies that perceptions of an item's value would be similar when the item was encountered as part of a choice or when it was encountered in a more neutral or goal-free setting. A number of recent fMRI papers have addressed this issue, finding direct evidence that the brain encodes preferences in a way that is relevant for choice even when participants are unconcerned with, or unaware of, any need to make a decision (Lebreton et al., 2009; Levy & Glimcher, 2011; Smith, Bernheim, Camerer, & Rangel, 2014; Tusche, Bode, & Haynes, 2010).

As a specific example, Tusche, Bode, and Haynes (2010) asked one group of fMRI participants to evaluate their preferences for cars they viewed, while a second group saw the cars incidentally during a different task. In both groups, activity in two brain areas (medial prefrontal cortex and insula) significantly predicted behavior when participants were later asked about their desire to purchase the cars. These findings suggest that even in the absence of an explicit decision framing, individuals formed an unconscious preference for the products they viewed, which was highly correlated with the decision value. By supporting psychological research on automatic preference formation, this work offers a useful scaffolding for validating and refining other consumer research models.

Last, neural research has been done on questions arising from the information processing literature suggesting the existence of "dual systems." In these theories, an emotional system (system 1) pushes one toward quick, intuitive and sometimes and suboptimal choices while a second, rational system (system 2) pushes one toward more deliberative and compensatory decisions (Evans, 2003; Kahneman, 2003; Petty & Cacioppo, 1986; Sloman, 1996). However, a neuroimaging investigation found that heuristic-simplifying choices were associated with activation of higher-order, cognitive brain systems, while deliberative choices (consistent with expected utility and cumulative prospect theory models) were associated with activation in lower-order, emotional brain systems (Venkatraman et al., 2009). These results suggest that the standard dual-systems framework may be a potentially misleading oversimplification.

Promise 3: Identifying New Processes in Consumer Decision Making

The new avenues of data provided by neuroscientific methods – and the ability they provide to visualize and track information processes – have tremendous potential for identifying new mechanisms and models in consumer psychology. In this section, we outline some of the research demonstrating this benefit.

A first contribution for identifying new decision processes has come from the study of the role of visual attention for consumer psychology (Milosavljevic & Cerf, 2008). Visual attention alters the quality of incoming information available for consumer decision making. Various studies have applied eye tracking to better understand how several aspects of visual attention affect consumer decision making, ranging from number and length of visual fixations (Krajbich, Armel, & Rangel, 2010; Krajbich, Lu, Camerer, & Rangel, 2012; Krajbich & Rangel, 2011), visual salience of stimuli (Milosavljevic, Navalpakkam, Koch, & Rangel, 2012; Pieters, Rosbergen, & Wedel 1999; Pieters & Wedel, 2004; Towal, Mormann, & Koch, 2013), and subjective meaning of stimuli influenced through branding (Philiastides & Ratcliff, 2013; Wedel & Pieters, 2000). As a whole, these papers highlight the important role that visual attention plays for understanding choices and choice biases. They further demonstrate the ways in which visual attention can be captured using eye tracking, how visual attention can be manipulated (e.g., length of exposure time, visual saliency of object; Itti, Koch, & Niebur, 1998) and also how visual attention as a mechanism can be integrated formally into models of consumer choice using evidence accumulation approaches such as drift diffusion models (Ratcliff, 1980).

A second area that has benefited from the use of neural methods to uncover new mechanisms is the psychology of price. For example, a recent fMRI study by Karmarkar, Shiv, and Knutson (in press) examined how early exposure to price information influences how product value is estimated as well as purchasing decision behavior. Learning price information before seeing a product, as opposed to afterwards, qualitatively changed the way that participants' brains responded to the products they wanted to buy as well as the products they didn't want. Specifically, differences in patterns of medial prefrontal cortex activity (an area correlated with perceptions of monetary value) suggested that seeing price first caused consumers to shift their decision-making process from a question of "Do I like it?" to a question of "Is it worth it?" An additional behavioral experiment supported this novel consumer theory by demonstrating that price-first situations increased consideration of products with a clearly defined "worth" or functional value. Putting price first also increased the correlation between stated willingness to pay and purchase decisions, suggesting that this simple shift in information sequence did indeed change the role of estimated (monetary) value and the overall decision process.

Another example, arising from a study by Mazar, Plassmann, Robataille, and Lindner (2014), provides novel insight on a differing dimension of the psychology of price. Using fMRI, the authors investigated whether paying a given price is similar to anticipating pain as suggested by behavioral economic theories of "pain of paying" (Prelec & Loewenstein, 1998). Their brain imaging results suggest that anticipating paying monetary prices and anticipating pain do indeed recruit similar neural systems, but they found an overlap only in higher-order, affective pain processing regions and not other regions of the "pain-matrix" in the brain. Building on this result, they conducted two behavioral follow-up studies manipulating affective versus somatosensory pain perception during purchasing decisions through priming and placebo studies and found further evidence for this new mechanism of how monetary payments are perceived. Their results indicate that "pain of paying" is not just a metaphor or a mere analytical process as standard economic theories suggest; it is indeed a painful experience, albeit a higher-order, affective experience.

The work described to this point describes several ways in which using neural techniques has proven useful to the field of consumer psychology. These examples also begin to demonstrate the development of consumer neuroscience as its own integrative field of study, as opposed to a collection of research motivated either by brain science or decision science. In the following sections, we explore topics that have become central to the study of consumer neuroscience in terms of present findings as well as future directions.

Neural Prediction of Preferences and Choice

Brain data, particularly from fMRI scans, can track a person's response to various attributes of a decision or decision target. Interestingly, this information is often encountered before a conscious decision is actually made. Due to this, one major and unique area of research that has emerged from the crossover between consumer psychology and neuroscience is the ability to use neural data to *predict* choice, both at the level of individuals and at the level of the population (see also Knutson & Karmarkar, 2014).

Individual-Level Choice Prediction

As is well known in the consumer behavior literature, individual differences, such as a person's thriftiness or need for cognition, can play an important moderating role in his or her decision processes, even when there are systematic biases evident from large-sample or population data. To better understand which elements of neural activity encode specific elements of the decision process, it is common for fMRI studies to model individual responses to various stimuli; these studies have demonstrated an ability to measure individual differences in sensitivity to factors such as anticipated monetary rewards (Knutson, Adams, Fong, & Hommer, 2001). Building on this, measuring activity in specific brain areas during one task has been shown to predict peoples' future behavior on other tasks hours, days, and even months into the future.

For example, Smith et al. (2010) found that activity from a section of vmPFC during exposure to social and monetary rewards predicted the likelihood of "buying" a socially rewarding visual experience just after the scanning session. Other studies focused on activity in brain areas correlated with a person's ability to imagine himself or herself in the future (Ersner-Hershfield, Wimmer, & Knutson, 2008) or imagine his or her enjoyment of an event in the future (Mitchell, Schirmer, Ames, & Gilbert, 2011) to predict the likelihood that their participants would choose a smaller immediate reward over a larger delayed one in decisions made days to weeks after the scanning session.

This predictive ability extends beyond decisions involving spending or money. It is possible to estimate the efficacy of a persuasive message on an individual's later behaviors, such as using sunscreen (Falk et al., 2010 or quitting smoking (Chua et al., 2011; Falk, Berkman, Whalen, & Lieberman, 2011) in advance by analyzing activity in prefrontal cortex. Neural data from the NAcc, which correlates well with more basic, primary reward responses, has also been shown to have predictive power for consumption behavior in regard to food consumption and sexual activities (Demos, Heatherton, & Kelley, 2012).

Population Choice Prediction

Individual-level findings have compelling uses in consumer welfare, but are restricted to predicting an individual's behavior from his or her own brain activity. However, recent research has expanded the generalizability of neural predictions, finding evidence for the usefulness of "neural focus groups." Berns and Moore (2012) scanned people while they were listening to song clips from relatively unknown artists. Three years later, those same songs had achieved varying levels of popularity (as measured by music sales data). The authors found that the participants' average neural activity in the NAcc during the songs was a significant predictor of the song's eventual popularity in the marketplace. Notably, they also found that people's behavioral responses – such as surveys where they rated how much they liked the songs – were not significant predictors, suggesting a distinct and significant benefit of the neural data. In a different study, activity in prefrontal cortex measured from a small group of individuals was similarly able to outperform survey measures in predicting the relative success of different anti-smoking message campaigns nationwide (Falk, Berkman, & Lieberman, 2012).

Predictions of Communication Efficacy

While many of the prediction studies discussed up to this point are focused on value and choice, communication is also an important part of the field. As we have seen, neural data are capable of representing the degree to which an individual finds a message persuasive, insofar as it is likely to influence behavior (e.g. Chua et al., 2011; Falk et al., 2010, 2011). In addition to this, methods have been developed that identify how well or cohesively the intent of a message is communicated. Work by Stephens, Silbert, and Hasson (2010) has shown that the degree of similarity between a source and a recipients' neural activity can indicate the degree to which the message has been "accurately" received. This kind of intersubject correlation (ISC) can also be used to examine how consistently information is processed across multiple individuals receiving the same message (Hasson, 2004). For example, while watching a media clip about a health threat (the H1N1 flu), individuals who perceived the flu as high risk showed a higher ISC in threat-assessment brain areas than individuals with low-risk perceptions (Schmalzle et al., 2013). While these studies focused more on how similarly a message was processed, or the fidelity of its transmission (how well it evoked the desired engagement; see Hasson et al., 2008), recent work has shown that the degree of ISC may even be able to predict population-level preferences for media, such as television shows (Dmochowski et al., 2014).

New Developments and Directions

Consumer neuroscience as a discipline, or even as a subdiscipline of consumer psychology, is still a young field. Even the foundational work has largely been published within the last twenty years. As a result, many of the findings already discussed could be considered "new." However, boosted by its connections to thriving communities in other disciplines, the pace of this research has been quite rapid, creating a platform with which to expand into new directions and/or add insights to existing topics using more of the neuroscience toolkit (Smidts et al., 2014). In this next section, we offer glimpses into some of these developing domains.

Improving Understanding of Demographic Differences

A topic of great interest to consumer researchers is the study of individual differences and their impact on decision behavior, and this is a field where neuroscience can add interesting new insights (Venkatraman et al., 2012).

Individual differences can arise from specific demographic factors such as socioeconomic status or culture. Powerful examples of this can be found in the study of economic choices made by individuals living under conditions of poverty. By measuring or experimentally altering levels of the hormone cortisol (which is released in response to stress), in various populations around the globe, it has been possible to identify links between poverty and stress and to tie those causally to changes in risk-taking behavior (Haushofer & Fehr, 2014).

Similarly cultural neuroscience studies have allowed researchers to better identify links among culture, cognitive and emotional processes, and behavior using neural data as a mediator (e.g., Kitayama & Park, 2010; Kitayama & Uskul, 2011). It is notable that this field of study generally can discriminate between culturally determined differences at the group level and the individual differences or variations that occur within these groups (Na et al., 2010). This suggests that neural data might be useful in identifying whether a particular difference, such as representations of the self, should be considered an individual difference or group difference.

Another demographic factor that has distinct influence on processes in consumer psychology is advanced consumer age (Carpenter & Yoon, 2012; Carstensen et al., 2011; Drolet, Schwarz, & Yoon, 2010; Yoon, Cole, & Lee, 2009). Neuroscientific methods can add important new perspectives to the study of aging consumers (Halfmann, Hedgcock, & Denburg, 2013). The idea behind a "consumer neuroscience of aging" is that the brain networks underlying consumer decision making, and their regulation by neurotransmitters such as dopamine and serotonin, undergo basic biological maturation. Such a maturation can also be linked to changes in plasticity due to the accumulation of experience or changes in motivational goals (Mohr, Li, & Heekeren, 2010; Samanez-Larkin, Li, & Ridderinkhof, 2013). Understanding constraints on brain resources due to aging contributes to better understanding the mechanisms underlying consumer psychology across the life span. For example, several studies have shown a change in the functioning of the mesolimbic dopamine system as one ages that mediates changes in aging consumers' behavior during financial decision making, cognitive control tasks, and intertemporal choice (Cassidy, Hedden, Yoon, & Gutchess, 2014; Denburg et al., 2007; Samanez-Larkin, Kuhnen, Yoo, & Knutson, 2010; Samanez-Larkin et al., 2009; Samanez-Larkin et al., 2011).

Improving Understanding of Individual Differences with Biological Markers

While the previous section discussed a top-down approach of how demographic-driven individual differences can be better understood via neuroscientific techniques, it is also possible to work from the bottom up, using differences in neurobiological markers to explain certain individual differences. Variations in brain structures such as gray matter volume can be linked to individual differences in brain function, personality, and behavior (DeYoung et al., 2010; Newman et al., 2007; Peinemann et al., 2005), possibly because they partly reflect the number and size of neurons and the complexity of their synaptic connections. Likewise, individual anatomical differences – for example, within reward-related dopaminergic pathways – have been linked to significant differences in behavioral effects, including variation of personality traits (Depue & Collins, 1999; Wansink, Payne, & North, 2007).

A recent consumer neuroscience study has applied an automated structural brain imaging approach in combination with traditional experiments to determine individual differences in expectancy effects of marketing actions such as pricing and branding (Plassmann & Weber, in press). Marketing expectancy effects – or sometimes called "Marketing Placebo Effects" – refer to the phenomenon that, for example, a high price tag of a wine changes not only reported measures of how much consumers like a wine but also change the underlying neurobiological processes, such as activity in the brain systems encoding taste pleasantness (Plassmann et al., 2008). Plassmann and Weber (in press) found evidence on both brain and behavioral levels that consumers high in reward seeking, high in need for cognition, and low in somatosensory awareness are more responsive to expectancy effects of marketing actions. Similarly, a study by Gilaie-Dotan and colleagues (2014) used neuroanatomy to estimate the risk attitudes of consumers. They found that the gray matter volume of a region in the right posterior parietal cortex was significantly predictive of individual risk attitudes such that participants with higher gray matter volume in this region exhibited less risk aversion.

It is also possible to examine more fundamental biological markers of individual differences via genetics. Studies on twins have suggested that certain aspects of consumer preferences are heritable and thus likely genetic (e.g., Simonson & Sela, 2011). More directly, neurogenetic studies have identified candidate genes or sequences with ties to decision-related individual differences such as risk taking or prosocial behavior (see Ebstein et al., 2010, for review).

Improving Understanding of "State-dependent" Differences

In this section, we highlight how neuroscience can also reveal variability in decision making that is dependent on being in a particular (temporary) state. When hungry, under stress, or sleep-deprived, we often make very different choices than when faced with the same options under more neutral physiological conditions. Pharmacological interventions and measurements offer an exciting new way to study these differences.

The idea behind this approach is that one potential source of state-dependent variability is the context-sensitive modulation of brain activity by so-called neuromodulators. The term *neuromodulators* refers to neurotransmitters and brain hormones and includes neurotransmitters such as dopamine (reward processing, motivation, and learning) and serotonin (regulation of mood, appetite and sleep, social preferences, memory and learning), as well as hormones such as testosterone, cortisol (stress processing) and oxytocin (social preferences and bonding; see Crockett & Fehr, 2014; Kable, 2011, for further detail).

Put simply, the levels of neuromodulators in the brain are regulated in response to specific states and events in the environment. Their activity in turn influences information processing in related brain systems (Cooper, Bloom, & Roth, 2003; Crockett & Fehr, 2014; Robbins & Arnsten, 2009). Thus, neuro-modulators can be thought of as encoding a context, very broadly defined as features of the external environment (e.g., stressors, competitors, potential mates, or riskiness of a decision) and also internal states (e.g., mood, reproduct-ive status, or hunger levels). Neuromodulators both signal the current context and shape neuronal activity to fit that context adaptively.

The functioning of these neurotransmitters and brain hormones can be integrated into consumer psychology research in at least two ways. The first is to establish associations between peripheral levels of the respective neuromo-dulator and consumer behavior. In the domain of impulsivity and time prefer-ences, a recent study investigated the link between participants' testosterone levels (measured from their saliva) and their preferences for smaller sooner over larger later rewards (Takahashi, Sakaguchi, & Oki, 2006). Interestingly, the study found an inverted-U relationship between delay discounting of gains and salivary testosterone levels, providing some of the first evidence that testoster-one might increase the discounting rate for gains over time in distinctly non-impulsive individuals, and also increase the discounting rate for gains over time in impulsive individuals. Another example associating neuromodulators with decision-making behavior is a recent study by Chumbley and colleagues (2014). The authors investigated the link between participants' endogenous cortisol levels (assayed using hair samples) and behavioral measures of loss and risk aversion. They found that the higher endogenous cortisol levels, the lower a participant's loss aversion, but *not* their risk aversion.

A second avenue for pursuing research with neuromodulators is to manipu-late neuromodulator systems, thus providing causal evidence for brain–behavior relationships. It is important to note that direct oral or intravenous administration of neuromodulators is not generally possible except for testoster-one and cortisol, because most of these molecules cannot cross the blood–brain barrier. For some neuromodulators such as oxytocin, a nasal administration, which bypasses this barrier, might be possible. However, the mechanisms by which intranasally administered neuromodulators might enter the brain remain unclear (Churchland & Winkielman, 2012). Instead, it is better understood how to directly stimulate or block neuromodulator *receptors*, which are the targets of these biochemical agents, along with other pharmacological agents. Such agents can be antagonists that impair neuromodulator functioning or agonists that increase neuromodulator functioning.

A study of relevance to consumer neuroscience by Pessiglione and colleagues (2006) has administered dopamine antagonists and agonists to impair and increase dopaminergic functioning in the brain during a preference learning task. The authors found a difference in how learning is guided by rewards depending on whether participants were treated with a dopamine agonist or antagonist. Their results indicate that decreasing and increasing dopaminergic functioning can account for how consumers learn to improve future decisions.

Overall, understanding the pharmacology underlying consumer behavior can generate exciting new avenues for consumer neuroscience that allows for establishing correlational and, more importantly, causal links between the brain and behavior.

Inferring Psychological Processes from Brain Imaging Data

Consumer neuroscience strives to understand the relationship between psychological processes relevant for consumer behavior and brain function. In an ideal world, the activation of a brain system such as the vmPFC and striatum would be indicative of the involvement of a specific psychological process, such as liking for a product. Such backward engineering from brain activity patterns to a psychological processes, or reverse inference (Poldrack, 2006, 2011a), is made particularly difficult by the fact that brain systems are involved in multiple processes, and a one-to-one brain-to-function mapping is rarely possible. The neuroimaging work described in this chapter has generally followed a different type of inference: the experimenter manipulates a specific psychological process, such as having participants think of how much they are willing to pay for a product, and then identifies the localized effects of that manipulation on brain activity, such as in the vmPFC (e.g. Hare et al., 2008; Plassmann, O'Doherty, & Rangel, 2007). This has been referred to as "forward inference" (Henson, 2006). However, the desire to reason backward from patterns of activation to infer the engagement of specific psychological processes is increasing in consumer neuroscience research since it could offer important new paths for theoretical advances. (Knutson & Karmarkar, 2014). In the following, we discuss two recent developments toward reaching the goal of "decoding" psychological processes from brain activations.

A Probabilistic Framework for Reverse Inference: Meta-Analysis

Meta-analyses across the increasing number of neuroimaging studies (Bartra, McGuire, & Kable, 2010; Clithero & Rangel, 2013; Yarkoni, Poldrack, Van Essen, & Wager, 2010) can provide statistical measures to quantify the validity of reverse inferences and show strong evidence for some brain behavior relationships for some cases (e.g., activation in the striatum and anticipated positive affect, Knutson & Greer, 2008) but much weaker for others (e.g., activation in the insula and feelings of love; Lindstrom, 2011; Poldrack, 2011b).

An interesting approach to synthesize maps of brain structure to brain function based on Bayesian statistics has been made by Yarkoni and colleagues (2011). Their "Neurosynth" framework (www.neurosynth.org) combines meta-analyses with text-mining techniques to provide several statistical measures for reverse inference. By taking advantage of large numbers of experiments studying varying facets of similar questions, this effort seems a very suitable way to address the problems that often arise from narrow attempts at reverse inference (for details, see Yarkoni et al., 2011).

A Formal Framework for Reverse Inference: Brain Decoding

Another recent approach provides the ability to formally test the inference of psychological states from neuroimaging data (Haynes & Rees, 2006; Norman, Polyn, Detre, & Haxby, 2006; Pereira, Mitchell, & Botvinick, 2009; Tong & Pratte, 2012). Such a "brain reading" approach uses tools from the field of machine learning to create statistical machines that can accurately decode the psychological state that is represented by a particular brain imaging data set. For example, in a decoding study of free decisions, such as deciding to press a button with one's left or right hand at a spontaneous point in time depending on one's urge to do so, participants showed expected evidence of motor preparatory activity a few seconds in advance of their action (Soon, Brass, Heinze, & Haynes, 2008). Interestingly, however, a bias in activity was observed in the prefrontal and parietal cortex up to 10 seconds prior to the participant's response. These findings suggest the existence of some sort of preconscious bias in the decision-making process (Soon et al., 2008).

On the whole, the discussed probabilistic and formal approaches attempting to infer psychological processes from brain data face several limitations and are still in their infancy (Poldrack, 2011a), but already show interesting future avenues for consumer neuroscience.

Conclusions

In the course of this chapter, we have provided an introduction to the use of neuroscientific methods in consumer psychology by giving an overview of the foundations of consumer neuroscience as well as current research and new developments in the field. These techniques are exciting and extremely powerful. However, as reflected by the responses to our survey of consumer neuroscience academics, they are most useful as a complement, rather than a substitute, to existing methodology. That is, the type of data provided by each technique has both benefits and drawbacks. The techniques may be well suited to providing insight into one type of question, but inappropriate (or overly costly) for others. Importantly, this chapter also demonstrates that the benefit of neuroscience is not limited to its tools. Adding this discipline can enrich theorizing in consumer psychology, allowing it the potential to become an important part of the field. Overall, consumer neuroscience allows behavioral researchers turn the "black box of the consumer's mind into an aquarium" (Smidts, 2005).

References

Aaker, J. L. (1997). Dimensions of brand personality. *Journal of Marketing Research, 34* (3), 347–356.

Allison, R. I., & Uhl, K. P. (1964). Influence of beer brand identification on taste perception. *Journal of Marketing Research, 1*(3), 36–39.

Ariely, D., & Berns, G. S. (2010). Neuromarketing: The hope and hype of neuroimaging in business. *Nature Reviews. Neuroscience, 11*(4), 284–292.

Bartra, O., McGuire, J. T., & Kable, J. W. (2010). The valuation system: A coordinate-based meta-analysis of BOLD fMRI experiments examining neural correlates of subjective value. *NeuroImage, 76*, 1–16.

Becker, G. M., Degroot, M. H., & Marschak, J. (1964). Measuring utility by a single-response sequential method. *Behavioral Science, 9*(3), 226–232.

Berns, G. S., & Moore, S. E. (2012). A neural predictor of cultural popularity. *Journal of Consumer Psychology, 22*(1), 154–160.

Cacioppo, J. T., Tassinary, L. G., & Berntson, G. (2007). *Handbook of Psychophysiology*. New York: Cambridge University Press.

Camerer, C. F., Loewenstein, G., & Prelec, D. (2004). Neuroeconomics: Why economics needs brains. *Scandinavian Journal of Economics, 106*(3), 555–579.

Carpenter, S. M., & Yoon, C. (2012). Aging and consumer decision making. *Annals of the New York Academy of Sciences, 1235*(1), 1–12.

Carstensen, L. L., Turan, B., Scheibe, S., Ram, N., Ersner-Hershfield, H., Samanez-Larkin, G. R., et al. (2011). Emotional experience improves with age: Evidence based on over 10 years of experience sampling. *Psychology and Aging, 26*(1), 21–33.

Cassidy, B. S., Hedden, T., Yoon, C., & Gutchess, A. H. (2014). Age differences in medial prefrontal activity for subsequent memory of truth value. *Frontiers in Psychology, 5*, 87.

Chua, H. F., Ho, S. S., Jasinska, A. J., Polk, T. A., Welsh, R. C., Liberzon, I., & Strecher, V. J. (2011). Self-related neural response to tailored smoking-cessation messages predicts quitting. *Nature, 14*(4), 426–427.

Chumbley, J. R., Krajbich, I., Engelmann, J. B., Russell, E., Van Uum, S., Koren, G., & Fehr, E. (2014). Endogenous cortisol predicts decreased loss aversion in young men. *Psychological Science, 25*(11), 2102–2105.

Clithero, J. A., & Rangel, A. (2013). Informatic parcellation of the network involved in the computation of subjective value. *Social Cognitive and Affective Neuroscience. 9*(9), 1289–1302.

Cooper, J. R., Bloom, F. E., & Roth, R. H. (2003). *The Biochemical Basis of Neuropharmacology*. Oxford: Oxford University Press.

Churchland, P. S., & Winkielman, P. (2012). Modulating social behavior with oxytocin: How does it work? What does it mean? *Hormones and Behavior, 61*(3), 392–399.

Crockett, M. J., & Fehr, E. (2014). Pharmacology of economic and social decision making. In P. Glimcher & E. Fehr (eds.), *Neuroeconomics: Decision-Making and the Brain* (pp. 259–279). London: Elsevier.

Demos, K. E., Heatherton, T. F., & Kelley, W. M. (2012). Individual differences in nucleus accumbens activity to food and sexual images predict weight gain and sexual behavior. *Journal of Neuroscience, 32*(16), 5549–5552.

Denburg, N. L., Cole, C. A., Hernandez, M., Yamada, T. H., Tranel, D., Bechara, A., & Wallace, R. B. (2007). The orbitofrontal cortex, real-world decision making, and normal aging. *Annals of the New York Academy of Sciences, 1121*, 480–498.

Deppe, M., Schwindt, W., Kugel, H., Plassmann, H., & Kenning, P. (2005). Nonlinear responses within the medial prefrontal cortex reveal when specific implicit information influences economic decision making. *Journal of Neuroimaging, 15*(2), 171–182.

Depue, R. A. R., & Collins, P. F. P. (1999). Neurobiology of the structure of personality: dopamine, facilitation of incentive motivation, and extraversion. *Behavioral and Brain Sciences, 22*(3), 491–469.

DeYoung, C. G., Hirsh, J. B., Shane, M. S., Papademetris, X., Rajeevan, N., & Gray, J. R. (2010). Testing predictions from personality neuroscience: Brain structure and the big five. *Psychological Science, 21*(6), 820–828.

Dmochowski, J. P., Bezdek, M. A., Abelson, B. P., Johnson, J. S., Schumacher, E. H., & Parra, L. C. (2014). Audience preferences are predicted by temporal reliability of neural processing. *Nature Communications, 5*, 1–9.

Drolet, A. L., Schwarz, N., & Yoon, C. (2010). *The Aging Consumer*. New York: Routledge.

Duckworth, K. L., Bargh, J. A., Garcia, M., & Chaiken, S. (2002). The automatic evaluation of novel stimuli. *Psychological Science, 13*(6), 513–519.

Ebstein, R. P., Israel, S., Chew, S. H., Zhong, S., & Knafo, A. (2010). Genetics of human social behavior. *Neuron, 65*(6), 831–844.

Erk, S., Spitzer, M., Wunderlich, A. P., Galley, L., & Walter, H. (2002). Cultural objects modulate reward circuitry. *Neuroreport, 13*(18), 2499–2503.

Ersner-Hershfield, H., Wimmer, G. E., & Knutson, B. (2008). Saving for the future self: Neural measures of future self-continuity predict temporal discounting. *Social Cognitive and Affective Neuroscience, 4*(1), 85–92.

Esch, F. R., Möll, T., Schmitt, B., Elger, C. E., Neuhaus, C., & Weber, B. (2012). Brands on the brain: What happens neurophysiologically when consumers process and evaluate brands. *Journal of Consumer Psychology, 22*(1), 75–85.

Evans, J. S. B. T. (2003). In two minds: dual-process accounts of reasoning. *Trends in Cognitive Sciences, 7*(10), 454–459.

Falk, E. B., Berkman, E. T., & Lieberman, M. D. (2012). From neural responses to population behavior: Neural focus group predicts population-level media effects. *Psychological Science, 23*(5), 439–445.

Falk, E. B., Berkman, E. T., Mann, T., Harrison, B., & Lieberman, M. D. (2010). Predicting persuasion-induced behavior change from the brain. *Journal of Neuroscience, 30*(25), 8421–8424.

Falk, E. B., Berkman, E. T., Whalen, D., & Lieberman, M. D. (2011). Neural activity during health messaging predicts reductions in smoking above and beyond self-report. *Health Psychology, 30*(2), 177–185.

Fazio, R. H., Sanbonmatsu, D. M., Powell, M. C., & Kardes, F. R. (1986). On the automatic activation of attitudes. *Journal of Personality and Social Psychology, 50*(2), 229–238.

Feldman, J. M., & Lynch, J. G. (1988). Self-generated validity and other effects of measurement on belief, attitude, intention, and behavior. *Journal of Applied Psychology, 73*(3), 421–435.

Gilaie-Dotan, S., Tymula, A., Cooper, N., Kable, J. W., Glimcher, P. W., & Levy, I. (2014). Neuroanatomy predicts individual risk attitudes. *Journal of Neuroscience, 34*(37), 12394–12401.

Halfmann, K., Hedgcock, W., & Denburg, N. L. (2013). Age-related differences in discounting future gains and losses. *Journal of Neuroscience, Psychology, and Economics, 6*(1), 42–54.

Hare, T. A., O'Doherty, J., Camerer, C. F., Schultz, W., & Rangel, A. (2008). Dissociating the role of the orbitofrontal cortex and the striatum in the computation of goal values and prediction errors. *Journal of Neuroscience, 28*(22), 5623–5630.

Hasson, U. (2004). Intersubject synchronization of cortical activity during natural vision. *Science, 303*(5664), 1634–1640.

Hasson, U., Landesman, O., Knappmeyer, B., Vallines, I., Rubin, N., & Heeger, D. J. (2008). Neurocinematics: The neuroscience of film. *Projections, 2*(1), 1–26.

Haushofer, J., & Fehr, E. (2014). On the psychology of poverty. *Science, 344*(6186), 862–867.

Haynes, J.-D., & Rees, G. (2006). Decoding mental states from brain activity in humans. *Nature Reviews. Neuroscience, 7*(7), 523–534.

Hedden, T., & Gabrieli, J. D. E. (2004). Insights into the ageing mind: A view from cognitive neuroscience. *Nature Reviews. Neuroscience, 5*(2), 87–96.

Hedgcock, W., & Rao, A. R. (2009). Trade-off aversion as an explanation for the attraction effect: A functional magnetic resonance imaging study. *Journal of Marketing Research, 46*(1), 1–13.

Henson, R. (2006). Forward inference using functional neuroimaging: Dissociations versus associations. *Trends in Cognitive Sciences, 10*(2), 64–69.

Huber, J., & Puto, C. (1983). Market boundaries and product choice: Illustrating attraction and substitution effects. *Journal of Consumer Research, 10*(1), 31–44.

Itti, L., Koch, C., & Niebur, E. (1998). A model of saliency-based visual attention for rapid scene analysis. *IEEE Transactions on Pattern Analysis and Machine Intelligence, 20*(11), 1254–1259.

Kable, J. W. (2011). The cognitive neuroscience toolkit for the neuroeconomist: A functional overview. *Journal of Neuroscience, Psychology, and Economics, 4*(2), 63–84.

Kahneman, D. (2003). A perspective on judgment and choice: mapping bounded rationality. *American Psychologist, 58*(9), 697–720.

Kang, M. J., Rangel, A., Camus, M., & Camerer, C. F. (2011). Hypothetical and real choice differentially activate common valuation areas. *Journal of Neuroscience, 31*(2), 461–468.

Karmarkar, U. R., Shiv, S., & Knutson, B. (in press). "Cost conscious? The neural and behavioral impact of price primacy on decision-making." *Journal of Marketing Research*.

Kitayama, S., & Park, J. (2010). Cultural neuroscience of the self: Understanding the social grounding of the brain. *Social Cognitive and Affective Neuroscience, 5*(2–3), 111–129.

Kitayama, S., & Uskul, A. K. (2011). Culture, mind, and the brain: current evidence and future directions. *Annual Review of Psychology, 62*(1), 419–449.

Klucharev, V., Smidts, A., & Fernández, G. (2008). Brain mechanisms of persuasion: How expert power modulates memory and attitudes. *Social Cognitive and Affective Neuroscience, 3*(4), 353–366.

Knutson, B., Adams, C. M., Fong, G. W., & Hommer, D. (2001). Anticipation of increasing monetary reward selectively recruits nucleus accumbens. *Journal of Neuroscience, 21*(16), 1–15.

Knutson, B., & Greer, S. M. (2008). Anticipatory affect: Neural correlates and consequences for choice. *Philosophical Transactions of the Royal Society B: Biological Sciences, 363*(1511), 3771–3786.

Knutson, B., & Karmarkar, U. (2014). Appetite, consumption, and choice in the human brain. In S. D. Preston, M. Kringelbach, & B. Knutson (eds.), *The Interdisciplinary Science of Consumption* (pp. 163–184). Cambridge, MA: MIT Press.

Knutson, B., Rick, S., Wimmer, G. E., Prelec, D., & Loewenstein, G. (2007). Neural predictors of purchases. *Neuron, 53*(1), 147–156.

Krajbich, I., Armel, C., & Rangel, A. (2010). Visual fixations and the computation and comparison of value in simple choice. *Nature, 13*(10), 1292–1298.

Krajbich, I., Lu, D., Camerer, C., & Rangel, A. (2012). The attentional drift-diffusion model extends to simple purchasing decisions. *Frontiers in Psychology, 3*, 193.

Krajbich, I., & Rangel, A. (2011). Multialternative drift-diffusion model predicts the relationship between visual fixations and choice in value-based decisions. *Proceedings of the National Academy of Sciences, 108*(33), 13852–13857.

Ladik, D. M. (2008). Where is the cutting edge? Presented at the AMA Summer Educators' Conference, San Diego, CA, USA.

Lebreton, M., Jorge, S., Michel, V., Thirion, B., & Pessiglione, M. (2009). An automatic valuation system in the human brain: Evidence from functional neuroimaging. *Neuron, 64*(3), 431–439.

Lee, L., Frederick, S., & Ariely, D. (2006). Try it, you'll like it the influence of expectation, consumption, and revelation on preferences for beer. *Psychological Science, 17*(12), 1054–1058.

Levy, D. J., & Glimcher, P. W. (2011). Comparing apples and oranges: Using reward-specific and reward-general subjective value representation in the brain. *Journal of Neuroscience, 31*(41), 14693–14707.

Lindstrom, M. (2011), "You love your iPhone. Literally." *New York Times*, October 10. Available at www.nytimes.com/2011/10/01/opinion/you-love-your-iphone-literally.html (accessed January 11, 2012).

Mazar, N., Plassmann, H., Robataille, N. & Lindner, A. (2014). Pain of paying – a metaphor gone literal: Evidence from neurobiology and behavioral decision making. INSEAD Working Paper.

McClure, S. M., Li, J., Tomlin, D., Cypert, K. S., Montague, L. M., & Montague, P. R. (2004). Neural correlates of behavioral preference for culturally familiar drinks. *Neuron, 44*(2), 379–387.

Milosavljevic, M., & Cerf, M. (2008). First attention then intention: Insights from computational neuroscience of vision. *International Journal of Advertising, 27*(3), 381–398.

Milosavljevic, M., Navalpakkam, V., Koch, C., & Rangel, A. (2012). Relative visual saliency differences induce sizable bias in consumer choice. *Journal of Consumer Psychology, 22*(1), 67–74.

Mitchell, J. P., Schirmer, J., Ames, D. L., & Gilbert, D. T. (2011). Medial prefrontal cortex predicts intertemporal choice. *Journal of Cognitive Neuroscience, 23*(4), 857–866.

Mohr, P. N. C., Li, S.-C., & Heekeren, H. R. (2010). Neuroeconomics and aging: Neuromodulation of economic decision making in old age. *Neuroscience & Biobehavioral Reviews, 34*(5), 678–688.

Na, J., Grossmann, I., Varnum, M. E. W., Kitayama, S., Gonzalez, R., & Nisbett, R. E. (2010). Cultural differences are not always reducible to individual differences. *Proceedings of the National Academy of Sciences of the United States of America, 107*(14), 6192–6197.

Newman, L. M., Trivedi, M. A., Bendlin, B. B., Ries, M. L., & Johnson, S. C. (2007). The relationship between gray matter morphometry and neuropsychological performance in a large sample of cognitively healthy adults. *Brain Imaging and Behavior, 1*(1–2), 3–10.

Norman, K. A., Polyn, S. M., Detre, G. J., & Haxby, J. V. (2006). Beyond mind-reading: Multi-voxel pattern analysis of fMRI data. *Trends in Cognitive Sciences, 10*(9), 424–430.

Peinemann, A., Schuller, S., Pohl, C., Jahn, T., Weindl, A., & Kassubek, J. (2005). Executive dysfunction in early stages of Huntington's disease is associated with striatal and insular atrophy: A neuropsychological and voxel-based morphometric study. *Journal of the Neurological Sciences, 239*(1), 11–19.

Pereira, F., Mitchell, T., & Botvinick, M. (2009). Machine learning classifiers and fMRI: A tutorial overview. *NeuroImage, 45*(1), S199–S209.

Pessiglione, M., Seymour, B., Flandin, G., Dolan, R. J., & Frith, C. D. (2006). Dopamine-dependent prediction errors underpin reward-seeking behaviour in humans. *Nature, 442*(7106), 1042–1045.

Petty, R. E., & Cacioppo, J. T. (1986). The elaboration likelihood model of persuasion. *Advances in Experimental Social Psychology, 19*, 123–162.

Philiastides, M. G., & Ratcliff, R. (2013). Influence of branding on preference-based decision making. *Psychological Science, 24*(7), 1208–1215.

Pieters, R., & Wedel, M. (2004). Attention capture and transfer in advertising: Brand, pictorial, and text-size effects. *Journal of Marketing, 68*(4), 36–50.

Pieters, R. Rosbergen, E. & Wedel, M. (1999). Visual attention to repeated print advertising: A test of scanpath theory. *Journal of Marketing Research, 36*(4), 424.

Plassmann, H., Ambler, T., & Braeutigam, S. (2007). What can advertisers learn from neuroscience? *International Journal of Advertising, 26*(2), 151–175.

Plassmann, H., O'Doherty, J. P., & Rangel, A. (2010). Appetitive and aversive goal values are encoded in the medial orbitofrontal cortex at the time of decision making. *Journal of Neuroscience, 30*(32), 10799–10808.

Plassmann, H., O'Doherty, J. P., & Rangel, A. (2007). Orbitofrontal cortex encodes willingness to pay in everyday economic transactions. *Journal of Neuroscience, 27*(37), 9984–9988.

Plassmann, H., O'Doherty, J. P., Shiv, B., & Rangel, A. (2008). Marketing actions can modulate neural representations of experienced pleasantness. *Proceedings of the National Academy of Sciences of the United States of America, 105*(3), 1050–1054.

Plassmann, H., Ramsøy, T. Z., & Milosavljevic, M. (2012). Branding the brain: A critical review and outlook. *Journal of Consumer Psychology, 22*(1), 18–36.

Plassmann, H., & Wager, T. D. (2014). How expectancies shape consumption experiences. In M. Kringelbach, B. Knutson, & S. Preston (eds.), *The Interdisciplinary Science of Consumption* (pp. 219–240). Cambridge, MA: MIT Press.

Plassmann, H. & Weber, B. (in press). Individual differences in marketing placebo effects: Evidence from brain imaging and behavioral experiments. *Journal of Marketing Research*.

Plassmann, H., Yoon, C., Feinberg, F. M., & Shiv, B. (2010). Consumer neuroscience. In J. Sheth & N. Malhotra, *Wiley International Encyclopedia of Marketing* (pp. 115–122). Chichester, UK: John Wiley & Sons, Ltd.

Poldrack, R. A. (2006). Can cognitive processes be inferred from neuroimaging data? *Trends in Cognitive Sciences, 10*(2), 59–63.

Poldrack, R. A. (2011a). Inferring mental states from neuroimaging data: From reverse inference to large-scale decoding. *Neuron, 72*(5), 692–697.

Poldrack, R. A. (2011b). NYT Op-Ed + fMRI = complete crap. Available at http://www.russpoldrack.org/2011/10/nyt-editorial-fmri-complete-crap.html (accessed January 11, 2012).

Prelec, D., & Loewenstein, G. (1998). The red and the black: Mental accounting of savings and debt. *Marketing Science 17*(1), 4–28.

Ratcliff, R. (1980). A note on modeling accumulation of information when the rate of accumulation changes over time. *Journal of Mathematical Psychology, 21*(2), 178–184.

Reimann, M., Zaichkowsky, J., Neuhaus, C., Bender, T., & Weber, B. (2010). Aesthetic package design: A behavioral, neural, and psychological investigation. *Journal of Consumer Psychology, 20*(4), 431–441.

Reutskaja, E., Nagel, R., Camerer, C. F., & Rangel, A. (2011). Search dynamics in consumer choice under time pressure: An eye-tracking study. *American Economic Review, 101*(2), 900–926.

Robbins, T. W., & Arnsten, A. F. T. (2009). The neuropsychopharmacology of fronto-executive function: Monoaminergic modulation. *Annual Review of Neuroscience, 32*(1), 267–287.

Rosbergen, E., Pieters, R., & Wedel, M. (1997). Visual attention to advertising: A segment-level analysis. *Journal of Consumer Research, 24*(3), 305–314.

Samanez-Larkin, G. R., Kuhnen, C. M., Yoo, D. J., & Knutson, B. (2010). Variability in nucleus accumbens activity mediates age-related suboptimal financial risk taking. *Journal of Neuroscience, 30*(4), 1426–1434.

Samanez-Larkin, G. R., Li, S.-C., & Ridderinkhof, K. R. (2013). Complementary approaches to the study of decision making across the adult life span. *Frontiers in Neuroscience, 7*, 243.

Samanez-Larkin, G. R., Mata, R., Radu, P. T., Ballard, I. C., Carstensen, L. L., & McClure, S. M. (2011). Age differences in striatal delay sensitivity during intertemporal choice in healthy adults. *Frontiers in Neuroscience, 5*, 1–12.

Samanez-Larkin, G. R., Robertson, E. R., Mikels, J. A., Carstensen, L. L., & Gotlib, I. H. (2009). Selective attention to emotion in the aging brain. *Psychology and Aging, 24*(3), 519–529.

Schaefer, M., Berens, H., Heinze, H. J., & Rotte, M. (2006). Neural correlates of culturally familiar brands of car manufacturers. *NeuroImage, 31*(2), 861–865.

Schaefer, M., & Rotte, M. (2007). Favorite brands as cultural objects modulate reward circuit. *Neuroreport, 18*(2), 141–145.

Schmalzle, R., Hacker, F., Renner, B., Honey, C. J., & Schupp, H. T. (2013). Neural correlates of risk perception during real-life risk communication. *Journal of Neuroscience, 33*(25), 10340–10347.

Simonson, I., & Sela, A. (2011). On the heritability of consumer decision making: An exploratory approach for studying genetic effects on judgment and choice. *Journal of Consumer Research, 37*(6), 951–966.

Sloman, S. A. (1996). The empirical case for two systems of reasoning. *Psychological Bulletin, 119*(1), 3–22.

Smidts, A. (2005). *Keynote Lecture.* Presented at the 2nd Conference on NeuroEconomics (ConNECs), Muenster, Germany (June 5).

Smidts, A., Hsu, M., Sanfey, A. G., Boksem, M. A., Ebstein, R. B., Huettel, S. A., Yoon, C., et al. (2014). Advancing consumer neuroscience. *Marketing Letters, 25*(3), 257–267.

Smith, A., Bernheim, B. D., Camerer, C. F., & Rangel, A. (2014). Neural activity reveals preferences without choices. *American Economic Journal: Microeconomics, 6*(2), 1–36.

Smith, D. V., Hayden, B. Y., Truong, T. K., Song, A. W., Platt, M. L., & Huettel, S. A. (2010). Distinct value signals in anterior and posterior ventromedial prefrontal cortex. *Journal of Neuroscience, 30*(7), 2490–2495.

Soon, C. S., Brass, M., Heinze, H.-J., & Haynes, J.-D. (2008). Unconscious determinants of free decisions in the human brain. *Nature Neuroscience, 11*(5), 543–545.

Stallen, M., Smidts, A., Rijpkema, M., Smit, G., Klucharev, V., & Fernández, G. (2010). Celebrities and shoes on the female brain: The neural correlates of product evaluation in the context of fame. *Journal of Economic Psychology, 31*(5), 802–811.

Stephens, G. J., Silbert, L. J., & Hasson, U. (2010). Speaker-listener neural coupling underlies successful communication. *Proceedings of the National Academy of Sciences, 107*(32), 14425–14430.

Takahashi, T., Sakaguchi, K., & Oki, M. (2006). Testosterone levels and discounting delayed monetary gains and losses in male humans. *Neuroendocrinology Letters, 27*(4), 439–444.

Tong, F., & Pratte, M. S. (2012). Decoding patterns of human brain activity. *Annual Review of Psychology, 63*(1), 483–509.

Towal, R. B., Mormann, M., & Koch, C. (2013). Simultaneous modeling of visual saliency and value computation improves predictions of economic choice. *Proceedings of the National Academy of Sciences, 110*(40), 15853–15854.

Tusche, A., Bode, S., & Haynes, J. D. (2010). Neural responses to unattended products predict later consumer choices. *Journal of Neuroscience, 30*(23), 8024–8031.

Venkatraman, V., Clithero, J. A., Fitzsimons, G. J., & Huettel, S. A. (2012). New scanner data for brand marketers: How neuroscience can help better understand differences in brand preferences. *Journal of Consumer Psychology, 22*(1), 143–153.

Venkatraman, V., Payne, J. W., Bettman, J. R., Luce, M. F., & Huettel, S. A. (2009). Separate neural mechanisms underlie choices and strategic preferences in risky decision making. *Neuron, 62*(4), 593–602.

Wansink, B., Payne, C. R., & North, J. (2007). Fine as North Dakota wine: Sensory expectations and the intake of companion foods. *Physiology & Behavior, 90*(5), 712–716.

Wedel, M., & Pieters, R. (2000). Eye fixations on advertisements and memory for brands: A model and findings. *Marketing Science, 19*(4), 297–312.

Willemsen, M. C., & Johnson, E. J. (2011). Visiting the decision factory: Observing cognition with MouselabWEB and other information acquisition methods. In M. Schulte-Mecklenbeck, A. Kühberger, & R. Ranyard (eds.), *A Handbook of Process Tracing Methods for Decision Research: A Critical Review and Users Guide* (pp. 19–42). New York: Taylor & Francis.

Yarkoni, T., Poldrack, R. A., Nichols, T. E., Van Essen, D. C., & Wager, T. D. (2011). Large-scale automated synthesis of human functional neuroimaging data. *Nature Methods, 8*(8), 665–670.

Yarkoni, T., Poldrack, R. A., Van Essen, D. C., & Wager, T. D. (2010). Cognitive neuroscience 2.0: Building a cumulative science of human brain function. *Trends in Cognitive Sciences, 14*(11), 489–496.

Yoon, C., Cole, C. A., & Lee, M. P. (2009). Consumer decision making and aging: Current knowledge and future directions. *Journal of Consumer Psychology, 19* (1), 2–16.

Yoon, C., Gutchess, A. H., Feinberg, F., & Polk, T. A. (2006). A functional magnetic resonance imaging study of neural dissociations between brand and person judgments. *Journal of Consumer Research, 33*(1), 31–40.

Zajonc, R. B. (1980). Feeling and thinking: Preferences need no inferences. *American Psychologist, 35*(2), 151–175.

7 Developmental Consumer Psychology

Children in the Twenty-First Century

Lan Nguyen Chaplin and Paul M. Connell

> Three year-old Amara can't identify money denominations, but she knows you exchange money for things you want, like food and toys. To Amara, brands are names of stores and commercials are entertaining and truthful. But for all the things she doesn't know, she has the admirable curiosity to ask one hundred questions a day.

> Armed with more consumption knowledge, seven-year-old Willhelm can correctly identify all money denominations but still thinks a box of Legos costing $189 is "not bad" since you get more than six hundred pieces. He recognizes some brands to be "expensive and for rich people" and that commercials try to get you to buy. What he doesn't know, he has the admirable curiosity to ask *almost* as many questions a day as he did when he was Amara's age.

Consumer socialization is defined as the process by which children acquire marketplace knowledge and skills (Ward, 1974) and is the cornerstone of developmental consumer psychology. The social and cultural benefits to understanding how children develop consumption knowledge, behaviors, and values are plentiful (see John 1999). However, top journals specializing in the consumer context such as the *Journal of Consumer Research (JCR)* and the *Journal of Consumer Psychology (JCP)* have published surprisingly little research in the area of developmental consumer psychology – fewer than twenty papers have been published in the last decade. The few studies that have been published in these leading journals have yielded a remarkable set of findings across a range of topics, including children's happiness with products and brands, brand understanding, materialism, consumption symbolism, and media effects on children.

We have three goals for this chapter. First, we present our view of twenty-first-century young consumers (from preschool age through adolescence) with an emphasis on cutting-edge research across disciplines (e.g., consumer research, child development, health and nutrition, public policy, media consumption). Given the growing presence of media in children's lives, we discuss many findings on media effects on children's consumption throughout the chapter, but we also discuss surprisingly underresearched topics such as children's understanding of money as well as children's happiness with possessions and experiences.

Second, in the spirit of emphasizing the most recent advances in developmental consumer psychology, we select three topics to discuss at a deeper level:

children's materialism, health-related risky behavior, and online risky behavior. These topics are of escalating interest and concern among parents, educators, researchers, and those in the public policy sector. We highlight important and unanswered questions in these areas.

Finally, we provide a future research agenda with a focus on three testable strategies to curb materialism and risky behaviors in children: (1) build their self-esteem, (2) encourage them to be grateful, and (3) foster their prospection abilities. We offer these strategies as alternatives or supplements to government interventions, which have proven to be very time consuming and difficult to implement. We also discuss two simple yet surprisingly underutilized strategies that may be effective in fostering children's self-esteem and prospection abilities: (1) encourage them to free play, and (2) allow them to safely experience failure.

This research agenda answers Olson and Dweck's (2008) call for developmental research to take a social-cognitive approach. For the purposes of this chapter, this means integrating cognitive development with social learning models to move the area of developmental consumer psychology forward (e.g., how parents or educators can help children develop and use cognitive defenses against advertising, online content, and other potentially risky sources of information). Throughout the chapter, we make suggestions for novel and engaging methodologies suitable for use with children across a wide age range.

Are Twenty-First-Century Children Savvy Consumers?

Children and adolescents spend more time consuming media than doing any other activity except for sleeping (Strasburger, 2011). They are consuming more types of media and using these different media simultaneously (e.g., watching television while "tweeting" a message from their Twitter account and posting a "selfie" on Instagram). And they are initiating media consumption at younger ages (Common Sense Media, 2011; Kaiser Family Foundation, 2010).

The proliferation of media technologies and children's increased use of them has raised the question of whether today's children are better able to cope with marketing messages than the children who served as participants in foundational research in the 1970s and 1980s (e.g., Brucks, Armstrong, & Goldberg, 1988; Butter, Popovich, Stackhouse, & Garner, 1981; Donahue, Henke, & Donahue, 1980; Robertson & Rossiter, 1974; Ward, Reale, & Levinson, 1972; Ward, Wackman, & Wartella, 1977). Because today's children have more experience with marketing messages disseminated across a growing number of media platforms, we often hear that they are savvier than children of yesteryear. But what does being media savvy mean in a consumption context? If it means having easy access to multiple media platforms, spending more time consuming media than ever before, and subsequently being oversaturated with marketing messages, then, yes, children today are savvier than children of the past and perhaps even adults. However, if being media savvy requires more advanced sociocognitive skills to make sense of the multitude of marketing messages across different media platforms (e.g., having more cognitive defenses, or developing advertising and other marketplace knowledge at an earlier age than what classic studies have found), the answer may not be as straightforward.

We begin a discussion on this intriguing issue by looking at two important subareas of developmental consumer psychology. The first has received a great deal of attention from researchers and the second has received surprisingly little attention: (1) the effects of advertising on children and (2) the meaning of money to children. It is important to start a discussion of this issue not only to help children successfully navigate their increasingly consumption-concentrated world but also due to the ethical implications of marketing toward children.

Effects of Advertising on Children

Recent replications corroborate classic findings that demonstrate children's inability to detect ads and defend themselves against marketing messages (e.g., Chan, 2000; Oates, Blades, & Gunter, 2002, 2003; Rozendaal, Buijzen, & Valkenburg, 2010). Moses and Baldwin (2005) argued that the findings of both classic studies from the 1970s and 1980s and their replications are consistent with developmental research on children's theory of mind (i.e., understanding the emotions and thoughts of others and being able to predict their behavior) and executive functioning (e.g., self-control, attention, information processing, and working memory). Between the ages of four to six, children develop the ability to understand others' motives and predict their behavior (Wellman, Cross, & Watson, 2001) and should therefore be able to understand that marketing activities are designed to persuade. However, their immature executive functioning limits their ability to defend effectively against advertisements even after they understand persuasive intent (Moses & Baldwin, 2005). Given that children today appear to have the same level of cognitive sophistication as children from decades ago, it seems that today's children are no better at detecting or defending themselves from ads than the children of decades ago. Perhaps the more appropriate question is, with children's cognitive abilities remaining the same but marketing messages increasing in number and dispersed across more media, are today's children even more vulnerable than they were decades ago? To answer this question, we look at research on the effects of television and new media advertising on children.

Television Advertising

The remarkable growth in media consumption, combined with a trend toward shorter television advertisements, has led to a rapid growth in the number of advertisements to which children of all ages are exposed (e.g., Kunkel, 2001; Moore, 2004; Powell, Szczypka, Chaloupka, & Braunschweig, 2007). The high rates of childhood obesity and associated health problems have also led to a great deal of recent research on the effects of advertising exposure on children's diets (mostly in health and dietetics journals). Research shows that foods high in fat, sugar, and salt comprise a high proportion of the total ads that children see (Powell et al., 2007). This is an issue of concern because children who see food ads are more likely to choose the advertised foods than children who have not seen the ads (Borzekowski & Robinson, 2001). Further, food advertising during television shows appears to prime children into eating more (Harris, Bargh, & Brownell, 2009). Thus, there is some evidence that advertising plays a prominent role in the prevalence of obesity in children (Gortmaker et al., 1996; McGinnis, Gootman, & Kraak, 2006).

Research has also been conducted to study the effects of advertising on teens' engagement in risky behaviors. This research has primarily appeared in health and psychology journals. Advertising of vices such as smoking and drinking alcohol has been shown to lead to increased consumption of them among teens (DiFranza et al., 2006; Morgenstern, Isensee, Sargent, & Hanewinkel, 2011). Consuming visual media such as television or films can exacerbate this problem. For example, watching films with sexual contact during adolescence has been shown to lower the age of initial sexual activity and increased risky sexual activity (O'Hara et al., 2012), watching television shows where the characters are drinking alcohol can increase the likelihood that adolescents will drink underage (Russell, Russell, Boland, & Grube, 2013) and being exposed to tobacco imagery in films can increase smoking susceptibility (Heatherton & Sargent, 2009; Pechmann & Shih, 1999).

New Media Advertising

Many social media sites display multiple advertisements such as banner ads and behavioral ads (ads that target people on the basis of their web-browsing behavior) that influence not only the buying tendencies of children but also their perceptions of what is common and acceptable. Young consumers are unaware that these ads are used to track their online activity and then target their profile to influence future purchasing decisions. Research on advertising in newer media (e.g., social media, text messaging, banner ads) suggests that children perform even worse at detecting ads in these newer media platforms than in traditional media such as television (Ali, Blades, Oates, & Blumberg, 2009), perhaps because of an increased blurring of ad and entertainment content (Moore, 2004). This is problematic because children and teenagers are exposed to a great quantity of alcohol and drug content online (e.g., posts with references to alcohol or drugs, images of alcoholic beverages) (\Moreno et al., 2009a). Pro-tobacco imagery through new media outlets is also highly prevalent (Freeman & Chapman, 2010; Kim, Paek, & Lynn, 2010; Primack et al., 2012; Seidenberg, Rodgers, Rees, & Connolly, 2012). And, studies have shown that exposure to references to these risky behaviors has a significant impact on adolescent behavior (Slater et al., 2007).

Thus, it appears that not only are children no better at effectively dealing with advertising today than they were in the past, but they also may actually be even more vulnerable to deceptive advertising. Clearly, children and adolescents need to be educated to become media-literate consumers and understand not only how to differentiate between advertising and entertainment content, but also learn how different types of advertisements in different formats can easily manipulate them (O'Keefe, Clarke-Pearson, & Council, 2011).

Children's Understanding of Money

Unlike the topic of the effects of advertising on children, surprisingly little is known about children's understanding of money, despite it also being a critical aspect of consumer psychology, not to mention social and cultural functioning. Researchers have examined whether children can identify different denominations and describe practical uses of money and whether they know about sources of money (Berti & Bombi, 1981; Webley, 2005). Children around age three are able to recognize that money is different from other objects and relate it to purchasing, but comprehending how bank notes are used to obtain goods does not emerge until around age six to eight. Children's understanding of how money is obtained comes later, as well as the relation between supply and demand (Webley, 2005; Leiser & Beth Halachmi, 2006; Thompson & Siegler, 2000).

Because researchers have primarily used interviews to study children's understanding of money, we know little about implicit associations that children form about money and how such associations might affect their behavior (Webley, 2005). Recently, researchers have demonstrated that children know more about money than they are able to verbalize in interviews. Sigelman (2012, 2013) found that children believe rich people are more competent and possess better skill sets than poor people. Gasiorowska, Zaleskiewicz, and Wygrab (2012) found that activating the idea of money affects the social behavior and social preferences of young children who do not understand the economic functions of money. Horwitz, Shutts, and Olson (2014) showed that children can be very sensitive to detecting who does and who does not have money. Additionally, Gasiorowska and colleagues (2015) used priming to show that children ages three to six acquire adult-like associations regarding money – reminders of money (as opposed to other concepts) produced behaviors such as being less helpful and performing better, replicating research that shows that when adults are reminded of money, they behave less prosocially and more agentically than they would at other times (Vohs, Mead, & Goode, 2006).

Although these recent studies suggest that children have a better understanding of money than we think, despite their lack of understanding of the economic functions of money and having so little experience handling money, little is known about whether they can apply their knowledge of money in a consumption context. We know that even when children have the mathematical knowledge to be able to select the superior price promotion, they still make mistakes (Boland, Connell, & Erickson, 2012). Similarly, although they may have some associations with money at a very young age, children may still have difficulty applying the associations they have made with money in a specific consumption context.

Summary and Future Research

Based on the studies reviewed thus far, several questions emerge: Until children become sophisticated consumers armed with cognitive defenses against marketing messages, what can be done to protect them? When and how do children's developing social-cognitive skills and marketplace knowledge, such as their understanding of money, impact their consumer attitudes, beliefs, and values?

With digital advertising potentially reaching an increasingly younger audience, some believe it is critical to establish ethical standards for what can and cannot be advertised to certain age groups (Montgomery & Chester, 2009). For example, some have suggested that limits be placed on advertising junk food and fast food to children and adolescents (Harris, Bargh, & Brownell, 2009), while others have argued that advertising healthy foods to children is acceptable since it can increase positive attitudes toward the food and children's willingness to choose healthy food as a snack (Strasburger, 2009). However, more research is needed to determine whether there are still some negative effects of viewing ads for healthy food. For example, young children may lack the cognitive sophistication to differentiate the health benefits from one product (drinking milk is healthy) to another (eating fast food is unhealthy) when both are in the same product category (food), have entertaining content, and are paired with likeable cartoon characters. And of course, there is the looming question of whether it is ethical to deliver *any* persuasive content, however well intended, to a population not well equipped with cognitive defenses. Perhaps the solution to protecting children and helping them grow up to be well-informed, responsible consumers is to supplement government intervention with actions that can be executed at home and in the classroom.

Recent research in cognitive development is paving the way for more work examining potential solutions for prompting children to use the cognitive defenses they have already developed more effectively. Researchers have found that by age four, children begin to gain abilities that, when properly cued, could help them overcome difficulties in recognizing which sources are trustworthy and when they should be skeptical. For example, by age four, children can recognize experts versus non-experts (Corriveau, Fusaro, & Harris, 2009) and use pointing as an indication of knowledgeability (Palmquist & Jaswal, 2012). Since recognizing a source as expert and knowledgeable enhances source credibility and makes marketing messages more believable, perhaps these techniques could be used to enhance the effectiveness of counter-messages for public service announcements (e.g., healthy vs. unhealthy foods).

Further research could also determine whether there are interventions that can encourage children to utilize their theory of mind, which begins to develop in infancy (Malle & Hodges, 2005; Moses & Baldwin, 2005), with a sharp increase between ages five and six (Baron-Cohen, Leslie, & Frith, 1985; Chaplin & Norton, 2015; Wellman, Cross, & Watson, 2001), to detect source biases and better cope with persuasive communications. For example, Chaplin and colleagues (2015b) found that telling a story by noting the motivations, emotions, and thoughts of characters (compared with telling a story simply by describing the chronology of events) resulted in a greater likelihood of using theory of mind abilities. Therefore, perhaps children's programming that includes the perspectives of others in narratives or short public service announcements containing such a narrative airing before a block of ads could enhance children's abilities to consider the perspective of the advertiser and better cope with the ads that follow.

When and how do children's developing social-cognitive skills and market-place knowledge impact their consumer attitudes, beliefs, and values? We put this broad yet intriguing question on the table and urge researchers to develop more specific research questions related to emerging consumer psychology topics discussed throughout this chapter. For example, great topics for future consideration include, what does money mean to children, and how does their understanding of money impact their product and brand choices, the value they place on material goods and experiences, and ultimately, their happiness?

Research topics along the lines of the aforementioned will contribute nicely to the growing body of research in developmental consumer psychology. Rather than elaborating on a longer list of possible topics, however, we encourage researchers to use this chapter as a guide to explore their own curiosities. We use the limited space in this chapter, instead, to discuss an important issue that researchers pursuing any developmental consumer psychology topic will face before they can move toward hypothesis testing: developing valid and reliable measures appropriate for children and adolescents.

Although retrospective methodologies show promise for identifying develop-mental patterns of consumer behavior (Braun-Latour & LaTour, 2004; Ellis, Holmes, & Wright, 2010; Connell, Brucks, & Nielsen, 2014; Richins & Chaplin, 2015), this approach may not be suitable for testing hypotheses related to newer phenomena such as new media's effects on twenty-first-century children's consumer attitudes, beliefs, and values. New measures more suitable for use with children would be useful to move the area of developmental consumer psychology forward.

Measuring young consumers' attitudes, beliefs, and values can be more difficult than measuring those of adults' for a number of reasons. First, children have short attention spans, limited reading comprehension skills, and under-developed verbal skills. Second, adolescents have little desire to talk to research-ers or to reveal personal information. It can be especially difficult to compare young consumers of different age groups to track developmental changes, due to differing age-related levels of social-cognitive sophistication in a single sample. Although documenting developmental changes is important to the field of consumer psychology, there are so few studies that sample a wide age range because it is extremely difficult to develop appropriate measures for use with very young children, tweens, and older teens in a single study.

Moving forward, there is a need to develop more age-appropriate, novel, and engaging stimuli to elicit thoughtful responses from a wide age range. Measures that are fun, engaging, and less reliant on verbalization skills (e.g., collages, sorting, reaction time) are likely to work well with a wide age range because the researcher is able to test a more diverse set of stimuli, tapping the interests of young children, tweens, as well as older teenagers. Therefore, engaging tasks akin to games or art projects are preferred over traditional ratings scales typically used with adults. However, when the use of validated rating scales is necessary, researchers could follow Chaplin and John's (2005) sorting method to administer surveys to children, where the authors printed each survey question on an index card and had children sort the cards into piles representing the rating scale (e.g., disagree a lot, agree a lot). This way, researchers would be able to administer a validated scale in an engaging way to capture children's interest and elicit thoughtful responses.

Although interviews capture only thoughts that children are able to verbalize, they do have the benefit of allowing children to describe their attitudes, beliefs, and values in their own words. Therefore, when researchers prefer interviews, we offer the following guidelines for eliciting more thoughtful responses from young children:

- Conduct interviews with young children in locations that are comfortable and familiar to them (e.g., an unused classroom at school or camp).
- Avoid interviews for sensitive topics, especially when sampling adolescents (e.g., self-esteem; peer pressure).
- Keep interviews brief and focused on one or two questions that are meaningful to children (e.g., "What makes you happy?" to measure materialistic values).
- Avoid questions that can have a right or wrong answer.
- Ask questions that allow children to feel they are teaching the researcher something, rather than being evaluated by an adult.

In this section, we have examined whether today's children are savvier consumers than the children of the past. For traditional media such as television, the body of evidence suggests that findings from seminal studies from the 1970s and 1980s hold true today. How children understand newer technologies is still poorly understood, but early evidence suggests that an increased blurring in the line between advertising and entertainment might make it even more difficult for children to defend against ads embedded within these media. We offered ideas informed by recent research findings into how parents and policy makers might help children use what knowledge they do have to attenuate their vulnerability to commercial messages. In addition, we explored how different research methodologies might be more effectively used to investigate this theoretically and practically important domain. In the next section, we discuss two additional theoretically and practically important domains where knowledge is nascent but rapidly advancing: materialism and risky behavior.

Recent Advances in Children's Consumer Psychology: Materialism and Risky Behaviors

Materialism and risky behavior may seem like strange bedfellows. However, these two areas of research actually share some commonalities that make them worthy of discussion at a deeper level in this chapter. Most notably, both have the potential to negatively impact children's self-worth, happiness, and well-being, which has generated concern from several constituents, including parents and those in the public policy sector. In addition, although materialism and risky behaviors may entail a wide range of undesirable consumption behaviors (from overspending, to smoking, to leaving a tarnished digital footprint), it is possible that the same intervention strategies could be employed to diminish these undesirable behaviors.

Materialism

Materialism has commonly been defined as the importance consumers place on material possessions as a means for reaching important life goals. Concern over levels of materialism among children has been escalating for the last decade. Materialism among adolescents is associated with mental health problems such as anxiety and depression (Cohen & Cohen, 1996; Schor, 2004), use of addictive substances such as alcohol and illegal drugs (Williams, Cox, Hedberg, & Deci, 2000), and selfish attitudes and behaviors (Kasser, 2005).

To date, research on youth materialism has examined several factors that have the potential to contribute to children's materialism, including parenting styles, disrupted family environments, materialistic parents, and heavy television viewing (Chaplin & John, 2010; Churchill & Moschis, 1979; Goldberg, Gorn, Perracchio, & Bamossy, 2003; Moore & Moschis, 1981; Moschis & Churchill, 1978; Moschis & Moore, 1979; Roberts, Tanner, & Manolis, 2005). Chaplin, Hill, and John (2014) have recently found that an impoverished environment fosters materialism in many young consumers. Although some work has been done on the causes (Chaplin & John, 2007) and consequences (Chaplin, John, Rindfleisch, & Froh, 2014a) of youth materialism, more work is needed to better understand the role of material goods to children. We know one thing is for certain: material possessions are important to children. Material possessions make children and adolescents happy, boost their self-esteem, and are used for self-development (Chaplin & John, 2005, 2007, 2010; Connell & Schau, 2012; Kasser, 2002; Kasser et al., 2014), all critical elements to a healthy development throughout childhood. What is less clear is the question of when and how children's desire for material goods can turn from being useful for healthy development to being potentially harmful. Research linking materialism and decreased prosocial behavior (e.g., generosity) in children is beginning to surface (Chaplin et al. 2014a), but more work is needed to understand fully the pros and cons of using material possessions to achieve desired goals.

Although most consumer research with children has focused exclusively on the importance of material goods in children's lives (Chaplin, Hill, & John, 2014; Chaplin & John, 2005, 2007, 2010; Chaplin & Lowrey, 2010; Goldberg et al., 2003; Kasser 2002), experiences can also be materialistic when they can be used to signal social status (e.g., going on an African safari, going to a Lady Gaga concert) (Shrum et al., 2013). Thus, experiences ought to be studied further to understand when, how, and why they become valuable to children. Recent research shows that younger children have a tendency to value possessions over experiences, but this preference gradually changes throughout childhood, culminating in a tendency to prefer experiences over possessions during adolescence (Chaplin et al., 2015b), similar to adults' preferences (Carter & Gilovich, 2012; Van Boven, 2005; Van Boven, Campbell, & Gilovich, 2010; Van Boven & Gilovich, 2003). Moving forward, it might be beneficial to study when children begin to use experiences in materialistic ways (e.g., deriving happiness from experiences because they signal social status) and to examine whether experience-focused materialism is associated with the same negative outcomes that have been linked to possession-focused materialism, such as decreased generosity and increased risky behaviors. One challenge for researchers is to develop more comprehensive and sensitive measurements of happiness that capture both the short term and long term and to measure both pleasure and deeper meanings of happiness derived from possessions versus experiences.

Health-Related Risky Behavior

Risky consumption habits are of concern to many stakeholders. Why teens engage in risky behaviors such as smoking just a few years after expressing nearly universally negative attitudes toward these behaviors has continued to puzzle researchers (Freeman, Brucks, & Wallendorf, 2005; Freeman, Brucks, Wallendorf, & Boland, 2009; Porcellato, Dugdill, Springett, & Sanderson, 1999). Perhaps it is because risk taking rises in adolescence and begins to decline after the early twenties (Mahalik et al., 2013), despite the fact that adolescents appear to understand the consequences of engaging in these behaviors (Steinberg, 2007). Or, perhaps, as Strasburger's (1995) "super-peer" theory states, the media are like powerful best friends and exert excessive pressure on children and teens to engage in risky behavior by depicting these behaviors as being normative (e.g., everyone drinks at a party). This conundrum has been informed by recent neurological and sociocognitive studies that suggest a "perfect storm" of developmental changes that occur in adolescence.

One of the key elements of this perfect storm is heightened sensation-seeking (pursuing highly arousing experiences as benign as riding a rollercoaster ride or as serious as drug use), which is at its peak between the ages of ten and fifteen

(Steinberg et al., 2008). While sensation-seeking rises dramatically in adolescence, self-regulation abilities and resources develop at a much slower rate and are not fully developed until the mid-twenties (Steinberg, 2005, 2007). This combination of heightened sensation-seeking with underdeveloped self-regulation has led some researchers to describe the transition from childhood into adolescence as "starting the engines without a skilled driver" (Dahl, 2001).

While neurological and hormonal research has provided important insights into why adolescents are more willing to take risks, it does not fully explain why teens turn to smoking, drinking, drugs, and sex. However, research on development of personality and self-concept provide additional insights. At approximately ages twelve through fourteen, salience of attributes and social skills that relate with one's social appeal to others is elevated (Damon & Hart, 1988; Harter, 2003) and neuroticism increases for girls (Soto, John, Gosling, & Potter, 2011). Of particular concern is girls' focus on weight and body image. For example, Larsen, Otten, and Engels (2009) found that the link between depression and smoking disappeared when controlled for weight concerns and dieting. The obsession with others' evaluations of oneself continues to increase in middle adolescence (approximately ages fifteen and sixteen) (Harter, 2003; Lapsley & Rice, 1988). Later in adolescence, emotional stability increases (Klimstra et al., 2009) and teens begin to become less obsessed with the opinions of others (Damon & Hart, 1988; Harter, 2003). However, by this point much of the damage has been done. In the United States, nearly nine out of ten smokers initiate use by age eighteen (U.S. Department of Health and Human Services, 2012), 54.1 percent of twelfth graders have been drunk at least once (Substance Abuse and Mental Health Services Administration, 2011), and 47.4 percent of surveyed high school students had engaged in sexual activity (Center for Disease Control, 2011). In addition, earlier initiation of risky behavior has been shown to be a risk factor for disordered behavior or health problems related to risky behavior later in life (Anthony & Petronis, 1995; DeWit, Adlaf, Offord, & Ongborne, 2000; O'Donnell, O'Donnell, & Stueve, 2001).

Online Risky Behavior

Today's youth have unprecedented access to new media. Research by the Pew Internet and American Life Project revealed that 93 percent of youth aged twelve to seventeen are online (Jones & Fox, 2009). It is no surprise that digital media have become an important source of information and is the new way of targeting children and teenagers (Montgomery & Chester, 2009). In fact, a large part of young consumers' social, emotional, and marketplace knowledge is developing while they are online or on their cellphones. However, because of their limited cognitive defenses, limited capacity for self-regulation, and heightened susceptibility to peer pressure, children and adolescents are at some risk as they experiment with social media. For example, because the media play a crucial role in the formation of body self-image and identity development, it may be responsible for contributing to unrealistic expectations resulting in a distorted body image (Strasburger, Jordan, & Donnerstein, 2010).

When consumers visit various websites, they can leave a trail of evidence of which sites they have visited, known as their "digital footprint." One of the biggest threats to people on social media is to their digital footprint and future reputations. Inexperienced and media-illiterate network navigation can put young consumers at risk for being targeted by marketers, but their reputation among family and friends and their prospects for future jobs and college acceptances may also be at risk (e.g., if the consumer posts about substance abuse or sexually suggestive content) (O'Keefe, Clarke-Pearson, & Council, 2011).

Media literacy requires having the ability to attend to, decode, and interpret an overwhelming number of messages dispersed across different media. To date, only the United Kingdom, Canada, and Australia mandate media education in their schools. Despite research indicating that teenagers respond to messages about the dangers of posting sexual references on social media by changing their online behavior accordingly, few schools in the United States incorporate media education into their curriculum (Moreno et al., 2009b). The research reviewed in this section suggests a need for media education at school and at home.

Summary and Future Research

More than fifty years of media research documents the significant influence of media on child and adolescent health (Pecora, Murray, & Wartella, 2006). We have discussed the most recent findings that highlight concerns in children's materialism and risky behavior. We have concluded that children and adolescents are at some risk as they overemphasize material possessions as a way to gauge self-worth and find happiness. In addition, their gravitation toward sensation-seeking combined with their limited cognitive defenses, limited capacity for self-regulation, and heightened susceptibility to peer pressure make experimenting with social media and health-related behaviors (sex, smoking, drugs, and alcohol) of great concern. Unfortunately, effective strategies for reducing materialism and risky behavior among children remain elusive. Calls for government to intervene by restricting television advertising and Internet marketing (Leave Our Kids Alone, 2013) and protecting the online privacy of children under the age of thirteen (the Children's Online Privacy Protection Act [COPPA]) have been numerous, but implementation of the suggested policies has been difficult and slow. For example, COPPA went into effect in April of 2000, years after young children were already registering to chat rooms and discussion boards. Calls for parents to educate their children about the marketplace and restrict media access may also be limited in their effectiveness. In short, parents, social scientists, and child advocates know there is a problem, but practical solutions have been slow to emerge. Thus, there is a need to explore the efficacy of alternatives or supplements to government intervention to reduce youth materialism and risky behavior.

Although there are many future research directions to take the topics of materialism and risky behaviors in children (e.g., antecedents, consequences, the development of better measures), given the mounting evidence linking materialism and risky behaviors to health and well-being concerns, we offer a future research agenda focused on practical interventions to tame these behaviors and values. Although government interventions are helpful, there may be simple and effective ways to tame these undesirable behaviors that require us to look no further than at home or school. We discuss these possibilities in the following subsections.

Self-Esteem

Prior research suggests that self-esteem is an antecedent to materialism and risky behavior among children and adolescents (Chaplin, Hill & John, 2014; Chaplin & John, 2007, 2010; Wild, Flisher, Bhana, & Lombard, 2004). However, two emerging streams of research suggest that the relationship between self-esteem and materialism may be more complicated than previously thought. First, Crocker and Park (2004) argue that *how* self-esteem is derived is as important as whether it is high or low. Research on contingences of self-worth suggests that self-esteem is drawn from a variety of sources (Burwell & Shirk, 2006; Crocker & Park, 2004; Park, Crocker, & Mickelson, 2004). Several domains are crucial to childhood self-esteem, including cognitive/scholastic competence, relationships with loved ones, social acceptance, physical/athletic competence, physical appearance, and behavioral conduct (e.g., Harter, 1985; Harter & Pike, 1984). Some of these sources of self-worth are less stable than others because they involve self-validation goals (Crocker & Park, 2004). When self-esteem is contingent on success or failure in one of these domains, it is less stable – success in one or more of these domains leads to increases in self-esteem while failures lead to decreases in self-esteem (Crocker & Knight, 2005). Because failures are likely to be more frequent in some of these domains (e.g., social acceptance), if self-esteem is largely derived from such an unstable source, then children and teens could develop materialistic or risk-taking tendencies in their quests to build positive images of themselves.

Second, there are two types of self-esteem, explicit and implicit self-esteem, that may impact behavior differently. Explicit self-esteem is defined as consciously reasoned evaluations of the self, whereas implicit self-esteem is defined as self-evaluations occurring outside of awareness or control (Greenwald & Banaji, 1995; Koole, Dijksterhuis, & van Knippenberg, 2001). Researchers have found that larger discrepancies between explicit and implicit self-esteem in either direction (high explicit/low implicit *or* low explicit/high implicit) lead to higher levels of materialism in adults (Park & John, 2011). More research is needed to determine whether this holds for children and how such discrepancies can affect their propensity to engage in risky behavior.

Because domains of self-esteem such as social approval, academic achievement, or physical appearance are likely to move children toward self-enhancement as a means to an end (e.g., buying popular brands or smoking to fit in), it would be fruitful for researchers to examine the effects of drawing from different domains of self-esteem (some explicit, some implicit) on the development of consumer values such as materialism and risky behavior. Moreover, understanding when the impact of discrepancies between explicit and implicit self-esteem on materialism begins and how it changes throughout childhood would help researchers understand why some children with high explicit self-esteem may express high levels of materialism or engage in risky behavior.

Children's increasing narcissism, which Twenge and colleagues (2008) argue is due to their parents' tendency to protect them from facing disappointments and failures, could have important implications for materialism and risky behavior. While narcissists have high self-esteem, it is highly volatile and easily threatened (Baumeister, Smart, & Boden, 1996). Thus, any threat to the ego could drive youth to self-verification motives, possibly resorting to materialistic behavior or risk taking for social approval or self-validation.

To date, research with children has been limited to examining the relationship between explicit self-esteem and self-verification motives such as materialism and risky behavior. Based on Park and John's (2011) findings, it would be worthwhile to examine whether self-esteem discrepancies in children are also a better predictor of materialistic orientations than explicit self-esteem alone, as it is in adults. We now know that implicit self-esteem decreases from ages eleven to eighteen (Cai, Wu, Luo, & Yang, 2014), but explicit self-esteem follows a different pattern. Explicit self-esteem drops during early adolescence and recovers late in adolescence (Harter, 2003). Therefore, it would be useful to try to capture vulnerabilities that older teens might experience if low implicit self-esteem is related to increased materialism or risk taking.

Gratitude

Showing gratitude is one of the most important yet least studied prosocial behaviors. Research indicates that grateful children are more generous and connected to their neighborhoods and communities, are in happier relationships with their family and friends, and have more self-discipline (Froh & Bono, 2014). How can gratitude be used to curb materialism and risky behavior?

Chaplin and colleagues (2015a) look to Values Theory (Bilsky & Schwartz, 1994) to argue for gratitude as a possible antidote for materialism. According to this theoretical framework, values are desirable, trans-situational goals that vary in importance and help guide people's lives. Moreover, this theory posits that some values are incompatible with each other; actions to fulfill one may conflict with actions to pursue another. One of the major conflicts is between orientations of *self-enhancement* (pursuing success and dominance over others) and *self-transcendence* (accepting others as equals and being concerned for their welfare) (Bilsky & Schwartz, 1994). Materialism is an example of a self-enhancement value, whereas gratitude is an example of a self-transcendent value (Burroughs & Rindfleisch, 2002; Kasser, 2005). Therefore, values theory suggests a negative correlation between gratitude and materialism because they represent opposing value systems.

Chaplin and colleagues (2015a) also show that an intervention designed to encourage feelings of gratitude among adolescents (keeping a gratitude journal) decreases materialistic tendencies and increases generosity toward others. Their findings provide help to parents, educators, and policy makers by redirecting their attention away from waiting for the government to intervene and instead taking a more proactive approach by looking for ways to instill gratitude both at home and at school. Although the work of Chaplin and colleagues (2015a) focuses on materialism, their gratitude intervention can be applied to other contexts as well. In the context of risky behavior, gratitude is associated with positive youth development and therefore should act as a buffer against risky behaviors (Ma, Kibler, & Sly, 2013). Indeed, it does. Researchers have found that gratitude protects against risky behaviors such as alcohol and drug use (Froh & Bono, 2014; Ma, Kibler, & Sly, 2013) as well as sexual activity (Ma, Kibler, & Sly, 2013). Thus, it would be important to find ways to encourage a grateful disposition in youngsters.

Prospection (Acting with the Future in Mind)

Prospection is defined as "our ability to 'pre-experience' the future by simulating it in our minds" (Gilbert & Wilson, 2007, p. 1352). Simulations of the future allow people to "preview" events and to "pre-feel" the pleasures and pains those events will produce. In fact, it has been suggested that thoughtful action is guided by assessing future possibilities rather than being driven by the past (Seligman, Railton, Baumeister, & Sripada, 2013).

There are a number of benefits to acting with the future in mind (Suddendorf and Busby, 2005). Of particular importance to consumer psychology, prospection benefits the self by aiding rational decision making and self-control (Seligman et al., 2013), which are critical to keeping children's tendencies toward materialism and risky behavior under control. More specifically, prospection abilities can help children and adolescents cope with a variety of consumption scenarios and choices, such as anticipating behaviors that will bring short-lived superficial peer acceptance versus long-term genuine peer acceptance or anticipating an undesirable future outcome as a result of engaging in risky behavior to feel good in the present. Prospection can be especially beneficial to adolescents, who often succumb to peer pressure because they are letting the past guide their present thinking (e.g., "a popular kid in school wore Pumas to school, so now that everyone has a pair, I need a pair"). What if the teenager simulated the future and anticipated how he would feel if he used the money he had been saving for a Father's Day gift on the trendy Pumas he won't even like? Would he still want to purchase the Pumas?

The evidence on children's prospection abilities shows that they are not good at being future-oriented (Atance & Meltzoff, 2005, 2006), which may explain why children appear to be so materialistic and engage in risky behavior. In the context of materialism, because marketing messages in the media encourage immediate gratification of pleasure, the ability to act with the future in mind should allow children to have more self-control over their desires to buy. With underdeveloped prospection abilities, young children will base their future choices on their present state (Atance & Meltzoff, 2006).

In the context of social media, prospection is important for children to navigate cyberspace safely. For example, children have a difficult time understanding that anything they post online can be forwarded, copied, and used by others almost instantly. Twitter, a microblogging site, has become part of today's teens' everyday routine to stay connected with friends and follow other users' activities. Although one can choose to keep tweets private, public tweets are preferred by teens (Lenhart, Purcell, Smith, & Zickuhr, 2013), which is worrisome if teens are unable or unwilling to anticipate consequences of their inappropriate public tweets. Prospection would also allow children to tailor their behavior to satisfy the challenges they face on a daily basis (e.g., manage peer pressure). The anticipation of consequences to mismanaging emotions would allow children to channel their present behavior in desired ways.

We know children have difficulty prospecting (Atance & Meltzoff, 2005, 2006; Russell, Alexis, & Clayton, 2010), but we have little knowledge of how to help children improve their prospection abilities. Moving forward, it would be useful to investigate how prospection abilities develop throughout childhood and to document the extent to which prospection can improve behavioral flexibility (the ability to plan for a range of events and emotions) across a range of consumer contexts (e.g., planning for the potential joy to be experienced when they buy the trendy shoes versus the disappointment they might face if the trendy shoes are out of stock; the excitement that comes with purchasing a new toy they have seen advertised for weeks and the possibility that the toy will not be as fun to play with as it is portrayed in the commercial). It would also be important to examine children's ability versus their willingness to act with the future in mind, as well as how their prospection abilities can be encouraged and improved. As is the case with other potential future research studies discussed in this chapter, the development of more engaging measures suitable for children will be needed before researchers can move forward with hypothesis testing.

In sum, adults are not always around to help children act with the future in mind, especially when they are online or around peers. Knowledge gained from prospection studies would inform us of how children's present consumer behaviors – such as brand choice, risky behavior, interpretation of marketing messages, and susceptibility to peer pressure to buy the latest trendy merchandise – may be impacted by their ability or willingness to be future-minded. Finally, if researchers can develop strategies to encourage and improve children's prospection abilities, they may be able to help children exercise more rational decision making and self-control across different consumption situations.

Building Self-Esteem and Encouraging Prospection through Free Play and Failure

We have discussed how self-esteem and prospection abilities can help curb undesirable values and behaviors such as materialism and risky behavior in children. But how can we help children build a stable self-esteem and a future-oriented mind? To answer this question, we argue for the importance of allowing children to *free play* and to experience *failure* safely. We also offer future research ideas focused on investigations that address how free play and failure can help build a stable self-esteem and a future-oriented mind, which we have argued earlier are important to decreasing materialism and risky behavior.

Free Play

As noted earlier, there is evidence that self-esteem is an antecedent to materialism and risky behavior among children and adolescents. How can free play curb these undesirable behaviors? Research suggests that free play can positively impact children's self-esteem. When people derive self-esteem from unstable sources that require self-validation, such as approval from peers, they might turn to marketplace symbols that convey social status as a means for building self-esteem and in turn develop materialistic values (Chaplin & John, 2010). However, when self-esteem is derived from more stable sources, such as parents or one's skills and competencies, self-esteem is more stable and there is less of a need to self-validate with external sources (Crocker & Park, 2004; Park, Crocker, & Mickelson, 2004) such as material goods or risky behavior.

Free play has a number of benefits and can draw children toward stable sources of self-esteem and in turn decrease their inclination to look to material possessions or engage in risky behaviors to boost their self-esteem or to self-validate. In addition to the fact that children report being happiest when at play (Csikszentmihalyi & Hunter, 2003), they develop physical and cognitive competencies, creativity, self-worth, and efficacy through play (Smith, 2005; Taylor & Kuo, 2006). Moreover, because free play does not have a specific aim (i.e., no benchmark for success), it allows children to behave without the worries of winning or disappointing someone, thus allowing them to experience positive emotions (Frederickson, 1998) rather than feeling bad about themselves for not having done better. In addition, play helps children develop intrinsic interests, learn how to make decisions, solve problems, exert self-control, follow rules, and regulate emotions (Johnson, 2014; Pellegrini, 2009), competencies associated with being future-minded. Play also helps children develop and maintain peer relationships (Johnson, 2014; Pellegrini, 2009), which is critical to a positive sense of self. In fact, free play is so critical to young children's development and physical and mental health (Burdette, & Whitaker, 2005; Fromberg & Bergen, 2006) that it is included in Article 31 of the United Nations Convention on the Rights of the Child.

The "broaden and build" model of positive emotions would also suggest that play fosters a stable self-esteem. It posits that feeling states such as joy and interest are experienced when people feel safe to experiment and explore (Frederickson, 1998). Moreover, positive emotions have been demonstrated to broaden cognition by enhancing creativity (Isen & Daubman, 1984; Isen, Johnson, Mertz, & Robinson, 1985; Isen, Niedenthal, & Cantor, 1992) and help build intellectual resources by enhancing learning (Masters, Barden, & Ford, 1979), in turn fostering a positive and stable self-esteem. Thus, although more research is needed, the evidence we have reviewed supports the notion that free play can be a simple and easy strategy to build children's self-esteem as a first step toward decreasing materialism and risky behavior.

Failure

Failure is an overlooked yet important factor in building self-esteem and encouraging prospection in children, which, as previously discussed, can curb materialism and risky behavior. Children develop a sense of competence by experiencing success, but to experience success, children must experience failure and figure out how to correct their mistakes in order to improve their perform-ance (Taylor, 2014). Research shows that unexpected incidents or failures are prerequisites for learning (Zakay, Ellis, & Shevalsky, 2004) because they induce a sense of discomfort, motivate learners to solve problems in order to perform better in the future, and fuel cognitive processes that stimulate growth (Kolb, 1984; Osterman, 1990).

Sadly, fear of failure among children is epidemic in America today (Taylor, 2010). This fear of failure is partially driven by the belief that if children fail, they will feel badly about themselves and will experience embarrassment, which many, especially parents, want to avoid. Because children are growing up in a culture of increasing competitiveness with a highly uncertain economic land-scape, parents are even more terrified of their children failing and will do what they can to help their child avoid failure. In order to increase their children's probability of future success, parents are enrolling children in more structured classes outside of school (Kohn, 2014). Although there can be many benefits to youngsters being involved in extracurricular activities, such as achieving higher grades (Darling, Caldwell, & Smith, 2005), these structured classes outside of school are also intruding on children's time for free play, which we have argued is important to developing a strong and stable sense of self. Given that interest in free play has waned over the years, it is not surprising that there has been a decline in play spaces offering children opportunities to test out their compe-tencies and imagination (Brussoni, Olsen, Pike, & Sleet, 2012).

In addition to cutting into their children's free play time by signing them up for structured classes to increase their chances of success, parents are over-indulging (Clarke, Dawson, & Bredehoft, 2014) and overcelebrating to spare their children from having to deal with making mistakes and feeling disap-pointed in their own shortcomings (Kohn, 2014). What are the potential consequences of overpraising children to protect them from dealing with failure? Research has shown that when children are showered with praise, they are less persistent in completing difficult assignments, are less willing to share their ideas, and have less confidence in their answers when they do share their ideas (Taylor, 2014).

The consequence of this overprotective approach will be a generation of young consumers who lack confidence in their abilities and therefore may find it easier to (1) gravitate toward materialism and risky behavior to develop self-worth than to rely on their competencies (2) blame others rather than to hold themselves accountable for their own actions (3) believe misleading marketing messages rather than be critical of them and (4) allow the past to guide their actions rather than the future. To be truly savvy consumers, children need to be confident, effective problem solvers. They must also be creative, critical, and future-oriented thinkers. Therefore, children should be taught to embrace failure as part of the learning process and not shy away from it. Clearly, more research is needed, but one way to help children deal with adversities such as failure is to encourage them to appreciate the people and resources they have to help them face challenges (Froh & Bono, 2014).

Future Research

As American children's freedom (to play and to fail) has declined, so has their creativity (Kim, 2011). This decline in creativity is noteworthy because Americans are known as the greatest innovators. Moving forward, it would be fruitful to study how protecting children from experiencing failure (e.g., the ever-growing prevalence of parents doing their children's homework for them) can negatively impact children's competencies, creativity, and self-worth. How might decreases in various competencies impact children's consumer knowledge (e.g., interpretation of marketing messages, beliefs about celebrity endorsements), attitudes toward products and brands, behaviors (e.g., brand choice, risky behaviors), values (e.g., materialism), and ultimately their happiness and well-being?

An intriguing future research idea would be to examine the benefits of different free play activities ranging from outdoor playspaces to unstructured indoor games and toys. In addition, it would be worthwhile to examine how free play alone versus with other children offers different learning experiences and benefits. Outcomes of interest might include creativity, self-control, resilience, and attitude toward experiencing failure (e.g., how a child deals with her Lego structure shattering into one hundred pieces when she accidentally pushes down on the final piece too hard), as well as ability to problem solve (rebuilding a Lego structure after another child knocks it over either accidentally or intentionally) and appreciation of success. More specific to developmental consumer psychology, researchers could examine how benefits from opportunities to free play (such as improved prospection abilities, critical thinking skills, and problem-solving abilities) across different activities (alone vs. with others) help to better equip children to interpret marketing messages critically, have more self-control over indulgent and unnecessary purchases, and problem solve when they encounter peer pressure to engage in risky behavior. We urge researchers to do more work not only on the benefits to encouraging children to free play, but also on how to maximize the benefits through the actual process of play.

Finally, it would be interesting to examine the role of prospection in dealing with failure as well as during the process of free play and how it might affect children's consumer decisions. For example, if children can anticipate failure, will they be more comfortable and successful overcoming failure when it happens, and, with this success, will they develop a stronger skill set (e.g., resilience, critical thinking, problem solving, self-control) needed to make good consumer decisions (e.g., avoid risky behavior, eat healthy food, tame materialistic temptations)?

Conclusion

Throughout this chapter, we have provided a glimpse into the consumer world of twenty-first century children, from their overexposure to traditional television advertising to uncensored online content saturated with images, videos, and other references to risky behavior (e.g., sex, drugs, alcohol, and smoking). We have delivered a summary of the most recent research findings related to the area of developmental consumer psychology, with a specific focus on materialism and risky behaviors, as well as issues of major concern to policy makers, parents, and others. Although traditional calls for government regulations are certainly important, policy changes can take a long time and may not go sufficiently far enough to provide needed protections. Thus, we have taken a different approach in this chapter and have offered several tractable interventions to pave the way for today's children to be more in control of navigating through their increasingly consumption-driven world. It is our hope that the studies reviewed and the directions for future research offered in this chapter excite researchers from all disciplines and levels of experience to collaborate and advance the area of developmental consumer psychology.

References

Ali, M., Blades, M., Oates, C., & Blumberg, F. (2009). Young children's ability to recognize advertisements in web page designs. *British Journal of Developmental Psychology, 27*, 71–83.

Anthony, J. C., & Petronis, K. R. (1995). Early-onset drug use and risk of later drug problems. *Drug and Alcohol Dependence, 40*, 9–15.

Atance, C. M., & Meltzoff, A. N. (2005). My future self: Young children's ability to anticipate and explain future states. *Cognitive Development, 20*(3), 341–361.

Atance, C. M., & Meltzoff, A. N. (2006). Preschoolers' current desires warp their choices for the future. *Psychological Science, 17*(7), 583–587.

Baumeister, R. R., Smart, L., & Boden, J. M. (1996). Relation of threatened egotism to violence and aggression: The dark side of high self-esteem. *Psychological Review, 103*, 5–33.

Baron-Cohen, S., Leslie, A. M., & Frith, U. (1985). Does the autistic child have a theory of mind? *Cognition, 21*, 37–46.

Berti, A. E., & Bombi, A. S. (1981). The development of the concept of money and its value: A longitudinal study. *Child Development, 52*(4), 1179–1182.

Bilsky, W., & Schwartz, S. H. (1994). Values and personality. *European Journal of Personality, 8*(3), 163–181.

Boland, W. A., Connell, P. M., & Erickson, L. M. (2012). Children's response to sales promotions and their impact on purchase behavior. *Journal of Consumer Psychology, 22*, 272–279.

Borzekowski, D. L., & Robinson, T. N. (2001). The 30-second effect: An experiment revealing the impact of television commercials on food preferences of pre-schoolers. *Journal of the American Dietetic Association, 101*, 42–46.

Braun-LaTour, K. A., & LaTour, M. S. (2004). Assessing the long-term impact of a consistent advertising campaign on consumer memory. *Journal of Advertising, 33*(2), 49–61.

Brucks, M., Armstrong, G. M., & Goldberg, M. E. (1988). Children's use of cognitive defenses against television advertising: A cognitive response approach. *Journal of Consumer Research, 14*, 471–82.

Brussoni, M., Olsen, L. L., Pike, I., & Sleet, D. A. (2012). Risky play and children's safety: Balancing priorities for optimal child development. *International Journal of Environmental Research and Public Health, 9*(9), 3134–3148.

Burdette, H. L., & Whitaker, R. C. (2005). Resurrecting free play in young children: Looking beyond fitness and fatness to attention, affiliation, and affect. *Archives of Pediatrics & Adolescent Medicine, 159*(1), 46–50.

Burroughs, J. E., & Rindfleisch, A. (2002). Materialism and well-being: A conflicting values perspective. *Journal of Consumer Research, 29*(3), 348–370.

Burwell, R. A., & Shirk, S. R. (2006). Self processes in adolescent depression: The role of self-worth contingencies. *Journal of Research on Adolescence, 16*, 479–490.

Butter, E. J., Popovich, P. M., Stackhouse, R. H., & Garner, R. K. (1981). Discrimin-ation of television programs and commercials by preschool children. *Journal of Advertising Research, 21*, 53–56.

Cai, H., Wu, M., Luo, Y. L., & Yang, J. (2014). Implicit self-esteem decreases in adolescence: A cross-sectional study. *PloS One, 9*(2), e89988.

Carter, T. J., & Gilovich, T. (2012). I am what I do, not what I have: The differential centrality of experiential and material purchases to the self. *Journal of Person-ality and Social Psychology, 102*(6), 1304–1317.

Center for Disease Control (2011). Youth risk behavior surveillance: United States. *MMWR 2012, 61*(SS-4).

Chan, K. (2000). Hong Kong children's understanding of television advertising. *Journal of Marketing Communications, 6*, 37–52.

Chaplin, L. N., Hill, R. P., & John, D. J. (2014) Poverty and materialism: A look at impoverished versus affluent children. *Journal of Public Policy & Marketing, 33* (1), 78–92.

Chaplin, L. N., & John, D. R. (2005). The development of self-brand connections in children and adolescents. *Journal of Consumer Research, 32*, 119–129.

Chaplin, L. N., & John, D. R. (2007). Growing up in a material world: Age differences in materialism in children and adolescents. *Journal of Consumer Research, 34*, 480–493.

Chaplin, L. N., & John, D. R. (2010). Interpersonal influences on adolescent materialism: A new look at the role of parents and peers. *Journal of Consumer Psychology, 20*(2), 176–184.

Chaplin, L. N., John, D. R., Rindfleisch, A. & Froh, J. (2015a). *Reducing Materialism in Adolescents.* Manuscript submitted for publication.

Chaplin, L. N., & Lowrey, T. M. (2010). The development of consumer-based consumption constellations in children. *Journal of Consumer Research, 36*, 757–777.

Chaplin, L. N., Lowrey, T. M., Ruvio, A., Shrum, L. J., & Vohs, K. D. (2015b). *Children's Developing Appreciation of Experiences.* Manuscript in preparation.

Chaplin, L. N., & Norton, M. (2015). Why we think we can't dance: Theory of mind and children's desire to perform. *Child Development, 86*, 651–658.

Churchill Jr., G. A., & Moschis, G. P. (1979). Television and interpersonal influences on adolescent consumer learning. *Journal of Consumer Research, 15*, 23–35.

Clarke, J. I., Dawson, C., & Bredehoft, D. (2014). *How Much Is Too Much? Raising Likeable, Responsible, Respectful Children – from Toddlers to Teens – in an Age of Overindulgence.* Boston: Da Capo Press.

Cohen, P., and Cohen, J. (1996). *Life Values and Adolescent Mental Health.* Mahwah, NJ: Erlbaum.

Common Sense Media (2011). Zero to eight: Children's media use in America. Available at www.commonsensemedia.org/research/zero-to-eight-childrens-media-use-in-america.

Connell, P. M., Brucks, M., & Nielsen, J. H. (2014). How childhood advertising exposure can create biased product evaluations that persist into adulthood. *Journal of Consumer Research, 41*, 119–134.

Connell, P. M. & Schau, H. J. (2012). Examining childhood consumption relationships. In S. Fournier, M. Breazeale, M. Fetscherin, & T. C. Melewar (eds.), *Consumer-Brand Relationships: Theory and Practice* (pp. 97–114). New York: Routledge/Taylor & Francis.

Corriveau, K. H., Fusaro, M., & Harris, P. L. (2009). Going with the flow: Preschoolers prefer nondissenters as informants. *Psychological Science, 20*, 372–377.

Crocker, J., & Knight, K. M. (2005). Contingencies of self-worth. *Current Directions in Psychological Science, 14*(4), 200–203.

Crocker, J., & Park, L. E. (2004). The costly pursuit of self-esteem. *Psychological Bulletin, 130*, 392–414.

Csikszentmihalyi, M., & Hunter, J. (2003). Happiness in everyday life: The uses of experience sampling. *Journal of Happiness Studies, 4*(2), 185–199.

Dahl, R. (2001). Affect regulation, brain development, and behavioral/emotional health in adolescence. *CNS Spectrum, 6*, 1–12.

Damon, W., & Hart, D. (1988) *Self-Understanding in Childhood and Adolescence.* Cambridge: Cambridge University Press.

Darling, N., Caldwell, L. L., & Smith, R. (2005). Participation in school-based extracurricular activities and adolescent adjustment. *Journal of Leisure Research, 37*, 51–75.

DeWit, D. J., Adlaf, E. M., Offord, D. R., & Ogborne, A. C. (2000). Age at first alcohol use: A risk factor for the development of alcohol disorders. *American Journal of Psychiatry, 157,* 745–750.

DiFranza, J. R., Wellman, R. J., Sargent, J. D., Weitzman, M., Hipple, B. J., & Winickoff, J. P. (2006). Tobacco promotion and the initiation of tobacco use: Assessing the evidence for causality. *Pediatrics, 117,* e1237–e1248.

Donohue, T. R., Henke, L. L., & Donohue, W. A. (1980). Do kids know what TV commercials intend. *Journal of Advertising Research, 20,* 51–57.

Ellis, A. W., Holmes, S. J., & Wright, R. L. (2010). Age of acquisition and the recognition of brand names: On the importance of being early. *Journal of Consumer Psychology, 20,* 43–52.

Frederickson, B. (1998). What good are positive emotions? *Review of General Psychology, 2,* 300–319.

Freeman, D., Brucks, M., & Wallendorf, M. (2005). Young children's understandings of cigarette smoking. *Addiction, 100,* 1537–1545.

Freeman, D., Brucks, M., Wallendorf, M., & Boland, W. (2009). Youths' understandings of cigarette advertisements. *Addictive behaviors, 34,* 36–42.

Freeman, B., & Chapman, S. (2010). British American tobacco on Facebook: Undermining article 13 of the global World Health Organization framework convention on tobacco control. *Tobacco Control, 19*(3), e1–e9.

Froh, J., & Bono, G. (2014). *Making Grateful Kids: A Scientific Approach to Helping Youth Thrive.* West Conshohocken, PA: Templeton Press.

Fromberg, D. P., & Bergen, D. (eds.). (2006). *Play from Birth to Twelve: Contexts, Perspectives, and Meanings,* 2nd ed. New York: Taylor & Francis.

Gasiorowska, A., Zaleskiewicz, T., Wygrab, S., (2012). Would you do something for me? The effects of money activation on social preferences and social behavior in young children. *Journal of Economic Psychology, 33,* 603–608.

Gasiorowska, A., Zaleskiewicz, T., Wygrab, S., Chaplin, L., & Vohs, K. D. (2014). *Children Become More Agentic but Less Helpful after Being Reminded of Money.* Manuscript submitted for publication.

Gilbert, D. T., & Wilson, T. D. (2007). Prospection: Experiencing the future. *Science, 317*(5843), 1351–1354.

Goldberg, M. E., Gorn, G. J., Peracchio, L. A., & Bamossy, G. (2003). Understanding materialism among youth. *Journal of Consumer Psychology, 13*(3), 278–288.

Gortmaker, S. L., Must, A., Sobol, A. M., Peterson, K., Colditz, G. A., & Dietz, W. H. (1996). Television viewing as a cause of increasing obesity among children in the United States, 1986–1990. *Archives of Pediatrics & Adolescent Medicine, 150,* 356–362.

Greenwald, A. G., & Banaji, M. R. (1995). Implicit social cognition: Attitudes, self-esteem, and stereotypes. *Psychological Review, 102*(1), 4–27.

Harris, J. L., Bargh, J. A., & Brownell, K. D. (2009). Priming effects of television food advertising on eating behavior. *Health Psychology, 28,* 404–413.

Harter, S. (1985). Competence as a dimension of self-evaluation: Toward a comprehensive model of self-worth. *Development of the Self, 2,* 55–121.

Harter, S. (2003). The development of self-representations during childhood and adolescence. In M. R. Leary & J. P. Tanguy (eds.), *Handbook of Self and Identity* (pp. 610–642). New York: Guilford Press.

Harter, S., & Pike, R. (1984). The pictorial scale of perceived competence and social acceptance for young children. *Child Development, 55*(6), 1969–1982.

Heatherton, T. F., & Sargent, J. D. (2009). Does watching smoking in movies promote teenage smoking? *Current Directions in Psychological Science, 18*, 63–67.

Horwitz, S. R., Shutts, K., & Olson, K. R. (2014). Social class differences produce social group preferences. *Developmental Science, 17*, 991–1002.

Isen, A. M., & Daubman, K. A. (1984). The influence of affect on categorization. *Journal of Personality and Social Psychology, 47*, 1206–1217.

Isen, A. M., Johnson, M. M. S., Mertz, E., & Robinson, G. F. (1985). The influence of positive affect on the unusualness of word associations. *Journal of Personality and Social Psychology, 48*, 1413–1426.

Isen, A. M., Niedenthal, P., & Cantor, N. (1992). The influence of positive affect on social categorization. *Motivation and Emotion, 16*, 65–78.

John, D. R. (1999). Consumer socialization of children: A retrospective look at twenty-five years of research. *Journal of Consumer Research, 26*, 183–213.

Johnson, L. (2014). A risk-free childhood is a bad start to life. *Financial Times*, April 22. Available at www.ft.com/intl/cms/s/0/a0ef5b8a-c719-11e3-929f-00144feabdc0.html#axzz353mOWohQ.

Jones, S., & Fox, S. (2009). *Generations Online in 2009*. Washington, DC: Pew Internet & American Life Project.

Kaiser Family Foundation (2010). Generation M: Media in the Lives of 8–18 Year-Olds – Report. Available at http://kff.org/other/generation-m-media-in-the-lives-of/.

Kasser, T. (2002). *The High Price of Materialism*. Cambridge, MA: MIT Press.

Kasser, T. (2005). Frugality, generosity, and materialism in children and adolescents. In K. A. Moore & L. H. Lippman (eds.), *What Do Children Need to Flourish?* (pp. 357–373). New York: Springer.

Kasser, T., Rosenblum, K. L., Sameroff, A. J., Deci, E. L., Niemiec, C. P., Ryan, R. M., Arnadottir, O., Bond, R., Dittmar, H., Dungan, N., & Hawks, S. (2014). Changes in materialism, changes in psychological well-being: Evidence from three longitudinal studies and an intervention experiment. *Motivation and Emotion, 38*, 1–22.

Kim, K. H. (2011). The creativity crisis: The decrease in creative thinking scores on the torrance tests of creative thinking. *Creativity Research Journal, 23*(4), 285–295.

Kim, K., Paek, H. J., & Lynn, J. (2010). A content analysis of smoking fetish videos on YouTube: Regulatory implications for tobacco control. *Health communication, 25*(2), 97–106.

Klimstra, T. A., Hale III, W. W., Raaijmakers, Q. A., Branje, S. J., & Meeus, W. H. (2009). Maturation of personality in adolescence. *Journal of Personality and Social Psychology, 96*, 898–912.

Kohn, A. (2014). Trophy furyz: What's behind claims that kids are coddled and over-celebrated? *New York Times,* May 4. Available at www.alfiekohn.org/miscellaneous/trophyfury.htm.

Kolb, D. A. (1984). *Experiential Learning: Experience as the Source of Learning and Development* (vol. 1). Englewood Cliffs, NJ: Prentice Hall.

Koole, S. L., Dijksterhuis, A., & van Knippenberg, A. (2001). What's in a name: Implicit self-esteem and the automatic self. *Journal of Personality and Social Psychology, 80*(4), 669–685.

Kunkel, D. (2001). Children and television advertising. In D. G. Singer & J. L. Singer (eds.), *Handbook of Children and the Media* (pp. 375–393). London: Sage.

Lapsley, D. K., & Rice, K. (1988). The "new look" at the imaginary audience and personal fable: Toward a general model of adolescent ego development. In D. K. Lapsley & F. Power (eds.), *Self, Ego, and Identity: Integrative Approaches* (pp. 109–129). New York: Springer.

Larsen, J. K., Otten, R., & Engels, R. C. (2009). Adolescent depressive symptoms and smoking behavior: The gender-specific role of weight concern and dieting. *Journal of Psychosomatic Research, 66,* 305–308.

Leave Our Kids Alone (2013). "We want an immediate end to all advertising aimed at children under 11," petition. Available at www.change.org/en-GB/petitions/the-uk-government-we-want-an-immediate-end-to-all-advertising-aimed-at-children-under-11 (accessed January 29, 2014).

Leiser, D., & Beth Halachmi, R. (2006). Children's understanding of market forces. *Journal of Economic Psychology, 27*(1), 6–19.

Lenhart, A., Purcell, K., Smith, A., & Zickuhr, K. (2013). *Social Media and Young Adults.* Washington, DC: Pew Internet & American Life Project.

Ma, M., Kibler, J. L., & Sly, K. (2013). Gratitude is associated with greater levels of protective factors and lower levels of risks in African American adolescents. *Journal of Adolescence, 36*(5), 983–991.

Mahalik, J. R., Coley, R. L., McPherran, C. L., Doyle, A. L., Markowitz, A. J., & Jaffee, S. R. (2013). Changes in health risk behaviors for males and females from early adolescence through early adulthood. *Health Psychology, 32,* 685–694.

Malle, B. F., & Hodges, S. D. (2005). *Other Minds: How Humans Bridge the Divide between Self and Others.* New York: Guilford Press.

Masters, J. C., Barden, R. C., & Ford, M. E. (1979). Affective states, expressive behavior, and learning in children. *Journal of Personality and Social Psychology, 37,* 380–390.

McGinnis, J. M., Gootman, J. A., & Kraak, V. I. (eds.). (2006). *Food Marketing to Children and Youth: Threat or Opportunity?* Washington, DC: National Academies Press.

Montgomery, K. C., & Chester, J. (2009). Interactive food and beverage marketing: Targeting adolescents in the digital age. *Journal of Adolescent Health, 45*(3), S18–S29.

Moore, E. S. (2004). Children and the changing world of advertising. *Journal of Business Ethics, 52,* 161–167.

Moore, R. L., & Moschis, G. P. (1981). The role of family communication in consumer learning. *Journal of Communication, 31*(4), 42–51.

Moreno, M. A., Briner, L. R., Williams, A., Walker, L., & Christakis, D. A. (2009a). Real use or "real cool": Adolescents speak out about displayed alcohol references on social networking websites. *Journal of Adolescent Health, 45*(4), 420–422.

Moreno, M. A., VanderStoep, A., Parks, M. R., Zimmerman, F. J., Kurth, A., & Christakis, D. A. (2009b). Reducing at-risk adolescents' display of risk behavior on a social networking web site: A randomized controlled pilot intervention trial. *Archives of Pediatrics & Adolescent Medicine, 163*(1), 35–41.

Morgenstern, M., Isensee, B., Sargent, J. D., & Hanewinkel, R. (2011). Exposure to alcohol advertising and teen drinking. *Preventive Medicine, 52,* 146–151.

Moschis, G. P., & Churchill Jr., G. A. (1978). Consumer socialization: A theoretical and empirical analysis. *Journal of Marketing Research, 15*(4), 599–609.

Moschis, G. P., & Moore, R. L. (1979). Decision making among the young: A socialization perspective. *Journal of Consumer Research, 6*(2), 101–112.

Moses, L. J., & Baldwin, D. A. (2005). What can the study of cognitive development reveal about children's ability to appreciate and cope with advertising? *Journal of Public Policy & Marketing, 24*, 186–201.

Oates, C., Blades, M., & Gunter, B. (2002). Children and television advertising: When do they understand persuasive intent? *Journal of Consumer Behaviour, 1*, 238–245.

Oates, C., Blades, M., Gunter, B., & Don, J. (2003). Children's understanding of television advertising: A qualitative approach. *Journal of Marketing Communications, 9*, 59–71.

O'Donnell, L., O'Donnell, C. R., & Stueve, A. (2001). Early sexual initiation and subsequent sex-related risks among urban minority youth: The reach for health study. *Family Planning Perspectives, 33*, 268–275.

O'Hara, R. E., Gibbons, F. X., Gerrard, M., Li, Z., & Sargent, J. D. (2012). Greater exposure to sexual content in popular movies predicts earlier sexual debut and increased sexual risk taking. *Psychological Science, 23*, 984–993.

O'Keefe, G. S., Clarke-Pearson, K., & Council on Communications and Media (2011). Clinical report: The impact of social media on children, adolescents, and families. *Pediatrics 127*(4), 800–804.

Olson, K. R., & Dweck, C. S. (2008). A blueprint for social cognitive development. *Perspectives on Psychological Science, 3*, 193–202.

Osterman, K. F. (1990). A new agenda for education. *Education and Urban Society, 22*, 133–152.

Palmquist, C. M., & Jaswal, V. K. (2012). Preschoolers expect pointers (even ignorant ones) to be knowledgeable. *Psychological Science, 23*, 230–231.

Park, J. K., & John, D. R. (2011). More than meets the eye: The influence of implicit and explicit self-esteem on materialism. *Journal of Consumer Psychology, 21*(1), 73–87.

Park, L. E., Crocker, J., & Mickelson, K. D. (2004). Attachment styles and contingencies of self-worth. *Personality and Social Psychology Bulletin, 30*, 1243–1254.

Pechmann, C., & Shih, C. F. (1999). Smoking scenes in movies and antismoking advertisements before movies: Effects on youth. *Journal of Marketing, 63*, 1–13.

Pecora, N., Murray, J. P., & Wartella, E. A. (eds.). (2006). *Children and Television: Fifty Years of Research.* New York: Routledge.

Pellegrini, A. (2009). *The Role of Play in Human Development.* New York: Oxford University Press. doi:10.1093/acprof:oso/9780195367324.001.0001.

Porcellato, L., Dugdill, L., Springett, J., & Sanderson, F. H. (1999). Primary school-childrens' perceptions of smoking: implications for health education. *Health Education Research, 14*, 71–83.

Powell, L. M., Szczypka, G., Chaloupka, F. J., & Braunschweig, C. L. (2007). Nutritional content of television food advertisements seen by children and adolescents in the United States. *Pediatrics, 120*, 576–583.

Primack, B. A., Carroll, M. V., McNamara, M., Klem, M. L., King, B., Rich, M., Chan, C. W., & Nayak, S. (2012). Role of video games in improving health-related outcomes: A systematic review. *American Journal of Preventive Medicine, 42*(6), 630–638.

Richins, M. L. & Chaplin, L. N. (2015). Material parenting: How the use of goods in parenting fosters materialism in the next generation. *Journal of Consumer Research, 41*(6), 1333–1357.

Roberts, J. A., Tanner Jr., J. F., & Manolis, C. (2005). Materialism and the family structure–stress relation. *Journal of Consumer Psychology, 15*(2), 183–190.

Robertson, T. S., & Rossiter, J. R. (1974). Children and commercial persuasion: An attribution theory analysis. *Journal of Consumer Research, 1* (1), 13–20.

Rozendaal, E., Buijzen, M., & Valkenburg, P. (2010). Comparing children's and adults' cognitive advertising competences in the Netherlands. *Journal of Children and Media, 4*, 77–89.

Russell, C. A., Russell, D. W., Boland, W. A., & Grube, J. W. (2013). Television's cultivation of American adolescents' beliefs about alcohol and the moderating role of trait reactance. *Journal of Children and Media, 8*(1), 5–22.

Russell, J., Alexis, D., & Clayton, N. (2010). Episodic future thinking in 3- to 5-year-old children: The ability to think of what will be needed from a different point of view. *Cognition, 114*(1), 56–71.

Schor, J. B. (2004). *Born to Buy.* New York: Scribner.

Seidenberg, A. B., Rodgers, E. J., Rees, V. W., & Connolly, G. N. (2012). Youth access, creation, and content of smokeless tobacco ("dip") videos in social media. *Journal of Adolescent Health, 50*(4), 334–338.

Seligman, M. E., Railton, P., Baumeister, R. F., & Sripada, C. (2013). Navigating into the future or driven by the past. *Perspectives on Psychological Science, 8*(2), 119–141.

Shrum, L. J., Wong, N., Arif, F., Chugani, S. K., Gunz, A., Lowrey, T. M., & Sundie, J. (2013). Reconceptualizing materialism as identity goal pursuits: Functions, processes, and consequences. *Journal of Business Research, 66*(8), 1179–1185.

Sigelman, C. K. (2012). Rich man, poor man: Developmental differences in attributions and perceptions. *Journal of Experimental Child Psychology, 113*(3), 415–429.

Sigelman, C. K. (2013). Age differences in perceptions of rich and poor people: Is it skill or luck? *Social Development, 22*(1), 1–18.

Slater, S. J., Chaloupka, F. J., Wakefield, M., Johnston, L. D., & O'Malley, P. M. (2007). The impact of retail cigarette marketing practices on youth smoking uptake. *Archives of Pediatrics & Adolescent Medicine, 161*(5), 440–445.

Smith, P. K. (2005). Social and pretend play in children. In A. D. Pellegrini & P. K. Smith (eds.), *The Nature of Play: Great Apes and Humans* (pp. 173–212). New York: Guilford Press.

Soto, C. J., John, O. P., Gosling, S. D., & Potter, J. (2011). Age differences in personality traits from 10 to 65: Big Five domains and facets in a large cross-sectional sample. *Journal of Personality and Social Psychology, 100*, 330–348.

Steinberg, L. (2005). Cognitive and affective development in adolescence. *Trends in Cognitive Sciences, 9*, 69–74.

Steinberg, L. (2007). Risk taking in adolescence new perspectives from brain and behavioral science. *Current Directions in Psychological Science, 16*, 55–59.

Steinberg, L., Albert, D., Cauffman, E., Banich, M., Graham, S., & Woolard, J. (2008). Age differences in sensation seeking and impulsivity as indexed by behavior and self-report: Evidence for a dual systems model. *Developmental Psychology, 44*, 1764–1778.

Strasburger, V. C. (1995). *Adolescents and the Media: Medical and Psychological Impact.* Thousand Oaks, CA: Sage.

Strasburger, V. C. (2009). Why do adolescent health researchers ignore the impact of the media? *Journal of Adolescent Health, 44*(3), 203–205.

Strasburger, V. C. (2011). Children, adolescents, obesity, and the media. *Pediatrics, 128*(1), 201–208.

Strasburger, V. C., Jordan, A. B., & Donnerstein, E. (2010). Health effects of media on children and adolescents. *Pediatrics, 125*(4), 756–767.

Substance Abuse and Mental Health Services Administration. (2011). *Results from the 2011 National Survey on Drug Use and Health: Volume I. Summary of National Findings.* Rockville, MD: Office of Applied Studies, NSDUH Series H-41, HHS Publication No. SMA 11-4658.

Suddendorf, T., & Busby, J. (2005). Making decisions with the future in mind: Developmental and comparative identification of mental time travel. *Learning and Motivation, 36*(2), 110–125.

Taylor, A. F., & Kuo, F. E. (2006). Is contact with nature important for healthy child development? State of the evidence. In C. Spencer & M. Blades (eds.), *Children and Their Environments: Learning, Using and Designing Spaces* (pp. 124–158). New York: Cambridge University Press.

Taylor, J. (2010). Prime family alert! Fear of failure is a childhood epidemic. *Huffington Post*, September 14. Available at www.huffingtonpost.com/dr-jim-taylor/parenting-alert-fear-of-f_b_709099.html.

Taylor, J. (2014). 5 "dangerous" things parents should do to their children. *Huffington Post*, January 10. Available at www.huffingtonpost.com/dr-jim-taylor/5-dangerous-things-parent_b_4562960.html.

Thompson, D. R., & Siegler, R. S. (2000). Buy low, sell high: The development of an informal theory of economics. *Child Development, 71*(3), 660–677.

Twenge, J. M., Konrath, S., Foster, J. D., Campbell, W. K., & Bushman, B. J. (2008). Egos inflating over time: A cross-temporal meta-analysis of the narcissistic personality inventory. *Journal of Personality, 76*, 875–902.

U.S. Department of Health and Human Services. (2012). *Preventing Tobacco Use among Youth and Young Adults: A Report of the Surgeon General.* Atlanta, GA: U.S. Department of Health and Human Services, Centers for Disease Control and Prevention, Office on Smoking and Health.

Van Boven, L. (2005). Experientialism, materialism, and the pursuit of happiness. *Review of General Psychology, 9*, 132–142.

Van Boven, L., Campbell, M. C. & Gilovich, T. (2010). Stigmatizing materialism: On stereotypes and impressions of materialistic and experiential pursuits. *Personality and Social Psychology Bulletin, 36* (4), 551–563.

Van Boven, L,. & Gilovich, T. (2003). To do or to have? That is the question. *Journal of Personality and Social Psychology, 85* (6), 1193–1202.

Vohs, K. D., Mead, N. L., & Goode, M. R. (2006). The psychological consequences of money. *Science, 314*, 1154–1156.

Ward, S. (1974). Consumer socialization. *Journal of Consumer Research, 1*(2), 1–14.

Ward, S., Reale, G., & Levinson, D. (1972). Children's perceptions, explanations, and judgements of television advertising: A further exploration. In E. A. Rubinstein, G. A. Comstock, & J. P. Murray (eds.), *Television and Social Behavior* (pp. 468–90). Washington, DC: U.S. Government Printing Office.

Ward, S., Wackman, D. B., & Wartella, E. (1977). *How Children Learn to buy: The Development of Consumer Information-Processing Skills.* Oxford: Sage.

Webley, P. (2005). Children's understanding of economics. In M. Barrett & E. Buchanan-Barrow (eds.), *Children's Understanding of Society* (pp. 43–65). New York: Psychology Press.

Wellman, H. M., Cross, D., & Watson, J. (2001). Meta-analysis of theory of mind development: The truth about false belief. *Child Development, 72*(3), 655–684.

Wild, L. G., Flisher, A. J., Bhana, A., & Lombard, C. (2004). Associations among adolescent risk behaviours and self-esteem in six domains. *Journal of Child Psychology and Psychiatry, 45*(8), 1454–1467.

Williams, G. C., Cox, E. M., Hedberg, V. A., & Deci, E. L. (2000). Extrinsic life goals and health risk behaviors in adolescents. *Journal of Applied Social Psychology, 30* (August), 1756–1771.

Zakay, D., Ellis, S., & Shevalsky, M. (2004). Outcome value and early warning indications as determinants of willingness to learn from experience. *Experimental Psychology, 51*(2), 150.

8 Consuming Brands

Jill Avery and Anat Keinan

Introduction

A world without brands would be a very boring world indeed. While consumers' utilitarian needs would continue to be satisfied by the functional attributes of the products and services they purchase and use, the ways in which consumers understand and relate to themselves and to others would be severely diminished if those same products and services were unbranded and generic. Consumers' symbolic needs would remain unsated, stripping away much of the joy of consumption.

Traditional definitions of branding often underestimate the value a brand has for infusing a choice situation with meaning. This chapter explores how people consume brands and presents three perspectives on the meaning of brands that have diverse theoretical roots in cognitive psychology, social psychology, and cultural sociology. These perspectives show that brands are important building blocks of the self and serve as relational partners, enabling people to build and enact meaningful lives. People consume brands to access the meaning contained within them and co-create that meaning through their consumption of and relationships with brands. This symbolic value often overshadows the more functional characteristics of the product (Levy, 1959). As consumers form relationships with brands, they extract the meanings embedded within them and use them in their own lives (Fournier, 1998). As they do so, they add new meanings to the brand, which becomes a cultural repository of co-created meaning (Holt, 2003; McCracken, 1986). Brands, thus, play an important role in documenting both individual experience and shared culture, serving as vessels for idiosyncratic and communal meanings.

Brands are, therefore, meaning-based assets, so brand management is actually a meaning management task. To understand brands as meaning-based assets, we must begin by deconstructing and reconstituting a definition of what a brand is. The American Marketing Association (AMA) proposes that a brand is "a name, term, design, symbol, or any other feature that identifies one seller's good or service as distinct from those of other sellers." This definition focuses only on the denotative property of brands. The AMA's definition defines what Douglas Holt calls a marker (Holt, 2003), a name or a label that serves to identify the product as belonging to a particular manufacturer. However, "brands are not about what you do, but what you enable people to do. Brands

are about people, not products. Brands are about customers, not companies . . .
a brand is fundamentally not about description, but enablement – what it does
for people, rather than what it is" (Fisk, 2015).

We, instead, propose that:

> A *brand* is a perceptual frame that consists of an individual schema and a
> collective cultural frame that enables a consumer to identify, classify, interpret,
> and utilize the meaning of an associated product or service in a way that
> differs from other similar products or services. This perceptual frame enables
> the consumer to choose, experience, and value the product or service as it is
> encountered in everyday life in a differential way, thereby transferring the
> meaning of the brand into their lives.

Under this definition, building a brand refers to the process of establishing
and maintaining a perceptual frame in the minds of consumers, both individually as well as collectively. This recognizes not only the denotative property of
brands but their connotative property as well. The definition attempts to
recognize that a brand's meaning is inherently social, such that a brand is
broadly recognized and collectively interpreted within a culture. It also clarifies
that a brand is, at the same time, inherently individualized and subjective.
Negotiating the collective meanings that swirl around the brand, each individual consumer jumps into the cultural discourse and emerges with a personalized, idiosyncratic understanding of it. This egocentric, yet culturally shaped,
frame can now be used as a heuristic to help the individual choose, experience,
and value the product or service, transferring the brand's meaning from the
object of consumption into his or her own life.

The definition presented here differentiates between a *marker* and a *brand* by
recognizing the role of meaning in affecting how consumers interpret and use
brands. It is not enough for a brand to merely label something, it must
also supply a way of viewing the world that enables the consumer to understand
and/or negotiate his or her environment (Mick & Buhl, 1992) differently.
The cultural aspect of the definition indicates that a brand must have history
to be a brand (Kapferer, 1992). The perceptual frame begins to take shape only
as a consumer either experiences the brand directly or is exposed to it through
marketing communications or social discourse. Hence, newly minted brands are
merely markers that have yet to be filled with meaning (Holt, 2003); their
perceptual frames are barren and not useful for consumers who lack awareness
of them. This definition also allows for the role of people other than the brand's
manufacturer in creating and maintaining a brand.

Finally, a brand is something that enables action: the consumer with a
perceptual frame is better able to recognize, recall, choose, experience, and
value a product than a consumer without one. This part of the definition
recognizes the economic value of a brand, in that it serves as a heuristic for
the consumer, lowering cognitive effort and search costs, adding utility to the
product experience, and reducing risk in the choice decision (Keller, 1998).
This differential response is what drives brand equity, the asset value of the
brand for the firm (Aaker, 1991).

Consuming Brands, Consuming Meaning

Consumer research contains three different streams that speak to brands as meaning-based assets, each approaching the topic from a different level of analysis. Cognitive psychology supports an intrapersonal interpretation of brands as associative networks in memory, social psychology supports a dyadic interpretation of brands as relational partners, and sociology supports a cultural interpretation of brands as repositories of shared meanings.

Brands as Cognitive Psychological Phenomena

Steeped in the tradition of cognitive psychology, David Aaker and Kevin Lane Keller laid the early theoretical groundwork for the intrapersonal interpretation. In early work, Aaker and Keller (1990) use a spreading-activation (Collins & Loftus, 1975) associative memory framework (Anderson, 1983; Wyer & Srull, 1989) to conceptualize brand meaning. What they call *brand knowledge* is the set of associations linked to a brand and the organization of those associations in an organized network in a consumer's memory. According to this line of research, brand managers create brand meaning by building associations between the brand and cognitive and affective attributes that are delivered to the consumer via the product experience itself or through marketing communications. These brand associations become linked to the brand in a consumer's memory and generate feelings, beliefs, and attitudes about the brand that drive preference and purchase. Through a process of spreading activation, the associative structure responds to a stimulus (either the brand itself or a perceived need in the product category) by bringing all connected associations to mind so that the consumer can use them as he or she cognitively processes the brand during a choice situation.

The meaning ascribed to the brand by its managers is theorized to be passively accepted by consumers, who process the incoming information and store it in their long-term memory. For a brand to be said to have meaning, it must have consumers who are aware of it and who have cognitively processed and stored knowledge about it (Keller, 1993). Since each consumer has a different history of usage with and exposure to the brand, brand meaning has a tendency to be idiosyncratic; however, given the centrally controlled meaning-creation mechanism and the tendency of marketers to keep projected brand meaning constant over the long term, many consumers come to share similar brand associations. However, the intra-individual organization of those associations is unique and therefore can be differentially measured by self-report, during which a consumer is probed to determine the strength of connection of each association to the brand, the favorability of the association to the consumer, and the uniqueness of the association to the brand. Keller (1993) terms the result of these three assessments *Customer-Based Brand Equity* (CBBE), a measure of the differential effect that a brand's meaning has on a customer's response to the brand in the marketplace. Brand meaning is a key component in Keller's brand equity pyramid model in which CBBE drives the consumer's cognitive responses (brand judgments) and affective responses (brand feelings) to the brand. Keller views brand meaning as relatively fixed, although he does recognize that it can be slowly changed over time via brand extension and/or repositioning of the brand by its managers.

Brands as Social-Psychological Phenomena

The second stream of research on brand meaning begins to move away from the cognitive psychological perspective and into a social psychological realm in which the consumer and the brand interact to create meanings in the context of a dyadic relationship. The concept of eisegesis, borrowed from the study of semiotics, helps delineate a dyadic process approach to brand meaning (Fournier, 1998; Mick & Buhl, 1992), in which marketers encode brands with denotative meaning and consumers actualize the meaning of brands by interpreting it through an egocentric lens. Marketers deliver a sign structure that is communicated to consumers via advertising and other brand communication vehicles. Consumers then take this sign structure and construct connotative brand meaning by interpreting it according to their psychological, sociocultural, and relational needs. Unlike the modernist flavor of Keller's conceptualization, this conceptualization reflects a postmodern branding paradigm (Holt, 2002) in which the consumer wrests control of brand meaning from the marketer and becomes an active participant and partner in the co-creation of brand meaning. Hence, rather than residing only within the head of the consumer, brand meaning now exists in the lived experience of the consumer as he or she relates with the brand. Given the shifting tides of a consumer's life projects and daily existence, brand meaning is dynamic and evolutionary, unlike the more static brand essence portrayed in Aaker's and Keller's conceptualization.

Three types of meaning lenses figure prominently in Mick, Buhl, and Fournier's conceptualizations. The psychological meaning lens shows the important role of identity building in the creation of brand meaning. Consumers' life themes and supporting life projects provide a frame, or a "horizon of structured expectations," through which consumers interpret brand meaning. Relationships with brands bring meaning to consumers as they are used as props to construct and maintain valued identities. Hence, brand meaning is highly personalized and idiosyncratic. The sociocultural lens shows that some parts of brand meaning can be shared across consumers, due to the fact that consumers interpret brand meaning with socially and culturally developed interpretation schemas that tend to be shared within a culture or a sociocultural cohort (Hirschman, 1981). The relational lens highlights that brands are meaningful only as part of a portfolio of products that the consumer uses; this total brand constellation provides meaning to the consumer, allowing for self-development, self-presentation, and an understanding of the world that surrounds him or her. These three lenses imbue the brand with a surrounding context in which the consumer–brand relationship plays out. This context includes both functional elements, as well as psychosocial and emotional elements that help support the relational bond.

Brands as Sociocultural Phenomena

The final research stream takes a cultural perspective for its level of analysis. In contrast to the idiosyncratic and personalized conceptualizations of the cognitive and social psychological perspectives, Douglas Holt's (2002, 2004) conceptualization of brand meaning emphasizes the collective meaning of a brand in a culture. His brand meaning is culturally shared and socially embedded, so that it becomes part of the fabric of a particular group's culture, such that brands become physical embodiments of cultural content. Brands are thus cultural artifacts that supply cultural meaning to consumers (McCracken, 1986). These cultural meanings fill up a brand over time and are supplied by product designers, advertisements for the brand, popular culture's usage of the brand, and the consumer's personal experiences with the brand. It is pumped into the brand by cultural gatekeepers and extracted by consumers through their ritual use of the products and services marked by it.

Brand meaning is not only collectively understood, but it is collectively authored as well; the brand's managers and its customers are joined by other cultural gatekeepers and influencers who all work together (or at odds with each other) to infuse the brand with meaning. Brand meaning is not inherent in the brand as it leaves the hands of the marketer; it is only through its travels through society and culture that a brand is filled up with stories, images, and associations that become known as its meaning. Meaning is only established once the stories, images, and associations are shared across people and are accepted as taken-for-granted truth (Holt, 2003). The individual consumer as meaning-maker is less in evidence in this conceptualization, as it is only through the collective actions of many that brand meaning emerges.

While Aaker's and Keller's (1990) definition of brand meaning answers the question, "What are you?" Holt's conceptualization emphasizes the question, "What do you stand for?" Brands holding culturally shared meaning usually derive their power from the myths that underlie their brand stories. These myths enable consumers to negotiate their lives, and successful ones indicate personal pathways to negotiating the ruling ideology in place in the culture. These myths, especially in lifestyle categories, can become more important than the functional, product-oriented brand associations so touted by Aaker and Keller.

Every manager dreams of building an iconic brand like Nike, Coke, or Apple. How do brands become iconic, that is, regarded as a representative symbol of the values of a culture? Holt's theory of cultural branding provides a roadmap (Holt, 2004; Holt & Cameron, 2010). According to Holt, iconic brands embed essential identity myths that consumers use to address identity desires and anxieties that arise in culture as a result of cracks in the dominant ideologies. Holt's theory recognizes that at any given time in a society, there are cultural contradictions between "what is" (the reality that most consumers live in that is filled with anxiety because they cannot live up to the dominant ideology) and "what could be" (a fantasized, mythical self that conquers the anxiety). Brands that deliver that "what could be" state to consumers via identity myths embedded in their brand stories will be powerful and resonant. Identity myth consumption allows consumers to create purpose in their lives, smooth over tensions that arise from cultural contradictions, and cement their desired identity in place when it is under stress.

Although brand meaning resides within the culture and exists only in its continuous circulation through society, Holt also recognizes its place in the mind of the consumer. Similar to Aaker and Keller, Holt views brand meaning as a perceptual frame that guides and enables consumer responses to products. Brand meaning colors how consumers experience, understand, and value the product.

Aaker's and Keller's conceptualization feeds into the current managerial thinking on branding and brand management by emphasizing (1) the brand manager as creator of brand meaning and (2) the maintenance of a consistent brand image over time. Holt's conceptualization challenges the way practitioners think about brand management and emphasizes the importance of thinking about brands as cultural artifacts of their times. This conceptualization recognizes that brand meaning is "sticky" due to the fact that meaning change may be driven only by collective action, which is difficult to kick-start when an established meaning is so immersed in the culture, as people are reluctant to challenge socially accepted conventions. However, it also recognizes that brand meaning must change, or the brand risks being left behind when culture moves on to new ideologies requiring new and different myths. Holt shows how consumers in a "post-" postmodern branding paradigm can use the brands and their embedded cultural meanings as original source materials for building and maintaining their identities (Holt, 2002; Thompson & Haytko, 1997).

While they approach the construct of brand meaning from different levels of analysis, these three research streams share some commonalities. First, all three conceptualizations characterize brand meaning as being a set of associations that the consumer cognitively connects with the brand. For Aaker and Keller, these associations are things that have been linked to the brand by the brand manager; for Mick and Fournier, these associations are things that the consumer has linked to the brand via his or her relationship with it; and for Holt, these associations are the collective myths, stories, and images that the culture has built that become attached to the brand in the consumer's mind. All three conceptualizations recognize that brand meaning provides a perceptual lens through which consumers experience the brand. Aaker's and Keller's web of associative meaning influences cognitive and affective responses to the brand, Mick's and Fournier's brand meaning provides the context for developing and living a relationship with the brand, and Holt's cultural meaning frames and filters the consumer's expectations and response to the brand. Finally, all three conceptualizations recognize the contribution and value of brand meaning to the lives of consumers. Aaker, Keller, and Holt talk about brand meaning as a heuristic, making product choices easier. Mick, Fournier, and Holt view brand meaning as a conduit the consumer uses to understand his or her world.

The major differences among the three theories lies in the creation of meaning, its management over time, and its residence. In Keller's and Aaker's world, the brand manager dictates meaning to passive consumers who use it to bring meaning to their lives. Mick and Fournier demonstrate the incredible meaning-creation power that individual consumers hold as they personalize brand meaning through interpreting it in the lived context of their relationships with brands. They specifically highlight the co-creation and co-ownership of meaning between the consumer and the brand manager. Holt widens the net for co-creation, citing multiple authorship origins for brand meaning and minimizing the individual contribution of any one consumer to the collective meaning.

While Holt's and Keller's views of brand meaning are relatively static, reflecting the difficulties of changing an established, shared meaning, Mick's and Fournier's view of meaning is much more amorphous and ephemeral, as it exists only in the relationship between one consumer and the brand. While Keller touts the "heritage" of a brand and warns against changing the brand's core, Holt warns of complacency and urges brand managers to anticipate cultural ideological shifts and to change brand meaning to accompany (or precede) them. Finally, major differences emerge when trying to pin down where brand meaning resides. Keller's and Aaker's cognitive structures, Mick's and Fournier's relational context, and Holt's brand culture all require different methods and a different ideological paradigm for unearthing the brand meaning that resides within them.

Brand Meaning and the Self: Brands as Identity Markers

All three perspectives support the idea that brands serve as important building blocks of the self. Our identities are built and communicated with the help of symbolic markers (Swann, 1983), such as brands. We can be whoever we want to be, merely by changing the things we buy and use (Firat & Venkatesh, 1995). Brands facilitate the presentation of the self to others by serving as conveyors of identity messages in social interaction (Dittmar, 1992; Douglas & Isherwood, 1979; McCracken, 1986; Solomon, 1983). Brands carry identity meanings, culturally shared stories, images, or associations that signal the identity of their users and help "set the stage for the multitude of social roles people must play" (Solomon, 1983, p. 320).

Possessions have long been recognized as symbolic markers used to establish identity, which bestow status or other identity traits on their owners (Levy, 1959), and research shows people choose and use possessions (and the brands that mark them) that reflect their actual or desired identities (Dittmar, 1992; Kassarjian, 1971; Sirgy, 1982), with the belief that the identity meanings attached to these possessions, by association, will transfer to the consumers who use them. Consumers not only use the identity meanings embedded in select possessions and brands to present their identities to others, but also to explore, fabricate, and enact their identities (R. Belk, 1988; Csikszentmihalyi & Rochberg-Halton, 1981; Douglas & Isherwood, 1979; Kleine, Kleine, & Kernan, 1993; Mick & Buhl, 1992; Solomon, 1983; Thompson & Haytko, 1997); hence, consumers attach considerable significance to the identity meanings their possessions and brands hold (Chan, Berger, & Van Boven, 2012; Dommer, Swaminathan, & Ahluwalia, 2013;Escalas & Bettman, 2003, 2005; ; Gao, Wheeler, & Shiv 2009; Park & John, 2010; White & Dahl, 2006, 2007).

Consumers choose brands to use as their identity markers based on the meanings they carry and the anticipated interpretation of those meanings by others. Brands serve as potent semiotic resources for identity building because large portions of brand meaning are communally shared among members of a culture (Hirschman, 1981), making brands an important signifying system for identity presentation in contemporary times. Those with whom we interact deduce who we are by observing the constellation of brands we use (Belk, 1978; Belk, Bahn, & Mayer, 1982; Calder & Burnkrant, 1977; Holman, 1981; Levy, 1959; Solomon, 1988; Solomon & Assael, 1987).

While some researchers argue that all brands carry symbolic meaning and are used by consumers for identity presentation (Kleine et al., 1993; Levy, 1981b), some brands, such as Harley-Davidson, Nike, and Apple, are classified as identity brands, brands that derive most of their value from what they symbolize and how they help consumers present their identities rather than from what they do (Holt, 2004; Park, Milberg, & Lawson, 1990). The meanings associated with identity brands contribute a large portion of the exchange value the products realize in the marketplace (Hirschman, Scott, & Wells, 1998).

Consumers choose brands that contain identity meanings that are congruent with a desired self-concept and avoid those that are incongruent. Research on consumer–brand identity congruence has primarily concentrated on choice: the "self-congruity hypothesis" has a long-standing history in marketing theory and claims that people choose brands that reflect their actual or desired self-concepts (Gardner & Levy, 1955; Kassarjian, 1971; Levy, 1959; Sirgy, 1982). Researchers who study personal or sociocultural life changes suggest that consumers whose identities change following major life events, such as getting married, having children, and getting divorced, will discard possessions or brands when they no longer deliver their newly desired identity. Schouten's (1991) study of plastic surgery recipients suggests that during times of life transition, consumers choose consumption items that are different from those they have chosen before. Other researchers conclude that consumers avoid possessions that are "not me" (Kleine, Kleine, & Allen, 1995) and dispose of or neglect possessions and brands that no longer reflect who they are following major life changes (Belk, 1988; Belk, Sherry, & Wallendorf, 1988; Fournier,

1998). Brands are shown to lose momentum and resonance with consumers when the identity meanings they offer fall out of step with changing societal-level identity needs (Holt, 2004).

Brand Meaning in Consumer–Brand Relationships: Brands as Relational Partners

In addition to their identity construction and enactment roles, brands serve important roles as relational partners. Traditionally, marketers have conceptualized consumers' relationships with brands in economic terms. Following neoclassical economic theory, consumers are viewed as rational, self-interested, economic beings who engage in relationships with brands purely to maximize the utility they receive from them. This behavior most resembles what psychologists label as exchange relationships in the human relationships realm. People engaged in exchange relationships operate under a quid-pro-quo agreement: "members assume that benefits are given with the expectation of receiving a benefit in return," (Clark & Mills, 1979, p. 12).

Fournier (1998) illustrates that consumer–brand bonds are extraordinarily diverse, and many are not merely exchange relationships driven by economic rules. Consumers do not purchase products just for the functional utility they provide; they purchase and use products in order to forge relationships with them, and these relationships provide their lives with meaning and purpose. Consumers form many different types of relationships with brands, many of them communal in nature. Aggarwal (2004) demonstrates that consumers can have both exchange and communal relationships with brands. Communal brand relationships are more emotional and less tactical than exchange relationships; consumers show less self-interest and demonstrate concern for the brand and a commitment to the long-term continuation of the relationship. Fournier further distinguishes among relational types and identifies fifteen different types of relationships, which include friendships, flings, marriages of convenience, and adversaries. These relationships vary along different dimensions: some are close and some are distant; some are more utilitarian and some are more emotionally laden; some are positive and some are negative; and in some, the consumer holds all of the power, while in others, the brand is more dominant.

Consumers transform brands into enlivened relational partners through a process of anthropomorphism, by attributing human characteristics, traits, motivations, and behaviors to brands to animate and humanize them (Aggarwal & McGill, 2012; Kervyn, Fiske, & Malone, 2012, Paharia, Keinan, Avery, & Schor, 2011). Brand meaning includes brand personality, the human traits consumers associate with the brand such as gender, age, lifestyle, and interests. Jennifer Aaker's work on brand personality (Aaker, 1997) categorizes brands into five different personality types: sincere, exciting, competent, sophisticated, and/or rugged. Different brand personalities invite different types of relating; for example, Aaker, Fournier and Brasel (2004) show that exciting brands yield relational trajectories more indicative of flings, while sincere brands yield relational trajectories more indicative of friendships and committed partnerships. As consumers relate to brands, they envision the brand as a relational partner and interpret its actions in line with the implicit rules of their specific relational type.

Communal Brand Meaning Making: Brands as Social Glue

Meaning making also occurs at a collective level, as brands are often the social glue that binds people together. Consumers' collective power to author brand meaning has been recognized by consumer researchers in studies of brand communities and subcultures of consumption (Kozinets, 2001; Muniz & O'Guinn, 2001; Muniz & Schau, 2005; Schouten & McAlexander, 1995), which situate authorship power in the group of active consumers who make up the brand community. A brand community is an organized group of consumers who participate in a structured set of social relations centered on their shared interest in a brand. Brand communities serve as both creators of brand meaning and also its arbiters, by generating and sharing brand stories; integrating and inculcating new members; and defining, enacting, and legislating brand meaning (Muniz & O'Guinn, 2001; Schau, Muniz, & Arnould, 2009). Brand communities practice and celebrate rituals and traditions that help create, interpret, perpetuate, and publicly affirm the meaning of the brand. These rituals and traditions set behavioral expectations for members, constraining their actions both within and outside the community.

Rather than passively accepting brand meaning, brand community members engage with it: interpreting it, massaging it, and negotiating it in a discursive and active process of meaning co-production, which generates an actualized meaning that may differ from the potential meaning put forth by marketers (Firat & Venkatesh, 1995; Holt, 2002; Thompson, Rindfleisch, & Arsel, 2006). If the marketer's espoused meaning is not consistent with the meaning embraced and needed by the brand community, the community will reject it and work to replace it with the community members' own meaning (Brown, Kozinets, & Sherry, 2003; Kozinets, 2001; Muniz & O'Guinn, 2001; Muniz & Schau, 2005). As such, the production of brand meaning can either be "a jointly told tale or a vicious verbal duel" (Brown, Kozinets, & Sherry, 2003) among the brand's marketers, the consumers in its brand communities, and other cultural producers. "When brand communities and subcultures are operative in a brand's 'meaning' ecology, managers no longer solely own the brand, its associations, or the right to position it for strictly commercial purposes," (Leigh, Peters, & Shelton, 2006, p. 492).

Managing Brands as Meaning-Based Assets

Brands are meaning-based assets, so brand management, at its core, requires meaning management. In this section, we use branding theory to inform the practice of brand management by addressing two key areas of inquiry: (1) how to build brand meaning and (2) how to change a brand's meaning over time.

Imbuing a Brand with Meaning

Crafting a brand identity is the first step in imbuing a brand with meaning. A manager's choice of brand elements – name, logo, colors, characters, symbols, taglines, and such – pours initial meaning into the brand's shell (Keller, 1993). However, it is usually through advertising and other marketing communications that a more sophisticated brand narrative is fashioned and told.

Consumer researchers have noted the importance of narrative for brand meaning (Escalas, 2004). Marketers have long recognized the value of a narrative structure for storytelling and frequently use it in advertising (Deighton, Romer, & McQueen, 1989; Mick, 1987; Puto & Wells, 1984; Stern, 1994). By presenting information about the brand in story form, marketers hope to engage consumers in narrative thought processing rather than analytical processing (Escalas, 2004). Narrative thought processing has been shown to be more persuasive than analytical processing, as it decreases negative cognitive attributions and generates strong affective responses (Green & Brock, 2000).

Many marketers imbue their brand stories with archetypal characters (e.g., the wise old man, the trickster, the siren) (Holt & Thompson, 2004; Levy, 1981a; Luedicke, Thompson, & Giesler, 2009), plots (e.g., David and Goliath, Romeo and Juliet, the classic Greek myths, the princess fairy tale) (Paharia et al., 2011), or metaphors (balance, control, container) (Zaltman, 2003; Zaltman & Zaltman, 2008) that we readily recognize from the stories of our childhood or our culture. This technique allows consumers to connect with the stories because they speak to our shared, common experience of being human. Stories using the archetypes and deep metaphors of contemporary culture resonate with consumers on a deeper level, tapping into our conscious, unconscious, and collective conscious minds, according to Jungian psychology (Jung, 1968).

One type of storytelling that has gained traction in the marketplace is the use of brand biography. Paharia and colleagues (2011) introduce the concept of brand biography to describe an emerging trend in branding where companies author a historical account of the events that have shaped the brand over time. Taking the form of a personal narrative, a brand biography chronicles the brand's origins, life experiences, and evolution. Brand biographies are initially authored by the brand's managers and are, therefore, a story selectively told, constructed and reconstructed as needed to promote the brand to consumers. As such, brand biographies are often delivered to consumers via packaging, advertising, branded websites, and other marketing communications. Brand biographies gain their rhetorical power from the fact that they are more than an arbitrary brand image constructed out of thin air, and they are also more than a simple recitation of facts about the brand (i.e., its country of origin or manufacture, the origins of its ingredients or its manufacturing process, or its year of inception). Rather, brand biographies link facts and events in the life of the brand to the experiences of the brand and its founders, selectively choosing anecdotes and incidents to include to narratively shape a coherent life story for the brand.

Brand biographies encourage narrative thought processing because their open-ended narrative structure nudges consumers to fill in the gaps in the brand's story and to causally link brand events and experiences to brand motives, personality, and developing character. Hence, brand biographies encourage and equip consumers to create narratively structured meaning for the brand.

The emergence of brand biographies in the marketplace demonstrates the continued anthropomorphism and animism of brands by marketers and consumers that has been discussed by researchers studying brand personality (Aaker, 1997) and consumer–brand relationships (Aggarwal, 2004; Fournier, 1998). Adding another facet to the "brand-as-person" concept, brand biographies allow the brand's story to be told in a dynamic and unfolding fashion over its lifetime. While brand personality describes a set of human characteristics associated with the brand that are largely static and enduring, a brand biography allows brands to be one thing when they are young and another when they are more mature. The brand's experiences and travels through its life can reveal its changing character to consumers. Furthermore, while brand personalities are often constructed on associations with fictitious concepts and characters, brand biographies are often based on the stories of real people, typically the brand's founders, giving them a tangibility and believability that make it easier for consumers to identify with the brand. Brand biographies capture the dynamism of a brand story over the course of a brand's life and offer consumers multiple points of entry to forge identification with the people behind the brand and with the brand itself (Avery, Paharia, Keinan, & Schor, 2010; Paharia et al., 2011).

Changing the Meaning of a Brand

History has proven that brands often follow an *S*-shaped life cycle, with distinct phases of development, introduction, growth, maturity, and decline. However, some brands seem to have extraordinary long lives, dominating their respective markets for over one hundred years. When managing brands over long periods of time, brand managers find that it is often challenging for the brand to remain relevant, given cultural changes, technological changes, competitive changes, and, most importantly, consumer changes in their markets. Managing brands over time often feels like walking a tightrope, balancing the need for the brand to stay true to its existing meaning while changing with the times to maintain its relevance. Brand managers need to constantly reinforce and fortify their existing brand meaning while looking for ways to leverage and capitalize on it.

Often, older brands need revitalization programs to help increase their relevance for existing customers and to attract new customers. As brands age over time, their narratives may become out of sync with changing consumers, competitors, and markets (Holt, 2004). When this happens, it is time for a brand repositioning. When tuning up their brand's positioning, brand managers have several options for change. They may choose to change the brand's target market by adding new user imagery. They may choose to change the brand's meaning narratives by adding or deleting brand associations or updating the brand personality to be more modern. They may change the brand's competitive set by adding new usage imagery or by redefining the competition. They may choose to update the brand's elements to be more current, changing the logo, tagline, colors, symbols, spokespeople, characters, and so on. Because it is an attempt to change the brand's meaning in the minds of its consumers, brand repositioning is often a dangerous proposition. Existing customers who are loyal to the brand are often resistant to change (Avery, 2007, 2012), while new customers are leery about the brand because they remember its past meaning incarnations.

Once managers build a strong brand, there is always the temptation to leverage that brand by using it to launch new products. Many brand managers use their existing brands to launch line extensions, extending an existing brand into new products in the same product categories, such as Diet Coke with Lime or Vanilla Coke, or brand extensions, extending into different categories. Despite the prevalence of brand extension as a dominant marketing strategy in today's marketplace, managers are plagued with doubts about its efficacy, happily reaping the short-term profits that brand extensions deliver, yet fearing that brand extensions may dilute parent brand value in the longer term.

While much research has been conducted to understand the parent brand and consumer factors that predict whether a brand extension will be successful (Broniarczyk & Alba, 1994; Monga & John, 2010; Rotemberg, 2013, Spiggle, Nguyen, & Caravella, 2012; Torelli & Ahluwalia, 2012; see Volckner & Sattler, 2006, for an overview), recent research examines the potential positive and negative feedback effects of brand extensions on their parent brands (Cutright, Bettman, and Fitzsimons 2013; Keller & Sood, 2001, 2003; Kirmani, Sood, & Bridges, 1999; Loken & John, 1993; Milberg, Park, & McCarthy, 1997; Moorthy, 2012; Sood and Keller 2012). Marketing managers risk changing the identity meaning of their brands when they launch brand extensions that appeal to new consumer segments. When new groups of consumers begin using a brand or when existing consumers stop using it, identity meanings may be affected (Shalev & Morwitz, 2012; White and Argo, 2011; White & Dahl 2006). Berger and Heath (2007, 2008) show that consumers abandon their preferences for and their usage of products and brands when undesirable social comparison groups begin using them.

A logical hypothesis stemming from this work is that consumers using a brand as an identity marker will discard the brand and distance themselves from it following a brand extension that changes the brand's identity meanings, as the brand no longer delivers the desired presentation of self. However, this hypothesis is consistent with a received conceptualization of brand meaning. Following marketer-authored brand meaning change, consumers would receive new brand meanings, evaluate whether they support the consumers' desired identities, and discard the brand if the brand meanings fail to do so. Avery (2007, 2012) instead proposes that discarding the brand is not the only strategy available to consumers of identity brands following brand meaning change. Instead, for some consumers, identity-threatening events in the life of the brand serve as an impetus for consumer meaning making, as consumers actively negotiate what the brand means to others to preserve its value as an identity marker for their presentation of self. Existing consumers can influence their social audiences' interpretation of the brand's evolving meaning by authoring and disseminating new meaning discourses about the brand that are supportive of their identity needs and suppressing those meaning discourses that are not. This alternative strategy is buttressed by work that emphasizes consumers' active negotiation and co-creation, rather than passive acceptance, of brand meaning (Firat & Venkatesh, 1995; Muniz & O'Guinn, 2001).

Bellezza and Keinan (2014) further examine how core consumers of selective brands react when non–core users obtain access to the brand. Contrary to the view that downward brand extensions and non–core users pose a threat to the brand, Bellezza and Keinan explore conditions under which these non–core users enhance rather than dilute the brand image. This research introduces a distinction between two types of non–core users based on how they are perceived by current users of core products: "brand immigrants," who claim to be part of the in-group of core users of the brand, and "brand tourists," who do not claim any membership status to the brand community. While brand immigrants pose a threat to the image and distinctiveness of selective brands, brand tourists can actually reinforce and enhance the brand's desirability and value in the eyes of core users. This "brand tourism effect" is mediated by the feelings of pride held by current core consumers for the brand; just as tourists boost the pride of citizens toward their home country and reinforce the attractiveness and the desirability of the place they visit, brand tourists serve as a source of pride and value for the brand.

In addition to the impact of brand extensions, recent research examines diverse corporate strategies and actions that could threaten the identity meanings and image of the brand (Aaker, Fournier, & Brasel, 2004; Johnson, Matear, & Thomson, 2011; Loken & John, 2009); for example, research examining consumer response to competitive behavior (Paharia, Avery, & Keinan, 2015), product versioning or deliberate subtraction of functionality (Gershoff, Kivetz, & Keinan 2012), the making of taboo trade-offs (McGraw Schwartz, & Tetlock, 2012), the enabling of user design (Fuchs, Prandelli, Schreier, & Dahl 2013), the soliciting of consumer input (Liu & Gal 2011), disclaimer speed (Herbst, Finkel, Allan, & Fitzsimons, 2012), and firm misappropriation (Fournier & Alvarez, 2013; Park, Eisingerich, & Park, 2013).

Promoting Meaningful and Relevant Branding Research

We conclude with a discussion of the importance of interdisciplinary branding research that combines lab and field studies with qualitative ethnographic approaches and aims to understand brands in social, cultural, and competitive context.

An Interdisciplinary Multimethod Approach to Branding Research

A 2014 editorial in the *Journal of Consumer Research* calls for building bridges within our field as well as across other disciplines, arguing that "consumption phenomena and problems are multifaceted and often cannot be fully addressed with only one theoretical base or methodology ... the most promising knowledge development in consumer research deserves, and requires, integration ..." (Peracchio, Luce, & McGill, 2014, p. 2). Branding, in particular, lends itself to interdisciplinary research, as it encompasses all aspects of our lives, including politics, economics, sports, religion, fashion, art, and popular culture (Kapferer, 2004). Accordingly, in recent years the consumption and marketing of brands have been explored from a variety of perspectives, including neuroscience and neurophysiology (Plassmann, Ramsøy, & Milosavljevic, 2012; Reinmann, Castaño, Zaichkowsky, & Bechara, 2012; Schmitt, 2012; Venkatraman, Clithero, Fitsimons, & Huettel, 2012), finance and accounting (Mizik & Jacobson, 2009; Stahl, Heitmann, Lehmann, & Neslin 2012), linguistics (Argo, Popa, & Smith, 2010), history (Koehn, 2001), religion (Izberk-Bilgin, 2012; Shachar, Erdem, Cutright, & Fitzsimons, 2011), and cultural studies and philosophy (Schroeder, Salzer-Mörling, & Askegaard, 2006).

Within consumer research, our understanding of the consumption of brands can greatly benefit from conversations across research traditions, combining the perspectives and methodologies of information processing and behavioral decision theory with those of consumer culture theory (Arnould & Thompson, 2005). Meaning creation and brand relationship development are highly complex process phenomena that do not lend themselves easily to simple cause-and-effect testing. There are multiple levels of analysis (individual, dyadic, and contextual) that one needs to take into account, levels that act and interact to produce outcomes, producing direct effects or combining in interactive ways to moderate or mediate each other. Therefore, merely looking at variables at one level of analysis can be misleading and incomplete. Secondly, studies of human relationships show that many cause-and-effect relationships actually consist of reciprocal determinism, where the "cause" causes the effect, but that the "effect" also causes the "cause" (Wieselquist, Rusbult, Foster, & Agnew, 1999). It is likely that consumers' relationships with brands follow a similar logic. Thirdly, meaning making processes and human relationships exhibit a sense of equifinality, in that there are many different ways of reaching a common outcome and there are multiple outcomes that can be reached given the same conditions (Sager, 1976). Therefore, there is no "one" path for meaning making or relationship development.

Moreover, brand meaning and consumer–brand relationships are idiosyncratic, in that each consumer has a unique relationship with each brand he or she uses that is based upon a shared history of usage of and exposure to the brand. Consumer–brand ties vary across consumer segments based on individual differences in involvement (Laurent & Kapferer, 1985) and differences in life themes (Fournier, 1998; Mick & Buhl, 1992) or salient identities (Kleine, Kleine, & Allen, 1995) that drive relational behavior. Given that idiosyncrasy is such an important facet of brand meaning and consumer–brand relationships, focusing solely on experimental and statistical methods that aggregate sameness, and eliminate differences, may miss an important part of the puzzle.

Understanding the Consumption of Brands within Social and Competitive Context

Meaning making and consumer–brand relationships are embedded in a web of social relationships that entangle the consumer (McAlexander, Schouten, & Koening, 2002). This web includes relationships between the consumer and other consumers in the brand community (Muniz & O'Guinn, 2001; Schouten & McAlexander, 1995), relationships between consumers and other people in their lives (Epp & Price, 2008; Fournier, 1998), relationships among brands in a competitive context (Paharia, Avery, & Keinan, 2015; Paharia et al., 2011), and relationships among brands in a particular consumers' use portfolio (Solomon, 1988). One brand is rarely the cornerstone of a consumer's identity; rather, it is the portfolio of brands, the brandscape (Sherry, 1987) or the consumption constellation (McCracken, 1988) that a consumer uses to define himself or herself. Studying brands in isolation ignores the cultural value of the brand and the sociocultural meaning consumers derive from consumer–brand relationships (Fournier, 1998).

In addition to exploring brands in a sociocultural context, recent research considers the impact of the competitive context on the evaluation and consumption of brands; for example, demonstrating that evaluations of the brand depend upon exposure to multiple brands (Yang, Cutright, Chartrad, & Fitzsimons, 2014), the competitive alternatives (Milberg, Sinn, & Goodstein, 2010), comparative advertising (Malaviya & Sternthal, 2009), exposure to competitive brand information (Meyvis, Goldsmith, & Dhar, 2012; Raju, Unnava, & Montgomery, 2009), order of entry (Cunha & Laran, 2009), the consumption of multiple products at the same time (Rahinel & Redden, 2013), and cross-category competition (Chernev. Hamilton, & Gal, 2011). Moreover, the way in which a brand frames its competitive context can affect brand attitudes and purchase; consumers increase their preference for small brands and decrease their preference for large brands when the two types of brands are framed as competing against each other (Paharia, Avery, & Keinan, 2015). This "framing the game" effect does not result from having a stronger competitor per se, but rather stems from the competition being made salient to the consumer. This research shows that brands themselves are embedded in a web of marketplace relationships with their competitors, and that this web provides meaning to consumers. Competitive contexts and the concerns that emerge from them differentially constrain and empower brands to claim meanings that can drive consumer preference.

In sum, a multimethod approach to investigating brands, embedded in the social, cultural, and competitive contexts, would further increase the impact of branding research, producing meaningful research (Dahl, Fischer, Johar, & Morwitz, 2014) that is useful and relevant to various audiences. The future of branding research and our ability to measure and understand the full psychological, economic, and sociocultural significance of brands relies upon researchers' willingness to both integrate different methodologies and disciplines and understand brands in their broader contexts.

References

Aaker, D. A. (1991). *Managing Brand Equity: Capitalizing on the Value of a Brand Name*. New York: Free Press.

Aaker, D. A., & Keller, K. L. (1990). Consumer evaluations of brand extensions. *Journal of Marketing, 54*, 27–41.

Aaker, J. L. (1997). Dimensions of brand personality. *Journal of Marketing Research, 34* (3), 347–56.

Aaker, J. L., Fournier, S., & Brasel, A. (2004). When good brands do bad. *Journal of Consumer Research, 31*(forthcoming), 1–24.

Aggarwal, P. (2004). The effects of brand relationship norms on consumer attitudes and behavior. *Journal of Consumer Research, 31*(1), 87–101.

Aggarwal, P., & McGill, A. L. (2012). When brands seem human, do humans act like brands? Automatic behavioral priming effects of brand anthropomorphism. *Journal of Consumer Research, 39*(2), 307–323.

Anderson, J. R. (1983). *The Architecture of Cognition*. Cambridge, MA: Harvard University Press.

Argo, J. J., Popa, M., & Smith, M. C. (2010). The sound of brands. *Journal of Marketing, 74*(4), 97–109.

Arnould, E. J., & Thompson, C. J. (2005). Consumer Culture Theory (CCT): Twenty years of research. *Journal of Consumer Research, 31*, 868–882.

Avery, J. (2007). Saving face by making meaning: The negative effects of consumers' self-serving response to brand extension. Doctoral dissertation, Harvard Business School.

Avery, J. (2012). Defending the markers of masculinity: Consumer resistance to brand gender-bending. *International Journal of Research in Marketing, 29*(4), 322–336.

Avery, J., Paharia, N., Keinan, A., & Schor, J. B. (2010). The strategic use of brand biographies. In R. W. Belk (ed.), *Research in Consumer Behavior* (vol. 10, pp. 213–229). Bingley, UK: Emerald Group Publishing Limited.

Belk, R. (1988). Possessions and the extended self. *Journal of Consumer Research, 15* (September), 139–165.

Belk, R. W. (1978). Assessing the effects of visible consumption on impression formation. In H. K. Hunt (ed.), *Advances in Consumer Research* (pp. 39–47). Ann Arbor, MI: Association for Consumer Research.

Belk, R. W., Bahn, K. D., & Mayer, R. N. (1982). Developmental recognition of consumption symbolism. *Journal of Consumer Research, 9*, 4–17.

Belk, R. W., Sherry, J. F., Jr., & Wallendorf, M. (1988). A naturalistic inquiry into buyer and seller behavior at a swap meet. *Journal of Consumer Research, 14*, 449–470.

Bellezza, S., & Keinan, A. (2014) Brand tourists: How non–core users enhance the brand image by eliciting pride. *Journal of Consumer Research, 41*(August), 397–417.

Berger, J., & Heath, C. (2007). Where consumers diverge from others: Identity signaling and product domains. *Journal of Consumer Research, 34*(2), 269–279.

Berger, J., & Heath, C. (2008). Who drives divergence? Identity signaling, out-group similarity, and the abandonment of cultural tastes. *Journal of Personality and Social Psychology, 95*(3), 593–607.

Broniarczyk, S. M., & Alba, J. W. (1994). The importance of the brand in brand extension. *Journal of Marketing Research, 31*(2), 214.

Brown, S., Kozinets, R. V., & Sherry, J. F., Jr. (2003). Teaching old brands new tricks: Retro branding and the revival of brand meaning. *Journal of Marketing, 67*, 19–33.

Calder, B. J., & Burnkrant, R. E. (1977). Interpersonal influence on consumer behavior: An attribution theory approach. *Journal of Consumer Research, 4*, 29–38.

Chan, C., Berger, J., & Van Boven, L. (2012). Identifiable but not identical: Combining social identity and uniqueness motives in choice. *Journal of Consumer Research, 39*(3), 561–573.

Chernev, A., Hamilton, R., & Gal, D. (2011). Competing for consumer identity: Limits to self-expression and the perils of lifestyle branding. *Journal of Marketing, 75* (3), 66–82.

Clark, M. S., & Mills, J. (1979). Interpersonal attraction in exchange and communal relationships. *Journal of Personality and Social Psychology, 37*(1), 12–24.

Collins, A. M., & Loftus, E. F. (1975). A spreading activation theory of semantic processing. *Psychological Review, 82*, 407–428.

Csikszentmihalyi, M., & Rochberg-Halton, E. (1981). *The Meaning of Things: Domestic Symbols and the Self*. New York: Cambridge University Press.

Cunha, M., Jr., & Laran, J. (2009). Asymmetries in the sequential learning of brand associations: Implications for the early entrant advantage. *Journal of Consumer Research, 35*(5), 788–799.

Cutright, K. M., Bettman, J. R., & Fitzsimons, G. J. (2013). Putting brands in their place: How a lack of control keeps brands contained. *Journal of Marketing Research, 50*(3), 365–377.

Dahl, D., Fischer, E., Johar, G., & Morwitz, V. (2014). Editorial: From the editors-elect: Meaningful consumer research. *Journal of Consumer Research, 41* (1), iii–v.

Deighton, J., Romer, D., & McQueen, J. (1989). Using drama to persuade. *Journal of Consumer Research, 16*(3), 335–343.

Dittmar, H. (1992). *The Social Psychology of Materials Possessions: To Have Is to Be*. New York: St. Martin's Press.

Dommer, S. L., Swaminathan, V., & Ahluwalia, R. (2013). Using differentiated brands to deflect exclusion and protect inclusion: The moderating role of self-esteem on attachment to differentiated brands. *Journal of Consumer Research, 40*(4), 657–675.

Douglas, M., & Isherwood, B. (1979). *The World of Goods.* New York: Basic.

Epp, A. M., & Price, L. L. (2008). Family identity: A framework of identity interplay in consumption practices. *Journal of Consumer Research, 35*(June), 50–70.

Escalas, J. E. (2004). Narrative processing: Building consumer connections to brands. *Journal of Consumer Psychology, 14*(1&2), 168–180.

Escalas, J. E., & Bettman, J. R. (2003). You are what they eat: The influence of reference groups on consumers' connections to brands. *Journal of Consumer Psychology, 13*(3), 339–348.

Escalas, J. E., & Bettman, J. R. (2005). Self-construal, reference groups, and brand meaning. *Journal of Consumer Research, 32*(3), 378–389.

Firat, F., & Venkatesh, A. (1995). Liberatory postmodernism and the re-enchantment of consumption. *Journal of Consumer Research, 22*, 239–267.

Fisk, P. (2015). Brand innovation: Embracing change to innovate your brand and accelerate growth. In K. Kompella (ed.), *The Brand Challenge.* London: Kogan Page, 41–82.

Fournier, S. (1998). Consumers and their brands: Developing relationship theory in consumer research. *Journal of Consumer Research, 24*(4), 343–373.

Fournier, S., & Alvarez, C. (2013). Relating badly to brands. *Journal of Consumer Psychology, 23*(2), 253–264.

Fuchs, C., Prandelli, E., Schreier, M., & Dahl, D. W. (2013). All that is users might not be gold: How labeling products as user designed backfires in the context of luxury fashion brands. *Journal of Marketing, 77*(5), 75–91.

Gao, L., Wheeler, S. C., & Shiv, B. (2009). The "shaken self": Product choices as a means of restoring self-view confidence. *Journal of Consumer Research, 36*(1), 29–38.

Gardner, B. B., & Levy, S. J. (1955). The product and the brand. *Harvard Business Review, 33*(2), 33–39.

Gershoff, A. D., Kivetz, R., & Keinan, A. (2012). Consumer response to versioning: How brands' production methods affect perceptions of unfairness. *Journal of Consumer Research, 39*(2), 382–398.

Green, M. C., & Brock, T. C. (2000). The role of transportation in the persuasiveness of public narratives. *Journal of Personality and Social Psychology, 79*(5), 701–721.

Herbst, K. C., Finkel, E. J., Allan, D., & Fitzsimons, G. M. (2012). On the dangers of pulling a fast one: Advertisement disclaimer speed, brand trust, and purchase intention. *Journal of Consumer Research, 38*(5), 909–919.

Hirschman, E. C. (1981). Comprehending symbolic consumption. In E. C. Hirschman & M. B. Holbrook (eds.), *Symbolic Consumer Behaviour* (pp. 4–6). Ann Arbor, MI: Association for Consumer Research.

Hirschman, E. C., Scott, L., & Wells, W. B. (1998). A model of product discourse: Linking consumer practice to cultural texts. *Journal of Advertising, 27*(1), 33–50.

Holman, R. H. (1981). Apparel as communication. In E. C. Hirschman & M. B. Holbrook (eds.), *Symbolic Consumer Behavior* (pp. 7–15). Ann Arbor, MI: Association for Consumer Research.

Holt, D. B. (2002). Why do brands cause trouble? A dialectical theory of consumer culture and branding. *Journal of Consumer Research, 29*(1), 70–90.

Holt, D. B. (2003). Brands and branding. *Harvard Business School Teaching Note* (N9–503–045).

Holt, D. B. (2004). *How Brands Become Icons: The Principles of Cultural Branding.* Boston: Harvard Business School Press.

Holt, D. B., & Cameron, D. (2010). *Cultural Strategy: Using Innovative Ideologies to Build Breakthrough Brands.* Oxford: Oxford University Press.

Holt, D. B., & Thompson, C. J. (2004). Man-of-action heroes: The pursuit of heroic masculinity in everyday consumption. *Journal of Consumer Research, 31*(2), 425–440.

Izberk-Bilgin, E. (2012). Infidel brands: unveiling alternative meanings of global brands at the nexus of globalization, consumer culture, and Islamism. *Journal of Consumer Research, 39*(4), 663–687.

Johnson, A. R., Matear, M., & Thomson, M. (2011). A coal in the heart: Self-relevance as a post-exit predictor of consumer anti-brand actions. *Journal of Consumer Research, 38*(1), 108–125.

Jung, C. G. (1968). *Man and His Symbols.* New York: Dell.

Kapferer, J.-N. (1992). *Strategic Brand Management: New Approaches to Creating and Evaluating Brand Equity.* New York: Free Press.

Kapferer, J.-N. (2004). *The New Strategic Brand Management: Creating and Sustaining Brand Equity Long Term.* London and Sterling, VA: Kogan Page.

Kassarjian, H. H. (1971). Personality and consumer behavior. *Journal of Marketing Research, 8*(4), 409–418.

Keller, K. L. (1993). Conceptualizing, measuring, and managing customer-based brand equity. *Journal of Marketing, 57*(1), 1–31.

Keller, K. L. (1998). *Strategic Brand Management: Building, Measuring, and Managing Brand Equity.* Upper Saddle River, NJ: Prentice Hall.

Keller, K. L., & Sood, S. (2001). *The Effects of Product Experience and Branding Strategies on Brand Evaluations.* University of California at Los Angeles Working Paper.

Keller, K. L., & Sood, S. (2003). Brand equity dilution. *Sloan Management Review, 45* (Fall)12–15.

Kervyn, N., Fiske, S. T., & Malone, C. (2012). Brands as intentional agents framework: How perceived intentions and ability can map brand perception. *Journal of Consumer Psychology: The Official Journal of the Society for Consumer Psychology, 22*(2) 166–176.

Kirmani, A., Sood, S., & Bridges, S. (1999). The ownership effect in consumer responses to brand line stretches. *Journal of Marketing, 63*, 88–101.

Kleine, R. E. I., Kleine, S. S., & Kernan, J. B. (1993). Mundane consumption and the self: A social-identity perspective. *Journal of Consumer Psychology, 2*(3), 209–235.

Kleine, S. S., Kleine, R. E., & Allen, C. T. (1995). How is a possession "me" or "not me"? Characterizing types and an antecedent of material possession attachment. *Journal of Consumer Research, 22*(December), 327–343.

Koehn, N. F. (2001). *Brand New: How Entrepreneurs Earned Consumers' Trust from Wedgwood to Dell.* Boston: Harvard Business Press.

Kozinets, R. V. (2001). Utopian enterprise: Articulating the meanings of Star Trek's culture of consumption. *Journal of Consumer Research, 28*(1), 67.

Laurent, G., & Kapferer, J.-N. (1985). Measuring consumer involvement profiles. *Journal of Marketing Research, XXII*, 41–53.

Leigh, T. W., Peters, C., & Shelton, J. (2006). The consumer quest for authenticity: The multiplicity of meanings within the MG subculture of consumption. *Journal of the Academy of Marketing Science 34*(4), 481–493.

Levy, S. J. (1959). Symbols for sale. *Harvard Business Review, 37*(4), 117–124.

Levy, S. J. (1981a). Interpreting consumer mythology: A structural approach to consumer behavior. *Journal of Marketing, 45*, 49–61.

Levy, S. J. (1981b). Symbols, selves, and others. In A. Mitchell (ed.), *Advances in Consumer Research* (vol. 10, pp. 542–543). Provo, UT: Association for Consumer Research.

Liu, W., & Gal, D. (2011). Bringing us together or driving us apart: The effect of soliciting consumer input on consumers' propensity to transact with an organization. *Journal of Consumer Research, 38*(2), 242–259.

Loken, B., & John, D. R. (1993). Diluting brand beliefs: When do brand extensions have a negative impact? *Journal of Marketing, 57*(3), 71–84.

Loken, B., & John, D. R. (2009). When do bad things happen to good brands? Understanding internal and external sources of brand dilution. In B. Loken, R. Ahluwalia, & M. J. Houston (eds.), *Brands and Brand Management: Contemporary Research Perspectives* (pp. 233–63). New York: Routledge.

Luedicke, M. K., Thompson, C. J., & Giesler, M. (2009). Consumer identity work as moral protagonism: How myth and ideology animate a brand-mediated moral conflict. *Journal of Consumer Research, 36*(April), 1016–1032.

Malaviya, P., & Sternthal, B. (2009). Parity product features can enhance or dilute brand evaluation: The influence of goal orientation and presentation format. *Journal of Consumer Research, 36*(1), 112–121.

McAlexander, J. H., Schouten, J. W., & Koening, H. F. (2002). Building brand community. *Journal of Marketing, 66*(1), 38–54.

McCracken, G. (1986). Culture and consumption: A theoretical account of the structure and movement of the cultural meaning of consumer goods. *Journal of Consumer Research, 12*, 71–84.

McCracken, G. (1988). *Culture and Consumption: New Approaches to the Symbolic Character of Consumer Goods and Activities*. Bloomington: Indiana University Press.

McGraw, A. P., Schwartz, J. A., & Tetlock, P. E. (2012). From the commercial to the communal: Reframing taboo trade-offs in religious and pharmaceutical marketing. *Journal of Consumer Research, 39*(1), 157–173.

Meyvis, T., Goldsmith, K., & Dhar, R. (2012). The importance of the context in brand extension: how pictures and comparisons shift consumers' focus from fit to quality. *Journal of Marketing Research, 49*(2), 206–217.

Mick, D. G. (1987). Toward a semiotic of advertising story grammars. In J. Umiker-Sebeok (ed.), *Marketing and Semiotics: New Directions in the Study of Signs for Sale* (pp. 249–278). Berlin: de Gruyter.

Mick, D. G., & Buhl, C. (1992). A meaning-based model of advertising experiences. *Journal of Consumer Research, 19*(3), 317–338.

Milberg, S. J., Park, C. W., & McCarthy, M. S. (1997). Managing negative feedback effects associated with brand extensions: The impact of alternative branding strategies. *Journal of Consumer Psychology, 6*(2), 119–140.

Milberg, S. J., Sinn, F., & Goodstein, R. C. (2010). Consumer reactions to brand extensions in a competitive context: Does fit still matter? *Journal of Consumer Research, 37*(3), 543–553.

Mizik, N., & Jacobson, R. (2009). Valuing branded businesses. *Journal of Marketing, 73*(6), 137–153.

Monga, A. B., & John, D. R. (2010). What makes brands elastic? The influence of brand concept and styles of thinking on brand extension evaluation. *Journal of Marketing, 74*(3), 80–92.

Moorthy, S. (2012). Can brand extension signal product quality? *Marketing Science, 31*(5), 756–770.

Muniz, A., & O'Guinn, T. C. (2001). Brand community. *Journal of Consumer Research, 27*, 412–432.

Muniz, A., & Schau, H. J. (2005). Religiosity in the abandoned Apple Newton brand community. *Journal of Consumer Research, 31*(4), 737–747.

Paharia, N., Avery, J., & Keinan, A. (2015). Positioning brands versus large competitors to drive sales. *Journal of Marketing Research, 51*(6) 647–656.

Paharia, N., Keinan, A., Avery, J., & Schor, J. B. (2011). The underdog effect: The marketing of disadvantage and determination through brand biography. *Journal of Consumer Research, 17*(5), 775–790.

Park, C. W., Eisingerich, A. B., & Park, J. W. (2013). Attachment–aversion (AA) model of customer–brand relationships. *Journal of Consumer Psychology, 23*(2), 229–248.

Park, C. W., Milberg, S., & Lawson, R. (1990). Evaluation of brand extensions: The role of product level similarity and brand concept consistency. *Journal of Consumer Research, 18*, 185–193.

Park, J. K., & John, D. R. (2010). Got to get you into my life: Do brand personalities rub off on consumers? *Journal of Consumer Research, 37*(4), 655–669.

Peracchio, L. A., Luce, M. F., & McGill, A. L. (2014). Building bridges for an interconnected field of consumer research. *Journal of Consumer Research, 40*(6), v–viii.

Plassmann, H., Ramsøy, T. Z., & Milosavljevic, M. (2012). Branding the brain: A critical review and outlook. *Journal of Consumer Psychology, 22*(1), 18–36.

Puto, C. P., & Wells, W. D. (1984). Informational and transformational advertising: The differential effects of time. In T. C. Kinnear (ed.), *Advances in Consumer Research* (vol. 11, pp. 638–643). Provo, UT: Association for Consumer Research.

Rahinel, R., & Redden, J. P. (2013). Brands as product coordinators: Matching brands make joint consumption experiences more enjoyable. *Journal of Consumer Research, 39*(6), 1290–1299.

Raju, S., Unnava, H. R., & Montgomery, N. V. (2009). The effect of brand commitment on the evaluation of nonpreferred brands: A disconfirmation process. *Journal of Consumer Research, 35*(5), 851–863.

Reimann, M., Castaño, R., Zaichkowsky, J., & Bechara, A. (2012). How we relate to brands: Psychological and neurophysiological insights into consumer–brand relationships. *Journal of Consumer Psychology, 22*(1), 128–142.

Rotemberg, J. J. (2013). Expected firm altruism, quality provision, and brand extensions. *Marketing Science, 32*(2), 325–341.

Sager, C. J. (1976). *Marriage Contracts and Couple Therapy*. New York: Brunner/Mazel.

Schau, H. J., Muniz, A. M. J., & Arnould, E. J. (2009). How brand community practices create value. *Journal of Marketing, 73*(September), 30–51.

Schmitt, B. (2012). The consumer psychology of brands. *Journal of Consumer Psychology, 22*(1), 7–17.

Schouten, J. W. (1991). Selves in transition: Symbolic consumption in personal rites of passage and identity reconstruction. *Journal of Consumer Research, 17*(4), 412–425.

Schouten, J. W., & McAlexander, J. H. (1995). Subcultures of consumption: An ethnography of the new bikers. *Journal of Consumer Research, 22*(June), 43–61.

Schroeder, J. E., Salzer-Mörling, M., & Askegaard, S. (eds.). (2006). *Brand Culture*. London:Routledge.

Shachar, R., Erdem, T., Cutright, K. M., & Fitzsimons, G. J. (2011). Brands: The opiate of the nonreligious masses? *Marketing Science, 30*(1), 92–110.

Shalev, E., & Morwitz, V. G. (2012). Influence via comparison-driven self-evaluation and restoration: The case of the low-status influencer. *Journal of Consumer Research, 38*(5), 964–980.

Sherry, J. F., Jr. (1987). *Cereal Monogamy: Brand Loyalty as Secular Ritual in Consumer Culture*. Paper presented at the annual conference of the Association for Consumer Research, Boston.

Sirgy, M. J. (1982). Self-concept in consumer behavior: A critical review. *Journal of Consumer Research, 9*(3), 287–300.

Solomon, M. R. (1983). The role of products as social stimuli: A symbolic interactionism perspective. *Journal of Consumer Research, 10*, 319–329.

Solomon, M. R. (1988). Mapping product constellations: A social categorization approach to symbolic consumption. *Psychology and Marketing, 5*, 233–258.

Solomon, M. R., & Assael, H. (1987). The forest or the trees? A gestalt approach to symbolic consumption. In J. Umiker-Sebeok (ed.), *Marketing and Semiotics: New Directions in the Study of Signs for Sale* (pp. 189–218). Berlin: Mouton de Gruyter.

Sood, S., & Keller, K. L. (2012). The effects of brand name structure on brand extension evaluations and parent brand dilution. *Journal of Marketing Research, 49*(3), 373–382.

Spiggle, S., Nguyen, H. T., & Caravella, M. (2012). More than fit: Brand extension authenticity. *Journal of Marketing Research, 49*(6), 967–983.

Stahl, F., Heitmann, M., Lehmann, D. R., & Neslin, S. A. (2012). The impact of brand equity on customer acquisition, retention, and profit margin. *Journal of Marketing, 76*(4), 44–63.

Stern, B. B. (1994). Classical and vignette television advertising dramas: Structural models, formal analysis, and consumer effects. *Journal of Consumer Research, 20*(4), 601–615.

Swann, W. B. J. (1983). Self-verification: Bringing social reality into harmony with the self. In J. Suls & A. G. Greenwald (eds.), *Psychological Perspectives on the Self* (vol. 2, pp. 33–66). Hillsdale, NJ: Lawrence Erlbaum Associates.

Thompson, C. J., & Haytko, D. L. (1997). Speaking of fashion: Consumers' uses of fashion discourses and the appropriation of countervailing cultural meanings. *Journal of Consumer Research, 24*, 15–42.

Thompson, C. J., Rindfleisch, A., & Arsel, Z. (2006). Emotional branding and the strategic value of the doppelganger brand image. *Journal of Marketing, 70*(1), 50–64.

Torelli, C. J., & Ahluwalia, R. (2012). Extending culturally symbolic brands: A blessing or a curse? *Journal of Consumer Research, 38*(5), 933–947.

White, K., & Argo, J. (2011). When imitation doesn't flatter: The role of consumer distinctiveness in responses to mimicry. *Journal of Consumer Research, 38*(4), 667–80.

White, K., & Dahl, D. W. (2006). To be or< i> not be? The influence of dissociative reference groups on consumer preferences. *Journal of Consumer Psychology, 16*(4), 404–414.

White, K., & Dahl, D. W. (2007). Are all out-groups created equal? Consumer identity and dissociative influence. *Journal of Consumer Research, 34*(4), 525–536.

Wieselquist, J., Rusbult, C. E., Foster, C. A., & Agnew, C. R. (1999). Commitment, pro-relationship behavior and trust in close relationships. *Journal of Personality and Social Psychology, 77*(5), 942–966.

Wyer, R. S., & Srull, T. K. (1989). Person memory and judgment. *Psychological Review, 96*(1), 58–83.

Venkatraman, V., Clithero, J. A., Fitzsimons, G. J., & Huettel, S. (2012). New scanner data for brand marketers: how neuroscience can help better understand differences in brand preferences. *Journal of Consumer Psychology, 22*, 143–153.

Volckner, F., Sattler, H. (2006). Drivers of brand extension success. *Journal of Marketing, 70*(April), 18–34.

Yang, L. W., Cutright, K. M., Chartrand, T. L., & Fitzsimons, G. J. (2014). Distinctively different: Exposure to multiple brands in low-elaboration settings. *Journal of Consumer Research, 40*(5), 973–992.

Zaltman, G. (2003). *How Customers Think: Essential Insights into the Mind of the Market*. Boston: Harvard Business School Press.

Zaltman, G., & Zaltman, L. (2008). *Marketing Metaphoria: What Deep Metaphors Reveal About the Minds of Consumers*. Boston: Harvard Business School Press.

9 User Design through Self-Customization

Claudia Townsend, Ulrike Kaiser, and Martin Schreier

Introduction

Open any introductory marketing textbook and you will learn that the role of the firm is to create, communicate, and deliver value to the consumer who, in turn, takes the passive role of paying and consuming. For many years, this was, in fact, how marketers, consumer researchers, and psychologists perceived these two roles; the notion of consumer input into value creation was almost entirely neglected.

This began to change when researchers in the area of innovation identified product users modifying and innovating on their own. In fact, von Hippel, De Jong, and Flowers (2012) found that in a representative sample of UK consumers, more than 6 percent had engaged in product modification or innovation during the prior three years, resulting in annual product development expenditures 1.4 times larger than the respective research and development (R&D) expenditures of all UK firms. More broadly, what emerged was the concept of "democratizing innovation," that getting users actively involved in the process of new product development (NPD) can be a great source of value to the consumer and, thus, the firm (von Hippel, 2005). Today, consumer input is a recognized force in new product development, so much so that the Marketing Science Institute (MSI) listed it as one of its top priorities for exploration for 2008 through 2010.

A parallel development in the marketplace has been that firms are going after smaller and more well-defined segments (Dalgic & Leeuw, 1994; Kotler & Armstrong, 2013). This is due to a number of factors, including the abundance of brands competing in many sectors; the rapid growth in media outlets, particularly online; and the increasing amount of information available on individual consumers. The result is that, in both media (Nelson-Field & Riebe, 2011) and products (Dalgic, 2006), the use of niche marketing is on the rise, while mass marketing is becoming an increasingly less viable option, particularly for new products.

These two developments, consumer involvement in design as well as smaller target markets, have resulted in the practice of self-customization, where instead of offering ready-made products, the firm equips consumers with the

Author note: The first and second authors contributed equally to this chapter.

tools to customize and design their own product. This can be viewed as the ultimate form of niche marketing, where the resulting segments consist of individuals. As such, there are many benefits to such an offering, including but not limited to greater customer involvement with the brand and product as well as a higher likelihood of the product matching the individual's needs and preferences. The integration of the Internet into marketing practices and most aspects of daily life has allowed this phenomenon to go mainstream, with innovative firms such as Dell and Nike leading the way in creating online platforms where consumers design their own products.

This chapter begins by offering a broad summary of self-customization – what it entails and how it is generally employed. Then we provide a summary of "what we know," recent research on relevant key concepts and issues, including self-customization's benefits and drawbacks. Academic research on customization has been mainly phenomenon-driven, with researchers drawing on a broad range of theories from innovation, management, marketing, psychology, and decision-making research. Early research in this area was primarily managerial in nature, focusing on the customization of functional product attributes with less focus on consumers' psychological response to aesthetic self-design. Thus, the discussion of "what we know" goes a bit far afield, offering insights even from areas where self-customization has not specifically been examined but that, presumably, have applicable findings.

Building on this, we then provide an overview of some important questions that are still unanswered. Indeed, given the relative novelty of both the practice of self-customization and also research on the topic in the context of consumer psychology, there is, in fact, a wealth of areas for future research. Finally, at the end of the chapter, we adopt a slightly different perspective on user design, exploring that of co-creation, in which consumers design products not just for themselves but for the general public. In consumer psychology co-creation is even less researched than self-customization, and thus it is a particularly rich area for future exploration.

More broadly, self-customization and also co-creation are exciting areas in which consumer psychologists can do innovative research in a real-world context that is evolving quickly with great opportunity for insights in a number of areas, such as decision making, creativity, and customer satisfaction. We hope this chapter provides both the groundwork to begin such exploration of consumers' changing role from passive to active as well as ideas of where exploration is most needed.

What Is Self-Customization?

Self-customization is defined as the process by which individual consumers, often using an online-based interface (also referred to as a "configurator" or "toolkit"), self-design their own products, which the manufacturer then produces to order (e.g., Salvador, Piller, & de Holan, 2009; von Hippel & Katz,

2002). Configurators or toolkits typically allow for trial-and-error experimentation and provide immediate, simulated feedback on the final product. Once the consumer is satisfied with his or her design choices, the design is transferred into the firm's production system and then delivered to the consumer (Randall, Terwiesch, & Ulrich, 2007). It has been proposed that self-customization "changes the rules substantially, allowing consumers to have much more control over the product's characteristics" (Moreau & Herd, 2010, p. 806). Instead of exploring consumer preferences and then developing a responsive product, a manufacturer equips consumers with the necessary tools so that even design novices can become the designers of their own products. The outcome is a product that, in most cases, is a better fit with the consumer's needs, with most consumers showing a clear preference for their own designs over professionally designed alternatives of equal quality (Franke & Piller, 2004).

Early conceptual work on the topic of mass customization started to emerge with the pioneering work of Gilmore and Pine (1996), Pine (1993), and von Hippel and co-authors (e.g., von Hippel & Katz, 2002). In the consumer behavior literature, the topic did not receive much attention until recently, when technological advances enabled more and more companies to implement mass customization systems successfully (e.g., for Nike sneakers, Adidas sunglasses, Dell computers, Mini cars, Chocri chocolates, just to mention a few of them). The focus of the following section is therefore on empirical studies published in the last five years, but we also draw from previous work and theory that offer insight on consumer response to customization.

What We Know

The value of mass customization is exemplified by the premium consumers will pay for these products. Not only do we see this in the marketplace with self-customized products such as Nike's ID and Adidas's customized eyewear demanding a significant price premium, but there is also evidence from the lab. Franke and Piller (2004) found mean willingness to pay for self-designed watches to be twice as much as a standard watch of equal quality and functionality. Subsequent studies found similar results across several consumer product categories, including T-shirts, scarves, and cell phone covers (Franke & Schreier, 2008; Franke, Schreier, & Kaiser, 2010; Schreier, 2006).

The broader question then becomes, how does this happen? What value does self-customization offer to the consumer? Changing the consumer's role from one of passive consumer to active designer of one's own products affects consumer behavior in several manners. In this section, we consider this and in doing so address the questions of why and when does self-customization create value and what are the mediators and moderators of the self-customization effect.

As a body of work, the research presented in the next section corroborates both anecdotal marketing findings as well as research on willingness to pay for self-customization (Franke & Piller, 2004; Franke, Schreier, & Kaiser, 2010), revealing that, while there may be some drawbacks to mass customization, overall the process offers value to the consumer.

Why and When Does Self-Customization Create Value?

Greater Likelihood of Preference Matching

The most straightforward benefit of a self-designed product is superior preference fit, defined as the degree of overlap between consumer preferences and product attributes (Randall, Terwiesch, & Ulrich, 2007; von Hippel & Katz, 2002). Indeed, in several studies the greater satisfaction reported by consumers for self-designed products over comparable off-the-shelf products can be attributed to the higher perceived utility and/or degree of match between products and preferences (Dellaert & Stremersch, 2005; Franke & Schreier, 2008; Franke, Schreier, & Kaiser, 2010). Because there tends to be significant heterogeneity in consumer preferences, in the absence of self-customization, matching these preferences becomes an arduous task for companies. Franke and Piller (2004) have demonstrated that a watch manufacturer would need 159 unique designs to meet perfectly (100 percent) the preferences of a sample of 165 students. Decreasing the goal to meet preferences at an 80 percent level (i.e., needs would be met on only four out of five dimensions for all consumers) reduces the number of unique designs needed to 134. The implication is, even for a small target audience, complete preference matching is likely not an attainable goal. Therefore, in the absence of self-customization, companies typically end up offering a selection of products that satisfy the preferences of the largest subtargets, though not perfectly, and leaving some consumers without any satisfactory option.

Preference Identification, Transfer, Forecasting, and Usage

However, such findings, and the practice of concept of self-customization in general, rely on three assumptions. The first is that, in contrast to companies, consumers have direct access to and complete knowledge of their own preferences. Second, a configurator allows them to transfer these easily into product specifications without bias or influence. Third, consumer preferences at the time of choice are the same as they will be at the time of consumption. All three of these assumptions have been questioned recently. While some of this research is not examining customization, it is highly relevant as it identifies manners in which customization may be falling short in providing value as well as how this deficiency may be overcome.

Preference Identification and Transfer

As discussed, preference fit is the most obvious benefit of customized products. Aside from supplying the number of products that would be needed in order to match preferences, companies would presumably have to undergo extensive market research in order to identify these consumer preferences. The assumption is that, in contrast, a consumer has direct and complete knowledge of his or her preferences. And yet there is ample evidence from the decision-making literature that this is often not the case. While Nisbett and Wilson's (1977) seminal work examined the ability to report on higher-order mental processes and not simple product preferences, their findings are relevant as they indicate the gap between what consumers actually know and what they feel they know and the questions they are likely to answer.

Additionally, research on constructed preferences, the idea that consumer preferences are not well defined but rather constructed during the process of choice, reveals either access to and/or the existence of some underlying fixed inclination often does not exist (Bettman, Luce, & Payne, 1998; Levin & Gaeth, 1988; Lichtenstein & Slovic, 2006; Simonson, 1989; Simonson & Nowlis, 2000) and, moreover, that the preference elicitation process can have strong influences on the choices made. This body of work reveals countless instances where irrelevant factors such as the framing or presentation of the options influences the choices made. For example, the impact a particular attribute has on choice can be influenced by whether options are evaluated simultaneously or separately (Hsee, 1996). When options are evaluated separately – for example, with a configurator that offers a default design from which consumers can opt to deviate – attributes that are hard to evaluate in isolation are weighted less in the decision. In contrast, in a joint evaluation – for example, with a configurator that offers different levels of an attribute from which to select – such attributes that are difficult to evaluate independently are weighted relatively more in the decision.

Another factor of the decision process that influences choice is how difficult the decision feels. When choices feel more difficult, consumers are more likely to defer choice or select the compromise option (Dhar & Simonson, 2003; Novemsky, Dhar, Schwarz, & Simonson, 2007). When using a self-customization configurator, choices can be easily changed to seem less difficult, such as by offering a deferral or no choice option (Dhar & Simonson, 2003), through the use of reference points for comparison (Luce, Bettman, & Payne, 1999), or even how easy it is to read the options (e.g., background/foreground contrast; Novemsky et al., 2007). Specific to the self-customization process, not only do consumers tend to select the compromise option more often when using the by-attribute method than the by-alternative method, but also they feel the process is less difficult and more satisfying (Valenzuela, Dhar, & Zettelmeyer, 2009). More broadly, Prelec, Wernerfelt, and Zettelmeyer (1997) show that consumers infer that the choice set, itself, offers information such as what the general range of preferences tends to be in the population. Altogether, the implication of this body of work is that, in many ways, the design of the configurator can influence the choices made and, more broadly, that consumers may not have well-defined preferences and thus fail to identify the customized option that fits their preferences.

Building off of such work on preference constructions as well as the findings by Nisbett and Wilson (1977), Simonson (2005) identifies two dimensions of consumer preferences that influence how useful customization can be. Specifically, customization is best when, first, consumers have stable well-developed preferences, and second, they have good insight into these preferences and are able to identify them clearly. Preferences tend to be more stable when they are at a broader rather than narrower level, such as across product categories rather than attributes (Simonson, 2005). Moreover, broadly speaking, preferences tend to be more permanent and less influenced by outside factors when consumers have greater prior knowledge and experience (Wedell & Bockenholt, 1990) and category familiarity (Coupey, Irwin, & Payne, 1998). These factors are also relevant in the more specific instance of self-customization, and thus this offers two boundary conditions for when self-customization might be optimal.

In fact, there is evidence specific to self-customization supporting this. Franke, Keinz, and Steger (2009) showed empirically that the benefits of customization are contingent on characteristics of the consumer – namely, level of insight into his or her own preferences and the ability to express those preferences (Franke, Keinz, & Steger, 2009). Relatedly, consumers with higher levels of product expertise find customization to be less complex than those with lower levels of expertise (Delleart & Stremersch, 2005). However, the self-customization process offers the additional benefit of trial-and-error learning whereby consumers gain the knowledge and familiarity needed to create and identify more stable preferences. In this sense, a consumer may come into the process with unstable preferences and/or low preference insight but, through the process of self-customization, define and identify his or her longer-term steady preference (Franke & Hader, 2013).

Preference Forecasting

Further complicating the matter is the delay between attribute choice and consumption. Thus, consumers need not only to be aware of their preferences but forecast what they will be in the future, and there can be errors in this process (Gilbert & Wilson, 2000). Moreover, consumers are aware of the potential for this error, anticipating post-purchase regret (Bell, 1982; Simonson, 1992). Larger assortments, as is innately the case with customization versus mass production, generally lead to higher anticipated regret as there are more alternative outcomes to consider (Heitmann, Herrmann, & Kaiser, 2007). More generally, there is less regret associated with a standard product option versus a customized one that can push consumers away from selecting customization (Syam, Krishnamurthy, & Hess, 2008). This effect may be mitigated by increasing the number of standard product options (Syam, Krishnamurthy, & Hess, 2008) and/or by offering default options within the self-customization process (Simonson, 1992).

Sense of Enjoyment and Accomplishment

Entirely separate from preference matching are benefits of the mere process of creation. This comes in two forms: an intrinsic effect of assembly effort and involvement in the creation process (Buechel & Janszewski, 2014) as well as a sense of accomplishment that results from creating the product oneself

(Franke, Schreier, & Kaiser, 2010; Norton, Mochon, & Ariely, 2012; Mochon, Norton, & Ariely, 2012).

At the most basic level, the process of creation can offer consumers enjoyment (Csikszentmihalyi, 1990; Dahl & Moreau, 2007). Using Dahl and Moreau's (2007) delineation of experiential creation, self-customization can be considered an activity high on the dimension of instruction, in that typically configurators offer a step-by-step process, and low on target outcome dictation, in that the final result is open to variation and not predefined. Dahl and Moreau (2007) hypothesize and show that this combination provides the highest level of enjoyment. Two other dimensions of the creation process that have been considered are that of the decision-making process and the production process. The work of Buechel and Janszewski (2014) reveals that integrating these processes rather than separating them increases engagement and thus overall satisfaction with the process. Together, this research reveals that the process of self-customization offers intrinsic enjoyment and moreover that it can be modified to ensure that this enjoyment is maximized.

Relatedly, customization offers a sense of accomplishment to consumers, who see themselves as the originator of the product (Franke, Schreier, & Kaiser, 2010; Mochon, Norton, & Ariely, 2012; Norton, Mochon, & Ariely, 2012). In the work by Franke, Schreier, and Kaiser (2010) on T-shirt design, participants were willing to pay 40 percent more for a T-shirt on which they had input, even though it was simply a replication of an existing design. Similarly, the IKEA effect demonstrates that participants see their own amateurish creations as similar in value to experts' creations and significantly more valuable than other amateurish creations, again even when no customization actually occurs (Norton, Mochon, & Ariely, 2012). In these cases, feelings of accomplishment mediated these effects (Franke, Schreier, & Kaiser, 2010; Norton, Mochon, & Ariely, 2012). Together, these works reveal that consumers derive value both from the process as well as from being the originator of their own work above and beyond self-customization's ability to match preferences.

Signaling to Self and Others

While all products offer consumers a chance to signal identity both to themselves as well as to others (Belk, 1988; Sirgy, 1982), self-customized products are particularly adept at signaling two traits. In some sense, these two traits parallel the two benefits identified thus far, that of preference matching and sense of accomplishment. Specifically, the customization aspect maps onto the desire to signal uniqueness, that one's self and preferences are different from others, while sense of accomplishment maps onto the desire to signal competency and one's efficacy.

Signal of Uniqueness

A specific aspect of self-expression that self-customized products are particularly able to communicate is that of individuation and uniqueness (Lynn &

Harris, 1997). Franke and Schreier (2008) report that consumers rate self-customized products to be more "unique," "one of a kind," and "special."

The uniqueness of the product naturally implicates this quality in the consumer as well (Belk, 1988; Sirgy, 1982). However, while uniqueness generally has a positive connotation and, in most Western cultures, is socially appreciated (Kim & Drolet, 2003), personal need for uniqueness varies across individuals (Snyder & Fromkin, 1977). It follows that the incremental value from individuality that self-customization offers varies with a consumer's need for uniqueness (Franke & Schreier, 2008). Indeed, Tian, Bearden, and Hunter (2001) found a greater propensity to own customized products (low-rider cars) among individuals who rated high on the consumer need for uniqueness scale.

Signal of Competency

While a self-customized product can signal a consumer's uniqueness through the individuality of the product, it also offers the signal of competency, and this signal can be seen as influencing consumer identity more directly than attributes of the product do. Dahl and Moreau (2007) found that "feelings of competence" were the most commonly mentioned motivation for engaging in creative tasks such as cooking, sewing, and jewelry making. Similarly, Mochon, Norton, and Ariely (2012) found that feelings of competence mediated the premium attached to a self-made LEGO car and that allowing consumers to affirm their competency in another manner reduced the premium allocated to a self-made IKEA storage box. While these examples are not of customization specifically, they share the qualities of self-involvement and effort that are inherent in self-customization. Thus, compared to mass-produced products, self-customization provides consumers with a manner in which to signal their competency and, moreover, this effect will be particularly strong when consumers, either chronically or due to situational factors, feel threatened in the areas of efficacy and competency.

What We Don't Know

In the previous section, we discussed why and when customization creates value, as exemplified by the price premium consumers are willing to pay. We have also pointed out some boundary conditions outside of which customization does not increase value. This discussion offered several implications and potential future research questions. However, given the novelty of the topic, we believe that there are additional areas for possible exploration. Next we discuss five broad directions for future research, areas where consumer psychologists have the opportunity to offer critical insight.

First, there are essentially two broad approaches to designing a customization interface. In one, customization is conceptualized as a structured choice activity; consumers are presented with a series of choices each relating to a different attribute and from which they select an attribute level. In the other, customization is less structured, thus this approach is often referred to as ill-structured (Franke, Keinz, & Schreier, 2009); consumers are offered a blank canvas with few or no limiting parameters for designing their product. The former is applicable only for simple customization, allowing for a low solution space. On the other hand, the latter is characterized by a virtually indefinite solution space, not restricting consumers by providing predefined choice options that can only be mixed and matched. We offer one call for action for each area.

Call for Action 1: How to Maximize Process and Outcome Satisfaction in the Structured Choice-Based Paradigm

Research on perceptions of variety, choice overload, as well as choices in sequence offer useful insights on how simple variations in the setup of a structured choice-based customization configurator can have strong effects on process and outcome satisfaction. We summarize this research before discussing some critical questions that are still unanswered and possible tools needed to answer them.

Variety Perceptions and Choice Overload

One factor that is known to influence satisfaction with the process as well as the likelihood of making a choice is the amount of perceived variety in the options. As discussed, customization effectively offers consumers an extremely large amount of variety from which to choose, making preference matching much more likely. While assortments that offer more perceived variety are generally preferred (Ratner & Kahn, 2002), this variety can be a liability if it leads to choice overload. When consumers find a choice decision complex or over-whelming, they are more prone to defer or opt out of choice (Iyengar & Lepper, 2000). Fortunately, there is a broad body of research on how to mitigate the negative effects of large assortments without decreasing the actual variety offered. The ultimate goal of these methods is to ensure that consumers recognize the variety available to them while minimizing perceptions of complexity. For example, Huffman and Kahn (1998) found that consumers are more likely to be satisfied by the process if the selector uses an attribute-based format (consumers sequentially evaluate each attribute, selecting a level for each they desire) rather than an alternative-based format (where consumers choose among full alternatives).

However, much of the research on variety perception and mitigating choice overload has not been considered in the context of customization, but rather when consumers face a typical alternative-based presentation of choice options. This, therefore, offers a broad array of findings that could potentially be considered in the customization context. Based on past research, one might consider how the organization of information on each option (Huffman & Kahn, 1998), whether options are presented in text or images (Townsend &

Kahn, 2014), how alignable the attributes are (Gourville & Soman, 2005), and how making a non-alignable attribute seem more alignable (e.g., highlighting the relative calorie content of flavors; Herrmann et. al., 2009) influence perceptions of variety, complexity, and satisfaction with the process and outcome. These are just some examples of findings that are likely relevant in the context of a customization configurator.

There is an additional note of caution on this issue of the potentially overwhelming variety offered by customization. With greater variety, consumers naturally increase their expectations for meeting their preferences, and this can result in lower satisfaction if the exact right match is not found (Diehl & Poynor, 2010). *Post hoc*, the mere knowledge that an option came from a larger rather than smaller assortment can decrease satisfaction with the same option. The implication is that product expectations are likely higher when the product results from a customization process than when it does not.

Thus, while self-customization creates great consumer value through the variety it offers and thus the ability to match preferences, with this variety comes potential for dissatisfaction both during the choice process and afterward. The result is that consumers may opt for a standard option over self-customization, may defer or opt out of choice when faced with the self-customization decision-making process, or ultimately be less satisfied with the same option if it resulted from self-customization as opposed to if it came from a smaller standard product assortment. Again, though, careful consideration of these issues when designing a choice-based configurator can help mitigate these effects.

Sequential Choice

Given that choice-based configurator design typically involves a series of decisions, research on multiple sequential choices is also relevant. On this topic Wilcox and Song (2011) identify that prior decisions can influence expectations of the difficulty of subsequent decisions, and this can influence how much consumers are willing to pay. In the context of a choice configurator, where the choice of attribute level influences price, this is relevant. Further analysis might consider whether there is also an effect on how such price premiums are perceived – whether having them at the beginning, middle, or end of the sequential process influences perceptions of their value. Relatedly, Khan and Dhar (2006) find a licensing effect in sequential choice in that a more virtuous selection in one choice can lead to more self-indulgence in later choices. This is, again, relevant when choice influences price but likely also when choices may be more hedonic versus utilitarian in nature. Additionally, there are likely implications for how to minimize the potential for guilt or other negative emotions in response to the multiple choices inherent in self-customization.

While the research on variety perception as well as on sequential choice offers an understanding of ways to prevent choice overload and how question order influences choice, there is still a great deal about how to maximize satisfaction with this process that is unknown. Consumer psychology could potentially offer a great deal of insight on this topic. To begin with, the creation or application of a tool or measure to measure affective response systematically over the course of engagement with a configurator would prove useful. If one were able to measure enjoyment implicitly, this could be critical in creating the optimal customization experience. Insights on feelings of progress, again perhaps with a systematic measure over the course of the process, as well as measures of attentional focus, such as via eye-tracking software, would also likely offer useful insight. Through such measures or otherwise, consumer psychologists might be able to offer insights on how small variations in the configurator might work to maintain motivation, prevent choice fatigue, and generally ensure that the user does not abandon the customization process.

Call for Action 2: How to Design the Interface in the Ill-Structured Open Paradigm

The research on preference construction, variety perception, and choice overload, as well as sequential choice, illustrates the substantial knowledge offering guidance for designing a choice-based configurator. However, less is known and applicable to the ill-structured, blank canvas paradigm. And yet, with the advent of three-dimensional printing, the ability to offer this almost limitless form of self-customization has opened up.

In a sense, a blank canvas–type configurator offers the greatest flexibility in outcome and thus the utmost variety. However, such a context is far removed from the typical choice task considered in research on variety and choice overload. As such, it is unclear whether such findings apply. Certainly a blank canvas with few parameters and little guidance might, indeed, seem overwhelming to consumers and cause them to turn away from the decision-making process. Thus, how to offer guidance in a manner that makes the consumer feel directed while minimizing feelings of constriction is an area for exploration. Work by Dahl and Moreau (2007) offers insight on this issue considering how instructional guidance and target outcomes determine perceived autonomy and competence. However, there are many more variables in a customization project that may influence perceptions of freedom versus constraint. These might include the amount of direction to give at the start of the design task, the appropriateness of guidance in the form of defaults or external feedback from peers (e.g., Franke, Keinz, & Schreier, 2009), or the variety of tools to offer. A good place to start for insights on this might be the rapidly growing body of work on creativity (Sternberg, 2004). Consideration of this research might offer solutions to such fundamental questions as how the open toolkit can be designed to inspire creativity and increase involvement while minimizing feelings of being overwhelmed. One can imagine that with an ill-structured problem, issues of motivation and persistence may also come into play, and these may in turn be influenced by the perceived goal. Specifically, customers may come into the process with the goal of creating something particularly

unique, ideal for themselves, or just meeting a minimal set of personal requirements. As such, individual differences such maximizer/satisficer tendencies
(Schwartz et al., 2002) may also play a role. There are numerous significant
questions that remain unanswered with little knowledge on how to optimize the
environment in an open blank canvas customization paradigm.

Call for Action 3: When Do People Self-Select to Customize?

Most studies discussed in the previous section used an experimental approach
and randomly assigned participants to either the treatment group (customization) or control group (standard choice). Participants were asked to customize a
product, and then they were asked about their preferences, purchase intention,
and other measures. A critical question is, however, when and why do consumers self-select to customize?

The limited work on this question reveals several situational and individual
differences. First, consumers who are made to feel less competent (given a hard
math problem) are more likely to select a product that requires assembly than
consumers who were given an easy math problem. The act of assembly offers
them an avenue for restoring feelings of competency (Mochon, Norton, &
Ariely, 2012). Customization likely offers the same competency boost and thus
would also be particularly appreciated by those who either chronically feel low
on this trait or are in a situation that inspires such feelings. Further, narcissistic
consumers who constantly seek self-enhancement might be particularly prone
to engage in self-customization. Lee, Gregg, and Park (2013) have shown that
narcissists tend to prefer products able to confer distinctiveness and satisfy their
need for uniqueness, such as limited editions or personalized products. In
particular, more narcissistic study participants rated a customizable shirt more
favorably than participants who scored lower on narcissism, and when given
the choice between a gift coupon and a leather case engraved with their
names, narcissists were more likely to opt for the personalized leather case
(Lee, Gregg, & Park, 2013). Another individual difference is how much utility
consumers gain from the unexpected benefit that may occur with the discovery
of a product feature not selected but attained. For those who highly value this
surprise, customization may not be ideal.

Despite such research, a broad understanding of what drives a customer to
select a self-customization option is not known. While the research, as discussed earlier in this chapter, reveals numerous benefits of customization, it is
unclear whether consumers are entirely aware of all of these benefits and, even
if so, for whom or in which consumption situations they are most pertinent.
No doubt there are individual, situational, as well as product categorical
factors that influence the perceived benefits of self-customization. It also seems
likely that the acceptance and desirability of customization varies across
cultures. Using insights from consumer psychology to provide an understanding of such issues would likely prove to be valuable to practitioners and
researchers alike.

Call for Action 4: How Customization Relates to Branding

Many examples we see today of brands that have successfully launched customizable products are large and established, such as Nike, Adidas, Oakley, or BMW Mini. However, there are also examples of large brands that have failed with such endeavors, such as Levi's and Mattel. Additionally, smaller brands (e.g., Timbuk2) or startup companies (e.g., Shoes of Prey) have successfully utilized customization without a preexisting established brand but by targeting a niche market. Aside from such anecdotes, to date there has been no systematic exploration of which brands might benefit most from customization and how the presence or absence of a strong brand affects the customization experience and the value of a customized product.

Brands offer guidance, convey quality and consistency, and minimize purchasing risks for consumers (Aaker, 1991). With customization, consumers take control over some of the aesthetic or functional aspects of a product that were traditionally exclusively under the control of the brand. Might customization weaken brand positioning by diluting key aspects of a brand's competencies? In other words, by giving consumers the option to create products that do not necessarily fit the brand image (e.g., color schemes that the brand would itself not advocate), does this temper brand message?

Surprisingly, there is only scarce research on the question of how customization relates to a brand's effectiveness, despite the topic's high managerial relevance. One of the few studies that exist is that by Moreau, Bonney, and Herd (2011), which posits that with branded products, consumers both benefit from the expected higher technical performance promised by the brand and the increased preference fit achieved by aesthetic self-customization. Self-customization of a strong brand is therefore more highly valued than self-customization of a comparable unbranded product if the brand is successful in signaling quality to consumers. In contrast, a recent study by Miceli, Raimondo, and Farace (2013) shows that in the presence of a strong brand, consumers prefer to select the modules provided by the firm over uploading their own graphics and pictures, whereas in the absence of a strong brand, consumers derive significant value by imbuing the product with personal symbols and pictures uploaded by the consumer. In this case, the implication is that customization may be valued more with weaker brands, though further exploration is needed.

A promising area for research is the question of how customization affects brand perceptions and long-term consumer–brand relationships. Extant research has maintained that customization is a viable strategy only if the incremental prices that customers are willing to pay for customized products exceed the incremental costs associated with custom production (Piller, Moeslein, & Stotko, 2004). Challenging this assumption, a study by Kaiser, Schreier, and Ofir (2012) suggests that customization might serve as an effective strategy to boost consumers' demand for a brand's other product offerings, even if such brand extensions are not customizable. The authors found that customers are willing to pay roughly 35 percent more for a noncustomized brand extension following a customization versus standard choice task. Consider Nike, which offers self-customization in a few, selected product categories (e.g., running shoes). Assuming that the self-customized products do not meet profit targets, Nike might consider discontinuing the self-customization offer. However, if customization delivers value beyond the focal self-customized product, by strengthening consumers' brand attachment, it might make sense to continue the specific mass customization track.

Call for Action 5: What Happens after the Design Process

The majority of the research on customization has focused on the design process itself and satisfaction with the outcome (immediately after having customized a product), with less insight into the consequences of self-customization. Beyond possible greater satisfaction due to preference matching and the potential for updates to the consumer's self-identify (e.g., accomplishment and uniqueness), what else might result?

First, it seems likely that customization might influence the self-concept in other manners. Future research could identify additional particular factors, like competence, that are influenced by customization, such as creativity or perception of category knowledge. Alternatively, larger self-related issues such as self-esteem might be helped or hindered by customization and could be explored. It would be particularly interesting to explore whether using customized products might have any downsides for consumers. For example, customization may increase narcissistic entitlement. Narcissists hold overtly positive self-views, expect special treatment, and believe they are entitled to more than others (Campbell et al., 2006; Exline et al., 2004). If the use of customized products is a constant reminder of one's uniqueness, then use may foster narcissistic behaviors such as overconfidence, egotism, and attention seeking.

Additionally, it seems likely that there are behavioral differences after purchase of a standard and customized product. The first broad area might be the utility that one derives from using a customized product. The difference in perceived value in the product may lead owners of customized products to use them more or less frequently than standard ones. Self-customized products can represent, or be associated with, desirable self-images (Belk, Bahn, & Mayer, 1982). Consequently, the use of a self-customized product, either to reaffirm positive aspects of an identity or to achieve aspirational aspects of an identity, could be motivational, independent of any functional benefits of product use or efficacy beliefs (Oyserman, 2009; Reed, Forehand, Puntoni, & Warlop, 2012; Sirgy, 1982). As a result, consumers might perform better with a customized versus standard product.

Alternatively, it seems likely that consumers feel a greater attachment to customized products, delaying or decreasing discard. This then has potential implications for motivating more environmentally friendly consumer behavior. Because of the inherent strength of customized products for self-expression, it seems probable that customized products are more likely to be publicly used and displayed than standard options. If this is the case, this makes the consumer more open to feedback from others. This then leads to questions around how reaction to feedback may differ. One could imagine that both positive and negative feedback have a greater impact on self-perception when the product is one that is the result of self-customization. Does such feedback then have a greater impact on self-perception or the perception of the feedback giver, or is there some alternative process that occurs? What these questions illustrate is that after purchase, very little is known about how self-customization influences both self-perception and behavior.

Outlook: Co-creation

So far, our literature review on user design has focused on self-customization where consumers design products for themselves. However, another aspect of consumers' changing role from passive to active is through co-creation, defined as "the practice of collaborative product development by firms and consumers" (Hoyer et al., 2010, p. 283). With co-creation, consumers do not (only) create ideas and designs for themselves, but for the broader market. To illustrate, consider apparel manufacturer Threadless (Ogawa & Piller, 2006). Instead of employing in-house graphic designers, Threadless relies on a large community of customers, including professional and hobbyist designers, who freely share their design ideas with the company for the purpose of offering them to the masses. Each week, Threadless solicits over one thousand new product designs from its customers, of which five to seven are released (O'Hern & Kahle, 2013). Customers also play a leading role in selecting the designs that will finally be manufactured by evaluating them via the company website.

Threadless is only one example of how firms increasingly outsource some of their core activities along the new product development process to consumers. In fact there are myriad ways in which consumers, or more generally "users," can co-create value with the firm, not only in new product development but also with other marketing activities, such as advertising (Thomson & Malaviya, 2013). This broad trend in co-creation has led to the development of new typologies that categorize various types and degrees of co-creation (e.g., Hoyer et al., 2010; O'Hern & Rindfleisch, 2010; Piller, Ihl, & Vossen, 2010).

It has been argued that co-creation potentially increases product quality and market acceptance and that it reduces costly product failures (Hoyer et al., 2010; Ogawa & Piller, 2006). Relatedly, research in innovation management has shown that users often innovate for themselves and that, contrary to conventional wisdom, many of those user innovations are commercially highly attractive (Lilien et al., 2002; von Hippel, 2005). One major promise of co-creation is thus to generate objectively better products. But how good are user-designed products really when systematically compared to professionally designed alternatives? Data from the Japanese company Muji, which draws on ideas by both users and professionals, demonstrate that user-designed products can outperform designer-generated products on key market performance metrics such as unit sales and average profit margins (Nishikawa, Schreier, & Ogawa, 2013). Poetz and Schreier (2012) report similar findings from a field experiment in which both users and professionals created ideas for an effective and relevant problem in the consumer goods market for baby products; user ideas scored significantly higher on novelty and customer benefit (but somehow lower on feasibility) compared to ideas generated by professionals.

It seems that under some conditions, user-generated products are indeed attractive to the broader market. However, subsequent research still needs to explore boundary conditions, the underlying processes, and potential downsides of user design. For example, in which product categories or for which product features (functional versus aesthetic) is co-creation most effective, and which consumers are most likely to come up with promising ideas? The few studies that exist have documented how consumer's expertise in analogous markets (Franke, Poetz, & Schreier, 2013) and a position of marginality (knowledge or experience on the fringe of an area rather than at its core; Jeppesen & Lakhani, 2010 positively influences problem solving and new product ideation in a given target market. Moreover, if firms increasingly draw on consumers as a source of innovation, the question arises whether consumers might feel a sense of exploitation at some point (Franke, Keinz, & Klausberger, 2013). Of equal practical importance is the question of how firms can maintain an ongoing supply of quality ideas from consumers over time. Data from Dell's Idea Storm community, for example, show that consumers with multiple ideas ("serial ideators") are more likely to come up with promising ideas than consumers with only one idea, though serial ideators are unlikely to repeat their success once their ideas have been implemented (Bayus 2013). Since more and more companies rely on consumer's ideas, more research on how to manage innovative user communities is needed.

Another largely unexplored research area is how consumers react to companies that market user-designed products to the masses. Consumers can be classified as participating (i.e., consumers who actively engage in co-creation activities) and nonparticipating users (i.e., consumers who "observe" that companies market user-designed products). Fuchs, Prandelli, and Schreier (2010) found that consumers who actively engage in co-creation (e.g., they select which products should be marketed) show higher demand for the underlying products than nonparticipating users, even though product evaluation was equally high. The reason for this demand effect is that co-creation results in higher psychological ownership of the selected products. As evidenced by two recent studies by Schreier, Fuchs, and Dahl (2012) and Fuchs, Prandelli, Schreier and Dahl (2013), co-creation also seems to have more subtle implications for the broader market. Threadless, Muji, LEGO, and other companies that sell products co-created by users typically stress that these products are designed by users. Threadless, for example, has the name of the user designer written on the tag inside the T-shirt, while LEGO prominently prints "designed by LEGO fans" on the product's packaging. How do nonparticipating users perceive products labeled as "user-designed"? Interestingly, Schreier, Fuchs, and Dahl (2012) have shown that marketing user designs does not decrease but actually increases consumers' perception of a firm's innovation ability, resulting in higher willingness to pay and higher word of mouth intentions.

While the topic of co-creation has received some attention in innovation or general management literature, research from a consumer behavior perspective is still scarce. We believe that there are plenty of opportunities for consumer researchers with unanswered questions such as how users perceive companies that sell products designed by users. More basically, an understanding of why consumers prefer products created by other users is needed. One could imagine this might be a way to infuse a brand or product with authenticity. Research also needs to address the boundary conditions, such as when consumers prefer not to buy co-created new products. For example, Fuchs and colleagues (2013) show that co-creation may backfire with luxury products. Research might also identify for which types of consumers user-designed products are most attractive. Finally, existing research focuses on co-creation in idea generation; co-creation in later stages of the new product development process is, to date, less studied.

Summary

The practice of involving the consumer in the design process is fairly recent, and thus it is not surprising that research on it is limited. What research does exist tends to focus on how to optimize the customization process as well as consumers' initial perceptions of its output. Moreover, most of this work has been focused on managerial implications with less emphasis on understanding the psychological processes behind the outcomes. Because of this, in order to give the reader a full picture of the state-of-the-art understanding of consumer psychology as it might apply to user design, we have gone beyond the most relevant literature and opted to cast a wide net in our literature review. We hope this provides readers with an understanding of not just what customization entails and what is currently known, but how consumer psychologists might offer further contributions. Indeed, there are a variety of substantial and important questions open for exploration – both where previous findings in consumer psychology might be applied to the practice of user design as well as where new theories might be necessary. We look forward to seeing future research that addresses such questions.

References

Aaker, D. (1991). *Managing Brand Equity: Capitalising on the Value of a Brand Name.* New York: Free Press.

Bayus, B. L (2013). Crowdsourcing new product ideas over time: An analysis of the Dell idea storm community. *Management Science, 59*(1), 226–244.

Belk, R. W. (1988). Possessions and the extended self. *Journal of Consumer Research, 15* (2), 139–168.

Belk, R. W., Bahn, K. D., & Mayer, R. N. (1982). Developmental recognition of consumption symbolism. *Journal of Consumer Research, 9*(1), 4–17.

Bell, D. (1982). Regret in decision making under uncertainty. *Operations Research, 30* (5), 961–981.

Bettman, J. R., Luce, M. F., & Payne, J. W. (1998). Constructive consumer choice processes. *Journal of Consumer Research, 25*(3), 187–217.

Buechel, E. C., & Janiszewski, C. (2014). A lot of work or a work of art: How the structure of a customized assembly task determines the utility derived from assembly effort. *Journal of Consumer Research, 40*(5), 960–972.

Campbell, K. W., Bonacci, A. M., Shelton, J., Exline, J. J., & Bushman, B. J. (2006). Psychological entitlement: Interpersonal consequences and validation of a self-report measure. *Journal of Personality Assessment, 83*(1), 29–45.

Coupey, E., Irwin, J. R., & Payne, J. W. (1998). Product category familiarity and preference construction. *Journal of Consumer Research, 24*(4), 459–468.

Csikszentmihalyi, M. (1990). *Flow: The Psychology of Optimal Experience.* New York: HarperCollins.

Dahl, D. W., & Moreau, C. P. (2007). Thinking inside the box: Why consumers enjoy constrained creative experiences. *Journal of Marketing Research, 44*(3), 357–369.

Dalgic, T. (2006). *Handbook of Niche Marketing: Principles and Practice.* New York: Emerald Group.

Dalgic, T., & Leeuw, M. (1994). Niche marketing revisited: Concept, applications and some European cases. *European Journal of Marketing, 28*(4), 39–55.

Delleart, B. G. C., & Stremersch, S. (2005). Marketing mass-customized products: Striking a balance between utility and complexity. *Journal of Marketing Research, 42*(3), 219–227.

Dhar, R., & Simonson, I. (2003). The effect of forced choice on choice. *Journal of Marketing Research, 40*(2), 146–160.

Diehl, K., & Poynor, C. (2010). Great expectations?! Assortment size, expectations, and satisfaction. *Journal of Marketing Research, 47*(2), 312–322.

Exline, J. J., Baumeister, R. F., Bushman, B. J., Campbell, K. W., & Finkel, E. J. (2004). Too proud to let go: Narcissistic entitlement as a barrier to forgiveness. *Journal of Personality and Social Psychology, 87*(6), 894–912.

Franke, N., & Hader, C. (2013). Mass or only niche customization? Why we should interpret configuration toolkits as learning instruments. *Journal of Product Innovation Management, 31*(5), 1–21.

Franke, N., Keinz, P., & Klausberger, K. (2013). "Does this sound like a fair deal?" Antecedents and consequences of fairness expectations in the individual's decision to participate in firm innovation. *Organization Science, 24*(5), 1495–1516.

Franke, N., Keinz, P., & Schreier, M. (2008). Complementing mass customization toolkits with user communities: How peer input improves customer self-design. *Journal of Product Innovation Management, 25*(6), 546–559.

Franke, N., Keinz, P., & Steger, C. J. (2009). Testing the value of customization: When do customers really prefer products tailored to their preferences? *Journal of Marketing, 73*(5), 103–121.

Franke, N., & Piller, F. (2004). Value creation by toolkits for user innovation and design: The case of the watch market. *Journal of Product Innovation Management, 21*(6), 401–415.

Franke, N., Poetz, M. K., & Schreier, M. (2013). Integrating problem solvers from analogous markets in new product ideation. *Management Science, 60*(4), 1063–1081.

Franke, N., & Schreier, M. (2008). Product uniqueness as a driver of customer utility in mass customization. *Marketing Letters, 19*(2), 93–107.

Franke, N., Schreier, M., & Kaiser, U. (2010). The "i designed it myself" effect in mass customization. *Management Science, 56*(1), 125–140.

Fuchs, C., Prandelli, E., & Schreier, M. (2010). The psychological effects of empowerment strategies on consumers' product demand. *Journal of Marketing, 74*(1), 65–79.

Fuchs, C., Prandelli, E. Schreier, M., & Dahl, D. W. (2013). All that is users might not be gold: How labeling products as user designed backfires in the context of luxury fashion brands. *Journal of Marketing, 77*(5), 75–91.

Gilbert, D., & Wilson, T. (2000). Miswanting: Some problems in the forecasting of future affective states. In J. Forgas (ed.), *Thinking and Feeling: The Role of Affect in Social Cognition* (pp. 178–197). Cambridge: Cambridge University Press.

Gilmore, J. H., & Pine II, B. J. (1996). The four faces of mass customization. *Harvard Business Review, 75*(1), 91–101.

Gourville, J. T., & Soman, D. (2005). Overchoice and assortment type: When and why variety backfires. *Marketing Science, 24*(3), 382–395.

Herrmann, A, Heitmann, M., Morgan, R. Henneberg, S. C., & Landwehr, J. (2009). Consumer decision making and variety of offerings: The effect of attribute alignability. *Psychology & Marketing, 26*(4), 333–358.

Heitmann, M., Herrmann, A., & Kaiser, C. (2007). The effect of product variety on purchase probability. *Review of Managerial Science, 1*(2), 111–131.

Hoyer, W. D., Chandy, R., Dorotic, M., Krafft, M., and Singh, S. S. (2010). Consumer co-creation in new product development. *Journal of Service Research, 13*(3), 283–296.

Hsee, C. K. (1996). The evaluability hypothesis: An explanation for preference reversals between joint and separate evaluations of alternatives. *Organizational Behavior and Human Decision Processes, 670*(3), 247–257.

Huffman, C. & Kahn, B. E. (1998). Variety for sale: Mass customization or mass confusion? *Journal of Retailing, 74*(4), 491–513.

Iyengar, S. S., & Lepper, M. R. (2000). When choice is demotivating: Can one desire too much of a food thing? *Journal of Personality and Social Psychology, 79*(6), 995–1006.

Jeppesen, L. B., & Lakhani, K. (2010). Marginality and problem-solving effectiveness in broadcast search. *Organization Science, 21*(5), 1016–1033.

Khan, U., & Dhar, R. (2006). Licensing Effect in Consumer Choice. *Journal of Marketing Research, 42*(2), 259–266.

Kim, H. S., & Drolet, A. (2003). Choice and self-expression: A cultural analysis of variety seeking. *Journal of Personality and Social Psychology, 85*(2), 373–382.

Kotler, P., & Armstrong, G. (2013). *Principles of Marketing,* 15th ed. Englewood Cliffs, NJ: Prentice Hall.

Lee, S. Y., Gregg, A. P., & Park, S. H. (2013). The person in the purchase: Narcissistic consumers prefer products that positively distinguish them. *Journal of Personality and Social Psychology, 105*(2), 335–352.

Levin, I., & Gaeth, G. (1988). How consumers are affected by the framing of attribute information before and after consuming the product. *Journal of Consumer Research, 15*(3), 374–378.

Lichtenstein, S., & Slovic, P., (2006). *The Construction of Preference,* Cambridge: Cambridge University Press.

Lilien, G. L., Morrison, P. D., Searls, K., Sonnack, M., & von Hippel, E. (2002). Performance assessment of the lead user idea-generation process for new product development. *Management Science, 48*(8), 1042–1060.

Luce, M. F., Bettman, J. R., & Payne, J. W. (1999). Emotional trade-off difficulty and choice. *Journal of Marketing Research, 36*(2), 143–159.

Lynn, M., & Harris, J. (1997). Individual differences in the pursuit of self-uniqueness through consumption. *Journal of Applied Social Psychology, 27*(21), 1861–1883.

Miceli, G. N., Raimondo, M. A., & Farace S. (2013). Customer attitude and dispositions towards customized products: The interaction between customization model and brand. *Journal of Interactive Marketing, 27*(3), 209–225.

Mochon, D., Norton, M., & Ariely, D. (2012). Bolstering and restoring feelings of competence via the IKEA effect. *International Journal of Research in Marketing, 29*(4), 363–369.

Moreau, C. P, Bonney, L., & Herd, K. B. (2011). It's the thought (and the effort) that counts: How customizing for others differs from customizing for oneself. *Journal of Marketing, 75*(5), 120–133.

Moreau, C. P., & Herd, K. (2010). To each his own? How comparisons with others influence consumers' evaluations of their self-designed products. *Journal of Consumer Research, 36*(5), 806–819.

Nelson-Field, K., & Riebe, E. (2011). The impact of media fragmentation on audience targeting: An empirical generalization approach. *Journal of Marketing Communications, 17*(1), 51–67.

Nisbett, R. E., & Wilson, T. D., (1977). Telling more than we can know: Verbal reports on mental processes. *Psychological Review, 84*(3), 231–259.

Nishikawa, H., Schreier, M., & Ogawa, S. (2013). User-generated versus designer-generated products: A performance assessment at Muji. *International Journal of Research in Marketing, 30*(2), 160–167.

Norton, M., Mochon, D., & Ariely, D. (2012). The IKEA effect: When labor leads to love. *Journal of Consumer Psychology, 22*(3), 453–460.

Novemsky, N., Dhar, R., Schwarz, N., & Simonson, I. (2007). Preference fluency in choice. *Journal of Marketing Research, 64*(3), 347–356.

Ogawa, S., & Piller, F. T. (2006). Reducing the risks of new product development. *MIT Sloan Management Review, 47*(2), 65–71.

O'Hern, M. S., & Kahle, L. R. (2013). The empowered customer: User-generated content and the future of marketing. *Global Economics and Management Review, 18*(1), 22–30.

O'Hern, M. S., & Rindfleisch, A. (2010). Customer co-creation: A typology and research agenda. *Review of Marketing Research, 6*, 84–106.

Oyserman, D. (2009). Identity-based motivation: Implications for action-readiness, procedural-readiness, and consumer behavior. *Journal of Consumer Psychology, 19*(3), 250–260.

Piller, F. T., Ihl, C., & Vossen. A. (2010). A typology of customer co-creation in the innovation. Available at SSRN: http://ssrn.com/abstract=1732127.

Piller, F., Moeslein, K., & Stotko, C. M. (2004). Does mass customization pay? An economic approach to evaluate customer integration. *Production Planning & Control, 15*(4), 435–444.

Pine II, J. B. (1993). *Mass Customization: The New Frontier in Business Competition.* Boston: Harvard Business School Press.

Poetz, M. K., & Schreier, M. (2012). The value of crowdsourcing: Can users really compete with professionals in generating new product ideas? *Journal of Product Innovation Management, 29*(2), 245–256.

Prelec, D., Wernerfelt, B., & Zettelmeyer, F. (1997). The role of inference in context effects: Inferring what you want from what is available. *Journal of Consumer Research, 24*(1), 118–125.

Randall, T., Terwiesch, C., & Ulrich, K. T. (2007). Research note: User design of customized products. *Marketing Science, 26*(2), 268–280.

Ratner, R. K., & Kahn, B. E. (2002). The impact of private versus public consumption on variety-seeking behavior. *Journal of Consumer Research, 29*(2), 246–257.

Reed II, A., Forehand, M., Puntoni, S., & Warlop, L. (2012). Identity-based consumer behavior. *International Journal of Research in Marketing, 29*(4), 310–321.

Salvador, F., Piller, F. T., & de Holan, P. M. (2009). Cracking the code of mass customization. *MIT Sloan Management Review, 50*(3), 71–77.

Schreier, M. (2006). The value increment of mass-customized products: An empirical assessment. *Journal of Consumer Behaviour, 5*(4), 317–327.

Schreier, M., Fuchs, C., & Dahl, D. W. (2012). The innovation effect of user design: Exploring consumers' innovation perceptions of firms selling products designed by users. *Journal of Marketing, 76*(5), 18–32.

Schwartz, B., Ward, A., Monterosso, J., Lyubomirsky, S., White, K., & Lehman, D. R. (2002). Maximizing versus satisficing: Happiness is a matter of choice. *Journal of Personality and Social Psychology, 83*(5), 1178–1197.

Snyder, C. R., & Fromkin, H. I. (1977). Abnormality as a positive characteristic: The development and validation of a scale measuring need for uniqueness. *Journal of Abnormal Psychology, 86*(5), 518–527.

Simonson, I. (1989). Choice based on reasons: The case of attraction and compromise effects. *Journal of Consumer Research, 16*(2), 158–174.

Simonson, I. (1992). The influence of anticipating regret and responsibility on purchase decisions. *Journal of Consumer Research, 19*(1), 105–119.

Simonson, I. (2005). Determinants of customers' responses to customized offers: Conceptual framework and research propositions. *Journal of Marketing; 69*(1), 32–45.

Simonson, I., & Nowlis, S. M., (2000). The role of explanations and need for uniqueness in consumer decision making: Unconventional choices based on reasons. *Research Papers 1610.* Stanford University: Graduate School of Business.

Sirgy, M. J. (1982). Self-concept in consumer behaviour: A critical review. *Journal of Consumer Research, 9*(3), 287–300.

Sternberg, R. J. (2004) (original 1999). *Handbook of Creativity.* Cambridge: Cambridge University Press.

Syam, N., Krishnamurthy, P., & Hess, J. D. (2008). That's what I thought I wanted? Miswanting and regret for a standard good in a mass customized world. *Marketing Science, 27*(3), 379–397.

Tevfik, D., & Leeuw, M. (1994). Niche marketing revisited: Concept, applications and some European cases. *European Journal of Marketing, 28*(4), 39–55.

Thomson, D. V, & Malaviya, P. (2013). Consumer-generated ads: Does awareness of advertising co-creation help or hurt persuasion? *Journal of Marketing, 77*(3), 33–47.

Tian, K. T., Bearden, W. O., & Hunter, G. L. (2001). Consumers' need for uniqueness: Scale development and validation. *Journal of Consumer Research, 28*(1), 50–66.

Townsend, C., & Kahn, B. (2014). The visual preference heuristic: The influence of visual versus verbal depiction on assortment processing, perceived variety, and choice overload. *Journal of Consumer Research, 40*(5), 993–1015.

Valenzuela, A., Dhar, R., & Zettelmeyer, F. (2009). Contingent response to self-customization procedures: Implications for decision satisfaction and choice. *Journal of Marketing Research, 46*(6), 754–763.

Von Hippel, E. (1986). Lead users: A source of novel product concepts. *Management Science, 32*(7), 791–806.

Von Hippel, E. (2005). *Democratizing Innovation.* Cambridge, MA: MIT Press.

Von Hippel, E., De Jong, J. P. J., & Flowers, S. (2012). Comparing business and household sector innovation in consumer products: Findings from a representative study in the United Kingdom *Management Science, 58*(9), 1669–1681.

Von Hippel, E., & Katz, R. (2002). Shifting innovation to users via toolkits. *Management Science, 48*(7), 821–833.

Wedell, D., & Bockeholt, U. (1990). Moderation of preference reversals in the long run. *Journal of Experimental Psychology: Human Perception and Performance, 16* (2), 429–438.

Wilcox, K., & Song, S. (2011). Discrepant fluency in self-customization. *Journal of Marketing Research, 48*(4), 729–740.

PART II

Interpersonal and Social Consumer Psychology

10 Identity-Signaling Behavior

David Gal

What do wearing a tie-dye shirt, driving a high-end sports car, carrying an intellectual book on a train, placing political signs on one's lawn, filling out a consumer survey, posting on Facebook, reading a Japanese manga, donating to a charitable cause, sharing a rumor, and choosing a healthy snack have in common? While the answer to this question might serve as a projective test to some, one answer is that they all can be considered forms of identity-signaling behavior.

In this chapter, identity-signaling behavior is defined as behavior motivated by the belief that the behavior will convey particular information about the individual to the self or to others. In this context, it is not imperative that others in fact observe the behavior, or even that the individual has a strong expectation others will observe the behavior. Rather, for the purpose of this chapter, it is sufficient that the individual anticipates how others would interpret the behavior if they were to observe it to constitute identity-signaling behavior motivated by others' perceptions of the behavior. This definition is consistent with the conception of social psychology as the study of how people's thoughts, feelings, and behaviors are influenced by the real or imagined presence of others (Allport, 1985).

Whereas identity-signaling behavior can involve self-signaling without regard to the perceptions of others (Bodner & Prelec, 2003), most identity-signaling behavior appears to reflect concern with signaling information about the self to others (Ross, 1971; Wicklund & Gollwitzer, 1982). This is reflected in findings that show that people are more likely to engage in signaling behavior when engaging in public or conspicuous behavior than in private or inconspicuous behavior (Bearden & Etzel, 1982; Ross, 1971). Likewise, individuals are more likely to engage in identity-signaling behavior in domains that they perceive can convey information about themselves to others (Berger & Heath, 2007; Shavitt, 1990; Shavitt & Nelson, 1999).

Research on identity-signaling behavior has a long history in consumer psychology research, with a number of well-known articles identifying identity-signaling motives as drivers of product and brand choice (Belk, 1988; Belk, Bahn, & Mayer, 1982; Fournier, 1998; Gardner & Levy, 1955; Holman, 1981; Levy, 1959; McCracken, 1986; Sirgy, 1982; Thompson & Hirschman, 1995). In an early article articulating the importance of the topic, Levy (1959) argued that consumers adopt brands not only for their functional benefits, but as a means to define their self-concept through the symbolic meaning with which brands are imbued. Similarly, McCracken (1989) described the process by which products become imbued with meaning and how consumers, in turn, construct their self-identity through acquiring and using brands with associations they wish to attach to the self.

Going further in connecting consumers with their possessions, Belk (1988) put forth the notion that people's possessions are part and parcel of the self. Consistent with this view, evidence shows that people tend to overvalue items in their possession relative to items outside their possession, and that this effect is driven by the extent to which people incorporate their possessions into their identity (Brenner, Rottenstreich, Sood, & Bilgin, 2007; Morewedge, Shu, Gilbert, & Wilson, 2009; Reb & Connolly, 2007; Shu & Peck, 2011; Strahilevitz & Loewenstein, 1998). Other researchers provided early evidence that product and brand choice are used by consumers to define themselves (Aaker, 1999; Escalas & Bettman, 2003, 2005; Kleine, Kleine, & Kernan, 1993), and that people use product and brand choices to evaluate those using them (Calder & Burnkrant, 1977; Douglas & Isherwood, 1978; Wernerfelt, 1990).

More recent research in consumer psychology has focused on distinguishing among the different motivations that drive identity-signaling behavior and on the unintended consequences of identity-signaling behavior. At the same time, identity-signaling behavior is still relatively underdeveloped as a research area, and many unanswered questions about the motives that lead to identity-signaling behavior and the consequences of such behavior remain, making the topic a potentially fruitful one for future research. The remainder of this chapter summarizes some of the key findings regarding the different motives identified as drivers of identity-signaling behavior and the unintended consequences resulting from identity-signaling behavior. The chapter then highlights potentially fertile areas for new research across these topic areas.

Drivers of Identity-Signaling Behavior

Identity-signaling behavior is not driven by a single desire; rather, many different motives likely lead people to engage in identity-signaling behavior. While various categorization schemes might be used to capture identity-signaling motives (see Swann, 1983), the current chapter delineates three broad categories of motives represented within the consumer psychology literature. In particular, a number of distinct findings can be classified into motives related to (a) need for belonging, (b) need for self-expression, and (c) need for self-enhancement.

Briefly, the need for belonging refers to people's basic need to belong to a group (Baumeister & Leary, 1995); the need for self-expression refers to the need to display aspects of one's actual self, rather than one's idealized self, to others (Bellah et al., 1985); and the need for self-enhancement refers to the need to enhance self-worth (Sedikides & Strube, 1995). These different motives are presented separately and can operate distinctly, yet these motives often overlap, such that identity-signaling behavior is often driven by some combination of these motives. Indeed, in much of the research on identity-signaling behavior, little distinction is drawn between these motives, with researchers often treating, for instance, self-expressive and self-enhancement motives for identity-signaling behavior synonymously.

Nonetheless, though the motives underlying identity-signaling behavior might overlap, they are also distinct, having different desired aims and resulting in different consequences for the individual. For example, whereas self-expression tends to be energizing, self-enhancement can be depleting, due to the latter requiring self-regulatory resources (Gal & Wilkie, 2010). Moreover, these motives can interact with each other in a variety of ways (e.g., White, Argo, & Sengupta, 2012). For example, signaling a social identity may be perceived as a form of self-enhancement and conformity if the individual views signaling the desired social identity as conflicting with the expression of his or her individuality. Conversely, signaling a social identity might be perceived as a form of self-expression among those whose individual identity is closely tied to the signaled social identity (as might particularly be the case among those with an interdependent sense of self; Kim & Sherman, 2007). In this section, the focus is on describing each of the three general motives underlying the afore-mentioned identity-signaling behavior. Later in the chapter, potential inter-actions of these motives and their implications will be discussed.

Need for Belonging

People have a basic need to belong to a group (Baumeister & Leary, 1995; Fiske, 2004). Research has shown that one means consumers use to identify their affiliation with a group is through acquiring and using products and brands that signal their belonging to the desired group (Escalas & Bettman, 2005). Products and brands can be used by consumers to signal membership in a particular social class, social group, professional group, family, society, or culture, among other groups (Braun & Wicklund, 1989; Escalas & Bettman, 2005; Kleine, Kleine, & Kernan, 1993; Laverie, Kleine, & Kleine, 2002; McShane, Bradlow, & Berger, 2012; Muniz & O'Guinn, 2001; Reingen, Foster, Brown, & Seidman, 1984; Wallendorf & Arnould, 1988; Wicklund & Gollwitzer, 1981). Moreover, others tend to use consumers' product and brand preferences as a means of assigning them to particular social groups (Douglas & Isherwood, 1978).

Though brands and products often signal membership in particular groups, the group memberships associated with brands and products are continuously evolving. One reason for this is because people wish to signal their belonging to desirable groups; as a consequence, people tend to avoid the use of products and brands that might serve to signal belonging to an undesirable group (Berger & Heath, 2007, 2008; Berger & Le Mens, 2009; Berger & Rand, 2008; White & Dahl, 2006, 2007). Thus, as increasing numbers of people adopt products or brands associated with membership in a desired group, the products or brands lose their distinctiveness in signaling membership in that group and the meaning of the products or brands shifts (Pronin, Berger, & Molouki, 2007; Thornton, 1996). Early group members may thus abandon the products or brands initially associated with the group in favor of alternative products or brands that are more distinctive (Berger & Heath, 2007).

In some cases, signaling a social identity may simply reflect a basic need to belong to a group; however, in other cases belonging motives may overlap with self-expressive or self-enhancement motives. For example, signaling a social identity might, in addition to the belongingness need, be motivated by a need to engage in self-expression to the extent that individuals view the social identity as overlapping with their own identity. Indeed, the idea that signaling a social identity is a form of self-expression is implicit to a large number of research articles that have examined the determinants of social-identity signaling (e.g., Berger & Heath, 2007; Berger & Schwartz, 2011; Berger & Ward, 2010; Sirgy, 1982).

Other research shows, in contrast, that people are motivated to signal their social identity through product or brand choices not to fulfill a need for self-expression, but as a means to conform to, or fit in with, a group with which they want to be affiliated (Bearden, Netemeyer, & Teel, 1989; Escalas & Bettman, 2005; Gal & Wilkie, 2010; McFerran, Dahl, Fitzsimons, & Morales, 2010). For example, research shows that people often use product or brand choices to conform to the majority, particularly when they feel socially isolated (Mead et al., 2011; Wang, Zhu, & Shiv, 2012). Thus, in such cases, signaling a social identity is not motivated by a need to engage in self-expression, but by a need to belong to the group and/or to enhance one's self-image through the group identity.

Need for Self-Expression

Self-expression can be defined as the expression or display of one's otherwise unobservable actual self or more tangibly as the expression of one's otherwise unobservable personality traits, values, beliefs, opinions, attitudes, and so forth (Bellah et al., 1985). Self-expression is widely recognized as a driver of consumer behavior, including product and brand choice (Aaker, 1999; Kassarjian, 1971; Kim & Drolet, 2003; Richins, 1994; Sirgy, 1982; Ward, 1974).

However, despite the widely accepted belief that self-expression is a driver of consumer behavior, consumer research attempting to demonstrate the role of self-expression in driving behavior has a mixed history. Early research in the 1960s and 1970s hypothesized that consumers use brands to express their identity, and thus that consumers would prefer brands with personalities that were congruent with their own ("self-congruity"). However, early evidence did not support this hypothesis (for summaries, see Kassarjian, 1971; Sirgy, 1982).

To explain the lack of a positive relationship between brand choice and identity, scholars posited that early investigations of self-expression via brands were based on a false premise, namely the idea of a stable individual identity (Kassarjian, 1971; Sirgy, 1982). In fact, subsequent research demonstrated that the self-concept is malleable and that different aspects of one's identity can be highlighted in different contexts (e.g., Markus & Kunda, 1986). To illustrate, aspects of one's identity that are likely to be accessible in a professional context, such as being diligent, might be less salient when in a social context, such as when having drinks with friends, where other aspects of one's identity, such as one's sense of humor, might be more salient.

In addition to the malleability of the self as an explanation for the failure of early self-expression research to identify a connection between individual personality and brand choice, researchers have proposed that different aspects of one's personality are likely to vary in importance to the self and hence in the degree to which one is motivated to express them (Markus, 1977; Visser, Krosnick, & Simmons, 2003). Thus, even if an individual possesses a particular trait, the individual will not be motivated to express that trait if the trait is not important to his or her identity. A further explanation put forth by researchers for the failure of early self-expression research to establish a link between individual personality and brand choice was that brand personality traits in early self-expression research were created ad hoc or adopted from human scales, such as from the big-5 personality inventory (Aaker, 1999), rather than from specific brand-personality scales. Lastly, it was argued that individual personality attributes might not be reflected in choice of brands because brand choice symbolism is not used simply to signal one's individuality but also to fulfill belonging and self-enhancement motives (Kassarjian, 1971; as also discussed in the other subsections of this section).

Consistent with many of these explanations for the failure of early self-expression research to identify a link between individual personality and brand choice, in an influential article, Aaker (1999) showed that consumers indeed prefer brands that match traits associated with their self-concept. The key differences between Aaker's (1999) research and the early self-expression research were that Aaker's investigation relied on the malleable conception of the self and used a brand personality typology systematically developed to apply to brands (Aaker, 1997). In particular, Aaker (1999) demonstrated that traits made accessible by situational cues and chronically accessible traits both positively influenced consumers' brand attitudes (see also Bhattacharjee, Berger, & Menon, 2014; Reed, Forehand, Puntoni, & Warlop, 2012).

Yet despite influential articles on the topic, and notable advances, the investigation of self-expression as a driver of consumer behavior, or of human behavior more generally, is relatively limited among both consumer psychologists and researchers from other disciplines. For instance, the work of Aaker (1999) focused on one important source of self-expression – expressing one's personality – but did not focus on other aspects of the individual, such as values, attitudes, or beliefs, that a consumer might similarly be motivated to express. With notable exceptions, such as Richins (1994), who showed that people's possessions reflected their material values, or Gal and Rucker (2011), who showed that people tend to express their attitudes and beliefs even when they are not asked about them, examinations of aspects of individuality that consumers are motivated to express other than personality traits are mostly absent from the literature.

Likewise, research on self-expression in consumer research has tended to focus on self-expression through brands or possessions, and has, with some exceptions (e.g., Gal & Rucker, 2011; Schau & Gilly, 2003), neglected the study of other forms of self-expression, such as the expression of consumer attitudes (e.g., in market research surveys or in the form of product or services reviews such as on Amazon and Yelp) or consumer-generated content, such as might be created by consumers on their personal websites or on social media.

In general, and again, despite notable individual articles, self-expression, for all intents and purposes, does not exist as a distinct research topic in social psychology or even consumer psychology, and a self-expression motive is often conflated with a self-enhancement motive or with a belonging motive. Indeed, belonging and self-enhancement motives sometimes do overlap with a self-expression motive; however, these motives are also distinct from self-expression and in many cases polar opposite in terms of their consequences (more on this later).

The relative absence of self-expression as a distinct research topic in psychology is somewhat surprising given (a) its apparent centrality to real-world consumer behavior and (b) the vast literatures on the other motives underlying identity-signaling behavior discussed in this chapter, namely the need to belong and the need to self-enhance. For example, no psychometric scale has been developed to measure the need for self-expression, whereas several such scales exist to measure belonging and self-enhancement motives. Thus, some basic questions about the nature of self-expression remain murky and unexplored, though initial answers are emerging.

Do People Have a Need to Self-Express?

One basic question is whether individuals, broadly, have a need to express themselves. As noted, early demonstrations consistent with the need for self-expression showed that consumers tend to pick brands with personalities that are congruent with active aspects of their own personality (Aaker, 1999). However, though such findings demonstrate the influence of brand personality on choice in a manner consistent with a self-expressive motive, the findings are also consistent with other motives, such as a need for consistency (as reflected in consistency between one's personality and the personality associated with one's possessions). Further, despite the importance of personality traits to one's identity, early research paid little attention to other aspects of one's identity, such as personal values, attitudes, and beliefs, that might be subject to self-expression. Moreover, early research often conflated a need for self-expression with other needs, such as the need to self-enhance or to belong (Sirgy, 1982).

Relatively recently, more direct evidence for a need to engage in self-expression is possible due to the Internet's democratization of the ability to create and disseminate content. The emergence of the Internet has given rise to systematic investigations of the motives underlying individuals' engagement in self-expressive activity through both personal websites and social media. Schau and Gilly (2003) found that people's postings on personal websites were motivated by a desire to express themselves, including expressions of their personality and values. Likewise, Back and colleagues (2010) showed that Facebook profiles reflect individuals' actual personality traits (rather than their idealized traits), and Toubia and Stephen's (2013) findings suggest that Twitter posters are driven to post by intrinsic expression motives in addition to image concerns.

Other relatively direct evidence for a need for self-expression is research showing that individuals actively choose to express themselves on issues that are personally important to them, even when they do not expect positive change to arise from their self-expression (Gal & Rucker, 2010; Visser, Krosnick, & Simmons, 2003). Gal and Rucker (2011) find, in fact, that individuals often attempt to convey attitudes on issues that they are not asked about through the judgments and preferences they express in response to unrelated questions, a phenomenon they term response substitution. For example, they find that respondents asked to evaluate a candy bar judge it less favorably when informed that it was made by a company engaging in immoral, compared to moral, business practices. This difference is attenuated when participants are made aware that they will have a subsequent opportunity to share any open-ended thoughts they might have about the company, which suggests that this difference in evaluation is, at least in part, due to a need to express their attitude toward the company (and not simply because the company's moral conduct affects their judgment of the candy bar). Moreover, the effect documented by Gal and Rucker (2011) holds when individuals are informed that their response will not be shared with, and will have no effect on, the behavior of the company. Thus, this finding suggests that respondents want to express their negative views of the company's moral conduct and choose to do so through providing a poor evaluation of the company's product.

Further supporting the conclusion that respondents' behavior in Gal and Rucker's (2011) study is driven by a need for self-expression, the effect is strongest among respondents who view company moral behavior as personally important to them (see Visser, Krosnick, & Simmons, 2003, for additional findings showing the influence of attitude importance on attitude-expressive behaviors). Thus, these findings suggest that individuals have a need to express themselves, even in the absence of positive consequences that might result from their actions, and that individuals will attempt to express their values and attitudes even if they are not asked about them.

If individuals indeed have a need to express themselves, then it might be expected, as is true for many psychological motives, that fulfilling the need to engage in self-expression will diminish the need to engage in self-expression subsequently. Consistent with this notion, recent work has examined how expressing preferences in one domain can influence preference expression in an unrelated domain (Chernev, Hamilton, & Gal, 2011). This work shows that expressing preferences for a self-expressive brand in one product category (e.g., computers) diminishes the valuation of self-expressive brands in unrelated product categories (e.g., shoes). This finding supports the view that self-expression, rather than being domain-specific or a chronic trait, is a general motivational force that can be temporarily satiated by fulfilling the need to engage in it. This finding also has important implications for brand management, as it suggests that brands compete not only with other brands within their own product category but across product categories for a share of the consumer's identity.

Why Do People Have a Need to Self-Express?

An even more fundamental question than whether people have a need to express themselves is why people might have a need for self-expression. Basic evolutionary motives have been put forth to explain the needs for belonging (Baumeister & Leary, 1995) and self-enhancement (Sedikides, Gaertner, & Toguchi, 2003), but it is not readily apparent how evolutionary motives would account for a need to engage in self-expression. However, at least two explanations have been put forth to account for a need for self-expression, namely (1) that self-expression fulfills a need for self-consistency and (2) that self-expression fulfills a need to view one's self in a positive light.

The first argument, that the need for self-expression stems from a need for consistency, stems from findings reflecting a need for consistency in greater recall for self-consistent (vs. inconsistent) information, less distortion of self-consistent (vs. inconsistent) information, and greater positive affect resulting from receipt of self-consistent (vs. inconsistent) information (Eisenstadt & Leippe, 1994). It is posited that self-consistency is valued because people innately like the predictable and familiar and dislike uncertainty (Swann, Stein-Seroussi, & Giesler, 1992). By engaging in self-expression, this line of argument suggests, people are being consistent with their internal selves, thus fulfilling the need for consistency and certainty.

The second argument, that self-expression stems from a need to view the self in a positive light, is based on the established idea that people have a strong desire to view themselves positively (e.g., Crocker & Park, 2004; Heine, Proulx, & Vohs, 2006), and thereby that they tend to construct positive self-concepts (Aronson, 1999). This line of argument suggests that self-expression tends to result in the expression of positive traits, which leads to pride and positive affect; on the other hand, for the same reasons, suppression of one's traits can lead to negative affect (Swann, De La Ronde, & Hixon, 1994). At its core, this argument seems to blur the distinction between self-expression and self-enhancement, suggesting that the need to express one's individuality is really just a need to enhance one's self-concept. Although self-expression might indeed be driven by self-enhancement motives in some cases, explaining all self-expressive behavior through a need to self-enhance seems to contradict the nature of self-expressive behavior as a need to display one's actual, inner self and is inconsistent with the idea that people display not only their positive qualities in self-expressive works (such as songs and poetry), but also their fears, personal tragedies, and imperfections (Dewey, 2005), and that people often express opinions or values of ambiguous valence (e.g., Gal & Rucker, 2011). Likewise, the logic behind the first explanation, that people engage in self-expression because of a need for consistency and certainty, is inconsistent with the idea that self-expressive behavior often includes the expression of emotions associated with uncertainty, such as sadness and fear (Tiedens & Linton, 2001), as depicted in self-expressive works of art and music (Dewey, 2005). If certainty and positivity were the goal, one might try to distract one's self from these emotions rather than to dwell on them and express them.

Further, both these arguments essentially dismiss the idea that people have an innate need to express their self and imply that the value of self-expressive behavior results from the cognitions attached to what is expressed rather than from the act of expression itself. Moreover, both these explanations focus on the expression of traits, but less on values, attitudes, beliefs, or emotions, that are the subject of much self-expressive behavior.

Thus, neither of the explanations posited to account for a need to engage in self-expressive behavior appears fully satisfactory. Perhaps another explanation is that, as fundamentally social beings, our individuality is fully realized only through the effects we have on others (i.e., on others' thoughts, actions, or behaviors). Indeed, the early-nineteenth-century German philosopher Hegel argued that self-consciousness is fundamentally dependent on "recognition" of the self by others, and that without others' recognition, one's acts have no meaning. Thus, in order to prove the certainty of one's existence, individuals must exert an influence on others (Hegel, 1807). At present, of course, such explanations remain within the realm of speculation.

Need for Self-Enhancement

Self-enhancement refers to people's motivation to enhance their self-worth (Sedikides & Strube, 1995).[1] Individuals are generally strongly motivated to maintain a positive self-image and to maintain and boost their self-esteem (Crocker & Park, 2004; Greenwald, Bellezza, & Banaji, 1988; Heine, Proulx, & Vohs, 2006; Tesser, 2000). Identity-signaling behavior can function to enhance self-worth through at least two major pathways: it can lead to social approval and it can lead to the generation of social proof.

---

[1] Self-protection, likewise, refers to individuals' motivation to maintain their self-worth, particularly in the face of threats, and is generally considered a form of the self-enhancement motive (e.g., Alicke & Sedikides, 2009).

Social Approval

Social approval tends to boost self-worth (Schlenker, 1980). As a result, people aspire to be liked, valued, appreciated, admired, and respected by others. To this end, people tend to present themselves in a manner that will generate a favorable impression of themselves in others' eyes (Baumeister, Tice, & Hutton, 1989; Schlenker, 1980). Flattery, mimicry, social conformity, and self-promotion are among the means by which individuals attempt to generate favorable impressions and thereby to enhance their self-concept (Fiske & Taylor, 1991).

Consumer researchers have shown that consumers also use identity-signaling behavior to fulfill self-enhancement motives. In particular, consumers use brands and possessions to signal an identity to others that they expect will result in social approval and thereby will enhance their self-concept. Aspects of identity consumers signal to generate favorable impressions, and thereby enhance their own self-image, include their cultural literacy, taste, and sense of style (Amaldoss & Jain, 2005; Twitchell, 2002).

The use of brands to signal an identity that will affect others' impressions, and thereby boost one's self-concept, can be traced to Veblen's (1899) idea of conspicuous consumption. Conspicuous consumption refers to the notion that individuals use costly markers of questionable practical utility, such as luxury brands or other high-priced products, to signal social status and wealth. Recently, research has shown that signaling status through wearing high-status brands indeed affects others' perceptions of the individual wearing the brand in a favorable manner (Gillath, Bahns, Ge, & Crandall, 2012; Nelissen & Meijers, 2011).

In addition to (or in concert with) establishing status in the eyes of others, consumer researchers have also shown that individuals often use products and brands to establish their uniqueness and distinctiveness in the eyes of others (Ariely & Levav, 2000; Berger & Heath, 2007; Griskevicius et al., 2006; Gross, 1977; Snyder, 1992; Snyder & Fromkin, 1977; Tian, Bearden, & Hunter, 2001). Consistent with the idea that signaling uniqueness enhances one's image, conformity can often be perceived as a sign of low social status (Berger & Ward, 2010; Feltovich, Harbaugh, & To, 2002; Han, Nunes, & Drèze, 2010; Mazzocco, Rucker, Galinsky, & Anderson, 2012), whereas uniqueness and lack of conformity can be viewed as a mark of status (Bellezza, Gino, & Keinan, 2014).

A question that arises is how consumers reconcile the motive to belong to a group (discussed previously) with the desire to signal uniqueness and status through a lack of conformity. Chan, Berger, and Van Boven (2012) addressed this question in a series of experiments that found that individuals pursue assimilation and differentiation goals on different choice dimensions. Individuals tend to conform on dimensions that are strongly tied to their group identity (e.g., a particular clothing brand) and to differentiate on dimensions that are less tied to their group identity (e.g., a particular color of clothing).

Social Proof

Closely related to the idea that individuals engage in identity-signaling behavior to gain social approval and thereby enhance their self-concept is the idea that individuals engage in identity-signaling behavior to gain social proof for a positive self-image. Research shows that the self-concept is malleable rather than fixed (Linville & Carlston, 1994; Markus & Kunda, 1986). This suggests that people's identity is inherently ambiguous and uncertain. Thus, if an individual can signal to, and thereby convince, others that the individual has desirable qualities, then the individual will be more likely to believe he or she has the desirable qualities himself or herself. In other words, an individual can boost his or her self-concept through others' perceptions of the individual's qualities because others' perceptions and beliefs function as a form of social proof (see Wicklund & Gollwitzer, 1982).

To elaborate, in the physical world, proof for a particular position is obtained through physical evidence. However, in the social world, physical and definitive evidence of one's identity is typically lacking. As a result, people tend to rely on the beliefs of others to form and validate their own beliefs (Cialdini et al., 1999; Festinger, 1954). Thus, by choosing a healthy option (Gal & Liu, 2011), donating to charity (Glazer & Konrad, 1996), attending a prestigious university (Spence, 1973), wearing a high status brand (Rucker & Galinsky, 2008, 2009), or conveying an exclusive piece of information (Berger & Schwartz, 2011), individuals can affect others' perceptions of themselves and thereby obtain social proof either to reaffirm their image of themselves (Akerlof & Kranton, 2000; Dolich, 1969; Escalas & Bettman, 2005; Niedenthal, Cantor, & Kihlstrom, 1985) or to boost their self-image (Ariely & Levav, 2000; Bellezza, Gino, & Keinan, 2014).

In addition to evidence from brand and product choice, research focused on consumer's dissemination of their beliefs provides relatively explicit evidence that individuals engage in identity-signaling behavior in order to obtain social proof and, in so doing, protect or boost their self-image. In a seminal case study in social psychology, Festinger, Riecken, and Schachter (1956) observed that members of a cult increased proselytization of their beliefs after an event that should have served to disconfirm their beliefs. Festinger and colleagues argued that this paradoxical effect occurred because the beliefs had become important to the cult members' identity. As a result, disconfirmation of the beliefs threatened the cult members' identity, inducing cult members to obtain social proof for their beliefs by convincing others as an attempt to protect their identity.

Bringing experimental scrutiny to this conclusion, Gal and Rucker (2010) found that individuals tend to express themselves on issues that are both important to them and in which their confidence is temporarily undermined. For example, Gal and Rucker (2010) found that Macintosh owners who believed in the superiority of Macs to PCs expressed greater likelihood of trying to persuade others to purchase a Mac when their confidence in the belief of the Mac's superiority was acutely undermined. Moreover, Gal and Rucker (2010) found that individuals' propensity to attempt to convince others of their beliefs was higher the more important the beliefs were to the individual. These findings suggest that a motive for expressing one's beliefs is to obtain social proof for those beliefs and thereby to bolster beliefs that are important to one's self-concept.

Response to Threat

Individuals are particular likely to engage in self-enhancement when their self-concept is threatened (Leary, Tambor, Terdal, & Downs, 1995; Steele, 1988; Tesser & Cornell, 1991). In the context of consumer behavior, research shows that people tend to respond to threats by buying products that symbolically compensate for the threatened aspect of their identity, a phenomenon termed compensatory consumption (for reviews, see Lee & Shrum, 2013; Rucker & Galinsky, 2013). For example, people are more likely to buy high-status products when they are temporarily induced to perceive themselves as having low power (Rucker & Galinsky, 2008, 2009), to buy products that signal their intelligence when their intelligence is threatened (Gao, Wheeler, & Shiv, 2009; Kim & Gal, 2014), and to buy products that offer variety when a sense of personal freedom or choice is threatened (Levav & Zhu, 2009).

Signaling personal values has also been shown to protect individuals from threat. In particular, research on self-affirmation shows that when individuals express personal values, their self-concept is relatively protected from threats (Gao, Wheeler, & Shiv, 2009; Sivanathan & Pettit, 2010; Steele, 1988; Townsend & Sood, 2012). For instance, Townsend and Sood (2012) showed that the purchase of aesthetically attractive products could protect individuals from self-threats because the choice of aesthetic products was an expression of a personal value of beauty. Similarly, Rucker, Galinsky, and Dubois (2012) show status objects restore a damaged sense of power. Although the precise mechanism by which self-affirmation protects an individual from self-threats is not fully understood, it is generally believed that self-affirmation provides a boost to self-worth by highlighting an aspect of one's identity from which one derives self-worth; in comparison to the highlighted attribute, the threat does not seem to reflect significantly on one's overall value as a person (Sivanathan, Molden, Galinsky, & Ku, 2008; Steele, 1988; Tesser, 2000).

Unintended Consequences of Identity Signaling

As discussed in the preceding sections, social identity-signaling behavior is governed by a number of motives, among which this chapter has discussed three, namely belonging, self-expressive, and self-enhancing motives. However, recent research has documented that engaging in identity-signaling behavior can also yield downstream consequences other than those intended by the actor engaging in the behavior.

One such consequence is depletion of regulatory resources. In particular, research has established that engaging in self-enhancing behavior typically requires self-regulation (Vohs, Baumeister, & Ciarocco, 2005). Thus, identity-signaling behavior motivated by the desire to enhance one's self-image can yield similar consequences to engaging in other self-regulatory behaviors, namely depletion of regulatory resources (Gal & Wilkie, 2010) and anger (Gal and Liu, 2011). For instance, Gal and Wilkie (2010) found that when men chose products they perceived to be masculine in order to signal their manliness rather than because they intrinsically preferred the more "masculine" products, they became depleted. This depletion resulted in diminished performance on a subsequent task.

Other research has focused on the idea that signaling one's identity leads one to act in a manner consistent with the activated identity (Kettle & Häubl, 2011; Oyserman, 2009; Shavitt, Torelli, & Wong, 2009). Early research showed that simply expressing attitudes verbally increased the degree to which individuals believed in the expressed attitudes (Higgins & Rholes, 1978) as can simply repeating one's attitude multiple times (Petrocelli, Tormala, & Rucker, 2007). Similarly, early research showed that when individuals made their attitudes public, their commitment to their attitudes increased (Kiesler, Roth, & Pallak, 1974; Kiesler & Sakumura, 1966).

More recently, Kettle and Häubl (2011) showed that signing one's name activates consumers' identity and leads them to act in a manner congruent with their identity. Similarly, research has found that engaging in self-expression by providing one's opinions and beliefs about particular attitude objects can affect people's subsequent attitudes and behaviors toward the attitude objects (Liu & Gal, 2011). In particular, the act of expressing attitudes and beliefs about an attitude object can activate novel thoughts about the attitude object that can lead to subsequent behavior consistent with the activated thoughts (Liu & Gal, 2011). For example, Liu and Gal (2011) found that the form in which people provided their beliefs about how an organization could best achieve its goals influenced their perceived relationship with the organization, which in turn affected their likelihood of transacting with the organization. For example, giving advice to a nonprofit organization led individuals to adopt the perspective of the organization receiving their advice, which in turn made them feel closer to the organization and ultimately to increase their willingness to donate to the organization. Conversely, stating their expectations of an organization led individuals to adopt distance from the organization, which decreased the closeness that individuals felt to the organization and thereby the likelihood that individuals would transact with the organization.

Future Directions

So far, this chapter has described three significant drivers of identity-signaling behavior as well as unintended consequences of engaging in such behavior. In so doing, the chapter has noted several unanswered or under-explored questions that might serve as potentially fruitful directions for future research. Among these, for example, were the possibility of generating a psy-chometric scale to measure self-expression as well as attempting to resolve the mechanism through which signaling one's values (e.g., self-affirmation) protects the self-concept. In this section, for the sake of brevity, the scope of discussion is limited to four additional potential opportunities for future research on identity-signaling behavior.

Disentangling Identity-Signaling Motives

Perhaps the key theme that has emerged from this review is that the various motives for identity-signaling behavior have been conflated in the literature. That is, any given behavior might be multiply determined or be susceptible to interpretation through multiple motives. This suggests that for identity-signaling behavior to develop as a research area, research is needed that disen-tangles the different motives underlying identity-signaling behavior and identi-fies the specific antecedents and consequences of identity-signaling behavior associated with the need to belong, the need to engage in self-expression, and the need to self-enhance, among others.

One important and related question that can be addressed by disentangling the various identity-signaling motives is that of when identity-signaling behav-ior serves as a means of self-expression (i.e., signaling an identity with the goal of expressing one's actual self) as opposed to as a means of self-enhancement (i.e., signaling an identity with the goal of generating a favorable impression). Self-determination theory, with its dichotomous conception of the motives underlying behavior, can help illuminate how these motives might be disentan-gled. In particular, self-determination theory suggests that choice tends to be either intrinsically motivated or extrinsically motivated (i.e., motivated by a need to conform to rigid or coercive internalized norms or demands; Moller, Deci, & Ryan, 2006; see also Laran & Janiszewski, 2011). Moreover, self-determination theory suggests that these motives can be disentangled experi-mentally through their different consequences, with intrinsically motivated behavior being cognitively energizing and extrinsically motivated behavior being cognitively depleting. Based on this theorizing, as noted previously, Gal and Wilkie (2010) showed that men's choices of masculine products were likely not always a form of self-expression but often a form of self-enhancement and conformity.

This paradigm, focused on whether identity-signaling behavior is energizing or depleting, can likely be extended to disentangling whether different forms of identity-signaling behavior reflect self-expressive or self-enhancing motives. For example, research might identify when prosocial behavior (e.g., composing an appeal for an environmental nonprofit organization) is self-expressive versus self-enhancive by examining the circumstances under which prosocial behavior is energizing versus depleting. Likewise, as other differences in consequences

associated with different identity-signaling motives are identified, new paradigms for disentangling the motives underlying specific forms of identity-
signaling behavior can emerge.

The Role of Culture

Another potentially fruitful area for future research is identifying the degree to
which different identity-signaling behaviors are universal versus culturally
determined. In particular, some researchers have argued that the need for self-
expression (Kim & Sherman, 2007) and self-enhancement (Heine, Lehman,
Markus, & Kitayama, 1999) might be culturally determined. In Western cultures, where consumers predominantly have an independent sense of self, choice
tends to be viewed as a sign of individual freedom, and thus individuals are
thought to use choice to express their inner self so as to realize this individuality
(Bellah et al., 1985). Likewise, individuals are thought to use choice to enhance
the self-concept (e.g., Heine et al., 1999). However, the majority of consumers
in Asian cultures tend to hold an interdependent sense of self, meaning that the
self tends to be viewed in relation to others (Kim & Sherman, 2007; Markus &
Kitayama, 1991; Triandis, 1989). In these cultures, the individual's sense of self
is both guided and constrained by social roles, obligations, and relationships
(Kim & Sherman, 2007). Thus, it has been argued, Asian consumers might view
choice more as a means of fitting in with the group than as a means to express
their individuality or to enhance their self-concept (Fiske, Kitayama, Markus,
& Nisbett, 1998; Kim & Drolet, 2003; Kim & Sherman, 2007).

Markus and Schwartz (2010) summarized the cross-cultural choice literature
and reached the conclusion that whereas choice is a form of positive self-
expression in Western cultures, in Eastern cultures, self-expression is less
valued, and choice is more likely to signal one's social relationships, roles,
memberships, norms, and obligations. Similar challenges were made to the
universality of a self-enhancement motive, with researchers arguing that individuals from Eastern cultures, given their interdependent sense of self, tend not
to have self-enhancement motives (Heine et al., 1999). This was a serious
challenge to the foundations of social psychology since the universality of a
self-enhancement motive has been central to the development of the field
(Aronson, 1992).

However, in response to such challenges, it has been argued that people
universally self-enhance on personally important dimensions, and that people's
sense of self simply determines what dimensions are important to them. Those
with an independent sense of self tend to view individual attributes as more
important to their identity, and hence they tend to enhance on individual
attributes, whereas interdependents tend to view collectivistic attributes as more
important to their identity and hence tend to self-enhance on collectivistic
attributes (Sedikides, Gaertner, & Toguchi, 2003). Likewise, the argument can
be made that those with an interdependent sense of self still have a need for self-
expression, but that such self-expression is more likely to take the form of

signaling a group identity. Such arguments can be subject to increasing experimental scrutiny as distinctions between the different identity-signaling motives are clarified and the specific antecedents and consequences associated with the different identity-signaling motives are ascertained.

Unexamined Forms of Identity-Signaling Behavior

Whereas the predominant focus of identity-signaling behavior research has been on product and brand choice, limited research has also examined other forms of identity-signaling behavior, including survey responses (e.g., Gal & Rucker, 2011), online content generation (e.g., Schau & Gilly, 2003), and word-of-mouth communications (Berger & Schwartz, 2011). Future research might identify other forms of identity-signaling behavior not as yet examined. For example, some research has argued that willingness-to-pay measures for the protection of public goods, such as to preserve a park or lake, used in contingent valuation studies are not truly reflective of individuals' willingness to pay to protect the goods, but of individual's attitudes toward the public good (Kahneman & Knetsch, 1992). However, whether such measures indeed reflect attitudes rather than participants' willingness to pay for the goods has received little empirical attention and is thus ripe for research attention.

Moreover, research might examine whether willingness to pay (and purchase likelihood) for private goods, such as new products and services, reflect identity-signaling motives rather than people's true willingness to pay for these goods. For example, a person's expression of his or her willingness to pay for a novel product might serve to signal that they are a hip, exciting person rather than reflecting their true willingness to pay for the product. Thus, future research might examine willingness to pay and other potential forms of identity-signaling behavior, including charitable giving and tipping behavior, that have to date been little explored in the context of identity-signaling research.

Other Motives for Identity-Signaling Behavior

This chapter has reviewed three broad motives for engaging in identity-signaling behavior, but many others likely exist, both identified and unidentified. For instance, research shows that people engage in identity-signaling behavior not only to enhance their self-concept but to verify it (Swann, 1983). Other research has shown that people engage in identity-signaling behavior because they believe signaling a particular identity will help them acquire things they desire from others. For instance, research has shown that signaling status can help people obtain favorable treatment (Nelissen & Meijers, 2011) as well as assist in mate acquisition (Griskevicius et al., 2007; Sundie et al., 2011) and that signaling anger can help people obtain a better outcome in a negotiation (Andrade & Ho, 2009). How such a motive interacts with the other motives described in this chapter is a potentially interesting question for future research.

Likewise, identifying previously unexamined motives for engaging in identity-signaling behavior seems to be a promising area for future research. For example, the section "Unintended Consequences of Identity Signaling" discussed the notion that engaging in identity-signaling behavior tends to lead to behavior congruent with the signaled identity. A question that arises is whether people proactively signal particular identities in order to regulate their own actions in a manner consistent with the signaled identity.

Conclusion

Despite a long history of research on identity-signaling behavior, the notion of identity-signaling behavior as a distinct area of study is still in its infancy. Indeed, until now, only limited reviews of the topic have appeared in the consumer psychology literature. Whereas some motives that drive identity signaling behavior, namely self-enhancement motives and the need to belong, have been the subject of extensive research, others that are perhaps most relevant to consumer psychology, such as self-expression motives, are surprisingly poorly explored. Moreover, the distinctions between and interactions among these different motives have received little attention. As such, the present chapter represents an initial attempt to survey the emergence of identity-signaling behavior as a coherent area of study not limited to consumer psychology, but one that spans economics, sociology, psychology, and consumer research.

Although identity-signaling behavior as a well-defined area of study is still developing, the number of papers that can be categorized as focusing on identity-signaling behavior is growing. Advancing identity-signaling research seems to be particularly well-suited to consumer psychologists, as identity-signaling behavior has not been extensively tackled by researchers in the closely related discipline of social psychology, and, at the same time, the topic is highly relevant to consumption. Indeed, identity-signaling behavior can be considered central to consumption given the view that much consumption is symbolic rather than functional (Holbrook & Hirschman, 1982). Thus, there is little doubt that the topic presents many opportunities for novel research, and it is expected that identity-signaling behavior will continue to develop as a topic area in consumer psychology and yield important new insights in the coming years.

References

Aaker, J. L. (1997). Dimensions of brand personality. *Journal of Marketing Research, 34* (3), 347–357.

Aaker, J. L. (1999). The malleable self: The role of self-expression in persuasion. *Journal of Marketing Research, 36*(1), 45–57.

Akerlof, G. A., & Kranton, R. E. (2000). Economics and identity. *Quarterly journal of Economics, 115*(3), 715–753.

Alicke, M. D., & Sedikides, C. (2009). Self-enhancement and self-protection: What they are and what they do. *European Review of Social Psychology, 20*(1), 1–48.

Allport, D. (1985). Distributed memory, modular subsystems and dysphasia. In S. P. Newman & R. Epstein (eds.), *Current Perspectives in Dysphasia* (pp. 32–60). Edinburgh: Churchil Livingstone.

Amaldoss, W., & Jain, S. (2005). Conspicuous consumption and sophisticated thinking. *Management Science, 51*(10), 1449–1466.

Andrade, E. B., & Ho, T. H. (2009). Gaming emotions in social interactions. *Journal of Consumer Research, 36*(4), 539–552.

Ariely, D., & Levav, J. (2000). Sequential choice in group settings: Taking the road less traveled and less enjoyed. *Journal of Consumer Research, 27*(3), 279–290.

Aronson, E. (1992). The return of the repressed: Dissonance theory makes a comeback. *Psychological inquiry, 3*(4), 303–311.

Aronson, E. (1999). The power of self-persuasion. *American Psychologist, 54*(11), 875–884.

Back, M. D., Stopfer, J. M., Vazire, S., Gaddis, S., Schmukle, S. C., Egloff, B., & Gosling, S. D. (2010). Facebook profiles reflect actual personality, not self-idealization. *Psychological Science, 21*(3), 372–374.

Baumeister, R. F., & Leary, M. R. (1995). The need to belong: Desire for interpersonal attachments as a fundamental human motivation. *Psychological Bulletin, 117* (3), 497–529.

Baumeister, R. F., Tice, D. M., & Hutton, D. G. (1989). Self-presentational motivations and personality differences in self-esteem. *Journal of Personality, 57*(3), 547–579.

Bearden, W. O., & Etzel, M. J. (1982). Reference group influence on product and brand purchase decisions. *Journal of Consumer Research, 9*(2), 183–194.

Bearden, W. O., Netemeyer, R. G., & Teel, J. E. (1989). Measurement of consumer susceptibility to interpersonal influence. *Journal of Consumer Research, 15*(4), 473–481.

Belk, R. W. (1988). Possessions and the extended self. *Journal of Consumer Research, 15* (2), 139–167.

Belk, R. W., Bahn, K. D., & Mayer, R. N. (1982). Developmental recognition of consumption symbolism. *Journal of Consumer Research, 9*(1), 4–17.

Bellah, R. N., Madsen, R., Sullivan, W. M., Swidler, A., & Tipton, S. M. (1985). *Habits of the Heart: Individualism and Commitment in American Life*. New York: Harper & Row.

Bellezza, S., Gino, F., & Keinan, A. (2014). The red sneakers effect: Inferring status and competence from signals of nonconformity. *Journal of Consumer Research, 41* (1), 35–54.

Berger, J., & Heath, C. (2007). Where consumers diverge from others: Identity signaling and product domains. *Journal of Consumer Research, 34*(2), 121–134.

Berger, J., & Heath, C. (2008). Who drives divergence? Identity signaling, outgroup dissimilarity, and the abandonment of cultural tastes. *Journal of personality and social psychology, 95*(3), 593 – 607.

Berger, J., & Le Mens, G. (2009). How adoption speed affects the abandonment of cultural tastes. *Proceedings of the National Academy of Sciences, 106*(20), 8146–8150.

Berger, J., & Rand, L. (2008). Shifting signals to help health: Using identity signaling to reduce risky health behaviors. *Journal of Consumer Research, 35*(3), 509–518.

Berger, J., & Schwartz, E. M. (2011). What drives immediate and ongoing word of mouth? *Journal of Marketing Research, 48*(5), 869–880.

Berger, J., & Ward, M. (2010). Subtle signals of inconspicuous consumption. *Journal of Consumer Research, 37*(4), 555–569.

Bhattacharjee, A., Berger, J., & Menon, G. (2014). When identity marketing backfires: Consumer agency in identity expression. *Journal of Consumer Research, 41*(2), 294–309.

Bodner, R., & Prelec, D. (2003). Self-signaling and diagnostic utility in everyday decision making. *Psychology of Economic Decisions, 1,* 105–126.

Braun, O. L., & Wicklund, R. A. (1989). Psychological antecedents of conspicuous consumption. *Journal of Economic Psychology, 10*(2), 161–187.

Brenner, L., Rottenstreich, Y., Sood, S., & Bilgin, B. (2007). On the psychology of loss aversion: Possession, valence, and reversals of the endowment effect. *Journal of Consumer Research, 34*(3), 369–376.

Calder, B. J., & Burnkrant, R. E. (1977). Interpersonal influence on consumer behavior: An attribution theory approach. *Journal of Consumer Research, 4*(1), 29–38.

Chan, C., Berger, J., & Van Boven, L. (2012). Identifiable but not identical: Combining social identity and uniqueness motives in choice. *Journal of Consumer Research, 39*(3), 561–573.

Chernev, A., Hamilton, R., & Gal, D. (2011). Competing for consumer identity: Limits to self-expression and the perils of lifestyle branding. *Journal of Marketing, 75*(3), 66–82.

Cialdini, R. B., Wosinska, W., Barrett, D. W., Butner, J., & Gornik-Durose, M. (1999). Compliance with a request in two cultures: The differential influence of social proof and commitment/consistency on collectivists and individualists. *Personality and Social Psychology Bulletin, 25*(10), 1242–1253.

Crocker, J., & Park, L. E. (2004). The costly pursuit of self-esteem. *Psychological Bulletin, 130*(3), 392–414.

Dewey, J. (2005). *Art as Experience.* New York: Berkley.

Dolich, I. J. (1969). Congruence relationships between self images and product brands. *Journal of Marketing Research, 6*(1), 80–84.

Douglas, M., & Isherwood, B. (1978). *The World of Goods: Towards an Anthropology of Consumption.* New York: Norton.

Eisenstadt, D., & Leippe, M. R. (1994). The self-comparison process and self-discrepant feedback: Consequences of learning you are what you thought you were not. *Journal of Personality and Social Psychology, 67*(4), 611–626.

Escalas, J. E., & Bettman, J. R. (2003). You are what they eat: The influence of reference groups on consumers' connections to brands. *Journal of Consumer Psychology, 13*(3), 339–348.

Escalas, J. E., & Bettman, J. R. (2005). Self-construal, reference groups, and brand meaning. *Journal of Consumer Research, 32*(3), 378–389.

Feltovich, N., Harbaugh, R., & To, T. (2002). Too cool for school? Signalling and countersignalling. *RAND Journal of Economics, 4*(33), 630–649.

Festinger, L. (1954). A theory of social comparison processes. *Human Relations, 7*(2), 117–140.

Festinger, L., Riecken, H. W., & Schachter, S. (1956). *When Prophecy Fails*. New York: Harper & Row.

Fiske, A. P., Kitayama, S., Markus, H. R., & Nisbett, R. E. (1998). The cultural matrix of social psychology. In D. T. Gilbert, S. T. Fiske, & G. Linzey (eds.), *Handbook of Social Psychology*, 4th ed. (pp. 915–981). Boston: McGraw-Hill.

Fiske, S., & Taylor, S. (1991). *Social Cognition*, 2nd ed.. New York, England: McGraw-Hill.

Fiske, S. T. (2004). *Social Beings: A Core Motives Approach to Social Psychology*. New York: John Wiley & Sons.

Fournier, S. (1998). Consumers and their brands: Developing relationship theory in consumer research. *Journal of Consumer Research, 24*(4), 343–373.

Gal, D., & Liu, W. (2011). Grapes of wrath: The angry effects of self-control. *Journal of Consumer Research, 38*(3), 445–458.

Gal, D., & Rucker, D. D. (2010). When in doubt, shout! Paradoxical influences of doubt on proselytizing. *Psychological Science, 21*(11), 1701–1707.

Gal, D., & Rucker, D. D. (2011). Answering the unasked question: Response substitution in consumer surveys. *Journal of Marketing Research, 48*(1), 185–195.

Gal, D., & Wilkie, J. (2010). Real men don't eat quiche: Regulation of gender-expressive choices by men. *Social Psychological and Personality Science, 1*(4), 291–301.

Gao, L., Wheeler, S. C., & Shiv, B. (2009). The "shaken self": Product choices as a means of restoring self-view confidence. *Journal of Consumer Research, 36*(1), 29–38.

Gardner, B. B., & Levy, S. J. (1955). The product and the brand. *Harvard Business Review, 33*(2), 33–39.

Gillath, O., Bahns, A. J., Ge, F., & Crandall, C. S. (2012). Shoes as a source of first impressions. *Journal of Research in Personality, 46*(4), 423–430.

Glazer, A., & Konrad, K. A. (1996). A signaling explanation for charity. *American Economic Review, 86*(4), 1019–1028.

Greenwald, A. G., Bellezza, F. S., & Banaji, M. R. (1988). Is self-esteem a central ingredient of the self-concept? *Personality and Social Psychology Bulletin, 14*(1), 34–45.

Griskevicius, V., Goldstein, N. J., Mortensen, C. R., Cialdini, R. B., & Kenrick, D. T. (2006). Going along versus going alone: When fundamental motives facilitate strategic (non)conformity. *Journal of Personality and Social Psychology, 91*(2), 281–294.

Griskevicius, V., Tybur, J. M., Sundie, J. M., Cialdini, R. B., Miller, G. F., & Kenrick, D. T. (2007). Blatant benevolence and conspicuous consumption: When romantic motives elicit strategic costly signals. *Journal of Personality and Social Psychology, 93*(1), 85–102.

Gross, H. E. (1977). Micro and macro level implications for a sociology of virtue: The case of draft protesters to the Vietnam War. *Sociological Quarterly, 18*(3), 319–339.

Han, Y. J., Nunes, J. C., & Drèze, X. (2010). Signaling status with luxury goods: The role of brand prominence. *Journal of Marketing, 74*(4), 15–30.

Hegel. (1807). *Phenomenology of Spirit*, A. V. Miller, trans. New York: OUP.

Heine, S. J., Lehman, D. R., Markus, H. R., & Kitayama, S. (1999). Is there a universal need for positive self-regard? *Psychological Review, 106*(4), 766–794.

Heine, S. J., Proulx, T., & Vohs, K. D. (2006). The meaning maintenance model: On the coherence of social motivations. *Personality and Social Psychology Review, 10*(2), 88–110.

Higgins, E. T., & Rholes, W. S. (1978). "Saying is believing": Effects of message modification on memory and liking for the person described. *Journal of Experimental Social Psychology, 14*(4), 363–378.

Holbrook, M. B., & Hirschman, E. C. (1982). The experiential aspects of consumption: Consumer fantasies, feelings, and fun. *Journal of Consumer Research, 9*(2), 132–140.

Holman, R. H. (1981). Product as communication: A fresh appraisal of a venerable topic. In B. M. Eris & K. J. Boering (eds.), *Review of Marketing* (pp. 106–119). Chicago: American Marketing Association.

Kahneman, D., & Knetsch, J. L. (1992). Valuing public goods: The purchase of Moral Satisfaction. *Journal of Environmental Economics and Management, 22*(1), 57–70.

Kassarjian, H. H. (1971). Personality and consumer behavior: A review. *Journal of Marketing Research, 8*(4), 409–418.

Kettle, K. L., & Häubl, G. (2011). The signature effect: Signing influences consumption-related behavior by priming self-identity. *Journal of Consumer Research, 38*(3), 474–489.

Kiesler, C. A., Roth, T. S., & Pallak, M. S. (1974). Avoidance and reinterpretation of commitment and its implications. *Journal of Personality and Social Psychology, 30*(5), 705–715.

Kiesler, C. A., & Sakumura, J. (1966). A test of a model for commitment. *Journal of Personality and Social Psychology, 3*(3), 349–353.

Kim, H. S., & Drolet, A. (2003). Choice and self-expression: A cultural analysis of variety-seeking. *Journal of Personality and Social Psychology, 85*(2), 373–382.

Kim, H. S., & Sherman, D. K. (2007). "Express yourself": Culture and the effect of self-expression on choice. *Journal of Personality and Social Psychology, 92*(1), 1–11.

Kim, S., & Gal, D. (2014). From compensatory consumption to adaptive consumption: The role of self-acceptance in resolving self-deficits. *Journal of Consumer Research, 41*(2), 526–542.

Kleine, R. E., Kleine, S. S., & Kernan, J. B. (1993). Mundane consumption and the self: A social-identity perspective. *Journal of Consumer Psychology, 2*(3), 209–235.

Laran, J., & Janiszewski, C. (2011). Work or fun? How task construal and completion influence regulatory behavior. *Journal of Consumer Research, 37*(6), 967–983.

Laverie, D. A., Kleine, R. E., & Kleine, S. S. (2002). Reexamination and extension of Kleine, Kleine, and Kernan's social identity model of mundane consumption: The mediating role of the appraisal process. *Journal of Consumer Research, 28*(4), 659–669.

Leary, M. R., Tambor, E. S., Terdal, S. K., & Downs, D. L. (1995). Self-esteem as an interpersonal monitor: The sociometer hypothesis. *Journal of Personality and Social Psychology, 68*(3), 518–530.

Lee, J., & Shrum, L. J. (2013). Self-threats and consumption. In A. A. Ruvio & R. W. Belk (eds.), *The Routledge Companion to Identity and Consumption* (pp. 216–224). New York: Routledge.

Levav, J., & Zhu, R. J. (2009). Seeking freedom through variety. *Journal of Consumer Research, 36*(4), 600–610.

Levy, S. J. (1959). Symbols for sale. *Harvard Business Review, 37*(4), 117–124.

Linville, P. W., & Carlston, D. E. (1994). Social cognition of the self. In P. G. Devine, D. L. Hamilton, & T. M. Ostrom (eds.), *Social Cognition: Its Impact on Social Psychology* (pp. 396–403). New York: Academic Press.

Liu, W., & Gal, D. (2011). Bringing us together or driving us apart: The effect of soliciting consumer input on consumers' propensity to transact with an organization. *Journal of Consumer Research, 38*(2), 242–259.

Markus, H. R. (1977). Self-schemata and processing information about the self. *Journal of Personality and Social Psychology, 35*(2), 63–78.

Markus, H. R., & Kitayama, S. (1991). Culture and the self: Implications for cognition, emotion, and motivation. *Psychological Review, 98*(2), 224–253.

Markus, H. R., & Kunda, Z. (1986). Stability and malleability of the self-concept. *Journal of Personality and Social Psychology, 51*(4), 858–866.

Markus, H. R., & Schwartz, B. (2010). Does choice mean freedom and well-being? *Journal of Consumer Research, 37*(2), 344–355.

Mazzocco, P. J., Rucker, D. D., Galinsky, A. D., & Anderson, E. T. (2012). Direct and vicarious conspicuous consumption: Identification with low-status groups increases the desire for high-status goods. *Journal of Consumer Psychology, 22*(4), 520–528.

McCracken, G. (1986). Culture and consumption: A theoretical account of the structure and movement of the cultural meaning of consumer goods. *Journal of Consumer Research, 13*(1), 71–84.

McCracken, G. (1989). Who is the celebrity endorser? Cultural foundations of the endorsement process. *Journal of Consumer Research, 16*(3), 310–321.

McFerran, B., Dahl, D. W., Fitzsimons, G. J., & Morales, A. C. (2010). I'll have what she's having: Effects of social influence and body type on the food choices of others. *Journal of Consumer Research, 36*(6), 915–929.

McShane, B. B., Bradlow, E. T., & Berger, J. (2012). Visual influence and social groups. *Journal of Marketing Research, 49*(6), 854–871.

Mead, N. L., Baumeister, R. F., Stillman, T. F., Rawn, C. D., & Vohs, K. D. (2011). Social exclusion causes people to spend and consume strategically in the service of affiliation. *Journal of Consumer Research, 37*(5), 902–919.

Moller, A. C., Deci, E. L., & Ryan, R. M. (2006). Choice and ego-depletion: The moderating role of autonomy. *Personality and Social Psychology Bulletin, 32*(8), 1024–1036.

Morewedge, C. K., Shu, L. L., Gilbert, D. T., & Wilson, T. D. (2009). Bad riddance or good rubbish? Ownership and not loss aversion causes the endowment effect. *Journal of Experimental Social Psychology, 45*(4), 947–951.

Muniz, A. M., & O'Guinn, T. C. (2001). Brand community. *Journal of Consumer Research, 27*(4), 412–432.

Nelissen, R., & Meijers, M. H. (2011). Social benefits of luxury brands as costly signals of wealth and status. *Evolution and Human Behavior, 32*(5), 343–355.

Niedenthal, P. M., Cantor, N., & Kihlstrom, J. F. (1985). Prototype matching: A strategy for social decision making. *Journal of Personality and Social Psychology, 48*(3), 575–584.

Oyserman, D. (2009). Identity-based motivation: Implications for action-readiness, procedural-readiness, and consumer behavior. *Journal of Consumer Psychology, 19*(3), 250–260.

Petrocelli, J. V., Tormala, Z. L., & Rucker, D. D. (2007). Unpacking attitude certainty: Attitude clarity and attitude correctness. *Journal of Personality and Social Psychology, 92*(1), 30–41.

Pronin, E., Berger, J., & Molouki, S. (2007). Alone in a crowd of sheep: Asymmetric perceptions of conformity and their roots in an introspection illusion. *Journal of Personality and Social Psychology, 92*(4), 585–595.

Reb, J., & Connolly, T. (2007). Possession, feelings of ownership, and the endowment effect. *Judgment and Decision Making, 2*(2), 107–114.

Reed, A., Forehand, M. R., Puntoni, S., & Warlop, L. (2012). Identity-based consumer behaviour. *International Journal of Research in Marketing, 29*(4), 310–321. doi: 10.1016/j.ijresmar.2012.08.002.

Reingen, P. H., Foster, B. L., Brown, J. J., & Seidman, S. B. (1984). Brand congruence in interpersonal relations: A social network analysis. *Journal of Consumer Research, 11*(3), 771–783.

Richins, M. L. (1994). Possessions and the expression of material values. *Journal of Consumer Research, 21*(3), 522–533.

Ross, I. (1971). Self-concept and brand preference. *Journal of Business, 44*(1), 38–50.

Rucker, D. D., & Galinsky, A. D. (2013). Compensatory consumption. In A. A. Ruvio & R. W. Belk (eds.), *The Routledge Companion to Identity and Consumption* (pp. 207–215). New York: Routledge.

Rucker, D. D., & Galinsky, A. D. (2009). Conspicuous consumption versus utilitarian ideals: How different levels of power shape consumer behavior. *Journal of Experimental Social Psychology, 45*(3), 549–555.

Rucker, D. D., Galinsky, A. D., & Dubois, D. (2012). Power and consumer behavior: How power shapes who and what consumers value. *Journal of Consumer Psychology, 22*(3), 352–368.

Schau, H. J., & Gilly, M. C. (2003). We are what we post? Self-presentation in personal web space. *Journal of Consumer Research, 30*(3), 385–404.

Schlenker, B. R. (1980). *Impression Management: The Self-Concept, Social Identity, and Interpersonal Relations*. Monterey, CA: Brooks/Cole.

Sedikides, C., Gaertner, L., & Toguchi, Y. (2003). Pancultural self-enhancement. *Journal of Personality and Social Psychology, 84*(1), 60–79.

Sedikides, C., & Strube, M. J. (1995). The multiply motivated self. *Personality and Social Psychology Bulletin, 21*(12), 1330–1335.

Shavitt, S. (1990). The role of attitude objects in attitude functions. *Journal of Experimental Social Psychology, 26*(2), 124–148.

Shavitt, S., & Nelson, M. R. (1999). The social identity function in person perception: Communicated meanings of product preferences. In G. R. Maio & J. M. Olson (eds.), *Why We Evaluate: Function of Attitudes* (pp. 27–57). Mahwah, NJ: Erlbaum.

Shavitt, S., Torelli, C. J., & Wong, J. (2009). Identity-based motivation: Constraints and opportunities in consumer research. *Journal of Consumer Psychology, 19*(3), 261–266.

Shu, S. B., & Peck, J. (2011). Psychological ownership and affective reaction: Emotional attachment process variables and the endowment effect. *Journal of Consumer Psychology, 21*(4), 439–452.

Sirgy, M. J. (1982). Self-concept in consumer behavior: A critical review. *Journal of Consumer Research, 9*(3), 287–300.

Sivanathan, N., Molden, D. C., Galinsky, A. D., & Ku, G. (2008). The promise and peril of self-affirmation in de-escalation of commitment. *Organizational Behavior and Human Decision Processes, 107*(1), 1–14.

Sivanathan, N., & Pettit, N. C. (2010). Protecting the self through consumption: Status goods as affirmational commodities. *Journal of Experimental Social Psychology, 46*(3), 564–570.

Snyder, C. R. (1992). Product scarcity by need for uniqueness interaction: A consumer catch-22 carousel? *Basic and Applied Social Psychology, 13*(1), 9–24.

Snyder, C. R., & Fromkin, H. L. (1977). Abnormality as a positive characteristic: The development and validation of a scale measuring need for uniqueness. *Journal of Abnormal Psychology, 86*(5), 518–527.

Spence, M. (1973). Job market signaling. *Quarterly Journal of Economics, 87*(3), 355–374.

Steele, C. M. (1988). The psychology of self-affirmation: Sustaining the integrity of the self. *Advances in Experimental Social Psychology, 21*, 261–302.

Strahilevitz, M. A., & Loewenstein, G. (1998). The effect of ownership history on the valuation of objects. *Journal of Consumer Research, 25*(3), 276–289.

Sundie, J. M., Kenrick, D. T., Griskevicius, V., Tybur, J. M., Vohs, K. D., & Beal, D. J. (2011). Peacocks, Porsches, and Thorstein Veblen: Conspicuous consumption as a sexual signaling system. *Journal of Personality and Social Psychology, 100*(4), 664–680.

Swann, W. B. (1983). Self-verification: Bringing social reality into harmony with the self. In J. Sulls & A. G. Greenwald (eds.), *Social Psychological Perspectives on the Self* (vol. 2, pp. 33–66). Hillsdale, NJ: Erlbaum.

Swann, W. B., De La Ronde, C., & Hixon, J. G. (1994). Authenticity and positivity strivings in marriage and courtship. *Journal of Personality and Social Psychology, 66*(5), 857–869.

Swann, W. B., Stein-Seroussi, A., & Giesler, R. B. (1992). Why people self-verify. *Journal of Personality and Social Psychology, 62*(3), 392–401.

Tesser, A. (2000). On the confluence of self-esteem maintenance mechanisms. *Personality and Social Psychology Review, 4*(4), 290–299.

Tesser, A., & Cornell, D. P. (1991). On the confluence of self-processes. *Journal of Experimental Social Psychology, 27*(6), 501–526.

Thompson, C. J., & Hirschman, E. C. (1995). Understanding the socialized body: A poststructuralist analysis of consumers' self-conceptions, body images, and self-care practices. *Journal of Consumer Research, 22*(2), 139–153.

Thornton, S. (1996). *Music Media and Subcultural Capital.* Middletown, CT: Wesleyan University Press.

Tian, K. T., Bearden, W. O., & Hunter, G. L. (2001). Consumers' need for uniqueness: Scale development and validation. *Journal of Consumer Research, 28*(1), 50–66.

Tiedens, L. Z., & Linton, S. (2001). Judgment under emotional certainty and uncertainty: The effects of specific emotions on information processing. *Journal of Personality and Social Psychology, 81*(6), 973–988.

Toubia, O., & Stephen, A. T. (2013). Intrinsic vs. image-related utility in social media: Why do people contribute content to Twitter? *Marketing Science, 32*(3), 368–392.

Townsend, C., & Sood, S. (2012). Self-affirmation through the choice of highly aesthetic products. *Journal of Consumer Research, 39*(2), 415–428.

Triandis, H. C. (1989). The self and social behavior in differing cultural contexts. *Psychological Review, 96*(3), 506–520.

Twitchell, J. B. (2002). *Living It Up*. New York: Columbia University Press.

Veblen, T. (1899). The preconceptions of economic science. *Quarterly Journal of Economics, 13*(4), 396–426.

Visser, P. S., Krosnick, J. A., & Simmons, J. P. (2003). Distinguishing the cognitive and behavioral consequences of attitude importance and certainty: A new approach to testing the common-factor hypothesis. *Journal of Experimental Social Psychology, 39*(2), 118–141.

Vohs, K. D., Baumeister, R. F., & Ciarocco, N. J. (2005). Self-regulation and self-presentation: Regulatory resource depletion impairs impression management and effortful self-presentation depletes regulatory resources. *Journal of Personality and Social Psychology, 88*(4), 632–657.

Wallendorf, M., & Arnould, E. J. (1988). "My favorite things": A cross-cultural inquiry into object attachment, possessiveness, and social linkage. *Journal of Consumer Research, 14*(4), 531–547.

Wang, J., Zhu, R. J., & Shiv, B. (2012). The lonely consumer: Loner or conformer? *Journal of Consumer Research, 38*(6), 1116–1128.

Ward, S. (1974). Consumer socialization. *Journal of Consumer Research, 1*(2), 1–14.

Wernerfelt, B. (1990). Advertising content when brand choice is a signal. *Journal of Business, 63*(1), 91–98.

White, K., Argo, J. J., & Sengupta, J. (2012). Dissociative versus associative responses to social identity threat: The role of consumer self-construal. *Journal of Consumer Research, 39*(4), 704–719.

White, K., & Dahl, D. W. (2006). To be or not be? The influence of dissociative reference groups on consumer preferences. *Journal of Consumer Psychology, 16*(4), 404–414.

White, K., & Dahl, D. W. (2007). Are all out-groups created equal? Consumer identity and dissociative influence. *Journal of Consumer Research, 34*(4), 525–536.

Wicklund, R. A., & Gollwitzer, P. M. (1981). Symbolic self-completion, attempted influence, and self-deprecation. *Basic and Applied Social Psychology, 2*(2), 89–114.

Wicklund, R. A., & Gollwitzer, P. M. (1982). *Symbolic Self-Completion*. Hillsdale, NJ: Lawrence Erlbaum Associates.

11 Coping Research in the Broader Perspective

Emotions, Threats, Mindsets, and More

DaHee Han, Adam Duhachek, and Nidhi Agrawal

Consumers face a wide variety of stressors every day. Some stressors come from "daily hassles" (Lazarus & Folkman, 1984, p.13), such as making difficult purchase decisions or experiencing poor service, and others originate from chronic illness, such as obesity or breast cancer, that requires consumers to make health and consumption decisions. Consumers cope with these stressors in multiple ways to alleviate stress and enhance mental and physical well-being. For example, when consumers are exposed to health messages that warn of the risk of heart disease due to obesity, some consumers "cope" with this stressful situation by making a plan to cut their daily food intake, while others cope by stopping themselves from being upset by distracting themselves from unpleasant thoughts due to the threatening health message. Given the seeming prevalence of coping episodes in consumers' everyday life, consumer researchers have recently begun to explore how consumers cope with stress stemming from a variety of distinct consumer-oriented stressors, such as long waiting times in negative service environments (Miller, Kahn, & Luce, 2008); purchasing, using, and disposing of products and services (Sujan, Sujan, Bettman, & Verhallen, 1999); adoption of new technology products (Cui, Bao, & Chan, 2009; Mick & Fournier, 1998); difficult decision making (Luce, Payne, & Bettman, 1999); or threatening health messages regarding the risk of disease (Lin, Lin, & Raghubir, 2003). Despite these recent developments in the consumer literature, the prospects for future research to build off these contributions loom larger than ever. The goal of the present chapter is to profile the existing coping research and to summarize the key findings and gaps in the literature. The chapter concludes with a discussion of fruitful future research questions for progress within the coping area.

In the present chapter, we organize our analysis around three objectives. First, we familiarize people with the general construct of coping and the antecedents and consequences of coping in the historical context of the literature. This section provides any researchers new to the study of coping, or its effects, a core foundation from which to build. Second, we provide a review of recent coping research most directly related to consumer behavior over the last ten years. Our emphasis on the last ten years is not only in the spirit of this handbook, but is a reflection of coping's recent emergence in the study of consumer psychology and consumer behavior. Our broad perspective conceptualizes coping as an individual variable and understands how it is influenced by social and situational factors. Finally, we emphasize important and unanswered questions for consumer coping. In doing so, we hope to use this important point to foster a next generation of coping-related research in consumer behavior.

Coping: An Introduction

The Definition of Coping and the Transactional Model of Appraisal

Coping scholarship has a strong tradition within several disciplines, with a great deal of work covering both theoretical and applied topics of interest to scholars working in psychology, sociology, anthropology, public health, political science, and business. A June 2014 Google Scholar search using the search term "coping" revealed nearly 2 million unique citations, with over two hundred thousand of those originating in the past five years. Thus, scholarship in this area is flourishing. Coping scholars define coping as the adaptive process involving cognitive or behavioral *efforts* to reduce stress stemming from stressful external and/or internal demands (Lazarus & Folkman, 1984). Stated more accurately, coping is defined as "cognitive and behavioral efforts to manage specific external and/or internal demands that are appraised as taxing or exceeding the resources of the person" (Lazarus & Folkman, 1984, p. 141). As Lazarus and Folkman suggest, a process approach to coping implies that coping has dynamic characteristics, which vary depending on the interactive relationship between a person and an environment. This approach posits that the person may have a personality or dispositional tendency to cope with stress in a specific way (e.g., using one form of coping), but his or her personality or dispositional tendency may change depending on the *particular context*. This definition takes an integrative view that characterizes coping as a function of personality-based factors *and* situational factors rather than a traditional view that describes coping as a trait (more will be said of this distinction subsequently).

Moreover, coping is a subset of adaptive processes to manage individuals' relationships with the environment and excludes automatized adaptive responses that do not require effort (Lazarus & Folkman, 1984). Thus, a key assumption of coping research is that these processes are conscious and deliberate (as opposed to non-conscious). Freud (1946) termed these latter non-conscious behaviors defense mechanisms, and these have traditionally been examined separately from coping. For example, when a person encounters a stressing environment for the first time, such as moving to a new town, a large amount of cognitive or behavioral effort is required to adapt to novel surroundings. However, as the person becomes experienced and has the opportunity to repeat key behaviors linked to stress (commuting, navigating a new city, etc.), these behaviors become automated. In other words, these actions no longer involve coping to the extent that they are not perceived as stressful, and the individual does not devote resources to thinking about how to adapt to them.

Although it is often hard to distinguish coping from automated adaptive thoughts or behaviors clearly, the definition based on Lazarus and Folkman (1984)'s view emphasizes distinct characteristics of coping, which involves cognitive and/or behavioral *efforts* to manage particular stressful situations that exceed the available resources of the person.

Since the term "coping" refers to "efforts," it should also be distinguished from outcomes. In other words, efforts to manage stress should be considered as coping regardless of their impact on subsequent adaptational outcomes. If an individual deliberately enacts responses to reduce stress, these are coping processes regardless of whether stress is alleviated. Therefore, one form of coping should not be regarded as inherently better or worse than another (Lazarus & Folkman, 1984). Finally, the term "coping" should not be equated with mastery over the environment (Lazarus & Folkman, 1984), as we use the word "reduce" instead of words such as "eliminate," because coping enables the person to "tolerate, minimize, accept, or ignore what cannot be mastered" (Lazarus & Folkman, 1984, p. 140). Coping is also distinct from key outcome variables such as self-efficacy (Bandura, 1982), positive emotions (Fredrickson, 2001; Fredrickson & Joiner, 2002; Tugade, Fredrickson, & Barrett, 2004), and subjective well-being (Burroughs & Rindfleisch, 2002; Diener, 1984; Kahneman, Diener, & Schwarz, 1999).

Using this process-based construct definition, Lazarus and Folkman (1984) proposed the transactional model of coping. It posits that an individual's engagement in one or more ways of coping is determined by two different kinds of cognitive appraisals, which are influenced by personality-based or situational factors. *Primary appraisals* entail judgments concerning whether a focal stimulus has motivational implications for an individual or is perceived as relevant to the individual's well-being (e.g., does this situation influence me?). If the focal stimulus has negative implications for the individual, it is perceived as a "stressor." *Secondary appraisals* are an evaluative process of whether the individual has an ability to employ a particular strategy or a set of coping strategies effectively and an evaluative process of future expectations regarding the consequences of using specific strategies. Note here that although the distinction between primary and secondary appraisals is meaningful, primary appraisals do not necessarily precede secondary appraisals. In other words, these two appraisals occur nearly simultaneously and co-determine the individual's emotional responses and coping (Lazarus & Folkman, 1984). Cognitive appraisal processes then elicit a broad range of emotions and, finally, those cognitive appraisals and emotional responses lead individuals to adopt specific coping strategies, which in turn influence subsequent stress and emotions (Duhachek, 2005; Duhachek, 2008; Lazarus & Folkman, 1984; Yi & Baumgartner, 2004).[1]

---

1 Although the transactional model of coping and previous research in the coping literature has emphasized the relationship between cognitive appraisals and emotions and the role of emotion in influencing coping tendencies and their outcomes, the current chapter will not discuss this link extensively. See Ellsworth and Smith (1988) for the relationship between cognitive appraisals and emotions, as well as Duhachek (2005) and Yi and Baumgartner (2004) for the relationship between emotions and coping.

Dimensional Structure of Coping: Problem-Focused Coping versus Emotion-Focused Coping

As long as scholars have taken an interest in coping, there has been a great deal of emphasis within the literature aimed at identifying the underlying structure of coping. These efforts at construct validation attempt to balance concerns of parsimony with nomothetic span. A key objective of this research has focused on identifying a core set of measures that captures a meaningful amount of variance in coping behavior. These efforts have produced several valid coping inventories, the most influential of which have been the Coping Strategies Indicator (CSI) (Amirkhan, 1990), the COPE inventory (Carver, Schieier, & Weintraub, 1989), the Coping Inventory for Stressful Situations (CISS) (Endler & Parker, 1990), the personal and contextual determinants inventory (Holohan & Moos, 1987), the Ways of Coping Questionnaire (WCQ) (Folkman & Lazarus, 1988), the emotional approach coping inventory (Stanton, Kirk, Cameron, and Danoff-Burg, 2000), and other situational inventories of coping (McCrae, 1984; Pearlin & Schooler, 1978; Stone & Neale, 1984; Sujan et al., 1999).

With respect to the dimensional structure of coping, the most influential and widely known perspective in consumer research is the two-dimensional framework proposed by Lazarus and Folkman (1984), which suggests that problem-focused coping and emotion-focused coping are superordinate dimensions that each broadly describe a variety of more specific behaviors. Since a complete review of previous research regarding the structure of coping is beyond the scope of this chapter, the current chapter will not discuss this issue in detail (see Duhachek & Oakley, 2007, and Skinner, Edge, Altman, & Sherwood, 2003, for comprehensive reviews).

Within Lazarus and Folkman's (1984) coping model, problem-focused coping is manifested in efforts to change a perceived cause of stress directly. For example, when a consumer reads a relevant health message that emphasizes her specific risk factors for heart disease, she may cope with the subsequent stress stemming from the threatening message by making a plan to work out regularly, by searching the information related to a certain disease, or by purchasing medicines or other products that she believes will lower her risk factors. In contrast, emotion-focused coping involves individuals' efforts to regulate their emotional responses to the source of stress. For instance, a consumer may try not to think about unpleasant thoughts related to potential heart disease or may vent his emotions in order to manage his anxiety by confiding in others capable of offering emotional support. Although both problem-focused coping and emotion-focused coping involve several different (lower-order) strategies, the most obvious distinction between two types of coping is that the former is directed at managing or solving the sources of stress while the latter is aimed at regulating emotional responses to the stress through cognitive processes so that "they can construe the cause of stress in different, less psychologically distressing terms" (Duhachek & Iacobucci, 2005, p. 53).

Another perspective that has received attention has produced an alternative superordinate distinction based on approach versus avoidance coping (Duhachek & Oakley, 2007). This classification (sometimes referred to as engagement versus disengagement coping) distinguishes between coping efforts directed toward the source of stress from efforts directed away from the source. Specifically, approach coping implies that consumers direct their coping efforts toward the source of stress. For example, when a consumer feels stressed because of being overweight, the consumer may cope with stress by reviewing what he or she ate last week, calculating calories, and making a list of food to be avoided in order to reduce the source of increasing weight. In contrast, avoidance coping means that consumers make an effort to be away from the source of stress. For example, when a consumer feels stressed due to being overweight, the consumer may cope with stress by distracting himself or herself and refusing to think about it too much.

Antecedents of Particular Coping Strategies: Dispositional Coping and Situation-Induced Coping

As noted previously, the transactional model of coping accounts for dispositional factors and situational factors that impact the employment of different coping strategies. Regarding the effects of personality-based factors on coping, previous research, which assumes that an individual copes with various stressful episodes in a highly invariant way over time (Duhachek, 2008), has examined how the "big five" personality factors of openness, conscientiousness, extraversion, agreeableness, and neuroticism have linked with specific forms of coping (Bolger & Zuckman, 1995). This literature has shown that extraversion and conscientiousness are associated with increased problem-focused coping and better adaptive outcomes, whereas neuroticism is associated with increased emotion-focused coping and less adaptive outcomes (see Carver & Connor-Smith, 2010, for a review). Other literature in this domain has examined how other factors, such as trait-based anxiety (Raffety, Smith, & Ptacek, 1997), depression-related personality types (Keller, Lipkus, & Rimer, 2002), optimism (Brissette, Sheier, & Carver, 2002), and core self-evaluation (Kammeyer-Mueller, Judge, & Scott, 2009) affect the use of specific coping strategies (see Connor-Smith & Flachsbart, 2007, for a recent meta-analysis). This stream of research shows that trait anxiety and depression are related to emotion-focused coping and negatively related to long-term adaption and psychological well-being, while optimism and core self-evaluation are positively related to problem-focused coping and long-term adaption.

Other Personality-Based Factors

In line with the coping literature in psychology, consumer researchers have begun to document the effects of personality-based factors on coping strategies and outcomes or the effects of consumers' dispositional tendencies toward specific coping strategies on well-being. For example, Duhachek and Iacobucci (2005) found that consumer assertiveness (i.e., "a tendency for consumers to stand up for their legitimate rights without violating the rights of others"; Richins, 1983, p. 74), marketing mavenism ("individuals who have information about many kinds of products, places to shop, and other facets of markets, and initiate discussions with consumers and respond to requests from consumers for market information"; Feick & Price, 1987, p. 85), and extraversion (a tendency for consumers to "like people and prefer large groups and gatherings ... [extroverts] like excitement and stimulation and tend to be cheerful in disposition"; Costa & McCrae, 1993, pp. 14–16) were positively associated with using active coping, which is a form of problem-focused coping strategies. In addition, Miller, Kahn, and Luce (2008, study 4) examined how consumers' predispositions toward particular coping strategies affected the level of consumers' stress in the context of waiting in negative service environments. Specifically, they found that participants who had a dispositional tendency to engage in avoidance-oriented coping, which is a form of emotion-focused coping, felt greater stress when they watched an aversive film and were then informed that they would be watching another aversive film as compared to those who had a dispositional tendency to use approach-oriented coping, which is a form of problem-focused coping. Duhachek and Kelting (2009) identified another unique coping trait factor, coping repertoire, defined as the number of different strategies consumers employ. Consumers with broader repertoires were found to have greater confidence in adjusting to stress episodes, as they had a broader array of strategies to bring to bear compared to consumers with a narrower band of coping behaviors in their repertoire.

Prior research has not only shown the effects of preexisting personality-based factors on coping and outcomes (e.g., psychological well-being) but also demonstrated the effects of individual's dispositional propensities to choose specific coping strategies on health outcomes (Carver, Scheier, & Weintraub, 1989; Endler & Parker, 1990). For example, Aldwin and Revenson (1987) suggest that individuals who have predispositions toward problem-focused coping strategies become stressed less frequently than those who use different coping strategies, while those tend to use emotion-focused coping are often observed to have a hard time promoting healthful adaptation (Raffety, Smith, & Ptacek, 1997; see Baker & Berenbaum, 2007, for the discussion). Carver and Connor-Smith (2010) emphasize that it is important to investigate how consumers' different dispositional coping tendencies might interact with environmental or stress-related factors to affect subsequent adaptation.

However, much of coping research has examined either disposition or situational factors independently rather than examining these factors jointly. Extant research has demonstrated that coping and outcomes are influenced by a variety of situational factors (e.g., Carver, Scheier, & Weintraub, 1989). Previous consumer research has explored the effects of situational factors on coping in a particular episode by following an assumption that an individual's propensity to cope in a specific manner is highly unstable (Carver & Scheier,

1994) and is largely influenced by the immediate situational factors that influence coping via the appraisal process (Duhachek, 2008; Schaubroeck & Merritt, 1997). For example, if consumers perceive a stressful situation as highly controllable, research has shown that they are more likely to use proactive coping, which is a form of problem-focused coping (Parkes, 1984; Schaubroeck & Merritt, 1997). In addition, Sujan et al. (1999) showed that if individuals' perceived self-efficacy was high, they were more likely to employ problem-focused coping, whereas if individuals' perceived self-efficacy was low, they were more likely to use emotion-focused coping. These findings demonstrate that the way that individuals cope with stress in a particular manner is determined by both dispositional factors and situational appraisals.

Other Situation-Induced Factors

Consumer researchers have also begun to investigate how situation-based factors influence the way consumers cope with stress. Duhachek (2005) investigated the effect of perceive self-efficacy on the adoption of specific coping strategies. In particular, participants were asked to imagine stressful encounters with a service company (e.g., "distressing event related to the bank, phone/cellular service, hotel, airlines, car/appliance repair, medical care provider, etc."; p. 44) and were then asked to report their level of self-efficacy. The findings indicated that participants were likely to engage in problem-focused coping in scenarios when perceived self-efficacy or controllability of the situation is high. In addition, Luce, Payne, and Bettman (1999) found that consumers had a tendency to engage in avoidant coping strategies when they encountered difficult decision making due to emotionally taxing attributes trade-offs (i.e., "the level of subjective threat a decision maker associates with making an explicit trade-off between two attributes"; p. 144). These findings thus suggest that efficacy and control are two important situational variables that drive coping processes.

Consequences of the Use of the Particular Coping Strategies

Previous coping research in psychology has focused on examining how the use of specific coping strategies determines clinical health outcomes (e.g., Florian, Mikulincer, & Taubman, 1995) such as cardiac failure (Penley, Tomaka, & Wiebe, 2002) or stress reduction (Gunthert, Cohen, & Armeli, 1999). In the consumer literature, Miller, Kahn, and Luce (2008) examined how different coping strategies affected stress levels as a function of the wait of duration for a negative service encounter. For those using approach (avoidance) coping strategies, longer (shorter) waiting times were found to increase stress levels. Duhachek, Agrawal, and Han (2012) found that problem-focused (emotion-focused) coping resulted from guilt (shame) appeals and led to increased persuasion of health messaging via a processing fluency mechanism. Despite these notable exceptions, there has been little research that investigates how the use of specific coping strategies results in different coping outcomes. Therefore, increased research attention is needed in this area to identify additional linkages between specific coping strategies and outcomes.

Recent Consumer Coping Research

Having provided an introduction to the construct of coping and how researchers have investigated the antecedents and consequences of the use of specific coping strategies, we now focus on our discussion of more recent consumer coping research.

Antecedents of the Use of the Particular Coping Strategies

More recently, coping theory has been extended to consider how consumers respond to a variety of factors, including a variety of psychological threats, motivational states, information processing states, and health research contexts. We briefly summarize this corpus of research.

Psychological Threats

Psychological threats (i.e., a discrepancy between where one wants to be and where one believes oneself to be on a dimension, such as perceiving oneself to be less intelligent than one desires) to one's sense of self are recognized to have transformative effects on consumer behavior (e.g., Cutright, 2012; Gao, Wheeler, & Shiv, 2009; Kim & Rucker, 2012; Mead et al., 2011; Rucker & Galinsky, 2008, 2009). It is our contention that investigations of these phenomena could be enhanced by considering a coping theoretical framework. If psychological threats are understood to be aversive episodes that cause consumers to feel stressed, coping theory suggests the experience of distinct psychological threats activates a need for coping. As threats vary in their scope, nature, and implications for the consumer, a host of distinct coping processes may be implicated. Thus far, the growing interest in how individuals "compensate" for these threats has only begun to identify threat-specific factors (e.g., Chae & Zhu, 2014; Cutright, 2012; Gao, Wheeler, & Shiv, 2009; Kim & Rucker, 2012; Mandel & Heine, 1999; Mead et al., 2011; Sharma & Alter, 2012; Rucker & Galinsky, 2008, 2009) and has not examined these phenomena from the framework of coping theory.

For example, when consumers' sense of their own existential security is threatened, they respond more favorably to luxury brands (Mandel & Heine, 1999). When people's sense of power is threatened, they respond more favorably to advertising that associates products with status, a known correlate of power (French & Raven, 1959), over advertising that emphasizes non-status aspects of the product (Rucker & Galinsky, 2008, 2009). When consumers' intelligence is threatened, they respond more favorably to a product associated with intelligence (Gao, Wheeler, & Shiv, 2009). And when consumers' perceived motivation is threatened, they consume more of a tea when the tea bag represented the tea as being associated with passion and excitement as opposed to calmness (Kim & Rucker, 2012). When feelings of personal control are threatened, consumers show a greater preference toward products with clear boundaries as a means of reasserting a sense of control (Cutright, 2012) and exhibit a greater tendency to display self-control failures (Chae & Zhu, 2014). In addition, consumers who feel rejected express a greater willingness to pay more for items that build social connections (Mead et al., 2011). Finally, when consumers' financial well-being is threatened, they prefer scarce products unavailable to other consumers to mitigate the sense of being deprived (Sharma & Alter, 2012).

Although this research has contributed to enhancing our understanding of the range of diverse specific consumer responses to a variety of discrete threats, this approach has seemed to lead researchers to stray away from examining commonalities across distinct threats. Rather, study of these threats has been conducted in silos and has led to the emergence of specific literatures surrounding threats such as mortality salience (Mandel & Heine, 1999), lack of power (Rucker & Galinsky, 2008, 2009), social rejection (Mead et al., 2011), one's financial well-being (Sharma & Alter, 2012), and ego threat (Cutright, 2012; Gao, Wheeler, & Shiv, 2009; Kim & Rucker, 2012).

To fill this gap, Han, Duhachek, and Rucker (2015) propose that across psychologically distinct threats there rests a common underpinning of the coping strategies that distinct threats provoke. Specifically, the authors argue that distinct threats can be linked either to approach motivations that tend to foster more problem-focused coping or avoidance motivations that tend to foster more emotion-focused coping. Consistent with these hypotheses, across a series of experiments, some threats (e.g., mortality salience, low intelligence) led participants to predominantly activate approach motivations and engage in problem-focused coping, whereas other threats (e.g., social rejection, low personal control) led participants to predominantly provoke avoidance motivations and employ emotion-focused coping.

Emotion

Consumers feel negative emotions in daily life. For example, consumers may feel guilty if they overeat, feel angry when they experience terrible service in a fancy restaurant, or feel sad when products that they are looking for are no longer available. Since negative emotions threaten consumers' psychological well-being, consumers usually engage in particular coping strategies to manage negative emotions. For example, when consumers have to use technological products, they can feel a variety of negative emotions, such as envy, foolishness, frustration, cautiousness, defeat, and betrayal, and tend to adopt different coping strategies depending on the stages of adoption of technological products (Mick & Fournier, 1998). When consumers feel conflicted or uncomfortable because they have to make judgments and choices involving difficult attribute trade-offs, they tend to cope with negative emotions associated with these judgments and choices by avoiding attribute trade-off making (Drolet & Luce, 2004) and by using effort- or conflict-reducing heuristics when the neutral option is not available (Nowlis, Kahn, & Dhar, 2002). In addition, when consumers feel anxious (sad), they tend to be risk-averse (reward-seeking) in a subsequent task, which is seemingly related but not directly related to the source or event that makes them feel anxious (sad), to address their negative emotional state (i.e., displaced coping; Raghunathan, Pham, & Corfman, 2006).

Consumers also engage in coping behavior (e.g., reframing a decision) when they feel regret because the utility from their purchase in a limited purchase opportunity context is low (Abendroth & Diehl, 2006). When consumers watch reality television programming, they engage in coping to reconcile the tensions between reality and fantasy (Rose & Wood, 2005). Consumers who feel ashamed due to their low literacy tend to restrict their choices to a safe and narrow set to cope with negative social evaluations (Adkins & Ozanne, 2005). When consumers feel fearful because of life-threatening illness, they cope with their negative emotional states and uncertainty via consumption (Pavia & Mason, 2004). Specifically, Pavia and Mason (2004) suggest that depending on the stage of coping with a severe illness, consumers engage in different consumption-oriented coping behaviors (e.g., consumers employ present-oriented consumption coping strategies in the earliest stage of coping with an illness and then engage in future-oriented consumption coping strategies to a greater extent after the medical treatments have ended and they believe they are cured).

Furthermore, consumer researchers have examined how different negative emotions activate distinct coping strategies. For example, Yi and Baumgartner (2004) found that anger and disappointment led consumers to engage in problem-focused coping (e.g., confrontive coping), while regret resulted in the use of emotion-focused coping (e.g., acceptance, positive reinterpretation). They also found that individuals who felt worried employed either problem-focused coping when the danger is tangible or emotion-focused coping when the threat is intangible. Duhachek (2005) found that consumers who felt threat emotions and high (low) self-efficacy were more likely to use expressive support-seeking coping (avoidant coping), while those feeling angry and highly self-efficacious tended to employ active coping. Passyn and Sujan (2006) found that straight fear appeals that induce feelings of low self-accountability resulted in greater action-facilitating coping and behavioral compliance when they were paired with guilt or regret that evoked feelings of high self-accountability. Duhachek, Agrawal, and Han (2012) showed that anti-drinking ads that evoke feelings of guilt (shame) led consumers to engage in problem-focused coping (emotion-focused coping).

Mental Depletion

Jia, Han, and Hirt (2015) examine the role that mental depletion plays in coping responses. Some may expect that when consumers are depleted, they may engage in more emotion-focused coping than problem-focused coping strategies because they lack the requisite resources to be able to cope (emotion-focused coping has been linked with low self-efficacy). Contrary to this intuition, the authors argue that depletion results in greater activation of problem-focused coping strategies. Recent research provides evidence that can support these hypotheses. That is, Schmeichel, Vohs, and Duke (2010) found that depletion leads people to adopt a more approach-rather than avoidance-oriented motivation. In addition, Han, Duhachek, and Rucker (2015) demonstrated that approach motivation results in problem-focused coping because people tend to adopt problem-focused coping strategies when they focus on positive outcomes or opportunities. Consistent with hypotheses, the findings indicate that depleted individuals prefer to engage in problem-focused coping.

Consequences of the Use of the Particular Coping Strategies

Stress Reduction in Negative Service Environments

Consumers encounter negative service environments every day. For example, they may feel stressed when they meet rude employees at the bank or when they are waiting for dental or medical appointments. Miller, Kahn, and Luce (2008) suggest that the valence of the event and consumers' coping orientation determine the effectiveness of different wait management strategies. That is, they propose that short waiting times are less effective for consumers who tend to use approach-oriented coping, which is a form of problem-focused coping, as compared to those who tend to use avoidance-oriented coping, a form of emotion-focused coping. As a result of the misappropriation of coping strategies, consumers consequently reported feeling greater stress. They reasoned that consumers engaging in approach-oriented coping (vs. avoidance-oriented coping) require a greater amount of time to implement their coping strategies (e.g., make a detailed plan to address stressful situation). Consistent with these hypotheses, they found that the use of problem-focused coping (vs. emotion-focused coping) resulted in greater stress reduction only when the waiting time was long.

Product Beliefs

Due to rapid technological advance, consumers often feel stressed when they have to decide whether to keep the current version of a product or upgrade to a new version. In this context, Cui, Bao, and Chan (2009) argue that consumers enact coping strategies to reduce stress and uncertainty, and those coping strategies influence attitude toward adoption and buying intention. Specifically, the authors hypothesize that problem-focused coping strategies (i.e., confrontational coping strategies) result in a more positive attitude toward adoption and buying intention than emotion-focused coping (i.e., avoidance coping strategies) because problem-focused coping strategies lead to more positive product beliefs (e.g., usefulness, ease of use, and fun). As hypothesized, the findings indicated that problem-focused coping resulted in more positive product beliefs, while emotion-focused coping led to negative product beliefs in the context of new product adoption. These findings show that the way that consumers cope with stress in a particular manner influences subsequent consumer attitude toward the products as well as consumers' psychological well-being in negative consumption contexts. A related study of technological adoption stress conducted by Mick and Fournier (1998) showed that consumers engaged in different sets of coping strategies depending on the stages of adopting new technology (i.e., pre-acquisition avoidance/confrontive and consumption avoidance/confrontive; Mick & Fournier, 1998, p. 133).

Psychological Construal Mindsets

Although previous research has enhanced our knowledge regarding the effects of consumers' specific coping strategies on related consumer outcomes, very little is yet known about how the use of particular coping strategies will affect subsequent information processing. To fill this gap, Han, Duhachek, and Agrawal (2015) propose unique consequences resulting from employment of either problem-focused or emotion-focused coping by building theory based on coping and Construal Level theories (Trope & Liberman, 2003, 2010). The authors propose that problem-focused coping provokes thoughts about potential actions one can initiate in response to stress. They further hypothesize that these strategies result in individuals thinking about their situation in concrete terms and processing information in a focused manner that is consistent with lower-level construals. In contrast, emotion-focused coping relies on the emotional consequences of the situation and how one may manage the emotions that will result. These strategies lead individuals to think about the situation in a more abstract and outcome-focused manner that is more consistent with higher-level construals. Thus, the authors posit that problem-focused coping activates lower levels of construal mindsets than emotion-focused coping.

To test these hypotheses, the authors manipulated consumer coping by asking participants to adopt either of two specific coping strategies (Miller, Kahn, & Luce, 2008) and measured their tendency to construe information at a high versus a low level using the twenty-five-item Behavioral Identification Form (BIF; Vallacher & Wegner, 1989). The results indicate that participants with problem-focused coping construed objects or actions in subsequent tasks at a more concrete low level while those with emotion-focused coping construed objects or actions in the subsequent task at a more abstract high level. These findings provide evidence that the way consumers cope with stress influences how they process subsequent information.

Effectiveness of Health Messaging

Coping is active when individuals feel negative emotions upon exposure to threatening health-relevant messaging. For example, when consumers are

Table 11.1 *Antecedents and Consequences of Different Coping Strategies*

Antecedents	→	Different Coping Strategies	→	Consequences
Personality-related factors Extraversion[1]/Conscientiousness[1] Optimism[2]/Core self-evaluation[3] Consumer assertiveness/Marketing mavenism/Extraversion[4] **Situational factors** High controllability[5]/High self-efficacy[6] **Psychological Threats** Mortality salience/Threat to intelligence[7] **Emotions** Anger/Disappointment[8]/Guilt[9] **Mental depletion** High depletion[10] **Motivation** Approach motivation[7]	→	Problem-focused coping (i.e., efforts to manage the source of stress)	→	Greater stress reduction when the waiting time is long[13] Positive product beliefs in the context of new product adoption[14] Low construal level mindset[15] Greater persuasion when shown the low construal level health message[15] Greater self-efficacy when shown the low construal level health message[15]
Personality-related factors Neuroticism[1]/trait-based anxiety[11] Depression-related personality types[12] **Situational factors** Low controllability[5]/low self-efficacy[6] **Psychological factors** Social rejection/ threat to personal control[7] **Emotions** Regret[8]/shame[9] **Mental depletion** Low mental depletion[10] **Motivation** Avoidance motivation[7]	→	Emotion-focused coping (i.e., efforts to manage emotional responses toward the source of stress)	→	Greater stress reduction when the waiting time is short[13] Negative product beliefs in the context of new product adoption[14] High construal level mindsets[15] Greater persuasion when shown the high construal level health message[15] Greater response efficacy when shown the high construal level health message[12]

Note: [1]Bolger & Zuckman, 1995; [2]Brissette, Sheier, & Carver, 2002; [3]Kammeyer-Mueller, Judge, & Scott, 2009; [4]Duhachek & Iacobucci, 2005; [5]Parkes, 1984; [6]Sujan et al., 1999; [7]Han, Duhachek, & Rucker, 2015; [8]Yi & Baumgartner, 2004; [9]Duhachek, Agrawal, & Han, 2012; [10]Jia, Han, & Hirt, 2015; [11]Raffety, Smith, & Ptacek, 1997; [12]...

confronted with a message warning them about the dangers associated with risky drinking, they may feel negative emotions such as guilt or shame as they consider their past behavior and may engage in coping processes in order to manage their emotions and stress. Since guilt and shame originate from harmful behaviors, marketers have tried to develop effective health advertisements such as anti-drinking ads or anti-smoking ads to enhance message compliance. In this context, previous health research has examined how different health message frames affect persuasion (Agrawal, Menon, & Aaker, 2007; Kees, Burton, & Tangari, 2010; Keller, Lipkus, & Rimer, 2003; Menon, Block, & Ramanathan, 2002).

Recently, Duhachek, Agrawal, and Han (2012) conjoined the coping literature and the health message framing literature to investigate the effectiveness of anti-drinking messages. Specifically, the authors propose that guilt appeals are more effective when they are paired with gain frames, whereas shame appeals are more effective when they are paired with loss frames. This argument is based on three important premises. First, the authors suggest that guilt is associated with high efficacy that leads people to rely on problem-focused coping aimed at taking actions to alter the stressful environment. Conversely, shame is associated with low efficacy that activates tendencies to rely on emotion-focused coping strategies aimed at regulating one's emotional responses. Second, the authors argue that gain appeals promote the use of problem-focused coping strategies because gain frames lead people to focus on the positive benefits of proactively following the action suggested, closely related with problem-focused coping's emphasis on action and benefits. In contrast, loss frames facilitate the use of emotion-focused coping strategies because loss frames lead people to focus more on the negative outcomes of not following the suggested actions, thus leading them to regulate their emotional responses with respect to the situation. Finally, since there is a fit between coping strategies favored by emotions and coping strategies facilitated by the message frame, this results in greater fluency and persuasion. That is, when the message frame requires the same coping strategies favored by the emotion, that frame activates or intensifies that coping strategies and makes it easier for individuals to understand the message and be persuaded by it.

Han, Duhachek, and Agrawal (2015) examine another form of match-driven persuasion effects in the context of coping and construal level. Previous consumer research has demonstrated that when consumers' mental representations of the target objects triggered by consumers' psychological states match with the construal level of advertising messages, consumers are more persuaded by the advertising claims (e.g., regulatory focus [Lee, Keller, & Sternthal, 2010]; self-view [Spassova & Lee, 2013]). Based on their findings, which show that problem-focused coping activates lower-level construal mindsets whereas emotion-focused coping provokes higher-level construal mindsets, the authors hypothesize that individuals who use problem-focused coping will be more persuaded by the low construal level message than high construal level message because problem-focused coping provokes low construal level mindsets.

In contrast, they posit that individuals who employ emotion-focused coping will be more persuaded by the high construal level message than the low construal level message because emotion-focused coping activates high construal level mindsets.

In one experiment, the authors induced participants to feel health-related stress using an episodic recall task. Subsequently, participants were asked to view fitness club ads that manipulated coping strategies (i.e., problem-focused vs. emotion-focused coping) and construal level (i.e., high construal level vs. low construal level) and asked to report their intention to sign up for the fitness club. The results revealed that participants who were shown the problem-focused coping ad indicated greater intention to join the fitness club when they were exposed to the ad message construed at a low level than the ad message construed at a high level. In contrast, participants who were exposed to the emotion-focused coping ad reported greater intention to join the fitness club when they were shown the high construal level ad than the low construal level ad.

Efficacy

As noted earlier in this chapter, previous research has shown that the degree of self-efficacy will influence the use of specific coping strategies (Duhachek, 2005; Sujan et al., 1999). That is, individuals who lack self-efficacy usually adopt emotion-focused coping whereas individuals who feel high self-efficacy usually employ problem-focused coping. While past work has investigated self-efficacy as the determinant of the use of particular coping strategies, recent work by Han, Duhachek, and Agrawal (2015) examined the role of self-efficacy (i.e., "an individual's belief regarding his/her ability to perform the proposed actions"; Bandura, 1982; Rogers, 1983), and response efficacy (i.e., "the degree to which an individual expects their response to the recommended actions to be effective"; Bandura, 1982; Rogers, 1983). Whereas most of the efficacy research in consumer behavior has examined self-efficacy, this research finds important differences between self-efficacy and response efficacy.

In particular, the authors argue that that a match between problem-focused coping and the low construal level of the health message results in greater self-efficacy. The authors reasoned that problem-focused coping activates low construal level mindsets and the health message construed at a low level will increase self-efficacy because the low construal level of the health message describes how people can execute the proposed actions in the ad (Trope & Liberman, 2003, 2010). According to the self-efficacy literature, providing information regarding detailed means to achieve a desired end state bolsters self-efficacy (Keller, 2006; Rogers, 1983).

In contrast, the authors argue that a match between emotion-focused coping and a high construal level message leads individuals to believe that the effectiveness of the actions suggested by the health program is greater (i.e., greater response efficacy). The authors reasoned that emotion-focused coping activates high construal level mindsets, and the health message construed at a high level will enhance response efficacy because the high construal level of the health message describes the desired outcomes by performing the suggested actions in the ad (Trope & Liberman, 2003, 2010). According to the response-efficacy literature, providing information that the recommended actions lead to the desired outcomes increases response efficacy (Keller, 2006; Rogers, 1975, 1983).

Consistent with these hypotheses, the authors found that the fit between problem-focused coping and a low construal level ad message activated greater self-efficacy, whereas the match between emotion-focused coping and a high construal level ad message generated greater response efficacy.

An Agenda for Future Research: Unanswered Questions

With the growing interest in consumer coping-related research, it is worthwhile to propose an agenda for future research in this domain. In our final section, we propose several areas of research that we believe to be important emerging themes for future research in consumer coping.

Coping as a Causal Factor

Previous research in this domain has heavily relied on self-reported retrospective accounts of coping (i.e., asking participants to answer coping questionnaires about past stress episodes) because researchers have been interested in identifying the antecedents of the use of specific coping strategies and thus measuring coping strategies as dependent variables. However, these approaches suffer from some key limitations. Because they rely on retrospection, they are especially prone to memory biases. Also, these designs are typically correlational, so it is impossible to impute causal significance to any of the linkages between coping and other factors under investigation. To overcome these limitations, a few researchers have developed the methods to manipulate different coping strategies (e.g., Han, Duhachek, & Agrawal, 2015; Miller, Kahn, & Luce, 2008) and have examined the consequences of the use of specific coping strategies, as well as potential interactions with antecedent factors. For example, Miller, Kahn, and Luce (2008) manipulated approach coping, which is a form of problem-focused coping, and avoidance coping, which is a form of emotion-focused coping, by asking participants to review coping materials. Specifically, participants were asked to read a story about retinitis pigmentosa (RP; blindness) and coping strategies related to RP. For example, the avoidance coping strategy material reads: "Avoidance coping responses include distraction, passivity, positive reinterpretation, wishful thinking, and venting negative emotion. These kinds of avoidance responses can be helpful because they allow time to integrate information" (Miller, Kahn, & Luce, 2008, pp. 641–2). After reading the coping materials, participants were asked to write how they would feel if they were diagnosed with RP and then to write in detail about either approach or avoidance coping depending their condition. They were further told to write about the benefits of this strategy in a manner that could motivate others to employ it. Han, Duhachek, and Agrawal (2015, study 1) adopted this method to successfully manipulate problem-focused coping and emotion-focused coping, respectively.

Han, Duhachek, and Agrawal (2015) demonstrated that consumer coping could also be manipulated within the presentation of an advertisement – a framing manipulation. Specifically, the authors developed and pretested different ad messages that differed in terms of the coping strategies. Both coping ad messages started with the headline describing the picture as "The SPEED Fitness CLUB for a Great Workout!" For the problem-focused coping ad, the message tagline read: "Join the Speed Fitness club and solve your problems." The accompanying text underneath this tagline read: "The Speed Fitness club will help you lose pounds, provide detailed diet and training plans, and help you become healthier!" For the emotion-focused coping ad, the message tagline read: "Join the Speed-Fitness club and Get Emotional Benefits!!" The accompanying text underneath the tagline read: "The Speed-Fitness club will help you become confident, happier, and healthier!"

Although past work has provided possible methods to manipulate distinct coping strategies, research is still needed to develop systematic methods to manipulate problem-focused versus emotion-focused coping strategies in consumer behavior contexts. For example, future research could develop advertisements designed to resonate with different coping strategies. In the context of service failure (e.g., when a bank website is not working properly), marketers can present two different coping messages (e.g., showing a message and a short clip that shows what the company is actually doing now to solve the problems or a list of actions that consumers can do to fix the problems vs. showing a message and a short clip that facilitates consumers managing their negative emotional responses). Depending on consumers' psychological states (e.g., feeling powerless, feeling negative emotions, etc.), marketers can present one of two coping messages.

Such research would further fill the gap existing in the current consumer coping literature by facilitating future research that investigates the subsequent consumer outcomes of the use of specific coping strategies and would provide tools to marketing practitioners and public policy makers who are interested in developing effective coping materials to enhance consumers' psychological well-being.

Sequence of the Use of Specific Coping Strategies

Past work on consumer coping has examined what kinds of factors will lead consumers to adopt either problem-focused coping or emotion-focused coping as well as what will happen if consumers use problem-focused coping or emotion-focused coping. However, it is possible that consumers may engage in one coping strategy first and then use another coping strategy later. For example, when a student set on exercising more feels stressed because he or she failed to go to the gym, the student may first engage in emotion-focused coping by letting his or her negative emotions out and then think about making a detailed plan to work out in the future. In contrast, another student who failed to pursue the same exercise goal may first engage in problem-focused coping by formulating a concrete plan to go to the gym regularly and then go out to socialize with friends to feel better during the weekend.

In this scenario, researchers could examine the following questions: (1) Which method (i.e., emotion-focused coping first, problem-focused coping second vs. problem-focused coping first, emotion-focused coping second) will be more effective to alleviate the health-related stress? (2) Which method will be more effective to motivate individuals to engage in subsequent behavior, such as going to the gym consistently on a regular basis? (3) Who will lose more weight? To our best knowledge, no research has examined how the sequence of the adoption of different coping strategies influences subsequent consumer-related outcomes such as stress reduction, motivations, and goal achievement. Understanding the effects of the sequence of the use of different coping strategies would greatly advance extant consumer coping theory.

Long-Term Effects of Coping

Previous consumer coping research has enhanced our understanding of the short-term consequences of the use of specific coping strategies. However, little is known about the long-term consequences of the use of particular coping strategies. For example, Han, Duhachek, and Agrawal (2015) found that the match between coping and the construal level of the health message led participants to show a greater intention to sign up for the fitness club featured in the ad. However, less is known about how the fit between coping and the construal level of the ad message will shape individuals' long-term behavior, such as going to a fitness club regularly; the degree of long-term weight loss; or long-term stress levels. While collecting longitudinal data is challenging, examining long-term effects of coping would provide great implications to consumers and public policy makers who are interested in enhancing consumers' psychological well-being.

Goal Failure and Subsequent Coping Strategies

Consumers set multiple goals and pursue them. They may eat healthy food to achieve their health goal, study hard to do well academically, or socialize actively with friends to accomplish their social goals. However, consumers often fail to achieve their goals. For example, some consumers who pursue a health goal cannot resist savory chocolate cakes, and others who plan to achieve academic goals make suboptimal choices rather than study. Given the prevalence of goal failure experiences, previous research has investigated the effect of initial goal failure on goal perseverance (Koo & Fishbach, 2008; Soman & Cheema, 2004; Wicklund & Gollwitzer, 1982). Past research demonstrates that goal failure can be represented in terms of lack of progress toward the end state and in terms of lack of commitment to the end state (Koo & Fishbach, 2008; Soman & Cheema, 2004; Wicklund & Gollwitzer, 1982) and that the way individuals interpret goal failure (i.e., lack of progress vs. lack of commitment) determines goal perseverance. The findings suggest that when people interpret failure experiences in terms of lack of progress toward a goal to which commitment remains intact, they are motivated to work harder toward the goal by perpetuating the goal-related behavior (Fishbach, Dhar, & Zhang, 2006), whereas when people represent goal failure in terms of lack of commitment to the goal, they are more likely to disengage from the goal (Soman & Cheema, 2004). Although previous research has enhanced our understanding of the effect of initial failure on goal perseverance, the existing research has not considered the process through which the different representations of goal failure influence the extent of goal perseverance.

To fill this gap, future research can rely on the coping literature. Specifically, goal failure experiences create stress because goal failure is an incident that is appraised as taxing and endangers individuals' well-being. Due to the taxing nature of goal failure experiences, consumers will engage in particular coping strategies (e.g., problem-focused coping or emotion-focused coping) to reduce stress related to goal pursuit failure. Therefore, it is possible that the different representations of goal failure will influence particular coping strategies that consumers will employ, which in turn determine the degree of goal perseverance. For example, individuals who represent goal failure as lack of progress will be more likely to engage in problem-focused coping because those individuals may activate approach motivations (Fishbach, Dhar, & Zhang, 2006), and approach motivations result in problem-focused coping (Han, Duhachek, & Rucker, 2015). In contrast, individuals who interpret goal failure as lack of commitment will be more likely to employ emotion-focused coping because those individuals may provoke avoidance motivations (Soman & Cheema, 2004), and avoidance motivations lead to emotion-focused coping (Han, Duhachek, & Rucker, 2015). Given that scant research has examined the role of coping in the context of goal failure and goal perseverance, it is worthwhile to investigate this area to integrate two different literatures.

Consumption as Coping

Consumers sometimes buy products impulsively to alleviate stress. For example, a consumer who feels angry because he or she made a mistake at work may buy luxurious shoes or chocolates to feel better. Another consumer who feels angry because of the mistake he or she made at work may buy books to study. Likewise, consumption can be a consequence of different coping strategies. Future research could examine which products represent problem-focused coping or emotion-focused coping. One possibility is that products associated with problem-focused coping involve products that induce high levels of efficacy (e.g., do it yourself products and services). Emotion-focused coping-related products might include personal consultants, life coaches, and other products and services where consumers turn over responsibility to achieve a goal to a product or service and exhibit greater response efficacy.

Additional Appraisals

Previous research has suggested the role of different appraisals in determining the use of different coping strategies (Lazarus & Folkman, 1984; Skinner & Brewer, 2002). That is, challenge appraisals (i.e., perceptions of opportunity in the stressful situation) result in problem-focused coping while threat appraisals (i.e., perceptions of potential danger in the stressful situation) lead to emotion-focused coping. Yi and Baumgartner (2004) suggest that when consumers attribute negative outcomes to others (e.g., when they feel angry), they tend to engage in problem-focused coping (e.g., confrontive coping), whereas when consumers blame the self for the negative outcomes (e.g., when they feel regretful), they tend to employ emotion-focused coping (e.g., acceptance and positive reinterpretation).

In addition to these appraisal dimensions (i.e., challenge vs. threats; self vs. other blame), future research could identify additional appraisal dimensions that determine the employment of specific coping strategies. For example, it is possible that consumers may employ different coping strategies depending on whether they feel certain or uncertain about what is happening in the negative situation. Also, it is probable that consumers may appraise negative outcomes to their specific behavior (e.g., "I did a bad thing"; local attribution) or to their global self (e.g., "I'm a bad person"; global attribution; Tangney & Dearing, 2002; Han, Duhachek, & Agrawal, 2014). Consumers who focus on their specific behavior may employ problem-focused coping whereas those who focus on their global self may emotion-focused coping, because fixing the specific behavior seems more changeable than changing the global self. Finally, the way consumers appraise stress can also influence the employment of different coping strategies. For example, Crum, Salovey, and Achor (2013) suggest that one's stress mindset (i.e., "the extent to which one holds the belief that stress has enhancing consequences for various stress-related outcomes [i.e., a 'stress-is-enhancing mindset'] or holds the belief that stress has debilitating consequences for those outcomes [i.e., a 'stress-is-debilitating mindset']," p. 716) affects individuals' coping responses. Although the authors propose that a stress-is-enhancing mindset will lead individuals to engage in actions to achieve enhancing consequences whereas a stress-is-debilitating mindset will lead individuals to avoid or manage the stress to reduce debilitating consequences, they did not examine the effects of different stress mindsets on the use of particular coping strategies directly. In addition, it is possible that individuals who hold a stress-is-debilitating mindset may actively avoid the stress by making plans to prevent debilitating outcomes (i.e., engage in problem-focused coping) or passively avoid the stress by doing nothing (i.e., emotion-focused coping). Future research could examine this relationship by measuring different coping strategies directly using existing coping scales (e.g., Duhachek, 2005 or Duhachek & Oakley, 2007).

Individual Differences

Although past research has explored the effects of consumers' personality or dispositional tendency on the use of particular coping strategies and on adaption outcomes (e.g., reduction of stress), research is still needed to link with other important personality constructs in the consumer literature. That is, given the findings of past research that has shown and validated an individual's propensity to engage in specific coping strategies as predictive of coping behavior and adaptation outcomes in the psychology literature (Carver, Scheier, & Weintraub, 1989; Endler & Parker, 1990), investigating consumers' dispositional coping tendencies has great implications in determining how consumers' predispositions toward certain coping strategies affect responses in the face of stressful events. Research along this line of inquiry has the potential not only to inform theory, but could also become a strategic decision variable for managers to consider when they plan and execute segmentation strategies to manage consumers' experienced stress (Miller, Kahn, & Luce, 2008). For example, the manager of an online shopping website (e.g., eBay) can show different types of messages while consumers are waiting for payment confirmation information, depending on consumers' tendency to employ specific coping strategies (e.g., problem-focused or emotion-focused coping). Therefore, future research could examine how consumers' dispositional tendencies toward particular coping strategies affect subsequent consumption behavior.

Cultural Differences

Culture influences the way consumers behave. To date, a great deal of research has examined how coping is affected by the cultural variable of individualism/collectivism. However, other cultural variables have been shown to exert an influence over consumer behavior. Recently, research has examined how power distance beliefs (PDB; the belief over the extent to which society should be organized hierarchically) affect charitable giving (Winterich & Zhang, 2014). Perhaps individuals in low PDB contexts would rely on more problem-focused coping because they might perceive a greater ability to impact change, whereas individuals in high PDB contexts might view such actions as less likely to produce change. Thus, individuals in these contexts may focus more on emotion-focused coping to change their reactions to environmental stressors.

Summary

The way consumers cope with stress influences a variety of consumer behaviors. Given the prevalence of consumer coping, researchers have investigated the antecedents and consequences of different types of consumer coping (see Table 11.1 for summary). In the current chapter, we have provided a brief introduction of the construct, reviewed recent findings in the last ten years of consumer coping-related research, and identified important issues that would be promising avenues for future research.

References

Abendroth, L. J., & Diehl, K. (2006). Now or never: Effects of limited purchase opportunities on patterns of regret over time. *Journal of Consumer Research, 33*(3), 342–351.

Adkins, N. R., & Ozanne, J. L. (2005). The low literate consumer. *Journal of Consumer Research, 32*(1), 93–105.

Agrawal, N., Menon, G., & Aaker, J. L. (2007). Getting emotional about health. *Journal of Marketing Research, 44*(1), 100–113.

Aldwin, C. M., & Revenson, T. A. (1987). Does coping help? A reexamination of the relation between coping and mental health. *Journal of Personality and Social Psychology, 53*(2), 337–348.

Amirkhan, J. H. (1990). A factor analytically derived measure of coping: The Coping Strategy Indicator. *Journal of Personality and Social Psychology, 59*(5), 1066–1074.

Baker, J. P., & Berenbaum, H. (2007). Emotional approach and problem-focused coping: A comparison of potentially adaptive strategies. *Cognition and Emotion, 21*(1), 95–118.

Bandura, A. (1982). Self-efficacy mechanism in human agency. *American Psychologist, 37*(2), 122–147.

Bolger, N., & Zuckerman, A. (1995). A framework for studying personality in the stress process. *Journal of Personality and Social Psychology, 69*(5), 890–902.

Brissette, I., Scheier, M. F., & Carver, C. S. (2002). The role of optimism in social network development, coping, and psychological adjustment during a life transition. *Journal of Personality and Social Psychology, 82*(1), 102–111.

Burroughs, J. E., & Rindfleisch, A. (2002). Materialism and well-being: A conflicting values perspective. *Journal of Consumer Research, 29*(3), 348–370.

Campbell, A. (1981). *The Sense of Well-being in America: Recent Patterns and Trends.* New York: McGraw-Hill.

Carver, C. S., & Connor-Smith, J. (2010). Personality and coping. *Annual Review of Psychology, 61*, 679–704.

Carver, C. S., & Scheier, M. F. (1994). Situational coping and coping dispositions in a stressful transaction. *Journal of Personality and Social Psychology, 66*(1), 184–195.

Carver, C. S., Scheier, M. F., & Weintraub, J. K. (1989). Assessing coping strategies: A theoretically based approach. *Journal of Personality and Social Psychology, 56*(2), 267–283.

Chae, B. G., & Zhu, R. J. (2014). Environmental disorder leads to self-regulatory failure. *Journal of Consumer Research, 40*(6), 1203–1218.

Connor-Smith, J. K., & Flachsbart, C. (2007). Relations between personality and coping: A meta-analysis. *Journal of Personality and Social Psychology, 93*(6), 1080–1107.

Costa, Jr., P. T., & McCrae, R. R. (1992). Psychological research in the Baltimore longitudinal study of aging. *Zeitschrift Fur Gerontologie, 26*(3), 138–141.

Crum, A. J., Salovey, P., & Achor, S. (2013). Rethinking stress: The role of mindsets in determining the stress response. *Journal of Personality and Social Psychology, 104*(4), 716–733.

Cui, G., Bao, W., & Chan, T. S. (2009). Consumers' adoption of new technology products: The role of coping strategies. *Journal of Consumer Marketing, 26* (2), 110–120.

Cutright, K. M. (2012). The beauty of boundaries: When and why we seek structure in consumption. *Journal of Consumer Research, 38*(5), 775–790.

Diener, E.(1984). Subjective well-being. *Psychological Bulletin, 95*(3), 542–575.

Diener, E. D., Emmons, R. A., Larsen, R. J., & Griffin, S. (1985). The satisfaction with life scale. *Journal of Personality Assessment, 49*(1), 71–75.

Drolet, A., & Luce, M. F. (2004). The rationalizing effects of cognitive load on emotion-based trade-off avoidance. *Journal of Consumer Research, 31*(1), 63–77.

Duhachek, A. (2005). Coping: A multidimensional, hierarchical framework of responses to stressful consumption episodes. *Journal of Consumer Research, 32*(1), 41–53.

Duhachek, A. (2008). Summing up the state of coping research: Prescriptions and prospects for consumer research. In C. P. Haugtvedt, P. M. Herr, & F. R. Kardes (eds.), *Handbook of Consumer Psychology* (pp. 1057–1077). New York: Psychology Press.

Duhachek, A., Agrawal, N., & Han, D. (2012). Guilt versus shame: Coping, fluency, and framing in the effectiveness of responsible drinking messages. *Journal of Marketing Research, 49*(6), 928–941.

Duhachek, A., & Iacobucci, D. (2005). Consumer personality and coping: Testing rival theories of process. *Journal of Consumer Psychology, 15*(1), 52–63.

Duhachek, A., & Kelting, K. (2009). Coping repertoire: Integrating a new conceptualization of coping with transactional theory. *Journal of Consumer Psychology, 19*(3), 473–485.

Duhachek, A., & Oakley, J. L. (2007). Mapping the hierarchical structure of coping: Unifying empirical and theoretical perspectives. *Journal of Consumer Psychology, 17*(3), 218–233.

Ellsworth, P. C., & Smith, C. A. (1988). Shades of joy: Patterns of appraisal differentiating pleasant emotions. *Cognition and Emotion, 2*(4), 301–331.

Endler, N. S., & Parker, J. D. (1990). Multidimensional assessment of coping: A critical evaluation. *Journal of Personality and Social Psychology, 58*(5), 844–854.

Feick, L. F., & Price, L. L. (1987). The market maven: A diffuser of marketplace information. *Journal of Marketing, 51*, 83–87.

Fishbach, A., Dhar, R., & Zhang, Y. (2006). Subgoals as substitutes or complements: The role of goal accessibility. *Journal of Personality and Social Psychology, 91*(2), 232–242.

Florian, V., Mikulincer, M., & Taubman, O. (1995). Does hardiness contribute to mental health during a stressful real-life situation? The roles of appraisal and coping. *Journal of Personality and Social Psychology, 68*(4), 687–695.

Folkman, S. & Lazarus, R. S. (1989). *Ways of Coping Questionnaire*. Palo Alto, CA: Consulting Psychologists Press.

Fredrickson, B. L. (2001). The role of positive emotions in positive psychology: The broaden-and-build theory of positive emotions. *American Psychologist, 56*(3), 218–226.

Fredrickson, B. L., & Joiner, T. (2002). Positive emotions trigger upward spirals toward emotional well-being. *Psychological Science, 13*(2), 172–175.

French, Jr., J. R., & Raven, B. (1959). The bases of social power. In D. Cartwright (ed.), *Studies in Social Power* (pp. 150–167). Ann Arbor, MI: Institute for Social Research.

Freud, A. (1946). *The Ego and Mechanisms and Defence*. New York: International University Press.

Gao, L., Wheeler, S. C., & Shiv, D. (2009). The "shaken self": Product choices as a means of restoring self-view confidence. *Journal of Consumer Research, 36*(1), 29–38.

Gunthert, K. C., Cohen, L. H., & Armeli, S. (1999). The role of neuroticism in daily stress and coping. *Journal of Personality and Social Psychology, 77*(5), 1087–1100.

Han, D., Duhachek, A., & Agrawal, N. (2015). Coping, construal and health messages: Response efficacy and self efficacy-based persuasion. Working Paper.

Han, D., Duhachek, A., & Agrawal, N. (2014). Emotions shape decisions through construal level: The case of guilt and shame. *Journal of Consumer Research, 41*(4), 1047–1064.

Han, D., Duhachek, A., & Rucker, D. D. (2015). Distinct threats, common remedies: How consumers cope with psychological threat. *Journal of Consumer Psychology*, http://dx.doi.org/10.1016/j.jcps.2015.02.001.

Holahan, C. J., & Moos, R. H. (1987). Personal and contextual determinants of coping strategies. *Journal of Personality and Social Psychology, 52*(5), 946–955.

Jia, L., Han, D., & Hirt, E. R. (2015). Mental depletion and coping. Working Paper.

Kahneman, D., Diener, E., & Schwarz, N. (eds). (1999). *Well-being: Foundations of Hedonic Psychology*. New York: Russell Sage Foundation.

Kammeyer-Mueller, J. D., Judge, T. A., & Scott, B. A. (2009). The role of core self-evaluations in the coping process. *Journal of Applied Psychology, 94*(1), 177–195.

Kees, J., Burton, S., & Tangari, A. H. (2010). The impact of regulatory focus, temporal orientation, and fit on consumer responses to health-related advertising. *Journal of Advertising, 39*(1), 19–34.

Keller, P. A. (2006). Regulatory focus and efficacy of health messages. *Journal of Consumer Research, 33*(June), 109–114.

Keller, P. A., Lipkus, I. M., & Rimer, B. K. (2002). Depressive realism and health risk accuracy: The negative consequences of positive mood. *Journal of Consumer Research, 29*(June), 57–69.

Keller, P. A., Lipkus, I. M., & Rimer, B. K. (2003). Affect, framing, and persuasion. *Journal of Marketing Research, 40*(1), 54–64.

Kim, S., & Rucker, D. D. (2012). Bracing for the psychological storm: Proactive versus reactive compensatory consumption. *Journal of Consumer Research, 39*(4), 815–830.

Koo, M., & Fishbach, A. (2008). Dynamics of self-regulation: How (un)accomplished goal actions affect motivation. *Journal of Personality and Social Psychology, 94*(2), 183–195.

Lazarus, R. S., & Folkman, S. (1984). *Stress, Appraisal, and Coping.* New York: Springer.

Lee, A. Y., Keller, P. A., & Sternthal, B. (2010). Value from regulatory construal fit: The persuasive impact of fit between consumer goals and message concreteness. *Journal of Consumer Research, 36*(5), 735–747.

Lin, Y. C., Lin, C. H., & Raghubir, P. (2003). Avoiding anxiety, being in denial, or simply stroking self-esteem: Why self-positivity? *Journal of Consumer Psychology, 13*(4), 464–477.

Luce, M. F., Payne, J. W., & Bettman, J. R. (1999). Emotional trade-off difficulty and choice. *Journal of Marketing Research, 36*(2), 143–159.

Mandel, N., & Heine, S. J. (1999). Terror management and marketing: He who dies with the most toys wins. In E. J. Arnould & L. M. Scott (eds.), *NA-Advances in Consumer Research* (vol. 26, pp. 527–532). Provo, UT: Association for Consumer Research.

McCrae, R. R. (1984). Situational determinants of coping responses: Loss, threat, and challenge. *Journal of Personality and Social Psychology, 46*(4), 919–928.

Mead, N. L., Baumeister, R. F., Stillman, T. F., Rawn, C. D., & Vohs, K. D. (2011). Social exclusion causes people to spend and consume strategically in the service of affiliation. *Journal of Consumer Research, 37*(February), 902–919.

Menon, G., Block, L. G., & Ramanathan, S. (2002). We're at as much risk as we are led to believe: Effects of message cues on judgments of health risk. *Journal of Consumer Research, 28*(March), 533–549.

Mick, D. G., & Fournier, S. (1998). Paradoxes of technology: Consumer cognizance, emotions, and coping strategies. *Journal of Consumer Research, 25*(2), 123–143.

Miller, E. G., Kahn, B. E., & Luce, M. F. (2008). Consumer wait management strategies for negative service events: A coping approach. *Journal of Consumer Research, 34*(February), 635–648.

Nowlis, S. M., Kahn, B. E., & Dhar, R. (2002). Coping with ambivalence: The effect of removing a neutral option on consumer attitude and preference judgments. *Journal of Consumer Research, 29*(3), 319–334.

Parkes, K. R. (1984). Locus of control, cognitive appraisal, and coping in stressful episodes. *Journal of Personality and Social Psychology, 46*(3), 655–668.

Passyn, Kirsten A., and Sujan, Mita (2006). Self-accountability emotions and fear appeals: Motivating behavior. *Journal of Consumer Research, 32* (4), 583–589..

Pavia, T. M., & Mason, M. J. (2004). The reflexive relationship between consumer behavior and adaptive coping. *Journal of Consumer Research, 31*(2), 441–454.

Pearlin, L. I., & Schooler, C. (1978). The structure of coping. *Journal of Health and Social Behavior, 19*, 2–21.

Penley, J. A., Tomaka, J., & Wiebe, J. S. (2002). The association of coping to physical and psychological health outcomes: A meta-analytic review. *Journal of Behavioral Medicine, 25*(6), 551–603.

Raffety, B. D., Smith, R. E., & Ptacek, J. T. (1997). Facilitating and debilitating trait anxiety, situational anxiety, and coping with an anticipated stressor: A process analysis. *Journal of Personality and Social Psychology, 72*(4), 892–906.

Raghunathan, R., Pham, M. T., & Corfman, K. P. (2006). Informational properties of anxiety and sadness, and displaced coping. *Journal of Consumer Research, 32* (4), 596–601.

Richins, M. L. (1983). Negative word-of-mouth by dissatisfied consumers: A pilot study. *Journal of Marketing, 47*, 68–78.

Rogers, R. W. (1975). A protection motivation theory of fear appeals and attitude change. *Journal of Psychology, 91*(1), 93–114.

Rogers, R. W. (1983). Cognitive and physiological processes in fear appeals and attitude change: A revised theory of protection motivation. In J. T. Cacioppo & R. E. Petty (eds.), *Social Psychophysiology* (pp. 153–176), New York: Guilford Press.

Rose, R. L., & Wood, S. L. (2005). Paradox and the consumption of authenticity through reality television. *Journal of Consumer Research, 32*(2), 284–296.

Rucker, D. D., & Galinsky, A. D. (2008). Desire to acquire: Powerlessness and compensatory consumption. *Journal of Consumer Research, 35*(August), 257–267.

Rucker, D. D., & Galinsky, A. D. (2009). Conspicuous consumption versus utilitarian ideals: How different levels of power shape consumer behavior. *Journal of Experimental Social Psychology, 45*(3), 549–555.

Schaubroeck, J., & Merritt, D. E. (1997). Divergent effects of job control on coping with work stressors: The key role of self-efficacy. *Academy of Management Journal, 40*(3), 738–754.

Schmeichel, B. J., Vohs, K. D., & Duke, S. C. (2010). Self-control at high and low levels of mental construal. *Social Psychological and Personality Science*, doi:10.1177/1948550610385955.

Sharma, E., & Alter, A. L. (2012). Financial deprivation prompts consumers to seek scarce goods. *Journal of Consumer Research, 39*(3), 545–560.

Skinner, N., & Brewer, N. (2002). The dynamics of threat and challenge appraisals prior to stressful achievement events. *Journal of Personality and Social Psychology, 83*(3), 678–692.

Skinner, E. A., Edge, K., Altman, J., & Sherwood, H. (2003). Searching for the structure of coping: A review and critique of category systems for classifying ways of coping. *Psychological Bulletin, 129*(2), 216–269.

Soman, D., & Cheema, A. (2004). When goals are counterproductive: The effects of violation of a behavioral goal on subsequent performance. *Journal of Consumer Research, 31*(June), 52–62.

Spassova, G., & Lee, A. Y. (2013). Looking into the future: A match between self-view and temporal distance. *Journal of Consumer Research, 40*(June), 157–171.

Stanton, A. L., Kirk, S. B., Cameron, C. L., & Danoff-Burg, S. (2000). Coping through emotional approach: Scale construction and validation. *Journal of Personality and Social Psychology, 78*(6), 1150–1169.

Stone, A. A., & Neale, J. M. (1984). New measure of daily coping: Development and preliminary results. *Journal of Personality and Social Psychology, 46*(4), 892–906.

Sujan, M., Sujan, H., Bettman, J. R., & Verhallen, T. (1999). Sources of consumers' stress and their coping strategies. In *Proceedings of European Advances in Consumer Research, 4*, 182–187.

Tangney, J. P. & Dearing, R. L. (2002). *Shame and Guilt*. New York: Guilford Press

Trope, Y., & Liberman, N. (2003). Temporal construal. *Psychological Review, 110*(3), 403–421.

Trope, Y., & Liberman, N. (2010). Construal-level theory of psychological distance. *Psychological Review, 117*(2), 440–463.

Tugade, M. M., Fredrickson, B. L., & Feldman Barrett, L. (2004). Psychological resilience and positive emotional granularity: Examining the benefits of positive emotions on coping and health. *Journal of Personality, 72*(6), 1161–1190.

Vallacher, R. R., & Wegner, D. M. (1989). Levels of personal agency: Individual variation in action identification. *Journal of Personality and Social Psychology, 57*(4), 660–71.

Wicklund, R. A., & Gollwitzer, P. M. (1982). *Symbolic Self-Completion.* Hillsdale, NJ: Erlbaum.

Winterich, K. P., & Zhang, Y. (2014). Accepting inequality deters responsibility: How power distance decreases charitable behavior. *Journal of Consumer Research, 41*(2), 274–293.

Yi, S., & Baumgartner, H. (2004). Coping with negative emotions in purchase-related situations. *Journal of Consumer Psychology, 14*(3), 303–317.

12 Power and Consumer Behavior

Derek D. Rucker and Adam D. Galinsky

The construct of power is part of the structural foundation of social psychology. Two of social psychology's most seminal works – Milgram's experiments on obedience to authority (Milgram, 1963) and Zimbardo's prison experiment (Zimbardo, 1973, 1974) – involved differences in power. In more recent years, the contemporary landscape of social psychology continues to feature power prominently. In one recent report, the number of power-related publications appearing in top social psychology journals has approximately doubled in the last five years compared to the previous five years (Galinsky, Rucker, & Magee, 2015).

Although work on power has spanned more than fifty years in social psychology, researchers have been largely silent in considering power's role in consumer behavior. As one relevant indicator, only in the last five years have papers on power begun to appear regularly in journals focused more on consumer behavior and consumption contexts such as the *Journal of Consumer Research* (e.g., Dubois, Rucker, & Galinsky, 2012; Jiang, Zhan, & Rucker, 2014; Jin, He, Zhang, 2014; Kim & McGill, 2011; Rucker & Galinsky, 2008; Rucker, Dubois, & Galinsky, 2011). The recent embrace of power by consumer researchers provides a foothold for the construct but also creates an important pivot point for the field. With power accepted as a topic important to consumer behavior, we explore what must be done to move the research agenda on power forward.

In the present chapter, we organize our analysis around three objectives. First, we familiarize readers with the general construct of power and the experimental approach used to study power. This section provides any researchers new to the study of power, or its effects on human behavior, a core foundation upon which to build. Second, we provide a review of power research most directly related to consumer behavior over the last five years. Our emphasis on the last five years is both in the spirit of this handbook and a reflection of power's recent emergence in the study of consumer psychology and consumer behavior. Finally, we emphasize important and unanswered questions for power in the study of consumer behavior. In doing so, we hope to utilize this pivot point to foster the next generation of power-related research in consumer behavior for seasoned and new researchers alike. As a whole, this chapter provides a nomological net or roadmap for the study of power built around antecedents, psychological processes, consequences, and future directions (see Figure 12.1).

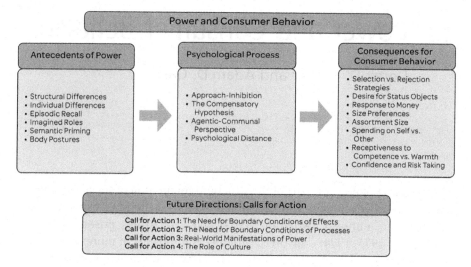

Figure 12.1 *A Nomological Net of the Emerging Study of Power in Consumer Behavior.*

Power: An Introduction

We formally define power, as it has been defined elsewhere, as *"asymmetric control over valued resources in a social relationship,"* (Magee & Galinsky, 2008; Galinsky, Rucker, & Magee, 2015). Central to this definition is the fact that power involves the hierarchical arrangement of two or more individuals based on a valued resource. The resource could be anything – physical control, money, or information – but at least one of the parties in the relationship must value the resource. This asymmetry allows the grouping of people, based on their relative possession of the resource and the value they place on that resource, into those with power and those without power. Once differences in power are created, they can produce transformative effects on human behavior.

As a construct, power can be distinguished from other important variables under the purview of consumer behavior. For example, power can be separated from both status and self-control. Although status was originally suggested as one basis of power (French & Raven, 1959) and can correlate with power (Kraus et al., 2012), recent theorizing has argued that status should be treated as conceptually distinct from power itself (for a discussion of status, see Chapter 13). Specifically, Magee and Galinsky (2008) note that whereas status reflects one's respect and admiration in the eyes of others, this respect may have little or no bearing on control over important resources, which is definitional to power. For example, a boss may have little status or respect from his employees, but can nonetheless control vital resources, such as the ability to delegate tasks, assign rewards, and offer punishments (see Fast, Halevy, & Galinsky, 2012). Similarly, self-control or willpower involves individuals' ability to resist temptation (Baumeister, Vohs, & Tice, 2007), but self-control is an intrapersonal construct that is self-focused and does not involve asymmetric control relative to another person.

Power as a Structural Difference

Early experiments on power examined the consequences of structural differences in power for behavior. Milgram's study on obedience to authority (Milgram, 1963) demonstrates that people succumb to the demands of an authority figure. In this research, a structural difference in power was created via the perception of the experimenter's authority. Because of this structural difference, participants acquiesced to the experimenter's request to administer increasingly violent shocks to a confederate. In addition, this research demonstrates that power is a perception that people make – people can perceive one has power over them – and thus may behave accordingly, even if no true physical power exists (i.e., participants could have physically stopped the experiment at any time).

Zimbardo's classic prison experiment (Zimbardo, 1973, 1974) also manipulated power though a structural difference. Zimbardo randomly assigned Stanford undergraduates to the role of guards or prisoners. The guards were given power over the prisoners – they could determine the prisoner's schedule and mete out punishments. Furthermore, although participants were randomly assigned to the roles, these assigned roles provoked a series of behaviors from the guards, such as taking away the prisoner's privileges and attempting to dehumanize the prisoners by having them refer to themselves only by their prisoner number. The roles also led to the prisoners attempting to exert their own form of power by engaging in hunger strikes and barricading themselves in their cells (though the costs were often borne by themselves).

Although these are both historic studies, a key difference exists between the Milgram and Zimbardo's experiments that carries with it an important implication for the study of power. Milgram examined immutable structural positions that produced differences in perceived power. That is, the experimenter conducting the study was perceived to possess power whereas participants were perceived to lack power. The roles were not randomly assigned; they were static products of the situation. In contrast, the Zimbardo experiment randomly assigned participants to positions with or without power. This point is important because it means that power does not need to be embedded in deep structural differences but can be created by temporary or assigned structural differences. Consistent with this idea, Anderson and Berdahl (2002) have developed a paradigm for manipulating power that involves randomly assigning participants to the role of a leader/boss or a subordinate/employee in a group task. This simple assignment creates a structural difference that can produce significant differences in how powerful individuals feel.

Power as a Psychological Experience

A sense of power not only arises from structural differences; situational factors can provoke a sense of power. Put differently, power is a psychological state – people can feel as if they have or lack power, even in the absence of any structural differences in a situation. Indeed, scholars have argued that structural differences in power may ultimately affect behavior through the psychological experience they produce (see Galinsky, Rucker, & Magee, 2015). As a consequence, any variable that triggers a differential experience of power may have the potential to impact behavior just as a structural difference in power would.

To illustrate, a commonly used procedure to manipulate power experientially is an episodic recall task. In this task, participants are instructed to recall a past experience to induce states of high or low power. For example, to induce a state of high or elevated power, people are asked to recall a time they possessed power over another individual or individuals in the form of controlling others' ability to obtain something they wanted. In contrast, to induce a state of low or reduced power, people are asked to recall a time an individual possessed power over them in the form of controlling the participants' ability to obtain something desired (for the original procedure, see Galinsky, Gruenfeld, & Magee, 2003). Note that this procedure fits the formal definition of power in that the manipulation focuses on asymmetric control over some resource of value. At the same time, such a manipulation has no objective bearing on the structural power an individual has in a subsequent task. However, this manipulation nonetheless activates a psychological mindset where individuals essentially feel more or less powerful, both as measured by participants' self-reported power as well as power coded by others (Galinsky, Gruenfeld, & Magee, 2003).

In addition to these experiments testing recall of past episodes, Dubois, Rucker, and Galinsky (2010) have shown that asking people to imagine possessing a future role can affect their sense of power. Specifically, participants were asked to imagine what it would be like to occupy the position of a boss in an organization or to occupy the position of an employee. Dubois and colleagues found that those who imagined occupying the position of a boss reported feeling more powerful than those who occupied the role of an employee. This situational prompt does not affect the actual power people have in a situation, but it nonetheless activates the psychological experience of power, and, as will be reviewed, this experience can have downstream consequences for consumer behavior.

Finally, power can be manipulated in a number of ways that can be decoupled from past or imagined structural differences altogether. For example, Bargh, Raymond, Pryor, and Strack (1995) demonstrated that power can be primed using sematic techniques such as having people complete words stems consisting of power-related concepts. In addition, Carney, Cuddy, and Yap (2010) demonstrated that people's sense of power can be affected by their body postures. Body postures that are expansive, such as leaning back in a chair with arms behind one's head, can trigger a state of high power, whereas body postures that are constrictive, such as slouching with one's hand between one's legs, can trigger a state of low power. These lines of research further support the idea that power is a psychological mindset or experience that can be activated independent of actual structural differences.

What We Know: Power and Consumer Behavior

Having provided a brief introduction to the concept of power and how researchers have examined differences in power, we now focus our discussion on the known relationships between power and important consumer-related outcomes. Given the breadth of the literature, we focus on findings most directly related to consumer outcomes, either in their context or their implications. Broader cognitive, perceptual, and behavioral consequences of power have been covered elsewhere (for reviews, see Fiske, 2010; Galinsky, Rucker, & Magee 2015; Magee & Galinsky, 2008).

Power Affects How Consumers Think: The Approach-Inhibition Model

Arguably the most influential model of power in the last decade is the approach-inhibition model (Keltner, Gruenfeld, & Anderson, 2003). This model proposes that having power activates approach-related tendencies whereas lacking power activates inhibition-related tendencies. Researchers have used the model to understand and explain a wide variety of behavior and consequences of power such as its effects on attention to rewards versus threats, automatic versus controlled information processing, disinhibited versus inhibited social behavior, and the experience of positive versus negative affect. Although a great deal of research in social psychology has been guided by this model (see Galinsky, Rucker, & Magee, 2015), only recently have efforts been made to apply it to the domain of consumer behavior.

Mourali and Nagpal (2013) examined the effects of power on consumers' use of selection versus rejection strategies in decision making. Based on the approach-inhibition model's notion that elevated levels of power predispose individuals toward approach, Mourali and Nagpal (2013) reasoned that high power would predispose people to strategies that involved selecting preferred options. In contrast, as low power predisposes people toward avoidance, the authors reasoned that low power would lead people to use strategies that involved eliminating undesirable options.

To test this idea, Mourali and Nagpal (2013) randomly placed participants into low-, high-, or baseline-power conditions using the episodic recall task. Specifically, participants wrote about a time someone had power over them (low power), they had power over another individual (high power), or they simply wrote about the events of the previous day (baseline). Next, participants were given information about twenty-four different brands of cars. They were told their objective was to narrow down their choice set and that they could do so using one of two strategies. The first strategy was described as picking out the cars they would consider buying (i.e., an inclusion strategy designed to resonate with approach). The second strategy was described as eliminating the cars they would not consider buying (i.e., an exclusion strategy designed to resonate with avoidance). Participants were asked to indicate what strategy they would use and then to use that strategy to reach a decision.

In the baseline condition, 58 percent of participants indicated a preference for the exclusion strategy. This preference increased to 66 percent for participants in the low-power condition and decreased to 32 percent in the high-power condition. Furthermore, when participants were asked what strategy they would choose if they could complete the task a second time, these differences became starker. In the baseline condition, 54 percent of participants indicated they would use the exclusion strategy, whereas 76 percent of participants in the low-power condition indicated they would use the exclusion strategy, and only 18 percent of participants in the high-power condition indicated they would use the exclusion strategy. Mourali and Nagpal (2013) also found that high-power participants were more satisfied with their decision when they had used an inclusion strategy, whereas low-power participants were more satisfied with their decision when they had used an exclusion strategy.

Power Affects What Consumers Value: The Compensatory Hypothesis

Among the first foray of power into the domain of consumer behavior came from work by Rucker and Galinsky (2008). In this research, the authors propose that low power is an aversive state that individuals seek to remedy (see also Worchel, Arnold, & Harrison, 1978). Importantly, the authors suggest that consumers' consumption choices could provide one means for people to restore a lost sense of power. Specifically, Rucker and Galinsky (2008) suggested that given that status correlates with and signals power (see French & Raven, 1959; Kraus et al., 2012; Magee & Galinsky, 2008), individuals may seek to compensate for a loss of power by obtaining objects associated with status. This core idea has produced one of the more extensive links between power and different consumption behaviors.

Desire for Status Products

In the original test of their compensatory hypothesis, Rucker and Galinsky (2008; see also Rucker & Galinsky, 2009) had participants complete an episodic recall task to manipulate power (see Galinsky, Gruenfeld, & Magee, 2003). In this task, participants recalled a past time when they had power over others (high power), others had power over them (low power), or they went to the grocery store (baseline condition). Subsequently, participants indicated their reservation price for a framed picture described either as being mass-produced and available to everyone (low-status picture) or as a limited edition and exclusive framed picture available only for a short period of time (high-status picture). Power had no effect on participants' reservation price for the low-status picture. In contrast, for the high-status picture, participants in a low-power state were willing to pay more compared to those in a high-power state or the baseline condition. Consistent with the compensatory hypothesis, in a subsequent study Rucker and Galinsky (2008) demonstrated that low-power participants, compared to high-power participants, were more likely to endorse the belief that acquiring a status-related object would give them more respect and power. Elsewhere, low-power participants have also been shown to express greater attraction to conspicuous consumption (wearing branded shirts and having bigger branded symbols on their shirts; see Rucker & Galinsky, 2009).

Response to Money

Because money is a resource, while not tantamount to power, it can be seen as one potential source of power. Furthermore, money can both facilitate the acquisition of status objects and represents status itself. Research has shown that power significantly affects both people's perception and physiological responses to money. Dubois, Rucker, and Galinsky (2010) examined the effects of power on people's perception of money. Based on past research demonstrating that desired objects are seen as bigger than they actually are (Bruner & Goodman, 1947), the authors reasoned that placing people in a low-power state would lead individuals to perceive monetary objects as larger than their actual size. Consistent with this logic, individuals induced into a low-power state, relative to individuals in a state of high power or a baseline condition, were more likely to exaggerate the size of money (e.g., the diameter of a quarter).

Research by Gal (2012) has also demonstrated evidence for a compensatory desire for money in the form of physiological responses. Specifically, postulating that people would salivate toward objects that fulfill activated goals, Gal first induced participants into a state of low or high power using the episodic recall task. Subsequently, participants were asked to place dental rolls in their mouth supposedly as part of an unrelated experiment. Finally, participants were asked to stare at a computer screen that either featured money on the screen or featured a neutral object (i.e., office furniture). After the experiment, the dental rolls were removed and weighed for saliva. Gal (2012) found that relative to a high state of power, a state of low power produced a greater salivary response when participants were exposed to money, but no differences emerged for the neutral object.

Size Preferences

The compensatory hypothesis has also been applied to products that are not normally related to status. Dubois, Rucker, and Galinsky (2012) examined how power affected participants' choice of products hierarchically arranged according to size. Specifically, consumers are often confronted with a choice of whether they want a small, medium, or large soft drink. Dubois, Rucker, and Galinsky (2012) reasoned that, although soft drinks lack an innate association with status, when presented within a hierarchically arranged assortment, the choice within a hierarchy provides an alternative means to signal status. Based on conventional naïve theories that bigger is better and that the more expensive options in a hierarchy are the best, participants who desire to signal status should be more likely to choose larger options. Consistent with hypotheses, across a series of experiments, a low-power state was associated with people choosing larger options within a hierarchy, and this outcome was mediated by a desire to increase one's standing.

Assortment Size

Understanding how power affects consumers' preferences has also been examined with regard to assortment size. Specifically, Inesi and colleagues (2011) proposed that because one consequence of being in a low-power state is a general decrease in one's sense of control over his or her environment, low power can lead individuals to prefer greater choice in their consumption to restore this missing sense of control. Consistent with this notion, Inesi and colleagues (2011) found that a low-power state led participants to prefer larger assortments to smaller ones and to expend more effort to obtain larger assortments over smaller assortments. For example, in one experiment participants in a low-power state, compared to a high-power state, indicated they would wait longer to buy ice cream from a store with fifteen different flavors compared to one with only three different flavors.

Power Affects Who Consumers Value: The Agentic-Communal Model

A second major finding at the intersection of power and consumer behavior is the idea that power affects whether people orient toward the self or others. Rucker, Galinsky, and Dubois (2012) reviewed several decades of research on power and found consistent support for the idea that having power tends to orient people toward the self, whereas lacking power tends to orient people toward others. Drawing on the seminal work of Bakan (1966), they suggest that high power tends to foster an agentic orientation where the self is viewed as more important and valued. Indeed, the very nature of high power is that it places an importance on one's own goals and objectives. In contrast, the authors suggest that low power tends to foster a communal orientation where others become valued. This hypothesis is rooted in the fact that being low power means one lacks access to valued resources and therefore is more dependent on others to access such resources. The core idea that high power leads to an agentic orientation whereas low power leads to a communal orientation has several critical implications for consumer behavior (for a deeper discussion of agency and communion, see Chapter 17).

Spending on Self versus Other

Rucker, Dubois, and Galinsky (2011) examined how states of power affected the amount of money participants were willing to spend on themselves versus others. For example, in one experiment participants were placed in a low- or high-power state by assigning them to the role of an employee (low power) or a boss (high power) in a subsequent task. However, prior to engaging in the task involving the role assignment, participants were given the opportunity to purchase a small bowl of chocolate. Participants were either told they could purchase the product for themselves (self-purchase) or told that they could purchase the candy for a friend (other-purchase). Rucker, Galinsky, and Dubois found, when buying the candy assortment for themselves, participants in the high-power condition ($1.73) spent more than participants in the low-power condition ($.88). But, when the same candy assortment was meant as a purchase for another person, participants in the low-power condition ($1.61) spent more than participants in the high-power condition ($.94). Furthermore, in another experiment, Rucker, Galinsky, and Dubois demonstrated that relative to baseline and low-power conditions, high power increased individuals' sense of self-importance, consistent with an increase in a sense of agency. In addition, relative to baseline and high-power conditions, low power increased individuals' dependence on others, consistent with an increase in a sense of communality. This work provides both a demonstration of the consequences of power spending for the self and others as well as evidence for an agentic-communal model of power.

Receptiveness to Competence versus Warmth

Based on the agentic-communal model, Dubois, Rucker, and Galinsky (2015) have recently examined the link between persuasive appeals that emphasize warmth as opposed to competence. Specifically, the authors proposed that high-power individuals would be more persuaded by messages that emphasized how skillful or talented (i.e., competent) an organization is over messages that emphasized how honest and trustworthy (i.e., warm) an organization is, with the opposite being true for low-power individuals. They based their prediction on the notion that the association between high power and agency would lead to a greater importance of competence-related information, whereas the link between low power and communality would lead to a greater importance of warmth-related information.

In a series of experiments, Dubois, Rucker, and Galinsky (2015) confirmed these predictions via manipulations of power, measures of social class, and people's self-reported role as a boss or an employee. Importantly, the authors showed that participants gave more money to the charity when the charity's appeal matched the type of information that participants valued. That is, low-power participants gave more money to a charity than high-power participants when a charity emphasized warmth. In contrast, high-power participants gave more money to a charity than low-power participants when a charity emphasized competence. This finding demonstrates that a sense of communality evoked by low power does not always lead to better outcomes for others. When people scrutinize information to decide whether or not to give, aligning arguments to the type of information they desire becomes important.

In addition, consistent with the notion that high power produces an agentic state focused on competence and what is best for the self, Rucker and Galinsky

(2009) proposed that high-power participants would be more responsive to persuasive appeals that emphasized the quality and performance of products. Across a series of experiments, Rucker and Galinsky (2009) found that people in an elevated state of power were more persuaded by appeals that emphasized performance and quality of a product compared to participants in a reduced state of power. In addition, Rucker and Galinsky (2009) replicated early work showing that participants in a reduced state of power were more persuaded by appeals linked to status than participants in an elevated state of power (see Rucker & Galinsky, 2008).

Confidence and Risk Taking

Consistent with the notion of agency, elevated power has also been linked to greater confidence (Briñol et al., 2007) as well as risk taking (Anderson & Galinsky, 2006). Briñol and colleagues (2007) examined the link between power and consumers' confidence in their thoughts. The authors reasoned that high power would lead people to be more confident than low power. Consequently, when power is induced after a message, individuals should be more confident in their subsequent thoughts and thus more likely to use those thoughts in forming their attitudes.

To test the idea that power increases confidence in one's thoughts, in one experiment Briñol and colleagues presented participants with a strong or weak message for a new mobile phone. After reading about the phone, participants listed their thoughts about the product but did not provide an evaluation. Next, participants took part in a presumably separate task where they were randomly assigned to either a manager role (high power) or a subordinate role (low power). The manager was seated in a taller and a better-looking chair than the subordinate, and then participants were instructed to have a conversation around work. Finally, participants provided their attitudes toward the mobile phone. Briñol and colleagues (2007) found that overall people liked the mobile phone better when the arguments supporting it were strong versus weak. Importantly, however, high-power participants showed an even greater difference between the strong and weak arguments. Given that participants had already listed thoughts, Briñol and colleagues (2007) suggested this was due to a greater reliance on their thoughts because of enhanced confidence in those thoughts. Briñol and colleagues (2007) also found that, when power was manipulated before a persuasive appeal, the powerful were less persuaded by strong appeals. The reasoning behind this effect again relates to confidence. Power that is activated before a persuasive appeal gives people confidence that their own beliefs are correct, which reduces the need to attend to the appeal and thus powerful individuals fail to realize how compelling strong arguments are.

Kim and McGill (2011) provide additional evidence for the idea of a link between power and agency in a series of experiments. Specifically, they examined consumers' risk perceptions as a function of anthropomorphism.

They reasoned that because power provides a sense of control and mastery over others – an aspect of agency – participants induced into a high state of power would be more likely to view themselves as having control over an outcome when the object they were interacting with was more human-like. For example, in one experiment participants were randomly assigned to low- or high-power states using the episodic recall task. Participants were subsequently shown a picture of a slot machine that was designed to be high in anthropomorphism (i.e., parts were arranged to give the appearance of eyes and a mouth) or low in anthropomorphism. Subsequently, participants were asked how risky they saw the slot game to be and how likely they would be to play. Kim and McGill (2011) found that participants in a high-power state viewed the game as less risky and were more likely to play than participants in a low-power state, but only when the object was high in anthropomorphism. High-power participants acted as if they believed they had more control over the outcome of the anthropomorphic slot machine and thus were more like to engage in the gamble.

What We Do Not Know: Unresolved Issues and Directions for Future Research

With the growth of interest in power-related research in consumer behavior, it seems apropos to set a research agenda for the future study of the topic. In our final section, and in the spirit of this handbook, we offer several areas of research that we view as both promising and important for the future study of power in consumer behavior. We refer to these as "calls to action" for the field, as we view these topics as broad questions and areas of investigation that no single scholar or paper will be able to answer alone. Instead, we hope that collectively, through the efforts of many consumer psychologists, we can piece together answers to these questions.

Call for Action 1: The Need for Boundary Conditions of Effects

Although we have identified a number of effects that link power to consumer behavior, by far and large, systematic efforts to identify boundary conditions of power on consumer behavior are scant. Our first call to action is to request a greater study of moderators to established power effects within the existing consumer behavior literature. Specifically, we suggest scholars pursue a study of the individual, the situation, the conceptualization of power, and individuals' awareness of their own power.

Individual Differences

At least two important directions exist for the study of power from an individual differences perspective. One critical direction is to understand what factors lead people to be more or less predisposed to be affected by their current power in a given situation. For example, prior research has shown that people vary in their dispositional level of power (Anderson & Berdahl, 2002; Anderson & Galinsky, 2006) and that an individual's dispositional level of power can produce similar effects as power manipulations (see Rucker & Galinsky, 2009). However, what is less known is whether certain individual difference factors lead people to be more or less likely to rely on their current sense of power.

As one example of how an individual difference may affect people's reliance on their level of power, consider self-monitoring (Snyder, 1974). Self-monitoring refers to people's propensity to rely on their own internal states versus factors in their environment. Research has shown, for example, that low self-monitors are more persuaded by the quality of a product (i.e., how it serves the self), whereas high self-monitors are more persuaded by the image of a product (i.e., how it represents the self to others; Snyder & DeBono, 1985). How might differences in self-monitoring interact with power? One possibility is that, as a social variable, high self-monitors might be especially sensitive to their level of power in a given situation and thus more likely to act based on the power they have. Thus, a power manipulation, such as the role one is assigned in a task (i.e., manager or subordinate), may be more likely to have an effect on high self-monitors compared to low self-monitors. Alternatively, to the extent people internalize power, people's generalized sense of power (Anderson & Berdahl, 2002) might be more likely to predict behavior among low self-monitors, as it would reflect their natural internal state. To date, the interaction among self-monitoring, situation levels of power, and chronic power has not been explored.

A second route is to consider whether power reveals the true nature of the self, making individual differences better predictors of the behavior of the powerful than the powerless. Because of the lack of dependency among the powerful, the constraints that normally govern thought, expression, and behavior may melt away, leaving the powerful to act in accord with their true essence. Numerous studies are consistent with the idea that power reveals the person. For example, power increases the correspondence between traits and behavior, such as communal orientations (Chen, Lee-Chai, & Bargh, 2001), empathy (Mast, Jonas, & Hall, 2009), propensity to sexually harass (Bargh, et al. 1995), social value orientation (Côté et al., 2011; Galinsky et al. 2008), political ideology (Chin, Hambrick, & Treviño, 2013), and trait affect (Anderson & Thompson. 2004). None of these studies, however, has investigated whether power makes individuals differences a stronger predictor of consumer behavior. Take the preceding example of self-monitoring – power could increase the tendency for low self-monitors to be persuaded by the quality of a product and high self-monitors to be persuaded by the image of a product.

These differential effects of individual differences –predicting who is sensitive to his or her level of power versus predicting when individual difference matters – open a number of research opportunities. Our proposition is for researchers to consider the myriad individual difference variables from the personality, social psychology, and marketing literatures and how they might influence, be affected by, or interact with power.

Situational Differences

Features of a situation also reflect a relatively unexplored area of research on the role of power. For example, research could explore what situational factors provoke people to be more or less inclined to rely on their power. Earlier we noted that anthropomorphic objects were more likely to lead power to have an effect on risk perception because people believed they could control the object (Kim & McGill, 2011). Building on this finding, one might imagine that power has a stronger influence in situations that involve interacting with another person (i.e., a Best Buy salesperson) versus those that do not (e.g., a purchase on Bestbuy.com). Or, within online contexts, people's behavior may be dependent on whether they are interacting with another person (e.g., bidding against another person on eBay) versus making a purchase from a website (i.e., amazon.com).

As another example, it is possible that situational cues serve to remind people about the amount of power they possess. Brands often engage in loyalty programs, and these programs may lead consumers to consider their relative standing. For example, airlines often have boarding groups that provide a direct representation of one's relative standing within the airline and the resources to which one has access. Understanding situational factors that heighten the accessibility of one's power may provide further insight into what brands and organizations can do to predict both the power of their consumers and the likelihood consumers' judgments will be influenced by power.

Conceptualization of Power

Another aspect that merits future research is an examination of the conceptualization of power with regard to factors that create and perpetuate power differences. For example, people can come into the possession of power, or perceive themselves to have acquired power, through a variety of means. Power can be earned or it can be taken; power can be legitimate or illegitimate. And once one has power, one may be secure in one's possession of power or one's hold on power may be precarious and unstable. How power is conceptualized or viewed by the power holder can have important effects on how that power affects subsequent behavior. For example, Lammers, Galinsky, Gordijn, and Otten (2008) have shown that when one's power is viewed as legitimate, elevated power leads to more approach than reduced power. However, when one's power is viewed as illegitimate, reduced power can lead to as much or even more approach than elevated power.

To date, the bulk of research has primarily manipulated power without giving much attention to how it is conceptualized. Yet scholars could systematically examine many factors. For example, take the research reviewed on powerlessness and the compensatory hypothesis. A core assumption of this work is that consumers view lacking power as aversive. However, what if consumers do not conceptualize reduced power as aversive and instead view elevated power as aversive? For instance, Josephs, Sellers, Newman, and Mehta (2006) proposed that low-testosterone people find being in a position of power uncomfortable. Specifically, low-testosterone individuals had a negative physiological reaction to being in the dominant position: they reported greater emotional arousal and showed worse cognitive functioning in a dominant position. Similarly, in some situations making decisions may be emotionally painful (Botti, Orfali, & Iyengar, 2009). Given that the aversive nature of low power is proposed to drive compensatory effects, changing the framing of how power is represented may reduce these compensatory efforts. Similarly, making a position of power aversive may produce compensatory efforts among those with power.

As another example, people might view the power they have as short- or long-lived. For example, people might feel powerful because they have won an award (e.g., employee of the month), but realize the award's meaning is ephemeral (someone else will win the award next month). Or they might feel powerful because they have been promoted to a more permanent position of power (i.e., sales manager). Considering power as enduring or ephemeral might affect people's behavior. For example, viewing a loss of power as short-lived may eliminate compensatory effects buttressed by the belief that power will return naturally. In contrast, viewing high power as short-lived may lead people to engage in maintenance strategies in an effort to hold onto the power for as long as possible. (see Maner & Mead, 2010).

Awareness

Little research has examined how participants' own awareness of their power affects how power guides their behavior. At one end of the spectrum, people may be fully aware of the power they possess as well as its effects. For example, individuals whose power derives from being a manager may both accurately assess their level power and recognize its effects (e.g., they know that their power leads them to take action and recognize that their power makes them more likely to take risks). An individual may also be aware of his or her compensatory responses; an individual who feels that he does not have power at work might buy status-related objects in a directed and volitional effort to impress his coworkers. At the other end of the spectrum, people may be largely unaware of their power or its effects. For example, individuals in positions of power might fail to take other's perspectives into account without realizing they are doing so. Or an individual who feels low in power might pay a premium for a prestige brand without realizing the underlying motives for his or her price point.

To date, very little work has made an effort to distinguish between more conscious versus unconscious effects of power. Studying the role of conscious awareness of power is important for at least three reasons. First, whether people are aware or unaware of their own power may have implications for how people behave in a given situation. For example, knowing one has power may lead one to feel more comfortable voicing an opinion (Anderson & Berdahl, 2002) than when the individual does not consciously realize he or she has power. Second, people's awareness of their own power may exacerbate or attenuate its effects. For example, the more conscious people are of their power, and the more desirable it is to have power in a situation, the more they may protect it (Maner & Mead, 2010). Third, when people are aware of the influence of power, they may try to correct for any unwanted influence of power (Wegener & Petty, 1995). For example, people may view paying a higher premium for the identical product due to its status as an unwanted bias that requires correction. This might be especially true if power is triggered from a situational manipulation and is temporary.

Call for Action 2: The Need for Boundary Conditions of Processes

A second important direction for the study of power in consumer behavior is with respect to moderators of the psychological processes that follow individual, structural, or situational differences in power. Specifically, several distinct processes have been proposed to underlie differences in the behavior of low- and high-power individuals. As previously reviewed, power has been related to consumer behavior primarily through the approach inhibition model (Keltner, Gruenfeld, & Anderson, 2003), the compensatory hypothesis (Rucker & Galinsky, 2008), and the agentic-communal perspective (Rucker, Galinsky, & Dubois, 2012). In addition, additional perspectives exist, such as power affecting behavior through psychological distance (Magee & Smith, 2013). Given that power can affect a number of processes, under what circumstances are the effects of power driven by one process versus another? This provides a substantial opportunity for enriching our theories of power as, in some cases, different processes may produce different effects. We provide two illustrative examples

Propensities versus Needs

Rucker, Galinsky, and Dubois (2012) discuss propensities versus needs as one moderator that may determine whether a state of low power influences behavior through a communal orientation or a compensatory motive. Specifically, they suggested that in the absence of any status cues, people's natural propensity in a low-power state is to be more communal. As a consequence, when provided with an explicit opportunity to buy a gift, low-power individuals spend more on a purchase when the recipient is another person as opposed to himself or herself. In contrast, as soon as the product is associated with status, the effect reverses: low-power individuals spend more on a purchase for themselves than another person. To explain this outcome, Rucker, Galinsky, and Dubois (2012) introduced the notion that power and powerlessness have both propensities and can activate certain needs. The authors suggested that propensities represent the more automatic or hard-wired effects of power on behavior. However, such propensities can be overridden when other goals are present in the context, such as the opportunity to elevate one's power via status. Their findings provide one such piece of evidence that helps to explain when power might affect behavior through distinct processes related to a communal perspective or a compensatory desire.

Elaboration Level

A large amount of research has spoken to the importance of consumers' elaboration level – or the amount of message-relevant thinking they engage in – and how it can affect how they respond to persuasion, aptly captured in the Elaboration Likelihood Model of Persuasion (see Petty & Briñol, 2012; Petty & Cacioppo, 1986). Specifically, people engage in different processes as a function of whether they think thoughtfully about information (i.e., high elaboration) or heuristically about information (i.e., low elaboration). For example, when people think carefully about a persuasive message, they are more likely to be persuaded by the central arguments of the message, that is, whether the information itself is compelling and persuasive. In contrast, when people think less thoughtfully, they are more likely to be persuaded by simple cues such as how attractive the source is, even when attractiveness has no bearing on the merits of the message. In addition, under high-elaboration conditions, people might sometimes be biased in their processing of information (i.e., focus on particular pieces of information). The key is that different processes (e.g., reliance on arguments versus heuristics) operate at different degrees of thinking or elaboration.

Despite this rather large literature in both psychology and marketing, relatively little work has applied elaboration to the theory to power. However, the notion of elaboration may serve as an important and powerful moderator of when different power processes operate. For example, some processes, such as the compensatory hypothesis, might be more likely to emerge under low or high elaboration depending on whether the effect itself is a result of a heuristic or a motivational bias. Alternatively, elaboration level may interact with how information is utilized based on the same process. For example, under low levels of elaboration, an agentic focus may lead information to be used as a simple cue for persuasion (i.e., "I am persuaded because that source seems competent"), whereas under high elaboration it may serve as a persuasive argument (i.e., "competence is the most important feature") or bias processing (i.e., "let me focus on the competence-related information"). Thus, even the same orientation may affect persuasion differently depending on the elaboration level of the audience. This observation presents an interesting opportunity for future research to explore how power operates at different levels of elaboration.

Call for Action 3: Real-World Manifestations of Power

One exciting element of consumer psychology has been the development of psychological perspectives to align with practical problems faced by brands and companies. That is, consumer psychology carries with it the prospect of informing critical decisions that may have millions, if not billions, of dollars attached to them. Beyond exploring basic effects in the power literature, we believe an exciting onus exists for consumer psychologists to demonstrate how power, as an individual difference, structural difference, or a situational state, plays out in real-world environments of practical importance.

Segmentation Strategies

A first approach to understand real-world manifestations of power would be to rely upon segmentations strategies. For example, power can sometimes arise from differences in one's social standing, where some individuals have more economic resources than others (see Rucker, Dubois, & Galinsky, 2011, for discussion; see also Dubois, Rucker, & Galinsky, 2015). As a consequence, differences in power might be predicted by people's zip codes. Although untested, people who live in relatively rich and prosperous neighborhoods might have chronically higher levels of power than those who live in poor and deprived neighborhoods. People could also be segmented not by their direct wealth but by whether they tend to occupy positions associated with power or not. Indeed, in recent work, Dubois, Rucker, and Galinsky (2015) found that individuals who self-reported to be bosses in their job behaved in a manner consistent with having power (e.g., valuing competence-related arguments), whereas those who self-reported to be employees in their job behaved in a manner consistent with lacking power (e.g., valuing warmth-related arguments). Thus, future research could look at individual variation in factors that affect power to find real-world proxies for consumers' level of power that could be used by brands.

A second form of segmentation strategy may rely not on individual differences but on situations that are linked to power. For example, when consumers call to negotiate a price decrease in their cable service because another carrier has approached them, this may be a situation where the consumer psychologically feels powerful. After all, he or she has an alternative, which provides a source of power in negotiations (see Galinsky, Rucker, & Magee, 2015). In contrast, when consumers experience a service failure (e.g., their cable goes out), they may feel relatively powerless compared to the cable provider. In such cases, practitioners might tailor the responses of their call centers to maximize the satisfaction of their consumers. As noted earlier, people may focus on their core competencies and skills when dealing with a consumer in a high-power state, but focus on their warmth and honesty when dealing with a consumer in a low-power state (Dubois, Rucker, & Galinsky, 2015).

Field Interventions

An alternative approach, which we believe is worth consideration, is for research-ers to begin to think about how brands can intervene to make consumers feel more or less powerful. That is, rather than rely on individual differences or occupational positions, the real-world importance of power could be demonstrated by showing it can be manipulated in the field. Within the work in power and consumer behavior, a few efforts have been made to show how power might be operational-ized in real-world contexts. For example, Rucker, Dubois, and Galinsky (2011) demonstrated it was possible to manipulate power via the tagline used in the copy of an advertisement. Specifically, to induce high power, they inserted a tagline that read, "Remember a time you felt powerful?" To induce low power, they instead used a tagline that read, "Remember a time you felt powerless?" In a variant of this technique, Dubois, Rucker, and Galinsky (2012) exposed participants to banner ads that reminded participants that "everyone feels powerful," or "everyone feels powerless." In both studies, the advertisement and banner produced the same effects as structural manipulations of power and episodic recall primes.

Of course, a limitation of these interventions is that they often lack the full press of factors involved in many marketing efforts such as the duration of the campaign, actions taken by competition, and long-term branding effects. Moving forward, we believe that future research will benefit from more field experiments that provide suggestive ways advertisers or marketers might affect power as well as more longitudinal and large-scale examinations of power.

Call for Action 4: The Role of Culture

The role of culture as a moderator and driver of the effects of power represents a final important area for future research. To date, few systematic efforts have been made to understand how culture interacts with power to affect the psych-ology and behavior of consumers. Even within the social psychology literature, efforts to understand the impact of culture on power are limited. In fact, the bulk of research has focused primarily on how power affects people in individu-alistic cultures (for a notable discussion, see Zhong, Magee, Maddux, & Galinsky, 2006). Within consumer behavior, a focus on the role of cultural is of particular importance given that brands are increasingly seeking to adopt a global focus (Matanda & Ewing, 2012).

As a starting point, research can develop and test hypotheses as to how the same power manipulation might produce differences in behavior based on how culture affects the way that power is acquired, exercised, and interpreted. As one example, cross-cultural research has suggested that individualistic cultures tend to be more exchange-focused in their relationships, whereas collectivist cultures tend to be more communally focused in their relationships (Triandis, 1989). This distinction in how people interact with others, especially those in their ingroups, may have implications for how power would affect people's behavior in each culture. For example, Torelli and Shavitt (2010) found that individualistic cultures viewed power as means to satisfy personal goals, whereas collectivist cultures viewed power as way to help and benefit others. In these studies, culture predicted what was considered to be an appropriate use of power and the type of power-related experiences people recalled.

Although not tested as a function of culture, research by Chen, Lee-Chai, and Bargh (2001) explored the interactive effects of power and people's natural disposition to be exchange-versus communal-focused. Whereas people might generally be more exchange-focused in individualistic cultures, Chen and colleagues preselected people based on their propensity to be exchange-focused or communally focused. Consistent with a large literature on power in individualistic cultures, people who were naturally exchange-focused behaved in accordance with their self-interest when primed with power. In contrast, people who were naturally communally focused behaved in a more generous way toward others when primed with power. These effects can be understood as arising due to power enhancing whatever goal people have in mind (see DeMarree et al., 2012; Galinsky, Rucker, & Magee, 2015; Guinote, 2007; Rucker, Galinsky, & Dubois, 2012). Because individualistic cultures tend to be more focused on self-interest, the activation of power should enhance self-interested goals as documented in extensive prior research (see Rucker, Galinsky, & Dubois, 2012, for a review). However, because collectivist cultures tend to be more communally focused with their ingroups (Triandis, 1989), the activation of power may lead to behavior toward ingroups that is more socially responsible and generous. Additional work on power and culture should explore how culture interacts with power to affect behavior in novel and unexplored ways.

Summary

Power has seen a recent surge of interest in the consumer psychology literature. In the present chapter, we have provided an overview of the construct, offered a summary of findings in the last five years of power-related research, and raised critical issues we hope will be addressed by future research efforts (see Figure 12.1 for the essence of this chapter). Consumer psychologists, as purveyors of both psychology and consumer behavior, are ideally positioned to build bridges that link power to important consumer behavior domains and to use the field of consumer behavior to ultimately shed light on the construct of power. We hope readers of this chapter will take it upon themselves to continue to contribute to work at the intersection of power and consumer behavior.

References

Anderson, C., & Berdahl, J. L. (2002). The experience of power: Examining the effects of power on approach and inhibition tendencies. *Journal of Personality & Social Psychology, 83*(6), 1362–1377.

Anderson, C., & Galinsky, A. D. (2006). Power, optimism, and risk-taking. *European Journal of Social Psychology, 36*(4), 511–536. doi: 10.1002/ejsp.324.

Anderson, C., & Thompson, L. L. (2004). Affect from the top down: How powerful individuals' positive affect shapes negotiations. *Organizational Behavior and Human Decision Processes, 95*(2), 125–139.

Bakan, D. (1966). Test of significance in psychological research. *Psychological Bulletin, 66*(6), 423–437. doi: 10.1037/H0020412.

Bargh, J. A., Raymond, P., Pryor, J. B., & Strack, F. (1995). Attractiveness of the underling: An automatic power–sex association and its consequences for sexual harassment and aggression. *Journal of Personality and Social Psychology, 68* (5), 768–781. doi: 10.1037/0022-3514.68.5.768.

Baumeister, R. F., Vohs, K. D., & Tice, D. M. (2007). The strength model of self-control. *Current Directions in Psychological Science, 16*(6), 351–355. doi: 10.1111/j.1467-8721.2007.00534.x.

Botti, S., Orfali, K., & Iyengar, S. S. (2009). Tragic choices: Autonomy and emotional responses to medical decisions. *Journal of Consumer Research, 36*(3), 337–352. doi: 10.1086/598969.

Brinol, P., Petty, R. E., Valle, C., Rucker, D. D., & Becerra, A. (2007). The effects of message recipients' power before and after persuasion: A self-validation analysis. *Journal of Personality and Social Psychology, 93*(6), 1040–1053. doi: 10.1037/0022-3514.93.6.1040.

Bruner, J. S., & Goodman, C. C. (1947). Value and need as organizing factors in perception. *Journal of Abnormal and Social Psychology, 42*(1), 33–44.

Carney, D. R., Cuddy, A. J. C., & Yap, A. J. (2010). Power posing: Brief nonverbal displays affect neuroendocrine levels and risk tolerance. *Psychological Science, 21*(10), 1363–1368. doi: 10.1177/0956797610383437.

Chen, S., Lee-Chai, A. Y., & Bargh, J. A. (2001). Relationship orientation as a moderator of the effects of social power. *Journal of Personality and Social Psychology, 80.* 173–187. doi:10.1037/0022-3514.80.2.173.

Chin, M., Hambrick, D. C., & Treviño, L. K. (2013). Political ideologies of CEOs: The influence of executives' values on corporate social responsibility. *Administrative Science Quarterly, 58*(2), 197–232.

Côté, S., Kraus, M. W., Cheng, B. H., Oveis, C., van der Lowe, I., Lian, H., & Keltner, D. (2011). Social power facilitates the effect of prosocial orientation on empathic accuracy. *Journal of Personality and Social Psychology, 101*(2), 217–232. doi: 10.1037/a0023171.

DeMarree, K. G., Loersch, C., Brinol, P., Petty, R. E., Payne, B. K., & Rucker, D. D. (2012). From primed construct to motivated behavior: Validation processes in goal pursuit. *Personality and Social Psychology Bulletin, 38*(12), 1659–1670. doi: 10.1177/0146167212458328.

Dubois, D., Rucker, D. D., & Galinsky, A. D. (2010). The accentuation bias: Money literally looms larger (and sometimes smaller) to the powerless. *Social Psychological and Personality Science, 1*(3), 199–205. doi: 10.1177/1948550610365170.

Dubois, D., Rucker, D. D., & Galinsky, A. D. (2012). Super size me: Product size as a signal of status. *Journal of Consumer Research, 38*(6), 1047–1062.

Dubois, D., Rucker, D. D., & Galinsky, A. D. (2015). The dynamic interplay of communicator and audience power in persuasion. Unpublished Manuscript, Northwestern University.

Dubois, D., Rucker, D. D., & Galinsky, A. D. (2015). Social class, power, and selfishness: When and why upper and lower class individuals behave unethically.
Journal of Personality and Social Psychology, 108(3), 436–449. doi: 10.1037/
pspi0000008.

Fast, N. J., Halevy, N., & Galinsky, A. D. (2012). The destructive nature of power
without status. *Journal of Experimental Social Psychology, 48*(1), 391–394.

Fiske, S. T. (2010). *Interpersonal Stratification: Status, Power, and Subordination*: New
York: John Wiley & Sons.

French, Jr., J. R. P., & Raven, B. (1959). The bases of social power. In D. Cartwright
(ed.), *Studies in Social Power* (pp. 150–167). Oxford: University of Michigan.

Gal, D. (2012). A mouth-watering prospect: Salivation to material reward. *Journal of
Consumer Research, 38*(6), 1022–1029. doi: 10.1086/661766.

Galinsky, A. D., Gruenfeld, D. H., & Magee, J. C. (2003). From power to action.
Journal of Personality and Social Psychology, 85(3), 453–466. doi: 10.1037/
0022–3514.85.3.453.

Galinsky, A. D., Magee, J. C., Gruenfeld, D. H., Whitson, J. A., & Lilenquist, K. A.
(2008). Power reduces the press of the situation: Implications for creativity,
conformity, and dissonance. *Journal of Personality and Social Psychology, 95*
(6), 1450–1466.

Galinsky, A. D., Rucker, D. D., & Magee, J. C. (2015). Power: Past findings, present
considerations, and future directions. In M. M. J. Simpson (assoc. ed.) & P.
Shaver (ed.), *APA Handbook of Personality and Social Psychology, vol. 3: Interpersonal Relationships*. Washington, DC: American Psychological Association.

Guinote, A. (2007). Power and goal pursuit. *Personality and Social Psychology Bulletin,
33*(8), 1076–1087. doi: 10.1177/0146167207301011.

Inesi, M. E., Botti, S., Dubois, D., Rucker, D. D., & Galinsky, A. D. (2011). Power and
choice: Their dynamic interplay in quenching the thirst for personal control.
Psychological Science, 22(8), 1042–1048. doi: 10.1177/0956797611413936.

Jiang, Y., Zhan, L., & Rucker, D. D. (2014). Power and action orientation: Power as a
catalyst for consumer switching behavior. *Journal of Consumer Research 41*(3),
183–196.

Jin, L., He, Y., & Zhang, Y. (2014). How power states influence consumers' perceptions
of price unfairness. *Journal of Consumer Research, 40*(5), 818–833.

Josephs, R. A., Sellers, J. G., Newman, M. L., & Mehta, P. H. (2006). The mismatch
effect: When testosterone and status are at odds. *Journal of Personality and
Social Psychology, 90*(6), 999–1013. doi: 10.1037/0022–3514.90.6.999.

Keltner, D., Gruenfeld, D. H., & Anderson, C. (2003). Power, approach, and inhibition.
Psychological Review, 110(2), 265–284. doi: 10.1037/0033–295x.110.2.265.

Kim, S., & McGill, A. L. (2011). Gaming with Mr. Slot or gaming the slot machine?
Power, anthropomorphism, and risk perception. *Journal of Consumer
Research, 38*(1), 94–107.

Kraus, M. W., Piff, P. K., Mendoza-Denton, R., Rheinschmidt, M. L., & Keltner, D.
(2012). Social class, solipsism, and contextualism: How the rich are different
from the poor. *Psychological Review, 119*(3), 27. doi: 10.1037/a0028756.

Lammers, J., Galinsky, A. D., Gordijn, E. H., & Otten, S. (2008). Illegitimacy moderates the effects of power on approach. *Psychological Science, 19*(6), 558–564.

Magee, J. C., & Galinsky, A. D. (2008). Chapter 8: Social hierarchy: The self-reinforcing
nature of power and status. *Academy of Management Annals, 2*(1), 351–398.

Magee, J. C., & Smith, P. K. (2013). The social distance theory of power. *Personality and Social Psychology Review, 17*(2), 158–186. doi: 10.1177/1088868312472732.

Maner, J. K., & Mead, N. L. (2010). The essential tension between leadership and power: When leaders sacrifice group goals for the sake of self-interest. *Journal of Personality and Social Psychology, 99*(3), 482–497. doi: 10.1037/A0018559.

Mast, M. S., Jonas, K., & Hall, J. A. (2009). Give a person power and he or she will show interpersonal sensitivity: The phenomenon and its why and when. *Journal of Personality and Social Psychology, 97*(5), 835–850. doi: 10.1037/A0016234.

Matanda, T., & Ewing, M. T. (2012). The process of global brand strategy development and regional implementation. *International Journal of Research in Marketing, 29*(1), 5–12. doi: 10.1016/j.ijresmar.2011.11.002.

Milgram, S. (1963). Behavioral study of obedience. *Journal of Abnormal and Social Psychology, 67*(4), 371–378. doi: 10.1037/h0040525.

Mourali, M., & Nagpal, A. (2013). The powerful select, the powerless reject: Power's influence in decision strategies. *Journal of Business Research, 66*(7), 874–880. doi: 10.1016/j.jbusres.2011.12.005.

Petty, R. E. & Briñol, P. (2012). The elaboration likelihood model. In P. A. M. Van Lange, A. Kruglanski, & E. T. Higgins (eds.), *Handbook of Theories of Social Psychology* (vol. 1, pp. 224–245). London: Sage.

Petty, R. E., & Cacioppo, J. T. (1986). The elaboration likelihood model of persuasion. In B. Leonard (ed.), *Advances in Experimental Social Psychology* (vol. 19, pp. 123–205). New York: Academic Press.

Rucker, D. D., Dubois, D., & Galinksy, A. D. (2011). Generous paupers and stingy princes: Power drives consumer spending on self versus others. *Journal of Consumer Research, 37*(6), 1015–1029.

Rucker, D. D., & Galinsky, A. D. (2008). Desire to acquire: Powerlessness and compensatory consumption. *Journal of Consumer Research, 35*(2), 257–267. doi: 10.1086/588569.

Rucker, D. D., & Galinsky, A. D. (2009). Conspicuous consumption versus utilitarian ideals: How different levels of power shape consumer behavior. *Journal of Experimental Social Psychology, 45*(3), 549–555. doi: 10.1016/j.jesp.2009.01.005.

Rucker, D. D., Galinsky, A. D., & Dubois, D. (2012). Power and consumer behavior: How power shapes who and what consumers value. *Journal of Consumer Psychology, 22*(3), 352–368. doi: 10.1016/j.jcps.2011.06.001.

Snyder, M. (1974). Self-monitoring of expressive behavior. *Journal of Personality and Social Psychology, 30*(4), 526–537.

Snyder, M., & DeBono, K. G. (1985). Appeals to image and claims about quality: Understanding the psychology of advertising. *Journal of Personality and Social Psychology, 49*(3), 586–597. doi: 10.1037/0022–3514.49.3.586.

Torelli, C. J., & Shavitt, S. (2010). Culture and concepts of power. *Journal of Personality and Social Psychology, 99*(4), 703–723. doi: 10.1037/A0019973.

Triandis, H. C. (1989). The self and social-behavior in differing cultural contexts. *Psychological Review, 96*(3), 506–520. doi: 10.1037/0033–295x.96.3.506.

Wegener, D. T., & Petty, R. E. (1995). Flexible correction processes in social judgment: The role of naive theories in corrections for perceived bias. *Journal of Personality and Social Psychology, 68*, 36–51.

Worchel, S., Arnold, S. E., & Harrison, W. (1978). Aggression and power restoration: The effects of identifiability and timing on aggressive behavior. *Journal of Experimental Social Psychology, 14*(1), 43–52.

Zhong, C. B., Magee, J. C., Maddux, W. W., & Galinsky, A. D. (2006). Power, culture, and action: Considerations in the expression and enactment of power in East Asian and Western societies. *Research on managing groups and teams, 9*, 53–73.

Zimbardo, P. G. (1973). On the ethics of intervention in human psychological research: With special reference to the Stanford prison experiment. *Cognition, 2*(2), 243–256. doi: 10.1016/0010–0277(72)90014-5.

Zimbardo, P. G. (1974). Obedience to authority. *American Psychologist, 29*(7), 566–567. doi: 10.1037/H0038158.

13 Social Hierarchy, Social Status, and Status Consumption

David Dubois and Nailya Ordabayeva

Introduction

Social hierarchy is a fundamental feature of most existing societies and organizations (Sidanius & Prato, 1999). Common to any hierarchical structure is the adoption of a ranking system, in which every individual occupies a specific position or social status relative to others. Although hierarchical ordering is a multifaceted construct (Weber, 1922/1978[1]), it typically stems from one or several attributes (e.g., race, gender, income, education, ancestry, occupation) that become status markers in social groups. This ordering simultaneously transforms every member into a sender and a recipient of status signals and guides individuals' actions vis-à-vis these signals. Because of their profound effects on individuals' thoughts, feelings, behaviors, as well as group dynamics, status and stratification processes have received significant interest in key areas of social sciences such as sociology (e.g., Podolny, 1993, 2005; Ridgeway et al., 2009), psychology (e.g., Fiske, 2010; Kraus et al., 2012a; Magee & Galinsky, 2008), economics (e.g., Frank, 2007), and even health care and epidemiology (e.g., Bobak et al., 1998; Marmot, 2004).

Although status processes deeply permeate both managers' and consumers' actions, research on these issues is relatively scant in consumer psychology and marketing.

To test this intuition, we conducted a systematic search of articles containing status-related words in their title (status, luxury, social hierarchy, socioeconomic status [SES], social class, conspicuous consumption, social rank) in thirty-two leading academic journals in marketing, social psychology, sociology, and marketing during the period between February 2011 and February 2014. Two notable observations merit discussion. First, in terms of the total number of articles, more articles included status-related constructs in their title in management (N = 78), social psychology (N = 74), and sociology (N = 104) than in marketing (N = 37; see Table 13.1). Second, among the articles obtained from our search, the use of "status" in the title was the lowest in marketing (43.9 percent) compared to management (94.8 percent), social psychology (67.5 percent), and sociology (68.2 percent; see Figure 13.1). These numbers suggest

---

1 Among key constructs that have been argued to form social hierarchy are social class and power (Weber, 1946). For a full discussion of power, see Chapter 12 of this handbook.

Table 13.1 *Number of Articles Including One of the Search Terms in Leading Marketing, Sociology, Social Psychology, and Management Journals, February 2011–February 2014*

Discipline \ Search Term	Marketing	Sociology	Social Psychology	Management
Status	29	71	50	74
Luxury	29	0	0	4
Social hierarchy	0	0	4	0
Socioeconomic status	1	12	6	0
Social class	0	21	8	0
Conspicuous consumption	7	0	2	0
Social rank	0	0	4	0
Total	**37**	**104**	**74**	**78**

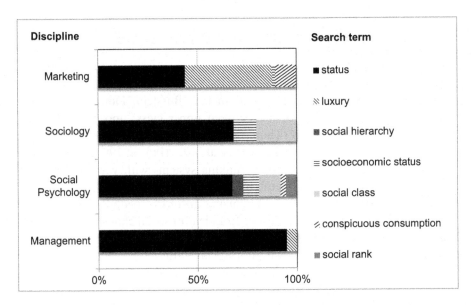

Figure 13.1 *Percentage of Articles Including One of the Search Terms in Leading Marketing, Sociology, Social Psychology and Management Journals, February 2011–February 2014.*

that although social status is a central construct in social sciences, marketing has contributed relatively less to research on status (see Figure 13.1 and Table 13.1).

Fortunately, interest in status in marketing may be growing, with a particular emphasis on how individuals' own status influences consumption of status goods and services (e.g., Dubois, Galinsky, & Rucker, 2012; Han, Nunes, & Drèze, 2010) and how the distribution of status within social groups can shed new light on consumption decisions (e.g., Kuksov & Xie, 2012; Ordabayeva & Chandon, 2011). Although these represent promising initial steps, we believe the status lens can significantly deepen our understanding of consumption phenomena, particularly given the profound changes taking place in social strata across the world (Piketty, 2014; Wilkinson & Pickett, 2010), and we outline a number of promising research avenues for future marketing research on status and social hierarchy.

We organize our review around three main objectives. First, we familiarize the reader with fundamental conceptual and empirical work on social hierarchy, and we delineate the relationships between social hierarchy and status processes. Second, we provide a review of recent social hierarchy and status research that is most relevant to consumer behavior. Specifically, we synthesize previous efforts to shed light on the forms and functions of status consumption before turning to the psychological, social, and economic antecedents and consequences of status consumption. Finally, we highlight key avenues for future research on social hierarchy and status in consumer behavior.

Basic Principles of Social Hierarchy and Status

Hierarchies are a salient feature of most societies and cultures across historical periods and civilizations. From the Athenians' stratification of society into Eupatrids, Metics, and Slaves (Pomeroy, Burstein, Donlan, & Robert, 2004) to the contemporary divide between upper class, upper middle class, middle class, and lower class (Thompson & Hickey, 2005), from Indian caste systems (Dumont, 1966) to the Tuareg social order (Prasse, 1995), most human societies have been characterized by ranking systems with various degrees of steepness. The prevalence of hierarchy has been argued to stem, in large part, from its superior effectiveness in organizing groups of people (Leavitt, 2005) and in reducing uncertainty that arises from fear of social chaos (Milner, 1994). Next we define social hierarchy and detail the functions of hierarchical structures before delineating their relation to social status.

Defining Social Hierarchy and Status

Defining Social Hierarchy

Social hierarchy typically refers to the ordering of individuals or groups within a population according to material or immaterial dimensions that are accepted as status markers within this population (e.g., Anderson & Brown, 2010; Gruenfeld & Tiedens, 2010; Magee & Galinsky, 2008). While some hierarchical orderings are explicitly communicated (e.g., through visible social codes or clothing styles), others are implicitly communicated (e.g., through subtle signals or behaviors; Berger & Ward, 2010). This distinction is particularly important in consumption contexts in which consumers use both implicit and explicit status signals.

Why Social Hierarchies?

Social scientists have argued that the pervasiveness of hierarchical structures reflects the superior organizational benefits that hierarchies provide to their members in three respects: (1) facilitating collective decision making, (2) motivating members to contribute to group success, and (3) coordinating individual behaviors so that members work *together* toward collective success (Frank, 1985; Gruenfeld & Tiedens, 2010; Leavitt, 2005; Magee & Galinsky, 2008). Together, these benefits reduce the uncertainty and fears associated with social chaos (Milner, 1994).

Decision-Making Benefit

By handing control over the group's resources to a few and giving them the power to determine how to manage these resources, hierarchies minimize conflict over the control of resources and facilitate group decision making (Van Vugt, Kaiser, & Hogan, 2008). These advantages are particularly relevant when the decisions that groups face are complex, provided groups choose competent individuals with superior abilities to take the lead (Van Vugt, 2006).

Motivational Benefit

High ranks are typically associated with desirable attributes such as admiration, autonomy, power, social support, and well-being (Frank, 1985; Keltner, Van Kleef, Kraus, & Chen, 2008; Willer, 2009). Because high ranks are typically attributed to individuals who contribute the most in groups (Hardy & Van Vugt, 2006; Willer, 2009), hierarchical structures activate individuals' status motivation across the strata: individuals higher in the hierarchy who enjoy tangible and intangible benefits are motivated to maintain their status, while individuals lower in the hierarchy aspire to climb the social ladder and improve their ranking (Kim, Park, & Dubois, 2014).

Coordination Benefit

Hierarchies tend to heighten coordination within groups by facilitating communication and reducing conflict (Berger, Zelditch, & Rosenholtz, 1980; Durkheim, 1893/1997; Tiedens, Unzetta, & Young 2007) compared with groups that do not have hierarchies (Greer & Caruso, 2007). For instance, hierarchies improve group functioning by speeding up the flow and integration of information (Scott, 1998). In addition, hierarchical differentiation among individuals helps create perceptions of differentiation in competence and power, which ease the implementation of group decisions (Magee, 2009; Todorov, Mandisodza, Goren, & Hall 2005).

Contingency Theories

Importantly, the extent to which hierarchies yield group benefits is contingent on the nature of the task pursued and on the properties of the hierarchies (for a discussion, see Anderson & Brown, 2010). To illustrate, Pfeffer and Langton's

(1993) study of nearly twenty thousand faculty members in six hundred academic departments found that greater wage differentials within academic departments predicted lower (rather than higher) levels of research productivity (i.e., publications).

Defining Social Status

Social status represents one's rank in a hierarchy and typically reflects the extent to which one is respected or admired by others (e.g., Ridgeway & Walker, 1995). In sociology, status has been argued to represent, along with class and power, a key pillar of social stratification (Weber, 1946; for a discussion of power, see Chapter 12 of this handbook). Social status may be *ascribed* (i.e., predetermined) or *achieved* (i.e., attained through merit). Historically, status was primarily ascribed: it was either acquired by birth (e.g., depending on the cast into which one was born) or by ordainment (e.g., by monarchs). To regulate status differences, societies often adopted strict norms and policies, such as sumptuary laws in medieval Europe that prescribed how individuals of different social ranks should dress (Berry, 1994). From the eighteenth century onward, however, the view that status might be achieved through merit gained momentum as traditional autocratic structures started to give way to egalitarian ideals (De Botton, 2004).

The distinction between *ascribed* and *achieved* status is important because the way consumers think about rank determines their preferences and consumption habits. Indeed, the idea that people may be able to climb the social ladder – that is, that *status can be achieved* – opens the possibility for people to engage in conspicuous consumption (i.e., to trade up) and thereby signal their social progress relative to others (Dubois, Rucker, & Galinsky, 2012; Ordabayeva & Chandon, 2011; Rucker & Galinsky, 2008). In contrast, ascribed status may encourage status signaling aimed at reinforcing one's status (e.g., within their own social class). Echoing the distinction between status attainment and status maintenance, evolutionary psychologists typically distinguish between strategies aimed at increasing an individual's dominance (i.e., by means of fear, intimidation, and force imposed on others) and those that build one's prestige (i.e., by means of sharing expertise and gaining the respect of others; Cheng et al., 2013; Henrich & Gil-White, 2001).

Defining Status Signals

To signal one's social standing effectively to others, status signals need to possess several key characteristics. First, status signals need to be costly or difficult to obtain such that their acquisition serves as a credible signal of one's superior resources or ability (Nelissen & Meijers, 2011). Luxury homes, expensive cars, and exclusive jobs often serve as costly signals because they require exceptional resources or ability (Dubois & Duquesne, 1993; Plourde, 2008). Often, products or people become associated with status through competitive processes (e.g., an exam, high standards). For instance, fashion houses implement a competitive process to attract and retain models, and in doing so build their prestige (Godart & Mears, 2009).

Second, status signals have in many cases limited practical value. According to the theories of costly signaling (Bliege, Bird, & Smith, 2005; Cronk, 2005; Miller, 2009; Saad, 2007) and conspicuous consumption (Veblen, 1899/1994), status signals are most effective when the owner incurs the expense for no other purpose than displaying rank. As Thorstein Veblen (1899/1994) described in *The Theory of the Leisure Class*, "the utility of [conspicuous leisure and conspicuous consumption] for the purposes of reputability lies in the element of waste that is common to both. In the one case it is a waste of time and effort, in the other it is a waste of goods" (p. 53). For him, the term "waste" is used because such "expenditure does not serve human life or human well-being on the whole" (p. 60).

Third, status signals are typically visible or recognizable by the members of the social group to whom one wishes to signal his or her status. This often results in highly conspicuous status signals (e.g., items with prominent logos of luxury brands). Yet in some cases, inconspicuous items may also signal status to the few who can recognize them (e.g., luxury items with subtle or no brand logos are recognized and appreciated only by experts; Berger & Ward, 2010; Han, Nunez, & Drèze, 2010).

Finally, there needs to be agreement among the members of a hierarchy about the value of a status signal (Berger, Ho, & Joshi, 2011). To illustrate, a consumer carrying a luxury handbag is seen as high-status only if observers also share the view that this luxury handbag grants status. Put simply, status signals act as a carrier of status only when they appear *legitimate* to both senders and recipients and guide their actions accordingly (Podolny, 1993, 2005; Saunder, 2006; Schmid, Mast, & Hall, 2004).

Importantly, status signals may vary across different groups. As a result, although a few traits such as wealth (Godoy et al., 2007) or physical attractiveness (Langlois et al., 2000) are universally recognized as markers of status, status signals typically depend on group norms as well as situational and cultural factors.[2] For example, large body size was once equated with high status among Western nobility (Diamond, 1997) but lost this association over time, except in a few contemporary cultures (e.g., in the South Pacific; Thompson, Crowin, & Sargent, 1997). Today, depending on group norms and circumstances, status can be derived from factors as diverse as academic achievement, one's skills as a sea turtle hunter, and even the ability to drink a lot of beer.

Common to all status signals is their adoption and abandonment by group members. As soon as one dimension – a characteristic or a resource – becomes increasingly socially valuable (e.g., when it is adopted by desirable individuals or groups), individuals naturally and spontaneously differentiate hierarchically

---

2 Throughout this chapter, we adopt a broad view of status, whereby the markers of status in a social group can stem from a broad set of characteristics. However, it should be noted that other research streams, including research following Weber's (1946) view on status, may have alternative views of status, in which the markers of status are more narrowly defined.

along that dimension and adopt it as a status signal. One study found that consumers seek status through the consumption of either small or large food portions depending on which portion size is believed to convey status (i.e., served at high-end restaurants; Dubois, Galinsky, & Rucker, 2012). In turn, as soon as a dimension loses its social value (e.g., when undesirable individuals or groups adopt it or when it stops being scarce because everyone has access to it), people no longer seek to differentiate along that dimension, which leads to its eventual abandonment as a status signal (Berger & Heath, 2007; Berger, Ho, & Joshi, 2011; McCracken, 1988).

Consequences of Social Status and Hierarchy

Basic Consequences of Social Status

Recent research demonstrates that having or lacking status can have profound effects on social dynamics by shifting how senders and recipients of status signals think, feel, and behave (Kraus et al., 2012a). This section delineates the important consequences of social status in three domains: how one is attended to and valued by others, how one behaves toward others, and how one self-regulates.

Attention and Value from Others

High-status individuals, compared to low-status individuals, typically enjoy greater attention and respect from others. They command greater influence and compliance (Masling, Greer, & Gilmore, 1955; Nelson & Berry, 1965), attain a greater number of interaction partners (Hardy & Van Vugt, 2006), receive more help and support (Van der Vegt, Oosterhof, & Bunderson, 2006), have more opportunities to develop their skills (Blau, 1955), and receive more praise or credit for their performance and successes (Fan & Gruenfeld, 1998; Podolny, 2005). These advantages and social benefits stem from a perception that high-status individuals are more competent even when they actually lack relevant expertise (Anderson & Kilduff, 2009).

Self-Attention and Self-Value

Status transforms how individuals think about themselves vis-à-vis others, which in turn has important behavioral consequences. A large body of evidence suggests that high status leads individuals to focus more on self (vs. others) and consequently to behave in ways that prioritize their individual well-being, even if such behavior comes at the expense of others. Specifically, upper-class individuals react with less empathy to the suffering of others compared to lower-class individuals, and they allocate more resources to themselves than to others (Piff et al., 2010; Stellar, Manzo, Kraus, & Keltner, 2012). In one study, participants who were induced to experience upper social rank (compared to lower social rank) believed that a smaller percentage of people's annual salary should be spent on charitable donations ($M = 2.95$ vs. 4.65 percent of annual income for high and low social rank, respectively) and reported trusting others less. However, this effect diminished when participants were primed to feel compassion, suggesting that high status may buffer individuals from being empathetic toward others (Piff et al., 2010).

Self-Regulation and Stress

Status affects individuals' ability to self-regulate, especially in domains where competency is challenged. For instance, low SES students, but not high SES students, consumed more candy after talking about their recent academic success (Johnson, Finkel, & Richeson, 2011). Given the inherently social nature of the process through which status is determined, one possibility is that individuals at the lower end of the strata feel rejected. Feelings of rejection in turn increase one's level of progesterone, which reflects the strength of an individual's motivation for social affiliation (Maner, Eckel, Schmidt, & Miller, 2010).

Basic Consequences of Social Hierarchy

How social hierarchies influence individuals' thoughts, feelings, and behaviors has been the subject of much debate across social sciences. In line with the subject matter of this chapter, here we focus on the consequences of social hierarchies' key characteristics for status competition.

Hierarchy Shape

Two key factors – the steepness of a hierarchy and the level of separation among its members – profoundly affect the extent to which individuals compete for status (Frank, 2007; Hopkins & Kornienko, 2004; Wilkinson & Pickett, 2010). The steepness of a hierarchy represents how densely or sparsely individuals are distributed across different tiers; the level of separation represents how far apart these tiers are from one another. Several studies have suggested that status competition intensifies as the hierarchy becomes steeper and the gap between top tiers and the rest of the hierarchy widens (Bagwell & Bernheim, 1996; Frank, 2007). This is because, as the top tiers of the hierarchy grow more distant, they enjoy a disproportionate share of status benefits, while those in bottom tiers fall behind and try to keep up through status spending (Christen & Morgan, 2005; Frank & Cook, 1995; Ireland, 1994). However, other work suggests that *reducing* gaps across tiers may also increase status spending, especially within lower tiers, because stacking individuals closer together increases the proportion of others who one can surpass by investing in status (Hopkins & Kornienko, 2004; Ordabayeva & Chandon, 2011).

Hierarchy Stability

Stability represents the extent and speed at which positions of high and low status in the hierarchy change over time (Sligte, Nijstad, & de Dreu, 2011; Tajfel, 1984; Tetlock, 1981). Stability of a social hierarchy significantly influences the nature of status competition. Stable hierarchies make it difficult for any individual or group to influence the pecking order. As a result, stable hierarchies often adopt views, laws, and policies that justify inequality and prevent status mobility. Notably, these laws reflect the view, prevalent during the Middle Ages, that everyone has a "natural" place and function in society, just as each organ in the body serves a unique function (de Botton, 2004, describing John of Salisbury's *Policraticus,* 1159). In contrast, unstable hierarchies increase high-status individuals' need to protect their privileged position (Tetlock, 1981) and to signal their status in response to potential threats of losing high status (Faddegon, Scheepers, & Ellemers, 2008). Studies of primate behaviors show that high-status primates placed in unstable hierarchies experience elevated levels of stress and health problems such as atherosclerosis (Sapolsky, 2005). Unstable hierarchies also increase low-status individuals' motivation to spend energy and resources on attaining and signaling higher status. Indeed, status competition has intensified continuously since societies adopted the principles of egalitarianism and meritocracy in the Age of Enlightenment, and most social hierarchies have grown more volatile and mobile (de Botton, 2004; Han, Nunez, & Drèze, 2010).

Hierarchy Origin
Social hierarchies vary in how they emerge and in how status is assigned to individuals or groups – through random generation (luck) or effort (de Botton, 2004). In turn, this influences what people think about hierarchies as well as their preferred organization. Specifically, randomly generated hierarchies are deemed unjust, and they fuel the desire to restore justice through redistribution of status benefits. As a result, individuals are more likely to favor policies that challenge and even penalize high-status members through measures such as taxation in randomly generated status distributions than in effort-based distributions (Zizzo & Oswald, 2001). Interestingly, beliefs about the origin and fairness of distribution vary by culture and may explain some cross-cultural differences in preferences for policies related to status competition. For example, people in the United States favor the view that one can earn his or her way to the top through effort, while those in France take the view that the most likely way to reach the top is by luck (e.g., birth, marriage, or lottery). This in part explains the greater support for redistribution policies, such as progressive income taxes, observed in France compared to the United States (Frank, Maddux, & Wertenbroch, 2013). Still, research on perceptions of the origins of social hierarchies as well as their influence on status competition is in its infancy.

Status Consumption in the Marketplace

Although marketing scholars have long recognized the influence of status motives on what, why, and how people buy (Levy, 1959), as illustrated at the outset of this chapter and in Figure 13.1 and Table 13.1, the relative amount of research in marketing on how status impacts consumer behavior is substantially smaller compared to other disciplines. Nonetheless, the presence of research on status consumption in marketing suggests that the time may be ripe for the field to expand this exploration. In this section, we define status consumption and review the findings on forms and functions of status consumption. We then delineate the psychological, social, and economic antecedents, as well as consequences of status consumption.

Forms and Functions of Status Consumption

We define status consumption as the acquisition, display, and/or use of items, behaviors, or attributes (e.g., sound or taste) that are implicitly or explicitly associated with a position in the social hierarchy. Status signals can be associated with low status or high status. For instance, talking in slang may be a signal of low status because the vocabulary is typically associated with low-ranked individuals. In contrast, wearing expensive jewelry may signal high status, and is therefore purchased and exhibited as such.

Forms of Status Consumption

Status consumption can take various forms. Consistent with the notion that status signals must often meet one or several criteria outlined previously (i.e., expensiveness, exclusivity, visibility, limited practicality, and identical interpretation by observers) in order to be deemed valuable, marketing researchers' investigation of status signals has focused on the specific product categories, items, and behaviors that are most associated with these characteristics. In the following subsections, we outline the main forms of status consumption that received attention in the literature.

Product Categories and Brands
A primary means of status consumption is the purchase and display of luxury products. Existing studies have particularly focused on categories such as cars (Griskevicius et al., 2007; Piff et al., 2011), homes (Solnick & Hemenway, 1998), luxury apparel (Ordabayeva & Chandon, 2011), accessories (Han, Nunes, & Drèze, 2010; Wilcox, Kim, & Sen, 2009), visible personal care items (Hill et al., 2012), electronics, and home decoration (Griskevicius, Tybur, & Van den Bergh, 2010). The consumption of high-end products and brands in these categories (e.g., those affiliated with top fashion houses and designers) is construed as a manifestation of status seeking, while the consumption of mass-produced brands (e.g., those often marketed at chain stores) is construed as a sign of little interest in status.

Product Attributes
In addition to product categories and brands, certain product attributes are naturally associated with status and can contribute to signaling high status alone or in combination.

Price

Premium price is typically associated with high status, while regular or low price is typically associated with low status. Indeed, an item's expensiveness credibly signals the buyer's ability to spend large amounts of resources. As such, the inclusion of price information in studies is often used to establish the status value of products (Griskevicius, Tybur, & Van den Bergh, 2010).

Size

Large size is typically associated with high status. For instance, in many species, dominant and high-status individuals are also larger in size (Sapolsky, 2005). In consumer settings, large size symbolizes status in many product categories, including homes, cars, and even food. For instance, Solnick and Hemenway (1998) showed that it is not just having a large home but having a larger home than one's neighbors that signals high status. However, recent evidence suggests that associations between size and status can be contextually constructed. Dubois, Galinsky, and Rucker (2011) found that low-status individuals typically choose larger snacks, as these are associated with greater status, resulting in greater calorie intake. In contrast, when the size-to-status relationship is negative (i.e., when smaller sizes are explicitly associated with high status), low-status consumers turn to small portion sizes to seek status, suggesting that cultural or contextual norms may change how people interpret size to infer high or low status.

In some contexts, large size may naturally signal low status. For instance, Han, Nunez, and Drèze (2010) coded the size of brand logos displayed on handbags of famous luxury brands (Chanel, Louis Vuitton, Gucci) and correlated logo size with product price. The results showed that, on average, an increase in logo size of one point on a seven-point (subjective) scale translated to a $122.26 price decrease for Gucci handbags and a $26.27 price decrease for Louis Vuitton handbags. Additional studies revealed that while low-status individuals choose and display products with large brand logos, high-status individuals recognize and prefer products with small or even no brand logos (Berger & Ward, 2010).

Group Membership

Consumers can derive status from their membership in communities and groups such as companies' loyalty programs. Significant investment in products allows individuals to climb the hierarchy and to enjoy the prestige and benefits that come with being a loyal customer, one of the benefits being the public display of preferential treatment relative to other (less loyal) consumers. Consumers prefer to attain and display their loyalty even if it does not yield any tangible benefits and instead yields tangible costs. For example, Ivanic and Nunes (2009) found that elite members of an airline's frequent flyer program preferred to stand in the elite line to board an airplane even when it was significantly longer and more time consuming than the regular line.

Disconformity

Individuals can signal status by displaying nonconforming consumption behaviors. For example, Belleza, Gino, and Keinan (2014) found that observers may ascribe high status to individuals who wear nonconforming clothes or engage in nonconforming behaviors (e.g., when an instructor wears red sneakers to teach a class at an elite institution). However, this happens only when individuals who display disconformity are considered to be part of an in-group. To illustrate, in one study conducted in Milan, the researchers found that shop assistants at luxury boutiques (members of an in-group) thought a potential client entering the store in gym clothes was more likely to be a VIP or a celebrity compared to someone wearing a suit. This is because shop assistants assumed nonconforming behavior signaled a consumer's autonomy and consequently greater status and competence. However, out-group members (i.e., regular pedestrians) did not share this assumption of status.

Roles of Status Consumption

Status consumption has a number of important roles. It enables individuals to associate with desirable groups, dissociate from undesirable groups, compensate for various psychological threats, and reduce the uncertainty in social and economic interactions. We briefly define each of these roles and elaborate on these in more detail in the subsections that follow.

Associative Role

Status consumption has been suggested to serve a bonding function (Aspers & Godart, 2013). That is, by imitating the status consumption behaviors of (desirable) individuals, the psychological tensions among individuals may decrease and individuals may be accepted as part of a social group or a community (Simmel, 1904/1957). Status consumption can thus facilitate the construction of social groups and inhibit the tensions within them.

Dissociative Role

Status consumption also has a dissociative role, as it helps individuals to signal how they are different from other (undesirable) groups in the social hierarchy (Bourdieu, 1984). For instance, Han, Nunes, and Drèze (2010) suggest that parvenus (defined as individuals with both high wealth and high need for status) use conspicuous products (with large logos) to dissociate themselves from individuals who have less wealth. Berger and Heath (2008) found that individuals try to dissociate from low-status groups (e.g., geeks) by abandoning the products that those groups consume.

Compensatory Role

A growing body of research suggests that status consumption helps individuals alleviate aversive psychological states such as the experience of low esteem or low power. For instance, Rucker and Galinsky (2008) found that consumers whose sense of power had been threatened were willing to pay more money for status-enhancing items relative to nonthreatened individuals. Exposure to threatening cues (related to economic recession and scarcity) boosts compensation through status consumption, and this tendency is more pronounced among certain individuals (e.g., those who grew up in unstable homes with low income; Griskevicius, Delton, Tybur, & Robertson, 2011).

Uncertainty Reduction

Finally, status signals reduce the uncertainty associated with a transaction or an interaction (e.g., Bothner, Podolny, & Smith, 2011). That is, status signals (e.g., a high price or an exclusive certification) grant additional informational value to a product or a service. This is particularly relevant in domains (such as wine or banking) where a high price or a prestigious award can partly compensate for consumers' inexperience in the domain and thereby encourage a preference for certain brands over others. For example, a customer might decide to contract a loan with a prestigious bank rather than a local bank due to the former's public image, even if the rates offered are similar (Podolny, 2005).

Antecedents of Status Consumption

Psychological Factors

Existing research on status consumption has mostly focused on how threats to one's self-concept or important goals (e.g., mating goal) affect status consumption. Self-threats can occur in a variety of domains (e.g., academic or economic performance) when one's position or performance is inferior to others, or when one is reminded of the difficulty to achieve a goal. When faced with threats, individuals experience psychological discomfort and use status consumption as a means to compensate (for reviews, see Lee & Shrum, 2013; Rucker & Galinsky, 2013). Underlying this tendency is the assumption that consuming status items can "buy" resources either to restore one's self-image or to replenish one's resources (e.g., to get access to reproductive opportunities). In the following subsections, we outline the role of specific self-threats.

Power Threat

A key driver of status consumption is a threat to one's sense of power (or asymmetric control over resources in social relationships; Rucker, Dubois, & Galinsky, 2011; Rucker, Galinksy, & Dubois. 2012). In a series of studies, Rucker and Galinsky (2008, 2009) showed that acquiring status-related items serves as a means to compensate for a lost sense of power. The authors manipulated participants' sense of power in a variety of ways (e.g., by instructing participants to recall a time they had power or lacked power, by assigning them to the role of a subordinate or a boss) and found that low-power individuals were willing to pay more for high-status products (e.g., a silk tie, a fur coat). However, no differences were observed for products that had no association with status (e.g., a washing machine, a ballpoint pen) compared to the baseline and the high-power conditions. Similarly, research found that certain ethnic minorities (e.g., Blacks and Hispanics) who occupy a lower position in the social hierarchy relative to the white majority often spend a greater percentage of their budget on conspicuous, visible items such as clothing, jewelry, and cars (Charles, Hurst, & Roussanov, 2009; Fontes & Fan, 2006; Ivanic, Overbeck, & Nunes, 2011). This occurs even after controlling for income disparities across populations and seems to be particularly pronounced when race is explicitly activated (i.e., when individuals are induced to think of negative race stereotypes; Ivanic, Overbeck, & Nunes, 2011).

Existential Threat

Exposing individuals to existential threats by reminding them of their mortality creates an aversive psychological state that leads them to reaffirm their cultural worldview, belief in their worth, and contribution to their culture (for a review, see Pyszczynski, Greenberg, & Solomon, 1999). One key response to such threats is status consumption (Arndt, Solomon, Kasser, & Sheldon, 2004; Burroughs et al., 2013; Mandel & Heine, 1999) because this signals that an individual is someone of value and worth to society as a whole. Consistent with this idea, Mandel and Heine (1999) found that making participants' mortality salient made them more receptive to status-enhancing products (e.g., a Rolex watch) but not to status-neutral products (e.g., Pringles potato chips).

Mating Threat

Status consumption may emerge in response to individuals' mating motives (for a review, see Chapter 5 in this handbook). For example, studies have demonstrated that activating mating goals among men increases their desire for luxury products – consistent with the notion that high-status products may facilitate reproductive opportunities (e.g., Hill et al., 2012; Griskevicius et al., 2007). Importantly, recent studies indicate that status signaling is particularly strong when individuals' mating prospects are threatened. For example, women engage in greater status consumption when their mating prospects are threatened by external economic conditions (Hill et al., 2012) or by the presence of other women (Wang & Griskevicius, 2014). Similarly, men turn to status consumption when their mating opportunities are endangered by the presence of many (vs. few) male competitors (Griskevicius et al., 2012).

Other Threats

A number of studies have documented that status consumption may also emerge as a result of various personal threats. Specifically, threats that individuals experience when growing up, such as parents' divorce (Rindfleisch, Burroughs, & Denton, 1997) or limited financial resources (Griskevicius et al., 2011), can enhance individuals' status-seeking behaviors. Furthermore, chronic as well as experimentally induced threats to one's sense of self-worth and social connections can trigger similar effects (Burroughs & Rindfleisch, 2012;

Chang & Arkin, 2002; Rindfleish, Burroughs, & Wong, 2009). For instance, Lee and Shrum (2012) showed that social exclusion may lead to greater status consumption but only when exclusion stems from being ignored (rather than rejected). This is because being ignored poses a threat to one's efficacy needs, which in turn motivates people to restore efficacy through status consumption (e.g., the acquisition of products with prominent brand logos). On the other hand, being rejected poses a threat to one's relational needs, which motivates people to restore social connections through pro-social acts.

Social Factors

Given the social nature of status competition, a key set of drivers of status consumption stem from social factors – those related to the characteristics of social groups and the nature of individuals' interactions with their social environment.

Presence of Others

The presence of others is a key precursor to status consumption because such consumption can signal one's relative rank only if others can observe it and agree on its meaning. To validate this assumption, a number of studies manipulated the private or public nature of the consumption environment in a hypothetical or a real setting and found that status consumption was more likely to occur in public, as opposed to private, settings (Berger & Heath, 2008; Dubois, Galinsky, & Rucker, 2012; Griskevicius, Tybur, & Van den Bergh, 2010). For example, Dubois, Galinsky, and Rucker (2012) assessed participants' preference for status products in three contexts with varying social presence (i.e., at home alone [private condition]; by oneself in public at a restaurant [public condition]; or at home with friends [social condition]), and found that the more social the consumption context, the more consumers preferred status products.

Relevance of Others

The identity of observers is another key determinant of status consumption. Specifically, consistent with social comparison theory (Festinger, 1954), status consumption is the highest in the presence of observers who are relevant to one's social identity. This means that individuals are more competitive in the presence of similar others. For example, in a series of studies conducted by Mandel, Petrova, and Cialdini (2006), undergraduate students compared themselves to students enrolled in either the same major or a different major. The results showed that preferences for status-enhancing luxury products were the strongest in the presence of others with the same (vs. different) major.

Furthermore, individuals engage in status consumption only when observers have a desirable identity (i.e., those whom one wishes to impress or with whom one wishes to affiliate). In a romantic context, this means that individuals will signal status in the presence of potential mates (Griskevicius et al., 2007). In a more general consumption context, status signals are adopted only when desirable groups (e.g., the "cool" kids on campus or members of an upper class) start using them (Berger & Heath, 2008; Han, Nunes, & Drèze, 2010), and they are abandoned when undesirable groups (e.g., the geeks on campus or members of a lower class) follow suit (Berger & Heath, 2008; Berger, Ho, & Joshi, 2011).

Finally, individuals are more likely to engage in status consumption when they are in a competitive social environment. To demonstrate this, Ordabayeva and Chandon (2011) asked participants to imagine that they were going to dinner with rival co-workers or childhood friends; they found that preferences for status-enhancing restaurants were the strongest when participants thought of rivals (vs. friends).

Number of others

The number of competitors affects the intensity of status competition and the amount of satisfaction that individuals derive from outcompeting others. Griskevicius and colleagues (2012) observed that a high proportion of men relative to women in various contexts increased status consumption (of categories such as jewelry and dining out). In a different set of experiments, Drèze and Nunes (2009) varied the number of status tiers in a consumption hierarchy (e.g., a frequent flyer program) and the number of people present in each tier. They found that those at the top of the hierarchy felt the most special when the number of tiers in the hierarchy as well as the number of people in the tier immediately below them was maximized. Finally, the number of observers influences how quickly status signals are adopted or abandoned. It seems that individuals are more likely to abandon status or identity signals when these are adopted by a large rather than a small number of individuals (Berger & Heath, 2007, 2008). This effect does not occur in product categories with little status value.

Economic Factors

The final set of drivers of status competition pertains to the characteristics of the economic environment. Specifically, a growing body of evidence underlines the importance of individuals' economic resources, economic expectations, and the degree of economic inequality.

Economic Resources

Inspired by Veblen, Duesenberry (1949) initiated a discussion about the economic precursors of status consumption (which he called "demonstration effects"). He argued that status consumption should increase with one's percentile or rank in the social hierarchy due to the greater economic resources available to those at the top compared to those at the bottom. More recently, researchers have qualified this prediction by demonstrating that status consumption can occur at all tiers in the hierarchy (Bloch, Rao, & Desai 2004; Moav & Neeman, 2008). In fact, individuals with scarce resources tend to allocate a greater percentage of their budget to status consumption than those with abundant resources (Bagwell & Bernheim, 1996; Dynan, Skinner, &

Zeldes, 2004). Researchers have argued that economically deprived individuals and households invest in status consumption because they do not want to fall behind others and lose face. Examples of such behavior are prevalent in many contexts. In the United States, members of certain ethnic minorities that have historically had limited access to economic resources are willing to pay more for status-enhancing products (Charles, Hurst, & Roussanov, 2009; Ivanic, Overbeck, & Nunes, 2011). Interestingly, merely remembering one's past deprivation (Griskevicius et al., 2011) or temporarily manipulating financial deprivation in an experimental setting (Ordabayeva & Chandon, 2011; Sharma & Alter, 2012) produced similar consequences.

Economic Expectations

The availability of resources at the societal level influences status consumption by shaping consumers' expectations of their economic well-being. Researchers have noted that as Western economies grew more prosperous over the past several decades, individuals have raised their level of aspiration and standards of living through the acquisition of status possessions (Kamakura & Du, 2012; Scitovsky, 1992). For example, Kamakura and Du (2012) reported that in the period spanning 1982 to 2003, spending on status-enhancing (positional) purchases such as apparel, jewelry and watches consistently grew during periods of economic expansion but shrunk during recessions. Recent findings suggest that economic downturns can also activate a need to engage in status consumption in certain product categories or populations. For instance, when Hill and colleagues (2012) measured women's interest in status-enhancing products and status-neutral products during recessionary periods or in the presence of recessionary (vs. neutral) cues in the lab, they found that women were more interested in conspicuous products in recessionary environments, because such products could potentially help them procure a better mate (at a time when high-status mates are scarce).

Economic Inequality

A final economic factor that shapes status competition is the distribution of economic resources in society. Analyses of secondary data and analytical models have found a positive link between status consumption and inequality of wealth or income in Western societies (e.g., Alpizar, Carlsson, & Johansson-Stenman, 2005; Clark & Oswald, 1998; Knell, 1999). To explain this link, researchers have argued that, as gaps across different tiers in the hierarchy become wider and high-status individuals pull away from the rest of the population, individuals at the low end of the hierarchy fall behind and use status consumption as a way to "keep up with the Joneses" (Christen & Morgan, 2005; Dupor & Liu, 2003; Frank, 1985). Recent studies, however, suggest that the role of inequality may be more nuanced. In a series of experiments, Ordabayeva and Chandon (2011) found that reducing inequality may increase, rather than decrease, status consumption among bottom-tier consumers, because by stacking people closer together, boosting equality increases the number of people that one can surpass through spending. Similarly, Hopkins and Kornienko (2004) used an analytical model to suggest that boosting equality might reduce the proportion of people stacked in the bottom tier and thereby leave bottom-tier consumers even further behind.

Consequences of Status Consumption

A large body of research testifies that having status deeply permeates consumer behavior. Earlier sections of this chapter outlined the broad consequences of having high or low social status. In this section, we focus on the specific implications of status *consumption* for consumers' feelings, behaviors, social interactions, and economic outcomes. Individuals engage in status consumption in pursuit of a host of tangible and intangible benefits (Huberman, Loch, & Onculer, 2004; Ivanic & Nunes, 2009). Status consumption therefore has important psychological, social, and economic consequences for individuals and groups, as well as society at large.

Psychological Consequences

Having status can have important psychological consequences for how individuals feel and behave.

Consumer Empowerment
Merely wearing status signals can provide a means of empowerment. Indeed, if they offer a way to climb the social ladder, people might wear status signals to transform how they feel and behave. Supporting this proposition, Dubois and Anik (2014) had women wear high heels or normal clothes and varied whether participants were in the presence of a female confederate, a male confederate, or no one. The results revealed that women wearing high heels exhibited greater action orientation, demonstrated greater abstraction, and took more risks (three measures associated with high power; Huang, Galinsky, Gruenfeld, & Guillory, 2011) compared to those wearing flat shoes. However, this happened only in the presence of another person, pointing to the social nature of social status.

Ethical Behavior
Recent research suggests that having status – as reflected in individuals' social class or possessions of status-enhancing items such as cars – can make people greedier and, as a result, boost their unethical behavior (Piff et al., 2011). The researchers assigned participants to high- and low-power roles or measured their status and repeatedly found that high-status individuals engaged more in cheating or lying behaviors than low-status individuals. Low status can also increase unethical behavior, especially when people feel devalued. For instance, Fast, Havely and Galinsky (2011) showed that people lacking status were more demeaning toward others because they felt disrespected and unappreciated, and

they engaged in aggressive compensatory behaviors aimed at boosting self-worth (Bushman & Baumeister, 1998; Henry, 2009).

Psychological and Physical Well-being

A large literature suggests that social status can have profound consequences for physiology and illness (for a review, see Marmot, 2004; Rivers & Josephs, 2010). For instance, Marmot and colleagues (1991) conducted a longitudinal study examining civil servants in the UK and found that their rank in the hierarchy significantly and negatively predicted their life expectancy, after controlling for variables such as predisposition, income, and education. One of the key drivers of the effect of status on health lies in the status-induced changes in levels of testosterone and cortisol, two hormones that shape physiology and behavior by regulating bodily functions. Both correlational (Lincoln, Guinness, & Short, 1972; Nelson, Pine, Leibenluft, & McClure, 2005) as well as experimental (Boksem et al., 2004; Christiansen, 1998) studies of male and female human and nonhuman participants found that high levels of testosterone are positively related to behaviors intended to achieve, maintain, or enhance status in the social hierarchy.

Social Consequences

Status consumption has important implications for consumers' social interactions and social well-being.

Social Interactions

Research suggests that status consumption changes the mindset that individuals adopt in their interactions with others. Ample evidence has shown that attaining or priming high (vs. low) status leads individuals to focus more on self (vs. others) in social interactions. Specifically, attaining high status can lead people to maximize their self-interest, even if it comes at the expense of others (Piff et al., 2011). For example, Piff and colleagues (2011) reported that drivers of high-status vehicles were more likely to cut off other drivers and pedestrians on the road than the drivers of low-status vehicles. In a different study, Chua and Zou (2009) exposed people to high-status or low-status products and found that exposure to high-status (vs. low-status) products led to a greater likelihood that individuals endorsed profit-maximizing business actions that could hurt the welfare of others (e.g., selling a new car that pollutes the environment).

Social Perceptions

Status consumption significantly shapes perceptions of individuals by others. Overall, people have a general tendency to ascribe extrinsic and self-interested motives to individuals who engage in high-status consumption compared to those who engage in status-neutral or experiential consumption. For example, Van Boven, Campbell, and Gilovich (2010) asked people to evaluate hypothetical individuals who engaged in status-seeking consumption (e.g., spending money on jewelry and apparel) or experiential consumption (e.g., spending on skiing and dining). The results showed that participants ascribed extrinsic motives and unfavorable traits (e.g., insecurity, selfishness) to status-seeking consumers, but intrinsic motives and favorable traits (e.g., open-mindedness, friendliness, intelligence) to experiential consumers. These conclusions were further supported by a recent study (Ferraro, Kirmani, & Matherly, 2013), in which participants first viewed the videos or pictures of a conspicuous or an inconspicuous stimulus (brand or consumer) and then indicated their attitudes toward the stimulus. Evaluations of the stimulus were less favorable in the conspicuous than in the inconspicuous condition.

Other findings, however, suggest that status consumption may also sometimes yield positive social perceptions, depending on context (e.g., Nelissen & Meijers, 2011). Specifically, the display of status consumption may be evaluated more positively in social interactions guided by exchange norms (e.g., when a service provider offers a good value for money and fosters a fair exchange with clients) compared to those guided by communal norms (e.g., when a service provider takes a personal interest in clients and fosters a harmonious working relationship with clients; Scott, Mende, & Bolton, 2013). This is because in exchange relationships, status consumption signals an individual's competence, while in communal relationships it signals an individual's lack of warmth.

Social Cohesion

Status disparity and consumption may influence social cohesion. Recent evidence has revealed that great disparity between the highest and the lowest levels of status in a given population can contribute to lower social cohesion, greater violence, and weaker trust among individuals (Wilkinson & Pickett, 2010). Some have even argued that low cohesion resulting from status disparity may contribute to ill health due to the association of low social status with such factors as weak social support and childhood attachment.

However, new studies suggest that status consumption can promote social connection when the benefits of high status extend to the members of the social group – a phenomenon referred to as the "entourage effect" (McFerran & Argo, 2013). In a series of experiments, researchers granted preferential treatment to randomly selected individuals at a real event (e.g., watching a sports game from a stadium's luxury box) or in a hypothetical scenario (e.g., imagining obtaining exclusive tickets to dinner with an admired political figure). Preferential treatment boosted participants' feeling of exclusivity and status more when they were allowed to bring along the members of their social group, and this happened due to the greater feeling of connection that participants felt with their group in the course of the exclusive experience.

Economic Consequences

Since the procurement of favorable economic outcomes is one of the prime rationales for status attainment and maintenance, it is not surprising that status consumption can also have important economic consequences for individuals, firms, and society at large.

Individual Outcomes

At the individual level, the consumption and display of status-enhancing products may lead to positive economic outcomes such as higher financial compensation, greater compliance, and favorable outcomes in negotiations. To illustrate, in several studies (Nelissen & Meijers, 2011), a confederate who wore a T-shirt either with a status-enhancing logo (Lacoste) or a status-neutral logo (Slazenger) approached participants with a series of requests (e.g., to fill in a survey, to make a hiring decision, to donate money to a charitable cause). The results revealed a higher agreement rate to fill in the survey (52.2 percent vs. 13.6 percent), higher financial compensation for a potential hire (€ 9.14 vs. € 8.36 per hour), and higher donation amounts (55 percent higher) when the confederate displayed a status-enhancing (vs. a status-neutral) logo. In a different experiment involving a market exchange, high-status sellers were able to set higher prices, and high-status buyers were able to obtain lower prices for a product than their low-status counterparts (Ball, Eckel, Grossman, & Zame, 2001). This happened regardless of whether status was publicly earned as a result of effort or assigned in a random draw.

Company Outcomes

Consumers' status motives can have significant implications for companies' economic outcomes. Since the ability to pay a premium for products is one of the ways in which consumers signal their status, the demand for status-enhancing products tends to increase with price (Amaldoss & Jain, 2005; Chao & Shor, 1998). This phenomenon (referred to as the "Veblen effect") allows companies to make significant margins from status-enhancing products, but only in the presence of both desirable opinion leaders (referred to as "snobs") who adopt these products and followers who are willing to imitate them in the marketplace (Amaldoss & Jain, 2005; Leibenstein, 1950). Notably, status can improve creativity inside companies, as high-status firms benefit from consumers' greater tolerance of their mistakes (Godart, Shipilov, & Claes, 2014).

It is important, however, for companies to track the balance of opinion leaders against followers who adopt their products, because excessive prevalence of high-status products among low-status individuals may have serious economic implications. On the one hand, it may dilute brand associations and brands' signaling value, which may lead to their abandonment by opinion leaders (Berger & Heath, 2008). On the other hand, the adoption of status-enhancing products by low-status individuals may make other consumers feel they have fallen behind and thereby increase public interest in these products (Shalev & Morwitz, 2012). Similarly, producers of status-enhancing products should carefully manage their portfolio of products since the presence of entry-level low-investment items (e.g., keychains, wallets) may change individuals' willingness to purchase high-ticket items (e.g., handbags; Patrick & Prokopec,

2012). Whereas the presence of entry-level status items enhances loyal customers' willingness to invest in the high-ticket items of the same brand, it deters occasional buyers from investing in high-ticket items since entry-level items satisfy these consumers' need for status.

Societal Outcomes

Status consumption has several important positive as well as negative consequences for economic outcomes at the societal level, both positive and negative. One the one hand, increases in status consumption are correlated with negative economic outcomes such as rising household debt, bankruptcy, and dissaving observed in Western societies (Christen & Morgan, 2005; Frank, 1985; Zhu, 2012). For example, Christen and Morgan (2005) have reported that the rise in household debt over the past several decades has been propelled significantly by the rise in nonrevolving debt (installment loans), which is often used to finance the purchase of status-enhancing products such as consumer durables.

On the other hand, status consumption can yield positive economic outcomes. For example, activating status concerns may promote sustainable consumption. In a series of experiments, Griskevicius, Tybur, and Van den Bergh (2010) showed that activating a status-seeking mindset by asking participants to imagine starting a new high-status job could boost subsequent preferences for sustainable products. This suggests that sustainable consumption may also serve as a status signal, and hence shifting the focus of status competition to sustainable consumption may promote sustainability and long-term economic well-being. Similarly, encouraging status competition by highlighting upward social comparisons in the domain of saving can boost collective levels of saving (Stilley, Winterich, & Nenkov, 2011).

Directions for Future Research on Status Consumption

We hope that the research on status reviewed in this chapter will spark the interest of young and seasoned scholars alike. This last section aims to identify key research questions that will further deepen our understanding of the role of status in marketing. In particular, we stress several avenues that future research can pursue in order to further examine the role of status at the micro level (how status affects consumer psychology) and at the macro level (how companies can manage status).

Psychology of Status

Identifying Forms of Status Consumption

Although studies often converge on their definition of status signals and consumption, many questions related to the very nature of status remain unanswered. It is clear that status is a multifaceted construct, and that status signals span a diverse set of behaviors (e.g., nonconforming behavior; Belleza, Gino, & Keinan, 2014), events (e.g., weddings, funerals; Banerjee & Duflo, 2007; Economist, 2007), activities and ideas (Veblen, 1899/1994). Yet the bulk of existing research has focused on a limited set of attributes and connotations of status consumption while overlooking how and why status signals vary across contexts and over time (but see Dubois, Czellar, & Laurent, 2005, for a cross-cultural study of attitudes toward luxury). For instance, luxury items can be purchased for utilitarian qualities (e.g., durability vs. status), enjoyed in private (vs. in public; Rucker & Galinsky, 2009), and in certain contexts they may signal low (vs. high) status (Griskevisius, Tybur, & Van den Bergh, 2010). We encourage future work to broaden the interpretations and operationalizations of status consumption used in the literature. Similarly, little is known about how individuals attribute status to specific items or behaviors. We believe it is important for future research to continue uncovering the different forms of status consumption and to identify mechanisms that lead to the legitimation and the delegitimation of various forms of status consumption.

Although several key defining dimensions of status signals have been identified (expensiveness, scarcity, visibility, limited practicality, and identical interpretation), little is known about how and why these dimensions might be differentially appealing to distinct audiences. Recent research suggests that various socioeconomic or cultural factors may affect the relative importance of each of these variables. For instance, one might predict that scarcity is a particularly effective signal of status for an audience of the financially deprived (Sharma & Alter, 2012). Studies also suggest that when one's power is threatened, the conspicuousness of items is positively associated with status (Dubois, Galinsky, & Rucker, 2012; Mazzocco, Galinsky, Rucker, & Anderson, 2012). Research has also suggested two distinct routes through which status can be attained or maintained: dominance and prestige (Cheng et al., 2013; Henrich & Gil-White, 2001). Yet little is known about when dominance versus prestige might be more effective at conveying status and why. We propose that future research efforts should be launched to disentangle the different status dimensions and to better understand how products acquire status associations in different populations and situations.

Roles of Status Consumption

As reviewed earlier in this chapter, one of the prime roles of status consumption is signaling status vis-à-vis others (desirable and undesirable social groups). Yet recent findings suggest that signaling is not only a social phenomenon; individuals may engage in certain behaviors to signal their favorable identity *to themselves* (Bodner & Prelec, 2003; Prelec & Bodner, 2003). For example, Dhar and Wertenbroch (2012) found that consumers derive greater utility from being able to signal to themselves their ability to withstand temptation by choosing a healthy food item from a mixed set (containing healthy and unhealthy options) compared to a homogeneous set (containing only healthy options). This raises an interesting question of whether consumers use certain strategies (behaviors or products) to elevate their status in their own (rather than others') eyes. It would be interesting for future research to explore whether, why, and when self status-signaling occurs and how it is different from social status-signaling.

Antecedents and Consequences of Status Consumption

Previous sections of this chapter have identified various antecedents of status consumption. While a considerable amount of effort has been directed at understanding the psychological, economic, and social drivers of status consumption, little is known about its cultural determinants. According to Hofstede's (1980) framework, cultures can be classified with respect to four basic dimensions: individualism or collectivism (the degree to which a culture reinforces individual or collective achievement and interpersonal relationships), power distance (the degree to which the social hierarchy and inequality are accepted in society), uncertainty avoidance (the level of acceptance of uncertainty and ambiguity in society), and masculinity (the degree of gender differentiation and reinforcement of gender roles in society). Among these dimensions, power distance is the most relevant for individuals' perceptions of and behaviors within the social hierarchy, with greater regard for hierarchy observed in high (vs. low) power distance cultures (Shavitt, Lalwani, Zhang, & Torelli, 2006). It is therefore likely that signaling status is more prevalent, visible, and elaborate in cultures with high (vs. low) power distance.

Likewise, the individualism (vs. collectivism) of a culture may have a strong influence on status consumption. Status consumption may be higher in individualist (vs. collectivist) cultures due to individuals' greater focus on self-enhancement (Gardner, Lee, & Gabriel, 1999; Markus & Kitayama, 1994). However, one could predict the opposite based on individuals' stronger referral to their social group and potentially stronger susceptibility to social comparison in collectivist (vs. individualist) cultures (Adams, 2005; Heine et al., 2008). We believe these questions represent fruitful avenues for future research.

Similar to the antecedents of status consumption, much still remains unknown about the consequences of status consumption with respect to how status consumption is perceived and appraised. For example, recent research suggests that individuals may behave differently toward others based on how they appraise the source of others' wealth (i.e., whether it was attained through work or luck; Frank, Werenbroch, & Maddux, 2013; Zizzo & Oswald, 2001). It is likely that different attributions of others' wealth that people construe from their observations of status consumption will lead to different reactions to status consumers. These reactions may also depend on the observers' own characteristics (i.e., their own status) as well as norms prevalent in the social and the cultural context (Scott, Bolton, & Mende, 2013). Examining these possibilities in the future would significantly advance our understanding of status and its dynamics.

Economics of Status

Managing Status

To date, very few academic studies have examined how the producers of status signals should manage their products. In particular, few studies have underlined the importance for status marketers of finding the right balance between expanding their customer base to new (less affluent) segments while preserving a prestigious brand image in the eyes of their core (more affluent) clientele. Preserving this balance is crucial when tracking the composition of companies' customer base (Amaldoss & Jain, 2005; Berger & Heath, 2007, 2008) and when managing the portfolio of low-ticket and high-ticket products (Patrick & Prokopec, 2012).

Apart from the issues of balance, however, little is known about the structure and the boundaries of optimal strategies for pricing, promoting, and distributing status signals. In a notable exception, researchers suggested that user-driven innovation may not be as effective in high-status product categories (e.g., luxury apparel) as it is in other contexts, because in high-status product categories, consumers trust the opinions of experts (i.e., renowned designers) more than the opinions of other users (Fuchs, Prandelli, Schreier, & Dahl, 2013).

Predicting Status

Finally, given that status products are social signals, more research is needed to predict how status consumption might change in response to social or economic evolutions in the marketplace. Evidence suggests that brands react to changes in the economic environment, specifically to shifts in the business cycle. In particular, status signals have grown more conspicuous (i.e., louder or larger in logo size) during the most recent recession (Nunes, Drèze, & Han, 2011). It would be important to understand further the predictive role of business cycle as well as of other economic factors, such as unemployment, availability of borrowing instruments (e.g., installment loans), import restrictions on foreign status signals, and word of mouth (WOM), since consumers tend to share a lot of information about their social rank and status consumption through WOM channels (Lovett, Peres, & Shachar, 2013). Last but not least, we believe it would be valuable to examine the link to status consumption of changes in social beliefs and collective mood, including individuals' beliefs about the social system and trust in public institutions.

Conclusion

Although seemingly underrepresented in marketing compared to other fields, status consumption has attracted recent interest from researchers in consumer behavior and marketing. The present chapter delineates the relationship between social hierarchy and social status, offers a multidisciplinary review of recent research in the area, and outlines what we believe are promising avenues for future research. Given that consumer settings are natural areas for the creation, growth, and use of status signals, marketing constitutes a particularly well-suited field of investigation for status research. We hope that this chapter will spark readers' interest in unpacking the processes underlying social hierarchy and status in consumption contexts.

Note on Search Sources

Included in our search were eight management journals (*Administrative Science Quarterly, Academy of Management Journal, Academy of Management Review, Journal of International Business Studies, Management Science, Organization Science, Organizational Behavior and Human Decision Processes*, and *Strategic Management Journal*), eight psychology journals (*Annual Review of Psychology Bulletin, American Psychologist, Journal of Applied Psychology, Journal of Experimental Social Psychology, Journal of Personality and Social Psychology, Personality and Social Psychology Bulletin*, and *Psychological Review*), eight sociology journals (*American Journal of Sociology, American Sociological Review, Demography Social Forces, Social Problems, Social Psychology Quarterly, Social Science Research*, and *Sociology of Education*), and eight marketing journals (*International Journal of Research in Marketing, Journal of Consumer Research, Journal of Consumer Psychology, Journal of Marketing, Journal of Marketing Research, Journal of Public Policy and Marketing, Journal of Retailing*, and *Marketing Science*). Selection of these journals was based on journal ranking information in their respective fields. The search was performed by compiling the results of multiple queries on Business Source Premier.

References

Adams, G. (2005). The cultural grounding of personal relationship: Enemyship in North American and West African worlds. *Journal of Personality and Social Psychology, 88*, 948–968.

Adler, N. E., Epel, E. S., Castellazzo, G., & Ickovics, J. R. (2000). Relationship of subjective and objective social status with psychological and physiological functioning: Preliminary data in healthy, white women. *Health Psychology, 19*(6), 586–592.

Alpizar, F., Carlsson, F., & Johansson-Stenman, O. (2005). How much do we care about the absolute versus relative income and consumption? *Journal of Economic Behavior & Organization, 56*(3), 405–421.

Amaldoss, W., & Jain, S. (2005). Pricing of conspicuous goods: A competitive analysis of social effects. *Journal of Marketing Research, 42*(1), 30–42.

Amaldoss, W., & Jain, S. (2007). Conspicuous consumption and sophisticated thinking. *Management Science, 51*(10), 1449–1466.

Anderson, C., & Brown, C. E., (2010). The functions and dysfunctions of hierarchy. *Research in Organizational Behavior, 30*, 55–89.

Anderson, C., & Kilduff, G. J. (2009). Why do dominant personalities attain influence in face-to-face groups? The competence-signaling effects of trait dominance. *Journal of Personality and Social Psychology, 96*(2), 491–503.

Arndt, J., Sheldon, K. M., Solomon, S., & Kasser, T. (2004). The urge to splurge: A terror management account of materialism and consumer behavior. *Journal of Consumer Psychology, 14*(3), 225–229.

Aspers, P., & Godart, F. (2013). Sociology of fashion: Order and change. *Annual Review of Sociology, 39*, 171–192.

Bagwell, L. S., & Bernheim, B. D. (1996). Veblen effects in a theory of conspicuous consumption. *American Economic Review, 86*(3), 349–373.

Ball, S., Eckel, C., Grossman, P. J., & Zame, W. (2001). Status in markets. *Quarterly Journal of Economics, 116*(1), 161–188.

Banerjee, A. V., & Duflo, E. (2007). The economic lives of the poor. *Journal of Economic Perspectives, 21*(1), 141–167.

Bellezza, S., Gino, F., & Keinan, A. (2014). The red sneakers effect: Inferring status and competence from signals of nonconformity. *Journal of Consumer Research, 41* (June), 35–54.

Berger, J., & Heath, C. (2007). Where consumers diverge from others: Identity-signaling and product domains. *Journal of Consumer Research, 34*(2), 121–134.

Berger, J., & Heath, C. (2008). Who drives divergence? Identity-signaling, outgroup dissimilarity, and the abandonment of cultural tastes. *Journal of Personality and Social Psychology, 95*(3), 593–607.

Berger, J., Ho, B., & Joshi, Y. (2011). Identity signaling with social capital: A model of symbolic consumption. Working Paper, Social Science Resource Network (SSRN).

Berger, J., & Fisek, M. H. (2006). Diffuse status characteristics and the spread of status value: A formal theory. *American Journal of Sociology, 111*(4), 1038–1079.

Berger, J., Fisek, M. H., Zelditch, M., & Norman, R. Z. (1977). *Status Characteristics and Social Interaction: An Expectation States Approach.* New York: Elsevier.

Berger, J., & Ward, M. (2010). Subtle signals of inconspicuous consumption. *Journal of Consumer Research, 37*(4), 555–569.

Berger, J., Zelditch, M., & Rosenholtz, S. J. (1980). Status organizing processes. *Annual Review of Sociology, 6*, 479–508.

Berry, S. T. (1994). Estimating discrete-choice models of product differentiation. *RAND Journal of Economics, 25*(2), 242–262.

Blau, P. M. (1955). *Dynamics of Bureaucracy.* Chicago: Chicago University Press.

Bliege Bird, R., & Smith, E. A. (2005). Signaling theory, strategic interaction, and symbolic capital. *Current Anthropology, 46*(2), 221–248.

Bloch, F., Desai, S., & Rao, V. (2004). Wedding celebrations as conspicuous consumption: Signaling social status in rural India. *Journal of Human Resources, 39*(3), 675–695.

Bobak, M., Pikhart, H., Hertzman, C., Rose, R., & Marmot, M. (1998). Socioeconomic factors, perceived control, and self-reported health in Russia: A cross-sectional survey. *Social Science & Medicine, 47*(2), 269–279.

Bodner, R., & Prelec, D. (2003). Self-signaling and diagnostic utility in everyday decision making. In Isabelle Brocas and Juan D. Carillo (eds.), *Psychology of Economic Decisions* (vol. 1, pp. 105–127). Oxford: Oxford University Press.

Boksem, M. A. S., Mehta, P. H., van den Bergh, B., van Son, V., Trautman, S. T., Roelofs, K., Smidts, A., & Sanfey, A. G. (2004). Testosterone inhibits trust but promotes reciprocity. *Psychological Science, 20*(10), 1–9.

Bothner, M., Podolny, J., & Smith, E. B. (2011). Organizing contests for status: The Matthew effect versus the Mark effect. *Management Science, 57*(3), 439–457

Bourdieu, P. (1984). *Distinction: A Social Critique of the Judgment of Taste* (R. Nice, Trans.). Cambridge, MA: Harvard University Press.

Burroughs, J. E., Chaplin, L. N., Pandelaere, M., Norton, M., Ordabayeva, N., Gunz, A., & Dinauer, L. (2013). Using motivation theory to develop a transformative consumer research agenda for reducing materialism in society. *Journal of Public Policy and Marketing, 32*(1), 18–31.

Burroughs, J. E., & Rindfleisch, A. (2012). What welfare? The mission of transformative consumer research and the foundational role of materialism. In C. Pechmann, D. Mick, J Ozanne, & S. Pettigrew (eds.), *Transformative Consumer Research for Personal and Collective Well Being* (pp. 249–266). Mahwah, NJ: Taylor & Francis.

Bushman, B. J., & Baumeister, R. F. (1998). Threatened egotism, narcissism, self-esteem, and direct and displaced aggression: Does self-love or self-hate lead to violence? *Journal of Personality and Social Psychology, 75*(1), 219–229.

Chang, L. C., & Arkin, R. M. (2002). Materialism as an attempt to cope with uncertainty. *Psychology & Marketing, 19*(5), 389–406.

Chao, A., & Schor, J. B. (1998). Empirical tests of status consumption: Evidence from women's cosmetics. *Journal of Economic Psychology, 19*(1), 107–131.

Charles, K. K., Hurst, E., & Roussanov, N. (2009). Conspicuous consumption and race. *Quarterly Journal of Economics, 124*(2), 425–467.

Cheng, J. T., Tracy, J. L., Foulsham, T., Kingstone, A., & Henrich, J. (2013). Two ways to the top: Evidence that dominance and prestige are distinct yet viable avenues to social rank and influence. *Journal of Personality and Social Psychology, 104*, 103–125.

Christen, M., & Morgan, R. M. (2005). Keeping up with the Joneses: Analyzing the effect of income inequality on consumer borrowing. *Quantitative Marketing and Economics, 3*, 145–173.

Christensen, V. (1998). Fishery-induced changes in a marine ecosystem: Insights for models of the Gulf of Thailand. *Journal of Fish Biology, 53*(Supplement A), 128–142.

Chua, R. Y. J., & Zou, X. (2009). The devil wears Prada? Effects of exposure to luxury goods on cognition and decision making. Working Paper, Harvard Business School.

Clark, A. E., & Oswald, A. (1998). Comparison-concave utility and following behaviour in social and economic settings. *Journal of Public Economics, 70*(3), 133–150.

Cronk, L. (2005). The application of animal signaling theory to human phenomena: Some thoughts and clarifications. *Social Science Information, 44*(4), 603–620.

de Botton, A. (2004). *Status Anxiety*. London: Hamish Hamilton.

Dhar, R., & Wertenbroch, K. (2012). Self-signaling and the costs and benefits of temptation in consumer choice. *Journal of Marketing Research, 49*(1), 15–25.

Diamond, J. M. (1997). *Guns, Germs and Steel: The Fates of Human Societies.* New York: W. W. Norton.

Drèze, X., & Nunes, J. C. (2009). Feeling superior: The impact of loyalty program structure on consumers' perceptions of status. *Journal of Consumer Research, 35*(April), 890–905.

Dubois, D., & Anik, L. (2014). Heels, status and power: Consequences of status consumption for thoughts. Working Paper, INSEAD.

Dubois, B., Czellar, S., & Laurent, G. (2005). Consumer segments based on attitudes toward luxury: Empirical evidence from twenty countries. *Marketing Letters, 16*(2), 115–112.

Dubois, B., & Duquesne, P. (1993). The market for luxury goods: Income versus culture. *European Journal of Marketing, 27*(1), 35–44.

Dubois, D., Galinsky, A. D., & Rucker, D. D. (2010). The accentuation bias: Money literally looms larger (and sometimes smaller) to the powerless. *Social Psychological and Personality Science, 4*(3), 199–205.

Dubois, D., Galinsky, A. D., & Rucker, D. D. (2012). Super size me: Product size as a signal of status. *Journal of Consumer Research, 38*(6), 1047–1062.

Duesenberry, J. (1949). *Income, Saving, and the Theory of Consumer Behavior.* Cambridge, MA: Harvard University Press.

Dumont, L. (1966). *Homo Hierarchicus: The Caste System and Its Implications.* Chicago: Chicago University Press.

Dupor, B., & Liu, W. (2003). Jealousy and equilibrium overconsumption. *American Economic Review, 93*(1), 423–8.

Durkheim, E. 1893/1997. The Division of Labor in Society. New York: The Free Press.

Dynan, K. E., Skinner, J., & Zeldes, S. P. (2004). Do the rich save more? *Journal of Political Economy, 112*(2), 397–444.

Economist (2007). Ghana: Bankruptcy and burials. May 24.

Faddegon, K., Scheepers, D., & Ellemers, N. (2008). If we have the will, there will be a way: Regulatory focus as a group identity. *European Journal of Social Psychology, 38*(5), 880–895.

Fan, E. T., & Gruenfeld, D. H. (1998). When needs outweigh desires: The effects of resource interdependence and reward interdependence on group problem solving. *Basic and Applied Social Psychology, 20*(1), 45–56.

Fast, N., Halevy, J. & Galinsky, A. D. (2011). The destructive nature of power without status. *Journal of Experimental Social Psychology, 48*(1), 391–394.

Ferraro, R., Kirmani, A., & Matherly, T. (2013). Look at me! Look at me! Conspicuous brand usage, self-brand connection, and dilution. *Journal of Marketing Research, 50*(4), 477–488.

Festinger, L. (1954). A theory of social comparison. *Human Relations, 7*(2), 117–140.

Fiske, S. T. (2010). *The Handbook of Social Psychology.* Hoboken, NJ: Wiley.

Fontes, A., & Fan, J. X. (2006). The effects of ethnic identity on household budget allocation to status conveying goods. *Journal of Family and Economic Issues, 27*(4), 643–663.

Frank, D., Wertenbroch, K., & Maddux, W. W. (2013). Fruits of labor or luck? Cultural differences in just world beliefs explain preferences for economic redistribution. Working Paper, INSEAD.

Frank, R. H. (1985). The demand for unobservable and other nonpositional goods. *American Economic Review, 75*(March), 101–116.

Frank, R. H. (2007). *Falling Behind: How Rising Inequality Harms the Middle Class.* Oakland: California University Press.

Frank, R. H., & Cook, P. J. (1995). *The Winner-Take-All Society: Why the Few at the Top Get So Much More than the Rest of Us.* New York: Penguin.

French, J. R. P., & Raven, B. (1959). The bases of social power. In D. Cartwright (ed.), *Studies in Social Power* (pp. 150–167). Ann Arbor, MI: Institute for Social Research.

Fuchs, C., Prandelli, E., Schreier, M., & Dahl, D. W. (2013). All that is users might not be gold: How labeling products as user-designed backfires in the context of luxury fashion brands. *Journal of Marketing, 77*(5), 75–91.

Gardner, W. L., Lee, A. Y., & Gabriel, S. (1999). "I" value freedom, but "we" value relationships: Self-construal priming mirrors cultural differences in judgment. *Psychological Science, 10*(4), 321–326.

Godart, F., & Mears, A. (2009). How do cultural producers make creative decisions? Lessons from the catwalk. *Social Forces, 88*(2), 671–692.

Godart, F., Shipilov, A., & Claes, K. (2014). Making the most of the revolving door: The impact of outward personnel mobility networks on organizational creativity, *Organization Science, 25*(2), 377–400.

Godoy, R., Seyfried, C., Reyes-Garcia, V., Tanner, S., McDade, T., Huanca, T., & Leonard, W. R. (2007). Signaling by consumption in a native Amazonian society. *Evolution and Human Behavior, 28*(2), 124–134.

Goodman, E., Huang, B., Adler, N. E., & Schafer-Kalkhoff, T. (2007). Perceived socioeconomic status: A new type of identity that influences adolescents' self-rated health. *Journal of Adolescent Health, 41*(5), 479–487.

Greer, L. L., & Caruso, H. M. (2007). Are high power teams really high performers? The roles of trust and status congruency in high power team performance. *Academy of Management Proceedings.*

Griskevicius, V., Delton, A. W., Tybur, J. M., & Robertson, T. E. (2011). The influence of mortality and socioeconomic status on risk and delayed rewards: A life history theory approach. *Journal of Personality and Social Psychology, 100* (6), 1015–1026.

Griskevicius, V., Kenrick, D. T., Miller, G. F., Sundie, J. M., Tybur, J. M., & Cialdini, R. B. (2007). Blatant benevolence and conspicuous consumption: When romantic motives elicit strategic costly signals. *Journal of Personality and Social Psychology, 93*(1), 85–102.

Griskevicius, V., Tybur, J. M., & Van den Bergh, B. (2010). Going green to be seen: Status, reputation, and conspicuous conservation. *Journal of Personality and Social Psychology, 98*(3), 392–404.

Griskevicius, V., White, A. E., Delton, A. W., Ackerman, J. M., Tybur, J. M., & Robertson, T. E. (2012). The financial consequences of too many men: Sex ratio effects on saving, borrowing, and spending. *Journal of Personality and Social Psychology, 102*(1), 69–80.

Gruenfeld, D. H., & Tiedens, L. Z. (2010). Organizational preferences and their consequences. In E. Aronson, & L. Garner (eds.), *Handbook of Social Psychology* (pp. 249–266). Oxford: Addison-Wesley.

Han, Y. J., Nunes, J. C., & Dréze, X. (2010). Signaling status with luxury goods: The role of brand prominence. *Journal of Marketing, 74*(4), 15–30.

Hardy, C. L., & van Vugt, M. (2006). Nice guys finish first: The competitive altruism hypothesis. *Personality and Social Psychology Bulletin, 32*(10), 1402–1413,

Heine, S. J., Takemoto, T., Moskalenko, S., Lasaleta, J., & Henrich, J. (2008). Mirrors in the head: Cultural variation in objective self-awareness. *Personality and Social Psychology Bulletin, 34*, 879–887.

Henrich, J., & Gil-White, F. (2001). The evolution of prestige: Freely conferred status as a mechanism for enhancing the benefits of cultural transmission. *Evolution and Human Behavior, 22*,165–196

Henry, P. J. (2009). Low-status compensation: A theory for understanding the role of status in cultures of honor. *Journal of Personality and Social Psychology, 97*(3), 451–466.

Hill, S. E., Rodeheffer, C. D., Griskevicius, V., Durante, K., & White, A. E. (2012). Boosting beauty in an economic decline: Mating, spending, and the lipstick effect. *Journal of Personality and Social Psychology, 103*(2), 275–291.

Hofstede, G. (1980). Culture and organizations. *International Studies of Management & Organization, 10*(4), 15–41.

Hopkins, E., & Kornienko, T. (2004). Running to keep in the same place: Consumer choice as a game status. *American Economic Review, 94*(4), 1085–1107.

Huang, L., Galinsky, A., Gruenfeld, D. H., & Guillory, L. E. (2011). Powerful postures versus powerful roles: Which is the proximate correlate of thought and behavior? *Psychological Science, 22*(1), 95–102.

Huberman, B. A., Onculer, A., & Loch, C. H. (2004). Status as a valued resource. *Social Psychology Quarterly, 67*(1), 103–114.

Humphreys, A., & Latour, K. A. (2013). Framing the game: Assessing the impact of cultural representations on consumer perceptions of legitimacy. *Journal of Consumer Research, 40*(4), 773–795.

Ireland, N. J. (1994). On limiting the market for status signals. *Journal of Public Economics, 53*(1), 91–110.

Ivanic, A., & Nunes, J. C. (2009). The intrinsic benefits of status. Working Paper, University of Southern California.

Ivanic, A. S., Overbeck, J., & Nunes, J. C. (2011). Status, race and money: The impact of racial hierarchy on willingness to pay. *Psychological Science, 22*(12), 1557–1566.

Johnson, S. E., Finkel, E. J., & Richeson, J. A. (2011). Middle class and marginal? Socioeconomic status, stigma, and self-regulation at an elite university. *Journal of Personality and Social Psychology, 100*(5), 838–852.

Kamakura, W. A., & Du, R. Y. (2012). How economic contractions and expansions affect expenditure patterns. *Journal of Consumer Research, 39* (2), 229–247.

Kasser, T., & Sheldon, K. M. (2000). Of wealth and death: Materialism, mortality salience, and consumption behavior. *Psychological Science, 11*(4), 348–351.

Keltner, D., Van Kleef, G. A., Kraus, M. W., & Chen, S. (2008). A reciprocal influence model of social power: Emerging principles and lines of inquiry. In M. P. Zanna (ed.), *Advances in Experimental Social Psychology 40*. Amsterdam: Elsevier, 151-192.

Kim, C. J., Park, B. S., & Dubois, D. (2014). Climbing up vs. not sliding down? The impact of political ideology on luxury consumption. Working Paper, INSEAD.

Knell, M. (1999). Social comparisons, inequality, and growth. *Journal of Institutional and Theoretical Economics, 155*(4), 664–695.

Kraus, M. W., Keltner, D., Rheinschmidt, M. L., Piff, P. K., & Mendoza-Denton, R. (2012a). Social class, solipsism, and contextualism: How the rich are different from the poor. *Psychological Review, 119*(3), 546–572.

Kraus, M. W., Keltner, D., Stellar, J. E., & Manzo, V. M. (2012b). Class and compassion: Socioeconomic factors predict responses to suffering. *Emotion, 12*(3), 449–459.

Kuksov, D., & Xie, Y. (2012). Competition in a status goods market. *Journal of Marketing Research, 50*(4), 609–623.

Langlois, J. H., Kalakanis, L., Rubenstein, A. J., Larson, A., Hallam, M., & Smoot, M. (2000). Maxims or myths of beauty? A meta-analytic and theoretical review. *Psychological Bulletin, 126*(3), 390–423

Leavitt, H. J. (2005). Hierarchies, authority and leadership. *Leader to Leader, 2005*(37), 55–61.

Lee, J., & Shrum, L. J. (2012). Conspicuous consumption versus charitable behavior in response to social exclusion: A differential needs explanation. *Journal of Consumer Research, 39*(3), 530–544.

Lee, J., & Shrum, L. J. (2013). Self-threats and consumption. In Ayalla A. Ruvio and Russell W. Belk (eds.), *The Routledge Companion to Identity and Consumption* (pp. 216–224) New York: Routledge.

Leibenstein, H. (1950). Bandwagon, snob, and Veblen effects in the theory of consumers' demand. *Quarterly Journal of Economics, 64*(2), 183–207.

Levy, S. J. (1959). Symbols for sale. *Harvard Business Review, 37*(4), 117–124.

Lincoln, G.A., Guinness, F., & Short, R. V. (1972). The way in which testosterone controls the social and sexual behavior of the red deer stag (cervus elaphus). *Hormones and Behavior, 3*(4), 375–396.

Lovett, M. J., Peres R., & Shachar R. (2013). On brands and word of mouth. *Journal of Marketing Research, 50*, 427–444.

MacCracken, G. D. (1988). *Culture and Consumption: New Approaches to the Symbolic Character of Consumer Goods and Activities.* Bloomington: Indiana University Press.

Magee, J. C. (2009). Seeing power in action: The roles of deliberation, implementation, and action in inferences of power. *Journal of Experimental Social Psychology, 45*(1), 1–14.

Magee, J. C., & Galinsky, A. D. (2008). Social hierarchy: The self-reinforcing nature of power and status. *Academy of Management Annals, 2*(1), 351–398.

Mandel, N., & Heine, S. J. (1999). Terror management and marketing: He who dies with the most toys wins. In E. J Arnould, & L. Scott (eds.), *Advances in Consumer Research 26.* Duluth, MN: ACR, 527-532.

Mandel, N., Petrova, P. K., & Cialdini, R. B. (2006). Images of success and the preference for luxury brands. *Journal of Consumer Psychology, 16*(1), 57–69.

Maner, J. K., Eckel, L. A., Schmidt, N. B., & Miller, S. L. (2010). The endocrinology of exclusion: Rejection elicits motivationally tuned changes in progesterone. *Psychological Science, 21*(4), 581–588.

Markus, H. R., & Kitayama, S. (1994). A collective fear of the collective: Implications for selves and theories of selves. *Personality and Social Psychology Bulletin, 20* (5), 568–579.

Marmot, M. G. (2004). *The Endocrinology of Exclusion: Rejection Elicits Motivationally Tuned Changes in Progesterone.* London: Bloomsbury.

Marmot, M. G., Feeney, A., Patel, C., Brunner, E., North, F., Smith, G. D., & Head, J. (1991). Health inequalities among British civil servants: The Whitehall II Study. *Lancet, 337*(June), 1387–1397.

Masling, J., Greer, F. L., & Gilmore, R. (1955). Status, authoritarianism and sociometric choice. *Journal of Social Psychology, 41*(2), 297–310.

Mazzocco, P. J., Galinsky, A. D., Rucker, D. D., & Anderson, E. T. (2012). Direct and vicarious conspicuous consumption: Identification with low-status groups increases the desire for high-status goods. *Journal of Consumer Psychology, 22*, 520–528.

McFerran, B., & Argo, J. J. (2013). The entourage effect. *Journal of Consumer Research, 40*(5), 871–884.

Miller, G. F. (2009). *Spent: Sex, Evolution, and Consumer Behavior.* New York: Viking.

Milner, M. (1994). Status and Sacredness: A General Theory of Status Relations and an Analysis of Indian Culture. New York: Oxford University Press.

Moav, O., & Neeman, Z. (2008). Conspicuous consumption, human capital and poverty. Discussion Paper No. 6864, Centre for Economic Policy Research, London EC1V 7RR, UK.

Nelissen, R. M. A., & Meijers, M. H. C. (2011). Social benefits of luxury brands as costly signals of wealth and status. *Evolution and Human Behavior, 32*(5), 343–355.

Nelson, E. E., Pine, D. S., Leibenluft, E., & McClure, E. B. (2005). The social re-orientation of adolescence: A neuroscience perspective on the process and its relation to psychopathology. *Psychological Medicine, 35*(2), 163–174.

Nelson, P. D., & Berry, N. H. (1965). Change in sociometric status during military basic training related to performance two years later. *Journal of Psychology: Interdisciplinary and Applied, 61*(2), 251–255.

Nunes, J. C., Drèze, X., & Young J. (2011). Conspicuous consumption in a recession: Toning it down or turning it up? *Journal of Consumer Psychology, 21*(2), 199–205.

Ordabayeva, N., & Chandon, P. (2011). Getting ahead of the Joneses: When equality increases conspicuous consumption among bottom-tier consumers. *Journal of Consumer Research, 38*(1), 27–41.

Patrick, V., & Prokopec, S. (2012). Can a successful brand extension dilute a luxury brand? How managing the "dream" matters. Working Paper, SSRN.

Pfeffer, J., & Langton, N. (1993). The effect of wage dispersion on satisfaction, productivity, and working collaboratively: Evidence from college and university faculty. *Administrative Science Quarterly, 38*(3), 382–407.

Piff, P. K., Keltner, D., Stancato, D. M., Cote, S., & Mendoza-Denton, R. (2011). Higher social class predicts increased unethical behavior. *Proceedings of the National Academy of Sciences, 109*(11), 4086–4091.

Piff, P. K., Cheng, B. H., Kraus, M. W., Keltner, D., & Cote, S. (2010). Having less, giving more: The influence of social class on prosocial behavior. *Journal of Personality and Social Psychology, 99*(5), 771–784.

Piketty, T. (2014). *Capital in the 21st Century.* Cambridge, MA: Harvard University Press.

Plourde, A. (2008). The origins of prestige goods as honest signals of skill and knowledge. *Human Nature, 19*(4), 374–388.

Podolny, J. M. (1993). A status-based model of market competition. *American Journal of Sociology, 98*, 829–872.

Podolny, J. M. (2005). *Status Signals: A Sociological Study of Market Competition.* Princeton, NJ: Princeton University Press.

Pomeroy, S. B., Roberts, J. T., Burstein, S. M., & Donlan, W. (2004). A brief history of ancient Greece: Politics, society, and culture. *Classical Review, 56*(1), 146–148.

Prasse, K. G. (1995). *The Tuaregs: The Blue People.* Copenhagen: Museum Tusculanum.

Prelec, D., & Bodner, R. (2003). Self-signaling and self-control. In D. Read, G. Lowenstein, & R. Baumeister (eds.), *Time and Decision* (pp. 277–298). New York: Russell Sage.

Pyszczynski, T., Greenberg, J., & Solomon, S. (1999). A dual-process model of defense against conscious and unconscious death-related thoughts: An extension of terror management theory. *Psychological Review, 106*(4), 835–845.

Ridgeway, C. L., Tinkler, J. E., Backor, K., Erickson, K. G., & Li, Y. E. (2009). How easily does a social difference become a status distinction? Gender matters. *American Sociological Review, 74*(1), 44–62.

Ridgeway, C. L., & Walker, H (1995). Status structures. In K. Cook, G. Fine, & J. House (eds.), *Sociological Perspectives on Social Psychology.* New York: Allyn and Bacon, 281-310.

Rindfleisch, A., Burroughs, J. E., & Wong, N. (2009). The safety of objects: Materialism, existential insecurity, and brand connection. *Journal of Consumer Research, 36*(1), 1–16.

Rindfleisch, A., Denton, F., & Burroughs, J. E. (1997). Family structure, materialism, and compulsive consumption. *Journal of Consumer Research, 23*(4), 312–325.

Rivers, J. J., & Josephs, R. A. (2010). Dominance and health: The role of social rank in physiology and illness. In A. Guinote, & T. K. Vescio (eds.), *The Social Psychology of Power.* New York: Guilford Press, 87-112.

Rucker, D. D., Dubois D. & Galinsky A. D. (2011). Generous paupers and stingy princes: Power drives spending on one's self versus others. *Journal of Consumer Research, 36*(7), 1015–1029.

Rucker, D. D., & Galinsky, A. (2008). Desire to acquire: Powerlessness and compensatory consumption. *Journal of Consumer Research, 35*(2), 257–267.

Rucker, D. D., & Galinsky, A. (2009). Conspicuous consumption versus utilitarian ideals: How different levels of power shape consumer consumption. *Journal of Experimental Social Psychology, 45*(3), 549–555.

Rucker, D. D., & Galinsky, A. (2013). *Compensatory Consumption.* In Russell W. Belk and Ayalla A. Ruvio (eds.), New York: Routledge, 207–15.

Rucker, D. D., Galinsky A. D. & Dubois D., (2012). Power and consumer behavior: Power shapes who and what we value. *Journal of Consumer Psychology, 22,* 352–368.

Saad, G. (2007). *The Evolutionary Bases of Consumption.* Mahwah, NJ: Erlbaum.

Sauder, M. (2006). Third parties and status position: How the characteristics of status systems matter. *Theory and Society, 35*(3), 299–321.

Sapolsky, R. M. (2005). The influence of social hierarchy on primate health. *Science, 308* (5722), 648–652.

Schmid Mast, M., & Hall, J. A. (2004). Who is boss and who is not? Accuracy of judging status. *Journal of Nonverbal Behavior, 28*(3), 145–165.

Scitovsky, T. (1992). *The Joyless Economy: The Psychology of Human Satisfaction.* Oxford: Oxford University Press.

Scott, J. C. (1998). *Seeing Like a State: How Certain Schemes to Improve the Human Condition Have Failed.* New Haven, CT: Yale University Press.

Scott, M. L., Bolton, L. E., & Mende, M. (2013). Judging the book by its cover? How consumers decode conspicuous consumption cues in buyer–seller relationships. *Journal of Marketing Research, 50*(3), 334–347.

Shalev, E., & Morwitz, V. G. (2012). Influence via comparison-driven self-evaluation and restoration: The case of the low-status influencer. *Journal of Consumer Research, 38*(5), 964–980.

Sharma, E., & Alter, A. L. (2012). Financial deprivation prompts consumers to seek scarce goods. *Journal of Consumer Research, 39*(3), 545–560.

Shavit, S., Lalwani, A. K., Torelli, C. J., & Zhang, J. (2006). The horizontal/vertical distinction in cross-cultural consumer research. *Journal of Consumer Psychology, 16*(4), 325–356.

Sidanius, J., & Pratto, F. (1999). *Social Dominance: An Intergroup Theory of Social Hierarchy and Oppression,* Cambridge: Cambridge University Press.

Simmel, G. (1094/1957). Fashion. *American Journal of Sociology, 62*(6), 541–558.

Sligte, D. J., Nijstad, B. A., & de Dreu, C. K. W. (2011). Power, stability of power, and creativity. *Journal of Experimental Social Psychology, 47*(5), 891–897.

Solnick, S. J., & Hemenway, D. (1998). Is more always better? A survey about positional goods. *Journal of Economic Behavior and Organization, 37*(3), 373–383.

Stellar, J. E., Keltner, D., Kraus, M. W., & Manzo, V. M. (2012). Class and compassion: Socioeconomic factors predict responses to suffering. *Emotion, 12*(3), 449–459.

Stilley, K., Nenkov, G. Y., & Winterich, K. P. (2011). You spend, I spend, but you save, I save: Effects of deliberative mindsets and social comparison on financial decisions. In D. W. Dahl, G. V. Johar, & S. M. J. van Osselaer (eds.), *Advances in Consumer Research, 38.* Duluth, MN: ACR.

Tajfel, H. (1984). *The Social Dimension.* Cambridge: Cambridge University Press.

Tetlock, P. E. (1981). Pre- to post-election shifts in presidential rhetoric: Impression management or cognitive adjustment. *Journal of Personality and Social Psychology, 41,* 207–212.

Thompson, S. H., Corwin, S. J., & Sargent, R. G. (1997). Ideal body size beliefs and weight concerns of fourth-grade children. *International Journal of Eating Disorders, 21*(3), 279–284.

Thompson, W. E., & Hickey, J. V. (2005). *Society in Focus.* Belmont, CA: Wadsworth.

Tiedens, L. Z., Young, M. J., & Unzueta, M. M. (2007). An unconscious desire for hierarchy? The motivated perception of dominance complementarity in task partners. *Journal of Personality and Social Psychology, 93*(3), 402–414.

Todorov, A., Mandisodza, A. N., Goren, A., & Hall, C. C. (2005). Inferences of competence from faces predict election outcomes. *Science, 308,* 1623–1626.

Van Boven, L., Campbell, M. C., & Gilovich, T. (2010). Stigmatizing materialism: On stereotypes and impressions of materialistic and experiential pursuits. *Personality and Social Psychology Bulletin, 36*(4), 551–563.

Van der Vegt, G. S., Oosterhof, A., & Bunderson, J. S. (2006). Expertness diversity and interpersonal helping in teams: Why those who need the most help end up getting the least. *Academy of Management Journal, 49*(5), 877–893.

Van Vugt, M. (2006). Evolutionary origins of leadership and followership. *Personality and Social Psychology Review, 10*(4), 354–371.

Van Vugt, M., Kaiser, R. B., & Hogan, R. (2008). Leadership, followership, and evolution: Some lessons from the past. *American Psychologist, 63*(3), 182–196.

Veblen, T. B. (1899). *The Theory of the Leisure Class: An Economic Study in the Evolution of Institution.* New York: Macmillan.

Wang, Y., & Griskevicius, V. (2014). Conspicuous consumption, relationships, and rivals: Women's luxury products as signals to other women. *Journal of Consumer Research, 40*(5), 834–854.

Weber, M. (1922) 1978. *Economy and Society: An Outline of Interpretive Sociology.* Berkeley: University of California Press

Weber, M., Gerth H. H., & Mills, C. W. (1946). *From Max Weber: Essays in Sociology.* New York: Oxford University Press.

Wilcox, K., Kim, H. M., & Sen, S. (2009). Why do consumers buy counterfeit luxury brands? *Journal of Marketing Research, 46*(2), 247–259.

Wilkinson, R., & Pickett, K. (2010). *The Spirit Level: Why Equality Is Better for Everyone.* London: Penguin.

Willer, R. (2009). A status theory of collective action. In E. Lawler & S. R. Thye (eds.), *Advances in Group Processes* (vol. 26, pp. 133–163). Bingley, England: Emerald.

Zhu, N. (2012). Household consumption and personal bankruptcy. *Journal of Legal Studies, 40*(1), 1–37.

Zizzo, D. J., & Oswald, A. J. (2001). Are people willing to pay to reduce others' incomes? *Annales d'Economie et de Statistique, 63–64* (July–December), 39–62.

14 Word of Mouth and Interpersonal Communication

Jonah Berger

Interpersonal communication is an integral part of everyday life. People swap stories with their friends, share information with their neighbors, and gossip with their co-workers around the water cooler. Consumers recommend new movies, complain about bad products, and suggest vacation destinations they think others will enjoy.

The person-to-person sharing of thoughts, opinions, information, news, and other content can be described as word of mouth. Broadly speaking, word of mouth is the informal communication between people about all sorts of goods, services, and ideas. It includes discussions of products (e.g., sneakers), brands (e.g., Nike), political candidates, ideas (e.g., environmental reform), and behaviors (e.g., smoking). It includes direct recommendations (e.g., "You should try this restaurant") and mere mentions (e.g., "We went to this restaurant for lunch").

Word of mouth is not just frequent, it is also important. What others talk about and share has a big impact on consumer behavior. Research finds that social talk shapes everything from where people eat (Godes & Mayzlin, 2009) and what consumers read (Chevalier & Mayzlin, 2006) to the drugs doctors prescribe (Iyengar, Van den Bulte, & Valente, 2010). McKinsey and Company (Iyengar, Van den Bulte, & Valente, 2010) argues that "word of mouth is the primary factor behind 20 to 50 percent of all purchasing decisions."

While interpersonal communication has been around for thousands of years, the rise of social media has focused even more attention on this area. Rather than just talking to one person over coffee, consumers can now share their thoughts with thousands of others in a matter of seconds. People can tweet, post, like, and share all sorts of opinions and information whenever they feel so inclined. Technology has accelerated the pace of communication and made it faster and easier to share with a large number of people very quickly. The fact that social media conversations leave a written record has also encouraged companies to realize the importance and power of interpersonal communication, causing many organizations to make word of mouth a key part of marketing strategy.

Jonah Berger is an Associate Professor of Marketing (jberger@wharton.upenn.edu) at the Wharton School, University of Pennsylvania and a visiting Professor at Cornell Tech.

This chapter provides an overview of recent research on word of mouth and interpersonal communication. First, I provide a simple framework that is useful for organizing much of the research in the area. Then, after reviewing relevant work in each part of the framework, I sketch out some potential directions for future research. Note that, as with any attempt to review a large and diverse research area, some choices must be made. Social networks research, for example, has discovered some exciting new developments that are relevant to the study of word of mouth. Given the focus on consumer psychology, however, this chapter focuses more on the psychological processes that underlie information transmission rather than sociological factors that impact information flows.

An Organizing Framework

In 1948, Harold Lasswell asked a question that outlines much of what has become communications science: Who says what to whom in what channel with what effect? Numerous models of communication have been proposed since then (e.g., Berlo, 1960; Schramm, 1954), but the major components have remained similar (see Figure 14.1).

There is a

1. Source, or communication sender (the "who" that is doing the sharing)
2. Message, or thing that is being communicated (the "what" that is being shared)
3. Audience, or person who is receiving the message (the "to whom")
4. Channel, or medium through which the message is being shared
5. Effect, or consequence of the communication

This framework is extremely useful in organizing word of mouth research. Consumers do not just communicate, they communicate *about something*, such as politics or different car brands. Why do people talk about some things more than others? What drives what people talk about?

Consumers also communicate *to someone*, such as friends or neighbors. How does to whom people are talking shape what they talk about?

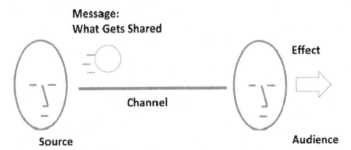

Message:
What Gets Shared

Effect

Channel

Source   **Audience**

Figure 14.1. *Visual Depiction of Key Communication Factors.*

Communication also happens *through a particular communication channel*, such as over the phone or face to face. How do people decide what channel to communicate through, and how does the channel influence what people communicate?

And finally, communication *has consequences*, impacting what the talker, or listener, thinks, does, or buys in the future. When does word of mouth have a larger impact on behavior and why?

This chapter considers the word of mouth message, audience, channel, and effect, reviewing relevant research and touching on potential directions for future work. While research has also looked at who is more likely to talk, given space constraints, I focus on the other four components in greater detail.[1] The chapter starts with what people talk about and why, then discusses how aspects of the audience and communication channel may shape what people share, and then examines the effects of word of mouth on consumer behavior. It closes with a discussion of fruitful questions for further research.

The Message: What People Talk about and Why

Seven key factors seem to underlie much of what people talk about and share: impression management, emotion regulation, information acquisition, social bonding, accessibility, useful information, and persuasion (Berger, 2014b). I discuss each in turn, focusing in particular on recent research in the area.

Impression Management

What people talk about and share is driven, in part, by impression management. A great deal of consumer research has shown that people make choices to communicate desired identities, and that others use people's choices to make inferences about them (Belk, 1988; Berger & Heath, 2007; Escalas & Bettman, 2003; Kleine, Kleine, & Kernan, 1993; Levy, 1959). Driving a BMW, for example, makes people seem wealthy, and wearing brands such as Nike, Abercrombie & Fitch, and American Apparel may make others think someone is sporty, preppy, or a hipster, respectively (see Chapter 13 in this handbook).

Just like the car people drive, or the clothes they wear, what people talk about and share shapes what others think of them. If someone is always talking about

---

1 Early adopters, opinion leaders, market mavens, and other people who believe that they have more knowledge or expertise tend to report sharing their opinion more often (Engel, Kegerreis, & Blackwell, 1969; Feick & Price, 1987; Katz & Lazersfeld, 1955). Personality factors also play a role, as more extroverted and less conscientiousness people are more likely to forward emails they receive from others (Chiu, Hsieh, Kao, & Lee, 2007), and neurotic people post more frequent (and more emotional) Facebook status updates (Buechel & Berger, 2014; see Wilson, Gosling, & Graham, 2012, for a broader discussion of factors driving Facebook use). Situational factors also shape who talks. Highly satisfied or dissatisfied customers seem to share more word of mouth (Anderson, 1998).

new restaurants, people will assume he or she is a foodie. If someone is always sharing articles about hot new technology, people will assume he or she is into that. Interpersonal communication serves as a signal of identity.

As a result, consumers are more likely to share things that make them look good (Chung & Darke, 2006; Hennig-Thurau, Gwinner, Walsh, & Gremler. 2004; Sundaram, Mitra, & Webster, 1998). More interesting products and brands (e.g., Apple rather than Windex) get more immediate word of mouth (Berger & Schwartz, 2011) and are discussed more online (Berger & Iyengar, 2013), and people report greater willingness to talk about more original products (Moldovan, Goldenberg, & Chattopadhyay, 2011). Similarly, more interesting or surprising newspaper articles are more likely to make the most emailed list (Berger & Milkman, 2012), and more extreme stories are more likely to be shared (Heath & Devoe, 2005) in part because they make people seem more interesting.

People are also more likely to talk about things that allow them to communicate specific desired identities. Premium brands are more likely to be discussed (Lovett, Peres, & Shachar, 2013) as are symbolic products (vs. more utilitarian ones; Chung & Darke, 2006). People also share word of mouth to compensate for lack of knowledge in a domain where they want to have more expertise (Packard & Wooten, 2013).

Impression management may also lead people to talk about positive things rather than negative ones. Most people prefer interacting with Positive Pollys rather than Negative Nellies (Bell, 1978; Folkes & Sears, 1977; Kamins, Folkes, & Pener, 1997), and sharing positive things puts others in a better mood, which should reflect positively on the sharer. As a result, particularly when their identity is on the line, people may be encouraged to pass on positive rather than negative stories and information (Tesser & Rosen, 1975). Indeed, more positive news articles are more likely to be highly shared (Berger & Milkman, 2012), and there are more positive than negative reviews (Chevalier & Mayzlin, 2006; East, Hammond, & Wright, 2007). That said, when talking about others, people may be more willing to share negative experiences because it makes them look relatively better by comparison (De Angelis et al., 2012).

Talking about unique or scarce goods is another way to foster positive impressions. Mentioning one's special hand-knit bowtie or talking about an experience that most others will never get to have allows people to differentiate themselves. Individuals with high needs for uniqueness, though, may strategically talk in ways that discourage adoption by others, thus allowing them to maintain their uniqueness. They may generate less positive word of mouth (Cheema & Kaikati, 2010) or share favorable word of mouth but mention how complex a new product is to use, thereby scaring others from adopting it (Moldovan, Steinhart, & Ofen, 2012).

Emotion Regulation

What people talk about and share is also driven by emotion regulation. Emotion regulation describes the ways people manage their emotional experiences

(Gross, 1998, 2008). If someone is sad because he or she was fired from a job, for example, that person may try to cope or manage that emotional experience by reminding himself or herself how many other good things are going on in the person's life.

Though emotions are often considered intrapersonal experiences, research on the social sharing of emotion (see Rimé, 2009, for a review) suggests that interpersonal communication plays an important role in emotional experiences. This work suggests that upward of 90 percent of all emotional experiences are shared with others (Rimé, Mesquita, Philippot, & Boca, 1991). When people get fired, they don't just cope by themselves in isolation; they reach out to others to help them manage their emotional experience.

Talking to others helps facilitate emotion regulation in a number of ways. First, interpersonal communication can generate social support. Particularly after a negative experience, connecting with others can provide comfort and solace (Rimé, 2007, 2009). Talking to someone else can make people feel cared for and less alone. Indeed, even the mere possibility of a response to an online post may be enough to generate perceived social support that improves well-being (Buechel & Berger, 2014).

Second, interpersonal communication also helps people make sense of what they are feeling. Particularly for negative emotional experiences, it is often unclear whether people feel angry, sad, or both. Talking to others can provide clarity, helping people understand what they feel and why (Rimé, Mesquita, Philippot, & Boca, 1991).

Third, sharing can reduce dissonance. People not only use social talk to help make better decisions (as discussed in the "Information Acquisition" section that follows), they also use communication to feel better about the decisions they have made. Consumers are often uncertain about whether they made the best decision. Was this really the best car to buy? Should I have put more money in my 401k? Talking with other scan help reduce feelings of doubt and bolster confidence in the choice (Engel, Blackwell, & Miniard, 1993).

Fourth, sharing fosters emotion regulation by enabling people to vent (Hennig-Thurau et al., 2004; Sundaram, Mitra, & Webster, 1998; though see Rimé, 2009). Complaining to a friend about a rude customer service represen-tative, for example, can provide catharsis that reduces the negative emotional impact (Pennebaker, 1999; Pennebaker, Zech, & Rimé, 2001). Indeed, research suggests that angry (Wetzer, Zeelenberg, & Pieters, 2007) and dissatisfied (Anderson, 1998) consumers often share word of mouth to vent.

Fifth, interpersonal communication also allows people to punish companies or organizations for negative experiences. Complaining helps people feel better, but it can also act to dissuade others from working with that company in the future. In this way, angry, frustrated, or dissatisfied consumers can share negative word of mouth to take revenge (Anderson, 1998; Wetzer, Zeelenberg, & Pieters, 2007).

Finally, while the preceding explanations have focused mostly on negative emotion, sharing can also allow people to rehearse and relive positive experiences (Hennig-Thurau et al., 2004; Rimé, 2009). Rehashing each detail of an exquisite meal or amazing vacation provides the opportunity to savor and ruminate on these positive events. Indeed, Langston (1994) found that sharing positive events enhanced positive affect (also see Gable, Reis, Impett, & Asher, 2004).

Consistent with these suggestions, research finds that most emotions increase sharing. More emotional social anecdotes (Peters, Kashima, & Clark, 2009), urban legends (Heath, Bell, & Sternberg, 2001), news stories (Berger & Milkman, 2012; Luminet et al., 2000), and emails (Chiu, Hsieh, Kao, & Lee, 2007) are more likely to be shared.[2]

High arousal emotions are particularly likely to be shared. In addition to differing in valence, emotions also differ on the level of physiological arousal, or the activation (i.e., increased heart rate, Heilman, 1997) with which they are associated. News that evokes more high arousal emotions, such as awe, anger, or anxiety, is more likely to be passed on (Berger & Milkman, 2012), and Super Bowl ads that elicit more biometric responses such as skin conductance receive more buzz (Siefert et al., 2009).

Information Acquisition

People also talk and share to acquire information. A consumer may be uncertain about which lawnmower to buy, or whether a particular recipe is easy to make, so he or she reaches out to others for assistance and advice (Dichter, 1966; Hennig-Thurau et. al., 2004; Rimé, 2009). For recommendations, suggestions about what to do, or simply another perspective (Fitzsimons & Lehmann, 2004; Tost, Gino, & Larrick, 2012; Zhao & Xie, 2011).

Consistent with this suggestion, one theory about the function of gossip is that it serves as a form of observational learning (Baumeister, Zhang, & Vohs, 2004). Rather than acquiring information through trial and error (which might be time consuming) or directly observing others (which might be similarly difficult), interpersonal communication allows people to learn from others' experiences. People can quickly and easily ask around to see what others are doing and acquire relevant information. Word of mouth also helps people solve problems that may come up after a decision is made. By talking to others, people can get a sense of how to resolve problems and find solutions.

People should be particularly likely to rely on word of mouth for information acquisition when decisions are risky, expensive, important, complex, or filled with uncertainty. For these types of decisions, people may feel a greater need to make the right choice or may need more help sorting through the information. As a result, they should be more likely to rely on others to help them. Indeed, some work finds that brands that involve more risk are discussed more (Lovett,

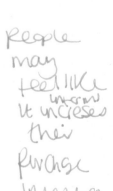

_____

2 That said, emotions such as shame and guilt, which make people look bad, may actually decrease sharing (Finkenauer & Rimé, 1998).

Peres, & Shachar, 2013). People should also be more likely to use word of mouth to acquire information when other sources are scarce or unavailable.

Social Bonding

A fourth reason people share word of mouth is to connect or bond with others (Rimé, 2009). In some ways, this social bonding motive can be seen as the most fundamental reasons for talking and sharing. People have a need for social relationships (Baumeister & Leary, 1995) and interpersonal communication helps fill that desire (Hennig-Thurau et al., 2004). In fact, some have argued that social bonding is the reason that language evolved in the first place (Dunbar, 1998, 2004). Animals used to pick nits out of each other's hair as a way of maintaining connection and dominance hierarchies. But as groups got larger, this became difficult, and so language evolved to allow humans to reinforce bonds and stay connected to a large set of others.

The term *phatic communication* (Malinowski, 1923) has been used to describe conversations whose function is to "create social rapport rather than to convey information," (Rettie, 2009, p. 1135). Indeed, some research suggests that over half of communication is phatic in nature (Rettie, 2009). Such conversations act to reinforce shared views and reduce loneliness and boredom.

One place the social bonding motive can be seen most clearly is people's tendency to talk about things they have in common with others (Clark, 1996; Stalnaker, 1978). Fast, Heath, and Wu (2009), for example, find that even controlling for actual performance, more famous baseball players are more likely to be mentioned in online discussion groups. Though one could argue that impression management plays a role here (i.e., other people are less likely to be interested in topics they know nothing about), social bonding does as well. Talking about topics that everyone can relate to increases the chance that others can weigh in and comment. This, in turn, should deepen the connection between conversation partners.

Indeed, some work shows that emotional sharing is particularly likely to deepen social connections (Peters & Kashima, 2007). Sharing an emotional story or narrative increases emotional synchrony between conversation partners (Barsade & Gibson, 2007). If someone tells someone else about something funny that happened, for example, both parties will laugh, and that shared experience will bring them closer together.

Accessibility

Accessibility also impacts what people talk about and share. Products, information, and conversation topics more broadly vary in their accessibility (Higgins & King, 1981; Wyer & Srull, 1981). Some things are more top-of-mind, while others are less so. But stimuli in the environment, such as sights, sounds, or smells, can act as cues, or triggers, activating associated concepts in memory and making them more accessible (Higgins, Rholes, & Jones, 1977).

This activation can then spread to related concepts through an associative network (Anderson, 1983; Collins & Loftus, 1975). So eating peanut butter not only makes peanut butter more top-of-mind, but it also makes its frequent partner jelly more accessible. A great deal of research has shown how accessibility affects judgment and choice (Feldman & Lynch, 1988; Hauser, 1978; Nedungadi, 1990; see Lynch & Srull, 1982, for a review).

Accessibility also shapes word of mouth. Consistent with the notion that people tend to talk about situation consistent topics (Landis & Burtt, 1924), people reported that 80 percent of word of mouth about a new coffee product was driven by related conversational or environmental cues (e.g., seeing an ad, but also simply drinking coffee or talking about food; Belk, 1978). Similarly, many word of mouth referrals seem to be driven by related topics happening to be discussed (Brown & Reingen, 1987). Cues can also be internal. People who care a lot about a particular brand or are heavily involved in a certain product category should have those constructs more chronically accessible, which should lead them to be more likely to be discussed.

More recent empirical work supports this suggestion, finding that products that are cued or triggered more frequently by the surrounding environment get 15 percent more word of mouth (Berger & Schwartz, 2011). Experimental evidence underscores this notion and shows that increasing the prevalence of triggers for a product increases the amount of word of mouth it receives (Berger & Schwartz, 2011). Similarly, research shows that compared to consumers' opinions, certainty information (i.e., consumers' feeling of certainty or uncertainty associated with an opinion) is less likely to be shared because it is less accessible (Dubois, Rucker, & Tormala, 2011).

The effect of public visibility on word of mouth may also be driven by accessibility. Some products and behaviors (e.g., shirts and greetings) are more public while others (e.g., socks and donations to charity) tend to be more private. This increased visibility, in turn, should increase the chance that others see and talk about those products. People talk about shirts more than socks, for example, because the former are more likely to be seen, made accessible, and discussed. Indeed, publicly visible products receive 8 percent more word of mouth (Berger & Schwartz, 2011).

Useful Information

Another factor that shapes interpersonal communication is useful information. Psychologists, sociologists, and folklorists have long theorized that people share rumors, folktales, and urban legends not only for entertainment, but also because they contain practically valuable information or social morals (Allport & Postman, 1947; Brunvand, 1981; Rosnow, 1980; Shibutani, 1966; Rosnow & Fine, 1976). People share rumors to help "understand and simplify complicated events" (Allport & Postman, 1947, p. 5), and tell legends "not only because of their inherent plot interest but because they seem to convey true, worthwhile and relevant information..." (Brunvand, 1981, p. 11). Indeed, there is some evidence that stories that are more useful (i.e., people would change their behavior upon hearing them) are more likely to be shared (Heath, Bell, & Sternberg, 2001).

Some consumer behavior research is consistent with these theoretical perspectives. Experimental work finds that people are more willing to share marketing messages that have more utilitarian value (Chiu et al., 2007) and suggests that usefulness may be particularly relevant in shaping the valence of word of mouth (Moldovan, Goldenberg, & Chattopadhyay, 2011). Empirical analyses find that more useful news articles are more likely to be highly shared (Berger & Milkman, 2012).

But while it is clear that people share useful information, the exact motive for sharing this type of content may be multiply determined. One reason people share useful information may be altruism, or the desire to help others (Dichter, 1966; Engel, Blackwell, & Miniard, 1993; Hennig-Thurau et al., 2004; Price, Arnould, & Deibler, 1995). Critical interviews, for example, suggest that over 20 percent of word of mouth conversations were motivated by the desire to help others avoid problems or make satisfying purchase decisions (Sundaram, Mitra, & Webster, 1998). Other potential drivers are more self-focused. Useful information has social exchange value (Homans, 1958), which can generate future reciprocity (Fehr, Kirchsteiger, & Riedl, 1998). People may also share useful content because it is self-enhancing and reflects positively on them (i.e., makes them seem as though they know useful things). Which of these motives is most important, and when, remains unclear.

Persuading Others

Finally, people share word of mouth to persuade others. People try to convince their spouses to see a particular movie or try to convince their office mates to go to a particular place for lunch. Relationship partners, for example, shift the language they use during arguments (i.e., words such as "we" and "us") when they are trying to convince others to do something. Similarly, across a wide range of areas, including purchase decisions (Kirchler, 1993) and health behaviors (Cohen & Lichtenstein, 1990; Tucker & Mueller, 2000), consumers report using interpersonal communication to influence others (Bui, Raven, & Schwarzwald, 1994; Roskos-Ewoldsen, 1997).

The Audience

Almost by definition, communication involves an audience. People do not just share something, they share that something with someone. But while the audience is an integral part of the communication process, less research has examined how the audience impacts communication. How does who people are talking to impact what they share?

Some key audience dimensions are tie strength, audience size, and status.

Tie Strength

Sometimes people talk to strong ties (i.e., friends, family members, or other people they know well), while other times people talk to weak ties (i.e., acquaintances or other people to whom we are not as closely tied; Brown & Reingen, 1987; Granovetter, 1973). Research finds that when people have a particularly valuable piece of information, they are more likely to share it with strong ties (Brown & Reingen, 1987). People are less likely to discuss controversial topics with weak ties (Chen & Berger, 2013), and word of mouth to weaker ties tends to be more positive (Dubois, Bonezzi, & De Angelis, 2013), potentially because people engage in more impression management with those they do not know as well. One might also imagine that people would be less likely to share embarrassing or personally damaging things with others they do not know as well.

That said, some work suggests that people also impression-manage with strong ties (Tesser & Campbell, 1982; Tesser & Paulhus, 1983). Strong ties are also more important to one's self-concept, making them potentially more relevant for impression management.

Audience Size

Most work on audience effects has examined tie strength, but some recent work has begun to look at audience size, or how the number of others with whom one is sharing affects what people talk about and share.

Talking with just one person can be described as narrowcasting, while talking with a larger group of others can be described as broadcasting. Some work finds that audience size impacts what people share by changing whether communicators focus their attention (Barasch & Berger, 2014). People naturally tend to focus on the self, but communicating with just one person heightens other-focus, which leads people to share less self-presenting content and more content that is useful to their audience. Other work finds that audience size impacts sharing through construal level (Joshi & Wakslak, 2013). When talking to larger groups, communicators tend to speak more abstractly to adopt a more universal perspective.

Tie Status

Even less work has examined tie status, but it should clearly impact sharing. Sometimes people communicate with high-status others, while other times they communicate with low-status others. One way this may shape word of mouth is through impression management. People care more what high-status others think, so they may be more likely to share things that make them look good. Indeed, some work finds that people are more likely to share positive information with others who are higher in the social hierarchy (DuPlessis & Dubois, 2014).

Overall, while existing work has found some interesting results, much more remains to be done regarding audience effects. One more general question is when the audience shapes what people share versus when what people want to share shapes the audience. In some cases the audience is fixed and people decide what to share. When someone runs into a colleague in the hallway, or is having dinner with a friend, who they are talking to is fixed, and that then impacts what gets shared. In other situations, the content is fixed, and that drives selection of the audience. When someone reads a news article, for example, they may then decide to reach out to any number of their social connections to share it with. Relevance should matter here, and content may even activate related social ties, making them more accessible (i.e., top-of-mind), which should facilitate the sharing process.

Communication Channels

Similar to audience effects, there has been relatively less attention to the role that communication channels play in word of mouth. Every time people share something, they share it through a particular channel (e.g., face to face, over the phone, online, etc.). Might the specific channel people communicate through impact what they talk about or share? And if so, how?

One way channels differ is whether they involve written or oral communication. While face-to-face communication is oral in nature, most online communication (e.g., social media and email) as well as texting involves writing instead. While this seems like a minor distinction, it can shape what people pass on. Oral communication is relatively synchronous. One person says something, and then the other responds relatively quickly. But written communication is more asynchronous, with longer gaps between conversation turns. This difference in synchrony, in turn, gives people more time to construct and refine what to say (Berger & Iyengar, 2013). More than 70 percent of Facebook messages, for example, are self-censored (Das & Kramer, 2013), where people edit what they are sharing until they like how it looks. Similarly, compared to requests made via voicemail, those made by email are seen as more polite, ostensibly because people have more time to compose and refine their request (Duthler, 2006). In a marketing context, written communication leads people to talk about more interesting products and brands for the same reason (Berger & Iyengar, 2013). The additional time allows people the opportunity to curate more carefully what they want to share.

Channels may also differ on a number of other dimensions that deserve further attention (see Berger, 2014a). While the audience is quiet salient in face-to-face communication, in most online communication social presence is greatly reduced. People cannot see their audience, which removes the ability to pick up on subtle cues such as body language. In addition, the lack of social presence may lull people into feeling like what they are sharing is private, even though many others may actually end up seeing it. Online channels can also provide anonymity. People can sometimes post without revealing their identity. Anonymity should likely reduce impression management concerns and free people up to say whatever they want.

Finally, some online communication channels, such as Facebook status updates, allow for undirected communication. Almost all other communication is directed. People pick someone to call on the phone, pick particular people to email, or pick someone to walk up to and talk to face to face. But Facebook status updates, or tweets, are undirected in nature. Rather than having to select a particular person (or people) to communicate with, people can reach out to a large group of individuals and see whether anyone responds. As a result, undirected communication may be particularly useful for people who are socially anxious (Buechel & Berger, 2014). It allows them to have the potential for social connection with reduced risk of being (or feeling) rebuffed.

Different communication channels may also have different impacts on behavior. Text-based communication, for example, does not release oxytocin and reduce stress in the same way that warm, interpersonal contact can (Seltzer, Prososki, Ziegler, & Pollak, 2012).

Word of Mouth Effects

Broadly speaking, word of mouth affects consumer behavior through two key routes (Van den Bulte & Wuyts, 2009). Word of mouth can inform people that a product or behavior exists (and make it more accessible or top-of-mind). This awareness function is particularly important for new, unknown, or low-risk products and ideas (Godes & Mayzlin, 2009).

Word of mouth can also have a persuasive function. It can change opinions about whether something is right or worth doing (similar to informational influence; Deutsch & Gerard, 1955), lead people to change their behavior to be liked or avoid being ostracized (similar to normative social influence; Deutsch & Gerard, 1955), and generate competitive concerns related to status. Word of mouth can also impact the social identity consumers' associate with a product or behavior, which may, in turn, affect likelihood of purchase or consumption (Berger & Heath, 2007, 2008). All of these more persuasive functions may be particularly important when the uncertainty is high (i.e., risk reduction).

Research on word of mouth effects can be broadly divided into quantitative research using field data and more behaviorally based experimental laboratory research.

Quantitative Research on Word of Mouth Effects

Across a variety of domains, quantitative research finds that word of mouth has a causal impact on individual behavior (e.g., purchase or new product adoption) and the firm more broadly (e.g., aggregate sales or financial performance).[3] Word of mouth has been shown to boost sales of books (Chevalier & Mayzlin, 2006), bath and beauty products (Moe & Trusov, 2011), and restaurants (Godes & Mayzlin, 2009) and speed the adoption and diffusion of new pharmaceutical drugs (Iyengar, Van den Bulte, & Valente, 2010). Other work suggests that word of mouth may boost sales of music (Dhar & Chang, 2009), movies (Chintagunta, Gopinath, & Venkataraman, 2010; Dellarocas, Zhang, & Awad, 2007; Duan, Gu, & Whinston, 2008; Liu, 2006), and video games (Zhu & Zhang, 2010) and increase microfinance loans (Stephen & Galak, 2012), television show viewership (Godes & Mayzlin, 2004), and sign-ups to a social network website (Trusov, Bucklin, & Pauwels, 2009). Some data even suggest that negative word of mouth may hurt stock prices (Luo, 2009) and stock returns (Luo, 2007).

Most studies that have collected word-of-mouth content have focused on online word of mouth, in part because it is easier to acquire. Online word of mouth includes consumer reviews and blog posts and can be decomposed into volume, valence, and variance (Dellarocas & Narayan, 2006; Moe & Trusov, 2011). Volume is the number of reviews or posts that a given item receives, where more postings are usually associated with increased sales. Valence is the average rating a product receives (e.g., 3.7 out of 5 stars; Dellarocas, Zhang, & Awad, 2007) or the number of reviews of different types (e.g., thirty-seven one-star reviews; Chevalier & Mayzlin, 2006), and more positive reviews are generally associated with increased sales (though see Berger, Sorensen, & Rasmussen, 2010). Finally, variance is either the statistical variance (Clemons, Gao, & Hitt, 2006) or entropy (Godes & Mayzlin, 2004) of the reviews.

One interesting question for future research is when and why different online word-of-mouth metrics have a stronger impact on (or are more predict- ive of) behavior, sales, or other relevant outcomes. Different papers have found different metrics to be more or less important. Some papers have found significant effects on both the volume and valence of reviews (Chevalier & Mayzlin, 2006; Dellarocas, Zhang, & Awad, 2007). Other papers have found effects only on either review volume (Duan, Gu, & Whinston, 2008; Liu, 2006) or review valence (Chintagunta, Gopinath, & Venkataraman, 2010), but not the other. While some of the difference may be due to the specific modeling framework used or dependent variable examined, the distinction between awareness and persuasion may also be important. Word of mouth may be

---

3 People may tend to behave similarly to their social ties, but in the field it is often unclear whether this correlation is driven by influence (i.e., one person affecting another's behavior), homophily (i.e., the fact that people tend to interact with similar others), or other factors (e.g., interdepend- ent sampling; Denrell & Le Mens, 2007). If someone goes to a movie his or her friend recommends, did he or she go *because* the friend recommended it, or would the person have seen it anyway simply because he or she likes those types of movies in the first place? This is an important issue that field work often deals with when trying to estimate the impact of word of mouth on behavior (see Aral, Muchnik, & Sundararajan, 2009).

valued or used differently depending on the novelty and risk involved with the thing being adopted (Godes & Mayzlin, 2009; Van den Bulte & Wuyts, 2009). For products that are relatively high-risk, or already quite well-known, the persuasive function of word of mouth should be particularly important. Thus valence should matter: positive word of mouth should increase choice, while negative word of mouth may decrease it. For low-risk or novel products, however, word of mouth should also impact behavior through increasing awareness. Here, volume should matter more than valence, and even negative word of mouth may boost choice (Berger, Sorensen, & Rasmussen, 2010).

Another rich area for behavioral research is the social dynamics of online reviews. Online review systems are organized in such a way that consumers are likely to see others' reviews before they write their own. How does the volume and valence of existing reviews impact (1) whether consumers write a review and (2) the nature of the review they write? Consumers might be more (or less) likely to post their opinion if there are few reviews about a product already, or if their opinion differs from the prevailing view. Similarly, existing reviews might generate either assimilation or contrast effects. Indeed, social dynamics may be one reason that the average product rating tends to decrease as more ratings arrive (Godes & Silva, 2012; Li & Hitt, 2008). Consequently, researchers have pointed out the importance of considering (and explicitly modeling) how existing reviews impact the arrival of new reviews (Moe & Schweidel, 2012; Moe & Trusov, 2011).

Behavioral Research on Word of Mouth Effects

Behavioral research on word of mouth has focused on when word of mouth may have a larger impact on behavior and why.[4]

Most of this work has looked at when and how word of mouth affects the word of mouth recipient.[5] One important factor is characteristics of the word of mouth source. People tend to listen more to credible sources, or those who are more trustworthy or have more expertise (Hovland & Weiss, 1951; Petty & Wegner, 1998; Pornpitakpan, 2004). Other important factors are the strength of the tie (i.e., friends vs. acquaintances, or strong vs. weak ties) and their similarity to the word-of-mouth recipient. Per dose or "instance" of word of mouth, strong ties may be more impactful (Bakshy, Rosenn, Marlow, & Adamic,

---

4 Though it focuses more on responses to persuasive messages in general, rather than word of mouth per se, the huge literature on attitude change (e.g., the elaboration likelihood model) is also relevant to considering when and why word of mouth may affect behavior. Though a comprehensive review of this literature is beyond the scope of this chapter, see Petty, Wheeler, & Tormala (2012) for a recent review.

5 Word of mouth also impacts the person who shares it. If the speaker uses a lot of explaining language when sharing, for example, the recipient will like a positive experience less and a negative experience more, impacting their likelihood of retelling that information again (Moore, 2012). Sharing self-relevant content online (e.g., Facebook status updates or tweets) can also aid in emotion regulation, helping neurotic individuals manage their emotions and repair well-being after negative emotional experiences (Buechel & Berger, 2012).

2012; Bond et al., 2012; Brown & Reingen, 1987) because people tend to trust them more and think they know more about their tastes and interests. That said, people have more weak ties, or acquaintances, so the overall impact of these types of individuals may be larger (Bakshy et al., 2012; for related discussions, see Brown & Reingen, 1987; Goldenberg, Libai, & Muller, 2001; Granovetter, 1973). Similarly, word of mouth from similar others may have a more positive effect (Brown & Reingen, 1987; Forman, Ghose, & Wiesenfeld (2008); also see Naylor, Lamberton, & Norton, 2011) because people think their tastes are similar (Brock, 1965). That said, word of mouth from dissimilar others may have benefits because these individuals have access to different information (Granovetter, 1973) and may be more familiar with alternative ways of thinking (Burt, 2004). Consequently, whether word of mouth from strong or weak ties and similar or dissimilar others is more impactful may depend on the particular situation.

Another important factor is the nature of the word of mouth itself. Word of mouth varies in its valence: people can recommend a restaurant, say they hated it, or merely mention that they went there. Recommendations likely have the most positive impact on behavior, but even mentions should have a positive effect if they increase product awareness or accessibility (see Lynch & Srull, 1982; also see Berger, Sorensen, & Rasmussen, 2010; Nedungadi, 1990; Stigler, 1961). In terms of absolute impact, negative word of mouth may have a stronger impact than positive word of mouth, in some cases (Basuroy, Chatterjee, & Ravid 2003; Chevalier & Mayzlin, 2006; see Chen & Lurie, 2014, for a potential behavioral explanation). Word of mouth also varies in its intensity or depth: people can talk briefly about an experience, or they can go on at length. Longer or more in-depth word of mouth discussions should have a stronger impact on behavior (though this may be mitigated for online word of mouth – see Godes & Mayzlin, 2004 – as people may not end up reading an entire post or review). Along these lines, face-to-face word of mouth may have a stronger impact than online or written word of mouth because it tends to be more engaging and vivid (Herr, Kardes, & Kim, 1991).[6] Whether the word of mouth is solicited also matters. Solicited advice seems to have a more positive impact than unsolicited advice (East, Hammond, Lomax, & Hardin, 2005) and unsolicited recommendations that go against an individual's opinion may even lead to reactance and strengthen the initial opinion (Fitzsimons & Lehmann, 2004). Finally, the level of certainty expressed along with an opinion can also have an effect, with uncertainty actually being beneficial in some cases (Karmarkar & Tormala, 2010).

The susceptibility of the word-of-mouth recipient is also important (Watts & Dodds, 2007). Just like some people may be more susceptible to catching a cold or a disease (e.g., because they have a weaker immune system), some people

---

6 More generally, chatter can evolve over a huge variety of online channels (e.g., Facebook, Twitter, blogs, etc.), and research might examine which of these channels actually influence sales rather than merely predict them.

may be more susceptible to, or prone to be affected by, social influence (Aral & Walker, 2012; Bearden, Netemeyer, & Tell, 1989; Godes, 2011). More susceptible individuals, for example, should be more likely to adopt new products or ideas if they hear about or see others using them. Though relatively little research has examined this issue, some data suggest that young people are more susceptible (Park & Lessig, 1977; Pasupathi, 1999), and people who perceive themselves as opinion leaders are less susceptible (Iyengar et al., 2011). Beyond individual differences, situational factors should also shape susceptibility. The closer people already are to taking some action, the more likely it is that a dose of word of mouth will push them over the edge. People who are searching online reviews, for example, are often close to being ready to make a purchase, and thus may be particularly susceptible to influence.

Another potentially interesting question is how multiple instances, or doses, of word of mouth aggregate over time. Research distinguishes between simple and complex contagions (Centola, 2010; Centola & Macy, 2007). In some cases, awareness may be all that is needed, and thus one dose of word of mouth may be enough to get people to adopt a product or idea (i.e., simple contagion). Being forwarded a link to a newspaper article once may get people to take a look. But for most products, ideas, or innovations, multiple sources of influence increase the likelihood of adoption (i.e., complex contagion). Trying a new surgical procedure, or even deciding to see a new movie, may require multiple sources of word of mouth before adoption occurs. In these situations, the persuasive impact of word of mouth may be more important.

Research has recognized that some products and behaviors require more doses of influence, and documented that multiple doses increase adoption, but little empirical work has examined this area. What types of products tend to require complex contagions (e.g., potentially newer or riskier ones; Woodside & Delozier, 1976)? How does the temporal distance between doses affect their overall impact (i.e., are two doses this week the same as one this week and one the next)? Are the behavioral processes behind these effects driven by memory, belief updating, or some other factor?

Research might also consider how doses of word of mouth combine with advertising to impact behavior (Goldenberg, Libai, & Muller, 2001). One possibility is that advertising helps spread general awareness and word of mouth, then persuades people to take action.

A related question is the effect of advertising on word of mouth. Advertising not only combines with word of mouth to impact sales, but may boost word of mouth as well (Moon, Bergey & Iacobucci, 2009; Onishi & Manchanda, 2012; Stacey, Pauwels, & Lackman 2012; Stephen & Galak, 2012).[7] What types

---

7 Note that word of mouth may also affect advertising. More word of mouth, for example, may allow companies to advertise less because everyone already knows about the product. Word of mouth might also impact the content of advertising. Companies and organizations sometimes design their ads based on the everyday language people are using to describe the product. Further, if consumers are already talking about certain features of a product, advertisers may want to highlight other features, or try to stamp out false word of mouth by sharing the truth.

of ads generate more word of mouth (Moldovan & Lehmann, 2010) or are more likely to be shared?

This is a particularly interesting question because some of the factors that make ads more likely to be shared may also make them less persuasive. One might imagine that consumers are hesitant to share advertisements that seem like direct influence attempts. At the same time, if advertisements make no attempt to be persuasive, they are less likely to benefit the brand. So it may be hard for ads both to be shared and to boost brand evaluation or choice. Indeed, research suggests that virality and ad persuasiveness are negatively correlated; every million more views an ad receives is associated with 10 percent lower persuasiveness (Tucker, 2014).

One way to address this conundrum may be to generate entertaining content in which the product or brand is integral to the narrative (i.e., BlendTec's Will it Blend campaign). Such ads are interesting enough to be shared, but provide enough information about the brand to boost brand evaluation, purchase likelihood, and choice after delay (Akpinar & Berger, 2014).

Finally, future work might more deeply examine the relative impact of word of mouth and advertising on behavior. Some research suggests that word of mouth referrals have a larger short-term effect and longer-term effects than media (Trusov, Bucklin, & Pauwels, 2009), and that while the per-event (e.g., one TV or blog post mention) sales impact of earned media is larger than that of social media, social media have a larger impact overall because the events are more frequent (Stephen & Galak, 2012). This work highlights that audience size (i.e., number of people reached) and per-person impact may be two key factors. Television ads, for example, tend to reach more people than most word of mouth conversations (though online ads may have similar reach). Advertising can also be used to reach many people faster than word of mouth usually can.

Compared to a dose of advertising, one might imagine that a dose of word of mouth is more likely to change behavior because it is more persuasive. People likely trust word of mouth more than they trust traditional marketing efforts, for a number of reasons. First, consumers recognize that advertisements are trying to persuade them and may react against this influence attempt (Friestad & Wright, 1994). Relatedly, word of mouth is usually more objective. Ads always say the product is good, so they are not very diagnostic. People's friends, however, tend to tell them the truth, so word of mouth is more trustworthy and more persuasive. Consequently, advertising may be most useful for spreading awareness, while word of mouth may be most useful for persuasion. Word of mouth is also usually more targeted than advertising. Ads try to appeal only to the target demographic, but word of mouth is even more focused. Consumers tend to seek out the people in their social network who would be most interested in a given piece of information, and that may be part of the reason referred customers are more profitable overall (Schmitt, Skiera, & Van den Bulte, 2011).

Directions for Future Research

Though there has been a great deal of exciting research on word of mouth that can be captured in the general framework depicted in Figure 14.1, much more remains to be done. The following subsections offer a sample of interesting questions that deserve further attention.

Why Does Arousal Boost Sharing?

Some research finds that content that induces high arousal emotion is more likely to be shared (Berger & Milkman, 2012; Siefert et al., 2009). Other work shows that even incidental arousal boosts sharing. Watching a scary movie, for example, or simply running in place increases people's willingness to share emotionally neutral news articles (Berger, 2011). These findings not only suggest that arousal increases sharing, but that arousal in one context can spill over and increase sharing of unrelated content.

But while the link between arousal and sharing is clear, the reason for this link is undetermined. One possibility is the link between arousal and action. Arousal is characterized by activity (Heilman, 1997). This excitatory state has been shown to increase all sorts of action-related behaviors, such as helping (Gaertner & Dovidio, 1977) and responding faster to offers in negotiations (Wood & Schweitzer, 2011). Researchers have even suggested that "the primary role of autonomic changes that accompany emotion is to provide support for action" (Davidson, 1993, p. 468). Consequently, arousal may boost sharing because sharing is an action. Arousal increases the activation necessary for action and increases sharing as a result.

A second possibility is that arousal increases sharing because sharing helps people down-regulate or up-regulate emotions, depending on which is needed. As discussed in the section "Emotion Regulation," sharing can help people regulate their emotions. Sharing negative emotions, for example, can help people vent and get rid of their anger. Sharing anxiety can help people find social support and feel better. At the same time, sharing high-arousal positive emotions might help people savor and extend those positive feelings. As a result, arousal might boost sharing as people attempt to down-regulate negative emotions and up-regulate positive ones.

A third possibility is that arousal generates an aversive state that people resolve through sharing. It is clear that negative high-arousal emotions such as anger and anxiety might benefit from resolution. Anxious people prefer to wait with others rather than alone (Schachter, 1959), and talking with others helps people vent their anger. But while positive emotions such as excitement or humor may seem like states that people would want to prolong, these may also have an overly active quality that people eventually would like to reduce. When exciting news happens, for example, people may feel the need to get it off their chest and cannot do that until they find someone to talk to about it.

When Do People Talk About?

Another potentially interesting question for further study is when people talk about. Sometimes people talk about things that happened in the past (i.e., what they had for lunch yesterday), while other times they talk about things that will happen in the future (i.e., what they are having for lunch tomorrow). Sometimes people talk about things that are temporally close (i.e., something that happened recently or will happen soon), while other times they talk about things that are temporally distant (i.e., something that happened a long time ago or will happen a while in the future). How does the temporal placement of an event impact its likelihood of being discussed? Are people more likely to talk about something before or after it happens?

One possibility is that things are less likely to be discussed the further away they are from now. While things that just happened are top-of-mind, events soon decay in memory, making it less likely they will be recalled and discussed. Similarly, while people may think ahead a little, temporally distant future events should be less accessible and thus less likely to be brought up.

Another possibility is that the future is talked about more than the past. A good deal of works shows that the future is more emotionally evocative than the past (Van Boven & Ashworth, 2007). Given that more emotional things are more likely to be discussed, the same event may be more likely to be talked about if it is in the future because it has greater emotional resonance.

How Does Content Breadth Impact Sharing?

Some topics or information have a broader potential audience than others. In the United States, for example, more people follow baseball than follow water polo. As a result, an article about baseball is likely relevant to more of someone's friends than an article about water polo. Similarly, more people in the United States eat pizza than eat Ethiopian food. As a result, an article about pizza is likely relevant to a broader audience of one's friends than an article about Ethiopian food.

Intuition would suggest that broadly relevant content should be more likely to be shared. There are more people one could share the article with, and as a result, they should be more likely to pass it on. Particularly on social media, where people broadcast content to a large and diverse audience, broadly relevant content seems like it should be more likely to be shared.

Narrowly relevant content, however, may benefit from stronger associations with particular individuals. While narrowly relevant content is, by definition, not as broadly interesting, it is more likely to be tied one or two particular individuals in one's social network. Further, because it is tied to fewer individuals, those ties are likely to be stronger (i.e., the fan effect; Anderson, 1974,

1983). Most people don't eat Ethiopian food, but because of that, it is more likely that a particular social tie (or two) is strongly activated when someone comes across an article about Ethiopian food. This stronger activation, in turn, may increase the likelihood that the article is shared, because people may use activation strength as a signal that content is worth sharing. Thus, while broadly relevant content *could* be shared with more people, narrowly relevant content may be more likely to be shared because it strongly activates a few people who might find the content highly relevant.

This discussion highlights the important distinction between sharing likelihood and number of shares overall. In this case, there is likely more overlap across people in what is broadly relevant than what is narrowly relevant. Most people have some friends who like pizza, but while some people may have a few friends who like Ethiopian food, and other people have a few friends who like water polo, most people may not have any friends who like either. Consequently, compared to broadly relevant topics, each person may be more likely to share whatever topic is narrowly relevant to them, but broadly relevant topics may get more overall shares because they could be shared by, and to, many more people. The underlying psychological driver of sharing is the same, but what it leads people to share may differ across different individuals.

How People Talk

Future research might also examine not just whether people talk about particular things but *how* they talk about them. Most research on word of mouth has focused on incidence or volume: whether a given topic or product is discussed or how frequently it is discussed. While such investigations are useful, they often ignore the multifaceted ways in which information can be shared. People can talk about the same topic for varying lengths of time, use different words, express greater certainty, and be more or less assertive. What shapes *how* people talk about a particular product or brand?

Some research has begun to focus on language use, examining personal pronoun usage (i.e., "I" vs. "you"; Packard, Moore, & McFerran, 2014; Packard & Wooten, 2013), language complexity (Packard & Wooten, 2013), and linguistic mimicry of conversation partners (Moore & McFerran, 2012). Customer service representatives tend to use "you" or "we" rather than "I" when talking to customers, for example, but using "I" actually enhances satisfaction and purchase intentions (Packard, Moore, & McFerran, 2014). Other work has examined how the use of explaining language impacts the word-of-mouth sharer. Much more research, however, remains to be done.

One could imagine, for example, that length of discussion depends on interest. The more involved people are in a given topic, the longer they should talk about it. Emotionality should have a similar effect. Controversy might also generate longer conversations (see Chen & Berger, 2013). The more room there is for debate, the more back and forth that should generate.

Conclusion

In conclusion, while interpersonal communication has always been an integral part of everyday life, the emergence of social media has only strengthened awareness of this important area. But while it is clear that word of mouth is frequent and important, less is known about the underlying consumer psychology. Why do people talk about and share some things rather than others? How does the audience people are communicating with and the channel they are communicating through shape what people share? And when and why does word of mouth have a larger impact on consumer attitudes and decision making? Great progress in this area has been made, but there are many more exciting questions to pursue.

References

Akpinar, Ezgi, & Berger, Jonah (2014). Valuable virality. Wharton Working Paper.

Allport, Gordon W., & Postman, Leo (1947). *The Psychology of Rumor*. New York: Henry Holt.

Anderson, John R. (1974). Retrieval of propositional information from long-term memory. *Cognitive Psychology, 6*, 451–474.

Anderson, John R. (1983). *The Architecture of Cognition*. Cambridge, MA: Harvard University Press.

Anderson, Eugene W. (1998). Customer satisfaction and word of mouth. *Journal of Service Research, 1*(1), 5–17.

Aral, Sinan, & Walker, Dylan (2012). Identifying influential and susceptible members of social networks. *Science, 337*(6092), 337–341.

Aral, Sinan, Lev Muchnik, & Arum Sundararajan (2009). Distinguishing influence based contagion from homophily driven diffusion in dynamic networks. *Proceedings of the National Academy of Sciences, 106*(51): 21544–21549.

Bakshy, Eytan, Rosenn, Itamar, Marlow, Cameron, & Adamic, Lada (2012). *The Role of Social Networks in Information Diffusion*. Paper presented at the 21st ACM World Wide Web Conference. Lyon, France, April, 16–20.

Barasch, Alix, & Berger, Jonah (2014). Broadcasting and narrowcasting: How audience size impacts what people share. *Journal of Marketing Research, 51*(3), 286–299.

Barsade, Sigal G., & Gibson, Donald E. (2007). Why does affect matter in organizations. *Academy of Management Perspectives, 21*, 36–59.

Basuroy, Suman, Chatterjee, Subimal, & Ravid, S. Abraham (2003). How critical are critical reviews? The box office effects of film critics, star power, and budgets. *Journal of Marketing, 67*, 103–117.

Baumeister, Roy. F., & Leary, Mark R. (1995). The need to belong: Desire for interpersonal attachments as a fundamental human motivation. *Psychological Bulletin, 117*, 497–529.

Baumeister, Roy F., Zhang, Liqing, & Vohs, Kathleen D. (2004). Gossip as cultural learning. *Review of General Psychology, 8*, 111–121.

Bearden, William O., Netemeyer, Richard G., & Teel, Jesse E. (1989). Measurement of consumer susceptibility to interpersonal influence. *Journal of Consumer Research, 15*(4), 473–481.

Belk, Russell W. (1978). Occurrence of Word of Mouth Buyer Behavior as a Function of Situation and Advertising Stimuli. In Fred C. Allvine (ed.), *Proceedings of the American Marketing Association's Educators Conference* (pp. 419–422). Chicago: American Marketing Association.

Belk, Russell W. (1988). Possessions and the extended self. *Journal of Consumer Research, 15*(September), 139–167.

Berger, Jonah (2011). Arousal increases social transmission of information. *Psychological Science, 22*(7), 891–893.

Berger, Jonah (2014a). Beyond viral: Social transmission in the Internet age. *Psychological Inquiry, 24*, 293-296.

Berger, Jonah (2014b). Word of mouth and interpersonal communication: A review and directions for future research. *Journal of Consumer Psychology, 24*(4), 586–607.

Berger, Jonah, & Heath, Chip (2007). Where consumers diverge from others: Identity-signaling and product domains. *Journal of Consumer Research, 34*(2), 121–134.

Berger, Jonah, & Heath, Chip (2008). Who drives divergence? Identity signaling, out-group dissimilarity, and the abandonment of cultural tastes. *Journal of Personality and Social Psychology, 95*(3), 593–607.

Berger, Jonah, & Iyengar, Raghuram (2013). Communication channels and word of mouth: How the medium shapes the message. *Journal of Consumer Research, 40*(3), 567–579.

Berger, Jonah, & Milkman, Katherine (2012). What makes online content viral. *Journal of Marketing, 49*(2), 192–205.

Berger, Jonah, & Schwartz, Eric (2011). What drives immediate and ongoing word of mouth? *Journal of Marketing Research, 48*(5), 869–880.

Berger, Jonah, Sorensen, Alan T., & Rasmussen, Scott J. (2010). Positive effects of negative publicity: When negative reviews increase sales. *Marketing Science, 29*(5), 815–827.

Berlo, David K. (1960). *The Process of Communication*. New York: Holt, Rinehart, & Winston.

Bond, Robert M., Fariss, Christopher J., Jones, Jason J., Kramer, Adam D. I., Marlow, Cameron, Settle, Jaime E., & Fowler, James H. (2012). A 61-million-person experiment in social influence and political mobilization. *Nature, 489*, 295–298.

Brock, Timothy C. (1965). Communicator-recipient similarity and decision change. *Journal of Personality and Social Psychology, 1*(6), 650–654.

Brooks, Alison Wood, & Schweitzer, Maurice E.. (2011)Can nervous Nelly negotiate? How anxiety causes negotiators to make low first offers, exit early, and earn less profit. *Organizational Behavior and Human Decision Processes, 115*, 43–54.

Brown, Jacqueline Johnson, & Reingen, Peter H. (1987). Social ties and word of mouth referral behavior. *Journal of Consumer Research, 14*(3), 350–362.

Brunvand, Jan H. (1981). *The Vanishing Hitchhiker: American Urban Legends and Their Meanings*. New York: Norton.

Buechel, Eva, & Berger, Jonah (2014). Facebook therapy: Why people share self-relevant content online. Working Paper, University of Miami.

Bui, Khanh-Van T., Raven, Bertram H., & Schwarzwald, Joseph (1994). Influence strategies in dating relationships: The effects of relationship satisfaction, gender, and perspective. *Journal of Social Behavior and Personality, 9*, 429–442.

Burt, Ronald S. (2004). Structural holes and good ideas. *American Journal of Sociology, 110*(2), 349–399.

Centola, Damon (2010). The spread of behavior in an online social network experiment. *Science, 329*(5996), 1194–1197.

Centola, Damon and Michael Macy (2007). Complex Contagions and the Weakness of Long Ties. *American Journal of Sociology, 113*, 702–34.

Chan, Cindy, & Berger, Jonah (2013). Arousal and social connection. Working Paper, Wharton.

Cheema, Amar, & Kaikati, Andrew M. (2010). The effect of need for uniqueness on word of mouth. *Journal of Marketing Research, 47*(3), 553–563.

Chen, Zoey, & Berger, Jonah (2013). When, why, and how controversy causes conversation. *Journal of Consumer Research, 40*(3), 580–593.

Chen, Zoey, & Lurie, Nicholas (2014). Temporal contiguity and the negativity bias in the impact of online word of mouth. *Journal of Marketing Research, 50*(4), 463–476.

Chevalier, Judith A., & Mayzlin, Dina (2006). The effect of word of mouth on sales: Online book reviews. *Journal of Marketing Research, 43*, 345–354.

Chintagunta, Pradeep K., Gopinath, Shyam, & Venkataraman, Sriram (2010). The effects of online user reviews on movie box-office performance: Accounting for sequential rollout and aggregation across local markets. *Marketing Science, 29*(5), 944–957.

Chiu, H-C., Hsieh, Y-C., Kao, Y-H., & Lee, M. (2007). The determinants of email receivers' dissemiating behaviors on the Internet. *Journal of Advertising Research, 47*(4), 524–534.

Christie, Israel C., & Friedman, Bruce H. (2004). Autonomic specificity of discrete emotion and dimensions of affective space: A multivariate approach. *International Journal of Psychophysiology, 51*, 143–153.

Chung, Cindy, & Darke, Peter (2006). The consumer as advocate: Self-relevance, culture, and word of mouth. *Marketing Letters, 17*(4), 269–279.

Clark, Herbert H. (1996). *Using Language.* Cambridge: Cambridge University Press.

Clemons, Erik K., Gao, Guodong, & Hitt, Lorin (2006). When online reviews meet hyper differentiation: A study of the craft beer industry. *Journal of Management Information Systems, 23*(2), 149–171.

Cohen, Sheldon, & Lichtenstein, Edward (1990). Partner behaviors that support quitting smoking. *Journal of Consulting and Clinical Psychology, 58*, 304–309.

Collins, Allan M., & Loftus, Elizabeth F. (1975). A spreading-activation theory of semantic processing. *Psychological Review, 82*(6), 407–428.

Das, Sauvik, & Kramer, Adam (2013). Self-censorship on Facebook. In *Proceedings of the 7th International Symposium on Usable Privacy (SOUP).* Association for the Advancement of Artificial Intelligence.

Davidson, Richard J. (1993). Parsing affective space: Perspectives from neuropsychology and psychophysiology. *Neuropsychology, 7*(4), 464–475.

De Angelis, Matteo, Bonezzi, Andrea, Peluso, Alessandro, Rucker, Derek, & Costabile, Michele (2012). On braggarts and gossips: A self-enhancement account of word of mouth generation and transmission. *Journal of Marketing Research, 49*(4), 551–563.

Dellarocas, Chrysanthos, & Narayan, Ritu (2006). A statistical measure of a population's propensity to engage in post-purchase online word of mouth. *Statistical Science, 21*(2), 277–285.

Dellarocas, Chrysanthos, Zhang, Xiaoquan, & Awad, Neveen (2007). Exploring the value of online product reviews in forecasting sales: The case of motion pictures. *Journal of Interactive Marketing, 21*(4), 23.

Denrell, J., & Le Mens, G. (2007). Interdependent sampling and social influence. *Psychological Review, 114*(2), 398–422.

Deutsch, Morton, & Gerard, Harold B. (1955). A study of normative and informational social influences upon individual judgment. *Journal of Abnormal and Social Psychology, 51*(3), 629–636.

Dhar, Vasant, & Chang, Elaine (2009). Does chatter matter? The impact of user-generated content on music sales. *Journal of Interactive Marketing, 23*(4), 300–307.

Dichter, Ernest (1966). How word of mouth advertising works. *Harvard Business Review, 44*, 147–166.

Duan, Wenjing, Gu, Bin, & Whinston, Andrew B. (2008). The dynamics of online word-of-mouth and product sales: An empirical investigation of the movie industry. *Journal of Retailing, 84*(2), 233–242.

Dubois, David, Bonezzi, Andrea, & De Angelis, Matteo (2013). The dangers of strong ties: How interpersonal closeness influences word of mouth valence. Working Paper, INSEAD.

Dubois, D., Rucker, D. D., & Tormala, Z. L. (2011). From rumors to facts, and facts to rumors: The role of certainty decay in consumer communications. *Journal of Marketing Research, 48*, 1020–1032.

Du Plessis, Christilene, & Dubois, David (2014). La vie en rose at the top? Why positive (negative) information goes up (down) in a hierarchy. Working Paper, INSEAD.

Dunbar, Robin (1998). *Grooming, Gossip, and the Evolution of Language.* Cambridge, MA: Harvard University Press.

Dunbar, Robin (2004). *The Human Story.* London: Faber and Faber.

Duthler, Kirk W. (2006). The politeness of requests made via email and voicemail: Support for the hyperpersonal model. *Journal of Computer-Mediated Communication, 11*(6), 500–521.

East, Robert, Hammond, Kathy, Lomax, Wendy, & Robinson, Helen (2005). What is the effect of a recommendation? *Marketing Review, 5*, 145–157.

East, Robert, Hammond, Kathy, & Wright, Malcolm (2007). The relative incidence of positive and negative word of mouth: A multi-category study. *International Journal of Research in Marketing, 24*(2), 175–184.

Engel, James E., Blackwell, Roger D., & Kegerreis, Robert J. (1969). How information is used to adopt an innovation. *Journal of Marketing Research, 9*(4), 3–8.

Engel, J. F., Blackwell, R. D., & Miniard, P. W. (1993). *Consumer Behavior,* 7th ed. Fort Worth, TX: Dryden Press.

Escalas, Jennifer E., & Bettman, James R. (2003). You are what they eat: The influence of reference groups on consumer connections to brands. *Journal of Consumer Psychology, 13*(3), 339–348.

Fast, Nathanael J., Heath, Chip, & Wu, George (2009). Common ground and cultural prominence: How conversation reinforces culture. *Psychological Science, 20*, 904–911.

Fehr, Ernst, Kirchsteiger, Georg, & Riedl, Arno (1998). Gift exchange and reciprocity in competitive experimental markets. *European Economic Review, 42*(1), 1–34.

Feick, Lawrence F., & Price, Linda L. (1987). The market maven: A diffuser of market-place information. *Journal of Marketing, 51*(January), 83–97.

Feldman, Jack M., & Lynch, Jr., John G. (1988). Self-generated validity and other effects of measurement on belief, attitude, intention, and behavior. *Journal of Applied Psychology, 73*(3), 421–435.

Finkenauer, Catrin, & Rime, Bernard (1998). Socially shared emotional experiences vs. emotional experiences kept secret: Differential characteristics and consequences. *Journal of Social Clinical Psychology, 17*, 295–318.

Fitzsimons, Gavan J., & Lehmann, Donald R. (2004). Reactance to recommendations: When unsolicited advice yields contrary responses. *Marketing Science, 23*(March–April), 82–94.

Folkes V. S., & Sears, D. O. (1977). Does everybody like a liker? *Journal of Experimental Social Psychology, 13*, 505–519.

Forman, Chris, Ghose, Anindya, & Wiesenfeld, Batia (2008). Examining the relationship between reviews and sales: The role of reviewer identity disclosure in electronic markets. *Information Systems Research, 19*(3), 291–313.

Friestad, Marian, & Wright, Peter (1994). The persuasion knowledge model: How people cope with persuasion attempts. *Journal of Consumer Research, 21*(June), 1–31.

Frenzen, Jonathan, & Nakamoto, Kent (1993). Structure, cooperation, and the flow of market information. *Journal of Consumer Research, 20*, 360–375.

Gable, Shelly L., Reis, Harry T., Impett, Emily A., & Asher, Evan R. (2004). What do you do when things go right? The intrapersonal and interpersonal benefits of sharing positive events. *Journal of Personality and Social Psychology, 87*, 228–245.

Gaertner, Samuel L., & Dovidio, John F. (1977). The subtlety of white racism, arousal, and helping behavior. *Journal of Personality and Social Psychology, 35*, 691–707.

Godes, David (2011). Invited comment on "opinion leadership and social contagion in new product diffusion." *Marketing Science, 30*(2), 224–229.

Godes, David, & Mayzlin, Dina (2004). Using online conversations to study word-of-mouth communication. *Marketing Science, 23*(4), 545–560.

Godes, David, & Mayzlin, Dina (2009). Firm-created word of mouth communication: Evidence from a field test. *Marketing Science, 28*(4), 721–739.

Godes, David, & Silva, Jose (2012) The dynamics of online opinion. Working Paper.

Goldenberg, Jacob, Libai, Barak, & Muller, Eitan (2001). Talk of the network: A complex systems look at the underlying process of word of mouth. *Marketing Letters, 12*(3), 209–221.

Granovetter, Mark S. (1973) The strength of weak ties. *American Journal of Sociology, 78*(6), 1360–1380.

Gross, James J. (1998). The emerging field of emotion regulation: An integrative review. *Review of General Psychology, 2*, 271–299.

Gross, James J. (2008). Emotion regulation. In M. Lewis, J. M. Haviland-Jones, & L. F. Barrett (eds.), *Handbook of Emotions* (pp. 497–512). New York: Guilford Press.

Hauser, John R. (1978). Testing the accuracy, usefulness, and significance of probabilistic models: An information-theoretic approach. *Operation Research Society of America, 26*(3), 406–421.

Heath, Chip, Bell, Chris, & Sternberg, Emily (2001). Emotional selection in memes: The case of urban legends. *Journal of Personality and Social Psychology, 81*, 1028–1041.

Heath, Chip, & DeVoe, Sanford (2005). Extreme comparisons: Biased information flows and social comparison theory. Working Paper, Stanford University.

Heilman, Kenneth M. (1997). The neurobiology of emotional experience. *Journal of Neuropsychiatry, 9*, 439–448.

Hennig-Thurau, Thorsten, Gwinner, Kevin, Walsh, Gianfranco, & Gremler, Dwayne (2004). Electronic word-of-mouth via consumer-opinion platforms: What motivates consumers to articulate themselves on the Internet? *Journal of Interactive Marketing, 18*(1), 38–52.

Hennig-Thurau, Thorsten, & Walsh, Gianfranco (2004). Electronic word of mouth: Consequences of and motives for reading customer articulations on the Internet. *International Journal of Electronic Commerce, 8*(2), 51–74.

Herr, Paul M., Kardes, Frank R., & Kim, John (1991). Effects of word of mouth and product-attribute information on persuasion: An accessibility-diagnosticity perspective. *Journal of Consumer Research, 17*(4), 454–462.

Higgins, E. Tory, & King, Gillian (1981). Accessibility of social constructs: information processing consequences of individual and contextual variability in personality, cognition, and social interaction. In Nancy Cantor & John Kihlstrom (eds.), *Personality, Cognition, and Social Interaction*, Vol. 14 (pp. 621–635). Hillsdale, NJ: Erlbaum.

Higgins, E. Tory, Rholes, William S., & Carl R. Jones (1977). Category accessibility and impression formation. *Journal of Social Psychology, 13*(2), 141–154.

Homans, George C. (1958). Social behavior as exchange. *American Journal of Sociology, 63*(6), 597–606.

Hovland, Carl I., & Weiss, Walter (1951). The influence of source credibility on communication effectiveness. *Public Opinion Quarterly, 15*(4), 635–650.

Iyengar, Raghuram, Van den Bulte, Christophe, & Valente, Thomas W. (2011). Opinion leadership and social contagion in new product diffusion. *Marketing Science, 30*(2), 195–212.

Joshi, P., & Wakslak, C. J. (2013). Communicating with the crowd: Speakers use abstract messages when addressing larger audiences. *Journal of Experimental Psychology: General, 143*(1), 351–362.

Kamins, M. A., Folkes, V. S., & Perner, L. (1997). Consumer responses to rumors: Good news, bad news. *Journal of Consumer Psychology 6*(2), 165–187.

Karmarkar, Uma R., & Tormala, Zakary L. (2010). Believe me, I have no idea what I'm talking about: The effects of source certainty on consumer involvement and persuasion. *Journal of Consumer Research, 46*, 1033–1049.

Katz, Elihu, & Lazarsfeld, Paul F. (1955). *Personal Influence*. Glencoe, IL: Free Press.

Kirchler, Erich (1993). Spouses' joint purchase decisions: Determinants of influence tactics for muddling through the process. *Journal of Economic Psychology, 14*, 405–438.

Kleine, III, Robert E., Kleine, Susan S., & Kernan, Jerome B. (1993). Mundane consumption and the self: A social identity perspective. *Journal of Consumer Psychology, 2*(3), 209–235.

Landis, Howard, & Burtt, Harold E. (1924). A study of conversation. *Journal of Comparative Psychology, 4*(1), 81–89.

Langston, Christopher A. (1994). Capitalizing on and coping with daily-life events: Expressive responses to positive events. *Journal of Personality and Social Psychology, 67*, 1112–1125.

Lasswell, Harold (1948). The structure and function of communication in society. In L. Bryson (ed.) *The Communication of Ideas* (pp. 117–129). New York: Institute for Religious and Social Studies.

Levy, Sidney J. (1959). Symbols for sale. *Harvard Business Review, 33*(March–April), 117–24.

Li, Xinxin, & Hitt, Lorin M. (2008). Self-selection and information role of online product reviews. *Information Systems Research, 19*(4), 456–474.

Liu, Yong (2006). Word of mouth for movies: Its dynamics and impact on box office revenue. *Journal of Marketing, 70*(3), 74–89.

Lovett, Mitch, Peres, Renana, & Shachar, Roni (2013). On brands and word of mouth. *Journal of Marketing Research, 50*, 427–444.

Luminet, Olivier, Bouts, Patrick, Delie, Frederique, Manstead, Antony S.R., & Rime, Bernard (2000). Social sharing of emotion following exposure to a negatively valenced situation. *Cognition & Emotion, 14*, 661–688.

Luo, Xueming (2007). Consumer negative voice and firm-idiosyncratic stock returns. *Journal of Marketing, 71*, 75–88.

Luo, Xueming (2009). Quantifying the long-term impact of negative word of mouth on cash flow and stock prices. *Marketing Science, 28*(1), 148–165.

Lynch, John G., & Srull, Thomas K. (1982). Memory and attentional factors in consumer choice: Concepts and research methods. *Journal of Consumer Research, 9*(1), 18–37.

Malinowski, B. (1923). The problem of meaning in primitive languages. In Christopher Ogden and Ivor Armstrong Richards (eds.), *The Meaning of Meaning,* London: Routledge.

McKinsey (2010). A new way to measure word of mouth marketing. *McKinsey Quarterly,* (April).

Moe, Wendy W., & Schweidel, David A. (2012). Online product opinion: Incidence, evaluation and evolution. *Marketing Science, 31*(3), 372–386.

Moe, Wendy W., & Trusov, Michael (2011). Measuring the value of social dynamics in online product forums. *Journal of Marketing Research, 48*(3), 444–456.

Moldovan Sarit, Goldenberg, Jacob, & Chattopadhyay, Amitava (2011). The different roles of product originality and usefulness in generating word of mouth. *International Journal of Research in Marketing, 28*, 109–119.

Moldovan, Sarit, & Lehmann, Donald R. (2010). The effect of advertising on word of mouth. In Margaret C. Campbell, Jeff Inman, & Rik Pieters (eds.) *Advances in Consumer Research* (vol. 37, pp. 119–121). Duluth, MN: Association for Consumer Research.

Moldovan, Sarit, Steinhart, Yael, & Ofen, Shlomit (2012). Share and scare: Solving the communication dilemma of early adopters with a high need for uniqueness. Working Paper.

Moon, Sangkil, Bergey, Paul K., & Iacobucci, Dawn (2009). Dynamic effects among movie ratings, movie revenues, and viewer satisfaction. *Journal of Marketing, 74*(1), 108–121.

Moore, Sarah G. (2012). Some things are better left unsaid: How word of mouth influences the storyteller. *Journal of Consumer Research, 38*(6), 1140–1154.

Moore, Sarah G., & McFerran, Brent (2012). Linguistic mimicry in online word of mouth. Working Paper, University of Alberta.

Moore, Sarah, Packard, Grant, & McFerran, Brent (2012). Do words speak louder than actions? Firm language in customer service interactions. Working Paper, University of Alberta.

Naylor, Rebecca Walker, Lamberton, Cait Poynor, & Norton, David A. (2011). Seeing ourselves in others: Reviewer ambiguity, egocentric anchoring, and persuasion. *Journal of Marketing Research, 48*, 617–631.

Nedungadi, Prakash (1990). Recall and consumer consideration sets: Influencing choice without altering brand evaluations. *Journal of Consumer Research, 17* (3), 263–276.

Onishi, Hiroshi, & Manchanda, Puneet (2012). Marketing activity, blogging and sales. *International Journal of Research in Marketing, 29*, 221–234.

Park, C. Whan, & Lessig, V. Parker (1977). Students and housewives: Difference in susceptibility to reference group influence. *Journal of Consumer Research, 4*(2), 102–110.

Pasupathi, Monisha (1999). Age differences in response to conformity pressure for emotional and nonemotional material. *Psychology and Aging, 14*(1), 170–174.

Packard, Grant, Gershoff, Andy, & Wooten, David (2012). Is immodesty a vice when sharing advice? Consumer responses to self-enhancing sources of word of mouth information. Working Paper, University of Michigan.

Packard, Grant, McFerran, Brent, & Moore, Sarah (2014). Putting the customer second: Personal pronoun use in customer-firm interactions. Working Paper, Laurier.

Packard, Grant, & Wooten, David B. (2013). Compensatory knowledge signaling in consumer word of mouth. *Journal of Consumer Psychology, 23*(4), 434–450.

Pennebaker, James W. (1999). The effects of traumatic disclosure on physical and mental health: The values of writing and talking about upsetting events. *International Journal of Emergency Mental Health, 1*(1), 9–18.

Pennebaker, James W., Zech, Emanuelle, & Rimé, Bernard (2001). Disclosing and sharing emotion: Psychological, social, and health consequences. In Margaret S. Stroebe, Robert O. Hansson, Wolfgang Stroebe, & Henk Schut (eds.), *Handbook of Bereavement Research: Consequences, Coping, and Care* (pp. 517–544). Washington, DC: American Psychological Association.

Peters, Kim, & Kashima, Yoshihasa (2007). From social talk to social action: Shaping the social triad with emotion sharing. *Journal of Personality and Social Psychology, 93*, 780–797.

Peters, Kim, Kashima, Yoshihasa, & Clark, Anna (2009). Talking about others: Emotionality and the dissemination of social information. *European Journal of Social Psychology, 39*, 207–222.

Petty, Richard E., & Wegner, Duane T. (1998). Attitude change: Multiple roles for persuasion variables. In D. Gilbert, S. Fiske, & G. Lindzey (eds.) *The Handbook of Social Psychology* (vol. 1, pp. 323–390). New York: McGraw-Hill.

Pornpitakpan, C. (2004). The persuasiveness of source credibility: A critical review of five decades' evidence. *Journal of Applied Social Psychology, 34*, 243–281.

Price, Linda L., Arnould, Eric J., & Deibler, Sheila L. (1995). Consumers' Emotional responses to service encounters: The influence of the service provider. *International Journal of Service Industry Management, 6*(3), 34–63.

Rettie, Ruth (2009). SMS: Exploring the interactional characteristics of near-synchrony. *Information, Communication, and Society, 12*(8), 1131–1148.

Rimé, Bernard (2007). Interpersonal emotion regulation. In J. J. Gross (ed.), *Handbook of Emotion Regulation* (pp. 466–485). New York: Guilford Press.

Rimé, Bernard (2009). Emotion elicits the social sharing of emotion: Theory and empirical review. *Emotion Review, 1*, 60–85.

Rimé, Bernard, Mesquita, Batja, Philippot, Pierre, & Boca, Stefano (1991). Beyond the emotional event: Six studies on the social sharing of emotion. *Cognition and Emotion, 5*, 435–465.

Roskos-Ewoldsen, David R. (1997). Implicit theories of persuasion. *Human Communication Research, 24*, 31–63.

Rosnow, Ralph L. (1980). Psychology of rumor reconsidered. *Psychological Bulletin, 87*, 578–591.

Rosnow, Ralph L., & Fine, Gary A. (1976). *Rumor and Gossip: The Social Psychology of Hearsay*. New York: Elsevier.

Schachter, S. (1959). *The Psychology of Affiliation*. Stanford, CA: Stanford University Press.

Schmitt, Philipp, Skiera, Gary A., & Van den Bulte, Christophe (2011). Referral programs and customer value. *Journal of Marketing, 75*, 46–59.

Schramm, W. (1954). How communication works. In W. Schramm (ed.), *The Process and Effects Of Communication* (pp. 3–26). Urbana: University of Illinois Press.

Seltzer, L. J., Prososki, A. R., Ziegler, T. E., & Pollak, S. D. (2012). Instant messages versus human speech: Hormones and why we still need to hear each another. *Evolution and Human Behavior, 33*(1), 42–45.

Shibutani, Tamotsu (1966). *Improvised News: A Sociological Study of Rumor*. Indianapolis, IN: Bobbs-Merrill.

Siefert, Caleb J., Kothuri, Ravi, Jacobs, Devra B., Levine, Brian, Plummer, Joseph, & Marci, Carl D. (2009). Winning the Super "Buzz" Bowl. *Journal of Advertising Research, 49*(3), 293–303.

Stacey, E. Craig, Pauwels, Koen H., & Lackman, Andrew (2012). Beyond likes and tweets: How conversation content drives store and site traffic. Working Paper.

Stalnaker, Robert C. (1978). Assertion. In P. Cole (ed.), *Syntax and Semantics 9: Pragmatics* (pp. 315–332). New York: Academic Press.

Stephen, Andrew T., & Galak, Jeff (2012). The effects of traditional and social earned media on sales: A study of a microlending marketplace. *Journal of Marketing Research, 49*(5), 624–639.

Stigler, George J. (1961). The economics of information. *Journal of Political Economy, 69*(3), 213–225.

Sundaram, Dilip S., Mitra, Kaushik, & Webster, Cynthia (1998). Word of mouth communications: A motivational analysis. *Advances in Consumer Research, 25*, 527–531.

Tesser, A., & Campbell, J. (1982). Self-evaluation-maintenance and the perception of friends and strangers. *Journal of Personality, 50*, 261–279.

Tesser, A., & Paulhus, D. L. (1983). The definition of self: Private and public self-evaluation management strategies. *Journal of Personality and Social Psychology, 44*, 672–682.

Tesser, Abraham, & Rosen, Sidney (1975). The reluctance to transmit bad news. In L. Berkowitz (ed.), *Advances in Experimental Social Psychology* (vol. 8, pp. 193–232). New York: Academic Press.

Tost, Leigh Plunkett, Gino, Francesca, & Larrick, Richard P. (2012). Power, competitiveness, and advice taking: Why the powerful don't listen. *Organizational Behavior and Human Decision Processes, 117*(1), 53–65.

Trusov, Michael, Bucklin, Randolph E., & Pauwels, Koen (2009). Effects of word of mouth versus traditional marketing: Findings from an Internet social networking site. *Journal of Marketing, 73*(5), 90–102.

Tucker, Catherine (2014). The reach and persuasiveness of viral video ads. *Marketing Science, 32*(2), 281–296.

Tucker, Joan S., & Mueller, Jennifer S. (2000). Spouses' social control of health behaviors: Use and effectiveness of specific strategies. *Personality and Social Psychology Bulletin, 26*, 1120–1130.

Van Boven, Leaf, & Ashworth, Laurence (2007). Looking forward, looking back: Anticipation is more evocative than retrospection. *Journal of Experimental Psychology: General, 136*(2), 289–300.

Van den Bulte, Christophe, & Wuyts, Stefan (2009). Leveraging customer networks. In Jerry Yoram Wind & Paul Kleindorfer (eds.), *The Network Challenge: Strategy, Profit and Risk in an Interlinked World* (pp. 243–258). Upper Saddle River, NJ: Wharton School Publishing.

Watts, Duncan J., & Dodds, Peter S. (2007). Influentials, networks, and public opinion formation. *Journal of Consumer Research, 34*(4), 441–458.

Wetzer, Inge M., Zeelenberg, Marcel, & Pieters, Rik (2007) Never eat in that restaurant, I did! Exploring why people engage in negative word of mouth communication. *Psychology & Marketing, 24* (8), 661–680.

Wilson, Robert E., Gosling, Samuel D., & Graham, Lindsay T. (2012). A review of Facebook research in the social sciences. *Perspectives on Psychological Science, 7*(3), 203–220.

Woodside, Arch G., & Delozier, M. Wayne (1976). Effects of word of mouth advertising on consumer risk taking. *Journal of Advertising, 5*(4), 12–19.

Wyer, Jr., Robert S., & Srull, Thomas K. (1981). Category accessibility: Some theoretical and empirical issues concerning the processing of social stimulus information. In E. Tory Higgins, C. P. Herman, & Mark P. Zanna (eds.), *Social Cognition: The Ontario Symposium* (vol. 1, pp. 161–197). Hillsdale, NJ: Erlbaum.

Zhao, Min, & Xie, Jinhong (2011). Effects of social and temporal distance on consumers' responses to peer recommendations. *Journal of Marketing Research, 48*(3), 486–496.

Zhu, Feng, & Zhang, Xiaoquan (2010). Impact of online consumer reviews on sales: The moderating role of product and consumer characteristics. *Journal of Marketing, 74*, 133–148.

15 Gift Giving

Morgan K. Ward and Cindy Chan

Across cultures and throughout history, gift giving has played a fundamental role in human interaction. Gifting is deeply embedded in our cultural conception of social norms and values. Stories and acts of gift giving help us understand ourselves with regard to our cultural ideals (e.g., the Statue of Liberty given by France defined America's values around immigration), religious beliefs (e.g., the Three Magi gave gifts of gold, frankincense, and myrrh to Jesus), and our own aspirations (e.g., in the classic *Wizard of Oz*, the "Wizard's" gifts emphasized valued personal characteristics – a medal for courage for the Lion, a diploma for knowledge for the Scarecrow, and a heart for the Tin Man). Thus, the symbolic meaning and social value of a gift can far exceed its mere physical attributes and monetary worth.

Gift exchange is an intrinsic element in maintaining cultural cohesiveness. It enables givers to define and strengthen their bonds with recipients via the choice of gifts that express their point of view on the relationship, the recipient, and the gift occasion. Much of the extant literature on gifting has studied the idiosyncratic set of practices and norms intended to preserve social bonds within a framework of ritualized occasions, such as birthdays or Christmas. Such research has examined how gifting provides relationship maintenance rites such as reciprocity and expressions of appreciation (Cheal, 1988) and reinforces established relationships (Bourdieu, 1977, 1986). Prior research further suggests that the rationale for gifting is that a prescribed cycle of reciprocal gift exchanges establishes predictable transactions between individuals (Sherry, 1983), thus ensuring that important relationships are regularly reaffirmed.

Although gifting may largely be thought of as a strategically engineered process, givers and recipients alike are deeply invested in the process of gift exchange. Givers often experience strong feelings of anxiety and excitement in anticipation of presenting a gift to the recipient (Wooten, 2000). Furthermore, one's response to the gift selected is as important as the gift itself, and recipients often regulate their responses to the gift in order to preserve close relational ties. Given the importance of appropriately responding to a gift, society strictly regulates the process of giving and receiving. For instance, children are closely instructed both how to purchase as well as how to receive a gift

Equal authorship.

properly (Kieras, Tobin, Graziano, & Rothbart, 2005; Saarni, 1984). Thus, as we will discuss, the importance of gift giving lies not in the particular item a gift giver selects for the recipient but rather in what the gift symbolizes to both the giver and recipient. In other words, it is a gift's important role in relationship maintenance and preservation that drives givers to look for the "perfect" gift and that incites strong emotional reactions during the search and purchase process.

The Gift Giver's Perspective

Researchers have debated givers' many motives when making their gift selections. Recent literature suggests that givers seek gifts that can effectively send signals to recipients about the nature of themselves as a relationship partner (Flynn & Adams, 2009; Gino & Flynn, 2011; Lerouge & Warlop, 2006; Ward & Broniarczyk, 2015), their perceptions of the recipient (Steffel & LeBoeuf, 2014; Ward & Broniarczyk, 2011), and the state of the relationship (Algoe, Haidt, & Gable, 2008; Giesler, 2006; Tuten & Kiecker, 2009). The universal dilemma faced by each gift giver when selecting a gift is that he or she must "attempt to infer the recipient's tastes, needs, desires, and reactions," and also "convey information about the giver and the giver-recipient relationship" (Belk, 1976). Indeed, while the presentation of an appropriate, desirable gift fortifies a relationship, the wrong one can undermine the relationship and embarrass the buyer (Belk & Coon, 1993; Dunn, Huntsinger, Lun, & Sinclair, 2008; Ruth, Otnes, & Brunel, 1999; Sherry, 1983, Sherry, McGrath, & Levy, 1993).

Given the importance of gift giving in establishing and preserving relationships, it is not surprising that givers often feel anxiety about their gift choices. Wooten (2000) found that givers' anxiety usually coincided with concerns about eliciting desired reactions from recipients. In essence, people get anxious when they are highly motivated to induce desired reactions from recipients but are doubtful of their ability to do so. Their authentic concern for how their gifts will be perceived illustrates just how important the practice of giving is to givers (Nguyen & Munch, 2011). In order to manage their negative emotions about gifting, givers look for strategies to mitigate their anxiety, such as deferring choice and extending their search (Ward & Broniarczyk, 2015), spending more resources on the gift (Flynn & Adams, 2009), purchasing gift cards (Offenberg, 2007), and customizing the gift (Moreau, Bonney, & Herd, 2011). Ideally, givers would be able to choose a gift that would fulfill all of their goals, but because givers' monetary and search resources are constrained, they often have to make trade-offs between their gifting goals. Recently, Marcoux (2009) found that feelings generated from participating in gift the economy can be so overwhelming that they incite people to turn to other markets as an escape. The pervasiveness of consumer anxiety over what gift to choose has increased retailers' sensitivity to gift purchase; to help alleviate givers' feelings of anxiety, retailers have created mechanisms such as gift registries and gift cards to ensure that the gifts chosen will be well received and mitigate the risk of offering the wrong item (Gino & Flynn, 2011; Ward & Broniarczyk, 2011).

In the following sections, we will examine how givers select gifts that they hope fulfill their often opposing relational objectives to convey information about their own identity, their knowledge of the recipient, and their feelings about the relationship. First, we will examine how and why givers choose self-signaling gifts – gifts that express important signals about who they are as individuals and as relationship partners. Such gifts may serve as a cue to remind the recipient about the giver (e.g., a gift that represents the giver's interests or identity) or as an affirmation of the giver's ability to be a good relationship partner (e.g., a gift that is well-suited for or well-liked by the recipient). Next, we will discuss how givers make gift choices that they hope accurately reflect their knowledge of the recipient. In particular, we will observe how well gift givers make these choices and what obstacles stand in the way of givers making successful choices on behalf of others. Finally, we will consider how close givers choose gifts that signal the nature of the relationship they have with the recipient and why these gifts facilitate and support their relationships.

Expressing the Giver's Ideals

Gift giving is a highly ego-involving activity (Belk, 1982) and is strongly related to the giver's own identity. Once an individual invests energy and cognitive resources in choosing a gift, the item becomes "charged" with the energy of that giver and thus serves as an effective reminder to the recipient of the giver's identity and his or her sentiments toward the recipient (Belk, 1976). A gift can be considered the "container for the being of the donor, who gives a portion of that being to the recipient" (Sherry, 1983, p. 159). Sherry (1983) contends that gift giving can be a self-verifying experience, as one's "self-identity may be confirmed by presenting it to others in the objectified form of a gift." Indeed, "keepsakes" (e.g., a locket with the giver's picture inside) or items of great sentimental value to the giver (e.g., a favorite lucky charm, a letterman jacket from a significant other) are given with the express purpose to remind the recipient of the giver when he or she sees or uses it.

The tradition of giving a gift that reflects the giver's identity and important values has been an effective method of passing on wealth to successive generations. Bradford (2009) examined how items were handed down within families and how this method of gift giving protected the items from being disposed of by the recipients. The author conducted qualitative interviews with thirty-eight informants and asked questions about gifts given from older to younger generations within a family. The author found that gift recipients are often considerate of givers' intentions when deciding what to do with the gift. These types of intergenerational gifts are sentimental in nature and are categorized as "inalienable wealth." Once a gift takes on inalienable qualities, it is prohibited from being treated as an economically viable product that could be sold and thus separated from the family.

While some givers may deliberately choose a self-signaling gift to remind the recipient of the giver's identity, others may unintentionally buy a self-signaling gift due to their conflation of the recipient's preferences with their own. According to LeRouge and Warlop (2006), when predicting a close friend's preferences, givers often ignore explicit information about the recipient's tastes and rely on more intimate information that is often found to be invalid or irrelevant. The researchers find that when predicting recipients' product attitudes, givers use their own preferences as a guide for what the recipient desires, often resulting in the choice of a gift that signals the givers' preferences rather than an item that matches the recipients' tastes.

Givers are inclined to offer gifts that allow them to express admirable qualities they hope to project, namely thoughtfulness and generosity. In order to express thoughtfulness, givers often show a particular concern for the intended recipient's preferences, likes, and dislikes. Belk explains that the giver's attentiveness to the recipient's needs and wishes is displayed in an object that is uniquely appropriate to that particular recipient (Belk, 1996). Ironically, many times, in an effort to express their sensitivity to the recipient's preferences, givers may make suboptimal decisions. For instance, Gino and Flynn (2011) found that in an effort to choose a gift that they felt would show their own thoughtfulness and sensitivity to the recipient's preferences, givers ignored the recipient's explicit preferences (expressed in the form of gift registries) and instead bought unsolicited gifts that they thought would be perceived as more thoughtful. The researchers explain that a giver's motive in making such gift choices was to choose items that signaled "sincere concern for the recipient because of the effort they [had] made to identify a seemingly appropriate gift, thus rendering the gift more personal and thoughtful."

Givers are also motivated to be seen by recipients as generous and tend to make product choices that signal this personal quality (Ellingsen & Johannesson, 2011; Flynn & Adams, 2009). Flynn and Adams (2009) show in three studies across a number of gifting contexts (e.g. birthday gifts, engagement rings) that givers predict more generously priced gifts will please recipients more than less costly items (although recipients did not show increased appreciation for more expensive gifts). Moreau, Bonney, and Herd (2011) reveal a similar finding in two studies that examined givers' preference for a giver-designed gift versus a gift created by a well-known brand. The researchers demonstrated that givers have a higher willingness to pay for gifts and desire to commit time and effort to customizing gifts for friends because they wish to offer something thoughtful and uniquely reflective of the friend, even though giver-designed gifts are less objectively appealing than items designed by well-known brands.

In sum, givers doggedly pursue their objective to signal their value as generous, sensitive friends by choosing unique items that truly express who they are to their intended recipients. Paradoxically, though, one consistent finding in the literature is that givers and recipients value different aspects of gifts. Ironically, in pursuit of choosing a meaningful gift, givers may fall short of their objective as they forgo an item that would be most appealing to the recipient for one that signals qualities about themselves to the recipient.

Communicating an Understanding of the Recipient

Givers are sensitive to recipients' preferences both so that they may purchase gifts that express something about themselves (as discussed previously) and because they are motivated to make selections that signal something about who they understand the recipient to be. Givers strategically look for clues that will provide insight into recipients' preferences in order to select an item that will be received enthusiastically and will express the giver's knowledge of the recipient. For instance, giving an item that is hard to find, one of a kind, or matches a little-known preference of the recipient is thought to endear the giver to the recipient more than an obvious or easily available choice. From the giver's perspective, the gift of an obscure book written by the recipient's favorite author shows his or her deep knowledge and attention to the recipient's particular preferences and would likely be met with more enthusiasm than a gift certificate to a bookstore.

Furthermore, recipients must not make their desires too transparent by asking for a certain gift, as ideally the giver can "infer the recipient's fondest desires without needing to be told" (p. 66), and thereby demonstrate the depth of his or her understanding and empathy with the recipient (Belk, 1996; Berg & McQuinn, 1986). However, some research concludes that givers fail to predict a familiar recipient's product attitudes properly despite extensive information they possess about this individual (Aron, Aron, Tudor, & Nelson, 1991; Gershoff & Johar, 2006; Marks & Miller, 1987). Lerouge and Warlop (2006) demonstrated this by having couples predict their partner's (vs. a stranger's) preferences. After each prediction, the partner's (vs. stranger's) actual preference was revealed, so as the study progressed, presumably each participant would better understand his or her partner's preference and gradually make better predictions. The results revealed the opposite finding: participants were better at predicting the stranger's tastes than their partner's tastes. Further, the accuracy of their predictions of their partners' tastes depended on the congruence between their own tastes and those of their partner rather than on their understanding of their partner's tastes, indicating that they were likely using their own tastes as a proxy for recipients' preferences.

The underlying motive for givers to predict recipients' tastes accurately is to clearly signal the intimacy of the relationship. Givers feel more similar to those with whom they have close relationships, and as such, the gifts they give may often be more reflective of the giver's tastes than the recipient's preferences (Lerouge & Warlop, 2006). Research conducted by Gershoff and Johar (2006) shows that close friends consistently overestimate their ability to predict a friend's preferences because they are motivated to believe that they have a deep and intimate knowledge of their close friends. Steffel and LeBoeuf (2014) find that givers faced with choosing for one (vs. many) recipients tend to over-individuate their gift choices (i.e., choosing gifts that are specifically appropriate for particular recipients based on their known preferences and values). In six studies, the researchers created two conditions in which the givers had the choice of a universally more desirable birthday card versus a less desirable birthday card. In conditions in which the givers selected cards for the recipients individually, givers chose the more liked card for both of the recipients. Conversely, when choosing for the two recipients simultaneously, givers purchase the better-liked card for the one that they thought would appreciate it more and the less-liked card for the other, thus avoiding purchasing the same gift for everyone. The researchers reveal that givers favor giving different (and potentially less-liked) gifts to each recipient, even when recipients will not compare gifts. Overindividuation seems to arise because givers try to be thoughtful by treating each recipient as unique. The outcome is that givers may sacrifice the appeal of the gift to achieve their goal of signaling their knowledge of the recipient.

Gift givers can feel conflicted not only when choosing for multiple recipients (Steffel & LeBoeuf, 2014), but also when choosing for an individual recipient whose preferences contradict their own (Ward & Broniarczyk, 2011). It is not uncommon, for example, for gift givers and recipients to hold opposing political views, be affiliated with rival schools, or root for competing sports teams. Ward and Broniarczyk (2011) showed in four studies that if givers are compelled to choose gifts for a close friend that run contrary to their own identities, they will feel a personal threat and subsequently behave in ways that will repair the damage to their identity, such as by distancing themselves from the gift or choosing highly identity-expressive items for themselves. For example, in the first study, gift givers were forced to choose a gift for a close friend that matched their friend's preferences but either threatened or matched their own identities. After examining the gift options, givers placed the threatening gifts physically farther away from themselves ($M = 16.14$ inches), compared to gifts that matched their own identities ($M = 14.17$ inches). The researchers concluded that subjects felt that by placing the identity-misaligned gifts farther from themselves, they were protecting themselves from the threat of having to choose an identity-contrary gift for a close friend.

The extant research clearly illustrates that givers are motivated to understand recipients' preferences in order both to please them as well as to demonstrate their own generosity, sensitivity and creativity as a giver. However, despite their best intentions, givers often make suboptimal choices and disappoint those closest to them with a gift that does not reflect recipients' preferences.

Conveying a Commitment to the Relationship

While some givers may choose gifts that are infused with their own identity or reflective of their interpretation of recipients' preferences, in many situations givers are motivated to offer an object that overtly represents the relationship between the giver and recipient. For instance, giving a gift that reminds the giver of how the two individuals are connected (e.g., a member of a team giving a team-representative item to a teammate) or the nature of the relationship (e.g., a husband purchasing lingerie for his wife) ultimately helps to reinforce the relationship.

The role of gifts in signaling relational intimacy has been discussed in past work on giving. For example, Belk (1979) proposed that "establishing, defining and maintaining interpersonal relationships" (p. 96) are major social functions of gift giving. Sherry (1983) presented similar thoughts in his discussion of the social dimensions of gift giving; he noted gift giving to be a reflection of social integration. Wolfinbarger (1990) corroborated that the gift giver communicates the importance of the relationship to the recipient via the signals implied by the gift. Finally, research by Rucker and colleagues (1991) indicates that an object is considered a "good gift" if it represents the giver's commitment to the relationship.

There are myriad ways that givers select gifts that signal the relational intimacy between givers and recipients. These gifts may express how the relationship meets certain culturally prescribed norms (Algoe, Haidt, & Gable, 2008; Bradford, 2009). For instance, researchers observing a gift exchange at a sorority found that although the gift occasion was a required ritual developed for existing members to welcome new members, the exchange effectively initiated longstanding social bonds between the new and existing sorority sisters (Algoe, Haidt, & Gable, 2008). Alternatively, gifts may be given without an explicit gift occasion in order to express the goals the giver has for the relationship (Saad & Gill, 2003). For instance, a suitor giving a surprise gift of theater tickets may signal his long-term romantic interests in the recipient. Lastly, gifts may also be a vehicle to express emotions and repair a relationship following a social inequity. In research by Chan, Mogilner, and Van Boven (2015), participants imagined a friend had spent the weekend helping them move into a new apartment. After imagining this situation, they were randomly assigned to a grateful, guilty, or control writing condition. In the grateful and guilty conditions, participants were instructed to write reasons they would feel grateful or guilty about the situation; in the control condition, they were instructed to write about their thoughts in the situation in an objective, unemotional way, such that someone reading it would not feel any emotion by reading what they wrote. Those who wrote about reasons they would feel either grateful or guilty were more likely to report they would give a gift to their friend (compared to those who wrote about the situation unemotionally). In sum, gifts can serve as a means for givers to communicate to recipients that they wish to foster and build their relationship.

An important aspect of choosing a gift that signals a close or intimate relationship is that the item expresses to both relational partners that the two individuals are so connected that the giver is capable of choosing a gift that is pleasing to the recipient without being told what to select (Camerer, 1988;

Gino & Flynn, 2011; Vanhamme & de Bont, 2008; Ward & Broniarczyk, 2015). Ward and Broniarczyk (2015) show in four studies that givers purposely avoid gifts requested by the recipient (in the form of gift registry items) in favor of nonrequested gifts that they believe better match the recipients' preferences. The researchers suggest that givers diverge from requested gifts because selecting such a gift would diminish their ability to express their understanding of and closeness with the intended recipient.

Across cultures, gifts are given to support important relationships. However, cultural idiosyncrasies may determine whether a gift is met with social approval and whether it will support or undermine relationships. For example, in China, gift exchanges must be conducted in front of a witness, whereas in Japan, gifts must be presented in private. In Saudi Arabia, gifts are presented and received with the right hand, and in Korea, presenting four of anything is bad luck. Importantly, although particular customs and norms vary across cultures, the fundamental reason to give gifts is the same: to encourage or cement social bonds. One notable difference between Eastern and Western cultures is the chronic self-construal of individuals from each culture. These differences play a significant role in how givers make and justify their gift purchases (Joy, 2001; Kimel, Grossmann, & Kitayama, 2012; Shen, Wan, & Wyer, 2011). For instance, in China – a highly interdependent culture – the "familial" self is promoted over the "private" self when gift giving. Furthermore, gift giving is influenced by Confucian ideals that encourage the individual to focus on developing internal moral constraints and squelching selfish behavior. Joy (2001) finds that the boundaries of the familial self are permeable and often include non-family members such as important romantic partners and, occasionally, close friends who become "like family." The implication for gift giving is that individuals look at their relationships along a continuum that includes "close friends," "good friends," "just friends," "hi-bye friends," and "romantic others," and select gifts that are specifically appropriate for the relationship. Thus, across contexts and cultures, givers strategically choose gifts that reflect the social closeness they feel to the recipient, their intentions for the relationship, and how they want to be perceived by the recipient.

Downstream Effects of Giving

Clearly, gifts are important vehicles with which givers express the degree and type of social connection that exists between relationship partners. While much of the focus of the prior research has been on how well a particular gift selection will please or displease the recipient, gift giving also has positive and negative implications for givers (Ward & Broniarczyk, 2011). For instance, givers may receive emotional benefits from gifting, such as the feelings of social closeness with the recipient that result from prosocial actions (Chan, Mogilner, & Van Boven, 2015; Zhang & Epley, 2012) and the pleasure of shopping for an important relationship partner (Babin, Gonzalez, & Watts, 2007). Lowrey, Otnes, and Ruth (2004) explore why givers are motivated to sacrifice their time and monetary resources to find a unique and special gift that expresses their emotions to recipients. The researchers conclude that when the appropriate gift is presented, the giver is rewarded when the relationship is strengthened and affirmed. Despite the pressure givers often feel to find an item that will enhance an important relationship, Babin, Gonzalez, and Watts (2007) find that the degree to which the giver "loves" the recipient and wants to express that sentiment via the gift predicts the hedonic value the giver experiences while shopping for the gift. Moreover, putting greater thought into a gift increases how connected a giver feels to the recipient (Zhang & Epley, 2012).

In sum, gifting is a complex social process in which givers are tasked with balancing their goals to express themselves and their perceptions of the recipient's preferences, as well as the relationship between them. Givers expend substantial resources of emotion, time, and money to purchase a gift that will enable them to perpetuate important relationships and are often anxious about the possibility of disappointing the recipient. However, despite their efforts to select the "perfect gift," givers often choose a gift that is less pleasing to the recipient in order to express personal sentiments to the recipient. Finally, it is not only recipients who benefit from gift exchange – givers themselves may also derive emotional and relational rewards through the act of giving.

The Gift Recipient's Perspective

Recipients also play a key role in a gift exchange. Recipients can ascribe meaning to the gifts they receive, interpreting them as a signal of what the giver thinks of them and their relationship (Belk & Coon, 1993). Furthermore, their perceptions of and response to a gift can determine whether the gift exchange is deemed successful and has important consequences for the giver–recipient relationship. Whereas some gifts can help the relationship to flourish, others may cause the relationship to falter or even fail altogether (Ruth, Otnes, & Brunel, 1999).

In the previous section, we reviewed research showing that gift givers invest a great deal of effort into selecting gifts that send a positive relational message to their recipients. But how are gift givers' efforts to find that perfect gift perceived by recipients? Are recipients more appreciative of receiving gifts that were thoughtfully selected for them? Is a bad gift cast aside with scorn and disregard for the gift giver? And which gifts do recipients consider to be more effective at strengthening their bonds with gift givers?

Recent research has revealed various discrepancies in how gift givers and recipients evaluate gifts. For example, gift givers believe that more thoughtful gifts will be better appreciated by recipients, but this is generally not the case (Flynn & Adams, 2009; Zhang & Epley, 2012). Although this may initially appear to be bad news for gift givers trying to convey their fondness for the recipient, we propose instead that these misaligned perceptions suggest that recipients are motivated to find and retain relational value in the gifts they receive. For example, recipients may look for cues that a gift giver has good intentions, or they may continue to link a gift to the giver long after receiving the gift. Recipients may also tailor their response to the gift to encourage a positive interaction during the gift exchange. In this section, we delve into recent research findings and discuss how recipients' reactions to gifts provide evidence that they wish to maintain positive relationships with their gift givers.

Appreciating Gifts

People tend to be very gracious gift recipients, and their reactions to gifts suggest that they are looking for the best in the gift giver. For example, recipients are generally appreciative of gifts they have received, regardless of how much they cost. Earlier in this chapter, we introduced Flynn and Adams' (2009) research in which they found that the price of a gift was not significantly associated with recipients' appreciation for the gift, despite gift givers' predictions that price and appreciation would be positively correlated. Indeed, they observed this effect even for the closely scrutinized gift of an engagement ring. In this study, the researchers recruited recently engaged couples and asked the men how much they had spent on their engagement ring and how much they thought their fiancée appreciated the ring; women responded to similar questions asking how much they estimated the ring cost and how much they appreciated the ring. Their results revealed that although men thought women would be more appreciative of a more expensive ring, the ring's price did not significantly predict how much it was appreciated by women. This effect also generalized to a broader array of gifts given or received for birthdays and when the researchers controlled for social desirability biases. The researchers concluded that recipients are therefore quite grateful for the gifts they receive, be they big or small.

There may be occasions, however, when recipients feel disappointed by a gift they have received but will try to disguise these feelings from the gift giver. For example, imagine a scenario in which a college student hoped that the large box under the Christmas tree contained the latest video gaming system, but upon unwrapping the gift box he instead found a new air purifier. He may then try his best to avoid looking crestfallen in front of the gift giver. These types of gracious, well-mannered responses to receiving gifts develop at a young age and require effort on the part of the recipient. Kieras and colleagues (2005) conducted a study among children between three and five years of age to test their reaction to desirable and undesirable gifts. They found that children who were better at regulating their emotional displays tended to score higher on measures of effortful control (consisting of a variety of behavioral tasks requiring them to suppress dominant responses). Consequently, children who were high in effortful control displayed more positive affect after receiving an undesirable gift than those who were low in effortful control. The findings that children are socialized at such a young age to be considerate of the gift giver and that recipients expend effort to regulate their emotional reactions are further indications that maintaining a positive relationship with the giver is important for recipients.

Other research shows that recipients' attempts to manage their relationships with bad gift givers go beyond regulating their emotional expressions; recipients also find ways to give bad gift givers the benefit of the doubt. Consistent with our premise that recipients are motivated to see the best in the gift giver, Zhang and Epley (2012) conducted four studies that revealed that recipients were often more appreciative of the gifts they received than givers predicted. Furthermore, when a gift was disliked, recipients gave credit to the gift giver for the thought that was put into their gift. The researchers argue that, contrary to the intuition that recipients appreciate good gifts, it is actually bad gifts that act as a trigger for recipients to consider how much thought and care the giver expended.

In one test of this effect, Zhang and Epley (2012) constructed an actual gift exchange among people attending a museum by randomly assigning them to be gift givers or recipients and then pairing them with a friend or family member or with a stranger who was also attending the museum. They asked gift givers to choose among a set of five gifts and manipulated whether the gifts were perceived to be relatively good or bad. Givers were instructed either to choose carefully and thoughtfully (thoughtful condition) or to not think hard about their choice and even choose randomly (thoughtless condition). Recipients were also made aware of the instructions provided to the giver. After recipients received their chosen gift, they rated how appreciative and grateful they felt (gift givers responded to similar questions asking them to predict their recipient's reactions to the gift). Their results showed that, on average, recipients tended to be more appreciative of their gifts than gift givers predicted. Among those receiving gifts from friends or family members, recipients appreciated good gifts, regardless of whether they had been chosen thoughtfully or thoughtlessly; for bad gifts, however, recipients took the giver's thoughtfulness into consideration and were more appreciative of bad thoughtful gifts than bad thoughtless gifts. As further support for the notion that recipients are driven by relational concerns, Zhang and Epley (2012) observed this interaction effect only when the gift was from an acquaintance of the recipient and not when the gift giver was a stranger. Among those receiving gifts from a stranger, good gifts were more appreciated than bad gifts, but there was no significant effect for the thought put into the gift.

The results of Zhang and Epley's (2012) research thus show that recipients tend to view gifts through a more positive lens than gift givers would believe. Recipients' reactions to bad gifts suggest they want to believe the gift giver has good intentions, particularly when their relationship with the gift giver is important to them.

Accepting, Consuming, and Discarding Gifts

Much of the prior research on gifting has focused on gift selection and exchange. However, the events surrounding gift acceptance, consumption, and disposal are important in understanding the role that gifts play in interpersonal interactions.

Fundamental cultural differences in the tendency to think of oneself as independent or interdependent affect people's disposition to accept a small gift. Asians, who are inclined to think of themselves in relation to others, are more likely than North Americans to invoke a reciprocity norm in exchanging gifts with casual acquaintances and may refuse small gifts if they cannot reciprocate in order to avoid the feeling of indebtedness (Shen, Wan, & Wyer, 2011). The norm of reciprocity has also played a significant role in Japan on Valentine's Day. Despite the fact that usually gifts must be reciprocated, until the 1950s Japanese norms for Valentine's Day demanded that women give men chocolates and other gifts, but men were not to present gifts to women. However, this holiday has been reconceived in the latter part of the century to be more equal, which also reflects Japan's changing social values and the strong norm of reciprocity (Minowa, Khomenko, & Belk, 2011).

Recipients continue to show concern for the gift giver after the gift is accepted, received, and in their possession. Bradford (2009) found that recipients of intergenerational gifts often seek to maintain the symbolism of these gifts and may even use them to connect past and future generations. For example, recipients described allocating inherited funds to specific savings accounts or business investments that would later be passed on to their children as a way of transmitting family values and preserving the legacy of older relatives. Such decisions are even made at the expense of recipients' current economic needs, showing that recipients can prioritize the relational value of a gift over its economic value.

Although recipients cherish some gifts for many years, they may not feel the same attachment to other gifts. Indeed, some undesirable gifts may never be taken out of their original box or packaging. Perhaps a recipient of a fancy new kitchen gadget simply has no interest in learning how to bake. Or a recipient's teenage obsession with a particular pop group has waned, but gifts of albums and concert tickets continue to arrive. In these cases, recipients may opt not to keep the gift they have been given, but research shows that they are still sensitive to the gift giver's feelings when deciding how to discard the unwanted gift. Adams, Flynn, and Norton (2012) conducted five studies examining the social taboo of regifting. They found that recipients are reluctant to regift their gift because they believe it would offend the gift giver, and recipients believe givers are entitled to have a say in how the gift is consumed. Indeed, gift recipients consider regifting to be as offensive as throwing the gift in the trash. In one study, the researchers asked participants to imagine they had received or given a wristwatch as a graduation gift. Recipients imagined they had regifted the watch or thrown it in the trash, and givers imagined their friend had discarded the watch through one of these two methods. They found that givers were more offended by the act of throwing the gift away, whereas recipients considered both to be equally offensive. Another study showed that recipients overestimated how offended gift givers would feel if their gift was regifted.

Therefore, even when gifts are undesirable to recipients, they are still mindful of the gift givers and the potential damage that regifting may cause to the relationship.

In summary, these articles demonstrate that recipients are motivated to view their gifts in a positive light and to express appreciation to the gift giver. Recipients try to be appreciative (Flynn & Adams, 2009; Zhang & Epley, 2012), well-mannered (Kieras et al., 2005), and considerate of the gift giver's intentions (Zhang & Epley, 2012), and these efforts are especially evident when the gift could otherwise threaten the relationship. Even when consuming or discarding a gift, recipients remain mindful of the gift giver's feelings and intentions. Overall, recipients therefore try to react to gifts in ways that are in the best interest of their relationship with the gift giver. Because failure to appreciate a gift can negatively affect relationships (Roster, 2006), recipients' abilities to view gifts through rose-colored glasses are helpful in achieving the interpersonal benefits of gifts. It therefore seems that gift givers' and recipients' differing perceptions about gifts may serve the same relational goal.

Building Relationships with Gifts

Gift givers and recipients go to great lengths to foster their relationships through gifts, and, as discussed earlier in this chapter, giving a gift can increase how close givers feel to their recipients. Research also shows that gifts can strengthen relationships from the perspective of the recipient (Algoe, Haidt, & Gable, 2008; Belk & Coon, 1993; Dunn et al., 2008; Ruth, Ontes, & Brunel, 1999), although recent work has found that not all gifts are equally effective in doing so (Baskin, Wakslak, Trope, & Novemsky, 2014; Chan & Mogilner, 2015; Chan, Mogliner, & Van Boven, 2015).

Baskin and colleagues (2014) conducted a series of experiments to examine how givers and recipients evaluated gifts that were more feasible (e.g., more convenient, easy to use, or practical) compared to those that were more desirable (e.g., higher quality or more attractive). They found that recipients tended to weigh the importance of feasibility more heavily than did gift givers, who tended to prioritize desirability. For example, in one study, the researchers recruited pairs of friends and assigned one friend to be the giver and the other to be the recipient. Givers chose between two pens to give to their recipients: Pen A (a desirable pen) or Pen B (a feasible pen). The desirable pen's description emphasized its aesthetic qualities, such as being fancy, state-of-the-art, and weighty, but also mentioned that it was not very portable or practical. The feasible pen's description emphasized its practical aspects, such as its long ink life and portability, but rated its aesthetics as medium. Recipients were told their friend had given them a gift and received one of the two pens (through random assignment – not based on their friend's choice), and they rated how much they liked the gift, how much the gift showed that their friend cared about them, and how much happier the gift made them feel. Their results showed that, although givers preferred to give the desirable pen, recipients who received a feasible pen reported marginally higher ratings for liking and significantly higher ratings for caring and happiness, compared to recipients of a desirable pen. Therefore, recipients considered feasible gifts to be a stronger relational signal than desirable gifts.

Gifts can also change how strong recipients feel their relationship with the gift giver is. For example, recent work by Chan and Mogilner (2015) shows that recipients of experiential gifts (e.g., sports games, concerts, and vacations) consequently feel closer to the gift giver than recipients of material gifts (objects for the recipient to keep, such as clothing, jewelry, and electronics). In one study, the authors tested this by recruiting pairs of friends and assigned one to be a giver and the other the recipient. Givers were provided with $15 and randomly assigned to purchase either an experiential or material gift over the next three days for their friend to consume on his or her own. Recipients completed an initial survey to measure the strength of their relationship with the gift giver. The following week, recipients completed a follow-up survey in which they described the gift they had received and rated the strength of their relationship with the gift giver. Results showed that receiving an experiential gift made recipients feel closer to the gift giver (measured as the difference between the pre- and post-gift relationship ratings), compared to receiving a material gift. Based on this and subsequent studies, the authors conclude that experiential gifts have this effect because of the greater emotion evoked when recipients consume the gift.

Other research has shown that the particular emotions conveyed by gift givers can differentially effect how much closer recipients feel to givers. Chan, Mogilner, and Van Boven (2015) examined the effectiveness of gifts that are given to remediate social inequities in a relationship, and found that recipients reported greater relationship improvements after receiving a gift that expressed gratitude rather than guilt. In one experiment, participants imagined that their roommate had left the kitchen in a mess, and they had cleaned up the kitchen for their messy roommate. Participants rated how close and connected they would feel to their roommate in this situation. Participants were next shown an image of a drink with a note attached that said either "thanks" or "sorry," and were asked to imagine their roommate had given them this gift. Participants then rated how close and connected they would feel to their roommate after receiving the gift. Results showed that participants who received a "thanks" gift reported the greatest improvement (change) in how close they felt to their roommate as a result of receiving the gift.

In summary, this recent research finds that feasible gifts tend to act as stronger relational signals than desirable gifts (Baskin et al., 2014), and gifts that are experiential in nature (Chan & Mogilner, 2015) or motivated by feelings of gratitude by the giver (Chan, Mogilner, & Van Boven, 2015) are more effective at improving how close recipients feel to the gift giver. These findings support earlier work, showing that gifts can signal how much the gift giver cares about the recipient and can change how recipients feel about their relationship with the gift giver; moreover, the findings provide a deeper understanding about why and how gifts have this effect on giver–recipient relationships.

Future Directions

Gift giving is inherently social, and in this chapter we have discussed how relational concerns can influence both the gift giver and the recipient. The social dynamics around and implications of gift giving, however, can often extend beyond a single act of gift giving and generate many important research questions. In this section, we turn to a discussion of some potential topics that would deepen our understanding of gift giving in social relationships.

Bidirectional Gift Exchanges

Most gift giving research has studied gift occasions where the exchange dyad consists of one gift giver and one recipient, but it is often the case that a person may be both a giver and recipient for a single gift occasion. For example, two friends may exchange Christmas gifts, or a husband and wife may exchange anniversary gifts. These types of bidirectional gift exchanges provide a number of opportunities for future research.

For instance, one area to be explored is how bidirectional gift exchanges affect gift givers' choice processes. Because givers' gift choices can change when choosing for multiple recipients (Steffel & LeBoeuf, 2014), givers may also choose differently when they know that they will also receive a gift from the recipient. Givers may experience heightened anxiety in these situations as they try to predict what the other person may give them and attempt to find an appropriately matched (or perhaps a better) gift. However, givers often mispredict what recipients would like and appreciate (Baskin et al., 2014; Flynn & Adams, 2009; Zhang & Epley, 2012), and it is also possible that they will mispredict what their gift exchange partners will give to them. For example, gift recipients may over- or under-predict how much the other person will spend. It would be interesting to understand how these mispredictions are forecast and how they might affect gift-giving strategies. Furthermore, it would be useful to examine whether differences exist in the value of the gifts that are exchanged and what effect these differences have on the relationship between consumers.

Gift exchange partners may employ tactics to mitigate conflicts or social inequities that arise as a result of imbalanced gift exchanges. For example, they could agree on specific gift rules (such as spending limits), they could involve each other in the choice process to signal their intentions, or they could agree to purchase and jointly consume the same gift (such as going out to dinner together or purchasing a new television for their home). These tactics may effectively ensure that the gifts given and received will be of similar value. At the same time, however, they can decrease the gift giver's freedom in gift choice and take much of the surprise out of the gift exchange for the recipient. Therefore, a question that arises is whether the net effect of these attempts to maintain social balance is a positive or negative one.

Finally, research could examine how being a gift giver affects how one evaluates the gifts received. Are givers also gracious recipients, appreciating gifts regardless of how much they cost (Flynn & Adams, 2009) or how good or bad they are (Zhang & Epley, 2012)? Or do they evaluate the gift they receive through a gift giver's lens, differentiating among gifts that are more and less expensive or thoughtful?

Long-Term Effects of Gifts

With most giving research focused on isolating and examining a single gift occasion, future research should also test the longer-term effects of gifts on relationships. This research could take several forms. First, research could examine the relational impact of a gift over time. How enduring are the relational effects of giving and receiving a single gift? And why might some gifts have longer-lasting relational benefits compared to other gifts? Second, research could examine how repeated gift exchanges over time affect relationships. Because gift giving can induce anxiety (Wooten, 2000), this negative emotion could chip away at a relationship with each anxiety-ridden gift exchange or drive people to opt out of giving altogether (e.g., Marcoux, 2009). On the other hand, these repeated exchanges could generate an upward spiral of gratitude and other positive emotions that promote relationship maintenance and building. Future research could thus examine these trade-offs to assess whether gifts result in a net benefit or deficit for relationships. Finally, research could examine how past gift exchanges within a relationship influence future exchanges. Specifically, could past exchanges in a relationship establish norms for future gift giving? Furthermore, could norms for gift giving drive givers' choices or create feelings of obligation, ultimately influencing recipients' expectations?

Much of the current research examines the choice and receipt of a particular gift but does not consider how the gift is regarded by the recipient over time. Gifts imbued with the qualities of the giver are meant to be a reminder to the recipient of the intentions of the giver (Bradford, 2009; Mauss, 1954), and recipients believe givers are entitled to have some input into how a gift is used or discarded (Adams, Flynn, & Norton, 2012). Future research might examine the duration for which items given as gifts maintain the link between the giver and the item in the minds of the recipients. That is, will the recipient ever actually feel he or she fully possesses the item? Or, perhaps after some time has passed, recipients may adapt to the items they receive and view them as indistinguishable from their many other possessions.

Individual Differences in Gift Givers and Recipients

Although there is some work examining individual differences in gift givers (e.g., Babin, Gonzalez, & Watts, 2007; Nguyen & Munch, 2011), none has examined what qualities about gift givers make them better or worse at gift selection. For example, it may be interesting to examine how givers' materialism may render them better gift givers. Specifically, one might hypothesize that more materialistic people – that is, individuals who are more likely to associate people with their material possessions – will be better at predicting what the recipient would like.

Along similar lines, it would be worth examining how empathy or one's likelihood to engage in perspective taking would influence one's ability to choose gifts that match recipients' preferences. Although common sense might predict that those personality attributes would be assets when selecting a gift, there is also reason to predict the opposite. Specifically, past research has shown that people tend to overestimate what they know about their friends' preferences (Dunning, Griffin, Milojkovic, & Ross, 1990; Swann & Gill, 1997). Given this finding, there is reason to believe that empathic givers might rely on their inferred knowledge of recipients' preferences to make a gift selection (rather than relying on recipients' explicitly stated preferences) and choose a gift that would be less desirable to recipients.

Alternatively, one might predict that perspective taking may lead to *less* thoughtful and generous behavior. Support for this line of reasoning lies both in the extant research on competitive games, which has shown that perspective taking can lead to more selfish behavior (Epley, Caruso, & Bazerman, 2006), and research showing that recipients equally appreciate more and less expensive gifts (Flynn & Adams, 2009). Taken together, one might hypothesize that individuals who have insight into recipients' appreciation for gifts may simply opt for cheaper items, as they realize these gifts will be appreciated equally as much as those that are expensive (Zhang & Epley, 2012). It would be informative to understand more thoroughly the personality traits and social skills that aid individuals in making better gift choices.

Finally, the relationship orientations held by givers and recipients could affect the success of a gift exchange in a number of ways. First, people who are more communally oriented in their relationships tend to be more responsive to their partners' needs (Clark & Mills, 1993); therefore, those with a communal orientation may be superior gift givers, selecting more thoughtful and better-liked gifts. Second, although prior research has documented that recipients' appreciation for gifts tends to be unrelated to the price of the gift (Flynn & Adams, 2009), recipients who are more exchange-oriented may be more sensitive to differences in the economic value of the gift and calibrate their appreciation for the gift. Finally, because exchange-oriented people "give benefits in response to benefits received in the past, or with the expectation of receiving benefits in the future" (Clark, Ouellette, Powell, & Milberg, 1987, p. 95), when choosing a gift, these givers may be more likely to reflect the value of a past gift received in the relationship.

Gift Giving in Consumer–Brand Relationships

Although much of this chapter has focused on the role of gifting in the context of interpersonal relationships, it should be noted that firms also leverage the relationship-building benefits of gift giving for more strategic reasons. People are highly responsive to receiving gifts and often respond to businesses who offer them gifts in the same way as they would to a friend. Firm managers are aware of the potent social dynamic resulting from the norms of reciprocity and may try use gifting strategies in order to facilitate communal versus exchange relationships with consumers (Gneezy & List, 2006; Falk, 2007; Kube, Maréchal, & Puppe, 2012). In cultivating a communal relationship, a business may be thought of as a "trusted friend" who the consumer is supportive of and loyal to rather than a business that the consumer can negotiate with or replace with a competitor. A deeper understanding of the potential for gifts to strengthen consumer–brand relationships remains a rich area for future study.

Summary

Researchers in the last decade have begun to examine the fundamental human drives that shape gift exchange. In this chapter, we have reviewed this literature through the lens of the particular relational goals that givers and recipients endeavor to fulfill when they are engaged in gift giving. Lastly, we have also suggested some related questions that future research might address. Although much of the earlier work on gifting came from social psychology, sociology, and economics, consumer researchers should continue to make important strides in this field of study to elucidate further how individuals choose products that appropriately embody their feelings and intentions for their relationship partners.

References

Adams, G. S., Flynn, F. J., & Norton, M. I. (2012). The gifts we keep on giving: Documenting and destigmatizing the regifting taboo. *Psychological Science, 23*(10), 1145–1150.

Algoe, S. B., Haidt, J., & Gable, S. L. (2008). Beyond reciprocity: Gratitude and relationships in everyday life. *Emotion, 8*(3), 425.

Aron, A., Aron, E. N., Tudor, M., & Nelson, G. (1991). Close relationships as including other in the self. *Journal of Personality and Social Psychology, 60*(2), 241.

Babin, B. J., Gonzalez, C., & Watts, C. (2007). Does Santa have a great job? Gift shopping value and satisfaction. *Psychology & Marketing, 24*(10), 895–917.

Baskin, E., Wakslak, C. J., Trope, Y., & Novemsky, N. (2014). Why feasibility matters more to gift receivers than to givers: A construal-level approach to gift giving. *Journal of Consumer Research, 41*(1), 169–182.

Belk, R. W. (1976). It's the thought that counts: A signed digraph analysis of gift-giving. *Journal of Consumer Research, 3*, 155–162.

Belk, R. W. (1979). Gift-giving behavior. In Jagdish N. Sheth (ed.), *Research in Marketing* (vol. 2, pp. 95–126). Greenwich, CT: JAI Press.

Belk, R. W. (1996). The perfect gift. In Cele Otnes and Richard F. Beltramini (eds.), *Gift Giving: A Research Anthology,* (pp. 59–84). Bowling Green, OH: Bowling Green University Popular Press.

Belk, R. W. (1982). Effects of gift-giving involvement on gift selection strategies. *Advances in Consumer Research, 9*, 408–412.

Belk, R. W., & Coon, G. S. (1993). Gift giving as agapic love: An alternative to the exchange paradigm based on dating experiences. *Journal of Consumer Research, 20*(3), 393–417.

Berg, J. H., & McQuinn, R. D. (1986). Attraction and exchange in continuing and noncontinuing dating relationships. *Journal of Personality and Social Psychology, 50*(5), 942.

Bourdieu, P. (1977). *Outline of a Theory of Practice (vol. 16).* Cambridge: Cambridge University Press.

Bourdieu, P. (1986). Force of law: Toward a sociology of the juridical field. *Hastings Law Journal, 38*, 805.

Bradford, T. W. (2009). Intergenerationally gifted asset dispositions. *Journal of Consumer Research, 36*(1), 93–111.

Camerer, C. (1988). Gifts as economic signals and social symbols. *American Journal of Sociology, 94*, S180–S214.

Chan, C., & Mogilner, C. (2015). Experiential gifts foster stronger relationships than material gifts. Unpublished manuscript.

Chan, C., Mogilner, C., & Van Boven, L. (2015). Gratitude, guilt, and gift giving. Unpublished manuscript.

Cheal, D. (1988). *The Gift Economy.* London: Routledge.

Clark, M. S., & Mills, J. (1993). The difference between communal and exchange relationships: What it is and is not. *Personality and Social Psychology Bulletin, 19*, 684–691.

Clark, M. S., Ouellette, R., Powell, M. C., & Milberg, S. (1987). Recipient's mood, relationship type, and helping. *Journal of Personality and Social Psychology, 53*(1), 94–103.

Dunn, E. W., Huntsinger, J., Lun, J., & Sinclair, S. (2008). The gift of similarity: How good and bad gifts influence relationships. *Social Cognition, 26*(4), 469–481.

Dunning, D., Griffin, D. W., Milojkovic, J. D., & Ross, L. (1990). The overconfidence effect in social prediction. *Journal of Personality and Social Psychology, 58*(4), 568–581.

Ellingsen, T., & Johannesson, M. (2011). Conspicuous generosity. *Journal of Public Economics, 95*(9), 1131–1143.

Epley, N., Caruso, N., & Bazerman, M. H. (2006). When perspective taking increases taking: Reactive egoism in social interaction. *Journal of Personality and Social Psychology, 91*(5), 872–889.

Falk, A. (2007). Gift exchange in the field. *Econometrica, 75*(5), 1501–1511.

Flynn, F. J., & Adams, G. S. (2009). Money can't buy love: Asymmetric beliefs about gift price and feelings of appreciation. *Journal of Experimental Social Psychology, 45*(2), 404–409.

Gershoff, A. D., & Johar, G. V. (2006). Do you know me? Consumer calibration of friends' knowledge. *Journal of Consumer Research, 32*(4), 496–503.

Giesler, M. (2006). Consumer gift systems. *Journal of Consumer Research, 33*(2), 283–290.

Gino, F., & Flynn, F. J. (2011). Give them what they want: The benefits of explicitness in gift exchange. *Journal of Experimental Social Psychology, 47*(5), 915–922.

Gneezy, U., & List, J. A. (2006). Putting behavioral economics to work: Testing for gift exchange in labor markets using field experiments. *Econometrica, 74*(5), 1365–1384.

Joy, A. (2001). Gift giving in Hong Kong and the continuum of social ties. *Journal of Consumer Research, 28*(2), 239–256.

Kieras, J. E., Tobin, R. M., Graziano, W. G., & Rothbart, M. K. (2005). You can't always get what you want effortful control and children's responses to undesirable gifts. *Psychological Science, 16*(5), 391–396.

Kimel, S. Y., Grossmann, I., & Kitayama, S. (2012). When gift-giving produces dissonance: Effects of subliminal affiliation priming on choices for one's self versus close others. *Journal of Experimental Social Psychology, 48*(5), 1221–1224.

Kube, S., Maréchal, M. A., & Puppe, C. (2012). The currency of reciprocity: Gift exchange in the workplace. *American Economic Review, 102*(4), 1644–1662.

Lerouge, D., & Warlop, L. (2006). Why it is so hard to predict our partner's product preferences: The effect of target familiarity on prediction accuracy. *Journal of Consumer Research, 33*(3), 393–402.

Lowrey, T. M., Otnes, C. C., & Ruth, J. A. (2004). Social influences on dyadic giving over time: A taxonomy from the giver's perspective. *Journal of Consumer Research, 30*(4), 547–558.

Marcoux, J. S. (2009). Escaping the gift economy. *Journal of Consumer Research, 36*(4), 671–685.

Marks, G., & Miller, N. (1987). Ten years of research on the false-consensus effect: An empirical and theoretical review. *Psychological Bulletin, 102*(1), 72.

Mauss, M. (1954). *The Gift: The Form and Reason for Exchange in Archaic Societies, W D.* New York and London: Norton 1990 [1950], 11.

Minowa, Y., Khomenko, O., & Belk, R. W. (2011). Social change and gendered gift-giving rituals: A historical analysis of Valentine's Day in Japan. *Journal of Macromarketing, 31*, 44–56.

Moreau, C. P., Bonney, L., & Herd, K. B. (2011). It's the thought (and the effort) that counts: How customizing for others differs from customizing for oneself. *Journal of Marketing, 75*(5), 120–133.

Nguyen, H. P., & Munch, J. M. (2011). Romantic gift giving as chore or pleasure: The effects of attachment orientations on gift giving perceptions. *Journal of Business Research, 64*(2), 113–118.

Offenberg, J. P. (2007). Markets: Gift cards. *Journal of Economic Perspectives, 21*(2), 227–238.

Roster, C. A. (2006). Moments of truth in gift exchanges: A critical incident analysis of communication indicators used to detect gift failure. *Psychology & Marketing, 23*(11), 885–903.

Rucker, M., Leckliter, L., Kivel, S., Dinkel, M., Freitas, T., Wynes, M., & Prato, H. (1991). When the thought counts: Friendship, love, gift exchanges and gift returns. *Advances in Consumer Research, 18*(1), 528–531.

Ruth, J. A., Otnes, C. C., & Brunel, F. F. (1999). Gift receipt and the reformulation of interpersonal relationships. *Journal of Consumer Research, 25*(4), 385–402.

Saad, G., & Gill, T. (2003). An evolutionary psychology perspective on gift giving among young adults. *Psychology & Marketing, 20*(9), 765–784.

Saarni, C. (1984). An observational study of children's attempts to monitor their expressive behavior. *Child Development, 55*(4), 1504–1513.

Shen, H., Wan, F., & Wyer, Jr., R. S. (2011). Cross-cultural differences in the refusal to accept a small gift: The differential influence of reciprocity norms on Asians and North Americans. *Journal of Personality and Social Psychology, 100*(2), 271.

Sherry, Jr., J. F. (1983). Gift giving in anthropological perspective. *Journal of Consumer Research, 10*(2), 157–168.

Sherry, Jr., J. F., McGrath, M. A., & Levy, S. J. (1993). The dark side of the gift. *Journal of Business Research, 28*(3), 225–244.

Steffel, M., & LeBoeuf, R. (2014). Overindividuation in gift giving: Shopping for multiple recipients leads givers to choose unique but less preferred gifts. *Journal of Consumer Research, 40*(6), 1167–1180.

Swann, Jr., W. B., & Gill, M. B. (1997). Confidence and accuracy in person perception: Do we know what we think we know about our relationship partners. *Journal of Personality and Social Psychology, 73*(10), 747–757.

Tuten, T. L., & Kiecker, P. (2009). The perfect gift card: An exploration of teenagers' gift card associations. *Psychology & Marketing, 26*(1), 67–90.

Vanhamme, J., & de Bont, C. J. (2008). "Surprise gift" purchases: Customer insights from the small electrical appliances market. *Journal of Retailing, 84*(3), 354–369.

Ward, M. K., & Broniarczyk, S. M. (2011). It's not me, it's you: How gift giving creates giver identity threat as a function of social closeness. *Journal of Consumer Research, 38*(1), 164–181.

Ward, M. K., & Broniarczyk, S. M. (2015). Ask and you shall (not) receive. Unpublished manuscript.

Wolfinbarger, M. (1990). Motivations and symbolism in gift-giving behavior. *Advances in Consumer Research, 17*(1), 699–706.

Wooten, D. B. (2000). Qualitative steps toward an expanded model of anxiety in gift-giving. *Journal of Consumer Research, 27*(1), 84–95.

Zhang, Y., & Epley, N. (2012). Exaggerated, mispredicted, and misplaced: When "it's the thought that counts" in gift exchanges. *Journal of Experimental Psychology: General, 141*(4), 667–681.

16 Interpersonal Influences in Consumer Psychology

When Does Implicit Social Influence Arise?

Kirk Kristofferson and Katherine White

Introduction

Imagine the following scenario: You are about to fly to Chicago to attend a conference, but boarding is delayed by ten minutes. Rather than open your laptop to begin that assignment or review that is due in two days, you head to the newsstand to find something to read. While perusing the latest issue of *People* (and by *People,* we of course mean *Businessweek*), you determine that this is the perfect distraction for the flight and decide to purchase it. So, you put back the magazine you were holding, grab an identical issue situated at the back of the stack, and head to the cash register to make your purchase. Most likely, many of us can relate to this purchase experience. But what if we asked you *why* you replaced the magazine you were reading with an identical one from the back of the stack? Most consumers would answer, "I don't know, I just did," but research has shown that people perceive that the item at the front is somehow *contaminated* by other people, even if they have not seen anyone touching it (Argo, Dahl, & Morales, 2006).

The influence that others in the environment have on our subsequent emotions, opinions, and behaviors has been shown to be extremely powerful. In fact, the most foundational investigations in social psychology have often highlighted the strong impact that another individual can have on people's attitudes and behaviors (e.g., Asch, 1956; Darley & Baston, 1973; Milgram, 1963; Sherif, 1936; Zimbardo, 1972). Following in these footsteps, consumer psychologists have made considerable contributions to understanding the impact of social factors on consumers' daily experiences and decisions. For example, research has investigated how consumers react to persuasive agents and draw inferences about their motives (Boush, Friestad, & Rose, 1994; Campbell, 1995, 1999; Friestad & Wright, 1994; Kirmani, 1990; Kirmani & Wright, 1989), and when and how this "persuasion knowledge" is used by the experienced consumer (Campbell & Kirmani, 2000; Kirmani & Campbell, 2004; Sujan, 1996). Recent work along these lines now goes beyond the effects of *explicit* social influence, by which we refer to purposeful and direct tactics utilized by those trying to influence others, including salespeople, advertisers, negotiators, and other agents in persuasive roles (e.g., Campbell & Kirmani, 2000; Menon & Kahn, 2003; Pechmann, Zhao, Goldberg, & Reibling, 2003).

The aim of the current chapter is to provide a framework for considering emerging research in consumer psychology that focuses on indirect or *implicit* forms of social influence in consumer contexts. We define "implicit social influence" as emerging when there is not an explicit or direct attempt to influence another, yet social elements or cues in the context itself subtly impact consumer attitudes and behaviors. For example, altering one's attitude or decision due to the presence or choices of other consumers in the environment is implicit in nature because influence occurs even though no direct attempts are present. This is contrasted with explicit forms of influence in which consumers are presented with tactics that seek to change attitudes and decisions directly, such as salesperson attempts and ad appeals (e.g., Campbell and Kirmani 2000; Cialdini 2009). Given the extensive work on explicit forms of social influence, the current chapter surveys work examining these implicit forms of social influence and suggests that four key motivations underlie consumer reactions to implicit social influence: association, uniqueness, self-enhancement, and self-presentation. For each motivation, we provide an in-depth review of recent findings in the consumer domain, elucidate the psychological processes driving such effects, and discuss conditions under which alternative responses might emerge. We think that these four motivations can exist in isolation; however, there are some situations under which more than one underlying motive is present and might account for the observed social influence. We also note that other motives may arise in social influence contexts (a point we return to in the discussion section). Nonetheless, we believe that association, uniqueness, self-enhancement, and self-presentation are the most commonly occurring motivations, and they provide the most parsimonious and encompassing explanations for these implicit forms of social influence. In addition, we find that examining social influence through the lens of these key drivers highlights gaps existing in the literature, and therefore we close with a discussion of unanswered research questions and directions for future study that we hope will motivate scholars to continue work in this burgeoning area.

The Desire for Association

One of the most fundamental human desires that defies gender, linguistic, and even cultural borders is the desire to associate, or feel a sense of connection, affiliation, and similarity with other people (Brewer, 1991; Leary, Tambor, Terdal, & Downs, 1995). In fact, researchers have suggested that the need to belong (Baumeister & Leary, 1995) and the need to feel a sense of assimilation and similarity with others (Brewer, 1991) are fundamental human motives. As such, even when no explicit attempt to change our behavior is made, it naturally follows that the motivation to fulfill this desire and need to connect and assimilate with those around us can leave us susceptible to implicit social influence.

Social Norms and Association

Social norms refer to "the customs, traditions, standards, rules, values, fashions and all other criteria of conduct that are standardized as a consequence of contact with individuals" (Sherif, 1936, p. 3). Although research has shown that the degree of normative influence exerted is affected by the number (Campbell & Fairey, 1989), uniformity (Valenti & Downing, 1975), expertise (Cialdini & Trost, 1998), and status level (Foushee, 1984) of those in the social environment, individuals often behave similarly to relevant others (Deutsch & Gerard, 1955). Cialdini and his colleagues (Cialdini, Kallgren, & Reno, 1991; Cialdini, Reno, & Kallgren, 1990; Reno, Cialdini, & Kallgren, 1993) highlight two types of social norms. First, descriptive norms convey information regarding what others commonly do. Second, injunctive norms convey information regarding what others approve and disapprove of. The past literature on social norms suggests that this type of information can have a powerful impact on individuals' attitudes and behaviors (e.g., Cialdini, Kallgren, & Reno, 1991; Cialdini, Reno, & Kallgren, 1990; Nolan, 2008; Schultz et al., 2007). Such norms serve as implicit forms of social influence because an explicit call to action need not be present for the norms to operate.

More recent research has extended our understanding of the conditions under which such normative influence is likely to arise (e.g., Goldstein, Cialdini, & Griskevicius, 2008; White & Simpson 2013). For example, Goldstein, Cialdini, and Griskevicius (2008) attempted to increase participation in an energy conservation program by encouraging hotel guests to reuse their towels. The guests were given different normative messages regarding the sustainable usage behaviors of others. These authors found that employing descriptive norms, such as noting that the majority of guests reuse their towels, led to higher reusage rates than standard appeals highlighting environmental protection. Furthermore, they found that if the message appealed to the consumer in a way that increased the psychological closeness of the message – in this case, by referring to the sustainable behaviors of other guests who stayed in the same room as the present consumer – sustainable reusage behaviors increased even more.

In another line of research examining consumers' sustainable disposal behaviors (such as "grasscycling" and composting other organic materials), White and Simpson (2013) find that people are often motivated to engage in the same behaviors as others, which is why descriptive norms are particularly powerful motivators of behavior they inform people of what might be appropriate in a given context. In addition, they find that injunctive norms can be particularly effective in encouraging similar behaviors when the collective level as opposed to the individual level of the self is activated. Taken together, these studies suggest that the desire to assimilate to the behaviors of others can drive consumers to engage in similar actions.

Association in Interpersonal Contexts

Although technology has expanded the methods of searching for and purchasing products (e.g., in online contexts), the retail environment remains a primary source of product information knowledge and acquisition (U.S. Census Bureau, 2014). In addition, it remains an environment where interpersonal interactions often occur. In such contexts, subtle elements in the social setting can exert an implicit social influence and impact subsequent consumer behaviors. For example, recent work shows that consumers are influenced by salespersons in indirect ways – such as consumers being influenced by their own past behavior toward salespersons (Dahl, Honea, & Manchanda, 2005), by the incidental similarity of the salesperson to the self (Jiang, Hoegg, Dahl, & Chattopadhyay, 2010), and by how consumers are treated by the salesperson (Ward & Dahl, 2014). In addition, consumers are influenced by individuals that they know (Luo, 2005), as well as by the mere presence of other, unknown consumers (Argo, Dahl, & Manchanda, 2005).

In one example of implicit social influence in retail contexts, Dahl, Honea, and Manchanda (2005) investigated the dynamics of consumer–salesperson interactions and proposed that consumers develop social connections with sales staff. Building upon the notion that consumers have a need to affiliate with others, the authors found that not purchasing a product after receiving help and making social conversation induces guilt among shoppers. This guilt, in turn, increased consumers' desire to purchase from the salesperson in the future. In this case, a positive social experience fostered affiliation toward the salesperson and led to increased willingness to purchase from that individual in the future. This work thus suggests that fostering positive relationships with consumers can have beneficial consequences in the future.

However, in other work, Ward and Dahl (2014) challenged the notion that providing friendly customer service is the best course of action and investigated whether negative customer sales experiences could have a positive influence on consumer brand attitudes and subsequent sales. Drawing on affiliation research showing that consumers will go to great lengths to reestablish social connections after rejection from an in-group (Williams, Cheung, & Choi. 2000; Williams & Somer, 1997);, Ward and Dahl (2014) found that participants who were treated rudely by salespeople from an aspirational brand (e.g., luxury: Gucci, Prada) actually displayed a more *positive* brand attitude and reported a *higher* willingness to pay toward the brand than did participants who were treated more neutrally.

Consumers are also influenced when shopping with peers in the environment. Luo (2005) found that the nature of the relationship one has with a shopping companion can impact consumption decisions. Specifically, this research found that shopping in the presence of peers increased the urge to purchase, but the presence of family members decreased it, especially when the group (peers or family) is cohesive because norms of responsibility became salient. Consumer researchers have further found that individuals are more positive about their evaluations and consume more of a product presented by a mimicker, especially when the mimicker is highly invested in the success of the product (Tanner et al., 2008).

Although the desire to associate is often paramount in contexts where the consumer interacts with known others such as salespeople and friends in the consumption environment, research has also shown that this desire is activated even in the mere presence of other, unknown consumers. For example, Argo, Dahl, and Manchanda (2005) asked participants to seek out and purchase batteries from their university bookstore. They varied the presence of others in the aisle (none vs. one vs. three) and examined the resulting feelings that participants had. The results revealed that consumers felt significantly more positive when a single individual was present than when no consumers were present or when three consumers were present. The authors argue that the presence of another person in the aisle may have satisfied participants' need for association and caused the decrease in negative (increase in positive) emotions between the other conditions. Moreover, Ferraro, Bettman, and Chartrand (2009) examined whether incidental exposure to a brand being used by a stranger could impact brand preference and found that repeated incidental exposure to a brand increased preference for that brand; however, this positive effect occurred only when association with the stranger was desirable (e.g., when the stranger was an in-group member).

The Impact of Feeling Excluded on Desire to Associate with Others

One compelling condition under which a desire to associate with others can emerge is when the individual feels excluded by others. Research in social psychology has developed innovative methods to induce feelings of social exclusion in laboratory settings, showing that individuals can respond in self-focused and destructive ways. For example, earlier work found that after being socially rejected, individuals behaved more aggressively (Twenge, Baumeister, Tice, & Stucke, 2001), were less cooperative with others (Twenge et al., 2003), displayed self-destructive behaviors (Twenge, Catanese, & Baumeister, 2002) and exhibited lower self-control (Baumeister, DeWall, Ciarocco, & Twenge, 2005). For example, in one series of studies, Baumeister and colleagues (2005) manipulated feelings of exclusion via interpersonal rejection by fellow participants. Upon arrival to the lab, participants engaged in a "get-to-know-you" activity for twenty minutes with fellow participants and then rated their desire to work with each individual on the next task. Participants in the exclusion (control) condition were told that no one (everyone) wanted to work with them on the next task, and as a result (but due to group size issues) they would have to complete it alone. Participants were then asked to taste unhealthy but tasty cookies and provide feedback. Excluded participants coped with their exclusion by consuming significantly more cookies than did affiliated participants.

More recent consumer research suggests that responses to social exclusion may sometimes be strategic in nature (Mead et al., 2011). Specifically, individuals may cope with exclusion by choosing to consume to foster relationships with others (Mead et. al., 2011), pursuing riskier but potentially more profitable financial opportunities (Duclos, Wan, & Jiang, 2013) and acting more dishonestly due to feelings of entitlement (Poon, Chen, & DeWall, 2013). In one example, Mead and colleagues (2011) found that consumers strategically tailor their consumption choices toward affiliating with others even at a cost of financial, physical, and ethical well-being. In a creative set of studies, Mead and colleagues (2011) found that, in comparison to nonexcluded participants, socially excluded participants showed a higher preference for membership-branded products (e.g., university logo), were willing to spend more on an unappealing food product (chicken feet) that was liked by a potential interaction partner, and showed a higher willingness to use cocaine when it would facilitate immediate acceptance by a social group. This work suggests that consumers choose products to increase the chances of making a connection – a deliberate and strategic course of action, and potentially carrying destructive consequences.

Lee and Shrum (2012) built upon this work and showed that the fundamental need being threatened through social exclusion is a key factor in predicting whether responses would be self-focused/self-serving or affiliation-focused/prosocial in nature. This research found that threats to efficacy needs, such as having a meaningful existence, led to self-focused responses, whereas threats to relational needs, such as self-esteem, led to the prosocial or affiliation-seeking behaviors such as were found in the work of Mead and colleagues (2011).

In sum, the desire to associate, connect, or assimilate with others in some way increases consumer susceptibility to interpersonal influence even when a source makes no explicit attempt to influence the consumer. This influence can take the form of (a) social norms present in the context; (b) the presence of others, including salespersons, peers, and strangers; or (c) exclusion by others. A second, somewhat opposing desire that affects the influence others have on our consumption behaviors is the need for uniqueness, or the desire to stand out in a crowd. We now turn to a discussion of this desire's impact on social influence and how the motives of affiliation and uniqueness operate separately and in tandem.

The Desire for Uniqueness

Although association is a strong driver of social influence, a separate, seemingly contradictory desire for differentiation or uniqueness from others is also present. Indeed, both of these two opposing motives are proposed to be powerful drives that consumers are impelled to restore to a state of balance (Brewer, 1991). Sometimes need for uniqueness is conceptualized as an individual difference variable (e.g., Tian, Beaden, & Hunter, 2001; Tian & McKenzie, 2001) and sometimes as a need arising out of elements of the social context that increase the desire to differentiate the self from others (e.g., Ariely & Levav, 2000; White & Argo, 2011). Recent work suggests that those motivated by a high need for uniqueness tend to opt for more unusual or counternormative options (e.g., Berger & Heath, 2007; Simonson & Nowlis, 2000; Tian, Bearden, & Hunter, 2001), and they seek to differentiate themselves from others when a sense of distinctiveness is threatened in some way (Irmak, Vallen, & Sen, 2010; Cheema & Kaikati, 2010; Ward & Berger, 2010; White & Argo, 2011).

Others' Choices as Threats to Consumer Distinctiveness

A condition under which uniqueness motives are evident is when a consumer's sense of distinctiveness is threatened in some way. One direct method of threatening uniqueness is a situation in which another consumer makes product choices identical to our own. How might we react? On the one hand, we may take this choice as a compliment, reinforcing our preference or selection as a "good choice." On the other hand, we may take it as a threat to our uniqueness and alter our consumption choices in favor of another product. In a classic example of this in the consumer domain, Ariely and Levav (2000) collected lunch receipts from more than two thousand diners and analyzed the variety of dishes selected based on group size. The results showed that as group size increased, the proportion of different dishes selected significantly increased. Thus, it appears as though consumers deliberately selected unique dishes to signal uniqueness, even at a potential cost of not choosing the best-tasting dish or their true preference.

More recent work has examined the pursuit of uniqueness in the context of mimicry, wherein another consumer copies a consumer's behaviors. Although mimicry can lead to positive outcomes (e.g., Tanner et al., 2008), as noted in the previous section, when mimicry poses a threat to distinctiveness, negative outcomes can arise. For example, White and Argo (2011) examined how consumers reacted after being mimicked by a similar other. They proposed and found that when consumers high in the need for distinctiveness were mimicked by a similar (versus dissimilar) other, this threatened their sense of uniqueness. This threat, in turn, led consumers to alter or give up their original product selection, even when the substitute product was less desirable. This effect was particularly pronounced when the product was symbolic in nature (i.e., it conveyed information about the consumer to others).

Not surprisingly, altering product choice to defend against infringement of one's own uniqueness has been documented in the domain of luxury brands. For example, in an investigation of conspicuous consumption, Berger and Ward (2010) explored how consumers alter their choices of product lines that carry items with more or less conspicuous brand logos. In this work, the authors focused on fashion, sampling high cultural-capital consumers. The results showed that "insiders" preferred less conspicuous brand cues to obvious cues in order to differentiate themselves from mainstream consumers. This choice was made with the awareness that these subtle products (e.g., black Louis Vuitton purse) would only be recognized by a select few.

Moreover, research by Irmak, Vallen, and Sen (2010) explored how Need for Uniqueness (NFU) is related to widespread adoption of new and innovative products by examining two social comparisons by which consumers infer product attitudes: introjection and projection. These authors argued that introjection, which is a reliance on other consumers' preferences to determine one's own, is more motivational in nature than projection, or relying on one's own preference to infer the preferences of others. Specifically, they show that as adoption of a product increases, high-NFU consumers will halt adoption of the product as they see it as infringing on their uniqueness.

Finally, work by Cheema and Kaikati (2010) investigates the effect of NFU in word of mouth, a topic we discuss in more detail in the final section of this chapter. This line of research argues that because others' adoption of publicly consumed products threatens a high-NFU person's individuality, such a person is less likely to provide positive word of mouth regarding products that he or she presently owns (vs. did not own or plan to buy). Interestingly, this effect did not hold for privately consumed products or when high-NFU individuals were asked to give details about products.

Overall, uniqueness threats can make consumers quite susceptible to various forms of implicit social influence. Throughout this section, we have also discussed the seemingly contradictory desires of affiliation and uniqueness. We now turn to the topic of identity to clarify the relationship between these two desires.

Consumer Identity Signaling

While research supports the impact of NFU as an individual factor, another example of consumer desire for uniqueness emerges in the domain of identity signaling, or making unique choices in product categories that signal one's identity to other people (Berger & Heath, 2007, 2008; see Chapter 10 in this volume). The identity-signaling model suggests that the number of consumers making similar product choices will influence consumers' divergent choices based on the social group to which they belong and the level with which the product signals their identity to others.

In one study, participants completed a survey on brand preferences in both symbolic and nonsymbolic product categories (e.g., favorite musical artist, toothpaste brand). They returned to the lab a few weeks later for a follow-up survey, but before completing the task they were asked to help the researchers with some data entry. The data they entered were the choices of other participants from the original preference survey they completed, but these surveys were altered to reflect the preferences of the participant. Put another way, participants were led to believe that the majority of participants had similar preferences to their own. They then proceeded to complete the preference survey again, and the dependent variable was the number of original preferences changed. A control condition was established in which participants received no exposure to other student preferences. Supporting the model, participants abandoned their original preferences significantly more in identity-signaling product categories. Although high-NFU participants diverged more than low-NFU participants when exposed to the other student preferences condition, no differences based on NFU emerged in the control condition.

The natural question, then, is how do consumers manage or balance their choices in identity-signaling product categories when they do not want to abandon their preferences? Certain brands are powerful symbols of the group to which one belongs and become central to consumer identity (e.g., Apple, Harley-Davidson). As such, switching products is not an option. How do consumers balance affiliation and uniqueness motives when more and more consumers are adopting their brand of choice? Luckily, recent consumer work helps to clarify how this influence operates.

Combining Association and Uniqueness Desires through Choice

Chen, Berger, and van Boven (2012) sought to understand how consumers walk the line between affiliation and uniqueness desires when making an individual product choice. They found that consumers can simultaneously pursue both goals, satisfying them in different ways. When the product category is strongly associated with the desired in-group's identity, consumers choose product attributes that conform to the majority on one dimension to signal identification with the group (e.g., brand), while differentiating themselves from other in-group members on other dimensions (e.g., color). In one study using automobile brands, consumers showed higher preference on the brand dimension for BMW when it was strongly linked to the in-group regardless of the preferences of others. However, within the in-group-associated brand (BMW), participants were less likely to choose the specific product type preferred by the majority. This suggests that facing the threat of increased adoption by accountants, Harley-Davidson riders will not switch to a Honda, but may trade in their Fatboy for a customized Street Bob.

Overall, the preferences and choices of other consumers have a strong influence on our perceived uniqueness and subsequent choices. Recent consumer research has helped clarify our understanding of how uniqueness and affiliation desires operate simultaneously to drive subsequent behavior.

The Desire to Self-Enhance

Self-enhancement refers to the desire "to enhance the positivity of the self-concept and to protect the self from negative information" (Sedikides, 1993, p. 18; see Sedikides & Strube, 1997, for review). To fulfill this desire, consumers can both seek out positive associations and avoid negative associations. For example, to feel more physically desirable, consumers have been shown to increase their preference for a product that has been touched by an attractive member of the opposite sex (Argo, Dahl, & Morales, 2006). On the other hand, consumers may attempt to fulfill this desire by reducing the relationship between the self and an undesirable group. This can be achieved by actively avoiding products that connect them to an undesirable group (White & Dahl, 2006). Although the previous discussion of uniqueness addressed differentiating oneself from others, it did not go as far as to suggest that one was actively *avoiding* a particular individual or group. To clarify, the desire for uniqueness motivates consumers to behave in ways that signal their individuality to themselves and others, whereas the desire to self-enhance motivates consumers to behave in ways that deliberately and visibly distance the self from an undesirable group (as well as increase associations with the favored group). While there may be overlap between the outcomes of these two motivations (desire for uniqueness and desire to self-enhance), we argue that the underlying motivations influencing the outcomes differ. Recent consumer research has made considerable contributions toward understanding the negative relationship portion of this desire.

Earlier research on association and dissociation for reasons of self-enhancement has examined this in the context of reference group influence. Reference groups refer to those groups or group members who are "psychologically significant for one's attitudes and behavior" (Turner, 1991, p. 5). The majority of reference-group research has focused on the role of membership (e.g., family, gender) and aspirational (e.g., celebrities, athletes) groups in influencing consumer preferences, showing that consumers often associate with positive referents (Bearden & Etzel, 1982; Childers & Rao, 1992; Escalas & Bettman, 2003, 2005; Folkes & Kiesler, 1991; Moschis, 1976; Park & Lessig, 1977). However, recent consumer research shows that not only are people motivated to associate with others in ways that maintain positive self-views (as might be attained by aligning the self with membership and aspirational reference groups), but they often are motivated to avoid negative self-associations as well (as might be accomplished by avoiding dissociative reference groups).

The Impact of Dissociative Reference Groups

An in-group or membership is a type of positive reference group that the individual belongs to, identifies with, is attracted to, and/or feels psychologically involved with (Turner, 1991). Dissociative (or negative) reference groups, on the other hand, are those groups an individual wishes to avoid being associated with (Dunn, White, & Dahl, 2012; Englis & Solomon, 1995). The act of dissociation is the avoidance or disparaging of products and brands that represent undesired groups or identities (Dunn, White, & Dahl, 2012).

To maintain a positive self-concept, consumers engage in behaviors that communicate and reinforce desired identities with their in-groups and differentiate their group from out-groups (Marques, Abrams, & Paez, 1998). White and Dahl (2006, 2007) show, however, that the desire to avoid the negative associations of dissociative outgroups can have compelling implications for consumer preferences via implicit social influence. In one study, participants were asked to make food selections from a banquet dinner menu (White & Dahl, 2006). Of interest was the selection of the main dish: either a ten-ounce or twelve-ounce steak. The key manipulation was the name of the smaller steak: chef's cut or ladies' cut. Note that for most males, the social category of being female is a dissociative reference group. The results showed that male participants were more likely to avoid and negatively evaluate the ten-ounce steak when it was associated with a dissociative reference group (women) than when it was associated with a neutral group (chefs). A subsequent investigation supported this avoidance strategy and found that Canadian consumers formed weaker brand connections with a brand symbolically representative of a dissociative out-group (American) than a neutral one (Belgian; White & Dahl, 2007).

Social Identity Threat

Another stream of research that highlights that consumers will often avoid negative associations in ways that help them to enhance and maintain positive self-views is work on social identity threat. For example, when one of an individual's social group memberships, such as male, golfer, Canadian, or teacher, becomes cast in a negative light, this can have implications for subsequent consumer evaluations and behaviors (e.g., Lee, Kim, & Vohs, 2011; White & Argo, 2009). In one example, Lee, Kim, and Vohs (2011) found that awareness of a negative in-group stereotype made consumers sensitive to whether service providers were in-group versus out-group members and lowered purchase intentions when the service provider was an out-group member.

Consumer research has uncovered factors that predict how and why consumers will attempt to self-enhance as a response when their own identities are threatened. One factor is the strength with which the individual sees the social identity as central to the self-concept, or collective self-esteem. White and Argo (2009) found that when an aspect of social identity was threatened (e.g., one's gender identity), high-collective-self-esteem individuals were less likely to distance themselves from the group than were low-collective-self-esteem individuals. This is because consumers with low collective self-esteem are more likely to focus on the individual (vs. collective) self, and they seek to protect self-worth when their identities are threatened.

A second factor that influences consumer responses to identity threat is self-construal. Self-construal refers to the extent to which the self is viewed as being separate and distinct from, or interconnected with, others (Singelis, 1994). Consumers with an independent self-construal focus on individual-level goals, while consumers with an interdependent self-construal value social identities and exhibit strong bonds to one's social groups (Trafimow, Triandis, & Goto, 1991). White, Argo, and Sengupta (2012) found that consumers primed with an independent self-construal tended to avoid identity-linked products when that identity was threatened because they were motivated to restore positive self-worth. Consumers primed with interdependent self-construals, however, expressed *higher* preferences for identity-linked products when that identity was threatened as a means of fulfilling belongingness needs.

In sum, the desire to self-enhance through increasing and decreasing the relationship between self and social identities can exert a strong influence on consumer behavior. Such responses represent a form of implicit social influence because individuals are responding to the situation or others on their own accord without explicit prompting. Do situations exist in which consumers may actually seek out dissociative reference groups? Recent research suggests that there are instances in which the desire to self-enhance is achieved through the reverse direction, such that consumers respond in ways that *increase* their affiliation with dissociative reference groups.

Shalev and Mortitz (2011) tested the theory that observing undesirable consumers (such as individuals with low socioeconomic status) using desirable products may actually increase preference for those products. This work proposes a social-influence model called comparison-driven self-evaluation and restoration (CDSER), which suggests that when consumers observe undesirable others using a high-status product, they infer that their relative standing on that desirable status trait is lower than originally believed to be. This lower perception, in turn, prompts consumers to approach (vs. avoid) the product used by the dissociative other by increasing preference and subsequent purchase. These findings are supported by work in the prosocial domain by White, Simpson, and Argo (2014), who show that when a consumer receives information about a dissociative out-group performing comparatively well on a positive behavior, the consumer is more likely to respond with positive intentions and actions when the setting is public as opposed to private. This influence occurs because learning of the successful performance of a dissociative out-group in public threatens the consumer's group-image and activates the desire to perceive the group-image in a positive light.

Individual Factors

The desire to self-enhance can also be activated upon encountering undesirable individuals in the consumption environment. Using a creative experimental method, McFerran, Dahl, Fitzsimons, and Morales (2010a) investigated how the body type of another individual influenced the amount of food consumers ate. Under the guise of evaluating a movie experience, participants came to the lab and were joined by a confederate. Although the same confederate was used in each experimental session, her body type was manipulated using a professionally constructed obesity prosthesis (a "fat suit"). The confederate was naturally a size zero, and in the thin condition she participated without the prosthesis. However, in the obese condition, the prosthesis increased her body dimension to size sixteen, thus causing her to appear obese. Participants first observed the confederate taking five heaping tablespoons of snacks and then were invited to take as much snack food as they wished, with the amount selected and consumed serving as dependent variables. The results showed that when another consumer (the confederate) chose a large portion, participants in the study chose less when the other consumer was obese than when she was thin. Given that obesity is viewed undesirably in Western cultures, consumers, to distance themselves from the undesirable other, took and consumed less food after seeing an obese consumer take a large amount. Interestingly, another effect emerged. When the other consumer chose a small portion, participants selected a larger portion when the other was obese than when she was thin, likely perceiving that if a desirably thin person can eat that much, they can as well.

A subsequent investigation examined the effects of the body type of serving staff on the amount of food ordered (McFerran et al., 2010b). These results found that non-dieters consumed more snacks when the server was thin, while dieters ate more when the server was obese. In addition, dieters were more persuaded by a heavy (vs. thin) server, choosing both a healthy and unhealthy snack more often when she recommended it.

Another factor shown to influence self-enhancement avoidance reactions to individuals is a consumer's level of body esteem. Dahl, Argo, and Morales (2012) explored how consumers react when other consumers or salespeople consume the same product they are interested in purchasing. The results showed that when an attractive target of comparison is consuming the same product as the consumer, the comparative difference in attractiveness – in this case, being less attractive – is highlighted for low-body-esteem consumers, leading to lower evaluations of the products.

Contagion Effects

One notable example of protecting the self from negative social information is contagion. Contagion occurs when a source and recipient come into direct or indirect contact (e.g., through touch), and the source transfers part or all of its "essence" to the recipient, and this essence remains even after contact is broken off (Nemeroff & Rozin, 1994; Rozin & Nemeroff, 1990). Argo, Dahl, and Morales (2006) manipulated the salience of contamination cues, such as the number of times an item was touched, and found that consumers perceived that the item in question was "contaminated" by other consumers, leading to a lower evaluation of the product. This lower evaluation was driven by increased feelings of disgust. In the desire to perceive the self as clean or "pure," consumers lower evaluations of products touched by others.

However, can owning a product contaminated by a stranger actually increase one's self-concept? Argo, Dahl, and Morales (2008) examined a situation in which this result occurs: highly attractive others. The authors found that product evaluations were higher when consumers perceived a product as having been physically touched by a highly attractive other, but only when the other was of the opposite sex. Newman, Diesendruck, and Bloom (2011) show further support for the presence of contagion in a study that examined why consumers express high demand for products owned and used by revered (e.g., film stars) or notorious (e.g., serial killers) celebrities. In this work, the authors show that while market factors do play a role in driving the prices paid for celebrity products, the critical factor is the essence transferred to these products through contagion.

The Desire to Look Good to Others

Impression management refers to the desire that individuals have to present themselves in a positive light to others (Goffman, 1959; Leary & Kowalski, 1990; Schlenker, 1980). By this definition, the presence of others in the social environment yields considerable influence on subsequent behavior. For example, positive social impressions facilitate rewarding social interactions (Chen, Schecter, & Chaiken, 1996), which increases consumer self-esteem (Baumeister & Leary, 1995). Moreover, successful impression management helps consumers avoid negative feelings associated with looking bad to others (e.g., embarrassment; Dahl, Manchanda, & Argo, 2001). Earlier research linked impression management motives to social anxiety (Schlenker & Leary, 1982), perceived exertion (Hardy, Hall, & Prestholdt, 1983), and self-handicapping (Kolditz & Arkin, 1982). Consumer researchers have made significant contributions in this area, highlighting the positive and negative impacts of the desire to look good to others.

Earlier consumer research showed that impression-management motives prompt consumers to alter their behaviors strategically in order to present themselves positively. When these motives are in conflict with honesty or rational economic gain, consumers are willing to trade off benefits in favor of portraying a positive image to others (e.g., lie about price paid, Sengupta, Dahl, & Gorn, 2002; coupon redemption, Ashworth, Darke, & Schaller, 2005). Specifically, Ashworth, Darke, and Schaller (2005) proposed that coupon use could convey a negative impression of cheapness and stinginess because it undermines positive impressions of financial wealth. In this work, the authors found that consumers were significantly less likely to redeem a coupon in public as opposed to private purchase situations, and this reluctance was driven by a fear of appearing cheap in front of others. Argo and Main (2008) extended these findings by proposing that the proximity to another consumer using a coupon may make *us* appear cheap. Argo and Main (2008) proposed that non-coupon-redeeming consumers experience stigma by association, or "a stigma that arises from one individual's behavior/trait/characteristic extending to negatively affect another person located nearby" (Goffman, 1963; Hebl & Mannix, 2003), when a consumer redeems a low-value coupon in close proximity. In this study, the researchers positioned two confederates in line at a retail store just ahead of a regular store patron. The first confederate purchased a pen and redeemed a low- or high-value coupon (experimental conditions) or paid the normal price (the control condition). When the actual store patron purchased their item, the cashier asked whether the consumer would answer a short survey, which was composed of questions measuring perceptions of others in the store. Results showed that the second confederate, who did not use a coupon, was stigmatized (perceived as cheap) significantly more when the first confederate redeemed a low-value coupon versus a high-value or no coupon. The authors showed that this stigma by association was stronger when a relationship existed between the two shoppers, but did not occur when the other consumer was located in a different cashier line or was highly attractive. Thus, it appears as though consumers not only need to work hard to manage their own impressions, they also have to be on guard against other consumers "cramping their style."

Kurt, Inman, and Argo (2011) build upon these findings by investigating the impact of impression-management motives when shopping with a friend. They find that consumers who are agency-oriented (operationalized as men in this research) spend significantly more when they shop with a friend (vs. alone), because they want to conform to their friend's expectations of them. Moreover, this effect is especially true for high self-monitors. Next, we turn to a research area that recent studies have shown to be strongly affected by the desire to manage impressions: prosocial behavior.

Prosocial Behavior

Early research in the domain of charitable giving showed that heightened public self-image concerns led to increased donor support (Glazer & Konrad, 1996; Satow, 1975). However, recent work in the prosocial domain provides evidence that the public nature of support does not uniformly increase donor support. White and Peloza (2009) find that the nature of charitable giving appeals – whether the benefits communicated are to others or to the self – is significantly affected by public self-image concerns. In this work, the authors find that when public self-image concerns are heightened, appeals that highlight the benefits to others (i.e., help those less fortunate) led to higher donation to the cause than appeals that highlight benefits to the self (i.e., networking opportunities).

Recent work investigating the social issue of slacktivism also highlights the impact that impression management can have on subsequent prosocial behavior. Slacktivism is defined as a willingness to perform a relatively costless, token display of support for a social cause, with an accompanying lack of willingness to devote significant effort to enact meaningful change (Kristofferson, White, & Peloza, 2014). Nonprofit organizations utilize a number of token-support campaigns (e.g., wearing a pin, liking a page on Facebook) in order to engage with consumers for the purpose of generating meaningful support for their causes. Given that these behaviors are observable to others, Kristofferson. White, and Peloza (2014) examined whether providing token support – which does little to advance the mission of the organization – led consumers to provide more meaningful support to the cause (e.g., activism, volunteering, financial donation) or not (e.g., slacktivism, no support). In one study that used the poppy pin to show support for Remembrance Day, participants received a free poppy and either displayed it publicly (on a jacket) or took it with them privately (in an envelope) before entering the student union building. Shortly after entering the building, a research assistant made a donation request on behalf of Canada's War Veterans. The results showed that public token supporters donated significantly less money to the cause when support was public than private. In fact, the amount of money public token supporters donated was no different from the amount donated by those in a control condition, who provided no token support. Subsequent studies showed that this lower support in the public condition was due to impression-management motives being satisfied. In effect, supporters realized that by wearing the pin, they communicated to others that they had *already* supported the cause. Preliminary results from our lab show that this pattern of behavior may extend to the communications of close others' prosocial behavior (Kristofferson & White, 2014). In one study, participants communicated or thought about the positive charitable behavior of a close other or acquaintance and later received a volunteer request. Results showed that participants who publicly communicated the positive behavior of a close other were less likely to volunteer to complete the survey than participants who thought about the close other's behavior, as well as those who communicated an acquaintance's prosocial behavior.

Recent research has shown one's level of moral identity – the extent to which moral traits are experienced as a central part of one's overall self-concept (Aquino et al., 2009; Aquino & Reed, 2002) – to be a strong predictor of charitable giving when impression-management motives are present (Reed & Aquino, 2003; Reed, Aquino, & Levy, 2007; Winterich, Zhand, & Mittal, 2012; Winterich, Mittal, & Aquino, 2013). Winterich, Mittal, and Aquino (2013) looked at how recognition of charitable donation affected subsequent support by examining the internalization and symbolization dimensions of moral identity. The results showed that public recognition increased subsequent charitable support among consumers with high moral-identity symbolization and low moral-identity internalization. Further, Lee, Winterich, and Ross (2014) qualify the prosocial support of high moral-identity consumers by showing that this relationship may not hold when recipients of benefits are responsible for their plight.

Overall, the awareness that one's actions are visible to others exerts a significant influence over one's subsequent choices. Recent consumer research has shown that the desire to present the self in a positive light influences consumer behavior in both positive and negative ways. We now turn to the final section of this chapter and discuss future directions for this exciting and promising research domain.

New Ways to Influence: Future Research Opportunities and Unanswered Questions

In this chapter, we propose a conceptualization of recent consumer research findings of social influence that involves four basic human psychological desires. Studying these desires can aid us in understanding and predicting consumer reactions. In addition, given the rapid technological changes and new types of social environments emerging in our society, we believe a fifth desire is potentially becoming increasingly important to understand and offers fruitful opportunities for consumer social-influence researchers: the desire to be *informed*. Evolving technology continues to change the ways that consumers interact with firms, social groups, peers, and even strangers with common interests. For example, brand communities previously confined to annual interpersonal events can now interact more frequently using multiple channels of engagement (Bagozzi & Dholakia, 2006). Along with generating additional desires, this technological advancement means that the current desires can and will be expressed in novel ways.

One area in which the desire to be informed can exert influence in the consumption environments is through word of mouth. While earlier word-of-mouth investigations focused on the impact of face-to-face consumer interactions (Westbrook, 1987), the rise in usage of social media and online forums creates opportunities for interaction among consumers from around the globe. Thousands of blogs, company and user forums, and online reviews provide consumers with information about and experience with products, brands, and customer experiences to which they previously would have never had access. Consumer research has only scratched the surface of understanding how these forms of interactions influence our behavior (see Chapter 14 in this handbook).

For example, whereas consumers once primarily relied on firm-to-consumer channels (such as retail sales staff and company websites) for information search, they now actively seek out and converse with current user forums. This two-way communication can influence consumers in a multitude of ways. Naylor, Lamberton, and Norton (2011) examined how the ambiguity of an online reviewer's identity impacted reviewer perception and persuasion, showing that consumers inferred that ambiguous reviewers had similar tastes to their own, which increased persuasion. Given that previous research has shown that consumers look to similar others to obtain accurate information about their current standing and needs (e.g., Collins, 1996; Festinger, 1957), this influence of potentially dissimilar others diverges significantly from past literature. Given this potentially undesirable influence, how can firms respond to this type of influence? How might firm intervention be perceived? Would the introduction of a self-interested party be viewed as supportive to consumers or be met with reactance?

Viewing word of mouth from the alternative perspective, what are the factors that drive consumers to participate in and initiate word-of-mouth communication? Berger (2014) suggests that the motivation behind creating word-of-mouth content is more self-serving than prosocial in nature. However, consumers seek out word-of-mouth communication from others under the assumption that the available information was shared to be helpful. How might knowledge of this self-serving motivation affect the consumption, adoption, and persuasion of this product information?

Future research should also examine how social interactions in the online world can influence consumer self-perceptions. Consumers interact with multiple others through various online channels, with connections varying in closeness: for example, one's closest circle includes family and close friends, while other connections are professional, interest-focused (e.g., running group, photography), and anonymous (e.g., user forums). How do these connections influence our feelings about ourselves? Wilcox and Stephen (2013) find that social-network usage increases self-esteem for those who focus on closer ties. Interestingly, this momentary increase in self-esteem reduces self-control in subsequent tasks. These authors also show that higher social-network usage is associated with higher levels of obesity and credit card debt. Clearly, our online behavior influences our lives in more ways than keeping up with our friends' travel photos. We call on future research to uncover these influences.

In addition, social-networking channels have made it increasingly easier to be instantly aware of offline activities that one could be engaging in. As such, an emerging social issue for high social-media users is the *fear of missing out* (FoMO), defined as a pervasive apprehension that others might be having rewarding experiences from which one is absent (Przybylski, Murayama, DeHaan, & Gladwell, 2013). Przybylski and colleagues (2013) demonstrated that FoMO was associated with lower mood and life satisfaction, as well as higher social-media usage. Interestingly, it was also associated with distracted driving and social-media usage during student classes. We urge consumer researchers to investigate this novel issue and to understand the potential consequences.

Summary

Social influence continues to be a fruitful and exciting area of interest for both consumer researchers and social psychologists. In the current chapter, we have introduced a framework that highlights four primary desires, the study of which can help us to understand underlying psychological processes and predict consumer responses. In doing so, we focus on recent research in consumer psychology and present vital questions that we hope future research will explore and address. The world is changing more rapidly than ever before, bringing with it new social interactions and potential for influence. We hope this chapter has helped provide a snapshot of current social-influence understanding as it pertains to implicit social influence and that it will motivate readers to continue to explore this fascinating aspect of consumer behavior. We also hope the introduction of this framework will encourage researchers to examine these and potentially other drivers of reactions to implicit social influence.

References

Amaldoss, W., & Jain, S. (2005). Pricing of conspicuous goods: A competitive analysis of social effects. *Journal of Marketing Research, 42*(1), 30–42.

Aquino, K., Freeman, D., Reed II, A., Lim, V. K. G., & Felps, W. (2009). testing a social-cognitive model of moral behavior: The interactive influence of situations and moral identity centrality. *Journal of Personality and Social Psychology, 97*(1), 123–141.

Aquino, K., & Reed II, A. (2002). The self-importance of moral identity. *Journal of Personality and Social Psychology, 83*(6), 1423–1440.

Argo, J. J., Dahl, D. W., & Manchanda, R. V., (2005). The influence of a mere social presence in a retail context. *Journal of Consumer Research, 32*(2), 207–212.

Argo, J. J., Dahl, D. W., & Morales, A. C. (2006). Consumer contamination: How consumers react to products touched by others. *Journal of Marketing, 70*(2), 81–94.

Argo, J. J., Dahl, D. W., & Morales, A. C. (2008). Positive consumer contagion: Responses to attractive others in a retail context. *Journal of Marketing Research, 45*(6), 690–701.

Argo, J. J., and Main, K. J. (2008). Stigma by association in coupon redemption: Looking cheap because of others. *Journal of Consumer Research, 35*(4), 559–572.

Ariely, D., & Levav, J. (2000). Sequential choice in group settings: Taking the road less traveled and less enjoyed. *Journal of Consumer Research, 27*(3), 279–290.

Asch, S. E. (1956). Studies of independence and conformity: I. A minority of one against a unanimous majority." *Psychological Monographs: General and Applied, 70*(9), 1–70.

Ashworth, L., Darke, P. R., & Schaller, M. (2005). No one wants to look cheap: Trade-offs between social disincentives and the economic and psychological incentives to redeem coupons. *Journal of Consumer Psychology, 15*(4), 295–306.

Baca-Motes, K., Brown, A., Gneezy, A., Keenan, E. A., & Nelson, L. D. (2013). Commitment and behavior change: Evidence from the field. *Journal of Consumer Research, 39*(5), 1070–1084.

Bagozzi, R. P., & Dholakia, U. M. (2006). Antecedents and purchase consequences of customer participation in small group brand communities. *International Journal of Research in Marketing, 23*(1), 45–61.

Baumeister, R. F., DeWall, N., Ciarocco, N. J., & Twenge, J. M. (2005). Social exclusion impairs self-regulation. *Journal of Personality and Social Psychology, 88* 4), 589.

Baumeister, R. F., & Leary, M. R. (1995). The need to belong: Desire for interpersonal attachments as a fundamental human motivation. *Psychological Bulletin, 117* (3), 497–529.

Bearden, W. O., & Etzel, M. J. (1982). Reference group influence on product and brand purchase decisions. *Journal of Consumer Research, 9*(2)(September), 183–194.

Berger, J. (2008). Who drives divergence? Identity signaling, outgroup dissimilarity, and the abandonment of cultural tastes. *Journal of Personality and Social Psychology, 95*(3), 593–607.

Berger, J. (2014). Word of mouth and interpersonal communication: A review and directions for future research. *Journal of Consumer Psychology, 24*(4), 586–607.

Berger, J., & Heath, C. (2007). Where consumers diverge from others: Identity signaling and product domains. *Journal of Consumer Research, 34*, 121–134.

Berger, J., & Heath, C. (2008). Who drives divergence? Identity signaling, outgroup dissimilarity, and the abandonment of cultural tastes. *Journal of Personality and Social Psychology, 95*(3), 593.

Berger, J., & Rand, L. (2008). Shifting signals to help health: Using identity signaling to reduce risky health behaviors. *Journal of Consumer Research, 35*, 509–518.

Berger, J., & Ward, M. (2010). Subtle signals of inconspicuous consumption. *Journal of Consumer Research, 37*(4), 555–569.

Bernieri, F. J. (1988). Coordinated movement and rapport in teacher–student interactions. *Journal of Nonverbal Behavior, 12*(2), 120–138.

Bloch, P. H. (1995). Seeking the ideal form: Product design and consumer response. *Journal of Marketing, 59*(3), 16–29.

Boush, D. M., Friestad, M., & Rose, G. M. (1994). Adolescent skepticism toward TV advertising and knowledge of advertiser tactics." *Journal of Consumer Research, 21*(June), 165–175.

Brewer, M. B. (1991). The social self: On being the same and different at the same time. *Personality and Social Psychology Bulletin, 17*(5), 475–482.

Brewer, M. B. (2003). Optimal distinctiveness, social identity, and the self. In M. Leary and J. Tangney (eds.), *Handbook of Self and Identity* (pp. 480–491). New York: Guilford Press.

Byrne, D., & Griffith, W. (1969). Similarity and awareness of similarity of personality characteristic determinants of attraction. *Journal of Experimental Research in Personality, 3*(3), 179–186.

Campbell, M. C. (1995). When attention-getting advertising tactics elicit consumer inferences of manipulative intent: The importance of balancing benefits and investments. *Journal of Consumer Psychology, 4*(3), 225–254.

Campbell, M. C. (1999). Perceptions of price unfairness: Antecedents and consequences. *Journal of Marketing Research, 36*(May), 187–199.

Campbell, M. C., & Kirmani, A. (2000). Consumers' use of persuasion knowledge: The effects of accessibility and cognitive capacity on perceptions of an influence agent. *Journal of Consumer Research, 27*(1), 69–83.

Campbell, J. D., & Fairey, P. J. (1989). Informational and normative routes to conformity: The effect of faction size as a function of norm extremity and attention to the stimulus. *Journal of Personality and Social Psychology, 57*(3), 457.

Chan, C., Berger, J., & Van Boven, L. (2012). Identifiable but not identical: Combining social identity and uniqueness motives in choice. *Journal of Consumer Research, 39*(3), 561–573.

Chartrand, T. L., & Bargh, J. A. (1999). The chameleon effect: The perception-behavior link and social interaction. *Journal of Personality and Social Psychology, 76*(6), 893–910.

Chartrand, T. L., Maddux, W. W., & Lakin, J. L. (2005). Beyond the perception-behavior link: The ubiquitous utility and motivational moderators of nonconscious mimicry. In Ran R. Hassin, James S. Uleman, & John A. Bargh (eds.) *The New Unconscious* (pp. 334–261). New York: Oxford University Press.

Cheema, A., & Kaikati, A. M. (2010). The effect of need for uniqueness on word of mouth. *Journal of Marketing Research, 47*(3), 553–563.

Childers, T. L., & Rao, A. R. (1992). The influence of familial and peer-based reference groups on consumer decisions. *Journal of Consumer Research, 19*(September), 198–211.

Cialdini, R. B. (2009). *Influence: Science and Practice.* Boston: Pearson Education.

Cialdini, R. B., & Goldstein, N. J. (2004). Social influence: Compliance and conformity. In S. T. Fiske, D. L. Schacter, & C. Zahn-Waxler (eds.), *Annual Review of Psychology* (vol. 55, pp. 591–621). Palo Alto, CA: Annual Reviews.

Cialdini, R. B., Kallgren C. A, & Reno, R. R. (1991). A focus theory of normative conduct: A theoretical refinement and reevaluation of the role of norms in human behavior. *Advances in Experimental Social Psychology, 24*(20), 1–243.

Cialdini, R. B., Reno, R. R., & Kallgren, C. A. (1990). A focus theory of normative conduct: Recycling the concept of norms to reduce littering in public places. *Journal of Personality and Social Psychology, 58*(6), 1015.

Cialdini, R. B., & Trost, M. R. (1998). Social influence: Social norms, conformity and compliance. In D. T. Gilbert, S. T. Fiske, & G. Lindzey (eds.) *The Handbook of Social Psychology*. 4th ed. (vol. 2, pp. 151–192). New York: McGraw-Hill.

Cialdini, R. B., Vincent, J. E., Lewis, S. K., Catalan, J., Wheeler, D., & Darby, B. L. (1975). Reciprocal concessions procedure for inducing compliance: The door-in-the-face technique. *Journal of Personality and Social Psychology, 31*(2), 206.

Chan, C., Berger, J., & Van Boven, L. (2011). Differentiating the "I" in "in-group": How identity-signaling and uniqueness motives combine to drive consumer choice. *Journal of Consumer Research, 39*(3), 561–573.

Chen, S., Shechter, D., & Chaiken, S. (1996). Getting at the truth or getting along: Accuracy-versus impression-motivated heuristic and systematic processing. *Journal of Personality and Social Psychology, 71*(2), 262.

Childers, T. L., & Rao, A. K. (1992). The influence of familial and peer-based reference groups on consumer decisions. *Journal of Consumer Research, 19*(2), 198–211.

Collins, R. L. (1996). For better or worse: The impact of upward social comparison on self-evaluations. *Psychological Bulletin, 119*(1), 51.

Colton, C. C. (1820). *Lacon* (vol. 1). London: Longman, Hurt, Rees, & Brown.

Dahl, D. W. Argo, J. J., & Morales, A. C. (2012). Social information in the retail environment: The importance of consumption alignment, referent identity, and self-esteem. *Journal of Consumer Research, 38*(5), 860–871.

Dahl, D. W. Honea, H., & Manchanda, R. V. (2005). Three Rs of interpersonal consumer guilt: Relationship, reciprocity, reparation. *Journal of Consumer Psychology, 15*(4), 307–315.

Dahl, D. W., Manchanda, R. V., & Argo, J. J. (2001). Embarrassment in consumer purchase: The roles of social presence and purchase familiarity. *Journal of Consumer Research, 28*(3), 473–481.

Darley, J. M., & Batson, C. D. (1973). "From Jerusalem to Jericho": A study of situational and dispositional variables in helping behavior. *Journal of Personality and Social Psychology, 27*(1), 100.

Deutsch, M., & Gerard, H. B. (1955). A study of normative and informational social influences upon individual judgment. *Journal of Abnormal and Social Psychology, 51*(3), 629.

Duclos, R., Wen Wan, E., & Jiang, Y. (2013). Show me the honey! Effects of social exclusion on financial risk-taking. *Journal of Consumer Research, 40*(1), 122–135.

Dunn, Lea, White, K., & Dahl, D. W. (2012). That is so not me: Dissociating from undesired consumer identities. In A. Ruvio & R. Belk (eds.) *The Routledge Companion to Identity and Consumption* (p. 273), New York: Routledge.

Edson Escalas, J., & Bettman, J. R. (2003). You are what they eat: The influence of reference groups on consumers' connections to brands. *Journal of Consumer Psychology, 13*(3), 339–348.

Englis, B. G., & Solomon, M. R. (1995). To be and not to be: Lifestyle imagery, reference groups, and the clustering of America. *Journal of Advertising, 24*(1), 13–28.

Escalas, J. E., & Bettman, J. R. (2005). Self-Construal, Reference Groups, and Brand Meaning. *Journal of Consumer Research, 32*(3), 378–389.

Ferraro, R., Bettman, J. R., & Chartrand, T. L. (2009). The power of strangers: The effect of incidental consumer brand encounters on brand choice. *Journal of Consumer Research, 35*(5), 729–741.

Festinger, L. (1957), *A Theory of Cognitive Dissonance* (vol. 2). Palo Alto, CA: Stanford University Press.

Folkes, V. S., & Kiesler, T. (1991). Social cognition: Consumers' Inferences about the self and others. *Handbook of Consumer Behavior, 3*, 281–315.

Foushee, H. C. (1984). Dyads and triads at 35,000 feet: Factors affecting group process and aircrew performance. *American Psychologist, 39*(8), 885.

Friestad, M., & Wright, P. (1994). The persuasion knowledge model: How people cope with persuasion attempts. *Journal of Consumer Research, 21*(June), 1–31.

Glazer, A., & Konrad, K. A. (1996). A signaling explanation for charity. *American Economic Review, 86*(4), 1019–1028.

Goffman, E. (1959). *The Presentation of Self in Everyday Life.* Garden City, NY: Anchor.

Goffman, E. (1963). *Stigma: Notes on the Management of Spoiled Identity.* New York: Simon & Schuster.

Goldstein, N. J., Cialdini, R. B., & Griskevicius, V. (2008). A room with a viewpoint: Using social norms to motivate environmental conservation in hotels. *Journal of Consumer Research, 35*(3), 472–482.

Granovetter, M. S., & Soong, M. (1986). Threshold models of interpersonal effects in consumer demand. *Journal of Economic Behavior and Organization, 7*(1), 83–99.

Hardy, C. J., Hall, E. G., & Prestholdt, P. H. (1983). *The Mediational Role of Social Influence in the Perception of Exertion.* Dissertation, Louisiana State University.

Hebl, M. R., and Mannix, L. M. (2003). The weight of obesity in evaluating others: A mere proximity effect. *Personality and Social Psychology Bulletin, 29*(1), 28–38.

Irmak, C., Vallen, B., & Sen, S. (2010). You like what I like, but I don't like what you like: Uniqueness motivations in product preferences. *Journal of Consumer Research, 37*(3), 443–455.

Jiang, L., Hoegg, J., Dahl, D. W., & Chattopadhyay, A. (2010). The persuasive role of incidental similarity on attitudes and purchase intentions in a sales context. *Journal of Consumer Research, 36*(5), 778–791.

Kirmani, A. (1990). The effect of perceived advertising costs on brand perceptions. *Journal of Consumer Research, 17*(September), 160–171.

Kirmani, A., & Campbell, M. C. (2004). Goal seeker and persuasion sentry: How consumer targets respond to interpersonal marketing persuasion. *Journal of Consumer Research, 31*(3), 573–582.

Kirmani, A., & Wright, P. (1989). Money talks: Perceived advertising expense and expected product quality. *Journal of Consumer Research, 16*(December), 344–353.

Kolditz, T. A., and Arkin, R. M. (1982). An impression management interpretation of the self-handicapping strategy. *Journal of Personality and Social Psychology, 43*(3), 492.

Krishna, A., & Morrin, M. (2008). Does touch affect taste? The perceptual transfer of product container haptic cues. *Journal of Consumer Research, 34*(6), 807–818.

Kristofferson, K., & White, K. (2015). I shared what you did last summer: vicarious impression management via the good deeds of others. Working Paper.

Kristofferson, K., White, K., & Peloza, J. (2014). The nature of slacktivism: How the social observability of an initial act of token support impacts subsequent prosocial action. *Journal of Consumer Research, 40*(6), 1149–1166.

Kurt, D., Inman, J. J., & Argo, J. J. (2011). The influence of friends on consumer spending: The role of agency-communion orientation and self-monitoring. *Journal of Marketing Research, 48*(4), 741–754.

La France, M. (1979). Nonverbal synchrony and rapport: Analysis by the cross-lag panel technique. *Social Psychology Quarterly, 42*(1), 66–70.

Lakin, J. L., & Chartrand, T. L. (2003). Using nonconscious behavioural mimicry to create affiliation and rapport. *Psychological Science, 14*(4), 334–336.

Lasaleta, J. D., Sedikides, C., & Vohs, K. D. (2014). Nostalgia weakens the desire for money. *Journal of Consumer Research, 41*(3), 713–729.

Leary, M. R., & Kowalski, R. M. (1990). Impression management: A literature review and two-component model. *Psychological Bulletin, 107*(1), 34.

Leary, M. R., Tambor, E. S., Terdal, S. K., & Downs, D. L. (1995). Self-esteem as an interpersonal monitor: The sociometer hypothesis. *Journal of Personality and Social Psychology, 68*(3), 518.

Lee, J., & Shrum, L. J. (2012). Conspicuous consumption versus charitable behavior in response to social exclusion: A differential needs explanation. *Journal of Consumer Research, 39*(3), 530–544.

Lee, K., Kim, H., & Vohs, K. D. (2011). Stereotype threat in the marketplace: Consumer anxiety and purchase intentions. *Journal of Consumer Research, 38*(2), 343–357.

Lee, S., Winterich, K. P., & Ross, Jr., W. T. (2014). I'm moral, but I won't help you: The distinct roles of empathy and justice in donations." *Journal of Consumer Research, 41*(3).

Lewin, K. (1935). *A Dynamic Theory of Personality*. New York: McGraw-Hill.

Luo, X. (2005). How does shopping with others influence impulsive purchasing? *Journal of Consumer Psychology, 15*(4), 288–294.

Marques, J., Abrams, D., & Paez, D. (1998). The role of categorization and in-group norms in judgments of groups and their members. *Journal of Personality and Social Psychology, 75*(4), 976–988.

McFerran, B., Dahl, D. W., Fitzsimons, G. J., & Morales, A. C. (2010a). I'll have what she's having: Effects of social influence and body type on the food choices of others. *Journal of Consumer Research, 36*(6), 915–929.

McFerran, B., Dahl, D. W., Fitzsimons, G. J., & Morales, A. C. (2010b). "Might an Overweight Waitress Make You Eat More? How the body type of others is sufficient to alter our food consumption. *Journal of Consumer Psychology, 20*(2), 146–151.

Mead, N. L., Baumeister, R. F., Stillman, T. F., Rawn, C. D., & Vohs, K. D. (2011). Social exclusion causes people to spend and consume strategically in the service of affiliation. *Journal of Consumer Research, 37*(5), 902–919.

Menon, S.,& Kahn, B. E. (2003). Corporate sponsorships of philanthropic activities: When do they impact perception of sponsor brand? *Journal of Consumer Psychology, 13*(3), 316–327.

Milgram, S. (1963). Behavioral study of obedience. *Journal of Abnormal and Social Psychology, 67*(4), 371.

Mooy, S. C., & Robben, H. S. J. (2002). Managing consumers' product evaluations through direct product experience. *Journal of Product & Brand Management, 11*(7), 432–446.

Moschis, G. P. (1976). Social comparison and informal group influence. *Journal of Marketing Research, 13*(August), 237–244.

Naylor, R. W., Lamberton, C., & Norton, D. A. (2011). Seeing ourselves in others: Reviewer ambiguity, egocentric anchoring, and persuasion. *Journal of Marketing Research, 48*(3), 617–631.

Nemeroff, C., & Rozin, P. (1994). The contagion concept in adult thinking in the United States: Transmission of germs and of interpersonal influence. *Ethos, 22*(2), 158–186.

Newman, G. E., Diesendruck, G., & Bloom, P. (2011). Celebrity contagion and the value of objects. *Journal of Consumer Research, 38*(2), 215–228.

Park, C. W., & Lessig, V. P. (1977). Students and housewives: Differences in susceptibility to reference group influence. *Journal of Consumer Research, 4*, 102–110.

Pechmann, C., Zhao, G., Goldberg, M. E., & Reibling, E. T. (2003). What to convey in antismoking advertisements for adolescents: The use of protection motivation theory to identify effective message themes. *Journal of Marketing, 67*(2), 1–18.

Peck, J., & Childers, T. L. (2006). If I touch it I have to have it: Individual and environmental influences on impulse purchasing. *Journal of Business Research, 59*(6), 765–769.

Poon, K., Chen, Z., & DeWall, C. N. (2013). Feeling entitled to more ostracism increases dishonest behavior. *Personality and Social Psychology Bulletin, 39*(9), 1227–1239.

Przybylski, A. K., Murayama K., DeHaan, C. R., & Gladwell, V. (2013). Motivational, emotional, and behavioral correlates of fear of missing out. *Computers in Human Behavior, 29*(4), 1841–1848.

Reed, II, A., & Aquino, K. F. (2003). Moral identity and the expanding circle of moral regard toward out-groups. *Journal of Personality and Social Psychology, 84*(6), 1270–1286.

Reed II, A., Aquino, K., & Levy, E. (2007). Moral identity and judgments of charitable behaviors. *Journal of Marketing, 71*(January), 178–193.

Reno, R. R., Cialdini, R. B., & Kallgren, C. A. (1993). The transsituational influence of social norms. *Journal of Personality and Social Psychology, 64*(1), 104.

Rozin, P., & Nemeroff, C. (1990). The laws of sympathetic magic: A psychological analysis of similarity and contagion, *Psychological Science, 1*(6), 383–384.

Satow, K. L. (1975). Social approval and helping. *Journal of Experimental Social Psychology, 11*(6), 501–509.

Schlenker, B. R. (1980). *Impression Management: The Self-Concept, Social Identity, and Interpersonal Relations.* Monterey, CA: Brooks/Cole.

Schlenker, B. R., & Leary, M. R. (1982). Social anxiety and self-presentation: A conceptualization model. *Psychological Bulletin, 92*(3), 641.

Schultz, P. W., Nolan, J. M., Cialdini, R. B., Goldstein, N. J., & Griskevicius, V. (2007). The constructive, destructive, and reconstructive power of social norms. *Psychological Science, 18*(5), 429–434.

Sedikides, C., & Strube, M. J. (1997). Self-evaluation: To thine own self be good, to thine own self be sure, to thine own self be true, and to thine own self be better. *Advances in Experimental Social Psychology, 29*, 209–269.

Sengupta, J., Dahl, D. W., & Gorn, G. G. (2002). Misrepresentation in the consumer context. *Journal of Consumer Psychology, 12*(2), 69–79.

Shalev, E., & Morwitz, V. G. (2011). Influence via comparison-driven self-evaluation and restoration: The case of the low-status influencer. *Journal of Consumer Research, 38*(5), 964–980.

Sherif, M. (1936). *The Psychology of Social Norms*. New York: Harper.

Simonson, I., & Nowlis, S. M. (2000). The role of explanations and need for uniqueness in consumer decision making: Unconventional choices based on reasons. *Journal of Consumer Research, 27*(1), 49–68.

Singelis, T. M. (1994). The measurement of independent and interdependent self-construals. *Personality and Social Psychology Bulletin, 20*(5), 580–591.

Snyder, C. R. (1992). Product scarcity by need for uniqueness interaction: A consumer catch-22 carousel? *Basic & Applied Social Psychology, 13*(1), 9–24.

Snyder, C. R., & Fromkin, H. L. (1977). Abnormality as a positive characteristic: The development and validation of a scale measuring need for uniqueness. *Journal of Abnormal Psychology, 86*(5), 518.

Snyder, C. R., & Fromkin, H. L. (1980). *Uniqueness*. New York: Plenum.

Sujan, H. (1996). Special session summary: Influence professionals. In Merrie Brucks and Deborah J. MacInnis (eds.), *Advances in Consumer Research* (vol. *24*, pp. 334–335). Provo, UT: Association for Consumer Research.

Tajfel, H., & Turner, J. C. (1979). *An Integrative Theory of Intergroup Conflict*. Monterey, CA: Brooks/Cole.

Tanner, R. J., Ferraro, R., Chartrand, T. L., Bettman, J. R., & van Baaren, R. (2008). Of chameleons and consumption: The impact of mimicry on choice and preferences. *Journal of Consumer Research, 34*(April), 754–766.

Tian, K. T., Bearden, W. O., & Hunter, G. L. (2001). Consumers' need for uniqueness: Scale development and validation. *Journal of Consumer Research, 28*(June), 50–66.

Tian, K. T., & McKenzie, K. (2001). The long-term predictive validity of consumers' need for uniqueness scale. *Journal of Consumer Psychology, 10*(3), 171–193.

Trafimow, D., Triandis, H. C., & Goto, S. G. (1991). Some tests of the distinction between the private self and the collective self. *Journal of Personality and Social Psychology, 60*(5); 649–655.

Turner, J. C. (1985). *Social Categorization and the Self-Concept: A Social Cognitive Theory of Group Behavior*. Greenwich, CT: JAI.

Turner, J. C. (1991). *Social Influence*. Buckingham, UK: Open University Press.

Twenge, J. M., Baumeister, R. F., DeWall, C. N., Ciarocco, N. J., & Bartels, J. M. (2007). Social exclusion decreases prosocial behavior. *Journal of Personality and Social Psychology, 92*(1), 56.

Twenge, J. M., Baumeister, R. F., Tice, D. M., & Stucke, T. S. (2001). If you can't join them, beat them: Effects of social exclusion on aggressive behavior. *Journal of Personality and Social Psychology, 81*(6), 1058–1069.

Twenge, J. M., Catanese, K. R., & Baumeister, R. F. (2002). Social exclusion causes self-defeating behavior. *Journal of Personality and Social Psychology, 83*(3), 606–615.

United States Census Bureau (2014). *Quarterly Retail E-Commerce Sales Report.* www.census.gov/retail/mrts/www/data/pdf/ec_current.pdf.

Valenti, A. C., & Downing, L. L. (1975). Differential effects of jury size on verdicts following deliberation as a function of the apparent guilt of a defendant. *Journal of Personality and Social Psychology, 32*(4), 655.

van Baaren, R. B., Holland, R. W., Kawakami, K., & van Knippenberg, A. (2004). Mimicry and prosocial behavior. *Psychological Science, 15*(1), 71–74.

van Baaren, R. B., Maddux, W. W., Chartrand, T. L., De Bouter, C., & van Knippenberg, A. (2003). It takes two to mimic: Behavioral consequences of self-construals. *Journal of Personality and Social Psychology, 84*(5), 1093–1102.

Ward, M. K. and Dahl, D. W. (2014). Should the devil sell Prada? Retail rejection increases aspiring consumers' desire for the brand. *Journal of Consumer Research, 41*(3), 590–609.

Westbrook, R. A. (1987). Product/consumption-based affective responses and post-purchase processes. *Journal of Marketing Research, 24*(3), 258–270.

White, K., & Argo, J. J. (2009). Social identity threat and consumer preferences. *Journal of Consumer Psychology, 19*, 313–325.

White, K., & Argo, J. J. (2011). When imitation doesn't flatter: The role of consumer distinctiveness in responses to mimicry. *Journal of Consumer Research, 38*(4), 667–680.

White, K., Argo, J. J., & Sengupta, J. (2012). Dissociative versus associative responses to social identity threat: The role of consumer self-construal. *Journal of Consumer Research, 39*(4), 704–719.

White, K., & Dahl, D. W. (2006). To be or not be? The influencer of dissociative reference groups on consumer preferences. *Journal of Consumer Psychology, 16*(4), 404–414.

White, K., & Dahl, D. W. (2007). Are all out-groups created equal? Consumer identity and dissociative influence. *Journal of Consumer Research, 34*, 525–536.

White, K., & Peloza, J. (2009). Self-benefit versus other-benefit marketing appeals: Their effectiveness in generating charitable support. *Journal of Marketing, 73*(4), 109–124.

White, K., & Simpson, B. (2013). The "dos and don'ts" of normative influence: When do (and don't) normative messages lead to sustainable consumer behaviors? *Journal of Marketing, 77*(2), 78–95.

White, K., Simpson, B., & Argo, J. J. (2014). The motivating role of dissociative outgroups in encouraging positive consumer behaviors. *Journal of Marketing Research, 51*(4), 433–447.

Wilcox, K., & Stephen, A. T. (2013). Are close friends the enemy? Online social networks, self-esteem and self-control. *Journal of Consumer Research, 40*(2), 90–103.

Williams, K. D., Cheung, C. K., & Choi, W. (2000). Cyberostracism: Effects of being ignored over the Internet. *Journal of Personality and Social Psychology, 79*(5), 748–762.

Williams, K. D., & Sommer, K. L. (1997). Social ostracism by coworkers: Does rejection lead to loafing or compensation? *Personality and Social Psychology Bulletin, 23*, 693–706.

Winterich, K. P., & Barone, M. J. (2011). Warm glow or cold, hard cash? Social identity effects on consumer choice for donation versus discount promotions. *Journal of Marketing Research, 48*(5), 855–868.

Winterich, K. P., Mittal, V., & Aquino, K. (2013). When does recognition increase charitable behavior? Toward a moral identity-based model. *Journal of Marketing, 77*(May), 121–134.

Winterich, K. P., Mittal, V., & Ross, Jr., W. T. (2009). Donation behavior toward in-groups and out-groups: The role of gender and moral identity. *Journal of Consumer Research, 36*(August), 199–214.

Winterich, K. P., Zhang, Y., & Mittal, V. (2012). How political identity and charity positioning increase donations: Insights from moral foundations theory. *International Journal of Research in Marketing, 29*(4), 346–354.

Wood, W., Lundgren, S., Ouellette, J. A., Busceme, S., & Blackstone, T. (1994). Minority influence: A meta-analytic review of social influence processes. *Psychological Bulletin, 115*(3), 323.

Zimbardo, P. (1972). *Interpersonal Dynamics in a Simulated Prison.* Fort Belvior, VA: Defense Technical Information Center.

17 Agency and Communion as a Framework to Understand Consumer Behavior

Didem Kurt and Jeremy Frimer

In his seminal work, Bakan (1966) proposed agency and communion as two pillars of human personality – they describe how people are different from one another and how these differences influence individual and social desires. Agency represents a desire for independence and separation from other organisms; communion represents a striving for connection and unity with other organisms. They reflect personal and social motives that can conflict, cooperate, or merely coexist, depending on the context or the person. These intriguing constructs attracted a considerable amount of attention among psychologists, resulting in significant theoretical and empirical advancement over the last fifty years. Building on this large body of literature, consumer researchers have started to examine the role of these two dimensions of human personality in various issues, including consumers' interactions with brands and other consumers in the marketplace. While doing so, they also contributed to the advancement of the agency-communion theory.

The goal of this chapter is to review this nascent literature and identify fruitful research opportunities. Four sections comprise this chapter. The first section provides a broad summary of agency and communion and discusses their relation to key behavioral outcomes such as motivation, memory, and prosocial behavior. The second section outlines the current state of consumer research on agency and communion and summarizes key findings. The third section highlights some of the methodological issues pertaining to the use and operationalization of agency and communion in the consumer behavior literature. The last section lays the groundwork for future research.

Agency and Communion Fundamentals

Agency is about getting ahead. To be agentic is to be competent, independent, competitive, ambitious, in control, and power seeking. Communion is about getting along. To be communal is to be warm, honest, compassionate, agreeable, and generous (Bakan, 1966). Agency and communion serve their respective adaptive functions by profiting the self and others, respectively (Abele & Wojciszke, 2007; Cislak & Wojciszke, 2008; Peeters, 2008).

Agency is self-profiting in that ambition, competence, and social power tend to directly gain the individual material wealth. Agency also has socially mediated benefits. In the eyes of others, agency is telling of a person's capacity for carrying out intentions. This perceived capacity earns agentic people respect and social status (Stopfer, Egloff, Nestler, & Back, 2013; Wojciske, Abele, & Baryla, 2009; cf. Carrier, Louet, Chauvin, & Rohmer, 2014) and passive facilitation (e.g., strategic associations; Cuddy, Fiske, & Glick. 2007, 2008). Managers prefer agentic employees, and, likewise, employees prefer agentic managers (Cislak, 2013). Thus, agency confers both material and social benefits to the individual.

Communion's other-profitability is also adaptive for the communal individual, albeit via social mechanisms. Communion is telling of others' intentions. People perceive communal people as allies and those low in communion as competitors (Cacioppo, Gardner, & Berntson, 1997). These attributions elicit active helping versus harming behavior (Cuddy, Fiske, & Glick. 2007, 2008). As the potential beneficiary of others' communal generosity, people seek and value communal people (Cislak & Wojciszke, 2008; Fiske, Cuddy, & Glick, 2007; Stopfer et al., 2013; Wojciske, Abele, & Baryla, 2009). Hence, communal people tend to have a favorable reputation, which secures their inclusion in harmonious social groups. Individuals in these groups tend to out-compete lone individuals (Haidt, 2012). Thus, communion too has its adaptive function.

Individual Differences in Agency and Communion

Origins

Agency and communion are only somewhat heritable (viz. 30 percent; Bleidorn et al., 2010) with male the more agentic gender, and female the more communal gender ($.4 < d < .8$; e.g., Lippa, 2001). In friendships, males tend to seek agency (e.g., status, physical fitness), and females tend to seek communion (e.g., intimacy, loyalty; Hall, 2011). Also, during interactions with same-sex friends males and females conform to the stereotype: males are more agentic, and females are more agreeable (Suh, Moskowitz, Fournier, & Zuroff, 2004).

However, careful empirical examinations found that the agency-masculinity and communion-femininity associations are mainly products of social roles, not sex. The male-agency and female-communion stereotypes break down with romantic partners wherein men are more communal than women (Suh et al., 2004). Regardless of gender, breadwinners tend to be agentic, and homemakers tend to be communal (Bosak, Sczesny, & Eagly, 2012). During interactions with people of varying social status, agency changes in both genders. For instance, males are more dominant with their supervisees than they are with their supervisors, but so are females (Moskowitz, Suh, & Desaulniers, 1994). Thus, agency and communion may be aligned with masculinity and femininity because of historical differences in the roles males and females played in society. Indeed, the agency-male and communion-female links weakened between the 1970s and 1990s (Holt & Ellis, 1998). Both genders have the capacity to adopt the agentic or communal personality.

Table 17.1. *Measures of Agency and Communion*

Measure	Illustrative Items/ Content	
	Agency	Communion
Self-Report Measures		
Sex-Role Inventory[1]	Self-reliant, athletic, assertive	Yielding, cheerful, shy
Personal Attributes Questionnaire[2]	Independent, active, competitive	Helpful, kind, aware of the feelings of others
Interpersonal Adjective Scale[3]	Ambitious–dominant	Warm–agreeable
Agency and Communion Values[4]	Competence, achievement, power	Forgiveness, altruism, loyalty
Warmth and Competence[5]	Capable, skillful, intelligent	Good-natured, trustworthy, tolerant
Agency and Communion[6]	Clever, efficient, ingenious	Fair, generous, honest
Implicit Measure		
Word Fragments Completion Task[7]	_ _ _erior, con_ _ _dent, _ _ ct _ ve	_ind, war_, gen_ _ _
Content Analysis		
Motives of Agency and Communion[8]	Self-mastery, status/victory, achievement, empowerment	Love, friendship, dialogue, care/help, community
Values Embedded in Narrative[9]	Power, status, possessions, achievement	Benevolence, universalism
Agency and Communion Dictionaries for LIWC[10]	Achieve, dominant, leader	Charitable, listen, understanding
Prosocial Words Dictionary for LIWC[11]	—	Care, give, help, gentle, protect

Note. [1]Bem (1974); [2]Spence, Helmreich, & Holahan (1979); [3]Wiggins (1979); [4]Trapnell & Paulhus (2012); [5]Cuddy, Fiske, & Glick (2007); [6]Wojciszke, Bazinska, & Jaworski (1998); [7]Bartz & Lydon (2004); [8]Mansfield & McAdams (1996); [9]Frimer & Walker (2009); [10]Hart et al. (2011); [11]Frimer et al. (2014).

Measurement

Three types of measures exist: (1) self-report, (2) cognitive accessibility, and (3) verbal content analysis (see Table 17.1). The self-report category represents the most commonly used approach in the literature. This category includes alternative scales, some of which derived from well-known personality inventories. Each of these scales consists of a set of related adjectives pertaining to agency and communion dimensions.

The cognitive accessibility measure asks participants to complete word fragments that can be accomplished with agentic (vs. neutral) and communal (vs. neutral) words. The accessibility of each dimension on the part of the respondent is measured by counting the number of agentic and communal words generated. While it is intuitive and easy to use, this measure has not been widely adopted in the literature.

Finally, content analysis involves a human coder counting themes, or a computer program counting particular words, that are agentic or communal in open-ended verbal responses.[1] Individual differences measured with scales vis-à-vis content analysis tend to correlate only weakly and predict different classes of behavior (McClelland, Koestner, & Weinberger, 1989; Thrash & Elliot, 2002), suggesting that scales and content analysis tap different psychological systems. An advantage of content-analytic methods is their ability to assess how agency and communion interact within the individual (e.g., whether a person construes agency as a means to an end of communion, e.g., Frimer et al., 2012). A disadvantage is coder bias (when human coded) or the ambiguity of linguistic markers of meaning (e.g., *fair* can mean *legitimate* or *blond hair*). Throughout the remainder of the chapter, we bracket these methodological heterogeneities and treat agency and communion as monolithic.

Behavioral Implications of Agency and Communion

Motivation and Emotion

Motivationally, agentics[2] desire to stand out and break from social norms. Reminding people of shaky, distant relationships increases the activation of agentic thought (Bartz & Lydon, 2004). When feeling threatened, agentics wish to distance themselves from others and become avoidant in their attachment style (Coolsen & Nelson, 2001). Moreover, agentics experience stress when trying to demonstrate competence (e.g., convey knowledge about a social issue), but not when arguing with a spouse (Smith et al., 1998). Among the elderly, agentics who experience threats to financial stability and social status are at a higher risk for suicide (Coren & Hewitt, 1999). Their expression of individuality can have ironic implications: In secular countries (e.g., Sweden, Germany) agentics tend to become religious (Gebauer, Paulhus, & Neberich, 2013). When online dating, agentics prefer status and attractiveness in their potential mates. This applies, however, only in countries that devalue status/attractiveness (e.g., France). Agentics' preferences for status/attractiveness and religiosity are a

---

1 For example, the following goal has communion content: "I want all children to have shelter from the elements. I need people to help by donating money, time, and resources to building shelters and helping relocate children who need help." In contrast, the following goal has agency content: "...to decide what career I want, and go to graduate school in that field. To do this I need to evaluate my interests, and look for graduate programs that are right for me." (Frimer, Schaefer, & Oakes, 2014, p. 796).
2 We use the term "agentics" to mean individuals who are more agentic than communal (i.e., relatively agentic). We use the term "communals" analogously (i.e., relatively communal).

product of their desire to stand out (Gebauer, Sedikides, Verplanken, & Maio, 2012).

Motivationally, communion is a desire to belong and conform to social norms. Reminding people of intimate, healthy relationships (by priming secure attachment) increased activation of communal thought (Bartz & Lydon, 2004). Under threat, communals tend to become clingy and seek to restore a close connection (viz. anxious-ambivalent attachment style; Coolsen & Nelson, 2001). For elderly communals, threats to social stability are risk factors for suicide (Coren & Hewitt, 1999). Communals experience stress when arguing with a spouse, but not when trying to demonstrate competence (Smith et al., 1998). When online dating, communals tend to value attractiveness/status in potential mates only when they live in countries where attractiveness/status are important social values (e.g., Italy; Gebauer, Leary, & Neberich, 2012). Out of their desire to belong to something greater than themselves, communals tend to be religious. However, the relationship that communals seek in religion may be human rather than spiritual. Communals are especially likely to be religious in countries where the social norm is religiosity (e.g., Turkey). In secular countries (e.g., Germany), the relationship between communion and religiosity vanishes (Gebauer, Paulhus, & Neberich, 2013).

Memory and Learning

Agency and communion are important channels through which information is organized, stored, and retrieved in memory. Agentic and communal individuals record more memories that are consistent with their respective orientation (Woike & Polo, 2001). When recalling past events, agentics recall moments of accomplishment, recognition, and failure. Communals recall experiences of love, friendship, and betrayal of trust (Woike, Gershkovitz, Piorkowski, & Polo, 1999). The structure of memories also depends on agentic and communal orientation. Agentics rely on contrasts and relative comparisons (i.e., differentiation), whereas communals use links and similarities (i.e., integration; Woike et al., 1999). When learning new information, agentics attend more to distinctions; communals are more attentive to connections and integrations (Woike, Lavezzary, & Barsky, 2001).

Health and Happiness

Both agency and communion tend to have positive implications for physical and emotional health. Agentics are physically active, eat healthily, have high self-esteem, and have few body shape concerns (Danoff-Burg, Mosher, & Grant, 2006; Mosher & Danoff-Burg, 2008; Wojciszke et al., 2011). For patients who suffered from a heart attack, agentics experience the least anxiety and depression during recovery (Helgeson, 1993). Among arthritics, agentics experience decreased distress, disability, and pain (Trudeau, Danoff-Burg,

Revenson, & Paget, 2003). These benefits may be sourced to agentics' belief in free will and their elevated sense of self-control (Baumeister & Brewer, 2012).

Agency is not beneficial for all health outcomes. When a friend discloses a problem, agentics exert control by offering advice, which induces stress in the friend (Fritz, Nagurney, & Helgeson, 2003). In contrast, communals are better at offering social support. When a friend discloses a problem, communals offer emotional support. Among spouses of heart attack sufferers, communals experience the least anxiety and depression (Helgeson, 1993). Communals are loyal and socially connected: they have relatively few sexual partners (Nagurney & Bagwell, 2009), and they tend to be happy (Fournier & Moskowitz, 2000).

In their extreme and pure forms, agency and communion seem to have uniformly negative health implications. Agency in the absence of communion – unmitigated agency – manifests as arrogance, boastfulness, and greed (Spence, Helmreich, & Holahan, 1979). Unmitigated agentics make unilateral decisions and exercise power over others (Buss, 1990). In a parallel vein, communion in the absence of agency – unmitigated communion – manifests as being spineless, servile, and gullible. Unmitigated communals are "doormats," placing the needs of others over their own (e.g., accepting verbal insults without retort; Helgeson, 1993; Helgeson & Fritz, 1998). Unmitigated agentics and unmitigated communals have difficult relationships and poor health outcomes (Helgeson & Fritz, 1999, 2000). Specifically, unmitigated agentics binge eat, drive recklessly, and abuse substances (Danoff-Burg, Mosher, & Grant, 2006). Unmitigated communals tend to engage in emotional eating and fasting (Mosher & Danoff-Burg, 2008).

Leadership and Prosocial Behavior

The stereotypical leader (e.g., manager) is more agentic than communal (Koenig, Eagly, Mitchell, & Risitkari, 2011). Indeed, agentics have successful careers, whereas communals have large families (Abele, 2003). Leaders achieve status using either a dominant style or the more liked prestigious style (combining their agency with communion; Cheng et al., 2013). Leaders of prosocial causes are both agentic and communal (Mansfield & McAdams, 1996; Matsuba & Walker, 2005; Walker & Frimer, 2007). These leaders combine their agency with their communion in their life stories and personal goals (Frimer & Walker, 2009; Frimer et al., 2011), framing their agency as a means to an end of a communal purpose (Frimer et al., 2012). This narrative framing of agency for communion is rare. Typical adults and even emerging communal leaders use agency for both agency and communion equally (Dunlop, Walker, & Matsuba, 2013).

Agency, Communion, and Social Judgment

When people evaluate the actions and characters of others, they make agentic and communal attributions, each of which can be positively or negatively valenced. These are at play both in judgments of individual persons and in judgments of groups (stereotypes).

Judging Individuals

The Double Perspective Model (Abele & Wojciszke, in press) posits that agency and communion play different roles in social judgment. For an agent trying to complete a task, agency is the more important motive because the active doer is concerned with efficient goal fulfillment. When describing goals or recalling doing something well, people describe their agency (e.g., efficiency; Abele & Wojciszke, 2007; Frimer, Schaefer, & Oakes, 2014). Also, priming positive agentic memories enhances self-esteem (Wojciszke, & Sobiczewska, 2013).

However, for an observer of another person's action, communion is more important than agency because the observer is concerned with the social consequences of the action, be they profitable for the observer or not. Thus, communion is the primary dimension of social judgment (Abele & Wojciszke, in press). Communal traits are more cognitively accessible, and people rate them as more important than agency (Abele & Wojciszke, 2007; Wojciszke et al., 2011). People process communal information faster and more automatically than agentic information (viz. mentioned first and faster recognition, categorization, and inference from behavior; Abele & Bruckmüller, 2011; Bi, Ybarra, & Zhao, 2013; Ybarra, Park, Stanik, & Lee, 2008). When recalling doing something well from the perspective of another person, people describe their communion (e.g., relatedness; Abele & Wojciszke, 2007). People prefer communion in others unless they are mutually interdependent (e.g., working together), in which case the preference is for agency (Abele & Brack, 2013).

Judging Groups: Stereotype and Prejudice

The Stereotype Content Model (e.g., Cuddy, Fiske, & Glick, 2008; Fiske, Cuddy, Glick, & Xu, 2002) and the BIAS map (Cuddy, Fiske, & Glick, 2007) posit that combinations of agency and communion describe stereotypes of various groups and can account for typical reactions toward these groups. Agency stereotypes elicit a desire to associate (or dissociate) with the group, whereas communion stereotypes elicit a desire to help (or harm) the group. Stereotypes of Asians, Jews, and the wealthy are agentic and not communal, eliciting envy and conflicting desires to associate with yet harm these groups (Wojciszke, Bazinska, & Jaworski, 1998). The disabled and the elderly are seen as communal and not agentic, eliciting pity and patronizing help and neglect. Stereotypically lacking agency and communion, the homeless and feminists elicit feelings of contempt, resulting in neglect and active harm. And housewives and the middle class are stereotypically both agentic and communal, eliciting admiration. People desire to both help and be socially connected to these groups (Cuddy, Fiske, & Glick, 2007).

Situational Flexibility of Agency and Communion

People have the capacity for both agency and communion; they transition flexibly between them from situation to situation. Agentic self-concept changes in response to successes and failure (e.g., Abele, 2003; Diekman & Eagly, 2000; Leszczynski, 2009; Moskowitz, Suh, & Desaulniers, 1994; Twenge, 1997). And communal self-concept increases when empathizing with another person (Uchronski, Abele, & Bruckmüller, 2013). People are more agentic on week-days, and more communal on weekends (Brown & Moskowitz, 1998; Uchronski, 2008). As people move through their careers, they become less agentic and more communal (Diehl, Owen, & Youngblade, 2004). Agency and communion vary depending on the situation.

To garner the benefits of both agency and communion, a common strategy is to behave agentically while maintaining a communal appearance. These mutu-ally conflicting motives turn social life into a kind of theatrical play, with vast differences between onstage and offstage performances (Goffman, 1959). On stage, people tend to become deceptively communal, claiming sanctimonious saint-like attributes and exaggerating their agreeableness and self-restraint (Gebauer, Sedikides, Verplanken, & Maio, 2012; Paulhus & John, 1998). Off stage (i.e., when feeling anonymous), people rarely engage in communal behav-ior (Hoffman, McCabe, & Smith, 1996; Shariff & Norenzayan, 2007) even if they committed themselves to doing so (Batson et al., 1997). To maintain this "moral masquerade" (Batson, 2008), people tend to present a communal self-identity and expend great efforts to repair deficiencies in communal reputation (e.g., Ybarra et al., 2012). People can also claim to be more agentic than they actually are to garner respect. Agentic deceivers make narcissistic superheroic revelations of their own social and intellectual status (Paulhus & John, 1998).

Mapping Consumer Behavior onto Agency and Communion

Agency and communion emerged as key themes in studies of consumer research during the last decade. A primary aim was to better understand the role of social forces (e.g., impression management, transmission by word of mouth) in consumer decision making. The goal of other studies was to further our understanding of the processes governing consumers' individual decision making (e.g., financial risk taking). The two fundamental modalities of human nature provide a useful framework for analyzing and interpreting differences in consumer behavior in socially dynamic settings, where individuals interact with other social actors or their choices are publicly observable to others. Agency and communion are also useful for understanding consumer behavior in socially isolated settings, where individuals are not subject to an explicit social influence. While the latter setting has received only limited attention of researchers to date, both contexts offer rich opportunities for understanding various dimensions of consumer decision making. Consistent with the spirit of this volume, we begin by identifying key theoretical and empirical advances in earlier research and then discuss relatively underresearched areas.

Agency, Communion, and Consumers' Interactions with Brands

Self-Identity and Consumption

Agentic and communal values are built into individuals' view of the self. As such, they are overarching concerns that motivate people in consumption episodes. Consumers' buying decisions, by their very nature, may be inherent manifestations of agency as they are ultimately intended to satisfy the needs of the self (Sedikides, Gregg, Cisek, & Hart, 2007). This view, however, does not fully explain many purchase situations in which consumer choices are imbued with concern for others.

Engaging in consumption activities may enable people to create a sense of self. In particular, consumers' prior experiences may accumulate as self-stories that help the individual define who they are and what they want (Escalas & Bettman, 2000). Escalas' (1996) brand story study provided evidence supporting this argument. Her analysis of consumers' brand stories revealed that brands helped people achieve their goals related to both agency (e.g., differentiating the self from others) and communion (e.g., connecting the self with others), strengthening the connection between the brand and one's sense of self.

Consumer–Brand Relationships

Marketers use agency and communion strategically to communicate and connect with consumer groups. Some brands aim to establish a communal relationship with consumers (Aggarwal, 2004); a common strategy is to offer certain benefits to show the brand's concern for customers' needs (rather than to get something in return). While such a strategy may increase customer loyalty, it also exposes the brand to the risk of violating norms of communal relationships (e.g., helping others without expecting monetary payments). Customers who feel a communal versus exchange relationship with a brand respond more negatively when the brand charges a fee for extra services linked to a prior transaction.

A key source of the appeal of luxury products to consumers is the agentic feelings (e.g., superiority and status) provided by such products. This effect is likely to fade as luxury brands attempt to establish a stronger connection with their customers via introducing user-created items (i.e., items designed by customers instead of the firm's internal designers). Labeling luxury fashion brands (e.g., Prada) as user-designed decreases demand for such products because such labels attenuate consumers' experience of agency (Fuchs, Prandelli, Schreier, & Dahl, 2013). On the other hand, labeling mainstream brands (e.g., Zara) as user-designed increases demand. Mainstream brand users may be less concerned about agentic feelings and place more emphasis on communal feelings, leading them to endorse more strongly the idea of user-design to foster a sense of connection to like-minded others.

The agentic orientation of narcissists manifests as instrumental relations with not only those around them but also with brands (Lambert & Desmond, 2013). Narcissists have little loyalty to brands and thus exhibit elevated brand-switching behavior. Their portfolio of brands changes as they encounter better ones; yet it consistently includes brands that communicate self-sufficiency, superiority, and status. In contrast, nonnarcissists adopt a communal orientation toward people and brands, leading them to establish deeper and long-lasting relations when dealing with both. The brand choices of nonnarcissists reflect the values they embrace in their personal relations, such as loyalty and modesty.

Advertising Strategies

Jorgenson's (1981) content analysis of more than five thousands ads that appeared in an American magazine targeting a primarily female audience for the period 1910 to 1979 revealed that communal themes were more prevalent than agentic themes. However, the ratio of communal themes to agentic themes decreased during the 1970s, consistent with the increasing emphasis on the self over those years. As people became more concerned with self-indulgence and differentiating themselves from others, marketers adjusted their messages to remain relevant.

Agentic and communal values embraced by consumers of different gender determine consumers' reactions to the self- and other-oriented advertising messages (Meyers-Levy, 1988). Males primed with agentic values exhibit a more favorable attitude toward a product than females primed with communal values when the product message is self-oriented (e.g., it kills germs and bacteria that cause decay), whereas the opposite is true when the message is other-oriented (e.g., it provides pleasing fresh breath). Nonetheless, the self-oriented message does not result in less favorable attitudes toward the product among females as compared to the other-oriented message, which is consistent with the argument that agentic values are increasingly embraced by female consumers.

Consumer-to-Consumer Interactions

Social Self-Threat

Social self-threat (e.g., being unloved and rejected by close others) influences how much consumers value the things they own (Dommer & Swaminathan, 2013). Both agentics and communals respond to social self-threat by attaching greater value to in-group items (i.e., a product with the home institution logo) as compared to generic items (i.e., a product with no logo). However, social self-threat causes agentics (but not communals) to devalue out-group items (i.e., a product with the rival institution logo). This finding is consistent with the argument that when it comes to items associated with out-groups, the link between possessions and the self is likely to be weaker, particularly among agentic individuals, as they have a tendency to separate themselves from others.

Social Presence

Agentics' drive to stand out alters their consumption when a peer is present (Kurt, Inman, & Argo, 2011). Agentics who are accompanied by a friend during a shopping trip spend more (e.g., choose a more expensive brand) than those who shop alone. On the contrary, the presence of a friend does not change spending among communals. The explanation for this observation is that the two groups have different impression-management concerns, leading them to adopt different self-presentation styles when shopping with friends. In particular, agency stresses self-promotion, leading agentics to pursue an acquisitive self-presentation style (i.e., getting ahead) through higher spending. Communals prefer a protective self-presentation style (i.e., getting along) by keeping their spending under control.

Word of Mouth

Consumers' willingness to exert social influence upon other consumers through word of mouth depends on their agency–communion orientation (Zhang, Feick, & Mittal, 2014). As the strength of the relation between the self and the recipient gets weaker, the likelihood of sharing a poor consumption experience with others diminishes among agentic individuals who are high in image impairment concern. That is, when image impairment concern is high enough, agency reduces people's tendency to prevent others from making a similar mistake unless others are very closely related to the self. This is because transmitting negative word of mouth involves the risk of looking foolish in the eye of the recipient (e.g., being seen as someone making bad purchase decisions). On the other hand, communal individuals are equally likely to tell their negative experiences to others regardless of the strength of their relationship to the recipient (e.g., a close friend vs. a casual acquaintance).

Charitable Donations

Agency and communion also determine the amount of money people spend to satisfy a sense of personal morality (Winterich, Mittal, & Ross, 2009). The amount of money donated to out-group targets (i.e., the victims of Indian Ocean Tsunami) increases with moral identity among communal (but not agentic) donors. When donation targets belong to an in-group (i.e., the victims of Hurricane Katrina), however, moral identity positively influences donations of agentic donors. The proposed explanation for this effect is that communion, which includes in-group others as a part of the self, allows for the expansion of the one's circle of moral regard to include members of other-groups. In contrast, agency limits the expansion of the boundaries of one's moral regard from the self to only those who are associated with the self in a meaningful manner (i.e., in-group others).

Agency and communion not only influence prosocial behavior but also impact how the beneficent feel afterward (Grant & Gino, 2010). Helping others causes the helper to experience stronger feelings of both agency (i.e., self-efficacy) and communion (i.e., social worth) when the beneficent received thanks for his or her efforts. However, only his or her level of communal feelings predicted whether the helper would engage in further prosocial behavior. That is, gratitude expressions motivate helpers to help more by increasing their perceived social value.

Agency, Communion, and Consumers' Interactions with Service Providers

Agency Is the Default

Agency may be the default in the various encounters of consumers with service providers. In-depth interviews with both bill collectors and consumer debtors suggest that agency characterizes the relationship between the two parties (Hill, 1994). Collectors tend to depersonalize and isolate themselves from debtors. By objectifying debtors, collectors may suppress empathic concerns for debtors, which may allow collectors to manipulate debtors to collect the desired amount without feeling guilt. This agentic approach, however, often escalates conflicts and sometimes leads to the use of excessive collection tactics.

Adding Communion to the Mix

Customer satisfaction is higher when the customer displays an agentic behavior pattern and the service provider exhibits a communal behavior pattern – or vice versa – in their interactions as compared to the case where both parties interact using the same style (Ma & Dube, 2011). For example, patrons at the dining room of a health care facility reported a lower level of satisfaction with the service when the patrons and servers both exhibited a dominant style. Reported satisfaction increased if either the patron or the server exhibited a submissive style. Similarly, when both the patron and the server exhibited agreeable behavior (vs. one party exhibiting quarrelsomeness), reported satisfaction was low. These findings suggest that agency and communion are complementary in social interactions, working together like yin and yang.

This compatibility of agency and communion – and incompatibility of agency and agency – in social relationships does not always apply and can sometimes reverse. When marketing their service, sellers may find that their self-promotion efforts backfire when trying to connect with clients with communal orientation. Scott, Mende and Bolton (2013) asked participants to read a magazine article about a lawyer and then indicate their interest in doing business with the lawyer. When the article emphasized the wealth of the lawyer, communal clients' interest in doing business with the lawyer declined. Contra the Ma and Dube (2011) study, this finding suggests that self-promotion (a key characteristic of agency) is incompatible with the communal orientation of some consumers and can thereby undermine the relationship between service providers and consumers.

Agency, Communion, and Material Wealth

Affluence

People often attribute greater agency to affluent individuals (Christopher & Schlenken, 2000) and expect that individuals with a high income to have agentic qualities, such as competence, and to have few communal qualities (Johannesen-Schmidt & Eagly, 2002). This suggests that when making attributions about others based on their income, agency and communion may function in a mutually exclusive manner. One explanation is that wealth and success typically breed self-promotion, a prevalent manifestation of agency. This movement may be at odds with communion's focus on avoiding separation and losses to maintain unity.

Issue Capability and Financial Risk Taking

Agency and communion may also influence how people gain affluence, through financial risk–taking behavior. Agency makes consumers sensitive to achievement of gains, whereas communion enhances consumers' sensitivity to avoidance of losses (He, Inman, & Mittal, 2008). As a result, higher issue capability (i.e., higher level of perceived resources or skills to resolve an issue) leads to greater risk seeking in investment decisions of agentic individuals, whereas the same effect was observed in insurance decisions of communal individuals. Specifically, issue capability increases agentics' willingness to invest their savings in the stock market instead of a savings account through shifting their focus more on the upside potential of their decision. While issue capability does not alter the likelihood of investing in the stock market among communals, it reduces their tendency to purchase insurance against potential losses (i.e., they take more risk).

Power and Financial Risk Taking

Having power or authority over others could serve many different purposes, agentic or communal. For example, managers can use their power to help their team function well together (communal purpose) or to gain accolades for themselves (agentic purpose). Agentic individuals tend not to think of social power in such a nuanced and contingent way. Rather, agentics default to the assumption that social power is, first and foremost, an opportunity for amassing personal wealth and expanding the boundaries of their power; communals do not make such a simplistic association. Supporting this perspective is evidence that feeling powerful induces greater financial risk taking among agentics when such risks provide high self-benefit (Kurt, 2015). In contrast, feeling powerful has no impact on the financial risk taking of communals. For agentics – and only for agentics – feelings of power, by default, are associated with the pursuit of self-enhancement through personal gain.

Not only does feeling powerful rather than powerless have differential impact on agentic and communal consumers, but it also facilitates agentic behavior on the part of consumers (for a detailed discussion, see Rucker, Galinsky, & Dubois, 2012, and Chapter 12 in this handbook). Consumers, when they feel powerful, report a higher level of self-importance (a typical characteristic of agency) and spend more money on the items they purchase for themselves than on the items they purchase for others (Rucker, Dubois, & Galinsky, 2011). That is, for those who feel powerful, self is associated with greater psychological utility as compared to others, resulting in higher monetary worth allocated to spending on the self rather than others.

Methodological and Analytic Issues in Consumer Research

The operationalization of agency and communion was a key issue emerging in our review of the extant consumer behavior literature. In this section, we briefly review how consumer researchers have measured agentic and communal orientations and how they have analyzed their data. We also discuss whether agency and communion are simply a variant of other related personality constructs that are of interest to consumer researchers.

Measuring and Manipulating Agency and Communion

Gender as a Proxy Measure

Using gender as a proxy for agency-communion orientation is quite common (e.g., Dommer & Swaminathan, 2013; He, Inman, & Mittal, 2008; Kurt, Inman, & Argo, 2011; Zhang, Feick, & Mittal, 2014). This approach has its roots in Bakan's (1966) observation that agency is more of a characteristic of males, whereas communion is more of characteristic of females. A key advantage of this approach is that it allows researchers to operationalize agency and communion in secondary datasets in which these dimensions were not explicitly measured (e.g., He, Inman, & Mittal, 2008; Kurt, Inman, & Argo, 2011). A major disadvantage of this approach, however, is that it relies on the questionable premise that all males are agentic and all females are communal. Dindia (2006, p. 11) summarized this issue as follows: "Women are more communal and men are more agentic, ... [but] they differ in degree, not kind."

Self-Report Inventories

Several researchers have used personality inventories to measure agentic and communal orientations directly.[3] Winterich, Mittal, and Ross (2009), for instance, employed the Bem's (1974) Sex Role Inventory, which contains twenty items related to each dimension. Others also used items selected from the Extended Version of Personal Attributes Questionnaire (Spence, Helmreich, & Holahan, 1979), which includes eight items on each dimension.

Because scoring high on agency does not necessarily imply a strong self-versus other-focus, as someone can score high on both agency and communion dimensions, some researchers adopted a "difference score" approach to assess the extent to which individuals endorse agentic versus communal values and thus have a truly self-rather than other-focus (e.g., Dommer & Swaminathan, 2013; Kurt, Inman, & Argo, 2011). This approach, which involves subtracting each respondent's communion score from his or her agency score, has a long tradition in the literature and recognizes that it is not the level of agency or communion but the difference between the two dimensions that determines one's self versus other orientation (e.g., Costos, 1986; Strahan, 1975; White, et al., 1986).

Experimental Manipulations

While acknowledging that priming agency and communion may be difficult (these characteristics are internalized through socialization at early ages; Eagly, 1987), researchers have nonetheless developed experimental manipulations for agency–communion orientation. These experimental manipulations typically involve asking participants to read statements about agentic and communal qualities (Myers-Levy, 1988), write a short paragraph explaining how they embody these qualities (Winterich, Mittal, & Ross, 2009), or perform a scrambled work task (Kurt, Inman, & Argo, 2011).

Agency–Communion and Related Constructs

Independence–Interdependence

Agency and communion are linked (but not identical) to other relationship orientation constructs used in the consumer behavior literature. Among these constructs stand out the independent and interdependent self-construals (Markus & Kitamaya, 1991; Singelis, 1994), which also reflect an emphasis on one's uniqueness and self-sufficiency versus connectedness and social synergy. Agency–communion differs from independent–interdependent self-construal

---

3 Content analysis also allows researchers to assess individuals' agentic and communal orientations. While this approach is gaining popularity in the psychology literature, it has not been adopted by consumer researchers yet. We urge future researchers to consider this alternative methodology as well (for an application, see Frimer et al., 2011).

in two important ways. First, agency–communion was conceptualized broad enough to capture such characteristics as self-confidence, competitiveness, and emotional expressivity besides independence versus interdependence. Agency, for instance, is about being independent from others but also getting ahead of them. Thus, while the independent self-construal may capture the self-sufficiency aspect of agency, it does not truly reflect one's desire to feel superior to others.

Second, agency–communion has its roots in personality psychology, whereas independent–interdependent self-construals originate from cultural psychology and are motivated by differences in interpersonal relations between Western and non-Western societies.[4] Accordingly, the former can be meaningfully used to motivate and explain variation in individuals' self- and other-oriented behavior within a particular culture. In contrast, the latter is a more appropriate construct to analyze cross-cultural differences in individuals' self versus other focus. That is, agentic qualities (e.g., decisiveness, competitiveness, leadership) and communal qualities (nurturance, emotional expressiveness) are part of every society regardless of whether a society is primarily independent (e.g., the United States) or interdependent (e.g., China). Accordingly, valuing independence over interdependence at a broader level does not necessarily imply that a person would embrace agency more than communion. For instance, people who belong to a primarily independent culture may prefer to nurture those around them in a way that those dependents will have the resources and ability to make their decisions independently in the future, whereas people from a primarily interdependent culture may exhibit nurturance in a way that it facilitates interdependence between the two parties. This, however, does not mean that the former group exhibits lower communion (and higher agency) than the latter group. It is just that communion may be practiced differently across cultures.

Exchange and Communal Relationship Styles

Relationship styles – exchange versus communal relationship (Clark & Mills, 1979) – also map onto agency–communion theory, particularly in the dimension of communion. This construct, however, has a narrower focus. Relationship styles primarily concern providing a benefit to a counterpart and the motivation behind this act. Undergirding these styles are implicit rules and norms that govern the process of giving benefits to others and receiving benefits from them. In exchange relationships, people benefit others with the expectation of the return of the favor. In communal relationships, people expect no such

---

4 For instance, the extent to which someone feels comfortable using one's first name soon after meeting a person (which is more of a characteristic of Westerners) is one of the dimensions of independence in Singelis' scale. Similarly, one's willingness to offer a seat to his or her professor on the bus (which is more of a characteristic of non-Westerners) relates to interdependence. In that sense, independent and interdependent self-construals are more closely related to the concepts of individualism and collectivism (e.g., Hofstede, 1984) than are agency and communion.

return on beneficence. The ultimate motivation in communal relationships is simply to respond the needs of others.

To map relationship styles onto agency and communion requires a distinction between means and ends (Frimer et al., 2012). Exchange relationships entail using communion (other-benefit) as a means to an end of advancing one's agency (the return on beneficence). In contrast, communal relationships entail treating communion (other-benefit) as an end in itself. Although communal relationship orientation captures communion's emphasis on attending to the needs of others and helping them, it is not broad enough to include such values as modesty, intimacy, and a sense of belonging. Hence, we urge researchers to consider the two sets of constructs (i.e., exchange and communal relationships and agency–communion) as complements rather than substitutes.

Directions for Future Research

In this section, we propose future research directions pertaining to consumer–brand relationships, social interactions in the marketplace, consumption through social media, and consumption habits.

Consumer–Brand Relationships

Brands as Servants or Partners

Consumers assign personality characteristics to brands (Aaker, 1997), partly because marketers present brands and products in a humanized form. Brand anthropomorphization often comes either in the form of a human partner or as a servant (Aggarwal & McGill, 2012). Just as agency and communion can explain stereotypical reactions to Asians, housewives, and the elderly (Cuddy, Fiske, & Glick, 2007), so too may agency and communion explain consumers' attitudes toward human brands. Specifically, we propose that agentic individuals will favor a servant brand over a partner brand because agentics prefer to be in control of others. We propose that communal individuals prefer partner brands because communals seek close, collaborative relationships. Parallel processes may be at play for product performance expectations and customer satisfaction.

Brand characteristics can determine whether pairing two brands (e.g., co-branding) invokes positive or negative reactions on the part of consumers. Here, competing hypotheses arise. If agency and communion function synergistically, consumers may respond positively when an agentic and a communal brand team up. On the other hand, if agency and communion are competitive in this context, then pairing agentic with agentic and communal with communal brands would elicit a more positive consumer response. Characteristics of the consumer may also influence reactions to co-branding. Joining forces with another brand may favorably affect the brand image among communal individuals. However, agentic individuals may respond negatively to this same pairing because they are concerned with separation and self-sufficiency. Testing these predictions has the potential to offer useful formulae for managers, particularly for those who primarily target either the agentic or communal segment of a consumer group.

Loyalty Programs

Loyalty programs represent an important aspect of consumer–brand relationships and offer various benefits to consumers, such as special discounts, shopping points, and reduced wait times. In exchange, companies gain access to valuable information about their customers' shopping habits. Signing up for loyalty programs thus involves an agreement to exchange of benefits between companies and consumers. These programs often differ in the degree to which they provide customers with communal vis-à-vis status-related benefits (e.g., birthday gifts vs. restricted check-in counters; Dréze & Nunes, 2009; Henderson, Beck, & Palmatier, 2011). This suggests that various steps of loyalty programs, from design to usage by customers, involve agentic and communal styles. We urge future research to examine how agentic and communal characteristics of customers and of loyalty programs influence the efficacy of loyalty programs at strengthening brand–customer relationships and customer satisfaction.

Product Disposal

Agentic individuals strive for material wealth (Frimer et al., 2011). Thus, agentics' willingness to dispose of an item may critically depend on the material value they obtain from its disposal. Agency is also about separation. This characteristic can facilitate the disposal process through reducing the pain of giving up an item, particularly when products take on an anthropomorphic quality (Chandler & Schwarz, 2010). However, agentic individuals may be less likely to dispose of an item that reflects their independent identity and helps them establish superiority over others. Communal individuals, on the other hand, may be reluctant to dispose of items that maintain or strengthen their connection to others. A related issue is the choice of disposition method. Agentics may tend to dispose of items through selling and replacing. Communals may be more inclined to gift, donate, or recycle their unwanted products. That is, both acquisition and disposition decisions of communals may be driven by their striving for connectedness with others.

Aesthetics

Seemingly disconnected areas of consumer behavior also offer fruitful opportunities for integrative research on agency–communion orientation. Aesthetics is one such area. Perhaps agentic individuals prefer particular colors or certain clothing designs that might help them stand out in a group and highlight their dominance. On the contrary, communal individuals may avoid unique colors or designs to ensure that their choices match those of the others around. Certain shapes that are inherently isolated and finite could induce feelings of agency (e.g., dots, lines), whereas others that have a more inclusive, connected nature could evoke feelings of communion (e.g., circles, ovals). If so, using agency- or communion-compatible shapes in an advertisement could improve the persuasiveness of the communicated message on the target group.

Social Interactions in the Marketplace

Consumer Choice in a Group Setting

Within group settings, people often change their consumption preferences based on prior selections of other group members, even at the expense of selecting nonfavorite items (e.g., Ariely & Levav, 2000; Quester & Steyer, 2010). Agency and communion offer a theoretically meaningful framework for future research aimed at extending this stream of literature. Insofar as "agency manifests itself in the formation of separations; communion in the lack of separations" (Bakan, 1966, p. 15), one's tendency to diverge from the previous choices of others may increase with agency. In contrast, communal individuals may be especially likely to conform to the group's most popular choice. However, one also needs to consider that agency involves putting pleasures of the self at the center stage. Therefore, deviating from others' choices at the cost of personal consumption satisfaction can create a tension between agentic individuals' eagerness to differentiate themselves from others and their desire to please the self.

Agentic and communal qualities of consumers may influence their risk-seeking tendency when making financial decisions in the presence of peers. Prior risky choices of other group members may induce greater financial risk taking among both agentic and communal individuals, but this effect may be more pronounced among agentics. That is, agentics' desire to get ahead of others may lead them to make riskier financial decisions than other members, while communal individuals' desire to get along with others may cause them to exhibit a risk-seeking behavior comparable to that of other members.

Interactions with Salespeople

Salespeople exert important social influence in the marketplace (e.g., Evans, 1963; Woodside & Davenport, 1974) but various consumer and salesperson characteristics moderate the efficacy of persuasion and selling tactics (e.g., Campbell & Kirmani, 2000). A customer's purchase decision, in part, depends on whether he or she considers salesperson a friend (Evans, 1963; Mayer & Greenberg, 1964). However, the specific behaviors that comprise "friendly" influence tactics of salespeople remain unclear. Future research should look into whether a friendly salesperson generates an impact similar to the presence of friends in a shopping trip on agentic and communal individuals' spending behavior. While agentics may alter their spending behavior to highlight their status vis-à-vis those around them, they may be less likely to establish friendly relations with salespeople due to their independent and self-reliant nature.

Lying

Consumers often tell white lies to service providers (e.g., providing positive verbal feedback about poor service; Argo & Shiv, 2010). The immediate function of these lies is to smooth over social interaction. However, the end result is that the liar behaves in such a way that benefits the wrongdoer (e.g., leaving a large tip to the server) at the expense of the consumer. We propose that communal individuals are especially prone to making white lies because they tend to place more emphasis on others' feelings and take actions that benefit others rather than the self.

Consumers also lie to other consumers (Argo, White, & Dahl, 2006) as a response to self-threatening social comparisons. That is, to avoid looking foolish, people tend to lie about the price they paid for a product when they find out that the other person actually paid much less for the same product. We propose that agentic individuals are more likely to engage in this sort of lying because doing so would enhance their self-image and maintain their perceived superiority over others. Further, customers sometimes provide misleading information to companies in the hopes of attaining material benefits for the self (Anthony & Cowley, 2012). We expect that this tendency may also be more pronounced among agentics.

Confrontation and Apology

Customers, salespeople, and cashiers experience confrontation over wait times, service quality, and pricing policies. Agentic and communal cues in the shopping environment can moderate the severity of confrontation. For instance, communal cues in a shopping environment may reduce consumers' tendency to engage in arguments with marketers because such cues prime consumers' motive to get along. Agentic cues, on the other hand, may exacerbate arguments by priming self-serving drives. Future research on this issue can examine implications that can potentially lessen the stressfulness of shopping environments.

Companies apologize to customers for product failures. Servers apologize to clients for service errors. And shoppers apologize for interrupting each other. Agency and communion may play a role in the causes and consequences of apology behavior in the marketplace. For example, agentic individuals may experience elevated self-worth after receiving an apology, whereas the same apology may increase a communal individual's sense of social-worth. Accordingly, the apology may help restore the relationship with a communal individual but not with agentic individuals.

Consumption through Social Media

Self-Presentation

With the increasing popularity of social networking sites such as Facebook and Twitter over the last few years, peer influence has had an increasing influence on consumer decision making. Individuals now share information with their friends digitally in the form of messages, photos, and videos. While people are increasingly using social networking channels, they differ widely in terms of volume, type, and quality of the digital content they generate and consume (Trusov, Bodapati, & Bucklin, 2010). Agentics and communals may present themselves differently online. We propose that agentic individuals tend to share experiences that highlight their individuality and superiority, whereas communal individuals' posts reflect their emotional expressivity and warmth. This tendency may in turn affect the traffic and attention their profiles attract, determining the success of their self-presentation efforts.

Similar to the effects of the physical presence of friends, the participation in social networking sites may alter consumer behavior. Agentic individuals may be more likely to self-promote through their spending decisions (e.g., going on an expensive trip, buying a new car, dining at a fancy restaurant, etc.). If so, the extensive use of online social networks coupled with agentics' desire to get ahead of others may have deleterious effects on agentic individuals' financial well-being.

Financial Risk Taking

Participation in online social networks can also impact people's sense of connectedness to and perceived support they receive from others. People who participate in online communities are willing to take greater financial risk than those who do not participate in an online community (Zhu, Dholakia, Chen, & Algesheimer, 2012). The authors explain this finding with the "cushion hypothesis" – individuals are more likely to make risky financial decisions when they feel that their peers and family members would cushion them in the event of a potential financial difficulty (Weber & Hsee, 1998). This effect may be more prevalent among communal individuals, who place emphasis on social relationships and connections with others. On the other hand, agentic individuals may rely on support from others less when making risky financial choices. Future research should explore this possibility.

Consumption Habits

Self-Control

Self-control failures result in habits of excessive, unhealthy eating and smoking (e.g., Baumeister, Heatherton, & Tice, 1994). While a great deal of research has examined the causes and consequences of such habits, little evidence exists regarding how consumers' self-focus versus other-focus influences their breakdowns in self-control. Both agentics and communals may exhibit high self-control, but for different reasons. Agency may protect individuals from picking up harmful habits because self-control and self-direction are key characteristics of agency (Helgeson, 1994; Helgeson & Lepore, 2004). On the other hand, communal individuals' other-focus may manifest as self-control when they are surrounded by supportive others. Thus, the presence or absence of others may influence agentics' and communals' self-control differently. Moreover, agentic and communal individuals may respond differently to self-control failures. The success-oriented nature of agentics may make them more sensitive to self-control failures, resulting in a loss of confidence and thus future ability to exert self-control.

The unmitigated forms of agency and communion may be linked to consumers' compulsive buying behavior. For example, when experiencing emotional stress, unmitigated communals may be prone to excessive gift giving, and unmitigated agentics may be prone to excessive self-gifting. This may help explain the well-established link between these unmitigated forms of agency and communion and poor social and health outcomes (Helgeson, 1994).

Multitasking

People who highly value achievement and success may attempt to create time by engaging in multiple activities at the same time (Cotte & Raneshwar, 2000), suggesting that multitasking pertains to agency. Communals could also multitask to free up time to spend with others. Hence, time consumption is another interesting setting in which to examine the role of agency and communion in consumer behavior. A related issue is paralysis in the face of decision making. Agency involves self-confidence and being decisive (Eagly, 1987). We reason that agentic individuals are less likely to experience "choice overload" (Iyengar & Lepper, 2000). Accordingly, when making a choice, they may rely less on justification-based mechanisms (e.g., picking utility over pleasure) when faced with a large set of alternatives (Sela, Berger, & Lie, 2009).

Conclusion

Half a century ago, Bakan (1966) introduced the concepts of agency and communion as the fundamental modalities that define and distinguish human beings. His seminal work sparked great interest among psychologists examining various dimensions of human behavior, contributing to a generation of research that produced a nuanced understanding of human decision making. While we trace the first use of these constructs in the consumer behavior literature to the 1980s, not until the twenty-first century did agency and communion gain popularity among consumer researchers.

A series of studies demonstrated the usefulness of agency and communion in understanding important differences in consumers' preferences and choices observed in both private and public settings. We categorized these studies under four broad topics: (1) consumers' interactions with brands, (2) consumer-to-consumer relations, (3) consumers' interactions with service providers, and (4) material wealth. Beyond offering valuable implications for research and practice, this stream of research has contributed significantly to the establishment of agency and communion as relevant constructs in consumer behavior. Our review demonstrates several fruitful avenues for future research. Broadly, we call for future research on the following topics: (1) consumer-brand relationships, (2) social interactions in the marketplace, (3) consumption through social media, and (4) consumption habits. We believe additional research on these topics would enhance the field's understanding of the role of interpersonal dynamics in consumption.

References

Aaker, J. L. (1997). Dimension of brand personality. *Journal of Marketing Research, 34,* 347–356.

Abele, A. E. (2003). The dynamics of masculine-agentic and feminine-communal traits: Findings from a prospective study. *Journal of Personality and Social Psychology, 85,* 768–776.

Abele, A. E., & Brack, S. (2013). Preference for other persons' traits is dependent on the kind of social relationship. *Social Psychology, 44,* 84–94.

Abele, A. E., & Bruckmüller, S. (2011). The bigger one of the "Big Two"? Preferential processing of communal information. *Journal of Experimental Social Psychology, 47,* 935–948.

Abele, A. E., & Wojciszke, B. (2007). Agency and communion from the perspective of self versus others. *Journal of Personality and Social Psychology, 93,* 751–763.

Abele, A. E., & Wojciszke, B. (in press). Communal and agentic content in social cognition: A dual perspective model. *Advances in Experimental Social Psychology.*

Aggarwal, P. (2004). The effects of brand relationship norms on consumer attitudes and behavior. *Journal of Consumer Research, 31,* 87–101.

Aggarwal, P., & McGill, A. L. (2012). When brands seem human, do humans act like brands? Automatic behavioral priming effects of brand anthropomorphism. *Journal of Consumer Research, 39,* 307–323.

Anthony, C. I., & Cowley, E. (2012). The labor of lies: How lying for material rewards polarizes outcome satisfaction. *Journal of Consumer Research, 39,* 478–492.

Argo, J. J., White, K., & Dahl, D. W. (2006). Social comparison theory and deception in the interpersonal exchange of consumption information. *Journal Consumer Research, 33,* 99–108.

Argo, J. J., & Shiv, B. (2010). Are white lies as innocuous as we think? *Journal of Consumer Research, 38,* 1093–1102.

Ariely, D., & Levav, J. (2000). Sequential choice in group settings: Taking the road less traveled and less enjoyed. *Journal of Consumer Research, 27,* 279–290.

Bakan, D. (1966). *The Duality of Human Existence: An Essay on Psychology and Religion.* Oxford: Rand McNally.

Bartz, J. A., & Lydon, J. E. (2004). Close relationships and the working self-concept: Implicit and explicit effects of priming attachment on agency and communion. *Personality and Social Psychology Bulletin, 30*, 1389–1401.

Batson, C. (2008). Moral masquerades: Experimental exploration of the nature of moral motivation. *Phenomenology and the Cognitive Sciences, 7*, 51–66.

Batson, C., Kobrynowicz, D., Dinnerstein, J. L., Kampf, H. C., & Wilson, A. D. (1997). In a very different voice: Unmasking moral hypocrisy. *Journal of Personality and Social Psychology, 72*, 1335–1348.

Baumeister, R. F., & Brewer, L. E. (2012). Believing versus disbelieving in free will: Correlates and consequences. *Social and Personality Psychology Compass, 6*, 736–745.

Baumeister, R. F., Heatherton, T. F., & Tice, D. M. (1994). *Losing Control: How and Why People Fail at Self-Regulation.* San Diego, CA: Academic Press.

Bem, S. L. (1974). The measurement of psychological androgyny. *Journal of Consulting and Clinical Psychology, 42*, 155–162.

Bi, C., Ybarra, O., & Zhao, Y. (2013). Accentuating your masculine side: Agentic traits generally dominate self-evaluation, even in China. *Social Psychology, 44*, 103–108.

Bleidorn, W., Kandler, C., Hülsheger, U. R., Riemann, R., Angleitner, A., & Spinath, F. M. (2010). Nature and nurture of the interplay between personality traits and major life goals. *Journal of Personality and Social Psychology, 99*, 366–379.

Bosak, J., Sczesny, S., & Eagly, A. H. (2012). The impact of social roles on trait judgments: A critical reexamination. *Personality and Social Psychology Bulletin, 38*, 429–440.

Brown, K. W., & Moskowitz, D. S. (1998). Dynamic stability of behavior: The rhythms of our interpersonal lives. *Journal of Personality, 66*, 105–134.

Buss, D. M. (1990). Unmitigated agency and unmitigated communion: An analysis of the negative components of masculinity and femininity. *Sex Roles, 22*, 555–568.

Cacioppo, J. T., Gardner, W. L., & Berntson, G. G. (1997). Beyond bipolar conceptualizations and measures: The case of attitudes and evaluative space. *Personality and Social Psychology Review, 1*, 3–25.

Campbell, M., & Kirmani, A. (2000). Consumers' use of persuasion knowledge: The effects of accessibility and cognitive capacity on perceptions of an influence agent. *Journal of Consumer Research, 27*, 69–83.

Carrier, A., Louvet, E., Chauvin, B., & Rohmer, O. (2014). The primacy of agency over competence in status perception. *Social Psychology, 45*, 347–356.

Chandler, J., & Schwarz, N. (2010). Use does not wear ragged the fabric of friendship: Thinking of objects as alive makes people less willing to replace them. *Journal of Consumer Psychology, 20*, 138–145.

Cheng, J. T., Tracy, J. L., Foulsham, T., Kingstone, A., & Henrich, J. (2013). Two ways to the top: Evidence that dominance and prestige are distinct yet viable avenues to social rank and influence. *Journal of Personality and Social Psychology, 104*, 103–125.

Christopher, A. N., & Schlenker, B. R. (2000). The impact of perceived material wealth and perceiver personality on first impressions. *Journal of Economic Psychology, 21*, 1–19.

Cislak, A. (2013). Effects of power on social perception: All your boss can see is agency. *Social Psychology, 44*, 138–146.

Cislak, A., & Wojciszke, B. (2008). Agency and communion are inferred from actions serving interests of self or others. *European Journal of Social Psychology, 38*, 1103–1110.

Clarks, M. S., & Mills, J. (1979). Interpersonal attraction in exchange and communal relationships. *Journal of Personality and Social Psychology, 37*, 12–24.

Coolsen, M. K., & Nelson, L. J. (2001). Desiring and avoiding close romantic attachment in response to mortality salience. *Omega: Journal of Death and Dying, 44*, 257–276.

Coren, S., & Hewitt, P. L. (1999). Sex differences in elderly suicide rates: Some predictive factors. *Aging & Mental Health, 3*, 112–118.

Cotte, J. & Ratneshwar, S. (2000). Time style and consuming time: Why we do what we do with our time. In S. Ratneshwar, D. G. Mick, & C. Huffman (eds.), *The Why of Consumption: Contemporary Perspectives on Consumer Motives, Goals, and Desires* (pp. 216–236). New York: Routledge.

Costos, D. (1986). Sex role identity in young adults: its parental antecedents and relation to ego development. *Journal of Personality and Social Psychology, 50*, 601–611.

Cuddy, A. C., Fiske, S. T., & Glick, P. (2007). The BIAS map: Behaviors from intergroup affect and stereotypes. *Journal of Personality and Social Psychology, 92*, 631–648.

Cuddy, A. C., Fiske, S. T., & Glick, P. (2008). Warmth and competence as universal dimensions of social perception: The stereotype content model and the BIAS map. In M. P. Zanna (ed.), *Advances in Experimental Social Psychology* (vol. 40, pp. 61–149). San Diego, CA: Elsevier Academic Press.

Danoff-Burg, S., Mosher, C. E., & Grant, C. A. (2006). Relations of agentic and communal personality traits to health behavior and substance use among college students. *Personality and Individual Differences, 40*, 353–363.

Diehl, M., Owen, S. K., & Youngblade, L. M. (2004). Agency and communion attributes in adults' spontaneous self-representations. *International Journal of Behavioral Development, 28*, 1–15.

Diekman, A. B., & Eagly, A. H. (2000). Stereotypes as dynamic constructs: Women and men of the past, present, and future. *Personality and Social Psychology Bulletin, 26*, 1171–1188.

Dindia, K. (2006). Men are from North Dakota, women are from South Dakota. In K. Dindia & D. J. Canary (eds.), *Sex Differences and Similarities in Communication* (pp. 3–20). Mahwah, NJ: Erlbaum.

Dommer, S. L., & Swaminathan, V. (2013). Explaining the endowment effect through ownership: The role of identity, gender, and self-threat. *Journal of Consumer Research, 39*, 1034–50.

Dréze, X., & Nunes, J. C. (2009). Feeling superior: The impact of loyalty program structure on consumers' perceptions of status. *Journal of Consumer Research, 35*, 890–905.

Dunlop, W. L., Walker, L. J., & Matsuba, M. (2013). The development of moral motivation across the adult lifespan. *European Journal of Developmental Psychology, 10*, 285–300.

Eagly, A. H. (1987). *Sex Differences in Social Behavior: A Social-Role Interpretation.* Hillsdale, NJ: Erlbaum.

Escalas, J. E. (1996). *Narrative Processing: Building Connections between Brand and the Self*. Dissertation, Duke University.

Escalas, J. E., & Bettman, J. R. (2000). Using narratives to discern self-identity related consumer goals and motivations. In S. Ratneshwar, D. G. Mick, & C. Huffman (eds.), *The Why of Consumption: Contemporary Perspectives on Consumer Motives, Goals, and Desires* (pp. 237–258). New York: Routledge.

Evans, F. B. (1963). Selling as a dyadic relationship: A new approach. *American Behavioral Scientist, 6*, 76–79.

Fiske, S. T., Cuddy, A. C., & Glick, P. (2007). Universal dimensions of social cognition: Warmth and competence. *Trends in Cognitive Sciences, 11*, 77–83.

Fiske, S. T., Cuddy, A. C., Glick, P., & Xu, J. (2002). A model of (often mixed) stereotype content: Competence and warmth respectively follow from perceived status and competition. *Journal of Personality and Social Psychology, 82*, 878–902.

Fournier, M. A., & Moskowitz, D. S. (2000). The mitigation of interpersonal behavior. *Journal of Personality and Social Psychology, 79*, 827–836.

Frimer, J. A., Schaefer, N. K., & Oakes, H. (2014). Moral actor, selfish agent. *Journal of Personality and Social Psychology, 106*, 790–802.

Frimer, J. A. & Walker, L. J. (2009). Reconciling the self and morality: An empirical model of moral centrality development. *Developmental Psychology, 45*, 1669–1681.

Frimer, J. A., Walker, L. J., Dunlop, W. L., Lee, B., & Riches, A. (2011). The integration of agency and communion in moral personality: Evidence of enlightened self-interest. *Journal of Personality and Social Psychology, 101*, 149–163.

Frimer, J. A., Walker, L. J., Lee, B. H., Riches, A., & Dunlop, W. L. (2012). Hierarchical integration of agency and communion: A study of influential moral figures. *Journal of Personality, 80*, 1117–1145.

Fritz, H. L., Nagurney, A. J., & Helgeson, V. S. (2003). Social interactions and cardiovascular reactivity during problem disclosure among friends. *Personality and Social Psychology Bulletin, 29*, 713–725.

Fuchs, C., Prandelli, E., Schreier, M., & Dahl, D. W. (2013). All that is users might not be gold: How labeling products as user designed backfires in the context of luxury fashion brands. *Journal of Marketing, 77*, 75–91.

Gebauer, J. E., Leary, M. R., & Neberich, W. (2012). Big two personality and big three mate preferences: Similarity attracts, but country-level mate preferences crucially matter. *Personality and Social Psychology Bulletin, 38*, 1579–1593.

Gebauer, J. E., Paulhus, D. L., & Neberich, W. (2013). Big two personality and religiosity across cultures: Communals as religious conformists and agentics as religious contrarians. *Social Psychological and Personality Science, 4*, 21–30.

Gebauer, J. E., Sedikides, C., Verplanken, B., & Maio, G. R. (2012). Communal narcissism. *Journal of Personality and Social Psychology, 103*, 854–878.

Goffman, E. (1959). *Presentation of Self in Everyday Life*. New York: Doubleday Anchor.

Grant, A. M., & Gino, F. (2010). A little thanks goes a long way: Explaining why gratitude expressions motivate prosocial behavior. *Journal of Personality and Social Psychology, 98*, 946–955.

Haidt, J. (2012). *The Righteous Mind: Why Good People Are Divided by Politics and Religion*. New York: Pantheon/Random House.

Hall, J. A. (2011). Sex differences in friendship expectations: A meta-analysis. *Journal of Social and Personal Relationships, 28*, 723–747.

Hart, C. M., Sedikides, C., Wildschut, T., Arndt, J., Routledge, C., & Vingerhoets, A. M. (2011). Nostalgic recollections of high and low narcissists. *Journal of Research in Personality, 45*, 238–242.

He, X., Inman, J. J., & Mittal, V. (2008). Gender jeopardy in financial risk taking. *Journal of Marketing Research, 45*, 414–424.

Helgeson, V. S. (1993). Implications of agency and communion for patient and spouse adjustment to a first coronary event. *Journal of Personality and Social Psychology, 64*, 807–816.

Helgeson, V. S. (1994). The relation of agency and communion to well-being: Evidence and potential explanations. *Psychological Bulletin, 116*, 412–428.

Helgeson, V. S., & Fritz, H. L. (1998). A theory of unmitigated communion. *Personality and Social Psychology Review, 2*, 173–183.

Helgeson, V. S., & Fritz, H. L. (1999). Unmitigated agency and unmitigated communion: Distinctions from agency and communion. *Journal of Research in Personality, 33*, 131–158.

Helgeson, V. S., & Fritz, H. L. (2000). The implications of unmitigated agency and unmitigated communion for domains of problem behavior. *Journal of Personality, 68*, 1031–1057.

Helgeson, V. S., & Lepore, S. J. (2004). Quality of life following prostate cancer: The role of agency and unmitigated agency. *Journal of Applied Social Psychology, 34*, 2559–2585.

Henderson, C. M., Beck, J. T., & Palmatier, R. W. (2011). Review of theoretical underpinnings of loyalty programs. *Journal of Consumer Psychology, 21*, 256–276.

Hill, R. P. (1994). Bill collectors and consumers: A troublesome exchange relationship. *Journal of Public Policy and Marketing, 13*, 20–35.

Hoffman, E., McCabe, K., & Smith, V. L. (1996). Social distance and other-regarding behavior in dictator games. *American Economic Review, 86*, 653–660.

Hofstede, G. (1984). *Culture's Consequences: International Differences in Work-Related Values*. Beverly Hills, CA: Sage.

Holt, C. L., & Ellis, J. B. (1998). Assessing the current validity of the Bem Sex-Role Inventory. *Sex Roles, 39*, 929–941.

Johannesen-Schmidt, M. C., & Eagly, A. H. (2002). Diminishing returns: The effects of income on the content of stereotypes of wage earners. *Personality and Social Psychology Bulletin, 28*, 1538–1545.

Jorgenson, D. O. (1981). Agency and communion trends in consumer goods advertising. *Personality and Social Psychology Bulletin, 7*, 410–414.

Iyengar, S. S., & Lepper, M. R. (2000). When choice is demotivating: Can one desire too much of a good thing? *Journal of Personality and Social Psychology, 79*, 995–1006.

Koenig, A. M., Eagly, A. H., Mitchell, A. A., & Ristikari, T. (2011). Are leader stereotypes masculine? A meta-analysis of three research paradigms. *Psychological Bulletin, 137*, 616–642.

Kurt, D. (2015). *Feeling Powerful and Chasing High Returns: The Interactive Effect of Power and Agency–Communion on Financial Risk Taking*. Working Paper, Boston University.

Kurt, D., Inman, J. J., & Argo, J. J. (2011). The influence of friends on consumer spending: The role of agency–communion and self-monitoring. *Journal of Marketing Research, 48*, 741–754.

Lambert, A., & Desmond, J. (2013). Loyal now, but not forever! A study of narcissism and male consumer-brand relationships. *Psychology & Marketing, 30*, 690–706.

Leszczynski, J. (2009). A state conceptualization: Are individuals' masculine and feminine personality traits situationally influenced? *Personality and Individual Differences, 47*, 157–162.

Lippa, R. (2001). On deconstructing and reconstructing masculinity–femininity. *Journal of Research in Personality, 35*, 168–207.

Ma, Z., & Dube, L. (2011). Process and outcome interdependency in frontline service encounters. *Journal of Marketing, 75*, 83–98.

Mansfield, E. D., & McAdams, D. P. (1996). Generativity and themes of agency and communion in adult autobiography. *Personality and Social Psychology Bulletin, 22*, 721–731.

Markus, H. R., & Kitayama, S. (1991). Culture and the self: Implications for cognition, emotion, and motivation. *Psychological Review, 98*, 224–253.

Matsuba, M., & Walker, L. J. (2005). Young adult moral exemplars: The making of self through stories. *Journal of Research on Adolescence, 15*, 275–297.

Mayer, D. & Greenberg, H. M. (1964). What makes a good salesman. *Harvard Business Review* (July–August), 119–125.

McClelland, D. C., Koestner, R., & Weinberger, J. (1989). How do self-attributed and implicit motives differ? *Psychological Review, 96*, 690–702.

Meyers-Levy, J. (1988). The influence of sex roles on judgment. *Journal of Consumer Research, 14*, 522–530.

Mosher, C. E., & Danoff-Burg, S. (2008). Agentic and communal personality traits: Relations to disordered eating behavior, body shape concern, and depressive symptoms. *Eating Behaviors, 9*, 497–500.

Moskowitz, D. S., Suh, E., & Desaulniers, J. (1994). Situational influences on gender differences in agency and communion. *Journal of Personality and Social Psychology, 66*, 753–761.

Nagurney, A., & Bagwell, B. (2009). Relations of the gender-related personality traits and stress to sexual behaviors among college students. *North American Journal of Psychology, 11*, 85–96.

Paulhus, D. L., & John, O. P. (1998). Egoistic and moralistic biases in self-perception: The interplay of self-deceptive styles with basic traits and motives. *Journal of Personality, 66*, 1025–1060.

Peeters, G. (2008). The evaluative face of a descriptive model: Communion and agency in Peabody's tetradic model of trait organization. *European Journal of Social Psychology, 38*, 1066–1072.

Quester, P., & Steyer, A. (2010). Revisiting individual choices in group settings: The long and winding (less traveled) road? *Journal of Consumer Research, 36*, 1050–1057.

Rucker, D. D., Dubois, D., & Galinsky, A. D. (2011). Generous paupers and stingy prices: Power drives consumer spending on self versus others. *Journal of Consumer Research, 6*, 1015–29.

Rucker, D. D., Galinsky, A. D., & Dubois, D. (2012). Power and consumer behavior: How power shapes who and what consumers value. *Journal of Consumer Psychology, 22*, 352–68.

Scott, M. L., Mende, M., & Bolton, L. E. (2013), Judging the book by its cover? How consumers decode conspicuous consumption cues in buyer–seller relationship. *Journal of Marketing Research, 50*, 334–347.

Sedikides, C., Gregg, A. P., Cisek, S., & Hart, C. M. (2007). The I that buys: Narcissists as consumers. *Journal of Consumer Psychology, 17*, 254–257.

Sela, A., Berger, J., & Lie, W. (2009). Variety, vice, and virtue: How assortment size influences option choice. *Journal of Consumer Research, 35*, 941–951.

Shariff, A. F., & Norenzayan, A. (2007). God is watching you: Priming God concepts increases prosocial behavior in an anonymous economic game. *Psychological Science, 18*, 803–809.

Singelis, T. M. (1994). The measurement of independent and interdependent self-construals. *Journal of Personality and Social Psychology, 20*, 580–591.

Smith, T. W., Gallo, L. C., Goble, L., Ngu, L. Q., & Stark, K. A. (1998). Agency, communion, and cardiovascular reactivity during marital interaction. *Health Psychology, 17*, 537–545.

Spence, J. T., Helmreich, R. L., & Holahan, C. K. (1979). Negative and positive components of psychological masculinity and femininity and their relationships to self-reports of neurotic and acting out behaviors. *Journal of Personality and Social Psychology, 37*, 1673–1682.

Stopfer, J. M., Egloff, B., Nestler, S., & Back, M. D. (2013). Being popular in online social networks: How agentic, communal, and creativity traits relate to judgments of status and liking. *Journal of Research in Personality, 47*, 592–598.

Strahan, R. F. (1975). Remarks on Bem's measurement of psychological androgyny: Alternative methods and a supplementary analysis. *Journal of Consulting and Clinical Psychology, 43*, 568–571.

Suh, E., Moskowitz, D. S., Fournier, M. A., & Zuroff, D. C. (2004). Gender and relationships: Influences on agentic and communal behaviors. *Personal Relationships, 11*, 41–59.

Thrash, T. M., & Elliot, A. J. (2002). Implicit and self-attributed achievement motives: Concordance and predictive validity. *Journal of Personality, 70*, 729–756.

Trapnell, P. D., & Paulhus, D. L. (2012). Agentic and communal values: Their scope and measurement. *Journal of Personality Assessment, 94*, 39–52.

Trudeau, K. J., Danoff-Burg, S., Revenson, T. A., & Paget, S. A. (2003). Agency and communion in people with rheumatoid arthritis. *Sex Roles, 49*, 303–311.

Trusov, M., Bodapati, A. V., & Bucklin, R. E. (2010). Determining influential users in internet social networks. *Journal of Marketing Research, 47*, 643–658.

Twenge, J. M. (1997). Changes in masculine and feminine traits over time: A meta-analysis. *Sex Roles, 36*, 305–325.

Uchronski, M. (2008). Agency and communion in spontaneous self-descriptions: Occurrence and situational malleability. *European Journal of Social Psychology, 38*, 1093–1102.

Uchronski, M., Abele, A. E., & Bruckmüller, S. (2013). Empathic perspective taking and the situational malleability of the communal self-concept. *Self and Identity, 12*, 238–258.

Walker, L. J., & Frimer, J. A. (2007). Moral personality of brave and caring exemplars. *Journal of Personality and Social Psychology, 93*, 845–860.

Weber, E. U., & Hsee, C. (1998). Cross-cultural differences in risk perception, but cross-cultural similarities in attitudes towards perceived risk. *Management Science, 44*, 1205–1217.

White, K. M., Speisman, J.C., Jackson, D., Bartis, S., Costos, D. (1986). Intimacy maturity and its correlates in young married couples. *Journal of Personality and Social Psychology, 50*, 152–162.

Wiggins, J. S. (1979). A psychological taxonomy of trait-descriptive terms: The interpersonal domain. *Journal of Personality and Social Psychology, 37*, 395–412.

Winterich, K. P., Mittal, V., & Ross, Jr., W. T. (2009). Donation behavior toward in-groups and out-groups: The role of gender and moral identity. *Journal of Consumer Research, 36*, 199–214.

Woike, B., Gershkovich, I., Piorkowski, R., & Polo, M. (1999). The role of motives in the content and structure of autobiographical memory. *Journal of Personality and Social Psychology, 76*, 600–612.

Woike, B., Lavezzary, E., & Barsky, J. (2001). The influence of implicit motives on memory processes. *Journal of Personality and Social Psychology, 81*, 935–945.

Woike, B., & Polo, M. (2001). Motive-related memories: Content, structure, and affect. *Journal of Personality, 69*, 391–415.

Wojciszke, B., Abele, A. E., & Baryla, W. (2009). Two dimensions of interpersonal attitudes: Liking depends on communion, respect depends on agency. *European Journal of Social Psychology, 39*, 973–990.

Wojciszke, B., Baryla, W., Parzuchowski, M., Szymkow, A., & Abele, A. E. (2011). Self-esteem is dominated by agentic over communal information. *European Journal of Social Psychology, 41*, 617–627.

Wojciszke, B., Bazinska, R., & Jaworski, M. (1998). On the dominance of moral categories in impression formation. *Personality and Social Psychology Bulletin, 24*, 1251–1263.

Wojciszke, B., & Sobiczewska, P. (2013). Memory and self-esteem: The role of agentic and communal content. *Social Psychology, 44*, 95–102.

Woodside, A. G., & Davenport, Jr., J. W. (1974). The effect of salesman similarity and expertise on consumer purchasing behavior. *Journal of Marketing Research, 11*, 198–202.

Ybarra, O., Chan, E., Park, H., Burnstein, E., Monin, B., & Stanik, C. (2008). Life's recurring challenges and the fundamental dimensions: An integration and its implications for cultural differences and similarities. *European Journal of Social Psychology, 38*, 1083–1092.

Ybarra, O., Park, H., Stanik, C., & Lee, D. (2012). Self-judgment and reputation monitoring as a function of the fundamental dimensions, temporal perspective, and culture. *European Journal of Social Psychology, 42*, 200–209.

Zhang, Y., Feick, L., & Mittal, V. (2014). How males and females differ in their likelihood of transmitting negative word of mouth. *Journal of Consumer Research, 40*, 1097–1108.

Zhu, R., Dholakia, U. M., Chen, X., & Algesheimer, R. (2012). Does online community participation foster risky financial behavior? *Journal of Marketing Research, 49*, 394–407.

18 Online Social Interaction

Andrew D. Gershoff and Ashesh Mukherjee

What Is Online Social Interaction?

We often interact with others in our social environment. These interactions have traditionally taken place in a face-to-face context, such as when we interact with loved ones at home, friends at a party, salespeople in a store, or colleagues at work. However, more recently, we have also begun to interact with others in an online setting. For example, we may read product reviews posted by others on review websites, post our status updates on social media websites, follow and comment on blog posts, provide online feedback to firms on corporate websites, join online brand communities, give advice to other consumers on product support websites, and interact with potential partners on dating websites. We formally define online social interaction as Internet-enabled communication and exchange activities involving both consumers and firms (Yadav & Pavlou, 2014). Here, consumers refer to people who purchase products and services for their own use, while firms refer to for-profit or not-for-profit organizations in the marketplace. Online social interactions are likely to occur even more frequently in the future since many consumers are now online more than ever, thanks to smartphones, tablets, laptops, and the availability of Wi-Fi networks at home and work and in public spaces. Given the ubiquity and importance of online social interactions in our daily lives, the broad purpose of this chapter is to synthesize what is known and unknown about the effects of online social interaction on consumer judgment and decision making. Specifically, this chapter is organized into the following three sections: (i) characteristics of online social interactions, (ii) past research on online social interactions, and (iii) future research on online social interactions. These sections have been developed to provide the reader with short, top-line summaries of key research findings, and also to identify promising directions for future research in this emerging topic area.

Characteristics of Online Social Interaction

As discussed earlier, consumers can interact with one another in the online or offline worlds. Thus, the first question we address in this section is, how does online social interaction differ from offline social interaction?

Subsequently, we delve deeper into the characteristics of online social interactions by outlining the key motivations that drive consumers to interact with others on the Internet.

Online versus Offline Social Interaction

Researchers interested in online social interaction should consider several key structural differences between online and offline communication. In the following subsections, we outline some of the differences that are relevant to consumer research in this domain.

Senders and Receivers

Relative to offline social interaction, the online environment expands reach between senders and receivers by increasing the ability to transmit content to either single or multiple receivers, who may be physically close or far, and who may be known or unknown to one another. Online senders and receivers also require access to specialized tools and knowledge of how to use them, creating demographic differences between online and offline interaction. For example, in the year 2013, more than 80 percent of the population used the Internet in developed countries such as United States and Japan, but fewer than 5 percent used it in less developed countries such as Ethiopia and Sierra Leone. Even within developed countries, differences in age and income exist – almost 90 percent of U.S. adults aged eighteen to twenty-nine years old regularly used the Internet in 2014, but only 56 percent of those sixty-five or older did so (Pew Research Center, 2014).

Communication Format

The communication format tends to differ across offline and online interaction. Compared to offline communication, which is often spoken, online communication is more often visual. This can occur in written form (Berger & Iyengar, 2013; Lovett, Peres, & Shachar, 2013) and also in the form of photographs via tools such as Instagram and Facebook or videos via tools such as YouTube and Vine. In addition, some websites process data about online social interaction before sharing it among users. For example, a consumer might post a product evaluation as a rating on a five-point scale, but receivers may only see this information after it has been aggregated with others' ratings as an average or as a visual distribution of ratings (Chintagunta, Gopinath, & Venkataraman, 2010; Clemons, Gao, & Hitt, 2006).

Distance and Timing

Compared to offline interactions, which may be in person or on the telephone, the online environment is better suited for communicating many types of messages over long distances. For example, unlike face-to-face or telephonic exchanges, online interactions allow for sharing large amounts of data, including lengthy documents, photographs, and video. The online context also gives users more control over the timing of social interactions in three distinct ways. First, unlike offline face-to-face or phone interactions, which typically happen at a given point in time, online social interactions offer greater flexibility, allowing an interaction to take place with simultaneous participation or over a longer period of time in which individuals exchange multiple messages. This gives individuals more time to think about message content and its potential effects on receivers. Second, unlike telephone conversations, which generally occur with just one other person, the online context allows for interaction with multiple others, either simultaneously or in a series of interactions. Third, online tools often allow users to communicate information about interaction timing, by displaying to others when they are available for interaction, when messages have been received, and when they are likely to respond.

Message Control

Compared to offline interaction, online interaction alters control over content, recipients, and uses of shared messages, in a number of ways. First, online interaction may increase a sender's control of what is communicated by offering tools that help build and craft messages prior to sharing with others. For example, Instagram and YouTube offer editing tools that give a user more choices about the look and feel of a photograph or video, so users can better convey their feelings or ideas. Services such as Snapchat increase senders' control over how long a message will be available after it is read before being automatically deleted. Other websites increase receivers' control by allowing them to search, sort, rearrange, and delete content according to their needs. For example, product rating sites such as Yelp and Epinions allow users to sort and filter based on product review scores and product attributes.

Conversely, the online environment can also diminish control over messages. Messages posted for specific others can be shared by others in ways that have unintended consequences for the sender (Soster, Boland, & Drenten 2014). Although this may occur offline as well, the online environment increases the ease, reach, and speed with which such messages can be passed on. In addition, messages intended for specific others may be accessed and used by marketers. For example, social networking sites such as Facebook and search sites such as Google often use information obtained about senders and receivers for marketing purposes (Story, 2008; Tate, 2011).

Motivations for Online Social Interaction

What influences whether or not consumers interact with one another online? Researchers in the fields of consumer behavior, psychology, and information systems have described a number of motivations underlying online social interaction. These include acquiring and sharing information, participation and belonging, influencing others, managing identity, engaging in creativity, seeking entertainment, and maintaining privacy.

Acquiring and Sharing

First, people engage in online social interaction as a way to acquire and share information that is of interest to them or of value to others (Belk, 2013). Consistent with this view, one survey found that more than 80 percent of respondents used social media as a means to gather information and educate themselves (Whiting & Williams, 2013). Another survey reported that people who stopped using Twitter did so primarily because they were able to get information they needed elsewhere (McDuling, 2014).

Belonging and Participating

The need to belong is an important motive driving human behavior. To satisfy this need, individuals seek out relationships that involve interaction (Baumeister & Leary, 1995). A number of studies have found that consumers engage in online social interaction to satisfy the need to belong, via activities such as online chatting (Zinkhan, Kwak, Morrison, & Peters, 2003), multiplayer online video games (Griffiths, Davies, & Chappell, 2004), participation in social networking sites (Hampton, Goulet, Rainie, & Purcell, 2011), and collaborative consumption (Belk, 2013; Lamberton & Rose, 2012).

Influencing Others

A third motivation for online social interaction is the desire to persuade or influence others' beliefs or opinions. For example, consumers often use inter-active websites and chatrooms to resolve complaints or bring an issue to the notice of a firm (Meuter, Ostrom, Roundtree, & Bitner, 2000). When complaints are not effective, consumers may use online tools for mobilizing others to join in organized protests (Ward & Ostrom, 2006).

Managing Identity

Consumers often use online social interactions to manage their identity as perceived by others. For example, a number of studies have shown that the desire to be perceived by others in a positive light influences online word of mouth (Barasch & Berger, 2014; Packard & Wooten, 2013; Wojnicki & Godes, 2011). In particular, Wojnicki and Godes (2011) showed that consumers writing product reviews sometimes modify what they write to signal their expertise or to try to appear more knowledgeable to others.

Expressing Creativity

Research suggests that the online environment can foster creativity by allowing people to collaborate for the generation of new ideas, products, and artistic works (Amabile, 1983; Hargadon & Bechky, 2006). Kozinets, Hemetsberger, and Schau (2008) describe "innovation-oriented online communities" that vary in their size and whether the problems they solve are abstract or specific in nature. Brand communities are another example of innovation-focused communities where consumers offer feedback to firms and assist in the collaborative design of new products (Fuchs, Prandelli, Schreier, & Dahl, 2013; Schau, Muñiz, & Arnould, 2009).

Seeking Entertainment

It cannot be overlooked that consumers' online interactions with others is often done for hedonic or pleasure-seeking reasons, as consumers share content that offers entertainment, diversion, or escape (Rosengren, Wenner, & Palmgren, 1985). Consistent with this view, research has identified the desire for entertainment as a key driver of participation in online communities (Cheung, Chiu, & Lee, 2011).

Maintaining Privacy

People have a need for uniqueness, which can be met by maintaining a certain level of privacy during online interactions (Chan, Berger, & Van Boven 2013). However, maintaining privacy can be a challenge because marketers, governments, and data intermediaries increasingly track and record online activities. Given this context, research has identified several types of privacy concerns involving the use of consumer information that influence willingness to participate online. These include use by organizations for marketing purposes; use by malicious individuals for purposes such as bullying, stalking, or character assassination; and use by criminal entities for purposes such as identity theft and financial fraud (Boyd & Ellison, 2008; Krasnova, Kolesnikova, & Guenther, 2009). These concerns imply a trade-off in online social interaction whereby consumers weigh the benefits of interaction against the costs in terms of lost privacy (Debatin, Lovejoy, Horn, & Hughes, 2009; Ibrahim, 2008). To resolve this trade-off, consumers might use cues such as brand familiarity to decide whether the risks of lost privacy are worth the benefits of online social interaction (Benedicktus, Brady, Darke, & Voorhees, 2010).

Past Research: Online Social Interaction

Although consumer researchers have begun to investigate many issues related to online social interaction, the topics that have received the most attention are online reviews and online communities. Hence we focus on and synthesize literature on these two topics, outlining research questions, describing theory and methods, and highlighting key results. Regarding methodology, both experimental and qualitative approaches have been used to study online social interactions. Experimental approaches have included surveys, interviews, controlled lab studies, and field experiments. Researchers have also examined secondary data in the form of textual analysis of online discussions on product forums, analysis of blog postings and replies, coding of reviews posted on Amazon, and sentiment analysis of postings on social media websites.

Online Reviews

Online reviews have been defined as consumer evaluations of products and services based on personal experience (Godes & Mayzlin, 2004). The Internet offers millions of these consumer-written reviews, which are hosted on review websites organized by category such as Tripadvisor for hotels and Rottentomatoes for movies, retailer websites such as Amazon and eBay, and firm websites such as Apple and Carnival Cruises. Building on the motivations for online social interaction discussed earlier, research indicates that posting of reviews can be influenced by motives such as highlighting perceived injustice, articulating advocacy positions, establishing unique identities, and reciprocating reviews posted by others (Cheema & Kaikati, 2010; Punj, 2012; Sen & Lerman, 2007; Ward & Ostrom, 2006).

A growing body of research indicates that online reviews have significant effects on consumer behavior. These effects have been documented both at the market level, in terms of sales and market share (e.g., Chen & Xie, 2005; Chevalier & Mayzlin, 2006; Ghose & Ipeirotis, 2011; Ho-Dac, Carson, & Moore, 2013; Park, Lee, & Han, 2007), and the individual level, in terms of product evaluation, source judgment, and choice (e.g., Dellarocas, Zhang, & Awad, 2007; Khare, Labrecque, & Asare, 2011; Mudambi & Schuff, 2010; Sen & Lerman, 2007; Zhu & Zhang, 2010). In the following sections, we first briefly outline the market-level effects of online reviews, followed by a more detailed analysis of the individual-level effects of online reviews.

Market-Level Effects of Online Reviews

A fundamental dimension on which online reviews vary is whether they are positive or negative in valence. Chevalier and Mayzlin (2006) investigated the effect of review valence on sales by analyzing online book reviews and sales at Amazon and Barnes & Noble. Contrary to much prior work on offline word of mouth, they found that positive reviews generally outnumbered negative reviews. Further, they found that although both positive and negative reviews influenced sales, negative reviews had a stronger effect on sales. An emergent finding in their research was that the length of a review had a significant effect on sales, implying that consumers pay attention to the written commentary and not just to the overall star rating of the review. We will expand on this finding later when discussing the individual-level effects of online reviews on consumers.

While Chevalier and Mayzlin (2006) examined the effects of review valence in isolation, Ho-Dac, Carson, and Moore (2013) examined the joint effects of review valence and brand equity on sales over time. Using Blu-ray and DVD sales data, they found that positive (negative) reviews increased (decreased) sales of brands with lower equity, but did not have a significant effect on sales of brands with higher equity. Further, since more sales led to a larger number of positive (but not negative) reviews, this created a positive feedback loop for sales of weak brands but not strong brands. Chen and Xie (2005) took a more strategic perspective by considering the optimum firm response to online reviews posted by consumers. In particular, these researchers asked the question, when should firms launch a marketing communication campaign to accompany online reviews posted by users? Based on a normative choice model, they concluded that firms should launch a campaign as soon as reviews become available when product cost is low and/or there are many expert product users. In contrast, when the product cost is high and/or users are mostly novices, it is best for the firm to reduce the amount of information provided to consumers in marketing communication campaigns.

Moe and Trusov (2011) further extended this line of research by considering the effect of social dynamics on review valence and sales. They reasoned that the valence of a review can be influenced by both a consumer's actual product experience as well as reviews of the product posted by others. Based on this argument, they modeled sales of more than five hundred different products as a function of posted product ratings while decomposing ratings into a baseline rating, the contribution of social influence, and random error. Results indicated that reviews had a direct effect on sales in the short run and also an indirect effect of sales in the long run by influencing future reviews.

Individual-Level Effects of Online Reviews

To understand individual-level effects of online reviews, it is useful to decompose reviews into their key components: summary ratings, such as stars or rating points on a scale; and written comments or detailed explanations by the reviewer. Based on this decomposition, we organize past research under the following three headings: summary ratings, written comments, and the interplay between ratings and comments. Within each section, we consider the effects of online reviews on judgments about the message (i.e., the product in the review) including evaluations of message informativeness and product quality, as well as judgments about the source (i.e., the person posting the review), including evaluations of likeability, credibility, and similarity of the poster. We further distinguish between the effects of online reviews on the reader of the review and the person posting the review.

Summary Ratings

Summary ratings from online reviews are widely used by consumers to make judgments because they are easy to process (Mudambi & Schuff, 2010; Zhu & Zhang, 2010). Since products often have multiple ratings that can differ substantially, an initial question in past research was, how do consumers integrate multiple ratings during judgment and choice? In an early article, West and Broniarczyk (1998) addressed this question by examining the effects of mean and variance of ratings on product evaluation. Based on prospect theory, they hypothesized that consumers would become risk seeking when the mean rating of a product is below the consumer's aspiration level for that product. As a result, consumers in this situation would prefer alternatives with higher rather than lower rating variance. Results of four studies using movie and restaurant ratings confirmed this hypothesis and identified aspiration level as a moderator of the effects of rating mean and variance on product evaluation. Park and Park (2013) extended this line of research by focusing on the effects of rating variance in conjunction with prior expectations, argument quality, and the number of reviewers. Based on attribution theory, these researchers showed that high-variance product ratings can undermine product evaluation when ratings are attributed to product performance. In contrast, when ratings are attributed to reviewer heterogeneity, high-variance ratings allow consumers to retain biased product evaluations consistent with their prior expectations.

Unlike the preceding studies that focused on product evaluation as the dependent variable, Gershoff, Mukherjee, and Mukhopadhyay (2003) focused on judgments of the reviewer such as trustworthiness, similarity of tastes, and probability of accepting advice. These researchers examined how reviewers were judged as a function of prior agreement between the consumer and the reviewer. Their key finding was that all prior agreements are not weighted equally. Specifically, when evaluating a rater for similarity of tastes, extreme agreement (e.g., agreement on five star and one star ratings) has a greater effect than moderate agreement (e.g., agreement on two-, three-, and four-star ratings), and positive agreement (e.g., agreement on five stars) has a greater effect than negative agreement (e.g., agreement on one star). An important contribution of the latter positivity effect is that it provides a counterpoint to a dominant finding in consumer research – exemplified by prospect theory – that negative information has a greater impact on judgments than positive information. In a follow-up article, Gershoff, Mukherjee, and Mukhopadhyay (2007) delved deeper into the psychological mechanism underlying the positivity effect in reviewer evaluation. They reasoned that the positivity effect arises from differences in the memory structure of likes versus dislikes, such that likes have consistently positive underlying attributes while dislikes are more ambiguous in terms of their underlying attribute valence. Based on this attribute ambiguity account, the authors identified three moderators of the positivity effect, namely number of attributes, number of alternatives, and revelation of reviewer attribute ratings. Finally, Zhang, Craciun, and Shin

(2010) showed that positivity and negativity effects in reviewer evaluation may depend on regulatory focus. Using data from laboratory experiments and actual online retailers, these researchers demonstrated that consumers who evaluate products associated with promotion goals perceive positive reviews to be more persuasive than negative ones (i.e., positivity bias). Conversely, consumers who evaluate products associated with prevention goals perceive negative reviews to be more persuasive than positive ones (i.e., negativity bias).

The aforementioned research examined the effects of past ratings on reviewer evaluation. In contrast, research by Gershoff, Mukherjee, and Mukhopadhyay (2008) and Naylor, Lamberton, and Norton (2011) examined the effect of personal characteristics on reviewer evaluation. In particular, Gershoff and colleagues (2008) focused on the false consensus effect whereby individuals tend to overestimate the likelihood of others sharing their opinions. Building on their earlier finding that the preference structure for likes is less ambiguous than the corresponding preference structure for dislikes, they showed in three studies that the false consensus effect for online reviews is stronger in the case of likes compared to dislikes. Naylor, Lamberton, and Norton (2011) examined the role of similarity between reviewers and consumers on dimensions such as age, gender, and hometown on judgments of common taste with reviewers. Building on the egocentric bias literature, these researchers showed that even reviewers who are ambiguous in terms of similarity are perceived to be trustworthy and persuasive, since consumers project their own preference structure onto ambiguous reviewers. These researchers also identified moderators of this egocentric reliance on ambiguous reviewers, such as accessibility of other-related thoughts and availability of external cues about reviewer heterogeneity.

Reviewer Comments

Online reviews often contain commentary in which reviewers offer their product impressions and reasons for their numerical rating. Since commentary is usually in the form of written text, research in this area has investigated the effects of textual variables such as figurative language (Kronrod & Danziger, 2013), dispreferred markers (Hamilton, Vohs, & McGill, 2014), level of abstraction (Schellekens, Verlegh, & Smidts, 2010), and emotional content (Yin, Bond, & Zhang, 2014).

Kronrod and Danziger (2013) focused on the use of figurative language in review commentary. Figurative language is the use of words and expressions to convey an additional connotation beyond their lexical sense (Fogelin, 1988). These additional connotations may be an alternative meaning (e.g., "climbing the wall"), metaphor (e.g., "the Ferrari of vacuum cleaners"), hyperbole (e.g., "the service person was a cell phone professor"), or idiomatic expression (e.g., "my car's a lemon"). Based on the theory of conversational norms, these researchers showed that figurative language in reviews leads to more favorable product evaluation in hedonic, compared to utilitarian, consumption contexts. Hamilton Vohs, and McGill (2014) examined another textual element of commentary, namely the use of dispreferred markers. Dispreferred markers refer to qualifiers that are sometimes added to negative reviews, such as "I'll be honest," "God bless it," or "I don't want to be mean, but...." Basing their study on politeness theory, these authors showed that consumers evaluate communicators who use dispreferred markers as more credible and likable than communicators who assert the same information without dispreferred markers. They also found that this dispreferred marker effect can spill over to influence product evaluation and willingness to pay.

Schellekens, Verlegh, and Smidts (2010) looked at another aspect of written commentary, namely the level of abstraction at which it is written. The abstractness of language can vary from more concrete (e.g., "This Parker pen sometimes does not write") to more abstract (e.g., "This Parker pen is not very good"), depending on whether the language describes specific actions or broad judgments. Based on linguistic categorization theory, the authors showed that consumers use more abstract terms when they describe experiences that are in line with their own attitude toward the product. On the receiver side, they show that abstract language in positive reviews leads readers to infer that the sender has a more favorable product attitude and a higher buying intent for the product under consideration. In contrast, they find an opposite pattern of results for negative reviews, such that concrete language leads to lower inferred product attitude and buying intent. Finally, Yin, Bond, and Zhang (2014) examined the effects of two negative emotions in online reviews, namely anxiety and anger, on perceived helpfulness of the review. Based on lab experiments and analysis of real reviews from Yahoo! Shopping, the authors showed that commentary conveying reviewer anxiety led to higher perceived helpfulness of the review compared to commentary marked by anger. Consistent with affect appraisal theory, this effect was found to be mediated by higher perceived effort expended by anxious reviewers compared to angry reviewers.

Ratings and Comments

Perhaps the most common type of review website is one that contains both ratings and commentary about products. He and Bond (2013) examined the relative value of ratings and comments for forecasting future product enjoyment. Based on an anchoring mechanism, these researchers showed that perceived similarity in preference structure between the reviewer and the consumer moderates the relative value of ratings and commentary for affective forecasting. Schlosser (2011) focused on a different issue related to ratings and comments, namely the perceived consistency between ratings and comments. Past research had indicated that two-sided reviews – that is, those that stated both pros and cons of the product – were likely to be considered more helpful and persuasive by consumers. In contrast, Schlosser (2011) showed that perceived consistency between ratings and commentary moderates this effect such that two-sided reviews are seen to be more helpful only when ratings are moderate since moderate ratings are consistent with the evaluative implications of both pros and cons in the commentary.

Continuing this line of research, Mudambi and Schuff (2010) and Schindler and Bickart (2012) examined usefulness or helpfulness of the review as the dependent variable. Mudambi and Schuff (2010) focused on the effects of rating extremity, commentary depth, and product type on perceived helpfulness of the review. Drawing on the paradigm of search and experience goods from information economics, these researchers found that reviews with extreme ratings are less helpful than reviews with moderate ratings for experience goods. Furthermore, commentary depth has a positive effect on the helpfulness of the review for both experience and search goods, and this effect is greater for search goods than experience goods. While Mudambi and Schuff (2010) argued for a monotonically positive effect of commentary depth on perceived helpfulness of the review, Schindler and Bickart (2012) argued for an inverted-U effect – such that moderate commentary depth (i.e., review length) is considered most useful when rating valence is positive but not when rating valence is negative. The flip side of perceived helpfulness is perceived dishonesty of the review – that is, the likelihood that the review is "fake" and has been planted by the firm or its competitors. Examining this issue, Bambauer-Sachse and Mangold (2013) found that activation of persuasion knowledge by contextual factors such as a large number of positive or negative reviews serves to weaken the impact of reviews on product evaluation.

Another stream of research on ratings and comments has focused on social influences during the posting of reviews. For example, Schlosser (2005) showed that posters can be influenced by prior negative reviews, adjusting their public attitudes downward in order to appear more discriminating to others. Consistent with this presentation bias, Schlosser (2005) found that posters present more than one side when publicly explaining their attitudes, and this effect persists despite posters' favorable product experiences and commitment to their attitudes. In a similar vein, Sridhar and Srinivasan (2012) examined the joint effects of others' ratings, own product experience, and firm response to product failure on product evaluation. Based on analysis of 7,499 actual online ratings of 114 hotels, these authors showed that high online product ratings by others is a double-edged sword, exacerbating the negative effect of product failure but strengthening the benefit of product recovery. Finally, Moore (2012) examined the effects of reviews not on the reader as in past research, but instead on the poster of the review. Using language processing theory, Moore (2012) showed that commentary containing more explaining language influenced posters through a process of sense making. As a result, explaining positive experiences led to a decrease in posters' evaluations of experiences, while explaining negative experiences led to an increase.

Online Communities

The Internet allows consumers to participate in online communities that provide a platform for interaction among its members. We focus on two important types of online communities that have received more research attention: brand communities and social networks. Brand communities are organized around an admired brand, while social networks are organized around the members in the network. Illustrative examples of brand communities are the Harley-Davidson owners' group (HOG), the BMW users' group, the Mac users' group, and the *Star Wars* fans group; examples of social networks are Facebook, Google +, Orkut, and Meetup. As discussed earlier, individuals could participate in online communities for utilitarian reasons such as gathering information about product usage and maintenance, as well as intellectual and social reasons such as learning, social support, and fellowship (Fournier, Senisper, McAlexander, & Shouten, 2001). Although we consider brand communities and social networks to be types of online communities, it should be noted that they can operate offline as well. For example, members of product user groups can communicate online through email, bulletin boards, and online discussion groups; in addition, these members can also meet face to face to engage in group activities such as picnics, concerts, drives, and boat trips. Hence insights from research on online brand communities and social networks could be extended to offline communities as well.

Brand Communities

Algesheimer, Dholakia, and Herrmann (2005) studied social influence in brand communities with data from car clubs in Europe. Drawing on theories of social identification and group-based decision making, these authors developed a structural model that tested the effects of brand community identification on outcomes such as membership duration and recommendation behavior. Results indicated that brand community identification has positive effects such as greater community engagement, as well as negative effects such as normative community pressure and reactance to community pressure. In addition, the authors also showed that the effects of community identification are moderated by customers' brand knowledge and the size of the brand community. While Algesheimer, Dholakia, and Herrmann (2005) demonstrated both positive and negative effects of brand communities, Zhu, Dholakia, Chen, and Algesheimer (2012) focused on an important negative effect of online community participation, namely risky financial behavior. These researchers found that participation in online financial communities, such as Prosper, was likely to increase people's risk-seeking tendencies in financial decisions because the presence of a community leads people to believe that they will receive help or support from other members should difficulties arise. The authors also identified a key boundary condition for this effect, namely tie strength between the target person and other members of the community.

A particular type of brand community is the peer-to-peer problem-solving (P3) community, where consumers post questions relating to a product and other consumers answer these questions. Mathwick, Wiertz, and Ruyter (2008) examined the formation of social capital in P3 communities, where social capital is defined as a collectively owned and intangible reserve of support that individuals and groups gain from their connections to one another. To understand the antecedents and consequences of social capital in P3 communities, the authors collected data from a virtual P3 community sponsored by a firm that develops software for digital media creation and web development. Extending social norm theory, the authors showed that social capital in this community was driven by the norms of voluntarism, reciprocity, and social trust. Results also indicated that social capital exerts a positive influence on the perceived value of informational resources available from the P3 community. Perceived value, in turn, increased commitment to the P3 community, and this effect was moderated by the length of membership in the community.

An important aspect of P3 communities is that they diffuse information among its members. Thus a key question in this context is, what is the process of consumer learning in knowledge-oriented P3 communities, and what are the consequences of such learning for decision making? Jayanti and Singh (2010) investigated this question by examining a health-focused P3 community for thyroid patients in the form of an electronic bulletin board. Guided by pragmatic learning theory, interpretive analysis of bulletin board postings indicated that social learning in online networks occurs in an uneven manner with some online interactions leading to leaps in generative learning while others lead to disengagement and lapses in learning. Another important aspect of brand communities is that they foster discussion between consumers, and Schlosser and Shavitt (2002) examined the effects of anticipating discussion on consumer judgment and decision making. These researchers argued that anticipating discussion shifts people's focus toward product attributes that people think will be important to others rather than attributes that are important to themselves. This shift in salience toward publicly relevant attributes, in turn, can lead to a shift in people's own attitudes.

Social Networks

Online social networks are becoming an increasingly important part of the daily life of consumers. The dominant social network today is Facebook, which is the most-visited website in the United States and has more than a billion users around the world. As a result, most research on social networks has examined Facebook or similar websites such as Myspace, Friendster, and Orkut. As discussed earlier, users could have different motivations for using social networks, ranging from desire to cultivate social connections, self-present to others, minimize loneliness, and relieve boredom (Nadkarni & Hofmann, 2012; Sheldon, Abad, & Hinsch, 2011; Wilson, Gosling, & Graham, 2012). In the following subsections, we summarize the effects of social networks organized under the subheadings of product-related and interpersonal judgments and decisions.

Product-Related Judgments and Decisions

Wilcox and Stephen (2013) examined the impact of social network use on self-control in the context of tempting products. They argued that social network use satisfies the need for affiliation and self-expression and hence is likely to increase one's self-esteem during the browsing episode. This momentary increase in self-esteem, in turn, is likely to reduce self-control through a licensing mechanism whereby individuals seek a reward for the virtuous accomplishment of positive self-regard. These researchers also showed that the effect of self-esteem on self-control is stronger for those with strong ties with others in their social network.

Unlike Wilcox and Stephen (2013), who focused on product evaluation and choice related to temptation, Hollenbeck and Kaikati (2012) looked at consumers' brand choices as an instrument for self-expression on Facebook. In contrast to past research in an offline environment indicating that brand choices are more likely to reflect ideal rather than actual consumer identity, Hollenbeck and Kaikati (2012) found that that brand choices displayed on social networks are more likely to reflect actual consumer identity. Their proposed explanation for this finding was that social networks such as Facebook are characterized by the presence of relatively close friends who provide accountability and feedback on one's profile and postings. As a result, an individuals' brand display on social networks is likely to be constrained to his or her actual identity known within the circle of friends.

Marketing communications can be embedded within a social network to create social media campaigns. For example, brands can create fan pages on Facebook or brand-focused discussion threads on blogs. The effectiveness of social media marketing has been examined by several researchers, such as de Vries, Gensler, and Leeflang (2012); Kozinets, Valck, Wojnicki, and Wilner (2010); and Naylor, Lamberton, and West (2012). Kozinets and colleagues (2010) examined brand communities in social networks through netnographic analysis of a social media campaign for mobile phones embedded in eighty-three prominent blogs. The key insight from this research was that marketing messages from a firm are systematically altered by the social network over time, following a four-step sequence of evaluation, embracing, endorsement, and explanation. de Vries, Gensler, and Leeflang (2012) focused on brand fan pages on social networks such as Facebook and set out to identify key drivers of brand fan page popularity as measured by the number of likes and comments. Based on analysis of 355 brand posts from 11 brands across 6 product categories, these researchers found that different drivers influence the number of likes and the number of comments. While vivid brand posts enhance the number of likes, interactive elements in the page such as questions from the brand increase the number of comments. Results also showed that positioning brand posts on top of the brand fan page enhances brand post popularity as measured by likes and comments. Naylor, Lamberton, and West (2012) extended this line of research by focusing on the effect of likes in brand pages on product evaluation. Specifically, they addressed the question, how does demographic similarity between the consumer and the person posting the likes influence product evaluation? The key finding in their research was that ambiguity, that is, lack of information about demographic similarity, led to product evaluations that were as positive as high demographic similarity, and low demographic similarity was associated with the lowest product evaluation. These results extend past research on the effects of similarity by showing that, at least in an online context, ambiguous similarity and high similarity have comparable effects on consumers. From a substantive standpoint, these results imply that managers would be better off withholding demographic information about their brand's fans if the fans are demographically different from the target consumer.

Interpersonal Judgments and Decisions

Past research has examined interpersonal effects of social network use on groups as well as individuals. In a group context of student–teacher interaction, Mazer, Murphy, and Simonds (2009) reported that students predict a positive classroom environment and high motivation when a teacher shares more personal information on his or her Facebook profile. Other research in an employment context has shown that information presented on Facebook can both help and hurt job candidates. For example, Bohnert and Ross (2010) reported that the chances of an applicant being offered a job increase when the job candidate's Facebook profile emphasizes family values and professionalism; conversely, if a profile contains inappropriate material, such as alcohol and drugs, then the candidate's prospects decrease. Further, female job candidates are penalized more than their male counterparts for inappropriate content on Facebook profiles (Peluchette & Karl, 2008). Other research in a group context has examined the process through which influential users of social networks can be identified (Trusov, Bodapati, & Bucklin, 2010). Using longitudinal data on browsing activity, Trusov, Bodapati, and Bucklin (2010) develop a technique for identifying users who most influence others' activity on social networks. In a similar vein, Li and Du (2011) proposed a method for identifying opinion leaders and "hot" blogs through analysis of written comments in the discussion threads.

From an individual perspective, research has examined people's concerns about privacy on social networks such as Facebook. Initial studies indicated a relatively low level of privacy concern, while more recent studies indicate that privacy concerns are on the rise. For example, an early study by Gross and Acquisti (2005) showed that Facebook users could be easily persuaded to hand over personal information, such as their current address and phone number, and that few Facebook users change the permissive default privacy settings on their Facebook account. In contrast, subsequent studies by Fogel and Nehmad (2009) showed that only a few Facebook users were willing to share personal information, and a significant minority had proactively changed their privacy settings (see also Christofides, Muise, & Desmarais, 2009; Dey, Jelveh, & Ross, 2012). Interestingly, research indicates a gap between reported privacy concerns and observed privacy behaviors on the part of social network users (Acquisti & Gross, 2006; Stutzman & Kramer-Duffield, 2010; Tufekci, 2008). For example, Acquisti and Gross (2006) found that the 16 percent of their respondents who reported being "very worried" about the possibility that a stranger knew where they lived and the location of their classes still revealed both pieces of information on their Facebook profile. Researchers have speculated that the reason for this disparity is that social network users underestimate the extent of damages that could arise from privacy violations (e.g., Krasnova, Kolesnikova, & Guenther, 2009). Finally, Weisbuch, Ivcevic, and Ambady (2009) compared interpersonal judgments in social networks versus the real world. Their key finding was a high level of consistency between impressions formed by face-to-face versus online interaction, such that people liked or disliked by interaction partners were also liked or disliked on the basis of their Facebook pages. Furthermore, social perceivers appeared to use similar criteria for forming impressions in both online and offline contexts, suggesting that the online context may have a relatively small effect on the fundamental processes of impression formation.

Future Research: Online Social Interaction

Since online social interaction is a relatively recent phenomenon, there are many unanswered questions about its effects on consumer judgment and decision making. We focus on two areas that we believe are most promising for future research: information sharing and online inferences. We briefly describe initial work in each area and then present ideas for future research.

Information Sharing

As noted earlier, the online environment makes it easy to share information and communicate with others. Information once shared, however, is often beyond the control of the sender and can be used by others in unintended and undesired ways. Research is only now emerging that examines how consumers decide what information to share and how they react to loss of control after sharing. In the following subsections, we discuss three related topics for future research, namely antecedents of sharing, consequences of sharing, and privacy concerns.

Antecedents of Sharing

It is not uncommon for people to use online channels for sharing content that is private in nature, intended for specific others and meant to be interpreted in a specific context. But after posting, the same content may be seen by unintended audiences, leading to unintended consequences. For example, people have reported being fired for posting comments about a superior's salary and for posting sexually suggestive photographs of themselves (Emerson, 2011). Emerging work in this area has begun to reveal why consumers share such information and their reactions to having that information seen by unintended audiences. For example, Wang and colleagues (2011) conducted a qualitative study that identified a number of reasons for posting sensitive content, including the desire to be perceived favorably by others, misjudgement of norms, failure to consider who might see the post, the likelihood of misinterpretation, the consequences of misinterpretation, and the author's emotional state at the time of posting. Researchers should build on this work to better understand the antecedents of sharing behavior for sensitive information. For example, it would be useful to examine whether consumers are aware of the costs and benefits of posting sensitive information and whether they systematically under-weight certain costs and overweight certain benefits in their decision to post (e.g., Fogel & Nehmad, 2009; Ibrahim, 2008). Potential factors that could influence the trade-off between costs and benefits include feelings of anonymity associated with online communication (Frost, Vermeulen, & Beekers, 2014) and lowered inhibition with strangers (Tice, Butler, Murayen, & Stillwell, 1995), both of which might lead to lower perceived risk.

Consequences of Sharing

Once information has been shared, the sender usually loses control over how it is subsequently used. In the following subsections, we discuss two future research topics worthy of study that relate to this loss of control, namely loss of control to others and loss of control to marketers.

Loss of Control to Others

In some cases, resharing of sensitive information can lead to a damaging effect on a persons' reputation or identity. For example, Soster, Boland, and Drenten (2014) have explored how explicit photographs sent by adolescent females go on to be reshared with others, resulting in damage to the young woman's reputation. Similarly, an entire genre of "fail" photographs and videos show people in embarrassing situations, such as falling down or having their clothing accidentally removed. Future research should explore what factors influence whether or not a person will share such content with others, given its potential to cause harm to the original subject. In particular, researchers might examine features of online interaction that lead to decreased empathy (Escalas & Stern, 2003) or increased schadenfreude (Sundie et al., 2009). In a similar vein, it could be beneficial for researchers to build on theories of dehumanization that describe denial of human traits and emotions to others and perception of others as objects (Haslam, 2006). It is possible that the virtual nature of online social interaction facilitates dehumanization. Consistent with this notion, Waytz and Epley (2012) found that individuals are more likely to hold dehumanized perceptions of distant others when they feel connected to close others. Extending this finding, one might predict that sharing sensitive content increases closeness between those who share while increasing dehumanization and harmful behavior toward the original subject or poster.

Loss of Control to Marketers

In addition to concerns about how consumers lose control of content to others, consumers are increasingly concerned with how their content and information could be used by firms in an exploitative manner (Culnan, 2000). For example, Facebook faced a public outcry when it altered the terms of service on its Instagram photo tool so that it could use an individual's personal photos in advertisements (Wortham, 2012). Similarly, Facebook suffered negative press and consumer backlash when it was revealed that it was showing only selected posts by friends as part of an experiment to increase user engagement (Goel, 2014). Initial research in this area suggests that consumers are less likely to react negatively depending on whether firms' use of personal information is relevant to the consumers' needs, is related to an ongoing relationship, is used in a way that honestly represents the consumer, and can ultimately be controlled by the consumer (Culnan & Armstrong, 1999).

Future research should build on these results to consider other factors that can influence consumer response to firms' use of personal information. For example, we would encourage future research to explore the expectations that consumers have about how firms will use their information. Many firms publish lengthy privacy policies that are often difficult for consumers to understand. One study found that it would take an average American consumer 244 hours to read all of the privacy policies on websites that he or she encountered in an average year (McDonald & Cranor, 2008). Given limited processing capacity, it is unlikely that consumers read these policies carefully and instead base their actions on implicit expectations about information by the firm (Rousseau, 2001). Future research could identify the exact nature of these expectations, as well as the processes through which these expectations are formed over time. For theoretical guidance, researchers may look to research in branding that has explored the formation of brand expectations and extend these theories to online social interaction with firms (e.g., Urban, Sultan, & Qualls, 2000).

Past research indicates that violations of psychological contracts in employer–employee relationships can lead to feelings of anger and betrayal (Robinson & Morrison, 2000). Thus future research could examine factors that lead to similar outcomes when firms are perceived to be misusing consumer information. Related prior work indicates that when consumers perceive an implicit promise has been broken, they tend to punish firms by avoiding products and discontinuing relationships even when doing so makes the consumer worse off (Gershoff & Koehler, 2011; Koehler & Gershoff, 2003). Similarly, it would be useful for future research to examine whether and when violations of implicit expectations regarding online social interaction influence consumer behavior toward the firm.

Privacy

As discussed earlier, research indicates a gap between reported privacy concerns and observed privacy behaviors on the part of consumers (e.g., Acquisti &

Gross, 2006). This gap manifests itself in the form of consumers who do not take advantage of options to protect their privacy (Debatin, Lovejoy, Horn, & Hughes, 2009) and consumers who share sensitive information without considering long-term consequences (Tufekci, 2008). Thus, an important direction for future research would be to identify factors that drive consumer adoption of online privacy protection tools. As a first step, researchers could examine the broader literature on attitude–behavior gap. For example, the attitude–behavior gap has been shown to be especially large in the context of organ donation, where many people say they are in favor of donation but relatively few choose to commit to making a donation. Further, it has been found that opt-outs compared to opt-ins serve to reduce the attitude–behavior gap for organ donation (Johnson & Goldstein, 2003). Research on the attitude–behavior gap in the context of privacy can build on these findings by investigating the role of factors such as default settings, exemplar settings, and policy length on the adoption of prudent privacy settings.

Online Inferences

A second broad area for future research deals with the inferences consumers make during online social interaction. For example, consumers could make inferences about the truth of a claim (Hawkins & Hoch, 1992) or the extent to which an opinion is shared by others (Gershoff, Mukherjee, & Mukhopadhyay, 2008). In the following subsections, we discuss three related topics for future research, namely the effects of repetition, reach, and homophily.

Repetition

After the Boston Marathon bombing, a large number of speculative messages were widely shared on Twitter and Reddit regarding the nature of the attack and the identity of the bombers (Starbird et al., 2014). In general, social media has increased the repetition of messages since forwarding or retweeting of messages accumulates quickly in a network of users. This means that individuals may be exposed to identical content many times, as identical messages are repeated by different sources. Thus one promising direction for future research would be to examine the effect of online message repetition on inferences of truth.

Prior work has shown that repeated exposure to a statement increases belief in its truth value (Bacon, 1979). Similarly, it has been shown that repeated exposure to an opinion or a position leads people to believe it is held by a greater proportion of the public (Weaver et al., 2007). These effects of repetition have generally been attributed to familiarity or fluency of processing of a repeated claim (Unkelbach, 2007). Future research can explore the role of fluency, as well as other mechanisms underlying the effect of repetition in an online environment. On one hand, the fluency mechanism predicts that the effect of repetition on truth would be stronger in an online context due to the increased frequency of exactly similar posts. On the other hand, it is also possible that consumers pay less attention to exactly similar messages since they convey less unique information. As a result, the "repetition = truth" effect could actually be reduced in an online environment. Another proposition that could be tested in future research is whether consumers learn the value or lack thereof of social media messages over time. Related research by Scholl, Greifeneder, and Bless (2014) indicates that reliance on fluency as a cue is learned, such that people rely more on fluency if they were successful by relying on it in the past. Thus future research can manipulate the value of repeated social media messages to investigate the process of consumer learning over time.

Reach

Unlike offline communication, online social interaction often includes information about the reach of sources. For example, each member of Twitter has a certain number of followers known to members of the network. Future research could investigate how reach of sources can influence inferences about the source as well as messages broadcast by the source. On one hand, it could be argued that sources with higher reach are seen as more reliable since they have received a vote of confidence from a large number of users (Wood, Pool, Leck, & Purvis, 1996). On the other hand, more recent research indicates that audience size can influence what information consumers are willing to share online (Barasch & Berger, 2014). Building on this research, it could be argued that greater reach will reduce perceived reliability of sources when individuals have a lay theory that sources with more followers are altering their messages to maintain their popularity or reach.

Homophily

The notion of homophily suggests that people prefer interacting with those who share their tastes and personal characteristics (Mcpherson, Smith-Lovin, & Cook, 2001). Some researchers have argued that homophily is likely to be strengthened in an online environment since it is easier to find and interact with others similar to oneself, and that this might lead to increased false consensus or exaggerated beliefs that others share their opinions (Sanger, 2013; Sunstein, 2009). In contrast, other researchers have argued that homophily may actually be weakened online since individuals seeking to validate the views of their in-group can seek to expose themselves to contrary views as a point of comparison (Bakshy, 2012; Bisgin, Agarwal, & Xu, 2012). Future research can investigate when people choose to interact with similar others online and when they choose to interact with dissimilar others. There are also some indications in past research that participating in online groups with similar others may not increase the false consensus effect. For example, Wojcieszak (2008) examined the radical beliefs of neo-Nazis and environmental extremists who participated in online forums, and she found no increase in false consensus compared to a non-online control group. Thus future research could seek to understand when and why false consensus is affected by online social interaction.

Conclusion

Online social interaction is becoming an important part of the everyday life of consumers. Consequently, investigators in different disciplines have begun to investigate research questions regarding the effects of online social interaction on individuals. In this chapter, we synthesized the extant literature on online social interaction from a consumer point of view and identified what we believe are some important and promising avenues for future research. We hope this compendium will provide a broad perspective and help researchers develop their own projects in this emerging area of research.

References

Acquisti, A., & Gross, R. (2006). Imagined communities: Awareness, information sharing, and privacy on the Facebook. In P. Golle & G. Danezis (eds.) *Proceedings of the 6th Workshop on Privacy Enhancing Technologies* (pp. 36–58). Cambridge, UK: Robinson College.

Algesheimer, R., Dholakia, U. M., & Herrmann, A. (2005). The social influence of brand community: Evidence from European car clubs. *Journal of Marketing, 69*(3), 19–34.

Amabile, T. M. (1983). *The Social Psychology of Creativity*. New York: Springer-Verlag.

Bacon, F. T. (1979). Credibility of repeated statements: Memory for trivia. *Journal of Experimental Psychology: Human Learning & Memory, 5*(3), 241–252. doi:10.1037//0278–7393.5.3.241.

Bakshy, E. (2012). *Rethinking Information Diversity in Networks. Facebook.* Retrieved from www.facebook.com/notes/facebook-data-team/rethinking-information-diversity-in-networks/10150503499618859.

Bambauer-Sachse, S., & Mangold, S. (2013). Do consumers still believe what is said in online product reviews? A persuasion knowledge approach. *Journal of Retailing and Consumer Services, 20*(4), 373–381. doi:10.1016/j.jretconser. 2013.03.004.

Barasch, A., & Berger, J. (2014). Broadcasting and narrowcasting: How audience size impacts what people share. *Journal of Marketing Research*, 140130091437001. doi:10.1509/jmr.13.0238.

Baumeister, R. F., & Leary, M. R. (1995). The need to belong: Desire for interpersonal attachments as a fundamental human motivation. *Psychological Bulletin, 117* (3), 497–529.

Belk, R. W. (2013). Extended self in a digital world. *Journal of Consumer Research, 40* (3), 477–500. doi:10.1086/671052.

Benedicktus, R. L., Brady, M. K., Darke, P. R., & Voorhees, C. M. (2010). Conveying trustworthiness to online consumers: Reactions to consensus, physical store presence, brand familiarity, and generalized suspicion. *Journal of Retailing, 86*(4), 322–335. doi:10.1016/j.jretai.2010.04.002.

Berger, J., & Iyengar, R. (2013). Communication channels and word of mouth: How the medium shapes the message. *Journal of Consumer Research, 40*(3), 567–579. doi:10.1086/671345.

Bisgin, H., Agarwal, N., & Xu, X. (2012). A study of homophily on social media. *World Wide Web, 15*(2), 213–232.

Bohnert, D., & Ross, W. H. (2010). The influence of social networking web sites on the evaluation of job candidates. *Cyberpsychology, Behavior and Social Networking, 13*(3), 341–347. Retrieved from www.ncbi.nlm.nih.gov/pubmed/20557256.

Boyd, D. M., & Ellison, N. B. (2008). Social network sites: Definition, history, and scholarship. *Journal of Computer-Mediated Communication, 13*, 210–230.

Chan, C., Berger, J., & Van Boyen, Leaf, (2012). Identifiable but not identical: Combining social identity and uniquenss motives in choice. *Journal of Consumer Research, 39*(3), 561–573.

Cheema, A., & Kaikati, A. M. (2010). The effect of need for uniqueness on word of mouth. *Journal of Marketing Research, XLVII*(June), 553–563.

Chen, Y., & Xie, J. (2005). Third-party product review and firm marketing strategy. *Marketing Science, 24*(2), 218–240. doi:10.1287/mksc.l040.0089.

Cheung, C. M. K., Chiu, P.-Y., & Lee, M. K. O. (2011). Online social networks: Why do students use Facebook? *Computers in Human Behavior, 27*(4), 1337–1343. doi:10.1016/j.chb.2010.07.028.

Chevalier, J. A., & Mayzlin, D. (2006). The effect of word of mouth on sales: Online book reviews. *Journal of Marketing Research, 345*(XLIII), 345–354.

Chintagunta, P. K., Gopinath, S., & Venkataraman, S. (2010). The effects of online user reviews on movie box office performance: Accounting for sequential rollout and aggregation across local markets. *Marketing Science, 29*(5), 944–957. doi:10.1287/mksc.1100.0572.

Christofides, E., Muise, A., & Desmarais, S. (2009). Information disclosure and control on Facebook: Are they two sides of the same coin or two different processes? *Cyberpsychology & Behavior, 12*(3), 341–345. doi:10.1089/cpb.2008.0226.

Clemons, E. K., Gao, G., & Hitt, L. M. (2006). When online reviews meet hyperdifferentiation: A study of the craft beer industry. *Journal of Management Information Systems, 23*(2), 149–171. doi:10.2753/MIS0742-1222230207.

Culnan, M. J. (2000). Protecting privacy online: Is self-regulation working? *Journal of Public Policy & Marketing, 19*(1), 20–26.

Culnan, M. J., & Armstrong, P. K. (1999). Information privacy concerns, procedural fairness, and impersonal trust: An empirical investigation. *Organization Science, 10*(1), 104–115.

De Vries, L., Gensler, S., & Leeflang, P. S. H. (2012). Popularity of brand posts on brand fan pages: An investigation of the effects of social media marketing. *Journal of Interactive Marketing, 26*(2), 83–91. doi:10.1016/j.intmar.2012.01.003.

Debatin, B., Lovejoy, J. P., Horn, A.-K., & Hughes, B. N. (2009). Facebook and online privacy: Attitudes, behaviors, and unintended consequences. *Journal of Computer-Mediated Communication, 15*(1), 83–108. doi:10.1111/j.1083-6101.2009.01494.x.

Dellarocas, C., Zhang, X. (Michael), & Awad, N. F. (2007). Exploring the value of online product reviews in forecasting sales: The case of motion pictures. *Journal of Interactive Marketing, 21*(4), 23–45. doi:10.1002/dir.20087.

Dey, R., Jelveh, Z., & Ross, K. (2012). Facebook users have become much more private: A large-scale study. In *2012 IEEE International Conference on Pervasive Computing and Communications Workshops* (pp. 346–352). Ieee. doi:10.1109/PerComW.2012.6197508.

Emerson, R. (2011). 13 controversial Facebook firings: Palace guards, doctors, teachers, and more. *Huffington Post.* Retrieved from www.huffingtonpost.com/2011/10/17/facebook-firings_n_1003789.html#s375205title=Teen_Fired_For.

Escalas, J. E., & Stern, B. B. (2003). Sympathy and empathy: Emotional responses to advertising dramas. *Journal of Consumer Research, 29*, 566–578.

Fogel, J., & Nehmad, E. (2009). Internet social network communities: Risk taking, trust, and privacy concerns. *Computers in Human Behavior, 25*(1), 153–160. doi:10.1016/j.chb.2008.08.006.

Fogelin, R. (1988). Hume and Berkeley on the proofs of infinite divisibility. *Philosophical Review, 97*(1), 47–69.

Fournier, S., Senisper, S., McAlexander, J. H., & Shouten, J. W. (2001). Building brand community on the Harley-Davidson posse ride. Harvard Business School case *9-501-015.*

Frost, J., Vermeulen, I. E., & Beekers, N. (2014). Anonymity versus privacy: Selective information sharing in online cancer communities. *Journal of Medical Internet Research, 16*(5), e126.

Fuchs, C., Prandelli, E., Schreier, M., & Dahl, D. W. (2013). All that is users might not be gold: How labeling products as user designed backfires in the context of luxury fashion brands. *Journal of Marketing, 77*(September), 75–91.

Gershoff, A. D., & Koehler, J. J. (2011). Safety first? The role of emotion in safety product betrayal aversion. *Journal of Consumer Research, 38*(1), 140–150. doi:10.1086/658883.

Gershoff, A. D., Mukherjee, A., & Mukhopadhyay, A. (2003). Consumer acceptance of online agent advice: Extremity and positivity effects. *Journal of Consumer Psychology, 13*(1–2), 161–170. doi:10.1207/S15327663JCP13–1&2_14.

Gershoff, A. D., Mukherjee, A., & Mukhopadhyay, A. (2007). Few ways to love, but many ways to hate: Attribute ambiguity and the positivity effect in agent evaluation. *Journal of Consumer Research, 33*(4), 499–505.

Gershoff, A. D., Mukherjee, A., & Mukhopadhyay, A. (2008). What's not to like? Preference asymmetry in the false consensus effect. *Journal of Consumer Research, 35*(1), 119–125. doi:10.1086/524416.

Ghose, A., & Ipeirotis, P. G. (2011). Estimating the helpfulness and economic impact of product reviews: Mining text and reviewer characteristics. *IEEE Transactions on Knowledge and Data Engineering, 23*(10), 1498–1512. doi:10.1109/TKDE.2010.188.

Godes, D., & Mayzlin, D. (2004). Using online conversations to study word-of-mouth communication. *Marketing Science, 23*(4), 545–560. doi:10.1287/mksc.1040.0071.

Goel, V. (2014). As data overflows online, researchers grapple with ethics. *New York Times,* August 12. Retrieved from www.nytimes.com/2014/08/13/technology/the-boon-of-online-data-puts-social-science-in-a-quandary.html.

Griffiths, M. D., Davies, M. N. O., & Chappell, D. (2004). Demographic factors and playing variables in online computer gaming. *CyberPsychology & Behavior, 7*(4), 479–487. doi:10.1089/cpb.2004.7.479.

Gross, R., & Acquisti, A. (2005). Information revelation and privacy in online social networks. *Proceedings of WPES'05* (pp. 71–80). Alexandria, VA: ACM. doi:10.1145/1102199.1102214.

Hamilton, R., Vohs, K. D., & McGill, A. (2014). We'll be honest, this won't be the best article you'll ever read: The use of dispreferred markers in word-of-mouth communication. *Journal of Consumer Research, 41*(1), 197–212.

Hampton, K. N., Goulet, L. S., Rainie, L., & Purcell, K. (2011). Social networking sites and our lives (pp. 1–85). Retrieved from http://pewinternet.org/Reports/2011/Technology-and-social-networks.aspx.

Hargadon, A. B., & Bechky, B. A. (2006). When collections of creatives become creative collectives: A field study of problem solving at work. *Organization Science, 17* (4), 484–500.

Haslam, N. (2006). Dehumanization: An integrated review. *Personality and Social Psychology Review, 10*, 252–264.

Hawkins, S. A., & Hoch, S. J. (1992). Low-involvement learning : Memory without evaluation. *Journal of Consumer Research, 19*(2), 212–225.

He, S. X., & Bond, S. D. (2013). Word-of-mouth and the forecasting of consumption enjoyment. *Journal of Consumer Psychology, 23*(4), 464–482. doi:10.1016/j.jcps.2013.04.001.

Ho-Dac, N. N., Carson, S. J., & Moore, W. L. (2013). The effects of positive and negative online customer reviews: Do brand strength and category maturity matter? *Journal of Marketing, 77*(November), 37–53.

Hollenbeck, C. R., & Kaikati, A. M. (2012). Consumers' use of brands to reflect their actual and ideal selves on Facebook. *International Journal of Research in Marketing, 29*(4), 395–405. doi:10.1016/j.ijresmar.2012.06.002.

Ibrahim, Y. (2008). The new risk communities: Social networking sites and risk. *International Journal of Media & Cultural Politics, 4*(2), 245–253.

Jayanti, R. K., & Singh, J. (2010). Pragmatic learning theory: An inquiry-action framework for distributed consumer learning in online communities. *Journal of Consumer Research, 36*(6), 1058–1081. doi:10.1086/648689.

Johnson, E. J., & Goldstein, D. (2003). Do defaults save lives? *Science, 302*, 1338–1339.

Khare, A., Labrecque, L. I., & Asare, A. K. (2011). The assimilative and contrastive effects of word-of-mouth volume: An experimental examination of online consumer ratings. *Journal of Retailing, 87*(1), 111–126. doi:10.1016/j.jretai.2011.01.005.

Koehler, J. J., & Gershoff, A. D. (2003). Betrayal aversion: When agents of protection become agents of harm. *Organizational Behavior and Human Decision Processes, 90*(2), 244–261. doi:10.1016/S0749-5978(02)00518-6.

Kozinets, R. V., Hemetsberger, a., & Schau, H. J. (2008). The wisdom of consumer crowds: Collective innovation in the age of networked marketing. *Journal of Macromarketing, 28*(4), 339–354. doi:10.1177/0276146708325382.

Kozinets, R. V, Valck, K. De, Wojnicki, A. C., & Wilner, S. J. S. (2010). Networked narratives: Understanding word-of-mouth marketing in online communities. *Journal of Marketing, 74*(March), 71–89.

Krasnova, H., Kolesnikova, E., & Guenther, O. (2009). "It won't happen to me!": Self-disclosure in online social networks. In *AMCIS 2009 Proceedings* (p. 343).

Kronrod, A., & Danziger, S. (2013). "Wii will rock you!" The use and effect of figurative language in consumer reviews of hedonic and utilitarian consumption. *Journal of Consumer Research, 40*(4), 726–739. doi:10.1086/671998.

Lamberton, C. P., & Rose, R. L. (2012). When is ours better than mine? A framework for understanding and sharing systems. *Journal of Marketing, 76*(July), 109–125.

Li, F., & Du, T. C. (2011). Who is talking? An ontology-based opinion leader identification framework for word-of-mouth marketing in online social blogs. *Decision Support Systems, 51*(1), 190–197. doi:10.1016/j.dss.2010.12.007.

Lovett, M. J., Peres, R., & Shachar, R. (2013). On brands and word of mouth. *Journal of Marketing Research, L*(August), 427–444.

Mathwick, C., Wiertz, C., & Ruyter, K. de. (2008). Social capital production in a virtual P3 community. *Journal of Consumer Research, 34*(6), 832–849.

Mazer, J. P., Murphy, R. E., & Simonds, C. J. (2009). The effects of teacher self-disclosure via Facebook on teacher credibility. *Learning, Media and Technology, 34*(2), 175–183. doi:10.1080/17439880902923655.

McDonald, A. M., & Cranor, L. F. (2008). The cost of reading privacy policies. *Journal of Law and Policy for the Information Society, 4*(3), 540–565.

McDuling, J. (2014). Why people quit Twitter. *Quartz*. Retrieved from http://qz.com/191524/why-people-quit-twitter/.

Mcpherson, M., Smith-Lovin, L., & Cook, J. M. (2001). Birds of a feather: Homophily in social networks. *Annual Review of Sociology, 27*(2001), 415–444.

Meuter, M. L., Ostrom, A. L., Roundtree, R. I., & Bitner, M. J. (2000). Self-service technologies: Understanding customer satisfaction with technology-based service encounters. *Journal of Marketing, 64*(3), 50–64.

Moe, W. W., & Trusov, M. (2011). The value of social dynamics in online product ratings forums. *Journal of Marketing Research, XLVIII*(June), 444–456.

Moore, S. G. (2012). Some things are better left unsaid: How word of mouth influences the storyteller. *Journal of Consumer Research, 38*(6), 1140–1154. doi:10.1086/661891.

Mudambi, S. M., & Schuff, D. (2010). What makes a helpful online review? A study of customer reviews on Amazon.com. *MIS Quarterly, 34*(1), 185–200.

Nadkarni, A., & Hofmann, S. G. (2012). Why do people use Facebook? *Personality and Individual Differences, 52*(3), 243–249. doi:10.1016/j.paid.2011.11.007.

Naylor, R. W., Lamberton, C. P., & Norton, D. (2011). Seeing ourselves in others: Reviewer ambiguity, egocentric anchoring, and persuasion. *Journal of Marketing Research, XLVIII*(June), 617–631.

Naylor, R. W., Lamberton, C. P., & West, P. M. (2012). Beyond the "like" button: The impact of mere virtual presence on brand evaluations and purchase intentions in social media settings. *Journal of Marketing, 76*(November), 105–120.

Packard, G., & Wooten, D. B. (2013). Compensatory knowledge signaling in consumer word-of-mouth. *Journal of Consumer Psychology, 23*(4), 434–450. doi:10.1016/j.jcps.2013.05.002.

Park, D.-H., Lee, J., & Han, I. (2007). The effect of on-line consumer reviews on consumer purchasing intention: The moderating role of involvement. *International Journal of Electronic Commerce, 11*(4), 125–148. doi:10.2753/JEC1086-4415110405.

Park, S.-B., & Park, D.-H. (2013). The effect of low-versus high-variance in product reviews on product evaluation. *Psychology and Marketing, 30*(7), 543–554. doi:10.1002/mar.

Peluchette, J., & Karl, K. (2008). Social networking profiles: An examination of student attitudes regarding use and appropriateness of content. *CyberPsychology & Behavior, 11*(1), 95–7. doi:10.1089/cpb.2007.9927.

Pew Research Center (2014). *The Web at 25 in the U.S* (pp. 1–40). Retrieved from www.pewinternet.org/files/2014/02/PIP_25th-anniversary-of-the-Web_0227141.pdf.

Punj, G. N. (2012). Do consumers who conduct online research also post online reviews? A model of the relationship between online research and review posting behavior. *Marketing Letters, 24*(1), 97–108. doi:10.1007/s11002-012-9205-2.

Robinson, S. L., & Morrison, E. W. (2000). The development of psychological contract breach and violation: A longitudinal study. *Journal of Organizational Behavior, 21*(June), 525–547.

Rosengren, K. E., Wenner, L. A., & Palmgren, P. (eds.) (1985). *Media Gratifications Research: Current Perspectives*. London: Sage.

Rousseau, D. M. (2001). Schema, promise and mutuality: The building blocks of the psychological contract. *Journal of Occupational and Organizational Psychology, 74*(4), 511–541. doi:10.1348/096317901167505.

Sanger, L. (2013). Internet silos. *Edge.org*. Retrieved from http://edge.org/response-detail/23777.

Schau, H. J., Muñiz, Jr., A. M., & Arnould, E. J. (2009). How brand community practices create value. *Journal of Marketing, 73*(September), 30–51.

Schellekens, G. A. C., Verlegh, P. W. J., & Smidts, A. (2010). Language abstraction in word of mouth. *Journal of Consumer Research, 37*(2), 207–223. doi:10.1086/651240.

Schindler, R. M., & Bickart, B. (2012). Perceived helpfulness of online consumer reviews: The role of message content and style. *Journal of Consumer Behaviour, 11*(March), 234–243. doi:10.1002/cb.

Schlosser, A. E. (2005). Posting versus lurking: Communicating in a multiple audience context. *Journal of Consumer Research, 32*(2), 260–265.

Schlosser, A. E. (2011). Can including pros and cons increase the helpfulness and persuasiveness of online reviews? The interactive effects of ratings and arguments. *Journal of Consumer Psychology, 21*(3), 226–239. doi:10.1016/j.jcps.2011.04.002.

Schlosser, A. E., & Shavitt, S. (2002). Anticipating discussion about a product: Rehearsing what to say can affect your judgments. *Journal of Consumer Research, 29*(1), 101–115.

Scholl, S. G., Greifeneder, R., & Bless, H. (2014). When fluency signals truth: Prior successful reliance on fluency moderates the impact of fluency on truth judgments. *Journal of Behavioral Decision Making, 27*(3), 268–280. doi:10.1002/bdm.1805.

Sen, S., & Lerman, D. (2007). Why are you telling me this? An examination into negative consumer reviews on the web. *Journal of Interactive Marketing, 21*(4), 76–94. doi:10.1002/dir.

Sheldon, K. M., Abad, N., & Hinsch, C. (2011). A two-process view of Facebook use and relatedness need-satisfaction: Disconnection drives use, and connection rewards it. *Journal of Personality and Social Psychology, 100*(4), 766–775. doi:10.1037/a0022407.

Soster, R. L., Boland, W. A., & Drenten, J. (2014). Digital consumption: adolescents cellphones, and the unintended creation of tethered identity. *Paper presented at American Psychological Association Annual Convention (Division 23),* Washington, DC, August.

Sridhar, S., & Srinivasan, R. (2012). Social influence effects in online product ratings. *Journal of Marketing, 76*(September), 70–88.

Starbird, K., Maddock, J., Orand, M., Achterman, P., & Mason, R. M. (2014). Rumors, false flags, and digital vigilantes: Misinformation on Twitter after the 2013 Boston Marathon bombing. In *iConference 2014 Proceedings.* iSchools. doi:10.9776/14308.

Story, L. (2008). How do they track you? Let us count the ways. *New York Times,* March 3. Retrieved from http://bits.blogs.nytimes.com/2008/03/09/how-do-they-track-you-let-us-count-the-ways/.

Stutzman, F., & Kramer-Duffield, J. (2010). Friends only: Examining a privacy-enhancing behavior in Facebook. In *Proceedings of the ACM Conference on Human Factors in Computing Systems* (CHI '10) (pp. 1553–1562). ACM Press.

Sundie, J. M., Ward, J. C., Beal, D. J., Chin, W. W., & Geiger-Oneto, S. (2009). Schadenfreude as a consumption-related emotion: Feeling happiness about the downfall of another's product. *Journal of Consumer Psychology, 19*(3), 356–373.

Sunstein, C. R. (2009). *Republic.com 2.0.* Princeton, NJ: Princeton University Press.

Tate, R. (2011). How Google spies on your gmail account (and how to stop it). *Gawker.* Retrieved from http://gawker.com/5800868/how-google-spies-on-your-gmail-account-and-how-to-stop-it.

Tice, D. M., Butler, J. L., Murayen, M. B., & Stillwell, A. M. (1995). When modesty prevails : Differential favorability of self-presentation to friends and strangers. *Journal of Personality and Social Psychology, 69*(6), 1120–1138.

Trusov, M., Bodapati, A. V, & Bucklin, R. E. (2010). Determining influential users in Internet social networks. *Journal of Marketing Research, XLVII*(August), 643–658.

Tufekci, Z. (2008). Grooming, gossip, Facebook and Myspace. *Information, Communication & Society, 11*(4), 544–564. doi:10.1080/13691180801999050.

Unkelbach, C. (2007). Reversing the truth effect: Learning the interpretation of processing fluency in judgments of truth. *Journal of Experimental Psychology: Learning, Memory, and Cognition, 33*(1), 219–230. doi:10.1037/0278–7393.33.1.219.

Urban, G. L., Sultan, F., & Qualls, W. J. (2000). Placing trust at the center of your Internet strategy. *Sloan Management Review, 42*(1), 39–48.

Wang, Y., Komanduri, S., Leon, P. G., Norcie, G., Acquisti, A., & Cranor, L. F. (2011). "I regretted the minute I pressed share": A qualitative study of regrets on Facebook. In *Symposium on Usable Privacy and Security (SOUPS) 2011* (pp. 1–13). Pittsburgh, PA.

Ward, J. C., & Ostrom, A. L. (2006). Complaining to the masses: The role of protest framing in customer-created complaint web sites. *Journal of Consumer Research, 33*(2), 220–230.

Waytz, A., & Epley, N. (2012). Social connection enables dehumanization. *Journal of Experimental Social Psychology, 48*(1), 70–76.

Weaver, K., Garcia, S. M., Schwarz, N., & Miller, D. T. (2007). Inferring the popularity of an opinion from its familiarity: A repetitive voice sounds like a chorus. *Journal of Personality and Social Psychology, 92*, 821–833.

Weisbuch, M., Ivcevic, Z., & Ambady, N. (2009). On being liked on the web and in the "real world": Consistency in first impressions across personal webpages and spontaneous behavior. *Journal of Experimental Social Psychology, 45*(3), 573–576. doi:10.1016/j.jesp.2008.12.009.

West, P. M., & Broniarczyk, S. M. (1998). Integrating multiple opinions: The role of aspiration level on consumer response to critic consensus. *Journal of Consumer Research, 25*(1), 38–51.

Whiting, A., & Williams, D. (2013). Why people use social media: A uses and gratifications approach. *Qualitative Market Research: An International Journal, 16*(4), 362–369. doi:10.1108/QMR-06-2013-0041.

Wilcox, K., & Stephen, A. T. (2013). Are close friends the enemy? Online social networks, self-esteem, and self-control. *Journal of Consumer Research, 40*(1), 90–103. doi:10.1086/668794.

Wilson, R. E., Gosling, S. D., & Graham, L. T. (2012). A review of Facebook research in the social sciences. *Perspectives on Psychological Science, 7*(3), 203–220. doi:10.1177/1745691612442904.

Wojcieszak, M. (2008). False consensus goes online: Impact of ideologically homogeneous groups on false consensus. *Public Opinion Quarterly, 72*(4), 781–791. doi:10.1093/poq/nfn056.

Wojnicki, A. C., & Godes, D. B. (2011). *Signaling Success: Strategically Positive Word of Mouth*. Working Paper, Rotman School of Management, University of Toronto.

Wood, W., Pool, G. J., Leck, K., & Purvis, D. (1996). Self-definition, defensive processing, and influence: The normative impact of majority and minority groups. *Journal of Personality and Social Psychology, 71*(6), 1181–1193. Retrieved from www.ncbi.nlm.nih.gov/pubmed/8979385.

Wortham, J. (2012). Facebook responds to anger over proposed Instagram changes. *New York Times*, December 18. Retrieved from www.nytimes.com/2012/12/19/technology/facebook-responds-to-anger-over-proposed-instagram-changes.html?_r=0.

Yadav, M. S., & Pavlou, P. A. (2014). Marketing in computer-mediated environments: Research synthesis and new directions. *Journal of Marketing, 78*(1), 20–40. doi:10.1509/jm.12.0020.

Yin, D., Bond, S. D., & Zhang, H. (2014). Anxious or angry? Effects of discrete emotions on the perceived helpfulness of online reviews. *MIS Quarterly, 38*(2), 539–560.

Zhang, J. Q., Craciun, G., & Shin, D. (2010). When does electronic word-of-mouth matter? A study of consumer product reviews. *Journal of Business Research, 63*(12), 1336–1341. doi:10.1016/j.jbusres.2009.12.011.

Zhu, F., & Zhang, X. (Michael). (2010). Impact of online consumer reviews on sales: The moderating role of product and consumer characteristics. *Journal of Marketing, 74*(March), 133–148.

Zhu, R. (Juliet), Dholakia, U. M., Chen, X. (Jack), & Algesheimer, R. (2012). Does online community participation foster risky financial behavior? *Journal of Marketing Research, XLIX*(June), 394–407.

Zinkhan, G. M., Kwak, H., Morrison, M., & Peters, C. O. (2003). Web-based chatting: Consumer communication in cyberspace. *Journal of Consumer Psychology, 13*(1–2), 17–27.

PART III

Societal Structures

19 Ethical Consumption

Rebecca Walker Reczek and Julie R. Irwin

In today's marketplace, goods that reflect an underlying concern with a specific ethical issue are more prevalent than ever before. Consumers who care about the environment are able to buy sustainable products ranging from "green" household cleaners to responsibly sourced building materials. Likewise, consumers who are concerned about the rights of workers in developing countries can choose to buy products certified as fair trade and/or recommended by organizations such as Human Rights Watch. However, the market share for many sustainable and ethically produced goods remains relatively small compared to that of their traditional competitors, suggesting that either (1) only a very small minority of consumers actually cares about ethicality in consumption contexts or (2) significant barriers exist to expressing one's concerns with ethical issues in the marketplace. In this chapter, we argue that it is primarily the latter driving the lower market share of products that reflect ethical values and that an understanding of consumer psychology can help remove these barriers to increase the likelihood that consumers will make purchases with ethical values in mind. To do so, we first conceptualize what we mean by ethical consumption, then review recent research identifying barriers to the expression of ethical values in purchase contexts, and, finally, outline a research agenda aimed at understanding and creating consumption contexts that will best allow consumers to express their most ethical selves.

Conceptualizing Ethical Consumption

We define ethical consumption as consumption activities that are consistent with conscience, values, and morals. This definition is consistent with the concept of ethical attributes that has been used in marketing and psychology research (e.g., Baron & Spranca, 1997; Ehrich & Irwin, 2005; Irwin & Baron, 2001; Irwin & Naylor, 2009; Luchs, Naylor, Irwin, & Raghunathan, 2010; Haws, Winterich, & Naylor, 2014; Peloza, White, & Shang, 2013). As such, ethical attributes and, hence, ethical consumption can relate to a variety of ethical issues, including the environment, labor practices, treatment of animals, and so on.

Additionally, ethical consumption includes all stages of the consumption cycle: acquisition, consumption, and post-consumption activities (Wells,

1993). In other words, one's conscience and therefore one's ethical values can affect choices about what brands or products to buy, how much of a product to use, and how to dispose of used goods. Ethical consumption choices can also include both choosing to engage in a particular behavior (e.g., choosing to buy a "green" household cleaner, choosing to donate or recycle used goods) and choosing to avoid another behavior (e.g., choosing not to buy a desirable pair of jeans made with sweatshop labor or choosing to use less of a given product in order to conserve resources).

Researchers have recently begun to determine the factors that drive ethical product usage. Notable examples of the work in this area include Lamberton and Rose's (2012) exploration of consumers' use of car sharing services, Ying-Ching and Chang's (2012) examination of usage quantity for sustainable goods, and Phipps and Brace-Govan's (2011) work on water conservation. Other researchers are investigating the drivers of ethical post-consumption activities such as recycling (Caitlin & Wang, 2013; Trudel & Argo, 2013) and creative reuse of products (Haws, Naylor, Coulter, and Bearden, 2012), a practice also known as upcycling (Gardiner, 2010). However, the majority of research on ethical consumption has focused on the drivers of ethical acquisition, specifically the purchase of goods that reflect an underlying concern with a specific ethical issue. Much of the interest in ethical consumerism lately has centered on "green" marketing, the marketing of environmentally friendly products (see Gershoff & Irwin, 2012, for a review). In this chapter, we discuss ethical consumerism for environmental and other ethical issues, and, in line with previous research, we focus primarily on the purchase of products that reflect ethical values.

Many consumers report that they care about ethical issues such as environmentalism and workers' rights and that they take these issues into account when making purchases. Some even report that they are willing to pay more for ethically produced goods (Trudel & Cotte, 2009). In keeping with these sentiments, a recent tracking poll by Mintel (2014) indicated that "nearly four in 10 Americans say they are dedicated to buying green products and services (i.e., either 'almost always' or 'regularly' buy green products)" (Mintel, 2014). Similarly, a recent Nielsen survey indicated that 50 percent of global consumers report that they are willing to pay more for products from socially responsible companies (Nielsen, 2013), and a majority of British consumers indicated that the Fairtrade certification mark makes them more likely to buy a product (Globescan, 2010). However, these self-reports of behavior do not appear to match reality. Products with positive ethical attributes are, in many product categories, not market leaders (Bonini & Oppenhein, 2008; Gleim, Smith, Andrews, & Cronin, 2013), and products with poor performance on ethical attributes continue to sell. Why does there appear to be a discrepancy between what consumers say they purchase and what sales figures suggest they actually buy?

Past research has addressed the causes of this gap by suggesting that consumers lie when they report their purchasing behavior. They may do so because they believe that reporting sustainable purchases is socially desirable (Luchs et al., 2010) or because of what Batson and colleagues (1999) term "moral hypocrisy," which is the reporting of values that one does not actually hold. Undoubtedly, such misrepresentation occurs, but other reasons might be behind this apparent attitude/behavior gap (Prothero et al., 2011). In fact, exploring why even consumers who care about the issues reflected in ethical attributes may not buy ethical products has been a fruitful avenue of research in recent years. In this chapter, we explore two types of barriers to ethical purchase behavior: (1) psychological barriers stemming from conflicting values and conflicting selves and (2) barriers that can be attributed to characteristics of the marketplace and their interaction with consumer psychology.

Psychological Barriers to Ethical Consumption: Conflicting Values and Conflicting Selves

After reaching a certain stage of moral development, most people have a general desire to be good, moral people (Kohlberg, 1984). In other words, most mature adults generally want to do the right thing and behave in an ethical and moral manner (Bandura, 1999; Bandura, Barbaranelli, Caprara, & Pastorelli, 1996) and, with the exception of sociopaths, have the general desire to be prosocial and to further the outcomes of creatures apart from themselves (Haidt, 2007). Given that this desire exists, it should feel good to express ethical values when making purchases in the marketplace. What stands between this feeling and actual purchasing behavior? In this section, we suggest that two related conflicts that consumers experience when considering ethical values in the marketplace lead them away from their ethical values. First, the trade-offs among attributes (such as price and quality) that consumers naturally engage in may be especially likely to lead them away from ethical product attributes. Second, the general conflict that consumers feel between their best, most ethical self and their more selfish, immediate self is constantly pulling them away from ethical behavior, and that pull is especially strong in many purchasing contexts.

Trade-offs between Ethical Attributes and Other Attributes

Work on attitude-behavior consistency (e.g., Verplanken & Holland, 2002) has shown that attitudes (e.g., an ethical value such as the desire to protect the environment) must be salient at the moment of action (e.g., the point of purchase) in order for them to affect the relevant action (e.g., choosing to buy a green laundry detergent over its traditional competitors). Importantly, though, more than one value may be salient at the time of purchase. For example, a consumer buying laundry detergent may care about the impact of his or her purchase on the environment but may also value frugality in purchasing. Because consumers expect sustainable products and fair trade goods to cost more than their traditional counterparts (Gleim et al., 2013), they may feel that there is a trade-off that must be made between ethicality and frugality. If this trade-off were usually made in a way that resolves the conflict in favor of ethicality, then there would be no ethical value/purchase inconsistency, but we argue that the opposite is the case.

Purchasing usually takes place in a retail space or online shopping environment in which price is very salient; pricing is presented everywhere in most shopping environments, and, when consumers are shopping, they are heavily influenced by price and price-related promotions (Chandon, Wansink, & Laurent, 2000; Dodds, Monroe, & Grewal, 1991; Wansink, Kent, & Hoch, 1998). Thus, the goal of frugality and concerns about price might naturally take precedence over ethicality in these contexts even if the consumer, overall, cares more about ethicality than about price, because in purchasing contexts the idea of frugality is more active. In fact, although one might expect that a conflict between frugality and ethical values would be less of an issue for consumers who value the ethical issue at hand especially highly, recent work on the nomological network underlying green consumption values (Haws, Winterich, & Naylor, 2014) shows that green consumption values are, in fact, correlated with frugality (Lastovicka, Bettencourt, Hughner, & Kuntze, 1999). Thus, greenness might itself prime frugality and may frequently present a value conflict for environmental consumers.

Lay theories about the correlation between ethical and nonethical attributes are another source of the potential conflict consumers may experience when trying to match their purchases to both their ethical and other values. Lay theories are common-sense explanations people use in their everyday lives to understand their environment that may or may not be scientifically accurate (Furnham, 1988). More generally, lay theories espousing the links between various phenomena have a powerful influence on human judgment and behavior (Molden & Dweck, 2006). We, along with our coauthors (Luchs et al., 2010), discovered one such lay theory that specifically pits ethical values against effectiveness. We found that consumers believe, at an implicit level, that sustainable products are not as strong and effective as their traditional counterparts. Thus, people are reluctant to purchase sustainable goods in product categories where strength is valued, an effect we term the "sustainability liability." Although consumers may not be willing to admit that they do not want to purchase sustainable products in product categories such as laundry detergent and hand sanitizer, projective techniques that reveal actual intentions by removing social desirability bias demonstrate that most consumers are, in fact, reluctant to choose green options in these categories. For example, in a field study, consumers chose a sustainable over a nonsustainable hand sanitizer to protect themselves against a flu virus (a context where strength and effectiveness are important) when being observed by an experimenter but chose a nonsustainable hand sanitizer when they thought they were unobserved (Luchs et al., 2010).

Although this "sustainable = less strong and effective" lay theory may or may not reflect the reality of the market (i.e., sustainable goods often are rated by *Consumer Reports* and other outlets as no less effective than their traditional counterparts), in many product categories, consumers face a perceived conflict between ethical values and other consumption goals because they subscribe to this belief at an intuitive level. In a follow-up to our work, Ying-Ching and Chang (2012) demonstrated that consumers who particularly value protecting the environment are even more prone to the sustainability liability, using a relatively greater quantity of a green versus nongreen hand sanitizer because they believed the green product was less effective. The sustainability liability has also been affirmed by new research showing that green products are considered less effective if the company intentionally makes the product more "green" (because consumers assume that doing so requires resource trade-offs) but not if the product is green as a result of an "unintended side effect" (Newman, Gorlan, & Dhar, 2014).

Put in the context of this chapter, the sustainability liability shows that an (often erroneous) assumption about the relationship between attributes is likely, at least for products for which strength is valued, to result in a lower attribute weight for ethical attributes. Ying-Ching and Chang's (2012) follow-up work further demonstrates that caring about the ethical value in question is not a protection from making these types of potentially incorrect lay theory-driven inferences.

The Ethical Self and the Selfish Self

There is a broader conflict at work in consumers than simply the weighting of attributes in decision trade-offs. Everyone has an ongoing conflict between the "angels" and "devils" (or at least the desire not to be an angel) of their nature. Although there are many terms for this ubiquitous conflict, we will use the terms the "want self" and the "should self" (Bazerman, Tenbrunsel, & Wade-Benzoni, 1998; Milkman, Rogers, & Bazerman, 2008). The want self is focused on the short term and achieving immediate gratification, which sometimes simply means avoiding having to deal with the complications of the should self, which considers the ethical impact of its actions. We propose that the internal conflict between want and should selves is triggered when consumers encounter desirable products that vary in their ethicality. We then explore the consequences of the conflicting desires stemming from these conflicting selves: the desire to make easy choices that please our want selves in the short run versus the desire to make good, moral decisions consistent with our should selves.

It stands to reason that behaving ethically would operate similarly to trying to exert self-control over visceral impulses, such as trying to avoid eating too many desserts (Baumeister, Muraven, & Tice, 2000; Redden & Haws, 2013), although we discuss later in this chapter the possibility that there may be differences between these two types of conflicts. Even if there are subtle differences among types of "angel" versus "devil" conflicts, it is clear from past research that allowing the should self to win against the prevalent and easy want self takes a certain amount of energy, whatever the "sin" that the want self desires. For example, Gino, Schweitzer, Mead, and Ariely (2011) demonstrate that resisting unethical behavior such as cheating both requires and depletes self-control resources. Barnes, Schaubroeck, Huth, and Ghumman (2011) show that a lack of sleep can make people behave less ethically as resources are depleted. Similarly, Kouchaki and Smith (2014) show that people behave more morally in the morning than in the afternoon because they are less depleted in the morning before their self-control resources have been worn down over the course of the day. This research is relevant to purchasing, both because most people would like to avoid feeling depleted and thus may avoid thinking about ethical issues in general, and because purchasing situations often involve time and resource constraints. Shoppers are often in a hurry, may have a lot to buy, and are frequently trying to satisfy multiple complex goals at once. Thus, in shopping contexts, there simply may not be enough resources left to attend to and process ethical attribute information.

Another reason that processing ethical attribute information can be depleting is that conflict between attributes with ethical implications and other attributes has the potential to lead to substantial negative affect (Luce, 1998; Luce, Payne, & Bettman, 2000). Ethical attributes are often linked to "protected" (Baron & Spranca, 1997; Irwin & Baron, 2001; Ritov & Baron, 1999) or "sacred" (McGraw & Tetlock, 2005; Tetlock, Kristel, & Elson, 2000) moral values, which are values that people are unwilling to trade off with other attributes, or at least that they indicate that they are unwilling to trade off with other attributes. Given their link to protected values, it is not surprising that decisions involving ethical attributes are often emotionally laden (Peloza, White, & Shang, 2013) and that asking people to make explicit trade-offs between ethical and other attributes may result in moral outrage (Baron & Spranca, 1997; Irwin, 1994; Irwin & Baron, 2001; Irwin & Spira, 1997; Tetlock, Kristen, & Elson, 2000). This moral outrage can lead consumers to such a sense of emotional overload that they are unable to rationally evaluate products that have ethical implications (e.g., Lichtenstein, Gregory, & Irwin, 2007).

As a result of the potential for depletion, intense negative emotions, and moral outrage that can stem from focusing on ethical values in the marketplace, we propose that consumers use coping strategies (Luce, 1998) to avoid having to consider negative ethical issues in purchase domains. Past research provides evidence for some specific coping mechanisms, including the use of rationalizations for the violation of ethical principles. For example, Paharia, Vohs, and Desphandé (2013) showed that (1) consumers use motivated reasoning to employ various political and economic rationalizations (e.g., "Sweatshops are the only realistic source of income for workers in poorer countries"; "Without sweatshops, poorer countries could not develop"; etc.) when considering going on a Caribbean vacation; and (2) these rationalizations drive intentions to patronize resorts that use sweatshop labor.

Other research suggests that consumers rely on willful ignorance as a coping mechanism, in both search and memory. Ehrich and Irwin (2005) demonstrated willful ignorance in search, by showing that, as a way to avoid the emotional costs of considering ethical attribute information in purchase contexts, consumers choose not to request ethical attribute information. Without this information, there is no need for trade-offs between the ethical attribute and other important attributes, an especially appealing prospect for consumers who particularly care about the ethical issue. However, Ehrich and Irwin (2005) also show that consumers will use ethical attribute information if is available without request. Given that consumers avoid ethical information if they can, but use it if it is available, marketers of ethically produced goods might conclude that the solution to willful ignorance is simply to provide ethical attribute information to the consumer. More recent research suggests that this solution may not work – consumers also exhibit willful ignorance in memory (Reczek, Irwin, & Ehrich, 2015). In a series of four studies on memory for attributes, we and our colleague established that there is a systematic pattern to memory for ethical attribute information: consumers have better memory for good versus poor performance on ethical attributes (a pattern not found for attributes without ethical implications). In other words, consumers engage in a form of motivated forgetting (see Dalton & Huang, 2014, for an example of a different type of self-protective motivated forgetting) to forget information that a product is unethical, thus avoiding any potential conflict they might experience between their want and should selves when they encounter a desirable but unethical product. They experience no conflict because they have forgotten that the product is unethical.

A question that remains about many of these coping mechanisms is whether they are consciously or unconsciously adopted. Future research should address this issue, as understanding the nature of these coping mechanisms may help guide marketing interventions to reduce consumers' tendency to rely on them. Future research should also explore other specific coping mechanisms consumers may employ. We suspect that consumers may lessen the weight they assign to ethical values when faced with a clear conflict between ethicality and frugality or ethicality and strength in order to allow themselves to resolve the conflict in favor of buying, for example, the more frugal or more effective option, but no research has addressed this issue to our knowledge.

Marketplace Barriers to Ethical Consumption

In addition to internal psychological barriers to ethical consumption, there are also barriers to making ethical purchases that can be attributed to characteristics of the marketplace itself and to the interaction of these characteristics with elements of consumer psychology.

Past research has shown that the weight placed on ethical attributes relative to other attributes appears to be especially prone to context effects, the specific way in which people's values are elicited. In other words, it is possible to shift how important ethicality is to the final decision just by asking the question in a different way. For example, people weight ethical attributes more when selling versus buying and, in general, when giving things up versus getting them (Irwin, 1994), in choice versus pricing tasks (Irwin & Baron, 2001; Irwin, Slovic,

Lichtenstein, & McClelland, 1993), in separate versus joint evaluation (Irwin et al., 1993; Sunstein, Kahneman, Schkade, & Ritov, 2002), and when attributes are presented separately versus jointly in conjoint tasks (Irwin & Spira, 1997).

This previous research is very important to understanding ethical consumption because purchasing itself is a context. People go to a shopping environment usually to buy (not sell), and when they are in a shopping situation, they are considering obtaining something and not losing it. Likewise, purchasing involves a strong sense of the price of a good because the money exchange is how the purchase takes place. Finally, in today's marketplace, consumers arguably rarely evaluate a potential purchase option singly. Instead, they typically consider items as part of a broader consideration set and thus are most likely to make a joint evaluation. Taken together, all of these aspects of the retail space work to push consumers away from their ethical values.

In addition, the way a consideration set (i.e., the set of items chosen from the larger market set for further consideration; Desai & Hoyer, 2000; Nedungadi, 1990) is formed can influence the degree to which ethicality impacts the option ultimately chosen to be purchased. We (Irwin & Naylor, 2009) demonstrated that consumers express ethical values more when forming consideration sets via exclusion (i.e., identifying the items from a broader set that the consumer is not interested in purchasing) than when forming consideration sets via inclusion (i.e., identifying the items from a broader set that the consumer is interested in purchasing). Further, when study participants were asked to judge the behavior of another decision maker, they indicated that the expression of ethical attributes is more compatible with (i.e., more justifiable in and morally relevant to) exclusion versus inclusion modes (Irwin & Naylor 2009). Unfortunately, consideration set formation is likely typically accomplished by inclusion, the context that does not favor ethicality. Inclusion appears to be the default mode when forming consideration sets from larger assortments (Heller, Levin, & Goransson, 2002; Levin, Prosansky, Heller, & Brunick, 2001), and larger sets are the norm in most offline and online retail contexts. Collectively, this research on context effects suggests that expressing ethical values is more likely and/or easier in some types of decision making contexts than others, but that marketplace reality often reflects the contexts in which ethical values are less likely to be expressed.

Consumers' perceptions about whether the marketplace is fair and just can also influence whether they express their ethical values when making purchases, as demonstrated by White, MacDonnell, and Ellard's (2012) exploration of the role of justice perceptions in consumer interest in purchasing fair trade coffee. These researchers demonstrated that when consumers perceive high levels of injustice (i.e., coffee growers living in extreme poverty) and believe that avenues for justice restoration are uncertain (because only 20 percent of the money paid for coffee by consumers goes to the growers), they are less likely to buy fair trade goods. Many societal problems related to ethical values (e.g., poor treatment of workers, environmental destruction) are characterized by a high level of injustice, and opportunities to remedy these situations are often unclear or unavailable. White, MacDonnell, and Ellard's (2012) research suggests that the more hopeless consumers feel about their ability to make a difference in changing any given ethical problem, the less likely they are to try to do so by expressing their ethical values in their purchase decisions. Producers of ethically produced goods may be inadvertently exacerbating this problem by communicating high need without clearly communicating avenues for how this need can be addressed. When the marketplace does not provide clear avenues to remedy ethical problems, consumers may simply give up.

Finally, consumers face a confusing information environment when it comes to making ethical purchases. As an example, unscrupulous marketers may try to make products appear more environmentally sustainable than they actually are, a practice commonly known as "greenwashing" (Delmas & Burbano, 2011; Nelson & Peterka, 2010). Recognizing this issue, the Federal Trade Commission (FTC) recently revised their "Green Guides" for marketers of environmentally friendly products (Federal Trade Commission [FTC], 2012). While the FTC guidelines are "designed to help marketers ensure that the claims they make about the environmental attributes of their products are truthful and non-deceptive" (FTC, 2012), they are still fairly general in nature and are guidelines rather than legally enforceable standards. Compared to the regulatory environment for food product labeling (in which the Nutrition Labeling and Education Act of 1990 mandates the information that must be communicated on all food packaging intended for individual retail sale), the legal requirements for labeling ethically produced goods are much less clear.

As a result, consumers may not always know when a good is an ethical choice, even if they want to express their ethical values through their purchases. There are a multitude of terms, from "green" to "organic" to "free trade" that may have different meanings for different consumers, depending on their level of expertise with respect to these issues. Recent research suggests that this lack of knowledge about specific terms related to ethical products can be a significant barrier to purchase (Gleim et al., 2013). Underscoring the importance of a lack of information/knowledge, in a recent survey of 1,022 Americans conducted by Opinion Research Corporation, 65 percent of Americans said that having one seal or label for all green products would give them more confidence that they were buying green (*Business News Daily*, 2010). Although the "Fair Trade" certification has fairly universal acceptance (at least in some countries; e.g., Britain; Globescan, 2010), there is no universally accepted "green" label in the United States, which may be a barrier to the purchase of ethical products, particularly for those lacking expertise in this domain. Interestingly, in the same Opinion Research Corporation poll, more Americans (41 percent) indicated that they thought the primary enforcer of green product claims should be "a third-party certification system like the Good Housekeeping Seal," than thought the FTC should be responsible (26 percent) (*Business News Daily*, 2010).

Of course, reactions to labels may have some unintended consequences; as we outlined earlier, consumers may decide to ignore or forget label information.

Also, the addition of a label may denigrate the value of other ethical attributes because the consumer psychologically combines all of the ethical information into a "super-attribute" as either good or bad (Jongmans, Jolibert, & Irwin, 2014). Nevertheless, it makes sense for the government to enforce the provision of this information much as they do for food products and potentially for marketers of ethical products to develop their own labeling system. Retailers such as Whole Foods have arguably succeeded in large part because inclusion in the Whole Foods portfolio of products suggests a label of approval via the company's strict ethical standards.

Increasing Ethical Consumption: Strategies and Avenues for Future Research

Overcoming Psychological Barriers to Increase Ethical Purchases

Although past research has identified a number of serious barriers to the purchase of ethical goods, this research can also suggest ways that the main barriers we have identified can be addressed. For example, ethical attributes are often seen as conflicting with other important product attributes, but knowing this fact suggests that consumers should be more likely to purchase ethical products when this conflict is resolved for them in some way.

Past work on the sustainability liability (i.e., the assumption that ethical products are not as strong and the resulting detrimental effect on purchase intentions) has demonstrated that giving consumers explicit reassurances that they do not have to trade ethicality off with other attributes reduces the liability, increasing purchase intentions toward ethical options (Luchs et al., 2010; Ying-Ching & Chang's, 2012). Using an explicit strength claim on a green product's package or in an ad (e.g., "guaranteed strong and effective") means consumers no longer have to rely on the lay theory that "ethical = less effective" to infer a product's strength. If marketers are aware that consumers may be reluctant to trust that an ethical product performs well on a particular attribute (e.g., strength, effectiveness, value), then explicitly communicating information about that attribute can reduce the conflict that consumers might otherwise feel without any reassurances from the marketer. Of course, a major caveat to this recommendation is that the information communicated must be true; otherwise, the claims would serve to increase concerns about greenwashing and activate the consumers' schemer schema (Friestad & Wright, 1994) with respect to ethical products.

Interestingly, Gupta and Sen (2013) suggest that, with time, assurances about an ethical product's strength may not be necessary. They argue that consumers' beliefs about how firm resources are allocated will change from believing that the development of an ethical product is a zero sum game, so that making a product more ethical means making it of lower quality, to a more synergistic belief, where "allocation of resources [is] a win-win affair wherein the resources devoted to one actually reflect positively on the firm's ability to achieve the other" (p. 118). This type of widespread belief change seems possible in light of the many firms that now express a commitment to corporate social responsibility throughout their business practices. Whether and when this shift will occur is an interesting and open question. Exploring how consumer beliefs will evolve for firms that have a spotty and sometimes contradictory track record on ethical issues (e.g., Wal-Mart, which has industry-leading sustainability practices but whose treatment of workers is ethically questionable for many consumers) is a fruitful avenue for future research.

In addition to explicit reassurances about attributes that consumers do not want to trade off with ethicality, another potential path to resolving conflict between ethical values and other goals consumers have in the marketplace might be to remind consumers that making ethical purchases can be compatible with their other consumption-related goals. For example, Griskevicius, Tybur, and Van den Bergh (2010) have shown that some consumers choose green options for status motives. Other types of goals may also be fulfilled by being more ethical so that buying ethical products can be seen as not only benefiting an abstract entity like the environment or society, but also as benefiting the individual in some way. It is likely that these benefits are product category–specific, so that, for example, fashion categories may be seen as more modern if they are more environmental, food may be seen as more delicious if it is harvested in a special way that results in better treatment of workers, and electronics may be seen as more interesting design-wise if they are powered in a sustainable way. Already companies such as Tesla and Cadillac have begun touting their more expensive hybrid cars as proper status symbols for people who want to distinguish themselves from the crowd. Presenting ethical products as a "win-win" (with both personal benefits to the self and broader societal benefits) may prove to be the most effective strategy for marketers to help consumers resolve the conflict they might otherwise feel when considering trading off ethical and other attributes.

In addition to suggesting strategies designed to reduce conflict between ethical values and other marketplace goals, past research indicates another strategy that may be effective in increasing interest in ethical goods: strengthening the should self. According to classic work on cognitive dissonance (e.g., Festinger, 1957), inner conflict stemming from conflicting motivations can be reduced by bolstering one of the motivations so that the strength of the conflicting motivations is unequal and thus no longer dissonant. In the context of this chapter, bolstering the desire to be ethical can help it "win" over the desire to avoid the potentially depleting task of considering ethical issues when making a purchase. Past research suggests multiple ways that this can be accomplished. For example, Reczek, Irwin, and Ehrich (2015) show that priming consumers' more ethical should selves reduces willfully ignorant memory and helps people to remember negative ethical attribute information. We demonstrate two ways that this can be accomplished: (1) by having participants read a set of "ethical rules" that most consumers follow when purchasing; and (2) by reminding consumers that their purchases are relevant to their identity and therefore say something about who they are as people (e.g., how ethical they are).

Similarly, Peloza, White, and Shang (2013) demonstrate that heightening "self-accountability," which they define as "the desire to live up to a salient, internally held self-standard," leads consumers to prefer products promoted using ethical appeals over products promoted with appeals focused on other types of self-benefits. Self-accountability focuses on comparing one's internal standards to one's actual behavior but can also be thought of as a way to strengthen the activation of the should self since it focuses on internal "ought" standards and whether these are being met. In one of their studies, Peloza, White, and Shang (2013) show that the presence of others heightens self-accountability, which is consistent with a growing literature demonstrating that social influence can also be a powerful way to strengthen one's desire to behave consistently with one's more ethical self. Arguably, social norms–based messages (Goldstein, Cialdini, & Griskevicius, 2008; Schulze et al., 2007; White & Simpson, 2013), which communicate information about the actions of others as a way to change behavior, are another way to activate the should self, but they do so by drawing a contrast not between one's internal standards and actual behavior but between one's own behavior and that of others.

Although Goldstein, Cialdini, and Griskevicius's (2008) exploration of the effectiveness of social norms–based persuasive messages suggests that information about the behavior of those most relevant to the current situation (e.g., other guests who have stayed in the same hotel room) is most effective at encouraging a specific sustainable behavior (i.e., reusing the towels in one's hotel room), White, Simpson, and Argo (2014) demonstrate that even information about the behavior of out-groups can influence consumers to behave more ethically in some circumstances. White and colleagues (2014) demonstrate that when consumers are told about the positive sustainable actions of a dissociative out-group, they are more inclined to engage in the same behavior in public (vs. private) settings. Marketers might be able to profitably activate the should self via marketing communications, using this research (and future research) as a guide, but more research is needed to untangle exactly which type of others should be referenced in an appeal to make it most effective at changing behavior.

Other research suggests that making a commitment to behave ethically in advance of the actual behavior may also strengthen the should self so that it is activated at the time of behavior. Recent work by Baca-Motes and colleagues (2013) draws from the literature on commitment, self-signaling, and the principle of consistency to demonstrate that making a commitment to engage in a sustainable behavior can also successfully increase the odds that consumers engage in that behavior. In a field study, consumers who made a specific commitment to reuse towels when checking in to a hotel were over 25 percent more likely to hang at least one towel for reuse during their hotel stay. This work is notable compared to the research on social norms because this method appears to activate the should self without a focus on the behavior of others or even on one's internal standards for what constitutes good, moral behavior and relies instead simply on one's need to be consistent. Potential conflict between ethicality and other goals may be avoided if a commitment is made to express ethical values before a potential conflict between ethical values and other goals is encountered. It is not known as yet whether this type of precommitment can be effective in other ethical contexts in which the commitment and the action and potential conflict may be separated by both time and place. The hotel context explored by Baca-Motes and colleagues may be the ideal format for such interventions since the behavior (reusing towels during a hotel stay) is proximate to the commitment in terms of both time (at check-in for the hotel) and location (at the same hotel). Whether a pledge to engage in ethical purchasing behavior over time across different shopping environments would be effective at increasing purchases of ethical products remains an open empirical question.

Finally, recent research suggests that consumer response to ethical products can differ a great deal based on individual differences such as underlying green consumption values (Haws, Winterich, & Naylor, 2014), the importance the individual consumer places on the particular ethical issue (Kronrod, Grinstein, & Wathieu, 2012), and even the individual's political ideology as a liberal or conservative. For example, Kidwell, Farmer, and Hardesty (2013) tested two types of persuasive appeals designed to encourage recycling, appeals that were consistent with the underlying moral foundations of either liberals or conservatives. In both the lab and a field study, consumers were more persuaded by appeals that matched their own political affiliation. Understanding how these and other individual difference variables drive interest in purchasing green products as well as responses to different types of ethical appeals is an important avenue for future research, as this research collectively suggests that different segments of consumers may experience more or less or even different types of value conflict when considering ethical purchases.

Restructuring the Marketplace to Increase Ethical Purchases

Understanding the ways that characteristics of the marketplace interact with consumer psychology can help researchers identify ways in which the marketplace can be restructured to make it easier for consumers to express their most ethical selves. For example, given that we show that consumers more easily express ethical values in exclusion tasks than inclusions tasks(Irwin & Naylor, 2009), marketers might encourage consumers to take a more exclusionary approach to shopping. For example, grocery stores might create sections of their stores that feature only sustainable products, similar to free-standing retail stores that feature only fair trade goods. Advocacy groups can create shopping guides, such as the "cruelty-free" shopping guide produced by People for the Ethical Treatment of Animals (PETA). Such guidelines could help consumers "exclude" entire sections and retail spaces of products as they construct their consideration sets, resulting in greater emphasis on ethics. Although these types of specialty retail sections, free-standing stores, and ethical shopping guides do exist, they are not currently the norm in most retail environments.

Recall that we outlined the ways in which shopping is focused on price and how price therefore becomes primed by shopping in a way that could work against ethical choices. There are ways instead to prime ethicality for shoppers. Baca-motes and colleagues' (2013) work on commitment suggests that retailers, marketers, or advocacy groups could ask consumers to sign ethicality pledges. The more specific these pledges are, the more likely they are to be effective. For example, if Whole Foods asked seafood shoppers to sign a pledge to buy only sustainable seafood, consumers would potentially be more likely to avoid nonsustainable seafood options not only while shopping at Whole Foods but also when buying seafood at other retailers and when ordering seafood in restaurants. Marketers and advocacy groups must be careful, though, to communicate that signing such pledges or making other types of commitments to ethical purchases is likely to make a difference. Otherwise, if consumers do not feel like doing so is actually a path to addressing the issue in a fair and just manner, they may not be motivated to participate, consistent with White, MacDonnell, and Ellard's (2012) work on belief in justice in ethical contexts.

Our research with our colleague Kristine Ehrich on willful ignorance in search (Ehrich & Irwin, 2005) and memory (Reczek, Irwin, & Ehrich, 2015) also suggests that (1) ethical attributes need to be clearly displayed in retail contexts so that consumers do not have to search for them (and hence cannot choose to be willfully ignorant); and (2) that people need multiple reminders about ethical attributes during the purchase process, perhaps by displaying this information throughout a retail environment or consistently during an online shopping experience, in order to prevent motivated forgetting of negative ethical attribute information.

In fact, providing more information to consumers about ethical products in general is particularly important, as evidenced by consumer concerns about greenwashing. Similar to the work done in food labeling (Andrews, Netemeyer, & Burton, 1998; Howlett, Burton, Bates, & Huggins, 2009; Kozup, Creyer, & Burton, 2003), new academic work is needed to understand what types of labels or other product packaging cues are most effective at (1) communicating information about product ethicality and (2) at increasing ethical choices. Such research will be of interest not only to marketing managers but also to policy makers at the FTC. Academic research exploring the type of information most effective at communicating information that a product is sustainable suggests that verbal versus numeric cues and a greater number of cues versus a smaller number of cues are most effective (Gleim et al., 2013), but more work remains to be done in this area, including addressing how to best communicate information about other types of ethical attributes.

Related to labeling and consumer information is the more philosophical question of what drives consumer perceptions that a product is ethical. Gershoff and Frels (2015) have begun this work by exploring inferences of overall product greenness based on the greenness of a single attribute. Based on literature on categorization, these authors propose and find that consumers perceive a product with a central green attribute as "greener" than one that has a more peripheral green attribute. These findings probably extend to other types of ethical attributes, but there are likely attribute and category effects as well as interactions with other variables such as managerial intentions (i.e., whether the attribute is green by design or by a fortuitous coincidence; Newman, Gorlin, & Dhar, 2014). Future research could also focus on how different elements of production influence perceptions that a product is ethical. For example, are products that are produced using sustainable practices (e.g., using energy saving production equipment) considered more or less green than those that have a sustainable component (e.g., part or all of the product is made with recycled material)? Are products that can be recycled seen as more or less green than those made from materials that have already been recycled? These and myriad other questions about the exact determinants of what makes consumers see a given product as ethical or as more ethical than another ethical alternative remain open for future inquiry.

Future research should also explore the interplay between firm and brand perceptions of ethicality. Presumably brands from firms that are considered more ethical are also considered more ethical, which begs the question of what determines firm ethicality. We think this is a particularly interesting question given that a firm's ethicality can be judged across a broad range of actions, and firms may be ethical in some domains and not in others. As discussed previously, Wal-Mart is actively invested in increasing sustainability throughout its supply chain. For example, it has partnered with the Environmental Defense Fund to reduce greenhouse gas emissions (Wal-mart, 2014). However, Wal-Mart's labor practices have, at times, been roundly criticized, even sparking protests (Greenhouse, 2012). How does a consumer who cares about both the environment and labor practices interpret this information to form an overall impression of Wal-Mart's ethicality? And how does this global impression influence a consumer's perceptions of the ethicality of the products on Wal-Mart's shelves? These types of questions must be answered as consumers come to expect more from firms than just being green or just treating workers fairly.

Suggestions for Future Theoretical and Practical Work

Throughout this chapter to this point, we have focused on the "should" aspects of human behavior that are linked to ethical consumption, the behaviors that appeal to the better angels of our nature. There are other types of "angel" behaviors that would not usually be considered ethical, specifically behaviors having to do with health (e.g., eating sensibly, working out regularly, flossing one's teeth) and safety (e.g., purchasing automobiles with airbags, practicing safe sex). These types of behaviors have received a great deal of attention because of their obvious public health implications, with overeating being especially popular as a topic in marketing (e.g., Van Ittersum & Wansink, 2012; Wansink & Chandon, 2014).

It is not clear whether health and safety "should" behaviors respond the same way to contextual variables as ethical behaviors do and, in turn, whether health and safety research can be applied fruitfully to ethical attributes. There is some indication of overlap. Environmental goods show a buying or selling price (and/or a gain/loss frame) discrepancy, with the "right thing" being favored more in selling and loss modes (Irwin, 1994) than in buying and gain modes. People are unlikely to agree to accept pollution, for example, for any amount of money even if they will not pay (or pay very much) to prevent pollution. Safety (e.g., Luce et al., 2000) and health (e.g., Chapman & Johnson, 1995) goods show the same pattern: people will demand a large amount of money to give up health or safety even when they will not pay much money to gain health or safety. Theoretical work on the cause of gain/loss preference reversals suggests that the same general processes – such as the activation of responsibility (Irwin, 1994), construal level (Irmak, Wakslak, & Trope, 2013), and differential focus on affect (e.g., Peters, Slovic, & Gregory, 2003) – would logically apply across all "should" considerations. On the other hand, it is likely that ethical considerations, which by definition do not benefit the self, activate some different psychological processes from health and safety considerations. There is very little current work on this issue, with the exception of a recent working paper (Berman & Small, 2015) that suggests that there may be differences in present versus future goals across types of "should" attributes.

Likewise, it bears mentioning that there is also a great deal of research on charitable donations, an issue that logically seems closely related to ethical consumption. People show many biases in how they view victims in need of help; they judge victims of catastrophic losses as more deserving than victims of chronic diseases (Small, 2010); favor identifiable victims over statistical victims (Small & Lowenstein, 2003); and, in general, respond with more care if the victims activate emotional responses (Slovic, Finucane, Peters, & McGregor, 2002). Intuitively it seems that the desire to purchase ethical goods must be linked to the same desire to help that drives charitable donations, but how this link should be made is as yet unclear. Our sense from looking at the whole of the ethical consumption literature is that many of the structural issues in the marketplace that push people away from ethical consumption may be absent in charitable donation contexts, and that the charitable context itself might be susceptible to unique counterintuitive contextual biases.

Some of the biases inherent in ethical consumption are driven by the sense among consumers that money and morality are incompatible. Charitable organizations and social marketing have been shown to suffer from a similar consumer belief. Consumers have stereotypes about for-profit firms and non-profits that suggest that those whose primary motive is to provide aid or to accomplish a societal good are seen as fundamentally different from those whose motive is profit (Aaker, Vohs, & Mogilner, 2010). Likewise, if profit concerns are linked to organizations that people feel should be driven by ethics, such as churches and pharmaceutical companies, then consumers tend to think badly of the organizations and find them to be less ethical (McGraw, Schwartz, & Tetlock, 2012). In general, the monetization of issues that people find morally important often makes them very angry (e.g., Lichtenstein, Gregory, & Irwin, 2007). This mechanism works for people, too: a person who behaves ethically combined with behaving in a self-interested way is actually rated as less ethical than a person who behaves only in a self-interested way (Newman & Cain, 2014). The incompatibility of money with ethics is a real concern both for marketers of ethical goods and for charitable enterprises. It is not clear how best to remove this barrier, but it is clear that many of the biases in consumer behavior where ethics are concerned are driven by the barrier. It is possible that time and consistently ethical actions by firms may provide a solution. If consumers consistently observe companies earning a profit while acting in the best interest of all of their stakeholders across a variety of domains, then the (probably unconscious) belief in an incompatibility between money and ethics may be diminished. In the mean-time, understanding this bias could help marketers offset the perhaps surpris-ingly negative reaction consumers have to the idea of making a profit and serving moral principles.

Summary

Despite the availability of ethical consumption options across the consumption cycle, consumers do not always choose ethical options even when they care about the underlying ethical issue. In this chapter, we have explored why even consumers who care about a given ethical issue do not necessarily make purchases that reflect their values, and we outline some of the main psychological drivers behind this inconsistency.

As we have shown, many of the barriers are natural components of human behavior, the structure of the marketplace, or both. People understandably feel conflict between doing the right thing and avoiding doing the right thing, because the right thing is often tedious, time consuming, resource depleting, and less fun. The marketplace is set up with a context that makes sense for purchasing, with a heavy emphasis on price (after all, we pay with price, not any other attributes), on comparing across many alternatives at once, on gaining versus losing, and on including into the set instead of excluding. Unfortunately, all of these contexts make it less likely that people will overcome their resistance to their "should" self and make the ethical purchase. We hope that this outline of relevant research on this topic will underscore these points and help market-ers avoid the despair that might come from seeing the lower market share numbers for ethical products. The lack of overall market share does not indicate a lack of consumer interest in being ethical. People in the United States alone gave over $400 billion dollars to charity in 2013 (White, 2014). Companies such as Toms, whose primary mission is to provide shoes for the needy, can thrive in the marketplace (e.g., with an estimated $250–300 million dollars in revenue in 2013; Chu, 2013). People do have ethical goals; the key is for marketers to help them accomplish these goals.

We expect research on ethical consumption to become increasingly popular and important as more marketers and consumers express interest in ethical options in the marketplace. However, this research should not be restricted to ethical purchases. We conclude this chapter with a reminder that ethical consumption includes ethical usage of products and other resources (which may include choosing not to buy products but to rent or share them instead), as well as ethical options for how to dispose of possessions once they are no longer needed. It is possible that ethical consumption habits after purchase could have as much of an impact as ethical choices in the marketplace.

References

Aaker, J., Vohs, K. D., & Mogilner, C. (2010). Nonprofits are seen as warm and for-profits as competent: Firm stereotypes matter. *Journal of Consumer Research*, *37*(2), 224–237.

Andrews, J. C., Netemeyer, R. G., & Burton, S. (1998). Consumer generalization of nutrient content claims in advertising. *Journal of Marketing*, *62*(4), 62–75.

Baca-Motes, K., Brown, A., Gneezy, A., Keenan, E. A., & Nelson, L. D. (2013). Commitment and behavior change: Evidence from the field. *Journal of Consumer Research*, *39*(5), 1070–1084.

Bandura, A. (1999). Moral disengagement in the perpetration of inhumanities. *Personality and Social Psychology Review*, *3*(3), 1193–1209.

Bandura, A., Barbaranelli, C., Caprara, G. V., & Pastorelli, C. (1996). Mechanisms of moral disengagement in the exercise of moral agency. *Journal of Personality and Social Psychology*, *71*(2), 364–374.

Barnes, C. M., Schaubroeck, J. M., Huth, M., & Ghumman, S. (2011). Lack of sleep and unethical behavior. *Organizational Behavior and Human Decision Processes*, *115* (2), 169–180.

Baron, J., & Spranca, M. (1997). Protected values. *Organizational Behavior and Human Decision Processes*, *70*(1), 1–16.

Batson, D. C., Thompson, E. R., Seuferling, G., Whitney, H., & Strongman, J. A. (1999). Moral hypocrisy: Appearing moral to oneself without being so. *Journal of Personality and Social Psychology*, *77*(3), 525–537.

Baumeister, R. F., Muraven, M., & Tice, D. M. (2000). Ego depletion: A resource model of volition, self-regulation, and controlled processing. *Social Cognition*, *18*, 130–150.

Bazerman, M. H., Tenbrunsel, A. E., & Wade-Benzoni, K. (1998). Negotiating with yourself and losing: Making decisions with competing internal preferences. *Academy of Management Review*, *23*(2), 225–241.

Berman, J. Z., & Small, D. A. (2015). Judgments of virtue in consumer behavior. Working Paper.

Bonini, S., & Oppenheim, J. (2008). Cultivating the green consumer. *Stanford Social Innovation Review*, *6*(4), 56–61.

Business News Daily (2010). Men less like to buy into "green" movement. Retrieved from www.businessnewsdaily.com/479-men-less-likely-to-buy-into-green-movement.html.

Catlin, J. R., & Wang, Y. (2013). Recycling gone bad: When the option to recycle increases resource consumption. *Journal of Consumer Psychology*, 23(1), 122–127.

Chandon, P., Wansink, B., & Laurent, G. (2000). A benefit congruency framework of sales promotion effectiveness. *Journal of Marketing*, 64(4), 65–81.

Chapman, G. B., & Johnson, E. J. (1995). Preference reversals in monetary and life expectancy evaluations. *Organizational Behavior & Human Decision Processes*, 62(3), 300–317.

Chu, J. (2013). Toms sets out to sell a lifestyle, not just shoes. *Fast Company*. Retrieved from www.fastcompany.com/3012568/blake-mycoskie-toms.

Dalton, A. N., & Huang, L. (2014). Motivated forgetting in response to social identity threat. *Journal of Consumer Research*, 40(6), 1017–1038.

Delmas, M. A., & Burbano, V. C. (2011). The drivers of greenwashing. *California Management Review*, 54(1), 64–87.

Desai, K. K., & Hoyer, W. D. (2000). Descriptive characteristics of memory-based consideration sets: Influence of usage occasion frequency and usage location familiarity. *Journal of Consumer Research*, 27(3), 309–323.

Dodds, W. B., Monroe, K. B., & Grewal, D. (1991). Effects of price, brand, and store information on buyers' product evaluations. *Journal of Marketing Research*, 28(3), 307–319.

Ehrich, K. R., & Irwin, J. R. (2005). Willful ignorance in the request for product attribute information. *Journal of Marketing Research*, 42(3), 266–277.

Federal Trade Commission (2012). FTC issues revised green guides. Retrieved from www.ftc.gov/opa/2012/10/greenguides.shtm.

Festinger, L. (1957). *A Theory of Cognitive Dissonance*. La Jolla, CA: Stanford University Press.

Friestad, M., & Wright, P. (1994). The persuasion knowledge model: How people cope with persuasion attempts. *Journal of Consumer Research*, 21(1), 1–31.

Furnham, A. (1988). *Lay Theories: Everyday Understanding of Problems in the Social Sciences*. Oxford: Pergamon.

Gardiner, B. (2010). Upcycling evolves from recyclying. Retrieved from www.nytimes.com/2010/11/04/business/energy-environment/04iht-rbogup.html?pagewanted=all&_r=0.

Gershoff, A. D., & Frels, J. K. (2015). What makes it green? The role of centrality of green attributes in evaluations of the greenness of products. *Journal of Marketing*, 79(1), 97–110.

Gershoff, A. D., & Irwin, J. R. (2012). Why not choose green? Consumer decision making for environmentally friendly products. In P. Bansal & A. J. Hoffman (eds.), *The Oxford Handbook of Business and the Natural Environment* (pp. 366–383). New York: Oxford University Press.

Gino, F., Schweitzer, M. E., Mead, N. L., & Ariely, D. (2011). Unable to resist temptation: How self-control depletion promotes unethical behavior. *Organizational Behavior and Human Decision Processes*, 115(2), 191–203.

Gleim, M. R., Smith, J. S., Andrews, D. & Cronin, Jr., J. J. (2013). Against the green: A multi-method examination of the barriers to green consumption. *Journal of Retailing*, 89(1), 44–61.

Globescan (2010). British sense of fair play helps workers in the developing world. Retrieved from www.globescan.com/news_archives/fairtrade_consu mer/.

Goldstein, N., Cialdini, R. B., & Griskevicius, V. (2008). A room with a viewpoint: Using social norms to motivate environmental conservation in hotels. *Journal of Consumer Research*, *35*(4), 472–482.

Greenhouse, S. (2012). Wal-Mart labor protests grow, organizers say. *New York Times*. Retrieved from www.nytimes.com/2012/10/10/business/organizers-say-wal-mart-labor-protests-spread.html.

Griskevicius, V., Tybur, J. M., & Van den Bergh, B. (2010). Going green to be seen: Status, reputation, and conspicuous conservation. *Journal of Personality and Social Psychology*, *98*(3), 392–404.

Gupta, R., & Sen, S. (2013). The effect of evolving resource synergy beliefs on the intentions-behavior discrepancy in ethical consumption. *Journal of Consumer Psychology*, *23*(1), 114–121.

Haidt, J. (2007). The new synthesis in moral psychology. *Science*, *316*, 998–1002.

Haws, K. L., Naylor, R. W., Coulter, R. A., & Bearden, W. O. (2012). Keeping it all without being buried alive: Understanding product retention tendency. *Journal of Consumer Psychology*, *22*(2), 224–326.

Haws, K. L., Winterich, K. P., & Naylor, R. W. (2014). Seeing the world through GREEN-tinted glasses: Green consumption values and responses to environmentally friendly products. *Journal of Consumer Psychology*, *24*(3), 336–354.

Heller, D., Levin, I. P, & Goransson, M. (2002). Selection of strategies for narrowing choice options: Antecedents and consequences. *Organizational Behavior and Human Decision Processes*, *89*(2), 1194–1213.

Howlett, E., Burton, S., Bates, K., & Huggins, K. (2009). Coming to a restaurant near you? Potential consumer response to nutrition information disclosures on menus. *Journal of Consumer Research*, *36*(3), 494–503.

Irmak, C., Wakslak, C. J., & Trope, Y. (2013). Selling the forest, buying the trees: The effect of construal level on seller-buyer price discrepancy. *Journal of Consumer Research*, *40*(2), 284–297.

Irwin, J. R. (1994). Buying/selling price preference reversals: Preference for environmental changes in buying versus selling modes. *Organizational Behavior and Human Decision Processes*, *60*(3), 431–457.

Irwin, J. R., & Baron, J. (2001). Response mode effects and moral values. *Organizational Behavior and Human Decision Processes*, *84*(2), 177–197.

Irwin, J. R., & Naylor, R. W. (2009). Ethical decisions and response mode compatibility: Weighting of ethical attributes in consideration sets formed by excluding versus including product alternatives. *Journal of Marketing Research*, *46*(2), 234–246.

Irwin, J. R., Slovic, P., Lichtenstein, S., & McClelland, G. H. (1993). Preference reversals and the measurement of environmental values. *Journal of Risk and Uncertainty*, *6*(1), 1–13.

Irwin, J. R., & Spira, J. S. (1997). Anomalies in the values for consumer goods with environmental attributes. *Journal of Consumer Psychology*, *6*(4), 339–363.

Jongmans, E., Jolibert, A., & Irwin, J. R. (2014). Toujours plus, toujours mieux? Effet contre-intuitif de l'évaluation des attributs environnementaux du produit par le consommateur. *Recherche et Applications en Marketing*, *29*(3), 10–33.

Kidwell, B., Farmer, R. A., & Hardesty, D. M. (2013). Getting liberals and conservatives to go green: Political ideology and congruent appeals. *Journal of Consumer Research*, *40*(2), 350–367.

Kohlberg, L. (1984). *The Psychology of Moral Development: The Nature and Validity of Moral Stages*. San Francisco: Harper and Row.

Kouchaki, M., & Smith, I. H. (2014). The morning morality effect: The influence of time of day on unethical behavior. *Psychological Science*, *25*, 95–102.

Kozup, J. C., Creyer, E. H., & Burton, S. (2003). Making healthful food choices: The influence of health claims and nutrition information on consumers' evaluations of packaged food products and restaurant menu items. *Journal of Marketing*, *67*(2), 19–34.

Kronrod, A., Grinstein, A., & Wathieu, L. (2012). Go green!! Should environmental messages be so assertive?? *Journal of Marketing*, *76*(1), 95–102.

Lamberton, C. P., & Rose, R. (2012). Yours, mine and ours: An investigation of consumers' propensity to participate in commercial sharing systems. *Journal of Marketing*, July, 109–125.

Lastovicka, J. L., Bettencourt, L. A., Hughner, R. S., & Kuntze, R. J. (1999). Lifestyle of the tight and frugal: Theory and measurement. *Journal of Consumer Research*, *26*(1), 85–98.

Levin, I. P., Prosansky, C. M., Heller, D., & Brunick, B. M. (2001). Prescreening of choice options in "positive" and "negative" decision-making tasks. *Journal of Behavioral Decision Making*, *14*(4), 279–293.

Lichtenstein, S., Gregory, R., & Irwin, J. R. (2007). What's bad is easy: Taboo values, affect, and cognition. *Judgment and Decision Making*, *2*(3), 169–188.

Loewenstein, G. (2006). Out of control: Visceral influences on behavior. *Organizational Behavior and Human Decision Processes*, *65*(3), 272–292.

Luce, M. F. (1998). Choosing to avoid: Coping with negatively emotion-laden consumer decision. *Journal of Consumer Research*, *24*(4), 409–433.

Luce, M. F., Payne, J. W., & Bettman, J. R. (2000). Coping with unfavorable attribute values in choice. *Organizational Behavior and Human Decision Processes*, *81*(2), 274–299.

Luchs, M., Naylor, R. W., Irwin, J. R., & Raghunathan, R. (2010). The sustainability liability: Potential negative effects of ethicality on product preference. *Journal of Marketing*, *74*(5), 18–31.

McGraw, P. A., Schwartz, J. A., & Tetlock, P. E. (2012). From the commercial to the communal: Reframing taboo trade-offs in religious and pharmaceutical marketing. *Journal of Consumer Research*, *39*(1), 157–173.

McGraw, A. P., & Tetlock, P. E. (2005). Taboo trade-offs, relational framing, and the acceptability of exchanges. *Journal of Consumer Psychology*, *15*(1), 2–15.

Milkman, K. L., Rogers, T., & Bazerman, M. H. (2008). Harnessing our inner angels and demons: What we have learned about want/should conflicts and how that knowledge can help us reduce short-sighted decision making. *Perspectives on Psychological Science*, *3*(4), 324–338.

Mintel (2014). Marketing to the green consumer. Retrieved from http://store.mintel.com/marketing-to-the-green-consumer-us-march-2014.

Molden, D. C., & Dweck, C. S. (2006). Finding "meaning" in psychology: A lay theories approach to self-regulation, social perception, and social development. *American Psychologist*, *61*(3), 192–203.

Nedungadi, P. (1990). Recall and consumer consideration sets: Influencing choice without altering brand evaluations. *Journal of Consumer Research*, *17*(3), 263–276.

Nelson, G., & Peterka, A. (2010). FTC proposes crackdown on "greenwashing." *New York Times*, October 6.

Newman, G. E. & Cain, D. A. (2014). Tainted altruism: When doing some good is evaluated as worse than doing no good at all. *Psychological Science*, *25*(3), 648–655.

Newman, G. E., Gorlin, M., & Dhar, R. (2014). When going green backfires: How firm intentions shape the evaluation of socially beneficial. Working Paper.

Nielsen (2013). 50% of global consumers surveyed willing to pay more for goods, services from socially responsible companies, up from 2011. Retrieved from www.nielsen.com/us/en/press-room/2013/nielsen-50-percent-of-global-con sumers-surveyed-willing-to-pay-more-fo.html.

Paharia, N., Vohs, K. D., & Deshpandé, R. (2013). Sweatshop labor is wrong unless the shoes are cute: Cognition can both help and hurt moral motivated reasoning. *Organizational Behavior and Human Decision Processes*, *121*(1), 81–88.

Peloza, J., White, K., & Shang, J. (2013). Good and guilt free: The role of self-accountability in influencing preferences for products with ethical attributes. *Journal of Marketing*, *77*(1), 104–119.

Peters, E., Slovic, P., & Gregory, R. (2003). The role of affect in the WTA/WTP disparity. *Journal of Behavioral Decision Making*, *16*(4), 309–330.

Phipps, M., & Brace-Govan, J. (2011). From right to responsibility: Sustainable change in water consumption. *Journal of Public Policy and Marketing*, *30*(2), 203–219.

Prothero, A., Dobscha, S., Freund, J., Kilbourne, W. E., Luchs, M. G., Ozanne, L., & Thøgersen, J. (2011). Sustainable consumption: Opportunities for consumer research and public policy. *Journal of Public Policy and Marketing*, *30*(1), 31–38.

Reczek, R. W., Irwin, J. R., & Ehrich, K. R. (2015). That's not how I remember it: Willfully ignorant memory for ethical product attribute information. Working Paper.

Redden, J. P., & Haws, K. L. (2013). Healthy satiation: The role of decreasing desire in effective self-control. *Journal of Consumer Research*, *39*(5), 1100–1114.

Ritov, I., & Baron, J. (1999). Protected values and omission bias. *Organizational Behavior and Human Decision Processes*, *79*(2), 79–94.

Schulze, P. W., Nolan, J. M., Cialdini, R. B., Goldstein, N. J., & Griskevicius, V. (2007). The constructive, destructive, and reconstructive power of social norms. *Psychological Science*, *18*(5), 429–434.

Slovic, P., Finucane, M., Peters, E., & MacGregor, D. G. (2002). The affect heuristic. in T. Gilovich, D. Griffin, & D. Kahneman (eds.), *Heuristics and Biases: The Psychology of Intuitive Judgment* (pp. 397–420). New York: Cambridge University Press.

Small, D. A. (2010). Reference-dependent sympathy. *Organizational Behavior and Human Decision Processes*, *112*, 151–160.

Small, D. A., & Loewenstein, G. (2003). Helping "a" victim or helping "the" victim: Altruism and identifiability. *Journal of Risk and Uncertainty*, *26*(1), 5–16.

Sunstein, C. R., Kahneman, D., Schkade, D. A., & Ritov, I. (2002). Predictably incoherent judgments. *Stanford Law Review*, *54*(6), 1153–1215.

Tetlock, P. E., Kristel, O. E., & Elson, B. S. (2000). The psychology of the unthinkable: Taboo trade-offs, forbidden base rates, and heretical counterfactuals. *Journal of Personality and Social Psychology, 78*(5), 853–870.

Trudel, R., & Argo, J. J. (2013). The effect of product size and form distortion on consumer recycling behavior. *Journal of Consumer Research, 40*(4), 632–643.

Trudel, R., & Cotte, J. (2009). Does it pay to be good? *MIT Sloan Management Review, 50*(2), 61–68.

Van Ittersum, K., & Wansink, B. (2012). Plate size and color suggestibility: The Delbouef illusion's bias on serving and eating behavior. *Journal of Consumer Research, 39*(2), 215–228.

Verplanken, B., & Holland, R. W. (2002). Motivated decision making: Effects of activation and self-centrality of values on choices and behavior. *Journal of Personality and Social Psychology, 82*(3), 434–447.

Wal-Mart (2014). The sustainability index. Retrieved from http://corporate.walmart.com/global-responsibility/environment-sustainability/sustainability-index.

Wansink, B., & Chandon, P. (2014). Slim by design: Redirecting the accidental drivers of mindless overeating. *Journal of Consumer Psychology, 24*(3), 413–431.

Wansink, B., Kent, R. J., & Hoch, S. J. (1998). An anchoring and adjustment model of purchase quantity decisions. *Journal of Marketing Research, 35*(1), 71–81.

Wells, W. (1993). Discovery-oriented consumer research. *Journal of Consumer Research, 19*(4), 489–503.

White, K., MacDonnell, R., & Ellard, J. H. (2012). Belief in a just world: Consumer intentions and behaviors toward ethical products. *Journal of Marketing, 76*(1), 103–118.

White, K., & Simpson, B. (2013). When do (and don't) normative appeals influence sustainable consumer behaviors. *Journal of Marketing, 77*(2), 78–95.

White, K., Simpson, B., & Argo, J. J. (2014). The motivating role of dissociative outgroups in encouraging positive consumer behaviors. *Journal of Marketing Research, 51*(4), 433–447.

White, R. (2014). U.S. charitable giving jumped 13% in 2013 to a record, report says. *Los Angeles Times,* January 13. Retrieved from http://articles.latimes.com/2014/jan/13/business/la-fi-mo-charitable-donations-record-2013-americans-20140113.

Ying-Ching, L., & Chang, C. A. (2012). Double standard: The role of environmental consciousness in green product usage. *Journal of Marketing, 76*(5), 125–134.

20 Government Efforts to Aid Consumer Well-Being

Understanding Federal Health Warnings and Disclosures

Jeremy Kees, Scot Burton, and J. Craig Andrews

Many products marketed in the United States and around the world can cause harm to consumers if misused. Of even greater concern, some products, such as combustible tobacco, can be inherently harmful to consumers even when used as intended (CDC, 2014a). Since the emergence of the modern-day Federal Trade Commission (FTC) and Food and Drug Administration (FDA) in the 1930s, the U.S. government has enacted legislation and regulations that help to protect consumers through information disclosures and/or warnings to identify potential risks. Laws and regulations involving consumer protection are directly related to the provision of objective and truthful information to consumers and how they, in turn, utilize this information. These laws are designed to prevent organizations from engaging in deceptive or unfair business practices and to help protect the rights of consumers. For example, in the United States, agencies such as the FDA, FTC, Consumer Product Safety Commission (CPSC), Federal Communications Commission (FCC), and others establish and enforce regulations that help to protect consumers. As part of this regulation, agencies often require marketers to provide disclosures or warnings on packaging or at the point of purchase, particularly for products in which safety or public health is an issue, such as for food, tobacco, and prescription drugs.

Federal agencies make decisions regarding whether or not a warning or disclosure is appropriate and how such information should be presented to consumers. To make these decisions, agencies require a clear understanding of how consumers acquire, process, and use warning and/or disclosure information. Furthermore, federal agencies take into account consumers' initial beliefs and knowledge regarding the product, potential individual differences among consumers, economic costs and benefits, and situational moderators.

At any point in time, agencies may be deluged with hundreds of current or emerging questions that present opportunities for consumer research. However, due to time and resource constraints, existing regulations and court decisions, and filing requirements for new regulations (e.g., Office of Management and Budget; *Federal Register* posting), the federal agencies are only able to address a small fraction of these questions and issues that often have important implications for consumer health and well-being. This situation therefore creates both an important need and rich opportunity for consumer researchers. In this chapter, we first introduce conceptual frameworks for the study of warnings and disclosures. We also review recent research on critical topical domains. We also highlight areas that offer substantial opportunity and need for additional study.[1]

Conceptual Frameworks for Studying Warnings and Disclosures

Several well-established information processing models can serve as useful guides for government agencies making decisions about the design of warnings and disclosures and the evaluation of intended and unintended outcomes for consumers and marketers. For instance, the Transtheoretical Model (i.e., "Stages of Change") (cf. Prochaska & DiClemente, 1983) measures one's progression through precontemplation, contemplation, preparation, action, maintenance, and possible relapse stages as a result of interventions to reduce product addictions (e.g., to nicotine, alcohol, prescription drugs, and other drugs). Similarly, Protection Motivation Theory (cf. Rogers, 1975) posits that we respond to interventions to change our behavior based on the perceived severity of a threatening event, the perceived probability of the occurrence (vulnerability), the efficacy of the recommended preventive behavior to reduce our risk, and our perceived ability to undertake the recommended preventive behavior (self-efficacy). These models have been useful in understanding situations in which the warning or disclosure presents an impending threat as part of the counterpersuasion process. However, sometimes warnings and disclosures can be beneficial even when they do not present an explicit impending threat directly to consumers. Thus, a broader model of consumer information processing may be more appropriate for the study of disclosures and warnings.

Perhaps the most broadly applicable framework to the study of warnings and disclosures is McGuire's Steps in Information Processing (1980). In this model, McGuire offers a helpful set of output variables into which effects on warnings and disclosures can be categorized: exposure, perception (attention), comprehension, agreement (attitude change), retention, retrieval, decision making (intentions), and action (behavior). These outcomes are specified by McGuire (1980) in his Communication-Persuasion Matrix and also include the following input variables: source, message, channel, receiver, and destination. More recently, the "Logic Model" (cf. Burke, 2007) has applied aspects of communication variables as inputs and information processing steps as outputs

---

1 Interested readers are referred to earlier and more detailed reviews of general warnings and disclosures research (cf. Andrews, 2011; Argo & Main, 2004; Bettman, Payne, & Staelin, 1986; Cox, Wogalter, Stokes, & Murff, 1997; Morris, Mazis, & Barofsky, 1980; Stewart & Martin, 1994), as our focus is on the application of federal agency health warnings and disclosures to the most current public policy issues.

and outcomes in planning and evaluation activities by federal and funding agencies. A similar, yet more succinct, model is Wogalter's (2006) Communication-Human Information Processing (C-HIP) Model. This is a helpful, alternative framework for considering public policy issues involving warnings and disclosures and for understanding their effects.

Based on these theoretical frameworks, we present a "Model of Consumer Responses to Warnings and Disclosures" in Figure 20.1 that identifies important outcome variables to consider when designing warning and disclosure programs. These include receiver outcome variables that are based on prior information processing and persuasion frameworks (e.g., Burke, 2007; McGuire, 1980; Petty & Cacioppo, 1986; Rogers, 1975; Wogalter, 2006). In addition, we identify specific individual and situational variables (e.g., prior expectations, complexity of choice, experience with the product, shopping environment) that have proven to be important in the disclosure and warning literature. Given this conceptual lens, we now examine graphic tobacco warnings, nutrition disclosures, and other federal agency applications of warnings and disclosures utilizing aspects of our model.

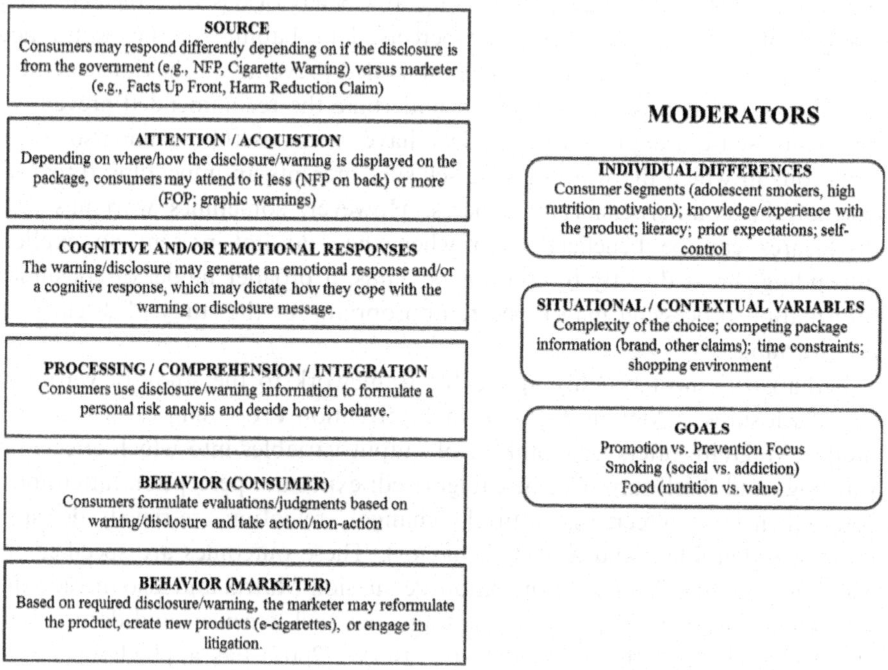

Figure 20.1 *A Model of Consumer Responses to Warnings and Disclosures.*
Note: The model is adapted from the following information processing and persuasion models: Logic model (Burke, 2007); Communication-Persuasion Model (McGuire, 1980); Protection Motivation Theory (Rogers, 1975); Elaboration Likelihood Model (Petty & Cacioppo, 1986); and the Communication-Human Information Processing (C-HIP) Model (Wogalter, 2006). The moderators identified represent a subset of the broad array of possible conceptual and practical moderators researchers may examine.

Tobacco – Established Products and New Frontiers

In the twentieth century, 100 million people died worldwide from tobacco-related diseases, and approximately 8 million deaths due to tobacco use are expected annually by 2030 (CDC, 2014a; Jha, 2009). In the United States, it has been fifty years since the first Surgeon General report on the health effects of smoking. Shortly after, in 1965, Congress passed the Federal Cigarette Labeling and Advertising Act (FCLAA), which required health warnings on all cigarette packages. Despite five decades of government regulation designed to warn consumers about the dangers of tobacco use, tobacco remains the leading cause of preventable disease and death in the United States, resulting in more than 480,000 deaths per year (DHHS, 2014). Along with antitobacco media campaigns, taxation, and restrictions on tobacco marketing, on-package warnings are an important mechanism to help curb tobacco use. Given the worldwide push for stronger and more graphic cigarette warning labels, and the rapidly changing regulatory environment for alternative tobacco products, tobacco is an important and fruitful area to study disclosures and warnings.

This section begins with a discussion of the most dangerous form of tobacco, combustible cigarettes, and the role that warnings play in discouraging cigarette smoking. Next, we will address alternative tobacco products (i.e., electronic cigarettes) and the role that disclosures and warnings play for these potentially "modified risk" tobacco products. Research needs are identified, and given the rapidly changing (and controversial) regulatory environment for tobacco, there are excellent opportunities to contribute to this very important area of study.

Cigarettes and Graphic Health Warnings

In 2009, Congress passed the Family Smoking Prevention and Tobacco Control Act (FSPTCA), which put tobacco legislation under the FDA's purview for the first time in American history (FSPTCA, 2009). The law also mandated the use of larger, more prominent graphic health warnings (GHWs) on cigarette packages. This law would have marked the first change in cigarette warnings in the United States since warnings were first required on cigarette packages in 1965 by the FCLAA. However, in 2012, a federal appellate court affirmed a lower court's decision to strike down the proposed rule. The court ruled that the new graphic warnings proposed by the FDA violated corporate free speech rights and that the FDA had failed to provide "a shred of evidence" that the new graphic warnings would reduce smoking rates. Yet, others have countered this assertion based on the existing research evidence on GHWs (Myers, 2013). While graphic cigarette warnings have been put "on hold" in the United States, some fifty-eight countries worldwide, covering about one-third of the world's population, have adopted graphic warnings since Canada became the first country to require them in 2000 (Hammond et al., 2004; World Health Organization, 2014). Some examples of these graphic health warnings are shown in Figure 20.2.

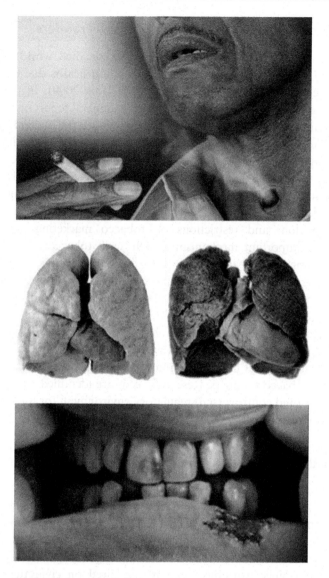

Figure 20.2 *Examples of Graphic Health Warnings.*

To date, there has been considerable research on the effects of GHWs (cf. Myers, 2013) that address a wide variety of outcomes in our model (see Figure 20.1). For example, in one of the first studies conducted after GHWs were required in Canada, Hammond and colleagues (2004) found that almost all Canadian smokers (91 percent) had read the warning labels and demonstrated a thorough knowledge of their content. A strong positive relationship was then observed between a measure of cognitive processing and smokers' intentions to quit and later cessation behavior. Eye-tracking studies have shown positive effects on viewing of the graphic warning text and dwell time in cigarette ads (Strasser et al., 2012). Other GHW eye-tracking research shows greater attention toward health warnings compared to brand information when shown on plain packs (i.e., without the colored logo associated with the brand name) versus regular branded packs, with effects observed among nonsmokers and weekly smokers, but not daily smokers (Munafo, Roberts, Bauld, & Leonards, 2011). Yet, interestingly, Maynard and colleagues (2014) found in an eye-tracking study that regular smokers fixated more on the branding rather than the health warning. This bias was smaller, but still evident, for "blank packs," where smokers preferentially attended to the blank region over the health warnings.

Other GHW research has examined further processing of the warnings beyond attention in experimental (causal) research. For example, using adult smokers from the United States and Canada, Kees, Burton, Andrews, and Kozup (2006) show that the addition of the GHW to the text-based warning significantly decreases the perceived attractiveness of the cigarette package. Similarly, Peters and colleagues (2007) find that the Canadian labels (combined text and GHWs) produced a greater negative response for U.S. adult smokers than the U.S. text warnings, without any signs of defensive or reactive responses. Later, Kees, Andrews, and Kozup (2010) discovered that the more graphic the warning, the greater the evoked fear, and fear acts as a mediator that explains increases in quit intentions for adult smokers. Romer, Peters, Strasser, and Langleben (2013) note that smoker self-efficacy in quitting is important in gauging the effects of the GHWs, as self-efficacy is lowest for new smokers and long-time smokers. Thus, they find that the GHWs are most effective for smokers with stronger quit-efficacy beliefs.

Additional research has shown that GHWs can lower intentions to smoke among young adult, occasional smokers (Blanton, Snyder, Strauts, & Larson, 2014), significantly reduce craving and electrophysiological brain responses to smoking cues (Wang et al., 2013), and influence affective and cognitive responses for adult smokers (Emery et al., 2013), as well as for young adult smokers and susceptible youth (Nonnemaker et al., 2010). Yet, given that 88 percent of current smokers begin during adolescence, an important population for the study of the GHWs is adolescent smokers (Kessler et al., 1997; Surgeon General Report, 2012). In a study of dual pathways to persuasion, Andrews, Netemeyer, Kees, and Burton (2014) find that both emotional responses (evoked fear) and beliefs from the GHWs affected adolescent smokers' thoughts of quitting. Evoked fear is found to have a stronger effect than beliefs in mediating the effects of GHWs on quit thoughts for adolescent smokers, yet this is reversed in a longitudinal study of young adult smokers. A recent examination of male, adolescent nonsmoker data (Pepper et al., 2013) reveals that the GHWs discouraged most male adolescents from wanting to smoke, but lung cancer warnings discouraged them more than addiction warnings. Finally, moderators can have an important impact on the effectiveness of the GHWs. For example, Andrews and colleagues (2014) show that smoking frequency for both adolescents and young adults moderated the impact of the GHW levels on quitting thoughts. In Zhao, Nan, Yang, and Iles (2014), warning message framing is an important moderator, with a loss frame found to be more effective than a gain frame. For text-only GHWs, message framing did not matter. Thus, in sum, as argued by Myers (2013), there is clear evidence across the stages of information processing indicating that the GHWs are effective.

Challenges in Developing Cigarette Warnings and Directions for Future Research

As noted previously, a specific challenge to developing effective cigarette warnings is the dearth of research examining the most important target audience for these types of warnings: adolescents. As noted previously, tobacco use is almost always initiated during adolescence. Each day, 3,200 adolescents under age eighteen smoke their first cigarette, and one-fifth of these youths become daily smokers (DHHS, 2014). From a persuasion standpoint, it is problematic that most of the 10 million adolescents in the United States who are open to trying smoking, or have already tried smoking, do not consider themselves smokers (FDA, 2014c). This segment also may not be particularly interested in the topic of tobacco risks and may not believe they will become personally addicted to tobacco (Arnett, 2000; Mayhew, Flay, & Mott, 2000). Thus, it is particularly challenging to develop warning messages to reach an audience who is not interested in the topic and likely does not feel like the message is relevant to them. Given these significant challenges, research is needed to understand how warnings can best reach this critical segment.

Consistent with the model of consumer responses to warnings and disclosures offered in Figure 20.1, the following questions are important to consider: Can cigarette warnings be designed to capture adolescents' attention? What types of warning will adolescents notice and comprehend? Is this segment more prone to a cognitive/factual appeal or can an emotional message be more effective? In one of the few studies examining the impact of graphic cigarette warnings on adolescent smokers, Andrews and colleagues (2014) find that highly graphic warnings were effective at impacting adolescent smokers' thoughts of quitting. Clearly, studies increasing our understanding of the breadth of adolescents' emotional and cognitive reactions to GHW's and plain packaging are needed. More generally, research addressing how cigarette warnings impact adolescent smokers and nonsmokers' beliefs about smoking and smoking behavior will be beneficial to policy makers and the public health community.

Time is also an important issue in considering the effects of labeling. The vast majority of studies that examine cigarette warning labels are cross-sectional in nature. These studies typically examine the impact of different types of warnings on short-term response outcome variables such as attitude, beliefs, affect, and intentions. While results from these studies are useful, some scholars note the potential for the warnings to become less effective or "wear out" after repeated exposure (Strahan et al., 2002). It is especially important from a regulatory perspective to understand what types of warnings have an effect that persists over time. While there have been studies that have examined the impact of antismoking media campaigns over time (e.g., Siegel & Biener, 2000), there have been very few studies that have studied the impact of warnings using a longitudinal design (Hammond et al., 2004). In one study that examines the impact of different graphic warning labels, Andrews and colleagues (2014) find that graphic warnings can have a carryover effect on thoughts of quitting smoking for young adult smokers after a one-week delay following exposure to the cigarette package warning. Currently, the FDA is conducting longitudinal research to measure the impact and effectiveness of "The Real Cost" antismoking campaign in which they will follow thousands of the same youths over a two-year period in seventy-five major media markets, assessing potential changes in their smoking behavior over time (FDA, 2014d). More longitudinal research is needed to understand the impact of cigarette warning labels on smoking behavior over time (see Figure 20.1) and the moderators impacting these effects.

Finally, there have been very few studies that can directly attribute cessation behaviors to cigarette warnings. Due to methodological challenges (e.g., intervening variables that are difficult to control), coupled with the nature of the regulated environment, the ability to demonstrate that any cigarette warning directly results in smoking cessation can be challenging. For a highly addictive behavior such as smoking, while some warnings may be able to encourage attempts to quit or the reduction of smoking frequency, they are unlikely to be the sole reason for cessation. Any research that can demonstrate a causal relationship between a warning and actual smoking behavior and demonstrate that the warning can singularly reduce smoking incidence (while controlling for other influential factors and possible intervening variables) would make an important contribution to the warnings literature. In the absence of research with smoking incidence as the outcome variable, studies could employ dependent variables, such as number of cigarettes smoked over time, calls to a quit line, and purchase of medications to assist with cessation.

Clearly, combustible tobacco products (e.g., cigarettes, cigars, cigarillos, hookah in which tobacco is burned and inhaled) are the most dangerous form of tobacco and pose the greatest risk to consumer health and well-being. It is in the best interest of public health to persuade smokers to quit. However, given the challenges associated with getting smokers to quit smoking altogether, there has been considerable debate within the public health community around the potential benefits of encouraging cigarette smokers to switch to a "less harmful" form of tobacco (Haar, 2014). If there is some health benefit to consumers switching from combustible cigarettes to an alternate form of tobacco, how might warnings and disclosures inform consumers of this benefit while still generally discouraging tobacco use, especially for potential new users? Can warnings and disclosures be designed both to persuade smokers to quit using tobacco and, in the absence of quitting, at least use a less dangerous form? Can disclosures on alternative tobacco products communicate the realistic (lower) risks of the product relative to combustible cigarettes, without the unintended consequences of attracting new or former tobacco users, contributing to adolescent nicotine use, or encouraging poly-use of tobacco products (Bombard, Pederson, Nelson, & Malarcher, 2007)? These are some of the issues we address in the next section.

New Frontiers: Modified Risk Tobacco Products

No tobacco product is safe. However, some forms of tobacco *may* be more dangerous to consumers' well-being than others. This is the premise for the provision under the Family Smoking Prevention and Tobacco Control Act (2009) that could potentially allow some modified risk tobacco products (MRTPs) to be marketed as "less harmful" or to "reduce the risk of tobacco-related disease" pending an MRTP application to the FDA's Center for Tobacco Products (FSPTCA, 2009). Examples of potential MRTPs include tobacco lozenges and e-cigarettes; the latter has grown from $2 million in sales in 2009 to $722 million in 2013 (*Wall Street Journal*, 2014). Any modified-risk claims would have to be backed by scientific evidence and would need to benefit the health of the population as a whole, taking into account both users and non-users of tobacco products. Gaining approval from the FDA to sell an MRTP would not signal that the product itself is safe or improves the health of the consumer. This designation would simply imply that the product has the potential to reduce tobacco-related harms compared with conventional tobacco products (i.e., combustible cigarettes). Furthermore, any potential MRTP must also contribute to reducing the overall rates of tobacco use and tobacco-related harm across the country.

There is a dearth of research regarding the actual and perceived health effects of MRTPs to guide federal regulatory decisions (IOM, 2011). In one of the few studies that examines the potential impact of tobacco harm reduction statements, Capella, Taylor, and Kees (2012) find that a disclosure suggesting that smokeless tobacco is less risky than cigarettes did not significantly impact consumers' relative risk perceptions of smokeless tobacco. The authors suggest that this lack of effect may be due to the presence of the mandated warning label that was present on the experimental stimuli or the lack of perceived credibility of the harm reduction statement, which was not attributed to the FDA in the studies. Thus, there is need for more research that examines how consumers may process any "harm reduction" disclosures for MRTPs, especially for absolute levels of safety and risk. Even if the evidence suggests that a modified risk tobacco product is safer than conventional tobacco products, will consumers interpret this information as suggesting that the product is objectively "safe" when it clearly is not? After all, such absolute health halos have occurred in the processing of relative nutrient content claims (cf. Andrews, Burton, & Netemeyer, 2000). Thus, it is unclear how the potential labeling of some tobacco products as less risky will impact consumers. These are the types of research questions that should be considered for various emerging alternative tobacco products.

The FDA is committed to "stopping practices that may cause people to start or continue using tobacco products that could lead to preventable disease and death," but at the same time the FDA's goal is to "reduce the number of tobacco-related deaths" (FDA 2012). While these two goals may seem aligned, an important question to be considered is whether or not the communication of MRTPs as less risky could result in a "net positive" effect of fewer total tobacco-related diseases and deaths. Could the number of smokers who switch exclusively to a less dangerous alternate tobacco product offset the number of potential new tobacco users who start using the MRTPs? Recent research shows that approximately 32.1 percent of adults in the United States use one or more tobacco product (with 18 percent smoking cigarettes), and 10.6 percent of adults are multi-users ("poly-users") of tobacco in the United States, including cigarettes, cigars, little cigars, electronic cigarettes, hookahs, smokeless tobacco, and snus (Lee, Hebert, Nonnemaker, & Kim, 2014). Given this usage pattern, the communication of benefits and risks to consumers by way of disclosures and warnings is an important topic in need of additional research.

Electronic Cigarettes

Perhaps the most popular tobacco product that has been promoted as having potential for harm reduction is electronic nicotine delivery systems (i.e., electronic cigarettes, or e-cigarettes) (Etter et al., 2011). These products tend to have a physical form that somewhat resembles a traditional cigarette, but they use electrical heating elements to vaporize a glycerol solution containing nicotine, which is inhaled by the user. E-cigarettes are aggressively marketed in the United States, and as a result consumer use of the products is increasing rapidly (Chen, 2013). In fact, youth exposure to television e-cigarette ads measured by target rating points (TRPs) increased 256 percent from 2011 to 2013 (Duke et al., 2014). Additionally, in a recent Congressional Report (2014), e-cigarette companies were cited for promoting their products at youth-oriented events and offering their e-cigarettes in flavors appealing to adolescents (e.g., Cherry Crush, Chocolate Treat).

While the FDA currently only regulates e-cigarettes that are marketed for therapeutic purposes, a proposed rule extends (or "deems") the agency's tobacco authority to cover e-cigarettes (FDA, 2014a). This proposed rule would prompt the FDA to implement regulatory tools such as age restrictions for minors and manufacturing standards. Importantly, the FDA also would regulate any modified risk claims that may suggest e-cigarettes can reduce tobacco-related disease and death, and any warnings that indicate that e-cigarettes are no less addicting than traditional tobacco. This is important, as e-cigarettes are commonly marketed as safer alternatives to combustible cigarettes and even as smoking cessation aids. U.S. sales of e-cigarettes have increased to $1.7 billion from almost nothing in a five-year period, and some estimate the market could expand to $10 billion in the next three years (Duprey, 2014). Given that e-cigarettes are an extremely high-growth tobacco product in the United States, much research (in both the social and hard sciences) is needed to understand the specific risks and how to communicate these risks to consumers.

At present, research is mixed in regards to the efficacy of e-cigarette in helping smokers quit. Siegel, Tanwar, and Wood (2011) conducted a study using 216 smokers who had purchased e-cigarettes for the first time. Results showed that 31 percent of the sample reported cigarette smoking abstinence after six months, and, of those who were not smoking, 34 percent reported being nicotine-free. Almost two-thirds of the sample reported a reduction in the number of cigarettes they smoked. In contrast, Bullen and colleagues (2013) found that of the 289 smokers who tried e-cigarettes as a means by which to quit smoking, only 7 percent had quit smoking after six months. Finally, after reviewing the existing clinical trials involving e-cigarettes as a cessation strategy, Grana, Benowitz, and Glantz (2014) concluded that e-cigarettes are not associated with successful cessation in general population-based samples of smokers. Regardless of whether or not e-cigarettes are, in fact, an effective method to quit smoking, smokers seem to perceive them as such. In fact, the majority of e-cigarette users report smoking reduction or cessation as their primary motivation for using the product (Goniewicz, Lingus, & Hajek, 2013). In a recent survey of over 1,500 smokers, those who tried e-cigarettes as a means by which to quit smoking reported a higher motivation to quit, higher quitting self-efficacy, and longer recent quit duration than did other smokers (Pokhrel et al., 2013).

One critical issue that is fruitful for future research is whether and how e-cigarettes can be marketed as a modified risk tobacco product or as a smoking cessation tool. Research in the *New England Journal of Medicine* suggests that e-cigarettes are likely to contain lower levels of toxins and carcinogens than combustible cigarettes (Cobb & Abrams, 2011). Yet, another well-controlled study of samples from twelve brands of e-cigarettes indicates that although levels of toxicants were 9 to 450 times lower than those of cigarette smoke, they still contained significantly higher levels of many carcinogenic and toxic compounds (e.g., formaldehyde, acetaldehyde, nitrosamines, cadmium, nickel, and lead) compared with Nicorette inhaler vapor (Goniewicz et al., 2013). Currently, U.S. tobacco marketers are not required to disclose the ingredients in their e-cigarette products, which have been found to deliver inconsistent levels of nicotine and contain some toxins (Riker, Lee, Darville, & Hahn, 2012). However, when the FDA implements regulations related to manufacturing standards for e-cigarettes, it should be possible to discern the level of risk of e-cigarettes relative to combustible cigarettes. Even given the uncertain science around the risks of e-cigarettes, from a public health perspective, it appears that society would in theory be better off if tobacco consumers used *only* e-cigarettes rather than combustible cigarettes (American Cancer Society, 2014). Of course, the potential for poly-use, nicotine poisoning among young children, and new and former tobacco users entering the market complicates the issue. Recently, a Centers for Disease Control and Prevention (CDC) study showed the percentage of e-cigarette users in high school more than doubled from 4.7 percent to 10 percent from 2011 to 2012, and more than 20 percent of middle-school students who reported using e-cigarettes claimed that they never had even tried traditional cigarettes (CDC, 2013).

It is unclear what (if any) messaging can be developed that would be effective at communicating the lower risk of e-cigarettes without the unintended consequence of attracting new tobacco users to the product as "dual-use" tobacco users, which would obviously be undesirable for public health. Recent research has confirmed that attracting new, young, tobacco users is a legitimate concern. Using data from the National Youth Tobacco Survey, Dutra and Glantz (2014) concluded that middle and high school students who use e-cigarettes are more likely to become regular smokers of combustible cigarettes. Other studies have found that e-cigarettes are perceived positively by young adults, and this segment is willing to experiment with the product (Choi et al., 2012).

Currently, e-cigarettes are not required to carry any warnings on packaging or advertising. As the FDA begins to create policy for e-cigarettes, research will be needed to guide these regulatory decisions. Should e-cigarettes carry the same Surgeon General warnings as more conventional tobacco products? While combustible cigarettes appear to warrant the strongest types of warnings about the health risks of smoking, will these types of warnings be appropriate for e-cigarettes, where the long-term health risks are not yet fully understood? While nicotine use should be discouraged, mandatory disclosures and warnings ought to be truthful, objective, and reflect what the scientific evidence tells us about the product risks. Research is needed to understand how consumers may respond to mild or ambiguous warnings about the uncertain long-term risks of e-cigarettes, as well as perceptions of health risks (beyond addiction) associated with combustible products.

Alternatively, given prior consumer testing with e-smokers ("vapers"), would a disclosure approach similar to qualified health claims on food products be more appropriate? In this scenario, the e-cigarette marketer would be allowed to claim that e-cigarettes are a safer form of nicotine consumption than combustible cigarettes, but would also be required to disclose that nicotine is highly addictive and that the long-term risks associated with the product are not understood. Of course, the critical research questions for any warning or disclosure approach would concern how young consumers, and other non-tobacco smokers considering trial, interpret the information. Will mild warnings or harm reduction claims (with risk disclosures) result in increased e-cigarette initiation rates and "duel use" of e-cigarettes and conventional tobacco products? In essence, is it possible to make truthful claims about the benefits of MRTPs (relative to conventional tobacco products) without experiencing the unintended consequence of drawing in new tobacco users? Finally, research would be needed to determine which segments may be most receptive to modified risk tobacco disclosures.

Obesity Trends: A Critical Global Issue

In the past fifty years, the prevalence of obesity among U.S. adults almost tripled, growing from approximately 13 to 36 percent (NIH, 2014).

Obesity is directly or indirectly related to chronic health conditions and diseases such as cancer, diabetes, and heart disease and is associated with some three hundred thousand deaths annually after adjustments for age and smoking factors (CDC, 2014b; U.S. Surgeon General, 2013). With more than two-thirds of Americans aged twenty years or older who are now overweight, there are dire concerns about the future impact on long-term consumer welfare. Estimates of the annual financial cost of obesity in the United States reach as high as $200 billion, which include direct medical costs, lost productivity costs, transportation costs, and human capital costs (Hammond & Levine, 2010).

Thus, U.S. agencies such as the FDA and USDA are concerned about the immediate and long-term consequences of obesity, which clearly represents a critical health issue to the well-being of many consumers. How nutrition information (e.g., calories, levels of saturated fat and sodium) is communicated and used by consumers in evaluations and decisions has become an increasingly crucial issue. Federal agencies such as the FDA should apply an appropriate conceptual lens as the agency considers the complex manner in which nutrition information is communicated, interpreted, and utilized by consumers. This includes information communicated through the two major sources of where and how consumers obtain their food: (1) nutrition disclosures relevant to purchases made at the retail stores and then subsequently prepared and consumed in the home, and (2) purchases of prepared foods from restaurants or other locations away from home.

Nutrition Disclosures on Product Packaging for Foods Consumed in the Home

U.S. consumers have had access to specific and thorough standardized nutrition information in the Nutrition Facts label found on the back or side of food packages since 1993. The disclosure of this information was mandated by the Nutritional Labeling and Education Act (NLEA) of 1990, and the FDA conducted qualitative and quantitative research to aid in the design of the Nutrition Facts disclosure. A primary objective of the NLEA was to help consumers make "more informed and healthier food choices in the context of their daily diet" (NLEA, 1990; *Federal Register,* 2010a).

However, as noted previously, since the time the standardized Nutrition Facts label was added to packages, we have seen concomitant increases in obesity rates among U.S. consumers. Thus, many would dispute whether the provision of information through FDA regulation has been effective in communicating the information to aid consumers in making food choices and whether it is capable of changing consumers' dietary habits (Heike & Taylor, 2012). Others note that not all consumers consult the label when making purchases (Choiniere & Lando, 2013), and that perhaps the obesity crisis would have been even more severe without standardized labeling (Andrews, Lin, Levy, and Lo, 2014). The model offered in Figure 20.1 includes the most significant issues related to how nutrition information disclosures are presented and subsequently processed by consumers in retail environments.

U.S. consumers have increasingly busy lifestyles, and at the retail shelf, nutrition and health-related evaluations and choices can be daunting. Despite the presence of the Nutrition Facts disclosure, one recent survey reported that many consumers still believe it is harder to identify healthier products while shopping at their grocery retailer than to do their own taxes (IFIC, 2012; Newman, Howlett, & Burton, 2014). This difficulty is impacted not only by the thousands of product alternatives crowding the retail shelf, but the fact that the Nutrition Facts label is found on the side or back of packages, a location that makes comparisons among multiple product alternatives difficult and time consuming. In addition, there can be more than fifty pieces of specific information available in the Nutrition Facts label. While the relatively comprehensive nature of the information disclosed is a benefit to certain consumer segments, it makes the acquisition, integration, and comparisons across products more time consuming and burdensome for the harried consumer. Many contend that the Nutrition Facts label is too complex and is more difficult than it need be for consumers to access the *most critical* nutrition information to evaluate product alternative healthfulness (Viswanathan & Hastak, 2002). There are also many cues offered on the package by food manufacturers to signal nutritional benefits that are much easier to access and in turn may be used to draw inferences about the perceived healthfulness of products. Unfortunately, these inferences may or may not be consistent with the objective healthfulness of the product (Andrews, Burton, & Kees, 2011; Kozup, Creyer, & Burton, 2003).

Such acquisition, integration and processing issues are important as the FDA is considering modifications to the communication of nutrition information that will increase the ease, or fluency, with which it may be accessed and potentially incorporated into consumer food judgments and decisions. These methods include the provision of front-of-package labeling and revision of the Nutrition Facts label (*Federal Register,* 2010b).

Front-of-Package Nutrition Disclosures

Over the past decade, consumers have encountered a plethora of front-of-package (FOP) nutrition labeling systems and icons, including Grocery Manufacturers of America and the Food Marketing Institute's Facts-Up-Front system, the United Kingdom's traffic light system, and Hannaford's Guiding Stars (Andrews et al., 2014; *Federal Register*, 2010b). As shown in Figure 20.3, generally, the systems can be divided into two broad types of disclosure systems: (1) evaluative or interpretive systems for the product that help with the evaluation task, and (2) nutrient-specific or reductive FOP systems that reduce and transfer important calorie and nutrient information from a nutritional panel from the back or side of the package. The evaluative/interpretive system can be further subdivided into systems that provide consumers either with an

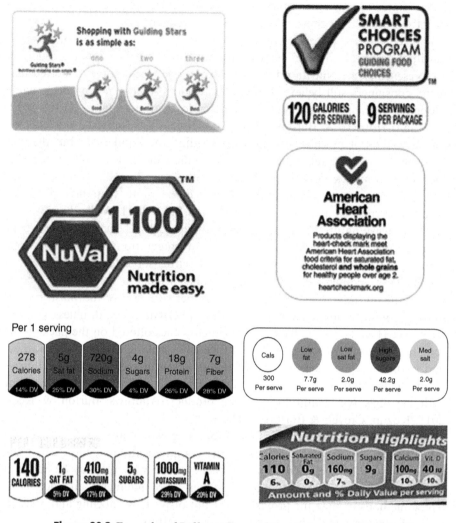

Figure 20.3 *Examples of Different Types of Front-of-package Nutrition Systems.*

overall evaluation of a product's healthfulness and systems that offer an evaluation of specific nutrients (e.g., saturated fat and sodium). Examples of the former include the NuVal nutrition scoring system (a 1–100 scale) or the Institute of Medicine's recommended format (products receive 0–3 stars). The latter includes the United Kingdom's traffic light system, which color-codes (red, amber, green) the disclosure for specific nutrients. The evaluative/interpretive systems usually require that the evaluation of the product or nutrient meets certain predetermined nutritional criteria to attain its score. In contrast, the nutrient-specific, reductive systems do not require any such additional evaluative criteria that must be determined. These systems have become popular with many manufacturers and trade groups and include the Facts-Up-Front icon and others using a Guideline Daily Amount (GDA)–type format.

In the past decade, an increasing amount of academic research has examined FOP labeling. While a complete review of this FOP literature is beyond the scope of this chapter (interested readers should see Andrews et al., 2014, and Hersey et al., 2013), some recent findings are consistent with the model offered in Figure 20.1. There is some evidence that FOP systems can increase attention to nutrition information and that there is some difference in the ease of processing information from different FOP nutrition disclosure systems (Hersey et al., 2013). For example, in a UK study it was found that a multiple traffic light format took the least time to interpret (the average time was 5.1 seconds) followed closely by the colored GDA (an average time of 5.4 seconds). The color-coding provided through quantitative scoring seems to aid attention and reduce the subsequent time for processing (Synovate, 2005; Hersey et al., 2013). Similarly, evaluative disclosures (e.g., traffic lights, number of stars, or 1–100 rating) seem to be *perceived* as requiring less time than GDA formats (Hersey et al., 2013). However, other research that compared a colored traffic light–style nutrient-specific disclosure to a no-color option found no differences between the evaluative/interpretive format (i.e., traffic lights) and the reductive format (i.e., no color) in self-reported attention paid to the disclosure or how easily consumers could judge the product's healthfulness (Kees, Stafford, & Cho, 2014).

It seems that consumers do like the general concept of some form of FOP labeling, and there are fairly consistent findings in the literature that consumers exposed to FOP labels perform better in understanding and identification of more healthful products than those exposed to no-FOP control conditions. Some studies have found that the use of evaluative formats with nutrient-specific traffic light formats is associated with a higher likelihood of identifying the healthier food choices compared to labels presenting non-evaluative GDA information (Hersey et al., 2013; Newman, Howlett, & Burton, 2014). However, a comprehensive Institute of Medicine report concluded that no FOP nutrition information system is superior to all others and that each has strengths and weaknesses (IOM, 2011).

Current and Future Research Needs on FOP Labeling

Despite an array of studies, there are substantial opportunities for future research to determine whether there is one specific FOP alternative that can *most effectively* serve needs across diverse situations, goal states, and consumer segments. In the model presented in Figure 20.1, we offer a brief overview of key variables of interest for FOP nutrition labeling: attention and acquisition of the information, processing and comprehension across individual differences and goals of various consumer segments, and broad effects and outcomes related to consumers' well-being (Andrews et al., 2014).

Research examining how contextual variables in a store/shopping environment are related to FOP attention, acquisition, and use is clearly needed.

Perceptually, what precise design elements, including color, location, size, and contrast, enhance initial awareness and acquisition of the information (Andrews et al., 2014)? How do different FOP label alternatives perform given variance in the number and positioning of manufacturer's nutrition claims, other promotion material, and level of package clutter?

There is also a dire need to examine what is occurring with shoppers at the store level. Clearly, while academic researchers have difficulty integrating controlled designs with the retail shopping experience, there is a dearth of studies involving consumer responses at the retail shelf. The need for policy-based decisions is obvious. For example, when consumers select a product at the store, observing their search behavior and choices and examining the role played by FOP information relative to other critical marketing variables are needed.

More controlled experiments may expand our understanding of hybrid systems. While evaluative systems may help in comprehension and judgments (Hersey et al., 2013; Newman, Howlett & Burton, 2014), they may at times create some bias depending on the specific objective nutrition profile and cutoff levels established (Andrews, Burton, & Kees, 2011; Andrews et al., 2014). Is there a hybrid system that, despite some additional complexity due to the expanded information conveyed, maximizes benefits while minimizing weaknesses of a single system?

Many questions that are critical to both policy and researchers relate to the long-term and broader effects of FOP labeling. To our knowledge, there is little research related to unintended consequences. For example, if an evaluative disclosure reveals a superior "three-star" product or traffic light format dominated by green, does this stimulate overconsumption by granting the license to consume (e.g., Wansink & Chandon, 2006)? While there is some evidence that the use of FOP labels by a retailer may positively affect healthful choices (Dzhogleva & Inman, 2013; Hersey et al., 2013), effects generally appear fairly small and are not always observed. Are there stronger behavioral effects of some FOP nutrition disclosure systems relative to others? Lastly, from a consumer health and welfare perspective, many researchers believe that the influence of mandates for labeling systems on new product development and reformulation will exceed effects on individual consumer behavior. If a standardized FOP system became required, how would it impact changes in the nutritional content of packaged foods, and would the more aggressive evaluative systems (traffic light, IOM stars) motivate the most substantial product modifications?

However, the questions and problems associated with obesity and the acquisition, use, and processing of nutrition information also concern perceived limitations of the Nutrition Facts label mandated in the United States. The FDA has already proposed changes to the Nutrition Facts label and research addressing these initial proposals, and the breadth of effects when implemented will also be an emerging research concern, with possible implications for consumer well-being (*Federal Register,* 2014).

Modifications to the Nutrition Facts Label

Proposed Regulatory Action Regarding Changes to the Nutrition Facts Label

In March 2014, the FDA requested comments on a number of proposed modifications to the Nutrition Facts label, including the enhancement of calorie information and adjustment of some of the serving size information (*Federal Register*, 2014). These changes represent the most substantial modifications since the introduction of the Nutrition Facts label twenty years ago. The impetus of this substantial proposed update to the Nutrition Facts disclosure on packaged foods is "to reflect the latest scientific information, including the link between diet and chronic diseases such as obesity and heart disease" (FDA, 2014b).

There are a number of important format changes between the current and proposed Nutrition Facts label that can be observed in Figure 20.3. This includes greater emphasis on the calorie content and servings per container by increasing the type size and placing the information in bold type. Clearly, the changes in prominence are designed to encourage attention, allow easier access, and spur its use in forming health-related judgments about products. Furthermore, there are proposed changes to serving sizes listed to reflect more accurately amounts people currently eat, relative to their dietary habits in the 1990s. Modifications proposed also include the presentation of calorie and nutrition information for the entire package of certain food products that could be consumed in a single sitting, including dual-column formats for both per serving and the entire package (*Federal Register*, 2014). Also, the modifications include switching the Daily Values (DVs) from the far-right to the far-left. While these are among the most prominent changes, the proposed rule lists some thirteen specific changes to the Nutrition Facts label, many of which can be directly observed in Figure 20.4. The FDA proposes that manufacturers have some two years after the effective date to comply with the final ruling.

Future Research Needs

Substantial research exists concerning the Nutrition Facts label that has examined alternative formats, effects on processing, evaluations of healthfulness and consumer choices, and macro-level influences of its implementation (see Drichoutis, Lazaridis, & Nayga, 2006, and Heike & Taylor, 2012, for comprehensive reviews). However, scant research has addressed these very specific changes proposed by the FDA and the White House (Harris, 2012). At this point, the FDA offers little direct evidence for effects, simply noting that it will "perform consumer research during this rulemaking process to evaluate how variations in label format may affect consumer understanding and use of the Nutrition Facts label" (*Federal Register*, 2014, p. 11882).

These modifications for the Nutrition Facts label offer an excellent example of how the consumer research community can provide assistance to

Nutrition Facts	
Serving Size 2/3 cup (55g)	
Servings Per Container About 8	

Amount Per Serving	
Calories 230	Calories from Fat 72

	% Daily Value*
Total Fat 8g	12%
Saturated Fat 1g	5%
Trans Fat 0g	
Cholesterol 0mg	0%
Sodium 160mg	7%
Total Carbohydrate 37g	12%
Dietary Fiber 4g	16%
Sugars 1g	
Protein 3g	
Vitamin A	10%
Vitamin C	8%
Calcium	20%
Iron	45%

* Percent Daily Values are based on a 2,000 calorie diet. Your daily value may be higher or lower depending on your calorie needs.

	Calories:	2,000	2,500
Total Fat	Less than	65g	80g
Sat Fat	Less than	20g	25g
Cholesterol	Less than	300mg	300mg
Sodium	Less than	2,400mg	2,400mg
Total Carbohydrate		300g	375g
Dietary Fiber		25g	30g

Nutrition Facts	
8 servings per container	
Serving size	2/3 cup (55g)

Amount per 2/3 cup	
Calories	**230**

% DV*	
12%	**Total Fat** 8g
5%	Saturated Fat 1g
	Trans Fat 0g
0%	**Cholesterol** 0mg
7%	**Sodium** 160mg
12%	**Total Carbs** 37g
14%	Dietary Fiber 4g
	Sugars 1g
	Added Sugars 0g
	Protein 3g
10%	**Vitamin D** 2mcg
20%	**Calcium** 260mg
45%	**Iron** 8mg
5%	**Potassium** 235mg

* Footnote on Daily Values (DV) and calories reference to be inserted here.

Figure 20.4. *Current Nutrition Facts Panel Compared to the Proposed 2014 Panel.*

Note: The proposed Nutrition Facts labels are available at www.fda.gov/Food/ GuidanceRegulation/GuidanceDocumentsRegulatoryInformation/LabelingNutrition/ ucm385663.htm#images.

policy-related decisions that appear in dire need of conceptually based empirical research. Over the next three to five years, there is substantial opportunity for research examining how each of the specific modifications (as compared to the current "control" Nutrition Facts label and other possible alternatives) may affect attention, processing, and integration into nutrient and product evaluations and influence choices among alternative choice sets. Which of the specific changes appear to have the greatest relative effects on product choices and evaluations? Subsequently, when the proposed changes are implemented in the future, what will be consumer reactions and effects in the marketplace? Will effects vary across individual difference variables (e.g., those low in nutrition consciousness and objective nutrition knowledge) and consumer segments at greater risk (e.g., high body mass index [BMI], low literacy, those suffering from diabetes or heart disease)? How do the changes to the Nutrition Facts label interact with alternative FOP labeling?

While revisions to both the Nutrition Facts label and front of the package may be beneficial to consumers' well-being, it may be argued that the information required to make an informed food choice is already available in the Nutrition Facts label for knowledgeable and motivated consumers (*if* the effort is expended to obtain it). However, for food consumed outside of the home, information has not been disclosed to consumers at the point of purchase, and changes to consumer lifestyles have made this an increasingly important issue.

Nutrition Disclosures for Foods Consumed Outside the Home

The NLEA (1990) exempted restaurants and other venues selling ready-to-consume prepared foods from nutrition labeling. However, U.S. consumers now consume some one-third of their total calories and spend almost one-half of their food budget on foods prepared outside the home, percentages that have grown substantially over the past forty years (*Federal Register,* 2011). Given these statistics and rising levels of obesity, Section 4205 of the U.S. Patient Protection and Affordable Care Act (2010) required chain restaurants with twenty or more outlets in the United States to provide nutrient content information for standard menu items. Given divergent labeling requirements for menu disclosures from an increasing number of states and localities, many major restaurant chains and the National Restaurant Association supported national legislation that would standardize labeling requirements. The FDA was charged with establishing the final rules, regulations, and outlets to be covered by the legislation, and the labeling changes are scheduled to occur in 2015 and 2016. Among the many difficulties encountered by the FDA were which retail establishments to include. The legislation called for calorie labeling for vending machines, restaurants, and "similar retail food establishments," yet determining what types of establishments should and should not be included as "similar" proved extremely problematic. Convenience stores, supermarkets, and take-out-only pizza chains lobbied for exemptions from the requirements. The final ruling included all of these outlets, but there are still on-going appeals.

Current Findings and Future Research Needs

Because a number of states and local governments have mandated calorie labeling for restaurant chains in the past seven years, several field- and lab-based experimental studies have been conducted. In a recent review that examined studies published between 2007 and 2013, it was concluded that despite some positive results concerning effectiveness in lab experiments (e.g., Burton,

Howlett, & Tangari, 2009), the market-based field studies suggest that calorie labeling generally will not reduce the total calories ordered across the general population (Kiszko, Martinez, Abrams, & Elbel, 2014). When considering the underlying model of when disclosures are likely to have effects, such macro-level findings should come as little surprise (Burton & Kees, 2012). That is, the conditions under which effects on a specific consumers' purchase appear relatively narrow; it is far more likely to find segments in which the labeling may have no effect, or even increase calories in an order, than the opposite.

For example, as suggested in our model, there is a hierarchical chain of very specific conditions, including attention and awareness, processing conditions, integration and evaluation, and situational and individual difference variables that need to be satisfied for consumers to be likely to reduce the caloric content for any specific order at a restaurant (Burton & Kees, 2012). As with any warning or disclosure, restaurant patrons must be aware of the disclosed calorie information. However, information acquisition in many menu board or drive-thru venues, when coupled with time constraints, may be fairly difficult. If consumers tend to order certain familiar items habitually, they may not even examine a menu board or menu. If found and considered, consumers must have the motivation and knowledge to process and incorporate the calorie information into judgments and choices. For the majority of consumers, food attributes such as taste, price, convenience, and meal size are more diagnostic and influential for decisions than is product healthfulness, and both perceptually and objectively these attributes may be negatively correlated to calorie levels. In fact, some may contend that the restaurant industry's success in designing and delivering convenient, reasonably priced, tasty fare has led to the tremendous increase in the food dollar captured and helped make calories and nutrition a tertiary concern for most consumers. It is also argued that for calorie labeling to have a favorable influence, the disclosed information must deviate from consumers' prior expectations (Burton, Creyer, Kees, & Huggins, 2006; Howlett, Burton, Bates, & Huggins, 2009). If calorie information merely confirms prior expectations, then little change in choice behavior is anticipated. In addition, there are situational influences in any restaurant setting and biases in processing that may reduce the likelihood of calorie labeling having a substantial influence (Burton & Kees, 2012; Chandon & Wansink, 2007).

Of course, there are also differences in calorie needs and wants that affect choices. For instance, twenty-year-old construction workers or high school athletes visiting a fast food restaurant for lunch may see a low calorie meal as insufficient for their specific dietary needs. They may use labeling to help identify a set of high calorie items required, given their daily activity level and caloric expenditure. Given the variety of motivations for food consumption (maximization of taste, value, convenience, emotional comfort), there are many segments of consumers for which calorie labeling is very unlikely to have intended effects.

Future research can consider the very refined, select segment of consumers who may be impacted by in-restaurant calorie labeling. The conceptualization regarding when and how disclosures are effective suggest possible four-way or higher interactions (e.g., calorie expectations × motivation × situation (time pressure, social) × disclosure) that may be considered. Calorie labeling is likely to positively affect the few rather than the many, and this presents intriguing research possibilities that can be explored.

Related to the preceding, situational variables such as the presentation of items and calories, the relationship of nutritional content to other critical evaluation attributes (price, perceived taste, size), and time pressure may all be interrelated in their effects (Parker & Lehmann, 2014). While the legislation requires that calorie labeling be used for chain restaurants and vending machines, at this point it appears it will also include a broader set of retailers, such as prepared food at grocery stores, convenience stores, take-out-only chains, and such. However, how the aspects of the legislation affect very different venues, such as buffets, fast food chains, casual dining table service restaurants, vending machines, and other venues covered will be of interest to numerous constituencies.

Also, as noted previously, one may consider across each type of venue the nature of the target market. Because goals and motives vary, interest in the nature of effects for the segment of twenty-year-old athletes relative to the segment of sedentary, overweight forty-five-to-sixty-five-year-old consumers suffering from heart disease will differ dramatically. Studies that have shown some increase in general calorie consumption probably mask significant differences for very refined segments. As with FOP labeling, how the required disclosures affect the modification and new product offerings of restaurant chains is of substantial interest.

In sum, while most of the market-based studies have focused on broad calorie consumption effects for the restaurant patron population (Kiszko et al., 2014), when the law is finally implemented, research should consider higher-order moderating effects (Burton & Kees, 2012) and longer-term consequences for consumers and firms.

Beyond Tobacco and Nutrition: Other Applications of Disclosures and Warnings

While we view tobacco and food as areas in which disclosures and warnings can have a broad impact on population well-being, there are other very important domains in which disclosures and warnings can have an important impact. One such area is consumer finance. Financial disclosures (e.g., mandatory mortgage loan disclosures, credit card disclosures, financial privacy notices) are a fundamental component of consumer protection policy for financial services (Durkin & Elliehausen, 2011). While financial disclosures are intended to provide consumers with basic information and facilitate comparisons among alternatives, sometimes there are unintended consequences (Navarro-Martinez et al., 2011). For instance, some research has documented that these disclosures can overwhelm consumers with information presented in complex formats, which only further confuses consumers (Lacko & Pappalardo, 2010; Woodward & Hall, 2010). Research is needed to better understand how to develop financial disclosures that consumers pay attention to, understand, and use in their decision making (Garrison, 2012). Indeed, the literature lacks conclusive evidence on how financial disclosures impact decisions and outcomes, especially in light of contextual, market, and individual difference factors (e.g., financial literacy) outlined in Figure 20.1 (Blumenthal & Perry, 2012).

Another domain in which disclosures can have a significant impact on consumer decisions and well-being is direct-to-consumer advertising (DTCA) of prescription drugs. When drug companies market directly to consumers, the FDA requires that the marketer balance information about how the drug can help treat certain conditions with a mandatory risk disclosure (i.e., fair balance; Aikin, O'Donoghue, Swasy, & Sullivan, 2001). While DTCA risk disclosures are predicated on the assumption that consumers appropriately interpret this information to make informed decisions (FDA, 2009a), similar to financial disclosures discussed previously, research has found that risk disclosures in DTCA are often ignored (Menon, Deshpandi, Perri, & Zinkhan, 2003), can lead to overestimation of product risk (Cox, 2010), and can adversely affect product use compliance (Wosinka, 2005). Similar to the other domains discussed in this chapter, and consistent with Figure 20.1, DTCA risk disclosures can be impacted by emotions (Cox, Cox, & Mantel, 2010), individual differences (Ahn, Park, & Haley, 2014), background noise and clutter (Andrews, 2011), and expert (physician) advice (Frosch & Grande, 2010).

The final topic that will be addressed in the chapter deals with the array of disclosures, disclaimers, and qualifiers that are required for food and supplement claims. For instance, some foods that make nutrient content claims (e.g., "low fat") are also required to carry a disclosure statement when that same food contains exceedingly high levels of another nutrient (e.g., "See nutrition information for sodium content"). For supplements, qualified health claims may make a statement that a product reduces the risk of a particular condition (i.e., coronary heart disease), but are also required to present a scientific certainty qualifier that the evidence behind the claim is preliminary, uncertain, or even unlikely to support the claim.

This domain is an excellent example of the difficulty of designing effective disclosures and warnings to communicate potential product risks without violating the rights of the marketer to communicate the benefits of its products. While there have been numerous studies to help inform the design of such food and supplement disclosures (Mason, Scammon, & Fang, 2007), federal agencies continue to struggle to develop effective disclosures. For instance, the FTC concluded that qualified health claims are not interpreted by consumers as intended (FTC, 2006). Much of the extant research suggests that the food and supplement disclaimer/disclosure environment is confusing to consumers

(Hasler, 2008) and sometimes can even result in the opposite of the desired effect (FDA, 2009b). As in the previously mentioned domains, and consistent with Figure 20.1, consumer research is critical in ensuring consumers pay attention to, process, and make appropriate decisions based on the information disclosures.

Conclusion

Across the different domains discussed in this chapter, it is clear that warnings and disclosures are an important regulatory tool for policy makers to impact consumer health and well-being. Federal laws and regulations mandate warnings and disclosures on product packaging, at the point of purchase, and/or in advertising to protect consumers from potentially danger-ous products. For some issues, there appears to be strong empirical support for a specific direction that would result in positive consumer and social outcomes (e.g., stronger cigarette warning labels in the United States). However, for most issues reviewed in this chapter, more research is needed to understand the optimum design of warnings and disclosures to facilitate consumer understand-ing and minimize unintended consequences.

The Model of Consumer Responses to Warnings and Disclosures offered in Figure 20.1 draws from a rich literature of consumer information processing (e.g., McGuire, 1980; Petty and Cacioppo, 1986; Rogers, 1975; Wogalter, 2006) to offer some of the key outcome variables, mediators, and moderators to consider when conducting warnings and disclosures research. These variables are important for researchers to consider given that developing effective warn-ings and disclosures requires a clear understanding of how consumers acquire, process, and use the information to shape their decisions. Particular attention should be paid to the potential moderating variables in the model. Consistent with marketing theory, any potential outcomes from exposure to a warning or disclosure will vary based on individual differences, situational factors, and consumer goals.

A considerable number of research questions are offered in this chapter, and we present an overview of some of these questions and issues in Table 20.1. Of course, for each of these questions there are potential moderating and mediating influences that may be considered and are of interest to consumers' well-being. Other questions could address effects across the various stages in our proposed model. While regulatory agencies are charged with crafting laws and rules to guide warning and disclosure policy, these agencies are limited in the research they are able to conduct. Thus, we hope this chapter encourages research from the academic community, which is critical to ensure that warning and disclosure regulation is grounded in well-designed empirical studies. Rigorous research using appropriate methodologies and relevant samples is important to ensure that warnings and disclosures have the greatest possible positive impact on consumer well-being.

Table 20.1 *Overview of Some Current Warning and Disclosure Issues and Examples of Possible Research Questions.*

Warning and Disclosure Challenges	Possible Research Question Recommendation
Graphic Health Warnings on Packages and in Advertising	What types of warnings are most effective for persuading adolescent smokers and nonsmokers? Can the effects of graphic health warnings persist over time or are they prone to "wear out"? How effective are graphic health warnings at influencing actual long-term smoking behavior?
Warnings for Modified Risk Tobacco Products	What are the trade-offs between effects of warnings on risks and use for MRTPs for adolescents and young non-users, relative to effects on smokers who may be attempting to curtail or eliminate cigarette consumption? How do consumers process "harm reduction" disclosures for MRTPs (e.g., will consumers understand these products to be "reduced" risk relative to combustible cigarettes or will they perceive them as completely "safe")?
Electronic Cigarette Warnings	What are the beliefs about risks associated with e-cigarettes compared to the objective research, and how would various warnings affect risk perceptions and usage? Can disclosures communicate the potential lower risk of e-cigarettes without the unintended consequence of attracting new or "dual use" tobacco users?
Front of Package Nutrition Disclosures	Is there one specific FOP alternative that would most effectively aid consumers in identifying the most healthful product in a choice set? Does this FOP affect choice and consumption levels of segments differing in motivation and knowledge, goal states, and BMIs? Is there a hybrid system that maximizes benefits while minimizing weaknesses of a single evaluative or reductive system? Would a mandated system have an effect on product reformulations and new (more healthful) products, and is there a specific FOP alternative that would lead to the greatest level of more healthful reformulations?
Modifications to the Nutrition Facts Disclosure	How do the combined and the individual recommended changes affect product perceptions and choices, relative to the current label? Which one change has the most substantial effect? Will consumers notice and act upon the inclusion of added sugars? Does moving the daily values (DVs) to the left of the label affect the accuracy of processing nutrients for those expecting them to be on the right? Do increases (decreases) in the serving size for specific products affect consumption levels?
Calorie Labeling in Chain Restaurants and Other Away-from-Home Venues	How does labeling affect choices and levels of consumption across item type, calorie expectations, consumer goals and motivation, situation, and consumer risk level?

Table 20.1 (*cont.*)

Warning and Disclosure Challenges	Possible Research Question Recommendation
Miscellaneous Applications for Warnings and Disclosures	How can the information be organized and presented in a manner that maximizes intended and minimizes unintended consequences? What are the different effects of labeling across different venues (fast food vs. dinner house chains, vending machines, and potentially convenience stores, grocery stores, and others that may be included)? How can disclosures for complex products (e.g., financial products, long list of harmful tobacco ingredients) be revised to communicate critical information without overwhelming and/or confusing consumers? What warning and/or disclosure formats are optimal for communicating risk for products that are extremely beneficial for some consumers (e.g., prescription drugs) without "overwarning"? Can disclosures be effective at informing consumers about products for which the scientific evidence is uncertain about the consumer benefits of the product (e.g., food/nutritional supplements)?

As a final note for academics with a strong interest conducting research that impacts public policy and federal regulation, there are opportunities to partner with government agencies. Many agencies within the FDA such as the Center for Food Safety and Applied Nutrition (CFSAN) and the Center for Tobacco Products (CTP) are understaffed with researchers to address the issues that are raised in this chapter (among many others that are important for consumer welfare). These agencies regularly bring in academics for semester or year-long appointments as Special Government Employees. For those who are unable to commit to a semester or longer, there are various important government committees that welcome academic members (e.g., the FDA Risk Communication Advisory Committee and the White House's Social and Behavioral Science Team). In our experience, agency officials welcome the help from the academic community in researching and understanding these very important policy issues.

References

Ahn, H., Park, J. S., & Haley, E. (2014). Consumers' optimism bias and responses to risk disclosures in direct-to-consumer. *Journal of Consumer Affairs, 48*(1), 175–194.

Aikin, K.J., O'Donoghue, A.C., Swasy, J.L., & Sullivan, H.W. (2001). Randomized trial of risk information formats in direct-to-consumer prescription drug advertisements. *Medical Decision Making, 31*(6), 23–33.

American Cancer Society (2014). E-Cigarettes – it's complicated. Accessed May 1, 2014. Retrieved from www.cancer.org/cancer/news/expertvoices/post/2014/06/24/e-cigarettes-its-complicated.aspx.

Andrews, J. C. (2011). Warnings and disclosures. In B. Fischhoff, N. Brewer, & J. Downs, (eds.), *Communicating Risk and Benefits: An Evidence-Based Users Guide* (pp. 149–161). Silver Spring, MD: U.S. Food & Drug Administration.

Andrews, J. C., Burton, S., & Kees, J. (2011). Is Simpler Always Better? Consumer Evaluations of Front-of-Package Nutrition Symbols. *Journal of Public Policy & Marketing, 30* (2), pp. 175–90.

Andrews, J. C., Burton, S., & Netemeyer, R.G. (2000). Are some comparative nutrition claims misleading? The role of nutrition knowledge, ad claim type, and disclosure conditions. *Journal of Advertising, 29*(3), 29–42.

Andrews, J. C., Lin, C. J., Levy, A. S., & Lo, S. (2014). Consumer research needs from the Food and Drug Administration on front-of-package nutritional labeling. *Journal of Public Policy & Marketing, 33*(1), 1.

Andrews, J. C., Netemeyer, R. G., Kees, J., & Burton, S. (2014). How graphic visual health warnings affect young smokers' thoughts of quitting. *Journal of Marketing Research, 51*(2), 165–183.

Argo, J. J., & Main, K. J. (2004). Meta-analyses of the effectiveness of warning labels. *Journal of Public Policy & Marketing, 23*(2), 193–208.

Arnett, J. J. (2000). Optimistic bias in adolescent and adult smokers and nonsmokers. *Addictive Behaviors, 25*(4), 625–632.

Ashley, D. L., & Backinger, C. L. (2012). The Food and Drug Administration's regulation of tobacco: The Center for Tobacco Products' Office of Science. *American Journal of Preventive Medicine, 43*(5 Suppl 3), S255.

Bettman, J. R., Payne, J. W., & Staelin, R. (1986). Cognitive considerations in designing effective labels for presenting risk information. *Journal of Public Policy & Marketing, 5*, 1–28.

Blanton, H., Snyder, L. B., Strauts, E., & Larson, J. G. (2014). Effect of graphic cigarette warnings on smoking intentions in young adults.. *PLoS One, 9*(5), e96315.

Blumenthal, P. M., & Perry, V. G. (2012). Understanding the fine print: The need for effective testing of mandatory mortgage loan disclosures. *Journal of Public Policy & Marketing, 31*(2), 305–312.

Bombard, J. M., Pederson, L. L., Nelson, D. E., & Malarcher, A. M. (2007). Are smokers only using cigarettes? Exploring current polytobacco use among an adult population. *Addictive Behaviors, 32*(10), 2411.

Bullen, C., Howe C., Laugesen M., McRobbie, H., Paraq, V., Williman, J., & Walker, N. (2013), Electronic cigarettes for smoking cessation: A randomized controlled trial. *Lancet, 382*(9905), 1629–1637.

Burke, Michael (2007). Tips for developing logic models. Paper presented at the 135th Annual Meeting of the American Public Health Association, Washington, DC, November 3–7. Retrieved from www.rti.org/pubs/apha07_burke_pos ter.pdf.

Burton, S., Creyer, E., Kees, J., & Huggins, K. (2006). Attacking the obesity epidemic: The potential health benefits of providing nutrition information in restaurants. *American Journal of Public Health, 96*(September), 1669–1675.

Burton, S., Howlett, E., & Tangari, A. (2009). Food for thought: How will the nutrition labeling of quick service restaurant menu items influence consumers' product evaluations, purchase intentions, and choices? *Journal of Retailing, 85*(3), 258–273.

Burton, S., & Kees, J. (2012). Flies in the ointment? Addressing potential impediments to population-based health benefits of restaurant menu labeling initiatives. *Journal of Public Policy & Marketing, 31*(2), 232–239.

Capella, M. L., Taylor, C. R., & Kees, J. (2012). Tobacco harm reduction advertising in the presence of a government-mandated warning. *Journal of Consumer Affairs, 46*(2), 235–259.

CDC (Centers for Disease Control and Prevention)(2013). *MMWR, 62* (35, September 6,), 729–730. Retrieved from www.cdc.gov/mmwr/preview/mmwrhtml/mm6235a6.htm.

CDC (2014a). Smoking & tobacco use: Fast facts, U.S. Department of Health and Human Services. Accessed May 16, 2014. Retrieved from www.cdc.gov/tobacco/data_statistics/ fact_sheets/fast_facts/index.htm.

CDC (2014b). Overweight and obesity. U.S. Department of Health and Human Services. Retrieved from www.cdc.gov/nccdphp/dnpa/obesity/index.htm.

Chandon, P., & Wansink, B. (2007). The biasing health halos of fast-food restaurant health claims: Lower calorie estimates and higher side-dish consumption intentions. *Journal of Consumer Research, 34*(3), 301–314. doi:10.1086/519499.

Chen, L. (2013). FDA summary on adverse events on electronic cigarettes. Nicotine and tobacco research. (Published online August 1.) doi: 10.1093/ntr/nts145.

Choi, K., Fabian, L., Mottey, N., Corbett, A., & Forster, J. (2012). Young adults' favorable perceptions of snus, dissolvable tobacco products, and electronic cigarettes: Findings from a focus group study. *American Journal of Public Health, 102*(11), 2088–2093.

Choinière, C. J., & Lando, A. (2013). 2008 health and diet survey. U.S. Food and Drug Administration. Accessed May 11, 2014. Available at www.fda.gov/Food/FoodScienceResearch/ConsumerBehaviorResearch/ucm193895.htm.

Cobb, N. K., & Abrams, D. B. (2011). E-cigarette or drug-delivery device? Regulating novel nicotine products. *New England Journal of Medicine, 365*(3), 193–195.

Committee on Energy and Commerce, U.S. House of Representatives. (2014). Gateway to addiction? A survey of popular electronic cigarette manufacturers and targeted marketing to youth. Retrieved from http://democrats.energycommerce.house.gov/sites/default/files/documents/Report-E-Cigarettes-Youth-Marketing-Gateway-To-Addiction-2014-4-14.pdf.

Cox, E. P., Wogalter, M. S., Stokes, S. L., & Murff, E. J. T. (1997). Do product warnings increase safe behavior? A meta-analysis. *Journal of Public Policy & Marketing, 16*(2), 195–204.

Cox, A. D., Cox, D., & Mantel S. P. (2010). Consumer response to drug risk information: The role of positive affect. *Journal of Marketing, 74*(July), 31–44.

Cox, W. A. (2010). Public disclosure requirements for buyers and sellers: Justifications for other than full and open competition. *Contract Management, 50*(2), 44.

Drichoutis, A. C., Lazaridis P., & Nayga, R. M. (2006). Consumers' use of nutritional labels: A review of research studies and issues. *Academy of Marketing Science Review, 9*, 1–22.

Duke, J. C., Lee, Y., Kim, A., Watson, K., Arnold, K., Nonnemaker, J., & Porter, L. (2014). Exposure to electronic cigarette television advertisements among youth and young adults. *Pediatrics, 143*(July), 1–8.

Duprey, Rich (2014). The e-cig market grows up. *Motley Fool,* March 26. Retrieved from www.fool.com/investing/general/2014/03/26/e-cig-market-grows-up.aspx.

Durkin, T. A., & Elliehausen, G. (2011). *Truth in Lending: Theory, History, and a Way Forward.* New York: Oxford University Press.

Dutra, L. M., & Glantz, S. A. (2014). Electronic cigarettes and conventional cigarette use among U.S. adolescents: A cross-sectional study. *JAMA Pediatrics, 168*(7), 610–617.

Dzhogleva, H., & Inman, J. (2013). Healthy choice: The effect of simplified POS nutritional information on consumer choice behavior. Working Paper.

Emery, L. F., Romer, D., Sheerin, K., Jamieson, K. H., & Peters, E. (2013). Affective and cognitive mediators of the impact of cigarette warning labels. *Nicotine & Tobacco Research,* August 14. doi:10.1093/ntr/ntt124.

Etter, J. F., Bullen, C., Flouris, A. D., Laugesen, M., & Eissenberg, T. (2011). Electronic nicotine delivery systems: A research agenda. *Tobacco Control, 20*(3), 243–248.

Family Smoking Prevention and Tobacco Control Act (FSPTCA) (2009). Pub. Law No. 625 110 U.S.C.. § 900-302.

FDA (Food and Drug Adminstration) (2009a). Patient and physician attitudes and behaviors associated with DTC promotion of prescription drugs – summary of FDA survey research results. Retrieved from www.fda.gov/downloads/Drugs/ScienceResearch/ResearchAreas/DrugMarketingAdvertisingandCommunicationsResearch/UCM152860.pdf%29.

FDA (Food and Drug Adminstration) (2009b). Experimental study of qualified health claims: Consumer inferences about monounsaturated fatty acids from olive oil, EPA and DHA Omega-3 fatty acids, and green tea. Retrieved from www.fda.gov/Food/IngredientsPackagingLabeling/LabelingNutrition/ucm207549.htm.

FDA (Food and Drug Adminstration) (2012). Less risky tobacco product? Only if the science says so. Retrieved from www.fda.gov/ForConsumers/ConsumerUpdates/ucm297895.htm.

FDA (Food and Drug Adminstration) (2014a). Extending authorities to additional tobacco products. Retrieved from www.fda.gov/TobaccoProducts/Labeling/ucm388395.htm.

FDA (Food and Drug Adminstration) (2014b). FDA proposes updates to nutrition facts label on food packages. Retrieved from www.fda.gov/NewsEvents/Newsroom/PressAnnouncements/ucm387418.htm.

FDA (Food and Drug Adminstration) (2014c). FDA to teens: Consider "real cost" of tobacco use. Retrieved from www.fda.gov/ForConsumers/ConsumerUpdates/ucm383887.htm.

FDA (Food and Drug Adminstration) (2014d). The real cost campaign. Retrieved from www.fda.gov/aboutfda/centersoffices/officeofmedicalproductsandtobacco/aboutthecenterfortobaccoproducts/publiceducationcampaigns/therealcostcampaign/default.htm.

Federal Register (2010a). Disclosure of nutrient content information for standard menu items offered for sale at chain restaurants or similar retail food establishments and for articles of food sold from vending machines. *Federal Register* 75:129 (July 7), 39026–39028.

Federal Register (2010b). Front-of-pack and shelf tag nutrition symbols; establishment of docket: Request for comments and information. *Federal Register, 75*:82 (April 29), 22602–22606.

Federal Register (2011). Food labeling: Nutrition labeling of standard menu items in restaurants and similar retail food establishments. *Federal Register, 76*(66, April 6), 19192–19236.

Federal Register (2014). Food labeling: Revision of the nutrition and supplement facts labels. *Federal Register, 79*(FR 11879, March 3), 11879–11987.

FTC (Federal Trade Commission) (2006). Comments of the staff in the matter of assessing consumer perceptions of health claims, public meeting; request for comments. Docket No. 2005N-0413. Accessed May 30, 2012. Retrieved from www.fda.gov/ohrms/dockets/dockets/05n0413 /05n-0413_emc0004-03.pdf.

Frosch, D., & Grande, D. (2010). Direct-to-consumer advertising of prescription drugs. *Leonard Davis Institute of Health Economics, 15*(3). Retrieved from http://ldihealtheconomist.com/media/direct-to-consumer-advertising-of-prescription-drugs.original.pdf.

Garrison, R. W. (2012). Natural rates of interest and sustainable growth. *Cato Journal, 32*(2), 423–437.

Goniewicz, M., Knysak, J., Gawron, M., Kosmider, L., Sobczak, A., Kurek, J., Prokopowicz, A., Jablonska-Czapla, M., Rosik-Dulewska, C., Havel, C., Peyton, J., & Benowitz, N. (2013). Levels of selected carcinogens and toxicants in vapour from electronic cigarettes. *Tobacco Control*, March 6, 1–7. doi:10.1136/tobaccocontrol-2012-050859.

Goniewicz, M., Lingas, E., & Hajek, P. (2013). Patterns of electronic cigarette use and user beliefs about their safety and benefits: An Internet survey. *Drug Alcohol Review, 32*(2), 133–140.

Grana, R., Benowitz, N., & Glantz, S. (2014). E-cigarettes: A scientific review. *Circulation, 129*, 1972–1986. Retrieved from http://circ.ahajournals.org/content/129/19/1972.full.

Haar, M. V. (2014) Update: Ongoing CTP regulatory issues. *Tobacco E-News*. Retrieved from www.cspnet.com/category-news/tobacco/articles/update-ongoing-ctp-regulatory-issues.

Hammond, D., Fong, G. T., McDonald, P. W., Brown, K. S., & Cameron, R. (2004). Graphic Canadian cigarette warning labels and adverse outcomes: Evidence from Canadian smokers. *American Journal of Public Health, 94*(8), 1442–1445. doi:10.2105/AJPH.94.8.1442.

Hammond, R. A., & Levine, R. (2010). The economic impact of obesity in the United States. *Diabetes, Metabolic Syndrome and Obesity: Targets and Therapy, 3*, 285–295. doi:10.2147/DMSOTT.S7384.

Harris, G. (2012). White House and the F.D.A. often at odds. *New York Times*, April 2. Retrieved from www.nytimes.com/2012/04/03/health/policy/white-house-and-fda-at-odds-on-regulatory-issues.html?_r=2&.

Hasler, C. M. (2008). Health claims in the United States: An aid to the public or a source of confusion? *Journal of Nutrition. 138*(6), 1216S.

Hersey, J. C., Wohlgenant, K. C., Arsenault, J. E., Kosa, K. M., & Muth, M. K. (2013). Effects of front-of-package and shelf nutrition labeling systems on consumers. *Nutrition Reviews, 71*(1), 1–14. doi:10.1111/nure.12000.

Hieke, S., & Taylor, C. (2012). A critical review of the literature on nutritional labeling. *Journal of Consumer Affairs, 46*(1), 120–156. doi:10.1111/j.1745-6606.2011.01219.x.

Howlett, E. A., Burton, S., Bates, K., & Huggins, K. (2009). Coming to a restaurant near you? Potential consumer responses to nutrition information disclosure on menus. *Journal of Consumer Research, 36*(3), 494–503. doi:10.1086/598799.

Institute of Medicine (2011). *Examination of Front-of-Package Nutrition Rating Systems and Symbols,* October 18. Retrieved from www.iom.edu/Activities/Nutrition/NutritionSymbols.aspx.

International Food Information Council (2011). *Front of Pack Labeling Consumer Research Project.* Retrieved from www.foodinsight.org/Content/3651/IFIC%20FOP%20SLIDES%20for%20WEB2011.pdf.

International Food Information Council (2012). *2012 Food & Health Survey: Consumer Attitudes toward Food Safety, Nutrition & Health.* Retrieved from www.foodinsight.org /Resources/Detail.aspx?topic=2012_Food_ Health_Survey_Consumer_Attitudes_ toward_Food_Safety_Nutrition_and_Health.

Jha, P. (2009). Avoidable global cancer deaths and total deaths from smoking. *Nature Reviews Cancer, 9*(9), 655–664. doi:10.1038/nrc2703.

Kees, J., Andrews, J. C., & Kozup, J. (2010). Understanding how graphic pictorial warnings work on cigarette packaging. *Journal of Public Policy & Marketing, 29*(2), 265–276. doi:10.1509/jppm.29.2.265.

Kees, J., Burton, S., Andrews, J. C., & Kozup, J. (2006). Tests of graphic visuals and cigarette package warning combinations: Implications for the Framework Convention on Tobacco Control. *Journal of Public Policy & Marketing, 25*(2), 212–223. doi:10.1509/jppm.25.2.212.

Kees, J., Stafford, M., & Cho, Y. (2014). Regulating front-of-package nutrition information disclosures: A test of industry self-regulation versus other popular options. *Journal of Consumer Affairs, 48*(1), 147–174.

Kessler, D. A., Natanblut, S. L., Wilkenfeld, J. P., Lorraine, C. C., Mayl, S. L., Bernstein, I. B., & Thompson, L. (1997). Nicotine addiction: A pediatric disease. *Journal of Pediatrics, 130*(4), 518–524. doi:10.1016/S0022-3476(97)70232-4.

Kiszko, K., Martinez, O., Abrams, C., & Elbel, B. (2014). The influence of calorie labeling on food orders and consumption: A review of the literature. *Journal of Community Health, 39*(6), 1248–1269.

Kozup, J. C., Creyer, E. H., & Burton, S. (2003). Making healthful food choices: The influence of health claims and nutrition information on consumers' evaluations of packaged food products and restaurant menu items. *Journal of Marketing, 67*(2), 19–34. doi:10.1509/jmkg.67.2.19.18608.

Lacko, James M., & Pappalardo, Janis K. (2010). The failure and promise of mandated consumer mortgage disclosures: Evidence from qualitative interviews and a controlled experiment with mortgage borrowers. *American Economic Review, 100*(2): 516–521.

Lee, S., Grana, R. A., & Glantz, S. A. (2014). Electronic cigarette use among Korean adolescents: A cross-sectional study of market penetration, dual use, and relationship to quit attempts and former smoking. *Journal of Adolescent Health: Official Publication of the Society for Adolescent Medicine, 54*(6), 684–690. doi:10.1016/j.jadohealth.2013.11.003.

Lee, Y. O., Hebert, C. J., Nonnemaker, J. M., & Kim, A. E. (2014). Multiple tobacco product use among adults in the United States: Cigarettes, cigars, electronic cigarettes, hookah, smokeless tobacco, and snus. *Preventive Medicine, 62*, 14–19. doi:10.1016/j.ypmed.2014.01.014.

Mason, M. J., Scammon, D. L., & Fang, X. (2007). The impact of warnings, disclaimers, and product experience on consumers' perceptions of dietary supplements. *Journal of Consumer Affairs, 41*(1), 74–99.

Mayhew, K. P., Flay, B. R., & Mott, J. A. (2000). Stages in the development of adolescent smoking. *Drug and Alcohol Dependence, 59*, 61–81. doi:10.1016/S0376-8716(99)00165-9.

Maynard, O. M., Attwood, A., O'Brien, L., Brooks, S., Hedge, C., Leonards, U., & Munafò, M. R. (2014). Avoidance of cigarette pack health warnings among regular cigarette smokers. *Drug and Alcohol Dependence, 136*, 170–174. doi:10.1016/j.drugalcdep.2014.01.001.

McGuire, W. J. (1980). The communication-persuasion model and health-risk labeling. In L. A. Morris, M. B. Mazis, & I. Barofsky (eds.), *Banbury Report 6: Product Labeling and Health Risks* (pp. 99–119). Cold Spring Harbor, NY: Cold Spring Harbor Laboratory.

Menon, A. M., Deshpande, A. D., Perri, III, M., & Zinkhan, G. M. (2003). Consumers' attention to the brief summary in print direct-to-consumer advertisements: Perceived usefulness in patient–physician discussions. *Journal of Public Policy & Marketing, 22*(2), 181.

Morris, L. A., Mazis, M. B., & Barofsky, I. (eds.), (1980). *Banbury Report 6: Product Labeling and Health Risks*. Cold Spring Harbor, NY: Cold Spring Harbor Laboratory.

Munafo, M. R., Roberts, N., Bauld, L., & Leonards, U. (2011). Plain packaging increases visual attention to health warnings on cigarette packs in non-smokers and weekly smokers but not daily smokers. *Addiction, 106*(8), 1505–1510.

Myers, M. (2013). *Government's Decision Not to Appeal Cigarette Warning Ruling Is Disappointing: FDA Should Quickly Develop New Set of Graphic Warnings*. March 19. Washington, DC: Campaign for Tobacco-Free Kids. Retrieved from www.tobaccofreekids.org/press_releases /post/2013_03_19_fda.

National Institutes of Health (2014). What are overweight and obesity? Retrieved from www.nhlbi.nih.gov/health/health-topics/topics/obe/.

Navarro-Martinez, D., Salisbury, L. C., Lemon K. N., Steward, N., Matthews, W. J., & Harris, A. J. L (2011). Minimum required payment and supplemental information disclosure effects on consumer debt repayment decisions. *Journal of Marketing Research, 48*, 60–77.

Newman, C. L., Howlett, E., & Burton, S. (2014). Shopper response to front-of-package nutrition labeling programs: Potential consumer and retail store benefits. *Journal of Retailing, 90*(1), 13–26. doi:10.1016/j.jretai.2013.11.001.

Nonnemaker, J., Farrelly, M., Kamyab, K., Busey, A., & Mann, N. (2010). *Experimental Study of Graphic Cigarette Warning Labels*. Research Triangle Park, NC: RTI International. Retrieved from www.tobaccolabels.ca/wp/wp-content/uploads/2013/12/USA-2010-Experimental-Study-of-Graphic-Cigarette-Warning-Labels-Final-Results-Report-FDA.pdf.

Nutrition Labeling and Education Act (NLEA) (1990). Public Law No. 101-535, 104 Stat. 2353 (codified in part at 21 U.S.C. 343).

Parker, J. R., & Lehmann, D. R. (2014). How and when grouping low-calorie options reduces the benefits of providing dish-specific calorie information. *Journal of Consumer Research, 41*(1), 213–235. doi:10.1086/675738.

Pepper, J. K., Cameron, L. D., Reiter, P. L., McRee, A., & Brewer, N. T. (2013). Non-smoking male adolescents' reactions to cigarette warnings: E65533. *PLoS One, 8*(8). doi:10.1371/journal.pone.0065533.

Peters, E., Romer, D., Slovic, P., Jamieson, K. H., Wharfield, L., & Mertz, C. K., (2007). The impact and acceptability of Canadian-Style cigarette warning labels among U.S. smokers and nonsmokers. *Nicotine & Tobacco Research, 9*(4), 473–481.

Petty, Richard E., & Cacioppo, John T. (1986). *Communication and Persuasion: Central and Peripheral Routes to Attitude Change.* New York: Springer-Verlag.

Pokhrel P., Pebbles F., Melissa A. L., Crissy T. K., & Herzog, T.A. (2013). Smokers who try e-cigarettes to quit smoking: Findings from a multiethnic study in Hawaii. *American Journal of Public Health, 103*, 9.

Prochaska, J. O., & DiClemente, C. C. (1983). Stages and processes of self-change of smoking: Toward an integrative model of change. *Journal of Consulting and Clinical Psychology, 51*(3), 390–395. doi:10.1037/0022-006X.51.3.390.

Riker, C. A., Lee, K., Darville, A., & Hahn, E. J. (2012). E-cigarettes: Promise or peril? *Nursing Clinics of North America, 47*(1), 159–171. doi:10.1016/j.cnur.2011.10.002.

Rogers, R. W. (1975). A protection motivation theory of fear appeals and attitudinal change. *Journal of Psychology, 91*(1), 93–114.

Romer, D., Peters, E., Strasser, A. A., & Langleben, D. (2013). Desire versus efficacy in smokers' paradoxical reactions to pictorial health warnings for cigarettes. *PloS one, 8*(1), e54937.

Siegel, M., & Biener, L. (2000). The impact of an antismoking media campaign on progression to established smoking: Results of a longitudinal youth study. *American Journal of Public Health, 90*(3), 380–386. doi:10.2105/AJPH.90.3.380.

Siegel, M. B., Tanwar, K. L., & Wood, K. S. (2011). Electronic cigarettes as a smoking-cessation: Tool results from an online survey. *American Journal of Preventive Medicine, 40*(4), 472.

Stewart, D. W., & Martin, I. M. (1994). Intended and unintended consequences of warning messages: A review and synthesis of empirical research. *Journal of Public Policy & Marketing, 13*, 1–19.

Strahan, E. J., White, K., Fong, G. T., Fabrigar, L. R., Zanna, M. P., & Cameron, R. (2002). Enhancing the effectiveness of tobacco package warning labels: A social psychological perspective. *Tobacco Control, 11*(3), 183–190. doi:10.1136/tc.11.3.183.

Strasser, A. A., Tang, K. Z., Romer, D., Jepson, C., & Cappella, J. N. (2012). Graphic warning labels in cigarette advertisements: Recall and viewing patterns. *American Journal of Preventive Medicine, 43*(1), 41–47. doi:10.1016/j.amepre.2012.02.026.

Surgeon General Report (2012). *Preventing Tobacco Use among Youth and Young Adults.* Retrieved from www.surgeongeneral.gov/library/reports/preventing-youth-tobacco-use/.

Synovate (2005). *Quantitative Evaluation of Alternative Food Signposting Concepts: Report of Findings.* Retrieved from http://webarchive.nationalarchives.gov.uk/20131104005023/www.food.gov.uk/multimedia/pdfs/signpostquanresearch.pdf.

U.S. Patient Protection and Affordable Care Act (2010). Public Law 111-148. Stat. 119 through 124.

U.S. Surgeon General (2013). *Overweight and Obesity: Health Consequences*. Retrieved from www.surgeongeneral.gov/library/calls/obesity/fact_consequences.html.

U.S. Department of Health and Human Services (2014). *The Health Consequences of Smoking – 50 Years of Progress: A Report of the Surgeon General*. Atlanta, GA: U.S. Department of Health and Human Services, Centers for Disease Control and Prevention, National Center for Chronic Disease Prevention and Health Promotion, Office on Smoking and Health.

Viswanathan, M., & Hastak, M. (2002). The role of summary information in facilitating consumers' comprehension of nutrition information. *Journal of Public Policy & Marketing, 21*(2), 305–318. doi:10.1509/jppm.21.2.305.17596.

Wall Street Journal (2014). Big tobacco's e-cigarette push gets a reality check. Retrieved from http://online.wsj.com/articles/big-tobaccos-e-cig-push-gets-a-reality-check-1409078319.

Wang, A., Romer, D., Elman, I., Turetsky, B., Gur, R., & Langleben, D. (2013). Emotional graphic cigarette warning labels reduce the electrophysiological brain response to smoking cues. *Addiction Biology* Available online December 15. doi: 10.1111/adb.12117.

Wansink, B., & Chandon, P. (2006). Can "low-fat" nutrition labels lead to obesity? *Journal of Marketing Research, 43*(4), 605–617. doi:10.1509/jmkr.43.4.605.

Wogalter, M. S. (2006). The communication-human information processing (C-HIP) model. In M. S. Wogalter (ed.), *Handbook of Warnings* (pp. 51–61). Mahwah, NJ: Lawrence Erlbaum Associates.

Woodward, R. E., & Hall, S. E. (2010). The burden of the nondiversifiable risk of entrepreneurship. *American Economic Review, 100*(3), 1163–1194.

World Health Organization (WHO) (2014). *WHO FCTC Health Warnings Database*. Geneva: WHO. Retrieved from www.who.int/tobacco/healthwarningsdatabase/en/.

World Health Organization (WHO) (2014). *Obesity and Overweight*. Geneva: WHO. Retrieved from www.who.int/mediacentre/factsheets/fs311/en/.

Wosinka, M. (2005). Direct-to-consumer advertising and drug therapy compliance. *Journal of Marketing Research, 42*(3), 323–332.

Zhao, X., Nan, X., Yang, B., & Iles, I. A. (2014). Cigarette warning labels: Graphics, framing, and identity. *Health Education, 114*(2), 101–117. doi:10.1108/HE-06-2013-0024.

21 Taxes and Consumer Behavior

Christopher Y. Olivola and Abigail B. Sussman

[I]n this world nothing can be said to be certain, except death and taxes.
– Benjamin Franklin, 1789

Introduction

At first glance, a chapter dedicated to taxes might seem like a strange addition to a handbook of consumer psychology. Yet, in many countries, taxes are an inescapable part of the purchasing experience, and they come in many forms: sales taxes, value added taxes (VAT), goods and services taxes (GST), and so on. The size and salience of taxes vary considerably across countries and even across states (within the United States). In many European countries, the taxes that consumers must pay when they purchase a taxable good are included in its listed price and therefore not explicitly visible. Consequently, these taxes are not very salient to European consumers. In the United States, by contrast, sales taxes are not listed in the prices of goods. Instead, they are explicitly added to the price that consumers must pay at the moment of purchase, and so are quite salient.

The government can leverage taxes to encourage spending in favored areas such as donations to charity and home purchases and to discourage spending in disfavored areas such as cigarettes and alcohol. In addition to shaping consumer behavior at the point of purchase, consumers' responses to taxes affect a variety of consequential decisions. For example, the presence and size of taxes can influence the jobs that consumers choose and the number of hours they work, and these factors can flow through to consumers' decisions to pay taxes that they have accrued (e.g., Jung, Snow, & Trandel, 1994; Kesselman, 1989; Pestieau & Possen, 1991, 1992; Watson, 1985; although see Parker, 2003, for a critique). Taxes can even alter consumers' decisions of how much to save and what they should be saving for (e.g., for education or retirement) (Bernheim, 2002). Decisions about earning and saving alter consumption choices by serving as critical inputs to the consumers' available budget. At each interaction with a tax, consumers' attitudes toward the government and tax authorities (i.e., those imposing the tax) can affect their decisions above and beyond the tax's economic value.

Given its pervasive importance, this chapter reviews the literature on the consumer psychology of taxes. We begin with a discussion of consumers' attitudes toward taxes and how they influence decisions to comply with tax payments that regulators can neither directly monitor nor enforce with certainty (e.g., taxes on income that is "off the books"). Next, we examine how taxes can shape consumer preferences and purchasing choices. We then consider key demographic variables that seem to moderate consumers' sensitivity to taxes. We conclude by discussing future directions of research and some unanswered questions.

For readers interested in the study of taxes more generally, there are several rich streams of research, stemming largely from economics, law, and political science, that are outside the scope of the current chapter. For example, there are numerous theories of optimal taxation (e.g., Bovenberg & Goulder, 1996; Chamley, 1986; Diamond & Mirrlees, 1971a, 1971b) and of taxes as tools for the redistribution of wealth (e.g., Alesina & Rodrik, 1994; Dixit & Londregan, 1998; McCaffery, 1994; Piketty, 1995). In this chapter, however, we will take a psychological perspective, focusing on research that is most directly relevant to consumers.

Tax Attitudes and Compliance

Tax noncompliance is a major problem for large governments, estimated at approximately $385 billion of uncollected tax revenue annually in the United States (IRS, 2012) and £42 billion in the United Kingdom (HMRC, 2012). Nonetheless, people pay more taxes than traditional economic models (e.g., Allingham & Sandmo, 1972) would predict given the low levels of enforcement and small penalties associated with tax evasion (e.g., Alm, McClelland, & Schulze, 1992; Andreoni, Erard, & Feinstein, 1998; Cullis, Jonesa, & Savoia, 2012; Spicer, 1986; Torgler, 2003). This gap between purely economic expectations and actual tax payments has encouraged closer examination of behavioral factors influencing a person's decision to comply (or not) with tax laws (beginning with Schmölders, 1959; for detailed reviews, see Pickhardt & Prinz, 2014, regarding the behavioral dynamics of tax evasion; Andreoni, Erard, & Feinstein, 1998, regarding tax compliance from an economic perspective; and Slemrod, 2007, regarding tax evasion from an economic perspective). Research has focused primarily on enforcement policies, moral obligation, and cultural and normative factors that influence attitudes toward, and decisions to comply with, tax payments (for reviews, see Alm, 2012; Jackson & Milliron, 1986; OECD, 2013; Torgler, 2007).

The basic economic consequences of getting caught and the threat thereof are effective at encouraging payment, even if they cannot fully explain observed tax compliance behavior (e.g., Orviska & Hudson, 2002; see Kirchler, Maciejovsky, & Schneider, 2003 for a discussion of differences in attitudes toward tax avoidance, tax evasion, and tax flight). Although enforcement works largely through economic incentives, psychological and behavioral factors, including emotions and interpretations of tax penalties, can also play a role. In addition to the financial consequences of incurring a penalty, exposing a cheater in public can have an additional cost of public shame (Bø, Slemrod, & Thoresen, 2015; Coricelli, Rusconi, & Villeval, 2014). However, Coricelli and colleagues (2014) find that taxpayers will cheat less when initial shaming is followed by forgiveness and reintegration into the community than when it is not followed by the opportunity for reintegration. In this case, the extreme negative emotions tied to cheating can actually lead to more of it. Additionally, differences in expectations about penalties and the likelihood of being caught can lead to differences in tax compliance. Uncertainty around the likelihood of an audit can lead to higher levels of tax compliance (Tan & Yim, 2014), as can over-weighting the low probability that there will be an audit (Alm, McClelland, & Schulze, 1992). Thus, a person's ability to learn about tax penalties is important for explaining tax compliance (Soliman, Jones, & Cullis, 2014).

Psychological Motivations for Tax Payments

In addition to the fear of an audit, tax payment patterns suggest that taxpayers have an intrinsic motivation to pay taxes in many situations (i.e., "tax morale"). According to the tax affinity hypothesis, individuals can derive utility from paying taxes due to benefits from pro-social behavior (e.g., Djanali & Sheehan-Connor, 2012). A variety of factors, including social norms (e.g., Cullis, Jonesa, & Savoia, 2012; Spicer, 1986), moral obligation (e.g., Bobek & Hatfield, 2003; Reckers, Sanders, & Roark, 1994; Shu et al., 2012), trust in government (e.g., Kasper, Kogler, & Kirchler, 2015; Scholz & Lubell, 1998; Torgler, 2003; Wahl, Kastlunger, & Kirchler, 2010), and beliefs about how tax-dollars are being spent (e.g., Hill, 2010; Lamberton, 2013; Lamberton, De Neve, & Norton, 2014; Sussman & Olivola, 2011), can influence a citizen's decision to pay taxes as well as his or her satisfaction from doing so.

Both personal norms (privately held ethical and moral convictions) and social norms (beliefs about others' behaviors and values) play a role in tax compliance. Appeals to a taxpayer's conscience (Schwartz & Orleans, 1967), wealth as a responsibility (Whillans, Wispinski, & Dunn, under review), anticipated guilt over noncompliance (Grasmick & Bursik, 1990; Scott & Grasmick, 1981), ethical convictions regarding taxes (Reckers, Sanders, & Roark, 1994), and general honesty (Porcano, 1988) have all been linked to more compliant behavior. Taxpayers are likely to believe that known others share their level of tax compliance (e.g., De Juan, Lasheras, & Mayo, 1994; Spicer & Lundstedt, 1976; Wallschutzky, 1984; Webley, Cole, & Eidjar, 2001).

Further, experimental studies have demonstrated that providing taxpayers with the information that people generally underestimate how much other taxpayers support compliance increased tax payments (Wenzel, 2005), whereas learning that others favor lower levels of penalties led to lower tax payments (Alm, McClelland, & Schulze, 1999). Although beliefs about tax compliance attitudes and behaviors among friends and similar others consistently mirror one's own behavior, beliefs about tax compliance among taxpayers in the general population have been shown to demonstrate the reverse pattern in some circumstances (Brooks & Doob, 1990; Hasseldine, Kaplan, & Fuller, 1994). Reconciling this discrepant pattern, Wenzel (2004) demonstrated explicitly that the effect of social norms is moderated by the strength of one's tie to the group whose behavior is known, with people assimilating tax compliance behavior to those with strong ties and differentiating themselves from those with weak ties.

Beliefs about the government and tax authorities can also influence people's willingness to comply with tax laws. In particular, higher levels of trust in the government can increase the likelihood of tax compliance (e.g., Scholz & Lubell, 1998), as can direct democratic rights (i.e., citizens' voice in the decision-making process; Torgler, 2003, 2007). Kirchler and colleagues (Kasper, Kogler, & Kirchler, 2015; Kirchler, 2007; Kirchler, Hoelzl, & Wahl, 2008; Kirchler, Muehlbacher, Kastlunger, & Wahl, 2010; Prinz, Muehlbacher, & Kirchler, 2014) detail a complex relationship between taxpayers' trust in the government and their expected level of enforcement of tax penalties, formalized in the slippery slope framework (Kirchler, Hoezl, & Wahl, 2008). When trust in the government and tax authorities is low, authorities need to exert power through higher fines and audit probabilities to increase compliance with tax laws. However, when trust in the government and tax authorities is high, other variables such as moral appeals, knowledge, attitudes, and fairness can lead to voluntary compliance, whereas high levels of penalties and enforcement can actually backfire and corrupt intrinsic motivation to pay taxes (e.g., Kirchler et al., 2010). When either trust in the government or the power of the government is at a maximum, people will comply with tax laws irrespective of the level of the other variable. Thus, these interactions matter most when levels of trust or power are) low (e.g., Kirchler, Hoezl, & Wahl, 2008).

Beliefs about Taxes

An understanding of the tax system (e.g., Eriksen & Fallan, 1996; Kasper, Kogler, & Kirchler, 2015) and how taxes are being used (e.g., Alm, McClelland, & Schulze, 1992; Hill, 2010) can serve as a critical component in considerations of one's moral obligation to pay taxes. Recent evidence suggests that people's attitudes toward taxes can become more favorable as their knowledge of the tax system increases. Eriksen and Fallan (1996) demonstrate that, as tax knowledge increases, people consider their own and others' tax evasion to be more serious and taxation to be more fair, while Kasper, Kogler, and Kirchler (2015) show that media coverage influences trust in tax authorities and perceived power of the government.

Taxpayers (as examined in the United States) believe that the government has a duty to ensure equal opportunity for all and view their taxes as part of this collective goal (Greenberg & Greenberg, 2013). More broadly, beliefs that taxes should be collected and distributed fairly and evenly can influence compliance, with equal treatment serving as a salient principal of fairness (Sausgruber & Tyran, 2014; see also Verboon & Van Dijke, 2007, for a discussion of the compatibility between self-interest motives and concerns about justice). Consistent with this pattern, the presence of sympathy or the priming of empathy can encourage tax compliance (Bazart & Bonein, 2014).

One factor hindering maximum tax compliance may be the disconnect between tax payments and the benefits provided by tax dollars. For example, one survey revealed that 53 percent of Americans who claimed they had never benefited from government social services had in fact taken out student loans, and 40 percent had Medicare (Mettler, 2011). Providing taxpayers with agency over how their tax dollars are being spent can also increase compliance and satisfaction with tax payments. Lamberton and colleagues (Lamberton, 2013; Lamberton, De Neve, & Norton 2014) have found that giving taxpayers the opportunity to allocate a small portion of their tax payments to specific budget categories or to signal their preferences for how they would like their tax dollars to be spent provides a stronger perceived coupling between payments and services received. Consequently, these interventions reduce antitax sentiment and hold satisfaction with tax payments stable as the value of tax payments increases. Consistent with this pattern, we have found that encouraging members of political parties favoring antitax policies to consider positive uses of their tax dollars can eliminate tax-averse tendencies (Sussman & Olivola, 2011).

How Taxes Shape Consumer Choices

A variety of factors influence consumer perceptions of, and attitudes toward, taxes. Perhaps most relevant from the perspective of consumer behavior researchers, taxes can also directly influence consumer choices in a variety of ways. In addition to shaping retail purchases (e.g., Einav, Knoepfle, Levin, & Sundaresan, 2014; Goolsbee, 2000; Manuszak & Moul, 2009; Sussman & Olivola, 2011), the presence of taxes – and the extent to which consumers are aware of them (e.g., Chetty, Looney, & Kroft, 2009; Goldin & Homonoff, 2013) – can also encourage behaviors valued by the government, such as charitable giving (e.g., Andreoni, 1993; Andreoni & Payne, 2011; Eckel, Grossman, & Johnston, 2005) and, the choice of certain financial products (e.g., Feenberg & Poterba, 1991; Sussman & Olivola, 2011), while discouraging disfavored behaviors such as eating unhealthy foods (Shah et al., 2014) and using plastic bags (e.g., Homonoff, 2013).

Retail Purchases

When consumers make decisions about which products to buy, elementary economics dictates that prices should matter. Holding the product constant, consumers should make purchasing decisions based on the overall prices that they will have to pay, regardless of the amount of tax included in that price, and when or how the tax is incurred. Indeed, the presence of taxes and additional costs therein do reduce consumer purchases holding all else constant (e.g., Ramsey, 1927). However, consumer responses are more complicated than basic economics might suggest (see Hines, 2007, for an economic, historical, and comparative analysis of consumption taxes in the United States versus internationally). In many cases, consumers respond more strongly to taxes than to equivalent financial costs or to positive incentives (e.g., subsidies, rebates, and bonuses), both because some consumers maintain an apparently intrinsic aversion to taxes (e.g., Sussman & Olivola, 2011), and because they respond more strongly to losses than to equivalent gains (e.g., Bracha & Cooper, 2014; Homonoff, 2013).

At a basic level, consumers strive to avoid additional financial costs, and taxes are included as part of this. One interesting area of investigation is online shopping behavior. As a general rule, online stores do not collect sales taxes unless they have a physical presence in a given state. Goolsbee (2000) shows that people who live in states with high sales taxes are significantly more likely to shop online and estimates that comparable online taxes could reduce the number of online buyers by nearly a quarter. Anderson, Fong, Simester, and Tucker (2010) examine cases where stores on the Internet open locations within a state and must begin charging sales taxes to all consumers in the state (see also Baugh, Ben-David, & Park, 2014). The authors show that when a store begins collecting taxes, its Internet sales decrease, but its catalogue sales remain unchanged. They attribute this difference to the ease of searching for alternatives online relative to through catalogues. In other words, when taxes are salient and also easily avoidable, consumers will alter their behavior to reduce or eliminate these costs. However, their efforts are limited by the availability of alternatives. Einav and colleagues (2014) show that consumers are more likely to purchase products from online retailers that do not have locations in their state. They estimate that every 1 percent increase in a consumer's state tax increases his or her online purchases by 2 percent but decreases the consumer's online purchases from retailers with a presence in their state by 3 to 4 percent (see also Hu & Tang, 2014).

However, in order for consumers to respond to a cost, they must first notice that they will be required to pay it. Chetty, Looney, and Kroft (2009) demonstrate that consumers underreact to taxes (relative to their dollar value) when these taxes are not salient. They find that posting price tags that explicitly state the amount of tax the consumer will need to pay reduces demand by 8 percent relative to incorporating the tax into the final price paid once the consumer reaches the register. Along a similar vein, consumers are less likely to respond to changes in toll amounts (i.e., alter their driving routes to avoid toll roads) when toll facilities adopt electronic toll collection, and the salience of paying the toll is minimized (Finkelstein, 2009). Finkelstein estimates that tolls are 20 to 40 percent higher than they would have been with manual collection. In addition to minimizing the salience of taxes by omitting them from price tags or through automaticity, complex tax systems have also been shown to reduce consumer response to amount (Abeler & Jäger, in press).

In contrast to underreacting to subtle forms of taxation, people can overreact to taxes when these are salient (Sussman & Olivola, 2011). For example, people report being more likely to purchase an item on sale when the sale is described as an "Axe the Tax" sale than when it is described as a "Customer Rewards" sale, holding the cost of the good and the amount of the discount constant. At the extreme of salient taxes, Cabral and Hoxby (2012) argue that the property tax is the most hated tax in part because it is the most salient tax that consumers pay. Goldin (2012) provides an overview of research suggesting that the salience of the monetary cost of a tax dramatically alters taxpayer behavior. Namely, consumers respond more strongly to a tax when the good's after-tax price is displayed more prominently (see also Goldin, 2014, for an economic discussion of optimal levels of tax salience).

Tax Deductions and Credits: Using Taxes to Encourage Behavior

In addition to serving as a form of neutral revenue for the government, tax policies can also be designed to encourage favored behaviors. An important example is the encouragement of charitable giving through tax deductions. Despite the presence of this policy, consumers underestimate their eligibility for tax benefits through charitable gifts as well as the size of these benefits (Goldin & Listokin, 2014). Since the government provides funds for many nonprofit organizations that originate through taxes, one question is whether this government funding crowds out (i.e., displaces) voluntary giving, as game theoretic analysis would suggest (e.g., Andreoni, 1993; Bergstrom, Blume, & Varian, 1986; Warr, 1982). Some existing research suggests that consumers continue to give voluntarily despite government funding (e.g., Andreoni, 1993; Gronberg, Luccasen, Turocy, & Van Huyck, 2012).

Neural evidence also supports this pattern, demonstrating that consumers derive benefit from voluntary donations above and beyond any satisfaction they experience from increases in public goods, such as those that occur through taxation (Harbaugh, Mayr, & Burghart, 2007). Consistent with strong responses to salient taxes observed in the context of consumer goods, Eckel, Grossman, and Johnston (2005) demonstrate that forced contributions through taxation do in fact crowd out private giving in instances where the source of the funding is made salient. In other words, when people are told explicitly that their tax dollars were contributed to a particular cause, they no longer want to give to that cause. In a review of field data estimates, Steinberg (1991) concludes that most studies reveal low levels of crowding out. However, the evidence is mixed (e.g., Manzoor & Straub, 2005, and Payne, 1998, are exceptions), and there may also be substantial but incomplete levels of crowding out (e.g., Andreoni, 1993; Chan, Godby, Mestelman, & Muller, 2002). Furthermore, Andreoni and Payne (2011) suggest that some apparent crowding out may actually be due to a reduction in fundraising efforts by the charity.

The government is able to use tax incentives to promote specific financial behaviors as well. For example, state and local governments can borrow money through tax-exempt municipal bonds. Consistent with responses to some of the neutral taxes described previously, consumers tend to respond more strongly than economic terms would dictate to this financial lever. From a rational economic perspective, a consumer choosing between a taxable corporate bond or a tax-exempt municipal bond with identical features (other than yield) should choose the bond with the higher after-tax yield, as determined by her personal marginal tax rate. The benefits to investors of holding tax-exempt municipal bonds increase with their marginal tax brackets.

However, Feenberg and Poterba (1991) show that nearly one-fifth of tax-exempt municipal bond interest goes to households with low marginal tax rates, for which the bonds appear to be suboptimal investments. They speculate that several factors could explain this behavior, including the sluggishness of portfolio adjustments to changing tax brackets or a desire to avoid paying taxes, even if that desire induces an economic cost (see Poterba, 2002, for an economic review of the role of taxes on household investment behavior, and Bernheim, 2002, for an economic review of the role of taxes on savings). In our own work, we provide support for the latter explanation of a non-economic desire to avoid taxes (Sussman & Olivola, 2011). Specifically, we found, in two studies, that people strongly prefer bonds with equivalent after-tax financial terms when they do not have to pay taxes on their earnings.

Sin Taxes: Using Taxes to Discourage Behavior

Just as tax deductions and exemptions can be used to encourage favored behaviors, governments often impose taxes with the goal of discouraging a range of disfavored behaviors, from increasing carbon emissions to smoking cigarettes to eating unhealthy foods. The existing evidence suggests that these taxes are generally effective at reducing undesirable behaviors, including the consumption of alcohol (see Wagenaar, Salois, & Komro, 2009, for a meta-analysis), sugary beverages (see Brownell et al., 2009, for a meta-analysis), and tobacco (see Chaloupka, Straif, & Leon, 2011). In fact, in the case of tobacco, comprehensive analyses demonstrate that tax increases are the most effective intervention to reduce demand (Jha & Chaloupka, 2000). While the effect of many of these taxes on overall consumer welfare (rather than consumption) remains unknown, there is evidence that the addition of taxes can at times increase consumer well-being, at least in the case of cigarette taxes (Gruber & Mullainathan, 2005; see O'Donoghue & Rabin, 2003, 2006, for a behavioral-economic perspective on optimizing sin taxes).

However, the majority of economic analyses of the effect of taxes on behavior change are silent about how much of this change results from purely economic factors relating to the cost of the tax versus from psychological reactions to its implementation. Although the government can turn to subsidies as an alternate financial lever, research suggests that taxes are more powerful tools for effecting behavior change than subsidies of equivalent value. For example, one recent investigation demonstrated that a five cent tax imposed on the use of each environmentally unfriendly disposable shopping bag significantly decreased consumers' reliance on disposable bags, whereas a five cent bonus for bringing reusable bags had no effect (Homonoff, 2013). Other research investigating the effects of taxes versus subsidies on food choice revealed a similar pattern, demonstrating that taxing unhealthy foods reduced the portion of fat purchased while subsidizing healthier foods had no effect on the nutrition quality of food purchased (Epstein, Dearing, Roba, & Finkelstein, 2010). Shah and colleagues (2014) further explored the interactions between psychological factors and costs associated with taxes in the domain of food choice. They found that explicitly informing restaurant patrons that certain foods were taxed for being unhealthy reduced consumption of less healthy foods above and beyond the additional financial cost imposed by the tax.

Many consumers display strong reactance to taxes. For example, DeCicca, Kenkel, and Liu (2013) provide evidence that consumers will travel across state borders to avoid taxes placed on cigarettes. Hardisty, Johnson, and Weber (2010) demonstrate sensitivity to the tax label itself, showing that consumers are more willing to pay an additional charge to make up for their environmental footprint when the charge is described as an offset rather than a tax (although this pattern is moderated by political party, as described later). Consistent with this finding, Swedes have been shown to prefer policies that function like a tax when these are not labeled as such (Brannlund & Persson, 2012). While this strong reaction to the tax label itself may be beneficial in that it discourages unwanted behaviors, it may also be unproductive from the standpoint of raising additional revenues.

Framing Effects

Although consumers' perceptions and responses to taxes reflect stable underlying attitudes, these can be amplified (or mitigated) by framing manipulations that highlight (or hide) the tax-related nature of the monetary cost imposed on purchases. Decades of research have convincingly demonstrated that simply manipulating the framing of choice sets (without altering their actual compositions) can dramatically alter people's preferences (Kahneman & Tversky, 2000; Tversky & Kahneman, 1981). Within the domain of tax-related judgments and decisions, there have been many studies examining how framing effects can influence tax compliance (e.g., Chang, Nichols, & Schultz, 1987; Cullis, Jones, & Savoia, 2012; Hasseldine & Hite, 2003; Schepanski & Shearer, 1995) and attitudes toward tax policies (e.g., Brannlund & Persson, 2012; Chow & Galak, 2012; LeBoeuf & Shafir, 2003; McCaffery & Baron, 2004; McCaffery & Slemrod, 2006; Reimers, 2009). In contrast, there has been much less research examining the effects of tax framing manipulations on consumers' purchasing decisions.

One set of studies showed that consumers respond more strongly to taxes on undesirable products than to subsidies on desirable products. Epstein and colleagues (2010) compared the effects of increasing the price of high-calorie-for-nutrient foods versus reducing the price of low-calorie-for-nutrient foods. They found that taxing less healthy foods led to the purchase of foods that were lower in calorie, lower in fat, and higher in protein (i.e., more healthy consumption). In contrast, subsidizing more healthy foods led consumers to purchase more calorific foods without reducing (or increasing) their consumption of fat and protein. Similarly, Homonoff (2013) found that a five-cent shopping bag tax reduced the use of disposable bags, whereas an equivalent five-cent bonus for using reusable bags had no effect. These results show that consumers are more averse to the prospect of losing money (i.e., taxes) than they are attracted to the prospect of gaining money (i.e., subsidies) (Bracha & Cooper, 2014; Tversky & Kahneman, 1991), in line with the predictions of several psychological theories (Kahneman & Tversky, 1979; Stewart, Chater, & Brown, 2006).

Another set of studies demonstrated that the "tax" label itself influences consumers' choices. Rivers and Schaufele (2014) provide evidence that taxing the consumption of gas causes a greater decline in the short-run consumption of gasoline than an equivalent increase in the market price of gasoline. They argue that this occurs because a carbon tax is more salient than equivalent market price movements and therefore more strongly affects demand for gasoline. Hardisty, Johnson, and Weber (2010) asked consumers to choose between two products that were nearly identical with the only difference being that one included a surcharge for emitted carbon dioxide, and was therefore more environmentally friendly but also more expensive. They found that conservative (Republican) consumers were less willing to pay for the more expensive and more environmentally friendly product when this surcharge was framed as a "carbon tax," compared to when it was labeled as a "carbon offset." Finally, our own studies have shown that consumers will go to greater lengths (literally) to avoid a tax-related cost on a product than they will to avoid an equivalent, or even larger, monetary cost that is unrelated to taxes (Sussman & Olivola, 2011). For example, participants were more likely to drive to a more distant store (adding twenty-five minutes to their travel time) to obtain an 8 percent tax-related discount on a television set than they were to drive the same distance to obtain a 9 percent discount on the same television model. In fact, the mere association with taxes influenced their purchasing choices: participants were willing to wait longer for a sales promotion, or to accept a lower discount, when it was labeled as an "axe-the-tax" sale than when it was labeled as "customer rewards" sale, even though neither promotion actually eliminated the underlying sales tax.

Consumer Demographics and Tax Behavior

Consumers do not respond uniformly to taxes: the impact of taxes and tax-related frames are more salient to some groups of consumers than others. Two variables, in particular, have been investigated as potential moderators of tax aversion: political orientation (whether a consumer identifies with a right-leaning versus left-leaning political ideology) and gender.

Political Orientation

Political orientation is an important, yet understudied, predictor of consumer behavior (Crockett & Wallendorf, 2004; Roos & Shachar, 2014). One salient example of this is political consumerism, whereby consumers express their political views through their purchase decisions, by deliberately abstaining from purchasing products that conflict with their political views (boycotting) and deliberately purchasing products that accord with their political views ("buycotting") (Katz, 2011; Newman & Bartels, 2011). Political orientation is also, of course, a strong predictor of attitudes toward taxes. Consumers who identify with right-leaning parties (such as the Republicans in the United States and the Tories in the U.K.) tend to be more opposed to taxes than those who identify with left-leaning parties (such as such as the Democrats in the United States and the Labour Party in the U.K.) (e.g., Alvarez & McCaffery, 2003; McGowan, 2000; although see Miles, 2014).

Not surprisingly, then, political orientation has been shown to be a strong predictor of how consumers respond to taxes. Interestingly, although right-leaning (conservative) consumers are less likely (than left-leaning/liberal consumers) to engage in political consumerism (Katz, 2011; Newman & Bartels, 2011), they are more responsive to taxes in their purchasing decisions. Studies have shown that right-leaning consumers are more averse to taxes on products than left-leaning consumers (Hardisty, Johnson, & Weber, 2010; Sussman & Olivola, 2011; Wahlund, 1992). Hardisty, Johnson, and Weber (2010) found that Republicans were less likely than Democrats to purchase a product that included a surcharge for emitted carbon dioxide, but *only* when this surcharge was labeled as a "carbon tax." In contrast, when it was labeled as a "carbon offset," Republican consumers were no less likely to purchase the product with the surcharge. Similarly, we found that consumers who identify with right-leaning political parties (Republicans and Libertarians in the United States, and the Tories in the U.K.) are more likely (than their left-leaning counterparts) to exhibit tax aversion (Sussman & Olivola, 2011). Moreover, reminding right-leaning consumers of the positive ways in which their taxes are being used by the government reduced their propensity to be tax-averse to the level of left-leaning consumers, whereas having them consider negative uses of their taxes further increased their tax aversion. Critically, the greater aversion to taxes among right-leaning consumers seems to be due to memory retrieval processes and cognitive accessibility rather than greater negative affective reactions to taxes (Hardisty, Johnson, and Weber, 2010; Sussman & Olivola, 2011), contrary to theories arguing that variations in political ideology, along the left–right (liberal–conservative) dimension reflect deep-seated, stable individual differences in physiological and psychological affective responses to negative stimuli (Hibbing, Smith, & Alford, 2014; Olivola & Sussman, 2014).

Gender

Another, perhaps less obvious, variable that has been thought to influence tax behavior is consumer gender. Several different streams of research point to this association.

First, a fairly sizable body of research suggests that people tend to associate tax policy with maleness. That is, taxes and fiscal policy are considered to be stereotypically "male" (as opposed to "female") issues (Alexander & Andersen, 1993; Kahn, 1993). This lay association between taxation and maleness is likely the product of a more general stereotype-based belief that male politicians are more suited to deal with "hard" issues, such as fiscal policy and taxation, while female politicians are assumed to be better at addressing "soft" issues, such as welfare, healthcare, and education (e.g., Alexander & Andersen, 1993; Chang & Hitchon, 2004; Huddy & Terkildsen, 1993). To the extent that these stereotypes reflect real gender differences or (more likely) that consumers internalize and respond to these stereotypes, we would predict that men would be more concerned about taxes and taxation. Consequently, male consumers would be more influenced by the presence of taxes than female consumers.

A second, and somewhat related, line of research on gender stereotypes suggests that consumers might associate maleness with opposition to taxation and femaleness with support for redistribution. Specifically, studies have found evidence that people stereotypically associate masculinity with independence and competitiveness, whereas they associate femininity with empathy and harmony maintenance (Kite, Deaux, & Haines, 2008; Lippa, 2005; Spence & Buckner, 1995). Consequently, people tend to view right-leaning parties (e.g., Republicans and Libertarians) and policies (e.g., lower taxes, greater military spending, and harsher crime punishment) as being more masculine, and they view left-leaning parties (e.g., Democrats and Socialists) and policies (e.g., increased welfare spending, greater investment in education, and better access to healthcare) as being more feminine (Winter, 2010). This second set of stereotypes would predict that male consumers would be more averse to taxes, compared to female consumers.

A third line of research concerns (actual) gender differences in attitudes toward risk and voluntary contributions. There is extensive evidence that women are generally more averse to risk and uncertainty than men (Borghans, Heckman, Golsteyn, & Meijers, 2009; Byrnes, Miller, & Schafer, 1999; Croson & Gneezy, 2009; Filippin & Crosetto, 2014), and this would help explain why they might be less likely to illegally evade taxes (for a discussion, see Kastlunger et al., 2010). Differential risk attitudes could not, however, explain why women would be less willing to *legally* avoid paying circumventable taxes (such as local sales taxes), which are arguably more relevant to everyday consumer behavior. In this respect, research concerning gender differences in voluntary contributions to collective goods is more pertinent. Here the evidence suggests that women are more likely than men to contribute to collective goods, but only when doing so guarantees positive returns to the contributor (Olivola et al.,

2014; Vesterlund, Babcock, & Weingart, 2014). In contrast, there is no clear evidence that women contribute more when the returns on investment are negative (Croson & Gneezy, 2009) or uncertain (Olivola et al., 2014).

Finally, a number of studies have found that women are more supportive of taxation and redistribution than men (Alvarez & McCaffery, 2003; Becchetti, Degli Antoni, Ottone, & Solferino, 2013). Conversely, male consumers are also more likely to condone tax evasion than their female counterparts (Baird, Zelin, Robert, & Brennan, 2011; Chung & Trivedi, 2003; Cullis, Jones, & Lewis, 2006; Kastlunger et al., 2010; Torgler & Valev, 2010).

Taken together, the preceding evidence leads to the prediction that male consumers are more attentive to the addition of taxes and more averse to tax-related costs. Consequently, we would predict that the consumption decisions of men are more sensitive to the presence and size of a tax on purchases. Specifically, the presence or addition of a tax on a product should more negatively affect the likelihood that men will purchase it, compared to women. However, the evidence for this is mixed, at best. For example, some studies have shown that male consumers are more responsive to cigarette taxes than women (Azagba & Sharaf, 2011; Chaloupka & Pacula, 1999; Hersch, 2000), while others have reached the opposite conclusion (Farrelly, Bray, Pechacek, & Woollery, 2001; Nonnemaker & Farrelly, 2011; Stehr, 2007). One study found that increasing the tax on beer decreased the incidence of child abuse by mothers, but not fathers (Markowitz & Grossman, 2000), which suggests that women are more responsive to taxes (on alcohol) than men are. But another more recent study found that (under some conditions) male restaurant patrons are more responsive to a surcharge on unhealthy foods than female customers (Shah et al., 2014).

We also looked at our own data (from Sussman & Olivola, 2011) to see whether male participants were more likely to demonstrate an irrational aversion to taxes (above and beyond other monetary costs). For each study, we defined the overall level of tax aversion as the difference between the proportion of participants who chose to avoid a cost that was (framed as being) related to taxes and the proportion of participants who chose to avoid a similar (or greater) cost that was unrelated to taxes. We calculated these tax aversion levels separately for male and female participants. For example, in our first study, we found that 75 percent of men assigned to the tax-related condition chose to avoid the cost, compared to 51 percent of those assigned to the tax-unrelated condition. The resulting level of tax aversion for the men in Study 1 would therefore be: 75% – 51% = +24%. Female participants in that same study were as likely as men to avoid the tax-related cost (76 percent), but more likely than them to avoid the tax-unrelated cost (63 percent). Consequently, their level of tax aversion was lower: 76% – 63% = +13%. We were able to calculate this tax aversion index for six studies reported in our paper (Studies 1, 2, 3a, 4 [U.S. sample], 4 [U.K. sample], and 5). These six tax aversion rates (listed by study order) were +24 percent, +9 percent, +63 percent, +28 percent, +18 percent, and +8 percent for male participants, and +13 percent, +10 percent, +65 percent, –4 percent, +11 percent, and +4 percent for female participants. In nearly every study, men and women both displayed tax aversion (the only exception being U.S. women in Study 4). As these numbers show, however, men were not consistently more tax-averse than women. In only four of the six studies did men seem to exhibit more tax aversion than women (in the narrow sense of being a larger number, not in the statistical sense of being a reliable difference). Moreover, in only one of these four studies (Study 4 [U.S. sample]) was the difference large (men were 32 percent more tax-averse than women). It is also worth noting that the lower levels of tax aversion among female participants in our studies were primarily driven by the fact that women were more willing than men to avoid the *non*-tax cost, rather than by a lower willingness to avoid the tax-related cost.

In sum, the evidence concerning the moderating effect of gender on responses to taxes seems to be mixed.

Other Demographic Variables

Although the moderating roles of political orientation and gender have been well studied, other demographic variables may also influence how sensitive and responsive consumers are to taxes. Examples include ethnicity, age, education, and wealth. For example, there is evidence that sensitivity to cigarette taxes is related to income, education, and ethnicity (Azagba & Sharaf, 2011; Chaloupka & Pacula, 1999; Goldin & Homonoff, 2013; Nonnemaker & Farrelly, 2011). More research is needed to examine whether (and how) these variables influence other consumption domains. In particular, researchers should consider systematically collecting these demographic variables in their studies and examining how they predict reactions and attitudes to taxes.

Unanswered Questions and Future Directions

In most countries, taxes are a prominent part of the consumption experience: they impact the prices of goods (e.g., sales taxes) and consumers' purchasing budgets (e.g., income taxes), and they shape consumers' attitudes. Despite their importance and ubiquity, there has been relatively little research on the consumer psychology of taxes, and most of this work is quite recent (e.g., Einav et al., 2014; Epstein et al., 2010; Hardisty, Johnston, & Weber, 2010; Homonoff, 2013; Shah et al., 2014; Sussman & Olivola, 2011). As a result, there are many unanswered questions that deserve attention. These, in turn, suggest rich possibilities for future research.

Political Orientation and Taxes

The evidence clearly shows that political orientation influences people's reactions to taxes, with right-leaning consumers more sensitive and averse to taxes (Hardisty, Johnston, & Weber, 2010; Sussman & Olivola, 2011). Yet, some of these studies also show that this tendency is surprisingly malleable (Sussman & Olivola, 2011). This raises a number of interesting questions about the stability of political beliefs and their impact on consumer choices (Olivola & Sussman, 2014), which deserve more attention. Furthermore, the findings of these studies suggest specific tools that governments could use to improve attitudes toward taxes and tax compliance. For example, reminding citizens of specific ways in which taxes benefit them, or asking them to consider several uses of their taxes that they endorse, could help reduce tax aversion (Sussman & Olivola, 2011), and thereby boost tax compliance, particularly among right-leaning consumers. This type of reminder could be included as part of an income tax form or added to billboards (e.g., near public schools or construction sites) and advertisements, to inform citizens of the many ways in which their tax dollars are being used effectively.

Gender and Taxes

As we discussed, the existing evidence concerning which gender (male or female consumers) is more sensitive and averse to taxes is quite mixed. Some studies have found that men are more responsive to taxes (e.g., Azagba & Sharaf, 2011; Chaloupka & Pacula, 1999; Hersch, 2000; Shah et al., 2014); others have found that women react more to taxes (Farrelly et al., 2001; Markowitz & Grossman, 2000; Nonnemaker & Farrelly, 2011; Stehr, 2007); and yet others have found no compelling evidence of a gender difference (e.g., our analysis of the data in Sussman & Olivola, 2011, described previously). Clearly, more research is needed, first to determine whether one gender is in fact more sensitive to taxes, generally, and second to identify the factors that moderate the relationship between gender and sensitivity to taxes (e.g., why women would be more sensitive to beer taxes but less sensitive to taxes on unhealthy foods; Markowitz & Grossman, 2000; Shah et al., 2014).

Implications for Companies

Given consumers' strong resistance to paying taxes and their overall negative reactions to taxes and the tax label itself, when these are applied to products (e.g., Hardisty, Johnson, & Weber, 2010; Rivers & Schaufele, 2014; Sussman & Olivola, 2011), companies need to learn how best to encourage consumers to purchase products even when they are heavily taxed. One interesting question is how the consumer response to taxes varies based on whether the tax is included in the initial listed price of a product or added later. Existing research on tax salience has demonstrated that consumers' immediate purchase decisions depend more strongly on the initial listed price, and thus shift more in response to taxes included in the initial listing (e.g., Goldin, 2012).

However, the longer-term implications for a company's relationship with consumers remain unexamined. For example, to the extent that consumers are negatively inclined towards the tax itself, they may attribute this negative response either to the government or to the company for imposing the tax. Separating a tax from the initial listed price and emphasizing that it is externally imposed could minimize the likelihood that consumers blame the company for the tax and leave them more likely to develop and maintain a positive impression of the company. Alternatively, while customers will be more likely to purchase the product once if the tax is not displayed initially, they may attribute more blame to the company for attempting to hide the initial cost, which could have downstream implications for subsequent interactions. More broadly, understanding the extent to which consumers attribute the complete final cost of a product to a company versus to the government, and the extent to which they respond to this distinction, would be a productive area for future exploration.

While consumers may be loath to pay their own (individual) taxes, this does not mean they will condone illegal tax evasion, or even legal tax avoidance, in others, especially among large, profitable corporations (Dyreng, Hoopes, & Wilde, 2014). Consequently, companies that (plan to) engage in tactics that (will) allow them to avoid paying corporate taxes, or that substantially reduce the amount of taxes they (will) have to pay, need to consider how this will be perceived by customers, investors, and the broader consumer population. Increases in profit are often seen by consumers as coming at the expense of society and can negatively impact a company's brand image independent of its tax contributions (Bhattacharjee, Dana, & Baron, under review). However, it would be worthwhile to explore how consumers' negative perceptions of taxes and company profits interact to shape their responses to a firm's plans to avoid taxes in order to increase profits. Consumers may sympathize with corporations for wanting to avoid taxes, or they may react negatively to the extent that they believe profitable (versus unprofitable) corporations should be held accountable for their profits.

Implications for Policy

From the perspective of the government, perhaps the most important outstanding question is how to improve consumers' relationship with taxes. Recent work has begun to explore how we can use behavioral insights such as social norms, coupling of tax payments to resources provided, and appeals to honesty to improve tax compliance (Lamberton, 2013; Lamberton, De Neve, & Norton, 2014; Shu et al., 2012; Sussman & Olivola, 2011). Future research should expand on what has already been studied, in an effort to further increase tax compliance (within the domain of tax collection). Additionally, researchers should examine whether similar interventions can be extended to consumer purchases, with the goal of minimizing tax aversion. Importantly, actions taken to improve consumers' overall relationship with taxes could have several positive consequences that cut across different areas. For example, given that consumers' compliance decisions appear to be responsive to changes in their knowledge concerning the government and the tax code (e.g., Eriksen & Fallan,

1996; Kasper, Kogler, & Kirchler, 2015), schools could include impartial education modules about taxes in order to increase this knowledge. Further, as we already suggested, broad media advertisements alerting consumers to the importance of their tax dollars and informing them of specific ways that their tax dollars are being used could help improve attitudes toward taxes.

Acknowledgments

The authors would like to thank Julia Park and Brian Huh for their assistance, Avni Shah for bringing a number of relevant references to our attention, and Cait Lamberton for providing many useful suggestions that helped us improve this chapter.

References

Abeler, J., & Jäger, S. (in press). Complex tax incentives. *American Economic Journal: Economic Policy*.

Alesina, A., & Rodrik, D. (1994). Distributive politics and economic growth. *Quarterly Journal of Economics, 109*(2), 465–490.

Alexander, D., & Andersen, K. (1993). Gender as a factor in the attribution of leadership traits. *Political Research Quarterly, 46*(3), 527–545.

Allingham, M. G., & Sandmo, A. (1972). Income tax evasion: A theoretical analysis. *Journal of Public Economics, 1*(3), 323–338.

Alm, J. (2012). Measuring, explaining, and controlling tax evasion: Lessons from theory, experiments, and field studies. *International Tax and Public Finance, 19*(1), 54–77.

Alm, J., McClelland, G. H., & Schulze, W. D. (1992). Why do people pay taxes? *Journal of Public Economics, 48*(1), 21–38.

Alm, J., McClelland, G. H., & Schulze, W. D. (1999). Changing the social norm of tax compliance by voting. *Kyklos, 52*(2), 141–171.

Alvarez, R. M., & McCaffery, E. J. (2003). Are there sex differences in fiscal political preferences? *Political Research Quarterly, 56*(1), 5–17.

Anderson, E. T., Fong, N. M., Simester, D. I., & Tucker, C. E. (2010). How sales taxes affect customer and firm behavior: The role of search on the Internet. *Journal of Marketing Research, 47*(2), 229–239.

Andreoni, J. (1993). An experimental test of the public-goods crowding-out hypothesis. *American Economic Review, 83*(5), 1317–1327.

Andreoni, J., Erard, B., & Feinstein, J. (1998). Tax compliance. *Journal of Economic Literature, 36*(2), 818–860.

Andreoni, J., & Payne, A. A. (2011). Is crowding out due entirely to fundraising? Evidence from a panel of charities. *Journal of Public Economics, 95*(5), 334–343.

Azagba, S., & Sharaf, M. (2011). Cigarette taxes and smoking participation: Evidence from recent tax increases in Canada. *International Journal of Environmental Research and Public Health, 8*(5), 1583–1600.

Baird, J. E., Zelin, I. I., Robert, C., & Brennan, P. J. (2011). Academic major, gender, personal values, and reactions to an ethical dilemma. *Journal of Business Case Studies, 2*(2), 73–82.

Baugh, B., Ben-David, I., & Park, H. (2014). The "Amazon Tax": Empirical evidence from Amazon and main street retailers. Working Paper, National Bureau of Economic Research.

Bazart, C., & Bonein, A. (2014). Reciprocal relationships in tax compliance decisions. *Journal of Economic Psychology, 40*(C), 83–102.

Becchetti, L., Degli Antoni, G., Ottone, S., & Solferino, N. (2013). Allocation criteria under task performance: The gendered preference for protection. *Journal of Socio-Economics, 45*, 96–111.

Bergstrom, T. C., Blume, L. E., Varian, H. R. (1986). On the private provision of public goods. *Journal of Public Economics, 29*(1), 25–49.

Bernheim, B. D. (2002). Taxation and saving. *Handbook of Public Economics, 3*, 1173–1249.

Bhattacharjee, A., Dana, J., & Baron, J. (under review). Can profit be good? Neglect of incentives and anti-profit beliefs.

Bø, E. E., Slemrod, J., & Thoresen, T. O. (2015). Taxes on the Internet: Deterrence effects of public disclosure. *American Economic Journal: Economic Policy, 7*(1), 36–62.

Bobek, D. D., & Hatfield, R. C. (2003). An investigation of the theory of planned behavior and the role of moral obligation in tax compliance. *Behavioral Research in Accounting, 15*(1), 13–38.

Borghans, L., Heckman, J. J., Golsteyn, B. H. H., & Meijers, H. (2009). Gender differences in risk aversion and ambiguity aversion. *Journal of the European Economic Association, 7*(2–3), 649–658.

Bovenberg, A. L., & Goulder, L. H. (1996). Optimal environmental taxation in the presence of other taxes: General-equilibrium analyses. *American Economic Review, 86*(4), 985–1000.

Bracha, A., & Cooper, D. (2014). Asymmetric responses to income changes: The payroll tax increase versus tax refund in 2013. *Economics Letters, 124*(3), 534–538.

Brannlund, R., & Persson, L. (2012). To tax, or not to tax: Preferences for climate policy attributes. *Climate Policy, 12*(6), 704–721.

Brooks, N., & Doob, A. N. (1990). Tax evasion: Searching for a theory of compliant behavior. In M.L. Friedland (ed.), *Securing Compliance: Seven Case Studies* (pp. 120–164). Toronto: University of Toronto Press.

Brownell, K. D., Farley, T., Willett, W. C., Popkin, B. M., Chaloupka, F. J., Thompson, J. W., & Ludwig, D. S. (2009). The public health and economic benefits of taxing sugar-sweetened beverages. *New England Journal of Medicine, 361*(16), 1599–1605.

Byrnes, J. P., Miller, D. C., & Schafer, W. D. (1999). Gender differences in risk taking: A meta-analysis. *Psychological Bulletin, 125*(3), 367–383.

Cabral, M., & Hoxby, C. (2012). The hated property tax: Salience, tax rates, and tax tevolts. Working Paper, National Bureau of Economic Research.

Chaloupka, F. J., & Pacula, R. L. (1999). Sex and race differences in young people's responsiveness to price and tobacco control policies. *Tobacco Control, 8*(4), 373–377.

Chaloupka, F. J., Straif, K., & Leon, M. E. (2011). Effectiveness of tax and price policies in tobacco control. *Tobacco Control, 20*, 235–238.

Chamley, C. (1986). Optimal taxation of capital income in general equilibrium with infinite lives. *Econometrica*, *80*(3), 607–622.

Chan, K. S., Godby, R., Mestelman, S., & Muller, R. A. (2002). Crowding-out voluntary contributions to public goods. *Journal of Economic Behavior & Organization*, *48*(3), 305–317.

Chang, C., & Hitchon, J. C. B. (2004). When does gender count? Further insights into gender schematic processing of female candidates' political advertisements. *Sex Roles*, *51*(3–4), 197–208.

Chang, O. H., Nichols, D. R., & Schultz, J. J. (1987). Taxpayer attitudes toward tax audit risk. *Journal of Economic Psychology*, *8*(3), 299–309.

Chetty, R., Looney, A., & Kroft, K. (2009). Salience and taxation: Theory and evidence. *American Economic Review*, *99*(4), 1145–1177.

Chow, R. M., & Galak, J. (2012). The effect of inequality frames on support for redistributive tax policies. *Psychological Science*, *23*(12), 1467–1469.

Chung, J., & Trivedi, V. U. (2003). The effect of friendly persuasion and gender on tax compliance behavior. *Journal of Business Ethics*, *47*(2), 133–145.

Coricelli, G., Rusconi, E., & Villeval, M. C. (2014). Tax evasion and emotions: An empirical test of re-integrative shaming theory. *Journal of Economic Psychology*, *40*(C), 49–61.

Crockett, D., & Wallendorf, M. (2004). The role of normative political ideology in consumer behavior. *Journal of Consumer Research*, *31*(3), 511–528.

Croson, R., & Gneezy, U. (2009). Gender differences in preferences. *Journal of Economic Literature*, *47*(2), 448–474.

Cullis, J., Jones, P., & Lewis, A. (2006). Tax framing, instrumentality and individual differences: Are there two different cultures? *Journal of Economic Psychology*, *27*(2), 304–320.

Cullis, J., Jones, P., & Savoia, A. (2012). Social norms and tax compliance: Framing the decision to pay tax. *Journal of Socio-Economics*, *41*(2), 159–168.

DeAngelo, H., & Masulis, R. W. (1980). Optimal capital structure under corporate and personal taxation. *Journal of Financial Economics*, *8*(1), 3–29.

DeCicca, P., Kenkel, D., & Liu, F. (2013). Excise tax avoidance: The case of state cigarette taxes. *Journal of Health Economics*, *32*(6), 1130–1141.

De Juan, A., Lasheras, M. A., & Mayo, R. (1994). Voluntary tax compliant behavior of Spanish income tax payers. *Public Finance*, *49*, 90–105.

Diamond, P. A., & Mirrlees, J. A. (1971a). Optimal taxation and public production I: Production efficiency. *American Economic Review*, *61*(1), 8–27.

Diamond, P. A., & Mirrlees, J. A. (1971b). Optimal taxation and public production II: Tax rules. *American Economic Review*, *61*(3), 261–278.

Dixit, A., & Londregan, J. (1998). Ideology, tactics, and efficiency in redistributive politics. *Quarterly Journal of Economics*, *113*(2), 497–529.

Djanali, I., & Sheehan-Connor, D. (2012). Tax affinity hypothesis: Do we really hate paying taxes? *Journal of Economic Psychology*, *33*(4), 758–775.

Dyreng, S., Hoopes, J. L., & Wilde, J. H. (2014). Public pressure and corporate tax behavior. Working Paper, Ohio State University.

Eckel, C. C., Grossman, P. J., & Johnston, R. M. (2005). An experimental test of the crowding out hypothesis. *Journal of Public Economics*, *89*(8), 1543–1560.

Einav, L., Knoepfle, D., Levin, J., & Sundaresan, N. (2014). Sales taxes and Internet commerce. *American Economic Review*, *104*(1), 1–26.

Epstein, L. H., Dearing, K. K., Roba, L. G., & Finkelstein, E. (2010). The influence of taxes and subsidies on energy purchased in an experimental purchasing study. *Psychological Science*, *21*(3), 406–414.

Eriksen, K., & Fallan, L. (1996). Tax knowledge and attitudes towards taxation: A report on a quasi-experiment. *Journal of Economic Psychology*, *17*(3), 387–402.

Farrelly, M. C., Bray, J. W., Pechacek, T., & Woollery, T. (2001). Response by adults to increases in cigarette prices by sociodemographic characteristics. *Southern Economic Journal*, *68*(1), 156–165.

Feenberg, D. R., & Poterba, J. M. (1991). Which households own municipal bonds? Evidence from tax returns. *National Tax Journal*, *44*(4), 93–103.

Filippin, A., & Crosetto, P. (2014). A reconsideration of gender differences in risk attitudes. Working Paper, University of Milan.

Finkelstein, A. (2009). EZ-Tax: Tax salience and tax rates. *Quarterly Journal of Economics*, *124*(3), 969–1010.

Goldin, J. (2012). Sales tax not included: Designing commodity taxes for inattentive consumers. *Yale Law Journal*, *122*(1), 258–301.

Goldin, J. (2014). Optimal tax salience. Unpublished Manuscript, Yale Law School and Princeton University.

Goldin, J., & Homonoff, T. (2013). Smoke gets in your eyes: Cigarette tax salience and regressivity. *American Economic Journal: Economic Policy*, *5*(1), 302–336.

Goldin, J., & Listokin, Y. (2014). Tax expenditure salience. *American Law and Economics Review*, *16*(1), 144–176.

Goolsbee, A. (2000). In a world without borders: The impact of taxes on Internet commerce. *Quarterly Journal of Economics*, *115*(2), 561–576.

Grasmick, H. G., & Bursik, Jr., R. J. (1990). Conscience, significant others, and rational choice: Extending the deterrence model. *Law and Society Review*, *24*(3), 837–861.

Greenberg, S. B., & Greenberg, A. (2013). Public interests project frequency questionnaire, October 21–26, 2003. *Greenberg Quinlan Rosner Research*.

Gronberg, T. J., Luccasen III, R. A., Turocy, T. L., & Van Huyck, J. B. (2012). Are tax-financed contributions to a public good completely crowded-out? Experimental evidence. *Journal of Public Economics*, *96*(7), 596–603.

Gruber, J. H., & Mullainathan, S. (2005). Do cigarette taxes make smokers happier? *B.E. Journal of Economic Analysis and Policy*, *5*(1), 1–45.

Harbaugh, W. T., Mayr, U., & Burghart, D. R. (2007). Neural responses to taxation and voluntary giving reveal motives for charitable donations. *Science*, *316*(5831), 1622–1625.

Hardisty, D. J., Johnson, E. J., & Weber, E. U. (2010). A dirty word or a dirty world? Attribute framing, political affiliation, and query theory. *Psychological Science*, *21*(1), 86–92.

Hasseldine, J., & Hite, P. A. (2003). Framing, gender and tax compliance. *Journal of Economic Psychology*, *24*(4), 517–533.

Hasseldine, D. J., Kaplan, S. E., & Fuller, L. R. (1994). Characteristics of New Zealand tax evaders: A note. *Accounting & Finance*, *34*(2), 79–93.

Her Majesty's Revenue and Customs [HMRC] (2012). Budget 2012. Retrieved from http://webarchive.nationalarchives.gov.uk.

Hersch, J. (2000). Gender, income levels, and the demand for cigarettes. *Journal of Risk and Uncertainty*, *21*(2–3), 263–282.

Hibbing, J. R., Smith, K. B., & Alford, J. R. (2014). Differences in negativity bias underlie variations in political ideology. *Brain and Behavioral Sciences, 37*(3), 297–307.

Hill, C. A. (2010). What cognitive psychologists should find interesting about tax. *Psychonomic Bulletin & Review, 17*(2), 180–185.

Hines, J. R. (2007). Taxing consumption and other sins. *Journal of Economic Perspectives, 21*(1), 49–68.

Homonoff, T. A. (2013). Can small incentives have large effects? The impact of taxes versus bonuses on disposable bag use. Working Paper, Princeton University.

Hu, Y. J., & Tang, Z. (2014). The impact of sales tax on internet and catalog sales: Evidence from a natural experiment. *International Journal of Industrial Organization, 32*, 84–90.

Huddy, L., & Terkildsen, N. (1993). Gender stereotypes and the perception of male and female candidates. *American Journal of Political Science, 37*(1), 119–147.

Internal Revenue Service [IRS] (2012). Tax gap for tax year 2006 overview. Retrieved from www.irs.gov/pub/newsroom/overview_tax_gap_2006.pdf.

Jackson, B. R., & Milliron, V. C. (1986). Tax compliance research: Findings, problems and prospects. *Journal of Accounting Literature, 5*, 125–166.

Jha, P., & Chaloupka, F. J. (2000). The economics of global tobacco control. *British Medical Journal, 321*, 358–361.

Jung, Y. H., Snow, A., & Trandel, G. A. (1994). Tax evasion and the size of the underground economy. *Journal of Public Economics, 54*, 391–402.

Kahn, K. F. (1993). Gender differences in campaign messages: The political advertisements of men and women candidates for US Senate. *Political Research Quarterly, 46*(3), 481–502.

Kesselman, J. R. (1989). Income tax evasion: An inter-sectoral analysis. *Journal of Public Economics, 38*, 137–182.

Kahneman, D., & Tversky, A. (1979). Prospect theory: An analysis of decision under risk. *Econometrica, 47*, 263–291.

Kahneman, D., & Tversky, A. (eds.). (2000). *Choices, Values, and Frames.* New York: Cambridge University Press.

Kasper, M., Kogler, C., & Kirchler, E. (2015). Tax policy and the news: An empirical analysis of taxpayers' perceptions of tax-related media coverage and its impact on tax compliance. *Journal of Behavioral and Experimental Economics, 54*, 58–63.

Kastlunger, B., Dressler, S. G., Kirchler, E., Mittone, L., & Voracek, M. (2010). Sex differences in tax compliance: Differentiating between demographic sex, gender-role orientation, and prenatal masculinization (2D:4D). *Journal of Economic Psychology, 31*(4), 542–552.

Katz, M. A. (2011). The politics of purchasing: Ethical consumerism, civic engagement, and political participation in the United States. Doctoral dissertation, Department of Sociology, Virginia Polytechnic Institute and State University.

Kirchler, E. (2007). *The Economic Psychology of Tax Behaviour.* Cambridge: Cambridge University Press.

Kirchler, E., Hoelzl, E., & Wahl, I. (2008). Enforced versus voluntary tax compliance: The "slippery slope" framework. *Journal of Economic Psychology, 29*(2), 210–225.

Kirchler, E., Maciejovsky, B., & Schneider, F. (2003). Everyday representations of tax avoidance, tax evasion, and tax flight: Do legal differences matter? *Journal of Economic Psychology*, *24*(4), 535–553.

Kirchler, E., Muehlbacher, S., Kastlunger, B., & Wahl, I. (2010). Why pay taxes? A review of tax compliance decisions. In J. Alm, J. Martinez-Vazquez, & B. Torgler (eds.), *Developing Alternative Frameworks for Explaining Tax Compliance* (pp.15–32). New York: Routledge.

Kite, M. E., Deaux, K., & Haines, E. L. (2008). Gender stereotypes. In F. L. Denmark & M. A. Paludi (eds.), *Psychology of Women: A Handbook of Issues and Theories*, 2nd ed. (pp. 205–236). Westport, CT: Praeger.

Lamberton, C. (2013). A spoonful of choice: How allocation increases satisfaction with tax payments. *Journal of Public Policy & Marketing*, *32*(2), 223–238.

Lamberton, C. P., De Neve, J., & Norton, M. I. (2014). Eliciting taxpayer preferences increases tax compliance. Working Paper, University of Pittsburgh.

LeBoeuf, R. A., & Shafir, E. (2003). Deep thoughts and shallow frames: On the susceptibility to framing effects. *Journal of Behavioral Decision Making*, *16* (2), 77–92.

Lippa, R. A. (2005). *Gender, Nature, and Nurture*, 2nd ed. Mahwah, NJ: Lawrence Erlbaum Associates.

Manuszak, M. D., & Moul, C. C. (2009). How far for a buck? Tax differences and the location of retail gasoline activity in Southeast Chicagoland. *Review of Economics and Statistics*, *91*(4), 744–765.

Manzoor, S. H., & Straub, J. D. (2005). The robustness of Kingma's crowd-out estimate: Evidence from new data on contributions to public radio. *Public Choice*, *123* (3–4), 463–476.

Markowitz, S., & Grossman, M. (2000). The effects of beer taxes on physical child abuse. *Journal of Health Economics*, *19*(2), 271–282.

McCaffery, E. J. (1994). The uneasy case for wealth transfer taxation. *Yale Law Journal*, *104*(2), 283–365.

McCaffery, E. J., & Baron, J. (2004). Framing and taxation: Evaluation of tax policies involving household composition. *Journal of Economic Psychology*, *25*(6), 679–705.

McCaffery, E. J., & Slemrod, J. (2006). Toward an agenda for behavioral public finance. In E. J. McCaffery & J. Slemrod (eds.), *Behavioral Public Finance* (pp. 3–31). New York: Sage.

McGowan, J. R. (2000). The effect of political affiliation on taxpayers' attitudes toward alternative tax systems. *Journal of the American Taxation Association*, *22*(1), 111–128.

Mettler, S. (2011). *The Submerged State*. Chicago: University of Chicago Press.

Miles, M. R. (2014). Process over outcome: How perceptions of procedural fairness influence conservative support for redistributive taxes. *Social Science Journal*, *51*(4), 615–626.

Newman, B. J., & Bartels, B. L. (2011). Politics at the checkout line: Explaining political consumerism in the United States. *Political Research Quarterly*, *64*(4), 803–817.

Nonnemaker, J. M., & Farrelly, M. C. (2011). Smoking initiation among youth: The role of cigarette excise taxes and prices by race/ethnicity and gender. *Journal of Health Economics*, *30*(3), 560–567.

O'Donoghue, T., & Rabin, M. (2003). Studying optimal paternalism, illustrated by a model of sin taxes. *American Economic Review*, *93*(2), 186–191.

O'Donoghue, T., & Rabin, M. (2006). Optimal sin taxes. *Journal of Public Economics*, *90*(10), 1825–1849.

OECD (Organization for Economic Co-operation and Development) (2013). What drives tax morale? Retrieved from www.oecd.org/ctp/tax-global/TaxMorale_march13.pdf.

Olivola, C. Y., Kim, Y., Merzel, A., Kareev, Y., Avrahami, J., & Ritov, I. (2014). Diffusion of responsibility across cultures and contexts: The impact of individual, cultural, and contextual factors on responses to the Volunteer's Dilemma Game. Unpublished Manuscript, Carnegie Mellon University.

Olivola, C. Y., & Sussman, A. B. (2014). Many behavioral tendencies associated with right-leaning (conservative) political ideologies are malleable and unrelated to negativity. *Brain and Behavioral Sciences*, *37*(3), 323–324.

Orviska, M., & Hudson, J. (2002). Tax evasion, civic duty and the law abiding citizen. *European Journal of Political Economy*, *19*(1), 83–102.

Parker, S. C. (2003). Does tax evasion affect occupational choice? *Oxford Bulletin of Economics and Statistics*, *65*(3), 379–394.

Payne, A. A. (1998). Does the government crowd-out private donations? New evidence from a sample of non-profit firms. *Journal of Public Economics*, *69*(3), 323–345.

Pestieau, P., & Possen, U. M. (1991). Tax evasion and occupational choice. *Journal of Public Economics*, *45*, 107–125.

Pestieau, P., & Possen, U. M. (1992). How do taxes affect occupational choice? *Public Finance*, *47*, 108–119.

Pickhardt, M., & Prinz, A. (2014). Behavioral dynamics of tax evasion – A survey. *Journal of Economic Psychology*, *40*, 1–19.

Piketty, T. (1995). Social mobility and redistributive politics. *Quarterly Journal of Economics*, *110*(3), 551–584.

Porcano, T. M. (1988). Correlates of tax evasion. *Journal of Economic Psychology*, *9*(1), 47–67.

Poterba, J. M. (2002). Taxation, risk-taking, and household portfolio behavior. *Handbook of Public Economics*, *3*, 1109–1171.

Prinz, A., Muehlbacher, S., & Kirchler, E. (2014). The slippery slope framework on tax compliance: An attempt to formalization. *Journal of Economic Psychology*, *40*, 20–34.

Ramsey, F. P. (1927). A contribution to the theory of taxation. *Economic Journal*, *37* (145), 47–61.

Reckers, P. M., Sanders, D. L., & Roark, S. J. (1994). The influence of ethical attitudes on taxpayer compliance. *National Tax Journal*, *47*(4), 825–836.

Reimers, S. (2009). A paycheck half-empty or half-full? Framing, fairness and progressive taxation. *Judgment and Decision Making*, *4*(6), 461–466.

Rivers, N., & Schaufele, B. (2014). Salience of carbon taxes in the gasoline market. Working Paper, University of Ottawa.

Roos, J. M. T., & Shachar, R. (2014). When Kerry met Sally: Politics and perceptions in the demand for movies. *Management Science*, *60*(7), 1617–1631.

Sausgruber, R., & Tyran, J. R. (2014). Discriminatory taxes are unpopular—even when they are efficient and distributionally fair. *Journal of Economic Behavior & Organization*, *108*, 463–476.

Schepanski, A., & Shearer, T. (1995). A prospect theory account of the income tax withholding phenomenon. *Organizational Behavior and Human Decision Processes, 63*(2), 174–186.

Schmölders, G. (1959). Fiscal psychology: A new branch of public finance. *National Tax Journal, 12*(4), 340–345.

Scholz, J. T., & Lubell, M. (1998). Adaptive political attitudes: Duty, trust, and fear as monitors of tax policy. *American Journal of Political Science, 42*, 903–920.

Schwartz, R., & Orleans, S. (1967). On legal sanctions. *University of Chicago Law Review, 34*, 282–300.

Scott, W. J., & Grasmick, H. G. (1981). Deterrence and income tax cheating: Testing interaction hypotheses in utilitarian theories. *Journal of Applied Behavioral Science, 17*(3), 395–408.

Shah, A. M., Bettman, J. R., Ubel, P. A., Keller, P. A., & Britton, J. E. (2014). Surcharges plus unhealthy labels reduce demand for unhealthy menu items. *Journal of Marketing Research, 51*(6), 773–789.

Shu, L. L., Mazar, N., Gino, F., Ariely, D., & Bazerman, M. H. (2012). Signing at the beginning makes ethics salient and decreases dishonest self-reports in comparison to signing at the end. *Proceedings of the National Academy of Sciences of the United States of America, 109*(38), 15197–15200.

Slemrod, J. (2007). Cheating ourselves: The economics of tax evasion. *Journal of Economic Perspectives, 21*(1), 25–48.

Soliman, A., Jones, P., & Cullis, J. (2014). Learning in experiments: Dynamic interaction of policy variables designed to deter tax evasion. *Journal of Economic Psychology, 40*, 175–186.

Spence, J. T., & Buckner, C. (1995). Masculinity and femininity: Defining the undefinable. In P. J. Kalbfleisch & M. J. Cody (eds.), *Gender, Power, and Communication in Human Relationships* (pp. 105–138). Hillsdale, NJ: Lawrence Erlbaum.

Spicer, M. W. (1986). Civilization at a discount: The problem of tax evasion. *National Tax Journal, 39*(1), 13–20.

Spicer, M. W., & Lundstedt, S. B. (1976). Understanding tax evasion. *Public Finance, 31*, 295–305.

Stehr, M. (2007). The effect of cigarette taxes on smoking among men and women. *Health Economics, 16*(12), 1333–1343.

Steinberg, R. (1991). Does government spending crowd out donations? *Annals of Public and Cooperative Economics, 62*(4), 591–612.

Stewart, N., Chater, N., & Brown, G. D. A. (2006). Decision by sampling. *Cognitive Psychology, 53*, 1–26.

Sussman, A. B., & Olivola, C. Y. (2011). Axe the tax: Taxes are disliked more than equivalent costs. *Journal of Marketing Research, 48*, S91–S101.

Tan, F., & Yim, A. (2014). Can strategic uncertainty help deter tax evasion? An experiment on auditing rules. *Journal of Economic Psychology, 40*(C), 161–174.

Torgler, B. (2003). To evade taxes or not to evade: That is the question. *Journal of Socio-Economics, 32*(3), 283–302.

Torgler, B. (2007). *Tax Compliance and Tax Morale: A Theoretical and Empirical Analysis.* Northampton, MA: Edward Elgar.

Torgler, B., & Valev, N. T. (2010). Gender and public attitudes toward corruption and tax evasion. *Contemporary Economic Policy, 28*(4), 554–568.

Tversky, A., & Kahneman, D. (1981). The framing of decisions and the psychology of choice. *Science, 211*(4481), 453–458.

Tversky, A., & Kahneman, D. (1991). Loss aversion in riskless choice: A reference-dependent model. *Quarterly Journal of Economics, 106*(4), 1039–1061.

Verboon, P., & Van Dijke, M. (2007). A self-interest analysis of justice and tax compliance: How distributive justice moderates the effect of outcome favorability. *Journal of Economic Psychology, 28*(6), 704–727.

Vesterlund, L., Babcock, L., & Weingart, L. (2014). Breaking the glass ceiling with "no": Gender differences in declining requests for non-promotable tasks. Unpublished Manuscript, Carnegie Mellon University.

Wagenaar, A. C., Salois, M. J., & Komro, K. A. (2009). Effects of beverage alcohol price and tax levels on drinking: A meta-analysis of 1003 estimates from 112 studies. *Addiction, 104*(2), 179–190.

Wahl, I., Kastlunger, B., & Kirchler, E. (2010). Trust in authorities and power to enforce tax compliance: An empirical analysis of the "Slippery Slope Framework." *Law & Policy, 32*(4), 383–406.

Wahlund, R. (1992). Tax changes and economic behavior: The case of tax evasion. *Journal of Economic Psychology, 13*(4), 657–677.

Wallschutzky, I. G. (1984). Possible causes of tax evasion. *Journal of Economic Psychology, 5*, 371–384.

Warr, P. G. (1982). Pareto optimal redistribution and private charity. *Journal of Public Economics, 19*, 131–138.

Watson, H. (1985). Tax evasion and labor markets. *Journal of Public Economics, 27*, 231–246.

Webley, P., Cole, M., & Eidjar, O.-P. (2001). The prediction of self-reported and hypothetical tax-evasion: Evidence from England, France and Norway. *Journal of Economic Psychology, 22*, 141–155.

Wenzel, M. (2004). An analysis of norm processes in tax compliance. *Journal of Economic Psychology, 25*(2), 213–228.

Wenzel, M. (2005). Misperceptions of social norms about tax compliance: From theory to intervention. *Journal of Economic Psychology, 26*(6), 862–883.

Whillans, A. V., Wispinski, N. J., & Dunn, E. W. (under review). Seeing wealth as a responsibility improves attitudes toward taxation.

Winter, N. J. (2010). Masculine Republicans and feminine Democrats: Gender and Americans' explicit and implicit images of the political parties. *Political Behavior, 32*(4), 587–618.

22 Moral and Political Identity

Karen Page Winterich, Vikas Mittal, and Karl Aquino

In the past several years, consumer researchers have examined many different identities, across individuals as well as within an individual. Identities such as gender (Shang, Reed, & Croson, 2008; Winterich, Mittal, & Ross, 2009), dependence (White, Argo, & Sengupta, 2012; Winterich & Barone, 2011; Zhang & Shrum, 2009), family (Reed, 2004), work (LeBoeuf, Shafir, & Bayuk, 2010), and global (vs. local, Zhang & Khare, 2009) have been found to influence consumer decisions. Starting from brand attitudes and choice, scholars have broadened the scope of the identity construct as an explanation for a richer set of consequences: political involvement (Huddy & Khatib, 2007), recycling (Kidwell, Farmer, & Hardesty, 2013), charitable giving (Winterich, Zhang, & Mittal, 2012), variety seeking (Fernandes & Mandel, 2014), and new product preferences (Khan, Misra, & Singh, 2013).

We continue this emerging research on consumer identity by focusing on two specific identities – moral and political. Surveys show that people's concept of morality and politics has strong influences in their everyday lives (Brooks, 2006; Kertzer, Powers, Rathbun, & Iyer, 2014; Lakoff, 2010); as such, both moral and political identity should be highly relevant in influencing, shaping, and explaining consumer-relevant attitudes, cognitions, and behaviors (Oyserman, 2009; Reed, Forehand, Puntoni, & Warlop, 2012).

More specifically, this chapter seeks first to examine and understand the constructs of moral identity and political identity in terms of their conceptualization and operationalization. Second, we provide an overview of the current state of the research on each identity, focusing on research in the past five to ten years that is pertinent to consumer psychology. Third, we consider how these constructs might jointly and interactively inform our thinking about consumer behavior. Lastly, we anticipate the direction these constructs will take in consumer psychology and identify areas for future research that we hope will lead to substantial advancement of the literature on identity-motivated processes.

We appreciate the assistance of Nivriti Chowdhry and thank Tatianna Aker, Kyuhong Han, and Daniel Zyung for their editorial assistance.

An Introduction to Moral and Political Identity

A person's identity is how a person views oneself (Ashforth & Mael, 1989; Bandura, 1991; Mischel & Shoda, 2008). From a sociocognitive perspective, a consumer's identity is "any category label to which a consumer self-associates either by choice or endowment" (Reed et al., 2012, p. 312). This self-conception is typically organized around a set of traits, associations, feelings, and behaviors that are consistent with the typical person in an identity category (Aquino & Reed, 2002; Reed et al., 2012). Said differently, an identity represents a person's associative cognitive network of ideas and associations, or a schema (Anderson & Bower, 1973). The ideas and associations within the schema can serve as powerful influences on subsequent thoughts, feelings, and actions (c.f, Aquino & Reed, 2002; Bem, 1981; Forehand, Deshpandé, & Reed, 2002).

Based on this broad conceptualization of identity, moral identity may be defined as "a self-conception organized around a set of moral traits" (Aquino & Reed, 2002, p. 1424), while political identity may be defined as a self-conception about the underlying goals and ideals of a political system (e.g., conservatism or liberalism; Grove, Remy, & Zeigler, 1974). As explained next, both identities operate around a set of psychological and social concepts that can also help understand the identities' influence in a consumer context. From a psychological perspective, these identities share several conceptual and empirical properties.

First, identities can be situationally activated through a prime that triggers one or more aspects of the identity schema (Reed, 2004). For example, reading a news article about how caring a stranger was to a child may temporarily activate a moral identity if caring for strangers is in one's schema for a moral identity. Similarly, for Americans, seeing an image of elephants (donkeys) could temporarily activate a conservative (liberal) identity given their association with the Republican (Democratic) parties. For Europeans, seeing the hammer and sickle (swastika or fasces) may temporarily activate a Communist (Facist) identity.

Second, consistent with the schema perspective, the strength of these identity-relevant associations reflects the degree to which a person's identity (moral or political) is chronically important and therefore accessible. Using the elephant example, some individuals have several schemas other than political identity associated with elephants that weaken this particular identity-relevant association. Consequently, their political identity, though able to be temporarily activated, is not as chronically important as it is for someone who, upon seeing an elephant, immediately thinks of the Republican Party and conservatives.

Third, these identities differ in self-importance. Self-importance refers to the extent or depth with which one associates a specific identity as part of oneself. An identity is more likely to be influential to the extent that the identity is important in defining oneself. The self-importance of an identity may vary from person to person (Aquino & Reed, 2002; Reed, 2004). For instance, the self-importance of a conservative political identity may vary from one conservative to another.

Fourth, from a social perspective, identities serve as powerful social categorization mechanisms. They provide a person with a basis for self-definition, guiding a person's processing of social information (Markus, 1977) and therefore implicitly triggering membership in certain social groups, often with some significant emotional value (Tajfel, 1972). Consequently, identities lead people to view themselves and others as belonging to an in-group versus out-group. This social categorization extends to individuals and other entities such as organizations and brands. Studies show that the same brand, when perceived as being used by out-group members, is evaluated less favorably than when used by in-group members (Choi & Winterich, 2013; White, Argo, & Sengupta, 2012).

What does this mean for understanding consumer behavior? A key tenet from this work is that consumers tend to think and behave in an identity-consistent manner (Blasi, 1984; Festinger, 1957). Why? First, psychologically it is easier for consumers to engage in behaviors that are consistent with their dominant schema, that is, activated identity, because it prevents dissonance that may arise from conflicting perceptions of the self (Bem, 1972). Second, a salient identity influences one's "ideal" self (Higgins, 1987), which results in consumers' motivation to achieve this ideal through consistent behaviors. Third, at the social level, consumers are motivated to convey their identities to others so others see them the same way as they see themselves, which is referred to as self-verification (Swann, 1983) or identity verification (Reed et al., 2012). Fourth, consumers regularly retrospectively assess their associations with their identity to reinforce their identity to the self (Winterich, Mittal, & Aquino, 2013). Given these multiple motivations for engaging in identity-consistent behaviors, consumers with a highly self-important or temporarily salient identity should be more motivated to act in ways that are consistent with their moral or political identity. We next discuss moral identity and political identity in terms of their conceptualization, operationalization, and measurement.

Moral Identity

Conceptualization of Moral Identity

The origins of moral identity can be traced to Kohlberg's theory of moral development in 1971. Blasi (1984) refined and clarified its definition later in his character perspective of morality. More recently, moral identity has been defined from a sociocognitive perspective by Aquino and Reed (2002). From such a perspective, a person characterized by a highly self-important moral identity should have more rapid access to thoughts regarding moral traits, such as fairness and generosity, as well as goals and behaviors of helping others than an individual whose moral identity has low self-importance. Aquino and Reed

(2002) note that being high in moral identity does not indicate whether or not one is a moral person in a normative sense, given that the definition of morality varies among individuals. Rather, it assesses how much importance individuals place on being moral based on their associations of morality.

Aquino and Reed (2002) conceptualize moral identity as having two dimensions: the private (internalization) dimension and the public (symbolization) dimension. Other theorists (e.g., Erikson, 1964; Fenigstein, Scheier, & Buss, 1975) have made similar claims about the dual aspects of personal identity. According to Aquino and Reed (2002), internalization is the subjective experience of having a moral identity (see also Blasi, 1984) and therefore captures the degree to which moral identity acts as a self-regulatory mechanism that guides behavior. One implication of the notion that the internalization aspect of moral identity represents a subjective experience is that people who are high in internalization should experience a motivation to engage in moral behavior regardless of the anticipated public or private nature of their acts because moral associations are chronically available to them in working memory (Winterich, Aquino, Mittal, & Swartz, 2013).

In contrast, the symbolization dimension captures the degree to which people tend to convey their moral identity externally through their actions in the world. The symbolization dimension is rooted in a symbolic-interactionist perspective (Mead, 1934) and is associated with a motivation for self-verification (Swann, 1983) and social reinforcement (Schlenker & Weigold, 1992; Shao, Aquino, & Freeman, 2008). Thus, a person who is high in moral identity symbolization is more likely to engage in visible activities that can convey, to others, his or her commitment to certain moral goals and ideals than someone low in symbolization, though this may occur only when the behavior is observable by others (Winterich et al., 2013). When the behavior is not likely to be observed by others, then the symbolization dimension becomes a relatively weaker predictor of behavior (Winterich et al., 2013).[1]

Assessing Moral Identity: Measurement and Operationalization

Historically, much of the work linking the concept of moral identity to moral behavior has been theoretical. Empirical research in this domain emerged only after Aquino and Reed (2002) developed a simple and effective scale to measure

---

1 In Aquino and Reed's (2002) model, an individual's symbolization may not regard his or her internalization such that while all individuals may have a base level of moral standards, some individuals may have higher levels of moral identity internalization, whereas others have higher levels of moral identity symbolization. Different levels of symbolization do not determine how important morality is to someone like different levels of internalization do. That is, the level of symbolization does not necessarily correspond to a person's level of internalization, although the two should be related, as indicated by their modest correlation is past studies (e.g., Aquino & Reed, 2002). Thus, when the terms "high" and "low" are used in theoretical arguments, comparisons are not being made regarding the strength of these elements of moral identity *across* dimensions (i.e., high internalization compared to high symbolization) but rather *within* each dimension.

the chronic Self-Importance of Moral Identity (SIMI) scale (see Appendix A). The SIMI scale first asks a respondent to consider nine traits – caring, compassionate, fair, friendly, generous, helpful, hardworking, honest, and kind – and then respond to ten items. Five items assess one's level of internalization (private MI), while the other five assess one's level of symbolization (public MI).

The SIMI scale taps the chronic accessibility of moral identity, which presumably has some stability over time. However, from a sociocognitive perspective, a consumer's moral identity can also be made temporarily accessible by exposure to situational cues (Aquino et al., 2009; Aquino, McFerran, & Laven, 2011; Lee, Winterich, & Ross, 2014). These two ways in which moral identity can become active in a person's working self-concept is consistent with general principles underlying identity salience effects (Reed, 2004; Reed et al., 2012) whereby a consumer's identity may be accessible as a result of either chronic identification or situational priming that temporarily activates an identity (Zhang & Khare, 2009). Differences in these two forms of identity activation can lead to different outcomes (Wheeler & Berger, 2007). A chronically important identity resides in a person's long-term memory, whereas a temporarily accessible identity is more similar to information stored in working memory (Wheeler, DeMarree, & Petty, 2008). Thus, it is likely that when an identity is made temporarily accessible it will exert a stronger effect on a person's imminent behavior immediately than one that is chronically self-important.

In general, both chronically and temporarily accessible identities yield consistent behavioral outcomes (Zhang & Khare, 2009). This, unsurprisingly, is also the case for moral identity: a chronically important moral identity and temporarily activated moral identity have similar effects. Relative to the effects of SIMI scale (chronic moral identity), Reed, Aquino, and Levy (2007) found similar effects when using a handwriting task to make moral identity temporarily accessible. Choi and Winterich (2013) replicated effects of chronic moral identity when eliciting moral identity temporarily via an advertisement in one study. Going a step further, Aquino and colleagues (2009) examined whether temporarily accessible moral identity interacts with chronic moral identity. They found that moral priming (i.e., making moral identity temporarily accessible) was more influential on people for whom moral identity has relatively low centrality. Thus, the moral self-schema can be accessible within the working self-concept, either temporarily or chronically, consistent with the sociocognitive perspective.

Finally, regarding measurement, an underinvestigated issue is the extent to which techniques that elicit prosocial behavior (i.e., foot-in-the-door, recognition, etc.) can themselves prime situational moral identity or reinforce chronic moral identity. Over time, one may conceivably see carryover effects – engaging in moral or prosocial activities would operationalize this construct temporarily and reinforce it chronically. For example, Winterich and Barone (2011) found that purchase of a product with a donation promotion increases moral identity, though they did not examine whether this effect could be maintained. Finally, it should be clarified that the majority of the existing primes have focused on moral identity internalization; primes regarding the symbolization dimension should be developed in future research.

Political Identity

Conceptualization of Political Identity

Political identity represents a person's beliefs about the underlying goals and ideals of a political system and their associations with these beliefs (Grove, Remy, & Zeigler, 1974). A person's political identity (Kelly, 1989; Yates & Youniss, 1998) has also been referred to as a person's constellation of political beliefs (Block & Block, 2006), political ideology (Jost, Glaser, Kruglanski, & Sulloway, 2003), and political orientation (Renshon, 1977). More overtly, it manifests as a person's identification with a major political party or the adoption of an ideological moniker as a term of self-description (Abrams, 1994; Duck, Hogg, & Terry, 1995; Huddy, 2001).

While many identities are fluid, changing over time and with social contexts, a person's political identity tends to be remarkably stable over time (Ethier & Deaux, 1994; Sears, 1983). Research shows that a person's political identity tends to develop during his or her childhood and reflects the attitudes, beliefs, and activities that emanate from a person's early socialization (Lane, 1959; Renshon, 1977). To be sure, political identities can and do evolve over time, particularly with younger individuals avoiding extreme political identities and developing stronger political identities over time with the accumulation of life experiences and through historical events such as war (Huddy, 2001; Laffan, 1996; Lipsman, 2007).

In Western countries, especially within the United States, there are two dominant political identities: liberal and conservative, which correspond to the Democratic and Republican parties, respectively (Brooks, 2006; Reyna, Henry, Korfmacher, & Tucker, 2006; Skitka & Tetlock, 1993). However, the liberal–conservative continuum for political views is not limited to the United States (Graham, Haidt, & Nosek, 2009).[2] Around the world, there are many more political parties than Democratic and Republican, but many of these parties correspond with a person's self-identification within the country's system and align with a liberal or conservative identity. As an example, within Brazil there are several political parties, with some of the largest including the Brazilian Social Democracy Party, based on social liberalism; the Democrats, based on

---

2 In some cases, researchers may also equate political identity with national identity, patriotism, and multiculturalism (Huddy, 2001). We acknowledge these alternative conceptualizations of political identity, but do not attempt to delve into this debate.

economic liberalism; and the Progressive Party, based on conservative ideals. Similarly, the largest political party in Russia, United Russia, is based on a conservative ideology.

Equating political identity with one's affiliation with a political party, as opposed to a deeper developmental process ascribed to a sociocognitive schema, also reflects a tension inherent in the different literatures examining this construct. While one perspective may view political identity as more of a socially constructed reality that is more likely to be externally ascribed, the other views it as more internally developed based on a person's cognitive schema. Clearly, and as described earlier, in developing an identity, both processes – public and private – are relevant. Thus, a person's political identity, like many identities, can be based on several factors, such as self-categorization or party affiliation, though the meaning ascribed by any and all of these evolves with historic cultural events such as invasion, unification, or separation of nations (Huddy, 2001). Deaux, Reid, Mizrahi, and Ethier (1995) examined the evolution and construction of several political identities such as conservative, environmentalist, liberal, pacifist, radical, and socialist. They found "predictions from social identity theory to be most applicable to ethnic, religious, [and] political" identities because they are more "collective in nature" than other individual aspects of identity (p. 286).

Early research argued that a person's political identity may be associated with his or her values (Barnea & Schwartz, 1998; Goren, Federico, & Kittilson, 2009; Layman, 1997; Rosenberg, 1956). More recently, the theoretical underpinnings of political identity have been comprehensively examined and understood in the context of Moral Foundations Theory (MFT) (Haidt & Joseph, 2004). Drawing upon traditional values research (Rokeach, 1973; Schwartz, 1992), MFT seeks to explain systematically the origins, development, and cultural variations in moral foundations. MFT views moral foundations as a coherent psychological system that guides cognitions, rather than as values or virtues. They are the "first draft" of the moral mind. MFT identifies five specific moral foundations – harm/care, fairness/reciprocity, in-group/loyalty, authority/respect, and purity/sanctity (Haidt & Graham, 2007). These foundations are subsumed into two super-ordinate foundations: (1) *individualizing*, which alludes to the protection and fair treatment of individuals; and (2) *binding*, which is based on authority, loyalty, tradition, and purity.

Empirical research shows that political identity systematically differentiates people's moral foundations (Haidt, 2012). Liberals place more importance on individualizing foundations (harm and fairness); conservatives, in contrast, place more importance on binding foundations (authority, loyalty, tradition, and purity) (Graham, Haidt, & Nosek, 2009; Haidt & Graham, 2007). To be sure, the individualizing foundations tend to be of greater relevance in general, but conservatives find binding foundations to be of greater relevance than liberals, and liberals find individualizing foundations to be of more relevance than binding foundations (Graham, Haidt, & Nosek, 2009; Winterich, Zhang, & Mittal, 2012).

Understanding the consequences of political identity from the lens of MFT provides a nuanced theoretical understanding of the observed effects. For example, research shows that conservatives tend to have more authoritarian personalities, and studies have found that authoritarianism is associated with religious fundamentalism and prejudice (Altemeyer, 1996). Such findings have led to a perception of "conservatives without conscience" (Dean, 2006). However, MFT also clarifies that conservatives value individualizing and binding foundations relatively equally. Thus, conservatives may still engage in moral behavior, such as protecting others and supporting fairness, though these behaviors may be limited to their group or those abiding by tradition based on the simultaneous importance of binding moral foundations. While these distinctions in moral foundations have been proposed to explain political disagreement, Frimer, Biesanz, Walker, and MacKinlay (2013) find that moral foundations between political identities are more similar than they are different, with differences arising primarily in regard to authority and loyalty, or the binding foundations.

Thus, a deeper foundation for understanding political identity and its impact on a variety of outcomes arises from its linkages to MFT. By understanding the underlying individualizing and binding foundations that are associated with the activated political identity, one can gain a more nuanced understanding of how and why political identity will manifest itself in terms of cognitions, attitudes, intentions, and behaviors.

Assessing Political Identity: Measurement and Operationalization

Unlike the commonly used SIMI scale for moral identity (Aquino & Reed, 2002), there is not a standard measure of political identity. Instead, there are several measures that can be used to assess political identity, which include measures of liberalism versus conservatism, support or opposition for political issues, and self-report of political ideology or party affiliation (see Appendix B). For example, Mehrabian (1996) developed a six-item conservatism–liberalism scale, which has been used to assess political identity (Winterich, Zhang, & Mittal, 2012). This scale includes items such as, "The major national media are too left-wing for my tastes." Additionally, research has assessed political identity by the extent to which an individual favors or opposes ongoing political issues such as abortion, gun control, capital punishment, and socialized healthcare (Kidwell, Farmer, & Hardesty, 2013; Nail et al., 2009). Other research has examined effects of political identity with simple self-report of political ideology, where 1 = strongly liberal, 4 = moderate, and 7 = strongly conservative (Graham, Haidt, & Nosek, 2009); or political party affiliation, where 1 = Democrat and 2 = Republican (Winterich, Zhang, & Mittal, 2012). These measures assess the chronic strength of one's political identity, but similar to moral identity and consistent with the sociocognitive perspective, it is important to consider whether a consumer's political identity can be made temporarily accessible by exposure to situational cues.

In some ways, the scales used by researchers also reflect the researcher's stance on the construct of political identity. Some researchers take the stance that a person's political identity is innate and fundamental to the individual (Kruglanski & Webster, 1996). Consistent with this notion, Kanai, Feilden, Firth, and Rees (2011) discovered structural differences in the neurobiology of liberals and conservatives. They identified that the right amygdala, the area of the brain responsible for processing basic emotional information such as fear and uncertainty and leading to heightened aggression under threat, was significantly larger for conservatives than liberals. Conversely, liberals were found to have a larger anterior cingulate cortex, the area of the brain responsible for overriding habitual processes as well as tolerating ambiguity, uncertainty, and conflict. Moreover, classic twin studies reveal that monozygotic twins (genetically identical) are more similar in their political attitudes than dizygotic (non-identical) twins (Alford, Funk, & Hibbing, 2005). Additionally, Hatemi and colleagues (2011) uncovered specific genetic markers that were predictive of political ideology. Specifically, results indicated that certain receptors (NMDA) were the most influential on political identity, as they are related to the organization of thoughts, abstract thought, information processing, and attitude formation and are instrumental in childhood development.

While a person's political identity may be relatively more stable than other identities, there are likely situations that can enhance or mitigate one's chronic political identity. Indeed, some research has been able to alter political identity temporarily (Eidelman, Crandall, Goodman, & Blanchar, 2012). For example, Fernandes and Mandel (2014) used a sentence scramble task to elicit a conservative or liberal identity. In other research, a threat to dispositional liberals elicited conservatism, as evidenced by dispositional liberals "thinking" like conservatives based on their attitudes toward capital punishment, abortion, and homosexuals (Nail et al., 2009). This research suggests that political identity is malleable, at least to some extent.

In consumer contexts, we believe that a situational activation of political identity may be strongest and most relevant for consumers whose political identity is not strongly formed. This possibility is of particular importance given that moderates are far more common than many may believe. Fiorina (2013) states that, regarding the United States, political independents and ideological moderates are far from disappearing. Though 23 percent of American liberals reported holding consistently liberal views and 20 percent of conservatives reported the same consistency pertaining to their political identity, this still leaves a majority of consumers not consistently identifying with either political identity (Murray, 2014), resulting in moderates competing with conservatives for the largest category of political self-identification (34 percent moderate vs. 38 percent conservative, 23 percent liberal; Jones, 2014). To the extent that moderates are more pliable in their political beliefs, consumer behaviors impacted by political identity may be heavily influenced by the decision-making context. For this literature to make substantial advances, future research should better articulate when and how political identity can be temporarily activated or altered.

With a basic understanding of both moral identity and political identity, we now focus on the current research regarding these two identities.

What We Know about Moral and Political Identity

Moral Identity

Many reviews exist to document the role of moral identity in motivating a wide array of behaviors in various social domains (Hardy & Carlo, 2005), including organizational settings (Shao, Aquino, & Freeman, 2008). We extend these reviews to the consumer behavior domain and present an updated summary of studies that have been conducted since the reviews by Hardy and Carlo (2005) and Shao, Aquino, and Freeman (2008).

Distinct Effects of Internalization and Symbolization

The majority of the papers using Aquino and Reed's (2002) SIMI scale show that the internalization and symbolization dimensions are positively correlated. This is expected if they are subcomponents of a higher-order construct. However, they can affect outcomes differently. In a study of consumers' comparative evaluations of the morality of giving time versus money to a socially desirable cause, symbolization did not predict differences in these evaluations in the same way as internalization did (Reed, Aquino, & Levy, 2007). Specifically, while internalization positively impacted corporations giving time over those giving money, symbolization did not affect perceptions of corporations based on giving time versus money. Similarly, Aquino, McFerran, and Laven (2011) also found that symbolization did not predict the extent to which people experienced moral elevation upon being exposed to acts of uncommon moral goodness as strongly as internalization. In contrast, Reynolds and Ceranic (2007) found that symbolization played more of a role in predicting charitable giving than did internalization, though this effect depended on the social consensus regarding the behavior. Wiltermuth, Monin, and Chow (2010) found that symbolization was a stronger predictor than internalization for whether individuals would praise others for positive moral behaviors. These differences in the relative predictive power of the two dimensions suggest that more precise theoretical models are needed to explain these effects.

Some studies have moved in this direction by examining the joint (interactive) effects of internalization and symbolization on moral outcomes. Skarlicki, Van Jaarsveld, and Walker (2008) found that employees with high symbolization moral identity are more likely to retaliate against customers unless the employees are also characterized by high internalization moral identity. More recently, Winterich and colleagues (2013) found that symbolization predicted prosocial behavior only when recognition was offered and consumers were low in moral identity internalization. In seeking to understand the mechanism for these distinct roles of moral identity, Winterich, Mittal, and Aquino (2013) demonstrated that social reinforcement underlies the effect of recognition on charitable giving for consumers with high moral identity symbolization and low moral identity internalization because recognition verifies moral identity to the self for these consumers; consumers with high moral identity internalization can achieve self-consistency through moral actions without recognition. Together, these studies show that the extent to which one dimension of moral identity impacts behavior may be dependent upon the other dimension.

Interaction with Other Social Identities

In addition to documenting how the two dimensions of moral identity interact, research has also begun to examine how moral identity interacts with other social identities. In one study, Winterich, Mittal, and Ross (2009) demonstrate that the effect of moral identity on donations is dependent on both gender and the group membership of the recipient. Relatedly, Winterich, Zhang, and Mittal (2012) found that the effect of political identity on charitable giving was dependent on moral identity as well as the moral relevance of the nonprofit organization.

Though recent and nascent, these results suggest that models recognizing the existence of multiple identities within the self-system and their interactions are a theoretically relevant and ecologically valid way of conceptualizing how the self can be motivated by various forms of identities and manifested as moral behavior. Indeed, the existence of multiple identities within the working self has been proposed before (Markus & Kitayama, 1991; Roccas & Brewer, 2002). Further investigating conditions under which the public and private dimensions of moral identity jointly affect consumer behaviors, and factors that may mediate this effect, is both theoretically warranted and practically useful for explaining consumer behavior.

Negative Effects of Moral Identity

Though moral identity is generally believed to positively impact prosocial behaviors while inhibiting antisocial behaviors, there are some studies that show exceptions to this positive pattern. One study found that people who place high importance on morality are more critical of the negative behavior of others, as they are more likely to condemn others' immoral behavior (Wiltermuth, Monin, & Chow, 2010). Barclay, Whiteside, and Aquino (2014) found that the moral identity dimensions interacted with the endorsement of the negative reciprocity norm to predict revenge, which has often been cast as an undesirable type of social behavior (Tripp & Bies, 2009). Specifically, for people who strongly endorsed a negative reciprocity norm, symbolization predicted revenge when individuals were the targets of mistreatment, whereas internalization predicted revenge when individuals observed mistreatment.

Although the two dimensions had distinct effects, moral identity was found to be directly associated with revenge. Whether revenge is always an antisocial or immoral response or whether it can actually be driven by prosocial motivation has been debated (Tripp, Bies, & Aquino, 2002). Nevertheless, any act of revenge necessarily inflicts harm on another party, and perhaps even on those who did not cause harm to the avenger – innocent parties whose sufferings we might refer to euphemistically as "collateral damage." Consistent with these less than desirable outcomes of moral identity, Lee, Winterich, and Ross (2014) found that moral identity internalization was negatively (rather than positively) related to donations when donation recipients were perceived as responsible for their plight. A provisional conclusion from these studies is that the positive effect of moral identity is dependent on the context in which the behavior occurs, which may determine whether having a strong moral identity predicts negative rather than positive effects. This possibility is supported by Passini's (2013) finding that moral identity limits prejudice only to the extent that the others are included in one's moral community to which moral values apply.

Consumption-Relevant Effects

Recent consumer research identifies effects of moral identity on consumer behaviors that go beyond morality. For example, Choi and Winterich (2013) show that moral identity influences brand evaluations. They found that the expansive nature of moral identity, referred to as the circle of moral regard, results in more abstract processing that leads to broader categorization and more favorable evaluations of brands associated with out-groups. These results suggest that moral identity may be associated with more abstract processing, which may result in moral identity impacting an array of outcomes that are influenced by information processing but need not have moral content (e.g., importance of central vs. peripheral features, feasibility vs. desirability, assimilation vs. contrast, and affect; Trope & Liberman, 2010). Moreover, it is possible that abstract processing could temporarily heighten moral identity salience, which can be explored in future research.

Vredeveld, Ross, and Coulter (2013) examined the role of moral identity in brand communities, finding that authentic brand users utilize moral identity to organize around the cause of anticounterfeits. Saatcioglu and Ozanne (2013) explored how moral identity shapes consumption practices within a marginalized working-class trailer-park neighborhood, finding that moral identities determine social status within this microcultural context. For example, "nesters" in the trailer park are very disciplined and individualistic in their hard work to provide for their family and more upward, but they are very critical of other park residents.

In conclusion, moral identity influences not only moral and immoral behaviors, but also consumption-relevant behaviors such as brand evaluations, interactions with brands and other consumers, and conspicuous consumption practices. Broadening our understanding of how moral identity influences other influential consumer and marketing-related constructs such as customer satisfaction (Mittal & Frennea, 2010), corporate social responsibility (Sen & Bhattacharya, 2001), service quality and service recovery (De Matos, Henrique, & Vargas Rossi, 2007), and online reviews and word of mouth activity (Zhu & Zhang, 2010) are critical future research areas.

Political Identity

Empirical research examining the outcomes of political identity has most clearly shown it to affect outcomes related to politics. These include, but are not limited to, people's voting behavior (Buttel & Flinn, 1978; Guth & Green, 1986), their support for leaders (Wyer et al., 1991), and their positions on social issues (Cohrs, Maes, Moschner, & Kielmann, 2007). In fact, an entire industry of consultants uses manifested political identity (party affiliation) to predict issues – policy, business, world, defense, science, religion, education, energy, and the like – germane to various stakeholders (e.g., RealClearPolitics, 2014). Within marketing, scholars have shown political identity to influence advertising and marketing activities (Gordon & Hartmann, 2013; Hoegg & Lewis, 2011; Phillips, Urbany, & Reynolds, 2008). For example, Crockett and Wallendorf (2004) found that political identity is expressed and constructed through contemporary consumption. Specifically, they studied African American consumers in a large, racially segregated Midwestern city in which they faced systemic disadvantages and engaged in provisioning. They found that consumers' political ideology guided their interpretation of which people and organizations should aid or antagonize in their provisioning.

More widely, political identity can affect factors such as delineation of in-groups (Fowler & Kam, 2007) and ideas about stakeholder rights and responsibilities. These factors can powerfully shape the context within which consumers evaluate brands, make choices, and consume. For example, Henry (2010) found that broad political ideologies influence consumer opinions of rights and responsibilities of various stakeholders, including consumers, businesses, and government participants. This shaping of opinions can powerfully affect not only brand evaluations but also consumer choices and consumption patterns. Next we examine several domains in which political identity affects consumers – directly and indirectly.

Financial Decision Making

Financial decisions are among the most critical decisions that consumers make apart from education and health. Research shows that political identity affects a variety of financial decisions, such as savings, charitable giving, and tax planning. Sussman and Olivola (2011) demonstrate that consumers desire to avoid taxes more than an otherwise equivalent cost. Based on this tax aversion, when savings are tax-related, consumers who most identify with antitax political parties (i.e., conservatives) have stronger preferences for savings compared to when savings are tax-unrelated. Importantly, when positive uses of tax payments are considered, tax aversion, even by conservatives, can be minimized. Thus financial service firms and policy makers can base strategies on consumers' political identity to motivate consumers to increase their savings.

Another major financial decision for most people is charitable giving, with individual consumers in the United States giving nearly $250 billion annually to charity (Giving USA Foundation, 2014). Recent research has shown how a consumer's political identity can affect their charitable behavior. Winterich, Zhang, and Mittal (2012) showed that people were more likely to give to charities whose positioning matched with the moral foundations underlying their own political identity. Another recent study by Kaikati, Torelli, and Winterich (2014) builds on the idea that conservatives are not only more rigid in their beliefs but also more prone to conformity in their behavior than liberals (Jost et al., 2003). Drawing from this research, Kaikati and colleagues (2014) find that conservatives are more likely to conform to perceptions of liberals as giving ("bleeding heart liberals") and increase their own donations in the presence of liberals who share a salient identity (i.e., college). Beyond the realm of savings, tax planning, and charitable giving, a broader array of financial decisions may be affected by political identity and the underlying moral foundations. This is an area for future research.

Sustainable Behavior

Political identity also impacts consumer beliefs about sustainability and government intervention. For example, Gromet, Kunreuther, and Larrick (2013) find that polarization of political ideologies on issues such as carbon emissions reduction and climate change impact choice such that conservatives were less likely to purchase an energy-efficient light bulb when it was labeled as environmentally friendly than when it was unlabeled. This choice was driven by differences in values on carbon emission reductions. When labels indicated a value on energy independence, choice was less polarized by political identity. More generally, conservatives are less responsive than liberals to government intervention: specifically, conservatives were found to have lower intentions to quit smoking and higher intentions to purchase unhealthy food than liberals when product warning labels were associated with the Food and Drug Administration (FDA) (Murdock, Irmak, & Thrasher, 2014). These effects occurred because high-reactance conservatives perceive the government regulations to signal that more restrictions may occur in the future, so they seek to counter these restrictions.

Kidwell, Farmer, and Hardesty (2013) found that political identity influenced sustainable behavior based on corresponding moral foundations. When persuasive appeals to enhance sustainable behavior were congruent with the moral foundations of one's political identity, they were substantially more effective.

For example, emphasizing the traditional aspects of America increased recycling among conservatives, whereas highlighting fairness and reducing harm to others increased recycling among liberals. Relatedly, Feinberg and Willer (2013) found that political polarization on environmental issues arose from liberals perceiving environmental issues in moral terms, specifically harm and care. However, when environmental issues were framed as purity concerns, effects of political identity on environmental attitudes were minimized. Given the importance of sustainable consumption in practice as well as in the literature, future research should continue to examine the relationship between political identity and green consumption values, attitudes, and behaviors (Haws, Winterich, & Naylor, 2014).

Consumer Judgments and Preferences

Political identity also influences consumer judgments more generally. For example, Farmer, Kidwell, and Hardesty (2014) found that liberals deliberate in their decision making to a greater extent than do conservatives. This distinction in the extent of deliberation resulted in conservatives preferring utilitarian, status quo, and feasible options more than liberals, who prefer hedonic, novel, and desirable options. In this regard, Duhachek, Tormala, and Han (2014) demonstrate that conservatives prefer advertising and product messages emphasizing stability, whereas liberals prefer those messages that highlight change. Similarly, Khan, Misra, & Singh (2013) found that conservatives prefer established national brands and are less likely to try newly launched products, which is consistent with conservative ideology regarding preference for the status quo and avoidance of uncertainty. Interestingly, conservatives may not always prefer the stable, low-variation option. Specifically, Fernandes and Mandel (2014) found that while the increased desire for control among conservatives decreases variety seeking, the social normative concerns of conservatives positively impacts variety seeking, ultimately resulting in a positive relationship between conservatism and variety seeking. Overall, this emerging stream of research indicates that the effects of political identity extend into a variety of attitudes, preferences, and behaviors associated with the consumer domain beyond political activism.

Moving Forward: Directions for Future Research

Interactive Effects of Moral and Political Identity

People possess multiple identities, and multiple identities can be simultaneously active; further, these identities can have a high degree of overlap, or they can be completely orthogonal (Roccas & Brewer, 2002). How do consumers reconcile the demands, goals, or expectations emanating from these identities? A host of activities, including, but not limited to, social information processing, judgment and decision making, and moral reasoning, may be used to reconcile these demands. Indeed, given that political identity has an underlying basis in moral foundations, there are good theoretical reasons to believe that for many people their political and moral identities are likely to have considerable overlap. While one may not be entirely embedded within the other, it is certainly conceivable that they interact with one another and consequently influence a variety of consumer-related outcomes.

Moral Foundations Theory

The moral foundations that are most salient in a liberal's moral schema differ from those in a conservative's schema, though Smith, Aquino, Koleva, and Graham (2014) show this can be altered by a person's moral identity. Recall that the binding foundations in MFT consist of the three subcomponents of in-group loyalty, respect for authority, and purity. Recall too that conservatives generally endorse the principles associated with the binding foundations more than liberals do. Among the consequences of people having a strong commitment to the binding foundations is that these values can motivate them to engage in the cooperative and self-sacrificing behaviors required to unite into collectives such as families, communities, and societies (Graham & Haidt, 2010; Norenzayan & Gervais, 2012). However, a darker side of such motivation is that they can lead people to harm those who may not be members of their collective – that is, the in-group. It is for this reason that a strong commitment to the binding foundations can be implicated as being a potential source of intergroup conflict, genocide, or terrorism. What Smith and his colleagues (2014) showed is that a salient moral identity can temper the more negative effects of binding foundations and may even lead people high in the binding foundations to show greater concern for out-group members. They argued that the psychological mechanism that produces this effect is due to the tendency of people who have a chronically accessible or highly salient moral identity to have a more expansive circle of moral regard (Reed & Aquino, 2003), which means that they will feel a greater obligation to show concern for a larger segment of humanity. These results suggest that moral identity may attenuate or amplify the effect of political identity, similar to how Winterich, Mittal, and Ross (2009) established that moral identity can alter the effect of gender identity on charitable giving.

As mentioned earlier, another study in a marketing context showed that moral identity can have a catalytic effect on how people's political identity affects their charitable giving. Specifically, Winterich, Zhang, and Mittal (2012) showed that the effectiveness of matching a charity's positioning to the moral foundations espoused by liberals or conservatives was stronger for those with higher moral identity than their counterparts. It is also possible that in certain situations it is political identity that can amplify and/or mitigate the effect of moral identity on consumer-relevant outcomes. For example, recognizing that moral identity can negatively impact prosocial behavior in specific contexts

(Lee, Winterich, & Ross, 2014), it is possible that a liberal's moral foundations would attenuate this negative effect of moral identity on charity recipients who are perceived as responsible for their plight.

These results posit a versatile theoretical model that includes both moral and political identities as assuming the role of a moderator. We think it more useful to take into account their joint effects, recognizing that in some situations it may be more meaningful to treat one as a moderator of the other and in others to reverse their roles. When would the joint effect of moral and political identity manifest? We suggest that the characteristics of specific issues (Dutton & Jackson, 1987) such as inequality or lack of purity or respect for tradition can act as relevant triggers to enhance or mitigate the joint effect of moral and political identity. More broadly, consumer issues that have a strong political and moral dimension and which evoke dimensions of justice and equity are more likely to be jointly affected by these two identities. Examples include environmentally responsible behaviors such as recycling (Kidwell, Farmer, & Hardesty, 2013), donation and prosocial behavior (Brooks, 2006), healthcare (Powers & Faden, 2008), religion (Wald & Calhoun-Brown, 2014), and corporate social responsibility (CSR; Sen & Bhattacharya, 2001). To the lay theorist, it may appear that those with a more liberal identity will respond more favorably to brands with higher levels of corporate social responsibility (Groening & Kanuri, 2013; Sen & Bhattacharya, 2001). However, one must consider both the social and financial aspects of CSR as well as one's political and moral identities such that some CSR efforts may better align with liberal moral foundations whereas others align with conservative moral foundations.

Joint effects may also exist, albeit to a lesser extent, for status consumption (such as luxury brands), financial decisions (particularly as related to taxation and monetary donations), word-of-mouth behavior (especially to out-groups and in digital forums), and social media consumption (Facebook, Twitter, etc.). The last two are of particular relevance because they can serve as mechanisms for verifying and reinforcing one's identity through socially scrutinized and publicly constructed activities. To the extent that a conservative political identity is based upon moral foundations emphasizing the in-group and because they are likely to evoke dimensions of justice and equity, conservatives may be more likely to engage in word of mouth, particularly in the case of product failure, if they see such word of mouth as a way of warning their friends and family (Zhang, Feick, & Mittal, 2014) and reinforcing their political and moral identities.

Role Identity

What factors can predict the relative importance of moral and political identity when they are simultaneously activated? One possible answer is a person's role identity (Stryker, 1980). Role identity refers to a person's self-perceptions in a particular social position in relation to others who occupy different roles within the same system (e.g., parent, employee, citizen). Though we occupy multiple roles that may coexist, these roles are arranged in order of salience at a given point in time; this role salience may determine the relative importance accorded to moral or political identity by a consumer.

For instance, younger people are typically more liberal, but as they gain more responsibility and their role within society changes, they become more conservative (Lipsman, 2007). So, based on a role identity explanation, we might predict that political identity might have greater self-importance than moral identity depending on the role a person occupies within a social system. Furthermore, if that particular role carries with it demands for loyalty to a group, respect for authority, and some degree of purity in one's actions (e.g., being employed in the military), it could increase commitment to the binding foundations, which, in turn, could lead them to adopt a more conservative political identity in contrast to a role (e.g., being a public defender) that requires a commitment to the individualizing foundations. We recognize in making this argument that the direction of causality may be such that people who are committed to either the binding or individualizing foundations can actively choose environments that are consistent with their preference. This does not invalidate our argument that what partly determines the relative salience of moral or political identity at a given point in time, such as when people make consumption choices, will be the salience of the social role that they identify themselves as occupying when the choice is being made. If the role that they happen to identify themselves with is associated with norms, values, or goals of their political identity, then this identity will be more salient than their moral identity and vice versa.

If the preceding arguments are correct, then future research should try to discover the array of consumer-relevant contextual factors, especially those that can be deliberately modified, which can affect the relative salience of these two identities within the working self. For example, how might marketing-mix factors such as advertising (content and medium), pricing, distribution, product design, product packaging, and brand influence social role perceptions and the activation of different identities associated with these roles? For example, in the United States, an advertisement for a car can remind some of their role as a parent or as a fun-loving person, and, in doing so, differentially impact the relative importance of the two identities.

At the post-consumption level, the joint influence of moral and political identity may impact how consumers react to service recovery efforts after service failure (Mittal & Frennea, 2010; Smith, Bolton, & Wagner, 1999). To the extent that liberals place more emphasis on justice associated with individualizing moral foundations, they may be less forgiving in the case of service failures if they happen to identify themselves with a social role that is associated with being liberal. Alternatively, if a person's role identity at the time of service happens to make moral concerns highly salient (e.g., they work in a caring profession), it could heighten the salience of their moral identity over their political identity, which could make them more forgiving of the service failure. To give another example of how roles might influence the relative salience of different identities, other research has found that conservatives tend to be less likely to aid those who are responsible for their own plight (Kaikati, Torelli, & Winterich, 2014; Reyna et al., 2006). However, it might be that if individuals happen to think about themselves in a social role (e.g., a parent) that has associated with it moral obligations and duties to care for the weak, this could make their moral identity more salient, and therefore conservatives, as suggested by the study of Smith and colleagues (2014), might be willing to aid even people held responsible for their negative outcomes.

Cultural Differences

While much of the empirical research on moral and political identity has been conducted in the United States, there is cultural variation in political and moral identities across different countries and cultures. In particular, how does the cultural variation in Hofstede's (2001) dimensions such as collectivism or power distance relate to political and moral identity? Given the potential overlap between binding moral foundations and collectivism (Triandis et al., 1988) or individualizing foundations and power distance (Hofstede, 2001), we can posit that political identity may have a weaker effect on consumer behavior in collectivistic cultures and in those with low power distance. If political identity is less salient in such cultures, is moral identity more influential? Alternatively, in war-torn countries in Africa, political identity may be more salient and thus more influential in consumer behavior, with moral identity playing only a secondary role.

More generally, how does the effect of moral identity and political identity differ across ethnic groups and regions within a country? In the United States, political identity tends to differ by geographic region, with more conservatives in rural areas and the South (Kotkin, 2012). Given these regional distinctions, corresponding role identities may heighten political identity and result in an overlap with global/local identity (Zhang & Khare, 2009). The importance of cultural factors on political and moral identity salience may be particularly important for evaluations influenced by country of origin (e.g., Swaminathan, Page, & Gurhan-Canli, 2007). In such judgments, a salient moral identity may attenuate country-of-origin effects due to the expansive boundaries, whereas a salient political identity may amplify country-of-origin effects, particularly for conservatives holding binding moral foundations, who may respond more strongly to "Made in the USA" product positioning, which also suggests financial support for the local rather than global economy.

Mechanisms

In understanding the joint effects of these two identities, future research should also explore the specific mediating processes through which these identities enact themselves. Elements of MFT certainly present a series of mechanisms to consider. In addition, our review of the empirical research shows the following set of mediators: inclusion of self with others (Winterich, Mittal, & Ross, 2009), psychological distance (Choi & Winterich, 2013), social reinforcement (Winterich et al., 2013), moral awareness (DeCelles, DeRue, Margolis, & Ceranic, 2012), moral elevation (Aquino, McFerran, & Laven, 2011), moral disengagement (Detert, Trevino, & Sweitzer, 2008), and affect (e.g., empathy and justice; Lee, Winterich, & Ross, 2014). This set of mediators is multifaceted to say the least, suggesting that the processes underlying our understanding of political and moral identity are not to be construed narrowly. Augmenting this set of mediators is a key research priority.

Correlates for Practice

Because these are influential identities, both practitioners and policy makers are in dire need to identify observable factors – demographics and behaviors – that can separate those placing high and low levels of importance on the identity. This may be a difficult task, especially when identities can evolve systematically over time as people age and mature. Understanding the lifecycle of identities could have important implications for marketers given that consumption patterns also evolve over time across consumer lifecycles (Du & Kamakura, 2006). Nonetheless, developing models that can statistically correlate antecedent demographics and behaviors to both political and moral identity is a key research area. This may also be important for bridging the gap between behavioral and quantitative researchers.

In summary, there are numerous areas for future research exploring how moral identity and political identity may jointly impact consumer decisions and behaviors. Moreover, consumers' roles and cultures as well as other factors are likely to influence the activation and joint influence of political and moral identities. Finally, understanding the factors that mediate the effect of these identities on key outcomes along with their demographic and behavioral antecedents represent key research opportunities.

Conclusion

In this chapter, we have provided an overview of moral identity and political identity, including their definition, conceptualization, measurement, and current methods of operationalization. We summarized current research and raised important areas for further research. Most importantly, we have discussed how future research may integrate the study of moral identity and political identity and articulated research questions to better understand the overlap of these identities and their impact on identity-consistent behavior. We hope this chapter offers interesting ideas for consumer psychologists seeking to add insights to this literature.

Appendix A

Aquino and Reed's (2002) Self-Importance of Moral Identity Instrument

Listed alphabetically below are some characteristics that might describe a person:

Caring, Compassionate, Fair, Friendly, Generous, Helpful, Hardworking, Honest, Kind

The person with these characteristics could be you or it could be someone else. For a moment, visualize in your mind the kind of person who has these characteristics. Imagine how that person would think, feel, and act. When you have a clear image of what this person would be like, answer the following questions using the scale below.

	Strongly Disagree						Strongly Agree
1. It would make me feel good to be a person who has these characteristics. (I)	1	2	3	4	5	6	7
2. Being someone who has these characteristics is an important part of who I am. (I)	1	2	3	4	5	6	7
3. I often wear clothes that identify me as having these characteristics. (S)	1	2	3	4	5	6	7
4. I would be ashamed to be a person who had these characteristics. (I/R)	1	2	3	4	5	6	7
5. The types of things I do in my spare time (e.g., hobbies) clearly identify me as having these characteristics. (S)	1	2	3	4	5	6	7
6. The kinds of books and magazines that I read identify me as having these characteristics. (S)	1	2	3	4	5	6	7
7. Having these characteristics is not really important to me. (I/R)	1	2	3	4	5	6	7
8. The fact that I have these characteristics is communicated to others by my membership in certain organizations. (S)	1	2	3	4	5	6	7
9. I am actively involved in activities that communicate to others that I have these characteristics. (S)	1	2	3	4	5	6	7
10. I strongly desire to have these characteristics. (I)	1	2	3	4	5	6	7

Note. I=Internalization item, S=Symbolization item, R=reverse-coded.

Appendix B

Measures of Political Identity

Conservatism–Liberalism Scale from Mehrabian (1996)

1. I am politically more liberal than conservative.(R)
2. In an election, given a choice between a Republican and a Democratic candidate, I will select the Republican over the Democrat.
3. Communism has been proven to be a failed political ideology.
4. I cannot see myself ever voting to elect conservative candidates. (R)
5. The major national media are too left-wing for my taste.
6. Socialism has many advantages over capitalism. (R)
7. On balance, I lean politically more to the left than to the right. (R)

(R) = Reverse coded

Political Ideology from Nail et al. (2009)

(1 = strongly against, 7 = strongly favor)

1. Capital punishment
2. Abortion (prolife)
3. Gun control (R)
4. Socialized health care (R)
5. Same-sex marriage (R)
6. Illegal immigration (R)
7. Democrats (R)

(R) = Reverse coded

Political Self-Identification from Graham, Haidt, and Nosek (2009)

On the scale below, please indicate the response which best represents your political identity.

1 = strongly liberal, 4 = neutral (moderate), 7 = strongly conservative

If you feel that you could not appropriately indicate your political identity on the above scale, please indicate the response below which best represents your political identity.*

Liberatarian, Other, Don't know/not political

*You do not need to answer this question if you feel your political identity was appropriately indicated in the above question.

Party Affiliation from Winterich, Zhang, and Mittal (2012)

Please indicate the political party with which you most identity:

- Democrat
- Republican

(Dummy coded: 0 = Democrat, 1 = Republican)

References

Abrams, D. (1994). Political distinctiveness: An identity optimising approach. *European Journal of Social Psychology, 24*, 357–365.

Alford, J. R., Funk, C. L., & Hibbing, J. R. (2005). Are political orientations genetically transmitted? *American Political Science Review, 99*(2), 153–167.

Altemeyer, B. (1996). *The Authoritarian Specter.* Cambridge, MA: Harvard University Press.

Anderson, J. R., & Bower, G. H. (1973). *Human Associative Memory.* Washington: V. H. Winston; distributed by the Halsted Press Division of Wiley, New York.

Aquino, K., Freeman, D., Reed, A., Lim, V. K., & Felps, W. (2009). Testing a social-cognitive model of moral behavior: The interactive influence of situations and moral identity centrality. *Journal of Personality and Social Psychology, 97*(1), 123–141.

Aquino, K., McFerran, B., & Laven, M. (2011). Moral identity and the experience of moral elevation in response to acts of uncommon goodness. *Journal of Personality and Social Psychology, 100*(4), 703–718.

Aquino, K., & Reed, II, A. (2002). The self-importance of moral identity. *Journal of Personality and Social Psychology, 83*(6), 1423–1440.

Ashforth, B. E., & Mael, F. (1989). Social identity theory and the organization. *Academy of Management Review, 14*(1), 20–39.

Bandura, A. (1991). Social cognitive theory of self-regulation. *Organizational Behavior and Human Decision Processes, 50*(2), 248–287.

Barclay, L. J., Whiteside, D. B., & Aquino, K. (2014). To avenge or not to avenge? Exploring the interactive effects of moral identity and the negative reciprocity norm. *Journal of Business Ethics, 121*(1), 15–28.

Barnea, M., & Schwartz, S. (1998). Values and voting. *Political Psychology, 19*(1), 17–40.

Bem, D. J. (1972). Self-perception theory. *Advances in Experimental Social Psychology, 6*, 1–62.

Bem, S. L. (1981). Gender schema theory: A cognitive account of sex typing. *Psychological Review, 88*(4), 354–364.

Blasi, A. (1984). Moral identity: Its role in moral functioning. In W. M. Kurtines & J. L. Gurwitz (eds.), *Morality, Moral Behavior, and Moral Development* (pp. 128–139). Hoboken, NJ: John Wiley & Sons.

Block, J., & Block, J. H. (2006). Nursery school personality and political orientation two decades later. *Journal of Research in Personality, 40*(5), 734–749.

Brooks, A. C. (2006). *Who Really Cares: The Surprising Truth about Compassionate Conservatism: America's Charity Divide–Who Gives, Who Doesn't and Why It Matters.* New York: Basic Books.

Buttel, F. M., & Flinn W. L. (1978) The politics of environmental concern: The impacts of party identification and political ideology on environmental attitudes. *Environment and Behavior, 10*(1), 17–36.

Choi, W. J., & Winterich, K. P. (2013). Can brands move in from the outside? How moral identity enhances out-group brand attitudes. *Journal of Marketing, 77* (2), 96–111.

Cohrs, J. C., Maes, J., Moschner, B., & Kielmann, S. (2007). Determinants of human rights attitudes and behavior: A comparison and integration of psychological perspectives. *Political Psychology, 28*(4), 441–469.

Crockett, D., & Wallendorf, M. (2004). The role of normative political ideology in consumer behavior. *Journal of Consumer Research, 31*(3), 511–528.

Dean, J. W. (2006). *Conservatives without Conscience.* New York: Viking.

Deaux, K., Reid, A., Mizrahi, K., & Ethier, K. A. (1995). Parameters of social identity. *Journal of Personality and Social Psychology, 68*(2), 280–291.

DeCelles, K. A., DeRue, D. S., Margolis, J. D., & Ceranic, T. L. (2012) Does power corrupt or enable? When and why power facilitates self-interested behavior. *Journal of Applied Psychology, 97*(3), 681–689.

De Matos, C. A., Henrique, J. L., & Vargas Rossi, C. A. (2007). Service recovery paradox: A meta-analysis. *Journal of Service Research, 10*(1), 60–77.

Detert, J. R., Trevino, L. K., & Sweitzer, V. L. (2008). Moral disengagement in ethical decision making: A study of antecedents and outcomes. *Journal of Applied Psychology, 93*(2), 374–391.

Du, R. Y., & Kamakura, W. A. (2006). Household life cycles and lifestyles in the United States. *Journal of Marketing Research (JMR), 43*(1), 121–132.

Duck, J. M., Hogg, M. A., & Terry, D. J. (1995). Me, us and them: Political identification and the third-person effect in the 1993 Australian federal election. *European Journal of Social Psychology, 25*, 195–215.

Duhachek, A., Tormala, Z., & Han, D. (2014). Stability vs. change: The effect of political ideology on product preference. Paper presented at the annual meeting of the Association for Consumer Research, October, Baltimore, MD.

Dutton, J. E., & Jackson, S. E. (1987). Categorizing strategic issues: Links to organizational action. *Academy of Management: The Academy of Management Review, 12*(1), 76.

Eidelman, S., Crandall, C. S., Goodman, J. A., & Blanchar, J. C. (2012). Low-effort thought promotes political conservatism. *Personality and Social Psychology Bulletin, 38*(6), 808–820.

Erikson, E. (1964). *Insights and Responsibility.* New York: W. W. Norton.

Ethier, K. A., & Deaux, K. (1994). Negotiating social identity when contexts change: Maintaining identification and responding to threat. *Journal of Personality and Social Psychology, 67*, 243–251.

Farmer, R., Kidwell, B., & Hardesty. D. (2014). Political ideology and consumer decision making. Paper presented at the annual meeting of the Association for Consumer Research, October. Baltimore, MD.

Feinberg, M., & Willer, R. (2013). The moral roots of environmental attitudes. *Psychological Science, 24*(1), 56–62.

Fenigstein, A., Scheier, M., & Buss, A. (1975) Public and private self-consciousness: Assessment and theory. *Journal of Consulting and Clinical Psychology, 43*(4), 522.

Fernandes, D., & Mandel, N. (2014). Political conservatism and variety-seeking. *Journal of Consumer Psychology, 24*(1), 79–86.

Festinger, L. (1957). *A Theory of Cognitive Dissonance.* Evanston, IL: Row Peterson.

Fiorina, M. P. (2013). America's missing moderates: Hiding in plain sight. *American Interest: Features: Policy, Politics, & Culture,* February 12. Retrieved from www.the-american-interest.com/articles/2013/02/12/americas-missing-moderates-hiding-in-plain-sight/.

Forehand, M. R., Deshpandé, R., & Reed, A., II (2002). Identity salience and the influence of differential activation of the social self-schema on advertising response. *Journal of Applied Psychology, 87,* 1086–1099.

Fowler, J. H., & Kam, C. (2007). Beyond the self: Social identity, altruism, and political participation. *Journal of Politics, 69*(3), 813–827.

Frimer, J. A., Biesanz, J. C., Walker, L. J., & MacKinlay, C. W. (2013) Liberals and conservatives rely on common moral foundations when making moral judgments about influential people. *Journal of Personality and Social Psychology, 104*(6), 1040–1059.

Giving USA Foundation (2014). *Giving USA 2014.* Glenview, IL: Giving USA Foundation.

Gordon, B. R., & Hartmann, W. R. (2013). Advertising effects in presidential elections. *Marketing Science, 32*(1), 19–35.

Goren, P., Federico, C. M., & Kittilson, M. C. (2009). Source cues, partisan identities, and political value expression. *American Journal of Political Science, 53*(4), 805–820.

Graham, J., & Haidt, J. (2010). Beyond beliefs: Religions bind individuals into moral communities. *Personality and Social Psychology Review, 14,* 140–150.

Graham, J., Haidt, J., & Nosek, B.A. (2009). Liberals and conservatives rely on different sets of moral foundations. *Journal of Personality and Social Psychology, 96*(5), 1029–1046.

Graham, J., Nosek, B. A., Haidt, J., Iyer, R., Koleva, S., & Ditto, P. H. (2011). Mapping the moral domain. *Journal of Personality and Social Psychology, 101*(2), 366–385.

Groening, C., & Kanuri, V. K. (2013). Investor reaction to positive and negative corporate social events. *Journal of Business Research, 66*(10), 1852–1860.

Gromet, D. M., Kunreuther, H., & Larrick, R. P. (2013). Political ideology affects energy-efficiency attitudes and choices. *Proceedings of the National Academy of Science, 110*(23), 9314–9319.

Grove, D. J., Remy, R. C., & Zeigler, L. H. (1974). The effects of political ideology and educational climates on student dissent. *American Politics Research, 2*(3), 259–275.

Guth, J. L., & Green, J. C. (1986). Faith and politics-religion and ideology among political contributors. *American Politics Quarterly, 14*(3), 186–200.

Haidt, J. (2012). *The Righteous Mind: Why Good People Are Divided by Politics and Religion.* New York: Pantheon.

Haidt, J., & Graham, J. (2007). When morality opposes justice: Conservatives have moral intuitions that liberals may not recognize. *Social Justice Research, 20*(1), 98–116.

Haidt, J., & Joseph, C. (2004). Intuitive ethics: How innately prepared intuitions generate culturally variable virtues. *Daedalus, 133*(4), 55–66.

Hardy, S. A., & Carlo, G. (2005). Identity as a source of moral motivation. *Human Development, 48*(4), 232–256.

Hatemi, P. K., Gillespie, N. A., Eaves, L. J., Maher, B. S., Webb, B. T., Heath, A. C., Medland, S. E., et al. (2011). A genome-wide analysis of liberal and conservative political attitudes. *Journal of Politics, 73*(01), 271–285.

Haws, K. L., Winterich, K. P., & Naylor, R. W. (2014). Seeing the world through GREEN-tinted glasses: Green consumption values and responses to environmentally friendly products. *Journal of Consumer Psychology, 24*(3), 336–354.

Henry, P. (2010). How mainstream consumers think about consumer rights and responsibilities. *Journal of Consumer Research, 37*(4), 670–687.

Higgins, E. T. (1987). Self-discrepancy: A theory relating self and affect. *Psychological Review, 94*(3), 319–340.

Hoegg, J., & Lewis, M. V. (2011). The impact of candidate appearance and advertising strategies on election results. *Journal of Marketing Research, 48*(5), 895–909.

Hofstede, G. (2001). *Culture's Consequences: Comparing Values, Behaviors, Institutions, and Organizations across Nations.* Thousand Oaks, CA: Sage.

Huddy, L. (2001). From social to political identity: A critical examination of social identity theory. *Political Psychology, 22*(1), 127–156.

Huddy, L., & Khatib, N. (2007). American patriotism, national identity, and political involvement. *American Journal of Political Science, 51*(1), 63–77.

Jones, J. (2014) Liberal self-identification edges up to new high in 2013. From www.gallup.com/poll/166787/liberal-self-identification-edges-new-high-2013.aspx.

Jost, J. T., Glaser, J., Kruglanski, A. W., & Sulloway, F. J. (2003). Political conservatism as motivated social cognition. *Psychological Bulletin, 129*(3), 339–375.

Kaikati, A., Torelli, C., & Winterich, K. P. (2014). Conforming conservatives: How norms of salient social identities overcome "heartless conservative" tendencies. Paper presented at the annual meeting of the Association for Consumer Research, October. Baltimore, MD.

Kanai, R., Feilden, T., Firth, C., & Rees, G. (2011). Political orientations are correlated with brain structure in young adults. *Current Biology, 21*(8), 677–680.

Kelly, C. (1989). Political identity and perceived intragroup homogeneity. *British Journal of Social Psychology, 28*(3), 239–250.

Kertzer, J. D., Powers, K. E., Rathbun, B. C., & Iyer, R. (2014). Moral support: How moral values shape foreign policy attitudes. *Journal of Politics, 76*(3), 825–840.

Khan, R., Misra, K., & Singh, V. (2013). Ideology and brand consumption. *Psychological Science, 24*(3), 326–333.

Kidwell, B., Farmer, A., & Hardesty, D. M. (2013). Getting liberals and conservatives to go green: Political ideology and congruent appeals. *Journal of Consumer Research, 40*(2), 350–367.

Kohlberg, L. (1971). From is to ought: How to commit the naturalistic fallacy and get away with it in the study of moral development. In T. Mischel (ed.), *Cognitive Development and Epistemology* (pp. 151–235). New York: Academic Press.

Kotkin, J. (2012). The Republican Party's fatal attraction to rural America. *Forbes*, March 4. www.forbes.com/sites/joelkotkin/2012/03/14/the-gops-fatal-attraction-to-rural-america/.

Kruglanski, A. W., & Webster, D. M. (1996). Motivated closing of the mind: "Seizing" and "freezing." *Psychological Review, 103*(2), 263–283.

Laffan, B. (1996). The politics of identity and political order in Europe. *JCMS: Journal of Common Market Studies, 34*(1), 81–102.

Lakoff, G. (2010). *Moral Politics: How Liberals and Conservatives Think,* 2nd ed. Chicago: University of Chicago Press.

Lane, R. E. (1959). *Political Life: Why People Get Involved in Politics.* Glencoe, IL: Free Press.

Layman, G. C. (1997). Religion and political behavior in the United States: The impact of beliefs, affiliations, and commitment from 1980 to 1994. *Public Opinion Quarterly, 61*(2), 288–316.

LeBoeuf, R. A., Shafir, E., & Bayuk, J. B. (2010). The conflicting choices of alternating selves. *Organizational Behavior and Human Decision Processes, 111*(1), 48–61.

Lee, S., Winterich, K. P., & Ross, W. (2014). I'm moral, but I won't help you: The distinct roles of empathy and justice in donations. *Journal of Consumer Research, 41*(3), 678–696.

Lipsman, R. (2007). *Liberal Hearts and Conservative Brains: The Correlation between Age and Political Philosophy.* Bloomington, IN: iUniverse, Inc., Ron Lipsman.

Markus, H. (1977). Self-schemata and processing information about the self. *Journal of Personality and Social Psychology, 35*(2), 63–78.

Markus, H. R., & Kitayama, S. (1991). Culture and the self: Implications for cognition, emotion, and motivation. *Psychological review, 98*(2), 224–253.

Mead, G. H. (1934). Mind, self, and society from the perspective of a social behaviorist. Chicago: University of Chicago Press.

Mehrabian, A. (1996). Relations among political attitudes, personality, and psychopathology assessed with new measures of libertarianism and conservatism. *Basic and Applied Social Psychology, 18*(4), 469–491.

Mischel, W., & Shoda, Y. (2008). Toward a unified theory of personality. In O. John, R. Robins, & L. Pervin (eds.), *Handbook of Personality* (pp. 208–241). New York: Guilford Press.

Mittal, V., & Frennea, C. (2010). *Customer Satisfaction: A Strategic Review and Guidelines for Managers.* MSI Fast Forward Series. Cambridge, MA: Marketing Science Institute.

Murdock, M., Irmak, C., & Thrasher, J. (2014). The effect of political ideology on reactions to warning labels and consumption regulations. Paper presented at the annual meeting of the Association for Consumer Research, October. Baltimore, MD.

Murray, A. (2014). The divided states of America. *Wall Street Journal,* June 12.

Nail, P. R., McGregor, I., Drinkwater, A. E., Steele, G. M., & Thompson, A. W. (2009). Threat causes liberals to think like conservatives. *Journal of Experimental Social Psychology, 45*(4), 901–907.

Norenzayan, A., & Gervais, W. (2012). The cultural evolution of religion. In E. Slingerland & M. Collard (eds.), *Creating Consilience: Integrating Science and the Humanities* (pp. 243–265). Oxford: Oxford University Press.

Oyserman, D. (2009). Identity-based motivation: Implications for action-readiness, procedural-readiness, and consumer behavior. *Journal of Consumer Psychology, 19*(3), 250–260.

Passini, S. (2013). What do I think of others in relation to myself? Moral identity and moral inclusion in explaining prejudice. *Journal of Community & Applied Social Psychology, 23*(3), 261–269.

Phillips, J., Urbany, J., & Reynolds, T. (2008). Confirmation and the effects of valenced political advertising: A field experiment. *Journal of Consumer Research, 34*(6), 794–806.

Powers, M., & Faden, R. (2008). *Social Justice: The Moral Foundations of Public Health and Health Policy*. New York: Oxford University Press.

RealClearPolitics, (2014). RealClearPolitics.com, accessed June 30.

Reed, A. (2004). Activating the self-importance of consumer selves: Exploring identity salience effects on judgments. *Journal of Consumer Research, 31*(2), 286–295.

Reed, A., & Aquino, K. (2003). Moral identity and the expanding circle of moral regard toward out-groups. *Journal of Personality and Social Psychology, 84*(6), 1270–1286.

Reed, A., Aquino K., & Levy, E. (2007). Moral identity and judgments of charitable behaviors. *Journal of Marketing, 71*(1), 178–193.

Reed, A., Forehand, M. R., Puntoni, S., & Warlop, L. (2012). Identity-based consumer behavior. *International Journal of Research in Marketing, 29*(4), 310–321.

Renshon, S. A. (1977). *Handbook of Political Socialization: Theory and Research.* New York: Free Press.

Reyna, C., Henry, P. J., Korfmacher, W., & Tucker, A. (2006). Examining the principles in principled conservatism: The role of responsibility stereotypes as cues for deservingness in racial policy decisions. *Journal of Personality and Social Psychology, 90*(1), 109–128.

Reynolds, S. J., & Ceranic, T. L. (2007). The effects of moral judgment and moral identity on moral behavior: An empirical examination of the moral individual. *Journal of Applied Psychology, 92*(6), 1610–1624.

Roccas, S., & Brewer, M. B. (2002). Social identity complexity. *Personality and Social Psychology Review, 6*(2), 88–106.

Rokeach, M. (1973). *The Nature of Human Values.* New York: Free Press.

Rosenberg, M. J. (1956). Cognitive structure and attitudinal affect. *Journal of Abnormal and Social Psychology, 53*(3), 367–372.

Saatcioglu, B., & Ozanne, J. L. (2013). A critical spatial approach to marketplace exclusion and inclusion. *Journal of Public Policy & Marketing, 32*(special issue), 32–37.

Schlenker, B. R., & Weigold, M. F. (1992). Interpersonal processes involving impression regulation and management. *Annual Review of Psychology, 43*(1), 133–168.

Schwartz, S. H. (1992). Universals in the content and structure of values: Theoretical advances and empirical tests in 20 countries. *Advances in Experimental Social Psychology, 25*(1), 1–65.

Sears, D. O. (1983). The persistence of early political predispositions: The roles of attitude object and life stage. *Review of Personality and Social Psychology, 4*, 79–116.

Sen, S., & Bhattacharya, C. B. (2001). Does doing good always lead to doing better? Consumer reactions to corporate social responsibility. *Journal of Marketing Research, 38*(2), 225–243.

Shang, J., Reed, A., & Croson, R. (2008). Identity congruency effects on donations. *Journal of Marketing Research, 45*(3), 351–361.

Shao, R., Aquino, K., and Freeman, D. (2008). Beyond moral reasoning: A review of moral identity research and its implications for business ethics. *Business Ethics Quarterly, 18*(4), 513–540.

Skarlicki, D. P., Van Jaarsveld, D. D., & Walker, D. D. (2008). Getting even for customer mistreatment: The role of moral identity in the relationship between customer interpersonal injustice and employee sabotage. *Journal of Applied Psychology, 93*(6), 1335–1347.

Skitka, L. J., & Tetlock, P. E. (1993). Providing public assistance: Cognitive and motivational processes underlying liberal and conservative policy preferences. *Journal of Personality and Social Psychology, 65*(6), 1205–1223.

Smith, A. K., Bolton, R. N., & Wagner, J. (1999). A model of customer satisfaction with service encounters involving failure and recovery. *Journal of Marketing Research, 36*(3), 356–372.

Smith, I. H., Aquino, K., Koleva, S., & Graham, J. (2014). The moral ties that bind . . . even to out-groups the interactive effect of moral identity and the binding moral foundations. *Psychological Science*, 0956797614534450.

Stryker, S. (1980). Toward an adequate social psychology of the self. *Contemporary Sociology, 9*(3), 383–385.

Sussman, A. B., & Olivola, C. Y. (2011). Axe the tax: Taxes are disliked more than equivalent costs. *Journal of Marketing Research, 48*(SPL), S91–S101.

Swaminathan, V., Page, K. L., & Gurhan-Canli, Z. (2007). "My" brand or "our" brand: The effects of brand relationship dimensions and self-construal on brand evaluations. *Journal of Consumer Research, 34*(2), 248–259.

Swann, W. B. (1983). Self-verification: Bringing social reality into harmony with the self. *Social Psychological Perspectives on the Self, 2*, 33–66.

Tajfel, H. (1972). Social categorisation (English manuscript of *La Categorisation Sociale*). In Moscovici, S. (ed.), *Introduction a la Psychologie Sociale* (vol. 1). Paris: Larousse.

Triandis, H. C., Bontempo, R., Villareal, M. J., Asai, M., & Lucca, N. (1988). Individualism and collectivism: Cross-cultural perspectives on self-in-group relationships. *Journal of Personality and Social Psychology, 54*(2), 323–338.

Tripp, T. M., & Bies, R. J. (2009). *Getting Even: The Truth about Workplace Revenge— and How to Stop It*. New York: John Wiley & Sons.

Tripp, T. M., Bies, R. J., & Aquino, K. (2002). Poetic justice or petty jealousy? The aesthetics of revenge. *Organizational Behavior and Human Decision Processes, 89*(1), 966–984.

Trope, Y., & Liberman, N. (2010). Construal-level theory of psychological distance. *Psychological Review, 117*(2), 440–463.

Vredeveld, A. J., Ross, W. T., & Coulter, R. A. (2013). Collective moral identity projects: Authentic brand users anti-counterfeit framework. Paper presented at the annual meeting of the Association for Consumer Research, October. Chicago, IL.

Wald, K. D., & Calhoun-Brown, A. (2014). *Religion and Politics in the United States*. Lanham, MD: Rowman & Littlefield.

Wheeler, S. C., & Berger, J. (2007). When the same prime leads to different effects. *Journal of Consumer Research, 34*(3), 357–368.

Wheeler, S. C., DeMarree, K. G., & Petty, R. E. (2008). A match made in the laboratory: Persuasion and matches to primed traits and stereotypes. *Journal of Experimental Social Psychology, 44*(4), 1035–1047.

White, K., Argo, Jennifer J., & Sengupta, J. (2012). Dissociative versus associative responses to social identity threat: The role of consumer self-construal. *Journal of Consumer Research, 39*(4), 704–719.

Wiltermuth, S. S., Monin, B., & Chow, R. M. (2010). The orthogonality of praise and condemnation in moral judgment. *Social Psychological and Personality Science, 1*(4), 302–310.

Winterich, K. P., Aquino, K., Mittal, V., & Swartz, R. (2013). When moral identity symbolization motivates prosocial behavior: The role of recognition and moral identity internalization. *Journal of Applied Psychology, 98*(5), 759–770.

Winterich, K. P., & Barone, M. J. (2011). Warm glow or cold, hard cash? Social identity effects on consumer choice for donation versus discount promotions. *Journal of Marketing Research, 48*(5), 855–868.

Winterich, K. P., Mittal, V., & Aquino, K. (2013). When does recognition increase charitable behavior? Toward a moral identity-based model. *Journal of Marketing, 77*(3), 121–134.

Winterich, K. P., Mittal, V., & Ross, Jr., W. T. (2009). Donation behavior toward in-groups and out-groups: The role of gender and moral identity. *Journal of Consumer Research, 36*(2), 199–214.

Winterich, K. P., Zhang, Y., & Mittal, V. (2012). How political identity and charity positioning increase donations: Insights from moral foundations theory. *International Journal of Research in Marketing, 29*(4), 346–354.

Wyer, R. S., Budesheim, T. L., Shavitt, S., Riggle, E. D., Melton, R. J., & Kuklinski, J. H. (1991). Image, issues, and ideology: The processing of information about political candidates. *Journal of Personality and Social Psychology, 61*(4), 533.

Yates, M., & Youniss, J. (1998). Community service and political identity development in adolescence. *Journal of Social Issues, 54*(3), 495–512.

Zhang, Y., Feick, L., & Mittal, V. (2014). How males and females differ in their likelihood of transmitting negative word of mouth. *Journal of Consumer Research, 40*(6), 1097–1108.

Zhang, Y., & Khare, A. (2009). The impact of accessible identities on the evaluation of global versus local products. *Journal of Consumer Research, 36*(3), 524–537.

Zhang, Y., & Shrum, L. J. (2009). The influence of self-construal on impulsive consumption. *Journal of Consumer Research, 35*(5), 838–850.

Zhu, F., & Zhang, X. (2010). Impact of online consumer reviews on sales: The moderating role of product and consumer characteristics. *Journal of Marketing, 74*(2), 133–148.

23 The Consumer Psychology of Online Privacy

Insights and Opportunities from Behavioral Decision Theory

Leslie K. John

As people spend more time shopping, gaming, and socializing online, and as data-gathering technology has become more sophisticated, consumer privacy has been dubbed "one of the most important issues facing management practice" (Awad & Krishnan, 2006, p. 14). The Internet, in its seemingly boundless capacity to facilitate information disclosure, dissemination, aggregation, and storage, has added great complexity to consumers' management of their personal data. Consumers face, on the one hand, risks of privacy invasions – from receiving spam e-mails to identity theft – and on the other, benefits such as improved convenience and personalization.

From a firm's perspective, the Internet has dramatically changed the way offerings are marketed. With respect to promotions, for example, in the past, marketers had strong control over the message and the medium. Marketers could "push" their promotions onto consumers, who had little say in when and how they were contacted. Today, however, people consume media on their own terms, rendering traditional methods of marketing communications – such as primetime television advertisements – less effective. Now more than ever, marketers must "be in the right place at the right time," which requires having detailed information on their customers. Fortunately for firms, just as the Internet has heightened the importance of understanding the customer, new Internet technologies have increased the ease of obtaining and using detailed customer data.

As a result, online advertising, and behavioral targeting in particular, has become of central importance to marketing. Behavioral targeting refers to the delivery of advertisements tailored to a user's revealed preferences (for an overview, see Gilbert, 2008). Unlike mere targeting, which refers to the traditional practice of tailoring messages to groups of consumers with similar interests and demographic characteristics, behavioral targeting is more invasive, since it is conducted at the individual level. Information is gleaned about the individual consumer by tracking his online behavior. This information is then used to show him customized advertisements.

How do consumers navigate the new complexities of information sharing in this context of unprecedented openness? How do firms maximize the new marketing capabilities afforded by new technologies, while respecting consumers' privacy? Behavioral decision theory (BDT) and, more broadly, social psychology provide answers. In this chapter, I first discuss how research in these fields can account for the privacy paradox – people's tendency to say they care about their privacy despite their willingness to reveal extremely sensitive personal information online. Drawing on this understanding, in the second section I show how this perspective can account for many of the seemingly paradoxical choices consumers make with respect to the management of their personal data and their reactions to behavioral targeting in particular. In doing so, I highlight recent research and venture into more speculative areas that represent opportunities for future inquiry. I conclude with a discussion of broad topics worthy of future research, including interventions to help consumers better navigate issues of online privacy.

Part 1: The Privacy Paradox Explained

In polls and surveys, consumers indicate profound and increasing concern for their privacy (ConsumersUnion.org, 2008; Federal Trade Commission, 2000, 2006; Jupiter Research, 2002; Goldfarb & Tucker, 2011a), and for good reason – it is fundamental to human development (Berscheid, 1977). Yet, from the posting of suggestive photographs on social networking sites (SNSs) to the impulsive broadcasting of illicit activities on Twitter, consumers' behavior often suggests a remarkable lack of concern for privacy. In addition to being inconsistent with stated attitudes, this behavior is also surprising because, as regularly highlighted in the media, there are very real dangers to online disclosure. For example, Virgin Atlantic flight attendants were fired after the company discovered that they had posted derogatory statements about the company on Facebook (Conway, 2008).

The privacy paradox (Norberg & Horne, 2007) – the discrepancy between people's stated and revealed preferences for privacy – has been documented empirically: those who indicate serious privacy concern nevertheless reveal intimate details of their lives for trivial rewards (Acquisti & Gross, 2009; Spiekermann, Grossklags, & Berendt, 2001; Tufecki, 2008). The paradox is also readily apparent in consumers' responses to behavioral targeting – consumers say they reject behavioral targeting, yet research suggests that it can be effective (Goldfarb & Tucker, 2011b; Lambrecht & Tucker, 2013). What accounts for this paradox? Behavioral decision theory provides some answers.

(In)tangibility

Privacy is a "faceless" issue – an amorphous concept, its definition long debated by scientists, philosophers, and legal scholars alike (Altman, 1975; Culnan & Armstrong, 1999; Jourard, 1966; Laufer & Wolfe, 1977; Margulis, 2003; Smith, Milberg, & Burke, 1996; Warren & Brandeis, 1890; Westin, 1991).[1] Research has shown that people's thoughts and behaviors are much more strongly

---

1 This chapter skirts discussion of how to define privacy and is based on the definition of privacy as concern over the security of one's personal information (Smith, Milberg, & Burke, 1996).

affected by issues that are specific and concrete relative to those that are abstract, such as privacy (Jenni & Loewenstein, 1997; Nisbett & Ross, 1980; Schelling, 1968). For example, people are more likely to donate to victims who are highly identifiable (and hence tangible) as opposed to those who are not (Cryder, Loewenstein, Scheines, 2013; Small & Loewenstein, 2003). The latter are mere statistics that fail to evoke the affective responses that stimulate giving.

Further contributing to its intangibility is the fact that the benefits of privacy are abstract and difficult to quantify. How much privacy have you lost if someone catches a glimpse of your naked body? What privacy intrusions have you prevented by providing a fictitious email address to a commercial website? The material value of privacy is extremely difficult to estimate (Hann, Hui, Lee, & Png, 2002a). Its psychological value is therefore likely to be even less well defined, causing consumers to prioritize other, more tangible considerations, which are often associated with sacrifices in privacy – for example, divulging personal data to receive store discounts.

Because privacy is an intangible, hard-to-quantify concept, concern for it is likely to be latent – privacy is not an issue that is typically at the forefront of people's minds. This can explain the incongruence between stated privacy attitudes and behaviors. By explicitly asking about the issue, public opinion polls rouse and hence are able to measure privacy concerns that often remain latent.[2] Privacy's intangibility can also explain why public outcry about privacy ebbs and flows with media coverage of salient privacy breaches. For example, after news of the National Security Agency's mass electronic surveillance data mining program broke in June 2013, people were less likely to enter privacy-sensitive search terms into Google (Marthews & Tucker, 2014).

Consistent with this line of thinking, consumers are much more willing to part with their information when it is collected covertly as opposed to overtly. For example, John, Acquisti, and Loewenstein (2011) asked New York Times readers (N = 890) whether they had engaged in a series of sensitive, if not also illegal, behaviors such as "Making a false insurance claim." The method of inquiry varied between subjects. In the overt inquiry condition, for each behavior subjects were asked, "Have you ever done this behavior?" and to rate its unethicality. In the covert inquiry condition, subjects had the choice of answering, "If you have ever done this behavior, how unethical do you think it was?" or, "If you have never done this behavior, how unethical do you think it would be, if you were to choose to do it?" Subjects in the covert inquiry condition were about 1.5 times more likely to admit to having engaged in the sensitive behaviors compared to those in the direct inquiry condition. Although the information requested was the same across conditions, covert inquiry made

2 Caveat: these polls are prone to overstating concern due to acquiescent response bias and the fact that there is no cost in saying you care about privacy. Conjoint analyses of concern for privacy are typically more compelling, although some go to extremes in attempting to quantify the unquantifiable (Hann, Hui, Lee, & Png, 2002a; Png, 2007).

the act of admission secondary – almost an afterthought – which increased self-disclosure by keeping privacy concern latent.

Broadly, intangibility accounts for why much of the covert tracking of individuals' online behavior, a necessary condition for behavioral targeting, fails to rouse concern. It also explains how, when it comes to the delivery of behaviorally targeted advertisements, overly personalized advertisements can backfire because they bring privacy concerns to the fore (White, Zahay, Thorbjorsen, & Shavitt, 2008). For example, the retail chain Target endured a public relations nightmare when it marketed diapers to a teen who the company (correctly) inferred to be pregnant due to her shopping patterns (Duhigg, 2012; Hill, 2012).

Multiple Motives: Balancing the Desire for Privacy with the Desire to Divulge

At the same time as they express grave concerns over their privacy, people also have a desire to divulge, and for good reason. A wealth of research has documented benefits of confiding in others. For example, disclosure yields health benefits, such as reduced blood pressure and increased blood hemoglobin (Pennebaker, 1984; Pennebaker, Kiecolt-Glaser, & Glaser, 1988; Smyth, 1998); professional benefits, such as better grades and employment (Spera, Buhrfeind, & Pennebaker, 1994); and psychological benefits, such as intimacy (Jourard, 1959; Mikulincer & Nachson, 1991; Reis & Shaver, 1988) and liking (Collins & Miller, 1994; Cozby, 1972). Moreover, recent neuroscientific research suggests that self-disclosure is intrinsically rewarding (Tamir & Mitchell, 2012).

What is the relationship between the desire to divulge and the desire for privacy? Most people at different times and in different situations experience each motivation; sometimes they experience both simultaneously. For example, a newly pregnant woman might have the urge to divulge her pregnancy, but at the same time wish to keep it private initially, until the risk of miscarriage is significantly reduced (or until the shotgun wedding). The notion that one can have simultaneous, seemingly contradictory, preferences for information to be both shared *and* withheld is characterized by multiple motive models of behavior (Loewenstein & O'Donoghue, 2005), which capture the familiar feeling of being of two minds. Applied to privacy, this perspective suggests that to understand variation in information revelation across situations, one must understand the operation of both motives – the desire to protect versus that to share information.

Multiple motives help to explain the privacy paradox. The Internet, perhaps more than any other communication medium, makes the desire to divulge salient. Facebook, for example, is riddled with cues that heighten the desire to disclose; users are perpetually posed the question, "What's on your mind?" and are peppered with prompts urging them to comment on others' postings. The desire for privacy, on the other hand, is simultaneously downplayed; privacy settings are accessible only by clicking on a cryptic-looking icon on a user's profile. Understood within this multiple-motive framework, the

Internet's tendency to heighten the desire to divulge while simultaneously downplaying the desire for privacy accounts for consumers' willingness to divulge in online contexts despite their privacy concern.

Preliminary evidence suggests that the success of behavioral targeting, and in particular dynamic retargeting (described later in this section) depends on the delicate interplay between two desires: personalization versus privacy (Tucker, 2014; Wathieu & Friedman, 2009). Consumers' desire for relevant, personalized content predicts that they will accept highly targeted (i.e., relevant) advertisements. And although salient advertisements are likely to be noticed, consumers' desire for privacy predicts that they will reject highly salient – and hence obtrusive – advertisements. What happens when an advertisement is both highly relevant *and* highly obtrusive? Goldfarb and Tucker (2011c) suggest that privacy concerns trump relevance concerns. Specifically, they found that con-textually targeted advertisements, ones that promote products that are highly relevant to the web page on which they appear, decrease in effectiveness as they become more obtrusive. For example, an advertisement for a vacation package presented on a travel news site will be effective when presented in a discreet, text-based format (i.e., when it is relevant but not obtrusive), as opposed to a more intrusive format, such as a large pop-up window (i.e., when it is both relevant and obtrusive). In other words, a multiple-motive framework accounts for why advertisements that are highly targeted *and* highly obtrusive are inef-fective when compared with those that have only one of these characteristics.

For its part, the effectiveness of dynamic retargeting is not yet well understood; a consideration of multiple motives could help. In dynamic retar-geting, consumers are shown an advertisement for an offering that they recently viewed. For example, if on Monday the consumer views a coat on Amazon.com, on Tuesday he is shown an advertisement for the identical product, though perhaps on a different website. A multiple motive account might suggest that the success of such dynamic retargeting depends on the likeness of the advertisement to the initially viewed offering, in this case, the coat viewed on Monday. It could be that dynamically retargeted ads of *similar* products are more effective than those of *identical* products. Although the latter satisfies the desire for personalization, it does so by potentially rousing privacy concerns – seeing the identical product makes it salient to the consumer that he is being tracked. Behaviorally retargeting similar, but not identical, advertisements may hit the "sweet spot" in appealing to these two motives. Future research is needed to better understand how behaviorally retargeted ads affect the delicate interplay of conflicting motives. Such an understanding will facilitate the design of advertisements that are more palatable from the consumer's stand-point, and in turn more effective from the marketer's standpoint.

Synthesis of Part 1

Taken together, intangibility and mixed motives account for the privacy para-dox and suggest that privacy is likely to be a domain characterized by great preference uncertainty. In the next section, I describe how this perspective accounts for a variety of seemingly inconsistent choices people make with respect to their privacy.

Part 2: How Behavioral Decision Theory Explains Privacy-Decision Making Phenomena

Context Effects

When people are uncertain of their preferences, inconsistencies in their judgments and decision making abound (Fox & Tversky, 1995; Hsee, Loewenstein, Blount, & Bazerman, 1999; Slovic, 1995). One way that people try to resolve this uncertainty is to rely on contextual cues. Importantly, the contextual cues that guide privacy concerns are often incommensurate with the prevailing costs and benefits of divulgence. This distortion can help account for the seemingly self-destructive, or at least inconsistent, choices consumers make. As I describe in the next three paragraphs, context effects account for why consumers' willingness to reveal personal data is (1) insensitive to cues to which they should be sensitive; (2) sensitive to cues to which they should be insensitive; and (3) responsive to contextual cues in exactly the wrong way. Compliance with marketers' requests for personal data can have negative outcomes for the consumer; for example, having one's identity stolen as a result of divulging one's social security number. As I explain in the following paragraphs, contextual cues can cause consumers to comply with requests for information in precisely the situations in which it is against their self-interest to do so, that is, in situations in which their information is more likely to be used for nefarious, as opposed to legitimate, purposes.

Privacy policies are contextual cues that should, but fail to, stimulate privacy concerns. A privacy policy is an institutionally provided statement detailing how consumer data are gathered, stored, and used. It therefore contains information relevant to the costs and benefits of disclosure. Consider the website realage.com, on which users divulge intensely personal health information in exchange for the simple knowledge of how their calendar age compares to their biological age. The privacy policy provides a long list of permissions that users implicitly provide. For example, users allow the company to "disclose your personally identifiable information" to "affiliates, strategic partners, agents, and third-party marketers" for "research, administrative, and/or business purposes" and "to offer you products." Translation: "you are giving us permission to do almost anything with your data" – for example, to sell personally identifying information of (self-identified) HIV patients to health insurance companies. The privacy policy thus contains information that should cause users to think twice about the relative imbalance of the benefits they glean versus provide to realage.com in complying with the site's requests for personal data. Whether it is because privacy policies are commonplace (leading to desensitization, discussed further in the "Comparative Judgments" subsection), or because they can be intimidatingly long (according to McDonald & Cranor, 2008, it would take Americans 54 billion hours annually to read the policy of each new site they visited), privacy policies usually go completely unread. As a result, they fail to rouse privacy considerations even when they should. Moreover, requests for consumers' information are typically decoupled from their accompanying privacy policy. When decontextualized in this manner, even the most diligently read policies fail to affect people's behavior (Adjerid, Acquisti, Brandimarte, & Loewenstein, 2013).

Peoples' willingness to part with their personal data has also been found to be affected by irrelevant factors, such as whether the disclosure experience is fluent. People disclose less when questions are presented in a disfluent manner (Alter & Oppenheimer, 2009), and curiously, emphasizing that a disclosure is *reversible* (e.g., that providing an email address to a mailing list can be "undone" by unsubscribing) *or* that it is *irreversible*, increases people's reluctance to part with their information (Peer, Acquisti, & Loewenstein, n.d.). Even though fluency and reversibility can be independent from the risks of disclosure, they can cue people to think about the sensitivity of their data and appear to increase the focus on privacy more generally.

It is also possible that the contextual cues guiding privacy decision making are inversely related to the objective dangers of divulgence. Thus, contextual cues can lead people to react in precisely the *wrong* way: to divulge when it is unsafe to do so and vice versa. For example, although it is more dangerous to divulge on unprofessional-looking websites (Cranor, 2002; Ivory & Hearst, 2002a, 2002b; Ivory, Sinha, & Hearst, 2001), their casual look and feel downplays privacy concerns and elicits disclosure (John, Acquisti, & Loewenstein, 2011). By contrast, recent research on the (in)effectiveness of the randomized response technique (RRT) provides empirical evidence of withholding in a context in which disclosure is relatively safe. The RRT is a method of asking sensitive questions, and although it increases objective privacy protection, its heavy-handedness can exacerbate the very concerns it is intended to assuage. The result is that people are ironically less willing to divulge using RRTs as opposed to when they are asked in a less privacy-protective manner (John, Loewenstein, Acquisti, & Vosgerau, n.d.). Similarly, heavy-handed confidentiality assurances can cause people to 'clam up' (Brandimarte, Acquisti, & Gino, n.d; Frey, 1986; John, Acquisti, & Loewenstein, 2008; Singer, Hippler, & Schwarz, 1992; Singer, von Thurn, & Miller, 1995). Assurances serve as a cue that triggers privacy concern, resulting in decreased disclosure in the face of increased protection.

Contextual cues can therefore influence privacy decision making in nonnormative ways, suggesting that people are vulnerable to making disclosures that they later stand to regret. Most notably, people can be induced to disclose in unsafe contexts and vice versa. Consistent with these findings, certain websites or programs (dubbed "foistware") offer a casual or fun service for free while surreptitiously installing tracking software, intentionally misleading users about the software's real purpose (e.g., zwinky.com).

Future research could examine how the effectiveness of dynamic retargeting depends on online context. I predict that such advertisements will be more effective when they are presented on the same website on which the product was initially viewed, as opposed to a site other than that from which it originated. Although in both cases a person's information typically passes through an infomediary, an advertising agency conducting real-time auctions for ad space, I predict that retargeted ads presented on the originator site will be perceived as contextually appropriate and hence less invasive.

Loss Aversion/Endowment

Loss aversion refers to how losses are more psychologically powerful than objectively equivalently sized gains (Kahneman & Tversky, 1979). Loss aversion gives rise to the endowment effect (Kahneman, Knetsch, & Thaler, 1990; Langer, 1975): the amount of money people are willing to accept (WTA) to sell a good is typically much higher than the amount they are willing to pay (WTP) to acquire it (according to standard economic theory, valuation should be independent from ownership).

These findings imply that privacy is valued more when a person stands to lose it than when she stands to acquire it. Acquisti, John, & Loewenstein (2013) tested this prediction in a field experiment in which shoppers were given a choice between two different gift cards: a "$12 identified card" that would link their names to their purchases for the gift card merchant to see; or a lower-valued but privacy-protective option: a "$10 anonymous card" that would *not* track their purchases. Some subjects were initially endowed with the $10 card and given the opportunity to switch easily to the $12 card. Other subjects were endowed with the $12 card and could switch to the $10 card. Thus, only the framing of the choice differed between conditions. Those initially given the $10 card faced a decision of whether they would accept $2 to *sell* their privacy by switching to the $12 card (which would track their purchases). In contrast, those initially given the $12 card decided whether they would pay $2 to *buy* privacy by switching to the $10 card (which would not track their purchases). In a third, control condition, subjects were not endowed with a card; they simply selected which of the two cards they wanted. Endowment exerted a large impact on privacy valuations: those who had been endowed with the $10, privacy-protective card were 5 times more likely to choose it relative to those who did not have privacy to begin with (i.e., those who had been endowed with the $12 card) and 1.5 times more likely to choose it relative to controls.

Broadly, loss aversion accounts for why privacy breaches generate outcry and for why privacy gains encourage apathy: breaches are akin to WTA (selling your privacy), and gains to WTP (buying privacy). Increasingly, the default privacy orientation in online contexts seems to be WTP, as new Internet technologies make information accessible by default. Perhaps more so now than ever before, privacy is something that people stand to gain rather than to lose. Consistent with this trend, people are generally unwilling to pay to obtain privacy-preserving technologies (Brunk, 2002; Romanosky & Acquisti, 2009; Stalder, 2002), and when they are, they will pay only a tiny premium (Tsai, Engelman, Cranor, & Acquisti, 2011).

Comparative Judgments

People tend to judge stimuli and make decisions in a comparative fashion (Kahneman & Miller, 1986). For example, Prospect Theory, Kahneman and Tversky's (1979) influential theory of decision making under risk, assumes that people make decisions on the basis of changes in, rather than absolute levels of, wealth. Theories of social utility capture the insight that people care about how their outcomes compare to others': a poor person in the United States might be objectively more affluent than a middle-class person in Bangladesh, but is likely to feel subjectively poorer (John, Loewenstein, & Rick, 2014; Loewenstein, Thompson, & Bazerman, 1989). Comparative judgments are especially likely when there is no objective basis for evaluation, which is also likely the case for privacy, given the extensive preference uncertainty with which it is associated.

Comparative judgments are the basis of "coherent arbitrariness" (Ariely, Loewenstein, & Prelec, 2003), which refers to how consumers' absolute valuations of goods, services, and experiences are often remarkably arbitrary, while their relative valuations tend to be stable and orderly. In the privacy context, people displaying coherent arbitrariness would judge the sensitivity or intrusiveness of an initial personal question in an idiosyncratic, subjective, and ultimately arbitrary fashion, but would judge the sensitivity of subsequent personal questions in a coherent manner relative to that first question. This prediction also arises from the "door-in-the-face" phenomenon (Cialdini et al., 1975; Tybout, Sternthal, & Calder, 1983), whereby people confronted with extreme requests are more likely to accede subsequently to moderate requests than those who are initially confronted with more minor requests. It is also broadly consistent with people's preference for sequences that improve rather than worsen (Loewenstein & Prelec, 1993).

This prediction was supported in a series of experiments in which changing degrees of privacy intrusions were simulated by altering the order in which subjects in an online questionnaire were asked questions of varying sensitivity (Acquisti, John, & Loewenstein, 2012). Subjects judged the severity of the privacy intrusions experienced in the present by comparing them to those they had experienced in the recent past. Questions of increasing sensitivity inhibited information disclosure, as if the contrast between the early and later questions accentuates privacy concern. Similarly, consumers' willingness to part with their personal data is impacted by changes in, rather than absolute levels of, the protectiveness of privacy policies. Consumers are more likely to trust a commercial website that has recently improved its privacy policy when compared to one that has always had an objectively superior policy (Brandimarte, Acquisti, & Loewenstein, 2012).

Coherent arbitrariness implies that although people are highly attuned to changes and deviations from common reference points, they tend to adapt to ongoing situations, getting used to and ceasing to notice them (Freedman & Fraser, 1966). This adaptation process occurs rapidly and operates by creating a new reference point to which subsequent changes are compared (Frederick & Loewenstein, 1999). As a result, people with chronic health conditions report happiness levels indistinguishable from healthy counterparts, and lottery winners are not happier than less wealthy individuals (Brickman, Coates, & Janoff-Bulman, 1978; Riis et al., 2005). Applied to privacy, adaptation suggests that privacy violations are sticky – once privacy is lost, it is difficult to regain.

Adaptation in the privacy domain can account for the recurrent pattern in which initial outrage over privacy invasions fades and ultimately turns into acceptance. For example, in September 2006, Facebook launched the "News Feed" feature, a running list of Facebook activities of a user's friends. By making available salient information that had previously been obscure, "News Feed" understandably generated backlash (Denham, 2009, p. 113; Parr, 2006; Zuckerberg, 2006). Over time, however, the outrage waned and people adapted to the change (Jesdanun, 2006). In fact, "News Feed" has since become a – if not *the* – central feature of Facebook.[3]

Adaptation is also readily apparent in the many cases in which people show little concern about dramatic violations of privacy if those violations have occurred for a long time. In Pittsburgh, the sale price of houses is easily available online, accessible by the address of the property or the name of the homeowner. New homeowners in Pittsburgh are often shocked when they discover that how much they paid is public knowledge. But over time, people stop caring about the public availability of this information because they adapt to it.

Broadly, the influence of comparative judgments on privacy concern can explain the success of Facebook's apparent "door-in-the-face" strategy of introducing reductions in user privacy. In December 2009, for example, the company reduced user privacy by making profiles public and web-searchable by default. Sure enough, uproar ensued (Bankston, 2009; BBCNews, 2009; Evangelista, 2010; O'Connell, 2009; Tate, 2009). Facebook reacted by improving the privacy policy, but only *slightly*. Users generally accepted the revised policy. According to coherent arbitrariness, the revised policy was accepted because it was evaluated relative to the initial one, which was weak; hence the revised policy represented an improvement. Had the revised policy been introduced initially, I suspect that it would not have been met with approval.

---

3 I once asked a Facebook engineer about the experiments run on its user base. The response was that the company typically tests the effect of only subtle changes to the interface, such as font size. The engineer went on to joke that the company would not do anything "anger-inducing like turning off 'News Feed.'" It seems that "News Feed" has become so accepted that users would get upset at its removal – a total reversal of the outcry it had initially generated.

Coupled with the endowment effect, comparative judgments suggest a vicious cycle of privacy erosion, because when information is public, people value privacy less, and when people value privacy less, they are more willing to part with it.

Illusion of Control

People overestimate the extent to which they can control events, an illusion that leads them to mistakenly act as if they can control random processes (Langer, 1975). For example, in the casino game of craps, people throw the dice harder when they want high numbers than when they want low numbers, as if they can control the outcome (Henslin, 1967). The Internet gives users unprecedented control over the posting of information, while at the same time reducing other types of control, such as secondary usage (e.g., the ability to sell information to third parties, known as data brokerage, a booming industry that fuels behavioral targeting). Brandimarte, Acquisti, & Loewenstein (2012) showed that the illusion of control leads people to confound control over the publication of information with control over its usage and dissemination, creating a false sense of security when the former is high. Strikingly, granting people control over publication leads to increased divulgence when the privacy risks associated with secondary usage are elevated. In sum, consumers' failure to discriminate among these different types of control impedes their ability to manage their personal data.

These findings help account for the popularity of and (over)divulgence on SNSs, which give users great control over posting (i.e., publication). The illusion of control also explains why Facebook's "News Feed" feature initially generated outcry. Although "News Feed" only highlights information that has already been made public, it may have caused backlash because it reduced control over posting.

The illusion of control also suggests that there may be unintended consequences of the Federal Trade Commission and the Organization for Economic Cooperation and Development's premise that consumer choice (i.e., control) is critical to effective industry self-regulation of consumer privacy in general and behavioral targeting in particular (Acquisti, Adjerid, & Brandimarte, 2013; FTC, 2012; OECD, 1980). Giving consumers control over a trivial aspect of their data could cause them to mistakenly believe that they control *all* aspects of their data. For better or for worse, it seems that proponents of industry self-regulation may have already realized this. On the Network Advertising Initiative's "Consumer Opt-Out" site, a consumer is informed of the advertising companies "customizing ads for your browser" (when I checked, I was being behaviorally targeted by 99 of 116 "participating companies").[4] The consumer can then select which companies to opt out of. Endorsing 99 opt-out checkboxes

---

4 www.networkadvertising.org/choices/.

made me feel in control, but as the fine print indicates, doing so prevents me from receiving targeted advertisements, *not* from being tracked. Ironically, opting out makes it harder for me to understand who is collecting my data and how they are using it: by having opted out of behavioral targeting, I no longer receive tailored ads, the residue of the fact that I am being tracked. Arguably, most people visit this opt-out site not because they dislike advertising that is relevant to them, but because they do not want their online activities recorded by third parties. If I am going to be tracked and if ads are unavoidable, I would like to at least have the benefit of receiving relevant ads.

Future research could look at how this illusion of control affects observers' impressions of disclosers. Consumers may confound control over *disclosing* an outcome with control over the outcome itself, causing them to "shoot the messenger." Suppose, for example, that a firm was forced to raise prices due to a factor out of its control (e.g., an increase in transportation costs). An illusion of control account might predict that consumers confound control over disclosing price increases with control over the price itself, in turn creating unwarrantedly negative impressions of the firm (i.e., more negative than those warranted by the price increase itself).

Norms

People's behavior conforms to that of others, a phenomenon documented in both the economics (Devenow & Welch, 1996) and psychology literatures (Asch, 1956). The importance of others' behavior is closely linked to research on social norms (Bicchieri, 2006), which amply demonstrates that people care about social norms and often infer those norms, at least in part, by observing others' behavior. Theories of social norms predict that people adapt their behaviors to conform to the behaviors of those around them, which also appears to be the case on the Internet, where people "move quickly, like a swarm of killer bees. They often behave in a mob-like fashion" (Solove, 2007, p. 101).

The influence of social norms on disclosure was illustrated in an experiment in which people were provided with simulated information on the societal acceptance of privacy invasions (Acquisti, John, & Loewenstein, 2012). The ostensible distribution of answers that others had provided to a number of highly intrusive questions was manipulated between-subjects. Subjects were more likely to admit to having engaged in sensitive, and in some cases illegal, behaviors when they were given information that led them to believe that others had engaged in those behaviors before them.

Herding phenomena help to explain over-divulgence on SNSs. Facebook, for example, facilitates herding by heightening the salience of others' disclosures. Upon logging in, the user immediately sees "News Feed." Only a small proportion of a user's network may have made recent disclosures, but Facebook's "News Feed" selectively highlights these episodes. "News Feed" therefore creates a norm of divulgence.

What happens when a person's online behavior violates established norms? People dislike norm violation and are willing to pay for norm enforcement (Fehr & Gaechter, 2002). Online, the costs of norm enforcement are reduced, which helps to explain the popularity of digital shaming – the malicious outing of norm violators (Solove, 2007). There are many websites devoted to this purpose; for example, on Bitterwaitress.com, waiters enter the names, locations, and descriptions of stingy customers into the "Shitty Tipper Database." Similarly, on dontdatehimgirl.com, women reveal the identities of philanderers. It is awkward to speak out against a norm violator in person; as these sites attest, it is easy to complain silently and anonymously online.

Traditional forms of communication (e.g., face-to-face, telephone, written letters) have strong social norms associated with them, which people are generally adept at following (Grice, 1975). People seamlessly match the tone and content of others' disclosures (Sedikides, Campbell, Reeder, & Elliot, 1999) and nonverbal behavior (van Baaren, Horgan, Chartrand, & Dijkmans, 2004); norm deviations are salient and eligible for social sanctions (Fehr & Gaechter, 2002). Thus, a natural starting point for consumers in navigating issues of privacy and disclosure in foreign, online contexts is to apply these well-established norms (Nissenbaum, 2004). But the problem is that "digital environments [...] confound the traditional ways in which we control our audiences and negotiate the boundary between the private and the public, the past and the future, disclosure and privacy" (Tufecki, 2008, p. 20). For example, the Internet makes information dissemination – through email, texts, blogs, or tweets – fast and easy. But at the same time, it has heightened the permanence of disclosures. Impulsive disclosures are forever catalogued in cyberspace (and, in the case of tweets, also in the Library of Congress! Lohr, 2010). Indeed, "what was once ephemeral, with evidence of it living only in the memory of the current witness – a conversation in a café, a cash purchase in a store, a nod toward an acquaintance while walking down the street – is increasingly enacted online, where it leaves a potentially lasting footprint" (Tufecki, 2008, p. 21).

What are the consumer privacy implications of this new permanence? For one, it can leave consumers vulnerable to making disclosures that they later stand to regret. Although it is sometimes possible to remove the information source (e.g., deleting a tweet), it is impossible to expunge its every trace. Moreover, the very content that people are most likely to regret (e.g., seductive photos posted when intoxicated) is often disproportionately likely to "go viral." Indeed, some have warned that the permanence of online disclosure means the "end of forgetting" (Rosen, 2010) or the "end of privacy" (Angwin, 2014; Nussbaum, 2007; Tanner, 2014). Today's youth are amassing digital "skeletons in the closet" that could haunt them in adulthood (Mayer-Schoenberger, 2011; Nussbaum, 2007). Political candidates are already subject to intense scrutiny; imagine the kind of scrutiny that could arise if digital records of their entire lives were available. Other commentators are less concerned about permanence, arguing that the sheer volume of publicly available information will make it possible to "hide in plain sight" (Mallon, 2014). But recent research suggests that concern is warranted. Disclosures of immoral acts have enduring (negative) impacts on impression formation, whereas observers quickly discount disclosures of moral acts (Brandimarte, Vosgerau, & Acquisti, n.d.). The long-term effects of online disclosure offer an important topic for future research.

The (mis)application of norms associated with traditional communication to digital environments has implications for behavioral targeting. Surveillance enables behavioral targeting and is conducted by two different technologies: web bugs and cookies. Both technologies track and record consumers' click-streams, but they may not be perceived as equally invasive. Whereas web bugs are embedded into web pages (and hence do not reside on one's computer), cookies are downloaded and housed on one's hard drive. If informed of this difference, consumers are apt to feel less comfortable with cookies than web bugs.[5] Because cookies are stored on one's own computer, they represent a violation of physical space and hence are likely to be deemed invasive.

Similarly, consumers' acceptance of surveillance might depend on the entity through which it is conducted. In traditional face-to-face communication, people are typically willing to share personal information only with those they trust (i.e., not strangers). Stemming from this fact, people disclose more when they communicate online as opposed to face to face (Tourangeau & Yan, 2007; Whitty & Joinson, 2009). Surveillance technologies operated by humans are therefore likely to be perceived as more invasive relative to those operated by machines or robots, even when both technologies collect the same information. Airport full-body scanners generate images that are monitored by humans; perhaps it is not a coincidence that they are loathed (Cooper, 2010). Many email clients such as Gmail present users with target advertisements based on the content of their emails. Interestingly, Google downplays the role of humans in describing how the ads are generated: "All targeting in Gmail is fully automated, and no humans read your email or Google Account information in order to show you advertisements or related information" (https://support.google.com/mail/answer/6603).

I recently conducted a simple experiment to test this notion – that surveillance is deemed relatively noninvasive if perceived to be conducted by inanimate agents. Subjects ($N = 174$) read a brief description of how email clients generate targeted advertisements. Half were told: "engineers have written computer programs that read through your email so that they can show you advertisements that you will find relevant" (animate condition); the others were told: "computer programs scan your email to automatically generate advertisements that you will find relevant" (inanimate condition). As predicted, the practice was deemed more intrusive in the animate condition ($M_{animate} = 7.2$ out of 9, $SD = 1.98$) relative to the inanimate condition ($M_{inanimate} = 6.3$ $SD = 2.4$; $t(172) = 3.14$, $p < .01$).

---

5 However, the names of these technologies may be a countervailing force in terms of consumer acceptance: A "cookie" sounds innocuous; a "web bug" sounds invasive.

In sum, traditional communication norms suggest that consumers' acceptance of new surveillance technologies depends on the manner in which it is conducted. Surveillance technologies that are objectively equally intrusive (in that they collect the same information) may not necessarily be perceived as such.

Isolation Errors/Myopia

Now perhaps more than ever before, people are bombarded with frequent requests for information. However, each request is often for only a small piece of information – a phone number here, a log-in ID there. Small but frequent requests for personal information give rise to isolation errors – the failure to appreciate the broader impact of one's choices, also referred to as "myopia" (Herrnstein & Prelec, 1991; Kahneman & Lovallo, 1999; Read, Loewenstein, & Rabin, 1999). They are also likely to place the discloser in "low-level construal mode," known to lead individuals to downplay abstract, big-picture goals such as the desire for privacy (Liberman & Trope, 2003).

Consistent with these tendencies, when they are online people only narrowly consider the consequences of divulgence, leading to an underappreciation of the emergent properties of information sharing, namely that separate, seemingly innocuous facts can be aggregated to reveal new information. For example, social security numbers can be predicted by combining a person's date and place of birth (both commonly divulged on Facebook) with an algorithm of the pattern by which SSNs are generated (Acquisti & Gross, 2009); medical records can be tracked down simply by knowing a person's birth date and zip code (Tanner, 2014). And as noted earlier in the case of Target, personal information can be inferred by aggregating information on shopping habits. Moreover, the new permanence of (online) disclosure means that a person's digital footprint grows over time. In part because of myopia, people are often surprised to learn how much of their personal information can be found online (Duhigg, 2012).[6] Similarly, people often fail to appreciate that such information can later be used for purposes other than those initially intended. Potential employers find "dirt" on applicants by "Googling" them; much of what is found has been disclosed by the applicants themselves (Clark, 2006; Grasz, 2009).

Future research could test whether isolation errors affect people's willingness to share personal information. For example, online, people tend to act as if they are divulging to a narrow audience, which can result in embarrassment or worse. Facebook is rife with examples of sensitive disclosures clearly intended for a small audience, but visible to the discloser's entire network. One woman

---

6 Axciom, the consumer-data aggregator giant, is now letting people read the information it has on them. But ironically, to obtain your report, you have to provide the company with more personal data (your name, address, email address, and last four digits of your social security number). One commentator noted that this is like "the Transportation Security Administration offering to show you the naked photos it takes at the airport—as long as you first agree to pose for some more photos" (Lewis, 2013).

posted inflammatory comments about her boss, whom she forgot was part of her network. She was fired as a result (Moult, 2009). Facebook seems by design to foster a narrow consideration of audience, creating an illusion of intimacy: when a user posts information, his friend list is hidden from view. At the moment of divulgence, the user's broader network is out of sight and out of mind. The result: people behave as if they are sending letters, when instead they are sending postcards.

Present-Biased Preferences

Present-biased preferences refer to the tendency to overweight immediate costs and benefits and to take a much more evenhanded approach to delayed costs and benefits (Frederick, O'Donoghue, & Loewenstein, 2002; Laibson, 1997; Loewenstein & Elster, 1992; O'Donoghue & Rabin, 1999). Present-biased preferences give rise to a variety of self-control issues that are readily apparent in the privacy domain (Acquisti, 2004).

The overweighting of immediate benefits leads to pre-operation – people are proactive in realizing the immediate benefits of information revelation (Rabin & O'Donoghue, 2000). Pre-operation explains why people are willing to divulge sensitive information in exchange for very small, but immediate, rewards (Chellappa & Sin, 2002; Hann, Hui, Lee, & Png, 2002b; Spiekermann, Grossklags, & Berendt, 2001). For example, 71 percent of people revealed their computer password for a meager chocolate bar (BBC News, 2004), and 85 percent provided information to shopping websites for a chance at a small prize (Jupiter-Research, 2002).

The overweighting of immediate costs leads to procrastination – people postpone taking actions to protect their privacy (O'Donoghue & Rabin, 2001). Unlike in offline contexts, where implementing privacy-preserving measures can be as simple as drawing the blinds or lowering one's voice, doing so online often requires mastering complicated new technologies (Whitten & Tygar, 2005), a costly activity that lends itself to perpetual deferral. At the same time, by making it easy to divulge, online contexts reduce the procrastination to share. This helps to explain why information spreads so readily over the Internet. Whereas online it is possible to forward a message to hundreds with the simple click of a mouse, offline it would require considerable effort to distribute the message physically by mail.

Several unique characteristics of online divulgence exacerbate the pernicious effects of present-biased preferences. First, the costs of online divulgence are often delayed; negative consequences – such as receiving spam email or, in the extreme, falling victim to identity theft – typically do not occur immediately after the disclosure episode but instead after considerable time has elapsed. Present-biased preferences lead individuals to favor the immediate gratification of divulgence despite its negative consequences because the latter are usually delayed and hence easily "written off." Unfortunately, however, when the future comes, people sometimes find themselves regretting their earlier disclosures. Secondly, the influence of present-biased preferences is heightened by the murky relationship between disclosure and its consequences. Disclosure is immediately rewarding psychologically, and often also economically, as when a consumer provides personal data in exchange for a discount. By contrast, the undesirable consequences of information sharing, such as identity theft, are difficult to attribute to a single disclosure episode. Both the coupling of disclosure to its benefits and the decoupling from its harms tend to aggravate the effects of present-biased preferences.

Together, these characteristics can account for consumers' great unwillingness to pay for privacy enhancing technologies. Whether it be time (in the case of privacy-enhancing web browsers such as DuckDuckGo, Tor, and PrivacyBird) or money (Tsai et al., 2011), the costs of adopting these technologies are immediate, and the benefits are delayed and amorphous.

Projection Bias

Projection bias refers to the misguided belief that future tastes will resemble current ones (Loewenstein, O'Donoghue, & Rabin, 2000). This bias suggests that people fail to appreciate that their valuation of privacy is likely to change over time and is readily apparent in the behavior of college students who post sensitive personal information only to regret it later, such as when seeking employment (Clark, 2006; Grasz, 2009) or when their parents join Facebook (myparentsjoinedFacebook.com). Projection bias, along with the heightened permanence of online information sharing, implies a systematic predisposition to overdisclose. A decision *not* to disclose is reversible, while the same cannot be said for a decision to disclose.

Overoptimism

People are generally overly optimistic about their likelihood of engaging in positive behaviors, such as donating to charity, exercising, or losing weight (Armor & Taylor, 2002; DellaVigna & Malmendier, 2006; Epley & Dunning, 2000; Weinstein, 1980). Applied to privacy, overoptimism suggests that people are likely to believe erroneously that they are invulnerable to privacy violations, which helps to explain why they fail to take privacy-protective actions. Consistent with this conjecture, 56 percent of respondents in a large survey were overly optimistic about their likelihood of avoiding identity theft (Romanosky, Sharp, & Acquisti, 2010).

Summary of Part 2

BDT principles account for the seemingly illogical decisions consumers make with respect to their online privacy. Privacy decision making is easily influenced by nonnormative factors, suggesting that people are vulnerable to making disclosure decisions that they later stand to regret.

Part 3: Broad Topics for Future Research

In Parts 1 and 2, I discussed how BDT principles can account for the privacy paradox and, more broadly, for the seemingly self-destructive choices consumers make with respect to the management of their personal data. Throughout, I have also highlighted opportunities for future research to further understand how consumers navigate the new complexities of information sharing in the digital age. In particular, I have identified areas for future research on digital advertising, a key marketing function that is affected by the shift toward openness. But BDT still has much to contribute. To conclude, I outline several other broad topics for future research.

A natural next step after having gained an understanding of consumers' online behavior with respect to their privacy is to develop ways to deal with personal information that are beneficial to firms and consumers alike. Several privacy advocates have recently proposed information provision as a means of helping people to make disclosure decisions that are in their best interest. Grimmelmann (2009, p. 1205), for example, argues that "teens and college students would be better off with a better understanding of the ways that persistent postings can return to haunt them." Similarly, one of the central tenets of the Federal Trade Commission's (2012) guidelines for consumer protection is information provision. These approaches imply that as long as people are aware of the costs and benefits of their online activities, they will be able to manage their personal data in a self-interested way. However, this approach is likely to be severely limited because biases in decision making tend to persist even when individuals are fully aware of their influence (Fischhoff, 1982; O'Donoghue & Rabin, 1999). On the other hand, recent research has shown that BDT principles can help people make better decisions (Loewenstein, John, & Volpp, 2013; Thaler & Benartzi, 2004; Volpp et al., 2008). In the following subsections, I outline two possible approaches to help people align their disclosure decisions with their own interests. These and similar ideas could be developed in future work.

Cue Realignment

Aligning contextual cues with the dangers of disclosure may improve privacy decision making. For example, privacy-preserving software could display behaviorally informed stimuli, such as a set of watchful eyes to signal dangerous websites. The feeling of being watched makes people self-conscious (Duval & Wicklund, 1972, p. 121) and could thus curb disclosure. Legal scholar Ryan Calo aptly notes that anthropomorphic design, "a form of 'visceral notice' – in the sense that the technique directly conveys the reality that user information is being collected, used, and often shared – could help shore up a failing regime of textual notice visceral notice that lines up our experience with actual information practice" (Calo, 2010, p. 848).

Cooling-Off Periods

Much as mandatory waiting periods for obtaining handguns are designed to prevent violence, cooling off periods may help people to avoid making disclosure decisions that they later stand to regret. On his blog, Thaler has written about the (currently fictional) "Civility Check" software "designed to prevent our hot-headed selves from causing unnecessary email disasters" (Thaler, 2009). Upon detecting inflammatory language (with the help of actual software like Tone Check; Wawro, 2008), the program could direct offending email to a temporary folder – a type of email purgatory. The email would be sent only upon confirmation by the user after several hours have passed, when he or she has presumably calmed down. Since this blog entry was written, a phone app called Drunk Text Savior has emerged, which scans text messages for cues of inebriation before they are sent. If detected, the program displays: "WARNING! You May Be Drunk! You have some warning signs in your text. Possibly too many drinks. Are you sure you want to send this text?"

Conflicting motivations are likely to pose a key barrier to implementing these types of interventions. Many online companies have strong interests in making information open and easily accessible and therefore are not motivated to increase consumers' privacy protection unless consumers demand it or it is required by law. Given our apathetic, often conflicting, attitudes toward privacy, it is unlikely that consumer demand for privacy protection will force companies to instate it. Government intervention may be necessary to regulate and protect consumers' privacy in the face of these forces. Yet there is still much to understand with respect to consumer behavior and online privacy, far beyond what can be understood through a BDT lens alone. To conclude, I highlight broad topics that are ripe for collaboration across different sub-disciplines within marketing and beyond.

Economic Benefits versus Consumer Satisfaction

Future research is needed to understand how marketers balance the economic benefits of obtaining and using consumers' personal data against consumers' often seemingly irrational responses. Understanding such trade-offs is integral to the success of a host of marketing functions, including pricing. The new availability of consumer data enables ever-finer price discrimination. The ride-sharing service Uber, for example, frequently implements surge pricing whereby the customer is informed that prices have increased due to high demand and is offered a new price (a multiple of the standard price). I have often wondered whether Uber uses my history of accepting or rejecting offers of various multiples to customize my prices. Even information that we leak through our online behavior could be rich pricing inputs for firms. For example, if you conduct several web searches for a specific flight, you may be signaling to the airline that you are eager to buy and hence willing to pay a premium. Although from a standard economics perspective price discrimination is beneficial both to firms (because it enables the highest rents to be extracted) and consumers (because it puts products into the hands of the people who value them most), the psychology of the matter is that it is perceived as unfair (Kahneman, Knetsch, & Thaler, 1986). How to balance the huge marketing opportunities of personal data against the desire to maximize customer satisfaction is an important topic for future research.

Interaction with Other Consumer Psychological Insights

This chapter has treated BDT principles as main effects, but there is still much to understand about how they interact with other psychological factors to explain consumers' online behavior with respect to their privacy. For example, common biases operate differently under the influence of different emotions (Lerner, Kassam, Li, & Valdesolo, 2015). Now more than ever before, through video and multimedia applications, the Internet is equipped to spark emotional reactions. This example points to the need to integrate the BDT perspective with other insights from psychology to form a unified framework for understanding consumer privacy. Such a framework would be helpful in understanding and predicting the impact of new Internet technologies that have yet to emerge in the constantly evolving online world.

Acknowledgments

I thank David John, Cait Lamberton, George Loewenstein, Michael Norton, and Evan Robinson for helpful comments on earlier versions of this chapter.

References

Acquisti, A. (2004). Privacy in electronic commerce and the economics of immediate gratification. Paper presented at the Proceedings of the ACM Conference on Electronic Commerce (EC'04).

Acquisti, Adjerid, & Brandimarte, L. (2013). Gone in 60 seconds: The limits of privacy, transparency, and control. *IEEE, 13*, 72–74.

Acquisti, A., & Gross, R. (2009). Predicting social security numbers from public data. *Proceedings of the National Academy of Sciences, 106*(27), 10975–10980.

Acquisti, A., John, L. K., & Loewenstein, G. (2012). The impact of relative standards on the propensity to disclose. *Journal of Marketing Research, April*, 160–174.

Acquisti, A., John, L. K., & Loewenstein, G. (2013). What is privacy worth? *Journal of Legal Studies, 42*(2), 249–274.

Acquisti, A., & Varian, H. (2002). Conditioning prices on purchase history. *Marketing Science, 24*(3), 367–381.

Adjerid, I., Acquisti, A., Brandimarte, L., & Loewenstein, G. (2013). Sleights of Privacy: Framing, disclosures, and the limits of transparency. In *Proceedings of the*

Ninth Symposium on Usable Privacy and Security, 9. New York: Association for Computing Machinery.

Alter, A. L., & Oppenheimer, D. M. (2009). Suppressing secrecy through metacognitive ease: Cognitive fluency encourages self-disclosure. *Psychological Science, 20* (11), 1414–1420.

Altman, I. (1975). *The Environment and Social Behavior.* Monterey, CA: Brooks/Cole.

Angwin, J. (2014). *Dragnet Nation: A Quest for Privacy, Security, and Freedom in a World of Relentless Surveillance.* New York: Henry Holt, Times Books.

Ariely, D., Loewenstein, G., & Prelec, D. (2003). Coherent arbitrariness: Stable demand curves without stable preferences. *Quarterly Journal of Economics, 118,* 73–106.

Armor, D. A., & Taylor, C. R. (2002). When predictions fail: The dilemma of unrealistic optimism. In T. Gilovich, D. Griffin, & D. Kahneman (eds.), *Heuristics and Biases: The Psychology of Intuitive Judgment.* Cambridge: Cambridge University Press.

Asch, S. E. (1956). Studies of independence and conformity: A minority of one against a unanimous majority. *Psychological Monographs, 70*(9), 118.

Asch, S. E. (1959). A perspective on social psychology. In S. Koch (ed.), *Psychology: A Study of Science* (vol. 3, pp. 363–383). New York: McGraw-Hill.

Awad, N. F., & Krishnan, M. S. (2006). The personalization privacy paradox: An empirical evaluation of information transparency and the willingness to be profiled online for personalization. *MIS Quarterly, 30*(1), 18–28.

Bankston, K. (2009). Facebook's new privacy changes: The good, the bad, and the ugly. Retrieved from www.eff.org/deeplinks/2009/12/Facebooks-new-privacy-changes-good-bad-and-ugly.

BBCNews (2004). Passwords revealed by sweet deal. Retrieved from http://news.bbc.co.uk/2/hi/technology/3639679.stm.

BBCNews (2009). Facebook faces criticism on privacy change. Retrieved from http://news.bbc.co.uk/2/hi/technology/8405334.stm.

Berscheid, E. (1977). Privacy: A hidden variable in experimental social psychology. *Journal of Social Issues, 33*(3), 85–101.

Bicchieri, C. (2006). *The Grammar of Society: The Nature and Dynamics of Social Norms.* Cambridge: Cambridge University Press.

Brandimarte, L., Acquisti, A., & Gino, F. (n.d.). Baring out with iron hands: Can disclosing make us harsher? Working Paper.

Brandimarte, L., Acquisti, A., & Loewenstein, G. (2012). Misplaced confidences: Privacy and the control paradox. *Social Psychological and Personality Science* (August), 340–347.

Brandimarte, L., Vosgerau, J., & Acquisti, A. (n.d.). Neither forgiven nor forgotten – moral acts depreciate over time, immoral acts do not. Working Paper.

Brickman, P., Coates, D., & Janoff-Bulman, R. (1978). Lottery winners and accident victims: Is happiness relative? *Journal of Personality and Social Psychology, 36*(8), 917–927.

Brunk, B. D. (2002). Understanding the privacy space. *First Monday,* 7.

Calo, R. (2010). People can be so fake: A new dimension to privacy and technology scholarship. *Penn State Law Review, 114*(3), 809–855.

Chellappa, R., & Sin, R. (2002). *Personalization versus Privacy: New Exchange Relationships on the Web*. Los Angeles: Marshall School of Business, University of Southern California.

Cialdini, R. B., Vincent, J. E., Lewis, S. K., Catalan, J., Wheeler, D., & Darby, B. L. (1975). Reciprocal concessions procedure for inducing compliance: The door-in the face technique. *Journal of Personality and Social Psychology, 31*, 206–215.

Clark, A. S. (2006). Employers look at Facebook, too: Companies turn to online profiles to see what applicants are really like. Retrieved from www.cbsnews.com/stories/2006/06/20/eveningnews/main1734920.shtml.

Collins, N. L., & Miller, L. C. (1994). Self-disclosure and liking: A meta-analytic review. *Psychological Bulletin, 116*(3), 457–475.

ConsumersUnion.org. (2008). Americans extremely concerned about Internet privacy. Retrieved from www.consumersunion.org/pub/core_telecom_and_utilities/006189.html.

Conway, L. (2008). Virgin Atlantic sacks 13 staff for calling its flyers "chavs." *The Independent*, November 1. Retrieved from www.independent.co.uk/news/uk/home-news/virgin-atlantic-sacks-13-staff-for-calling-its-flyers-chavs-982192.html.

Cooper, H. (2010). Administration to seek balance in airport screening. Retrieved from www.nytimes.com/2010/11/23/us/23tsa.html.

Cozby, P. C. (1972). Self-disclosure, reciprocity, and liking. *Sociometry, 35*(1), 151–160.

Cranor, L. (2002). Web Privacy with P3P. Sebastopol, CA: O'Reilly & Associates.

Cryder, C. E., Loewenstein, G., & Scheines, R. The donor is in the details. *Organizational Behavior and Human Decision Processes, 120*(1), 15–23.

Culnan, M. J., Armstrong, P. K. (1999). Information privacy concerns, procedural fairness, and impersonal trust: An empirical investigation. *Organization Science, 10*(1), 104–115.

DellaVigna, S., & Malmendier, U. (2006). Paying not to go to the gym. *American Economic Review, 96*(3), 694–719.

Denham, E. (2009). *Report of Findings into the Complaint Filed by the Canadian Internet Policy and Public Interest Clinic (CIPPIC) against Facebook Inc. under the Personal Information Protection and Electronic Documents Act*. Ottawa: Privacy Commissioner of Canada.

Devenow, A., & Welch, I. (1996). Rational herding in financial economics. *European Economic Review, 40*, 603–615.

Duhigg, C. (2012). How companies learn your secrets. *New York Times Magazine*, February 16. Retrieved from www.nytimes.com/2012/02/19/magazine/shopping-habits.html.

Duval, S., & Wicklund, R. A. (1972). *A Theory of Objective Self-Awareness*. New York: Academic Press.

Epley, N., & Dunning, D. (2000). Feeling "holier than thou": Are self-serving assessments produced by errors in self- or social prediction? *Journal of Personality and Social Psychology, 79*(6), 861–875.

Evangelista, B. (2010). Canada's privacy commissioner launches new Facebook probe. sfgate. Retrieved from www.sfgate.com/cgi-bin/blogs/techchron/detail?entry_id=56175.

Federal Trade Commission (2000). *Privacy Online: Fair Information Practices in the Electronic Marketplace*. Washington, DC: Federal Trade Commission.

Federal Trade Commission (2006). *The Identity Theft Report.* Washington, DC: Federal Trade Commission.

Federal Trade Commission (2012). *Protecting Consumer Privacy in an Era of Rapid Change.* Retrieved from ftc.gov/os/2012/03/120326privacy report.pdf.

Fehr, E., & Gaechter, S. (2002). Altruistic punishment in humans. *Nature, 415,* 137–140.

Fischhoff, B. (1982). Debiasing. In D. Kahneman, P. Slovic & A. Tversky (eds.), *Judgment under Uncertainty: Heuristics and Biases* (pp. 422–444). Cambridge: Cambridge University Press.

Fox, C. R., & Tversky, A. (1995). Ambiguity aversion and comparative ignorance. *Quarterly Journal of Economics, 110*(3), 585–603.

Frederick, S., & Loewenstein, G. (1999). Hedonic adaptation. In D. Kahneman & E. Diener (eds.), *Well-being: The Foundations of Hedonic Psychology* (pp. 302–329). New York: Russell Sage Foundation.

Frederick, S., O'Donoghue, T., & Loewenstein, G. (2002). Time discounting and time preference: A critical review. *Journal of Economic Literature, 40*(2), 351.

Freedman, Jonathan L., & Fraser, Scott C. (1966). Compliance without pressure: The foot-in the door technique. *Journal of Personality and Social Psychology, 4*(2), 195–202.

Frey, J. H. (1986). An experiment with a confidentiality reminder in a telephone survey. *Public Opinion Quarterly, 50,* 267–269.

Gilbert, F. (2008). Beacons, bugs, and pixel tags: Do you comply with the FTC behavioral marketing principles and foreign law requirements? *Journal of Internet Law, 11*(11), 3–10.

Goldfarb, A., & Tucker, C. (2011a). Shifts in privacy concerns. Available at SSRN: http://ssrn.com/abstract=1976321 or http://dx.doi.org/10.2139/ssrn.1976321.

Goldfarb, A., & Tucker, C. (2011b). Privacy regulation and online advertising. *Management Science, 57*(1), 57–71.

Goldfarb, A., & Tucker, C. (2011c). Online display advertising: Targeting and obtrusiveness. *Marketing Science, 30,* 389–404.

Grasz, J. (2009). 45% employers use Facebook-Twitter to screen job candidates. *Oregon Business Report* (August). Retrieved from http://oregonbusinessreport.com/2009/08/45-employers-use-Facebook-twitter-to-screen-job-candidates/.

Grice, Paul (1975). Logic and conversation. In P. Cole & J. Morgan (eds.), *Syntax and Semantics* (vol. 3: Speech Acts, pp. 41–58). New York: Academic Press.

Grimmelmann, J. (2009). Saving Facebook. *Iowa Law Review, 94,* 1137–1206.

Hann, I.-H., Hui, K.-L., Lee, T. S., & Png, I. P. L. (2002a). The value of online privacy: Evidence from the USA and Singapore. Paper presented at the Twenty-Third International Conference on Information Systems, Barcelona.

Hann, I.-H., Hui, K.-L., Lee, T. S., & Png, I. P. L. (2002b). Online information privacy: Measuring the cost-benefit trade-off. Paper presented at the Twenty-Third International Conference on Information Systems, Barcelona.

Henslin, J. M. (1967). Craps and magic. *American Journal of Sociology, 73*(3), 316–330.

Herrnstein, R. J., & Prelec, D. (1991). Melioration: A theory of distributed choice. *Journal of Economic Perspectives, 5*(3), 137–156.

Hill, K. (2012). How Target figured out a teen girl was pregnant before her father did. Forbes.com, February 16. Retrieved from www.forbes.com/sites/kashmirhill/2012/02/16/howtarget-figured-out-a-teen-girl-was-pregnant-before-her-father-did/.

Hsee, C., Loewenstein, G., Blount, S., & Bazerman, M. (1999). Preference reversals between joint and separate evaluations: A review and theoretical analysis. *Psychological Bulletin, 125*(5), 576–590.

Ivory, M. Y., & Hearst, M. A. (2002a). Improving web site design. *IEEE Internet Computing, 6*(2, Special Issue on Usability and the Web), 56–63.

Ivory, M. Y., & Hearst, M. A. (2002b). Statistical profiles of highly rated web sites. Paper presented at the Conference on Human Factors in Computing Systems, Minneapolis.

Ivory, M. Y., Sinha, R. R., & Hearst, M. A. (2001). Empirically validated web page design metrics. Paper presented at the Conference on Human Factors in Computing Systems, Seattle.

Jenni, K. E., & Loewenstein, G. (1997). Explaining the "identifiable victim effect." *Journal of Risk and Uncertainty, 14*, 235–257.

Jesdanun, A. (2006). Facebook offers new privacy options. Associated Press.

John, L. K., Acquisti, A., & Loewenstein, G. (2008). Inconsistent preferences for privacy. Paper presented at Behavioral Decision Research in Management Conference, Rady School of Management, University of California, San Diego.

John, L. K., Acquisti, A., & Loewenstein, G. (2011). Strangers on a plane: Context-dependent willingness to divulge sensitive information, *Journal of Consumer Research, 37*, 858–873.

John, L. K., Loewenstein, G., Acquisti, A., & Vosgerau, J. (n.d.). The Psychology of randomized response techniques and why they backfire. Working Paper.

John, L. K., Loewenstein, G., & Rick, S. (2014). Cheating more for less: Upward social comparisons motivate the poorly compensated to cheat. *Organizational Behavior and Human Decision Processes, 123*, 101–109.

Jourard, S. N. (1959). Self-disclosure and other-cathexis. *Journal of Abnormal and Social Psychology, 59*, 428–431.

Jourard, S. N. (1966). Some psychological aspects of privacy. *Law and Contemporary Problems, 31*(2), 307–318.

Jupiter Research. (2002). Seventy percent of US consumers worry about online privacy, but few take protective action. Retrieved from www.prnewswire.com/news-releases/70-of-us-consumers-worry-about-online-privacy-but-few-take-protective-action-reports-jupiter-media-metrix-77697202.html.

Kahneman, D., Knetsch, J., & Thaler, R. (1986). Fairness as a constraint on profit seeking: Entitlements in the market. *American Economic Review, 76*(4), 728–741.

Kahneman, D., Knetsch, J., & Thaler, R. (1990). Experimental test of the endowment effect and the Coase Theorem. *Journal of Political Economy, 98*(6), 1325–1348.

Kahneman, D., & Lovallo, D. (1999). Timid choices and bold forecasts: A cognitive perspective on risk taking. *Management Science, 39*(1), 17–31.

Kahneman, D., & Miller, D. T. (1986). Norm theory: Comparing reality to its alternatives. *Psychological Review, 93*, 136–153.

Kahneman, D., & Tversky, A. (1979). Prospect theory: An analysis of decision making under risk. *Econometrica, 47*, 263–291.

Laibson, D. (1997). Golden eggs and hyperbolic discounting. *Quarterly Journal of Economics, 112*(2), 443–478.

Lambrecht, A., & Tucker, C. (2013). When does retargeting work? Information specificity in online advertising. *Journal of Marketing Research, 50*(5), 561–576.

Langer, E. (1975). The illusion of control. *Journal of Personality and Social Psychology*, *32*(2), 328.

Laufer, R. S., & Wolfe, M. (1977). Privacy as a concept and a social issue: A multidimensional developmental theory. *Journal of Social Issues*, *33*(3), 22–24.

Lerner, J. S., Kassam, K., Li, Y., & Valdesolo, P. (2015). Emotion and decision making. *Annual Review of Psychology*, *66*, 799–823.

Lewis, A. (2003). Please, tell us more. *Wall Street Journal*. Retrieved from www.wsj.com/articles/SB10001424127887324123004579057350800192892.

Liberman, N., & Trope, Y. (2003). Temporal construal theory of intertemporal judgment and decision. In G. Loewenstein, D. Read, & R. Baumeister (eds.), *Time and Choice: Economic and Psychological Perspectives on Intertemporal Choice*. New York: Sage.

Lichtenstein, S., & Slovic, P. (2006). *The Construction of Preference*. New York: Cambridge University Press.

Loewenstein, G., & Elster, J. (eds.). (1992). *Choice over Time*. New York: Russell Sage Foundation.

Loewenstein, G., John, L. K., & Volpp, K. (2013). Protecting people from themselves: Using decision errors to help people help themselves (and others). In E. Shafir (ed.), *The Behavioral Foundations of Public Policy* (pp. 361–379). Princeton, NJ, and Oxford: Princeton University Press.

Loewenstein, G., & O'Donoghue, T. (2005). *Animal Spirits: Affective and Deliberative Processes in Economic Behavior*. Pittsburgh, PA: Carnegie Mellon University.

Loewenstein, G., O'Donoghue, T., & Rabin, M. (2003). Projection bias in predicting future utility. *Quarterly Journal of Economics*, *118*(4), 1209–1248.

Loewenstein, G., & Prelec, D. (1993). Preferences for sequences of outcomes. *Psychological Review*, *100*(1), 91–108.

Loewenstein, G., Thompson, L., & Bazerman, M. H. (1989). Social utility and decision making in interpersonal contexts. *Journal of Personality and Social Psychology*, *57*, 426–441.

Lohr, S. (2010). Library of Congress will save tweets. *New York Times*, April 15, B2.

Mallon, H. W. (2014). Hiding in plain sight: Privacy on the Internet. Retrieved from http://helenwmallon.com/hiding-in-plain-sight-privacy-on-the-internet/.

Margulis, S. T. (2003). On the status and contribution of Westin's and Altman's theories of privacy. *Journal of Social Issues*, *59*(2), 411–429.

Marthews, Alex, & Tucker, Catherine. (2014). Government surveillance and Internet search behavior. Available at SSRN: http://ssrn.com/abstract=2412564.

Mayer-Schoenberger, V. (2011). *Delete: The Virtue of Forgetting in the Digital Age*. Princeton, NJ: Princeton University Press.

McDonald, A. D., & Cranor, L. F. (2008). The cost of reading privacy policies. *I/S: A Journal of Law and Policy for the Information Society*, *4*(22), 543–568.

Mikulincer, M., & Nachson, O. (1991). Attachment styles and patterns of self-disclosure. *Journal of Personality and Social Psychology*, *61*(2), 321–331.

Moult, J. (2009). Woman "sacked" on Facebook for complaining about her boss after forgetting she had added him as a friend. Mail Online, August 14. Retrieved from www.dailymail.co.uk/news/article-1206491/Woman-sacked-Facebook-boss-insult-forgetting-added-friend.html.

Nisbett, R. E., & Ross, L. (1980). *Human Inference: Strategies and Shortcomings of Social Judgment*. New Jersey: Prentice Hall.

Nissenbaum, H. (2004). Privacy as contextual integrity. *Washington Law Review*, *79*(1), 119–157.

Norberg, P. A., Horne, D. R., & Horne, D. A. (2007). The privacy paradox: Personal information disclosure intentions versus behaviors. *Journal of Consumer Affairs*, *41*(1), 100–126.

Nussbaum, Emily (2007). Say everything. *New York Magazine*, February 12. Retrieved from http://nymag.com/news/features/27341/.

O'Connell, H. (2009). What does Facebook's privacy transition mean for you? Retrieved from http://dotrights.org/what-does-Facebooks-privacy-transition-mean-you.

O'Donoghue, T., & Rabin, M. (1999). Doing it now or later. *American Economic Review*, *89*(1), 103–124.

O'Donoghue, T., & Rabin, M. (2001). Choice and Procrastination. *Quarterly Journal of Economics*, *116*(1), 121–160.

Organization for Economic Cooperation and Development (1980). OECD guidelines on the protection of privacy and transborder flows of personal data, 23. Retrieved from www.oecd.org/sti/ieconomy/oecdguidelinesontheprotectionofprivacyand transborderflowsofpersonaldata.htm#memorandum.

Parr, B. (2006). Students against Facebook News Feed (official petition to Facebook). Retrieved from www.Facebook.com/group.php?gid=2208288769.

Peer, E., Acquisti, A., & Loewenstein, G. (n.d.). The impact of reversibility on the decision to disclose personal information. Working Paper.

Pennebaker, J. (1984). Confiding in others and illness rate among spouses of suicide and accidental-death victims. *Journal of Abnormal Psychology*, *93*(4), 473–476.

Pennebaker, J. W., Kiecolt-Glaser, J. K., & Glaser, R. (1988). Disclosure of traumas and immune function: Health implications for psychotherapy. *Journal of Consulting and Clinical Psychology*, *56*(2), 239–245.

Png, I. P. L. (2007). *On the Value of Privacy from Telemarketing: Evidence from the "Do Not Call" Registry*. Singapore: National University of Singapore.

Rabin, M., & O'Donoghue, T. (2000). The economics of immediate gratification. *Journal of Behavioral Decision Making*, *13*, 233–250.

Read, D., Loewenstein, G., & Rabin, M. (1999). Choice bracketing. *Journal of Risk and Uncertainty*, *19*(1–3), 171–197.

Reis, H. T., & Shaver, P. (1988). Intimacy as an interpersonal process. In S. Duck (ed.), *Handbook of Personal Relationships* (pp. 367–389). Chichester, England: Wiley.

Riis, J., Loewenstein, G., Baron, J., Jepson, C., Fagerlin, A., & Ubel, P. (2005). Ignorance of hedonic adaptation to hemodialysis: A study using ecological momentary assessment. *Journal of Experimental Psychology: General*, *134*(1), 3–9.

Romanosky, S., & Acquisti, A. (2009). Privacy costs and personal data protection: Economic and legal perspectives. *Berkeley Technology Law Journal*, *24*(3), 1061–1101.

Romanosky, S., Sharp, R., & Acquisti, A. (2010). Data breaches and identity theft: When is mandatory disclosure optimal? Presentation for the Ninth Workshop on the Economics of Information Security (WEIS), June 7, Arlington, VA.

Rosen, J. (2010). The web means the end of forgetting. *New York Times Magazine*, July 21. Retrieved from www.nytimes.com/2010/07/25/magazine/25privacyt2.html?pagewanted=all&_r=0.

Schelling, T. C. (1968). The life you save may be your own. In S. Chase (ed.), *Problems in Public Expenditure Analysis* (pp. 113–146). Washington, DC: Brookings Institute.

Sedikides, C., Campbell, W. K., Reeder, G. D., & Elliot, A. J. (1999). The relationship closeness induction task. *Representative Research in Social Psychology, 23*, 1–4.

Singer, E., Hippler, H.-J., & Schwarz, N. (1992). Confidentiality assurances in surveys: Reassurance or threat? *International Journal of Public Opinion Research, 4*, 256–268.

Singer, E., von Thurn, D. R., & Miller, E. R. (1995). Confidentiality assurances and response: A quantitative review of the experimental literature. *Public Opinion Quarterly, 59*, 66–77.

Slovic, P. (1995). The construction of preference. *American Psychologist, 50*(5), 364–371.

Smith, H. J., Milberg, S. J., & Burke, S. J. (1996). Information privacy: Measuring Individuals' Concerns about Organizational Practices. *MIS Quarterly, 20*(2), 167–196.

Smyth, J. M. (1998). Written emotional expression: Effect sizes, outcome types, and moderating variables. *Journal of Consulting and Clinical Psychology, 66*, 174–184.

Solove, D. (2007). *The Future of Reputation: Gossip, Rumor, and Privacy on the Internet.* New Haven, CT: Yale University Press.

Spera, S. P., Buhrfeind, E. D., & Pennebaker, J. W. (1994). Expressive writing and coping with job loss. *Academy of Management Journal, 37*, 722–733.

Spiekermann, S., Grossklags, J., & Berendt, B. (2001). E-privacy in 2nd generation E commerce: Privacy preferences versus actual behavior. Paper presented at the Conference on Electronic Commerce, Association for Computing Machinery, Tampa, FL.

Stalder, F. (2002). The failure of privacy enhancing technologies (PETs) and the voiding of privacy. *Sociological Research Online, 7*(2). Retrieved from www.socreson line.org.uk/7/2/stalder.html.

Tamir, D. I., & Mitchell, J. P. (2012). Disclosing information about the self is intrinsically rewarding. *Proceedings of the National Academy of Sciences, 109*(21), 8038–8043.

Tanner, A., (2014). *What Stays in Vegas: The World of Personal Data – Lifeblood of Big Business – and the End of Privacy as We Know It.* New York: PublicAffairs.

Tate, R. (2009). Facebook's great betrayal. Retrieved from http://gawker.com/5426176/Facebooksgreat-betrayal.

Thaler, R. (2009). Civility check has been here all along. Retrieved from http://nudges.wordpress.com/a-civility-check-has-been-here-all-along/.

Thaler, R., & Benartzi, S. (2004). Save more tomorrow: Using behavioral economics to increase employee saving. *Journal of Political Economy, 112*(1), S164–S187.

Tourangeau, R., & Yan, T. (2007). Sensitive questions in surveys. *Psychological Bulletin, 133*(5), 859–883.

Tsai, J. Y., Engelman, S., Cranor, L., & Acquisti, A. (2011). The effect of online privacy information on purchasing behavior: An experimental study. *Information Systems Research, 22*(2), 254–268.

Tucker, C. (2014). Social networks, personalized advertising, and privacy controls. NET Institute Working Paper No. 10–07; MIT Sloan Research Paper No. 4851–10. Available at SSRN: http://ssrn.com/abstract=1694319.

Tufecki, Z. (2008). Can you see me now? Audience and disclosure regulation in online social network sites. *Bulletin of Science, Technology, & Society, 28*(1), 20–36.

Tversky, A., & Kahneman, D. (1974). The framing of decisions and the psychology of choice. *Science, 211*(4481), 453–458.

Tversky, A., & Kahneman, D. (1991). Loss aversion in riskless choice: A reference dependent model. *Quarterly Journal of Economics, 106*(4), 1039–1061.

Tversky, A., Slovic, P., & Kahneman, D. (1990). The causes of preference reversal. *American Economic Review, 80*(1), 204–217.

Tybout, Alice M., Sternthal, Brian, & Calder, Bobby J. (1983). Information availability as a determinant of multiple request effectiveness. *Journal of Marketing Research, 20*(August), 280–290.

Van Baaren, R., Horgan, T., Chartrand, T. L., & Dijkmans, M. (2004). The forest, the trees, and the chameleon: Context dependency and nonconscious mimicry. *Journal of Personality and Social Psychology, 86*, 453–459.

Volpp, K., John, L., Troxel, A. B., Norton, L., Fassbender, J., & Loewenstein, G. (2008). Financial incentive-based approaches for weight loss: A randomized trial. *Journal of the American Medical Association, 300*(22), 2631–2637.

Warren, S. D., & Brandeis, L. D. (1890). The right to privacy. *Harvard Law Review, 4* (5), 193–220.

Wathieu, L., & Friedman, A. 2009. An empirical approach to understanding privacy concerns. ESMT Working Paper 09–001, ESMT European School of Management and Technology, Berlin.

Wawro, A. (2008). ToneCheck email plugin is like spellcheck for your emotions. *PC World Communications*. Retrieved from http://tech.ca.msn.com/pcworld-art icle.aspx?cp-documentid=27941607.

Weinstein, N. (1980). Unrealistic optimism about future life events. *Journal of Personality and Social Psychology, 39*(5), 806–820.

Westin, A. F. (1991). *Harris-Equifax Consumer Privacy Survey 1991.* Atlanta, GA: Equifax, Inc.

White, T. B., Zahay, D. L., Thorbjorsen, H., & Shavitt, S. (2008). Getting too personal: Reactance to highly personalized email solicitations. *Marketing Letters, 19*, 39–50.

Whitten, A., & Tygar, J. D. (2005). Why Johnny can't encrypt: A usability evaluation of PGP 5.0. In L. Cranor & G. Simson (eds.), *Security and Usability: Designing Secure Systems that People Can Use* (pp. 679–702). Sebastopol, CA: O'Reilly and Associates.

Whitty, M. T., & Joinson, A. N. (2009). *Truth, Lies, and Trust on the Internet.* New York: Routledge.

Zuckerberg, M. (2006). An open letter from Mark Zuckerberg. Retrieved from http://blog.Facebook.com/blog.php?post=2208562130.

24 Consumers and Healthcare

The Reluctant Consumer

Janet A. Schwartz

Healthcare is often thought of as a negative service; no one wants to get hurt or be sick, and it is unpleasant to contemplate and prepare for the reality that this can happen. Adding to that burden is the degree of uncertainty surrounding whether and when shocks, either chronic or acute, to health will occur. Consumer decisions affecting health can range from routine choices about whether to have salad for lunch, get a flu shot, or select a primary care doctor, to more serious and consequential choices about what is the right insurance to have, when to seek medical care, and what the best treatment is for a serious illness such as cancer.

Consumers have greatly benefited from recent advances in medical knowledge about the causes of disease and how to prevent or treat it. Technology now gives consumers the ability to manage uncertainty and negative health outcomes with unprecedented access to excellent sources of information, advice, and feedback. At the same time, the responsibility of making wise healthcare decisions has increasingly shifted to individuals, making them more accountable than ever for their personal choices and spending. So while today's consumer is better informed and more autonomous than those in previous generations, making good health and healthcare choices can still be rife with complexity and difficult trade-offs. Given the theoretical and practical implications for both consumer welfare and public policy, understanding how people navigate the medical marketplace is an important focus for psychologists. To that end, this chapter outlines our understanding of factors that shape consumer health decisions. We begin with individual awareness and perception of health risks, which serve as the foundation for almost any model of health behavior. Next, we explore how risk perceptions lead people to approach the trade-offs they believe are necessary to manage the risks of poor health outcomes. The final section explores how the cognitive factors underlying health decisions combine with significant social, emotional, and environmental forces to guide prevention behaviors, and ultimately health outcomes. Throughout, domains in which consumer research has already made a contribution are noted, along with important areas that warrant future research.

Understanding Health Risk

A dominant approach to studying health has been to examine risk perceptions, because they are the primary drivers of behavioral change (Brewer et al., 2007). In health, risk is typically defined as a likelihood that an unfavorable event involving injury or loss will occur. In order for people to make a conscious decision to be healthier, they must know and believe they are at some risk of experiencing a negative event. Theoretical models of health risk perception continue to provide fertile ground for researchers in all domains of health, including psychology, public policy, medicine, and consumer behavior. Early models such as the Health Belief Model (Becker, 1974) provided a view that increased risk perceptions facilitated behaviors that either promote good health or prevent bad health. Unfortunately, it is not this simple; a great deal of subsequent research showed that people do not always behave more healthfully when well informed of the risks (Ajzen, 1985, 1991). Cigarette smoking may be one of the best examples illustrating this point. The causal relationship between cigarette smoking and poor health outcomes is definitive, and the warnings are impossible to ignore. Despite broad consumer knowledge of the potential harms, cigarette smoking remains the leading cause of preventable death in the United States, where almost one in five of all American adults smoke (CDC, 2014a).

Later models of health risk perception attempted to better account for changes, or lack thereof, in behavior by considering how people's attitudes and intentions were shaped by risk information. Fishbein and Ajzen's (1975) Theory of Reasoned Action posited that changes in behavior must follow actual intentions to change. These intentions are driven by attitudes that often have complex and subjective structure that incorporates perceptions regarding the importance of the problem, the risk of a negative event, and observable norms drawn from the actions of others. In this model, a person's decision to use tobacco despite knowing the risks may be attributed to her not thinking that the risks are important enough to act on and/or observing social cues among those around who suggest the behavior is acceptable. Although the Theory of Reasoned Action is more sophisticated than the Health Belief Model in capturing the nuances that guide health risk perceptions, an intention–behavior gap still exists. That is, some people know the risks of certain behaviors, think they are important to address, see that others act healthfully, and may even express intentions to change, but *still* do not alter their behavior.

A classic experiment demonstrating a gap between intentions and behaviors was conducted by Leventhal, Singer, and Jones in 1965; almost fifty years later, the findings are still relevant to today's consumer health researchers. In their study, employees at Yale University were randomly assigned to two groups in an intervention targeting increased take-up of tetanus shots. Both groups were given the same information in a postcard about the risks of tetanus and the benefits of the vaccine. The key manipulation was that while both groups were encouraged to get the shot, one group's postcard was enhanced with a campus map that highlighted the health center's location and specified an exact time to go. When the researchers followed up with employees several weeks later, they found two interesting results. The first was that both groups, regardless of whether their postcard was enhanced, were equally knowledgeable about the risk of getting tetanus and the benefits of the vaccine. The second was that despite equally positive attitudes and intentions to vaccinate among the two groups, only 3 percent of the plain postcard group reported getting the shot as compared to 28 percent of the enhanced postcard group. Findings like these are very difficult to explain by models that assume that awareness, attitudes, and intentions are the primary drivers of behavior. Both groups appeared equally convinced that getting tetanus shot was the right thing to do, but the critical factor in closing the intention–behavior gap had nothing to do with increasing awareness and risk perceptions.

Health risk models are still evolving (see Menon, Raghubir, & Agrawal, 2008, for a comprehensive overview of the various models of health risk perception) in ways that improve our knowledge of the complex cognitive, emotional, and social factors that shape health attitudes, intentions, and behaviors. For example, the Theory of Planned Behavior expands on previous models to incorporate one's sense of personal control in health decisions (Ajzen, 1991). While this and many health risk perception models are excellent at capturing the processes that underlie health attitudes and intentions, closing the intention–behavior gap remains a perplexing problem. Experimental evidence over many health intention–behavior studies suggests that relatively large changes in intentions may lead to only very small changes in behaviors (Webb & Sheeran, 2006). In short, there is still much work for psychologists to do.

This reality creates opportunity and challenges for consumer researchers who strive to advance both theory and practice. From a theoretical perspective, health risk models are rich in their ability to illuminate the processes by which health attitudes and intentions are shaped. From a practical perspective, however, such illumination does very little for either consumer welfare or public policy if those intentions do not result in meaningful behavioral change. As demonstrated by the tetanus shot study (Leventhal, Singer, & Jones, 1965), sometimes closing the intention–behavior gap has less to do with making people aware of their health risks or creating better attitudes toward vaccination and more to do with making it easier for consumers to do what is right. Increasingly, consumer health research is called upon to understand not only changes in attitudes and intentions, but also how those psychological forces translate, or fail to translate, into real health behaviors.

Consumer health research has identified that one problem with leveraging risk to motivate intentions and behavior is a fundamental assumption that risks are perceived accurately. Many early models of health risk perception operated from the normative perspective that people objectively incorporate risk information, and that this information was evaluated independently of the other important attributes (e.g., Ajzen 1985, 1991; Becker, 1974; Fishbein & Ajzen, 1975). Of course, these models have subsequently evolved and adapted to reflect the now more common empirical finding that behaviors stem from how much a person *feels* that she or he is at risk, sometimes regardless of the actual risk (Weinstein, 1982). Put another way, health risk assessments, just like those in other domains, are often subjective and malleable (Tversky &

Kahneman, 1986), so exposing people to risk can be scary and alienating rather than informative and actionable (Keller & Block, 1995; Menon, Block, & Ramanathan, 2002; Menon, Raghubir, & Agrawal, 2008). The subjective nature of risk has provided ample research opportunities in the domain of consumer psychology. Marketing healthcare products, services, and even public health messages often involves promises that the risk of poor health outcomes will be reduced by taking some medication, starting a program, or stopping a behavior. A variety of relevant and irrelevant factors can influence people's perceptions of risk (Brewer, Chapman, Schwartz, & Bergus, 2007), their subsequent intentions to change, and ultimately their behaviors (Brewer et al., 2007).

Exposing people to information on health risks as a means of improving informed decision making can certainly be effective in reducing harmful behaviors. To date, empirical evidence strongly supports the notion that risk perceptions provide the best foundation for theoretical models of health behavior (Brewer et al., 2007). Returning to the example of cigarette smoking, many American consumers either quit or never started smoking after the Surgeon General's landmark warning in 1964 (42 percent of American adults smoked cigarettes in 1965, compared to 18 percent today; CDC, 2014a). Highlighting the health-related risks of cigarette smoke to both smokers and those around them continues to play a prominent role in public health. At the same time, the decline in smoking rates in the United States from 42 percent to 18 percent has been a gradual one, and risk awareness is accompanied by many other regulatory measures such as heavy taxation, advertising and marketing restrictions, and outright smoking bans in many public and private places. Social pressure and the stigmatization of smoking have also played a significant role in reducing smoking rates by making it culturally unacceptable (McBride, Emmons, & Lipkus, 2003). Nevertheless, the fact that many people do not take action in the face of undeniable risks leads to a stream of empirical research questioning why.

Research dedicated to understanding how risk exposure influences health intentions and behaviors reveals complex answers (Rothman & Salovey, 1997). For example, highlighting risk can backfire by making people fearful and even less likely to act (e.g., Keller and Block, 1996). Some people may stop processing information because it is too cognitively taxing to integrate (Luce, 1998) or too emotionally difficult to contemplate (Raghunathan & Trope, 2002). The downstream consequences of a heightened sense of risk or fear are not trivial, as they can influence subsequent attitudes and perceptions about those risks and the quality of medical procedures that detect them (Kahn & Luce, 2003; Luce & Kahn, 1999). Others may exhibit self-positivity bias in which they are motivated to believe that they are less at risk of developing health problems than the average person in their circumstances (Raghubir & Menon, 1998; Weinstein, 1982, 1984). The impact of emotions, experience, and the natural desire to regulate our mood can lead to risk underestimation and overestimation in a variety of consumer domains, but the biasing effects can be particularly strong when outcomes are salient and stakes are high (Vosgerau, 2010). This is often the case in health.

In some cases, appealing to consumers in ways that encourage overestimation errors improves health behaviors. That is, antismoking appeals might be more effective in warning male smokers that they are twenty-three times more likely to get lung cancer than nonsmokers, than warning them that they have a 16 percent chance (though it is higher, almost 25 percent, for heavy smokers) of getting lung cancer (American Lung Association, n.d.). Both illustrations are accurate, but describing them in relative versus absolute terms makes people feel at greater risk (Malenka et al., 1993). With something as irrefutably harmful as cigarette smoking, there may be little disadvantage to framing or manipulating information in ways that exacerbate risk and consequently make people less likely to smoke or more likely to quit. With other health behaviors, however, taking advantage of natural biases in risk estimation does not always lead consumers down a better path. For example, pharmaceutical companies often frame the clinical benefits of medication in relative versus absolute terms because consumers (and their doctors) are much more likely to see benefit in a medication that reduces their risk by 50 percent than a medication that drops it from 4 percent to 2 percent. Because risk perceptions can drive behavior, subtle changes in framing can lead to the overutilization of drugs that come with side-effects and costly copays but provide only marginal health benefits.

Finally, the framing of risk messages can become controversial when scientific evidence emerges to question the value of certain medical products and procedures. Mammogram adherence is a very timely example. Research has shown (e.g., Banks et al., 1995) that women are more compliant with recommendations to have routine screening for breast cancer with loss-framed appeals (e.g., a yearly mammogram reduces your chances of dying) than gain-framed appeals (e.g., a yearly mammogram increases your chances of living). Recently, however, the value of mammograms as a screening tool has been called into question, and guidelines for screening have been significantly revised (U.S. Preventive Services Task Force, 2009). Mammograms are not perfect in detecting real cancers (some cases are missed) and can sometimes find tumors that are not there (false alarms). Some tumors may not be life threatening if left untreated, or perhaps would be found early by a woman or her doctor during an exam. After reviewing the results of many large-scale longitudinal studies on whether mammograms indeed save lives, the Task Force concluded that while some women will be saved, some will still go undiagnosed, and many women are unnecessarily treated as the result of routine screening. Thus, while loss-framed risk appeals for mammogram adherence may increase screening rates, there is now some debate as to whether more screening actually improves health outcomes. When scientific evidence refutes long-held beliefs or clashes with strong cultural norms that tell us screening reduces risks and saves lives, there is understandable confusion among consumers about what to do. Confusion and anxiety are further increased when experts disagree about the implications of the findings, or people believe that insurers will revisit decisions about whether certain tests should continue to be covered. Mammograms are not the only routine screening tests that have come under scrutiny, and consumer psychology will play an important role in shaping how both risk perceptions and behaviors change as the value of certain elements of preventive screening is empirically validated.

As a whole, we see that risk perceptions play a complex role in shaping health attitudes and behaviors, and that as researchers it can be difficult to predict a priori whether positive or negative effects on attitudes and behaviors will result from highlighting risk to consumers. Whether this ultimately engages or alienates them varies a great deal across the seriousness of afflictions, message framing, and individual mood, motivation, and coping styles (Ruiter, Abraham, & Kok, 2001). These findings create challenges for those striving toward a unifying theory of health behaviors that accurately incorporates the role of risk and for those tasked with creating effective health messages that leverage risk awareness to motivate the right kind of behavior. In the next section, we will explore how consumers' perceptions of risk illuminate the trade-offs they face in making health decisions.

Trade-offs in Health and Healthcare

As fundamental as risk perceptions are to understanding health behavior, these decisions are also characterized by the trade-offs people confront in an effort to minimize those risks. Increasingly, these trade-offs involve the price of health goods and services. In most consumer domains, cost is an obvious factor when buying ordinary goods like laptops, smart phones, and car insurance. Factoring prices into consumer health decisions, however, is a scant and relatively recent addition to the literature. Many early models, such as the Health Belief Model or Theory of Reasoned Action and their antecedents (e.g., Theory of Planned Behavior; Ajzen, 1991), were flexible enough to consider cost as a barrier to healthcare consumption, but surprisingly few studies really confront the complex psychology of making trade-offs between health and money.

To give some historical perspective, consider the now famous RAND Health Insurance Experiment (Manning et al., 1987), which began in the early 1970s and lasted longer than a decade. American families were randomly assigned to different levels of health insurance out-of-pocket cost sharing (ranging from no cost sharing at all, to being responsible for 95 percent of costs up to $1,000 – the equivalent of almost $6,000 today). The purpose of the RAND study was to measure the impact of cost sharing on healthcare consumption and medical outcomes. The results showed that, perhaps not so surprisingly, those with little or no cost sharing were more likely to seek services and had a greater number of services per user than those in the higher cost-sharing groups. The more surprising result was that when higher levels of cost sharing led participants to cut back on healthcare services, they were *equally likely* to cut back on necessary and unnecessary treatments. Higher levels of cost sharing, particularly among the poor, led fewer people to seek medication, reduced medication adherence rates, and caused the complete discontinuation of medication for important ailments such as hypertension (i.e., high blood pressure). Poor adherence to blood pressure medication increases an individual's risk of developing complications such as kidney disease or stroke – both of which are difficult and expensive to treat. The fact that consumer cost sharing indiscriminately reduced consumption poses challenges for policy makers who want to remove barriers to seeking treatment that saves lives and minimizes long-term costs, but puts some restrictions on the overuse of treatment that has no real benefit or downstream cost savings.

The RAND findings had a tremendous impact on shaping today's insurance plan designs, including their complicated array of cost sharing fees such as premiums, copays for doctor visits and medicines, deductibles, and many other out-of-pocket expenses. These fees are designed to facilitate the use of necessary treatment and prevent the overuse of unnecessary medical treatment. In reality, however, cost-sharing measures often prevent the utilization of necessary treatment, and we still lack a complete understanding of why this occurs (Goldman, Joyce, & Zheng, 2007). That is, we do not know whether cost drives people away via a conscious calculation of value, such as when a consumer decides that a blood pressure medicine's price is too high given its potential reduction in risk for a negative outcome. Alternatively, self-positivity bias could provide an affective buffer against the pain of paying, such as when a consumer decides not to purchase a $25 medication because he or she is not really at risk. Many other psychological forces could also be at work. Consumer psychology's role in uncovering the processes by which individuals evaluate price information and reach a decision about whether to seek treatment, continue therapy, or choose the appropriate level of insurance coverage is thus crucial to improving policies that guide people toward more cost-effective choices.

Generally speaking, people are strongly averse to the notion that preserving health comes at some monetary value. Research has shown that, in matters of improving health and extending life, most people want broad accessibility for those who need medical care, regardless of their ability to pay (Fiske & Tetlock, 1997). This communal sharing orientation (Fiske, 1992) is echoed in some aspects of healthcare (e.g., free childhood vaccination and orphan drug programs), but can be sharply contrasted with the efficient market pricing forces that are also commonplace (e.g., tiered-pricing schemes for prescription medications). Whether one is an individual, a caretaker, or an insurance administrator, deciding how much money to spend on better health and longer life can be considered a taboo trade-off that violates sacred values (Tetlock, 2003; Tetlock et al., 2000). People are reluctant to contemplate these decisions (some may even outright refuse to do so) and become morally suspect of those who do (Baron & Spranca, 1997; McGraw & Tetlock, 2005). With specific regard to pricing healthcare goods and services, consumers can equate high prices with real intentions to harm because they simply put medicine out of reach for some but not others. This is considered rationing and is perceived as grossly unfair (Campbell, 1999) to the end that it leads to consumer outrage and backlash. Such public response is not trivial, especially if it draws the attention of the media and policy makers – so marketing practices in the highly regulated healthcare industry fall under a different type of scrutiny than practices in some other consumer domains (McGraw, Schwartz, & Tetlock, 2012).

The reality of the medical marketplace, however, is that exchanges of money and health routinely take place (Tetlock, 2003). As consumers share a greater burden of and responsibility for healthcare costs, they must confront these difficult trade-offs. For their part, consumer researchers recently uncovered some interesting insights into the psychology of trading money for health. For example, one study (McGraw, Schwartz, & Tetlock, 2012) showed that consumers' concerns about a profits-driven medication price increase were mitigated when the company reframed its pricing strategy as simply passing high research and development costs on to consumers. This was compared to the relative outrage consumers felt when the price increase was justified as the reward for bringing value and innovation to the marketplace. Interestingly, the relational framing of price increases as either communal sharing or market pricing was very influential on perceptions of price fairness for therapeutic medicines (e.g., heart medication), but not for cosmetic medications such as antiwrinkle treatments or everyday utilitarian goods such as computer software. This finding is consistent with the notion that for sacred values such as health, people tolerate price increases in the name of communal sharing (we *do* share the financial responsibility of making life-saving medicine accessible to everyone), but reject them in the name of market pricing (access to medication is restricted to those who can pay). For non-sacred goods, however, people show relative indifference to how pricing policies are established, presumably because no taboo trade-off has been made. That is, the rhetoric surrounding the taboo topic of paying for healthcare is crucially important to the public's tolerance of these exchanges.

While people have a general distaste for trade-offs involving health and money, the reality that these trade-offs happen can leave them naturally wondering what prices reflect. Consumer research has, of course, long examined price signaling, and specifically has explored what inferences people draw. Unsurprisingly, consumers believe that price and quality are positively correlated, and this perception is strongest when products are unfamiliar (Monroe & Krishnan, 1985; Rao, 2005; Rao & Monroe 1988, 1989). In healthcare, consumers may be unfamiliar with products and services until they become sick or injured, a time that leaves little room for comparison shopping. Under exigent circumstances, people may be forced to make or accept choices about treatment and defer strategies for payment until the emergency is resolved. Finally, marketing efforts are often directed toward healthcare professionals rather than end-use consumers. As such, a person may not know that an inexpensive but equally effective generic alternative to a branded drug exists unless a healthcare professional informs the patient. Recent changes to laws in the United States under the Patient Affordable Care Act of 2010 demand greater price transparency in healthcare, with the hope that access to better information about prices will lead to better decision making (e.g., Emanuel et al., 2012). These changes provide an ongoing and excellent opportunity for consumer researchers to investigate how prices affect health risk perceptions, attitudes, and behaviors.

In some cases, recent research has shown that people make price-quality inferences about healthcare goods and services much the same way they do in other domains. That is, inferences drawn from prices impact both expectations and experiences of product efficacy. In one study, for example, researchers gave participants randomly assigned to two groups the exact same energy drink, but varied the descriptions to show one with a high retail price and the other with a low retail price. Participants sampled the drinks and then waited a few minutes (for the drink to "take effect") before doing an anagram test. Those in the high price group solved significantly more anagrams than those in the low price group (Shiv, Carmon, & Ariely, 2005). This price "placebo effect" has also been shown to occur with medicine where participants in a mock clinical trial experienced greater pain relief from an electric shock with a high-priced analgesic than a low-priced analgesic. In both conditions, the pain reliever was actually a placebo that offered no real analgesic benefit (Waber, Shiv, Carmon, & Ariely, 2008). Others have shown that medication placebo effects can even be produced through mere direct-to-consumer advertising (Kamenica, Naclerio, & Malani, 2013). Taken together, this nascent body of research investigating how prices influence expectations and health outcomes suggests that people do not just think expensive medications work better, they actually experience more improvement. If expectations and experiences favor expensive goods and services, then making trade-offs between health and money become that much more challenging at both the individual and policy level.

Research examining the impact of prices on expectations and experience in healthcare has real implications for consumer welfare and public policy, as individuals, benefits providers, and governments try to rein in costs. Generic medications, for example, have the same chemical structure and safety record as their branded counterparts, but come at a direct savings to consumers in the form of lower out-of-pocket costs. The average employer-insured American can expect a generic medication copay to cost $10 compared to $25 to $80 for branded medications (Hoadley, Summer, Hargrave, & Cubanski, 2013). Prices are considerably higher without coverage, and uninsured consumers can expect to pay $33 and $268 for generics and brands, respectively (www.healthcostin stitute.org). Research has shown that although a majority of consumers (70 percent) report that generics work just as well and have better value than branded equivalents, fewer than 40 percent would rather take a generic over a branded medication (Shrank et al., 2009). The reasons underlying brand preferences for medication, and the extent to which they may be different from those in other consumer domains, are not well understood and warrant further investigation.

One contributing factor is that market forces and their impact on consumers are sometimes different in healthcare than for other goods and services. For example, while insurers and some policy makers work to drive consumers toward cost-effective choices, regulations that provide extended patent protection to pharmaceutical companies can limit them to relatively few affordable options. Moreover, because consumers are prescribed medications by their doctors, biases in perceptions about efficacy may be exacerbated by an expert's endorsement or the patient's desire to not go against the advice of a trusted medical professional (Schwartz, Luce, & Ariely, 2011). Further complications arise when doctors themselves show common choice biases (Schwartz & Chapman, 1999; Redelmeier & Shafir, 1995), including conflicts of interest that put their own financial interests before the well-being of their patients (Cain & Detsky, 2008).

Price-driven expectations are not limited to mere perceptions about quality or experienced efficacy, but can also reflect the reality of tiered-pricing policies for different types of medications. Sometimes price differences for the same medication are volume-based, such as when one insurance company negotiates a better rate for one cholesterol-lowering medication than another. Other price differences may be tied to disease severity or consequences of living without treatment. Some European nations take this communal sharing approach to medication tiered-pricing (Fraeyman et al., 2013). For example, in Belgium and France, insulin, which some diabetics need in order to live, has no copay, but therapeutic medications for conditions such as hypertension and cosmetic afflictions have progressively larger levels of cost sharing (Drummond & Towse, 2012). While such policies reflect society's communal sharing values that life-saving medications should be accessible, the flip side is that people might use prices to make inferences about potential risk and disease severity.

Consumer research has shown that as medication prices for therapeutic goods such as vaccines increase, perceptions of health risks decrease (Samper & Schwartz, 2012). That is, high-priced flu vaccines make people feel like they are less likely to get the flu than with low-priced flu vaccines, even when participants' out-of-pocket costs are controlled across conditions. As with many other findings in healthcare, this result has both practical and theoretical implications. From a practical perspective, we see that transparency and cost sharing does not always produce desired behaviors of reducing overconsumption and improving underconsumption. From a theoretical perspective, we have a better understanding of why: people expect important medications to be reasonably priced (or even free) and come to rely on price as one indicator of their personal risk. Put another way, when people see that prices are high, they believe the risk of getting sick is not high enough to warrant a pricing subsidy, and, importantly, may not be high enough for them to act.

Difficult trade-offs are in no way limited to taboo exchanges between secular goods such as money and sacred goods such as health. Imagine, for example, comparing drugs that vary in effectiveness but also vary in the risk of inducing unpleasant and dangerous side-effects. Much research has examined how these exchanges, often referred to as tragic trade-offs because they pit sacred values such as efficacy and safety against each other, affects healthcare choices. Decisions involving taboo and tragic trade-offs are emotionally charged and create more negative emotion than routine trade-offs (Tetlock et al., 2000). Negative affect has a general tendency to hinder information processing (Luce, 1998; Luce, Bettman & Payne, 1997) because the desire to make accurate decisions can be trumped by the competing goal of restoring oneself to a positive mood (Raghunathan & Trope, 2002). In pursuing this goal, consumers may engage in a variety of self-regulatory measures that circumvent difficult trade-offs but do not necessarily improve their health. Sometimes people flatly refuse to contemplate these decisions (Baron & Spranca, 1997) or passively accept options that make them feel less culpable (Ritov & Baron, 1999). Alternatively, they may adopt a more deliberate strategy that weights the sacred value (e.g., efficacy) more heavily when it is contrasted with a non-sacred value (e.g., money) or even another sacred value such as side-effects (Luce, Payne, & Bettman, 1999). Put differently, treatment efficacy becomes much more important to people when they are confronted with price trade-offs compared to when they are not. Finally, negative affect produced by difficult trade-offs can also exacerbate self-positivity bias, whereby an individual is convinced that his or her relative risk is not great enough to warrant further treatment considerations (Weinstein, 1984). While all of these behaviors can be adaptive in restoring one to a positive mood, they are maladaptive from the perspective that they lead individuals toward inaction that could delay necessary treatment and risk their condition(s) worsening and becoming more difficult or expensive to treat (Luce, 1998, 2005).

In sum, consumer psychology reveals that people's thoughts and behaviors regarding the trade-offs required to minimize health risks and poor health outcomes are complicated. This is particularly true when it becomes apparent that achieving better health will come at the expense of other things – such as effort, time, money, and even some other element of health or well-being. Consumer-driven healthcare policies are often designed with a rational consumer in mind – one who accurately incorporates risk information, easily makes trade-offs between steadily weighted attributes, and, to some end, does this with little regard for emotion or context. Empirical evidence from the consumer psychology literature, however, often highlights how people struggle to approach the trade-offs rationally. These insights into how people think about what it will take to be healthier sets the stage for the next section, in which the focus shifts from thoughts to behaviors, with an eye on closing the intention–behavior gap.

Prevention

One of the best ways to avoid thinking about or experiencing unpleasant health events and their associated costs is simply not to get injured or sick. Of course, this is impossible. For most people, health risks are a combination of genetic and environmental influences. Some of these influences are out of our control – the best we can do is to be prepared. Other risks can be mitigated or managed with good behavior. Good behavior usually means limiting a lot of the things we love (television binge watching and ice cream) and developing a taste for things we do not (elliptical trainers and kale). The trade-offs people face in terms of what they want right now and what is good for them in the future are often regulated by self-control. Failures of self-control, ranging from lack of awareness that self-control is necessary to conscious decisions to behave in ways that can compromise future well-being, are key contributors to poor health outcomes. As such, understanding health risks and the trade-offs necessary to mitigate their effects bring us to health prevention and how people actually behave. Because we know that awareness and good intentions do not always lead to better behavior, much research has been dedicated to understanding how to close the gap by helping people exercise self-control.

The individual and societal health consequences of poor self-control are far-reaching and difficult to address (Moffitt et al., 2011). From both a theoretical and practical perspective, understanding self-control processes is an increasingly important research topic for consumer health researchers. Engaging in preventive health behaviors such as exercise, balanced nutrition, and smoking cessation helps ward off disease and premature death, but also requires ongoing and persistent self-control. Psychological research has long shown that activating and maintaining prolonged self-control can be difficult and exacting (Baumeister, Bratslavsky, Muraven, & Tice, 1998; Hagger, Wood, Stiff, & Chatzisarantis, 2010; Muraven & Baumeister, 2000); at the same time, it may be the crucial to closing the intention–behavior gap in health.

A challenge for self-control in health is that it is not always easy to see how any one instance of indulgence today leads to bad outcomes far in the future (Metcalfe & Mischel, 1999). People who develop Type 2 Diabetes from poor diet and exercise habits or lung cancer from smoking cannot identify the one meal or cigarette that made them sick. Moreover, the effects of bad habits on health accumulate over time and have only some likelihood of occurring – the majority of smokers do not develop lung cancer (American Lung Association, n.d.). Good health in exchange for good behavior is not guaranteed either. This further pits the angst of forgoing immediate temptation or suffering an uncomfortable procedure against an intangible and elusive future reward (Frederick, Loewenstein, & O'Donoghue, 2002). Given the reality of the present and the uncertainty of the future, it is understandable that health attitudes and behaviors can be misaligned. Research on intertemporal choice has long shown that people give much more weight to their current circumstances than to future outcomes (Loewenstein & Prelec, 1992), and that this is particularly true in health (Chapman, 1998). This is not to say that people do not care about their future selves – they do (Bartels & Rips, 2010) – but self-positivity biases and motivated reasoning (Kunda, 1990) allow people to rationalize that one dessert or cigarette today will not do any harm tomorrow, and that makes abstaining from the surrounding temptations more difficult.

Bypassing the Need for Self-Control

One way to get people to behave better is to make it easier to do the right thing. Sometimes a simple change to the physical environment provides the cue to action, and behavior falls in line. Recall that in the tetanus shot study discussed earlier, the key to increasing vaccination rates was giving people explicit instructions about where and when to go, rather than relying solely on risk perceptions to motivate healthy behavior (Leventhal, Singer, & Jones, 1965). In effect, removing the additional effort needed to make an appointment and determine how to get there reduces some of the demand on self-control resources required to plan and execute a relatively unpleasant task. Recent research, particularly from the behavioral sciences, has shown that small changes to the physical or choice environment can have profound influences on behavior, particularly when they remove effort or make exercising self-control more immediately rewarding (Thaler & Sunstein, 2008).

One powerful environmental influence on behavior is defaults. In their classic study, Johnson and Goldstein (2003) found stark differences in organ donation consent rates across European nations. These differences existed even among countries that were culturally similar, and persisted despite some large-scale awareness-based intervention efforts campaigning to register potential donors. The relative differences could thus not be attributed to strong cultural norms against the notion of organ donation or lack of awareness that there was a need for viable organs. In fact, the key difference in consent rates simply came down to the default assumptions. In countries with high consent rates, people were presumed to be donors and could register to opt out, but the opposite was true in countries with low consent rates, where people were presumed not to be donors and could register to opt in. In essence, no one registers, so the countries with opt-out policies have larger pools of donors than countries with opt-in policies by default.

Default effects can improve a variety of consumer health behaviors ranging from health insurance plan choices (Samuelson & Zeckhauser, 1988) and increased influenza vaccination rates (Chapman, Li, Colby, & Yoon, 2010) to cost savings with mandatory generic substitutions of branded prescription medications (Shrank et al., 2010). Changing defaults often requires little effort on the part of consumers and at the same time offers substantial capacity to reduce out-of-pocket fees to individuals, lost-productivity hours to employers, and lower payment costs for private and public benefits providers. Importantly, this can be achieved without compromising health outcomes (in many cases, health outcomes improve, e.g., Johnson & Goldstein, 2003) and operates in line with consumers' intentions to do what is right. Since research has shown that many people know that generic medications provide greater value than branded equivalents, would likely choose to become organ donors if no default was provided, would prefer more cost-effective insurance plan selections, and have good preventive health intentions to get flu vaccines, making these options the default better aligns people's behaviors with their goals. Some of these measures are easy for providers to implement and can be a cost-effective way to help consumers close the intention–behavior gap.

Defaults have also shown considerable power in the domain of eating and could prove to have an impact in efforts to reduce overweight and obesity rates. As with smoking, being overweight or obese is linked to poor self-control and has considerable individual and societal costs (Finkelstein, DiBonaventura, Burgess, & Hale, 2010; Finkelstein, Trogdon, Cohen, & Dietz, 2009). More than one-third of American adults are obese, which puts them at some risk of developing a weight-related disease such as hypertension or diabetes (Ogden, Carroll, Kit, & Flegal, 2014). The primary cause of obesity is overeating (Cutler, Glaeser, & Shapiro, 2003), and the role of defaults in curbing overeating is of considerable interest to consumer psychologists. Recent interventions with default effects in nutrition have shown that defaults can promote healthy eating by simply moving healthy and lower-calorie items to eye level (Thorndike et al., 2012), where consumers' attention is naturally drawn (Dreze, Hoch, & Purk, 1995), or making unhealthy foods more difficult to obtain than healthy foods (Wisdom, Downs, & Loewenstein, 2010). Such designs take advantage of the fact that busy consumers are drawn to convenience, and their "choices" are often not the result of strong preferences or careful deliberations, but merely reflect what they see first or can grab the most quickly. Simply putting healthy options in place of less healthy options can significantly reduce the number of calories people buy and consume and, importantly, may do so without depleting self-control resources.

Others have shown that defaults may work to reduce overeating by more complicated mechanisms than effort reduction. Consumer researchers have prolifically demonstrated that overconsumption is driven by portion sizes, packaging, and even cultural norms (Chandon, 2013; Chandon & Wansink, 2012; Wansink & Chandon, 2014), all of which can serve as a type of default. These cues are powerful enough to induce "mindless" eating whereby people overconsume partially because self-control is never activated or is activated only after caloric needs are met. This suggests that satiety is a psychophysical phenomenon where perceptions of fullness and hunger are regulated by external environmental cues in addition to internal hormonal cues such as glucose levels. As such, consumers are likely to report feeling more satiated when served small portions in small containers than when that same portion is served in a larger container. This important insight suggests that several avenues for reducing caloric intake can be achieved with changes to default serving sizes that induce satiety and bypass the explicit need for self-control or by encouraging self-control before it becomes difficult to activate.

Adherence to cultural norms is just one of many types of defaults that can shape health behaviors. Smoking, for example, has largely been banned in and around public spaces, office buildings, hospitals, stadiums, universities, and even bars and restaurants. In many places, smokers are relegated to specific areas that may be 500 yards or more from buildings. Taken together, these policies invoke a strong cultural norm that smoking is unacceptable. Cultural norms also influence eating behavior. Americans in particular feel compelled to eat everything they have been served, and are unlikely to report feeling satiated until plates and containers are empty (Wansink, Payne, & Chandon, 2007). When cultural norms and market forces combine to push people toward indulgence rather than restraint, as is often the case with "value-sized" meals, free refills, and all you can eat buffets, consumers have a difficult time exercising self-control or even knowing when to stop eating. Recent research, however, suggests that while food marketing efforts are traditionally known for encouraging overconsumption, there is no reason that insights into the processes driving consumption and satiety could not also be effective in promoting healthier nutrition choices (Chandon & Wansink, 2012). In sum, a defining feature of default effects is taking advantage of our propensity to do nothing and simply maintain the status quo, move along the path of least resistance, or follow the herd. Such inertia typically threatens health, but consumer psychology has shown that well-constructed defaults can sometimes leverage laziness into something healthful. An ongoing effort for consumer researchers interested in studying the effects of defaults on health behaviors is to identify the circumstances under which defaults are most effective and where they may be limited or even potentially harmful. If defaults are best in situations that harness inertia, then their power may be concentrated in one-time or infrequent decisions rather than choices that require ongoing action and persistent self-control.

Some attention to any adverse effects of defaults is also warranted. For example, automatic enrollment into prescription refills is a type of default that could improve medication adherence for health conditions such as hypertension that require ongoing therapy. At the same time, any changes in medications or instructions to discontinue a particular drug would result in people having to take action to cancel ongoing prescriptions. Since such action is unlikely, there is some risk that patients could continue to pay for medications they are not using or become confused and continue medications that are no longer necessary. Likewise, we know from the persuasion literature that when encouraging consumers to follow the behaviors of others, others must be behaving well (Cialdini, 1984). If descriptive norms suggest poor adherence to recommended guidelines and people are inclined simply to follow suit, then health outcomes are unlikely to improve using this approach. Finally, some research in changing defaults in eating environments suggests that while making healthy options easier to access works in the short term, people tend to compensate with extra calories later (Wisdom, Downs, & Loewenstein, 2010). Understanding the boundaries of different types of defaults in the complex psychology of consumer health behavior is a crucial direction for future research.

Incentives Matter

Sometimes closing the intention–behavior gap requires substantially more than a change to the physical environment, and the reality may be that defaults and other changes that prod people along can take us only so far. There are situations where it is almost impossible to circumvent the need for action or self-control. In fact, some of society's most perplexing and costly health problems, such as preventable diseases related to tobacco use, obesity, and lack of exercise, may all be representative of these situations.

As an aside, let us imagine for a moment that we were able to use defaults to help at-risk people, by providing automatic enrollment in gym memberships and commercial programs such as Smoke Enders and Weight Watchers. This one-time decision to enroll would undoubtedly be easier and provide some motivational spark, but the real question is how long that would last when people have to confront their cigarette cravings, abstain from foods they love, and spend time on the treadmill day after day. Empirically, the answer to that question can be disheartening. Systematic reviews of commercial weight loss programs in both the United States and the United Kingdom reveal very modest results on weight loss, high attrition rates, and that more than 50 percent of those who did achieve some weight loss during the program gained it back within two years (Truby et al., 2006; Tsai & Wadden, 2005). This suggests that while defaults might be very good at getting people into programs that promote good health, keeping them engaged through the challenges of smoking cessation, better nutrition, and exercise might require an approach that does not rely on inertia.

An increasingly popular approach activating and maintaining self-control in the health domain is the broad use of financial incentives offered to motivate consumers to be healthier. Under the Patient Affordable Care Act of 2010, the government has made provisions for both employers and insurers to promote healthy behavior through the use of financial incentives. These incentives come in the form of discounts on health insurance premiums for engaging in health wellness and screening activities, subsidies for weight loss or smoking cessation programs, discounted gym memberships, or even cash and gifts for achieving or maintaining a healthy weight or blood pressure levels. From a behavioral perspective, this is an attractive way to make healthy behaviors have more tangible and immediately rewarding results.

Empirical research has shown that incentives can work and demonstrate a positive effect in many important domains, such as weight loss (John et al., 2011; Volpp et al., 2008a), smoking cessation (Volpp et al., 2006; Volpp et al., 2009), exercise (Charness & Gneezy, 2009), and medication adherence (Volpp et al., 2008b). Promising results from this growing area of research find that almost all of these very challenging behaviors can be temporarily improved with the use of financial incentives. Some studies have even shown that the effects can last after the financial incentive has stopped, suggesting that rewards can play an important role in helping consumers develop healthier lifestyle habits. From a cost-containment perspective, this could be good news because it suggests that financial incentives could be a short-term measure that has long-term benefits (Charness & Gneezy, 2009; Volpp et al., 2009). Other studies, however, have shown that bad behavior returns soon, if not immediately, after incentives are removed (e.g., John et al., 2011; Volpp et al.,

2008a, 2008b). If financial incentives are effective at changing behavior only so long as they stay in place or require some escalation of payments to keep people motivated, then important policy questions arise about their large-scale economic feasibility (Gneezy, Meier, & Rey-Biel, 2011). Another challenge exists in the self-selection biases among those who choose to take part in incentive programs. If such schemes are attractive only to those who are healthy and have good self-control to begin with, then there is some danger that these systems are ultimately shifting a greater burden of the healthcare costs to those most at risk.

Healthier by Precommitment

In some situations, people can avoid temptation or confront their self-control problems head on, but in others they cannot. Self-control problems can vary across people and situations, which further highlights that there is no one-size-fits-all approach to improving health behaviors. Some people are attracted to incentives that make exercising self-control more immediately beneficial and do quite well with this approach. Others may choose a different approach whereby they acknowledge their difficulty exercising self-control and elect to restrict their environments to avoid procrastination, being tempted, being unable to act on their impulses, and so on (e.g., Ariely & Wertenbroch, 2002). The insight that people are sophisticated about their self-control problems (O'Donoghue & Rabin, 1999, 2001) creates a promising approach to health interventions. It suggests that consumers will welcome marketplace opportunities to restrict their behaviors even if that means forgoing discounts and paying penalties. The notion that consumers will pay more to avoid the temptation that comes with an abundance of vices goes against marketplace norms and rational economics, both of which assume that consumers are only looking to maximize value. From a psychological perspective, this behavior makes more sense and signals that self-aware consumers recognize the gap between their intentions and behaviors and search for ways to close them. Precommitment strategies can range from simple rules, such as not keeping ice cream in the house, to more complex, financially binding contracts that require self-funded monetary deposits that cannot be reclaimed without biometric verification that a health goal, such as a healthy body mass index (BMI), has been achieved.

These commitment devices are colloquially referred to as Ulysses Contracts in reference to Homer's hero (1991), who instructed his crew to tie him to the mast of his ship so that he could not be lured into the sea by the call of the sirens. Ulysses wanted to hear their enchanting song, but not be able to act on his impulses to leap into the water, where he would certainly drown. Incidentally, while Ulysses wanted to be tied to the mast, he also instructed his crew to stuff wax in their ears and go below deck so they could not even hear, and thus not be tempted by, the sirens. Both approaches were effective and elegantly illustrate that self-control can be achieved by creating environments that limit temptation or restrict impulsive behavior.

The commercial success of commitment devices, both light and restrictive, shows some empirical promise. First, evidence suggests that some consumers spontaneously restrict their environments, such as when they prefer to pay a premium for smaller packages of vice goods, such as cigarettes, rather than receive a bulk discount (Wertenbroch, 1998). Others have shown that simply prompting people to downsize portions in a fast-food setting is effective and significantly reduces caloric intake, even if the smaller portions are not discounted (Schwartz, Riis, Elbel, & Ariely, 2012). Yet another study found that smokers who committed to a six-month financial deposit contract, where they put their own money on the line, had significantly lower smoking rates one year later than smokers who did not precommit (Giné, Karlan, & Zinman, 2010; see also Donatelle et al., 2004).

Finally, research has shown that precommitment can be successfully implemented on a large-scale basis (Schwartz et al., 2014). Members of a large health rewards program engaged in a six-month commitment contract to increase the percentage of healthy foods purchased at the grocery store. Those who met the goal kept their 25 percent grocery discount, while those who did not forfeited their savings for that month. The results showed a significant increase in healthy food purchases among those who precommitted (relative to a control group who could not make a financially binding commitment and those who declined to precommit) for each of the six months of the study and for a full six months after the penalty was removed (Mochon et al., 2015). Taken together, these results suggest that self-aware consumers have an appetite for incentive designs that help them restrict their impulses, even if there is no financial reward and only the threat of a loss.

Improving health outcomes with defaults, financial incentives, and commitment devices that circumvent self-control, or make it easier to activate and maintain, is a promising and exciting area of research. Many tests of behavior in both the lab and the field have now shown that these approaches can effectively improve targeted behaviors, and can even be combined for greater effect. Less attention, however, has been paid to their scalability and any potential negative side-effects of targeting self-control through the use of financial incentives. Crucial issues such as these arise as theoretical insights from the laboratory and the results of small-scale studies are tested in the much more dynamic marketplace. One concern with approaches that explicitly target self-control is that people will become depleted in one domain, such as eating, only to be indulgent in another, such as exercise. If people can be encouraged to eat healthier, but as a result stop exercising, then the overall impact of nutrition interventions on self-control in eating may be diminished. Evidence of such balancing behaviors in the field is mixed, but promising in that while some studies show compensation (Wisdom, Downs, & Loewenstein, 2010), others show no evidence of compensation (Schwartz et al., 2012) and even some positive spillover where better nutrition behavior leads to more exercise

(Mochon et al., 2015). Future research will continue to assess the net impact of measures that activate and maintain self-control and how best to bring them to scale in large insurance schemes.

Consumers, Health Technology, and Privacy

A great place to take the pulse of today's health consumer is the Internet. Specifically, much can be learned from the app marketplaces, where more than 2,500 health and fitness apps are available to Apple (www.apple.com/iphone-5s/app-store/) and Android smart phone users (www.appbrain.com). Some apps are practically oriented and provide consumers with immediate information about risks, symptoms, treatments, and medication side-effects (including costs). Others help people manage doctors' appointments, provide medication and refill reminders, plan exercise routes, and even find a low-calorie meals or yoga classes within a five-minute walk. Many more are dedicated to making the daily challenge of healthcare more fun by offering consumers feedback on their progress toward achieving health goals, giving points or financial rewards, and offering opportunities to challenge their friends and family members also to meet their goals.

A perfunctory scan of these markets reveals how much insight from the behavioral sciences has been incorporated into health and fitness apps. For the sophisticated consumer, there are even commitment devices where users can designate their forfeited funds to friends, family, charities, or even "anti-charities" if they are concerned that donating to a charity they love is too much of a reward for not going to the gym (e.g., www.stickk.com). A spate of new wearable monitoring devices can tell people they were not active enough, slept poorly, or forgot to take their medication. The boom in health- and fitness-related technology, and its impact on improving health behaviors and outcomes, creates many exciting avenues of research for consumer psychologists.

It is worthwhile to note that as technology advances and tries to make it easier to close the intention–behavior gap and makes it more fun to be healthy in our everyday lives, there is a potential downside to divulging so much information. Consumers may not be aware that their Internet search and shopping behaviors and habits are being tracked or the extent to which this information is available to – and can be used by – advertisers, insurers, or employers (Singer, 2014). Under the Health Insurance Portability and Accountability Act (1996), or HIPPA, American consumers have largely been protected from discrimination on the basis of medical history by restrictions to the access and use of private and individually identifiable health information, but these protections might not hold when people implicitly or explicitly volunteer information about their consumption behaviors, health habits, or medical problems. The extent to which consumers are willing to trade off privacy for convenience and savings has begun to pique the interest of consumer welfare advocates and policy makers and is also likely to have an important impact on our psychological understanding of how consumers navigate the medical marketplace.

In closing, decades of research show us that good health decisions start with awareness and perceived risks, move to choices about what trade-offs are necessary to mitigate those risks, and then require some action that prevents poor health outcomes. There are many obstacles along the way, and well-intentioned consumers often fail to align their healthy attitudes with their actual behaviors. This chapter outlines what psychology has already learned about each stage and where more research is needed to help consumers close the intention–behavior gap.

References

Affordable Care Act. (2010). Patient Protection and Affordable Care Act. *Public Law* (111–148).

Ajzen, I. (1985). From intentions to actions: A theory of planned behavior. In *Action Control: From Cognition to Behavior* (pp. 11–39). Heidelberg, Germany: Springer.

Ajzen, I. (1991). The theory of planned behavior. *Organizational Behavior and Human Decision Processes, 50*(2), 179–211.

American Lung Association (n.d.). Lung cancer fact sheet. Retrieved June 22, 2014, from www.lung.org/lung-disease/lung-cancer/resources/facts-figures/lung-cancer-fact-sheet.html.

Apple (n.d.). Apple – iPhone 5s – App Store. Retrieved June 30, 2014, from www.apple.com/iphone-5s/app-store/.

Ariely, D., & Wertenbroch, K. (2002). Procrastination, deadlines, and performance: Self-control by precommitment. *Psychological Science, 13*(3), 219–224.

Banks, S. M., Salovey, P., Greener, S., Rothman, A. J., Moyer, A., Beauvais, J., & Epel, E. (1995). The effects of message framing on mammography utilization. *Health Psychology, 14*(2), 178–184.

Baron, J., & Spranca, M. (1997). Protected values. *Organizational Behavior and Human Decision Processes, 70*(1), 1–16.

Bartels, D. M., & Rips, L. J. (2010). Psychological connectedness and intertemporal choice. *Journal of Experimental Psychology: General, 139*(1), 49–69.

Baumeister, R. F., Bratslavsky, E., Muraven, M., & Tice, D. M. (1998). Ego depletion: Is the active self a limited resource? *Journal of Personality and Social Psychology, 74*(5), 1252–1265.

Becker, M. H. (1974). *The Health Belief Model and Personal Health Behavior*. Thorofare, NJ: C. B. Slack.

Brewer, N. T., Chapman, G. B., Gibbons, F. X., Gerrard, M., McCaul, K. D., & Weinstein, N. D. (2007). Meta-analysis of the relationship between risk perception and health behavior: The example of vaccination. *Health Psychology, 26*(2), 136.

Brewer, N. T., Chapman, G. B., Schwartz, J. A., & Bergus, G. R. (2007). The influence of irrelevant anchors on the judgments and choices of doctors and patients. *Medical Decision Making, 27*(2), 203–211.

Cain, D. M., & Detsky, A. S. (2008). Everyone's a little bit biased (even physicians). *Journal of American Medical Association, 299*(24), 2893–2895.

Campbell, M. C. (1999). Perceptions of price unfairness: Antecedents and consequences. *Journal of Marketing Research, 36*(2), 187–199.

CDC (Centers for Disease Control and Prevention). (2014a). Adult cigarette smoking in the United States: Current estimates. February 14. Retrieved June 21, 2014, from www.cdc.gov/tobacco/data_statistics/fact_sheets/adult_data/cig_smoking/.

CDC (Centers for Disease Control and Prevention). (2014b). Adult obesity facts. March 28. Retrieved June 28, 2014, from www.cdc.gov/obesity/data/adult.html.

Chandon, Pierre (2013). How package design and packaged-based marketing claims lead to overeating. *Applied Economic Perspectives and Policy, 35*(1), 7–31.

Chandon, P., & Wansink, B. (2012). Does food marketing need to make us fat? A review and solutions. *Nutrition Reviews, 70*(10), 571–593.

Chapman, G. B. (1998). Sooner or later: The psychology of intertemporal choice. *Psychology of Learning and Motivation, 38*, 83–113.

Chapman, G. B, Li, M., Colby, H., & Yoon, H. (2010). Opting in versus opting out of influenza vaccination. *Journal of the American Medical Association, 304*(1), 43–44.

Charness, G., & Gneezy, U. (2009). Incentives to exercise. *Econometrica, 77*(3), 909–931.

Cialdini, R. B. (1984). *Influence*. New York: Morrow.

Cutler, D. M., Glaeser, E. L., & Shapiro, J. M. (2003). Why have Americans become more obese? *Journal of Economic Perspectives, 17*(3), 93–118.

Donatelle, R. J., Hudson, D., Dobie, S., Goodall, A., Hunsberger, M., & Oswald, K. (2004). Incentives in smoking cessation: Status of the field and implications for research and practice with pregnant smokers. *Nicotine & Tobacco Research, 6*(Supp 2) 163–179.

Dreze, X., Hoch, S. J., & Purk, M. E. (1995). Shelf management and space elasticity. *Journal of Retailing, 70*(4), 301–326.

Drummond, M., & Towse, A. (2012). Is it time to reconsider the role of patient co-payments for pharmaceuticals in Europe? *European Journal of Health Economics, 13*(1), 1–5.

Emanuel, E., Tanden, N., Altman, S., Armstrong, S., Berwick, D., de Brantes, F., & Spiro, T. (2012). A systemic approach to containing health care spending. *New England Journal of Medicine, 367*(10), 949–954.

Finkelstein, E. A., DiBonaventura, M. D., Burgess, S. M., & Hale, B. C. (2010). The costs of obesity in the workplace. *Journal of Occupational and Environmental Medicine, 52*(10), 971–76.

Finkelstein, E. A., Trogdon, J. G., Cohen, J. W., & Dietz, W. (2009). Annual medical spending attributable to obesity: Payer and service-specific estimates. *Health Affairs, 28*(5), 822–831.

Fishbein, M., & Ajzen, I. (1975). *Belief, Attitude, Intention, and Behavior: An introduction to Theory and Research*. Reading, MA: Addison-Wesley.

Fiske, A. P. (1992). The four elementary forms of sociality: Framework for a unified theory of social relations. *Psychological Review, 99*, 689–723.

Fiske, A. P., & Tetlock, P. E. (1997). Taboo trade-offs: Reactions to transactions that transgress the spheres of justice. *Political Psychology, 18*(2), 255–297.

Fraeyman, J., Verbelen, M., Hens, N., Van Hal, G., De Loof, H., & Beutels, P. (2013). Evolutions in both co-payment and generic market share for common medication in the Belgian Reference Pricing System. *Applied Health Economics and Health Policy, 11*(5), 543–552.

Frederick, S., Loewenstein, G., & O'Donoghue, T. (2002). Time discounting and time preference: A critical review. *Journal of Economic Literature, 40*(2), 351–401.

Giné, X., Karlan, D., & Zinman, J. (2010). Put your money where your butt is: A commitment contract for smoking cessation. *American Economic Journal: Applied Economics, 2*(4), 213–235.

Gneezy, U., Meier, S., & Rey-Biel, P. (2011). When and why incentives (don't) work to modify behavior. *Journal of Economic Perspectives, 25*(4), 191–209.

Goldman, D. P., Joyce, G. F., & Zheng, Y. (2007). Prescription drug cost sharing: Associations with medication and medical utilization and spending and health. *Journal of the American Medical Association, 298*(1), 61–69.

Hagger, M. S., Wood, C., Stiff, C., & Chatzisarantis, N. L. D. (2010). Ego-depletion and the strength model of self-control: A meta-analysis. *Psychological Bulletin, 136*, 495–525.

Health Care Cost Institute (n.d.). Spending on prescriptions in 2011. Retrieved June 30, 2014, from www.healthcostinstitute.org/files/HCCI_IB4_Prescriptions.pdf.

Health Insurance Portability and Accountability Act. (1996). *Public Law* (104–191).

Hoadley, J., Summer, L., Hargrave, E., & Cubanski, J. (2013). *Medicare Part D prescription drug plans: The marketplace in 2013 and key trends, 2006–2013.* Menlo Park, CA: Henry J. Kaiser Family Foundation. Retrieved June 24, 2014, from http://kff.org/medicare/issue-brief/medicare-part-d-prescription-drug-plans-the-marketplace-in-2013-and-key-trends-2006-2013/.

Homer. (1991). *The Iliad.* (B. Knox, ed. R. Fagles, trans.) New York: Penguin Classics.

John, L. K., Loewenstein, G., Troxel, A. B., Norton, L., Fassbender, J. E., & Volpp, K. G. (2011). Financial incentives for extended weight loss: A randomized, controlled trial. *Journal of General Internal Medicine, 26*(6), 621–626.

Johnson, E. J., & Goldstein, D. (2003). Do defaults save lives? *Science, 302*(5649), 1338–1339.

Kahn, B. E., & Luce, M. F. (2003). Understanding high-stakes consumer decisions: Mammography adherence following false-alarm test results. *Marketing Science, 22*(3), 393–410.

Kamenica, E., Naclerio, R., & Malani, A. (2013). Advertisements impact the physiological efficacy of a branded drug. *Proceedings of the National Academy of Sciences, 110*(32), 12931–12935.

Keller, P. A., & Block, L. G. (1995). When to accentuate the negative: The effects of perceived efficacy and message framing on intentions to perform a health-related behavior. *Journal of Marketing Research, 32*(2), 192–203.

Keller, P. A., & Block, L. G. (1996). Increasing the persuasiveness of fear appeals: The effect of arousal and elaboration. *Journal of Consumer Research, 22*(4), 448–459.

Kunda, Z. (1990). The case for motivated reasoning. *Psychological Bulletin, 108*(3), 480.

Leventhal, H., Singer, R., & Jones, S. (1965). Effects of fear and specificity of recommendation upon attitudes and behavior. *Journal of Personality and Social Psychology, 2*(1), 20.

Loewenstein, G., & Prelec, D. (1992). Anomalies in intertemporal choice: Evidence and an interpretation. *Quarterly Journal of Economics, 107*, 573–597.

Luce, M. F. (1998). Choosing to avoid: Coping with negatively emotion-laden consumer decisions. *Journal of Consumer Research, 24*(4), 409–433.

Luce, M. F. (2005). Decision making as coping. *Health Psychology, 24*(4), 23.

Luce, M. F., Bettman, J. R., & Payne, J. W. (1997). Choice processing in emotionally difficult decisions. *Journal of Experimental Psychology: Learning, Memory, and Cognition, 23*(2), 384–405.

Luce, M. F., & Kahn, B. E. (1999). Avoidance or vigilance? The psychology of false-positive test results. *Journal of Consumer Research, 26*(3), 242–259.

Luce, M. F., Payne, J. W., & Bettman, J. R. (1999). Emotional trade-off difficulty and choice. *Journal of Marketing Research, 36*(2), 143.

Malenka, D. J., Baron, J. A., Johansen, S., Wahrenberger, J. W., & Ross, J. M. (1993). The framing effect of relative and absolute risk. *Journal of General Internal Medicine, 8*(10), 543–548.

Manning, W. G., Newhouse, J. P., Duan, N., Keeler, E. B., & Leibowitz, A. (1987). Health insurance and the demand for medical care: Evidence from a randomized experiment. *American Economic Review, 77*, 251–277.

McBride, C. M., Emmons, K. M., & Lipkus, I. M. (2003). Understanding the potential of teachable moments: The case of smoking cessation. *Health Education Research, 18*(2), 156–170.

McGraw, A. P., Schwartz, J. A., & Tetlock, P. E. (2012). From the commercial to the communal: Reframing taboo trade-offs in religious and pharmaceutical marketing. *Journal of Consumer Research, 39*(1), 157–173.

McGraw, A. P., & Tetlock, P. (2005). Taboo trade-offs, relational framing, and the acceptability of exchanges. *Journal of Consumer Psychology, 15*(1), 2–15.

Menon, G., Block, L. G., & Ramanathan, S. (2002). We're at as much risk as we are led to believe: Effects of message cues on judgments of health risk. *Journal of Consumer Research, 28*(4), 533–549.

Menon, G., Raghubir, P., & Agrawal, N. (2008). Health risk perceptions and consumer psychology. In C. P. Haugtveldt, P. Herr, & F. Kardes (eds.), *Handbook of Consumer Psychology* (pp. 981–1010). New York and London: Lawrence Erlbaum Associates.

Metcalfe, J., & Mischel, W. (1999). A hot/cool-system analysis of delay of gratification: Dynamics of willpower. *Psychological Review, 106*(1), 3–19.

Mochon, D., Schwartz, J., Maroba, J., Patel, D., & Ariely, D. (2015). Gain without pain: The extended effects of a behavioral health intervention. Unpublished manuscript, Tulane University.

Moffitt, T. E., Arseneault, L., Belsky, D., Dickson, N., Hancox, R. J., Harrington, H., Caspi, A., et al. (2011). A gradient of childhood self-control predicts health, wealth, and public safety. *Proceedings of the National Academy of Sciences, 108*(7), 2693–2698.

Monroe, K. B., & Krishnan, R. (1985). The effect of price on subjective product evaluations. In J. Jacoby & J. C. Olson (eds.), *Perceived Quality: How Consumers View Stores and Merchandise* (pp. 209–232). Lexington, MA: LexingtonBooks.

Muraven, M., & Baumeister, R. F. (2000). Self-regulation and depletion of limited resources: Does self-control resemble a muscle? *Psychological Bulletin, 126*(2), 247.

O'Donoghue, T., & Rabin, M. (1999). Doing it now or later. *American Economic Review, 89*(1), 103–124.

O'Donoghue, T., & Rabin, M. (2001). Choice and procrastination. *Quarterly Journal of Economics, 116*(1), 121–60.

Ogden, C. L., Carroll, M. D., Kit, B. K., & Flegal, K. M. (2014). Prevalence of childhood and adult obesity in the United States, 2011–2012. *Journal of the American Medical Association, 311*(8), 806–814.

Raghubir, P., & Menon, G. (1998). AIDS and me, never the twain shall meet: The effects of information accessibility on judgments of risk and advertising effectiveness. *Journal of Consumer Research, 25*(1), 52–63.

Raghunathan, R., & Trope, Y. (2002). Walking the tightrope between feeling good and being accurate: Mood as a resource in processing persuasive messages. *Journal of Personality and Social Psychology, 83*(3), 510–525.

Rao, A. R. (2005). The quality of price as a quality cue. *Journal of Marketing Research, 42*(4), 401–405.

Rao, A. R., & Monroe, K. B. (1988). The moderating effect of prior knowledge on cue utilization in product evaluations. *Journal of Consumer Research, 15*(2), 253–264.

Rao, A. R., & Monroe, K. B. (1989). The effect of price, brand name, and store name on buyers' perceptions of product quality: An integrative review. *Journal of Marketing Research, 26*(3), 351–357.

Redelmeier, D. A., & Shafir, E. (1995). Medical decision making in situations that offer multiple alternatives. *Journal of the American Medical Association, 273* (4), 302–305.

Ritov, I., & Baron, J. (1999). Protected values and omission bias. *Organizational Behavior and Human Decision Processes, 79*(2), 79–94.

Rothman, A. J., & Salovey, P. (1997). Shaping perceptions to motivate healthy behavior: The role of message framing. *Psychological Bulletin, 121*(1), 3.

Ruiter, R. A., Abraha M. C., & Kok, G. (2001). Scary warnings and rational precautions: A review of the psychology of fear appeals. *Psychology and Health, 16*(6), 613–630.

Samper, A., & Schwartz, J. A. (2012). Price inferences for sacred versus secular goods: Changing the price of medicine influences perceived health risk. *Journal of Consumer Research, 39*(6), 1343–1358.

Samuelson, W., & Zeckhauser, R. (1988). Status quo bias in decision making. *Journal of Risk and Uncertainty, 1*(1), 7–59.

Schwartz, J. A., & Chapman, G. B. (1999). Are more options always better? The attraction effect in physicians' decisions about medications. *Medical Decision Making, 19*(3), 315–323.

Schwartz, J., Luce, M. F., & Ariely, D. (2011). Are consumers too trusting? The effects of relationships with expert advisers. *Journal of Marketing Research, 48*, S163–S174.

Schwartz, J., Mochon, D., Wyper, L., Maroba, J., Patel, D., & Ariely, D. (2014). Healthier by precommitment. *Psychological Science, 25*, 538–546.

Schwartz, J., Riis, J., Elbel, B., & Ariely, D. (2012). Inviting consumers to downsize fast-food portions significantly reduces calorie consumption. *Health Affairs, 31*(2), 399–407.

Shiv, B., Carmon, Z., & Ariely, D. (2005). Placebo effects of marketing actions: Consumers may get what they pay for. *Journal of Marketing Research, 42*(4), 383–393.

Shrank, W. H., Choudhry, N. K., Agnew-Blais, J., Federman, A. D., Liberman, J. N., Liu, J., Fischer, M. A., et al. (2010). State generic substitution laws can lower drug outlays under Medicaid. *Health Affairs, 29*(7), 1383–1390.

Shrank, W. H., Cox, E. R., Fischer, M. A., Mehta, J., & Choudhry, N. K. (2009). Patients' perceptions of generic medications. *Health Affairs, 28*(2), 546–556.

Singer, N. (2014). When a health plan knows how you shop. *New York Times*, June 28. Retrieved June 29, 2014, from www.nytimes.com/2014/06/29/technology/when-a-health-plan-knows-how-you-shop.html?hp&action=click&pgtype=Homepage&version=HpSumSmallMediaHigh&module=second-column-region®ion=top-news&WT.nav=top-news&_r=0.

Tetlock, P. E. (2003). Thinking the unthinkable: Sacred values and taboo cognitions. *Trends in Cognitive Sciences, 7*(7), 320–324.

stickK (n.d.). Who's stickKing? Change starts now. Retrieved June 30, 2014, from www.stickk.com.

Tetlock, P. E., Kristel, O. V., Elson, S. B., Green, M. C., & Lerner, J. S. (2000). The psychology of the unthinkable: Taboo trade-offs, forbidden base rates, and heretical counterfactuals. *Journal of Personality and Social Psychology, 78*(5), 853.

Thaler, R. H., & Sunstein, C. R. (2008). *Nudge: Improving Decisions about Health, Wealth, and Happiness*. New Haven, CT: Yale University Press.

Thorndike, A. N., Sonnenberg, L., Riis, J., Barraclough, S., & Levy, D. E. (2012). A 2-phase labeling and choice architecture intervention to improve healthy food and beverage choices. *American Journal of Public Health, 102*(3), 527–533.

Truby, H., Baic, S., DeLooy, A., Fox, K. R., Livingstone, M. B. E., Logan, C. M., Millward, D. J., et al. (2006). Randomised controlled trial of four commercial weight loss programmes in the UK: Initial findings from the BBC "diet trials." *British Medical Journal, 332*(7553), 1309–1314.

Tsai, A. G., & Wadden, T. A. (2005). Systematic review: An evaluation of major commercial weight loss programs in the United States. *Annals of Internal Medicine, 142*(1), 56–66.

Tversky, A., & Kahneman, D. (1986). Rational choice and the framing of decisions. *Journal of Business, 59*(4), 251–278.

U.S. Preventive Services Task Force. (2009). Screening for breast cancer: US Preventive Services Task Force recommendation statement. *Annals of Internal Medicine, 151*(10), 716–726.

Volpp, K. G., John, L. K., Troxel, A. B., Norton, L., Fassbender, J., & Loewenstein, G. (2008a). Financial incentive–based approaches for weight loss. *Journal of the American Medical Association, 300*, 2631–2637

Volpp, K. G., Levy, A. G., Asch, D. A., Berlin, J. A., Murphy, J. J., Gomez, A., Lerman, C., et al. (2006). A randomized controlled trial of financial incentives for smoking cessation. *Cancer Epidemiology Biomarkers & Prevention, 15*, 12–18.

Volpp, K.G., Loewenstein, G., Troxel, A. B., Doshi, J., Price, M., Laskin, M., & Kimmel, S. E. (2008b). A test of financial incentives to improve warfarin adherence. *Biomedical Central Health Services Research, 8*(1), 272.

Volpp, K. G., Troxel, A. B., Pauly, M. V., Glick, H. A., Puig, A., Asch, D. A., DeGuzman, J., et al. (2009). A randomized, controlled trial of financial incentives for smoking cessation. *New England Journal of Medicine, 360*(7), 699–709.

Vosgerau, J. (2010). How prevalent is wishful thinking? Misattribution of arousal causes optimism and pessimism in subjective probabilities. *Journal of Experimental Psychology: General, 139*(1), 32.

Waber, R. L., Shiv, B., Carmon, Z., & Ariely, D. (2008). Commercial features of placebo and therapeutic efficacy. *Journal of the American Medical Association, 299*(9), 1016–1017.

Wansink, B. (2004). Environmental factors that increase the food intake and consumption volume of unknowing consumers. *Annual Review Nutrition, 24*, 455–479.

Wansink, B., & Chandon, P. (2014). Slim by design: Redirecting the accidental drivers of mindless overeating. *Journal of Consumer Psychology, 24*(3), 413–431.

Wansink, B., Payne, C. R., & Chandon, P. (2007). Internal and external cues of meal cessation: The French paradox redux? *Obesity, 15*(12), 2920–2924.

Webb, T. L., & Sheeran, P. (2006). Does changing behavioral intentions engender behavior change? A meta-analysis of the experimental evidence. *Psychological Bulletin, 132*(2), 249–268.

Weinstein, N. D. (1982). Unrealistic optimism about susceptibility to health problems. *Journal of Behavioral Medicine, 5*(4), 441–460.

Weinstein, N. D. (1984). Why it won't happen to me: Perceptions of risk factors and susceptibility. *Health Psychology, 3*(5), 431.

Wertenbroch, K. (1998). Consumption self-control by rationing purchase quantities of virtue and vice. *Marketing Science, 17*(4), 317–337.

Wisdom, J., Downs, J. S., & Loewenstein, G. (2010). Promoting healthy choices: Information versus convenience. *American Economic Journal: Applied Economics, 2*(2), 164–178.

25 Social Class and Scarcity

Understanding Consumers Who Have Less

Anuj K. Shah

More than 4 billion people in the world earn less than $10 a day (World Bank, 2014). And despite having limited funds, the world's poor often have to pay more for various goods and services. Grocery staples might be 20 percent more expensive in poor communities, credit can be more than 5,000 percent more costly, and cashing paychecks generates enough fees to support billion dollar businesses (Mendel, 2005; Prahalad & Hammond, 2002; Talukdar, 2008). With such a large swath of the population facing such striking challenges, this raises the question of how consumers think and decide when resources are scarce. Of course, social scientists have studied poverty for as long as there have been social sciences, but our understanding of human behavior in these contexts has largely been shaped by work in economics, sociology, anthropology, and political science. Psychologists and decision-making researchers have only more recently begun a systematic study of how poverty and other conditions of scarcity affect behavior.

Initially, psychological and behavioral economic theories responded to more standard economic views of poverty. One standard view suggested that the poor adapted to their environment over time and behaved optimally or rationally within its constraints. But the behavioral view highlighted how poor individuals make the same kinds of mistakes and exhibit the same biases that wealthy individuals do (Bertrand, Mullainathan, & Shafir, 2006). This approach showed how decision making in the context of poverty could be improved with nudges such as smart defaults, channel factors, and even interventions that considered a person's identity. This approach still overlooked an important fact: it assumed that the psychology of scarcity was no different from the psychology of abundance. The heuristics and biases were the same, but simply more costly for the poor.

However, recent research suggests that scarcity creates its own psychology and mindset (Mullainathan & Shafir, 2013). A better understanding of how this mindset plays out in consumer contexts has the potential to improve consumer welfare. Further, because psychological research in this area is still young, there remain many open questions. This chapter describes the questions being asked, those that remain, and the frameworks being developed to answer those questions.

The first section of this chapter focuses on how the fundamental experience of scarcity – having too few resources to meet all of one's needs – has profound consequences for how people think and decide. The second section takes a broader view by considering the psychology of social class that emerges as poor individuals navigate a unique set of social roles and expectations. Each section describes the methods used to study these questions and then covers a series of empirical results on how cognition and behavior change under various forms of scarcity. Finally, this chapter concludes with an eye to the many unanswered questions in this domain and promising avenues for future consumer research, including interventions that can improve decision making in the context of poverty.

The Scarcity Mindset

To understand the scarcity mindset, first imagine how we manage expenses when resources are abundant. In this case, basic expenses such as groceries and utility bills do not require much attention, effort, or creativity to handle. Instead, these expenses come and go and rarely linger on the mind. Under scarcity, though, the world has a different texture. These expenses are no longer easily dispatched. Instead, each one becomes urgent and pressing and difficult to manage. Groceries, utility bills, and rent payments loom larger, and they capture our attention. Because of this, we focus more on how to solve these problems. That is, the scarcity mindset essentially consists of greater focus (Mullainathan & Shafir, 2013; Shah, Mullainathan, & Shafir, 2012).

This section will first describe how scarcity-induced focus cascades through behavior. Then, it will also explore how scarcity affects psychological and physiological well-being and broader social judgments as well. First, however, to better understand the empirical findings that follow, it is worth noting the methods used to study the scarcity mindset.

Empirical Approaches

Perhaps the most ecologically valid approach to studying scarcity consists of testing how fluctuations or cross-sectional differences in resources (e.g., income, caloric intake) affect behavior (e.g., Binkley & Bejnarowicz, 2003; Goldin & Homonoff, 2013; Hall, 2008; Mani, Mullainathan, Shafir, & Zhao, 2013; Shah, Shafir, & Mullainathan, 2015). However, this approach makes it difficult to establish causality. To remedy this issue, researchers have developed various techniques for creating scarcity in the lab. One approach endows participants with varying levels of resources to manage. Participants' cognition and behavior with those resources can then be measured (Shah, Mullainathan, & Shafir, 2012; Spiller, 2011).

It is also possible to prime a scarcity mindset more broadly. For example, some work has demonstrated that episodic recall of times when people feel financially deprived can activate the scarcity mindset (Sharma & Alter, 2012). More indirect primes might simply ask people how they would navigate an easy or difficult financial situation, where the latter is more likely to induce feelings of scarcity

(Mani et al., 2013). Importantly, many of these approaches show that relative or perceived scarcity and objective scarcity similarly shape behavior.

Scarcity and Focus

To appreciate just how general the relationship between scarcity and focus is, first consider a clever experiment done in a context far removed from that of poverty. Specifically, consider how thirst affects where our mind focuses. Aarts, Dijksterhuis, and De Vries (2001) had participants consume either salty treats (to induce thirst) or control treats that would not create thirst. Participants then completed a lexical decision task in which some words were drinking-related (e.g., juice, soda) and some were not (e.g., chair, table). Thirsty participants were significantly quicker to recognize drinking-related words. These results show how unmet needs capture the mind and elicit greater focus when people face scarcity. Even more compelling is the fact that there are analogues of this phenomenon when people are short on money. For example, Mullainathan and Shafir (2013) asked Boston commuters the starting fare on a taximeter. Lower-income respondents answered correctly more than 30 percent of the time, whereas wealthier participants were correct only 12 percent of the time. Similarly, poorer participants exiting a supermarket are better able to name the prices of the items that they just purchased than are wealthier participants. And this greater focus also makes low-income participants less susceptible to certain pricing strategies. In supermarkets, for instance, some products get more expensive when they are bought in bulk (i.e., there is a "quantity surcharge"). Of course, most consumers remain unaware of this pricing trick, instead expecting that they are saving money when they buy larger quantities. However, poorer consumers are less susceptible to quantity surcharges (Binkley & Bejnarowicz, 2003). Similarly, poorer consumers are less influenced by "hidden" taxes that are not included in the posted price (Goldin & Homonoff, 2013).

These findings also generalize to subjective feelings of scarcity. In one study, for instance, participants were asked to recall a time when they felt financially worse (or better) off than their peers. They then completed a visual discrimination task where they had to identify the stimulus that was least prevalent in an array. The stimuli in the discrimination task were unrelated to the experience of financial deprivation. Still, participants who felt subjectively deprived were better able to identify the scarce stimuli. These results are notable because they show that when resources are limited, people might focus on scarcity more generally rather than just on unmet needs or the scarce resource itself (Sharma & Alter, 2012).

Consequences of Scarcity-Induced Focus

As consumers shift their focus under scarcity, this can similarly alter their preferences. Sharma and Alter (2012) followed up the preceding findings to test whether participants experiencing financial deprivation might actually prefer less-available items to mitigate feelings of deprivation. Participants first indicated their subjective financial well-being across a series of questions. They were then given the opportunity to consume M&Ms. One color of M&Ms was relatively abundant, while another color of M&Ms was scarce. Participants who felt financially deprived consumed a larger proportion of the scarce M&Ms than did participants who felt financially well off. Thus, under scarcity, it seems that attention shifts and preferences follow attention.

Importantly, because scarcity elicits greater focus and engagement on some problems and some needs, people will necessarily neglect other demands on their budget (Shah, Mullainathan, & Shafir, 2012). By focusing intently on how to deal with a utility bill, we might neglect or forget about a credit card payment coming due. Indeed, attentional neglect of this sort often occurs in low-income settings. Low-income homeowners might neglect routine maintenance as they instead focus on more pressing needs. Neglected, these routine repairs become major projects later on (Acquaye, 2011).

Lab experiments highlight this tension more clearly. In one study, participants played a video game called Angry Blueberries, in which they had to shoot blueberries at waffles scattered throughout each round (Shah, Mullainathan, & Shafir, 2012). Participants were either given a small number of blueberries per round (i.e., "poor participants") or they were given a large number of blueberries (i.e., "rich participants"). Some participants could use only the blueberries allotted per round. Other participants could "borrow" blueberries from future rounds at interest, meaning they would have fewer blueberries for future rounds. Interestingly, poor participants spent more time aiming each shot than did rich participants. That is, they were more focused. They also used their blueberries more efficiently, earning more points per shot than did rich participants. Critically, however, this increase in focus on the current round came at a cost down the road. When allowed to borrow, poor participants borrowed significantly more blueberries from future rounds than did rich participants. As a result, poor participants overborrowed, earning fewer points when they had the flexibility to borrow than when they could not borrow. Further, this overborrowing among the poor seemed to have been driven by their increased focus. When poor participants spent more time aiming each shot on a given around (i.e., were more focused), they borrowed significantly more from future rounds.

This increase in focus also taxes cognitive capacity and mental bandwidth. In a seminal study, participants were recruited while in a shopping mall to complete several cognitive tasks (Mani et al., 2013). Some of these tasks measured fluid intelligence (e.g., Raven's Progressive Matrices), while others measured cognitive control (e.g., Hearts and Flowers). Before participants completed these tasks, they were asked to imagine that their car suddenly needed to be repaired. Some participants imagined that the repair would be relatively inexpensive. Other participants imagined that the repair would constitute a significant cost. Participants thought aloud about how they would handle this expense. They then completed the cognitive tasks. High-income participants performed equally well on the cognitive measures regardless of whether they had imagined a small expense or a large expense. And when low-income participants considered the small expense, they were hardly different from wealthier participants. But when they considered the large expense, low-income participants performed significantly worse on the subsequent cognitive tasks. The greater focus required from them had the side-effect of reducing their mental bandwidth. These bandwidth taxes are even evident when people are not told to explicitly think about different expenses. For example, sugar cane farmers in India show diminished mental bandwidth just before they harvest their crop (i.e., financially lean times) as opposed to after the harvest (i.e., relatively abundant times).

It is also worth noting how these results might shift the conversation about why the poor focus too much on some problems, borrow too much from the future, and seem to have limited bandwidth. While some have argued that all of these problems can be attributed to some personal failing that perpetuates conditions of scarcity, the preceding studies clearly suggest that the causal arrow can run in the opposite direction: scarcity leads to these cognitions and behaviors (Mullainathan & Shafir, 2013).

The Nature of Scarcity-Induced Focus

The preceding studies simply suggest that scarcity elicits greater focus. But a growing body of research helps unpack the nature of this focus in more detail. While consumers do not usually think about opportunity costs unless prompted (Frederick et al., 2009), the scarcity mindset leads people to think more carefully about trade-offs and opportunity costs. As mentioned previously, scarcity necessarily means that competing expenses and unmet needs will accumulate and linger on the mind. As a result, scarcity will provide many accessible comparisons that will frame the value of an item. For example, the cost of a utility bill will be measured not just in dollars or cents, but also in terms of how it compares to monthly fuel expenses or school fees. To demonstrate how scarcity leads people to consider opportunity costs, Spiller (2011) had participants complete a shopping task where they had several "days" during which they could buy items. If participants spent too much money on one day, then they would have less money for shopping on future days. Participants could also preview the products available on future days if they wished. That is, participants could consider the opportunity cost of spending money today (by attending to what would be available in the future). Participants were given budgets that were framed as relatively small (i.e., weekly budgets) or large (i.e., monthly budget). Under relative scarcity, participants were more likely to consider opportunity costs.

This simple result has striking consequences for the way consumers think about the value of things. Numerous results from the decision-making literature have shown that preferences and perceptions of value are often malleable. For example, in Thaler's (1985) "beer on the beach" problem, people are willing to pay more for a beer that will be delivered to them from a luxury resort than from a grocery store. It is the same beer, consumed on the same beach, and yet people offer more money when they know it comes from the resort. Why? Because it is difficult to have a clear sense of what small expenses are worth, people look for contextual cues that guide their valuation (Tversky & Kahneman, 1981). When these cues shift, so do preferences. In this case, the beer's point of purchase provides a cue (albeit an irrelevant one) to how much one should pay.

But if scarcity leads people to think about opportunity costs, then that means they not only ask themselves "What should I pay for this item?" but also "What must I give up in order to buy it?" Thinking about these trade-offs provides a more consistent frame for deciding what an item is worth. The trade-offs, for instance, do not depend on where the beer is purchased. Spending $5 means giving up a cup of coffee or a sandwich, and that is true regardless of whether the beer comes from a resort or a grocery store.

Because these trade-offs offer a more stable frame for perceiving value, scarcity might actually make consumers less susceptible to certain context effects. In recent work, for instance, participants were asked what they would be thinking of when naming their willingness to pay in the preceding scenario. Wealthier participants were more likely to say they would use location as the relevant contextual cue. Poorer participants were more likely to say they would think about items they could not buy if they bought the beer (Shah, Shafir, & Mullainathan, 2015). As a result, wealthier participants offered higher prices for the beer when it came from the resort, but poorer participants were less influenced by the external context and named similar prices for both points of purchase (Mullainathan & Shafir, 2013; Shah, Shafir, & Mullainathan, 2015). In similar work, Hall (2008, 2012) asked participants whether they would be willing to travel for a discount on a purchase. The absolute value of the discount was always the same (e.g., $50), but the original price of the purchase was low or high. When the original price is low, the discount represents a larger percentage off. And usually, people's preferences for the discount depend on its relative size (Tversky & Kahneman, 1981). But poorer participants' preferences were more stable and depended on the absolute value of the discount. This may have been because the opportunity cost of not taking the discount depends only on the discount's absolute value, not its relative size. Taken together, these results suggest that the scarcity mindset is characterized by a greater focus on trade-offs and opportunity costs, which can lead to substantial differences between how consumers decide under scarcity versus abundance.

The unmet needs and obstacles that scarcity creates can also shift the way people construe their world more generally. Roux and Goldsmith (2014), for instance, draw on research that shows that people think more abstractly when they encounter obstacles. They show that the obstacles scarcity creates lead to similar shifts in construal. Participants first completed an episodic recall task where they thought about times when resources were scarce.

Then participants completed a survey where they could describe an action either in abstract, high-level terms or in concrete, low-level terms. For example, "locking a door" could be described as "securing the house" (high-level) or "putting a key in the lock" (low-level). Participants who thought about scarcity were more likely to describe actions in abstract, high-level terms.

Scarcity and Impatience

The obstacles that scarcity creates may also change the way people value the future. For example, field data suggest that lower incomes lead to steeper discount rates (Tanaka, Camerer, & Nguyen, 2010). In lab experiments, when participants are led to believe that they have relatively little discretionary income, they also discount future outcomes more steeply (Callan, Shead, & Olson, 2011). And when participants experience negative income shocks in the lab, they discount more steeply as well (Haushofer & Fehr, 2014). When and why might scarcity lead people to value the future less? Some evidence suggests that scarcity elicits a physiological stress response. For example, when farmers in Kenya experience negative income shocks (because of drought), their cortisol levels rise. The increase in stress, in turn, might lead to steeper discounting (Haushofer & Fehr, 2014). Aside from the relationship between scarcity and discount rates, however, the fact that scarcity undermines physiological well-being raises the question of how it affects psychological well-being more broadly.

Scarcity and Well-being

The canonical results in this area suggest that income matters relatively little for well-being, at least once basic needs are met. To the extent that income does matter, it might matter more within countries than across countries (Easterlin, 1974). And relative income may matter more than absolute income (Oswald & Clarke, 1996). More recent research, however, suggests that both absolute and relative income matter even once basic needs are met (Sacks, Stevenson, & Wolfers, 2012). Poorer individuals report lower life satisfaction. Wealthier individuals, meanwhile, can derive additional life satisfaction from a variety of other sources, such intimate connections and autonomy. But poorer individuals derive no additional benefit from these factors unless they are first able to meet essential consumption needs (Martin & Hill, 2012). The negative relationship between income and well-being also seems exacerbated in societies where there is greater income inequality. Under these conditions, lower-income individuals report that they trust people less and see society as less fair, which subsequently undermines their happiness (Oishi, Kesebir, & Diener, 2011). Given the importance that these social judgments play in determining happiness, how else might scarcity affect the way we see others and interact with those around us?

Scarcity and Social Decision Making

Recent research has primarily approached this question by considering the ways that scarcity affects moral judgment. Pitesa and Thau (2014) found that lower-income participants rated moral transgressions more harshly than did wealthier participants. But other research has shown that financial deprivation might make consumers more likely to transgress and more tolerant of transgressions (Sharma, Mazar, Alter, & Ariely, 2014). In one study, participants first played a game where they either earned money or lost money. Participants then moved on to a simple task where they encountered a conflict of interest. On the one hand, participants were told to respond as accurately as possible to a visual discrimination task. On the other hand, they were paid more if they responded in a biased way. That is, participants could earn more by lying about what they saw. In fact, participants who had been financially deprived in the first phase of the study were more likely to cheat on the second phase of the study, and these results hold when subjective feelings of deprivation are manipulated instead of objective deprivation. Moreover, subjectively deprived participants were less harsh in their judgments of similarly deprived individuals who stole. Although these results seem at odds with each other, Pitesa and Thau (2014) conducted a follow-up study where they found that subjective feelings of deprivation only affect the way that people judge *harmful* transgressions and only when people feel vulnerable. If theft seems relatively harmless (compared to violent transgressions) or people feel somewhat insulated from the thefts, then that could explain the discrepancy in these results. Further, stealing might be uniquely acceptable because it directly alleviates financial deprivation (Sharma et al., 2014).

Related research has focused on how scarce environments make people more self-oriented (Roux & Goldsmith, 2012). For instance, when participants imagine a world with limited resources, they are less likely to donate to charity. But if participants believe that other-oriented behavior will ultimately benefit the self in the future, then participants are more likely to act "generously" toward others.

The growing literature on resource scarcity currently offers several clear messages. First, scarcity elicits greater focus. As a result of this focus, some capacities improve in the short run under scarcity. People might spend more efficiently or be more aware of what they are spending. And they might be better able to think about trade-offs and the opportunity costs of transactions. But this increase in focus is effortful. It taxes mental bandwidth and increases physiological stress, which can in turn lead people to discount the future more steeply. This constellation of negative effects may undermine well-being more generally. And scarcity might simultaneously lead people to judge others more harshly (if their actions feel like a direct threat) while also making people more likely to cheat or otherwise take self-oriented actions.

Of course, focusing only on financial or material dimensions misses the broader context that surrounds consumers who have less. A lack of money or other resources often accompanies other features of social class, such as one's education, social rank, and neighborhood (Kraus & Stephens, 2012). Some might even argue that differences in social class are on par with broader cultural differences (Kraus, Piff, & Keltner, 2011). The next section explores the research emerging on the psychology of social class.

The Psychology of Social Class

Early theories of social class imagined a "culture of poverty" where counterproductive behaviors, deviant values, and dysfunctional traits were common and were passed between generations (Lewis, 1968). Recent work on social class, however, takes a different approach. It does not define social class as a stable set of traits. Rather, it suggests that the conditions people encounter in their daily lives – especially experiences with their social rank – create a cognitive repertoire that guides thought and behavior (Kraus et al., 2012).

There are two features of poverty that seem to exert the greatest influence over social class. First, poverty leads to unreliable environments (Steele & Sherman, 1999). Second, people have to be more aware of and prepared to respond to these environments. They must be more aware of their surroundings because they cannot insulate themselves from them (Kraus et al., 2012). As described in this section, these two factors lead people to care more about trust and to adopt a more interdependent mindset.

Critically, this cognitive repertoire does not only depend on objective features of social rank (e.g., education, neighborhood), but rather it is also shaped by the local context and subjective feelings and perceptions of one's rank. In fact, perceived social class and objective socioeconomic status are only moderately correlated, suggesting that subjective social class is a separable construct (Kraus et al., 2012). Because the study of social class explicitly considers both objective and subjective dimensions, there are different methods that researchers use to develop convergent evidence in this domain.

Empirical Approaches

Measures of objective social class typically include three factors: income, education, and occupation. Income most directly tracks a person's access to material resources. Greater education exposes people to different social networks and cultural norms. Also, higher-status jobs often afford more autonomy, while lower-status jobs might require more supervision and routine (Kraus & Stephens, 2012). To measure subjective social class, researchers typically rely on the MacArthur Scale of Subjective Socioeconomic Status (Adler, Epel, Castellazzo, & Ickovics, 2000), where people rank themselves on a ladder with ten rungs. To manipulate subjective social class, researchers often shift the social comparisons that participants make. When comparing themselves to someone lower on the ladder, participants' feelings and actions align with higher social class repertoires (and vice versa when comparing themselves to someone higher on the ladder). Despite being distinct constructs, both objective and subjective social class often exert similar influences.

Social Class, Trust, and Uncertainty

As mentioned previously, poverty introduces unreliability and uncertainty into many situations. As a result, poverty creates a psychology where trust is a precious commodity and people prefer to not depend on others financially (Steele & Sherman, 1999). For instance, Hall (2008) found that trust matters more for poorer individuals when they make monetary decisions. Participants were asked to imagine selling an item to either an individual whom they knew and who has been a family friend for years, or they imagined selling an item to someone who lived nearby but whom they did not know well. Participants then chose which payment option they would prefer: one where the buyer offered more money over the course of four payments, or one where the buyer offered less money up front. High-income respondents predominantly chose the higher-paying option, regardless of whether they knew the buyer. Low-income respondents also chose the higher-paying option when they knew the buyer. But when low-income respondents did not know the buyer, they chose the lower-paying option because they could obtain money up front and would not have to trust the person to continue making payments. In fact, wealthier participants self-reported that they cared more about the financial outcomes of a transaction, whereas poorer individuals reported that they cared more about being able to trust the other party involved in the transaction.

Because poorer consumers confront volatility and unreliability on a regular basis, this might lead them to prefer financial options that cost more money but allow them to avoid committing to something well in advance. For example, rent-to-own contracts are remarkably common in low-income settings. Under these contracts, consumers pay a small, fixed-amount over the course of many weeks. As a result, they pay much more than list price for the product. But poorer consumers prefer these arrangements, in part, because they are "escapable" and allow consumers to change course should they encounter income shocks (Zikmund-Fisher & Parker, 1999).

Social Class, Interdependence, and Control

This volatility comes not just from a lack of money but also from institutions and other people. Whereas wealthier individuals can leverage institutional power for their benefits, poorer individuals cannot and might instead be *influenced* by institutions. Some research suggests that this leads to decreased feelings of personal control. In one study, participants reported their subjective social status as well as how much they agreed with statements like, "Whatever happens in the future mostly depends on me," and, "There is little I can do to change many of the important things in my life" – those who reported lower subjective status reported feeling less personal control. Moreover, lower-status individuals considered more contextual explanations for events whereas higher-status individuals focused on dispositional attributions (Kraus, Piff, & Keltner, 2009).

Because poorer individuals might not have the means to insulate themselves from threats or shocks, they have to be more aware of their environment, including other people (Kraus et al., 2012). For example, subjective social class was manipulated by having participants compare themselves to people who were below them in social rank or above them in social rank. Participants were then asked to name the emotions on faces displaying nervousness, hostility, playfulness, and other expressions. Those with subjectively lower status performed better, suggesting that lower social status leads to greater empathic accuracy (Kraus, Cote, & Keltner, 2010). In further work, participants were paired up and told to get to know their partner through a series of discussion questions. These interactions were recorded and then coded based on whether participants showed that they were engaged (e.g., nodding head, raising eyebrows) or disengaged (e.g., doodling, fiddling). Participants with lower socioeconomic status were consistently more engaged than participants with higher socioeconomic status (Kraus & Keltner, 2009). This series of results suggests that lower status makes people more attuned to their settings, while perhaps also feeling more at the whim of the environment.

To some extent, this focus on the environment can increase compassion and prosociality among individuals with lower social class (Kraus, Cotes, & Keltner, 2010). For instance, in a dictator game, lower social class participants made more generous offers to their partners. Participants who were made to feel as if they had lower social rank donated more to charity. Finally, because the environment and context matter so much in lower social classes, people may feel more compelled to blend in with their setting rather than trying to stand out. Indeed, in a study where participants were given a chance to choose a unique pen or a more common pen, lower social class participants were more likely to choose the common pen (Stephens, Markus, & Townsend, 2007). Note that these results stand slightly in contrast to some of the aforementioned results where resource scarcity led people to be more self-oriented (Roux & Goldsmith, 2012). This discrepancy might be due to differences in how people think when focused specifically on a lack of material resources rather than on the broader context of social class.

Social Class and Social Comparison

As some of the preceding results show, subjective social class – especially relative rank – can influence thoughts and behavior as much as objective social class. In one study, relative rank mattered more than social class. Participants compared themselves to either people below them or above them in rank. Those who compared themselves to people lower than them reported greater subjective well-being. More striking, relative rank had a stronger effect on subjective well-being than did socioeconomic status (Anderson, Kraus, Galinsky, & Keltner, 2012).

In fact, people are remarkably averse to occupying the lowest tier in society. For instance, a survey of Americans showed widespread support for increasing the minimum wage. However, people who earned just above the minimum wage were least supportive, presumably because the wage increase would not affect them, but would instead improve the lot of those just below them, reducing (or eliminating) the gap between themselves and the bottom tier. And in a lab experiment, participants in a multiplayer game were randomly assigned different endowments (e.g., $1, $2, ... $6). For each participant (except those at the extremes), there was always one person who earned $1 more and one person who earned $1 less. Participants were then given an additional $2 to distribute to another player who was either just above them or just below them in rank (based on the initial endowments). Many participants redistributed the $2 to participants who were below them. However, those who were in second-to-last place were least likely to do so, presumably because this would have resulted in them moving to last place (Kuziemko, Buell, Reich, & Norton, 2014).

Consumers incorporate these comparisons into how they spend. For example, during recessions people spend less on positional goods because they do not need to spend as much to keep up with others (who will also have had to reduce their spending; Kamakura & Du, 2012). Poor individuals might be prone to conspicuous consumption, choosing to spend in a way that makes them seem wealthier than their peers, rather than spending on nutrition or education or even saving the money (Moav & Neeman, 2012). These social comparisons can also lead poor consumers to play the lottery more often (Haisley, Mostafa, & Loewenstein, 2008). Poor consumers tend to see lotteries as one of the few ways for them to compete on equal footing with higher-status individuals (i.e., winning the lottery is one of the few positive life outcomes where the wealthy do not have a built-in advantage). Indeed, when subjective feelings of lower social status are induced in consumers, they purchase lotteries at a higher rate, and this is particularly true when their attention is drawn to the fact that wealthier consumers do not have a better chance at winning the lottery than they do.

Clearly, more than just material resources shape how consumers behave when they face scarcity. Instead, consumers carry with them a set of expectations, thought patterns, and beliefs that emerge from the broader contexts surrounding resource scarcity. These cognitive repertoires lead people to pay more attention to the environment (and others in the environment), to care more about trust and uncertainty, and to focus on social comparisons as they approach the bottom rungs of a social group. The research summarized in the preceding sections provides the outlines of a framework that can be leveraged against many more questions in future work. The next section covers a few of these promising avenues for additional research.

Toward a Better Understanding of Having Less

Although this chapter has primarily focused on monetary scarcity and the context of poverty, additional research suggests that the scarcity mindset similarly arises when we lack other resources, such as time or calories. But which features of the scarcity mindset generalize across resources and which are specific to money?

Scarcity across Resources

Some research suggests that scarcity of one resource can activate the scarcity mindset with other resources. For example, when people are hungry, they also become stingier and are less likely to donate to charity (Briers, Pandelaere, Dewitte, & Warlop, 2006). Also, people sometimes treat time losses like monetary losses (Leclerc, Schmitt, & Dube, 1995). But other research finds that these resources differ (Okada & Hoch, 2004; Sani & Monga, 2008; Zauberman & Lynch, 2005). Specifically, people treat money differently because its value is less ambiguous than the value of other resources, such as time. Future research should categorize resources along different dimensions (e.g., ambiguity of value, ease of exchange) and systematically explore how these dimensions shape behavior. This taxonomy is also essential for determining how different forms of scarcity change the way people think and behave. It may be that scarcity of some resources captures attention more than others, for instance.

Focusing on Scarcity

This raises an additional question worth pursuing. Namely, when do people recognize scarcity in the first place? Much of the research so far suggests that scarcity makes people myopic. It focuses people on making ends meet today at the expense of thinking about tomorrow. But the poor do save for the future (Collins, Morduch, Rutherford, & Ruthven, 2010). However, they do not put their savings into some general account, but rather earmark it for a specific expense in the future (e.g., an appliance, a child's wedding). Saving for specific expenses suggests that consumers recognize that funds are lacking for future priorities. Further research should explore when people recognize scarcity in the moment versus when they anticipate scarcity in the future. Moreover, some of the preceding results suggest that the poor discount the future more steeply. But what is the nature of this "discounting"? It seems like there might be two possibilities: (1) the poor consider the future and value it less; or (2) the poor are not attending to the future at all because current demands are too pressing. Teasing apart these mechanisms could help develop more effective interventions to increase savings among the poor.

It is also worth noting that many of the preceding studies suggest that the scarcity mindset can be momentarily activated. That is, the same person can look entirely different depending on whether resources are momentarily scarce or abundant. But some researchers argue that repeated exposure to scarcity gradually changes and shapes psychological systems, perhaps leading to more permanent changes in the way people behave.

Acquiring the Scarcity Mindset

For instance, Chakravarti (2006) suggests that prolonged deprivation reduces autonomy and lowers motivation. As a result, people adapt to scarcity in a few ways. First, they become better at handling low-value decisions, but are less capable of handling high-value decisions. Poor consumers might spend too long deliberating the trivial. Second, the poor might eventually become resigned to their circumstances or suffer from learned helplessness. And third, the capacity to aspire might be less developed among the poor. Similarly, Griskevicius and colleagues (2013) argue that people develop life-history strategies that are either fast (e.g., myopic, impulsive, risk taking) or slow (e.g., far-sighted, risk avoiding). People develop these strategies in response to environmental circumstances, with fast strategies being a common response to scarcity. And these life-history strategies seem stable enough to be triggered easily. For example, participants of high and low socioeconomic status were either primed with pictures of economically depressed areas or were primed with control pictures. When shown the economically depressed pictures, low socioeconomic status participants subsequently behaved more impulsively and took more risks.

Naturally, this raises the question of which features of the scarcity mindset are stable and which are deployed in response to specific circumstances. Furthermore, what features of the environment affect whether people acquire a stable scarcity mindset or one that is more temporary? Perhaps when people believe their circumstances are less changeable, they imprint the scarcity mindset more deeply.

Ultimately, to better understand which features of the scarcity mindset are stable and which are not, we first need a more detailed taxonomy of these features. To accomplish this, consumer researchers may need to rely on ethnographic approaches more than experimental research. For example, through a series of qualitative interviews, Underlid (2007) found that poor respondents feared the future because of the overwhelming insecurity they faced on a daily basis. Indeed, exploratory research such as this might be most important at this stage because the field is still at the beginning of understanding the psychology of scarcity and social class.

As we broaden our conceptual understanding of these contexts, it also becomes possible to study practical approaches for helping consumers who confront scarcity. Future work should directly tackle the challenge of translating the aforementioned theoretical concepts and frameworks into interventions that can alleviate some of difficulties facing the poorest and most vulnerable members of society.

Intervening on the Scarcity Mindset

Research on scarcity-induced focus suggests that interventions will be particularly effective if they disrupt attentional tunneling and help reorient poor consumers' attention to neglected priorities. For example, one intervention reoriented attention using simple text message reminders to save money for the future. Participants who received text message reminders increased their savings rate by 6 percent relative to those who did not receive these reminders (Karlan, McConnell, Mullainathan, & Zinman, 2010). The effectiveness of this intervention suggests that additional gains could be made by looking for other ways to disrupt the attentional set that scarcity induces. But this also raises a conceptual question about which features of the environment (or which personal goals) are most likely to be neglected when scarcity shifts attention. That is, future research will first need to map out where attentional neglect will be most likely and most costly under scarcity, and then additional work will need to develop targeted attentional interventions.

Because of scarcity's effects on mental bandwidth, poor consumers might find it particularly difficult to navigate even small obstacles or hassle factors during the day. A compelling study examined whether poor consumers would follow-up on a two-hour workshop about banking to open their own bank account. Although 90 percent of participants reported wanting to open a bank account after the workshop, only 50 percent did. Why might this be? Participants could not open the bank account immediately. Instead, they had to carve out the time and mental energy from another day to do so. These small hassles become magnified because scarcity tires the mind. In fact, more participants followed through when the workshops were tweaked so that attendees they could immediately begin the paperwork to open accounts (Bertrand, Mullainathan, & Shafir, 2006). Failure to open bank accounts is just one example of a host of behaviors among the poor that might be stem from taxed bandwidth. For example, the poor miss more medical appointments (Karter et al., 2004), show worse medical adherence (DiMatteo, 2004), speak to their children less or snap at their children more (McLoyd, 1998), and are less focused at work (Kim & Garman, 2004). Many of these behaviors have been attributed to the dispositions or personality traits of the poor, but if these result from limited bandwidth, then simple channel factors might substantially change behavior.

Finally, future research should consider which context and framing effects are reduced under the scarcity mindset. Such work could guide the approaches policy makers use to nudge low-income consumers. For example, not all frames are created equal for the poor. In nudging consumers to rely less on payday loans, one could frame the loan's interest rate in terms of the rate per pay period (e.g., 20 percent) or the rate per year (e.g., more than 500 percent). The latter frame seems more startling, but is in fact no more effective. Instead, poor consumers respond more to a different frame: describing the cost of the loan in absolute dollar terms (Bertrand & Morse, 2011). Perhaps this frame does a better job of highlighting the opportunity costs of the loans, which resonates more with the scarcity mindset.

Intervening on Social Class and Identity

Still stronger interventions might consider the broader context surrounding scarcity. For example, because poor individuals often lack the autonomy or agency that wealthy individuals have, they might experience some degree of fatalism. Some have suggested that the poor struggle with the capacity to aspire or set visionary goals (Bernard, Dercon, Orkin, & Taffesse, 2014), but carefully designed interventions can reverse this pattern. For example, one group of participants in rural parts of Ethiopia were shown a documentary of people from similar communities who succeeded without help from others. Participants who saw this documentary (as opposed to a control documentary) had stronger aspirations and saved more money for the future. Future research should first explore the goals and aspirations that poor individuals hold. Of course, these might vary widely across contexts, but there may be common threads. Research could then consider why scarcity undermines aspirations and which behaviors benefit most from improving aspirations.

Related to this point, poor individuals face many forms of stigma. Alleviating that stigma might remove one barrier to advancement. Hall, Zhao, and Shafir (2013) found compelling evidence for this when they had participants in a soup kitchen either complete an affirmation manipulation (e.g., discussing a time they felt successful) or a control exercise (e.g., describing a meal). Affirmed participants were more likely to later take up useful financial information and performed better on subsequent measures of cognitive capacity. That is, removing the stigma of being poor alleviated some of the bandwidth tax of being poor. Future research might explore other positive effects of affirmation among the poor. Translating these concepts into more direct interventions to remove the stigma of being poor would also increase the welfare of low-income consumers.

But this work highlights a much more powerful point. The poor experience not just a poverty of resources but also a poverty of bandwidth (Mullainathan & Shafir, 2013). Addressing the lack of bandwidth might be an easier way to improve the lives of the poor. Importantly, this approach requires a broader understanding of the inputs into mental bandwidth. While most of the research on the scarcity mindset highlights how income is a strong input, this is also the hardest factor to change (except through unconditional cash transfers). But a host of other factors associated with poverty might also reduce bandwidth. For instance, the poor experience more pain and worse health, both of which have not just physical effects but also psychological effects. They, too, capture the mind and serve as distractions. The poor also experience more social isolation and conflict, which seem likely to tax bandwidth. But these inputs might be far easier to alleviate and might offer stronger levers for improving the lives of the poor in the future.

Concluding Remarks

The study of poverty and other conditions of scarcity is not new. But the turn toward developing a psychology of scarcity is fairly recent. And while the preceding research represents a series of promising first steps, there remains significant work to better develop frameworks for understanding how consumers behave when money is short and when navigating the social context of having less. Such frameworks will necessarily combine insights from cognitive and social psychology while also incorporating ideas from economics, sociology, and public policy. This topic is profoundly important, given the number of people in the world facing some form of scarcity. There is much to gain from research that more deeply explores the lives of consumers who have less.

References

Aarts, H., Dijksterhuis, A., & De Vries, P. (2001). On the psychology of drinking: Being thirsty and perceptually ready. *British Journal of Psychology, 92*, 631–642.

Acquaye, L. (2011). Low-income homeowners and the challenge of home maintenance, *Community Development, 42*, 16–33.

Adler, N. E., Epel, E. S., Castellazzo, G., & Ickovics, J. R. (2000). Relationship of subjective and objective social status with psychological and physiological functioning: Preliminary data in healthy, white women. *Health Psychology, 19*, 586–592.

Anderson, C., Kraus, M. W., Galinksy, A. D., & Keltner, D. (2012). The local ladder effect: Sociometric status and subjective well-being, *Psychological Science, 23*, 764–771.

Bernard, T., Dercon, S., Orkin, K., & Taffesse, A. S. (2014). The future in mind: Aspirations and forward-looking behavior in rural Ethiopia. *Center for the Study of American Economies Working Paper Series* 2014–16.

Bertrand, M., & Morse, A. (2011). Information disclosure, cognitive biases, and payday borrowing. *Journal of Finance, 66*, 1865–1893.

Bertrand, M., Mullainathan, S., & Shafir, E. (2006). Behavioral economics and marketing in aid of decision-making among the poor. *Journal of Public Policy and Marketing, 25*, 8–23.

Binkley, J. K., & Bejnarowicz, J. (2003). Consumer price awareness in food shopping: The case of quantity surcharges. *Journal of Retailing, 79*, 27–35.

Briers, B., Pandelaere, M., Dewitte, S., & Warlop, L. (2006). Hungry for money: The desire for caloric resources increases the desire for financial resources and vice versa. *Psychological Science, 17*, 939–943.

Callan, M. J., Shead, N. W., & Olson, J. M. (2011). Personal relative deprivation, delay discounting, and gambling. *Journal of Personality and Social Psychology, 101*, 955–973.

Chakravarti, D. (2006). Voices unheard: The psychology of consumption in poverty and development. *Journal of Consumer Psychology, 16*, 363–376.

Clark, A. E., & Oswald, A. J. (1996). Satisfaction and comparison income. *Journal of Public Economics, 61*, 359–381.

Collins, D., Morduch, J., Rutherford, S., & Ruthven, O. (2010). *Portfolios of the Poor: How the World's Poor Live on $2 a Day*. Princeton, NJ: Princeton University Press.

DiMatteo, M. R. (2004). Variations in patients' adherence to medical recommendations: A quantitative review of 50 years of research. *Medical Care, 42*, 200–209.

Easterlin, R. (1974). Does economic growth improve the human lot? Some empirical evidence. In P.A. David & M. W. Reder (eds.), *Nations and Households in Economic Growth: Essays in Honour of Moses Abramowitz* (pp. 89–125). New York: Academic Press.

Frederick, S., Novemsky, N., Wang, J., Dhar, R., & Nowlis, S. (2009). Opportunity cost neglect. *Journal of Consumer Research, 36*, 553–561.

Goldin, J., & Homoff, T. (2013). Smoke gets in your eyes: Cigarette tax salience and regressivity. *American Economic Journal: Economic Policy, 5*, 302–336.

Griskevicius, V., Ackerman, J. M., Cantu, S. M., Delton, A. W., & Robertson, T. E. (2013). When the economy falters do people spend or save? Responses to resource scarcity depend on childhood environments. *Psychological Science, 24*, 197–205.

Haisley, E., Mostafa, R., & Loewenstein, G. (2008). Subjective relative income and lottery ticket purchases. *Journal of Behavioral Decision Making, 21*, 283–295.

Hall, C. C. (2008). Decisions under poverty: A behavioral perspective on the decision making of the poor. Retrieved from ProQuest Dissertations and Theses. (Accession Order No. 304507599.)

Hall, C. C. (2012) Behavioral decision research, social class and implications for public policy. In H. R. Markus & S. T. Fiske (eds.), *Facing Social Class: How Societal Rank Influence Interaction* (pp. 175–194). New York: Russell Sage Foundation.

Hall, C. C., Zhao, J., & Shafir, E. (2013). Self-affirmation among the poor: Cognitive and behavioral implications. *Psychological Science, 25*, 619–625.

Haushofer, J., & Fehr, E. (2014). On the psychology of poverty. *Science, 344*, 862–867.

Kamakura, W. A., & Du, R. Y. (2012). How economic contractions and expansions affect expenditure patterns. *Journal of Consumer Research, 39*, 229–247.

Karlan, D., McConnell, M., Mullainathan, S., & Zinman, J. (2010). Getting to the top of mind: How reminders increase saving. NBER Working Paper 16205.

Karter, A. J., Parker, M. M., Moffet, H. H., Ahmed, A. T., & Ferrara, A. (2004). Missed appointments and poor glycemic control: An opportunity to identify high-risk diabetic patients. *Medical Care, 42*, 110–115.

Kim, J., & Garman, E. T. (2004). Financial stress, pay satisfaction, and workplace performance. *Compensation and Benefits Review, 36*, 69–76.

Kraus, M. W., Cote, S., & Keltner, D. (2010). Social class, contextualism, and empathic accuracy. *Psychological Science, 21*, 1716–1723.

Kraus, M. W., & Keltner, D. (2009). Signs of socioeconomic status: A thin-slicing approach. *Psychological Science, 20*, 99–106.

Kraus, M. W., Piff, P. K., & Keltner, D. (2009). Social class, sense of control, and social explanation. *Journal of Personality and Social Psychology, 97*, 992–1004.

Kraus, M. W., Piff, P. K., & Keltner, D. (2011). Social class as culture: The convergence of resources and rank in the social realm. *Current Directions in Psychological Science, 20*, 246–250.

Kraus, M. W., Piff, P. K, Mendoza-Denton, R., Rheinschmidt, M. L., & Keltner, D. (2012). Social class, solipsism, and contextualism: How the rich are different from the poor. *Psychological Review, 119*, 546–572.

Kraus, M. W., & Stephens, N. M. (2012). A road map for an emerging psychology of social class. *Social and Personality Psychology Compass, 6*, 642–656.

Kuziemko, I., Buell, R. W., Reich, T., & Norton, M. I. (2014). "Last place aversion": Evidence and redistributive implications. *Quarterly Journal of Economics, 129*, 105–149.

Leclerc, F., Schmitt, B. H., & Dube, L. (1995). Waiting time and decision-making: Is time like money. *Journal of Consumer Research, 22*, 110–119.

Lewis, O. (1968). The culture of poverty. In Daniel P. Moynahan (ed.), *On Understanding Poverty: Perspectives from the Social Sciences* (pp. 187–200). New York: Basic Books.

Mani, A., Mullainathan, S., Shafir, E., & Zhao, J. (2013). Poverty impedes cognitive function. *Science, 341*, 976–980.

Martin, K. D., & Hill, R. P. (2012). Life satisfaction, self-determination, and consumption adequacy at the bottom of the pyramid. *Journal of Consumer Research, 38*, 1155–1168.

Mendel, D. (2005). Double jeopardy: Why the poor pay more. *Advocasey, 7*, 5–22.

McLoyd, V. C. (1998). Socioeconomic disadvantage and child development. *American Psychologist, 53*, 185–204.

Moav, O., & Neeman, Z. (2012). Savings rates and poverty: The role of conspicuous consumption and human capital. *Economic Journal, 122*, 933–956.

Mullainathan, S., & Shafir, E. (2013). *Scarcity: Why Having Too Little Means So Much.* New York: Times Books.

Oishi, S., Kesebir, S., & Diener, E. (2011). Income inequality and happiness. *Psychological Science, 22*, 1095–1100.

Okada, E. M., & Hoch, S. J. (2004). Spending time versus spending money. *Journal of Consumer Research, 31*, 313–323.

Pitesa, M., & Thau, S. (2014). A lack of material resources causes harsher moral judgments. *Psychological Science, 25*, 702–710.

Prahalad, C. K., & Hammond, A. (2002). Serving the world's poor, profitably. *Harvard Business Review, September*, 4–11.

Roux, C., & Goldsmith, K. (2012). On the consequences of a scarcity mindset: Why thoughts of having less can lead to taking (and giving) more. SSRN Paper # 2147919.

Roux, C., & Goldsmith, K. (2014). When reminders of resource scarcity promote abstract thinking. SSRN Paper # 2255636.

Sacks, D. W., Stevenson, B., & Wolfers, J. (2012). The new stylized facts about income and subjective well-being. *Emotion, 12*, 1181–1187.

Saini, R., & Monga, A. (2008). How I decide depends on what I spend: Use of heuristics is greater for time than for money. *Journal of Consumer Research, 34*, 914–922.

Shah, A.K., Mullainathan, S., & Shafir, E. (2012). Some consequences of having too little. *Science, 338*, 682–685.

Shah, A. K., Shafir, E., & Mullainathan, S. (2015). Scarcity frames value. *Psychological Science.* doi: 10.1177/0956797614563958.

Sharma, E., & Alter, A. L. (2012). Financial deprivation prompts consumers to seek scarce goods. *Journal of Consumer Research, 39*, 545–560.

Sharma, E., Mazar, N., Alter, A., L, & Ariely, D. (2014). Financial deprivation selectively shifts moral standards and compromises moral decisions. *Organizational Behavior and Human Decision Processes, 123*, 90–100.

Spiller, S. A. (2011). Opportunity cost consideration. *Journal of Consumer Research, 38*, 595–610.

Steele, C., & Sherman, D. A. (1999). The psychological predicament of women on welfare. In D. A. Prentice & D. T. Miller (eds.), *Cultural Divides: Understanding and Overcoming Group Conflict* (pp. 393–428). New York: Russell Sage Foundation.

Stephens, N. M., Markus, H. R., & Townsend, S. S. M. (2007). Choice as an act of meaning: The case of social class. *Journal of Personality and Social Psychology, 93*, 814–830.

Talukdar, D. (2008). Cost of being poor: Retail price and consumer price search difference across inner-city and suburban neighborhoods. *Journal of Consumer Research, 35*, 457–471.

Tanaka, T., Camerer, C. F., & Nguyen, Q. (2010). Risk and time preferences: Linking experimental and household survey data from Vietnam. *American Economic Review, 100*, 557–571.

Thaler, R. H. (1985). Mental accounting and consumer choice. *Marketing Science, 4*, 199–214.

Tversky, A., & Kahneman, D. (1981). The framing of decisions and psychology of choice. *Science, 211*, 453–458.

Underlid, K. (2007). Poverty and experiences of insecurity: A qualitative interview study of 25 long-standing recipients of social security. *International Journal of Social Welfare, 16*, 65–74.

World Bank. (2014). *World Development Indicators*. Washington, DC: World Bank.

Zauberman, G., & Lynch, J. G. (2005). Resource slack and propensity to discount delayed investments of time versus money. *Journal of Experimental Psychology – General, 134*, 23–37.

Zikmund-Fisher, B. J., & Parker, A. M. (1999). Demand for rent-to-own contracts: A behavioral economic explanation. *Journal of Economic Behavior & Organization, 38*, 199–216.

26 Consumer Sharing

Collaborative Consumption, from Theoretical Roots to New Opportunities

Cait Lamberton

Imagine a consumer needing a tool to fix her sink. She may go to her local big box store, where she spends $50 to obtain the tool. She fixes her sink. The barely used tool, tucked away in a garage corner, becomes immediately obsolete. A few weeks later, her neighbor makes the same trip to the big box store, buys the same tool, and similarly exiles it to the garage immediately afterward. In this scenario, we observe four things: While the big box store may be pleased with its income, (1) had the neighbors connected, time and money could have been saved; (2) if either had not had enough money to buy the tool, both would still have broken sinks; (3) the unused tools sitting in garages offer utility that no one is enjoying; and (4) a buildup of unused tools is likely headed for the landfill. These conditions magnified to scale can lead to a state referred to as "hyperconsumption" – the excess purchase of largely unused items – and be destructive to consumers, the economy, and the environment (Albinsson, Wolf, & Kopf, 2010).

Collaborative consumption systems aim to remedy these conditions, connecting individual needs with unused, or "slack" (Benkler, 2004), resources held by others. When individuals collaborate, they can gain access to needed goods or services without incurring the cost of sole ownership. If our hypothetical neighbors had taken advantage of such a system, both would experience at least as much overall utility, less waste, and perhaps foster a rewarding interpersonal relationship. Thus, from tool libraries (www.localtools.org) to meal sharing (www.mealsharing.com) to work barter (www.taskrabbit.com) to peer-to-peer car or ride sharing systems (e.g., Uber, Lyft, relayrides.com), we might anticipate that collaborative consumption systems offer unique financial and social benefits to consumers and, by extension, to society. Such possibilities prompted *Time Magazine* to highlight collaborative consumption as one of ten ideas that would change the world (Walsh, 2011).

However, substantial confusion exists about the nature of collaborative consumption systems and the sustainability of their benefits. Neal Gorenflo, founder of shareable.com, declared collaborative consumption "dead" in 2013, lamenting the decrease in potential for "transformative social experience" that he argues is central to a sharing economy (Gorenflo, 2013). Rather, he argues that collaborative consumption companies have increasingly come to resemble traditional competitive marketplace firms: car sharing becomes equivalent to car rental or taxi hire, couchsurfing becomes an ad hoc hotel, and job sharing devolves into a potentially exploitative temp service. Such shifts led economics journalist Matthew Yglesias to proclaim that the term "sharing economy" is a misnomer (Yglesias, 2013), as these platforms promote renting, buying, and selling in ways that are barely different from standard market exchange. So, at present we may have more questions than answers about collaborative consumption: Why do consumers decide to collaborate, and what determines whether they stay in or exit such a system? Are economic, psychological, or social benefits most important to consumers? More generally, how can we design collaborative systems that prompt sustained, productive participation and promote consumer well-being?

If we look to academic research for answers, we may conclude that current theory is too diffuse to provide deep insights. A search of AcademicOneFile using the keyword "collaborative consumption" yields 44 peer-reviewed journal articles, spread across communication, business, consumer behavior, information technology, corporate governance, economics, environmental protection, political science, psychology, ethics, and transportation. The keywords "sharing economy" yield 149 peer-reviewed journal articles, again dispersed across geography, law, economics, business, sociology, art, international development, education, computer science, and information systems. Much of this work provides interesting domain-specific examination, exploring specific contexts such as book sharing (Guercini, Corciolani, & Dalli, 2014), Freecycle.org (e.g., Nelson, Rademacher, & Paek, 2007), toy libraries (Ozanne & Ballantine, 2010), flea markets and clothing exchanges (e.g., Denegri-Knott & Molesworth, 2009; Sherry, 1990) and car sharing (e.g., Bardhi & Eckhardt, 2012). While each piece provides a valuable perspective, we find no generalizable framework for collaborative consumption. Perhaps most problematically, we can say little about the ways that collaborative consumption projects should be designed or the outcomes that might be expected from a collaborative system.

In this chapter, I argue that to build an appropriate framework for understanding collaborative consumption in its contemporary form, we need to consider the deep and nuanced literature on human cooperation as well as work specific to modern sharing systems. Though it is beyond the scope of this chapter to provide an exhaustive discussion, snapshots from leading thinkers in multiple traditions allow us to conceptualize modern collaborative consumption systems and offer predictions about their optimal design and trajectory. At the same time, this review highlights the failure of any one perspective to address completely the dynamics of contemporary collaborative consumption. As such, collaborative consumption presents a rich opportunity to apply consumer psychology's multidisciplinary perspective in a domain of theoretical and practical importance.

Defining Contemporary Collaborative Consumption

While the term "collaborative consumption" first appeared in Felson and Spaeth's 1978 paper, "Community Structure and Collaborative

Consumption: A Routine Activity Approach," the most useful definitions of contemporary collaborative consumption come primarily from descriptive practitioner work. Rachel Botsman defines it as: "An economic model based on sharing, swapping, trading, or renting products and services, enabling access over ownership" (Botsman, 2013). For its reliance on technology-mediated connection between participants, collaborative consumption has also been called, "the mesh economy" (Gansky, 2010) or "the peer economy." Because of its emphasis on joint access as opposed to sole ownership, collaborative consumption is also sometimes referred to as part of "the sharing economy" (Gorenflo, 2013). When it represents rejection of materialistic acquisition via a competitive market, collaborative consumption is also associated with "unconsumption" (Albinsson & Perera, 2012) and "anti-consumption" (Ozanne & Ballentine, 2010). As an alternative to the extractive capitalist economy, collaborative consumption is often included in the set of "transition initiatives" (Hopkins, 2011), which shift individuals away from traditional consumption paradigms toward localized systems that pool resources, reduce waste, and are argued to be highly resilient and sustainable.

Part of the reason that collaborative consumption goes by many names is likely because of its breadth. Rachel Botsman and Roo Rogers' landmark book *What's Mine Is Ours* (2010) outlines four components of the sharing economy:

1. Design, production and distribution of goods through collaborative networks
2. Maximum utilization of assets through efficient models of redistribution and shared access
3. Person-to-person banking and crowd-driven investment that decentralize finance
4. Open education and person-to-person learning models that democratize education

Rogers and Botsman also note three systems that are included in collaborative consumption: redistribution markets, such as sites that allow consumers to resell used goods; collaborative lifestyles, where non-product assets such as space and skills are traded in new ways; and product service systems, where consumers can pay to access a service without having to take sole ownership. It should be noted that while collaborative consumption may contain prosocial elements, it is different from simple altruism, gift giving, or prosocial behavior in general: participants in collaborative consumption efforts expect bilateral or multilateral exchange of some sort, though the precise nature of that exchange is open to definition.

Importantly, the collaborative consumption movement as a whole has spurred innovative efforts to decentralize production, democratize consumption, and redistribute goods as described by Botsman and Rogers (Schwartz, 2013). Researchers interested in the movement's macroeconomic consequences will ultimately have the opportunity to evaluate the success of these efforts. However, a consumer psychologist reviewing this material can do little to infer consumers' reasons to pursue collaborative consumption. Perhaps most troubling is that in their focus on contemporary phenomena, this work overlooks decades of rigorous research in human cooperation, of which modern collaborative systems represent a novel, but clearly related, manifestation. Disjointed from such traditions, it is very difficult to talk about collaborative consumption in general or to forecast its future. Thus, to understand these "new economy" phenomena (Alperovitz, 2013), we begin with our understanding of the deepest roots of human cooperation – literature that explores collaborative consumption when it was, in fact, a matter of life and death.

Views from Anthropology and Evolutionary Psychology: Collaboration Is for Survival

Collaboration may be one of humanity's oldest and most native modes of production and exchange. Evidence for cooperation as an innate capacity comes from studies of group hunting and subsequent food sharing in simple economies, where working together likely represented an adaptive evolutionary advantage (Axelrod, 1984; Cosmides & Tooby, 1992). In this literature, scholars recognize that food sharing, or any type of resource sharing at all, is distinct to and may be hardwired in humans (Ridley, 1996).

However, such collaboration could be argued to be irrational: Why would a hunter-gatherer relax control of her food in response to the needs of others, when doing so reduces her own consumption potential? This decision can be argued to be rationally "anomalous" (Dawes & Thaler, 1990). Thus, a great deal of work has been devoted to a question that remains relevant for the design of collaborative consumption systems: What prompts consumers – of anything – to forego sole ownership?

Researchers examining simple economies have identified four motivations for sharing that may be particularly relevant for modern collaborative consumption (see Jaeggi & Gurven, 2013 for a review of underlying literature):

Kin Selection-Based Nepotism

Anthropologists argue that individuals should share when doing so promotes the survival of individuals who are genetically similar to themselves. Hamilton (1964) postulated that an individual should give resources to kin when the benefits to a recipient (B), weighted by their relatedness to the self (r), outweigh the cost of giving (C) (that is, $rB > C$). This thinking suggests that even though a person may bear a cost for submitting his or her goods or resources to a collaborative system, to the extent that doing so increases the likelihood of individuals who share a maximal number of traits with that person, it may be worthwhile.

How could this be applied to modern collaborative consumption? On one hand, one can see evidence of kin selection in the market: cell phone plans offer "friends and family" plans that presume that sharing with these more-related individuals will be more attractive than sharing with strangers. On the other hand, though, kin selection fails to fully explain many behaviors. For example, I may decide that some family members (but not others) should pay rent for sharing my home, particularly after a certain age or the cost incurred due to their residence. Kin selection theory can do little to address cases of different treatment for similarly related individuals. In addition, some collaborative consumption platforms are attractive precisely because they bring strangers together to share resources – it is their ability to connect unrelated individuals that makes them appealing, not their reinforcement of existing relationships (Tanz, 2014). Further, determinations of "relatedness" may be quite malleable, likely expanding beyond immediate genetic connections and perhaps into other types of interconnections. In fact, sharing itself may alter perceptions of relatedness, making it difficult to treat as an exogenous factor (Belk, 2010). Thus, though cooperation consistent with kin selection theory may appear in some modern systems, it is difficult to say whether its role is central or not.

Costly Signaling

More easily applied to modern collaborative consumption is the concept of costly signaling. Under costly signaling, individuals might share in order to display their own ability to acquire a difficult-to-obtain resource or to signal their interest in engaging in cooperation, more generally, with their sharing partners. Costly signaling can conceivably promote sharing when producers maintain a high degree of control over their resources.

Though costly signaling has been given more attention in animal behavior than in human psychology (as noted, as an exception, by Griskevicius et al., 2007), we see that it may operate in collaborative contexts. Kickstarter's platform (www.kickstarter.com) offers an opportunity for costly signaling. Here, individuals can create accounts and share their resources with a wide range of causes, from artistic endeavors to community gardens. In doing so, they both provide financial and moral support, signaling their willingness to associate with a cause.

It may be that costly signaling also encourages consumers' participation in platforms like www.mealshare.org – if one has a particular culinary skill, he may wish to invite others into his home to appreciate the results of his efforts. Doing so may provide an evolutionary advantage, building a system of relationships that insulate one from risk and potentially attracting mates. However, we do not know how collaborative consumption of a good may change its function as a signal: If I become a driver for Uber, allowing strangers to ride all over town in my car, does the fact that I drive a fancy car remain a meaningful signal? If I invest a lot of resources in a community garden, do I still get to claim that its produce serves as a personal signal for me? Is the signal's value spread across collaborators, or does each collaborator get to claim the signal, making it super-additive? Thus, though we may expect that the opportunity to engage in costly signaling may help promote some collaborative behaviors, we lack grounds to pinpoint this as a primary, or well-understood, driver.

Tolerated Scrounging

At some point, a primary producer or acquirer may be unable to consume everything she owns. If it becomes too costly to defend this excess resource, she may allow others to use it (Winterhalder, 1996). Here, participation is determined by need – individuals who need a resource can take up the excess – in a process called tolerated scrounging. Gleaning programs (USDA, 2014) are a good contemporary example of tolerated scrounging. Here, organizations or individuals can "collect … excess fresh foods from farms, gardens, farmers markets, grocers, restaurants, state/county fairs, or any other sources in order to provide it to those in need." Many questions arise with regard to tolerated scrounging: How is "need" assessed? What is the status of the "gleaned" good – how is it valued by donors or recipients? When will individuals who hold excess goods be willing to be "scrounged" from, and when will they want to hold this excess for future use or simply as a symbol of plenty? Are all individuals sensitive to the needs of others, or might some require overt "begging" to share with others, as suggested by primatologists (Jaeggi, Stevens, & Van Schalk, 2010)? Though the opportunity to provide our excess to others in need may well be part of collaborative consumption systems, here again we need more work to understand its importance.

Reciprocal Altruism

Perhaps most clearly relevant to modern collaborative consumption, reciprocal altruism recognizes that individuals may choose to share primarily when they have benefited from sharing in the past and have a reasonable expectation of doing so in the future (Trivers, 1971). Reciprocal altruism, it can be argued, underlies all trade, as individuals provide goods of one type and receive, in exchange, the goods of another (Hill & Kaplan, 1993). Unlike other collaborative motivations, reciprocal altruism is contingent; people will enter their goods into a sharing system only if they anticipate future return.

Participation in large-scale sharing systems such as zipcar.com rely on reciprocal altruism. If I pick up a clean shared vehicle on time, I should return it clean and on time for the next user. If I do, I will anticipate the same when I use the car in the future. The same holds for bike-sharing systems: If I borrow a bike, I will return it to an authorized location. In turn, I anticipate that others will do the same, making a bike available for me in the future. Participants in food co-ops share a similar philosophy: If I put my time into the operation of the co-op, others will as well. Because we all give of our time, we all share lower food costs.

However, if reciprocity is not observed, the system has to engage in punishment in order to right itself. Modern examples of this phenomenon have clearly identified both the importance of reciprocal altruism and chronicled responses to punishment mechanisms. For example, the Park Slope Food Co-Op in Brooklyn, New York, is notably successful, offering outstanding products at low costs. These costs can be explained by the fact that over 70 percent of the co-op's labor is covered by members. However, the co-op is also notoriously harsh in its treatment of individuals who fail to complete their share of the work required of them – forcing "repayment" in multiples of the amount of work or time missed (Ain, 2009.) While such punishment-driven reciprocity may make sense based on anthropological models, it also may alienate individuals who simply cannot reciprocate, due to work schedules or family demands.

These four motivations for collaboration are thus reflected in modern collaborative consumption systems, and the rich literature pertaining to each should be considered by theorists working in this domain. Each provides frameworks to explore theoretically interesting questions in contemporary settings. However, as Rand and Nowak (2013) note, "The simplicity of the strategy space of most evolutionary models does not reflect the intricacy of human psychology and decision-making" (p. 422). For example, anthropological and evolutionary perspectives have little to say about the way that multiple motivations to collaborate may interact with one another: Participating in a credit union could be based in reciprocal altruism, in that I anticipate that membership will allow me to borrow at a low interest rate in the future, but it may also be driven by the desire to signal to others in my profession that I identify strongly with the group. Tax-funded social safety net programs may be seen as a form of tolerated scrounging, in that members of a given society assent to pay a portion of their taxes for redistribution to those in need, but it may also be motivated by a culture that promotes interdependence among individuals. Further, for most consumer psychologists, the methods used in this work are difficult to replicate – few have the resources or training to engage in lengthy interview or participant-observer experiences with somewhat isolated tribes. Even if this were possible, it would be unclear how such insights could be translated to most consumers' experiences.

Fortunately, experimental economics builds on concepts from anthropology and provides methods that may help us to work with these constructs quite successfully. We turn to this literature next, both in order to enrich our understanding of these motivations and gain methods that may be more adaptable to consumer psychology research.

Views from Economics: Collaboration Is for Utility

Economists have a long tradition of using games to explore complex human interactions. One of the most famous of these games, the Prisoner's Dilemma (Rapoport & Chammah, 1965), is particularly relevant to situations involving mutual sacrifice and joint outcomes, such as those seen in collaborative consumption.[1] This method allows us to see how individuals make decisions to collaborate or defect while also providing a useful platform for the integration of new factors and contextual variables.

In a two-player Prisoner's Dilemma game, two individuals are faced with some version of the following scenario:

Two members of a criminal gang are arrested and imprisoned. Each prisoner is in solitary confinement with no means of speaking to or exchanging messages with the other. The police admit they lack enough evidence to convict the pair on the principal charge. They plan to sentence both to a year in prison on a lesser charge. Simultaneously, the police offer each prisoner a Faustian bargain. Each prisoner is given the opportunity either to betray the other, by testifying that the other committed the crime, or to cooperate with the other by remaining silent. Here is how it goes:

- If A and B both betray the other, each of them serves two years in prison.
- If A betrays B but B remains silent, A will be set free and B will serve three years in prison (and vice versa).
- If A and B both remain silent, both of them will serve only one year in prison (on the lesser charge).

Each individual has the option to defect, implicating the other prisoner, which would rationally lead to the shortest prison sentence for an individual, or to cooperate, by remaining silent. Despite researchers' a priori belief that defection should strongly dominate in a one-shot game, up to 50 percent of individuals studied chose to cooperate (Rapoport & Chammah 1965; Rapoport, 1995). When the game is played for multiple rounds, participants can learn, develop norms, and punish defectors (for examples, see Axelrod 1984; Axelrod & Hamilton, 1981). In such cases, the tendency may be to lock in on a cooperative strategy – and this tendency increases when participants gain more knowledge about one another or can coordinate their efforts (Wichman, 1970; and see Rapoport, 1995, for a longitudinal review of Prisoners' Dilemma research).

An *N*-person Prisoner's Dilemma is called a Public Goods Game (Fehr & Gintis, 2007) and can be structured to bear substantial greater resemblance to a collaborative consumption context.[2] In Public Goods Games, individuals

1 Other coordination games can also be used to explore individuals' decisions in joint-outcome situations. For example, the "chicken game" (Rapoport & Chammah, 1966; and see Wang et al., 2013, for a recent application) which makes the outcome of the game for one participant dependent on the behavior of another, offers another method for exploring dyadic behavior. In the chicken game, two individuals are walking on a path toward one another. Swerving is characteristic of a "chicken," or loser – and if both participants swerve, there is no payoff. However, if one participant swerves and the other does not, the non-swerving individual is the winner. If both partners do not swerve, they are both damaged (as they walk into one another).
2 The name of this game highlights the fact that the primary form of collaborative consumption for most individuals is donation to the public good via taxes. However, the fact that people do not choose to cooperate, but are instead required to do so, may change the extent to which it is viewed as inherently collaborative (see Lamberton, 2013). Thus, the extent to which a framework

voluntarily divide an initial pool between themselves and a "public account," which is shared with other players. (See Davis & Holt, 1994, and Ledyard, 1995, for in-depth discussions of Public Goods Games.) "Interest" on the public account is provided by multiplying the amount in the pool by some factor of two and redistributing the public account to all participants. Importantly, individuals receive from the public account whether or not they contributed, creating the possibility of free-riding. Past work has argued that individuals' decision to contribute to the public account is driven by anticipated reciprocation (Falk & Fischbacher, 2006). However, it has also been observed that when play is anonymous, individuals may drift toward free-riding (Fehr & Gintis, 2007), creating a classic "Tragedy of the Commons" problem (Hardin, 1968), where everyone withdraws but there is insufficient donation to sustain positive utility for all participants.

However, as the anthropologists suggested, anticipated reciprocity is only one possible motivator for collaboration. Croson's (2007) work causally disentangles the reasons why one might contribute to a public good, that is, why people may choose to contribute to a shared pool rather than keep resources for themselves. She discusses three specific theories. First, commitment theories suggest that individuals will behave in accordance with the Kantian imperative, that is, they will contribute the amount they believe everyone else will contribute. If everyone adheres to such a belief, public goods will be sufficiently funded. Such theories, she points out, have been used to explain water conservation, voting, and tax evasion tendencies.

A second explanation for participation in a public good is altruism. Here, a given individuals' contribution will be negatively correlated with others'; if others cannot contribute much, I will feel that I should contribute more, so that others can consume at an acceptable level. Under "impure altruism," this desire may be accompanied by a simultaneous benefit to the individual, perhaps in the "joy of giving" or "warm glow." Such motivations have been said to underlie hospitals' provision of services and contribution to charities. Further, in an echo of anthropology scholars and Gintis, Bowles, Boyd, and Fehr (2003), a third main motivation lies in reciprocity – the belief that I should reciprocate others' behavior, and they will reciprocate mine. Reciprocity has been used to explain tax evasion behaviors, workplace cooperation, and labor market behavior.

In her investigation, Croson finds evidence that reciprocity, rather than altruism or commitment, drives cooperative behaviors. This conclusion can be drawn based on the patterns of giving in a Public Goods Game – contribution tends to be positive and is positively correlated with other participants' giving. Such a pattern makes sense when one both trusts that others will match her own contributions and feels that they should match the contributions of others.

for collaborative consumption should also be applicable to consumers' motivations to pay taxes remains an interesting, and unresolved, question.

What happens when individuals do not experience reciprocation, in other words, when one donates to a shared good but does not receive back in kind? Can a collaborative system survive such a dynamic? Reinforcing the importance of punishment seen in anthropological work, economics research suggests that a system may survive defection if punishment and rewards can be used to maintain cooperation among members (West, Griffin, & Gardner, 2007). More specifically, individuals value punishment as protection from personal losses associated with others' defection. In addition, the threat of punishment can be used as a means of obtaining better outcomes (Krasnow, Cosmides, Pederson, & Tooby, 2012). As discussed by Gintis and colleagues (2003), the tendency to punish others for nonreciprocation and reward others for cooperation, even at an unrecoverable cost to oneself, underlies the principle of *strong reciprocity*.

Gintis and colleagues (2003) present experimental evidence that supports the argument that strong reciprocity can explain how a group of self-regarding individuals reaches stability. As they note, the punishment inherent in strong reciprocity is an inherent part of cooperative systems that may be observed in Western culture, such as penalties for tax noncompliance (Andreoni, Erard, & Feinstein, 1998) and efforts to protect environmental public goods or take other collective actions (Acheson, 1988; Ostrom, 1990[3]). In addition to possible economic gains, the economics literature highlights another reward of cooperation: the opportunity to build a positive reputation. That is, people may cooperate most fully when doing so will promote their own reputation and allow them to remain among individuals with desired characteristics or goods. Building a reputation, particularly over repeated interactions, provides a means of generating "social income" that motivates continued, visible cooperation (e.g., Becker, 1974).

Contemporary sharing systems' monitoring systems also suggest that a combination of punishment and observable reputation-building opportunities may be useful in sustaining collaborative consumption systems. For example, the punishment mechanisms used by the Park Slope Food Co-Op discussed previously may help motivate some degree of reciprocity, but likely would be even more effective if in addition to exiling noncooperators, particularly active contributors could gain rewards in the form of visible credit for their efforts. Reputation-building mechanisms such as Trustcloud have formalized the ability of collaborative consumers to gain trust from one another (Botsman, 2013). Trustcloud's tool (found at https://trustcloud.com/measure-trust) allows consumers to aggregate their interactions, that is, to verify identity, capture the responsiveness and consistency of communications, and integrate ratings and endorsements in peer-to-peer transactions as part of a portable trust profile. Importantly, such quantitative means of monitoring and displaying one's past

---

3 For a deeper look into game-theoretic work focusing on the positive resolution of common pool resource problems, particularly as related to natural resources, see Elinor Ostrom's work, notably Ostrom (1994). Among other things, this work sets out design principles for common pool resource institutions, most of which are relevant to political institutions.

collaborative behavior allow individuals to push beyond the bounds of kin sharing discussed by anthropologists – we may be willing to collaborate with strangers if they have a reputation for fair contributions to past collaborations, and we may collaborate well if we recognize that doing so provides us important social currency.

While experimental economic frameworks provide elegant methods for exploring sharing systems and reinforce the importance of some elements of collaborative consumption as identified in anthropological and evolutionary work, questions still persist about consumers' motivations for joining or remaining in a real-world collaborative system. We have also explored few benefits of collaborative consumption – so we can say little about when it should or should not be recommended for consumers. To build further on these theoretical cornerstones, we now add the complexity of insights from social psychology.

Insights from Cognitive and Social Psychology: Collaboration Is for Motivation

Morton Deutsch's early work offers a natural bridge from experimental economics to social psychology, as his early work in fact used a Prisoner's Dilemma framework. However, Deutch proposed that cooperation should be conceptualized in terms of individual motivation, or in consumer psychology language, goal pursuit. (Deutsch, 1958). Therefore, in his theory, competition is defined as the pursuit of one individual's goal at the expense of another's. That is, in pure competition, there is a negative value attached to another person's desired outcomes. Egoistic motives vary slightly from those in competition – one focuses only on his or her own goal attainment, but attaches no particular importance to whether others' goals are affected or not. By contrast, pure cooperation is characterized by the positive interdependence of individuals' goals – others' desired outcomes have a positive weight in decision making. Further, Deutsch's empirical work (see Deutsch, 2011, for a review) establishes that the benefits of collaboration extend beyond economic utility or the avoidance of punishment: cooperators develop trust, empathy, and positive affect. Interestingly, this positive affect may explain why cooperators develop more mutually beneficial solutions than do competitors when placed in a negotiation situation (De Dreu, Wingart, & Kwon, 2000).

A second major psychological theory adds yet more variables to the decision to cooperate: the loftiness of one's aspiration and willingness to relinquish one's goal. In Dual Concern Theory, individuals may be other-concerned, self-concerned, or somewhere in-between. Self-concern is related in some research to a high level of aspiration and unwillingness to yield to others (Kelley, Beckman, & Fischer, 1967). Other-concern is associated with a desire to cooperate (Pruitt & Lewis, 1975), and, like Deutsch's cooperation, yields a positive mood (Carnevale & Isen, 1986). Echoing kin selection theory, other-regarding cooperation tends to be more prevalent in interactions with friends rather than strangers (Fry, Firestone, & Williams, 1983).

Interestingly, however, empirical investigation also suggests that a collaborative system made up simply of other-regarding individuals will not be sustainable. Rather, other-regarding individuals also need to have a high resistance to yielding for cooperation to lead to develop integrative, mutually beneficial outcomes (DeDreu, Wingart, & Kwon, 2000). That is, the prosocial individual must be concerned about the desires of others, but must also be interested in promoting his or her own. When this occurs, cooperative systems can yield "win-wins" – creative, positive outcomes for all members.

Thus, Deutsch's theory would argue that collaborative consumption will be most attractive when consumers feel that they share positively related goals – when they do not feel that consumption involves a zero-sum game where another's "win" implies my "loss." Dual Concern Theory would suggest that successful collaborative consumption systems would prime the idea of cooperation consistently, perhaps through branding or slogans; promote positive mood among participants; and allow individuals either to cooperate with individuals they know or build a community among cooperators where such relationships can be formed. At the same time, however, this theory would encourage cooperators to stick to their own guns – not to simply give into the demands of those around them. If they were to do that, the cooperative system would likely collapse, as power and resources aggregated in the hands of only those who had higher resistance to yielding – and who may be self-concerned as well.

Social psychologists have also asked when collaboration as opposed to competition will lead to better outcomes, in general (see Johnson et al., 1981, and Stanne, Johnson, & Johnson, 1999, for meta-analytic reviews). Here, two key factors emerge. First, cooperation leads to better performance than competition when tasks are inherently interdependent – when labor can be divided and individuals can simultaneously progress en route to a shared goal. For example, well-coordinated group meals offer a perfect opportunity for cooperation, as each participant's contribution to a potluck furthers the group's goal. When interdependent motor tasks are considered, cooperation provides a substantial boost to performance relative to competition, with an average effect size of 1.67 (Stanne, Johnson, & Johnson, 1999). However, when individuals are engaging in independent tasks, cooperation has virtually no effect on performance relative to competition.

But all cases of competition and cooperation are not this pure, and not all competition is the same. Mixed forms of cooperation and competition have been variously referred to as "intergroup competition": when one cooperates with some individuals in the interest of triumphing over groups of others. Tauer and Harackiewicz (2004) report that on cognitive tasks, intergroup competition can enhance individual and group productivity (e.g., Erev, Bornstein & Galili, 1993; Mulvey & Ribbens, 1999), suggesting that pitting collaborative systems against one another may lead to greater productivity in the market as a whole.

That is, collaborative systems may have a worthwhile place – and be most beneficial – when they exist within a competitive market. "Inappropriate" competition has also been distinguished from "appropriate" competition – where competition is fair, progress is transparent, and all competitors have realistic chances of winning. Stanne, Johnson, and Johnson (1999) also found that in the few studies where competition was "appropriate," there was not a significant difference between competition and cooperation; the primary differences emerged when competition was structured in such a way that it was inherently unfair or lacked in transparency. Given recognition of growing inequality in the current economy (Desilver, 2014), perceptions that our market's competition structure is unfair may also motivate consumers to explore collaborative opportunities.

Psychologists also lend the insight that under certain circumstances, cooperation can enhance participants' motivation to pursue a goal. First, cooperation may enhance intrinsic motivation by increasing perceptions of relatedness to others. This finding suggests that rather than being dependent on the proximity of those around us to spur cooperation, as suggested by anthropology research, cooperation can in fact reduce the psychological proximity of those with whom we share. As this happens, we may become more committed to the collaborative effort. Second, if cooperation provides clear feedback – that is, if cooperators can clearly see how their combined efforts paid off – it may also enhance motivation to continue (Deci & Ryan, 1991; Ryan & Deci, 2000a, 2000b). Thus, providing clear communications about a system's successes and growth may also help consumers persist.

Finally, personality researchers and social psychologists have identified contextual and individual differences that may govern the tendency to participate in collaborative consumption. Interdependence theory (Kelley & Thibout, 1985; Rusbelt & VanLange, 1996) builds on a decision matrix reminiscent of those used in game theory, such that we can examine combinations of possible choices by two individuals who have the opportunity to cooperate or defect. The way matrices evolve depends not only on the power dynamics and correlation of goals between partners, but also on characteristics of the situation in which they make their decisions. For example, some situations involve little information about collaborators' preferences – these situations tend to lend themselves to either misunderstanding or information seeking (Erber & Fiske, 1984; Ickes & Simpson, 1997), both of which can shape future decisions to cooperate.

Individuals' attachment styles may also influence individuals' propensity to participate in sharing systems. For example, individuals who have a secure attachment style (Bowlby, 1969) may feel more comfortable in situations of dependence and may be less likely to exploit others with whom they cooperate (Baldwin et al., 1996; Simpson, Rholes, & Phillips. 1996; Tidwell, Reis, & Shaver, 1996). Further, some individuals simply tend to hold a more cooperative orientation from childhood forward; these individuals tend to grow more cooperative over time. By contrast, individuals who hold an inherently competitive orientation will perceive even neutral interactions as competitive and expect that others do the same, prompting others to behave competitively toward them (Messick & McClintock, 1968; Van Lange, 1999). Many other individual differences can also shape individuals' responses to cooperative situations, including gender (Van Vugt, De Cremer, & Janssen, 2007) trait self-control (Dzhogleva & Lamberton, 2014), and social norms (see Rusbelt & Van Lange, 2003, for a review). Finally, momentary affect can promote or impede collaborative behaviors. For example, Polman and Kim (2013) find that anger, disgust, and sharing can all influence the tendency to contribute to a shared pool of resources.

We can integrate these findings about goal pursuit and motivation into our framework: indeed, cooperation may be for utility. The maximal utility of cooperation is most likely to emerge when consumers can coordinate their efforts toward a shared goal, when the alternate competitive structure is inherently unfair or nontransparent, and when it is possible to see the relationship between one's contribution and the group's progress. Further, cooperation may have different effects based on many different factors of the individual and his or her group, and segmenting based on individual differences may also help us identify consumers among whom collaboration will be more or less attractive. Thus, we can continue to develop our stock of guides for individuals wishing to design successful systems and for consumers considering participation.

However, we are still missing critical information if we want to be able to make comprehensive recommendations: What types of goods are most amenable to collaborative consumption? And, returning to our initial discussion, when and why would a collaborative consumption platform begin to shift toward a competitive system?

Insights from Law and Consumer Research: Collaboration Is for Community

To make such concrete prescriptions, we next turn to frameworks that explicitly focus on sharing and collaborative consumption. While it is difficult to cover this literature completely, here I focus on some of the most generative, broad work in this area. The interested reader may wish to explore the works that have cited these important papers since their publication, to consider domain-specific applications and counterpoints to their findings.

Some of the most practical thinking about collaborative consumption has come from the legal domain. In his landmark paper, Benkler (2004) begins by discussing two examples of collaboration that defy previous frameworks from anthropology or experimental economics: the SETI@home distributed computing platform and carpooling. The SETI@home platform, at that time, constituted the world's fastest supercomputer and was based on the computers of more than 4 million volunteers, and carpooling, which was involved in about one-sixth of U.S. commuting trips. Both, Benkler notes, "rely on social relations and an ethic of sharing, rather than on a price system, to mobilize and allocate resources" (p. 275.)

Unlike the goods studied in economics and economics, however, both of these collaborative systems involve privately owned (not public) goods, are not limited to tightly knit communities, and include repeat interaction across many contexts. Further, SETI@home introduces the idea of a "greater good" that can be met by collaboration – the combined power of participants' computers can accomplish something that none could do alone. However, there is no direct benefit to participants other than the satisfaction of being part of this shared discovery process. Carpooling, by contrast, reflects an aversion to waste – which, while noted by anthropologists, was not shown to be a primary motivator of behavior in their work. Thus, while these contemporary sharing systems aim to extract unused utility from an economy, they also appear to have the potential for a richer set of motivations than can be captured by utility or individual goal pursuit alone.

Benkler specifies that the most sharable goods are "lumpy" and of "mid-grained granularity." Lumpy goods are provisioned in discrete units rather than as a continuous flow. For example, when one buys a car, she acquires a "lump" of space for five passengers. One cannot simply use one seat, separate from bringing along the four seats with which it is packaged. The four seats therefore represent wasted capacity, called "slack." Mid-grained granularity suggests that goods are well-distributed in a society (i.e., most people have them), and most people have an amount of slack that is large enough to make it worth contributing to a shared pool, but small enough that they do not feel they should retain personal control. To the extent that technology keeps connection and transaction costs low, collaborative systems can therefore extract unused utility from a society in ways that are more efficient than either the traditional market or the state can offer.

Though Benkler focuses on collaborative systems that exist among otherwise unconnected individuals, he also discusses the importance of social norms in perpetuating collaboration. People decide who can be included and excluded in access to a good, after all. Further, social exchanges lack the "crispness" characteristic of market transactions: We do not always know exactly how much we will receive in return for our investment, as we might when purchasing a bond or stock. Rather, the exact units of exchange may be coarsely or subjectively defined by participants, again depending on social norms for governance.

Importantly, the slippery slope from collaborative consumption toward a standard capitalist market system can be explained in Benkler's terms. As collaborative consumption systems grow, the drive for efficiency of exchange grows. This is most easily done via posted pricing and contract-driven exchange, which also helps promote a feeling of fairness and trust among partners. Individuals who have relatively little slack to enter into the collaboration will be less likely to participate, as the monetary return for them seems trivial in relation to the transaction costs necessary to participate. Because fewer individuals contribute their slack resources, the supply may be inadequate for all participants who would like to take part. Thus, pricing systems may be created that manage supply by excluding those who cannot pay to obtain the shared resources, in effect restricting access to those who can or will pay – even if this means all resources are not used and not all needs are met. As such, a collaborative system becomes a market system, acquiring its attendant waste and failure to meet all needs.

Consumer researcher Russell Belk's (2010) view of sharing also argues that we must begin to think beyond purely economic or rational models of sharing if we are to understand its impact on consumers and society. Belk first acknowledges prior work in anthropology and sociology. This work, as he notes, suggests that collaborative consumption may be fundamentally self-interested, as it operates by prompting an obligation of reciprocity. Further, he discusses scholarship that characterizes the sharing of paychecks, sexual relations, and the maintenance of shared space within a family as part of a contractual agreement, which, over time, we may describe as marriage (Ruskola, 2005). In short, such work reduces collaborative consumption to a means of survival or maximum joint utility, not strikingly different from the viewpoints from anthropology or economics.

Belk challenges this perspective, arguing that sharing can constitute something profoundly different from an alternate form of exchange. In this sense, he aligns with social psychologists who similarly considered that intangible benefits are key elements of cooperation (e.g. Fiske, 1991; Woodburn, 1998). The "more," to Belk, involves feelings of "solidarity and bonding" and "caring" created by shared goods (Belk, 2010, p. 717). Belk, too, can explain the potential for slippage from collaboration toward competition: As sharing systems grow, they may lose the sense of community that was their hallmark when smaller; they become more about "sharing out" – a way of dividing a resource among separate entities that does not "extend the boundaries of the self" – as opposed to "sharing in," which instead expands the domain of common property and integrates others into the self (p. 726). Because of a shift from sharing in to sharing out, a sense of community can be lost. Belk suggests that this disjointed sharing experience is precisely what distinguishes Felson and Spaeth's (1978) "collaborative consumption" work, focusing on car sharing, from sharing as experienced in families or tightly knit communities.

Other work also reinforces the idea that collaborative consumption has at its heart a drive for community and connection (Albinsson & Perera, 2012). Further, these authors note that many collaborative consumption systems have arisen as overt rejections of a capitalist economic model that tolerates, and even promotes, overconsumption and other unsustainable practices (see also Cherrier, 2009). Such collaborative systems challenge the suggestion that reciprocity and balanced exchange underlie sharing systems, as collaborative consumption often persists with the exchange of nominal or nonexistent amounts of money or valued goods. Rather, membership may be sustained primarily by ideology or shared values, even if a given participant is solely a donor and withdraws very little of the shared resources. Indeed, some quantitative work echoes the idea of "anti-industry utility" in promoting illegal movie sharing (Hennig-Thurau, Henning, & Sattler, 2007), but it is unclear whether this motivation exists in all domains (Lamberton & Rose, 2012).

If collaborative consumption generates interpersonal connection, it stands to reason that it may also affect other facets of consumer experience. As collaborative consumption systems mature, it becomes possible to capture data on the ways that participation in such systems can shape consumers' vocabulary and cognitive and social structures over time. Fascinating new work examining data from the car-sharing system Uber (Giesler and Versiu, 2014) suggests that these changes may be quite profound, affecting multiple aspects of consumer experience and behavior. Importantly, this new wave of research takes us far beyond prior conceptualizations of cooperation, which presented the individual as a stable part of a fixed system, where an individual actor made predictable decisions in a family, economic game, goal structure, or decision-making context. While some learning could occur, we did not observe wholesale changes to consumers' processing or discourse. As consumers participate in collaborative consumption experiences over time, we can expect that both consumers and systems will jointly influence one another.

Key Constructs and Open Questions

Returning to the opening anecdote, we may ask: What does all of this tell us about how and why neighbors might share a tool rather than buying it themselves? Rather than having a lack of theory to guide us, this integrative review demonstrates that if we draw from multiple perspectives on human cooperation, we are able to sketch out parameters that may help us understand optimal design of collaborative consumption systems and their likely outcomes. Further, unanswered questions in recurrent themes prompt us to push for deeper understanding – presenting vast opportunity for consumer researchers.

Balancing Economic and Social Goals

This review has highlighted the fact that collaboration can meet numerous goals, from the very utilitarian (survival and economic utility) to those focused more on intangible outcomes (psychological experiences, conformity with social norms, social connectedness, or the "warm glow" of working with others.) While some proponents of collaborative consumption place primary value on social and psychological outcomes (e.g., Gorenflo, 2013), others appear comfortable focusing on the gains in economic efficiency and financial well-being provided by collaboration (e.g., Botsman & Rogers, 2010). The clear indication of our review is that economic, psychological, and social motivation may all be powerful collaboration cues. To attract and sustain participation, research needs to identify both optimal and tolerable balances of various benefits of collaboration for different types of consumers in different sharing domains.

The lamented drift of collaborative consumption systems toward competitive marketplace structures is also not without explanation by academic research. Rather, the work discussed would anticipate that when systems originally designed to foster interpersonal connectedness become very large or complex, they may also become less transparent or be perceived as unfair. Simultaneously, in a large system the drive for efficiency might trump social concerns, make trust more difficult, connect less-related individuals, and lead to a need for a more externally regulated system of punishment and reward. Thus, the marketization of collaborative consumption should not be unexpected. What we still do not know is whether such shifts can or should be prevented, if our goal is to support consumers' overall well-being. Can such shifts be made acceptable to consumers through appropriate communications? Or should some systems be protected from a pro-market shift, such that critical social benefits remain paramount?

The Limits of Reciprocity

Our review also suggests that collaborative consumption systems are likely to be most successful when participants anticipate not only providing to, but also benefiting from, the cooperative effort. By contrast, if individuals are concerned that, either because of free-riding, a lack of communication, or a sense of competition for resources, they will not receive any benefit, they lean toward sole ownership.

However, even this conclusion leaves many questions open, as reciprocity itself is a complex construct (see Molm, 2010, for a discussion). What degree of economic reciprocation is necessary in our contexts? In its simplest forms, the required return on one's contribution appears to be far from direct: In hunter-gatherer and agricultural-forager populations, the correlation between giving and receipt is between .10 and .65 – an acquirer giving away 1 percent of his production could expect only .33 percent in return (Gurven, 2004). But how do modern consumers think about the necessity of reciprocation, and how does this vary across contexts, consumers, and situations? Further, over what time horizon will individuals require reciprocity for it to be deemed appropriate, and not warrant punishment or defection? (See Gurven, 2004, p. 551, for a discussion.) When can social utility compensate for low levels of economic reciprocity? Can the reliance on social utility to offset economic loss ever become exploitative?

The importance of addressing these questions in terms of a modern collaborative consumption context is quite clear. Perhaps a consumer opts to enter her tools into a tool library. Perhaps she does so because she is an avid woodworker and has a basement full of often-unused tools. However, she may find that as her interest and investment has surpassed that of many other participants, when she needs a specific, high-end tool, she is still faced with the need to acquire it herself. Such "apex donators" may sense little reciprocation in a collaborative consumption system – but will they mind? Given the importance of their resources in a healthy collaborative resource pool, can they be encouraged to maintain participation, perhaps by prompting the adoption of altruistic motives or generation of a longer-term horizon?

The Role of Trust and Punishment

One means of maintaining both the intangible and economic benefits of collaborative consumption is to foster trust among collaborators – a theme that also echoes across multiple disciplines. As discussed, technology helps collaborators build reputations and provide grounds for trust, even among strangers. Some work suggests that individuals differ in their "trust threshold" – they may simply need more or less trust to collaborate, or this may vary by context (Tanz, 2014). However, much remains to be learned about other ways to build enduring trust among collaborators. How much, and what type, of reputational evidence is needed for trust to emerge? How can trust, once violated, be regained in these contexts? What attribution processes do participants use when trying to understand a violation of trust in a collaborative consumption effort?

If a platform wishes to generate trust extrinsically, one option is to put in place punishment mechanisms, which also appear across theoretical perspectives. However, we should also note that such explicitly enumerated punishment mechanisms may be among the very elements that reduce the social benefit of collaboration. First, it may be argued that social exchange differs from market exchange in the absence of such precise, tit-for-tat arrangements (Benkler, 2004). Adding such mechanisms may shade the system inexorably toward contractually governed market experiences. Second, even in relatively simple economics games, punishment can change peoples' perceptions of the system and one another: a punisher's reputation can be damaged, leading to alienation by other players (Ostrom, 1994). So is there a role for punishment in modern collaborative consumption contexts, or should "carrots" rather than "sticks" be used to prompt appropriate participation? Can we propose creative ways that noncontractually-defined collaborative consumption systems can maintain trust among members, or is some form of punishment simply necessary?

The Dynamics of the Collaborative Group

Another pervasive theme in this review is the importance of the group with whom one shares. We will share with those like us: those who have goals that are positively correlated with our own, with whom we can communicate, and whom we trust. At the same time, however, some work suggests that if individuals anticipate high similarity in use, they may anticipate higher competition for scarce resources and opt to lower this risk via more costly sole ownership (Lamberton & Rose, 2012). Indeed, complementarity in use may be preferable in modern collaborative consumption settings, such that one has slack available at the time when others are in need, and vice versa. Also, we know that perceptions of interpersonal similarity are highly subject to contextual cues, even in shared spaces such as online communities (e.g., Naylor, Lamberton, & West, 2011). Future research may explore the way that similarity and relatedness are evaluated and the effects they produce at different points in a collaborative system's development – it may be that while important initially as a means of establishing trust, homophily decreases in importance as individuals shift their focus to the collaboration's efficiency.

Technology

Throughout the literature reviewed, we see that communication among collaborators, transparency, monitoring, trust and reputation building, alignment of potentially proximally distal "slack" with needs, coordination of goals, and community building can all foster healthy collaborative consumption systems. Without the advances in technology of the last few decades, collaborative consumption almost certainly could not have boomed as it has, as technology facilitates coordination and reduces many aspects of the transaction's costs. However, technology can do many things – and just as not all of them may be beneficial to individuals, they may not all be beneficial for collaborative consumption systems. Concerns that technology may isolate people (Greengard, 2011) or facilitate dishonest behavior (Citera, Beauregard, & Mitsuya, 2005) may raise the questions of whether highly technology-dependent forms of collaborative consumption are ideal. Further, access to technology is not universal, which may reduce access to collaborative systems for the consumers who may most benefit. Future work can explore the influence of different technologies on these frameworks and various types of collaborative systems. It may be that heavily technology-mediated collaborative systems provide distinctly different benefits and present different dangers than do more human-to-human collaborations, but that they also present different types of risks and shortcomings.

The Primacy of Ownership and the Emergence of a Sharing Ethic

Whether intrinsically or culturally motivated, it appears that there may simply be mindsets that make individuals less attached to the idea of personal ownership. In Benkler's (2004) terms, they may adopt a "sharing ethic." Some research suggests that a shift in the zeitgeist has reduced individuals' attachment to ownership (e.g., Chen, 2009) while other work points out that the lines between ownership and possession may not be completely clear in all cases (Jenkins, Molesworth, & Scullion, 2014). Some work suggests that engagement in alternative forms of exchange may also be associated with greater civic engagement, hinting that if a sharing ethic is adopted, it may also foster other positive outcomes (Nelson, Rademacher, & Paek, 2007). Yet, Rachel Botsman suggests that many companies reject collaborative consumption opportunities in the belief that "Owning something is the holy grail" (quoted in Gardner, 2013). How can a collaborative ethic be fostered in individuals or a community? If the connection to sole ownership is weakened, how can we avoid the diffusion of responsibility that may occur (e.g., Darley & Latané, 1968) and instead foster an ethic of responsible collaboration?

New Domains

A broader consideration of collaborative consumption in the scope of this volume suggests that theoretical frameworks for its study should be flexible enough to address domains that lie even outside Botsman and Rogers' broad descriptions. For example, we may consider the way that consumers evaluate healthcare. As Schwartz (Chapter 24 in this volume; also McGraw, Schwartz, & Tetlock, 2012) discusses, sacred values such as health may prompt the tolerance of price increases if such expenditures are framed in terms of communal sharing. However, consumers may reject similar price increases if they are framed in terms of market pricing. Can collaborative consumption lower price sensitivity, and should it? Further, studies of income inequality suggest that we may find more willingness to collaborate among lower-income consumers (Chapter 25 in this volume), but policy makers should also be sensitive to the possibility of exploitation among this segment – having relatively little personal slack, a system that does not ensure reciprocation or contain enough excess to cover needs could create more danger than security. In addition, we may connect the idea of collaborative consumption to ethical consumption more broadly. Rather than focusing on specific attributes of products (Chapter 19 in this volume), it may be that a collaborative mode of acquisition raises perceptions of a given act of consumption as ethical. However, this may be an unhelpful placebo – simply because I gain use of a gas-guzzling SUV via a car-sharing system does not reduce the vehicle's environmental impact. Likely, to design collaborative systems that avoid such perverse psychological effects, we will need to understand how consumers think about collaborative consumption as part of a portfolio of consumption decisions.

Are All Outcomes of Collaborative Consumption Positive?

If properly structured and applied to appropriate tasks, it seems that collaboration can decrease waste, increase productivity and efficiency, accomplish tasks larger than could be carried out by a single individual, build positive affect, and create connections. Further, the individuals who start such sharing platforms can make a great deal of money: AirBnb's market value was estimated at $13 billion (Lorenzetti, 2014), while Uber was "rumored" to have a value between $3.5 billion and $10 billion (Saitto, 2014). However, we also recognize that some dangers exist in collaboration, from free-riding to exploitation of other-centric consumers by self-focused individuals. For example, individuals who rely on collaborative consumption platforms for regular income, such as Uber and Lyft drivers or Taskrabbit helpers, face substantial uncertainty due to changes in the systems in which they work, the lack of protective regulation, and the idiosyncrasies of demand and payment from other participants (Singer, 2014).

In addition, some experts argue that collaborative consumption offers a deceptively appealing band-aid for systemic economic crises (Cagle, 2013). Because people can help cover the cost of their rent by leasing out a room in their home via AirBnb, the pressure for policy makers to avoid addressing untenable increases in housing costs may decrease. Similarly, because under-employed individuals can make extra money "on the side" by driving for Uber in the evenings, calls for attention to income inequality and excess student loan debt may stay muffled a bit longer. But what psychological costs are incurred by the individual who becomes reliant on others and loses control of his or her own space? What costs, in terms of stress, health, family wellness, and foregone opportunities for additional training or pursuit of other job options, will the part-time Uber driver incur? Can the creation of a "freelancers union" (Horowitz, 2014) protect the economic and health interests of these collaborative consumption participants without undermining the distinct social benefits of volitional cooperation?

There are many other questions open to consumer psychologists' exploration, and much nuance to be added to this conceptual landscape. As a discipline that has historically been interdisciplinary, and as the bulk of collaborative consumption systems involve elements with which consumer psychologists are intimately concerned, we may be particularly well positioned to develop a rigorous framework for understanding these current phenomena. Further, this approach may be able to help us both better understand the nature of collaboration in present-day consumption and design systems in ways that tap the greatest amount of potential – in terms of economic, social, and psychological outcomes.

References

Acheson, J. (1988). *The Lobster Gangs of Maine*. Hanover, NH: University Press of New England.

Ain, A.J. (2009). Flunking out at the food co-op. *New York Times*, October 25. Retrieved from www.nytimes.com/2009/10/25/nyregion/25coop.html?pagewanted= all&_r=1&.

Albinsson, P.A. & Perera, B. Y. (2012). Alternative marketplaces in the 21st century: Building community through sharing events. *Journal of Consumer Behaviour, 11* (4), 303–15.

Albinsson, P.A., Wolf, M., & Kopf D.A. (2010). Anti-consumption in East Germany: Consumer resistance to hyperconsumption. *Journal of Consumer Behaviour, 9*(6), 412–425.

Alperovitz, G. (2013). *What Must We Then Do? Straight Talk about the Next American Revolution*. White River Junction, VT: Chelsea.

Andreoni, J., Erard, B., & Feinstein, J. (1998). Tax compliance. *Journal of Economic Literature, 36.* 818–60.

Axelrod, R. (1984). *The Evolution of Cooperation.* New York: Basic Books.

Axelrod, R. (1986). An evolutionary approach to norms. *American Political Science Review, 80,* 1095–1111.

Axelrod, R., & Hamilton, W. (1981). The evolution of cooperation. *Science, 211,* 1390–1396.

Baldwin, M.W., Keelan, J.P.R., Fehr, B., Enns, V., & Koh-Rangarajoo, E. (1996). Social-cognitive conceptualization of attachment working models: Availability and accessibility effects. *Journal of Personality and Social Psychology, 71,* 94–109.

Bardhi, F., & Eckhardt, G.M. (2012). Access-based consumption: The case of car sharing. *Journal of Consumer Research, 39*(4), 881–898.

Becker, G. (1974). A theory of social interaction. *Journal of Political Economy, 82,* 1063–1093.

Belk, R. (2010). Sharing. *Journal of Consumer Research, 36* (5), 715–734.

Benkler, Y. (2004). Sharing nicely: On shareable goods and the emergency of sharing as a modality of economic production. *Yale Law Journal. 114*(2), 273–358.

Botsman, R. (2013). The sharing economy lacks a shared definition. Retrieved from www.collaborativeconsumption.com/2013/11/22/the-sharing-economy-lacks-a-shared-definition/.

Botsman, R., & Rogers, R. (2010). *What's Mine Is Yours: The Rise of Collaborative Consumption.* New York: Harper Collins.

Bowlby, J. (1969). *Attachment and Loss, vol. 1: Attachment.* New York: Basic Books.

Cagle, S. (2013). The sharing economy, from soup to nuts. Retrieved from http://grist.org/basics/the-sharing-economy-from-soup-to-nuts/.

Carnevale, P.J., & Isen, A.M. (1986). The influence of positive affect and visual access on the discovery of intergrative solutions in bilateral negotiation. *Organizational Behavior and Human Decision Processes, 37*(1), 1–13.

Chen, Y. (2009). Possession and access: Consumer desires and value perceptions regarding contemporary art collection and exhibit visits. *Journal of Consumer Research, 35*(April), 925–940.

Cherrier, Helene (2009). Anti-consumption discourses and consumer-resistant identities. *Journal of Business Research, 62*(2), 181–190.

Citera, M., Beauregard, R., & Mitsuya, T. (2005). An experimental study of credibility in e-negotiations. *Psychology & Marketing, 22*(2), 163–179.

Cosmides, L., & Tooby, J. (1992). Cognitive adaptations for social exchange. In J. Barkow, L. Cosmides, & J. Tooby (eds.), *The Adapted Mind: Evolutionary Psychology and the Generation of Culture.* Oxford: Oxford University Press.

Croson, R. T. A. (2007). Theories of commitment, altruism and reciprocity: Evidence from linear public goods games. *Economic Inquiry, 45*(2), 199–216.

Darley, J. M. & Latané, B. (1968). Bystander intervention in emergencies: Diffusion of responsibility. *Journal of Personality and Social Psychology, 8,* 377–383.

Davis, D., & Holt, C. (1994). *Experimental Economics.* Princeton, NJ: Princeton University Press.

Dawes, R. M., & Thaler, R. H. (1990). Anomalies: Cooperation. *Journal of Economic Perspectives, 2*(3), 187–197.

De Dreu, C. K. W., Wingart, L. R. & Kwon, S. (2000). Influence of social motives on integrative negotiation: A meta-analytic review and test of two theories. *Journal of Personality and Social Psychology, 78*(5), 889–905.

Denegri-Knott, J., & Molesworth, M. (2010). Love it. Buy it. Sell it. Consumer desire and the social drama of ebay. *Journal of Consumer Culture, 10*(1), 56–79.

Deci, E., & Ryan, R. (1991). A motivational approach to self: Integration in personality. In R. Dientsbier (ed.), *Perspectives on Motivation. Nebraska Symposium on Motivation* (pp. 237–288). Lincoln, NE: University of Nebraska Press.

Desilver, D. (2014). Americans agree inequality has grown, but don't agree on why. Pew Research Center, April 28. Accessed online at www.pewresearch.org/fact-tank/2014/04/28/americans-agree-inequality-has-grown-but-dont-agree-on-why/.

Deutsch, M. (1949). A theory of cooperation and competition. *Human Relations, 2*, 199–231.

Deutsch, M. (1958). Trust and suspicion. *Journal of Conflict Resolution, 2*, 265–279.

Deutsch, M. (2011). Cooperation and competition, In P.T. Coleman (ed.), *Conflict, Interdependence and Justice: The Intellectual Legacy of Morton Deutsch* (pp. 23–40). New York: Springer.

Dzhogleva, H., & Lamberton, C. (2014). Should birds of a feather flock together? Understanding self-control decisions in dyads. *Journal of Consumer Research, 41*(2), 361–380.

Erber, R., & Fiske, S. T. (1984). Outcome dependency and attention to inconsistent information. *Journal of Personality and Social Psychology, 47*, 709–726.

Erev, I., Bornstein, G., & Galili, R. (1993). Constructive intergroup competition as a solution to the free rider problem: A field experiment. *Journal of Experimental Social Psychology, 29*, 463–478.

Falk, A., & Fischbacher, U. (2006). A theory of reciprocity. *Games and Economic Behavior, 54*, 293–315.

Fehr, E., & Gintis, H. (2007). Human motivation and social cooperation: Experimental and analytical foundations. *Annual Review of Sociology, 33*, 43–64.

Felson, M., & Spaeth, J.L. (1978). Community structure and collaborative consumption. *American Behavioral Scientist, 21*, 614–624.

Fiske, A.P. (1991). *Structures of Social Life: The Four Elementary Forms of Social Relations.* New York: Free Press.

Fry, W. R., Firestone, I. J., & Williams, D. L. (1983). Negotiation process and outcome of stranger dyads and dating couples: Do lovers lose? *Basic and Applied Social Psychology, 4*, 1–16

Gansky, L. (2010). *The Mesh: Why the Future of Business Is Sharing.* New York: Penguin.

Gardner, J. (2013). The sharer barer: Rachel Botsman on the new democracy. *London Standard*, June 27. Retrieved from www.standard.co.uk/lifestyle/london-life/the-sharer-barer-rachel-botsman-on-the-new-democracy-8676228.html.

Giesler, M., & Veresiu, E. (2014). Building a sharing economy: The case of Uber. Working Paper, Schulich School of Business, York University, Canada, M3J1P3.

Gintis, H., Bowles, S., Boyd, R., & Fehr, E. (2003). Explaining altruistic behavior in humans. *Evolution and Human Behavior, 24*, 153–172.

Gorenflo, N. (2013). Collaborative consumption is dead, long live the real sharing economy. Pando.com, March 19. Retrieved from http://pando.com/2013/03/19/collaborative-consumption-is-dead-long-live-the-real-sharing-economy/.

Greengard, S. (2011). Living in a digital world. *Communications of the ACM, 54*(10), 17–19.

Griskevicius, V., Tybur, J. M., Sundie, J. M., Cialdini, R. B., Miller, G. F., & Kenrick, D. T. (2007). Blatant benevolence and conspicuous consumption: When romantic motives elicit strategic costly signals. *Journal of Personality and Social Psychology, 93*(1), 85–102.

Guercini, S., Corciolani, M., & Dalli, D. (2014). Gift-giving, sharing and commodity exchange at Bookcrossing.com: New insights from a qualitative analysis. *Management Decision, 52*(4), 755–776.

Gurven, M. (2004). To give and give not: The behavioral ecology of human food transfers. *Behavioral and Brain Sciences, 27*, 543–583.

Hamilton, W.D. (1964). The genetical evolution of social behavior I & II. *Journal of Theoretical Biology, 7*, 1–52.

Hardin, G. (1968). The tragedy of the commons. *Science, 162*(3859), 1243–1248.

Hennig-Thurau, T., Henning, V., & Sattler, H. (2007). Consumer file sharing of motion pictures. *Journal of Marketing, 71*(4), 1–18.

Hill, K., & Kaplan, H. (1993). On why male foragers hunt and share food. *Current Anthropology, 34*, 701–710.

Hopkins, R. (2011). *The Transition Companion*. White River Junction, VT: Chelsea Green.

Horowitz, S. (2014). America, say goodbye to the era of big work. Retrieved from www.latimes.com/opinion/op-ed/la-oe-horowitz-work-freelancers-20140826-story.html.

Ickes, W., & Simpson, J. A. (1997). Managing empathic accuracy in close relationships. In W. Ickes (ed.), *Empathic Accuracy* (pp. 218–250). New York: Guilford Press.

Jaeggi, A. V., & Gurven, M. (2013). Natural cooperators: Food sharing in humans and other primates. *Evolutionary Anthropology, 22*, 186–195.

Jaeggi, A. V., Stevens J. M. G., & Van Schalk, C. P. (2010). Tolerant food sharing and reciprocity is precluded by despotism among bonobos but not chimpanzees. *American Journal of Physical Anthropology, 143*, 41–51.

Jenkins, R., Molesworth, M., & Scullion, R. (2014). The messy lives of objects: Interpersonal borrowing and the ambiguity of possession and ownership. *Journal of Consumer Behaviour, 13*(2), 131–139.

Johnson, D., Maryuama, G., Johnson, R., Nelson, D., & Skon, L. (1981). Effects of cooperative, competitive and individualistic goal structures on achievement: A meta-analysis. *Psychological Bulletin, 89*, 47–62.

Kelley, H. H., Beckman, L. L., & Fischer, C. S. (1967). Negotiating the division of reward under incomplete information. *Journal of Experimental Social Psychology, 3*, 361–389.

Kelley, H. H., & Thibaut, J. W. (1985). Self-interest, science, and cynicism. *Journal of Social Clinical Psychology, 3*(1), 2b–32.

Krasnow, M. M., Cosmides, L., Pederson, E. J., & Tooby, J. (2012). What are punishment and reputation for? *PLoS ONE, 7*(9), e45662.

Lamberton, C. (2013). A spoonful of choice: How allocation increases satisfaction with tax payments. *Journal of Public Policy & Marketing, 32*(2), 223–238.

Lamberton, C., & Rose, R. (2012). When is ours better than mine? A framework for understanding and altering participation in commercial sharing systems. *Journal of Marketing, 76*(4), 109–125.

Ledyard, J. O. (1995). Public goods: A survey of experimental research. in J. Kagel & A. Roth (eds.), *Handbook of Experimental Economics.* Princeton, NJ: Princeton University Press.

Lorenzetti, L. (2014). Airbnb's valuation set to reach $13 billion after employee stock sale. *Fortune,* October 24. Retrieved from http://fortune.com/2014/10/24/airbnbs-valuation-set-to-reach-13-billion-after-employee-stock-sale/.

McGraw, P. A., Schwartz, J. A., & Tetlock, P. E. (2012). From the commercial to the communal: Reframing taboo trade-offs in religious and pharmaceutical marketing. *Journal of Consumer Research, 39*(1), 157–173.

Messick, D. M., & McClintock, C. G. (1968). Motivational bases of choice in experimental games. *Journal of Experimental Social Psychology, 4*(1), 1–25.

Molm, L. D. (2010). The structure of reciprocity. *Social Psychology Quarterly, 73*(2), 199–131.

Mulvey, P. W., & Ribbens, B. A. (1999). The effects of intergroup competition and assigned group goals on group efficacy and group effectiveness. *Small Group Research, 30*(6), 651–677.

Naylor, R. W., Lamberton, C. P., & West, P. M. (2011). Beyond the "like" button: The impact of mere virtual presence on brand evaluations and purchase intentions in social media settings. *Journal of Marketing, 76*(6), 105–120.

Nelson, M. R., Rademacher, M. A., & Paek, H. (2007). Downshifting consumer = upshifting citizen? An examination of a local freecycling community. *American Academy of Political and Social Science, 511,* 141–156.

Nowak, M.A. (2006). Five rules for the evolution of cooperation. *Science, 314,* 1560–1563.

Ostrom, E. (1990). *Governing the Commons: The Evolution of Institutions for Collective Action.* Cambridge: Cambridge University Press.

Ozanne, L. K. & Ballentine, P. W. (2010). Sharing as a form of anti-consumption? An examination of toy library users. *Journal of Consumer Behaviour, 9*(6), 485–498.

Polman, E., & Kim, S. H. (2013). Effects of anger, disgust and sadness on sharing with others. *Personality and Social Psychology Bulletin, 39*(12), 1683–1692.

Pruitt, D. C., & Lewis, S. A. (1975). Development of integrative solutions in bilateral negotiation. *Journal of Personality and Social Psychology, 31,* 621–633.

Pruitt, D. G., & Rubin, J. Z. (1986). *Social Conflict: Escalation, Stalemate, and Settlement.* New York: Random House.

Rand, D. G., & Nowak, M. A. (2013). Human cooperation. *Trends in Cognitive Sciences, 17*(8), 413–425.

Rapoport, A. (1995). Prisoner's Dilemma: Reflections and recollections. *Simulation Gaming, 26,* 489–503.

Rapoport, A., & Chammah, A. M. (1965). *Prisoner's Dilemma.* Ann Arbor: University of Michigan Press.

Rapoport, A., & Chammah, A. M. (1966). The game of chicken. *American Behavioral Scientist, 10*(3), 10–28.

Ridley, M. (1996). *The Origins of Virtue: Human Instincts and the Evolution of Cooperation.* New York: Viking.

Rusbelt, C. E., & van Lange, P. A. M. (1996). Interdependence processes. In E. T. Higgins & A. W. Kruglanski (eds.), *Social Psychology: Handbook of Basic Principles* (pp. 564–596). New York: Guilford Press.

Rusbelt, C. E., & van Lange, P. A. M. (2003). Interdependence, interaction and relationships. *Annual Review of Psychology, 54*, 351–375.

Ruskola, T. (2005). Home economics: What is the difference between a family and a corporation? In M. Ertman & M. Williams (eds.), *Rethinking Commodification: Cases and Readings in Law and Culture* (pp. 324–344), New York: New York University Press.

Ryan, R., & Deci, E. (2000a). Intrinsic and extrinsic motivations: Classic definitions and new directions. *Contemporary Educational Psychology, 25*, 54–67.

Ryan, R., & Deci, E. (2000b). Self-determination theory and the facilitation of intrinsic motivation, social development, and well-being. *American Psychologist, 55*, 68–78.

Saitto, S. (2014). Uber said to be in funding talks for more than $10B value. *Bloomberg Business*, May 15. Retrieved from www.bloomberg.com/news/articles/2014-05-15/uber-said-to-be-in-funding-talks-for-more-than-10b-value.

Schwartz, A. (2013). The top 11 collaborative consumption stories of 2013. Fastcoexist.com, December 13. Retrieved September 29, 2014, from www.fastcoexist.com/3023086/the-top-11-collaborative-consumption-stories-of-2013.

Sherry, Jr., J. (1990). A sociocultural analysis of a Midwestern American flea market. *Journal of Consumer Research, 17*(1), 13–30..

Simpson, J. A., Rholes, W. S., & Phillips, D. (1996). Conflict in close relationships: An attachment perspective. *Journal of Personality and Social Psychology, 71*, 899–914.

Singer, N. (2014). In the sharing economy, workers find both freedom and uncertainty. *New York Times*, August 16. Retrieved from www.nytimes.com/2014/08/17/technology/in-the-sharing-economy-workers-find-both-freedom-and-uncertainty.html

Stanne, M. B., Johnson, D. W., & Johnson, R. T. (1999). Does competition enhance or inhibit motor performance: A meta-analysis. *Psychological Bulletin, 125*(1), 133–154.

Tanz, Jason (2014). How Airbnb and Lyft finally got Americans to trust each other. Wired.com, April 23. Retrieved from www.wired.com/2014/04/trust-in-the-share-economy/.

Tauer, J. M., & Harackiewicz, J. M. (2004). The effects of cooperation and competition on intrinsic motivation and performance. *Journal of Personality and Social Psychology, 86*(6), 849–861.

Thompson, L. (1990). Negotiation behavior and outcomes: Empirical evidence and theoretical issues. *Psychological Bulletin, 108*, 515–532.

Tidwell, M. C. O., Reis, H. T., & Shaver, P. R. (1996). Attachment, attractiveness and social interaction: A diary study. *Journal of Personality and Social Psychology, 71*, 729–745.

Trivers, R. L. (1971). The evolution of reciprocal altruism. *Quarterly Review of Biology, 35*, 35–57.

U.S. Department of Agriculture. (2014). Let's glean! United We Serve toolkit. Retrieved September 30, 2014, from www.usda.gov/documents/usda_gleaning_toolkit.pdf.

Van Lange, P. A. M. (1999). The pursuit of joint outcomes and equality in outcomes: An integrative model of social value orientation. *Journal of Personality and Social Psychology, 77*, 337–334.

Van Vugt, M., De Cremer, D., & Janssen, D.P. (2007). Gender differences in cooperation and competition. *Psychological Science, 18*(1), 19–23.

Walsh, B. (2011). Today's smart choice: Don't own. Share. *Time, 177*(12), 62.

Wang, Y., Roberts, K., Yuan, B., Zhang, W., Shen, D., & Simons, R. (2013). Psychophysiological correlates of interpersonal cooperation and aggression. *Biological Psychology, 93*(3), 386–391.

West, S. A., Griffin, A. S., & Gardner, A. (2007). Social semantics: Altruism, cooperation, mutualism, strong reciprocity and group selection. *European Society for Evolutionary Biology, 20*, 415–432.

Wichman, H. (1970). Effects of isolation and communication in a two-person game. *Journal of Personality and Social Psychology, 16*, 114–30.

Winterhalder, B. (1996). Social foraging and the behavioral ecology of intragroup resource transfers. *Evolutionary Anthropology, 5*(2), 46–57.

Woodburn, J. (1998). Sharing is not a form of exchange: An analysis of property-sharing in immediate-return hunter-gatherer societies. In C. M. Hann (ed.), *Property Relations: Renewing the Anthropological Tradition* (pp. 48–53). Cambridge: Cambridge University Press.

Yglesias, M. (2013). There is no "sharing economy." Slate.com, December 26. Retrieved from www.slate.com/blogs/moneybox/2013/12/26/myth_of_the_sharing_econo my_there_s_no_such_thing.html.

27 Globalization, Culture, and Consumer Behavior

Carlos J. Torelli and Shirley Y. Y. Cheng

As globalization increases, the world is becoming smaller and the consciousness of the world as a whole is intensifying rapidly. With the rapid growth of global linkages and global consciousness, the marketplace is also growing in cultural diversity both in terms of the demand side (i.e., consumer markets) and the supply side (i.e., brand offerings). Increased cultural diversity in the demand side of the market is fueled by the emergence of a robust middle class in emerging economies (such as those of China, Russia, Brazil, and India), the immigration patterns changing the cultural landscape of developed markets (e.g., growth of Hispanics in the United States or that of Muslim populations in Europe), and the increased cultural curiosity of worldwide consumers thanks to Internet connectivity, social media platforms, and global travel.

The supply side of the market is witnessing the emergence of global brands from every corner of the developed and developing world. Specifically, the last decade has witnessed a tremendous growth in the number of new American and European brands successfully establishing a global presence in emerging markets. For instance, one may consider the American brand Jack Daniel's success in China and Europe, which has helped the company to sell more whiskey abroad than in the United States (Kiley, 2007). Or consider the high-stakes expansion of Spanish phone company Telefónica into Latin America, which has been instrumental for helping the company become the largest telecommunications company in Europe (O'Brien, 2012). More importantly, brands from emerging markets have also recently emerged as global challengers. Consider, for example, the leadership position achieved in recent years by Chinese Lenovo Group in the personal computer industry, overtaking competitors Hewlett-Packard and Dell in worldwide sales (Hachman, 2014), the recent entry of India's Tata Group into the luxury cars segment via the acquisition of the Jaguar and Land Rover brands, or the growth of Brazilian's Embraer in the Western-dominated aerospace industry.

As a result of these global market trends, a wide range of brands bring a variety of cultures to a consumer population that is also growing culturally diverse. How do these cultural changes impact extant models of consumer behavior? How do consumers of different cultures interact with the cultural meanings in brands and products? How can marketers incorporate cultural factors into their decision making? What are the future challenges that marketers will face in a culturally diverse marketplace? This chapter provides answers to these important questions. It starts by defining culture and identifying the key cultural dimensions used to predict consumer behavior. This discussion followed by an exploration of the psychological processes underlying the culturally patterned responses of consumers. Special emphasis is given to how these responses are dynamically constructed and are often instrumental for fulfilling cultural identity goals. Finally, the chapter discusses how marketers can leverage their cultural understanding for building stronger brands, as well as identifies knowledge gaps for guiding a future research agenda.

Culture: Basic Principles

What Is Culture?

Culture consists of shared elements that provide the standards for perceiving, believing, evaluating, communicating, and acting among those who share a language, a historical period, and a geographic location (Triandis, 1989, 1996). As a collective phenomenon, culture consists of shared meanings that provide a common frame of reference for a human group to make sense of reality, coordinate their activities, and adapt to their environment (Shore, 2002; Sperber, 1996). A group of individuals who share the same standards form a cultural category or group. A cultural group can reside within a single country, extend across several country boundaries, and/or coexist within the same nation with other cultural groups. In other words, cultural groups and nations are not necessarily the same thing. However, for historical and geographical reasons, nations and cultures can often overlap (Hofstede, 1980). Thus, culture can be studied across nations or across individuals within nations.

Where Does Culture Exist?

As a collective phenomenon, culture exists in different forms. Culture is subtly reflected in thinking styles, ideas, beliefs, and values that are shared by members of a social group. At such individual level, culture can exist in two related, yet different, forms. First, culture can be present as values and beliefs that are endorsed by individuals, such as individualist versus collectivist cultural orientations (Triandis, 1989). Second, culture can exist in the form of intersubjective perceptions of culture – beliefs and values that members of a social group perceive to be widespread in their society (often referred to as *intersubjective culture*) (Chiu et al., 2010). In other words, culture can be evident in a distinctive pattern of beliefs, thinking styles, and values that are endorsed by individuals in a given group, as well as in the shared understanding that group members have about how widespread these beliefs, thinking styles, and values are.

Culture not only exists "in the head" of individuals as values and beliefs, but is also externalized into material objects, social practices, and social institutions

(Kitayama, Duffy, & Uchida, 2007). For instance, the Japanese tea ceremony embodies the recognition of the beauty of nature and life that characterizes Japanese culture (Watanabe, 1974). Similarly, because arranged marriages reflecting the values of parental control, ancestral lineage, and sense of kinship have been a distinct element in Indian culture, this social practice is distinctively represented in the matchmaker (or *nayan*) (Rao & Rao, 1982).

What Is Culture For?

As a provider of a common frame of reference for understanding reality, culture facilitates social interactions and solves coordination problems (Kashima, 1999). This basic function served by culture is obvious to those who have struggled understanding how things are done in a foreign cultural environment. However, beyond this obvious social coordination purpose, culture also serves several functions for the individual. First, participation in a culture helps to fulfill the need to belong – a fundamental human motive (Hong, Roisman, & Chen, 2006). People reminded of their cultural tradition tend to see themselves as members of a group rather than as individuals (Briley & Wyer, 2002). Moving away from a personal toward a social identity implies a depersonalization of the self, as well as a realization that one shares a set of characteristics with other group members. This implies a shift in which *I* becomes *we*, as the individual becomes sensitive to the similarities shared with others in the social group (Brewer, 1991), which triggers a tendency to evaluate more favorably ingroup (vs. outgroup) members (Turner, Brown, & Tajfel, 1979). Providing a positive group identity increases the identification that one has with the group, as well as strengthens the bonds and facilitates the cooperation between group members.

The sense of reality provided by culture also serves an epistemic function for the individual. Humans are the only living organisms aware of the inevitability of death and hence subject to the experience of existential terror (Becker, 1973). The mere thought of death can trigger this existential terror creating psychological distress in the individual. Defending one's cultural worldview is one of the strategies used by people to alleviate this existential terror (Greenberg, Solomon, & Pyszczynski, 1997). By living up to the standards provided by culture, the individual experiences a sense of epistemic security and symbolic immortality (Solomon, Greenberg, & Pyszczynski, 1991).

How to Study Culture?

The previous discussion highlights how complex it is to study culture and how cross-cultural research can be conducted at multiple levels of analysis. A first dichotomy in the study of culture is whether it should be studied inside the person (i.e., focusing on beliefs, values, and interpretive frameworks for making sense of reality) or outside the person (i.e., analyzing practices, objects, or institutions shared by a group) (Triandis, 2007). A second issue when studying culture is deciding the social level of analysis: across nations, across ethnic groups within nations, across individuals within nations (focusing on cultural orientation), and even across situations within individuals through the priming of cultural frames.

Regardless of how culture is studied, differences emerge in relation to the standards, behaviors, and practices adopted by cultural groups throughout the world. Cross-cultural psychologists who study these differences attempt to identify the constructs underlying these cultural variations in psychological functioning (i.e., cultural syndromes; Triandis, 1996). Understanding these cultural distinctions has been demonstrated to have important implications for advertising content, persuasiveness of appeals, consumer motivation, consumer judgment processes, and consumer response styles. We turn to these issues next.

Does Culture Impact Consumer Behavior?

Research in the last three decades has demonstrated how culture impacts basic psychological domains such as self-definition, perception, knowledge organization, self-presentation, motivation, and self-regulation (Shavitt, Lalwani, Zhang, & Torelli, 2006; Shavitt, Torelli, & Riemer, 2010; Triandis, 1995). A great deal has also been learned in recent years about the role of culture in consumer psychology (for reviews, see Briley, Wyer, & Li, 2014; Shavitt, Lee, & Torelli, 2008). For instance, in the persuasion domain, extensive research has clearly established that the content of and responses to advertising appeals are culturally influenced. Some cultures are more likely to use certain kinds of ad appeals than are other cultures (e.g., Alden, Hoyer, & Lee, 1993; Han & Shavitt, 1994b; Hong, Muderrisoglu, & Zinkhan, 1987; Kim & Markus, 1999). Culturally matched ad appeals are more likely to be effective than mismatched appeals (e.g., Aaker & Maheswaran, 1997; Han & Shavitt, 1994b; Zhang & Gelb, 1996). A consumer's culture or cultural orientation also influences the nature of information processing that accompanies a message (Aaker & Maheswaran, 1997; Aaker & Sengupta, 2000; Alden, Stayman, & Hoyer, 1994; Shavitt, Nelson, & Yuan, 1997), the role of affect in that processing (Aaker & Williams, 1998), as well as the types of goals that motivate consumers (Aaker & Lee, 2001).

Although most of the cross-cultural research in consumer behavior has focused on culture as an aspect of consumers, recent research has started to acknowledge that culture is also present in products and brands. As such, consumers respond to the cultural meanings in brands and form bonds with these brands due to their ability to fulfill cultural identity goals (for reviews, see Torelli, 2013; Torelli & Cheng, 2015). Considering culture as an aspect of products and brands adds to the traditional view of culture as an aspect of consumers and highlights the fact that culture exists both "in the head" and "in the world," and as such should be incorporated in models of consumer behavior.

Key Cultural Dimensions Driving Consumer Behavior

Individualism–Collectivism Classification

The constructs of *individualism* (IND) and *collectivism* (COL) represent the most broadly used dimensions of cultural variability for cross-cultural comparison (Gudykunst & Ting-Toomey, 1988). In individualistic cultures, people value independence from others and subordinate the goals of their ingroups to their own personal goals. In collectivistic cultures, in contrast, individuals value interdependent relationships to others and subordinate their personal goals to those of their ingroups (Hofstede, 1980, 2001; Triandis, 1989). The key distinction involves the extent to which one defines the self in relation to others. In individualistic cultural contexts, people tend to have an independent self-construal (Markus & Kitayama, 1991) whereby the self is defined as autonomous and unique. In collectivistic cultural contexts, people tend to have an interdependent self-construal (Markus & Kitayama, 1991) whereby the self is seen as inextricably and fundamentally embedded within a larger social network of roles and relationships.

National cultures that celebrate the values of independence, as in the United States, Canada, Germany, and Denmark, are typically categorized as individualistic societies in which an independent self-construal is common. In contrast, cultures that nurture the values of fulfilling one's obligations and responsibilities over one's own personal wishes or desires, including most East Asian and Latin American countries, such as China, Korea, Japan, and Mexico, are categorized as collectivistic societies in which an interdependent self-construal is common (Hofstede, 1980, 2001; Markus & Kitayama, 1991; Triandis, 1989).

Vertical–Horizontal Distinction

Individualism and collectivism are broad concepts that attempt to summarize a host of differences in focus of attention, self-definitions, motivations, emotional connections to in-groups, as well as belief systems and behavioral patterns (Oyserman, Coon, & Kemmelmeier, 2002). Describing a delineation of different "species" of individualism and collectivism, Triandis and his colleagues noted that, nested within individualism and collectivism categories, some societies are horizontal (valuing equality), whereas others are vertical (emphasizing hierarchy) (Singelis, Triandis, Bhawuk, & Gelfand, 1995; Triandis & Gelfand, 1998).

The vertical–horizontal distinction emerges from the observation that American or British individualism differs from, say, Australian or Norwegian individualism in much the same way that Chinese or Japanese collectivism differs from the collectivism of the Israeli Kibbutz. Whereas individuals in horizontal societies value equality and view the self as having the same status as others in society, individuals in vertical societies view the self as differing from others along a hierarchy and accept inequality (Triandis, 1995). Thus, combining the horizontal–vertical distinction with the individualism–collectivism classifications produces four cultural orientations: horizontal individualist, vertical individualist, horizontal collectivist, and vertical collectivist.

In vertical individualist societies (e.g., the United States and the United Kingdom), people tend to be concerned with self-enhancement values of power and achievement – distinguishing themselves from others via competition, achievement, and power. In contrast, in horizontal individualist cultures (e.g., Sweden, Denmark, Norway, and Australia), people prefer to view themselves as equal to others in status and avoid status differentiation. Rather than standing out, the focus is on openness values, or values of stimulation and self-direction – expressing one's uniqueness and establishing one's capability to be successfully self-reliant. In vertical collectivist societies (e.g., Japan and India), people are concerned with conservation values of tradition, conformity, and security – they believe in the importance of existing hierarchies, emphasize the subordination of their goals to those of their ingroups, and endorse traditional family values. Finally, in horizontal collectivist cultural contexts (e.g., the Israeli Kibbutz or some rural communities in Latin America), individuals endorse self-transcendence values that promote the welfare of others – the focus is on sociability and interdependence with others within an egalitarian framework (Shavitt, Torelli, & Riemer, 2010).

The horizontal–vertical distinction resembles the *power distance* continuum at the national level (Hofstede, 1980, 2001). However, there are important conceptual and structural differences between the horizontal–vertical distinction and power distance. From a conceptual standpoint, the horizontal–vertical distinction refers to differences in the acceptance of hierarchies as being valid or important in one's society. Power distance reflects the degree to which the less powerful members of organizations and institutions in a society perceive and accept inequalities in power (Hofstede, 2001). From a structural standpoint, power distance is conceptualized as a single dimension (from high to low power distance index [PDI]; Hofstede, 1980, 2001). The horizontal–vertical classification represents distinct categories that are conceptualized as nested within collectivism and individualism classifications and that have divergent validity (Triandis & Gelfand, 1998). Although Hofstede (1980) conceptualized IND and power distance as distinct dimensions, data do not appear to support the independence of these dimensions at the national level. The high correlation between power distance and IND, before controlling for country wealth, obtained with his operationalization, suggests that there may be overlap between these two constructs (e.g., Earley & Gibson, 1998; Smith, Dugan, & Trompenaars, 1996), leading to an association of high-PDI societies with VC and low-PDI societies with HI (Singelis et al., 1995).

Cultural Patterns in Consumer Behavior

Attention, Perception, and Information Processing

The considerable social differences that exist among different cultures affect how people perceive the world around them. Because collectivistic cultures emphasize a view of the self in relation to others (i.e., interdependent self-construal), knowledge about the social surroundings becomes very important, and particularly about others in direct interaction with the self. Perceiving the self as embedded within a larger social context forces people to attend to the relationships among the self, others, and the environment. Thus, interdependent people from collectivistic cultures (e.g., East Asians) have a tendency to attend to the social and environmental context as a whole, and especially to relationships between focal objects and the environment, and to predict events on the basis of such relationships. This way of thinking is often referred to as *holistic* thinking style (Nisbett, Peng, Choi, & Norenzayan, 2001). Being more sensitive to the relationships between objects and the environment affords an advantage in detecting broader connections between objects. Indeed, because Easterners pay more attention to the environment, they are more able to identify relationships between a parent brand and a newly introduced extension based on complementarity of use or overall reputation. For example, Indian consumers (collectivists) perceive a higher fit between the product and the parent brand and evaluate more favorably a Kodak filing cabinet than American (individualists) consumers do. This effect occurs because of the complementarity of use connection between Kodak and filing cabinets (e.g., filing cabinets can be used to store pictures) that Indian consumers are able to detect (Monga & John, 2007).

In contrast, individualistic cultures promote an independent view of the self. Viewing the self as a separate entity free of social constraints fosters a decontextualized view of the world that focuses on focal objects and their attributes. Independent people from individualistic cultures (e.g., Americans) have a tendency to focus on the attributes of an object, separate from its context, in order to assign it to a category, and to use rules about the category to explain and predict the object's behavior (Nisbett et al., 2001). Westerners also tend to judge brand extensions on the basis of their similarity with the products already sold by the brand or on the extent to which the attributes of the parent brand transfer to the new product (Monga & John, 2007).

Focusing on the vertical and horizontal distinctions, nested within the broader individualism–collectivism classification, affords a more nuanced understanding of the way in which people from different cultures perceive the world. As stated earlier, individualists have a tendency to assign objects to categories and to make predictions about these objects based on category attributes. Thus, when presented with information about a focal object, individualists often focus on information that is consistent with the stereotype of the category to which the object belongs, and ignore information that is inconsistent – often referred to as *stereotyping processing*. This processing tendency is particularly acute among powerful individuals who rely on such processing strategies as a way of defending one's powerful status by reasserting control (Fiske, 1993). Recent research shows that such stereotyping tendencies are more common among vertical individualists. Because these individuals are concerned with competition, power, and rising in status above others, they think of power as something to be used for their personal advancement.

In turn, situations that heighten a sense of power make these individuals more likely to engage in stereotyping processing. For instance, vertical individualists presented with an advertisement for an upscale, status-enhancing financial advisory service recognize better, in a subsequent recognition task, information *congruent* with the stereotypical image of the status product (e.g., "financial experts graduated from the top-tier universities in the country") relative to their recognition of *incongruent* information (e.g., "When you visit Interbank offices, you will feel the warmth of your own home") (Torelli & Shavitt, 2011).

Because collectivists rely less on categories, their perceptions are often based on a holistic view that considers all aspects of the target object. Such an other-centered processing style involves an effort in individuating and understanding others – often referred to as *individuating processing*. This processing tendency is particularly evident among powerful individuals who feel responsible toward others (Overbeck & Park, 2001). Recently, these individuating tendencies have been linked to people with a horizontal collectivistic orientation. Because these individuals are concerned with interdependence and sociability under an egalitarian framework, they think of power as something to be used for having positive impacts on undifferentiated others. In turn, situations that heighten the nurturing effects that one can have on others make these individuals more likely to engage in individuating processing. For instance, horizontal individualists presented with an advertisement for a nurturing dog food recognize better, in a subsequent recognition task, information *incongruent* with the stereotypical image of the nurturing product (e.g., "It has been reported that the company recently influenced distributors to stop carrying competitors' products") (Torelli & Shavitt, 2011).

Self-Presentation

Self-presentation pervades all aspects of human behavior. In trying to look good in their interactions with others, people often embellish their representations to convey a desired image rather than an accurate representation of one's personality (Paulhus, 1984). Because what constitutes a desirable image of the self can vary by culture, people of different cultures present themselves to others in varied ways (Lalwani, Shavitt, & Johnson, 2006). In individualistic cultures, people strive to present themselves as self-reliant, confident, and skillful. This often results in an exaggeration of one's abilities or in a tendency to describe oneself in inflated and overconfident terms – also referred to as *self-deceptive enhancement*. In contrast, people in collectivistic cultures strive to present themselves as sensitive and socially appropriate – also referred to as *impression management* (Paulhus, 1998). For example, having an independent view of the self makes people more likely to choose to take a test that would showcase their self-reliance, whereas having an interdependent view of the self makes it more likely to choose to take a test that showcases one's social sensitivity (Lalwani & Shavitt, 2009).

Examination of horizontal versus vertical categories yields more nuanced insights into the self-presentation styles of people from different cultures. As stated earlier, people in horizontal individualistic cultures are especially motivated to view themselves as separate from others, self-reliant, and unique. In contrast, people from vertical individualistic cultures are concerned with competition and achieving a higher status. Thus, horizontal individualism (but not vertical individualism) fosters a self-presentation style aimed at establishing a view of oneself as capable of being successfully self-reliant (Lalwani, Shavitt, & Johnson, 2006). In contrast, vertical individualism (but not horizontal individualism) promotes a self-presentation style aimed at establishing one's achievements, status, and power (Torelli, 2013). For example, horizontal individualists express more confidence that they can make the right decision about whether to accept a future job and are more likely to anticipate performing well on the job, whereas vertical individualists are more likely to inflate their income and their success at influencing others.

People from horizontal collectivistic cultures are especially motivated to maintain strong and benevolent social relations and therefore to appear socially appropriate in their responses (Lalwani, Shavitt, & Johnson, 2006). In contrast, people from vertical collectivistic cultures are concerned with serving and sacrificing for the ingroup, and hence to appear as being dutiful and responsible (Torelli, 2013). For example, horizontal collectivists are more likely to deny that they would gossip about coworkers on a job, plagiarize a friend's paper for a course, or damage someone's furniture without telling them, whereas vertical collectivists are more likely to inflate their self-reported success at fulfilling their duties in close relationships with others (e.g., being a more responsible parent, friend, or spouse).

Content of Message Appeals

Most research on cultural influences on judgment and persuasion suggests that the prevalence or the persuasiveness of a given type of appeal matches the cultural value orientation of the society. For instance, American advertisers are often exhorted to focus on the advertised brand's attributes and advantages (Ogilvy, 1985) – something consistent with the individualistic tendency to focus on the attributes of objects that characterizes American culture.

In contrast, advertisements in Japan tend to focus on "making friends" with the audience and showing that the company understands their feelings (Javalgi, Cutler, & Malhotra, 1995) – something consistent with the collectivistic tendency to focus on relationships that characterizes Japanese culture. Similarly, a content analysis of magazine advertisements revealed that in South Korea, compared to the United States, advertisements are more focused on family well-being, interdependence, group goals, and harmony, whereas they are less focused on self-improvement, ambition, personal goals, independence, and individuality (Han & Shavitt, 1994a).

The content of advertisements can also reflect the vertical or horizontal tendencies of the cultures. Although advertisements from both South Korea and Thailand (both collectivistic) contain more group-oriented situations than those from Germany and the United States (both individualistic), relationships between the central characters in advertisements that used humor were more often unequal in cultures characterized as having higher power distance (i.e., relatively vertical cultures, such as South Korea) than in those labeled as lower in power distance (such as Germany), in which these relationships were more often equal (Alden, Hoyer, & Lee, 1993). Such unequal relationships portrayed in the advertisements reflect the hierarchical interpersonal relationships that are more likely to exist in vertical societies.

Persuasiveness of Advertising Messages

The persuasiveness of advertising appeals appears to mirror the cultural differences in their prevalence. Appeals to individualistic values (e.g., "Solo cleans with a softness that you will love") are more persuasive in the United States, whereas appeals to collectivistic values (e.g., "Solo cleans with a softness that your family will love") are more persuasive in South Korea. However, this effect is much more evident for products that are shared (laundry detergent, clothes iron) than for those that are not (chewing gum, running shoes) (Leclerc, Schmitt, & Dubé, 1994). Individualists and people with an independent self-construal are persuaded by information that addresses their promotion regulatory concerns, including messages about personal achievement, individuality, uniqueness, and self-improvement. In contrast, collectivists and people with an interdependent self-construal are persuaded by information that addresses their prevention regulatory concerns, including messages about harmony, group goals, conformity, and security (Aaker & Lee, 2001).

A focus on the vertical or horizontal versions of individualism and collectivism provides a more nuanced understanding of the persuasiveness of advertising appeals. Specifically, although appeals to self-enhancement values (emphasizing individual concerns with status achievement) and openness values (emphasizing individual concerns with being free and living an exciting life) seem equally appropriate in individualistic cultures (i.e., both primarily refer to individual interests), appeals to openness values are more appealing for consumers with a horizontal individualistic orientation, but less so for those with a vertical individualistic orientation. In contrast, appeals to self-enhancement values are more appealing for consumers with a vertical individualistic orientation, but less so for those with a horizontal individualistic orientation (Torelli et al., 2012). Similarly, although appeals to self-transcendence values (emphasizing collective concerns with the welfare of others and of nature) and conservation values (emphasizing collective concerns with maintaining traditions) seem equally appropriate in collectivistic cultures, appeals to self-transcendence values are more appealing for consumers with a horizontal collectivistic orientation, but less so for those with a vertical collectivistic orientation. In contrast, appeals to conservation values are more appealing for consumers with a vertical collectivistic orientation, but less so for those with a horizontal collectivistic orientation (Torelli et al., 2012).

The Presence of Culture in Products and Brands

Brands as Cultural Symbols

As stated earlier, culture not only exists in the values, beliefs, and thinking styles of individuals, but also manifests itself in objects such as brands and products. Brand meanings originate in the culturally constituted world and move into brands through several instruments, such as advertising, the fashion system, and reference groups (McCracken, 1986). As a result, brands can acquire cultural meanings (Aaker, Benet-Martinez, & Garolera, 2001) and become associated with the abstract characteristics that define a cultural group. There is evidence that consumers attribute cultural significance to certain commercial brands (Aaker, Benet-Martinez, & Garolera, 2001). For example, some brands in the United States are associated with ruggedness (e.g., Harley-Davidson's associations with strength, masculinity, and toughness), whereas some brands in Japan are associated with peacefulness, and ruggedness and peacefulness are abstract dimensions characteristic of American and East Asian cultures, respectively. Brands that acquire cultural meanings can reach the level of a cultural symbol. This happens when the brand is consensually perceived to symbolize the abstract image that characterizes a certain cultural group (Torelli, Keh, & Chiu, 2010). To the extent that these brands are associated with knowledge about the culture, they can reach an iconic status and act as cultural reminders (see Betsky, 1997; Ortner, 1973). Encountering such iconic brands can serve as subtle cultural primes that can lead to culturally patterned responses (Torelli & Cheng, 2011).

The Dynamic Constructivist View of Culture

The notion that brands can bring to mind their attendant cultural knowledge is consistent with the dynamic constructivist view of culture. According to the dynamic constructivist theory of culture (Chiu & Hong, 2007; Hong, Morris, Chiu, & Benet-Martinez, 2000), culture is stored in memory as an associative network of knowledge. It is internalized in the form of a loose network of domain-specific knowledge structures consisting of a central concept (e.g., American culture) and its associated categories (e.g., individualist values of freedom and self-reliance), implicit theories (e.g., an individual's behavior originates in internal dispositions), and cultural icons (e.g., the Statue of Liberty or the American flag) (Hong et al., 2000; Torelli & Ahluwalia, 2012; Torelli & Cheng, 2011). These knowledge structures guide cognition and behavior only when they come to the fore in an individual's mind – either because they are chronically accessible or activated by environmental stimuli (Hong et al., 2000; Lau, Chiu, & Lee, 2001; Sechrist & Stangor, 2001; Trafimow, Silverman, Fan, & Law, 1997).

As part of the cultural knowledge network, a culturally symbolic brand connects to the central cultural concept (e.g., Harley-Davidson's symbolism of American culture) as well as the values, beliefs, ideas, and other shared elements that form part of the culture (e.g., American cultural values of free-dom and independence; Torelli & Cheng, 2011). Like other cultural icons, a culturally symbolic brand can activate its associated cultural knowledge and lead to culturally appropriate behaviors (Chiu, Mallorie, Keh, & Law, 2009; Torelli & Ahluwalia, 2012; Torelli, Chiu, Keh, & Amaral, 2009a). For instance, after encountering American iconic brands such as Coke or Levi's (vs. non-iconic brands such as Dasani or New Balance), American participants feel more comfortable and are more successful explaining to others what it means to be an American (Torelli et al., 2009a).

Biculturalism and Cultural Activation

With globalization, the number of individuals with direct or indirect knowledge about two (bicultural) or more cultures (multicultural) as opposed to a single culture (monocultural) is rapidly on the rise (Lau-Gesk, 2003; Maheswaran & Shavitt, 2000). Tremendous growth in international travel and Internet access increases the availability that people have to information about lifestyles, customs, and developments around the world. With increasing exposure to foreign cultures, so-called monocultural individuals who have not lived for extended periods in a foreign culture can internalize certain aspects of these cultures through international travel and media exposure and hence exhibit cultural priming effects similar to those exhibited by traditional biculturals (Alter & Kwan, 2009).

According to the dynamic constructivist theory of culture, biculturalism and multiculturalism are conceptualized as having more than one set of cultural knowledge representations. The most critical evidence is the frame-switching effect observed among bicultural individuals when interacting with culturally charged stimuli. For these individuals, exposure to symbols of one culture can prime them to adopt its associated cultural frame to the exclusion of the other (also known as "frame switching"; e.g., Briley, Morris, & Simonson, 2005; Hong et al., 2000; Ng, 2010). For instance, priming Singaporean consumers with American (Singaporean) cultural icons induces impatience (i.e., promotion focus) and thus leads to higher willingness to pay for expedited shipping (Chen, Ng, & Rao, 2005). Similarly, Hong Kong Chinese participants presented with a McDonald's advertisement (vs. an advertisement containing Chinese symbols) prefer an individualist message over a collectivist one (Chiu et al., 2009).

Iconic Brands and the Fulfillment of Cultural Identity Goals

Consumers often buy brands as a way of signaling to the self and others those aspects of their personality that are self-defining (Levy, 1959; Sirgy, 1982). For instance, a consumer might buy a Harley motorcycle as a way of signaling the importance of being free and independent (core associations with the Harley-Davidson brand) in his self-definition. However, another consumer might buy the same product due to its meanings for American culture (because of the consensual belief that Harley-Davidson is an American icon). In the latter case, the consumer uses the brand to symbolize to the self and others a cultural identity (Swaminathan, Page, & Gürhan-Canli, 2007; Torelli, 2013). A cultural identity relates to the membership in a particular cultural, or subcultural, group that is clearly distinguishable from other cultural groups (Chiu & Hong, 2006). As discussed earlier, culturally symbolic brands are public expressions of the abstract meanings of a cultural group. Because culturally symbolic brands symbolize the beliefs, ideas, and values of a cultural group, consumers with a heightened need to symbolize a cultural identity will judge culturally symbolic brands as highly instrumental for fulfilling such needs. By being a patron of a culturally symbolic brand, one can emphasize the possession of the cultural identity and the alignment with and adherence to the culture.

Making salient a cultural identity triggers favorable attitudes toward objects that are identity-congruent. For instance, when making an ethnic identity salient (e.g., Asian), consumers evaluate more favorably advertisements that are targeted to the ethnic ingroup (e.g., by means of the copy or the images in the ad) (Forehand, Deshpandé, & Reed, 2002) or that include a spokeperson from the ethnic ingroup (Forehand & Deshpandé, 2001) than when the identity is not made salient. Because commitment to a cultural identity makes the identity more likely to be salient in different contexts, highly identified consumers are especially motivated to favor culturally symbolic brands (over nonsymbolic ones) to fulfill their salient cultural identity needs (Torelli, Chiu, & Keh, 2010; Torelli et al., 2009a; Torelli, Chiu, Keh, & Amaral, 2009b).

A salient cultural identity increases the desirability of brands that symbolize it, which causes consumers to evaluate more favorably and to be willing to pay more for culturally symbolic brands (Torelli, Chiu, & Keh, 2010). Furthermore, because a salient social identity brings to mind identity-consistent decisions that do not require further reflection, the higher valuation of culturally symbolic brands occur rather automatically and without conscious deliberation. In other words, consumers process information about a culturally symbolic brand easily and feel that it is right to favor the brand. In turn, this feeling results in a pleasing processing experience and an accompanying enhanced brand valuation (Torelli & Ahluwalia, 2012). Over time, continued reliance on culturally symbolic brands for fulfilling salient cultural identity needs can result in the development of strong self-brand relationships (Torelli, Chiu, & Keh, 2010). In turn, forming a strong bond with a culturally symbolic brand, due to its cultural identity meaning, can shield the brand against negative publicity when cultural identity needs are salient (Swaminathan, Page, & Gürhan-Canli, 2007).

Culture Mixing and Its Consequences

In globalized markets, symbols of different cultures often occupy the same space at the same time. Unlike the situation investigated in most monoculture priming research (e.g., Hong et al., 2000), exposure to symbols of multiple cultures, or *culture mixing*, activates not only one but two or more cultural representations at the same time. Recent research has found some distinctive effects of culture mixing that are different from the effects of typical cultural priming (i.e., single culture priming). Specifically, culture mixing draws attention to cultural differences, resulting in the expectation that cultures are discrete entities with relatively impermeable boundaries. For instance, compared to showing American participants with culture-neutral products that carried prototypic British brand names (monocultural priming), showing them iconic Mexican products that carry British brand names (culture mixed product) activates representations of Mexican and British cultures at the same time and increases perceived differences between cultures (Torelli et al., 2011). This effects emerges not only for the target cultures (e.g., Mexican and British), but also for other cultures (e.g., Puerto Rican and Canadian). Culture mixed products can also trigger negative consumer reactions. For instance, American participants evaluate less favorably a culture mixed product, such as Sony cappuccino machines (the Sony brand is iconic of Japan, whereas cappuccino machines are iconic of Italy), than a monocultural product, such as a Sony toaster oven (only the Japanese Sony is culturally symbolic), in spite of the similar levels of moderate fit of the two products with the Sony brand (Torelli & Ahluwalia, 2012). This unfavorable evaluation is driven by the subjective experience of disfluency triggered by the simultaneous activation of two different cultural schemas.

Recent studies (Chen & Chiu, 2010; Cheng, 2010; Cheng, et al., 2011; Chiu & Cheng, 2007; Torelli & Ahluwalia, 2012; Torelli et al., 2011) have uncovered two factors that foster negative reactions toward culture mixing: salience of intercultural competition and culture defense mindset. First, salient intercultural competition highlights the ingroup–outgroup boundary and heightens a sense of distrust of outgroups (Insko & Schopler, 1998; Turner et al., 1987). This should result in more unfavorable attitudes toward potential cultural mixing and exclusionary reactions toward other cultures. Cheng and colleagues (2011) investigated this notion with Chinese consumers during the 2008 Beijing Olympics. Mainland Chinese participants evaluated brands that symbolize either Chinese (e.g., LiNing) or American cultures (e.g., Nike) before and after the Beijing Olympics. Before the Olympics, only respondents who were highly identified with Chinese culture showed favoritism for Chinese-(over American-) symbolic brands. However, as the Olympics progressed, presumably because of the salient rivalry between the United States and China, participants who were both high and low in their identification with Chinese culture exhibited favoritism of Chinese-(over American-) symbolic brands. This finding suggests that, in face of salient intercultural competition, people shifted their preferences in favor of brands that symbolize the local culture over brands that symbolize a competing foreign culture.

Second, resistance to culture mixing can be fostered by a culture defense mindset, such as that triggered by thoughts of one's own death (Torelli et al., 2011). When reminded of their mortality, people adhere to and defend their cultural worldview as a way to achieve symbolic immortality (Greenberg,

Porteus, Simon, & Pyszczynski, 1995). This in turn encourages aggression against those who violate the cultural worldview (McGregor et al., 1998) and evokes intolerance of using cultural icons in an inappropriate way (e.g., using the crucifix as a hammer; Greenberg et al., 1995). Extending this notion to culture mixed situations, Torelli and colleagues (2011) show that people are particularly intolerant of contamination of brands that symbolize their culture when they are under the joint influence of culture mixing and mortality salience. Upon inducing (vs. not) mortality salience, American participants were asked to evaluate a marketing plan of Nike (an American icon), which involved some questionable actions to increase its competitiveness in a foreign market (e.g., eliminating the "Swoosh" symbol and replacing the Nike brand name with the Arabic word for "Sportsmanship" to penetrate the Middle East market). Results showed that, only upon making mortality salient, participants evaluated the marketing plan less favorably after evaluating culture mixed products (e.g., a Chinese brand of breakfast cereal) than after evaluating monocultural products (e.g., an American brand of breakfast cereal).

Future Research Directions

Identifying Novel Cultural Dimensions

In trying to further refine predictions about how consumers from different cultures will react to alternative market offerings, researchers focus on uncovering the cultural dimensions that will provide the highest predictive power. As discussed earlier, the individualism–collectivism classification and the distinction between vertical and horizontal cultural orientations (or the related dimension of power distance) have captured most of the research attention. In combination, these cultural constructs have afforded a more nuanced understanding of consumer behavior (Shavitt et al., 2006). What other cultural dimensions have the potential to provide even further refinements?

A neglected source of cultural variation that has such potential is the distinction between cultures that are "tight" – have strong norms and a low tolerance of deviant behavior – and those that are "loose" – have weak norms and a high tolerance of deviant behavior (Gelfand et al., 2011). This distinction has important implications for a variety of psychological domains. For instance, tight societies have a much higher degree of situational constraint that restricts the range of behavior deemed appropriate across everyday situations, whereas loose societies afford a much wider range of permissible behavior across everyday situations. Accordingly, individuals in tight (vs. loose) cultures are more prevention-focused (i.e., concerned with avoiding mistakes) and have higher self-regulatory strength (i.e., higher impulse control) (Gelfand et al., 2011). Research should be conducted to link the cultural dimensions of tightness and looseness with consumer behavior aligned with these culturally distinctive self-regulatory tendencies.

Another source of cultural variability likely to provide novel insights is that of religious beliefs. Interestingly, cross-cultural research has paid very little attention to the thorough cultural psychology theory of Max Weber in his *Protestant Ethic and the Spirit of Capitalism* (Weber, 2002). Recent research has started to unlock some of the potential in this theory for uncovering the link among sublimation, culture, and creativity (Kim, Zeppenfeld, & Cohen, 2013). Specifically, it has been found that Protestants (vs. Catholics and Jews) are more likely to sublimate unacceptable sexual desires and suppressed anger and to harness their anxieties about depravity to productive ends. Protestants (vs. Catholics and Jews) produced more creative artwork (sculptures, poems, collages, cartoon captions) when they were induced to feel unacceptable sexual desires or forced to suppress their anger. Activating anger or sexual attraction was not enough; it was the forbidden or suppressed nature of the emotion that gave the emotion its creative power. These findings emphasize the importance of adding to our understanding of the conscious cultural mind (e.g., values, attitudes, and beliefs) the perspective from subconscious processes where cognitions and emotions move in and out of consciousness. Future research aimed at this objective has the potential to unearth interesting cross-cultural effects.

A More Detailed Understanding of Biculturals' Responses

The review in this chapter highlights the fact that research on culture and consumer behavior has gradually moved from predicting cross-cultural differences in consumer behavior to examining the coexistence of two or more cultures within a consumer or within a market offering. As an increasing number of consumers acquire knowledge of multiple cultures, several important questions arise: How is knowledge about different cultures acquired and organized in consumers' minds? Would the way in which people organize cultural knowledge in memory influence their consumption behavior? Answering these questions might require expanding existing cultural frameworks (e.g., the dynamic constructivist approach to culture) to develop a more holistic view of biculturalism and multiculturalism.

For instance, research on frame switching often treats bicultural or multicultural knowledge as "cold" representations that follow the cognitive principles of activation and application. One fruitful avenue for future research is to focus more on the motivations brought to mind by priming a given cultural frame and its accompanying cultural identity. Recent research suggests that making a cultural identity salient triggers a motivational pull toward identity-congruent judgments and behaviors (i.e., identity-based motivation; Oyserman, 2009; Oyserman, Fryberg, & Yoder, 2007). When situations cue an identity, the cued identity triggers a general readiness to make sense of the world in identity-congruent terms, including the norms and goals associated with that identity. What motivations would guide behavior when more than one view of "who I am" (i.e., more than one cultural identity) is salient? In this context, what factors might impact the extent to which the motivation triggered by one cultural frame would dominate the one associated with the other?

Recent research suggests that the way in which cultural frames are organized in memory can impact the motivations triggered by exposure to cultural primes. Mok and Morris (2013) demonstrate that bicultural individuals can show assimilative or contrastive responses to culture priming depending on how knowledge about the two cultural identities is organized in memory. In their studies, Asian (American) primes increased preference for individualistic (collectivistic) appeals among Asian Americans who keep the two cultural identities as separate, and incompatible, representations of the self (i.e., non-integrated biculturals). For these individuals, cultural cues that prime one cultural identity are perceived as a threat to the other cultural identity. In response to the threat, these individuals assimilate their behavior to the *unprimed* cultural identity as an attempt to affirm such identity. This finding points to the motivational conflict that bicultural individuals might experience when reacting to cultural cues in the environment. It also highlights the context-dependence of bicultural individuals' behaviors.

Focusing on the identity aspects of cultural knowledge facilitates integrating the cultural literature with that on identity processes. Given that people strive to maintain a positive and optimally distinctive identity, when cultural cues bring to mind two contrastive identities (e.g., being Asian and being American), people might emphasize the one that helps them achieve positive distinctiveness for the situation at hand – and hence suppress the other. For example, maintaining positive distinctiveness might motivate an American Chinese bicultural individual exposed to a bicultural product (e.g., a Chinese breakfast cereal) to assimilate to his American cultural identity when in a Chinese-majority group.

The preceding discussion underscores the importance of further investigating the cognitive and motivational principles governing activation and application of cultural knowledge. It also highlights the distinction between cultural knowledge acquired by a substantial cultural immersion (e.g., growing up in a culture and developing a cultural identity) or by more superficial encounters via international travel and indirect cultural contacts. In general, cultural knowledge acquired through substantial cultural immersion seems more likely to be identity-relevant. Thus, activation and application of this knowledge would not only have cognitive consequences (as is also the case for cultural knowledge acquired through briefer encounters) but also motivational consequences. Further exploring these issues seems worthy of research.

How Do Iconic Cultural Brands Emerge?

Although prior research has identified the cultural priming effect of culturally symbolic brands, little is known about how brands emerge as cultural symbols. Unlike some cultural icons such as the American national flag that are created to symbolize a nation, brands and products are originally created for commercial purposes. Yet, some brands or products gradually become widely regarded as cultural icons. Torelli and colleagues (Torelli, 2013; Torelli, Chiu, & Keh, 2010; Torelli & Stoner, 2015) identify some of the factors that contribute to a brand's cultural symbolism (or its cultural equity). They propose that country (or region) of origin associations, globalness associations (i.e., perceiving the brand as being global), embodiment of abstract cultural characteristics, and cultural authority are four building blocks of cultural symbolism. However, little is known about the sociological or psychological processes that determine how these factors are integrated into a consensual view of brands as symbols of a culture.

In addition, because cultural symbolism emerges from a consensual understanding of the brand's cultural significance, culturally symbolic brands are the result of co-creation processes between marketers and consumers. Although marketers might spend time and resources in positioning brands as cultural symbols, not all attempts will succeed. It seems then important to study the psychological conditions that would facilitate, or hinder, the emergence of cultural symbols within a group. It is well known that culture fulfills a variety of psychological needs, such as the need for epistemic and existential security (Chiu & Hong, 2006; Fu et al., 2007; Torelli et al., 2011). How do these psychological needs influence the emergence of culturally symbolic brands? Would brands be more likely to acquire cultural meanings when existential threats are more salient (i.e., during times of war)? Future research may begin to examine the psychological factors that foster the emergence of iconic brands.

Cultural Meaning of Brands in a Global Value Chain

Most contemporary products emerge from a global value chain in which manufacturing and brand ownership are spread throughout different cultures. To take advantage of lower labor or logistic costs, companies that own brands with symbolic meanings for a given culture often shift (parts of) their manufacturing process to locations in contrastive, foreign cultures (e.g., China for Western-iconic brands). Companies are aware of the potential confusion in consumers' minds from this cultural mixing of brand ownership and product manufacturing. For instance, Apple now uses the "Designed by Apple in California" slogan, and Chrysler (American iconic brand owned by Italy's Fiat) uses the "Imported from Detroit" slogan in trying to assure consumers of their cultural roots. However, little is known about how consumers process and organize in their minds the cultural mixing of brand ownership and product manufacturing.

Past research has investigated some of the implications of manufacturing location changes for consumers' judgments about product quality. For instance, Johansson and Nebenzahl (1986) found that because consumers value Japanese carmakers for their particular production systems and management techniques, for these carmakers, shifting manufacturing to other locations threatens quality perception. Han and Terpstra (1988) further concluded that quality perception is influenced more by the manufacturing country-of-origin than brand name origin. Similarly, Häubel (1996) found that brand name origin has a direct impact on attitude toward the product, whereas the manufacturing country of origin impacts attitude toward the product through its effect on product quality evaluation. These findings converge on the notion that manufacturing country of origin, if different from brand origin, can have a substantial impact on attitude toward the product.

However, this prior research has focused exclusively on judgments about quality and has failed to consider consumers' more subjective feelings toward the cultural meanings in brands (Torelli & Ahluwalia, 2012). How and to what extent does combining brand and manufacturing countries of origin influence consumers' perceptions about the cultural symbolism of a brand? For example, would Ford or Apple become less iconic of America to the extent that people focus more on the shifting of their manufacturing outside of the United States? How would this impact the more emotional responses by consumers? Future research investigating these issues would provide a more holistic understanding of consumer behavior in the globalized marketplace.

Cultural Identities at Multiple Levels of Categorization

As stated earlier in the chapter, several cultures can coexist within the same region, and the geographic borders that delineate a region might or might not coincide with country boundaries (Triandis, 1995). Furthermore, it is often the case that different cultures that coexist within a common region might compete with each other, collaborate with each other, or interact with each other within a hierarchical arrangement of social groups. For instance, we can consider the United States as a region in which individuals share the same American culture.

However, we can easily identify subgroups of individuals in the United States that share distinctive cultural elements (e.g., white Americans, black Americans, Latinos, or Native Americans). We refer to the patterns of cultural meanings shared by these subgroups as subcultures within the overarching American culture. These subcultures often compete with each other for the allocation of economic resources but also cooperate with each other in shaping a common American identity. How does the dynamic construction of cultural identities at different levels of group categorization (i.e., sub-level or supra-level) impact consumer behavior? How do different sub-groups nested within a supra-level cultural identity negotiate to define the standards that will define the culture? What cultural standards (i.e., from different subgroups) are more likely to be transferred to brands and products to endow them with cultural meanings? How do members of different subgroups react to iconic brands of other subgroups?

These are important questions that ask for multidisciplinary research integrating knowledge from sociology, anthropology, and psychology. Generally speaking, supra-level cultures seem to be defined in terms of the characteristics of the more (as opposed to less) dominant groups, and symbols of such dominant groups are more likely to be explicitly used as elements in broad-level cultural discussions (Zerubavel, 1996). For example, symbols and historical events linked to white Americans are more likely to be distributed through museums, shrines, and parks than those linked to African Americans or Native Americans (Myers, 2006), reflecting the higher status and power historically enjoyed by white Americans relative to other ethnic groups. This shapes an intersubjective understanding in American culture that "American = white" – an implicit shared belief that affirms the status distinction among ethnic groups in America by attributing Americanness exclusively to the dominant ethnic group (Caucasians) (Devos & Banaji, 2005). Extending these notions to brands, one could argue that brands that symbolize more (vs. less) dominant groups would find it easier to develop an iconic status at the superordinate cultural level. This would align with the observation that brands such as Harley-Davidson and Ford, which have been traditionally associated with white male Americans, are revered as American icons. However, brands such as Coca-Cola and McDonald's, which are less distinctively associated with white America, have also managed to reach an iconic status in American culture. Further research should investigate the dynamic development of cultural meanings at different levels of group categorization.

The previous discussion about subgroups nested within a country-level identity (e.g., American identity) can extend to supra-level cultural identities encompassing more than one country-based cultural group. For instance, researchers often consider that East Asians share common cultural meanings rooted in Confucianism (Nisbett, 2003; Triandis, 1995) or deliberate about the emergence of an overarching European identity (Checkel & Katzenstein, 2009; Cinnirella, 1997). Nevertheless, Chinese, Korean, and Japanese cultures have their distinct cultural elements (e.g., the notion of *amae* in Japan [Doi, 1973], or that of *chong* in Korea [Kim & Choi, 1994]) in the same way that Spanish and Danish cultures share unique cultural scripts (e.g., the *Janteloven* in Denmark [Nelson & Shavitt, 2002], or the cultural script of *simpatía* in Spain [Triandis, Marín, Lisansky, & Betancourt, 1984]). Do people identify with these supra-level regional identities? How does identification with the supra-level regional identity impact consumers' attitudes toward brands that symbolize other subgroups nested within the regional identity? What role do potential intergroup rivalries play in shaping these attitudes?

Because people can define themselves in terms of either subgroup or superordinate identities depending on the context, there is reason to believe that consumers can factor in their sense of belongingness to a supra-level cultural group when interacting with brands that symbolize an outgroup. Specifically, when members of different subgroups (e.g., Koreans and Japanese) are induced to think of themselves as a single superordinate group (e.g., recategorization as East Asians) rather than two separate groups, attitudes toward former outgroup members can become more positive (i.e., pro-ingroup bias; Gaertner et al., 1993). However, when recategorization as a superordinate social identity becomes a threat to positivity and distinctiveness, such recategorization processes can backfire and increase intergroup bias (Crisp, Stone, & Hall, 2006).

It seems then worthy to investigate the factors and psychological processes that impact people's reactions toward brands that symbolize outgroup cultures that are nested within the same supra-level cultural identity.

Multiculturalism and the Global Mindset

Due to the rise in globalization, people are increasingly recognizing the commonalities rather than dissimilarities among people around the world and are also more interested in global events. This interest is being stimulated by the instantaneous access that consumers have to news, stories, and developments taking place in every corner of the world, as well as by increased intercultural contact due to a flourishing global tourism and travel industry. The emergence of a global culture, characterized by cosmopolitanism and a zest for wide international experience, is evident in the growing number of individuals who identify themselves with people from around the world (Arnett, 2002). These individuals seem to develop a bicultural identity in which their membership to the local culture coexists with their belongingness to the global culture. The values of the global culture are based on individualism, openness to change, and tolerance of differences (Friedman, 2000), which are those that prevail in the countries that have the greater influence in feeding globalization processes (i.e., the West, especially the United States). However, globally savvy individuals in the Western world often exhibit cultural framing effects that characterize biculturals from a collectivistic background (i.e., East Asian immigrants; Alter & Kwan, 2009). It seems then possible that a global mindset might look different in the minds of individuals with different cultural backgrounds. For a Westerner, a global identity might be more similar to the local identity than for an Easterner. If so, Westerners (vs. Easterners) might find it easier to integrate a global and a local identity. For Easterners, there may be more confusion in trying to develop a bicultural identity that lets them participate in both the local and the global culture. Future research should investigate these issues by trying to uncover the psychological processes underlying the fulfillment of global identity goals among consumers of different cultures, as well as to more clearly delineate the psychological characteristics of a global mindset as manifested in different cultures.

References

Aaker, J. L., Benet-Martinez, V., & Garolera, J. (2001). Consumption symbols as carriers of culture: A study of Japanese and Spanish brand personality constucts. *Journal of Personality and Social Psychology, 81*, 492–508.

Aaker, J. L., & Lee, A. Y. (2001). "I" seek pleasures and "we" avoid pains: The role of self-regulatory goals in information processing and persuasion. *Journal of Consumer Research, 28*, 33–49.

Aaker, J. L., & Maheswaran, D. (1997). The effect of cultural orientation on persuasion. *Journal of Consumer Research, 24*, 315–328.

Aaker, J. L., & Sengupta, J. (2000). Addivity versus attenuation: The role of culture in the resolution of information incongruity. *Journal of Consumer Psychology, 9*, 67–82.

Aaker, J. L., & Williams, P. (1998). Empathy versus pride: The influence of emotional appeals across cultures. *Journal of Consumer Research, 25*, 241–261.

Alden, D. L., Hoyer, W. D., & Lee, C. (1993). Identifying global and culture-specific dimensions of humor in advertising: A multinational analysis. *Journal of Marketing, 57*, 64–75.

Alden, D. L., Stayman, D. M., & Hoyer, W. D. (1994). Evaluation strategies of American and Thai consumers. *Psychology & Marketing, 11*, 145–161.

Alter, A. L., & Kwan, V. S. (2009). Cultural sharing in a global village: Evidence for extracultural cognition in European Americans. *Journal of Personality and Social Psychology, 96*, 742–760.

Arnett, J. J. (2002). The psychology of globalization. *American Psychologist, 57*, 774–783.

Becker, E. (1973). *The Denial of Death*. New York: Free Press.

Betsky, A. (1997). *Icons: Magnets of Meaning*. San Francisco: Chronicle.

Brewer, M. B. (1991). The social self: On being the same and different at the same time. *Personality & Social Psychology Bulletin, 17*, 475–482.

Briley, D. A., Morris, M. W., & Simonson, I. (2005). Cultural chameleons: Biculturals, conformity motives, and decision making. *Journal of Consumer Psychology, 15*, 351–362.

Briley, D. A., & Wyer, Jr., R. S. (2002). The effect of group membership salience on the avoidance of negative outcomes: Implications for social and consumer decisions. *Journal of Consumer Research, 29*, 400–415.

Briley, D. A., Wyer, Jr., R. S., & Li, E. (2014). A dynamic view of cultural influence: A review. *Journal of Consumer Psychology, 24*, 557–571.

Checkel, J. T., & Katzenstein, P. J. (2009). *European Identity*: Cambridge: Cambridge University Press.

Chen, H., Ng, S., & Rao, A. R. (2005). Cultural differences in consumer impatience. *Journal of Marketing Research, 42*, 291–301.

Chen, X., & Chiu, C.-Y. (2010). Rural-urban differences in generation of Chinese and Western exemplary persons: The case of China. *Asian Journal of Social Psychology, 13*, 9–18.

Cheng, S. Y. Y. (2010). Social psychology of globalization: Joint activation of cultures and reactions to foreign cultural influence. Unpublished dissertation, University of Illinois at Urbana–Champaign.

Cheng, S. Y. Y., Rosner, J. L., Chao, M. M., Peng, S., Chen, X., Li, Y., Kwong, J. Y. Y., Hong, Y.-y., & Chiu, C.-Y. (2011). One world, one dream? Intergroup consequences of the 2008 Beijing Olympics. *International Journal of Intercultural Relations, 35*, 296–306.

Chiu, C.-Y., & Cheng, S. Y. Y. (2007). Toward a social psychology of culture and globalization: Some social cognitive consequences of activating two cultures simultaneously. *Social and Personality Psychology Compass, 1*, 84–100.

Chiu, C.-Y., Gelfand, M. J., Yamagishi, T., Shteynberg, G., & Wan, C. (2010). Intersubjective culture: The role of intersubjective perceptions in cross-cultural research. *Perspectives on Psychological Science, 5*, 482–493.

Chiu, C.-Y., & Hong, Y.-Y. (2006). *Social Psychology of Culture*. New York: Psychology Press.

Chiu, C.-Y., & Hong, Y.-Y. (2007). Cultural processes: Basic principles. In T. E. Higgins & A. W. Kruglanski (eds.), *Social Psychology: Handbook of Basic Principles* (pp. 785–806). New York: Guilford Press.

Chiu, C.-Y., Mallorie, L., Keh, H. T., & Law, W. (2009). Perceptions of culture in multicultural space: Joint presentation of images from two cultures increases in-group attribution of culture-typical characteristics. *Journal of Cross-Cultural Psychology, 40*, 282–300.

Cinnirella, M. (1997). Towards a European identity? Interactions between the national and European social identities manifested by university students in Britain and Italy. *British Journal of Social Psychology, 36*, 19–31.

Crisp, R. J., Stone, C. H., & Hall, N. R. (2006). Recategorization and subgroup identification: Predicting and preventing threats from common ingroups. *Personality and Social Psychology Bulletin, 32*, 230–243.

Devos, T., & Banaji, M. R. (2005). American = white? *Journal of Personality and Social Psychology, 88*, 447–466.

Doi, T. (1973). *The Anatomy of Dependence*. Tokyo: Kodansha International.

Earley, P. C., & Gibson, C. B. (1998). Taking stock in our progress on individualism-collectivism: 100 years of solidarity and community. *Journal of Management, 24*, 265–304.

Fiske, S. T. (1993). Controlling other people: The impact of power on stereotyping. *American Psychologist, 48*, 621–628.

Forehand, M. R., & Deshpandé, R. (2001). What we see makes us who we are: Priming ethnic self-awareness and advertising response. *Journal of Marketing Research, 38*, 336–348.

Forehand, M. R., Deshpandé, R., & Reed, A. (2002). Identity salience and the influence of differential activation of the social self-schema on advertising response. *Journal of Applied Psychology, 87*, 1086–1099.

Friedman, T. L. (2000). *The Lexus and the Olive Tree: Understanding Globalization*. New York: Anchor.

Fu, J. H.-y., Morris, M. W., Lee, S.-l., Chao, M., Chiu, C.-y., & Hong, Y.-y. (2007). Epistemic motives and cultural conformity: Need for closure, culture, and context as determinants of conflict judgments. *Journal of Personality and Social Psychology, 92*, 191–207.

Gaertner, S. L., Dovidio, J. F., Anastasio, P. A., Bachman, B. A., & Rust, M. C. (1993). The common ingroup identity model: Recategorization and the reduction of intergroup bias. *European Review of Social Psychology, 4*, 1–26.

Gelfand, M. J., Raver, J. L., Nishii, L., Leslie, L. M., Lun, J., Lim, B. C., Duan, L., Almaliach, A., Ang, S., Arnadottir, J., Aycan, Z., Boehnke, K., Boski, P., Cabecinhas, R., Chan, D., Chhokar, J., D'Amato, A., Ferrer, M., Fischlmayr, I. C., Fischer, R., Fülöp, M., Georgas, J., Kashima, E. S., Kashima, Y., Kim, K., Lempereur, A., Marquez, P., Othman, R., Overlaet, B., Panagiotopoulou, P., Peltzer, K., Perez-Florizno, L. R., Ponomarenko, L., Realo, A., Schei, V., Schmitt, M., Smith, P. B., Soomro, N., Szabo, E., Taveesin, N., Toyama, M., Van de Vliert, E., Vohra, N., Ward, C., & Yamaguchi, S. (2011). Differences between tight and loose cultures: A 33-nation study. *Science, 332*, 1100–1104.

Greenberg, J., Porteus, J., Simon, L., & Pyszczynski, T. (1995). Evidence of a terror management function of cultural icons: The effects of mortality salience on the inappropriate use of cherished cultural symbols. *Personality and Social Psychology Bulletin, 21*, 1221–1228.

Greenberg, J., Solomon, S., & Pyszczynski, T. (1997). Terror management theory of self-esteem and cultural worldviews: Empirical assessments and conceptual refinements. In M. P. Zanna (ed.), *Advances in Experimental Social Psychology* (vol. 29, pp. 61–139). San Diego, CA: Academic Press.

Gudykunst, W. B., & Ting-Toomey, S. (1988). *Culture and Interpersonal Communication*. Newbury Park, CA: Sage.

Hachman, M. (2014). Lenovo widens lead as PC market decline slows. pcworld.com, downloaded on September 3, 2014.

Han, C. M., & Terpstra, V. (1988). Country-of-origin effects for uni-national and bi-national products. *Journal of International Business Studies, 19*, 235–255.

Han, S.-p., & Shavitt, S. (1994a). Persuasion and culture: Advertising appeals in individualistic and collectivistic societies. *Journal of Experimental Social Psychology, 30*, 326–350.

Han, S.-p., & Shavitt, S. (1994b). Persuasion and culture: Advertising appeals in individualistic and collectivistic societies. *Journal of Experimental Social Psychology, 30*, 326.

Häubl, G. (1996). A cross-national investigation of the effects of country of origin and brand name on the evaluation of a new car. *International Marketing Review, 13*, 76–97.

Hofstede, G. H. (1980). *Culture's Consequences: International Differences in Work-Related Values*. Newbury Park: Sage.

Hofstede, G. H. (2001). *Culture's Consequences : Comparing Values, Behaviors, Institutions and Organizations across Nations*. Thousand Oaks, CA.: Sage.

Hong, J. W., Muderrisoglu, A., & Zinkhan, G. M. (1987). Cultural differences and advertising expression: A comparative content analysis of Japanese and U.S. magazine advertising. *Journal of Advertising, 16*, 55–62, 68.

Hong, Y.-Y., Morris, M. W., Chiu, C.-Y., & Benet-Martinez, V. (2000). Multicultural minds: A dynamic constructivist approach to culture and cognition. *American Psychologist, 55*, 709–720.

Hong, Y.-Y., Roisman, G. I., & Chen, J. (2006). A model of cultural attachment: A new approach for studying bicultural experience. In M. H. Bornstein & L. Cote (eds.), *Acculturation and Parent-Child Relationships: Measurement and Development* (pp. 135–170). Hillsdale, NJ: Lawrence Erlbaum Associates, Inc.

Insko, C. A., & Schopler, J. (1998). Differential distrust of groups and individuals. In C. Sedikides, J. Schopler, & C. A. Insko (eds.), *Intergroup Cognition and Intergroup Behavior* (pp. 75–107). New Jersey: Lawrence Erlbaum Associates.

Javalgi, R. G., Cutler, B. D., & Malhotra, N. K. (1995). Print advertising at the component level: A cross-cultural comparison of the United States and Japan. *Journal of Business Research, 34*, 117–124.

Johansson, J. K., & Nebenzahl, I. D. (1986). Multinational production: Effect on brand value. *Journal of International Business Studies, 17*, 101–126.

Kashima, Y. (1999). Culture, groups, and coordination problems. *Psychologische Beitrage, 41*, 237–251.

Kiley, D. (2007). Jack Daniel's international appeal. businessweek.com, downloaded on September 3, 2014.

Kim, E., Zeppenfeld, V., & Cohen, D. (2013). Sublimation, culture, and creativity. *Journal of Personality and Social Psychology, 105*, 639–666.

Kim, H. S., & Markus, H. R. (1999). Deviance or uniqueness, harmony or conformity? A cultural analysis. *Journal of Personality & Social Psychology, 77*, 785–800.

Kim, U., & Choi, S.-H. (1994). Individualism, collectivism, and child development: A Korean perspective. In P. M. Greenfield & R. R. Cocking (eds.), *Cross-cultural Roots of Minority Child Development* (pp. 227–257). Hillsdale, NJ: Lawrence Erlbaum Associates.

Kitayama, S., Duffy, S., & Uchida, Y. (2007). Self as cultural mode of being. In D. Cohen & S. Kitayama (eds.), *Handbook of Cultural Psychology* (pp. 136–174). New York: Guilford Press.

Lalwani, A. K., & Shavitt, S. (2009). The "me" I claim to be: Cultural self-construal elicits self-presentational goal pursuit. *Journal of Personality and Social Psychology, 97*, 88–102.

Lalwani, A. K., Shavitt, S., & Johnson, T. (2006). What is the relation between cultural orientation and socially desirable responding? *Journal of Personality and Social Psychology, 90*, 165–178.

Lau, I. Y.-m., Chiu, C.-Y., & Lee, S.-l. (2001). Communication and shared reality: Implications for the psychological foundation of culture. *Social Cognition, 19*, 350–371.

Lau-Gesk, L. G. (2003). Activating culture through persuasion appeals: An examination of the bicultural consumer. *Journal of Consumer Psychology, 13*, 301–315.

Leclerc, F., Schmitt, B. H., & Dubé, L. (1994). Foreign branding and its effects on product perceptions and attitudes. *Journal of Marketing Research, 31*, 263–270.

Levy, S. J. (1959). Symbols for sale. *Harvard Business Review, 37*, 117–124.

Maheswaran, D., & Shavitt, S. (2000). Issues and new directions in global consumer psychology. *Journal of Consumer Psychology, 9*, 59–66.

Markus, H. R., & Kitayama, S. (1991). Culture and the self: Implications for cognition, emotion, and motivation. *Psychological Review, 98*, 224–253.

McCracken, G. (1986). Culture and consumption: A theoretical account of the structure and movement of the cultural meaning of consumer goods. *Journal of Consumer Research, 13*, 71–84.

McGregor, H. A., Lieberman, J. D., Greenberg, J., Solomon, S., Arndt, J., Simon, L., & Pyszczynski, T. (1998). Terror management and aggression: Evidence that mortality salience motivates aggression against worldview-threatening others. *Journal of Personality and Social Psychology, 74*, 590–605.

Mok, A., & Morris, M. W. (2013). Bicultural self-defense in consumer contexts: Self-protection motives are the basis for contrast versus assimilation to cultural cues. *Journal of Consumer Psychology, 23*, 175–188.

Monga, A. B., & John, D. R. (2007). Cultural differences in brand extension evaluation: The influence of analytic versus holistic thinking. *Journal of Consumer Research, 33*, 529–536.

Myers, J. P. (2006). *Dominant-Minority Relations in America: Linking Personal History with the Convergence in the New World*. Boston: Allyn and Bacon.

Nelson, M. R., & Shavitt, S. (2002). Horizontal and vertical individualism and achievement values: A multimethod examination of Denmark and the United States. *Journal of Cross-Cultural Psychology, 33*, 439–458.

Ng, S. (2010). Cultural orientation and brand dilution: Impact of motivation level and extension typicality. *Journal of Marketing Research, 47*, 186–198.

Nisbett, R. E. (2003). The geography of thought: How Asians and Westerners think differently … and why. New York: Free Press.

Nisbett, R. E., Peng, K., Choi, I., & Norenzayan, A. (2001). Culture and systems of thought: Holistic versus analytic cognition. *Psychological Review, 108*, 291–310.

O'Brien, K. J. (2012). Telefónica's 20-year gamble pays off. nytimes.com, downloaded on September 3, 2014.

Ogilvy, D. (1985). *Ogilvy on Advertising*. New York: Vintage.

Ortner, S. B. (1973). On key symbols. *American Anthropologist, 75*, 1338–1346.

Overbeck, J. R., & Park, B. (2001). When power does not corrupt: Superior individuation processes among powerful perceivers. *Journal of Personality and Social Psychology, 81*, 549–565.

Oyserman, D. (2009). Identity-based motivation: Implications for action-readiness, procedural-readiness, and consumer behavior. *Journal of Consumer Psychology, 19*, 250–260.

Oyserman, D., Coon, H. M., & Kemmelmeier, M. (2002). Rethinking individualism and collectivism: Evaluation of theoretical assumptions and meta-analyses. *Psychological Bulletin, 128*, 3–72.

Oyserman, D., Fryberg, S. A., & Yoder, N. (2007). Identity-based motivation and health. *Journal of Personality and Social Psychology, 93*, 1011–1027.

Paulhus, D. L. (1984). Two-component models of socially desirable responding. *Journal of Personality and Social Psychology, 46*, 598–609.

Paulhus, D. L. (1998). Interpersonal and intrapsychic adaptiveness of trait self-enhancement: A mixed blessing? *Journal of Personality and Social Psychology, 74*, 1197–1208.

Rao, P., & Rao, N. (1982). *Marriage, the Family and Women in India*. New Delhi: South Asia Books.

Sechrist, G. B., & Stangor, C. (2001). Perceived consensus influences intergroup behavior and stereotype accessibility. *Journal of Personality & Social Psychology, 80*, 645–654.

Shavitt, S., Lalwani, A. K., Zhang, J., & Torelli, C. J. (2006). The horizontal/vertical distinction in cross-cultural consumer research. *Journal of Consumer Psychology, 16*, 325–356.

Shavitt, S., Lee, A. Y., & Torelli, C. J. (2008). Cross-cultural issues in consumer behavior. In M. Wanke (ed.), *Social Psychology of Consumer Behavior* (pp. 227–250). New York: Psychology Press.

Shavitt, S., Nelson, M. R., & Yuan, R. M.-L. (1997). Exploring cross-cultural differences in cognitive responding to ads. In M. Brucks & D. J. MacInnis (eds.), *Advances in Consumer Research* (vol. 24, pp. 245–250): Provo, UT: Association for Consumer Research.

Shavitt, S., Torelli, C. J., & Riemer, H. (2010). Horizontal and vertical individualism and collectivism: Implications for understanding psychological processes. In M. J. Gelfand, C.-Y. Chiu, & Y.-y. Hong (eds.), *Advances in Culture and Psychology* (vol. 1, pp. 309–350). New York: Oxford University Press.

Shore, B. (2002). Taking culture seriously. *Human Development, 45*, 226–228.

Singelis, T. M., Triandis, H. C., Bhawuk, D., & Gelfand, M. J. (1995). Horizontal and vertical dimensions of individualism and collectivism: A theoretical and measurement refinement. *Cross-Cultural Research: The Journal of Comparative Social Science, 29*, 240–275.

Sirgy, M. J. (1982). Self-Concept in Consumer Behavior: A Critical Review. *Journal of Consumer Research, 9*, 287–300.

Smith, P. B., Dugan, S., & Trompenaars, F. (1996). National culture and the values of organizational employees: A dimensional analysis across 43 nations. *Journal of Cross-Cultural Psychology, 27*, 231–264.

Solomon, S., Greenberg, J., & Pyszczynski, T. (1991). A terror management theory of social behavior: The psychological functions of self-esteem and cultural worldviews. In M. P. Zanna (ed.), *Advances in Experimental Social Psychology* (vol. 24, pp. 93–159). San Diego, CA: Academic Press.

Sperber, D. (1996). *Explaining Culture: A Naturalistic Approach*. Massachusetts: Blackwell.

Swaminathan, V., Page, K. L., & Gürhan-Canli, Z. (2007). "My" brand or "our" brand: The effects of brand relationship dimensions and self-construal on brand evaluations. *Journal of Consumer Research, 34*, 248–259.

Torelli, C. J. (2013). *Globalization, Culture, and Branding: How to Leverage Cultural Equity for Building Iconic Brands in the Era of Globalization*. New York: Palgrave Macmillan.

Torelli, C. J., & Ahluwalia, R. (2012). Extending culturally symbolic brands: A blessing or a curse? *Journal of Consumer Research, 38*, 933–947.

Torelli, C. J., & Cheng, S. Y. Y. (2011). Cultural meanings of brands and consumption: A window into the cultural psychology of globalization. *Social and Personality Psychology Compass, 5*, 251–262.

Torelli, C. J., & Cheng, S. Y. Y. (2015). Culture and brand iconicity. In S. Ng & A. Y. Lee (eds.), *Handbook of Culture and Consumer Behavior* (vol. 1, pp. 274–296). New York: Oxford University Press.

Torelli, C. J., Chiu, C.-Y., & Keh, H. T. (2010). Cultural symbolism of brands in globalized economy. Paper presented at the Global Brand Management Conference, Istanbul, Turkey.

Torelli, C. J., Chiu, C.-Y., Keh, H. T., & Amaral, N. (2009a). Brand iconicity: A shared reality perspective. *Advances in Consumer Research, 36*, 108–111.

Torelli, C. J., Chiu, C.-Y., Keh, H. T., & Amaral, N. (2009b). Cultural symbolism of brands: A shared reality perspective. Unpublished manuscript, University of Minnesota.

Torelli, C. J., Chiu, C.-Y., Tam, K.-p., Au, A. K. C., & Keh, H. T. (2011). Exclusionary reactions to foreign cultures: Effects of simultaneous exposure to cultures in globalized space. *Journal of Social Issues, 67*, 716–742.

Torelli, C. J., Keh, H. T., & Chiu, C.-Y. (2010). Cultural symbolism of brands. In B. Loken, R. Ahluwalia, & M. J. Houston (eds.), *Brands and Brand Management: Contemporary Research Perspectives* (pp. 113–132). New York: Routledge.

Torelli, C. J., Ozsomer, A., Carvalho, S., Keh, H. T., & Maehle, N. (2012). Brand concepts as representations of human values: Do cultural congruity and compatibility betweeen values matter? *Journal of Marketing, 76*, 92–108.

Torelli, C. J., & Shavitt, S. (2011). The impact of power on information processing depends on cultural orientation. *Journal of Experimental Social Psychology, 47*, 959–967.

Torelli, C. J., & Stoner, J. L. (2015). Managing cultural equity: A theoretical framework for building iconic brands in globalized markets. *Review of Marketing Research, 12*, 83–120.

Trafimow, D., Silverman, E. S., Fan, R. M.-T., & Law, J. S. F. (1997). The effects of language and priming on the relative accessibility of the private self and the collective self. *Journal of Cross-Cultural Psychology, 28*, 107–123.

Triandis, H. C. (1989). The self and social behavior in differing cultural contexts. *Psychological Review, 96*, 506–520.

Triandis, H. C. (1995). *Individualism & Collectivism*. Boulder, CO: Westview Press.

Triandis, H. C. (1996). The psychological measurement of cultural syndromes. *American Psychologist, 51*, 407–415.

Triandis, H. C. (2007). Culture and psychology: A history of the study of their relationship. In S. Kitayama & D. Cohen (eds.), *Handbook of Cultural Psychology* (pp. 59–76). New York: Guilford Press.

Triandis, H. C., & Gelfand, M. J. (1998). Converging measurement of horizontal and vertical individualism and collectivism. *Journal of Personality and Social Psychology, 74*, 118–128.

Triandis, H. C., Marín, G., Lisansky, J., & Betancourt, H. (1984). Simpatía as a cultural script of Hispanics. *Journal of Personality and Social Psychology, 47*, 1363–1375.

Turner, J. C., Brown, R. J., & Tajfel, H. (1979). Social comparison and group interest in ingroup favouritism. *European Journal of Social Psychology, 9*, 187–204.

Turner, J. C., Hogg, M. A., Oakes, P. J., Reicher, S. D., & Wetherell, M. S. (1987). *Rediscovering the Social Group: A Self-Categorization Theory*. Oxford: Blackwell.

Watanabe, M. (1974). The conception of nature in Japanese culture. *Science, 183*, 279–282.

Weber, M. (2002). *The Protestant Ethic and the Spirit of Capitalism (P. Baehr, ed.)*. New York: Penguin.

Zerubavel, E. (1996). Social memories: Steps to a sociology of the past. *Qualitative Sociology, 19*, 283–299.

Zhang, Y., & Gelb, B. D. (1996). Matching advertising appeals to culture: The influence of products' use conditions. *Journal of Advertising, 25*, 29–46.

Name Index

Subject Index

Lightning Source UK Ltd.
Milton Keynes UK
UKOW05f0326190717
305607UK00011B/126/P